PHYLOGENY AND CLASSIFICATION OF BIRDS

PHYLOGENY AND CLASSIFICATION OF BIRDS

A Study in Molecular Evolution

Charles G. Sibley and Jon E. Ahlquist

Yale University Press   New Haven & London

Designed by James J. Johnson.
Set in Times and Gill San types by
The Composing Room of Michigan, Inc.
Printed in the United States of America.

*The paper in this book meets the guidelines for
permanence and durability of the Committee on
Production Guidelines for Book Longevity of the
Council on Library Resources.*

10 9 8 7 6 5 4 3 2 1

Library of Congress Cataloging-in-Publication Data

Sibley, Charles Gald, 1917–
    Phylogeny and classification of birds : a study in
molecular evolution / Charles G. Sibley and Jon E.
Ahlquist.
        p.   cm.
    Includes bibliographical references and index.
    ISBN 0–300–04085–7 (alk. paper)

    1. Birds—Genetics.   2. Nucleic acid hybrid-
ization.   3. Birds—Classification.   I. Ahlquist,
Jon E.   II. Title.
QL696.5.S53   1991
598.23′8—dc20   90–35938
                                                        CIP

We Dedicate This Book to Those Who Helped

Contents

PART II

Figures

Tables

Preface

This is a book about birds. It may seem to be mostly about DNA, but Jon Ahlquist and I used DNA hybridization only as the means to an end. The goals of our study were the reconstruction of the phylogeny of the groups of living birds and the derivation of a new classification based on the phylogeny. Others will judge how successful we have been in achieving those goals; we think we made some discoveries and produced new evidence of avian evolution. Our data are not perfect and we did not subject them to every available statistical analysis; that we should have done many things better is undeniable, but hindsight is always crystal-clear. We urge critics to set up their own laboratories, collect the necessary specimens, and improve on our work. We did what we could with the methods and resources available. We are satisfied with the results, but we know that many questions remain unanswered and that we have raised new ones. That is progress; perfection is for the future.

This book has a phylogeny. It originated on September 11, 1955, when I completed *A Synopsis of the Birds of the World: A Manual of Systematic Ornithology.* This was a mimeographed book of 151 pages prepared as a text and laboratory syllabus for the course in systematic ornithology that I taught at Cornell (1955–64) and Yale (1965–85). The *Synopsis* was assembled from the classical publications of Nitzsch, Huxley, Beddard, Garrod, Gadow, Sharpe, Ridgway, Stresemann, Wetmore, Peters, Mayr and Amadon, and others; the bibliography contained 22 citations, with others cited in the text.

Capsule reviews of the history of avian systematics were important parts of the two monographs based on our studies of the egg-white proteins (Sibley 1970, Sibley and Ahlquist 1972). The bibliography expanded to 315 citations in the 1970 paper on the passerines, and to 1100 in the 1972 non-passerine monograph. Most of these reviews and citations are included in this book. I haven't counted the publications cited herein, but there must be about 2000.

The text includes references and quotations from the works of ornithologists from Linnaeus to the present. This aspect alone should make it useful to those without access to such classics as the *Catalogue of Birds in the British Museum*, Sharpe's *Hand-List*, Gadow's *Vögel*, Stresemann's *Aves*, and Peters' *Check-list of Birds of the World*.

Our studies of the egg-white proteins produced few answers to questions about the systematic relationship of birds, but they introduced us to laboratory procedures that facilitated the transition from proteins to DNA in 1973, as noted in chapter 1.

We have dedicated this book "To Those Who Helped." They are named in the Acknowledgments. Without their help there would have been nothing to write about.

The laboratory work was under Jon's direction, and he took over the data analysis in December 1979, when the Yale Computer Center would no longer accept the non-magnetic teletype tapes from our gamma counter. I obtained the specimens and financial support, wrote the papers, and dealt with academic responsibilities. We share credit and criticism equally for all aspects.

I began to enter the text on a computer in August 1983, and the book will be printed from my computer files by electronic typesetting. Many authors acknowledge the person who typed the manuscript; well, I typed this one and I have lost count of how many times I revised sections and how many reams of printouts were replaced. Those who predicted that the computer revolution would end the use of paper were poor prophets. Jon and I wrote different sections and we have lost track of which one composed the first draft of most of them. I produced the figures of the melting curves with Microsoft EXCEL, and Jon used Joe Felsenstein's PHYLIP for the FITCH and KITSCH trees. Jon made the UPGMA trees, by hand, from matrices that we both developed longhand. In 1986, we made enlarged copies of the 33 UPGMA pages and presented them as a poster at the 19th International Ornithological Congress in Ottawa, Canada. Bob Raikow dubbed this 50-foot-long poster "The Tapestry"—it is depicted in figures 353–385.

The Latin and English names of birds are the same as those in *Distribution and Taxonomy of Birds of the World* (Sibley and Monroe 1990)—discrepancies are unintentional. Some of the spellings of English names of birds, e.g., "Grey" instead of "Gray," are the results of an attempt to standardize the spellings in English-speaking countries. Burt Monroe participated in discussions with colleagues in those countries and compromises were necessary. The two books complement one another and use the same classification. Burt joined us in the development of the classification and provided advice on various aspects of the presentation.

The Introduction and the chapters pertaining to the structure, function, and biochemistry of DNA were read by Sidney Altman, Roy Britten, Richard Harrison, and John Kirsch. We appreciate their comments and corrections, but we accept responsibility for errors. Sid was co-winner of the 1989 Nobel Prize for chemistry; Roy discovered repeated DNA and is the acknowledged guru of DNA hybridization; Rick, a product of Paul Doty's Harvard laboratory where the reassociation reaction of single-stranded DNA was discovered, uses biochemical methods in his studies of crickets and crabs; and John is using DNA hybridization to reconstruct mammalian phylogeny. Robert Raikow commented on several sections, including the chapters pertaining to methods and principles of classification. Bob is a comparative morphologist and a cladist who once told me that he would welcome a trustworthy phylogeny of birds to aid his understanding of avian morphology.

It has been a pleasure and an education to work with the editors of Yale University Press: Edward Tripp (Editor-in-Chief, now Editor-at-Large), friend and guide; Jay Williams, now in New York; and Stacey Mandelbaum, who coordinated the project, checked everything, and kept us on schedule during the final months. A special thanks to Lorraine Atherton of Austin,

Texas, who was engaged as the free-lance manuscript editor by Yale University Press. Lorraine read every word of the text and her eye for detail, knowledge of English grammar, and interest in natural history improved every aspect of the presentation. Katherine Klain (Corte Madera, California) drew figures 1A, 1B, 2, and 3. Jon Ahlquist made figures 4–17.

I cannot count the ways in which my wife, Frances, has aided and abetted this project, but she knows and so do I.

Charles G. Sibley
Tiburon, California
May 7, 1990

Acknowledgments

At least 300 persons contributed to the research on which this book is based. Many helped in the field at some time during the 23 years between 1963 and 1986. Others assisted in the laboratory for various periods between 1973 and 1986. The following alphabetical list of the names of "Those Who Helped" is an inadequate expression of our gratitude and we apologize to those we may have overlooked.

H. Abdulali, J. S. Adams, David Ainley, S. Allen-Stotz, Peter Ames, P. D. Anderson, Anthony Archer, Miguel Avedillo, Barbara Baechler, Russell Balda, Rob Barker, George Barrowclough, Sandy Bartle, Rollin Bauer, G. Baylis, Bruce Beehler, Jacques Begaud, William Belton, Anthony Bledsoe, Walter Bock, B., P., and H. Bomford, José Borrero, José Borrero, Jr., Rudyerd Boulton, D. Braun, H. Bregulla, Bevan Brown, W. F. Bruce-Miller, R. Bruggers, Alan Brush, Milan Bull, Ralph Bulmer, Alan Burger, Tony Bush, John Calaby, C. Camillari, David Candy, R. Cassidy, Tamar Cassidy (Salinger), Mark Clayton, Fergus Clunie, John Colebrook-Robjent, Charles Collins, J. R. Contreras, John Cooper, Kendall Corbin, J. Cox, R. L. Crawford, Frank Crome, Tim Crowe, Juan Cuello, R. Cunningham-van-Someren, Doyle Damman, Stephen Davies, Jared Diamond, Annabelle Dod, Douglas Dorward, Robert Dowsett, John E. duPont, Henry J. Eckert, John Engbring, Stephen Ervin, G. Falxa, Tibor Farkas, V. Fayad, Andrew Ferguson, Camille Ferry, Kenneth Fletcher, D. Foote, Alec Forbes-Watson, Julian R. Ford, Douglas Forsell, J. Forsyth, A. Fuller, Sean Furniss, P. Galindo, Plácido Garayalde, Steve Garber, Aldegundo Garza de Leon, P. Gertler, C. Gilbert, Peter Ginn, Steven Goodman, E. Grai, Gilbert Grant, Gary Graves, Llewellyn Grimes, Ian Grimwood, G. Gunnell, Jurgen Haffer, Svein Haftorn, Yngvar Hagen, Tas Hammersley, L. Hammonds, Graham Harrington, T. Harris, Ed N. Harrison, Nancy Harrison, John Hechtel, Herbert Hendrickson, Peter Hillard, E. Hird, H. Hoffman, Holger Holgersen, J. Holly, Glen Holmes, Harry Hoogstraal, George Hunt, Charles Huntington, R. Hutchings, Michael P. Stuart Irwin, Susan Jackson, Joseph Jehl, Rolf Jensen, Eric Johnson, B. Kaghan, P. V. G. Kainady, Alan Kemp, Joan Kennard (Mrs. F. H. Sheldon), Lloyd Kiff, D. Klein, Carl Koford, Eric Koford, Joris Komen, Stan Koster, M. Kroese, Arlene Kumamoto, Robert

Kyongo, Scott Lanyon, Wesley Lanyon, H. T. Laycock, Bernd Leisler, Thomas Lemke, Gary Lester, Seymour Levy, Richard Liversidge, Geoffrey and Diana Lodge, Hans Löhrl, Michel Louette, George H. Lowery, Jr., G. H. Lunn, Charles Luthin, A. Mack, Roy Mackay, Gordon Maclean, G. Magellson, Philip Maher, Stephen Marchant, R. Margalef, Jean Mariaux, A. J. Marshall, F. Martinsen, Ian Mason, J. S. McIlhenny, John McKean, Gathorne Medway, E. Méndez, D. Meyer, A. L. A. Middleton, S. G. Moore, Gerard Morel, Michael Morrison, J. and P. Morrissey, N. Myburgh, René de Naurois, Terry Oatley, B. Odum, Penny Olsen, Storrs Olson, Carol O'Neill, John O'Neill, Timothy Osborne, J. A. Ottenwalder, David Owen, Shane Parker, Roy Parker, Theodore Parker, III, Sam Patten, David Paton, Joan Paton, Robert Payne, William Peckover, L. Pedler, Luis Peña G., Derek Pomeroy, H. Douglas Pratt, Dieter Prestel, Stephen Pruett-Jones, Gordon Ragless, Galen Rathbun, John Ratti, B. Reid, Nick Reid, James V. Remsen, Perry and Alma Ribeira, B. Riekert, M. Robbins, William Robertson, Colin Roderick, Wynne Rohan-Jones, Gerry Rose, Stephen Rothstein, B. Rowe, Ian Rowley, A. Ruschi, Ward C. Russell, Oliver Ryder, N. John Schmitt, Richard Schodde, D. A. Schroeder, Karl Schuchmann, Thomas Schulenberg, H. and L. Schweppe, Richard Semba, D. L. Serventy, Lucia Severinghaus, Frederick Sheldon, Lester Short, Harry Shugg, Barbara Sibley, Carol Sibley, Dorothy Sibley, Frances Sibley, Fred C. Sibley, Roy Siegfried, W. H. Sloan, David Snow, S. Somadikarta, Lawrence Spear, Jeffrey Spendelow, Alexander Sprunt, IV, D. Stegmann, George A. Smith, Graeme Smith, Thomas B. Smith, P. Stone, Bernard Stonehouse, Glen Storr, Stuart Strahl, Joseph Strauch, Jr., Dan Tallman, Peter Taylor, Warren Thomas, Frank Todd, Melvin Traylor, Jr., Wayne Trivelpiece, E. Graham Turbott, N. Van Derheyden, C. R. Veitch, Carl Vernon, R. H. Watten, Shirley Webb, David Wells, John Weske, L. Wessels, Kai Westerskov, Nathaniel and Eugenia Wheelwright, Andrew Williams, Gordon Williams, John Williams, David Wingate, K. Wohl, Hans Wolters, John Womersley, D. Scott Wood, Eric Worrell, Douglas Wysham, Robert Zink, Virginia Zinsmeister, and Richard Zusi.

In the laboratory we were assisted by Chris Barkan, Anthony Bledsoe, Lisa Foret, Rosemary Gatter, Lisa Kugelman, Michelle Mattie, Leslie Merritt, Edmund Nowicki, Marge Pitcher, Peter Separak, Fred Sheldon, Fred Sibley, Nick Snow, Louise Tiglio, Linda Wallace, and Lise Woodard. Steven Pitcher, Temple F. Smith, and Dan H. Moore, II (Calico Computing, Livermore, California) provided computer assistance. Dan Moore wrote the macros that simplified the work with the Micosoft EXCEL program that produced the melting curves. Joseph Felsenstein and George Wilson provided the PHYLIP program and advice for its use.

We gratefully acknowledge the help and cooperation of the Louisiana State University Museum of Natural Sciences, the Los Angeles Zoo, San Diego Zoological Garden, San Antonio Zoological Garden, the Western Foundation of Vertebrate Zoology, National Zoological Gardens of Pretoria, South Africa, the South African Department of Environmental Affairs and South African Scientific Committee for Antarctic Research, Kruger National Park of South Africa, the National Parks and Wildlife departments of Malaysia (David Jenkins, Patrick Andau, Lamri Ali), the Department of Environment and Conservation of Papua New Guinea (K. Kisokau, I. Ila), Department of Conservation of New Zealand, the Vogelspark Walsrode, the Alpha Helix Program of the Scripps Institution of Oceanography, and the departments of conservation and wildlife in many other countries and states that provided permits and assistance, including the U.S. Fish and Wildlife Service and the U.S. Department of Agriculture.

We gratefully acknowledge the support of the William Robertson Coe Fund for Ornithology of Yale University, and grants from the U.S. National Science Foundation, Alfred P. Sloan Foundation, National Geographic Society, and private donors.

Part One

Introduction

Comparative biochemistry, immunology, protein sequencing, and early DNA studies have for the most part corroborated earlier evolutionary findings, and at the same time provided new understanding of molecular processes in evolution. Of these approaches, the comparison of DNA seems most promising since a relatively precise quantitative comparison can be made of all of the genetic material of different species.

David E. Kohne 1970:328

Single-copy DNA hybridization is quicker than DNA sequencing and the results are more conclusive since the whole genome is averaged.

Roy J. Britten (pers. comm.), March 1987

The plants and animals of Earth evolved from a single origin of life and they have had a single evolutionary history, or phylogeny. The reconstruction of this phylogeny has been a challenge to biologists since Darwin (1859) recognized the principle of descent with modification. The pattern of descent is genealogical; organisms are related to one another by the degree to which they share genetic information.

The pattern of phylogeny is like that of a huge bushy tree with a short trunk that branched again and again, until the uppermost branches end in terminal twigs. The height of the tree is relative to time, but the tree has a ragged top because different branches evolve at many different rates; the lengths of the branches reflect those rates. Each branch node records a divergence event when one species split into two. The horizontal spread of the branches represents the diversity of life, and the topmost twigs are the individual organisms living today. The branches below the living twigs at the top are dead; they represent the ancestors, which, except for fossil remains, are invisible to us. Most of the branches are broken off below the top; they are the extinct lineages.

The challenge is to reconstruct the branching pattern of the tree and, if possible, to date each branching event. If we could do these things for all organisms we would have reconstructed the phylogeny of life on Earth. Our present goal is to reconstruct the small cluster that represents the phylogeny of the approximately 10,000 living species of birds.

We begin the process at the top of the avian branch by clustering individuals into larger and larger groups, based on some hypothesis about what constitutes a valid basis for such clustering. Evolution provides the hypothesis: we will cluster on the basis of genealogical relationship, that is, we will use evidence of the degrees of genetic relatedness among individual birds. The first clusters contain the members of the same population; populations are

3

clustered into species, and so on, gradually working downward through the branches, and backward in time, until we reach the branching at which the ancestor of the avian lineage diverged from its sister reptilian lineage, an event that probably occurred in the Jurassic Period, at least 150 million years ago.

The topmost clusters are relatively easy to define because closely related organisms share so many characteristics. We can usually determine the closest relatives of each species from such evidence as the ability to interbreed, anatomical similarities, and behavior. We make few mistakes at this level, but as we descend the tree the evidence becomes progressively more difficult to decipher. Evidence of the relationships among the older branches is always present in some form in their living descendants; the problem is to interpret that evidence correctly. Morphology is an obvious source of evidence of genealogical relationship because we can expect related organisms to be similar in structure. This is usually true, but morphological characters are prone to convergent evolution, which may cause unrelated species to come to look alike to the human eye because their bodies have been adapted to cope with the same environmental demands. For example, swifts and swallows are superficially similar because both are specialized to feed on flying insects, but swifts are more closely related to hummingbirds and nightjars than to swallows, and swallows are more closely related to the other passerines (e.g., warblers, thrushes, sparrows) than to swifts. In early classifications swifts and swallows were placed together, and the debate about their relationships extended into the late 1800s, long after Darwin had provided the basis for understanding convergent evolution.

Thus, morphological similarity is not a universally safe basis for deciding degrees of genealogical relationship. We must be certain that the similarities we employ are due to common ancestry. Similarities due to convergence are analogies, those due to inheritance from a common ancestor are homologies. Only homologous similarities may be used to reconstruct phylogenies.

Divergent evolution between closely related species may also complicate the interpretation of morphological characters. There are many examples, including the toucans and New World barbets, or the storks and New World vultures. Our eyes tell us that the members of these pairs are unlike one another in their external appearances, but there are morphological characters, as well as genetic similarities, that testify to the close relationship between them.

Convergence and divergence can be far more subtle than these examples, and they are hazards in all comparisons of morphological characters, whether in living or fossil organisms. The fossil record for most groups is fragmentary, and for some it is nonexistent. Partial phylogenies for some groups have been reconstructed from fossils, and it is possible to date most fossils with reasonable accuracy, but a dated fossil only records the time the individual organism perished, not the time that its lineage diverged from that of its next nearest relatives.

Morphological comparisons and fossils have provided the evidence to reconstruct many portions of the phylogeny of birds. The avian fossil record is fair for the past few million years, but less complete than that for other groups of vertebrates at older levels. Many birds are small, bird bones are fragile, and most birds die in circumstances not conducive to preservation. Convergence is common because the morphology of most birds is constrained by the requirements of flight. Nonetheless, we can be certain that all parrots are more closely related to one another than any parrot is to hawks, pigeons, or ducks. Similarly, morphological similarities among hawks, or pigeons, or ducks, and many other groups indicate that the members of such groups have descended from a recent common ancestor, that is, they are monophyletic clusters of species. However, we encounter difficulties when we assess the evidence for the older branches that must link the more recent branches together. Are parrots more closely related to hawks than to pigeons? Are ducks more closely related to pheasants than to grebes? Relevant fossils are usually lacking and morphological comparisons reveal little or produce conflicting opinions from different studies of the same groups or even the same characters. The branches occurred long ago and adaptive changes, extinctions, and convergence may have erased or confused the phylogenetic trail. Since we are trying to reconstruct the genealogy of living birds it makes sense to look for evidence in the genetic material, the DNA. It seems reasonable that a method that measures genealogical distances should provide evidence for the reconstruction of phylogeny. We believe that DNA-DNA hybridization is such a method.

DNA-DNA hybridization measures degrees of genealogical relationship among species by comparing their DNAs. If such comparisons are made among species representing all, or most, of the groups of living birds they reveal the branching pattern of the phylogeny because the net effect of genetic evolution is sure to be divergence. Genetic divergence takes time, thus the degrees of difference among the DNAs of living birds are relative to the length of time since their lineages diverged from their most recent common ancestor. To convert the relative times provided by measurements of DNA differences into absolute time poses difficult problems. There are few trustworthy calibration points and the rates of DNA evolution may differ in different lineages. Fortunately, differences in rates seem to be small among avian lineages, but different rates of genetic evolution produce branches of different lengths and make the assignment of dates to branchings tentative and subject to correction.

In some cases the DNA hybridization distances may be calibrated against dated geological events that caused branching events in the ancestry of living taxa. For example, the opening of the Atlantic Ocean in the Cretaceous must have split many widespread Gondwanaland species into African and South American populations. Although the rates of genetic evolution differ in different lineages, the differences are detectable by appropriate comparisons among species that are known to have branched at different relative times. Dated fossils of undoubted identity must be consistent with the datings based on geological events, but they should be used with caution as the basis for dating phyletic divergences because, as noted above, a dated fossil provides only the approximate time the organism died, not the date of the divergence of its lineage from that of its sister lineage. If the DNA-based phylogeny is correctly calibrated such fossils must have an age equal to or younger than the divergence time proposed for their lineage by the DNA comparisons. There is considerable evidence that the average rate of DNA evolution is correlated with several demographic factors, including the age at which a species begins to breed, generation time, clutch size, and longevity. These properties are, in some way, related to the accession rate of genetic mutations.

A phylogeny based on DNA distance measures is a diagram of the degrees of genetic divergence among the included taxa. It is, therefore, a suitable basis for a classification that reflects the branching pattern.

There is but one true phylogeny, and its reconstruction is a scientific activity because it involves the construction of a hypothesis and the testing of that hypothesis. The best test for DNA hybridization data is probably the degree of congruence between them and long sequences of nucleotides from the same taxa. Few such comparisons are yet possible because there are not many comparable DNA sequences available, but the meagre evidence supports the prediction that DNA hybridization data and sequence data will give the same answer to a given question (Koop et al. 1989). Other useful criteria include (1) the validity of the technique by which the data are produced, (2) tests of the statistical significance of the data, and (3) congruencies with independent sources of evidence, for example, Earth history and morphological characters. Of these, congruence is the most important.

A simple test of congruence is whether the clusters of species produced by the DNA comparisons are congruent with the clusters based on morphological characters. For example, do all ducks, geese, and swans cluster together, or are there some ducks that cluster with the pigeons, hawks, or pheasants? The answer is clear; the DNA comparisons reconstruct essentially the same clusters that have long been recognized. Ducks cluster with ducks, pigeons with pigeons, hawks with hawks, and pheasants with pheasants. With few exceptions, the DNA comparisons "see" the same clusters of closely related species that the human eye sees. The incongruencies occur mainly at the older levels in the avian tree where the effects of convergence and divergence have had more time to evolve characteristics that act to conceal the evidence of relationships from the human eye. Thus, lack of congruence does not prove that the DNA data are wrong, only that they disagree with the evidence available to the eye. Since the DNA comparisons are able to recognize the obviously correct clusters of species, and because they are blind to morphological divergence and convergence, it is logical to assume that they can discern the correct clusters at all levels in the phylogeny of birds. However, the DNA-DNA hybridization technique, as applied to birds, cannot reach back much beyond 100 million years; thus it may not be applicable to the complete reconstruction of the phylogenies of groups that contain branches older than the middle to early Cretaceous. Fortunately, this includes the branchings among the groups of living birds.

Birds are often cited as the best-known group of animals because all but a small percentage of the living species have been discovered, described, and named, but our understanding of their phylogeny and classification has been no better than for other groups of organisms. There have always been uncertainties in the traditional classifications of birds, and in recent years numerous misconceptions have been revealed. Many problems have been identified and defined, but the attempts to solve them often produce more polemics than proofs.

The same difficulties plague the systematics of all groups of organisms and affect other areas of biology that depend to some degree on phylogeny and classification. Students of comparative morphology, behavior, physiology, ecology, or biochemistry lack a trustworthy taxonomic frame of reference within which to interpret their own data, and even the most vigilant may be led astray by erroneous classifications. Some fields are especially affected. For example, biogeography requires accurate taxonomic information, and the complexities of ecology are made more difficult by the lack of classifications that reflect the phylogenies of plants and animals.

In recent years the concepts and methods of systematic biology have been the subjects of many publications, and various new procedures for data production and analysis have been proposed. The debates among the evolutionists, cladists, and numerical taxonomists, which have occupied many pages in *Systematic Zoology* and other periodicals, have enlightened and/or agitated the participants and bystanders. Although methods and theories have been modified, the source of data has remained much the same as in the past, namely, gross morphology. Morphological comparisons have brought us a long way toward our goal, and they still have much to contribute, but some problems seem insoluble by reliance on morphological characters alone because they do not provide a complete or necessarily accurate reflection of genetic evolution. Furthermore, as adaptive evolution proceeds it erases the phylogenetic trail; morphological differences become so great that the clues to relationship may become indecipherable or lost. Although morphology is usually a trustworthy index to affinity at the lower taxonomic levels, it can be misleading when used to delineate the higher categories and to link them to one another, as noted above. These problems defeat the most talented and zealous systematists, and even the most logical procedures, the most sophisticated methods of data analysis, or a multiplicity of characters cannot avoid all of the hazards that result from the evolutionary process. It is, therefore, not surprising that new data from comparative morphology often add fuel to the debates, rather than reduce the uncertainties. Hull (1988) provides an excellent account of the history of systematic biology, with special attention to the recent conflicts among and within the three schools—evolutionists, numerical taxonomists, and cladists.

To circumvent the inherent difficulties of morphological characters, a search developed for sources of data that would provide a different view of the process of evolution and its effects. This has led to the development of techniques for the comparison of structures at the molecular level, including proteins and the nucleic acids, DNA and RNA.

The ideal method would provide a complete and accurate reading of the sequence of all of the nucleotides in the DNA, a procedure for comparing such sequences among species, and an accurate calibration of the data against absolute time. From such data we could expect to reconstruct the phylogeny of any and all groups of living organisms. But the genomes of higher organisms contain millions or billions of nucleotide pairs and the determination of many complete sequences is impractical, although possible. If the technique could be speeded up so that nucleotide sequences could be determined at the rate of one base per second, it would take just under 90 minutes to determine the sequence of the virus ϕ-X174, which is 5386 nucleotides long. At a rate of one base per second, only 49 days would be required to read out the 4.2 million nucleotides of the bacterium *Escherichia coli*, but 95 years to record the complete DNA sequence of the ca. 3 billion nucleotides in the nucleus of a human cell. In spite of the difficulties, there are rapidly developing plans to sequence the human genome. One would involve 580 laboratories, cost $290 million, and be completed in one year (Palca 1986, Lewin 1986). Some Japanese scientists have proposed the development of a "super-sequencer" and a "large DNA sequencing centre or 'factory'" to sequence the human genome at the rate of "300,000 bases per day, or one base every 0.28 s." The minimal cost is estimated as 10 U.S. cents per base, or U.S. $35 million (Wada 1987). Other proposals are being made by various agencies of government and private organizations, including the U.S. Department of Energy and the Howard Hughes Medical Institute. The potential rate of production continues to increase and the cost per base to decrease. It is likely that the human genome will be completely sequenced by the year 2000, at a possible cost of $3 billion (L. Roberts 1988). In 1989 a special human genome project under the direction of James Watson (of Watson and Crick fame) was established within the National Institutes of Health. Nearly every current issue of *Science* or *Nature* includes information about this subject.

Many things will be learned from the complete human genome sequence but it alone will provide no evidence bearing on the phylogeny of man or other animals. Fortunately, even 50,000 bases may be enough to solve most of the problems of interest to systematists and this may be the future of phylogeny reconstruction. However, the technique of DNA-DNA hybridization is currently available and relatively inexpensive. With it we can achieve a reasonable approach to the ideal by taking advantage of the structural and chemical properties of the genetic material to compare the homologous nucleotide sequences of different species and to measure the degree of difference between them.

The DNA-DNA hybridization technique solves the convergence problem by the stringency of the conditions of the experiments, homologous sequences are self-identifying, relative rates of genomic evolution can be determined, and the median, modal, or average difference between the genomes of different species can be measured. Trees may be produced by computer programs that either do or do not assume equal rates of evolution, and computer programs produce melting curves that provide graphic evidence of the relationships among taxa.

The search for more and better data continues and this study is an example of the quest. This book describes the application of a method, DNA-DNA hybridization, to the solution of a problem: the reconstruction of the phylogeny of the living birds of the world and the development of a classification based on that phylogeny. An introduction to the structure and chemistry of DNA provides background information relating to the technique, and reviews of taxonomic history demonstrate the problems, methods, and opinions that have characterized and influenced the development of ideas about the phylogeny, relationships, and classification of birds.

CHAPTER ONE

A Brief History

Aristotle, Pliny, William Turner, Pierre Belon, Conrad Gesner, Ulisse Aldrovandi, and other early ornithologists organized their writings around classifications based on habitat, food habits, and the functional aspects of morphology. The first important classification that also used such characters as the structure of the beak, feet, and body size was produced by Willughby and Ray (1676), whose *Ornithologiae* influenced the classification of birds developed by Linnaeus for his *Systema Naturae* (e.g., 1758). Anatomical characters became the principal basis for all levels of classification (E. Stresemann 1975).

The advent of Darwinian concepts in 1859 provided a theoretical framework for all systematists. The ornithologists, led by Thomas Henry Huxley, embraced evolution by natural selection and set out to support their faith with facts as they sought a "natural system" that would be a synopsis of evolutionary history. Darwinism provided the stimulus and the guide that caused comparative morphology to flourish during the second half of the nineteenth century and the early years of the twentieth. By 1893, when Hans Gadow published his system, the shape of classifications in use today had been formed. Gadow was influenced by the monumental work of the anatomist Maximilian Fürbringer (1888), whose massive volumes must have seemed to signal an end to the need for more studies, but some problems, especially those due to convergent evolution, proved to be durable. In 1930, when Alexander Wetmore produced the first of the five editions (1930, 1934, 1940, 1951, 1960) of his classification of the birds of the world, he acknowledged his debt to Gadow's arrangement and departed little from it. Erwin Stresemann (1934) also based his classification on those of Gadow and Fürbringer, and the classifications of Peters (1931) and of Mayr and Amadon (1951) were derived from Gadow, via Wetmore and Stresemann. Mayr and Amadon were also influenced by the opinions of Hartert (1910). Thus, the classifications of birds in use for the past century have been based primarily on morphological characters and have undergone little revision since Gadow proposed his arrangement in 1892 and 1893. The classifications used by Richard Bowdler Sharpe and his co-authors for the *Catalogue of Birds in the British Museum* and the *Hand-List of Birds* were eclectic assemblages that seem to have had less influence than the works of Gadow and Fürbringer.

Gadow's classification has endured in the modified form of Wetmore's arrangement, but it has not been universally accepted as beyond improvement. Stresemann (1959) was pessimistic and critical when he noted that "as far as the problem of relationships of the orders of birds is concerned, so many distinguished investigators have labored in the field in vain, that little hope is left for spectacular breakthroughs. . . . Science ends where comparative morphology, comparative physiology, comparative ethology have failed us after nearly 200 years of efforts. The rest is silence."

But the silence had already been broken by the revolution in molecular biology that had been gathering strength for many years and recently had exploded with the determination of the amino acid sequence of the protein insulin by Sanger and Tuppy (1951), and the structure of DNA by Watson and Crick (1953). The "spectacular breakthroughs," for which Stresemann had little hope, had already occurred, but their application to systematics and evolutionary biology had barely begun in 1959.

Fundamental scientific discoveries are soon followed by the development of experimental techniques that make it possible to apply the new concept to the solution of other problems. The discovery that protein molecules are chains of twenty kinds of amino acids synthesized in a specific sequence on a genetically determined template spawned a host of new techniques and refinements of old ones. Some systematists had been aware of the possibility of using protein comparisons since the early years of the century when Nuttall (1904) and others applied immune reaction techniques to problems of evolutionary relationship. In the years following Sanger and Tuppy's proof of the polypeptide structure of proteins a few systematists used such techniques as electrophoresis, chromatography, serology, and protein sequencing to obtain data for classification (e.g., Sibley 1960, Alston and Turner 1963, Wright 1974; Sibley et al. 1974 reviewed avian examples).

Protein molecules reflect genetic information, but each protein is equivalent in information content to one gene, and less than 10% of the genome is expressed in the amino acid sequences of proteins. Clearly, it would be advantageous to obtain comparisons reflecting the information in a larger portion of the genome.

DNA: The Genetic Material

The story of the discovery of DNA, and the subsequent history of DNA research, has been told many times, including the accounts by Cairns et al. (1966), Judson (1979), Davis (1980), and Adams et al. (1981). The following synopsis was distilled from the historical essays by Fruton (1972), and Portugal and Cohen (1977).

In 1869 a young Swiss organic chemist, Friedrich Miescher, a post-doctoral student in the laboratory of Felix Hoppe-Seyler, isolated a substance that he called "nuclein" from the nuclei of pus cells. Miescher (1871, 1879), and others, also found nuclein in the erythrocytes of birds and snakes, in yeast cells, in the spermatozoa of salmon, and in the nuclei of the cells of many other organisms. Miescher continued his study of nuclein at the University of Basel, where he was appointed Professor of Physiology in 1872, a post he retained until his death in 1885.

The composition of nuclein proved to be complex, but the components were gradually isolated and identified by a series of investigators and by 1889 Richard Altmann had obtained protein-free nucleins containing phosphorus, which he called "nucleic acids."

Albrecht Kossel (1853–1927) began his studies of nuclein in the 1870s. Much of Kossel's work concerned the composition of the nucleic acids, especially the bases. With his colleague A. Neumann, Kossel discovered adenine in 1885, thymine in 1893, and cytosine in 1894. The fourth DNA base, guanine, has an avian connection—it was so named because it was discovered in Peruvian guano, in 1844. Kossel (1893) also found that the carbohydrate components of the nucleic acids are pentose sugars. By 1910, when Kossel was awarded the Nobel Prize, the two purines (adenine and guanine) and three pyrimidines (thymine, cytosine, and uracil), as well as phosphoric acid and a pentose sugar, had been recognized as constituents of the nucleic acids.

The yields of adenine, thymine, guanine, and cytosine seemed so close to a 1:1:1:1 ratio that P. A. Levene (1909) and Levene and W. A. Jacobs (1912) proposed that nucleic acids are composed of identical repeating "tetranucleotide" units arranged in a linear sequence. Levene's tetranucleotide hypothesis eventually proved to be wrong, but he also determined the structures of the sugar components of DNA and RNA, established the nature of nucleosides and nucleotides, and discovered the correct internucleotide linkage.

By 1920 the prevailing view was that the nucleic acids of plants and animals differ by the presence of uracil in plants and thymine in animals and by differences in the pentose sugars. (It is now known that these differences characterize DNA and RNA, not plants vs animals.) Both plants and animals were thought to have tetranucleotide nucleic acids.

During the 1930s nucleic acids were assumed to be simple linear tetranucleotides, not macromolecules, but by 1946 it was realized that carefully prepared nucleic acids are large molecules of high molecular weight.

The demise of the tetranucleotide hypothesis came during 1946–1950 when Erwin Chargaff and his associates (e.g., 1950) performed the first precise quantitative analyses of the constituents of DNA. They showed that adenine, guanine, cytosine, and thymine are not present in equimolar proportions, as required by the tetranucleotide hypothesis, but that DNA preparations from different species vary widely, and that the molar ratios of adenine:thymine and of guanine:cytosine are equal. Chargaff (1950:206) concluded: "The deoxypentose nucleic acids extracted from different species thus appear to be different substances or mixtures of closely related substances of a composition constant for different organs of the same species and characteristic of the species. The results serve to disprove the tetranucleotide hypothesis. Whether this is more than accidental, cannot yet be said—that in all deoxypentose nucleic acids examined thus far the molar ratios of total purines to total pyrimidines, and also of adenine to thymine and of guanine to cytosine, were not far from 1." The A = T and G = C ratios became known as Chargaff's Rules.

Thus, in the early 1950s, DNA was known to be "a high molecular weight polymer with phosphate groups linking deoxyribonucleosides between 3′ and 5′ positions of the sugar groups. The sequence of bases was unknown, although some quantitative regularities in base composition had been observed. While the detailed chemical structure of DNA had been determined, its molecular geometry remained a mystery" (Portugal and Cohen 1977:202).

The solution to the mystery of the molecular geometry of DNA began in 1912 with the development of the technique of X-ray diffraction by Max von Laue. The property that makes X-rays able to penetrate solid matter is their wavelength, which is shorter than that of visible light. When X-rays are directed at a crystalline substance at a known angle, the rays are diffracted by the lattice formed by the atoms of the crystal. The effect is similar to that of interference patterns formed when visible light is diffracted by optical gratings. The patterns of spots and lines are photographed and, by mathematical analysis, they reveal the three-dimensional structure of the crystal. The method became, and remains, the primary procedure to visualize the structure of crystals, or of fibers.

The X-ray diffraction patterns of DNA fibers produced by William Astbury and Florence Bell (1938), Maurice Wilkins et al. (1951), and Rosalind Franklin and R. G. Gosling (1953a,b) were to provide some of the most important evidence for the construction of the correct three-dimensional model of DNA by James D. Watson and Francis H. C. Crick. Watson, an American geneticist (and amateur ornithologist), and Crick, a British physicist, developed their collaboration by chance when, in 1951, Watson went to the Cavendish Laboratory at Cambridge University as a post-doctoral fellow. Crick was completing his Ph.D. and they were assigned to the same office. They shared an interest in the problem of DNA structure, and over the next two years, they assembled the evidence for their model of DNA. The scientific and sociological history of the discovery of the Watson-Crick model has been discussed and dissected by various authors, including Watson (1968). Judson's (1979) account is possibly the most detailed and objective.

Watson and Crick (1953) described their model of DNA as

two helical chains each coiled round the same axis. . . . each chain consists of phosphate di-ester groups joining β-D-deoxyribofuranose residues with 3′,5′ linkages. The two chains (but not their bases) are related by a dyad perpendicular to the fibre axis. Both chains follow right-handed helices, but owing to the dyad the sequences of the atoms in the two chains run in opposite directions. . . . the bases are on the inside of the helix and the phosphates are on the outside . . . , the sugar being roughly perpendicular to the attached base. There is a residue on each chain every 3.4 A. in the z-direction. We have assumed an angle of 36° between adjacent residues in the same chain, so that the structure repeats after 10 residues on each chain, that is, after 34 A. The distance of a phosphorus atom from the fibre axis is 10 A. As the phosphates are on the outside, cations have easy access to them. . . .

The novel feature . . . is the manner in which the two chains are held together by the purine and pyrimidine bases. The planes of the bases are perpendicular to the fibre axis. They are joined together in pairs, a single base from one chain being hydrogen-bonded to a single base from the other chain, so that the two lie side by side with identical z-co-ordinates. One of the pair must be a purine, the other a pyrimidine for bonding to occur. . . .

If it is assumed that the bases only occur in the structure in the most plausible tautomeric forms . . . it is found that only specific pairs of bases can bond together. These pairs are: adenine (purine) with thymine (pyrimidine), and guanine (purine) with cytosine (pyrimidine).

In other words, if an adenine forms one member of a pair, on either chain, then . . . the other member must be thymine; similarly for guanine and cytosine. . . . However, if only specific pairs of bases can be formed, it follows that if the sequence of bases on one chain is given, the sequence on the other chain is automatically determined.

It has been found . . . that the ratio of the amounts of adenine to thymine, and . . . of guanine to cytosine, are always very close to unity for deoxyribose nucleic acid. . . .

It has not escaped our notice that the specific pairing we have postulated immediately suggests a possible copying mechanism for the genetic material.

Subsequent X-ray diffraction, and other experimental evidence, supported the Watson-Crick structure. The discovery of the structure of DNA set off a burst of research that has never abated. The revolution in molecular biology had begun.

In 1989 (Beebe et al.) direct observation of the structure of native DNA was achieved with the scanning tunneling microscope (STM). The resolution was such that the major and minor grooves could be distinguished and the pitch of the helix could be measured. G. Lee et al. (1989) used the STM to measure the effects of dehydration on A-form and B-form DNAs and were able to detect variations in helical pitch as small as 1 angstrom. Arscott et al. (1989) examined the Z form of DNA and found "good agreement with models derived from X-ray diffraction." It may soon become possible to read the sequence of bases with this instrument.

Watson, Crick, and Wilkins shared the Nobel Prize for chemistry in 1962. Rosalind Franklin, equally deserving, had died in 1958. Linus Pauling, who had suggested a different model for DNA, stated his belief that "the discovery of the double helix and the developments that resulted from the discovery constitute the greatest advance in biological science and our understanding of life that has taken place in the last hundred years" (Portugal and Cohen 1977:271). This statement is unlikely to be disputed, although the *Origin of Species* was published 94 years before the Watson-Crick model.

The Function of DNA

After Miescher's discovery in 1869, the physiology of the cell nucleus and of nuclein were widely discussed and various functions were suggested. With the development of cytology (1870–1890) the specific staining reaction of the chromosomes was used to study their behavior during cell division, and a relationship between nuclein and heredity was proposed by several cytologists. Hertwig (1885:290) believed that it was "highly probable that nuclein is the substance that is responsible not only for fertilization, but also for the transmission of hereditary characteristics." Edmund B. Wilson (1895:4), one of the leading biologists of the time, expressed a common view when he called attention to the chemical similarity between Miescher's nuclein and the chromosomal substance, chromatin: "The precise equivalence of the chromosomes contributed by the two sexes is a physical correlative of the fact that the two sexes play, on the whole, equal parts in hereditary transmission, and it seems to show that the chromosomal substance, the chromatin, is to be regarded as the physical basis of inheritance. Now chromatin is known to be closely similar to, if not identical with a substance known as nuclein . . . which analysis shows to be a tolerably definite chemical compound of nucleic acid (a complex organic acid rich in phosphorus) and albumin [protein]. And thus we reach the remarkable conclusion that inheritance may, perhaps, be effected by the physical transmission of a particular compound from parent to offspring."

Others had come to the same conclusion, although there was no consensus about the exact role of nuclein in heredity. However, Strasburger (1909:108) argued that "chromatin cannot itself be the hereditary substance, as it . . . leaves the chromosomes, and the amount of it is subject to considerable variation in the nucleus, according to its stage of development."

Chromatin lost favor as the genetic material after 1910, and the protein components of cell nuclei were most often considered to be the carriers of hereditary traits. Proteins were known to be complex macromolecules, clearly capable of encoding a vast amount of genetic information, while the nucleic acids were believed to be simple, repeated tetranucleotides. Thus, the tetranucleotide theory of DNA structure caused the "genes are proteins" theory to be widely accepted for more than thirty years.

In 1944 the nucleic acids were proved to be the genetic material when Oswald T. Avery and his colleagues Colin MacLeod and Maclyn McCarty showed that highly purified DNA preparations could transform specific strains of pneumococcal bacteria from one type into another. "Biologists have long attempted by chemical means to induce in higher organisms predictable and specific changes which thereafter could be transmitted in series as hereditary characters. Among micro-organisms the most striking example of inheritable and specific alterations in cell structure and function that can be experimentally induced and are reproducible under well defined and adequately controlled conditions is the transformation of specific Types of Pneumococcus" (Avery et al. 1944:137). The history of this discovery, which proved that genes are made of DNA, has been recorded by one of the participants (McCarty 1985).

Doubts remained for a few years, but by the early 1950s there was general agreement that DNA, not protein, is the material basis of heredity. The demonstration by Alfred Hershey and Martha Chase (1952) that viruses infect bacteria by injecting DNA into their cells convinced most of the skeptics.

Molecular genetics now rapidly grew through interaction of a succession of new concepts and new methods. . . . The results have provided deep insights into many aspects of DNA structure and function. Today we know about how genes are replicated enzymatically, maintain extraordinary fidelity, occasionally mutate, are transcribed into RNA, are expressed as protein sequences via a genetic code, are regulated in their expression, recombine into new arrangements, exchange between a virus and a cell chromosome, and expand in number as more complex organisms evolve. In short, the structure of DNA provides for biology, as the structure of the atom does for chemistry, a set of principles and properties that account for an enormous variety of phenomena, and for the emergence of an enormous variety of arrangements of matter. Studies in molecular genetics have also filled in the missing elements in Darwin's theory of evolution, providing a detailed physical basis for heredity and for its variation. In addition, molecular genetics has provided direct support for the Darwinian picture: divergence in DNA sequence among species shows the predicted parallel to evolutionary distance. . . . Accordingly, the implications . . . are inescapable. Except for those skeptics who are willing to discard rationality, Darwin's theory has become Darwin's law (Davis 1980:79).

Discovery and Development of DNA-DNA Hybridization

The recognition of DNA as the genetic material opened a new field of biochemical genetics, and among many discoveries was the propensity of the single strands of DNA to form correctly base-paired double-stranded structures by reassociating with their homologous, complementary partners (Doty et al. 1960, Marmur and Doty 1961). The story has been told by Judson (1979) in his entertaining and informative book about the discoverers and discoveries of the properties of DNA:

When a solution of DNA was heated nearly to boiling and then cooled suddenly, the hydrogen bonds between the purine-pyrimidine pairs that held the two strands of the double helices together were ruptured and the strands unwound and floated loose. The change could be demonstrated in several ways: for example, the viscosity of the solution decreased drastically as the structure collapsed, and the bases were now exposed to attack by chemicals to which the double helix was virtually impervious.

A similar unfolding and loss of structure had long been known to afflict proteins when they were heated in solution, and was called "denaturation." But denaturing of DNA was first noted by Julius Marmur and Paul Doty, of Harvard, in 1959. . . . Marmur . . . made the interesting discovery that when he cooled a solution of denatured DNA slowly, the single strands spontaneously reconstituted double helices. At least, some of them did. When the DNA came from bacteriophage [a virus], which have very little DNA, reconstitution of double-helical molecules was quick and nearly total. When the DNA came from bacteria, which each have thirty times as much as a phage, renaturation was slower and restored about half the double helices. When it came from calf thymus cells, which have five thousand times more nucleotides than bacteria, renaturation took place hardly at all. Marmur reasoned that for successful reunion, two single strands in the solution had to find each other that were perfectly complementary, or very nearly so, in their base sequences. Thus, Marmur also discovered that reconstitution would take place only between DNA strands that came from the same or closely related organisms. Renaturation has since become the indispensable technique for testing or detecting complementary sequences (Judson 1979:455).

This remarkable property made it possible to form "hybrid" DNA molecules from the single strands of two different species and to determine the degree of genetic similarity between them, thus providing a measure of the changes in the two genomes that had occurred since the two species diverged from their most recent common ancestor. This discovery was translated into the technique of DNA-DNA hybridization, which was applied successfully to studies of viruses (Schildkraut et al. 1962) and bacteria (Schildkraut et al. 1961, McCarthy and Bolton 1963). The slow and incomplete reassociation that Marmur and Doty found with the DNA from calf thymus cells was due to the much greater complexity of eukaryotic genomes and to the long chains of DNA that are produced by gentle extraction and purification. It soon became clear that it is necessary to shear long-chain DNA into shorter fragments to obtain faster reassociation between homologous sequences and to simplify the process by separating linked sequences.

The first DNA hybrids between higher organisms were made by Ellis Bolton, Bill Hoyer, Richard Roberts, Brian McCarthy, Roy Britten, David Kohne, and other members of the Department of Terrestrial Magnetism at the Carnegie Institution of Washington, using their DNA-agar method. In this procedure long fragments of single-stranded DNA of one species are immobilized in a dilute agar gel so they cannot reassociate among themselves. Short fragments of the radiolabeled DNA of the same species (homoduplex) or of another species (heteroduplex) are then passed through the porous gel under conditions that promote the reassociation of the labeled fragments with homologous sequences of the immobilized DNA. The amount of radioactivity retained by the material in the agar gel is a measure of the percentage of hybridization between the DNAs of the two species (Hoyer et al. 1964, Hoyer and Roberts 1967).

These early attempts to apply the method to the DNAs of higher organisms were sometimes equivocal. The reason became clear in 1964 when Britten and Waring (1965) discovered that higher plants and animals have two principal types of DNA, the single strands of which reassociate at vastly different rates. One type, the "repetitive" or "multiple-copy" sequences, occurs in numerous copies in each genome, while the "single-copy" or "unique" sequences are present as one copy per genome. Because each repeated sequence has so many potential partners, they reassociate more rapidly than do the single-copy sequences. In the early DNA hybridization experiments, using total DNA, only the repeated sequences were detected. This sometimes gave erratic results and obscured the information in the single-copy sequences, which have proved to be the most useful for studies of phylogeny.

A major improvement was provided by the introduction of hydroxyapatite (HAP) thermal chromatography (Bernardi 1965, Miyazawa and Thomas 1965). HAP is a form of calcium phosphate. Under certain conditions double-stranded DNA will bind to HAP, but single strands will not. If a sample of fragmented single-stranded DNA is allowed to reassociate long enough for most of the repeated sequences to form double-stranded molecules, but not long enough for the single-copy sequences to do so, the two sets may be separated by HAP chromatography. The double strands, which are the repeated sequences, bind to the HAP, but the single strands (the single-copy sequences) do not and can be washed off and collected. Thus, HAP chromatography makes it possible to separate most of the repeated DNA from the single-copy DNA. The single-copy DNA can then be radiolabeled and used as the "tracer" in DNA-DNA hybrids.

In 1965 Britten and Kohne (1966) used HAP thermal chromatography to make the first single-copy DNA comparisons between the single-copy tracer DNA of the House Mouse (*Mus musculus*) and the unlabeled ("driver") DNA of the Norway Rat (*Rattus norvegicus*). Their method is the basis for the DNA-DNA hybridization procedures in use today.

By the late 1960s the technique had developed to the point that a high degree of confidence in it was justified, but its application to systematics was restricted because it was necessary to grow living cells in tissue culture to incorporate a radioactive label into the DNA of one of the two species to be compared. This constraint was removed when in vitro labeling with isotopic iodine was developed (Commorford 1971). With that step it became possible to prepare DNA-DNA hybrids from the genetic material of any two species from which suitably preserved tissues can be obtained. Thus, by the early 1970s the technique was ready for exploitation by systematic biologists.

At Cornell University in 1957, Sibley and Paul Johnsgard, then a graduate student, began using electrophoresis to compare avian proteins in an effort to learn more about the genetics of naturally hybridizing bird populations. The available techniques lacked the necessary resolution for this task, but the electrophoretic patterns seemed promising as evidence of relationships among the higher categories (e.g., Sibley 1960). For the 16th International Congress of Zoology, held in Washington, D.C., in late August 1963, Sibley had organized a symposium titled "New Techniques for Systematics." Present was Ellis Bolton, one of the group that developed the DNA-agar method. After the symposium, Bolton suggested to Sibley that he should consider the use of "DNA hybridization" and a visit to the Carnegie Institution followed the same day. Thus, Sibley was introduced to the DNA-agar method by Bolton, Bill Hoyer, and the other pioneers, named above. Sibley and Kendall Corbin, then a graduate student, worked with the DNA-agar method in 1963–64, but had little success because of the then unsolved problems caused by repeated sequences and in vivo isotopic labeling. In 1965, Sibley moved to Yale University and, with the collaboration of Corbin (as a post-doctoral fellow), returned to work on avian proteins. Ahlquist, who had participated in the protein work at Cornell as an undergraduate, came to Yale as a graduate student in 1966. He received the Ph.D. in 1974 with a thesis on shorebird relationships based on protein comparisons (Ahlquist 1974a,b).

In October 1973, Sibley learned of the new developments in DNA hybridization methods from Gerald F. Shields, who had just completed his doctoral studies using the HAP technique for a study of several species of passerine birds (Shields and Straus 1975). Kohne et al. (1972) had also used the method to compare the DNAs of several primates. The technique was now so promising that during 1974 Sibley and Ahlquist stopped work with proteins and prepared to use the HAP method for comparisons of avian DNAs. We produced our first HAP DNA-DNA hybrids on January 30, 1975, and continued without interruption for 11.5 years, until July 23, 1986. With the help of several laboratory assistants, graduate students, and post-doctoral fellows, we produced 30,054 DNA hybrids in 1209 experimental sets, most of which were composed of a tracer-tracer (homoduplex) hybrid and 24 tracer-driver (heteroduplex) hybrids. A semi-automatic instrument was constructed to perform thermal chromatography ("melts") on 25 hybrids simultaneously (Sibley and Ahlquist 1981a). It was this instrument that made it possible to produce the large number of DNA-DNA hybrids.

The 30,054 DNA hybrids included 26,554 among birds, 3150 among mammals (primates, rodents, shrews), and 350 among reptiles and frogs. François Catzeflis made the rodent and shrew comparisons and Ulrich Joger performed the reptile and frog comparisons. Frederick Sheldon (1987a,b) compared the DNAs of many species of herons, and Anthony Bledsoe (1988b) compared the DNAs of the New World nine-primaried oscines. Over 500 DNA hybrids among species of primates, mainly hominoids, were produced (Sibley and Ahlquist 1984a, 1987d; Sibley et al. 1990).

The comparisons presented in this volume used about 1700 of the ca. 9700 species of living birds, representing all but three of the 171 groups recognized as "families" by Wetmore (1960). Of these, 346 were used as tracers. Not all experiments were successful, but ca. 24,000 avian hybrids were good enough to provide useful information. The field work required to obtain the blood and/or tissue samples of nearly 2000 species of birds also required substantial effort. More than 200 persons participated in the field and/or laboratory work, and we have dedicated this book to them. The laboratory studies were carried out at Yale University.

Some of the properties of DNA are important in relation to the DNA-DNA hybridization technique, some are not. The technique views double-stranded DNA molecules as units with different chemical bonding energies, proportional to the degree of base pairing between the two strands. The genetic information encoded in the sequences of bases and the structure and function of the various subunits of the genome are irrelevant; only the base pairing between the complementary bases and the interactions between the vertically stacked bases in homologous sequences are detected and measured.

DNA-DNA comparisons contain evidence of phylogeny because genetic information is encoded in base sequences and genetic evolution is recorded in the form of changes in base sequences over time. DNA-DNA hybridization works because mismatches between bases in DNA-DNA hybrids reduce the melting temperature of each hybrid duplex molecule in proportion to the number of base sequence differences that have evolved since the two species whose DNAs form the duplex last shared a common ancestor.

One of the most interesting and controversial facets of molecular evolution concerns the rate, or rates, at which base changes are incorporated into the genomes of organisms. Is there a single, universal "molecular clock," many such clocks, or is the idea of regularity in the accumulation of base changes only a myth?

In birds we have found that the average genomic rate of base changes is correlated with the age at first breeding. What we observe suggests that birds apparently accumulate selectively neutral, or near neutral, mutations at a rate that is inversely related to the age at first breeding. Thus, birds that begin to breed at the age of one year (over 80% of all species) have a faster rate than those that do not begin to breed until two years old, and so on. Species that breed more often than once per year (e.g., the estrildine finches) have a faster rate than those that begin to breed at one year of age. Since the age at maturity is proportional to the generation time, it appears that the rate of accession of mutations is adjusted by natural selection to be approximately constant per generation. This subject is controversial and the answer or answers are not yet clear. It is discussed in chapters 12 and 13.

The effects of differences in ages at first breeding are seen as differences in branch lengths when dendrograms are constructed from DNA-DNA hybridization data. Ages at first reproduction longer than one or two years produce shorter branches relative to outgroup species, and shorter-than-one-year species produce longer branches in such comparisons. The correlation between branch lengths and delayed maturity is clear; we have found no species with delayed maturity which did not also have shorter branch lengths when compared with related species that breed at one year of age. The relative positions of melting curves also reflect different ages at first breeding.

The effect of delayed maturity became apparent after we had made a large number of DNA-DNA comparisons among the larger species of non-passerine birds, most of which do not begin to breed until more than one or two years of age. Our earlier work was with passerines, most of which breed at the age of one year, and we had found that all passerines appear to be evolving at, or close to, the same average genomic rate. From this we assumed that there is a uniform average rate in birds, which is approximately true for birds with the same age at maturity. Thus, there seem to be as many average genomic rates of evolution in birds as there are differences in generation times, but it must be emphasized that the differences among all birds are relatively small. They do not approach the disparity among mammals in which small rodents are evolving about 10 times as fast as hominoid primates (Catzeflis et al. 1987).

The DNA-DNA hybridization technique is based on the properties of chemical bonds that are broken by heat. The technique may appear complex when the details are examined and the procedures are described, but it is essentially an extremely simple method because it is objective and quantitative. To understand and evaluate the results of DNA-DNA hybridization it is necessary to be somewhat familiar with the properties of DNA and the techniques by which the data are produced and analyzed. In the following pages we review a small sample of the enormous literature on the structure and properties of DNA; the dissociation, reassociation, and thermal stability of DNA duplexes; the sequence organization of the genome; and other subjects with varying degrees of pertinence to the DNA hybridization technique. These sections are intended to provide background information, to answer questions that may arise in the minds of readers, and to offer an introduction to a vast literature for those wishing to use the DNA-DNA hybridization technique. Molecular biology and the biochemistry of DNA are among the most rapidly developing fields of science, and some of the material in these sections will be outdated by the time this book appears.

CHAPTER TWO

Structure and Properties of DNA

Deoxyribonucleic acid (DNA) is the genetic material of most of the organisms on Earth. The exceptions are certain viruses, which have ribonucleic acid (RNA) as the hereditary material. Each single strand of the double helix of the Watson-Crick structure of DNA is a chain of four kinds of chemical units, the nucleotides. Each nucleotide is composed of three subunits: a five-carbon (pentose) deoxyribose sugar, a phosphate group, and a nitrogenous base. The structures of the sugar and the phosphate group are the same in all nucleotides, but there are four types of bases that characterize the four kinds of nucleotides. Each base is a ring composed of carbon and nitrogen atoms. The bases, adenine (A), guanine (G), thymine (T), and cytosine (C), are of two types; adenine and guanine are purines, with fused five- and six-member rings; thymine and cytosine are pyrimidines, which have a six-member ring. A nucleoside consists of a base plus a pentose sugar. The four nucleosides are adenosine, guanosine, cytidine, and thymidine. In RNA the sugar is ribose, and uracil (U) occurs in place of thymine. The nucleoside of uracil is uridine.

The backbone of a DNA chain consists of an alternating series of pentose sugar and phosphate groups in which the 5′ carbon of one pentose ring is bonded to the 3′ carbon of the adjacent pentose ring by a phosphate group. Thus, the phosphate-sugar series consists of 5′–3′ linkages, and the chain has directionality; one end is the 5′ end, the other is 3′. When base sequences are written the one-letter symbols A, G, T, and C are arranged with the 5′ end at the left, e.g., 5′G-A-C-T-A-T-G-G-A-etc. 3′.

In double-stranded DNA the four types of bases form complementary pairs composed of a purine and a pyrimidine: an adenine in one chain always pairs with a thymine in the other chain, and guanines pair only with cytosines. This A-T (or T-A) and G-C (or C-G) base pairing means that the two strands of the double helix are complementary base sequences. The base sequence of one strand runs in the 5′ to 3′ direction, and the other from 3′ to 5′. The two strands spiral around one another, forming the famous double helix described by Watson and Crick (1953). (Fig. 1a.)

The A-T and G-C compositions of the base pairs are dictated by the structural and

DNA
DOUBLE
HELIX

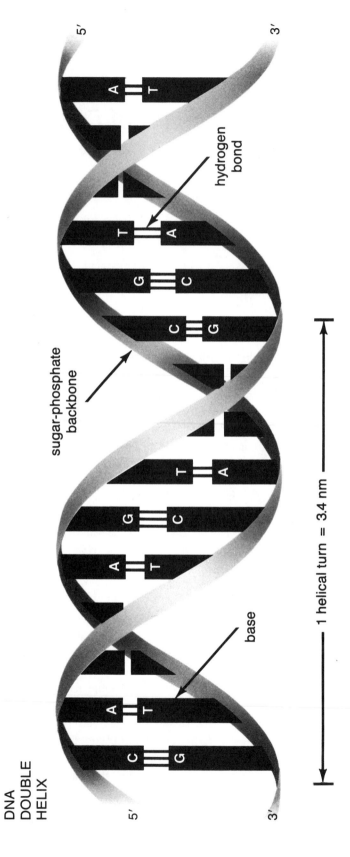

FIGURE 1a. DNA Structure, double helix.

chemical constraints imposed by the geometry of the double helix. Of the six possible combinations of the four bases, only the Watson-Crick configuration of A-T and G-C pairs is symmetric in relation to the helical structure and other properties of the two sugar-phosphate backbones, and to one another. If other combinations occur (A-G, T-G, C-T, C-A) the symmetry is distorted and hydrogen bonding is prevented. Thus, mismatched base pairs reduce the total bonding energy between the two strands.

Stabilizing Forces: Hydrogen Bonding and Base Stacking

The structural and functional aspects of the DNA helix depend on two kinds of interactions between the bases: those in the horizontal plane due to hydrogen bonding, and those in the vertical plane due to base stacking.

HYDROGEN BONDING

Hydrogen bonds are formed when a hydrogen atom (H) acts as a connector between two atoms of higher electronegativity. The strength of H-bonds depends on charges located on the participating atoms. H-bonds between DNA bases involve nitrogen (N) and oxygen (O) atoms, as diagrammed in Fig. 1b. A-T base pairs are held together by two H-bonds, G-C pairs by three H-bonds.

The bonding energies of H-bonds are 3-6 kcal/mole, while those of covalent bonds are 83-99 kcal/mole; thus, H-bonds are 20 to 30 times weaker than the covalent bonds that link the atoms of the nucleotides together (Saenger 1984:117). Because the weakest bonds in the DNA structure are those holding the base pairs together, they rupture ("melt") first when DNA is heated in solution. This is important for the success of the DNA-DNA hybridization technique because it makes it possible to separate duplex DNA into single strands without damaging the rest of the molecule. Because A-T base pairs are linked by two hydrogen bonds they melt at a lower temperature than do the three-bonded G-C pairs. A-T pairs have a total bonding energy of -7.00 kcal/mole; G-C pairs of -16.79 kcal/mole (Saenger 1984:131). Thus, in a solution containing ca. 0.05 sodium (Na^+) a sequence composed only of A-T base pairs melts at ca. 54°C and a sequence composed of G-C base pairs melts at ca. 105°C. Sequences composed of mixtures of A-T and G-C pairs melt between these extremes as a function of their composition. For example, avian DNAs, which are composed of about 42% G-C pairs and 58% A-T pairs, have a median melting temperature (T_m) of 86–87°C. (See "Base Composition" in chapter 5.)

The lability of hydrogen bonds is also fundamental for the function of DNA as the genetic material. In the living organism duplex DNA is separated into single strands by the action of enzymes during the replication process. As Watson and Crick (1953:737) noted, the double-stranded structure, made up of complementary hydrogen-bonded base pairs, suggested "a possible copying mechanism for the genetic material."

Westheimer (1987) examined the question of "why Nature chose phosphates" as dominant elements of "the living world":

Phosphate esters and anhydrides dominate the living world but are seldom used as intermediates by organic chemists. Phosphoric acid is specially adapted for its role in nucleic acids because it can link two nucleotides and still ionize; the resulting negative charge serves both to stabilize the diesters against

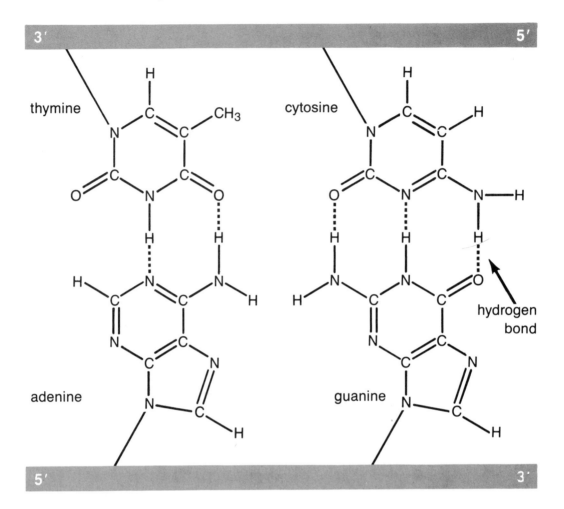

FIGURE 1b. DNA Structure, hydrogen bonding between base pairs.

hydrolysis and to retain the molecules within a lipid membrane. A similar explanation for stability and retention also holds for phosphates that . . . serve as energy sources. . . . No other residue appears to fulfill the multiple roles of phosphate in biochemistry. . . .

The genetic materials DNA and RNA are phosphodiesters. . . . Why did nature choose phosphates? . . .

Granted that phosphates are ubiquitous in biochemistry, what do they do? The answer is that they can do almost everything. . . .

The existence of a genetic material such as DNA requires a compound for a connecting link that is at least divalent. In order that the resulting material remain within a membrane, it should always be charged, and therefore the linking unit should have a third, ionizable group. The linkage is conveniently made by ester bonds, but, in order that the ester be hydrolytically stable, that charge should be negative and should be physically close to the ester groups. All these conditions are met by phosphoric acid, and no alternative is obvious. . . .

We can understand the choices made both by chemists and by the process of natural selection. They are both correct (pp. 1173, 1177).

BASE-STACKING INTERACTIONS

The paired bases are flat structures that lie nearly perpendicular to the axis of the DNA helix. In the double helical configuration the bases are stacked, one above the next, "like coins in a roll." Stacking is important for the stabilization of the helical structure and adjacent bases are stacked such that their planes are parallel at the van der Waals distance of ca. 3.4 angstroms (Saenger 1984:132).

The hydrogen bonding between base pairs depends on base composition, but base-stacking energies are influenced by both composition and sequence. The melting temperature of a DNA sequence is remarkably sensitive to the base-stacking forces which differ for most dimeric combinations of bases, and hence for all longer sequences. Purine-purine stacks are the most stable, pyrimidine-purine stacks less so, and pyrimidine-pyrimidine stacks are least stable. Table 1 presents the 10 stacking energies for 16 dimers.

Nussinov (1984) analyzed the stacked dinucleotide preferences in sequences comprising more than 500,000 bases. Consistent preferences in stacked doublets were observed in the ca. 122 kb prokaryotic set, the 290 kb eukaryotic set, and the 85 kb mitochondrial set. In eukaryotes purine-purine (A,G) and pyrimidine-pyrimidine (C,T) stacked dinucleotide pairs are

TABLE 1. Total Stacking Energies in Kilocalories per Mole of Dimer, for 16 Possible Dimers in the B-DNA Arrangement. The upper left base in each dimer is 5', the upper right base 3'. From Saenger 1984:139.

Stacked Dimers		Stacking Energies
C-G G-C		−14.59
C-G A-T	T-A G-C	−10.51
C-G T-A	A-T G-C	−9.81
G-C C-G		−9.69
G-C G-C	C-G C-G	−8.26
T-A A-T		−6.57
G-C T-A	A-T C-G	−6.57
G-C T-A	T-A C-G	−6.78
A-T A-T	T-A T-A	−5.37
A-T T-A		−3.82

preferred over purine-pyrimidine and pyrimidine-purine pairs, and there are numerous preferences between any two nucleotides. For example, CT>AC; CC>GT; TG>GA; TT>TA; AA>AT; and CA>TC. Hierarchies are also apparent, e.g., TG>CC>AC>TA>CG; CT->TC>AT>TA>CG; GG>GC>GT>TA>CG; and AA>GA>AC>TA>CG. The average frequencies of the 16 dimeric doublets in eukaryotic nuclear DNAs are given in Table 2.

Since the dimer preference patterns have been conserved throughout evolutionary history their occurrence is presumably based on a common functional requirement. The low frequency of the CG doublet may be related to its known propensity as a mutational hot spot and methylation site. Other dimer preferences are probably related to structural requirements, for example, nucleosome packaging and steric strain relationships. Hanai and Wada (1988) analyzed 112 human DNA sequences with respect to dinucleotide frequency and amino acid composition of the proteins coded for by the DNA.

The forces that stabilize paired and stacked bases include an electrostatic interaction component, a van der Waals component (including London dispersion forces), a polarization component, and a hydration component. The base-dependent interactions involved in the calculation of energy differences between the helical duplex and the single-stranded random coil states are base-pairing, base-stacking, base-backbone, and possibly cation interactions in the grooves of the helix. The only experimental quantity available to determine the parameters of these interactions is the median melting temperature (T_m) of DNA duplexes (Ornstein and Fresco 1983).

Ornstein and Fresco (1983) used the T_ms for 20 DNA duplexes with different repeating base sequences to develop an "empirical potential method" to compute the apparent enthalpies for the melting transition from the double-stranded helix to single-stranded random coils.

Table 2.   Average Dinucleotide Frequencies of Occurrence in Nuclear DNAs of Eukaryotes.
From Nussinov 1984:115.

Doublet	Frequency
TG	1.26
CT	1.24
AA	1.16
CA	1.14
AG	1.11
CC	1.08
GG	1.08
TT	1.07
GA	1.05
GC	1.03
TC	1.03
AC	0.90
GT	0.86
AT	0.85
TA	0.65
CG	0.54

Enthalpy (H) is a measure of the total heat content of a system and ΔH is the difference between the initial and final states. Thus, average ΔH is a measure (in kcal/mole base pair) of the energy required for melting base sequences.

Ornstein and Fresco (1983) found that their calculated average ΔH value is linearly correlated with T_m (coefficient of correlation, r, = 0.99) for a large array of sequences of different lengths and compositions. A chain length greater than 60 bp produces a T_m within 2–3°C of that of much larger polymers, for example, 600 bp. Below ca. 60 bp there is an exponential dependence of T_m on chain length. For DNA sequences of various lengths and compositions between ca. 200 and 400 bp, the T_ms are less than 1°C below that of a duplex of 10^5 bp (or greater) in length, and chain lengths between 400 and 600 bp were calculated to have T_ms only 0.3–0.5°C below that of a duplex of infinite length (i.e., 10^5 bp or greater).

For DNA sequences greater than ca. 100 bp, the T_m varies with the composition of the constituent duplexes, as in Table 3.

T_ms also vary with the composition of the complementary dinucleotide fragments, as indicated in Table 4. Hall et al. (1980) showed that a sequence of 60 bp has a T_m 8°C below that of a 500 bp fragment. For a DNA sequence with an average composition the T_m reduction equals 500 divided by the length in bp.

The base-stacking and base-pairing energy values for various complementary dinucleotide fragments are given in Table 5.

In Tables 1–5 it is apparent that T_ms and bonding energies are related to G-C content, as Marmur and Doty (1959) first showed for natural DNAs. However, the data presented by Ornstein and Fresco (1983) "also emphasize that nearest-neighbor stacking interaction, i.e., sequence, makes an additional substantial contribution that moderates significantly the primary dependence on G-C content" (p. 1996). In fact, it is possible to have combinations of complementary dinucleotide fragments with 0%, 50%, and 100% G-C content that have the same stability, which clearly demonstrates "the important role of sequence-dependent stacking of base pairs." It is also evident from the data in Table 4 that for CDFs with the same G-C content, the purine (3'–5') pyrimidine CDF is always more stable than the reverse pyrimidine (3'–5') purine CDF. This trend is apparently related to the differential overlap of the aromatic rings.

Ornstein and Fresco (1983:1980) concluded that "stacking rather than base-pairing

TABLE 3. T_ms (in 0.05 M Na$^+$) for DNA Duplexes of Various Chain Lengths and Compositions. From Ornstein and Fresco 1983:1989.

Duplex	T_m °C	Chain Length, Base Pairs
d(G-C)$_n$: d(G-C)$_n$	105	457
d(A-C)$_n$: d(G-T)$_n$	83	292
d(G-A-T)$_n$: d(A-T-C)$_n$	76	354
d(A-G)$_n$: d(C-T)$_n$	75	667
d(A)$_n$: d(T)$_n$	61	5000
d(A-T)$_n$: d(A-T)$_n$	54	2800

TABLE 4. Normalized T_ms and Contributing Complementary Dinucleotide Fragments (CDFs) for DNA Duplexes. From Ornstein and Fresco 1983:1991.

T_m °C	Contributing CDFs
105.5	[C-G/G-C] + [G-C/C-G]
95.5	[G-C/G-C]
95.1	[G-C/A-T] + [C-G/G-C] + [A-T/C-G]
90.6	[G-C/G-C] + [T-A/G-C] + [G-C/T-A]
83.8	[C-G/A-T] + [A-T/C-G]
76.7	[A-T/G-C] + [T-A/A-T] + [G-C/T-A]
75.9	[A-T/A-T] + [C-G/A-T] + [A-T/C-G]
75.3	[G-C/A-T] + [A-T/G-C]
72.7	[G-C/A-T] + [T-A/G-C] + [A-T/T-A]
71.1	[T-A/T-A] + [C-G/T-A] + [T-A/C-G]
61.1	[A-T/A-T]
56.9	[A-T/A-T] + [T-A/A-T] + [A-T/T-A]
54.1	[T-A/A-T] + [A-T/T-A]

Normalized T_m = corrected for chain-length variation.
In each pair, e.g., G-C/C-G, then Gs are 3', the Cs 5', etc.

interactions appear to contribute most to the differential stabilities of duplexes with different sequences."

These data and conclusions are important for DNA-DNA hybridization because they show that the melting behavior of a DNA-DNA duplex is a sensitive indicator of its base sequence.

"Breathing" and Branch Migration

If double-stranded DNA is dissolved in tritiated water (H_2O in which the hydrogens are radiolabeled with tritium, ^3H, forming ^3H_2O), there is a rapid exchange between the hydrogen-

TABLE 5. Component and Total Calculated Δ Enthalpy Values (ΔH_{calc}) of DNA Complementary Dinucleotide Fragments (CDFs). From Ornstein and Fresco 1983:1993.

CDF	Energies in kcal/mole base pair		
	Stacking	Base Pairing	Total
C-G/G-C	−24.69	−4.64	−29.33
C-G/A-T	−24.78	−3.77	−28.55
G-C/A-T	−24.52	−3.77	−28.29
G-C/G-C	−23.48	−4.64	−28.12
T-A/A-T	−24.77	−2.89	−27.66
G-C/C-G	−22.98	−4.64	−27.62
G-C/T-A	−22.43	−3.77	−26.20
C-G/T-A	−22.42	−3.77	−26.19
A-T/A-T	−23.18	−2.89	−26.07
A-T/T-A	−21.25	−2.89	−24.14

bonded protons of the bases and the $^3H^+$ ions in the water. This indicates that the hydrogen bonds between one, or a few, base pairs are opening and closing at frequent intervals, forming transient, short, single-stranded "bubbles" in the double helix. This phenomenon is called breathing, and it is thought to enable regulatory proteins to interact with the DNA base sequence. As might be expected, breathing occurs most often in regions of low bonding energies, such as A-T-rich sequences. This may be the basis for the functions of the "TATA box" and the AATAAA poly (A) signal during the transcription process. (See chapter 3.)

The breathing motion of a single base pair apparently induces, or permits, the double helix to bend or kink at that point. The breathing frequency of a stable duplex DNA involves about 1% of the bases at any moment, and the enthalpy of the base-pair opening is ca. 5 kcal. The opening of base pairs in double-stranded DNA is a prerequisite for replication and transcription and is possibly a factor in the recognition, flexibility, and structure of DNA.

The breathing process opens the double helix at intervals, and this permits the process of branch migration to occur. Branch migration is the displacement of one base-paired strand in a double helix by another strand that is also able to pair with the same complementary strand. Branch migration replacement is thought to occur during the formation of DNA-DNA hybrids when a single-stranded fragment replaces one of the two fragments that have formed a double helix. This is possible if the invader fragment is a better match for the complementary strand than the fragment that is replaced, i.e., if the invader provides a more favorable bonding energy level than the strand it replaces. The result is that the perfection of base pairing continues to improve during the time that single strands are incubated together when DNA-DNA hybrid duplexes are being formed (Manning 1983, Freifelder 1983:116, 737). Guéron et al. (1987) determined base-pair lifetimes as ca. 10 milliseconds at room temperature, suggested that there is a single mode of base-pair opening, and that the other base of an open pair probably functions as the catalyst for proton exchange.

Chromosomes and Nucleosomes

In the nuclei of the cells of higher organisms the DNA occurs in the chromosomes. Each chromosome contains one molecule of DNA in a continuous chain of nucleotides. For example, in each of the 46 human chromosomes the DNA molecule is ca. 4 centimeters long, thus the total length of the duplex DNA in one somatic cell is nearly 2 meters, packed into a nucleus that is 0.5 micrometer in diameter. This is equivalent to a fine thread 0.1 millimeter in diameter and 100 kilometers long, squeezed into a sphere 25 centimeters in diameter (Saenger 1984:8). The DNA in the nucleus of the average avian cell is ca. two-thirds as long as that in a human cell.

DNA strands examined under the electron microscope appear to be composed of a series of beadlike particles connected by short DNA strands. The beads, called nucleosomes, consist of the DNA strand complexed with a set of five proteins, the histones. Each nucleosome consists of two parts, a core particle and a linker segment which connects adjacent core particles.

The detailed structure of the histone proteins in the core particle of the red cell DNA of the Domestic Fowl (*G. gallus*) has been determined by X-ray crystallography at a resolution of 3.3 angstroms (Burlingame et al. 1985). The four core histones are complexed in an (H2A-

H2B-H3-H4)$_2$ octamer around which about 165 base pairs of DNA are wrapped in two superhelical turns. Histone 1 appears to be bound to the outside of this particle and to interact with the linker DNA, which leads to the next nucleosome. The octamer is a prolate ellipsoid 110 angstroms long and 65–70 angstroms in diameter, and "its general shape is that of a rugby ball." The octamer is tripartite, consisting of a central (H3-H4)$_2$ tetramer flanked by two H2A-H2B dimers. "The DNA helix, placed around the octamer in a path suggested by features on the surfaces of the protein appears like a spring holding the H2A-H2B dimers at either end of the (H3-H4)$_2$ tetramer."

Some of the details of this structure of the histone core have been challenged by Klug et al. (1985) and Uberbacher and Bunick (1985). Uberbacher et al. (1986) found that the conformation of the histone octamer depends upon the specific salt used as the solvent. In 2 M sodium chloride the octamer is similar in size and shape to the histone component of crystallized core nucleosomes; in 3.5 M ammonium sulfate the octamer is an ellipsoid approximately 114 by 62 angstroms. Thus, the rugby-ball shape described by Burlingame et al. (1985) is due to the particular salt conditions used.

The linker DNA varies in length from 14 bases in the fungus *Aspergillus* to 102 in the sea urchin *Strongylocentrotus*. The length of the linker segment also varies within species, for example, from 52 to 58 bases in different tissues of the Norway Rat (*Rattus norvegicus*). In the Domestic Fowl (*G. gallus*) the linker segment in oviduct cells contains 56 bases and in the erythrocytes 67–72. Thus, the total nucleosome length (core plus linker) varies from at least 154 to 241 bases in different organisms (Kornberg 1974, Chambon 1978, Botchan and Watson 1978, Dubochet and Noll 1978, Olins and Olins 1978, Isenberg 1979, Adams et al. 1981:90, Lewin 1983:457, Klug and Butler 1983, Saenger 1984:439).

A sixth type of histone, H5, occurs in the erythrocytes of birds, amphibians, and fish. It is similar to H1 in structure and function and occupies the same position as H1 in the nucleosome. The genes coding for H1 and H5 have homologous segments, indicating that they evolved from a common ancestral gene following an ancient gene duplication (Ruiz-Carillo et al. 1983).

The nucleosomes organize the DNA into a structure about one-sixth as long as the extended DNA strand. The strings of nucleosomes are then folded again into 20–30 nanometer diameter chromatin fibers that fold the DNA by another factor of 5 to 10. The chromatin fibers are further folded to make up the chromosomes.

Burlingame et al. (1985:553) suggest that the structure of nucleosomes "may modulate protein-protein and protein-DNA interactions . . . resulting in coupled conformational changes in the protein-DNA complex . . . [which] may ultimately be manifested as functional transitions in the chromosome."

The Genetic Code

At least two kinds of genetic information are encoded in the base sequences of nuclear DNA. Structural genes specify the sequence of amino acids in structural proteins and regulatory genes control the expression of the genetic message via regulatory proteins.

The genetic code that directs the sequential assembly of amino acids to form a protein chain is composed of triplets of the four kinds of bases, thus there are 64 possible combinations, or codons. Since there are only 20 different amino acids that enter into the structure of proteins, there are more codons than would seem to be needed. In most cases an amino acid is coded for by more than one codon, i.e., the code is redundant (Table 6). Three of the codons (TAA, TAG, TGA) are STOP signals for the termination of the translation of a base sequence—a gene—into a messenger RNA sequence. (See chapter 3.)

Thus, the genetic message is written in the linear sequence of bases and it is interpreted indirectly via the extrinsic process of protein synthesis involving messenger RNA, ribosomes, transfer RNAs, and a series of enzymes (Fig. 2). Perhaps the most remarkable feature of the genetic code of the nuclear genome is its virtual universality; the same triplet codons specify the same amino acids in viruses, bacteria, and the nuclear DNAs of higher organisms. This indicates that the genetic code must have been established early in the evolution of life on Earth (Lewin 1983:72). Exceptions to the universality of the code are known in several microorganisms and a yeast. In the ciliate protozoa (e.g., *Paramecium*) TAA and TAG codons specify

TABLE 6. The Genetic Code of Eukaryotic DNA. Each of the 64 codons is composed of three bases, of which 61 code for amino acids and 3 are STOP codons that signal chain termination. The table is read from left (5′) to right (3′), e.g., a triplet in which A is the first base, G the second, and C the third codes for serine, GCC = alanine, etc. The STOP codons are TAA, TAG, and TGA. The code is degenerate because most of the 20 amino acids are designated by more than one triplet; serine, argenine, and leucine are each coded for by 6 codons, 15 amino acids are coded for by 2, 3, or 4 codons, and only tryptophan and methionine by single codons.

First Base	Second Base				Third Base
	T	C	A	G	
T	Phe	Ser	Tyr	Cys	T
	Phe	Ser	Tyr	Cys	C
	Leu	Ser	STOP	STOP	A
	Leu	Ser	STOP	Trp	G
C	Leu	Pro	His	Arg	T
	Leu	Pro	His	Arg	C
	Leu	Pro	Gln	Arg	A
	Leu	Pro	Gln	Arg	G
A	Ile	Thr	Asn	Ser	T
	Ile	Thr	Asn	Ser	C
	Ile	Thr	Lys	Arg	A
	Met	Thr	Lys	Arg	G
G	Val	Ala	Asp	Gly	T
	Val	Ala	Asp	Gly	C
	Val	Ala	Glu	Gly	A
	Val	Ala	Glu	Gly	G

PROTEIN SYNTHESIS

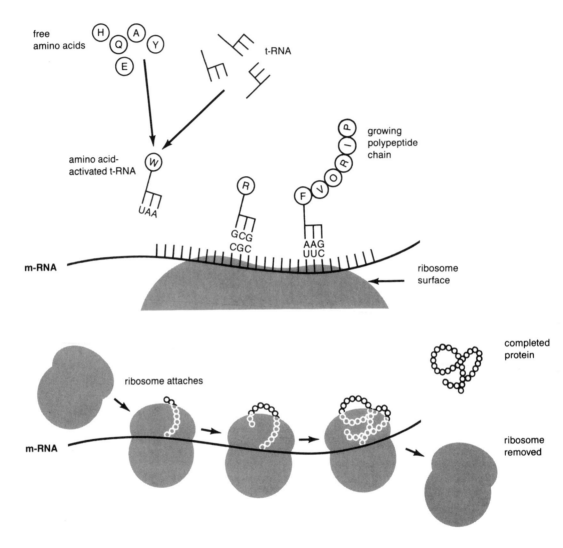

FIGURE 2. Protein synthesis. Messenger RNA (mRNA) is synthesized by transcription as a complementary copy of one strand of DNA. Translation of the mRNA sequence depends on base pairing between codons of the mRNA and complementary anticodons of transfer RNA (tRNA) molecules. The tRNAs carry amino acids. The mechanics of ordering the tRNAs on the mRNA are accomplished by ribosomes that attach to the mRNA and move along it synthesizing the polypeptide chain.

glutamine, instead of STOP as in eukaryotes (review by Grivell 1986). Termination codons are also used to code for amino acids in *Mycoplasma* and *Tetrahymena*. In *E. coli* the TGA termination codon codes for selenocysteine. In the non-spore-forming yeast *Candida cylindracea* the universal codon for leucine, CTG, codes for serine. In mitochondrial DNA there are several departures from the nuclear code (Kawaguchi et al. 1989).

CHAPTER THREE

Gene Structure and Function

A gene is a sequence of nucleotides that codes for the sequence of amino acids in a protein. There are many genes in each chromosome and it is estimated that the minimum number of genes in the mammalian genome is about 30,000; the maximum estimate is ca. 90,000 (Cavalier-Smith 1985:84). Thirty thousand genes would account for only 1% to 3% of the total DNA; the other 97% or more is non-coding DNA which may have structural functions or compose introns, pseudogenes, and the accessory sequences associated with genes but is not transcribed into messenger RNA. Polymorphic loci and repeated sequences also account for some of the discrepancy. The fruit fly, *Drosophila*, has a genome about one-twentieth the size of that of a mammal but containing possibly 10,000 genes, thus a mammalian genome is unlikely to be more than about six times as complex as that of an insect (Alberts et al. 1983:406). The protein-coding sequences may account for as much as 10% of the single-copy fraction of the genome.

With the development of nucleic acid sequencing techniques in the 1970s it became possible to determine the detailed structure of individual genes, and a large number have been sequenced. The techniques were described by Maxam and Gilbert (1980) and Sanger (1981). Lewin (1983:54–61), Alberts et al. (1983:189–190), and Stryer (1988) provide brief descriptions. Fig. 3 is a diagram of the structure and organization of a typical eukaryotic gene.

Introns and Exons

One of the early tenets of molecular genetics was that the sequence of amino acids in a protein is colinear with the sequence of nucleotides in the gene coding for that protein. Colinearity is the rule in the prokaryotic genomes of bacteria, but the genes of eukaryotes are composed of two kinds of subunits: those that code for the protein sequence and those that do not. Early evidence from electron microscopy was confirmed by Jeffreys and Flavell (1977), who showed that the base sequence coding for the β-globin chain of the European Rabbit

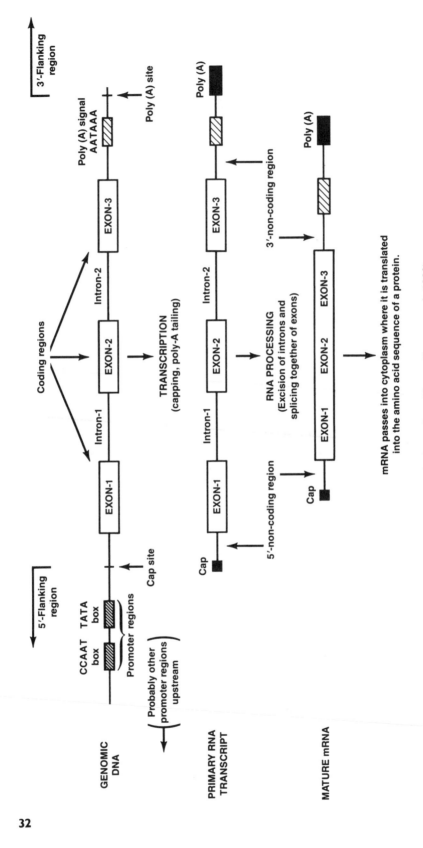

FIGURE 3. RNA processing in a eukaryotic protein coding gene. (Redrawn from Hewett-Emmett et al. 1982)

(*Oryctolagus cuniculus*) is split by a 600-base insert that is transcribed into messenger RNA (mRNA) but not translated into the amino acid sequence of the protein. A similar intervening sequence of ca. 550 bases was found to interrupt the β-globin gene of the House Mouse (*Mus musculus*) (Tilghman et al. 1978). It is now apparent that intervening sequences, or introns, are a common element of the protein-coding genes of eukaryotes. Thus, a eukaryotic gene is composed of two major subunits. The exons are the regions that code for the protein product; therefore they are transcribed into mRNA and translated into the amino acid sequence of a protein. The introns are transcribed but are later spliced out of the precursor of the mRNA to produce a messenger RNA that consists only of the exons. Colinearity still exists between the exons and the amino acid sequence of the protein, but the base distances in the gene may not correspond to the distances within the protein. Some eukaryotic genes are not interrupted by introns and are colinear with their protein product, but the majority contain from one to many intervening sequences.

Many protein-coding structural genes are much longer than their mRNAs, and the total precursor mRNA sequence is known as heterogeneous nuclear RNA, or hnRNA. The average length of mRNAs is about 2 kb, but hnRNAs are known to range up to 22 kb. The reduction in size from that of hnRNA to mRNA is partially due to the processing of the introns, but this accounts for only part of the difference. The hnRNA exists in the form of an extended RNA chain within the nucleus, associated with several proteins. The mRNA is derived from hnRNA (Lewin 1983:420).

M. W. Smith (1988) made a statistical analysis of the size distributions of exons, introns, and other gene parts. The frequency distributions of the sizes of seven gene parts were most normal when transformed to fit a lognormal distribution. The average length of introns was 603 bp and of exons 138 bp. The mRNA untranslated region following the termination codon averages 205 bp, and the average length of the region preceding the start codon is 62 bp. The average mRNA (972 bp) plus intervening DNA (3174 bp) sums to within 300 bp of the transcription unit which averages 4448 bp. Smith concluded that "These nonrandom patterns in gene structure demonstrate that models of gene evolution must incorporate selective processes."

Transcription and Translation

See Fig. 3. The genetic message is read and transcribed into mRNA by an enzyme, RNA polymerase, that begins its task by recognizing and binding to specific sites upstream (i.e., toward the 5' end of the sequence) from the "cap site" where the transcription of the DNA sequence into mRNA will begin. Two DNA sequence elements are required for the regulation of genes that encode mRNA in eukaryotes: promoters and enhancers. Promoter regions are typically about 100 bp in length and a typical promoter for RNA polymerase binding includes an AT-rich region composed of specific, short base sequences that recur in all (or most) eukaryotic genes. One such "consensus" site, located 25–30 bases upstream from the cap site, has the sequence TATTAA or TATA and is called the TATA box, or the Goldberg-Hogness box. The TATA box functions primarily to ensure that transcripts are accurately initiated. Another upstream promoter element (UPE), 70–80 bases upstream, has the sequence CCAAT. This and other UPEs increase the rate of transcription. Additional recognition sites may be present still farther upstream. The TATA box is flanked by two GC-rich regions. If the segment containing the TATA box is experimentally altered, transcription levels decline, and new mRNAs are synthesized whose starting sites are displaced from the normal one. The distance between the TATA box and the UPEs is also critical, suggesting that regulatory proteins bound to the UPE interact with a protein (or proteins) bound to the TATA box (Hewett-Emmett et al. 1982, Maniatis et al. 1987).

The RNA polymerase copies the sequence of one DNA strand of the gene by adding nucleotides to the mRNA strand that are complementary to those in the DNA strand. Transcription begins at the cap site and proceeds in the 3' direction via the exons and introns and beyond the poly (A) sequence (AATAAA) for some 11–30 bases to the poly (A) site where transcription stops and the poly (A) tail is added. The cap is attached to the first nucleotide at the 5' end of the primary transcript, which is usually an adenine-cytosine dinucleotide. Capping involves the addition of 7-methylguanosine triphosphate to the adenine. The cap is added to the free 5' end of the growing mRNA chain before the RNA polymerase has transcribed more than about 20 bases. The function of the cap is not clear, but it may serve to promote translation. The poly (A) tail, composed of a series of ca. 200 adenine nucleotides, is added to the 3' end of the mRNA transcript after the RNA chain is cut about 20 nucleotides downstream from the AATAAA poly (A) sequence. The long string of adenines may protect the mRNA transcript from attack by cytoplasmic enzymes. Wickens and Stephenson (1984) found that mutations in the AATAAA (AAUAAA in mRNA) sequence prevent cleavage of the mRNA precursor in simian virus 40 (SV 40). If cleavage is prevented a new 3' terminus cannot be formed, and the mRNA transcript is not transported from the nucleus to the cytoplasm.

As the RNA polymerase travels from 5' to 3' the RNA separates from the DNA as the primary RNA transcript is synthesized, but the RNA molecule does not separate completely until the 3' end is formed. Thus, the capped and tailed primary RNA transcript contains the exons, introns, and the 5' and 3' non-translated regions. The RNA transcript is a sequence of bases complementary to the DNA coding sequence, but the thymines in the DNA are represented by uracils in the RNA. The other three bases—guanine, cytosine, and adenine— are the same in DNA and RNA.

The RNA transcript is then processed, which involves the excision of the introns, the splicing together of the exons, and the addition of the poly (A) sequence. (Breathnach and Chambon 1981, Hewett-Emmett et al. 1982, Darnell 1982, 1983, 1985, Padgett et al. 1984, Felsenfeld 1985, Stryer 1988). The details of the process are complex, involving the formation of a multicomponent complex, the spliceosome, which contains at least five small nuclear ribonucleoprotein particles (snRNPs, or snurps), U1, U2, U4, U5, and U6. The U stands for uracil, a major component of the snRNA. A complex containing precursor RNA and the four most abundant snRNP particles is involved in the formation of the spliceosome, which functions in the removal of introns from the coding regions of mRNA precursors. The snRNPs in the spliceosome may act to align the phosphate esters to be broken and joined. Several other snRNPs have been identified in mammalian cell nuclei. These may also take part in mRNA processing (Grabowski and Sharp 1986, Sharp 1987, Maniatis and Reed 1987, Steitz 1988). The introns remain in the nucleus, where they are digested and recycled.

Most genes follow this general pattern and process, but there are exceptions to some of the steps, and some structures may be absent. The various processes are catalyzed by enzymes, most of which are proteins, but there are also RNA catalysts (ribozymes) involved in the splicing of exons (Zaug and Cech 1986, Cech 1986, 1987, Westheimer 1986). For example, in bacteria, ribonuclease P (p-rRNA) is a ribonucleoprotein that cleaves precursors to transfer RNA (tRNA) molecules to yield the correct 5' terminal sequences of the mature tRNAs. The RNA portion of ribonuclease P acts as a catalyst in this reaction, apparently because it has the ability to form specific hydrogen bonds with a complementary sequence of nucleotides in the tRNA molecule and thereby to create a stretch of double or triple helix. Such a helical region may provide a mechanism for specific substrate recognition through base pairing, governed by the rules unique to interactions between nucleic acid sequences. In the splicing reaction of eukaryotic mRNAs it is probable that an RNA catalyst serves as a substrate to bring the splicing junction sequences of introns into the close proximity required for splicing to occur (Guerrier-Takada et al. 1983, Guerrier-Takada and Altman 1984, Altman 1984). For the discovery and analysis of the role of ribozymes, Altman and Cech were awarded the 1989 Nobel Prize in chemistry.

The mature mRNA transcript passes through pores in the nuclear membrane into the cytoplasm, where it becomes associated with ribosomes and the exons are translated into the amino acid sequence of a protein. The 5' and 3' non-translated regions are transcribed into mRNA but are not translated into an amino acid sequence. The translation of the mRNA into a polypeptide is mediated by some 45 to 50 different tRNAs that correspond to one or more of the triplet codons of the genetic code. Each tRNA is a complex structure of ca. 75–90 nucleotides. A set of 20 enzymes, the tRNA synthetases, each specific for one of the 20 amino acids, comprises the critical components that recognize and bind to the mRNA triplet codon for a given amino acid. Each tRNA and its synthetase recognize each other by details of their structures that are complex and specific (Rould et al. 1989; Waldrop 1989).

Gilbert (1986) suggested that the precursors of living systems were first RNA, then proteins, and finally DNA. In the first stage RNA molecules may have performed catalytic activities to assemble themselves into self-replicating patterns that could recombine and mutate to develop new functions and adapt to new niches. Next, RNAs began to synthesize proteins, which became more effective as enzymes and took over that role. Finally, DNA evolved and became the principal repository of information, copied from RNA by reverse transcription. After double-stranded DNA evolved there was a stable linear information store, error-correcting, but still capable of mutation and recombination. Gilbert concluded that "The relic of this process is the intron/exon structure of genes, left imprinted on DNA from the RNA molecules that earlier encoded proteins, a residue of the basic mechanism of RNA recombination."

Doolittle (1987) reviewed the evidence of the origin and function of introns and summarized two major theories: "(1) introns were introduced into the genomes of eukaryotes after the eukaryotes arose from the prokaryotes, and introns have served to 'speed' evolution; and (2) introns are relics of precellular genome-assembly processes and have since been eliminated from prokaryotes. Current data support the second view, suggesting that although introns have played an important role in evolution of new functional proteins, this role cannot be seen as an adaptation, at least at the level of organisms within a species. A scheme for the origin of genomes is suggested by the potential for self-replication shown by some contemporary introns."

Genes of the Avian Egg-white Proteins

The genes that code for the egg-white proteins provide examples of the structure and other properties of most genes. The avian oviducal genes are under hormonal control and the base sequences that code for the egg-white proteins ovalbumin, conalbumin (ovotransferrin), lysozyme, and ovomucoid have been determined in the Domestic Fowl (*G. gallus*) (Kato et al. 1978, McReynolds et al. 1978, O'Malley et al. 1979, Chambon et al. 1979, Breathnach and Chambon 1981).

OVALBUMIN

The ovalbumin gene is composed of eight exons and seven introns. The eight exons contain a total of 1158 bases, the 5' non-coding region contains 64 bases, and the 3' non-coding region, 637 bases. Thus, the mRNA mature transcript contains 1859 bases, of which 1158 are translated into the 386 amino acids of the ovalbumin molecule. The seven introns are composed of ca. 5690 bases, and the entire ovalbumin gene contains ca. 7550 bases. The introns account for 75% of the base sequence (O'Malley et al. 1979).

The 5'-to-3' sequence of the subunits of the ovalbumin gene, and the approximate number of bases in each, are given in Table 7. Chambon et al. (1979) obtained slightly different values for some of the sequences, but the overall agreement with the O'Malley et al.

TABLE 7. Sequence of Subunits of the Ovalbumin Gene

Region	Approximate Length, Base Pairs
1. 5' non-coding region	64
2. Exon 1	15
3. Intron A	1600
4. Exon 2	160
5. Intron B	230
6. Exon 3	70
7. Intron C	590
8. Exon 4	130
9. Intron D	380
10. Exon 5	150
11. Intron E	860
12. Exon 6	140
13. Intron F	295
14. Exon 7	90
15. Intron G	1740
16. Exon 8	400
17. 3' non-coding region	637
	Total 7551 bases

(1979) data is excellent. McReynolds et al. (1978) presented the complete sequence of the ovalbumin gene.

Sequencing of extensive regions near the ovalbumin gene revealed two related genes, X and Y. These two genes are homologous to the ovalbumin gene but are expressed at a much lower rate. All three genes of the ovalbumin family have eight exons, which vary somewhat in length and show varying degrees of sequence similarity. Although the locations of the splicing junctions between introns and exons have been well conserved, the introns and the sequences coding for the 3' non-coding regions of the mRNAs have diverged more rapidly than the exons. The conalbumin gene in *Gallus* contains at least 16 introns and the lysozyme gene has three introns.

OVOMUCOID

The *Gallus* ovomucoid gene, from the cap site to the end of the 3' non-coding region, is 5545 bases long and, like the ovalbumin gene, contains eight exons and seven introns. O'Malley et al. (1979:287) made an electron micrograph of the hybrid molecule formed between the ovalbumin gene and its mRNA transcript. The exons are spliced together, end to end, forming a double-stranded segment with the mRNA from which the non-transcribed single-stranded introns loop out from the hybrid segment. The relative lengths of the intron loops correspond to their lengths in base pairs. Table 8 lists the 5'-to-3' sequence of the subunits of the ovomucoid gene and the approximate number of bases in each (based on Kato et al. 1978, O'Malley et al. 1979, Stein et al. 1980, Catterall et al. 1980).

Of the 5545 bases in the primary mRNA transcript, 4724 are in the seven introns, 191

TABLE 8. Sequence of Subunits of the Ovomucoid Gene

Distance from Cap Site, Base Pairs	Region	Approximate Length, Base Pairs
0	5' non-coding	53
53	Exon 1	58
111	Intron A	900
1011	Exon 2	20
1031	Intron B	725 Domain I
1756	Exon 3	137 Domain I
1893	Intron C	450 Domain I
2343	Exon 4	58 Domain I
2401	Intron D	264 Domain II
2665	Exon 5	137 Domain II
2802	Intron E	760 Domain II
3562	Exon 6	67 Domain II
3629	Intron F	1150 Domain III
4779	Exon 7	110 Domain III
4889	Intron G	475 Domain III
5364	Exon 8	43 Domain III
5407	3' non-coding	138
		Total 5545 bases

are the non-translated 5' and 3' regions, and 630 comprise the eight exons. The 630 exon bases are translated into the 210 amino acids of the primary ovomucoid protein sequence, which includes the 24 amino acid residues coded for by the 58 bases of exon 1 plus the first 14 bases of exon 2. These 24 amino acid residues are deleted from the mature protein after secretion, thus the functional ovomucoid molecule is a sequence of 186 amino acid residues, coded for by the last two codons of exon 2, plus exons 3–8, inclusive, i.e., 558 bases. Only 10% of the primary mRNA transcript codes for the protein product. The 24-residue sequence coded for by exons 1 and 2 is a "signal peptide" that is presumably involved in gene regulation.

DOMAINS

See Table 8. The mature ovomucoid protein is divided into three functional domains, designated I, II, and III. Each domain can bind one molecule of trypsin or other serine protease, and each contains three disulphide bonds in almost identical positions.

Domain I consists of 65 amino acids, II of 68, and III of 51. The sequences of I and II are more similar to one another (46%) than either is to that of III (30%, 33%), suggesting that the three domains are the result of two doubling events in the ancestral gene. The first doubling produced the ancestor of III and that of I+II. The second doubling of the I+II sequence gave rise to I and II. Thus, III has been evolving independently from I and II longer than they have from one another (Kato et al. 1978, Stein et al. 1980). The three tandem domains are therefore homologous sequences, derived from a common ancestral sequence by duplication and divergence.

The three domains are also delineated in the base sequence of the gene. The primary mRNA transcript of each domain is composed of two introns and two exons. The splicing junctions between domains are always between codons, but the intra-domain splicing junctions are within a codon, between the second and third bases of the triplet. When the introns are spliced out, the split codons are reunited in the mature transcript.

The internal introns are at identical positions within the three domains, indicating that their positions have been conserved since the duplication events that occurred millions of years ago.

In the primary mRNA transcript, domain I begins at base No. 132, which is 1032 bases downstream from the cap site, including the introns. Domain I begins with intron B (725 bp), which is inserted between bases 131 and 132 (the last base of exon 2 and the first base of exon 3). The amino terminus of the mature protein begins with an alanine-glutamine (Ala-Glu) dipeptide (bases 126–131, GCT-GAG), which is the only part of exon 2 that is translated into the sequence of the ovomucoid protein. The first amino acid in domain I is a valine coded for by a GTG codon at positions 132–134. Thus, domain I includes introns B and C and exons 3 and 4 and is composed of 1370 bases in the gene, of which 195 are translated into the 65 amino acids of domain I in the mature ovomucoid protein.

Domain II includes introns D and E and exons 5 and 6 and is composed of 1228 bases, of which the 204 in the exons are translated into the 68 amino acids of the domain in the protein.

Domain III includes introns F and G and exons 7 and 8. Thus, it is composed of 1778 bases in the gene, of which 153 are translated into the 51 amino acids of domain III in the ovomucoid protein. See Catterall et al. (1980:484) for the complete sequence of the ovomucoid mRNA and the sequence of the ovomucoid protein.

Breathnach and Chambon (1981:353–360) summarized some of the aspects of gene structure, as follows:

The widespread occurrence of introns and the location of neighboring genes at distances comparable to or larger than their lengths, accounts in part for the C-value paradox* of higher eukaryotic genomes; (in the 40-kb ovalbumin gene family region apparently not more than 9% of the DNA codes for protein.) From one gene to another and for the same length of mature mRNA, the number and lengths of introns and exons are variable, and there is no apparent rule. Total intron length can represent more than 95% of a gene. . . . Introns are mostly localized in amino acid coding regions. . . . There is no evidence as yet that any intron or exon from a given gene could be found as such elsewhere in the genome, if one excludes the genes that belong to the same family. However, introns (but not exons) can contain highly or middle repetitive sequences, as shown in the case of the X . . . and conalbumin . . . genes. These intronic repeated sequences appear to evolve rapidly, since, for instance, the repeated sequences that are present in the X gene are not found in the other two members of the ovalbumin family. . . . The comparison of members of a given gene in different species has led to the conclusion that protein-coding sequences evolve slowly, mainly by point mutations. Noncoding sequences (introns and very often 3'-untranslated regions) evolve much more rapidly . . . by deletion and insertion events that are most probably selected against in the coding regions. Therefore split genes appear to be made up of rather stable protein-coding elements embedded in a rapidly changing environment. . . . The evolutionary advantage of the splicing mechanism is clear: it allows the creation of new genes by "fusion" of the duplicated domain-encoding DNA segments into one transcription unit and subsequent splicing of the RNA to yield a new mRNA, without waiting for an exact deletion of the spacer DNA that separates the duplicated DNA segments. . . . The chicken ovomucoid gene may have evolved by triplication of an ancestral protein-coding DNA segment split by one intron, and there is evidence that the conalbumin gene evolved by duplication from an ancestral gene with seven or eight exons. The lack of homology between the various exons of some genes, like the ovalbumin gene, definitely does not exclude the possibility that they originated through multiple ancient duplication events that may be difficult or impossible to recognize due to sequence drift during the course of evolution.

*"C-value paradox" refers to the wide variation in genome size among organisms of similar morphological complexity. See "Genome Size" in chapter 5. Reviews by Marx (1978), Chambon (1978), Crick (1979), Abelson (1979), and Kolata (1980). Stryer (1988) described and illustrated gene structure and function.

CHAPTER FOUR

Genetic Regulation

Regulation in Prokaryotes

The control of the expression of genetic information differs in prokaryotes and eukaryotes. In prokaryotes, regulation is organized to produce a maximum growth rate when conditions are optimal and to respond quickly to changing conditions.

In bacteria, blocks of genes can be turned off by the binding of a repressor protein to a sequence of bases, the operator. The genes are reactivated when specific small molecules bind to the repressor and remove it from the operator. The recognition process between repressor and operator is probably mediated by the formation of hydrogen bonds between the amino acids of the repressor protein and specific base pairs of the operator DNA sequence. Thus, the interaction between repressor and operator is intrinsic and depends on the structural and chemical properties of the control protein and the DNA helix.

THE *LAC* OPERON

Genetic regulation was first studied in detail by Jacob and Monod (1961) in the intestinal bacterium *Escherichia coli*. Their operon model was developed from a study of the control of the metabolic degradation of the sugar lactose in *E. coli*. Three genes are involved in the metabolism of lactose, one of which codes for the enzyme β-galactosidase. The lactose operon, or *lac* operon, is composed of three genes which occur next to one another in the bacterial chromosome and are transcribed together. Transcription begins when the enzyme RNA polymerase binds to a sequence of nucleotides, the *lac* promoter, located near one end of the operon. The *lac* operator sequence is close to the promoter, and the *lac* repressor protein can bind to the operator. When the repressor and operator are bound together, the polymerase cannot attach to the promoter and the *lac* operon cannot be transcribed into mRNA. This condition is in effect when there is no lactose in the cell. When molecules of lactose enter the cell a modified form of lactose acts as an inducer by binding to the repressor in such a way that the repressor no longer can bind to the operator. This frees the promoter to interact with the polymerase, and transcription of the gene for β-galactosidase begins. The details are more complex than this simplified description, but the principle of regulation by induction is demonstrated; the presence of lactose turns the *lac* operon on, the absence of lactose turns it off. Thus, the synthesis of proteins is controlled by a feedback system dependent on the sequence of nucleotides in the DNA (Freifelder 1983:540, Lewin 1983:219).

There seems to be a common pattern by which regulatory proteins in bacteria and viruses recognize their target DNA sequences. The three-dimensional structures of co-crystals, composed of a regulatory protein bound to its target DNA sequence, have been determined by X-ray crystallography. In viruses the proteins are dimers, consisting of two identical amino acid chains that fit neatly into two successive sites along the major groove of the B-DNA double helix.

J. E. Anderson et al. (1987) described and figured the crystal structure of a specific complex between the DNA-binding domain of bacteriophage 434 repressor and a synthetic 434 operator DNA sequence, which shows the interactions that determine sequence-dependent affinity. The repressor recognizes its operators by its complementarity to a particular DNA conformation as well as by direct interaction with base pairs in the major groove.

Gellert and Nash (1987) described experiments showing that in prokaryotes, "some site-specific recombination systems require the interacting DNA sequences to have a specific relative orientation. This means that DNA segments can sense each other's direction even though they may be separated by many thousands of base pairs."

Regulation in Eukaryotes

In multicellular eukaryotes gene regulation must control morphology through cellular differentiation and embryonic development, as well as cell growth and multiplication. In adult higher organisms growth must be turned off and the activities of different cell types regulated at different times and in various ways. Thus, the regulatory mechanisms are more complex than in bacteria and viruses.

REGULATORY PROTEINS

Much of the control of gene expression in eukaryotes involves regulatory proteins that interact with genes or gene segments. Although little is yet known about the regulatory proteins of eukaryotic organisms, some may be quite different from those of prokaryotes. One eukaryotic regulatory protein that has been characterized (TFIIIa) is involved in gene transcription. It consists of one protein chain of nearly 350 amino acids, 300 of which form a long DNA-binding region, which attaches to ribosomal RNA genes. Other eukaryotic regulatory proteins may be more like those of prokaryotes (review, Marx 1985).

Regulation is often achieved by the control of transcription at the level of initiation. This process seems to be controlled mainly or entirely by specific proteins that recognize unique sites on the DNA and bind to them. The base sequence of a local region, the topography of the major and minor grooves of the DNA helix, the presence of a methyl group on thymine bases, and other structures (zinc fingers, leucine zippers, helix-turn-helix) appear to provide the specificity required for recognition sites where regulatory proteins may interact with the DNA to control the activity of individual genes (Schleif 1988a, Ptashne 1988, B. W. Mathews 1988, P. J. Mitchell and Tjian 1989).

Regulation may also be achieved via the transmission of long-range effects in DNA. Crothers and Fried (1982) proposed several mechanisms of long-range transduction in which, for example, DNA configuration may be altered by interaction with a regulatory protein at one site and the effect transmitted to a second site. Torsional stress, bending stress, packing forces, and other phenomena may be involved in such regulatory effects. The common thread is that all such mechanisms are sequence dependent.

Ptashne (1986) reviewed the evidence of gene regulation by proteins acting at various distances from the transcription site and suggested that

regulatory proteins recognize specific sites in DNA using structures that are complementary to the ordinary helix. . . . Second, DNA-bound regulatory proteins influence transcription by excluding binding of other proteins (for example by competing with polymerase for an essential site) or . . . by touching another DNA-bound protein. . . . [In some cases] one DNA-bound repressor helps another to bind, and the latter in turn helps polymerase to bind and begin transcription, and these cooperative efforts are mediated by protein-protein interactions. . . . these descriptions hold whether the interacting proteins are adjacent on DNA or . . . separated—in the latter case the DNA between the separated sites loops out to allow the protein-protein interactions. Should looping prove to be a general phenomenon in gene regulation at a distance . . . a protein bound at a distal site might help another protein to bind at a proximal site and the latter might then directly activate or repress a gene . . . [or] a bound activator protein might be constrained and rendered inactive by interaction with another protein bound at a distal site. Proteins binding within the loop might break it, thereby relieving the negative or positive effect of the interaction. Proteins bound to the same DNA sites might have quite different effects on gene regulation depending upon the nature of their interaction with other proteins. Our problem is no longer to invent a possible mechanism; rather, it is to see how far one operative idea, looping, will carry us (pp. 700–701).

Schleif (1987) suggested that DNA loops so that regulatory proteins located at some distance from the site of regulation can participate by contact with other regulatory proteins at the site of activity, and for the cooperativity generated by multiple-site binding.

Dandanell et al. (1987) noted that "regulation of transcription initiation by proteins binding at DNA sequences some distance from the promoter region itself seems to be a general phenomenon in both eukaryotes and prokaryotes. Proteins bound to an enhancer site in eukaryotes can turn on a distant gene."

Maniatis et al. (1987) reviewed the regulation of gene expression and noted that the DNA

sequences required for eukaryotic gene expression . . . are modular in nature, consisting of short (10- to 12-base pair) recognition elements that interact with specific transcription factors [proteins]. Some transcription factors have been extensively purified and the corresponding genes have been cloned, but the mechanisms by which they promote transcription are not yet understood. Positive and negative regulatory elements that function only in specific cell types or in response to extracellular inducers have been identified. A number of cases of inducible and tissue-specific gene expression involve the activation of preexisting transcription factors, rather than the synthesis of new proteins. This activation may involve covalent modification of the protein or an allosteric change in its structure. The modification of regulatory proteins may play a central role in the mechanisms of eukaryotic gene regulation.

ENHANCER ELEMENTS

The rate of transcription of some genes is regulated by the stimulating effect of special sequences called enhancers. Their absence retards transcription, their presence increases it. Enhancers are specific for the cell type in which they occur, and they can exert their influence when positioned either close to or at distances of up to several kb from the target gene, even if their orientation is reversed. Enhancers may transmit the stimulatory signal via a modification of the supercoiling of the DNA helix, or by acting as the entry site for RNA polymerase, which then travels along the DNA until it encounters a promoter region. Enhancers probably work by the binding of a specific protein that is present only in those cells requiring expression of the genes controlled by that enhancer (Khoury and Gruss 1983, Felsenfeld 1985:64–65).

Schleif (1988a) reviewed the phenomenon of DNA looping and its relationship to enhancer sequences that may lie hundreds or thousands of nucleotides away from the genes whose transcription they affect. He suggested "two reasons for the existence of DNA looping. First, . . . [it provides] a convenient mechanism for achieving high affinity binding via the binding site cooperativity inherent in the systems. Second, looping facilitates regulating gene activity when more than several regulatory proteins are involved. One or two proteins can bind to DNA alongside RNA polymerase, but having RNA polymerase respond to still more regulatory proteins generates complications. Looping permits additional regulatory proteins to be placed at a substantial distance away from the RNA polymerase and still influence the initiation process. . . . DNA looping provides a . . . simple explanation for the action-at-a-distance phenomenon that is found in prokaryotic and eukaryotic cells. It is a logical and versatile mechanism for regulating gene activity."

It is also clear that genes can be turned off for long periods of time but not be eliminated from the genome. This may involve a repressor protein that prevents transcription (see "Dormant Genes" in chapter 8), or be related to the packing of genes into chromatin, to patterns of DNA methylation (see below), or to the inheritance of rearranged DNA sequences.

Gene activator proteins provide positive regulation in eukaryotes by binding to specific ligands that change the activator's affinity for DNA and thus turn genes on or off. Other methods of known or possible gene regulation include changes in the form of the DNA helix, the action of hormones, methylation, gene amplification, and transposable elements.

VARIANT FORMS OF THE DNA HELIX

Studies of the X-ray diffraction patterns of DNA fibers have shown that DNA can exist in two principal forms, B and A. The B form is assumed under conditions of high hydration (92% relative humidity) and is the form thought to prevail in the living cell. The A form occurs at low hydration (75% relative humidity). Both forms have the same helical ladder shape, and both have a major groove and a minor groove formed by the stereochemical geometry of the sugar-phosphate backbones and the stacked base pairs.

The nitrogen and oxygen atoms on the floor of the major groove can form hydrogen bonds with the side chains of the amino acids of a protein; thus the base sequence of the DNA carries a message that can be read by specific proteins acting as control elements. At each rung of the helical ladder the four types of base pairs present four possible patterns to a repressor or other control protein. Although less informative, the minor groove also contains the potential for information transfer.

X-ray diffraction studies of crystallized synthetic base sequences revealed additional details about the A and B forms and led to the discovery of other configurations designated C, D, E, and Z (for zigzag), which occur under special conditions or in particular base sequences. A, B, and Z are of principal interest in relation to the control of genetic expression.

A- and B-DNAs are right-handed helices, with average helical twists between bases of 33.1 and 35.9 degrees respectively, corresponding to 10.9 and 10.0 base pairs per 360-degree rotation. In A-DNA the average helix rise per base pair is 2.92 angstroms; in B-DNA the average rise is 3.36 angstroms. These average values demonstrate some of the differences between the A and B forms, but there is a surprisingly large variation in the helical twist values that is correlated with the base sequence, suggesting that the control proteins recognize particular base sequences. The range in helical twist values in A-DNA is from 16.1 to 44.1 degrees, with a standard deviation of 5.9. In B-DNA the range is 27.7 to 42 degrees, standard deviation 4.3. B-DNA is 20 angstroms in diameter. Most of the helix in the living cell is in the B form at any one time.

The Z form is a left-handed, tightly wound helix, 18 angstroms in diameter, with 12.0 base pairs per turn, and the sugar-phosphate backbone follows a zigzag path. Z-DNA is found only in alternating purine-pyrimidine sequences (such as CGCG bases, which have the highest bonding energies) and is believed to occur only in short segments of the DNA helix. Z-DNA has only one deep groove, corresponding to the minor groove of B-DNA. The concave major groove of B-DNA forms the convex outer surface of the Z-DNA conformation. The conversion from B-DNA to Z-DNA involves a series of complex rearrangements that change the positions of the bases relative to the sugar-phosphate backbone.

There are other variations in the angles, twists, and inclinations of the bases, all of which suggest that base sequences influence local helical structure and that this in turn may control the expression of genetic information (Zimmerman 1982, Rich 1982, Dickerson et al. 1982, Dickerson 1983a,b, Udvardy and Schedl 1983, Saenger 1984, Rich et al. 1984).

Saenger et al. (1986) suggested that the different forms of the DNA helix are the result of the principle of hydration economy. In the B form the phosphate groups are far apart (6.6 angstroms) and individually hydrated; in the A and Z forms the phosphate groups are closer together (5.3 and 4.4 angstroms) and bridged by water molecules. Thus, the A and Z forms are more economically hydrated than the B form, and as a result, the A and Z forms are stable under a water deficit and the B form is stable under a water excess. Frank-Kamenetskii (1986) noted that another explanation, shared by many investigators, is that the "high-salt B-Z transition is governed by electrostatic interactions of phosphate groups with each other and with the salt ions. In such a . . . model, water does not play a structural role and only dampens the interactions between charges." The hydration economy model is a factor in the interactions that govern the stability of the double helix and "its importance can no longer be ignored."

Shakked et al. (1989) crystallized an eight-base-pair sequence of DNA in various forms and showed that different conformations of the double helix depend on hydration, molecular packing, and temperature. The different forms "have implications on the modes of DNA recognition by proteins."

HORMONAL REGULATION

Hormones are important regulators of gene activity in eukaryotes. The steroid hormones (e.g., estrogen, testosterone) act by turning on the transcription of a gene. The mechanism is not completely understood, but apparently a hormone molecule enters a target cell and forms a complex with a cytoplasmic receptor molecule. The hormone-receptor combination enters the nucleus, binds to a specific site in the chromatin, and initiates the transcription of the target gene.

For example, the transcription of the genes that code for the egg-white proteins of birds is induced by estrogen acting on the cells of the avian oviduct. In the oviduct of a young female Domestic Fowl (*G. gallus*) there is no detectable egg-white synthesis and there is only about one mRNA molecule per cell. However, if the bird is injected with estrogen the columnar epithelial cells of the oviduct respond by increasing the number of mRNA molecules in each cell to ca. 100,000, and the synthesis of the egg-white proteins continues as long as estrogen is supplied. When the hormone is discontinued, the mRNA population drops to ca. 30 molecules per cell, and egg-white protein synthesis decreases (Harris et al. 1975, Lewin 1980:726, Freifelder 1983:950–952).

The COUP (chicken ovalbumin upstream promoter) transcription factor (COUP-TF) exists in various tissues and is necessary to the expression of the avian ovalbumin gene. It binds to the ovalbumin promoter and, in conjunction with a second protein (S300-II) stimulates initiation of transcription. Homologs of COUP-TF occur in other species, including mammals, and it is a member of "the steroid/thyroid hormone/vitamin receptor superfamily . . . [which] contains proteins which bind and activate distal promoter elements of eukaryotic genes" (Wang et al. 1989). Darnell (1982, 1983, 1985) reviewed the mechanisms of transcriptional control in eukaryotes.

The synthesis of the yolk proteins is also regulated by hormones. In all oviparous vertebrates the yolk proteins are derived from a common precursor, vitellogenin, which is synthesized under estrogen control in the liver of the mature female, secreted into the bloodstream, transported to the ovary, and cleaved into the yolk proteins phosvitin and lipovitellin.

The initial stimulus presumably comes from the environment. In birds the annual photoperiod is known to stimulate the hypothalamus of the brain to secrete small peptides (neurohumors) which move to the anterior pituitary via hollow neurons and a special portal vein system. The neuropeptides induce the cells of the anterior pituitary to synthesize several hormones, including the gonadotrophins. These, in turn, induce the ovarian follicle cells to produce estrogen. In this cascade there are several steps involving hormonal induction of gene activity. For additional details see Wahli et al. (1981), Freifelder (1983:960), and Wynshaw-Boris and Hanson (1983).

METHYLATION

The methylation of DNA is also involved in the control of gene expression. Methylation is carried out by specific enzymes (methyltransferases) that add a methyl group (CH_3) to carbon–5 of cytosine residues or carbon–6 of adenine residues. Only cytosines tend to be methylated in eukaryotes, and in animals the cytosines are mainly those immediately followed by guanines. In animal DNAs, 2% to 5% of the cytosines are methylated, and the amount and pattern are species specific. The mechanism of methylation is uncertain, but it is probable that, like most regulatory systems, it exerts its effect by altering the interactions between DNA and the proteins that bind to it. It is clear that active genes are less methylated than inactive genes and that inactive genes can be activated by demethylation. The methylation of a few specific CG sites will abolish the activity of a gene, and methylated genes are inherited by successive generations, which may explain the occasional expression of dormant genes in individual animals or under special conditions (see "Dormant Genes" in chapter 8). Loss of methylation, which can result from DNA damage, may lead to heritable abnormalities, and these may be important in the development of cancer and aging. In the fruit fly genus *Drosophila* there are no methylated cytosines in its DNA, which suggests that DNA methylation is but one of the mechanisms that can create inherited patterns of gene regulation in eukaryotes (Razin and Friedman 1981, Flavell and Thompson 1983, Doerfler 1983, Lewin 1983:492, Alberts et al. 1983:460–462, Felsenfeld 1985:67–68, Holliday 1987, 1989).

GENE REARRANGEMENTS

Two major mechanisms for the control of gene expression are DNA inversion and DNA transposition. In DNA inversion a segment of DNA reverses its position in the sequence and is rejoined by site-specific recombination, disconnecting or connecting a gene to sequences required for its expression. In DNA transposition a gene moves into an expression site where it displaces its predecessor by gene conversion. Rearrangements altering gene expression have mainly been found in some unicellular organisms. They allow a fraction of the organisms to preadapt to sudden changes in environment, i.e., to alter properties such as surface antigens in the absence of an inducing stimulus. The antigenic variation that permits the causative agents of certain diseases to elude host defense mechanisms is controlled in this way.

DNA rearrangements are of two types, programmed and incidental. Incidental rearrangements arise from errors in replication, repair, or recombination; from the movements of mobile elements (transposons); or from the insertion or excision of plasmid DNA, viral DNA, or other immigrant DNA. Most incidental rearrangements are deleterious to the individual affected by them. Programmed rearrangements are part of the normal developmental program of an organism. The process is carried out by specific enzymes and is developmentally regulated. Such rearrangements occur in three categories: (1) amplification or deletion of genes, (2) assembly of genes from gene segments, and (3) rearrangements that alter gene expression (Borst and Greaves 1987).

HEAT SHOCK

Some genes can be activated by heat. For example, in *Drosophila* the increase in temperature "from 25°C to 37°C induces the rapid production of a small number of specific proteins which alter the cellular metabolic machinery and seem to allow cells to survive the environmental insult. The heat shock products appear to be induced in all tissues both adult and embryonic as well as in several stable *Drosophila* cell lines. Synthesis of most other mRNAs is suppressed during heat shock. Normal patterns of RNA synthesis return within several hours after the animals are returned to 25°C" (Bryan and Destree 1983:54).

Gene amplification is another method of gene regulation; see "Gene Amplification" in chapter 7. Transposable elements, or transposons, also function in gene regulation; see "Possible Functions of Repeated Sequences" in chapter 6 and "Transposable Elements" in chapter 7.

DNA Damage and Repair

Damage to a normal coding sequence may result in phenotypic changes that cause harm to the individual and/or its offspring. Therefore, it is not surprising that mechanisms to repair alterations in base sequences have evolved. Much of the damage to DNA can be repaired because of the double-stranded structure of DNA, thus information lost by one strand is still present in the complementary sequence of the other strand. Damage to DNA is any modification "that alters its coding properties or its normal function in replication or transcription. Some minor base modifications may result in an altered DNA sequence while other types of damage may distort the DNA structure and interfere with replication. To be repairable, damage must be recognized by a protein that can initiate a sequence of biochemical reactions leading to its elimination and the restoration of the intact DNA structure" (Hanawalt et al. 1979:786).

Damage may be caused by replication errors, environmental agents such as mutagenic chemicals and ionizing radiation, or the inherent chemical instability of the structure of DNA. The defects may be in the form of (1) a base change in one strand resulting in a base-pair mismatch, (2) a missing base in one strand, (3) an altered base that is changed into a different chemical structure, (4) a single-strand break, (5) a double-strand break, or (6) formation of a covalent cross-link between paired bases.

Each of these alterations can be corrected by one of several repair mechanisms. The damaged bases may be excised, reconstructed, or disregarded. If the damage is not repaired, i.e., disregarded, the mutation is incorporated into the genome.

The repair mechanisms involve specific enzymes (e.g., DNA ligase and polymerases) that recognize the defects and, in most cases, repair the damage. Thus, only a small percentage of the defects become mutations that permanently alter the base sequence.

DNA mismatch correction is a strand-specific process involving recognition of non-complementary Watson-Crick nucleotide pairs and participation of widely separated DNA sites. In *E. coli* several mismatch repair systems are known, one of which involves DNA methylation patterns, the products of four mutator genes, a single-strand DNA binding protein, several enzymes, adenosine triphosphate (ATP), and the four deoxynucleoside triphosphates. In cell-free extracts under in vitro conditions, these components can process seven of the eight base-base mismatches in a strand-specific reaction that is directed by the state of methylation of a single d(GATC) sequence located 1 kb from the site of the mispaired bases (Lahue et al. 1989).

Hanawalt et al. (1978, 1979), R. L. Adams et al. (1981:286–304), Lewin (1983:553–569), Freifelder (1983:316–338), Haseltine (1983), Friedburg (1985), Radman and Wagner (1988), and Stryer (1988:677) provide reviews and additional information on DNA repair.

CHAPTER FIVE

DNA Reassociation and Thermal Stability

Measurement Methods

Several methods have been used to measure the rate and extent of dissociation, reassociation, and the thermal stability of DNA-DNA duplexes.

OPTICAL HYPOCHROMICITY

When a solution of DNA is heated its physical properties, such as optical density, light scattering, and viscosity, undergo dramatic changes. The changes occur over a narrow temperature range as the hydrogen bonds between base pairs melt and the double helix is disrupted into single strands that form random coils. The midpoint of the transition is the melting temperature, or T_m. T_m may also be defined as the half value of complete denaturation.

The melting of native DNA displays cooperative behavior, that is, the melting of one segment influences the melting of adjacent segments. The longer the DNA chain, the higher the temperature required to reach the T_m, because the stability of the double helix is proportion to the chain length. Short helices will melt at lower temperatures because their cooperativity is lower. The melting temperatures of double helices also increase with the ionic strength of the medium and with the GC-AT ratio of the DNA (Marmur and Doty 1962, Schildkraut and Lifson 1965, Saenger 1984:143).

The heterocyclic rings of the nucleotides absorb ultraviolet (UV) light with a maximum at 260 nanometers. When the double helix is in its ordered state the aromatic rings of the nucleotides are stacked, like "coins in a roll" (Saenger 1984:132), and they absorb ca. 40% less UV than does a mixture of free nucleotides of the same composition. This hypochromic effect, which results from the stacked arrangement of the bases, is a sensitive measure of the physical state of the DNA. When the temperature is raised, and the helix is disrupted at the T_m, the UV absorption suddenly increases as the rings of the nucleotides become exposed. The increase in optical density, or hyperchromicity, signals the change from the ordered to the disordered state.

Optical hypochromicity was used in the early studies by Doty et al. (1959a), Marmur and Doty (1961b, 1962), and Marmur et al. (1963b) and is still an important procedure. Thus, with a spectrophotometer, it is possible to follow the time course of reassociation of single-stranded DNA in solution by monitoring the decrease in optical density as reassociation proceeds (Crothers et al. 1965, Wetmur and Davidson 1968, Wetmur 1976, Lewin 1980:504, Saenger 1984:143).

DNA-AGAR METHOD

Long strands of single-stranded DNA are embedded in a dilute, porous agar gel, and short fragments of radiolabeled DNA are passed through the gel under conditions favoring reassociation. The formation of duplexes is measured as the percentage of labeled DNA that hybridizes with the long-stranded DNA immobilized in the gel. This technique was developed by Bolton and McCarthy (1962), McCarthy and Bolton (1963), and Hoyer et al. (1964). Hoyer and Roberts (1967) reviewed this and related methods. This method is no longer used, but it was the first procedure with which eukaryotic genomes were compared.

MEMBRANE FILTER METHOD

Single-stranded DNA is immobilized on a nitrocellulose filter which is then treated to prevent further adsorption of DNA to its surface. Radiolabeled DNA fragments in solution are then added, and the extent of reassociation is measured as the amount of radioactivity remaining on the filter after unbound DNA has been washed off (D. Gillespie and Spiegelman 1965, Denhardt 1966).

HYDROXYAPATITE COLUMN METHOD

The hydroxyapatite (HAP) method is currently popular and was used in our studies. HAP is a crystalline form of calcium phosphate which, under certain conditions of salt concentration and temperature, will bind double-stranded DNA molecules longer than ca. 50 base pairs. Single-stranded DNA will not bind to HAP under those conditions. The properties of HAP permit it to be used in chromatographic columns to separate duplexes from simplexes during the thermal chromatography of DNA-DNA hybrids. HAP columns are also used to measure reassociation rates under different conditions of temperature and salt concentration and to follow the kinetics of reassociation of the slowly reassociating middle repetitive and single-copy sequences. Procedures for HAP chromatography have been described by Bernardi (1965), Miyazawa and Thomas (1965), Britten and Kohne (1968), Kohne (1970), Kohne and Britten (1971), N. C. Goodman et al. (1973), Martinson (1973a-d), Britten et al. (1974), Martinson and Wagenaar (1974), Angerer et al. (1976), Young and Anderson (1985), Werman et al. (1990), and Sibley and Ahlquist (1981a, 1983, 1986, and this volume).

S-1 NUCLEASE

The resistance of DNA duplexes to single-strand specific nucleases may be used to assay the kinetics of reassociation. For example, the S-1 nuclease of *Aspergillus oryzae* will remove the single-strand tails and non-complementary segments from partially duplex structures. The nuclease procedure measures the fraction of nucleotides in duplex at each point in the reassociation reaction. This is also approximately true for the optical hypochromicity assay. The HAP procedure measures only the fraction of DNA fragments that are completely single-stranded. The S-1 nuclease method and its application to the reassociation kinetics of DNA have been described by M. J. Smith et al. (1975), S. J. Miller and Wetmur (1975), Britten and Davidson (1976), Benveniste (1985), Benveniste and Todaro (1975, 1976) and Caccone and Powell (1989).

Factors Determining the Rate and Extent of Reassociation and the Thermal Stability of DNA-DNA Hybrids

When two single strands of DNA containing homologous nucleotide sequences come together in a solution of low or moderate salt concentration they will form a double helix with the complementary bases paired. The initial collision between complementary sequences is a nucleation event that results in the hydrogen bonding of one, two, or three base pairs at the site of contact, followed by the rapid "zippering" of the other matched bases. The first base pair is energetically unstable, but after three consecutive stacked base pairs have created a nucleus, the pairing of additional stacked bases leads to favorable negative contributions to free energy. From then on the growth of the double helix is spontaneous, due mainly to the geometrical constraints of the stereochemistry of the sugar-phosphate backbone. Thus, base-pair stacking and hydrogen-bonding interactions are responsible for the cooperative behavior of nucleic acid helix formation (Saenger 1984:141–143).

This process has been called reassociation, renaturation, reannealing, and hybridization. The term "hybridization" is sometimes reserved for a DNA-RNA duplex, but it is also widely used for DNA-DNA duplexes, especially if the two DNAs are from different species. Herein we will distinguish between homoduplex DNA hybrids, which result from reassociation between conspecific DNA strands, and heteroduplex DNA hybrids between the DNAs of different species. In some experiments it is useful to specify that homoduplex hybrids have been formed between DNA strands from the same individual and heteroduplex hybrids from DNA strands from two different individuals of the same species. The words "homologous" and "heterologous," borrowed from the vocabulary of immunology, are often used as synonyms for "homoduplex" and "heteroduplex," but we will restrict the word "homology" and its derivatives to the meaning defined in chapter 8.

CRITERION

The extent and rate of the reassociation reaction are determined primarily by the combination of incubation temperature and salt concentration. The incubation temperature determines the extent of reassociation because it is proportional to the level of sequence mismatch that will be tolerated for the formation of a stable duplex. This relationship has been designated as the criterion; the criterion determines the degree of complementarity which two nucleic acid sequences must have to interact and form a stable double-stranded molecule. "The criterion is that set of experimental conditions which defines the difference between the temperature of incubation and the melting temperature of precisely paired polynucleotides of the kind being studied. The criterion thus establishes the minimum degree of base pairing that can be recognized. The term is also used when some other condition (e.g., hydroxyapatite or enzyme treatment) discriminates against imperfectly base-paired structures, and thus mimics the effect of increasing incubation temperature" (Davidson and Britten 1973:566).

Or, criterion is "most precisely defined as the difference between the temperature of incubation (T_i) and the melting temperature $[T_m]$ in the incubation solvent of perfectly base-paired DNA of the type (base composition and fragment size) being studied. The term is rarely used with this precision . . . but always implies that imperfectly complementary strand pairs are discriminated against at some level of sequence matching, fixed by the criterion. Usages such as 'stringent' or 'open' criteria are descriptively useful. The rate of reassociation is reduced as the T_i approaches the T_m and the reassociation may be incomplete for pairs which melt near the criterion. Thus, incubation at open criterion followed by shift to stringent criterion during assay may not yield the same result as incubation at the stringent criterion" (Britten et al. 1974:366).

Wetmur (1976:347–348) defined criterion "as the difference in temperature between T_m and the renaturation temperature. Stringent (small) or open (large) criteria are chosen depending upon the amount of mismatched sequences that may be permitted in a particular experiment with eukaryotic DNA. . . . Where mismatched products of closely related sequences are to be permitted, an open criterion of about 25°C will in general give the maximum renaturation rate. If an open criterion is chosen, there is a range of about 10°C within which the rate constants obtained will be essentially independent of temperature. Most experiments have been performed under these conditions."

These conditions produce an optimal incubation temperature of 60°C in a salt solution such that the T_m of a homoduplex hybrid is at or close to 85°C. In practice the criterion is defined in terms of the incubation temperature, the salt concentration of the solvent, and the average length of DNA fragments. The standard criterion conditions for reassociation are 60°C, 0.12 M phosphate buffer (PB) (0.18 M Na^+), and 450 base fragments. The criterion conditions impose a lower limit on the T_m of mismatched duplexes because the sequences included in the measurement are only those that are sufficiently complementary in their base sequences to form stable duplexes, while the more divergent sequences, which cannot form stable duplexes, are excluded. When the extent of reassociation (% hybridization) is incomplete for this reason, the measured depression in the T_m underestimates the amount of divergence between the DNA sequences of the two species (Angerer et al. 1976:218). It is possible to circumvent this problem with the $T_{50}H$ statistic which, in effect, reconstitutes the missing portion of the melting curve by extrapolation to its intercept with the 50% level of hybridization. For a definition of $T_{50}H$ and for the procedure for calculating $T_{50}H$ and $\Delta T_{50}H$, see chapter 11.

REASSOCIATION KINETICS

The kinetics of reassociation of single-stranded DNA were discussed by Doty et al. (1960), Marmur and Doty (1961), Marmur et al. (1963b), Wetmur and Davidson (1968), Britten and Kohne (1968), Kohne (1970), Lee and Wetmur (1972a,b), Bonner et al. (1973),

Britten et al. (1974), M. J. Smith et al. (1975), Britten and Davidson (1976), Wetmur (1976), Britten and Davidson (1985), and Young and Anderson (1985). McCarthy and Church (1970) considered the factors affecting the specificity of nucleic acid hybridization reactions, and Kennell (1971) reviewed the principles and practices of nucleic acid hybridization. Straus (1976) examined the factors affecting DNA reassociation, especially with reference to repeated sequences, and Southern (1974) reviewed the structure, organization, biochemistry, and evolution of eukaryotic DNA. Thompson and Murray (1981) discussed the nuclear genome, especially in plants, and Preisler and Thompson (1981a) analyzed reassociation kinetics in the repeated sequences of plants. Britten and Davidson (1985) presented a synopsis of "hybridisation strategy" including definitions of terms and the equations for the kinetics of reassociation. Werman et al. (1990) provided information and protocols for DNA hybridization.

The salt concentration, incubation temperature, DNA concentration, and fragment size are the most important factors that must be controlled to achieve reproducible rates of reassociation. The base composition, solvent viscosity, genome size, sequence divergence, and presence of single-strand tails also affect reassociation and thermal stability. These factors are discussed below.

In principle, DNA reassociation should follow second-order kinetics, but because there is a high probability that two single strands will form a duplex that is not completely base-paired, the kinetics are more complex. The rate of reassociation will vary according to the composition of the DNA and the conditions of its environment.

SALT CONCENTRATION

The ionic strength of the solvent is important because DNA molecules are charged and, therefore, likely to repel one another. The presence of salt masks this repulsion; hence the monovalent cation concentration, usually in the form of sodium (Na^+), has a major effect on the rate of reassociation. If the concentration of sodium ion is below 0.01 M, reassociation is blocked. In 0.12 M sodium phosphate buffer (abbreviated NaPB or PB) (0.18 M Na^+) and an incubation temperature of 60°C, the relative reassociation rate has been set, arbitrarily, at 1.0. According to Angerer et al. (1976:215) the same criterion is obtained in 1.0 M NaCl at 70°C. In general, the higher the cation concentration, the faster the rate of reassociation. In 0.48 M PB (0.72 M Na^+) the relative rate is 5.65, and in 1.0 M PB (1.5 M Na^+) the relative rate is 8.4 (Britten et al. 1974:364, Young and Anderson 1985:63). Incubation in 1.0 M NaCl accelerates the rate 25 times that in 0.12 M PB. Wieder and Wetmur (1981, 1982) discussed the acceleration of renaturation in various solvents. For example, a 100-fold increase in reassociation rate may be achieved with a solvent containing 35–40% dextran sulphate in 1 M NaCl at 70°C. Much higher rates are attained in a phenol aqueous emulsion by the PERT method of Kohne et al. (1977).

TEMPERATURE

If the native double-stranded DNA of any eukaryote is dissolved in 0.12 M PB and heated, the different sequences will melt as a function of their hydrogen bonding strengths and base-stacking interactions. The dissociation of the A-T-rich sequences begins at approximately 80°C, the sequences with intermediate ratios of A-T and G-C base pairs melt between 84° and 90°C, and the G-C-rich sequences do not melt until ca. 95°C. Thus, the thermal transition of native DNA spans ca. 15°C and the melting curve is a plot of the distribution of A-T:G-C base pairs, plus a contribution from the stacking energies resulting from the base sequence.

When an individual segment of double-stranded DNA is heated in solution the hydrogen bonds in the double helix are ruptured and the DNA collapses into two single-stranded molecules. The temperature at which this occurs is the transition temperature, or melting temperature—the T_m. The T_m of the melting curve of a sample of native DNA is the temperature at which 50% of the total base pairs have melted. The T_m of the native DNAs of various groups of eukaryotes is usually between 83° and 90°C in 0.12 M PB. In birds the T_m of native DNA is ca. 87°C, and for reassociated homoduplexes composed of sheared fragments, the T_m is ca. 85–86°C. For homoduplexes the T_m and the $T_{50}H$ are identical. Figs. 4 and 5 show the relationships among the T_m, $T_{50}H$, and mode of frequency distribution and cumulative melting curves.

The T_m is related to the G+C content because the triple hydrogen bonding between G-C base pairs confers extra stability on the DNA helix. In standard saline citrate (0.15 M NaCl, 0.015 M citrate, pH 7) the relationship is expressed by the equation

$$\%GC = (T_m - 69.3)2.44$$

For example, a T_m of 86°C indicates a %GC of 40.75.

If the %GC is known, the T_m may be calculated (Marmur and Doty 1962)

$$T_m = 0.41(\%GC) + 69.3$$

Homologous sequences of single-stranded DNA will reassociate if they are incubated in a salt solution at a suitable temperature and for a sufficient length of time. If other conditions are held constant the rate of reassociation increases as the incubation temperature is decreased below the T_m, reaching a maximum rate about 25°C below the T_m, then decreasing with a further decrease in temperature (Wetmur and Davidson 1968, Wetmur 1976). Thus, for native DNA, for homoduplex DNA hybrids, and for heteroduplex DNA hybrids between closely related species, the incubation temperatures producing the highest rates of reassociation are between 55° and 70°C. The optimum incubation temperature for most conspecific DNAs is 25°C below the T_m, or 60°C. However, in many experiments widely divergent species are compared and the rate of reassociation depends, in part, on the degree of sequence divergence, the reason for which will be discussed below (see "Effects of Sequence Divergence"). Therefore, DNA-DNA hybrids between closely related and distantly related species cannot both be at the optimum incubation temperature when they are incubated together in the same experimental set. However, the optimum incubation temperature is displaced downward by only half as much as the T_m—i.e., if the T_m of a DNA hybrid is 10°C lower than that of native DNA, the optimum incubation temperature is decreased by only 5°C. This is a minor effect because, at a 60°C incubation temperature, the rate of reassociation of a DNA hybrid with a 75°C T_m is ca. 97% of the rate for a homoduplex hybrid.

At 60°C at least 75–80% of the base pairs must be hydrogen bonded to produce a stable duplex molecule (Britten et al. 1974). At higher temperatures (i.e., more stringent criteria) the

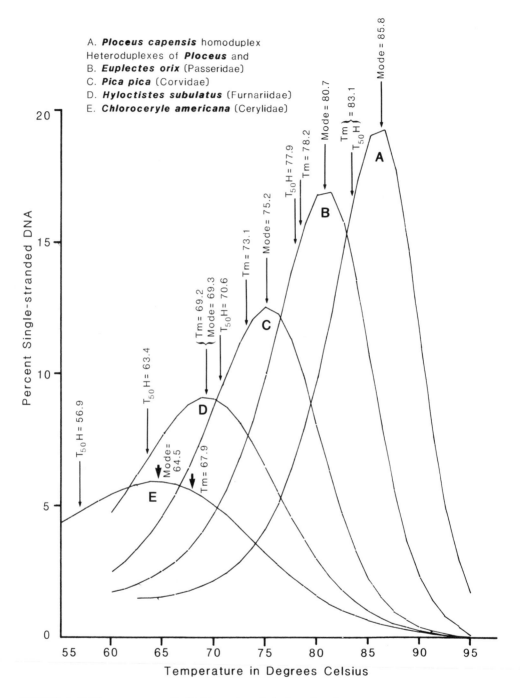

FIGURE 4. Differences among $T_{50}H$, T_m, and mode indicated on frequency distributions of DNA-DNA hybrid melting curves.

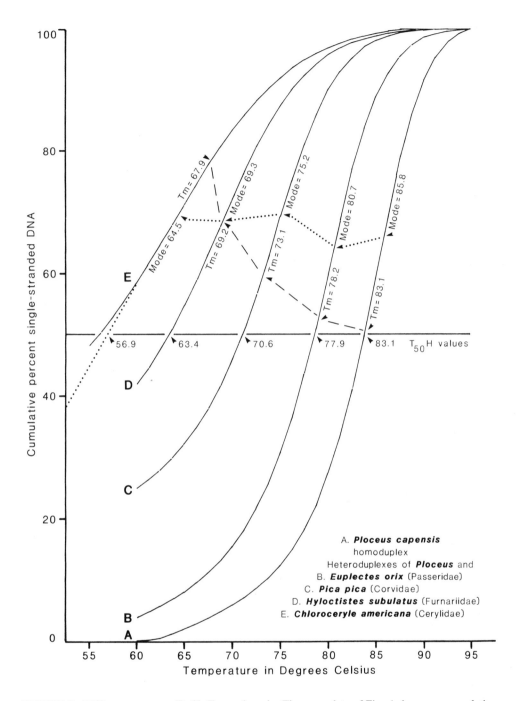

FIGURE 5. Differences among $T_{50}H$, T_m, and mode. The same data of Fig. 4 shown on cumulative distributions.

base pairing must be even more complete. This indicates that the more stringent criterion of the higher temperature selects the better-matched sequences from a population with a wide range of base-pair divergence (Hall et al. 1980).

At lower incubation temperatures the stringency is reduced and fewer matched bases are required for the formation of stable duplexes. At ca. 35–40°C only one base pair out of four must be hydrogen bonded to produce a thermally stable molecule. Because of the four-base genetic code, that level of complementarity is achieved by random reassociation and the entire genome reassociates rapidly, but homology is lost and the duplexes are genetically meaningless. This places the lower bound on the degree of sequence divergence that can be measured by the DNA-DNA hybridization technique. However, with hybrids incubated at standard criterion conditions, valid comparisons can be made between living lineages that diverged more than 100 million years ago and, with a relaxed criterion, e.g., 50°C, probably up to 150 million years ago. With an incubation temperature of 60°C in 0.48 M NaPB we have obtained valid distance measures between the most divergent taxa of living birds and have detected sequences with at least 70–75% of their bases paired in DNA-DNA hybrids between birds and reptiles (Fig. 6).

To obtain the maximum discrimination between single-stranded and double-stranded DNA during HAP chromatography, the column temperature and phosphate ion concentration must be varied together. For example, at 60°C and 0.12 M PB, single-stranded DNA is almost perfectly separated from double-stranded DNA. However, if the temperature is lowered to 50°C to obtain a greater extent of reassociation, the phosphate ion concentration must be increased to 0.14 M to maintain maximum discrimination (Britten et al. 1974:385–387).

CONCENTRATION OF DNA

To initiate the formation of a stable duplex DNA molecule, a random collision between homologous, complementary single strands must occur. Thus, the rate of reassociation obeys the law of mass action and depends on the concentration of each different nucleotide sequence present in the reaction mixture. Relatively simple genomes, such as those of viruses or bacteria, reassociate rapidly because they contain fewer different sequences than those of eukaryotes. In the complex genomes of higher organisms a given sequence will encounter many non-complementary sequences before colliding with an acceptable partner, hence the more copies of a given sequence that are present, the higher the probability that each of them will find a complementary sequence in the shortest length of time. Conversely, those sequences present at a low level of concentration will require more time to encounter complementary partners.

The product of the initial concentration of DNA and the length of time during which the mixture is incubated is the controlling parameter for estimating the completion of the reassociation reaction. For this reason the term "C_ot value" has been defined for the study of DNA reassociation and the formation of DNA hybrids. C_o is the initial concentration of single-stranded DNA in moles of nucleotide per liter, and "t" is the incubation time in seconds (Britten and Kohne 1968). A C_ot value of 1.0 is attained if single-stranded DNA is incubated for one hour at 60°C in 0.12 M PB at a concentration of 83 micrograms/ml which corresponds to an optical density of ca. 2.0 at 260 nanometers. C_ot is approximately equal to one-half of the

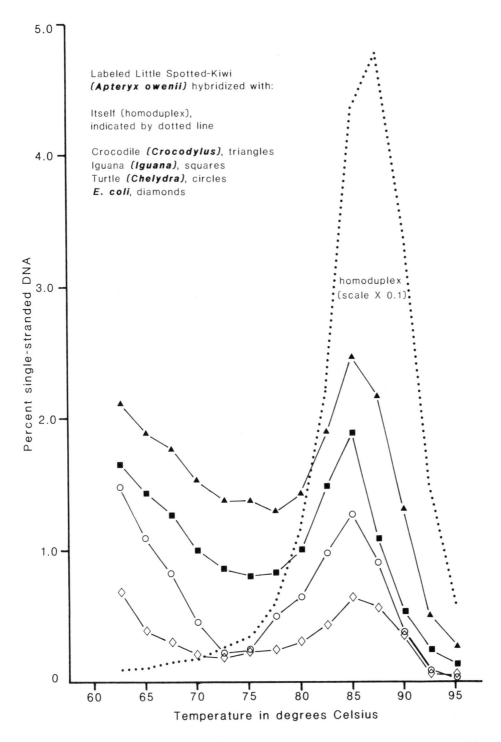

FIGURE 6. Bird-reptile DNA-DNA hybrids. Each heteroduplex curve represents the average of five hybrids. The peak near 85°C is due to tracer-tracer hybridization, thus only the low temperature portion of the curves reflects heteroduplex formation. Note decreasing amount of heteroduplex formation with reptiles of presumed greater divergence from birds. The homoduplex curve is shown at 0.1 scale.

optical density at 260 nanometers times hours. A $C_o t$ of 1×10^{-3} is achieved in 15 seconds at standard criterion and a concentration of 2.05×10^{-2} mg/ml. A $C_o t$ of 20,000 could be reached in 120 hours in 0.48 M PB using a concentration of 2.52 mg/ml. "$C_o t$" is usually written, and pronounced, "Cot."

The time course of reassociation may be presented as a Cot plot, which illustrated in Fig. 7. The reassociation kinetics of the DNA of an organism may be characterized as the Cot value at which the reassociation reaction is half completed (Cot $1/2$) under controlled conditions. The observed rates range over at least eight orders of magnitude, so it is necessary to use a logarithmic scale to present the measurements of reactions over extended periods of time and wide ranges of concentration. The time course of an ideal second-order reaction would produce a plot in which the slope of the central two-thirds of the curve is close to a straight line. The slope may be evaluated from the ratio of Cot values at its two ends. If this ratio is much over 100, it means that two or more frequency classes of DNA sequences, with different rates of reassociation, are present.

The reassociation rate constant, k, is the reciprocal of the Cot $1/2$. The equation for the reaction is

$$C/C_o = 1/(1 + k \text{ Cot})$$

where, C is the concentration of remaining single-stranded DNA and Co the initial concentration of single-stranded DNA, both in moles of nucleotides per liter, as noted above. The value of the reassociation rate constant, k, depends on the incubation conditions and the complexity of the DNA; more specifically, it depends on the relative concentration of complementary regions in the DNA at which nucleation can occur and lead to reassociation (Britten et al. 1974:367, Wetmur 1976, Young and Anderson 1985).

Britten and Davidson (1985) note that the expected value of k for standard conditions can be calculated by

$$k = R/G$$

where R is the rate constant ($M^{-1} \times \text{sec}^{-1}$) irrespective of complexity, and G is the genome size (number of nucleotides). R is independent of complexity but dependent on ionic strength, temperature, fragment length, etc. A typical value is $10^6 M^{-1} \times \text{sec}^{-1}$ for reassociation under standard conditions, i..e, 500 base fragments in 0.18 M Na^+ at the optimum temperature assayed by HAP binding. The value of k for the genome of λ phage with a complexity of 48.5 kb is 21; for the single-copy genome of a bird, assuming a complexity of 10^9, the value of k is ca. 10^{-3}.

Because the rate of reassociation depends on the concentration of each different nucleotide sequence, it is obvious that if many copies of some sequences are present they will reassociate more rapidly than sequences present as fewer copies. The occurrence and frequency of repetition of multiple sequences is discussed in chapter 6. Straus (1976), Thompson and Murray (1981), and Jelinek and Schmid (1982) reviewed this subject. Fig. 8 is a diagram of the sequence complexity of the avian genome.

The procedure for preparing a Cot plot and its use in the preparation of single-copy tracers are described in chapter 10.

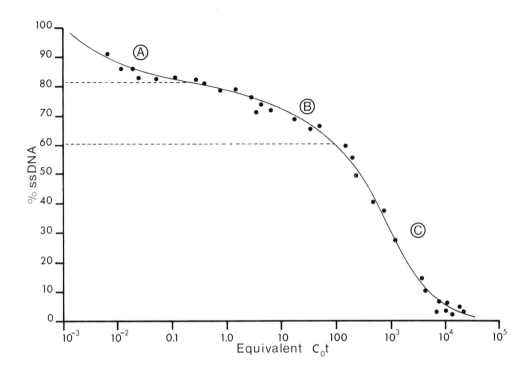

FIGURE 7. Cot curve of Herring Gull (*Larus argentatus*) DNA. *A*, *B*, and *C* are the highly repeated, the moderately repeated, and the single-copy fractions respectively.

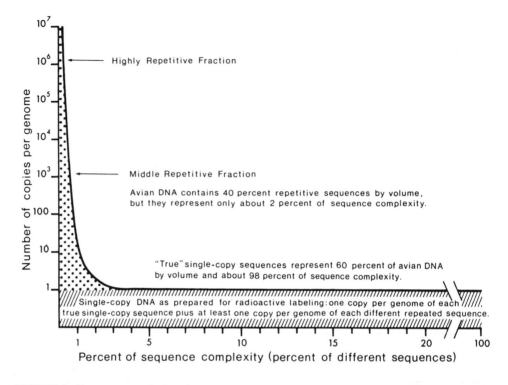

FIGURE 8. Sequence complexity of the avian genome.

FRAGMENT SIZE

The length of the DNA strands affects the rate and extent of reassociation. Long single strands encounter diffusion problems that reduce the probability of a collision between complementary sequences, and because of the interspersion of repeated sequences in eukaryotes, long-stranded DNA can form large concatenates, or networks, during reassociation. If a repeated single-stranded sequence forms a duplex with a complementary sequence in a different position in the genome, the nearby sequences are likely to be unrelated and, because of steric hindrance, cannot reassociate with their complements. Thus, long strands will be held together by a few, relatively short paired regions. The result is a large network of DNA that is mostly single-stranded.

A second complication in the reassociation of long-stranded DNA is that the longer the strand, the higher the probability that it will contain a repeated sequence. If long strands are used in the preparation of single-copy tracer DNA a large percentage of the single-copy sequences will be linked to a repeated sequence. The repeated sequences will tend to reassociate among themselves, which may distort the results based on counts of radioactivity. This may cause the delta values to be smaller than they should be and divergent taxa to seem more closely related than they actually are.

An excessive number of short-stranded fragments also presents problems. Duplexes of less than ca. 50 bases do not bind to HAP and will elute in the first washoff, thus reducing the percentage of hybridization. If a large number of fragments shorter than ca. 100 bp are present in the tracer DNA, the shape of the melting curve will be affected and the T_m of the homoduplex will be lower than desirable. Short-stranded tracers produce melting curves with a rapidly rising "foot" region because the short duplexes melt more readily at the lower temperatures than longer duplexes with the same percentage of base pairing. Ideally, a tracer preparation should contain no fragments shorter than 100 bp, and few below 200 bp.

To achieve controlled, reproducible rates of reassociation, in which all complementary sequences can form duplexes, long-stranded native DNA is sheared into smaller fragments which can interact, regardless of their original position in a long sequence of bases (Britten and Waring 1965, Britten and Davidson 1971, Britten et al. 1974, Straus 1976). The procedure for shearing long DNA strands into fragments of an optimal range of sizes is described in chapter 10.

For most DNA-DNA hybridization experiments the ideal population of DNA fragments has an average length of ca. 500 bases with a range between ca. 200 and 800 bp. The reassociation of such fragments, when assayed by HAP chromatography, displays second-order kinetics. The rate-limiting event is the initial collision (nucleation) between two complementary, or partly complementary, single strands at a point where a few base pairs are in correct complementary register, followed by the rapid zippering reaction of the remaining complementary base pairs of the two strands, as described above.

The rate of reassociation is proportional to the square root of the length of complementary DNA fragments of equal length or, if the fragments are unequal, to the square root of the shorter of two reacting single strands (Wetmur 1976). This relationship holds for fragment lengths from ca. 100 to 10,000 bases, thus for all fragments likely to be used in DNA-DNA comparisons. Wetmur and Davidson (1968), Kohne (1970), Lee and Wetmur (1972a), Britten et al. (1974), Wetmur (1976), Hall et al. (1980), Grula et al. (1982), and Britten and Davidson (1985:7) provide additional information on this subject.

The effect of fragment size on the extent of reassociation is illustrated by an example from a study of sea urchin DNAs by Angerer et al. (1976:218, 221). In one experiment the single-copy tracer DNA of *Strongylocentrotus purpuratus* was sheared into 450 bp fragments and reassociated with the whole, sheared DNA of *S. franciscanus*. In a second experiment the tracer DNA was sheared into 230 bp fragments. The 450 bp fragments reassociated to 62%, the 230 bp fragments to 51%. Thus, in general, longer labeled fragments have higher normalized reassociations when assayed by HAP chromatography.

Britten et al. (1974:367) noted that the effect of fragment size on thermal stability may be expressed as

$$T_n - T_m = B/L$$

where T_n is the melting temperature of long-stranded DNA, T_m that of the fragments, L the fragment length, and B a constant. They suggested that a value for B equal to 650 in 0.18 M Na$^+$ was the "best compromise" of several estimates.

Hall et al. (1980:98) used alkaline agarose and sucrose electrophoretic gradients, and DNA fragments of known size produced by digestion with restriction endonucleases, to calculate the effect of fragment length on thermal stability as

$$T_m \text{ reduction} = 500/\text{fragment length in nucleotide pairs}$$

Ornstein and Fresco (1983) found that a chain length greater than 60 bp will have a T_m within 2–3°C of that of much longer fragments. For lengths between 200 and 400 bp the reduction in T_m compared with much longer sequences is less than 1.0°C, and fragments between 400 and 600 bp have T_ms only 0.3–0.5°C below duplexes of infinite length. (See chapter 2.)

A disparity between the average lengths of the tracer and driver fragments in a DNA-DNA hybrid may introduce a small amount of experimental error. For example, if the tracer fragments are substantially longer than those of the driver it is possible for hybrids to form in which there are long single-strand tails of tracer which include labeled sites. Such duplexes will bind to HAP, but when they dissociate they contribute an excessive number of radioactive counts to the data. This can result in unequal reciprocal values and lower delta values if the period of reassociation is short. However, if the reassociation is long enough to permit the formation of hyperpolymers by the base pairing of the single-strand tails of different partial duplexes, the effect is minimal when assayed on HAP. Thus, although the control of fragment size is important for accurate results, a long period of reassociation will reduce the effect of unequal fragment lengths between tracer and driver sequences. Single-strand tails may be removed with S–1 nuclease.

BASE COMPOSITION

As noted in chapter 2, there are two hydrogen bonds between A-T base pairs, and three between G-C pairs. Thus, G-C pairs melt at a higher temperature than A-T pairs, and the T_m of a double-stranded DNA sequence depends, in part, on its A-T:G-C ratio. Base stacking also contributes to helix stability. In a solvent of 0.15 M sodium chloride plus 0.015 M sodium citrate, a synthetic polynucleotide sequence composed only of G-C base pairs has a T_m ca. 106°C, and one composed only of A-T base pairs has a T_m ca. 66°C (Marmur and Doty 1962). These values vary by several degrees depending on the properties of the solvent, especially the concentration of sodium ion (Na^+). Therefore, it is necessary to specify the type and molarity of the buffer. The thermal transition of such uniform DNAs would be abrupt, rather than having the relatively broad transition of ca. 15°C characteristic of natural DNAs that contain both A-T and G-C base pairs.

The melting curve of native double-stranded DNA is a cumulative plot of the melting of different regions of differing average base composition, with the A-T rich regions melting at the lower temperatures and the G-C rich regions melting at the higher temperatures. Thus, an A-T rich DNA will have a lower T_m than one that is G-C rich. For example, in a solvent of 0.15 M sodium chloride plus 0.015 M sodium citrate, the T_ms and percentage of G+C ranged from 84°C for a 38% G+C composition to 97°C for a 67% G+C content (Marmur and Doty 1959, 1962; Mandel and Marmur 1968). Thus, a change of 1% in G+C content causes a change of ca. 0.45°C in the T_m. DNAs with higher G+C ratios also reassociate slightly faster than those with a lower G+C content because the triple hydrogen bonds between G-C bases form stronger pairs during the nucleation event between complementary sequences (Wetmur and Davidson 1968, Laird 1971).

The melting behavior of interspecific duplexes formed by DNA-DNA hybridization depends on the A-T:G-C content and on the base pair mismatches that have accumulated since the two species diverged from their most recent common ancestor. The sigmoid shape of the cumulative melting curve of a DNA-DNA hybrid is a function of the base composition, but the difference between the melting curve of a heteroduplex hybrid and that of the comparable homoduplex hybrid is due to base pair mismatches between the DNAs of the two species forming the heteroduplex.

There is considerable variation in the amounts of A+T and G+C among organisms. These amounts are expressed as the molar ratio, A+T:G+C, or more simply as the percent G+C (the %A+T obviously equals 100 minus the %G+C). The %G+C is related to the ratio of A+T to G+C. If x = %G+C, then $100 - x/x$ = A+T:G+C; for example, $100 - 43/43$ = 1.32.

In the fungi the %G+C ranges from 25 to 97, but in most groups it is much less; 22% in the slime mold *Dictyostelium* and 73% in the bacterium *Mycobacterium phlei*. Other bacteria have %GC values as low as 34; thus the bacteria have a range of at least 39%. The wood-rotting fungus *Schizophyllum commune* has a %GC of ca. 57, plus a small amount of DNA with a %GC of 22.1, and a satellite with 27% GC that composes 2% of the whole-cell DNA (Ullrich et al. 1980a). In the insects and other invertebrates, the %GC ranges from ca. 32–42 (Berry 1985). In the vertebrates the %GC ranges at least from 36.2 in a minnow (*Cyprinus*) to 46.3 in a frog (*Rana*). In 14 genera of mammals the range is from 38% to 54%, with both extremes recorded from human tissues, indicating either intraspecific variation or, more likely, measurement error. For calf (*Bos taurus*) thymus cells the ratio has been calculated by 18 different authors whose results range from 40% to 45%. The G+C content in the Domestic Fowl (*G. gallus*) has been measured at least eight times with results ranging from 42% to 45%, average 43% (Shapiro 1976). In *G. gallus* Shapiro (1976) and Adams et al. (1981:36) found a 43%

G+C, but Stefos and Arrighi (1974) measured the *Gallus* %G+C as 37.8 based on T_m, and 39.6 based on buoyant density.

As noted above, the G+C content is related to the T_m as expressed by the equation

$$\%GC = (T_m - 69.3)2.44$$

In our data the T_ms of the best homoduplex avian hybrids are usually 85–86°C; thus the G+C content in birds is essentially the same as in mammals, ca. 40–44%.

In 2.4 M tetraethylammonium chloride (TEACL) DNA melts at ca. 62°C, the effect of base composition on melting temperature is suppressed, and the melting transition is abrupt, ca. 1.5°C. This makes it possible to detect small differences between the melting curves of closely related DNAs. Using TEACL as the solvent, Britten et al. (1979) demonstrated a 4% base-pair mismatch between the genomes of individual Purple Sea Urchins (*Strongylocentrotus purpuratus*), due to the summation of genetic polymorphisms. Other species of sea urchins had less polymorphism. Britten et al. (1979:222) examined DNA sequence polymorphism in a few other species and reported that "Within the limit of sensitivity of this technique, approximately 0.5°C, no polymorphism has been recognized for human DNA, *Mus musculus* DNA, or Eastern song sparrow [*Melospiza melodia*] DNA." Other studies using TEACL as the solvent include Hall et al. (1980), Hunt et al. (1981), Grula et al. (1982), Hunt and Carson (1983), Powell et al. (1986), Caccone and Powell (1987, 1989), and Caccone et al. (1987). Werman et al. (1990) provide a protocol for the TEACL method.

The physical chemistry of the thermal transition of DNA from the double-stranded to the single-stranded condition has been studied by Crothers et al. (1965) and Hayes et al. (1970). Bloomfield et al. (1974) reviewed the physical chemistry of nucleic acids. Adams et al. (1981) and Saenger (1984) provide reviews.

VISCOSITY

The rate of reassociation is inversely proportional to solvent viscosity in high salt solvents at all criteria. This observation supports the rate-temperature profile theory, which provides for only one mechanism for the reaction at all temperatures. The alternative theory, involving different mechanisms for reassociation reactions at open and stringent criteria, is not supported by experimental results. The exact nature of the viscosity effect on the rate of base-pair formation has not been established, although it is probable that the reorientation of the bases and concurrent base stacking and hydrogen bonding may be a diffusion-limited process. When high concentrations of dextran polymers are added to reassociation mixtures, the rate is accelerated because the added polymers increase the effective concentration of the DNA, hence the rate of reassociation. Rate acceleration may be useful for decreasing the time necessary for hybridizing highly complex eukaryotic DNAs (Chang et al. 1974, Wetmur 1976:350–351).

Solvent concentration may be the same in all DNA-DNA comparisons, but the DNA concentrations may vary and produce a range of viscosities, as may protein and polysaccharide impurities. To avoid the effects of different viscosities DNA hybrids may be diluted to a final concentration of 2 mg/ml.

GENOME SIZE

The "genome size" is the DNA in a haploid set of chromosomes. The haploid quantity of nuclear DNA is expressed as the C-value, measured in picograms (pg). One pg equals 10^{-12} grams, and one pg of DNA contains 0.965×10^9 nucleotide pairs, equal to 6.1×10^{11} daltons. One dalton equals the mass of one hydrogen atom, which equals 1.66×10^{-24} grams. The relative molecular weights of the four 5' monophosphate nucleotides (adenosine, thymidine, cytidine, and guanidine) are 347.25, 322.23, 322.22, and 363.25, respectively. Thus, the mean molecular weight per nucleotide is 339.0. The formation of a nucleotide pair involves the loss of a water molecule, so the mean molecular weight per nucleotide pair is ca. $339 \times 2 - 18$, or 660. The use of this factor assumes equal amounts of the four nucleotides, which is not true, so the mean value provides only an approximation.

If the molecular weights of nucleotides are based on the weights of the component atoms (C, H, O, N, P), a sugar plus a phosphate unit equals 356 (178×2); cytosine plus guanine H-bonded together equals 260, and adenine plus thymine equals 259. For an A-T base pair plus a sugar-phosphate the molecular weight is 616, and for a G-C pair plus a sugar-phosphate, 615. Segal (1976:135) notes that the average molecular weight of a complementary pair of deoxynucleotide residues is about 618.

Nuclear DNA amounts are measured by several methods and all are subject to error; thus, the amounts cited herein are estimates, not precise measurements. Bennett and Smith (1976:236–239) discussed this problem.

The information content of the genome is characterized by its sequence complexity, defined as the total length of different DNA sequences measured in nucleotide pairs (NTP) (Britten 1971). In higher organisms the sequence complexity is approximately equal to the number of NTP in one copy of each single-copy sequence plus one copy of each different repeated sequence (Britten et al. 1974:368). See "The Complexities of the Genome" at the end of this chapter.

The rate of reassociation is inversely proportional to the sequence complexity of the genome. For example, the single-copy genome of the bacterium *Escherichia coli* has a sequence complexity of ca. 4.5×10^6 NTP and that of the Domestic Cow (*Bos taurus*) has a sequence complexity of 3.2×10^9 NTP, or about 700 times that of *E. coli*. Under the same conditions the DNA of *E. coli* was half reassociated in eight hours, but it would take ca. 500 times as long, or about 167 days, for the single-copy sequences of *Bos* to attain the same level of reassociation (Britten and Kohne 1968; Kohne 1970:336). (*E. coli* is closer to 4.2×10^6 NTP, *fide* Zimmermann and Goldberg 1977.)

The quantity of DNA in the cells of eukaryotes varies widely, and organisms with similar levels of morphological complexity can have remarkably different C-values. This disparity, known as the C-value paradox, is illustrated by the Amphibia, in which the range of C-values is large and includes some of the highest C-values among animals. Hilder et al. (1983) reviewed previous studies and measured the amount of 5S-ribosomal DNA in the African Clawed Frog (*Xenopus laevis*), which has 3 pg and 9000 copies of 5S-rDNA; the Crested Newt (*Triturus cristatus*) with 23 pg, 32,000 copies; and the Axolotl (*Ambystoma mexicanum*), 38 pg, 61,000 copies. D. D. Brown and Sugimoto (1973) found 3 pg and 9000 copies in *Xenopus borealis*, and Pukkila (1975) measured 45 pg and 300,000 copies in the Newt (*Notophthalmus viridescens*).

There is a trend of increasing 5S gene copy-number with increasing C-values, but the correlation coefficient, r, is only 0.75. The differences between the two *Xenopus* are striking.

At least in part, the trend may be related to the need to supply more ribosomes to the larger cells associated with larger genomes, particularly during oogenesis and embryonic cleavage. It appears that when the demand for gene products cannot be met by increasing the rate of production per gene, or the time in which the product can accumulate, the copy-number of genes can be increased. The poor correlation suggests that while there may be a minimum number of copies of the 5S gene required in proportion to C-value, there is no precise constraint on the maximum number.

At least some genes have the capacity to amplify (i.e., increase the number of copies) in response to external challenges, thus adding to the C-value within a single generation (Schimke 1982, J. W. Roberts et al. 1983, and see "Gene Amplification" in chapter 7). Thus, differences in the number of copies of repeated sequences account for at least some of the differences in C-values between closely related taxa (Hutchinson et al. 1980).

Several aspects of cell structure and function seem to be correlated with C-values. There is a linear relationship between cell area, cell volume, and amount of DNA (Szarski 1974, Olmo and Morescalchi 1975, Cavalier-Smith 1985). In some plants there is an inverse correlation between C-value and minimum mitotic cell cycle time (Van't Hoff and Sparrow 1963, Bennett 1972). In some amphibia the developmental rate and DNA quantity are correlated (Goin et al. 1968). The exceptions to these observations suggest that they may be coincidental, not general.

The quantity of DNA in the genome has been determined for more than a thousand species of plants and animals. In general, total DNA content increases from the lower to the higher invertebrates, and closely related organisms tend to have similar amounts of DNA, although there are some notable exceptions.

The single-stranded genome of the bacterial virus φ-X174 is composed of 5386 nucleotides, and their complete sequence is known (Sanger et al. 1977; M. Smith 1979). This virus infects the intestinal bacterium *E. coli*, which has a genome of 4.2 million NTP, or 780 times the size of φ-X174. Some salamanders have ca. 8×10^{10} nucleotides per genome, and the psilopsids, a group of primitive plants, have ca. 2.9×10^{11}, which is 690,000 times the size of the genome of *E. coli*.

Expressed in picograms, the range in C-values is from ca. 0.00000585 pg for a virus, 0.007 pg for a bacterium, and 0.05–0.09 pg in the fungi, to ca. 300 pg in the psilopsids (Hinegardner 1976, Ullrich and Raper 1977, Ullrich et al. 1980a).

Plants

The ferns have from 6 to ca. 100 pg, and the psilopsids from ca. 129 to more than 300 pg (Sparrow et al. 1972). Bennett and Smith (1976) listed the C-values for 753 species of angiosperms, which range from 0.2 to 127.4 pg, but most species of flowering plants have less than 10 pg. In most species the DNA amount is constant, but many exceptions are known, and some congeneric species differ widely. For example, in different species of the leguminous genus *Vicia* the nuclear DNA content differs by up to seven-fold, even among diploid species in which 2n equals 14 (Chooi 1971, Bennett and Smith 1976:267–269).

The smallest known angiosperm genome is that of *Arabidopsis thaliana*, which has only 0.2 pg of DNA (7×10^7 bp) (Meyerowitz and Pruitt 1985).

Invertebrates

The C-values of invertebrates range from 0.05 pg in sponges to 15.8 in the crustaceans, but most groups have between 0.1 and 7.5 pg (Hinegardner 1976). The Virginia Oyster (*Ostrea virginica*) has 0.69 pg, the Surf Clam (*Spisula solidissima*) 1.2 pg, the Horseshoe Crab (*Limulus polyphemus*) 2.8 pg, a nemertean worm (*Cerebratulus lacteus*) 1.4 pg, and a jellyfish (*Aurelia aurita*) 0.73 pg (Goldberg et al. 1975). The Sea Hare (*Aplysia californica*), a large opisthobranch gastropod, has 1.8 pg (Angerer et al. 1975), and the Purple Sea Urchin (*Strongylocentrotus purpuratus*), 0.89 pg (Hinegardner 1974a, 1976).

Most insect tissues are polyploid and the amount of DNA per nucleus is difficult to measure. However, insect genome sizes seem to be similar to those of most other eukaryotes, with ca. 0.5 pg per haploid nucleus as an average. Of the insect genomes that have been examined none has an excessive amount of DNA (Berry 1985).

Vertebrates

FISH. The sharks and rays have 2.8–9.8 pg, the lungfish (Dipnoi) have one of the largest genomes with 80–140 pg, the coelacanth *Latimeria* has 7 pg, and the teleosts have 0.39–4.4 pg, with a modal value ca. 1.0 pg. The Alligator Gar (*Lepisosteus osseus*) genome contains ca. 1.1×10^9 bp, or ca. 1.1 pg of DNA, a loach (Cobitididae) has 1.4 pg, a sturgeon (*Acipenser*) 2 pg, and salmon (*Salmo*) 3 pg (Hinegardner 1976, Vladychenskaya et al. 1983).

AMPHIBIA. The anuran amphibians (frogs, toads) have relatively standard genomes of 1.2–7.9 pg. C-values for 120 species of frogs and toads range from 1 to 10 pg, with a modal value of 2.5 pg. Only three species of the discoglossid genus *Bombina* have more than 7 pg (Olmo 1973).

Like the lungfish, the urodele amphibians (salamanders) have extremely large genomes, ranging from 18 to nearly 100 pg. The C-value varies among congeneric species, and even between different populations, or possibly individuals, of the same species. For example, the five species of *Ambystoma* range from 22 to 52 pg, the four species of *Desmognathus* from 18 to 22 pg, and the three species of *Necturus* from 68 to 95 pg (Olmo 1973, Hinegardner 1976).

Mizuno and Macgregor (1974) compared the genome sizes, karyotypes, and sequence frequencies of 15 of the 17 North American species of the salamander genus *Plethodon*. All species have 14 chromosomes and nearly identical karyotypes, but the C-values range from 18 pg in the eastern *P. cinereus* group to 33–69 pg in western species. *P. vandykei*, of western Washington, with 69 pg, has more than three times the DNA of *P. cinereus*, but the two species are as morphologically similar as any two species in the genus. The differences in C-values were found to be in the repeated fraction, but the single-copy fraction in all amphibian species is essentially the same size. See additional comments on this study in chapter 6.

Birstein (1982) reviewed the structural characteristics of amphibian genomes, including genome size, chromosome number, banding patterns, and genome organization. Birstein noted that differences in genome size among related species of anurans and urodeles are "due to the different content of highly repetitive and intermediate sequences, the amount of unique sequences being equal" (p. 78). For example, in anurans, the African Clawed Frog (*Xenopus laevis*) has 3 pg of DNA per genome, and a Common Toad (*B. bufo*) 7 pg, but both have ca. 1.5

pg of single-copy DNA. Similarly, two salamanders, *Triturus cristatus* and *Necturus maculosus*, have 23 and 52 pg respectively, but both have ca. 11 pg of single-copy DNA.

REPTILES. Olmo (1976) determined the nuclear DNA content of 49 species of reptiles, representing the Chelonia (turtles), Crocodylia, and Squamata (lizards, snakes). The 12 species of turtles range from 4.6–9.1 pg, average 6.6; the single crocodilian (*Caiman crocodylus*) has 5.4 pg; 30 lizards range from 4.0 to 7.8, average 5.3; and six species of snakes have 3.5–6.3, average 5.3 pg. The 49 species range from 3.5 to 9.1 pg, with a modal value ca. 5.5.

BIRDS. The C-values of 23 species of birds, representing seven orders and 17 families, were determined by Bachmann et al. (1972b). They range from 1.6 pg in the Budgerigar (*Melopsittacus undulatus*) to 2.2 in the Palm Warbler (*Dendroica palmarum*). However, the average for the eight non-passerines is 1.90 pg and for the 15 passerines 1.92 pg. For all 23 species the average is 1.91 pg. The modal C-value is 1.8 pg, which is equivalent to 1.74×10^9 NTP. The single-copy fraction is ca. 60%, or 1.04×10^9 NTP.

The ratio between the largest and smallest known avian genomes is 1.3:1; thus the genomes of these 23 species range over ca. 30% in size. However, as suggested by Stefos (1971), the differences are probably due to varying amounts of highly repetitive sequences and the sequence complexity is far more equivalent than the total DNA amounts might seem to indicate. Since most of the copies of repeated sequences are removed during the preparation of single-copy tracers, the differences in the total amounts of DNA may have little, if any, effect on the reassociation or thermal stability of avian DNA-DNA hybrids.

MAMMALS. Bianchi et al. (1983) measured the C-values in five species of South American cricetid rodents: four species of *Akodon* and *Bolomys obscurus*. The range was 2.23 to 3.23 pg. Within *A. molinae* the range was 2.87–3.23, correlated with the 2n chromosome number, which ranges from 42 to 44.

Manfredi Romanini (1985) reported the nuclear DNA content of ca. 200 species of mammals. The 2C-values averaged 7.25 pg (C, 3.6 pg) and 80% of the species examined ranged from 6 to 9 pg (C, 3–4.5 pg).

Sherwood and Patton (1982) measured the C-values in two subgenera, five species, and 21 subspecies of pocket gophers (*Thomomys*). They found (1) extensive interspecific variation with some congeners identical in C-values and others differing by as much as 230%, (2) C-values differing to 35% within species, and (3) significant differences in C-values between different populations of the same subspecies with apparently similar karyotypes. In *Thomomys bottae* there is a high correlation ($r = -0.94$) between the C-value and the number of acrocentric (uniarmed) chromosomes per karyotype for most of the populations and subspecies examined. A one-picogram change in cellular DNA content is associated with a change in arm number of 17, which is an average of 0.06 pg of DNA per heterochromatic arm. Clearly, the variation in the karyotypes reflects actual differences in the C-values.

Within the subspecies and populations of *T. bottae* the 2C-values range from 8.42 to 11.43 pg (C-values, 4.21–5.72) and average 9.79 pg (average C-value, 4.90). This contrasts with the smaller genomes of the *T. talpoides* group, which have diploid genomes averaging ca. 4.95 pg (C, 2.47 pg).

The extensive variations in C-values in *Thomomys* indicate that single C-values cannot be assumed to characterize a species, or even a population within a species. Sherwood and Patton (1982:177) conclude that "DNA amount is a feature of the genome like nucleotide sequence and sequence arrangement for which variability continues to represent an enigma."

Nei (1975) and Hinegardner (1976) reviewed the literature on genome size and discussed the evolutionary significance of changes in DNA quantity and sequence complexity. In view of the discoveries of intraspecific variation described by Sherwood and Patton (1982), it seems prudent to assume that previous conclusions about the evolutionary significance of genome size should be considered premature. (See "Gene Amplification" in chapter 7.)

Cavalier-Smith (1982) examined the relationships among genome size, cell volumes, and growth rates. He assumed that "The mass of DNA in a haploid nucleus is usually constant in any one species" (p. 273) and that "C-values are generally positively correlated with cell and nuclear volumes" (p. 274). Cavalier-Smith (1982:298) concluded that "The primary cause of the . . . vast spectrum of eukaryote genome sizes is the evolution of a great variety of cell volumes, coupled with . . . a DNA replication pattern that allows large amounts of DNA to be replicated in a relatively shorter time than in prokaryotes."

There are positive correlations between DNA content and cell volume in many organisms, but as noted above, Bianchi et al. (1983) and Sherwood and Patton (1982) have demonstrated that there is extensive variation in C-values within species and even within subspecies.

Among the papers reporting genome size data are those of Mirsky and Ris (1949, 1951), Ohno et al. (1964), Beçak et al. (1964), Atkin et al. (1965), Ohno and Atkin (1966), Hinegardner (1968, 1974a,b), Pedersen (1971), Hinegardner and Rosen (1972), Britten and Davidson (1971, 1976), Bachmann et al. (1972a,b), Sparrow et al. (1972), Olmo (1973, 1976), Wallace and Morowitz (1973), Rees (1974), and Sparrow and Nauman (1976). Nagl (1978) discussed variation in nuclear DNA, especially in relation to changes during ontogeny and phylogeny. Cavalier-Smith (1985) edited a volume on the evolution of genome size.

The size of the genome is important in DNA hybridization because the larger genomes contain large amounts of repeated DNA, hence they pose a problem for the production of single-copy tracers. Any species with a genome larger than ca. 5 pg will have to be reassociated for a long time to reach a Cot $\frac{1}{2}$ value in the range of the single-copy fraction. Differences in genome size may affect reciprocity.

EFFECTS OF SEQUENCE DIVERGENCE

When, for any reason, two populations derived from a common ancestor become reproductively isolated, their nucleotide sequences begin to diverge as each population incorporates different base substitutions. The degree of sequence divergence is a measure of genealogical distance that can be determined by the extent of reassociation (% hybridization) and the thermal stability of hybrid DNA-DNA duplexes formed from the two diverging genomes. Bonner et al. (1973) examined the reduction in the rate of reassociation resulting from sequence divergence and concluded that the rate is reduced by a factor of two for each 10°C reduction in melting temperature due to sequence divergence.

It is possible to increase the extent of reassociation by lowering the incubation temperature, but duplex formation is still limited to those sequences that form stable duplexes at that temperature. At 60°C ca. 75–80% of the bases must be correctly paired to form a stable duplex. Thus, for closely related species the percentage of hybridization will be high, but for more widely diverged species the base-pair complementarity will be reduced in proportion to their genetic differences and a smaller percentage of the two genomes will form stable duplexes. Furthermore, the duplexes that are formed represent the more conserved sequences, i.e., those that have changed least since the lineages diverged. The result is that the percentage of hybridization decreases, but the thermal stability (as T_m) of the duplexes that form remains high. The effect is to truncate the melting curve, leaving only those hybrids composed of sequences that have retained a high enough degree of complementarity to be stable at the incubation temperature.

An example illustrating these factors was explored by Angerer et al. (1976) in a study of sea urchin relationships. The single-copy tracer DNA of *Strongylocentrotus purpuratus* was hybridized (70°C, 1.0 M NaCl) with the driver DNAs of two congeners, *S. franciscanus* and *S. drobachiensis*, and with the DNA of a much more distantly related species, *Lytechinus pictus*. The *S. purpuratus* tracer DNA had normalized hybridization percentages and ΔT_m values with the other three species as follows: *S. drobachiensis*, 68%, 2.5°C; *S. franciscanus*, 51%, 3.5°C; and *L. pictus*, 12%, 7.5°C.

It is obvious that the percentages of hybridization and the ΔT_m values are not decreasing at the same rate. The discrepancy is especially large for *L. pictus*, which differs from *S. purpuratus* by 88% of its single-copy sequences at 70°C, but the 12% that does react shows a ΔT_m of only 7.5°C. Thus, the sequences that formed duplexes have a relatively high thermal stability, indicating that these sequences have changed little since the two lineages diverged. Angerer et al. (1976) suggested that possibly 5% of these genomes have undergone almost no sequence divergence.

This example also illustrates the effect of a stringent criterion (70°C) on the reassociation of the DNAs of widely diverged species. However, if the stringency had been reduced by using a 55°C incubation temperature, a much larger percentage of the two genomes would have formed stable duplexes, resulting in a larger ΔT_m for the hybrid between *S. purpuratus* and *L. pictus*. This shows the effect of divergence on T_m, which measures the median melting temperature only of those sequences that actually form duplexes. The ΔT_m values are therefore poor measures of the true amount of sequence divergence, except for comparisons between closely related species. The $\Delta T_{50}H$ statistic, which is a measure of the median sequence divergence of the total genome, is recommended for DNA-DNA hybrid comparisons, especially between distantly related taxa. However, $T_{50}H$ values are partly dependent on the accuracy of the percent of hybridization, which is a difficult measurement to obtain accurately. T_m and $T_{50}H$ are approximately equal at low delta values (< 5°C). The T_{mode} is sometimes used, but Werman et al. (1990) state, "There does not appear to be any range of distance where the T_{mode} is the most accurate estimator of evolutionary distance." Unfortunately, there is no perfect single measurement for the comparison of DNA melting curves. See chapter 11 for definitions of these measurements.

In a study of the same sea urchin taxa named above, Hall et al. (1980) measured the thermal stability of heteroduplexes in 2.4 M tetraethylammonium chloride (TEACL), which suppresses the effect of base composition on melting temperature. They also corrected for the lengths of duplexes after treatment with S–1 nuclease and found that the degree of base substitution was significantly larger than indicated by the earlier measurements of Angerer et al. (1976). By the TEACL method the delta median ($\Delta T_{50}H$) for the hybrids between *S. purpuratus* and *S. franciscanus* on HAP was 15 and by the S–1 procedure, 21. Corrections for intraspecies polymorphism (Britten et al. 1978) and fragment length suggested that the single-copy difference between these two congeners is ca. 19% and the divergence time, from fossils, was ca. 20 million years ago (MYA); thus, the average genomic rate of evolution is ca. 0.5%/MY (19/40 = 0.48). The corrections brought the two sets of data (Angerer et al. 1976, Hall et al. 1980) into agreement. Hall et al. (1980) confirmed the ca. 5% conserved sequences among the species of *Strongylocentrotus* and *Lytechinus pictus* and calculated an approximate delta median of 7.7 for hybrids between *S. purpuratus* and *S. drobachiensis*, and of 51 for *purpuratus* × *Lytechinus* hybrids. The latter had a normalized reaction of 22%, compared with 83% for *purpuratus* × *drobachiensis* and 64% for *purpuratus* × *franciscanus*.

The differences between the results of these two studies illustrate some of the problems involved in making single-copy DNA comparisons between widely divergent taxa, or between those with excessive amounts of intraspecies polymorphism. Fortunately, birds have much lower levels of intraspecific polymorphism, and no living lineages diverged from one another more than ca. 100–125 MYA.

Bonner et al. (1973) also found that the reassociation of interspecific DNA-DNA hybrids is discriminated against because the driver sequences reassociate rapidly among themselves, thus reducing the number of potential complementary partners for the tracer fragments. This effect is proportional to the degree of divergence between the two genomes, hence most severe between distantly related species.

It is difficult to compensate for the effects of sequence divergence, but the best results are obtained if DNA-DNA hybrids are incubated long enough to permit the complete reassociation of all tracer fragments in homoduplex hybrids and of all heteroduplexes that are stable at the incubation temperature. For most DNA-DNA hybrids among birds, incubation to Cot 16,000 satisfies these requirements.

RELATIONSHIP BETWEEN DELTA VALUES AND
PERCENTAGE OF BASE-PAIR MISMATCH

The lower thermal stability of reassociated DNA duplexes, compared to that of native DNA, is due to base-pair mismatches between the reassociated strands. The difference between the median melting temperature (T_m or $T_{50}H$) of a homoduplex DNA-DNA hybrid and that of a heteroduplex hybrid is the ΔT_m (or $\Delta T_{50}H$), which provides an index to the thermal stability of the hybrid duplexes. Several estimates of the relationship between the T_m and the percentage of mismatched base pairs have been made. Bautz and Bautz (1964), Uhlenbeck et al. (1968), and Laird et al. (1969) reported a 1.4–1.5°C reduction in the T_m for each 1% of unpaired bases for DNAs with ca. 42% G+C and fragments of ca. 450 bp. Bonner et al. (1973) pointed out certain problems with the earlier estimates and concluded: "At the moment it appears that the best value of the conversion factor for naturally occurring sequence divergence is approximately 1 deg. C drop per 1% unpaired bases" (p. 124), and "By best present estimates, 10 deg. C reduction in T_m corresponds to about 10% unmatched bases" (p. 132).

Similarly, Wetmur (1976:353) concluded that the melting temperature is reduced ca.

1.1°C per percent base pairs modified. Alonso et al. (1986:16) found that a ΔT_m of 1.0 the three genes coding for actin in the House Mouse (*Mus musculus*) was correlated with a 1.3% difference in base sequence.

Caccone et al. (1988) concluded from a study based on 906 bp of the rRNA-coding region of mtDNA for several species of *Drosophila* that ΔT_m 1.0 indicates a base-pair mismatch of 1.7%.

The T_m statistic is bound from below by the incubation temperature because it is the median temperature of the actual melting curve, which is composed only of those duplexes that are thermally stable at the incubation temperature, e.g., 60°C. Thus, the T_m is an accurate measure of the median temperature of the complete melting curve only for homoduplexes. For heteroduplexes, whose melting curves are truncated in proportion to sequence divergence, the accuracy of the T_m declines. Up to ca. ΔT_m 10 the accuracy is acceptable, but the regression between T_m and percent hybridization is curvilinear and it reaches an asymptote beyond ca. ΔT_m 15. By contrast, the $T_{50}H$ statistic, which is approximately the median temperature of the complete melting curves at all degrees of sequence divergence, continues to increase with sequence divergence and hence with base-pair mismatch. Because $\Delta T_{50}H$ values track the median sequence divergence they should be close to 1:1 (or 1:1.7) vs percentage of base-pair mismatch for all degrees of divergence, but we do not have experimental evidence for this statement.

The avian genome contains ca. 1.7×10^9 NTP, of which ca. 60%, or 1.0×10^9 NTP, is single-copy. Thus, a $\Delta T_{50}H$ of 1.0, based on a single-copy tracer, is the result of mismatches between 1% of 10^9, or ca. 10×10^6 bases. Or, if Caccone et al. (1988) are correct, $\Delta T_{50}H$ 1.0 is the result of 1.7% mismatch, or ca. 17×10^6 bases.

THE COMPLEXITIES OF THE GENOME

Britten (1971) defined three kinds of complexity with reference to DNA sequences: sequence complexity, kinetic complexity, and genetic complexity.

Sequence complexity is the total length of different DNA sequences, measured in nucleotide pairs. It is equal to the genome size for organisms that have only single-copy, or simple sequence, DNA, such as viruses and bacteria. In these, the sequence complexity is the number of NTP per virus particle or bacterium. For organisms with repeated DNA sequences the measurement of sequence complexity is difficult, in part because it depends on the criterion at which the measurement is made. If the base sequence of an entire eukaryotic genome were known, the sequence complexity would be one copy of each different sequence. Thus, identical copies of repeated sequences would be counted as one, regardless of copy number. Even this definition is inadequate, because the members of a repeated "family" differ by various amounts, and the concept of "identical" sequences becomes difficult, or impossible, to define. Thus, sequence complexity is the ideal quantity, but kinetic complexity is the measurable quantity.

Because the rate of reassociation is the only method available to measure the complexity of repeated sequences, Britten (1971) defined kinetic complexity as the sequence complexity calculated from the results of a measurement of the rate of reassociation of a DNA preparation. Britten et al. (1974:368) defined the kinetic complexity, G_i, as:

$$G_i = K_i \times \text{correction factors} \times G_{coli}/K_{coli}$$

K_i is the measured rate constant, G_{coli} is the size of the simple sequence genome of the bacterium *Escherichia coli*, and K_{coli} is the rate constant for *E. coli* DNA, used as the reference DNA. The correction factors allow for the effects of base composition and sequence divergence on the rate of reassociation.

The sequence complexity of single-copy DNA is approximately equal to the kinetic complexity—i.e., when total nuclear DNA is reassociated, the Cot $^1/_2$ of the slowly reassociating component is proportional to the nuclear DNA content of haploid cells. However, this will change with the criterion; thus the apparent sequence complexity of the single-copy DNA is equal to the amount that is observed under the conditions of measurement.

Genetic complexity is a measure of the functional sequences of the genome. The extent of transcription of DNA into RNA forms a probable lower limit to genetic complexity, but the true extent of functional sequences is unknown and the definition itself assumes that some sequences have no function, which may or may not be true. It is clear that only a modest percentage of the nuclear genome is transcribed, but that does not prove that only transcribed sequences are functional. Therefore, at this time the genetic complexity of the genome is unknown.

Britten (1971:506) concluded "this somewhat abstract discussion on a practical note. The physical separation of repeated from nonrepeated DNA is limited unless very special techniques are available. One copy, at least, of each of the families of repetitive sequences will remain in the nonrepeated fraction. At this degree of purification the sequences of course will be observably nonrepetitive. In the animals that have been examined such sequences do not appear to represent a significant fraction of the total nonrepeated DNA nor do they contribute appreciably to the total complexity."

Thus, so-called "single-copy tracer" preparations contain representatives of all sequences that are kinetically different under the criterion conditions employed. It is likely that at least 10 copies per genome of each repeated sequence are present in tracers prepared at the standard criterion, and somewhat more if the stringency is relaxed. However, this is a small percentage of the total DNA because only about 3% to 5% of the kinetically different sequences are represented in the repeated fraction of the genome. Fig. 8 is a diagram of the sequence complexity of the avian genome.

CHAPTER SIX

The Sequence Organization of the Genome

A 10% fraction of the DNA of the mouse—called the mouse satellite—has played an important role in the development of our study of repeated DNA sequences. In the early summer of 1964 the success of the DNA-agar system for the study of animal DNA suggested to Britten the existence of repeated DNA. As a result Britten and Waring (Year Book 64) started studying mouse DNA and discovered in the fall of 1964 that the satellite reassociated very rapidly. It was intuitively recognized that this was an example of repetition. Subsequently, measurement of the actual rate of reassociation and its variation with DNA concentration showed that this was true, and that a short nucleotide sequence was repeated about a million times in mouse DNA. Having this extreme example in our pocket, so to speak, made the more modest degrees of repetition (tens and hundreds of thousands) more believable and gave momentum to the studies which led to the recognition of their general occurrence.

Britten and Kohne 1967:74

In classical genetics the word "gene" refers to the unit of heredity expressed in the phenotype and passed on from parent to offspring. At the molecular level a gene is a segment of DNA composed of a specific sequence of nucleotides that is transcribed into messenger RNA (mRNA) and translated into the amino acid sequence of a protein molecule. As described in chapter 3, a gene consists of the exons after the introns have been spliced out. The coding sequence consists of the sequence of nucleotides that includes the introns, exons, and other segments associated with them. Furthermore, only a relatively small percentage of the eukaryotic genome seems to code for proteins, different sets of genes are active at different stages of ontogeny, and the function of much of the genome is not yet known. Thus, for the purposes of this brief description of DNA sequence organization, the word "gene" is best replaced by the non-committal words "sequence," "base sequence," or "nucleotide sequence," which designate a linear segment of DNA without reference to its size, function, or location in the genome.

Each chromosome contains a continuous stretch of DNA in which the different sequences are arranged in tandem. DNA sequences vary in the number of similar, or identical, copies, from one per genome to millions of copies per genome, and the pattern of interspersion of sequences of different frequency classes differs in different organisms. These properties affect DNA-DNA hybridization, so it is important to examine the frequency of repetition of sequences, the occurrence of families of repeated sequences, the patterns of interspersion of the different frequency classes, and other aspects of sequence organization.

Frequency of Sequence Repetition

The approximate number of copies of a base sequence may be determined by measuring the rate of reassociation, which depends on the concentration of complementary sequences, as described above. Thus, the rate of reassociation is roughly proportional to the number of copies of a given sequence that are present. At the standard criterion (60°C; 0.12 M PB) the kinetics of reassociation, monitored by optical hypochromicity and/or HAP chromatography, provide the data for a Cot plot describing the time course of the reaction. The shape of the Cot curve reveals the presence of different frequency classes, and the time required for half-reassociation (Cot $^1/_2$) indicates the approximate number of copies in each frequency class. For details, see "Concentration of DNA" in chapter 5.

There are two main frequency classes of DNA sequences. Those sequences that occur with a frequency of one per genome are the single-copy, unique, or non-repetitive sequences. Since DNA is double-stranded, the single-copy sequences actually occur as a pair of complementary copies. Those sequences that occur with a frequency greater than one (or two) copies per genome are the repeated, repetitive, redundant, or multiple-copy sequences.

There is no definable boundary between single-copy and repeated sequences because the definition of frequency classes depends on the conditions of reassociation. For example, if the salt concentration is held constant (e.g., 0.12 M PB) and the temperature is varied, the ratio between single-copy and repeated sequences changes accordingly. At a high incubation temperature, e.g., 70°C, a larger percentage of the genome will appear to be composed of single-copy sequences than at a lower temperature, e.g., 60°C. As the incubation temperature is reduced, fewer matched base pairs are required to form a stable duplex and more sequences behave as repeated DNA until, at ca. 35–40°C, only one complementary base pair out of four (i.e., 25% of the bases in a DNA fragment) is required to form a stable duplex. This permits random reassociations between non-complementary sequences, and the entire genome reassociates rapidly, thus appearing to consist entirely of repeated DNA sequences. Conversely, if a highly stringent incubation temperature is used, e.g., 80°C, little or no repetitive DNA is observed because only perfectly base-paired duplexes will be stable. At 80°C ca. 95–98% of the bases must be complementary to form a stable hybrid.

For example, if the single-stranded DNA of the Domestic Cow (*Bos taurus*) is reassociated at 78°C in 0.12 M PB, only those duplexes that are perfectly or almost perfectly complementary will be stable, and duplexes less than ca. 95% complementary will be unstable. Under these conditions the sequences of a repetitive family will reassociate only with their exact complements, and less than 10% of the genome will appear to be composed of repeated DNA sequences. However, if the incubation temperature is 36°C below the T_m of native DNA (ca. 50°C), 55% of the genome will appear to be composed of repeated sequences because the lower stringency permits the formation of partially mismatched duplexes.

For these reasons it is important to specify the criterion conditions of incubation temperature and salt concentration when repetition frequencies are reported (Britten and Davidson 1971). Burr and Schimke (1980) reviewed the reassociation behavior of DNA under conditions of reduced stringency, including avian examples. Britten and Kohne (1968), Straus (1976), Thompson and Murray (1981), and Jelinek and Schmid (1982) reviewed the literature on repeated DNA.

Frequency Classes

The nuclear DNA of eukaryotes may be divided into several repetition classes, distinguished by their different rates of reassociation under the same criterion conditions. There is no sharp distinction between frequency classes, and there may be a continuum from the single-copy class to the highly repetitive classes (Thompson and Murray 1981). For convenience, the frequency classes have been designated as follows:

1. Single-copy, or unique, sequences occur (approximately) once per haploid set of chromosomes (genome) and reassociate at the slowest rate, proportional to the sequence complexity of the genome.

2. Low-frequency repeated sequences, characterized by a repeat frequency of up to 40 copies per genome, have been reported by Deininger and Schmid (1979).

3. Intermediate, middle, or moderately repetitive sequences occur at frequencies of ca. 1000 to 100,000 copies per haploid genome.

4. Highly repetitive sequences occur at the highest frequencies, up to millions of copies per genome. They are sometimes short sequences of fewer than 10 bases. Some are satellite DNAs which have base compositions such that they form satellite bands during density gradient centrifugation. See "Satellite DNA" in this chapter.

5. Foldback, or palindrome, sequences are complementary but inverted sequences that occur adjacent to one another in the same DNA strand and form hairpin or foldback structures during reassociation. Also called zero-time binding fraction, or inverted repeats, these sequences reassociate even faster than the highly repeated sequences. The foldback sequences may vary in length from a few to more than 15,000 bases, and the spacer region separating the two complementary sequences of the foldback region varies from 100 to more than 30,000 bases. The DNA in the repeated sections contains highly repetitive, middle repetitive, and single-copy sequences in about the same proportion as in total DNA, with a somewhat greater percentage of middle repetitive sequences. Cech et al. (1973) and Cech and Hearst (1975, 1976) studied the foldback sequences in the House Mouse (*Mus musculus*).

The formation of stem-loop structures by inverted repeats influences the spatial configuration of sequences in both RNA and DNA. In DNA the function of stem-loops is unknown, but they may be used as regulatory signals in developmental arrangements or in transcription (Moore et al. 1984). Harford (1977) reviewed satellite DNAs.

Examples of Sequence Frequency Classes

Repeated DNA sequences were discovered when it was found that 10% of the DNA of the House Mouse (*Mus musculus*) reassociated at an extremely rapid rate (Britten and Waring 1965, Waring and Britten 1966, Britten and Kohne 1967, 1968). This was a satellite DNA consisting of about a million copies per genome of a short base sequence. Subsequent studies on many groups of plants and animals have shown that repeated nucleotide sequences apparently occur in all eukaryotes (Britten and Davidson 1971, 1976, Davidson and Britten 1973, Britten et al. 1974, Galau et al. 1976, Straus 1976, Miklos and Gill 1982).

It is important to note that the percentage of single-copy sequence DNA, when assayed by HAP chromatography, depends on the fragment size and interspersion pattern of single-copy and repeated sequences, as well as on the criterion conditions. Differences in these factors produce different estimates of the percentages of frequency classes. Following are some examples of the occurrence of single-copy and repeated DNAs in various organisms.

PROKARYOTES

The bacteria and blue-green algae have relatively simple genomes composed only of single-copy DNA, but the genomes of all eukaryotes (protozoa, fungi, plants, animals) contain both single-copy and repeated sequences.

PROTISTA

The protozoa tend to have a large percentage of single-copy DNA and one repeated fraction with a relatively low copy number. In *Paramecium aurelia* (50°C, 0.12 M PB, 500 base fragments) 85% is single-copy, and the repeated fraction is composed of 53–76 copies in different strains. Under the same conditions, various strains of *Tetrahymena pyriformis* have 70–95% single-copy, and the repeated fraction varies from 25 to 33 copies. In *Acanthamoeba castellanii* 70% is single-copy and the 30% repeated sequences are present as ca. 30 copies per genome (Allen and Gibson 1972, Jantzen 1973, review by Straus 1976:14).

The chloroplast DNA of the unicellular green alga *Chlamydomonas reinhardtii* is composed of 70% single-copy and a repeated fraction of more than 1000 copies (Wells and Sager 1971).

FUNGI

The fungi have small genomes (ca. 0.05 pg) with 2% to 42% repeated sequences. The genome of the fungus *Aspergillus nidulans*, at 60°C in 0.12 M PB, contains 97–98% single-copy sequences and only 2–3% repeated DNA. The complexity of the repeated fraction is 11,000 base pairs with ca. 60 copies per haploid set. The total genome contains 2.6×10^7 base pairs, or 0.028 pg of DNA (Timberlake 1978). The genome of the wood-rotting fungus *Schizophyllum commune* contains ca. 3.6×10^7 base pairs, of which 80–90% is single-copy and 10% is repeated (Ullrich et al. 1980a). The ascomycete bread mold *Neurospora crassa* has 80% single-copy DNA and a 60-copy repeated fraction (Brooks and Huang 1972).

SLIME MOLDS

Dictyostelium discoideum (56°C, 0.12 M PB) has ca. 60% single-copy and 28% repeated DNA with ca. 113 copies (Firtel and Bonner 1972), and *Physarum polycephalum* has 58% single-copy and a 42% repeated fraction composed of ca. 15,000 copies (Fouquet et al. 1974).

PLANTS

The repetitive frequencies in plants range from 20 to 300,000 copies per genome, with most components present as a few thousand copies or less. In seven species of conifers,

Miksche and Hotta (1973) found that 70–80% of the genomes reassociated as repeated sequences. The genome of Parsley (*Petroselinum sativum*) has 5% of a very rapidly reassociating component, 13% of a highly repeated fraction consisting of ca. 136,000 copies, 48% of a middle repetitive fraction of 3000 copies, 16% with ca. 42 copies, and ca. 18% that behaves as single-copy. The Garden Pea (*Pisum sativum*) genome is composed of 4% highly repetitive sequences, 46% with 10,000 copies, 33% with 300 copies, and ca. 17% single-copy (Thompson and Murray 1981:13). "While the data . . . provide a useful indication of the range of repetition . . . found among higher-plant DNAs, it is important to recognize that the values . . . are at best crude approximations. . . . Whether . . . plant DNA sequences are actually present in a small number of discrete frequency classes . . . is also questionable. . . . the results are best interpreted by assuming an essentially continuous distribution of repetition frequencies instead of the simple two-class model" (Thompson and Murray 1981:13–15).

Murray et al. (1981) found that the presumptive single-copy fraction of *Pisum sativum* contains substantial mismatch at the standard criterion. They concluded that "virtually all" of the "single copy" DNA is composed of extensively diverged "fossil repeats," which are members of ancient families of repeated sequences. The true single-copy fraction apparently accounts for only a few percent of the *Pisum* genome.

About 46%, or 2.1×10^7 NTP, of the much smaller genome of the Mung Bean (*Vigna radiata*) is composed of true single-copy sequences. The Garden Pea genome is nine times larger than that of the Mung Bean, thus if even 3% of the Garden Pea genome is true single-copy it would consist of ca. 1.4×10^7 NTP. Therefore, the actual quantities of true single-copy sequences are comparable, and the large differences in genome size are due to the repeated fractions.

The small genome of the angiosperm *Arabidopsis thaliana* contains only 7×10^7 bp, of which 10–14% are highly repeated or inverted repeat sequences, and 23–27% are middle repetitive sequences. Thus, the single-copy component contains ca. 4.4×10^7 bp, or 63% of the genome (Meyerowitz and Pruitt 1985).

INVERTEBRATES

The sequence organizations of five marine invertebrates were determined by Goldberg et al. (1975) using 300 and 3000 bp fragments, 60°C, and 0.12 M PB (0.18 M Na⁺).

Oyster (*Ostrea [Crassostrea] virginica*): 60% single-copy with two repeated fractions of 40 and 3700 copies; 35% of the repeats are in 200–400 bp fragments.

Surf clam (*Spisula solidissima*): 75% single-copy; one repeated fraction with 30 copies; 60% of repeats in 200–400 bp fragments.

Horseshoe crab (*Limulus polyphemus*): 70% single-copy; repeats of 50 and 2000 copies; 75% in 200–400 bp fragments.

Nemertean worm (*Cerebratulus lacteus*): 60% single-copy; repeats of 40 and 1200 copies; 55% in 200–400 fragments.

Jellyfish (*Aurelia aurita*): 70% single-copy; one repeated class of 180 copies; 60% in 200–400 bp fragments.

In a sea hare (*Aplysia californica*), a large nudibranch gastropod, Angerer et al. (1975) found 55% single-copy; repeated fractions of 85, 4600, and 7 million copies, with 60% in the 200–400 bp fragments.

In a squid (*Loligo*) Davidson et al. (1975a) found 75% single-copy; repeated fractions of 100, 4100, and 230,000 copies, with 60% in the 200–400 bp fragments.

The Purple Sea Urchin (*Strongylocentrotus purpuratus*) has 75% single-copy; 100- and 1500-copy repeats, with 75% in the 200–400 bp fragments (Graham et al. 1974).

For 26 repeat families of the Purple Sea Urchin Klein et al. (1978) used cloned repeated sequence probes to measure repetition frequencies which varied up to several thousand copies per genome. Intrafamilial sequence divergence estimates were based on the thermal stability of heteroduplexes between the genomic DNA and the cloned fragments. The difference was <4°C for three of 18 families, and <10°C for 13 of these families. The 13 families lack detectable highly divergent sequence relatives, and the results do not change at a low criterion of 55°C in 0.18M Na$^+$. Five of the 18 cloned families showed greater sequence divergence, and the average sequence divergence of the total short repetitive sequence fraction matched the average of the divergences of the cloned repeat sequences.

D. M. Anderson et al. (1981) studied three of the Purple Sea Urchin repeat families used by Klein et al. (1978). These three families were defined by homology to a specific cloned probe of 100 to several hundred nucleotides in length. Several methods were used to determine the organization of each repeat family, and elements of one of the families were found embedded in longer repeat sequences which often occur in small clusters. Members of the second family also occur in a long repetitive sequence but usually occur singly in any given region of the DNA. The third repeat family was only 200 to 300 nucleotides long and generally terminated by single-copy DNA. These three repeat sequence families apparently constitute sets of homologous sequences that relate to distant regions of the DNA.

Scheller et al. (1981) also used three repetitive sequence families isolated from recombinant libraries to study sequence relationships. One large, divergent family was shown to consist of an assemblage of many small repeat sequence subfamilies. Each subfamily includes fewer than 40 members, which are not contiguous in the genome but are closely related colinear sequence elements several kb in length. The different subfamilies share only small sequence subelements which, in each subfamily, occur in a different linear order surrounded by different sequences. Other families have other characteristics. Highly homologous sequences were found to have been conserved among sea urchin species, which diverged ca. 200 MYA, although only about 10% of the single-copy DNA of these species is now complementary enough to form duplexes at the standard criterion.

Posakony et al. (1981) studied the sequences of eight cloned repeats which were so divergent that they would not hybridize at the standard criterion. They found that the number and order of internal sequence subelements differ among family members and that fine-scale rearrangement and sequence divergence have occurred during the evolution of at least one of the families.

The fruitfly (*Drosophila melanogaster*) has 75% single-copy and a repeated fraction with 35 copies, of which 10% is in the 200–400 bp fragments (Manning et al. 1975).

VERTEBRATES

Fish

Hanham and Smith (1980) measured the reassociation kinetics of three species of salmon (*Oncorhynchus keta, O. kisutch, O. nerka*) with HAP chromatography of 450 bp fragments in 0.12 M PB at 60°C. Approximately 60% of the genomes are repeated sequences, of which ca. 4% is a fast fraction composed of ca. 100,000 copies, 15–20% is an intermediate fraction repeated tens of thousands of times, and 35–40% is a slowly reassociating component containing hundreds of copies per genome. The single-copy sequences comprise 30–40%.

Gharrett et al. (1977) examined the reassociation properties of the DNAs of ten species of fish: nine teleosts and a lamprey (*Entosphenus tridentatus*). Reassociations of ca. 400 bp fragments were followed by spectrophotometry at 60°C in a perchlorate buffer that produced a relative reassociation rate of 13. In all species they found a single-copy fraction and a fraction composed of sequences repeated more than 500 times. The size of the repeated fraction varied, and some species had an intermediate fraction repeated ca. 100 times. The repeated fraction varied from 34–62% of total DNA, and sequence complexity varied from 0.75 to 1.62×10^9 bp in the teleosts and 2.26×10^9 bp in the lamprey.

Similarities between base sequences were examined by comparing the Cot curve of a mixture of DNAs from two species to the separate Cot curves of those same species. The results were in accordance with other evidence of taxonomic relationships.

Vladychenskaya et al. (1983) studied the genome of the Alligator Gar (*Lepisosteus osseus*) using fragments 2100 and 300 bp long, reassociated at 60° and 67°C in 0.12 and 0.40 M sodium phosphate buffer, respectively. Long (> 2000 bp), slightly divergent sequences predominate, with few short repeats alternating with unique sequences.

Amphibia

Mizuno and Macgregor (1974) compared the genome sizes, karyotypes, and DNA sequences of 15 of the 17 species of the lungless salamander genus *Plethodon* that occur in North America. The 10 species of southeastern Canada and the eastern United States fall into two groups: (1) the small eastern species composed of *P. cinereus* and its relatives, *richmondi, hoffmani,* and *nettingi,* and (2) the large eastern species, *wehrlei, punctatus, ouachitae, yonahlossee, glutinosus,* and *jordani.* One species, *P. neomexicanus,* is isolated in the Jemez Mountains of New Mexico, and six species occur in the Pacific Northwest from Vancouver Island to northwestern California, namely, *elongatus, vehiculum, dunni, gordoni, larselli,* and *vandykei.*

All species have 14 chromosomes and "remarkably similar" karyotypes, but the genome sizes range from ca. 20 pg in the small eastern species and 20–36 pg in the large eastern species to 33–69 pg in the western species. *P. larselli* has 48 pg and *P. vandykei* 69 pg, or more than three times the amount of DNA in the genome of *P. cinereus.*

The genome of *P. cinereus* was examined by HAP chromatography (65°C, 0.12 M PB). A highly repetitive fraction comprises ca. 30% and completes its reassociation by Cot 10. An intermediate fraction makes up ca. 15% and is completely reassociated by Cot 1000, and the unique sequences comprise 40% and reassociate above Cot 1000. Thus, between 45% and 60% of the *P. cinereus* genome reassociates by Cot 1000, in contrast to the genomes of the western species, *vehiculum* and *dunni,* in which 80% completes reassociation by Cot 1000 and is therefore composed of repetitive sequences.

DNA-DNA hybrids showed that closely related species of *Plethodon* have 60–90% of their repeated sequences in common. The two groups of eastern species have 40–60% in common, but the eastern and western groups have less than 10% in common. DNA-DNA hybrids between the unique fractions gave the same pattern of relationships as did the repeated sequences, but the degrees of difference were much less. As much as 40% of the unique sequences of *P. cinereus* are represented in the western species, and 70% in the large eastern species.

Mizuno and Macgregor (1974) concluded that the smaller genomes of the *cinereus* group represent the primitive condition and that saltatory replication of repetitive sequences produced the larger genomes of the western species after they diverged from the eastern group. Thus, the differences in total amounts of nuclear DNA are due to the amplification of repeated DNA. Homologies among the unique sequence DNA have been retained in the genomes of all of the species of *Plethodon* tested, but no detectable part of them was found in the repeated DNA of any species. This indicates that the amplification events occurred long ago and that the repeated fractions have been diverging, forming families of repeats which have become so different from ancestral unique sequences that homologies no longer can be detected by the methods employed.

Mizuno et al. (1976) found that *Plethodon cinereus* and *P. dunni* share a set of evolutionarily stable (i.e., conservative) intermediate repetitive sequences which are also present in the genomes of other species of *Plethodon*, although most repeated DNAs differ among these species. The shared repeated sequence of *Plethodon* could not be detected in other plethodontids or in more distantly related salamanders.

The reassociation kinetics (60°C, 0.12 M PB, HAP assay) of the DNAs of the Tiger Salamander (*Ambystoma tigrinum*) and the Mudpuppy (*Necturus maculosus*) were studied by Straus (1971). These urodeles have large haploid genomes of 33 pg and 78 pg, respectively, or 32×10^9 and 76×10^9 nucleotide pairs. From other studies (e.g., Mizuno and Macgregor 1974) it would be expected that most of the DNA in such large genomes consists of repeated sequences, and Straus found this to be true. In fact, he was unable to detect any single-copy DNA in either species, although it is certainly present. Straus calculated that the Cot $1/2$ of the unique sequences of *Ambystoma* would be 20,500, and of *Necturus* 49,000. Obviously, it would take a very long period of reassociation to obtain a sample of the unique sequences with little contamination by repeated DNA.

Ambystoma has a slowly reassociating component comprising 27% with a repetition frequency of 54 copies, a moderately repeated fraction (37%, 3480 copies), and a highly repetitive component (6.1%, 2.5×10^6 copies). *Necturus* has a slow component (20%, 334 copies), a middle repetitive component (54%, 49,800 copies), and a highly repetitive fraction (13.6%, 6.7×10^6 copies). Such large genomes also have more families of repeated sequences.

The anuran amphibians have much smaller genomes than do the urodeles. As noted above (see "Genome Size" in chapter 5) the C-values for 120 species of frogs and toads range from 1 to 10 pg, with a modal value at 2.5 pg (Olmo 1973).

Straus (1971) examined the genomes of three anurans: a spadefoot toad (*Scaphiopus couchi*), the Giant Toad (*Bufo marinus*), and the Green Frog (*Rana clamitans*). The reassociation kinetics (60°C, 0.12 M PB, HAP assay) showed that the genome of *Scaphiopus couchi* contains 60% unique sequences, 23% of an intermediate fraction with a repetition frequency of 100 copies, and 3.5% of a fraction with 5360 copies. *Bufo marinus* has only 26% unique sequences, 14% of a slowly reassociating component with a frequency of 35 copies, a middle repetitive fraction comprising 27% with 100 copies, and a highly repeated component making up 26% and 48,200 copies. *Rana clamitans* has 22% unique sequences, 40% with 93 copies, 27% with 4080 copies, and 9% with 71,700 copies.

The African Clawed Toad (*Xenopus laevis*) has 75% single-copy DNA and three repeated fractions of 100, 2100, and 290,000 copies, with 75% of the repeats in sequences 200–400 bp long, averaging ca. 300 bp. The repeats account for ca. 18% of the genome, or ca. 4.9×10^8 nucleotides. Thus, the genome contains ca. 1.6×10^6 300-bp repeated sequence elements. The major frequency of repetition averages 2000 copies of each sequence, so there are about 800 distinct repetitive sequence families. There is also a complex class of long repeated sequences (Davidson et al. 1973, Galau et al. 1976).

Chamberlin et al. (1975) studied the sequence organization of the genome of *Xenopus laevis* with the electron microscope. They found that direct measurement of visualized duplexes showed that the mean length of interspersed repetitive sequence elements is 345 bases, thus confirming the less precise, but generally accurate, estimate based on reassociation (Davidson et al. 1973).

These data from the Amphibia demonstrate that animals with large genome sizes generally have higher frequencies of sequence repetition than those with smaller genomes. The large genomes apparently result from increases in the number of copies of a small percentage of the genome. This point is of special importance when considering the sequence complexity of the single-copy fraction vis-à-vis the repeated fraction.

Reptiles

Epplen et al. (1979) used 300-base fragments reassociated at 60–65°C in 0.04–0.55 M PB, and HAP chromatography, to determine the frequency classes in three reptiles. The Reticulated Python (*Python reticularis*) had 71% single-copy, 17% middle repetitive, and 12% highly repeated sequences. In *Caiman crocodilus* the values were 66%, 21%, and 13%, and for the Box Turtle (*Terrapene carolina*), 54%, 19%, and 27%.

Birds

Several studies of the sequence frequency classes of the Domestic Fowl (*G. gallus*) have been made. Sanchez de Jiménez et al. (1974) found that the single-copy fraction comprises 70–80% of the genome at 66°C, 0.12 M PB, and that the same ratio of single-copy to repeated sequences occurs in all tissues of the body. Arthur and Straus (1978) (60°C, 0.12 M PB) reported that the unique sequences make up 80%, an intermediate repeated component 11%, and the highly repeated sequences 7–8%. The intermediate fraction is repeated ca. 640 times. Epplen et al. (1978) used 0.04 M PB at 60°C and fragments of ca. 230 bases. Under these conditions they found that the *Gallus* genome consists of 68% unique, 10% intermediate repeated, and 20% highly repeated sequences.

Stefos and Arrighi (1974) used the livers of female Domestic Fowl as the source of DNA and found that the repeated fraction composed 17%, in two subfractions, localized in the microchromosomes and the W chromosome.

The different conditions used in these several measurements presumably account for some of the variations reported, but these examples show that it is difficult to obtain a precise measurement of the percentages of frequency classes. The variation may also indicate that the amplification of genes varies within species of birds, as it does in mammals (Sherwood and Patton 1982, reviewed below).

Epplen et al. (1978) also measured the percentages of the frequency classes in the Muscovy Duck (*Cairina moschata*) and the Rock Pigeon (*Columba livia*). In the Muscovy Duck the unique fraction comprises 73%, intermediate repeated sequences 13%, highly repeated 14%. The Rock Pigeon had 60% unique, 11% intermediate, and 15% highly repeated.

The reassociation kinetics of the DNAs of eight species of passerine birds were examined by Shields and Straus (1975). They used fragments averaging 345 bases in length, reassociated in 0.12 M PB at 60°C, and assayed on HAP columns. They found that the single-copy sequences compose 60–65% of the genome, an intermediate repeated class makes up 16%, and the highly repeated sequences 20%. These values were found in the juncos (*Junco*), White-throated Sparrow (*Zonotrichia albicollis*), Tree Sparrow (*Spizella arborea*), Song Sparrow (*Melospiza melodia*), Cardinal (*C. cardinalis*), Purple Finch (*Carpodacus purpureus*), House Sparrow (*Passer domesticus*), and Hermit Thrush (*Catharus guttatus*). In *Junco hyemalis* the intermediate repetitive class is repeated ca. 200 times and the highly repeated sequences ca. 370,000 times (Straus 1976). We have found similar percentages in various species of birds. For example, the 500-base fragments of Herring Gull (*Larus argentatus*) DNA, reassociated at 60°C in 0.12 M and 0.48 M PB, consist of ca. 60% single-copy, 22% intermediate repetitive, and 18% highly repeated sequences (Sibley and Ahlquist 1983:253). (Fig. 7.)

From these measurements, it seems probable that the avian genome, under standard criterion conditions, consists of ca. 60–70% single-copy, 13–20% intermediate repeated, and 16–20% highly repeated sequences.

Mammals

The reassociation kinetics of eight genera of rodents were studied by Santiago and Rake (1973) using 400–500-base fragments incubated at 65°C in a solvent consisting of 50% formamide and 5× SSC (0.75 M NaCl, 0.08 M Na citrate). The reactions were monitored spectrophotometrically at 270 nm. Each species has two repeated fractions, but there is considerable variation among them in the number of copies and percentages of each fraction. The highly repetitive fraction composes 10–13% of total DNA and is present in frequencies from 6700 copies in the Eastern Chipmunk (*Tamias striatus*) to 100,000 copies in the House Mouse (*Mus musculus*). The average number of copies in the eight species is 28,200. Even confamilial genera differ greatly in the number of copies—e.g., in the two sciurids, the chipmunk (*Tamias*) has 6700 and the squirrel (*Sciurus*) 24,300. Among the four cricetids (*Cricetus, Gerbillus, Peromyscus, Microtus*) the variation is from 10,000 to 19,400 copies, and the two murids (*Mus, Rattus*) have 100,000 and 40,000 copies respectively. The intermediate repetitive fraction makes up 11% to 31% of total DNA, averaging 17%, and is present in frequencies from 92 to 380 copies, averaging 170. The single-copy sequence component varies from 58% to 77%, averaging 71%.

Pearson et al. (1978) analyzed the sequence organization of the Norway Rat (*Rattus norvegicus*) genome using fragments of various sizes, S–1 nuclease digestion of single-strand tails, and HAP chromotography at 60°C in 0.12 M PB, or at 70°C in 0.48 M PB. One-kilobase fragments showed that 20% of *Rattus* sequences are 3000-fold repeated, and 4-kb fragments display two repetitive fractions. Ca. 60% of the repeated sequences are 200–400 bp long; the remainder are longer than 1500 bp. Repeated sequences are interspersed among 2500 bp single-copy sequences in more than 70% of the genome, and there are ca. 350 different 3000-fold repeats interspersed among 600,000 single-copy sequences.

Ginatulina et al. (1982) analyzed the genomes of eight species of the ground squirrel genus *Citellus* (*Spermophilus*). A "very fast" component comprised 6–20%, a "fast" fraction 12–14%, an intermediate component 10–20%, and a slow (single-copy) fraction 47–67%. They found no obvious relationships between the parameters of reassociation kinetics and the taxonomic status of species within the genus, or with chromosome number.

Britten and Smith (1970) found 65% single-copy sequences in the genome of the Domestic Cow (*Bos taurus*) and two repeated fractions with 60,000 and 1 million copies, of which 55% are in 200–400-bp-long sequences. There may also be repeated fractions with fewer than 10,000 copies present.

In human DNA Schmid and Deininger (1975) found that repeated sequences are distributed throughout 80% or more of the genome and that ca. 52% of the genome consists of short single-copy sequences ca. 2 kb in length, interspersed with repetitive sequences ca. 0.4 kb long. A portion of the genome is also occupied by an interspersed arrangement of longer single-copy sequences of unknown length. The sequence organization is of the Xenopus type. Inverted repeats are randomly positioned so that all three sequence classes are interspersed in a portion of the genome.

Satellite DNA

DNA satellites have been found in many plants and animals. Because some satellite DNAs may be separated from the rest of the genome by density gradient centrifugation, they have been the subjects of many studies. In the House Mouse (*Mus musculus*) the satellite DNA is localized in the centromeric heterochromatin (Pardue and Gall 1970, Jones 1970). In other organisms satellites may be located in other regions, e.g., the arms of the chromosomes.

In some organisms the satellite DNAs are similar to one another or to those in related species. For example, in the fruitfly *Drosophila virilis* there are three satellites that differ from one another by a single base substitution. The repeating unit of one of the satellites is seven bases long (Gall and Atherton 1974). In *D. melanogaster* three of the five satellites differ from one another by single bases and variable arrangements of AT and AAT sequences (Peacock et al. 1974). The III satellite in human DNA hybridizes with the A satellite of the chimpanzee (*Pan*), indicating shared sequences (Prosser et al. 1973). Southern (1974) reviewed additional examples.

Satellite DNAs may differ within a single species and between closely related species. For example, the satellites of three species of the Old World rodent genus *Apodemus* differ in density, quantity, and rates of reassociation (Hennig and Walker 1970). Substantial differences in the highly repetitive DNAs of species of *Mus* have also been demonstrated (Sutton and McCallum 1972; Rice 1972; Rice and Straus 1973).

In the kangaroo rats (*Dipodomys*) and some other rodents, the satellite DNAs differ from both of the patterns described above. The three satellites in *D. ordii* are unrelated to one another, but one of them is similar in base sequence to a satellite in the Guinea Pig (*Cavia porcellus*). Most of the 22 species of *Dipodomys* have three satellites, but there is a wide range in the relative amounts in different species. These satellites have been studied by Hatch and Mazrimas (1970, 1974), Mazrimas and Hatch (1972, 1977), Fry et al. (1973), Salser et al. (1976), Hatch et al. (1976), and Fry and Salser (1977).

In the salamander *Plethodon cinereus* the satellite represents about 2% of the nuclear DNA and is localized near the centromeres in all 14 chromosomes. The *P. cinereus* satellite sequences are present in various smaller amounts in other closely related species of *Plethodon* but absent in others. *P. dorsalis* has three satellites, none of which seem to contain sequences homologous to those of *P. cinereus* (Macgregor et al. 1973).

When repetition frequency classes are determined by reassociation kinetics the satellite DNA appears as part of the highly repetitive class. Further comments on satellite DNAs are presented in chapter 7.

Interspersion Patterns

In most eukaryotic genomes the repeated sequences are interspersed with single-copy sequences in an alternating, but not necessarily regular, pattern. The approximate interspersion pattern is revealed by the reassociation behavior of DNA fragments of different lengths. For example, fragments 2–3 kb long are allowed to reassociate to a low Cot value, such that only the rapidly reassociating repetitive sequences will have time enough to form duplexes. The double-stranded fraction is then separated from the single-stranded by HAP chromatography. Although the repeated sequences may actually comprise only 20–40% of total DNA, it is found that 80–100% of these long fragments bind to the HAP column, thus behaving as if they were repeated sequences. This means that the single-copy sequences are interspersed among the repeated elements, at least at intervals of every 2–3 kb.

Similar experiments, using fragments of various lengths, have shown that most animal genomes are arranged in at least two dispersed interspersion patterns, known as the Xenopus pattern and the Drosophila pattern, after the organisms in which they were discovered (Davidson et al. 1973; Manning et al. 1975). The apparent dichotomy between these two patterns may be oversimplified. Intermediate interspersion patterns have been found in some plants, and a continuum of patterns may actually occur (Thompson and Murray 1981).

In some organisms, some repeated sequences are not dispersed throughout the genome but occur in clusters of various sizes. Jelinek and Schmid (1982) reviewed the occurrence of repeated sequences in eukaryotes.

XENOPUS PATTERN

In most organisms most of the dispersed repeated sequences occur in short stretches of 100–400 bp, which are interspersed with single-copy sequences of ca. 1–2 kb. Approximately 50–80% of the DNA in such organisms has the short-period interspersion pattern. The remainder of the repeated DNA is arranged in long stretches, greater than 1–2 kb, which are not interrupted by unique sequences. All repetition frequency classes are found in both long and short interspersion elements, although the highly repeated fraction may be absent from the short sequence elements.

The copies making up the short repetitive elements have diverged as much as 10–30% in sequence homology among themselves, but the sequences composing the long elements appear to differ by less than 2%, possibly because of an artifact caused by cross-linked DNA in the long S–1 nuclease resistant fraction (R. J. Britten, pers. comm.).

The short-period interspersion pattern of dispersed repeats has been found in the African Clawed Frog (or Toad) *Xenopus laevis* (Davidson et al. 1973, 1974; Chamberlin et al. 1975) and in several marine invertebrates, including molluscs (*Spisula, Crassostrea, Aplysia, Loligo*), an arthropod (*Limulus*), a nemertean (*Cerebratulus*), a coelenterate (*Aurelia*), and an echinoderm (*Strongylocentrotus*) (Davidson et al. 1975b; Angerer et al. 1975; Graham et al. 1974; Galau et al. 1976; Goldberg et al. 1975).

In the Purple Sea Urchin (*Strongylocentrotus purpuratus*) ca. 50% of the genome consists of a short-period interspersion pattern with repeated segments of 300–400 bases interspersed with single-copy sequences of ca. 1 kb. Another 20% or more consists of a longer-period interspersed pattern. Approximately 22% may be uninterrupted single-copy DNA or may have more widely spaced interspersed repeats (Graham et al. 1974).

The Xenopus type of sequence arrangement is also present in the Housefly (*Musca domestica*) (Crain et al. 1976b), Silkmoth (*Antheraea pernyi*) (Efstradiatis et al. 1976), Norway Rat (*Rattus norvegicus*) (Bonner et al. 1974), Man (Deininger and Schmid 1976, 1979), and several genera of plants, including cotton (*Gossypium*) (Walbot and Dure 1976) and tobacco (*Nicotiana*) (Zimmerman and Goldberg 1977).

Bozzoni and Beccari (1978) compared the clustered and repeated sequences in four species with different amounts of nuclear DNA: two anurans (*Xenopus laevis*, 3 pg, *B. bufo*, 7 pg) and two urodeles (*Triturus cristatus*, 23 pg, *Necturus maculosus*, 52 pg). They found that the number of long repetitive sequences is roughly proportional to genome size in all four species, while the number of ca. 300 bp repeats is greatly increased in the species with the larger genomes.

In three reptiles (*Python reticularis, Caiman crocodilus, Terrapene carolina*) Epplen et al. (1979) found an appreciable amount of short-period interspersion.

The short-period pattern apparently occurs in some, but not all, birds. Ginatulin and Ginatulina (1979) found the short-period pattern in the Royal Albatross (*Diomedea epomophora*) and the Common Murre (*Uria aalge*). In these species they report that 300 bp repeats are interspersed with 150 bp single-copy sequences.

Wilkes et al. (1978) used electron microscopy to determine the size and arrangement of repeated and foldback sequences in the DNA of the Norway Rat (*Rattus norvegicus*). The average size of a class of numerous short, repeated sequences is 400 bp. The average spacing between interspersed repeats is ca. 1500–1800 bp, and there are ca. 1.9×10^5 foldback pairs per genome, spaced an average of 9700 bp apart. Repeated, foldback, and single-copy sequences are interspersed in at least half of the Norway Rat genome.

Ginatulin et al. (1983) analyzed the sequence organization of five species of the ground squirrel genus *Citellus* (*Spermophilus*) by reassociation kinetics of fragments of various lengths and the size distribution of S–1 nuclease–resistant duplexes of repeated DNA. Only 15% of the genomes consisted of short single-copy and repeated sequences interspersed with a period of less than 2–3 kb. Most of the genome is composed of moderately long (3–15 kb) and very long (more than 15 kb) sequences. The five species formed two groups: the short-tailed species (*pygmaeus*, *major*, *fulvus*) have 17–24% moderately long single-copy sequences, and the long-tailed species (*parryi*, *undulatus*) only 1–7% of such sequences. The same division was found for the very long single-copy sequences. Repeated sequences vary in length from 70 bp to several kb; those of more than 12 kb are most common and some contain 70–150 bp. About one-third of the repeats in *parryi* (10% of the genome) are short sequences; the other species have only 1–4% of the genome represented by such sequences. These ground squirrel species do not fall clearly into either the Xenopus type or the Drosophila type. About 15% of their genomes tend to be of the Xenopus type, the remainder of the Drosophila type. The genomes of *fulvus* and *major* are close to the Drosophila type; most of the genomes of *parryi* and *undulatus* are organized into the very long interspersion pattern. These two groups are placed in different subgenera on morphological evidence. *C. pygmaeus* is placed in a third subgenus. Thus, great differences in genomic organization occur within this genus, and the authors speculate "that such differences in sequence organization arose . . . as a result of the redistribution of the single-copy sequences within the genome" (p. 127). It is unusual to find such large differences between closely related species. These results may have been caused by steric hindrance due to the use of long DNA sequences with the S–1 nuclease method.

DROSOPHILA PATTERN

A somewhat different pattern of interspersion has been found in at least four insects: a fruitfly (*Drosophila melanogaster*) (Manning et al. 1975, Crain et al. 1976a), a midge (*Chironomus tentans*) (Wells et al. 1976), the Honeybee (*Apis mellifera*) (Crain et al. 1976b), and a flesh fly (*Sarcophaga bullata*) (Samols and Swift 1979). In these species both single-copy and repeated sequences are clustered in regions of greater than 4 and 13 kb, respectively. Some single-copy sequences are as long as 35 kb. *Drosophila* DNA has an average repetitive sequence element of 5.6 kb and *Chironomus* an average of 4.3 kb. This contrasts with the 300-base average of the Xenopus pattern. The long repeats in these insects are flanked on either side by shorter repeats of ca. 255–400 bp.

The insects have rather small genome sizes, and it has been suggested that the long-period pattern evolved from the short-period pattern (Crain et al. 1976b, Davidson et al. 1977). However, Arthur and Straus (1978) found that the sequence organization of the Domestic Fowl (*G. gallus*) is more like that of *Drosophila* than that of *Xenopus*, although the avian genome contains ca. 20 times as much DNA as does that of *Drosophila* (Hinegardner 1976).

In their study of the sequence organization in *Gallus*, Arthur and Straus (1978) used a series of five fragment sizes from 320 to 4500 bases in length and examined the reassociation kinetics at 60°C in 0.12 M PB with HAP assay. They found that the repeated and single-copy sequences are not extensively interspersed and that the length of the repeated element is ca. 3.4 kb.

In the Domestic Fowl, Eden and Hendrick (1978) and Eden (1980) found a long-period pattern in which 2–4 kb repeats are interspersed with ca. 4.5 kb single-copy segments in more than 40% of the genome. Longer single-copy sequences occur in the rest of the genome, and there are no 200–400 bp interspersed repeats. Some repeats in *Gallus* are clustered in arrays as long as 20 kb that may be extensively methylated, but with specific undermethylated regions (Eden et al. 1981). Epplen et al. (1978) used 220–230-base fragments to determine the interspersion patterns in the Muscovy Duck (*Cairina moschata*), Domestic Fowl (*G. gallus*), and Rock Dove (*Columba livia*). In *Cairina* only 12%, and in *Gallus* 28%, of the single-copy sequences are interspersed with repetitive elements in 2–3 kb fragments. In *Gallus* the single-copy sequences alternating with middle repetitive sequences are at least 2.3 kb long, and the interspersed middle repetitive segments are at least 1.5 kb long. In *Cairina* the middle repeated sequences are smaller.

CLUSTERED PATTERN

Eukaryotic DNAs also contain clustered repeats, some composed of simple sequences of from three to ten bases long, repeated 10^6 to 10^7 times. Others are hundreds of bases long and repeated millions of times per genome. Many of the clustered sequences are satellites (see "Satellite DNA" in this chapter, and chapter 7).

The simple, tandemly repeated, satellite sequences are present in centromeric and telomeric heterochromatin and are usually not transcribed. However, satellite DNAs in the Crested Newt (*Triturus cristatus*) and the Spotted Newt (*Notophthalmus viridescens*) are transcribed during the lampbrush chromosome stage of oogenesis (Varley et al. 1980a,b, Diaz et al. 1981, Stephenson et al. 1981).

Long repeats also occur in clusters. For example, in the basidiomycete fungus *Schizophyllum commune* the repeated DNA is in possibly 16 clusters, averaging 225 kb in length (Ullrich et al. 1980b).

At another extreme of sequence organization, the interspersed repeats in the aquatic fungus *Achlya* are longer than 27 kb and are interspersed by single-copy sequences of more than 135 kb (Hudspeth et al. 1977, Pellegrini et al. 1981). In a nematode (*Panagrellus silusiae*) Beauchamp et al. (1979), using 2000 bp fragments, found no interspersion.

Possible Functions of Repeated Sequences

The widespread occurrence of repeated sequences and evidence of interspersion suggested to Britten and Davidson (1969) that some repeats might be related to the regulation of gene activity. They developed a model of regulatory network evolution and explored the organization of animal genomes for supporting evidence (Britten and Davidson 1971, 1976, Britten 1972, Davidson and Britten 1973, 1979, Britten et al. 1972, Davidson et al. 1971, 1973, 1975a,b). These important papers contain significant data and the Britten-Davidson model stimulated many other studies of interspersion patterns and other aspects of genome organization. However, it gradually became clear that there are several patterns of interspersion, some of which do not fit the model. In addition, other regulatory systems were discovered (see chapter 4) and some repeated sequences have been shown to code for proteins, hence they are behaving as structural genes themselves. At least one aspect of the Britten-Davidson model has proved to be relevant to the control of gene activity; transposable elements, which constitute a class of middle repetitive sequences, have been shown to be involved in genetic regulation. Davidson (1982) commented on the concept of "regulatory network evolution."

About 10 years ago Britten and I proposed that there are genomic regulatory networks which functionally relate physically distant genes, and that these networks are constructed of interspersed repetitive DNA sequences. We argued that evolutionary change in the location of members of given repeat sequence families could give rise to significant new biological structure and function, by creating new ontogenetic regulatory connections among preexistant structural genes. We assumed that a continuing evolutionary process exists by which new families of repetitive sequence are created and dispersed about the genome and suggested that the changing pattern of sequence homologies within the genome could provide the structural basis for the appearance of new regulatory networks based on interspersed repeat sequences. . . . During the last decade many new findings and hypotheses relevant to [these ideas] have emerged. . . . The most relevant data concern the genomic sequence organization of animal genomes. . . . it has been discovered that repetitive sequences are indeed interspersed among other DNA sequences in all or most metazoan genomes, including our own. . . . in several cases . . . it is clear that repeat sequences are located in the vicinity of structural genes, though in other cases they are not. The key point is [that] the . . . function of the interspersed repeat sequences . . . remains unknown. [But] a major aspect of the model . . . is probably correct . . . that repetitive families expand and "diffuse" rapidly around the genome during evolution . . . giving rise to new networks of sequence homologies . . . "nomadic" repeat sequences. . . . transposons come and go. . . . data for both sea urchins and Drosophila show that there is a large scale and comparatively rapid appearance of repetitive sequences at novel genomic sites during evolution.

Davidson and Posakony (1982) concluded from a review of repeated sequence transcripts in development that "Despite their ubiquity, their quantitative prominence, their apparent developmental regulation and the amount of interest they have aroused, the repetitive sequence transcripts of animal cells remain a phenomenon in search of a physiological meaning."

Jelinek and Schmid (1982:816) reviewed the occurrence of repeated sequences and concluded:

Thus, various patterns of dispersed repeats can be distinguished in the DNAs of a variety of different eukaryotic organisms, and although the short-period interspersion pattern of dispersed repeats exists in the DNAs of the majority of organisms examined, it appears not to be an obligatory attribute of eukaryotic DNAs. There is no reason to believe that the different arrangements of dispersed repeats perform common functions in DNAs of the various organisms in which they are present. It is, however, plausible to imagine that the interspersed repeats in organisms with similar DNA sequence organizations may serve common functions and/or reflect a common dispersal mechanism. Because short-period interspersed repeats are present in most eukaryotic DNAs examined, and among single copy sequences that contain protein coding sequences, they possibly function in the control of gene expression, and therefore have been extensively investigated. . . . Despite considerable effort the biological function(s), if any, of these dispersed repeats remain obscure.

Thompson and Murray (1981) also reviewed the structure and function of the nuclear genome and concluded that "most of the interspersed repetitive DNA in larger eukaryotic genomes probably does not function in gene regulation. While some of the interspersed repetitive sequences in plant and animal genomes could function in gene regulation, this model cannot explain the origin and evolution of the very large amounts of interspersed repetitive DNA frequently observed in large genomes, especially those of many higher plants."

One class of repeated sequences is known to act as regulatory elements. These are the transposable elements, or transposons. (See "Transposable Elements" in chapter 7.) Gene amplification, induced by a challenge from outside the genome, produces multiple copies of a sequence, the product of which is required in a greater quantity during some phase in the life of an organism. (See "Gene Amplification" in chapter 7.)

CHAPTER SEVEN

The Families of Repeated DNA

The thermal stability of reassociated DNA strands depends on the precision of base pairing. If there are no mismatched bases in a reassociated duplex its thermal stability will be close to that of native DNA, but the presence of non-complementary base pairs lowers the melting temperature. For example, the totally single-copy genome of the bacterium *Escherichia coli* melts with a T_m ca. 90°C, the sheared DNA of *E. coli* has a T_m ca. 88°C, and the sheared, dissociated, and reassociated DNA has a T_m ca. 87°C. These small differences indicate that there is virtually no mispairing of bases when the simple sequence genome of *E. coli* is sheared and reassociated (Britten and Kohne 1968).

However, if the equivalent experiment is conducted with the DNA of any eukaryote containing repeated sequences, the T_m of the sheared, dissociated, and reassociated DNA will be several degrees below that of the native DNA. Furthermore, if the repeated sequences are examined by HAP chromatography a wide range of thermal stabilities will be found. Some of the repeated sequences will have high melting temperatures close to that of native DNA, indicating that they are perfectly base paired, other sequences will show a small reduction in T_m, and some will have greatly depressed T_ms, indicating extensive base mismatching.

The wide range of thermal stabilities is the evidence that the repeated sequences consist of several subsets, or families, in each genome. Many studies have shown that the member sequences of each family are similar enough to reassociate with one another under fairly stringent conditions, but that they are not identical to one another in base sequence. A range of similarities can be detected among the member sequences of a family and, as expected, the degree of similarity depends on the criterion conditions.

The Alu Family

The existence of families of dispersed repeated DNA sequences was first detected by observations of thermal stabilities (Britten and Kohne 1968; Rice 1972). These data have been confirmed and extended by other techniques that have led to the discovery of several well-defined families, of which the Alu family in primate and rodent genomes is an outstanding example (Schmid and Jelinek 1982, Jelinek and Schmid 1982, Lewin 1983:378, Britten et al. 1988).

The human genome consists of ca. 3×10^9 bp, of which ca. 20–30% are in the repeated fraction. Repeated human DNA includes: (1) dispersed sequences of 100–300 bp in the short-period (Xenopus) interspersion pattern; (2) clustered repeats not interspersed with single-copy sequences; (3) repeated sequences longer than 300 bp; (4) long single-copy sequences not interspersed with repeated sequences, and (5) inverted repeats. Many of the inverted repeats in primate and rodent DNAs make up the Alu family of interspersed repeats, which includes a significant proportion of the total short-period interspersed repeated sequences.

The Alu family derives its name from the fact that its members are cleaved at the same site by the restriction endonuclease Alu I, an abbreviation based on the name of the bacterium *Arthrobacter luteus*, from which the endonuclease is obtained. The Alu family accounts for at least 3–6% of the human genome, or ca. 100 million to 200 million bases. The repeating unit is ca. 300 bp in length and there are nearly a million copies interspersed throughout the human genome with an average spacing of ca. 4 kb. The Alu family accounts for most of the interspersed 300 bp repeats in the human genome.

The Alu family is abundant and widely dispersed in the genomes of the hominoids. The number of Alu-family repeats in the human genome is ca. 910,000; in the Common Chimpanzee, 330,000; Gorilla, 410,000; and Orangutan 580,000. Thermal stability measurements show that although the families of repeats are moderately divergent in sequence, little net sequence change has occurred during the evolution of the higher apes, including Man. Most or all of the members of these families of repeats are interspersed throughout the genome. Therefore, a large number of insertions and/or deletions of these sequences must have occurred during the evolution of the hominoids (Hwu et al. 1986). Britten et al. (1988) discussed the evolution of human *Alu* sequences, noting that a series of conserved genes is the primary source of the Alu family and that these genes have probably replaced each other in overlapping relays during the evolution of the primates.

The Alu family is also abundant and widely dispersed in the genome of the African Green Monkey (*Cercopithecus aethiops*) and, presumably, in other cercopithecoids. In the Thick-tailed Galago (*Galago crassicaudatus*), a prosimian, Daniels and Deininger (1983) found two distinct, highly repetitive families of sequences related to the human Alu family. One of these is apparently homologous to the human Alu family, but one of the monomers of the other family shows only limited homology to the human *Alu* sequence, or to the other monomer in the galago. This suggests that the non-homologous half must have evolved in the galago lineage after it branched from the lineage leading to the anthropoids. Alu-equivalent families are known in other mammals.

The human *Alu* sequence of ca. 300 bases is composed of two ca. 130 bp, directly repeated monomers, with a 31 bp insertion in one of them. In rodents, the sequence equivalent to the primate Alu family is a monomer, ca. 130 bp long, that is homologous to the dimeric *Alu* sequences of primates but with several differences in the base sequences. "Presumably these rodent and primate sequences are descendants of a common ancestral sequence that has been well preserved during recent evolution" (Schmid and Jelinek 1982:1067).

The Alu family is the single most abundant family of interspersed repeats in the mammalian genomes that have been examined and as such have been the most completely described. Whether they function in the control of gene activity as has been suggested, but not demonstrated for short-period interspersed repeats in general (Davidson and Britten 1973), remains to be determined. From sequence analyses, they appear to be mobile elements, possibly the most successful such elements in primate and rodent genomes. It has been suggested that the low molecular weight RNA's transcribed from them may function in their dispersal to new chromosomal locations. . . . If Alu family members are nothing more than mobile DNA elements, then like other mobile DNA elements they may have profound influences on gene expression at some of their sites of insertion into chromosomal DNA. The properties of Alu family members may also be attributes of other families of short-period dispersed repeats in both mammalian and non-mammalian species (Schmid and Jelinek 1982:1069–1070).

The Vitellogenin Family

The yolk proteins of oviparous vertebrates are derived from a common precursor, vitellogenin, which is synthesized in the liver of the adult female, transported to the ovary, and cleaved into the yolk proteins, lipovitellin and phosvitin. In the African Clawed Frog (*Xenopus laevis*) there are at least four distinct, but related, vitellogenin genes that form the vitellogenin gene family. There are two main groups of sequences, A and B, which differ in ca. 20% of their base sequences. A and B are composed of subgroups (A1, A2; B1, B2), which differ by ca. 5%. There are 33 introns in A and B that occur at homologous positions relative to the 34 exons. Many of the introns contain repeated elements, and the introns that apparently have arisen by duplication have diverged extensively by events that include deletions, insertions, and duplications (Wahli et al. 1981).

There are many other gene families in the vertebrates, including the actin, histone, and globin families.

Drosophila Gene Families

Another example is provided by the middle repetitive DNA sequences of six species of the *Drosophila melanogaster* subgroup, namely, *D. melanogaster, mauritiana, simulans, teissieri, yakuba*, and *erecta*. Several of these species interbreed and produce viable offspring; *mauritiana* interbreeds with all the others. Crosses between *mauritiana* and *simulans* produce some fertile progeny.

Dowsett (1983) found that of the 28 repeated sequence families in the *D. melanogaster* genome, only two are present in the other five species. *D. erecta* lacks most of the *melanogaster* families but has another set of repetitive families that are absent from the *melanogaster* genome. Others of these six species possess some of the *melanogaster* and *erecta* families but lack others. Dowsett (1983:104) concluded that most "middle repetitive families are highly unstable components of the *Drosophila* genome over short periods of evolutionary time." This contrasts with the finding that all of 12 arbitrarily chosen single-copy probes were "sufficiently conserved across these species to be clearly detectable by the same criteria" used to detect the middle repetitive sequences (Dowsett 1983:107).

Thus, it is clear that gene amplification events can occur in a random pattern among the members of a closely related group of taxa. This is one of the reasons it is important to remove most of the repeated sequences from radiolabeled DNAs used as tracers when the DNA-DNA hybridization technique is used to reconstruct phylogenies.

Satellite Sequences as Repeated DNA Families

The highly repeated, short-sequence elements of the DNA satellites of the kangaroo rat genus *Dipodomys* have been the subject of a series of studies by Mazrimas, Hatch, Salser, Fry, and their colleagues.

The 21 species of the heteromyid rodent genus *Dipodomys* occur in the arid and semiarid regions of western North America from southern Canada to central Mexico and from the Great Plains to the Pacific coast. *D. ordii*, the most widely distributed species, ranges from the Great Plains to eastern Oregon and Nevada, and from southwestern Saskatchewan to western Texas and north central Mexico (Honacki et al. 1982).

D. ordii has three satellite fractions that make up 52% of total nuclear DNA. The HS-β satellite consists of ca. 11% of total DNA, is repeated ca. 40 million times per genome, and is composed of a basic sequence of 10 bases with several mutational variations. The basic repeating sequence is 5'ACACAGCGGG3'. The major variations have the same sequence for the first six bases with the differences only among the last four. There are at least four major variants present in frequencies ranging from 33% to 15% of that of the basic sequence, and several others represented by smaller percentages (Fry et al. 1973).

The HS-α satellite of *D. ordii* makes up 19% of the total DNA and occurs in at least 12 variants, which are present in different amounts. The variants differ by one or two base substitutions from the dominant six-base sequence, 5'TTAGGG3', which makes up 25% of the HS-α satellite. None of these 12 HS-α variants is related to the other two DNA satellites in this species or in other species of *Dipodomys*. However, the major six-base sequence is identical to the repeating unit of the Guinea Pig (*Cavia porcellus*) α satellite (Southern 1970). The Botta Pocket Gopher (*Thomomys bottae*) and the Antelope Ground Squirrel (*Ammospermophilus leucurus*) also have α satellite sequences in common with the kangaroo rats. This indicates that the short repeated sequences of at least some satellite DNAs persist over long periods of time because the ancestors of these four species probably diverged from one another during the Eocene, ca. 40–50 MYA (Fry and Salser 1977; Salser et al. 1976; Mazrimas and Hatch 1977).

The MS satellite makes up ca. 22% of the total nuclear DNA in *D. ordii*, and its basic repeat sequence is only three nucleotides long, 5'AAG3'. There are about 500 million copies of this sequence and its variants per genome! The variants CAG and GAG are the most common, with ACG and AGG less so (Salser et al. 1976).

The relative proportions of these three satellites to one another and to the intermediate-density and principal fractions vary widely among the species of *Dipodomys*, and also among different subspecies of *D. ordii*, *D. spectabilis*, and *D. heermanni*. Other aspects of the genome, including chromosome number, proportions of uni-armed and bi-armed chromosomes, and total nuclear DNA, also vary widely and the variations are correlated with one another. These correlations suggest that such variations reflect adaptive responses to environmental challenges (Hatch et al. 1976).

Some families of repeated sequences are present in the genomes of many species, and the closer two species are related the greater the similarity between their repetitive sequences. There are also families of repeated sequences restricted to a single species or found only in a few closely related species. For example, the satellite DNA of the House Mouse (*Mus mus-*

culus) comprises ca. 10% of total DNA and is repeated about one million times. The T_m of the reassociated *Mus* satellite is only 5°C below that of the native satellite, which indicates that the copies form a family of similar, but not identical, sequences.

The *Mus musculus* satellite reassociates with the repetitive sequences of *Mus caroli* and *Mus cervicolor*, but the T_ms of the hybrids are as much as 25°C below that of native *Mus* DNA. Thus, although the satellite sequences within each species are quite similar, they differ markedly between these congeners (Rice and Straus 1973). This may be an example of concerted evolution. (See "Concerted Evolution of Repeated Sequence Families" in this chapter.)

When *Mus musculus* satellite DNA is hybridized with the repeated fraction from other rodent genera (*Apodemus, Rattus, Peromyscus, Cricetus, Cavia*) at 60°C, 0.12 M PB, there is little cross reaction.

Gillespie (1977) compared the highly repetitive sequences of 30 species, representing 19 genera, of Old World primates, including Human, Common Chimpanzee, gibbons, several baboons, macaques, monkeys, a lemur, and a slow loris. To obtain maximum sensitivity he incubated the tracer DNAs at 70°C in 0.12 M PB and removed the duplex fraction that had reassociated by Cot 5 (ca. 18 hrs) by HAP chromatography above 80°C. This yielded a fast repeat, high T_m (FRHT) class of well-matched repeated DNA sequences, which must represent the most recently amplified families. Furthermore, if such sequences were amplified in only one of two species after they had diverged from their most recent common ancestor, the new family would be present in one of the species, but in the other species would be represented by a single-copy sequence that would not be detectable in the low Cot hybridizations.

These assumptions were supported by the experiments, and the grouping of the species and genera was in accordance with the commonly accepted phylogeny of these taxa. As one example, human FRHT sequences occur in at least three sets: one not shared with the Common Chimpanzee; one shared with the Common Chimpanzee but not with the gibbons; and one shared with chimpanzees and gibbons but missing from the DNAs of the Old World monkeys, lemurs, and lorises.

The existence of FRHT classes of DNA presents a potential problem for the use of DNA-DNA hybridization in phylogeny reconstruction. If the labeled taxon in a DNA hybrid has a recently amplified sequence, the well-matched members of this FRHT family will reassociate among themselves and might be a significant component of the data. This could result in unequal reciprocal values. The solution is to use low stringency conditions (e.g., 50°C, 0.48 M PB) during the preparation of single-copy tracers to ensure that most of the copies of repeated sequences are removed before radiolabeling.

Miklos and Gill (1982) summarized and reviewed the data for highly repeated DNA sequences that exist in long tandem arrays. Sequence complexities are known to vary from 2 bp to at least 359 bp among invertebrates, and from 3 bp to 2350 bp in mammals, with considerable sequence variation within species. Alterations in the basic repeating unit vary from 1 bp to at least 98 bp in length, and involve single-base changes, deletions, and additions. Tandemly repeated arrays are constantly subjected to cycles of amplification and deletion with no apparent somatic effects.

The function or functions of DNA satellites remain obscure and "the main characteristic of satellites is their extensive variation" within and between species. "Repeated arrays are continually generated, expanded, reduced and dispersed as a natural consequence of the . . . machinery of eukaryotic cells" (Miklos and Gill 1982:24–25).

For those interested in using DNA-DNA hybridization to reconstruct phylogenies the lesson is, again, obvious. To obtain comparable, reproducible results, most of the copies of repeated sequences must be removed from DNAs to be used as tracers; i.e., only the single-copy fraction provides unequivocal evidence of the evolutionary history of lineages. The single-copy fraction also contains copies of all repeated sequences, thus the complexity of the entire genome is represented in a so-called single-copy preparation.

Gene Amplification

The observations described above indicate that families of repeated DNA sequences arise at intervals during the evolution of a lineage by the saltatory replication or amplification of a single-copy sequence. At first this adds to the total quantity of nuclear DNA but not to its sequence complexity. Subsequent variation among the sequences composing a family occurs as mutations are fixed in some of the originally identical sequences, followed by further amplification of the altered sequences. This process increases the sequence complexity of the genome.

The function of amplified sequences is obscure in some cases, but several examples show that amplification apparently is a response to an increased demand for the product of the gene that is amplified. Schimke (1982:1) described the process:

There comes a time in the life of every organism . . . when that organism must modulate the amount of a specific protein, whether in response to nutritional changes in the environment, in response to environmental agents that inhibit their growth (antibiotics, toxic agents, various drugs), or as a part of a developmental process. In most instances, organisms have evolved such that the expression of specific genes is regulated to increase or decrease transcription of a particular gene, hence, the existence of repressors, inducers, operons, and the like in prokaryotes and various hormonal modulations of gene expression in higher organisms. An alternative solution to the synthesis of increased amounts of a protein is the presence of multiple copies of a particular gene. We see this solution in the presence of multiple ribosomal genes in virtually all organisms, multiple tRNA genes, multiple histone genes, etc.

J. M. Roberts et al. (1983) expressed the same idea: "Gene amplification is a frequent mechanism by which cells meet the demand for increased quantities of specific gene products. . . . In somatic cells gene amplification may permit cells to overcome deficiencies in essential enzymatic activities. . . . During development individual genes, or sets of genes may be specifically amplified at precise developmental stages. . . . The changes in gene number observed in somatic cells . . . have also been exploited in evolutionary time to generate stable multigene families present in the chromosomes of the gamete as well as the somatic cells."

The first evidence of selective amplification of specific genes was found by Brown and Dawid (1968) in the ribosomal genes of the oocytes in the African Clawed Frog (*Xenopus laevis*). After fertilization the number of ribosomes increases during the period when protein synthesis is occurring at a rapid rate.

In *Drosophila* during certain stages of ovarian follicle cell development, four genes coding for chorion (eggshell) proteins are amplified from 16- to 60-fold. The amplified regions extend 45–50 kb on either side of the chorion genes (Spradling and Rubin 1981).

There is substantial evidence that gene amplification can be induced by an environmental challenge, such as a toxic substance. For example, Schimke et al. (1978) found that cultured mouse (*Mus*) cells developed resistance to the drug methotrexate, which is used in the treatment of malignant tumors. Methotrexate, an analog of folic acid, kills malignant cells by inhibiting the activity of the enzyme dihydrofolate reductase (DHFR), resulting in the prevention of the synthesis of proteins and nucleic acids. However, prolonged use of methotrexate often results in the development of drug-resistant tumors generally associated with an increase in DHFR, which is correlated with an increase in the number of DHFR genes. The amplification occurs in steps, beginning with an initial selection of those cells with the highest levels of DHFR production, followed by gene amplification. Resistance to antibiotics and insecticides may result from the same mechanism (Alt et al. 1978, Tlsty et al. 1982, P. C. Brown et al. 1983, and various papers in Schimke 1982).

Gene amplification is exploited by the pharmaceutical industry to produce large quantities of antibiotics, enzymes, and hormones in bacteria. With recombinant DNA techniques a gene can be inserted into a bacterium and induced to amplify a hundred-fold or more (Demain 1981:992).

It seems possible that induction by environmental challenges such as extreme temperatures, diseases, parasites, etc., may account for some of the variations in repeated DNA content observed in closely related but ecologically and/or geographically separated organisms such as the *Plethodon* salamanders, kangaroo rats, and pocket gophers. In the kangaroo rat genus *Dipodomys*, Mazrimas and Hatch (1972) reported a significant relationship between the amount of satellite DNA and the phylogeny of the group. They studied 12 of the 21 species and found that the amount of satellite DNA, expressed as a fraction of total nuclear DNA, is correlated directly with the number of subspecies and the chromosome fundamental number and inversely correlated with the extent of specialization for saltatory locomotion. They suggested that these correlations indicate that changes in the amount of repetitive DNA promote genetic flexibility, which permits or facilitates selective responses to changeable environments. Although the amounts of satellite DNAs vary, the sequences tend to be highly conserved in *Dipodomys* (Mazrimas and Hatch 1977).

Fry and Salser (1977) suggested a causal relationship between the abundance and distribution of highly conserved sequences of satellite DNA and speciation. Their argument was based on the discovery that the satellite DNAs of closely related species of kangaroo rats differ more among themselves than from those of other rodent genera that may have diverged from *Dipodomys* 40 million to 50 million years ago. In other organisms, however, the sequences of satellites found within and between species are closely related, for example, in the *Drosophila virilis* species group (Gall and Atherton 1974).

Hatch et al. (1976) examined the correlations among total quantity of DNA, satellite DNA, and variations in the number and structure of the chromosomes in *Dipodomys*. These properties vary between species and, to some degree, within species. The principal findings were (1) that the interspecific variations in diploid chromosome number cluster at 52–54, 60–64, and 70–72; (2) that high total nuclear DNA is associated with high chromosome number and with relatively large amounts of satellite DNA; and (3) that a high ratio of HS satellite DNA to intermediate-density DNA was correlated with a predominance of metacentric and submetacentric chromosomes (high fundamental number). They concluded that "the relationships of satellite DNA to karyotype structure reveal a new level of hierarchy in the genome that appears capable of exerting global control over environmental adaptation and the evolution of new species. This mechanism is consistent with recent hypotheses that changes in the macro-structure of the genome are more important than point mutations in facilitating the rapid phases of animal evolution" (p. 155).

The correlations reported by Hatch et al. (1976) seem to be consistent with proposals that chromosomal rearrangements may be speciation mechanisms in some groups of organisms (White 1969, 1973, 1978a, Bush 1975, Bush et al. 1977, Wilson et al. 1975, Levin and Wilson 1976). These authors suggested that translocations, fusions, inversions, and changes in chromosome number may, under certain conditions, result in rapid speciation. The key factor in animals may be the type of social behavior that produces small effective populations and inbreeding. Bush et al. (1977) found a correlation between rates of speciation and rates of chromosomal evolution in 225 species of vertebrates, and Levin and Wilson (1976) reported the same correlation in seed plants.

White (1978b) reported that genetic isolation between small, local *Mus musculus* populations in Italy and Switzerland is correlated with chromosomal rearrangements. The resulting process of "stasipatric" speciation (White 1968, 1969) may protect the co-adapted gene complexes of locally adapted populations from disruption by introgression. This process would be most likely to occur in organisms of limited vagility, such as small mammals, lizards, and wingless insects. It would be expected to be rare in highly mobile animals, including most birds. In these, allopatric speciation is clearly the dominant mode.

Sherwood and Patton (1982:176) came to a different conclusion when they found "no consistently demonstrable differentiation, either morphologically or ecologically, which is associated with different karyotypes or amounts of DNA in the diploid genome" of Botta's Pocket Gopher (*Thomomys bottae*), one of the most sedentary small mammals. They found "no obvious relationship between formal systematic species status and cellular DNA content differences" and noted that quantitative genome change "is neither necessary for speciation nor apparently an expected characteristic of the process of divergence." They concluded that their "*Thomomys* data do not support the conclusions" of Hinegardner (1976) that "low DNA values, specialization and speciation all tend to go together."

Thus, although gene amplification has been shown to be related to the demand for an increase in the product of an amplified gene, there is no consistent relationship between genome size or satellites and speciation.

Concerted Evolution of Repeated Sequence Families

The existence of families of repeated DNA sequences is indicated by the range of thermal stabilities over which repeated sequences dissociate, as described above. Although there are various degrees of base-pair mismatch among the members of most repeat families, some are essentially homogeneous within species, but exhibit differences between closely related species. The high degree of base sequence homology between related species indicates that the family of repeats originated in a recent common ancestor, and it is no surprise to find differences between species, but how has homogeneity been preserved within each species? Apparently, "each individual member of a gene family does not necessarily evolve independently of the others. Through genetic interactions among its members, the family may evolve together in a concerted fashion, as a unit" (Arnheim 1983:38).

For example, the genes coding for the 18S and 28S ribosomal RNAs in the African clawed frogs (*Xenopus*) are present as hundreds of copies. Each gene consists of a transcribed segment (exon) and a non-transcribed spacer segment (intron). Within each of two species (*X. borealis, X. laevis*) both segments are homogeneous. However, between the two species the transcribed segments are nearly identical, but the non-transcribed segments differ substantially. Similar patterns have been found in several other genes in various species.

Thus, gene duplication, or amplification, is not necessarily followed by the evolution of variation. Instead, a homogeneous multigene family may evolve. "This suggests that eukaryotes have devised a mechanism for maintaining the homogeneity of multigene families, presumably to avoid the serious selective disadvantages of sequence heterogeneity in abundant structural RNAs. In effect, homogenization of multiple gene copies enables the cell to reduce a multigene family to a single-copy gene on which natural selection can act as on any true single-copy locus" (Weiner and Denison 1982:1142).

At least four possible mechanisms have been proposed to explain the homogeneity of some repeated DNA families in eukaryotes. The four models are (1) the master-slave hypothesis, (2) unequal crossing over, (3) democratic gene conversion, and (4) saltatory replication or gene amplification (Weiner and Denison 1982).

All four mechanisms may occur, but gene conversion and amplification seem to fit more of the known cases of concerted evolution. In gene conversion: "Two partially homologous DNA sequences are thought to pair . . . in a heteroduplex that is subsequently repaired and resolved. The result is a nonreciprocal exchange of sequence information between loci that are genetically homologous. In truly democratic gene conversion, each locus would serve as the template for repair in half of the conversion events. [However, conversion may not be truly democratic and some loci] . . . serve more than half of the time as the template for repair of the heteroduplex. . . . even a small conversional advantage will cause a single gene to dominate a multigene family after many successive rounds of mutual interconversion" (Weiner and Denison 1982:1142).

Saltatory replication, or gene amplification, may also homogenize multigene families:

If any individual member of a preexisting multigene family were to undergo a massive expansion, the amplified gene copies would constitute a significant fraction of the total number of genes in the multigene family. . . . In this way, the sequence divergence that necessarily accumulates in any multigene family would be overwhelmed periodically by random amplification of a single functional member of the family.

Given the facility with which cells can amplify a single-copy gene into a tandemly repeated array, we may safely assume that many if not most DNA sequences within the genome are continually subject to transient amplification. Most of these amplifications will be genetically invisible in the absence of selective conditions, but occasionally such an amplified array might be retained if it conferred a growth advantage on the cell. This may be the mechanism by which saltatory replications effectively homogenize multigene families (Weiner and Denison 1982:1144).

Arnheim (1983:61) concluded that "selectively advantageous mutations . . . could be fixed in the multiple copies of . . . genes by gene conversion. Gene correction mechanisms not only fix neutral mutations, thus maintaining homogeneity among family members, but also provide an efficient way of fixing selectively advantageous mutations in multigene systems."

How will DNA-DNA hybridization view the results of concerted evolution? A homogeneous family of repeated sequences will behave during reassociation like any set of identical, or nearly identical, repeats. They will reassociate rapidly and be perceived by the technique as a set of highly repetitive or middle repetitive sequences, depending on copy number. At least one copy, and probably 10–20 copies, per genome, of each such sequence will be present in a tracer prepared from a DNA sample containing such sequences. Thus, concerted evolution presents no special problem to the interpretation of the data of DNA-DNA hybridization, although the extra copies are a small factor in the size of the experimental error.

Conservation of Repeated Sequences

Concerted evolution explains the homogeneity of repeated sequences within species, but repeated sequences may also be conserved in different species. For example, Moore et al. (1978) estimated the frequency of occurrence of certain repeated sequence families in three species of sea urchins, *Strongylocentrotus purpuratus*, *S. franciscanus*, and *Lytechinus pictus*. For nine cloned repeated sequence elements from *S. purpuratus*, the ratio of the repetition frequency in *S. purpuratus* to that in *franciscanus* ranged from ca. 20 to ca. 1. Estimates of frequency changes in many repetitive families were made by measuring the reassociation of labeled repeat fractions of each species with total DNA of the other two species. In all cases the rate of reassociation was slower for interspecific comparisons than for intraspecific comparisons. Thus, it appears that the dominant repetitive families in each species are present at lower frequencies in the DNAs of related species. Most repeat families have changed in frequency and sequence, although some have changed little in sequence but greatly in frequency.

Conservation of repeated sequences was also shown by Lima-de-Faria et al. (1984) for five species of deer (Cervidae). The 2n chromosome number is 70 in the Reindeer (*Rangifer tarandus*), Old World Elk or Moose of North America (*A. alces*), and Roe Deer (*C. capreolus*); 68 in the Fallow Deer (*D. dama*, or *Cervus dama*), and only 6 in the Indian Muntjac (*Muntiacus muntjak*). However, all five species share homologies between certain highly repetitive sequences. The three species with 70 chromosomes are more similar to one another than to the other two, but the sequence homologies have been conserved although the chromosome number has been drastically reduced in the Muntjac.

Transposable Elements

Most of the DNA in the genomes of prokaryotes and eukaryotes seems to be composed of static nucleotide sequences that change their positions only over long spans of time, but certain sequences, known as mobile genetic elements, transposable elements, jumping genes, or transposons, can move from one site to another within the genome. The process of transposition is detected by the appearance of a segment of DNA, which is known to occupy a certain site, at a second site with which the transposon is not homologous. The element that moves is a copy of the original sequence, which remains at the original position. Transposable elements were first detected in maize by Barbara McClintock (e.g. 1952, 1965) from phenotypic evidence. The molecular mechanism of transposition was first discovered in bacteria and later in yeast and *Drosophila*. Transposons are presumed to occur generally in eukaryotes.

Transposons are repeated sequences, usually of several hundred to a few thousand bases in length. For example, the copia element in *Drosophila melanogaster* is ca. 5 kb long and occurs as 20–60 copies per genome. Transposons probably account for a large percentage of the repetitive sequences in *Drosophila* and possibly in other eukaryotes. The Alu family may be composed of transposable, 300-bp middle repetitive elements. It accounts for 3–6% of the total human nuclear genome and perhaps 10–20% of all repeats in the human genome (see the introduction to this chapter). Adams et al. (1981), Freifelder (1983), Lewin (1983), and Shapiro (1983) provide reviews.

Campbell (1983) considered the evolutionary significance of transposons and concluded (p. 278) that: "Movable elements are found in organisms of all types and have doubtless caused some chromosomal changes of evolutionary importance. Chromosomal rearrangements can also arise by less specific mechanisms that do not depend on specific elements. . . . a role in evolution to which movable elements are especially suited . . . is the dissemination of . . . regulatory sites around the genome. Controlled gene rearrangements are observable in diverse organisms [and could] constitute the . . . mechanism whereby specialized cells of higher eukaryotes acquire their . . . stable properties. Movable elements might be (1) the agents of some such rearrangements; (2) the evolutionary precursors of the cellular agents; (3) derivatives of the normal agents, which serve no useful function to the organism but are tolerated by it; or (4) all of the above."

Fedoroff (1984) reviewed the discovery of transposons in maize and speculated that they may be of great significance in evolution because:

their properties appear to make them suitable agents for modifying . . . the expression of genes [and] the structure of genes and genomes. . . . it is known that transposable elements are activated when the genome is stressed and chromosome breakage is taking place. . . . once the elements are activated they can promote many kinds of mutations and chromosomal rearrangements. It is as if transposable elements can amplify a small genetic disturbance, turning it into a genetic earthquake. Perhaps such genetic turbulence is an important source of genetic variability, the raw material from which natural selection can sift what is useful for the species. Moreover, evidence is accumulating that in addition to turning genes off transposable elements can turn them on or amplify their expression. There is reason to suspect they can reprogram genes as well, changing when and where in the organism a gene is active. This is indeed the stuff of remodeling and rebuilding, of organismic evolution.

Lloyd et al. (1987) noted that: "At least 15% of most eukaryotic genomes is composed of interspersed repetitive DNA sequences . . . the function of which is largely unknown. Many of these repetitive sequences are transposable elements, with the ability to . . . replicate and insert into new positions in the genome, thus increasing their copy number. Transposable elements can generate DNA rearrangements, including (1) placing new promoters in front of genes that they insert next to . . . (2) causing inversions and deletions of flanking sequence owing to recombination between elements . . . (3) cooperating to levitate large blocks of DNA to new positions in the genome . . . and (4) producing mutations by inserting into genes. . . . Transposable elements, therefore, generate genetic variation for natural selection to act on. Indeed, transposable elements may provide a prime force in molding genomes during evolution."

The Alu family (discussed above) of nearly a million interspersed repeated sequences apparently has been inserted into the genomes of the primates by retroposition. Using high criterion conditions for hybridization, Britten et al. (1989) found that precise hybrids formed between a significant cloned fraction of human *Alu* repeated sequences and DNA of an Old World monkey (Mandrill, *Papio sphinx*) but not with the DNA of a New World Spider Monkey (*Ateles*). The Old World monkeys (Cercopithecoidea) are known to be more closely related to the ape-human lineage than are the New World monkeys (Ceboidea). Britten et al. noted: "Human and mandrill are moderately distant species with a single-copy DNA divergence of about 6%. Nevertheless, their recently inserted *Alu* sequences arise by retroposition of transcripts of source genes with nearly identical sequences. Apparently a gene present in our common ancestor at the time of branching was inherited and highly conserved in sequence in both the lineage of Old World monkeys and the lineage of apes and man."

Thus, regardless of their origin or functional significance, transposons evolve like other sequences and contain information about the phylogeny of organisms. In the DNA-DNA hybridization technique transposons may be expected to behave like other repetitive sequences; thus, most of the copies would be removed in the preparation of tracers. Because the DNA is sheared into fragments, each sequence is free to find its complementary partner during reassociation. Therefore, there is no reason to assume that transposable sequences present a special problem during the hybridization procedure or in the interpretation of the data.

Genomes of Cellular Organelles

A varying, but usually small, percentage of eukaryotic genetic information resides outside the nucleus in the chloroplasts and mitochondria of most plants and the mitochondria of most animals. The exceptions are more than a thousand species of protozoa and a few species of fungi that lack mitochondria (Cavalier-Smith 1987, Vossbrinck et al. 1987).

These cellular organelles contain genomes composed primarily or entirely of single-copy DNA in a circular sequence. Usually, there are several copies of the genome per organelle and from a few to several hundred organelles per cell. Thus, the organelle genomes constitute a repeated sequence fraction of DNA in whole-cell DNA preparations.

The mitochondrial genetic code differs from the nuclear code in at least five codons in some organisms, and the mitochondrial DNA (mtDNA) codons in different organisms are not identical (Kroon 1983).

The endosymbiotic theory of the origin of mitochondria and chloroplasts suggests that they were derived from the blue-green algae (Cyanobacteria), primitive prokaryotes with properties similar to those of the organelles of higher organisms. Curtis and Clegg (1984:296) compared the sequences of apparently homologous genes in cyanobacteria and higher plants and concluded that the comparisons "strongly support the inference that these genes derived from a common ancestor. Estimates of divergence times between cyanobacterial and chloroplast genes, while still tentative, also suggest that divergence occurred after the evolution of the eukaryotic cell. . . . These data may therefore be taken as support for the endosymbiotic origin of the chloroplast genome. Further support for the endosymbiotic theory can be found in comparisons of 16S rRNA sequences from *Escherichia coli*, cyanobacteria, and chloroplast DNA (Tomioka and Sugiura 1983)."

Chloroplast genomes in the lower eukaryotes (e.g., *Euglena, Chlamydomonas*) contain up to 200 kb, and in most higher plants (e.g., *Zea, Spinacia, Nicotiana*) ca. 150 kb.

Curtis and Clegg (1984) reviewed comparative data on the evolution of chloroplast genes. The chloroplasts of most plants have similar structural organizations, and sequence divergence is similar in higher plants and blue-green algae. In angiosperms there is a large duplicated region of reverse, or inverted, orientation, separated by two regions of single-copy DNA. Some chloroplast tRNA genes contain introns. The estimated rate of nucleotide substitution for synonymous codons is ca. 1.1 per nucleotide per 10^9 years, thus, ca. 100-fold less than similar estimates for primate mtDNA by W. M. Brown et al. (1982). Whitfield and Bottomley (1983) reviewed the organization and structure of chloroplast genes.

Plant mitochondrial genomes are known to range from ca. 15 kb in the unicellular green alga *Chlamydomonas* to 66 kb in the bread mold *Neurospora*, 84 kb in the yeast *Saccharomyces*, 110 kb in the Garden Pea *Pisum sativum*, and 2400 kb in the muskmelon or canteloupe *Cucumis melo*. Thus, in most of the higher plants, with their large nuclear genomes, the organelle genomes provide only a small percentage of total cellular DNA, but there are some large mtDNA genomes, as in *Cucumis melo*, above. Lewin (1980, 1983) and Tzagoloff (1982) reviewed organelle structure and function.

Ohyama et al. (1986) sequenced the chloroplast DNA of the liverwort *Marchantia polymorpha* and deduced the gene organization. The genome contains 121,024 base pairs and codes for 128 possible genes that code for ribosomal RNAs, transfer RNAs, and open reading frames for proteins. Seven of the latter show high homology to unidentified reading frames found in human mitochondria.

Animal mtDNA genomes are smaller than those of most plants and consist of a single closed-circular, duplex, DNA molecule of 15,700 to 23,000 base pairs that appears to be entirely single-copy. Most groups have 16 to 17.5 kb of mtDNA. Some individuals of the lizard *Cnemidophorus exsanguis* have 22.2 kb, whereas most have 17.4 kb. The difference is due to a tandem duplication of a 4.8 kb region that includes regulatory sequences and transfer and ribosomal RNA genes (Moritz and Brown 1986).

Genome size is not correlated with taxonomic groups; in fact, there is substantial variation within some taxa, e.g., *Drosophila* (Solignac et al. 1986). The mtDNA genome is present only in female gametes, therefore it is maternally inherited. In mammals the mtDNA genome appears to evolve much faster than the average rate of the nuclear genome (W. M. Brown 1983), but in *Drosophila* the two genomes seem to evolve at rather similar rates. Solignac et al. (1986) found that the mtDNA rate in members of the *Drosophila melanogaster* group is "barely double that of nuclear DNA." Powell et al. (1986) reported that the rates of nucleotide substitution in *Drosophila* mtDNA and nuclear DNA are similar.

The avian mtDNA genome is ca. 16,000–17,000 bp in length (Glaus et al. 1980, Ovenden et al. 1987).

The percentage of GC is similar to but more variable than that of the nuclear genome, ranging from 37% to 50% in the vertebrates. In birds, the Domestic Mallard (*Anas platyrhynchos*) has ca. 50% GC, and the Domestic Fowl (*G. gallus*) has 46% GC. W. M. Brown (1983) presents additional details and references.

Glaus et al. (1980) compared the restriction endonuclease cleavage maps of the mtDNAs of five species of galliforms. They concluded that the five species are "closely related," but did not attempt to construct a phylogeny.

Avise (1986), Avise et al. (1979a,b, 1983, 1984a,b, 1986), Avise and Lansman (1983),

Avise and Saunders (1984), Bermingham et al. (1986), Bermingham and Avise (1986), Chapman et al. (1982), Douglas and Avise (1982), Laerm et al. (1982), Lamb and Avise (1986), Lansman et al. (1981, 1983a,b), Ferris et al. (1981a,b, 1982), and Kessler and Avise (1984, 1985a,b) have used mtDNAs in comparative studies of various vertebrates.

Avise and Nelson (1989) compared the mtDNAs of specimens representing the populations of the Seaside Sparrow (*Ammodramus maritimus*) that occur along the Atlantic and Gulf of Mexico coasts of the United States with the mtDNA of the last surviving individual of the subspecies *nigrescens*, the Dusky Seaside Sparrow. This population of the east coast of central Florida had once been considered to be a full species and as its numbers declined it was placed on the endangered species list. Attempts were made to save the *nigrescens* genotype by crossing it with birds from the Gulf coast population of western Florida (*peninsulae*). Avise and Nelson found a substantial genetic gap between the Atlantic and Gulf coast populations but a close relationship between *nigrescens* and the other Atlantic coast populations. They concluded that "applied management strategies for the seaside sparrow [were] based on a morphological taxonomy that does not adequately reflect evolutionary relationships." Their data showed that "by the criterion of mtDNA sequence, the last *A. m. nigrescens* appears to have been a routine example of the Atlantic coast phylad of seaside sparrow."

Ovenden et al. (1987) used six restriction endonucleases to digest the mtDNAs of six species of the Australian parrot genus *Platycercus*. The resulting fragments were compared by electrophoresis, the data were analyzed by several methods, and trees were constructed. They found that the phylogenies produced from the mtDNA genomes agreed well with the current classification of the genus, except for *P. icterotis* which did not cluster with "either of the superspecies of *Platycercus* and . . . should probably be placed in a third group."

Ball et al. (1988) compared the restriction-site variation in the mtDNAs of 127 Red-winged Blackbirds (*Agelaius phoeniceus*) collected from 19 breeding localities in Canada, the United States, and Mexico. They found 34 mtDNA genotypes, but differences among the populations were minor, in contrast to the substantial amount of morphological geographic variation in this species.

S. A. Anderson et al. (1981) determined the sequence and organization of the 16,569 bp in the human mtDNA genome. In the known functional regions, 13 genes code for proteins, 22 for transfer RNAs, and two for the 12S and 16S ribosomal RNAs.

Each cell in higher animals contains several hundred mitochondria; thus, the mtDNA in whole-cell DNA preparations will behave as a family of rapidly evolving middle repetitive sequences during DNA-DNA hybridization. Since the mtDNA genome of animals contains only 15,000–20,000 bases, it has a sequence complexity of about 0.001 of 1% of that of the avian nuclear genome; thus, it is a minor component of the total DNA per cell and should not have a detectable effect on the data of DNA-DNA hybridization.

In at least a few organisms the mtDNA is a substantial percentage of whole-cell DNA. For example, 28% of the DNA of the cellular slime-mold *Dictyostelium discoideum* is mtDNA (Firtel and Bonner 1972), and 26% is mtDNA in the nematode *Ascaris lumbricoides* (Tobler et al. 1972). Kroon (1983), Jacobs et al. (1983), and J. W. Roberts et al. (1983) provide additional information about the mitochondrial genome.

CHAPTER EIGHT

Homology

There are three sources of structural and functional similarities between organisms: convergence, parallelism, and common ancestry. Convergent evolution and parallel evolution produce analogous similarities; common ancestry produces homologous similarities. Convergence may be defined as the independent evolution of similar derived states from different precursors or by different genetic or developmental processes. Parallelism is the independent origin of similar derived states from the same precursor or by similar developmental or genetic processes. The general term for both phenomena is homoplasy. The problems of homoplasy are further complicated by evolutionary reversals, which give rise to secondarily derived, apparently primitive, similarities. Some definitions of homology follow:

The occurrence of convergence and various other kinds of similarity not resulting from common descent demonstrates that in the construction of classifications one must distinguish several kinds of similarities. Only similarities between homologous characters are of taxonomic importance. . . . Homologous features (or states of the features) in two or more organisms are those that can be traced back to the same feature (or state) in the common ancestor of these organisms (Mayr 1969:84–85).

A character of two or more taxa is homologous if this character is found in the common ancestor of these taxa, or, two characters (or a linear sequence of characters) are homologues if one is directly (or sequentially) derived from the other(s) (Wiley 1981:121–122).

Homology is . . . the most important principle in all comparative biology. . . . homology is the only method of comparing attributes of different species. . . . any comparative method in conflict with the concept of homology is . . . subject to question. . . . [in two organisms those features are homologous which] can be traced phylogenetically to the same feature . . . in the immediate common ancestor of both organisms (Bock 1973:386).

Homology . . . is resemblance (more precisely, correspondence) caused by a continuity of information. . . . For molecular biologists . . . a good touchstone is that homology is always an inference, never an observation. What we observe is similarity or identity, never homology (Van Valen 1983).

Two structures are called homologous if they represent corresponding parts of organisms which are built according to the same body plan. The existence of corresponding structures in different species is explained by derivation from a common ancestor that had the same structure as the two species compared. . . . Homology is assessed regardless of shape or function. Only morphological equivalence in terms of relative position, structure, and connections with nerves and blood vessels counts (Wagner 1989:51).

Wagner (1989) reviewed the homology concept in relation to morphology, with special attention to developmental pathways and morphogenesis. He concluded that the "biological validity of the homology concept revolves around . . . the relationship between phylogenetic and iterative homology, the question of individuality of repeated organs, the nature of continuity, and the variability of development."

Patterson (1988) summarized his discussion of the concept of homology in classical and molecular biology as follows:

Hypotheses of homology are the basis of comparative morphology and comparative molecular biology. The kinds of homologous and nonhomologous relations . . . are explored through the three tests that may be applied to a hypothesis of homology: congruence, conjunction, and similarity. The same three tests apply in molecular comparisons and in morphology, and in each field they differentiate eight kinds of relation. . . . The unit or standard of comparison differs in morphology and in molecular biology; in morphology it is the adult or life cycle, but with molecules it is the haploid genome. In morphology the congruence test is decisive in separating homology and nonhomology, whereas with molecular sequence data similarity is the decisive test. Consequences of this difference are that the boundary between homology and nonhomology is not the same in molecular biology as in morphology, that homology and synapomorphy can be equated in morphology but not in all molecular comparisons, and that there is no detected molecular equivalent of convergence. Since molecular homology may reflect either species phylogeny or gene phylogeny, there are more kinds of homologous relation between molecular sequences than in morphology. The terms paraxenology and plerology are proposed for two of these kinds—respectively, the consequence of multiple xenology and of gene conversion (p. 603).

From his study of the problem, Patterson (1988) concluded

that the criterion used to define homology—i.e., the criterion of common ancestry—is a theoretical concept. Like truth, we must approximate it as best we can, and we have no touchstone to tell whether we have found it. The criteria we use to recognize homology are the same in morphology and molecular biology. But because molecular sequences are one-dimensional, recognition of molecular homology is a statistical problem, and the limit between homology and nonhomology is set by the resolving power of statistical procedures. In morphology, homologies concern three- or four-dimensional structures, and recognition of homology is a problem of systematics. In morphology the limit between homology and nonhomology is set by the resolving power of systematics, the confidence with which we can resolve monophyletic groups by congruence of features; and so in morphology it is legitimate to equate homology and synapomorphy. In molecular phylogenetics, there is no exact equation between homology and synapomorphy, first because the operational limit between molecular homology and nonhomology is statistical, and second because the theoretical criterion of homology—i.e., the criterion of common ancestry—does not distinguish between taxon lineages and gene lineages, which may ramify between and within taxa (p. 621).

Patterson's last sentence applies to short DNA sequences of a few thousand bases but not to DNA hybridization which compares all or most of the two genomes in a DNA-DNA hybrid.

The concept of homology is equally important when dealing with molecules and their attributes as sources of phylogenetic information. With reference to genes and proteins Fitch (1976:161) defined homology "as similarity arising by virtue of common ancestry, as opposed to analogy which is similarity arising by virtue of convergent evolution." This definition is the same as those applied by many authors to morphological characters. However, for genes and proteins, Fitch noted that "There are two kinds of homology that are important to distinguish. Two different gene products existing in the same organism may have a common ancestral gene that, either through gene duplication or translocation, gave rise to independent genes evolving side by side in a single line of descent. Such genes are said to be paralogous. Two different gene products whose difference is a consequence of independence arising from speciation are said to be orthologous because there is an exact phyletic correspondence between the history of the genes and the history of the taxa from which they derive."

The distinction between paralogous and orthologous genes is useful with reference to gene products, i.e., proteins, but does not affect the interpretation of DNA-DNA hybridization data because both types will contain base sequences that reflect the amount of genetic divergence that has occurred since two lineages last shared a common ancestor. In the broadest sense, all genes may be homologous because it is probable that all genes, in all organisms, have originated by gene duplication and subsequent base sequence divergence. This hypothesis assumes that the genes in living species have been derived from pre-existing nucleotide sequences, back to the primordial gene(s) that accompanied the origin of life on Earth.

Duplicate (or repeated) sequences diverge from their most recent common ancestral sequence, and from one another, by the incorporation of different base substitutions, deletions, and insertions. Eventually such homologous sequences will acquire so many mismatched bases that they will not form thermally stable heteroduplex molecules at the standard criterion of 60°C. At that point, such sequences may be said to have become part of the single-copy fraction and to have been added to the sequence complexity of the genome. They may still form stable duplexes under less stringent conditions, e.g., 50°C and 0.14 M PB, but as divergence continues, they will eventually behave as non-homologous sequences, even at the most relaxed conditions of stringency. Thus, the degree of base-pair complementarity, by which homologous genes are identified, gradually declines as a function of time. However, homologies between genes that began their divergence hundreds of millions of years ago can still be recognized from their base sequences, or from the amino acid sequences of the proteins for which they code.

For example, the immunoglobulin genes of the vertebrates are the descendants of an ancestral gene of ca. 330 base pairs that existed in some pre-vertebrate lineage more than 500 million years ago. By duplication and divergence this gene produced the immunoglobulin family which, in the mammals, consists of ten members that make up five (or six) immunoglobulin molecules. In birds, there are four immunoglobulins, in reptiles three, and in amphibians two. In the fishes there is only one, the IgM type, from which the others apparently evolved (Barker and Dayhoff 1976:165; Marchalonis 1977). Evidence of the presence of homologs of the insulin gene and the genes for other hormones has been found in many organisms from bacteria, protozoa, and fungi to the insects and vertebrates (Doolittle 1979; Kolata 1982). The brain peptides of vertebrates (e.g., serotonin, enkephalin, oxytocin) have homologs in plants, protozoa, and invertebrates. In many cases the homologous peptides have different functions and occur in different tissues in different organisms (Krieger 1983).

In recent years the word "homology" has been misused by many authors to express the percentage of sequence identity between DNA sequences. For example, a 20% identity in the sequences of two genes is described as 20% homology. In this form, homology simply means similarity without the vital implication of common ancestry. Reeck et al. (1987) protested this erroneous usage and appealed for the proper expression of this important word and concept. Lewin (1987) reviewed the problem.

Roth (1988:7) introduced the concept of genetic piracy as the principle that "genes, previously unassociated with the development of a particular structure, can be deputized in evolution, that is, brought in to control a previously unrelated developmental process, so that entirely different suits of genes may be responsible for the appearance of the structure in different contexts." This idea is supported by the many examples of homologous genes that perform different functions in distantly related taxa. It may present a problem for morphological systematics but not for molecular comparisons of genes or genomes.

Examples of Molecular Homology

THE HOMEO BOX

A remarkable example of homology involves the several genes that determine body segmentation in insects, annelids, and vertebrates. In *Drosophila*, the genes of the Antennapedia and Bithorax complexes determine the structure and diversity of the body segments. Both gene clusters are located on the right arm of the third chromosome. A mutant of Antennapedia causes legs to grow in place of antennae, and the mutant Ophthalmoptera induces wings to grow in place of eyes. Such mutations, which produce structures usually found in other positions, are called homeotic. The genes in *Drosophila* that determine body segments share a conserved sequence of 183 nucleotides called the homeo box (often spelled "homoeo" in British usage).

Studies of the expression of Antennapedia suggest that this gene specifies mainly the second thoracic segment. Schneuwly et al. (1987) showed that the transformation of antennae into the second pair of legs "is due to the ectopic overexpression of the *Antp*+ protein." This was determined by "heat induction at defined larval stages." Heat-shock induces the expression of some genes; in this case it showed that "*Antp* controls the developmental pathway leading to the second thoracic segment and specifies not only the ventral parts (the mesothoracic legs) but also the dorsal parts (the scutum)." Brownlee (1987) provided a popular account of homeo box studies in *Drosophila*.

In the Red Flour Beetle (*Tribolium castaneum*) Beeman (1987) discovered a cluster of homeotic genes that are ordered along the second linkage group in a sequence identical to that of the body segments in which they act. The domain of function of this gene cluster spans ca. 15 segments in the head, thorax, and abdomen and includes elements apparently homologous to the Antennapedia and Bithorax genes in *Drosophila*. Mutations at one end of the cluster affect the mouthparts; at the other end they affect the posterior abdominal segments. Thus, there is colinearity between the gene position in the linkage group and the morphological effect.

Homologous homeo box sequences have also been detected in the genomes of other organisms, including an African clawed frog (*Xenopus*), the House Mouse, and Man (Alberts et al. 1983:840, McGinnis et al. 1984a–c, Gehring 1985, Jackson et al. 1985, Simeone et al. 1986, Snow 1986).

Gaunt et al. (1986), using in situ DNA hybridization, showed "that expression of the mouse homoeobox gene . . . is spatially restricted in the developing embryo and that localization of expression is already evident within the germ layers before their morphological differentiation. These findings support the suggestion that the homoeobox genes of mammals, like those of *Drosophila*, may be important in pattern formation."

There is even a segment of a gene in the yeast *Saccharomyces cerevisiae* that is weakly homologous to a portion of the homeo box of higher eukaryotes (McGinnis et al. 1984a, Shepherd et al. 1984, Porter and Smith 1986). Holland and Hogan (1986) found sequences that hybridize to *Drosophila* and House Mouse homeo box probes in arthropods, annelids, molluscs, chordates, echinoderms, and brachiopods. More divergent reactions were obtained when the probes were hybridized with nemerteans and tapeworms. Neither probe hybridized with the DNAs of a flatworm (*Schistosoma*), two nematodes, yeast, or a slime mold. These results show the wide homology of the homeo box sequences and have implications for invertebrate phylogeny.

Gehring (1987) summarized "homeo boxes in the study of development": "The body plan of *Drosophila* is determined to a large extent by homeotic genes, which specify the identity and spatial arrangement of the body segments. Homeotic genes share a characteristic DNA segment, the homeo box, which encodes a defined domain of the homeotic proteins. The homeo domain seems to mediate the binding to specific DNA sequences, whereby the homeotic proteins exert a gene regulatory function. By isolating the *Antennapedia* gene, fusing its protein-coding sequences to an inducible promoter, and reintroducing this fusion gene into germline flies, it has been possible to transform head structures into thoracic structures and to alter the body plan in a predicted way. Sequence homologies suggest that similar genetic mechanisms may control development in higher organisms."

A large and expanding literature on homeotic genes indicates that sequence homologies may be ancient in origin, highly conserved, and widely distributed among organisms, although their morphological expressions may not be recognized as homologous. Homeo box genes produce proteins that bind to specific DNA regions and act as transcription factors, as described in chapter 4. As more is learned about this system additional complexities are found, including the POU domain (Sturm and Herr 1988), "a bipartite DNA-binding structure." In the roundworm *Caenorhabditis elegans*, Bürglin et al. (1989) estimate that "the number of homoeobox-containing genes is at least 60, constituting ca. 1% of the estimated total number of genes." (Reviews by Robertson 1988, Marx 1988 and 1989, and Lewis 1989.)

HEMOGLOBINS

Homologies between genes extend to even more distantly related organisms. For example, the hemoglobins are oxygen-transporting proteins in the eukaryotes, but heme proteins with similar functions are also found in bacteria (Wakabayashi et al. 1986, Perutz 1986) and plants (Landsmann et al. 1986). The filamentous bacterium *Vitreoscilla* synthesizes a heme protein that has a 24% sequence homology with lupine (*Lupinus*) leghemoglobin, which may enable the organism to survive in oxygen-limited environments (Wakabayashi et al. 1986:481). The leghemoglobins of the legumes are well-known, but homologous genes have also been found in non-leguminous plants. Landsmann et al. (1986:166) "conclude that the globin gene family may be widespread in modern plants, that plant haemoglobins may have a cryptic function in non-symbiotic tissue and that plant haemoglobins have evolved by vertical descent, probably from an ancestor common to modern plants and animals."

Bogusz et al. (1988) isolated a hemoglobin gene from *Trema tomentosa*, a non-nodulating member of the Ulmaceae. "The gene has three introns located at positions identical to those in the haemoglobin genes of nodulating plant species, strengthening the case for a common origin of all plant haemoglobin genes. The data argue strongly against horizontal . . . transfer from animals to plants."

Homologous genes are the evidence that gene duplication, followed by the modification of one or both of the duplicate genes, is a common evolutionary strategy. Li (1983) suggested that

Gene duplication is probably the most important mechanism for generating new genes and new biochemical processes that have facilitated the evolution of complex organisms from primitive ones. . . . The existence of numerous systems of homologous proteins or genes in higher organisms also indicates that gene duplication has occurred frequently in the evolutionary process. . . .

Gene duplication seems to have been important even in the refinement of genes in evolution. Many proteins of present-day organisms show internal repeats of amino acid sequences (for example, serum albumin) and these repeats often correspond to the functional or structural domains of the proteins. . . . This observation suggests that the genes coding for these proteins were formed by internal gene duplication and that the function of the genes was improved by increasing the number of active sites or stability of the proteins produced. The recent finding that eukaryotic genes generally consist of several exons and introns . . . and that exons often correspond to functional or structural domains of proteins . . . also suggests that many genes in present-day organisms were formed by duplication of primordial genes that probably existed in the early stage of life and were presumably small in size and simple in function (pp. 14–15).

Pseudogenes

Although gene duplication (or amplification) provides the opportunity for one of the two (or more) copies to evolve a new function, a duplicate gene may also become nonfunctional if it accumulates mutations that prevent it from performing the normal function or a modification of it. Many such pseudogenes have been discovered by DNA sequencing studies of eukaryotic genomes and they appear to incorporate base changes more rapidly than do functional genes, which are constrained by natural selection. This discovery has important implications for the neutral mutation hypothesis (Li 1983:15–16).

Dormant Genes

There is also evidence that genes may be turned off for long periods of time without being eliminated from the genome or undergoing loss of function. For example, Kollar and Fisher (1980) showed that the embryonic epithelial tissue of the Domestic Fowl (*G. gallus*), when grafted to the embryonic molar mesenchyme of the House Mouse (*Mus musculus*), can produce a variety of dental structures, including perfectly formed mammalian teeth. Thus, the loss of teeth in birds, ca. 100 million years ago, probably did not result from a loss of genetic coding for specific protein synthesis but from an alteration in the tissue interactions required for odontogenesis. Phenotypic change does not necessarily involve an equivalent change at the genetic level. Silent genes that retain their function over millions of years are probably conserved by selection, otherwise they would be destroyed by drift. This implies that they retain some degree of function, although not expressed in a way obvious to the human eye.

There are many other examples of the activation of dormant genes that indicate that the regulatory molecules responsible for the transcription of those genes in one cell type can activate the silent genes in another cell type. Some specialized cells can be induced to undergo gene activation and to change their phenotype. Examples include the regeneration of the lens from pigment cells of the iris epithelium in adult urodeles, the regeneration of urodele limbs after amputation, and the activation of the dormant genes in avian erythrocytes when fused with HeLa cells in tissue culture. DiBerardino et al. (1984) cite additional examples and conclude that: "The ability of some specialized cells to undergo gene activation and change phenotype indicates that all cell specializations do not necessarily involve irreversible genetic changes. . . . Of the various methods for achieving stability of the differentiated state, only DNA loss would appear to be irreversible. All other putative mechanisms should be modifiable. . . . it is possible that the molecular mechanisms that confer genetic and cellular stability . . . can be reversed by intra- and extra-cellular regulatory molecules."

The expression of some dormant genes can be induced by exogenous hormones. For example, Jannett (1975) showed that the presence, degree of development, or absence of hip glands in microtine rodents is mediated solely by the male sex hormone, testosterone. Many species of microtines normally have skin glands on the posterolateral areas of the body which are usually more developed in adult males than in females. Some species lack these glands, but subcutaneous testosterone implants induce their development.

Raikow (1975) and Raikow et al. (1979) have shown that the genes controlling the expression of certain limb muscles in birds can be turned off for long periods during their evolutionary history and turned back on in one or a few species. In some cases a muscle reappears only in one or a few individuals or only on one side of the body of an individual bird. The presence of such anomalies in the few specimens available for dissection indicates that they must be of frequent occurrence. There seems to be no significant correlation between the occurrence of these muscles and the taxonomic relationships of the birds in which they have been found. Raikow et al. (1979:206) concluded that "The most widely accepted idea of homology today is that it is based on descent from a corresponding condition in a common ancestor. This implies continuity of developmental genetic control. If this definition of homology is accepted it would appear that re-established characters should be considered homologous, in a special sense, to their corresponding ancestral features. We have shown that there is reason to believe that the loss of a structure in the phenotype does not necessarily mean that the genetic information controlling its development has also been eliminated from the genome. This hypothesis is . . . consistent with current ideas of developmental genetics, especially in relation to the possible temporary inactivation of regulatory genes."

Blackburn (1984) commented on the same phenomenon from the point of view of the reversibility of evolution, i.e., the reappearance of characters many generations after their apparent loss in fossil ancestors. He concluded, "How, then, are we to detect and characterize such reversals? The systematist is in much the same situation in attempting to judge the probability that a given character state complex has arisen convergently. Intuition no longer seems adequate to the problem, for as we now know, minor genotypic changes can have unexpectedly large phenotypic consequences. The implications of recent genetic advances do not seem to have been fully recognized in systematics; I am frequently struck by the casualness with which developmental biologists dismiss the same phenotypic changes to which systematists attach great importance" (p. 244).

Hall (1984) reviewed the developmental mechanisms underlying the formation of atavisms, i.e., the reappearance of a lost character typical of remote ancestors. He noted examples from several groups of animals, including those in birds described by Raikow and his colleagues. Hall (1984) concluded that "Atavisms . . . are the outward and visible sign of a hidden potential for morphology change possessed by all organisms. Neither basic capacity to form the organ nor patterning information is lost. Modification of components of inductive tissue interactions helps to explain how organs are lost during evolution. . . . retention of the basic mechanism explains how structures can be revived as atavisms. . . . Frequency of atavisms thus provides an indication of the degree of modification or loss of the underlying developmental programme" (p. 119).

For morpho-taxonomists, the problem is to decide how to detect the presence of a dormant homologous gene, or genes, coding for a character that is expressed in some, but not all, of the members of a monophyletic taxon. If such structures are viewed as shared derived characters, the resultant branching pattern will reflect the distribution of the expressed genes but not the true phylogeny of the group.

Thus, totally new genes do not arise de novo, but are produced by the duplication and divergence of pre-existing genes, and dormant genes may be re-awakened. It is obvious that these facts are of paramount importance for the concept of DNA sequence homology and for the understanding and interpretation of the data of DNA-DNA hybridization. They also indicate that the occurrence or distribution of a given morphological character, in at least some taxa, may have little to do with monophyly but may represent the pattern of activation of a gene that is present in all but silent in some. Such a pattern of gene expression may be related to functional requirements, or constraints, rather than to the phylogeny of the group.

It is clear that inability to distinguish between similarities due to the effects of convergent evolution and those resulting from common ancestry is a hazard for systematists using morphological characters. Is it also a problem for those using DNA-DNA hybridization? Fortunately, it is not, because the conditions of the experiments preclude the formation of thermally stable duplexes between non-homologous sequences. At 60°C two base sequences must be at least 75–80% base paired to form a stable duplex, and only homologous sequences have this high degree of complementarity. Even at lower incubation temperatures, e.g., 45°C, homology is required for the formation of stable DNA-DNA hybrids. Neither is there a problem with dormant genes because they will be detected by the DNA hybridization technique. To put it another way: DNA-DNA hybridization depends only on the intrinsic properties of DNA and is not affected by gene regulation.

It seems clear that only complementary sequences can form stable duplexes at incubation temperatures above ca. 45°C, but is it not possible for complementarity to occur by chance between non-homologous sequences? It is unfashionable in science to preclude anything as impossible, but Nei (1975:17) pointed out that "the number of ways in which a sequence of 1000 nucleotides of DNA can be produced is about 10^{602}. Therefore it is extremely improbable that two unrelated organisms would by chance have selected and manufactured two structures with a degree of similarity as great as that observed" in the DNA sequences of related organisms. Even if the improbable occurred, and two non-homologous sequences achieved 80% complementarity, it would be such a rare event that the presence of such sequences would have no discernible effect on the results of DNA-DNA hybridization. It is pertinent to note that 10^{602} is several times greater than the number of fundamental particles in the Universe. For the ca. 500 base fragments we use for DNA hybridization there are 10^{301} different arrangements. There are only 10^{70} electrons in the Universe.

DNA hybridization distinguishes homology from analogy because it compares enormously complex sets of hundreds of millions of unit characters and *complexity* offers the best guide to homology (Hecht and Edwards 1977, Ghiselin 1984, Gould 1985). It measures the net divergence of the entire single-copy genome, which is ca. 10^9 nucleotide pairs in birds. At the incubation temperature of 60°C, more than 75% of the bases must be correctly paired to form a stable duplex. *Only* homologous sequences are likely to have this degree of complementarity. Although a rigorous analysis of the probability of convergence under different models of DNA evolution has not been developed, a first approximation might apply a random model in which the probability of identical substitutions at each base position in two species is 1/4. For a 500 base-pair sequence, the probability of convergence at 75% of the base positions is 1/4 raised to the power of 375, a vanishingly small product. This . . . illustrates the enormous complexity contained in a single, 500 base-pair strand, and it suggests that genome-wide homoplasy [convergence] is extremely improbable (Ahlquist et al. 1987:557).

Thus, for DNA-DNA hybridization, the homology problem is solved by the criterion conditions of the experiments and the enormous complexity of the genome; the problem of convergence disappears.

Although exact convergence of nucleotide sequences is highly improbable, the chance occurrence of enough sequence similarity to produce detectable hybrids must be considered. Britten and Roberts (1971) calculated the probability of such accidental sequence similarities and provided a series of probability curves for varying lengths of fragments and different percentages of mismatch.

To demonstrate the improbability of such accidental sequence similarities Britten and Roberts (1971:502–503) considered

a hypothetical experiment in which the homology is being measured between two genomes that are unrelated except by chance. We assume that both are the size of a typical mammalian genome, about 3×10^9 nucleotide pairs. If the experimental criterion were such that there was a probability of 10^{-12} for chance relationship then about 0.3% (3×10^{-12}) of the DNA of one species would bind to that of the other. . . . It does not appear likely under usual experimental conditions that a probability of 10^{-12} would arise. For example, a stretch of nucleotides 40-long with 80% matching would probably melt at least 40° below native DNA. Also, other examples (such as 55% matching for 120 bases) would appear to be unstable. . . . It might be suggested that repeated sequences could to some extent be due to accidental sequence homology rather than to past events of multiplication. . . . a simple argument shows that this cannot be the case. Suppose, for example, that at some experimental criterion, chance sequence relationship had a probability of 10^{-7} in a genome of 3×10^9 nucleotides. One would expect under these conditions that each sequence would show relationship to about 300 other sequences. Most of the DNA would appear repetitive. However, under such conditions the DNA of all other species would also show a chance relationship of the same order of magnitude. In other words, if repetition were due to chance relationship almost complete cross reaction would be observed with all higher organism DNA.

Needless to say, this is not the case.

Genetic homology extends to the chromosomal level of structure, as shown by the conservation of the high-resolution banding patterns of chromosomes. Sawyer and Hozier (1986) found that the G-banding patterns of the chromosomes of human and mouse (*Mus musculus*) show "regions of subbanding homology . . . known to have conserved gene assignments, an indication that . . . extensive regions of the mammalian genome may remain intact after 60 million years of species divergence."

CHAPTER NINE

Comparative DNA-DNA Studies

DNA-DNA hybridization and other molecular methods have been used to compare the genomes of a wide array of organisms from viruses to vertebrates. This chapter provides an introduction to the literature. The coverage is not exhaustive, but the references in the cited papers should lead a reader to most of the pertinent publications before 1990.

Viruses

Some of the earliest DNA-DNA comparisons were among the related T2, T4, and T6 bacteriophages (Schildkraut et al. 1962). Cowie and McCarthy (1963), Cowie (1964), Cowie and Hershey (1965), and Cowie and Avery (1971) also compared viral nucleic acids. Hoyer and Roberts (1967) reviewed these early studies.

Bacteria

The first DNA-DNA comparisons were made between bacteria by Schildkraut et al. (1961, 1962). Bolton and McCarthy (1962) described the DNA-agar technique, and McCarthy and Bolton (1963) used it to compare the RNAs and DNAs of ten species of bacteria. Marmur et al. (1963a) used DNA-DNA hybridization for bacterial taxonomy, and Kingsbury (1967) examined DNA homologies among species of the bacterial genus *Neisseria*.

Bendich and McCarthy (1970a) used RNA-DNA hybridization to compare the members of a diverse group of organisms, including bacteria, plants, and animals. Brenner et al. (1969, 1976) and Hawke et al. (1981) used HAP chromatography for extensive DNA-DNA comparisons of bacteria. Sanderson (1976) examined genetic relatedness in enterobacteria with several techniques, including nucleic acid reassociation. He concluded that "a revision of the Enterobacteriaceae" would be based on DNA reassociation "with other criteria of genetic relatedness and presently used classical criteria playing a supporting role."

Schleifer and Stackebrandt (1983) reviewed several methods for comparisons of bacterial molecular structure, including DNA-DNA hybridization. They concluded that "DNA-DNA homology studies" are useful only for comparisons "between closely related organisms" (p. 172). This indicates that the concepts of the bacterial genus and species are quite different from those of vertebrates. It is not surprising that there are large genetic distances between morphologically similar bacterial lineages that diverged hundreds of millions of years ago.

Farmer et al. (1985) reviewed the biochemical identification of the Enterobacteriaceae, including the use of DNA-DNA hybridization.

Carl Woese and his colleagues have reconstructed ancient branching patterns from comparisons of the sequences of the slowly evolving 16S ribosomal RNAs. Three primary lineages of organisms have been proposed: Archaebacteria, Eubacteria, and Eukaryotes. Fox et al. (1980), Woese (1981), and Stackebrandt and Woese (1981) reviewed these studies. The tree proposed by Woese was challenged by Lake (1986), who based his phylogeny on characters of the photocytes and eocytes of bacteria. Lake (1988), "using evolutionary parsimony, a . . . rate-invariant treeing algorithm," proposed that the eukaryotic ribosomal rRNA genes evolved from the eocytes, "a group of extremely thermophilic, sulphur-metabolizing, anucleate cells." The reconstructed tree contains five main groups in two divisions: one (Parkaryotes) contains the Eubacteria, Halobacteria, and Methanogens; the other (Karyotes) includes the Eocytes and Eukaryotes. The phylogeny "implies that the last common ancestor of extant life, and the early ancestors of eukaryotes, probably lacked nuclei, metabolized sulphur and lived at near-boiling temperatures."

Meyer et al. (1986) presented evidence against the use of bacterial amino acid sequence data for the construction of "all-inclusive phylogenetic trees."

Field et al. (1988) used "a rapid sequencing method for ribosomal RNA" to resolve the evolutionary relationships among Metazoa. "Representatives of 22 classes in 10 animal phyla were used to infer phylogenetic relationships, based on . . . comparisons of the 18S ribosomal RNA sequences."

Fungi

Szecsi and Dobrovolszky (1983, 1985a,b) compared the DNAs of species of *Fusarium* and cited other papers containing data on DNA properties and homologies in fungi. Other studies of fungi include those by Kurtzman et al. (1983), Ellis (1985), and Gueho et al. (1985).

Plants

Bolton and Bendich (1965) and Bendich and Bolton (1967) used the DNA-agar method to compare several plant DNAs. Bendich and McCarthy (1970a) examined the homologies of ribosomal RNAs of a diverse array of plants and (1970b) compared the DNAs of several cereal grains.

Chang and Mabry (1973) used DNA-DNA and RNA-DNA hybridization in comparisons among ten species of Centrospermae. Stein and Thompson (1975, 1979) and Stein et al. (1979) compared the DNAs of species of the fern family Osmundaceae. Belford and Thompson (1979) compared the DNAs of several species of *Atriplex* and proposed a phylogeny.

Hake and Walbot (1980) hybridized the DNA of maize (*Zea mays*) with those of related grasses, including *Tripsacum*, teosinte, and popcorn. Evans et al. (1983) examined the repeated DNA sequences in nine species of *Allium*, including some thermal stability measurements of heteroduplexes.

Thompson and Murray (1981) reviewed the structure and function of the nuclear genome of plants, and Preisler and Thompson (1981a,b) examined evolutionary sequence divergence in repeated DNA families of higher plants. Belford et al. (1982) described DNA hybridization techniques for the study of plant evolution. Hori et al. (1985) constructed a phylogenetic tree for green plants from comparisons of 28 5S rRNA sequences. Antonov (1986) reviewed the literature on the structure and evolution of plant genomes.

Clegg (1987) organized a symposium on plant molecular evolution that includes five contributions pertaining to the nuclear, chloroplast, and mitochondrial genomes of plants.

Invertebrates

The first comparisons of invertebrate DNAs were among species of *Drosophila* (Laird and McCarthy 1968, Entingh 1970). DNA comparisons among several species of Hawaiian *Drosophila* have been made by Hunt et al. (1981) and Hunt and Carson (1983). Riede et al. (1983) used blot hybridization to compare a ca. 10 kb cloned fragment of the *D. virilis* genome with the DNAs of four other species of the *virilis* group.

The single-copy tracer DNA of *Drosophila melanogaster* was compared with the driver DNAs of six other species of *Drosophila* by Zweibel et al. (1982). The DNA relationships were partly congruent with a phylogeny based on morphology, but there were also some discrepancies. The gene for alcohol dehydrogenase (ADH) from *D. melanogaster* was also hybridized with the genomes of the other species and the results agreed with the single-copy comparisons, "demonstrating that a single gene can reflect divergence of the entire genome." However, this does not prove that the rate of evolution of a single gene is the same as the average rate of the entire genome.

Solignac et al. (1986) compared the mtDNAs of species of the *D. melanogaster* subgroup.

Powell et al. (1986) found that the rates of nucleotide substitution in the mtDNA and nuclear DNA of *Drosophila* are similiar. Caccone et al. (1987) studied intraspecific DNA divergence in *Drosophila mercatorum*, and Caccone and Powell (1987) used DNA-DNA hybridization to examine evolutionary divergence in cave crickets.

Teshima (1972) used the nitrocellulose filter technique of D. Gillespie and Spiegelman (1965) to compare the DNAs of five species of blackflies (Diptera: Simuliidae). Sohn et al. (1975) criticized Teshima's technique and used the HAP column method to compare the DNAs of six species of blackflies.

Petrov and Aleshin (1983) compared the DNAs of eleven species of dragonflies (Odonata) representing six traditional families. They assumed "an equal rate of divergence of the unique DNA sequences in different phyletic lines" and concluded that the "level of homology" of some of the differences they observed between dragonfly families were as great as between the "orders of the chordate animals." This demonstrates the lack of categorical equivalence in the classifications of different groups of organisms.

Jordan and Brosemer (1974) determined the genome size, sequence complexity, and G+C content of three species of bees but did not compare them by DNA-DNA hybridization.

Many of the important publications by Roy Britten, Eric Davidson, and their associates have used sea urchin (Echinoidea) DNAs to explore various aspects of the animal genome. Some of their papers include DNA-DNA comparisons, e.g., Angerer et al. (1976) and Hall et al. (1980).

Harpold and Craig (1978) also compared sea urchin DNAs and calculated the average rate of divergence as 0.22%/MY. Britten (1986:1393) calculated the comparable sea urchin rate as 0.26%/MY, or 0.13%/MY for each lineage since the divergence from the most recent common ancestor. We found the average divergence rate in the higher primates to be 0.24%/MY (Sibley and Ahlquist 1987d).

M. J. Smith et al. (1982) examined single-copy DNA homologies in six species of sea stars (Asteroidea). A. B. Smith (1988) used numerical cladistics to reconstruct the phylogeny and divergence times of 21 genera of the sea urchin order Camarodonta. He proposed more recent divergence times for the camarodont families than those used in the molecular studies cited above and calculated the single-copy rate of divergence as 0.65–0.85°C/MY. The sequence data on histone genes indicated a rate of silent substitution of 0.70–0.85%/MY. The results were consistent with a constant-rate model, but did not offer proof for a constant rate.

For ancient divergences the highly conserved nucleotide sequences of the 5S rRNA molecule have been used. For example, Ohama et al. (1984) compared the 5S rRNA sequences of a mesozoan (*Dicyema misakiense*) with those of an acorn worm (*Saccoglossus*), a bryozoan (*Bugula*), and an octopus (*Octopus*). The phylum Mesozoa contains ca. 50 known species of small, ciliated, endoparasites lacking most of the standard organ systems. Some authors consider them to be secondarily simplified flatworms; others view them as a separate multi-cellular group derived from the protists. The phylogenetic tree reconstructed by Ohama et al. (1984) from the 73 5S rRNA sequences presently available "suggests that the mesozoan is the most ancient multicellular animal identified so far; its emergence time being almost the same as that of flagellated or ciliated protozoans. The branching points of planarians and nematodes are a little later than that of the mesozoan, but are clearly earlier than other metazoan groups including sponges and jellyfishes. Many metazoan groups seem to have diverged within a relatively short period."

Vertebrates

The first comparisons among vertebrate DNAs were those reported by Hoyer et al. (1964), who used the DNA-agar method to compare several mammals and one fish. These early studies used total DNA for both tracer and driver, and prepared tracers at a low Cot value, thus, only the repeated sequences formed hybrids. However, the broad relationships among the taxa were correctly indicated. The authors concluded that "The caliber of these preliminary results warrants the optimistic view that future developments will provide a fruitful addition to our criteria for the classification of living forms." Hoyer and Roberts (1967) reviewed the studies based on the DNA-agar method, including data not otherwise published.

Mednikov (1980) reviewed the studies of various groups of vertebrates by himself and his associates at Moscow State University.

FISH

Schmidtke et al. (1979) and Schmidtke and Kandt (1981) examined single-copy DNA relationships in polyploid species of teleost fishes, Hanham and Smith (1980) compared the DNAs of three species of salmon, and Gharrett et al. (1977) compared the Cot curves of nine teleosts and a lamprey. Mednikov et al. (1977) used Denhardt's (1966) nitrocellulose filter method to compare the DNAs of several genera of fishes.

Kedrova et al. (1983) compared the single-copy DNA of the Alligator Gar (*Lepisosteus osseus*) with the driver DNAs of fishes representing various degrees of divergence. They concluded that the "Acipenseriformes, Crossopterygimorpha, Chondrichthyes, Lepisosteiformes, and . . . Teleostei . . . correspond in rank to classes of vertebrates."

AMPHIBIA

Birstein (1982) reviewed several aspects of the amphibian genome and provided an extensive bibliography. Toivonen et al. (1983) reported on the ribosomal RNAs in polyploid hylid frogs.

BIRDS

Schultz and Church (1972) compared the repeated sequences of the DNAs of six species of galliform birds, and Shields and Straus (1975) compared the single-copy DNAs of eleven species of passerines. Our comparative studies of avian DNAs are covered in this volume. See citations to Ahlquist, Bledsoe, Sheldon, and Sibley. Mindell and Honeycutt (1989) mapped ribosomal DNA restriction sites in 10 species from eight orders of birds to "assess the level of variation and to determine phylogenetic relationships." Ingold et al. (1989) used DNA hybridization for a study of 14 species of cranes. Krajewski (1989) made more than 1200 comparisons among the same 14 species studied by Ingold et al.

MAMMALS

Britten and Waring (1965) discovered repeated sequences in the House Mouse (*Mus musculus*) in 1964. Kohne (1970) reviewed the structure and properties of eukaryotic DNA, the DNA-DNA hybridization technique, and comparative studies on primates and other mammals. Kohne (1971), Kohne et al. (1971, 1972), Hoyer et al. (1972), Benveniste and Todaro (1974, 1976), and Bonner et al. (1980, 1981) compared the DNAs of several primates. Sibley and Ahlquist (1984a) developed a complete matrix of DNA-DNA comparisons among the hominoid primates and proposed a phylogeny with dated divergence nodes. Sibley and Ahlquist (1987d) reported on the results from an expanded data set for the hominoids, which gave the same tree as the 1984a study. Felsenstein (1987) made a statistical analysis of the Sibley and Ahlquist data. Caccone and Powell (1989) used the TEACL method to compare the DNAs of the hominoids. They obtained virtually identical delta values and the same branching pattern as Sibley and Ahlquist (1984a, 1987d). Sibley et al. (1990) reanalyzed their earlier data using only the raw counts without corrections for aberrant values. They concluded that the chimpanzee-human clade was revealed but that the confidence limits were reduced. The melting curves indicated that the chimpanzees are more closely related to Man than to the Gorilla but that the Gorilla is more closely related to the chimpanzees than to Man. This suggests slightly different average genomic rates of evolution along the chimpanzee and human lineages after their divergence.

Springer and Kirsch (1989) investigated rates of single-copy DNA evolution in phalangeriform marsupials and found a "counterexample to the . . . view that rates of change in DNA sequences are inversely correlated with generation time."

The papers on rodent DNAs by Rice (1971a–d, 1972, 1974), Rice and Paul (1972), Rice and Esposito (1973), and Rice and Straus (1973) contain many comparative data. Brownell (1983) compared the DNAs of 16 rodent species and proposed a phylogeny. Catzeflis et al. (1987) compared several species of muroid rodents and showed that their genomes are evolving much faster than those of hominoids and birds. Catzeflis et al. (1989) examined the relationships among the chromosomal species of Eurasian mole rats (*Spalax ehrenbergi*).

A series of studies on the evolution of viral genes included DNA comparisons among various mammals. Benveniste and Todaro (1975) labeled the single-copy DNAs of Domestic Pig (*Sus scrofa*) and House Mouse (*Mus musculus*) and compared them with several rodents and artiodactyls. They also compared the tracer DNA of the Domestic Cat (*Felis catus* or *silvestris*) with those of 12 other felids, Mink (*Mustela vison*), rodents, primates, a pig, cow, rabbit, and a bat. Benveniste et al. (1977) compared the DNAs of three species of *Mus* with those of other rodents, and Sherr et al. (1978) used Mink tracer DNA in comparisons with three other mustelids, Raccoon (*Procyon lotor*), Domestic Dog (*Canis familiaris* or *lupus*), African Lion (*Panthera leo*), Spotted Hyena (*C. crocuta*), two rodents, a rabbit, cow, baboon, and human.

Benveniste (1985) reviewed DNA hybridization studies on several mammalian groups and reported on the contributions of retroviruses to the study of mammalian evolution. He noted that different studies, using slightly different methods of DNA-DNA hybridization, had produced virtually identical delta values for the same comparisons among primate groups. Retroviruses are genetically transmitted and have been conserved during the course of evolution in several vertebrate lineages. They can also transfer their genes between distantly related species and become integrated into the germ line of the new host. Benveniste found that a delta value of "1°C corresponds to approximately 4.4 million years of evolution. This value is in excellent agreement with that obtained by Sibley and Ahlquist (1983, 1984)" (p. 372).

CHAPTER TEN

Materials and Methods

Collection and Preservation

DNA can be extracted from the nuclei of all cells, but nucleate red blood cells provide the best and most convenient source. Thus, for all vertebrates except mammals, erythrocytes are to be preferred over other tissues. For mammals, the soft organ tissues or white blood cells are the most convenient sources of DNA.

Blood samples may be collected with a hypodermic syringe and needle using an anticoagulant-preservative solution (APS) composed of 10% (w/v) EDTAP (dipotassium ethylene diamine tetra-acetate), 0.5% sodium fluoride, and 0.5% thymol. Use only distilled or deionized water to prepare APS. Avoid water that may contain dissolved metals. Disodium EDTA is less soluble than the dipotassium form, and it may be necessary to warm the water to achieve complete solution. A 10% solution of EDTA is nearly saturated, and undissolved EDTA may be present. EDTA chelates metallic ions; thus it prevents clotting and inhibits the activity of deoxyribonuclease (DNase), which degrades DNA by enzymatic cleavage of the nucleotide strands. Sodium fluoride and thymol inhibit DNase and prevent the growth of bacteria and fungi. A 10% solution of EDTA alone may be used, especially if it is possible to refrigerate the sample until the DNA can be extracted.

Allow blood cells to sediment by gravity or gentle centrifugation (2000 rpm, 5 min), decant the supernatant plasma and APS, and refill the container with fresh APS. Preserved blood cells may be stored at ambient temperatures for long periods of time without damage to the DNA. Other anticoagulants, such as heparin or oxalate, may be used to collect the blood, but they will not provide protection for long-term storage unless the samples are frozen.

For vertebrates with nucleate red cells, 10 ml of whole blood contains enough DNA for many comparisons and even 1 ml will yield enough DNA for several. If mammalian blood is centrifuged, or the cells are allowed to sediment by gravity, the nucleate white blood cells form a buffy coat on the surface of the mass of red cells. The white cells from 100–200 ml of whole blood will yield enough DNA for a series of DNA hybrids.

Tissues, especially those of the soft organs (liver, spleen, heart, lungs, kidneys, brain, etc.) are good sources of DNA. Tissues contain fewer cells per unit of volume than blood, and additional steps are required to obtain highly purified DNA. Muscle tissue is less productive because the individual cells tend to be large and the connective tissue is more difficult to disintegrate. It is sometimes difficult to obtain long-chain DNA from tissues.

As soon after death as possible remove the soft organs and larger muscles and immerse them in 90–96% ethyl alcohol (ethanol) or 2-propanol in a large-mouthed container. Cut the immersed organs into small pieces, ca. 5–10 mm in diameter. Transfer the pieces to a container (bottle, vial, plastic bag) full of 90–96% alcohol. The volume of alcohol should be at least twice that of the tissues. When possible, replace the ethanol after a few hours. This procedure will ensure that dilution by the tissue fluids does not lower the concentration of the alcohol and permit damage to the DNA.

Note: Do **not** use methyl alcohol (methanol).

After several days in alcohol, the tissues may be transferred to a leak-proof plastic bag with enough liquid alcohol to keep them moist. Refrigeration is unnecessary. As for blood, save as much as possible. The yield of DNA is usually lower for tissues than for blood cells, and some tissue samples do not produce long-chained DNA, for reasons that remain obscure.

Note: For unknown reasons, the tissues of cold-blooded vertebrates, especially fishes, often do not produce long-chain DNA from samples preserved in alcohol. It seems best to freeze the tissues until ready to proceed with extraction.

Arrighi et al. (1968) described a method for extracting DNA from tissues preserved in various fixatives. They found that 2-propanol and ethanol are most effective and convenient; methanol presents problems and should be avoided if possible, and formalin interferes with DNA isolation. For additional details see Sibley and Ahlquist (1981d), but note the modifications given above.

The DNA-DNA Hybridization Technique

The following sections describe the steps in the DNA hybridization method used to produce the data reported in this book. The "how to" format is for the convenience of those who wish to use these procedures. Methods for the extraction and purification of DNA are based on Marmur (1961), modified by our experience. Blood cells and tissues differ in their ease of extraction, hence separate protocols are presented.

REAGENTS

Following are the formulas for reagents and solutions. The first name or abbreviation given is used throughout. Formula weights (F.W.) are approximate for the necessary degree of accuracy. References to "water" mean deionized or distilled water.

$2\times$ SSC (double-strength saline–sodium citrate solution): 17.54 g (grams) sodium chloride (NaCl, F.W. 58) plus 8.82 g sodium citrate ($Na_3C_6H_5O_7$–$2H_2O$, F.W. 294) in 1 liter of water.

SDS (sodium dodecyl sulfate, F.W. 288): Prepare a 5% (w/v) solution, e.g., 5 g in 100 ml water. Use electrophoresis-purity grade, which dissolves quickly and is more stable than the economy grade marketed as sodium lauryl sulfate.

SELF-DIGESTED PROTEASE (sometimes called Pronase, a proprietary name of Calbiochem): Sigma proteinase Type XIV (P–5147), also called Pronase E, is a mixture of proteolytic enzymes isolated from the bacterium *Streptomyces griseus*. Prepare a solution by adding 10 milligrams (mg) of proteinase per milliliter of water (e.g., 100 mg in 10 ml water) in a serum bottle fitted with a sleeve-type rubber stopper, dissolve using a vortex mixer, and place in a water bath at 37°C for 1 hour. This self-digestion step allows the proteases to hydrolyze DNase in the preparation. Freeze and thaw as needed.

PHENOL: Add water to a jar of phenol crystals, allow to stand overnight, and stir gently with a glass rod to mix. Use as needed, adding more water as the solution is used until no crystals remain. Some investigators add a buffer solution to the phenol to neutralize the pH; others recrystallize commercial liquefied phenol to remove impurities.

CHLOROFORM–ISOAMYL ALCOHOL: Chloroform is $CHCl_3$; isoamyl alcohol is also sold as isopentyl alcohol or methyl–1-butanol. Mix chloroform and isoamyl alcohol in a 24:1 ratio (v/v), e.g., 240 ml of chloroform and 10 ml of isoamyl alcohol.

Comment: Phenol and chloroform are hazardous chemicals. Phenol is extremely caustic and chloroform is a possible carcinogen; both can be absorbed through the skin. Wear disposable gloves, work in a suitable fume hood, and use a remote pipetting device. Avoid splashes of phenol; the liquid evaporates leaving tiny crystals that can cause a painful burn. Store used reagents awaiting removal from the laboratory in amber glass jars with wide mouths and resistant lids (Bakelite) or in similar polyethylene containers. Chloroform and phenol may be mixed, but chloroform attacks many plastics and phenol corrodes metals. Do not fill glass waste containers to more than three-quarters of capacity, and leave the lid loose to avoid a buildup of pressure that could shatter the glass. Store waste phenol and chloroform in a fume hood with the door raised a few inches to provide a draft.

0.02 M SODIUM ACETATE: Use the anhydrous powder CH_3COONa, F.W. 82; 1.64 g/liter.

PHOSPHATE BUFFERS (PB); composed of equimolar amounts of sodium phosphate monobasic monohydrate (NaH_2PO_4–$2H_2O$, F.W. 138) and sodium phosphate dibasic anhydrous (Na_2HPO_4, F.W. 142):
  0.48 M PB = 33.12 g/liter monobasic plus 34.08 g/liter dibasic.
  0.12 M PB = 8.28 g/liter monobasic plus 8.52 g/liter dibasic.
  These buffers are excellent media for the growth of microorganisms; do not leave solutions at room temperature for more than ca. five days. Store in the cold.

HEAT-TREATED RNASE, used to hydrolyze RNA in DNA preparations: Use a moderate grade of purity (e.g., Sigma ribonuclease A, R4875). Prepare a 10 mg/ml solution in a serum bottle as for Pronase. Place the dissolved sample in a water bath at 80°C for 5 min to inactivate DNase.

7.2 M SODIUM PERCHLORATE ($NaCl_4$, F.W. 122): Dissolve 175.7 g in 20 ml water, starting with ca. 8 ml of water; add as much sodium perchlorate as possible while heating gently. It is possible to dissolve 175.7 g of perchlorate in a final volume of 20 ml. When completed, transfer solution to a volumetric flask and cool to room temperature; the volume will decrease. Add water to make up to 20 ml. Filter the solution before use. Attach a 10 ml disposable syringe barrel to a 25 mm filter holder (Nucleopore) fitted with a polycarbonate filter with 0.2 micrometer pore diameter. Add the desired quantity of solution to the syringe barrel and gently force it through the filter with the syringe plunger.

IODINATION BUFFER, used during radiolabeling of DNA. Dissolve the following ingredients in one liter of water:

ca. 0.4 M NaCl (23.38 g).

0.01 M sodium phosphate monobasic (0.69 g).

0.01 M sodium phosphate dibasic (0.71 g).

ca. 2×10^{-4}M disodium EDTA (F.W. 372) (0.074 g).

EQUIPMENT AND SUPPLIES FOR EXTRACTION OF DNA

Centrifuges

A. A tabletop, semi-portable model equipped with a swinging-bucket rotor and sealed bucket assembly. For example, the DuPont/Sorvall GLC series, with the HL–4 bucket assembly, consisting of 4 twin-trunnion rings with 8 **tapered** 50 ml buckets, inserts for conical tubes, and screw caps. This centrifuge may be used for all operations involving volumes of solutions from ca. 7 to 50 ml. When loaded, the GLC will attain a maximum speed of 3000 rpm, a safe range for the tubes described below.

B. A small centrifuge that develops ca. 1500 rpm. For example, the Damon-IEC Whisperfuge. The rotor of this model takes twelve 7 ml vials (described below). Small-diameter tubes are held securely by removable spring clips. The plastic tube holders are attacked by chloroform, so the vials should be capped before centrifugation.

Centrifuge tubes

A. An all-purpose tube. For example, the Falcon 2070, 50 ml, conical, graduated tube with a screw cap. Used in DNA preparation up to and including shearing of DNA into fragments. These tubes are made of polypropylene and are damaged by chloroform, but may be washed and used until they develop stress fractures. Screw caps are necessary because the tubes are used in shakers, etc. A DNA preparation may be stored in a capped tube for weeks with minimal evaporation. These tubes are tapered, hence they require the special tapered centrifuge buckets, noted above.

B. Glass scintillation vials, 7 ml capacity, with resistant plastic screw tops with foil liners. Used after sonication and for long-term storage over chloroform of whole, sheared

DNAs. Sample numbers may be written on the caps. Chloroform evaporates from stored samples and must be added about once a year.

PROCEDURE FOR EXTRACTING DNA FROM BLOOD CELLS

Birds have from 1.9 million red cells per cubic millimeter of blood in an Ostrich (*Struthio camelus*) to about 4 million in a Rock Pigeon (*Columba livia*), with an average of ca. 3 million per cubic mm (Sturkie 1954:3). The DNA content per cell in birds varies from ca. 1.6 pg to 2.2 pg, averaging ca. 1.9 pg (Bachmann et al. 1972b). The average potential yield of DNA from 1 ml of avian blood is 6 milligrams, and it is possible to recover 4–5 milligrams after losses during extraction. The quantity of DNA released from more than 5 ml of red blood cells is so large that it is necessary to use several centrifuge tubes to hold the viscous solution following nuclear lysis. The following procedure is optional for 1–5 ml of red cells and may be scaled down for smaller samples. Blood cells may be stored in APS for many years without damage to the DNA.

1. Transfer the blood sample from the collection vial to a centrifuge tube and rinse the vial with deionized water to remove all cells. Add 30–40 ml of water to the cells, cap the tube, and shake it by hand or on a vortex mixer to disperse the cells. In most samples lysis of the cells will have occurred during storage in APS, but the deionized water will lyse any that remain intact. Centrifuge the cells for 10 min at 3000 rpm. The cell coats and nuclei will form a pellet or pad at the bottom of the tube. Decant and discard the supernatant aqueous layer, which contains mainly hemoglobin and plasma proteins. The conical shape of the bottom of the tube acts to pack the cell pad tightly enough so the supernatant may be decanted without disturbing the pad. If the supernatant is reasonably clear proceed to step 2; if not, the washing step may be repeated one or more times.

If a blood sample has dried out during storage it is usually possible to recover undamaged DNA: add some $2\times$ SSC, allow the sample to rehydrate in the cold overnight, and proceed with the washing step, as above.

2. To the packed cells add twice their volume of $2\times$ SSC and suspend the cells in solution by shaking on a vortex mixer, then add SDS to a final concentration of 2% to lyse the nuclei. For example, to a 2 ml pad of red cells add 4 ml of $2\times$ SSC and 4 ml of 5% SDS. The release of DNA from the lysed nuclei is indicated by a dramatic increase in the viscosity of the solution. The preparation may become so viscous as to inhibit further mixing. Add $2\times$ SSC in small amounts until the solution will swirl when placed on a vortex mixer.

3. Add the self-digested protease, ca. 1 mg/ml of solution. The example above would require about 1 ml. Mix thoroughly and place in a water bath at 37°C overnight. Part of the viscosity is due to proteins which will be digested by the protease. At the end of the incubation no granular material should remain. If some undigested cells remain they can be removed after the next step, washed, and treated again.

4. The digest should be about the consistency of heavy cream; if it is too viscous, add small amounts of $2\times$ SSC while mixing. If the digest is light-colored and translucent, proceed with the addition of chloroform–isoamyl alcohol, otherwise add ca. 10 ml phenol and shake for 2–5 min. The phenol forms an emulsion and the solution will become milky. The emulsion does not settle into discrete layers by gravity, and centrifugation may not be effective. When

this occurs, add at least 10 ml of chloroform-isoamyl and shake an additional 5 min. This will reduce the emulsion and remove phenol from the aqueous phase. Centrifuge at 3000 rpm for 10 min. The phenol and chloroform act to denature and remove proteins from the DNA; the isoamyl alcohol reduces the foaming of the SDS detergent and aids in separation of proteins from the DNA.

5. The sample will separate into three layers. The upper, aqueous phase, contains the DNA; the lower phase contains the chloroform plus phenol, which are miscible. The lower phase may be variously colored depending on how much pigmented material has been extracted. There is also a middle layer of varying thickness containing the remaining phenol emulsion plus the denatured and SDS-complexed proteins. This middle layer may still contain DNA, especially if it is thick. With a Pasteur pipette remove the lower phase, taking care not to disrupt the middle layer. To the material that remains, add two volumes of chloroform-isoamyl and shake for 10 min. If using a vortex mixer do not exceed 40 ml total volume in a 50 ml tube or the necessary vortex will not form. Centrifuge again, remove the lower phase, and repeat 2–3 more times. For the last extraction the shaking should be continued for at least 2 hours.

Note: Such lengthy extractions require three pieces of equipment: (1) A four-place vortex test-tube mixer (e.g., Scientific Industries, Model K–500–4) equipped with spring clips and rubber cups to hold tubes securely. The clips may be moved vertically on a support rod. This mixer is especially useful for small samples. Various sizes of rubber cups are available for a range of tube diameters. (2) An orbital sanding machine mounted upside down. The bottom plate, which normally holds the sandpaper, is removed and a wire basket (test-tube basket) is installed in its place to hold the sample tubes. Foam rubber is used to immobilize the tubes in the wire basket and the speed of orbital movement is adjusted with a voltage regulator. The sanders are reliable but, after extended use, may require replacement of motor brushes and the rubber legs that connect the platen to the transmission housing. The sander was used because there seems to be no commercially available shaker with the ideal properties for this purpose, viz., vigorous high-speed motion in a small, slightly eccentric orbit. (3) A reciprocating laboratory shaker that provides moderate shaking at ca. 200 cycles/min for long periods of time and that can be fitted with clips to hold different sizes of Erlenmeyer flasks. This requires transfer of the DNA preparation and hence some losses of DNA. It is difficult to secure ground glass stoppers in the glass flasks or screw caps on polyethylene flasks. The phenol corrodes parts of the shaker and fumes require placing the shaker in a hood or with other adequate ventilation.

6. After the last extraction, centrifuge the sample, remove the bottom layer of chloroform, and centrifuge again. This will cause the whitish middle layer to form a pellet at the bottom of the tube. The aqueous phase may then be poured into a test tube or small beaker and chilled on ice or in a freezer. Add two volumes of cold 95% ethanol. If the ethanol is added carefully it can be layered over the aqueous phase without mixing. At the interface the precipitating DNA can be seen as whitish strands. Gently mix the solution by swirling a glass rod through the interface. The DNA will spool out on the glass rod as a gelatinous mass composed of the DNA strands holding a large volume of ethanol by capillary action. When the two layers have been mixed and no more DNA is being taken up on the glass rod, place the rod upright with the mass of DNA plus ethanol in the air to allow the ethanol to drain off and evaporate. Alternatively, the DNA-ethanol mass may be blotted with a piece of filter paper or

tissue to remove most of the ethanol. During this process the DNA will lose most of its original volume and form a sticky cap at the end of the glass rod. After about an hour the DNA is ready to be rehydrated in the appropriate buffer.

Note: Spooling out is not essential for the recovery of DNA. It is also possible to add the ethanol, shake briefly, and collect the DNA by centrifugation. However, a sample that spools out is certain to be long-stranded and the subsequent steps may be carried out without modification. DNA may also be precipitated by the addition of 2-propanol (isopropyl alcohol). DNA will begin to precipitate in 2-propanol when about half as much 2-propanol as there is DNA solution has been added, making this a useful method when the total volume must be kept minimal.

7. RNA is removed from the DNA preparation by digestion with ribonuclease (RNase). After spooling out and removal of the ethanol, the typical DNA mass will be ca. 1–2 cubic millimeters in size and whitish to brownish in color; the whiter the greater the purity. To rehydrate the DNA preparatory to RNase treatment, remove it from the glass rod with a blunt forceps and place the mass of DNA in 10 ml of 2× SSC. It will take from several hours to overnight for the DNA to swell as it rehydrates. Occasional shaking will disperse the DNA in the buffer, but shaking will not aid in rehydration. If, after shaking, air bubbles remain trapped in the DNA, rehydration is not complete and an additional 10 ml of 2× SSC may be added. The concentration of the DNA should be 1–2 mg/ml.

Comment: This is the first point in the procedure at which it is appropriate to measure the amount of DNA present. Before this the turbidity of the solution and the presence of phenol would produce inaccurate values. Phenol absorbs strongly in the ultraviolet near 270 nanometers (nm), which is close to the absorbance peak of the nucleic acids at 260 nm. The phenol should be eliminated by the combination of multiple chloroform extractions and spooling out or precipitation.

If the odor of phenol can be detected in the DNA preparation, or if the concentration of DNA as determined by spectrophotometry seems too high, the sample should be extracted with ether to remove the phenol. Any spooled DNA with a concentration above 8 mg/ml, or a sheared preparation of greater than 15 mg/ml, should be suspect, especially if it is watery. Add ca. one volume of diethyl ether (ether for anesthesia, **not** petroleum ether) and shake vigorously for ca. 10 seconds in a fume hood; avoid sparks or flame. Allow the sample to settle. The phenol readily enters the ether phase, which is the upper layer. Because ether is somewhat miscible in aqueous solutions, a sharp demarcation between the layers is not present. Decant as much of the ether as possible without losing any of the DNA, then extract once with chloroform to remove excess ether. Another way is to bubble air through the sample. To avoid contaminating the sample with foreign substances in the air supply, place a Drierite cartridge between the air valve and the pipette that enters the solution.

The concentration of nucleic acids is given by:

$$C = \frac{A^{260}(M)(d)}{E}$$

where C is the concentration in mg/ml; A^{260} is the absorbance at 260 nm; M is the average molecular weight of nucleotides in the sample, which is 320; d is the dilution at which the absorbance is measured; E is the molar extinction coefficient, which = 6420 for nucleic acids with ca. 43% GC.

A spectrophotometer measures light absorbed by a solute, in this case nucleic acids, as compared with a sample of the solvent without the solute. To measure the absorbance of a sample of DNA, pipette 2 ml of the buffer into each of two 1 cm cuvettes. Use the same buffer in which the DNA was rehydrated. A typical DNA preparation will need to be diluted 400-fold to be within the range of the spectrophotometer. Add 5 microliters of the DNA solution to one of the cuvettes (a 1:400 dilution), place a small piece of Parafilm over the mouth of the cuvette and invert it several times to disperse the DNA. Place the blank cuvette in the spectrophotometer and set the absorbance to zero, then take a reading of the cuvette containing the DNA. The absorbance may be entered into the equation and the concentration calculated. For example, if the $A^{260} = 0.125$,

$$C = \frac{0.125(320)(400)}{6420}$$

or 2.5 mg/ml.

If the DNA was dissolved in 10 ml of buffer, the amount of DNA in the preparation would be 25 mg, except that RNA has not yet been removed. The amount of RNA in avian erythrocytes varies from 7% to 17% (Bruns et al. 1965, Attardi et al. 1966), and it is usual to lose about 20% of the material that absorbs at 260 nm when the RNase step is performed.

8. Place a 10 mg/ml solution of RNase (as for Pronase) in a water bath at 80°C for 5 min to inactivate DNase. (RNase free of DNase activity is available, but expensive.) To the DNA preparation in $2\times$ SSC, add an amount of RNase equivalent to 0.1 mg/ml. In this example, 0.1 ml of the RNase solution would be adequate. Incubate at 37°C for 1 hour, extract the sample with chloroform (to denature the RNase), precipitate with ethanol or 2-propanol (the ribonucleotides will stay in solution), centrifuge, and suspend the pellet of DNA in 0.02 M sodium acetate. Take another spectrophotometric reading and adjust the amount of sodium acetate to obtain a 20 ml volume at a concentration of 2 mg/ml.

PROCEDURE FOR EXTRACTING DNA FROM TISSUES

DNA may be extracted from tissues by gently blending ethanol-preserved material in a Waring blender, but the yields tend to be low and there is a risk of strand scission because of the shearing forces. A better method is to use liquid nitrogen, as follows:

1. Starting material: 6–8 grams, wet weight, of soft tissues preserved in ethanol. Trim excess fat and connective tissue.
2. Freeze-dry for ca. 48 hours.
3. Place freeze-dried tissue in liquid nitrogen in a laboratory mortar for 5–10 seconds; not more than 30 seconds is ever necessary to freeze a sample.
4. Grind frozen tissue with pestle in liquid nitrogen to produce a fine powder. This should take about 30 seconds.
5. Transfer powder to a 50 ml centrifuge tube. Remove all powder with a fine brush.

6. Add 20 ml of 0.08 M NaCl, 0.01 M disodium EDTA. Adjust to pH 8.0.
7. Suspend material using a vortex mixer and let stand for 20–30 min.
8. Centrifuge for 10 min at 3000 rpm.
9. Decant supernatant.
10. For each 5 ml of packed cells add 20 ml of 0.15 M NaCl, 0.01 M disodium EDTA. Adjust pH to 8.0.
11. Suspend cells and let stand 10–20 min.
12. Add sodium dodecyl sulfate (electrophoresis-quality SDS) to ca. 3% (wt:vol) and proceed as with extraction described above for red blood cells.

The yield of spoolable DNA after RNase treatment should be between 2 and 12 mg/g of **dry** powder, depending on the extent of degradation before extraction. Ca. 50% of the material absorbing at 260 nm will be lost following RNase digestion.

SHEARING OF DNA INTO FRAGMENTS

To be able to remove the excess copies of repeated sequences and to obtain reproducible rates of reassociation, it is necessary to shear the purified long-stranded DNA into shorter fragments. Ideally, the range in fragment sizes is between ca. 200 and 800 bases, with an average near 500. As discussed in chapter 5 under "Fragment Size," an excessive number of short fragments may affect the shape of the melting curve and the value of the T_m. Fragments less than 100 bases in length tend to form duplexes that melt at the lower temperatures, producing a rapidly rising "foot" region and a homoduplex T_m below 85°C. Thus, the distribution of fragment sizes is as important as the average size of the population of fragments.

Several methods have been used to shear DNA, including the French press, the Virtis high-speed blender, and high-frequency sound. We prefer sonication because it is fast, requires little cleanup between samples, and results in minimal loss of DNA, but it also produces many short fragments. A suitable sonicator is the Branson Sonifier Cell Disruptor, Model W–350, equipped with a one-eighth-inch-diameter microtip.

To shear long-chain DNA into shorter fragments, place 20 ml of a DNA solution at a concentration of 2 mg/ml in 0.02 M sodium acetate in a 50 ml polyethylene centrifuge tube immersed in an ice bath. Position the sonifier probe 1.0 cm from the bottom of the tube and sonicate the sample at a power setting of 3 for eight minutes. Add ca. 0.5 grams of solid sodium acetate to make the sample 0.3 M with respect to sodium acetate, and place on a vortex mixer to dissolve. Add one volume of ice-cold 2-propanol while shaking, then allow the sample to precipitate in a freezer for ca. 1 hour. The sodium acetate helps to aggregate the fragments.

Note: The high energy output of the sonifier damages the probe, breaking off microscopic particles of stainless steel. This erosion can be seen as pits on the bottom of a probe and as they increase in size they will alter the frequency of the sound being produced. If the erosion proceeds long enough fine particles of steel may cause sonicated DNA samples to appear grayish after precipitation. The tip of the probe may be filed to remove the pits, a procedure necessary once a week under normal use. Use a fine file and hone the tip smooth and flat on an oilstone. It is possible to file off ca. 1 cm from the tip of a probe before reaching the point where the diameter of the probe increases. At this point the probe must be discarded because its sound frequency will change. To check the output power of the sonifier set up the centrifuge tube and probe as usual, but place them on the pan of a top-loading balance. Zero the balance, turn on the sonifier, and measure the downward pressure exerted by the vibrating probe (Hoyer et al. 1973). The Branson instrument has a pulsed output to minimize heat buildup in the sample, and several sound-dispersive horns are available for various applications.

Centrifuge the sample at 3000 rpm for 10 minutes to form a dense pellet of the precipi- tated DNA fragments. Pour off the propanol and place the test tube inverted over a paper towel for about 1 hour to drain off the remaining fluid. (The DNA pellet will not fall out.) Rehydrate the sheared DNA in 2 ml of 0.48 M PB and place it in a 7 ml glass vial over 1 ml of chloroform. Add more 0.48 M PB if the sample is too viscous, but maintain a concentration of at least 2 mg/ml. Preparations are stored at concentrations of 5–10 mg/ml. Rehydration may also be done in 10^{-4} EDTA, which will dissolve more of the DNA than will 0.48 M PB.

The sonicates may be extracted several more times with chloroform-isoamyl. During sonication additional proteins may settle at the interface between the DNA and the chloroform, and further incubation with protease and/or RNase may be necessary. These steps are carried out in 7 ml glass vials and centrifuged in the Whisperfuge. The following steps should be repeated until no visible middle layer remains:

1. Extract with chloroform.
2. Centrifuge at 1500 rpm for 5 min.
3. Remove chloroform with a Pasteur pipette.
4. Centrifuge, remove sample, leaving pellet behind.
5. Transfer DNA to a new vial.
6. If precipitation is necessary, use ice-cold propanol.

Purified DNA samples should have absorbance ratios of A^{260}/A^{230} 2.2, and A^{260}/A^{280} 1.8. A sample is pure enough for use in DNA-DNA hybrids if it shows no rise in the baseline when heated to 60°C and melts sharply with a hyperchromicity of at least 28% after denatura- tion, i.e.,

$$\frac{A^{260}(100°C) - A^{260}(60°C)}{A^{260}(100°C)} \times 100 = 28\% \text{ or more}$$

The two ratios are indices to protein contamination of the sample, and the hyper- chromicity is due to RNA. The single-stranded RNA, when melted, loses only its base- stacking bonds, producing a straight diagonal line when absorbance is plotted against tempera- ture (Bloomfield et al. 1975), and the change in absorbance is less than when DNA duplexes are melted. RNA contamination therefore reduces hyperchromicity and lowers the slope of the melting curve. Some spectrophotometers automatically plot a scan of absorbance from 220 nm to 320 nm, as well as a melt of temperature vs absorbance.

SIZING FRAGMENTS

To determine the sizes of sheared DNA fragments the sample is compared by electro- phoresis to a set of standards of known length. These markers are restriction enzyme digests of bacteriophage or plasmid DNAs selected according to the needs of the problem. Three restriction enzymes, HindIII, BstNI, and HaeIII (New England Biolabs, Beverly, Massachusetts), have been used in our studies.

The following protocol applies to the IBI (International Biotechnologies, Inc., New Haven, Connecticut) Model QSH gel electrophoresis apparatus. Several manufacturers make equipment suitable for the electrophoresis of DNA; there is some variation in the amounts of reagents and procedures for casting the gels.

Stock Solutions

TBE BUFFER 10×.

1.0 M Tris base, 121.1 g
1.0 M boric acid, 61.8 g
0.02 M disodium EDTA, 7.44 g
Deionized water to make one liter

For a working solution of 1× dilute 100 ml of the 10× buffer to one liter with deionized water.

LOADING BUFFER.

Ficoll, 3.0 g
Bromphenol blue, 0.024 g
Disodium EDTA, 1.86 g
Deionized water to make 10 ml.

ETHIDIUM BROMIDE. Prepare 100 ml of a solution at a concentration of 10 mg/ml in deionized water. Store in the cold. Wear gloves when handling powder or solutions of ethidium bromide, a known carcinogen.

To separate fragments in the range of 0.5 to 10 kb prepare a 1.5% agarose solution (IBI Ultra Pure Agarose):

1. Combine 40 ml of 1× TBE and 0.6 g of agarose.

2. Heat to boiling; cool to 60°C.

3. Add 20 microliters of ethidium bromide solution; pour the combination into the gel-forming apparatus; insert the comb, and allow the agarose to solidify.

4. Only 3 micrograms of DNA are needed per sample well, thus most DNA samples must be diluted to avoid overloading of the gel. For example, one microliter of DNA at a concentration of 5 mg/ml should be diluted with 9 microliters of 0.48 M PB to produce a concentration of 0.5 micrograms/microliter; 6 microliters of this solution contains the 3 micrograms needed for each well.

5. The sample wells made by the 7-tooth comb can contain 33 microliters. For a set of two gels (14 samples) dilute 28 microliters of loading buffer with 224 microliters of deionized water.

6. Combine 18 microliters of diluted loading buffer, the appropriate volume of the

DNA sample (e.g., 6 microliters), and 9 microliters of deionized water to make 33 microliters, and place in a sample well in the gel.

7. Fill the buffer reservoir with enough $1\times$ TBE to reach the ends of the gels without covering the gels.

8. Connect the power leads with the anode opposite the wells and pre-run the gel at 100 volts for 5 min to move the DNA into the gel matrix.

9. Disconnect the power, cover the gels with $1\times$ TBE, and run at 100 volts, 50–60 milliamperes, for about one hour or until the bromphenol blue dye has migrated to the opposite end of the gel.

10. Remove the gel and place it in deionized water. The DNA may be visualized and photographed over an ultraviolet light source (wear protective goggles). The ethidium bromide intercalates with the secondary and tertiary structure of DNA; it is this concentration of dye that makes the bands visible.

If the distribution of fragment sizes shows a large fraction below 200 bases in length, the short-stranded DNA should be removed. This may be done by electrophoretic separation and extraction of the desired size classes, by fractionation on a chromatographic column, or other methods. We used sonicated DNAs without removing the short strands, and the melting curves show the results; some homoduplex curves are excellent with T_ms at 86°C or higher, many have T_ms ca. 85°C, and too many have T_ms below 85°C. We recommend that tracers be sized to remove the short strands and, ideally, the driver DNAs also should have the short strands removed. The relative positions of the melting curves are not affected by short-stranded tracers, but the calculation of delta values will be. Corrections may be made to compensate for the variation between experiments caused by tracer sizes, but it is preferable to prepare better tracers than to correct for the effects of short fragments.

REASSOCIATION KINETICS

The kinetics of reassociation and the factors that determine the rate of reassociation are discussed in chapter 5. See "Concentration of DNA" in chapter 5 for a discussion of Cot.

Following is a description of the preparation of a Cot plot.

To separate the single-copy sequences from the total DNA and to determine the optimal conditions for the formation of DNA-DNA hybrids, it is necessary to examine the kinetics of reassociation of the DNAs being compared. The data are presented as a Cot plot of the percentage of single-stranded DNA versus the log Cot (see Fig. 7). Cot is the initial concentration of moles of nucleotides per liter times the time of incubation in seconds, or Cot = Msl^{-1}.

To determine the lower values of Cot a known quantity of sheared DNA, dissolved in 0.12 M PB, is melted in a spectrophotometer cuvette, then cooled to 60°C while recording the decrease in absorbance as the strands reassociate. This procedure is used for Cot values from 10^{-3} to 1.0. For Cot values from 1.0 to 10^4, samples of known concentration in 0.48 M PB are placed in 1 ml serum bottles, heated to 100°C for 5 min, and incubated at 60°C for various lengths of time. After incubation, the samples are quick-frozen in dry ice plus acetone and stored at −40°C until analysis. The higher salt concentration of 0.48 M PB increases the rate of reassociation 5.65 times the rate in 0.12 M PB. The values are corrected and plotted as equivalent Cot (Ecot).

After all the samples have been collected, each sample is thawed, diluted to 0.12 M PB, and applied to a column of hydroxyapatite (HAP) at 60°C. Under these conditions double-stranded DNA binds to the HAP, but single-stranded DNA may be washed from the column with 0.12 M PB. A second wash with 0.48 M PB will remove the double-stranded molecules of DNA. The quantities of single- and double-stranded DNA are measured spectrophotometrically, as described above.

PREPARATION OF SINGLE-COPY TRACER DNA

No facet of the DNA hybridization technique elicits more questions than the use of single-copy tracer DNA. A common misperception is that removal of most of the copies of repeated sequences discards a substantial percentage of the information content of the genome. The following discussion is intended to dispel this erroneous idea and to explain how tracer DNAs are prepared.

At 60°C in 0.12 M PB, the single-copy sequences of birds make up ca. 60–70% by volume of nuclear DNA, and the repeated sequences ca. 30–40%. However, under these conditions, the single-copy fraction contains 95–98% of the different sequences, i.e., of the sequence complexity, and the repeated fraction contains only 2–5% of the different sequences. If the total genome were to be used in the preparation of the radioactive tracers for DNA-DNA hybrids the repeated fraction would contribute 30–35% of the counts, although containing only 2–5% of the genetic information. In addition, as Kohne et al. (1971:490) pointed out:

The fraction containing repeated sequences is diverse even within one species, and the differences observed between the repeated sequences of two species cannot be assumed to have occurred since the time of divergence of those species.

Nonrepeated [single-copy] DNA sequences, on the other hand . . . [occur] only one time per haploid cell. Reassociated, nonrepeated DNA has a thermal stability that indicates that essentially perfect nucleotide pair matching is present. Nonrepeated DNA sequences held in common between species must be the descendants of the same ancestor sequence that was present in the most recent common ancestor. Nonrepeated DNA is therefore highly suitable for determining the extent of nucleotide change since the divergence of two species.

Kohne (1970:361) also noted that "Hybridization experiments using nonrepeated DNAs provide information concerning the rate of nucleotide substitution during evolution. Similar experiments using the repeated fraction provide a different type of information, namely information concerning the rate at which new DNA was incorporated into the genome by formation of new families of repeated sequences."

The evidence of gene amplification has continued to accumulate since Kohne (1970) and Kohne et al. (1971) recognized the significance of repeated DNA sequences in relation to DNA-DNA hybridization. The discovery by Sherwood and Patton (1982) of the large differences in genome size between closely related populations, subspecies, and species of pocket gophers (*Thomomys*) is but one of many examples. The removal of most of the copies of the repeated sequences from the tracer DNA is therefore necessary to obtain a true measure of nucleotide sequence evolution, i.e., the accumulation of sequence differences since the two species being compared diverged from their most recent common ancestor.

It is technically impossible to remove all of the repeated DNA copies by reassociation, without also removing all of the single-copy fraction; therefore, the so-called single-copy tracer preparations used in DNA-DNA hybridization actually contain at least one copy per genome of each repeated sequence that is kinetically different under the experimental conditions. Grula et al. (1982:666) found that their 600-base tracers, reassociated to Cot 200, had 6% or less repetitive sequence contamination. In fact, it is probable that ca. 10–20 copies per genome of each repeated sequence are actually present in most tracer preparations. Thus, single-copy tracers contain 100% of the sequence complexity of the genome, as determined by the criterion conditions.

A frequent question concerns the possibility that repeated sequences alone might yield an answer different from that obtained using single-copy tracer DNA. Since the repeated fraction contains only 2–5% of the sequence complexity of the genome, it may be expected to be less informative than the single-copy fraction. However, 2% of the average avian genome contains ca. 34 million nucleotides. In our experience with a single example (Sibley and Ahlquist 1981a:320–321) we found no discrepancy between the results using single-copy vs repeated DNA tracers. However, Eden et al. (1978) reported an unexpected result in some avian comparisons that we suspect was due to the misidentification of one of their preparations. We have compared the same taxa and found no anomalies. With Kohne et al. (1971) and others, we conclude that single-copy tracers are imperative for studies of phylogeny and taxonomic relationships.

Because repeated sequences reassociate more rapidly than single-copy sequences, the two frequency classes may be separated. The Cot curve indicates the length of time that whole, sheared, single-stranded DNA must be incubated to allow most of the repeated sequences to find complementary partners, while most of the single-copy fragments remain single-stranded.

To obtain a single-copy fraction containing a minimal percentage of repeated DNA sequences, it is necessary to permit reassociation to proceed to a Cot value of at least 200, and preferably higher. Reassociation to a Cot of 1000 at 50°C produces a single-copy fraction that probably contains fewer than 20 copies of each repeated sequence that is kinetically different under these conditions. As noted above, all preparations of single-copy DNA contain representatives of every repeated sequence family.

To prepare single-copy DNA, 1 or 2 mg of sheared, whole, DNA in 0.48 M PB is boiled at 100°C for 2–5 minutes, then incubated at 50°C to an equivalent Cot (Ecot) of 1000. The sample is then diluted to 0.12 M with respect to phosphate and applied to a chromatographic column containing 2.5 ml of HAP in 0.12 M PB. The column is allowed to equilibrate to 50°C and is then washed with 20 ml of 0.12 M PB to elute the single-stranded (single-copy) DNA. The amount of single-stranded DNA in the eluate is measured spectrophotometrically and the sample is dialyzed overnight against deionized water, after which it is freeze-dried.

RADIOIODINE (^{125}I) LABELING

Several different isotopes may be used to label DNA fragments for the preparation of tracers. For the studies reported in this book single-copy DNAs were radiolabeled with iodine 125 (^{125}I) using a procedure based on the methods described by Commorford (1971), Davis (1973), Tereba and McCarthy (1973), Orosz and Wetmur (1974), Scherberg and Refetoff (1975), Altenburg et al. (1975), Anderson and Folk (1976), Prensky (1976), and Chan et al.

(1976). Ertl et al. (1970) discussed the physical and biological attributes of ^{125}I. Friedlander et al. (1981:94) described other technical details.

Radioactive iodine labels DNA by a substitution reaction in which an atom of radioiodine replaces a hydrogen atom at the fifth carbon position on the cytosines. (The uracils of RNA may be labeled, but at a lower efficiency). The reaction takes place in an acid solution which promotes the protonation of the 5,6-carbon double bond. The addition of thallic ion (Tl^{-3}) initiates the reaction by converting I^- to I_2 and IOH, the latter of which reacts to form an unstable intermediate, 5-iodo–6-hydroxydihydrocytidine. A further heating at neutral pH dehydrates the intermediate to form the stable product 5-iodocytidine. All protocols for iodination of DNA are based on the method proposed by Commorford (1971). The range of conditions over which iodination may be carried out are given by Prensky (1976:136–137), as follows:

Iodide ion, 3.0×10^{-5} to 1.0×10^{-4} M
Cytosine (as DNA), 0.05×10^{-4} to 1.0×10^{-3} M
Thallic ion (Tl^{+3}), 4–10 times the I^- conc.
Sodium acetate buffer, 0.03–0.2 M
pH, 4.0–5.0
Temperature, 30–80°C

Of these conditions, the pH, temperature, and presence of thallic ion potentially can damage the single-stranded DNA by deamination or depurination. The reaction barely occurs at or above pH 5.0; as the pH is decreased toward 4.0 the reaction rate increases, but so does the probability of strand scission. Prensky (1976:137) recommended pH 4.7; we have found pH 4.5 to be optimal. In choosing a temperature, the efficiency of incorporaton of iodine must be balanced against possible damage to the DNA; 60°C is commonly used and seems optimal.

The reaction mixture introduced by Chan et al. (1976) differs from that of Prensky in using sodium perchlorate $(NaClO_4)$ to keep low-complexity nucleic acids in the single-stranded state during iodination and to protect the DNA from strand scission. The sodium perchlorate reduces the rate of iodine incorporation from that obtained under low salt (ca. 0.1 M) conditions but provides greater uniformity in the homoduplex $T_{50}H$ values. The Chan et al. (1976) procedure involves the addition of 7.2 M sodium perchlorate to the sodium acetate buffer to give a final concentration of 5.8 M sodium perchlorate at pH 4.5.

Extreme care must be observed when using any isotope of iodine because it will accumulate in the thyroid if volatile particles are breathed or enter the body via the skin or mouth.

PREPARATION OF DNA-DNA HYBRIDS

DNA hybrids are formed from a mixture composed of 1 part (200 nanograms) of single-copy tracer and 1000 parts (200 micrograms) of sheared, whole (driver) DNA, at a concentration of 2 mg/ml in 0.48 M PB. The amounts of tracer and driver DNAs are calculated from their concentrations. Typical amounts for the tracer are 3.0–5.0 microliters. For driver DNA at a concentration of 5.0 mg/ml, 40 microliters would be needed. Since the hybrid mixture is to contain 100 microliters, the remaining 60 microliters would be 0.48 M PB.

The hybrid combinations are placed in 1 ml stoppered serum vials, heated to boiling for 5 minutes (**not more**), and placed in a temperature-controlled water bath at 60°C for 120 hours (Cot 16,000). After incubation, the buffer in each hybrid vial is diluted to 0.12 M PB by adding 300 microliters of deionized water. The hybrids are then placed on HAP columns in a temperature-controlled water bath at 55°C. The temperature is then raised in 2.5°C increments to 95°C. At each of the 17 temperatures, the single-stranded DNA produced by the melting of labile duplexes is eluted in 20 ml of 0.12 M PB.

Chromatographic columns for the preparation of single-copy DNAs and for the thermal elution of DNA-DNA hybrids were made from the barrels of 10 ml disposable polyethylene syringes fitted with a disc of porous polyethylene as a support for the HAP. Blunt tubing adaptors (14 gauge, 3/4 inch, Becton and Dickinson #2804), on which were placed a length of silicone tubing, were attached to the Luer-lock portion of each syringe. These columns were eluted in a semi-automatic instrument (DNAlyzer) described and illustrated in Sibley and Ahlquist (1981a).

Hydroxyapatite (Bio-Gel HTP, Bio-Rad Laboratories) was prepared by suspending 100 grams in ca. 1 liter of 0.12 M PB, allowing the HAP to settle for 5 minutes, then decanting the fines (the smallest particles). The volume of PB was adjusted so that 10 ml of the slurry decanted by a volumetric dispenser yielded 2 ml of wet, packed HAP.

After thermal chromatography was completed, the vials containing the eluates were placed in a gamma counter and the amount of radioactivity in each vial was counted and recorded. These raw counts formed the basis for the production of melting curves and for the calculation of distance values between the homoduplex and each of the heteroduplexes in each experimental set. The procedures are described in chapter 11.

For future studies using DNA-DNA hybridization we recommend that fragments less than 100 bp in length be removed from tracer and driver preparations, and that tritiated oligonucleotide tracers be used. The TEACL method (Caccone and Powell 1989, Werman et al. 1990) is useful for closely related taxa, but we continue to prefer HAP for systematic studies involving a wide range of taxa. Werman et al. (1990) provide protocols for all methods of DNA-DNA hybridization.

CHAPTER ELEVEN

Data Analysis

Definitions

Some of the following definitions have been discussed elsewhere in this book. They are repeated here for convenience.

HOMODUPLEX DNA HYBRID. A DNA-DNA duplex molecule formed from labeled and unlabeled DNA of the same individual.

HETERODUPLEX DNA HYBRID. A DNA-DNA duplex molecule composed of one strand of radioactively labeled DNA of one species and an unlabeled strand of DNA of a different species.

TRACER. DNA that has been labeled with a radioactive nuclide; so called because its presence and behavior may be followed or traced during subsequent events.

DRIVER. In a hybrid mixture the driver is the unlabeled DNA; so called because its high concentration promotes, or drives, the reassociation reaction.

COUNTS. As used here meaning "radioactivity," but not referring specifically to radioactive disintegrations per minute (dpm) or counts of radioactivity per minute (cpm).

THERMAL ELUTION CURVE OR MELTING CURVE. A frequency distribution of radioactive counts versus temperature in degrees Celsius, representing the dissociation of DNA duplexes over a temperature gradient. The same count data may be summed incrementally to produce a sigmoid curve of the cumulative distribution, as in Figs. 18 to 324.

PERCENTAGE OF HYBRIDIZATION. The percentage of labeled DNA that forms hybrid molecules, or duplexes, with unlabeled DNA during a reassociation reaction.

NPH, NORMALIZED PERCENTAGE OF HYBRIDIZATION. The percentage of hybridization of a heteroduplex DNA hybrid divided by that of the homoduplex hybrid $\times$ 100.

T_m. The temperature in degrees Celsius at the median of a thermal elution curve; i.e., the temperature at which one-half of the hybridized DNA has dissociated. This is the "melting temperature" often reported in the literature.

MODE. The temperature in degrees Celsius at the highest point of the frequency distribution in a thermal dissociation curve. This value is found by fitting a distribution function to the experimental data and solving for the mode of the fitted distribution.

$T_{50}H$ (OR $T_{50}R$). The temperature in degrees Celsius in an ideal, normalized cumulative frequency distribution at which 50% of all potentially hybridizable single-copy DNA sequences are in the hybrid form and 50% have dissociated. Operationally, this represents the temperature at which the 50th percentile intercepts a cumulative distribution or extrapolated portion thereof. Also called T_mR by Benveniste and Todaro (1976).

DELTA VALUES. The difference in degrees Celsius between the various parameters of the distribution of radioactive counts of a homoduplex DNA hybrid and any heteroduplex hybrid formed from the same labeled DNA. For example, ΔT_m, Δ mode, or $\Delta T_{50}H$.

FREE IODINE. ^{125}I that is bound to something other than the cytosines in DNA, such as iodide salts or iodinated fragments of proteins.

Calculations

The data from the thermal chromatography of DNA-DNA hybrids are in the form of counts of radioactivity vs temperature. The counts were measured by a gamma counter that detects and records the amount of radioiodine (^{125}I) attached to the single strands of DNA eluted from the HAP columns at each of seventeen, 2.5°C temperature increments, from 55°C to 95°C. The counts in each of the 17 samples from each hybrid are summed to give the total counts for that hybrid. The DNA-DNA hybrids were incubated at 60°C; the melting cycle on the HAP columns was begun at 55°C; and the material eluted at 55, 57.5, and 60.0°C is unbound free ^{125}I and counts attached to small fragments and short duplexes. The counts in the first three elutions are also summed; they represent the DNA that did not bind to the HAP at 60°C.

The counts in the first three elutions are not critical in the case of homoduplexes or heteroduplexes formed with drivers closely related to the tracer species, but in the weakly base-paired heteroduplexes formed with drivers distantly related to the tracer species, a high percentage of tracer is not bound to HAP and might contaminate the 62.5°C eluate if the thermal elution was started at 60°C and eluted only once. This could cause a spuriously high percentage of hybridization. Eluting more than once at 60°C is not sufficient because the passage of additional buffer through the column will dissociate duplexes that are marginally stable at 60°C, thus reducing the percentage of hybridization (Fig. 9).

The three initial elutions also remove free iodine and other labeled contaminants from

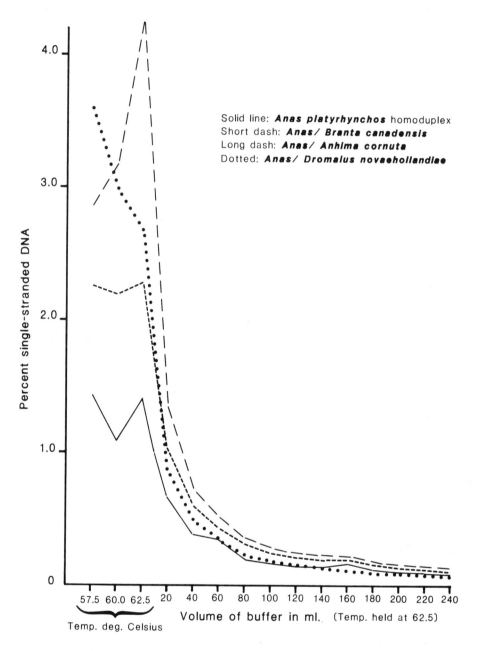

FIGURE 9. Effect of buffer volume on elution of DNA from hydroxyapatite. The temperature was raised from 55 to 62.5°C, then held constant while 240 ml of buffer was passed over the columns in 20 ml aliquots. Each curve represents the average of five hybrids.

the column. The so-called free iodine is mainly $Na^{125}I$. Iodinated protein fragments and labeled oligonucleotides too small to form stable hybrids may also be removed. Much of the free iodine is removed by dialysis; the amount remaining can be determined by thin-layer chromatography using methanol:acetone (1:1, v:v) as the solvent. The labeled DNA remains at the origin, and free iodine migrates with the solvent front. The thin-layer chromatogram can be cut up and the portions assayed for radioactivity.

Each tracer includes some free iodine even after dialysis. This is used only when determining the efficiency of hybridization of the homoduplex. To correct for the percent counts attributable to free iodine, multiply the percent free iodine times the total counts and subtract the value from the total counts in the first three elutions. This is possible because thin-layer chromatography shows that little free iodine remains in the eluates above 60°C.

The percentage of hybridization is given by:

$$\%H = (counts\ bound/total\ counts)100$$

Counts bound are the total counts above 60°C. For the homoduplex this value is set to 100%. A normalizing factor (NF) for the homoduplex is computed as:

$$NF = 1/fraction\ hybridized$$

The NPH of a heteroduplex is:

$$NPH = [(\%H\ of\ the\ heteroduplex)/(\%H\ of\ homoduplex)]100$$

The normalized percent counts is given by:

$$NPC = [(counts\ at\ temperature\ x)/(total\ counts)]NF$$

The general equation for the calculation of $T_{50}H$ is:

$$T_{50}H = [(50 - y_1)/(\Delta y/\Delta T)] + T_1.$$

in which y_1 and T_1 are, respectively, the percent counts and temperature at the beginning of the curve segment. The change in percent counts over the temperature increment is given by Δy, and ΔT is the temperature increment, which for our data is 2.5°C.

An example of the calculations is given in Table 9. The line segment used is the one with the steepest slope. For homoduplexes this is normally the line segment closest to the 50th percentile. For hybrids having an NPH less than 50, using the line segment with the greatest slope reduces variation because the effect of the low-temperature portion of the curve is eliminated.

Figures 4 and 5 show examples of frequency and cumulative distributions of melting curves with mode, T_m, and $T_{50}H$ indicated. All curves are asymmetrical. In frequency distributions the ascending slope (lower temperatures) is less steep than the descending slope (high temperatures). As genetic distance from the homoduplex increases, the temperature at the mode of the distribution decreases, the maximum heights of the curves decrease, and the curves become broader and more symmetrical. These effects are caused by increasing base-pair mismatches in the duplexes. The areas under the curves reflect NPH more than do the heights of the distributions. The cumulative distributions show a decreasing slope with increasing genetic distance, and their origins (at 60°C) reflect NPH, by definition. Obviously, the cumulative distributions converge at 95°C.

TABLE 9. Thermal Elution Data and Values Computed from Them.

A. Homoduplex of labeled single-copy DNA of the Lesser Melampitta (*Melampitta lugubris*) hybridized with itself. CPC indicates the cumulative percent counts at each temperature.

T(C)	Counts		NPC	CPC
55.0	131203 ⎫			
57.5	7442 ⎬	143494		
60.0	4849 ⎭		0.00	0.00
62.5	6607 ⎫		1.24	1.24
65.0	7534		1.41	2.65
67.5	8414		1.58	4.23
70.0	9485		1.78	6.01
72.5	11535		2.16	8.17
75.0	14541		2.73	10.90
77.5	21281 ⎬	533335	3.99	14.89
80.0	35519		6.66	21.55
82.5	58603		10.99	32.54
85.0	91010		17.06	49.60
87.5	122147		22.90	72.50
90.0	86740		16.08	88.58
92.5	43258		8.11	96.69
95.0	17661 ⎭		3.31	100.00
Total	676829		100.00	

NPH = 100.00 $T_{50}H$ = 85.00 Δ = 0.00

B. Heteroduplex of labeled *Melampitta lugubris* hybridized with the Eastern Whipbird (*Psophodes olivaceus*).

T(C)	Counts		NPC	CPC
55.0	140117 ⎫			
57.5	30026 ⎬	178847		
60.0	8704 ⎭		6.12	6.12
62.5	12670 ⎫		2.34	8.46
65.0	15466		2.86	11.32
67.5	19396		3.58	14.90
70.0	24195		4.47	19.37
72.5	35558		6.57	25.94
75.0	48389		8.94	34.88
77.5	70047 ⎬	508325	12.94	47.82
80.0	85185		15.73	63.55
82.5	79659		14.71	78.26
85.0	57294		10.58	88.84
87.5	37432		6.91	95.75
90.0	15409		2.85	98.60
92.5	5492		1.01	99.61
95.0	2133 ⎭		0.39	100.00
Total	687172		100.00	

NPH = 93.88 $T_{50}H$ = 77.80 Δ = 7.20

Comparisons of Mode, T_m, and $T_{50}H$

Each of the single-number distance statistics has advantages and disadvantages for the estimation of genetic relatedness among taxa. Some of these have been discussed by Springer and Krajewski (1989), Sheldon and Bledsoe (1989), Bledsoe and Sheldon (1989), Sarich et al. (1989), and Marks et al. (1989). Not all of these individuals are in agreement, nor do they possess the full data base of avian DNA hybridization on which the following summary statements are based. For several reasons we have used and continue to prefer the $T_{50}H$.

THE MODE

The mode represents a true statistical parameter of a distribution.

The mode must be determined by an objective curve-fitting procedure to be valid, therefore all data points contribute to its determination.

Methods for testing goodness-of-fit between the distribution function and experimental values are usually included in data analyses based on the mode.

Calculation of the mode is independent of the percentage of hybridization.

Within the experimental domain (60–95°C) the mode is more or less linear with the observed differences among the curves.

The mode is difficult to estimate when a true inflection of the melting curve is not within the experimental domain, thus the range of the mode is limited to ca. Δ 20.

Curves of different shapes or different percentages of hybridization can have the same mode, thus the potential exists for the loss or non-indexing of genetic information.

Finally, differences among modes may not track with differences in genetic information across the genome. Werman et al. (1990) state that "There does not appear to be any range of distance where the T_{mode} is the most accurate estimator of evolutionary distance. It changes more slowly with distance for closely related species and is difficult to determine with any accuracy. It may not change at all for very closely related species, depending on the amount of slowly changing DNA sequences. There is only a narrow range of distances where it could be used at all and there the accuracy is less than the other methods."

THE T_M

The T_m represents a true statistical parameter, the median, of a thermal elution curve. Since the curves are not normally distributed, the T_m does not equal the mode. For a homoduplex the T_m and $T_{50}H$ are the same.

The T_m has been the most widely used single-number statistic for describing melting curves.

The T_m is easily determined from the cumulative distribution by hand or by a programmable calculator.

For good data and over its range of effectiveness (ca. Δ 15) T_m is correlated with NPH.

Measurement errors are minimized because the T_m is usually located in the region of the cumulative distribution where there is minimal variation in the slope.

Differences in shapes of curves due to experimental error may result in T_m values that are different even though the NPH is the same. On the other hand curves may cross each other and thus have the same T_m even though the NPH may be different.

T_m cannot discriminate among high delta values because it cannot be lower than the criterion temperature. This produces a compression of T_m values as the distance from the homoduplex T_m increases. In practice, T_m values do not even approach the criterion temperature. Although it is obvious to the eye that cumulative distributions differ, the differences are not reflected by increasing ΔT_m values. Distantly related taxa cannot be distinguished with confidence on the basis of T_m, and this has led to the erroneous assertion that any delta values above 15, regardless of the distance measurement used, cannot be trusted. Fig. 5 illustrates the compression effect on the T_m.

THE $T_{50}H$

Unlike mode and T_m, $T_{50}H$ is not a true statistical parameter of the experimental portion of a melting curve.

Like the T_m, $T_{50}H$ is based on the cumulative melting curve and is easy to calculate.

By definition the $T_{50}H$ maximizes the range of delta values over which it can be used. The mode has a less effective range, and the T_m has the least range of the three distance measures being compared.

The $T_{50}H$ corresponds well to the observable properties of increasingly dissimilar melting curves; i.e., when there are visible differences between curves, the $T_{50}H$ reflects them.

Extrapolation provides high $\Delta T_{50}H$ values, at least to ca. $\Delta 30$. Such high values may overestimate the true genetic dissimilarity (i.e., $\Delta T_{50}H$ may not be linear with genetic tance), but this is not known for certain.

$T_{50}H$ is correlated with NPH and is sensitive to errors in measuring NPH, but the effect is minimized by calculating the $T_{50}H$ using the steepest slope of the cumulative distribution, thereby eliminating the variation present in the low-temperature end of a curve. Variation in NPH may be minimized by careful sizing of tracer and driver DNA fragments and maintenance of constant tracer:driver length ratios.

The error in the measurement of $T_{50}H$ is alleged to increase with genetic distance, but this is not necessarily true, at least out to $\Delta 30$. Some data sets have small standard deviations even for high delta values. The utility of $T_{50}H$ depends ultimately on the quality of the thermal elution curves and this depends on the quality of the samples hybridized and the precision with which the thermal elution is carried out.

Development of Matrices

When the desired comparisons have been made, the distance data are arrayed into a matrix of values. A complete matrix is one in which all taxa have been labeled and compared to one another as drivers. Such a matrix is characterized by a diagonal line of zero distances representing the homoduplex hybrids; thus the number of cells containing non-zero distances is ($N2 - N$). When the reciprocal comparisons (i.e., those above and below the diagonal) are found to be the same or nearly the same, they may be averaged to produce a folded matrix. See Table 10 for examples of data matrices.

If a matrix lacks a value in one or more cells it is incomplete. If comparisons are lacking in one direction only, folding will produce a complete matrix. Some types of cluster analysis do not require a complete matrix, although the topology of the resulting tree may be altered if the missing values are required to establish a node in the branching sequence. Some algorithms contain methods for estimating the values of missing cells.

Ideally, matrices are composed only of comparisons among single species used both as drivers and tracers, but many of the cells in our matrices include measurements from different species if the data show that they can be pooled. An advantage of using a matrix of single species is that a less complicated statistical model can be developed. However, because of the way our data were gathered, the cells in our matrices may include measurements derived from hybrids involving several tracers and drivers. This was inevitable because the data were obtained over many years and because considerable time often elapsed before a problem could be identified and investigated. During this time DNA of some species was used up and could not be obtained again. Additional species were obtained which changed the scope of coverage or the focus of a study.

Pooling of several species into the same cell of a matrix is appropriate if the species are members of a monophyletic lineage and the rates of genome evolution are identical or nearly so. In most cases we have pooled only closely related species, as indicated by morphology and by the DNA hybridization data. The validity of new clusters revealed by the DNA data can be tested by comparison to an out-group. The use of an out-group can also establish uniformity of rates within a group because the reciprocal comparisons serve as a relative rate test. Combining several species in one cell of a matrix may reduce errors from variation among single preparations of a species. That is, it may provide a more accurate average of the distance between the groups.

Properties of Distance Measures

To be useful in phylogeny reconstruction a desirable property of distance measures is that they be metric. The four conditions for metricity given by Sneath and Sokal (1973:120) are

1. $d(A,A) = 0$
2. $d(A,B) = d(B,A)$
3. $d(A,C) < d(A,B) + d(B,C)$
4. $d(A,B) > 0$

Relationship 1 states that identical taxa are identical. By definition labeled DNA and unlabeled DNA of the same individual are identical, hence the distance between the two preparations of DNA is 0. It is possible for DNAs of different individuals of the same species (or pooled from different populations of the same species) to be non-identical due to intra-species polymorphisms (e.g., Britten et al. 1978), but for birds these differences are small and there is no evidence that they have affected our data.

Relationship 2 pertains to reciprocity, or symmetry; that is, the distance from labeled A to unlabeled B should be the same as the distance from labeled B to unlabeled A. In most cases reciprocity of measurements is acceptable within the limits of experimental error. The main causes of true non-reciprocity are differences in genome size or genomic non-equivalence. Within a closely knit taxonomic group such as birds differences in genome size are likely to be caused by differences in the amounts of repetitive DNA. This has not been demonstrated in birds, although it is known for some mammals (e.g., Sherwood and Patton 1982). Differences in the amounts of repetitive DNAs should be minimized by relaxing the criterion at which single-copy sequences are separated from repeated sequences. Genomic equivalence means that among the species being compared all sequences are orthologous. Gene duplication and gene deletion (or insertion and deletion of small numbers of nucleotides) are the causes of genomic non-equivalence. Genomes of equal size should be equivalent, so paralogy is unlikely to be a problem.

Relationship 3 is the triangle inequality. This means that the distance between A and C cannot be greater than the sum of the distances from A to B and B to C. The conformity of data to the triangle inequality can be tested over a data matrix, and in most instances data are found to obey it.

Relationship 4 means that if A and B differ in their character states (gene sequences), the distance between them must be greater than zero. This obviously is realized in any data set, but negative branches may occur in trees constructed from data which are not strictly metric.

These relationships have been discussed by Bledsoe and Sheldon (1989), who also introduce the property of additivity (Buneman 1971) as a requirement for accurate phylogenetic reconstructions. Considering four taxa (A, B, C, D), additivity implies that

$$d(A,B) + d(C,D) \leq max [d(A,C) + d(B,D), d(B,C) + d(A,D)]$$

Average Linkage (UPGMA) Clustering

To produce a tree from a matrix it is necessary to employ some method of clustering. One of the simplest and most useful is average linkage, also known as UPGMA, for "unweighted pair-group method using arithmetic averages" (Sokal and Michener 1958). Clustering begins with the two taxa separated by the shortest distance in the matrix. They are joined at a branch half the distance between them, combined into a single group relative to the other groups in the matrix, and the distances between them and the other groups are calculated by averaging. The pair of taxa having the next-shortest distance between them are combined, and the distances between them and the remaining taxa are recalculated. The procedure is repeated until all taxa have been clustered. Several pairs of taxa may cluster before forming larger units. The procedure is sequential, agglomerative, hierarchical, and non-overlapping.

An example of clustering a matrix of data by UPGMA is shown in Table 10(A-I). At the point represented by Table 10(I) it is not necessary to reduce the matrix further because the remaining clusters can be discerned. The thrushes join at 8.5, followed by the starlings and mockingbirds at 9.1 (average of 9.2 + 9.0), *Cinclus* at 9.7 (average of 9.2 + 9.7 + 10.1), and the Bombycillidae at 10.6 (average of 10.9, 10.4, 10.6, 10.6). If the various nodes are assembled in order of increasing distances and each branch is assigned one-half of the nodal distance value, the tree in Fig. 10 is obtained.

The average linkage method and its application to DNA hybridization distance measurements was studied by Degens and colleagues. They refined the algorithms to include a bootstrap measure of fit for clusters, weighted three-objects variance estimators, and improvements for robustness. The relevant papers are Degens (1983a,b; 1985), Degens and Lausen

TABLE 10. Average Linkage Clustering.

A. The data in the matrix below are taken from Sibley et al. (1987) and represent values related to the starling-mockingbird problem. They are distances involving the species used both as tracers and drivers.

Bombycilla	0.0											
Phainopepla	5.2	0.0										
Dulus	6.9	6.4	0.0									
Cinclus	10.9	10.8	11.0	0.0								
Turdus	10.2	10.6	10.4	9.2	0.0							
Myadestes	10.5	10.3	10.4	9.2	7.9	0.0						
Erithacus	10.8	10.4	11.3	9.4	8.7	8.1	0.0					
Melaenornis	10.8	10.8	9.8	10.0	8.7	8.5	7.1	0.0				
Sturnus	10.9	10.9	10.7	10.3	8.6	9.4	9.2	8.8	0.0			
Lamprotornis	10.6	10.6	10.2	10.0	9.8	9.1	9.1	8.9	3.8	0.0		
Dumetella	10.4	11.2	10.3	9.9	9.2	8.8	9.3	8.7	6.1	5.6	0.0	
Mimus	10.9	11.0	10.8	10.3	8.9	9.4	8.9	8.2	6.2	5.5	2.7	0.0
Toxostoma	10.5	10.3	10.5	10.0	9.0	9.1	9.4	8.9	6.0	5.3	2.6	2.1	0.0

B. The smallest value in the matrix is between *Mimus* and *Toxostoma* at Δ 2.1. We join the two taxa at that distance and average the values between them and the remaining taxa (i.e., the two rows) to give a new matrix as shown below in which M. + T. = *Mimus* plus *Toxostoma*.

Bombycilla	0.0										
Phainopepla	5.2	0.0									
Dulus	6.9	6.4	0.0								
Cinclus	10.9	10.8	11.0	0.0							
Turdus	10.2	10.6	10.4	9.2	0.0						
Myadestes	10.5	10.3	10.4	9.2	7.9	0.0					
Erithacus	10.8	10.4	11.3	9.4	8.7	8.1	0.0				
Melaenornis	10.8	10.8	9.8	10.0	8.7	8.5	7.1	0.0			
Sturnus	10.9	10.9	10.7	10.3	8.6	9.4	9.2	8.8	0.0		
Lamprotornis	10.6	10.6	10.2	10.0	9.8	9.1	9.1	8.9	3.8	0.0	
Dumetella	10.4	11.2	10.3	9.9	9.2	8.8	9.3	8.7	6.1	5.6	0.0
M. + T.	10.7	10.6	10.6	10.2	9.0	9.2	9.2	8.6	6.1	5.4	2.6	0.0

C. The smallest value is 2.6 between *Dumetella* and the cluster just formed of *Mimus* and *Toxostoma*, thus *Dumetella* joins them at that value. We form a new OTU (D. + M. + T.) and average the values to the remaining taxa to produce a new matrix.

Bombycilla	0.0									
Phainopepla	5.2	0.0								
Dulus	6.9	6.4	0.0							
Cinclus	10.9	10.8	11.0	0.0						
Turdus	10.2	10.6	10.4	9.2	0.0					
Myadestes	10.5	10.3	10.4	9.2	7.9	0.0				
Erithacus	10.8	10.4	11.3	9.4	8.7	8.1	0.0			
Melaenornis	10.8	10.8	9.8	10.0	8.7	8.5	7.1	0.0		
Sturnus	10.9	10.9	10.7	10.3	8.6	9.4	9.2	8.8	0.0	
Lamprotornis	10.6	10.6	10.2	10.0	9.8	9.1	9.1	8.9	3.8	0.0
D. + M. + T.	10.6	10.9	10.4	10.0	9.1	9.0	9.2	8.6	6.1	5.5	0.0

(continued)

TABLE 10. (*Continued*)

D. Inspection of the matrix in (C) shows the next smallest value to be Δ 3.8 between *Sturnus* and *Lamprotornis*; they are joined at 3.8. We average the values between these two genera and all remaining taxa to produce a new OTU (S. + L.) and a new matrix.

Bombycilla	0.0								
Phainopepla	5.2	0.0							
Dulus	6.9	6.4	0.0						
Cinclus	10.9	10.8	11.0	0.0					
Turdus	10.2	10.6	10.4	9.2	0.0				
Myadestes	10.5	10.3	10.4	9.2	7.9	0.0			
Erithacus	10.8	10.4	11.3	9.4	8.7	8.1	0.0		
Melaenornis	10.8	10.8	9.8	10.0	8.7	8.5	7.1	0.0	
S. + L.	10.8	10.8	10.4	10.2	9.2	9.2	9.2	8.8	0.0
D. + M. + T.	10.6	10.9	10.4	10.0	9.1	9.0	9.2	8.6	5.8	0.0

E. The next cluster is formed by *Bombycilla* and *Phainopepla* joining at Δ 5.2. Averaging the columns containing the distances from them reduces the matrix further.

B. + P.	0.0							
Dulus	6.6	0.0						
Cinclus	10.8	11.0	0.0					
Turdus	10.4	10.4	9.2	0.0				
Myadestes	10.4	10.4	9.2	7.9	0.0			
Erithacus	10.6	11.3	9.4	8.7	8.1	0.0		
Melaenornis	10.8	9.8	10.0	8.7	8.5	7.1	0.0	
S. + L.	10.8	10.4	10.2	9.2	9.2	9.2	8.8	0.0
D. + M. + T.	10.8	10.4	10.0	9.1	9.0	9.2	8.6	5.8	0.0

F. The starlings (S. + L.) and mockingbirds (D. + M. + T.) now join at a value of 5.8, and the averaging procedure is repeated to yield:

B. + P.	0.0						
Dulus	6.6	0.0					
Cinclus	10.8	11.0	0.0				
Turdus	10.4	10.4	9.2	0.0			
Myadestes	10.4	10.4	9.2	7.9	0.0		
Erithacus	10.6	11.3	9.4	8.7	8.1	0.0	
Melaenornis	10.8	9.8	10.0	8.7	8.5	7.1	0.0
Star. + Mock.	10.8	10.4	10.1	9.2	9.1	9.2	8.7	0.0

G. Next join *Dulus* to *Bombycilla* plus *Phainopepla* at a distance of 6.6 and average the columns.

B. + P. + D.	0.0						
Cinclus	10.9	0.0					
Turdus	10.4	9.2	0.0				
Myadestes	10.4	9.2	7.9	0.0			
Erithacus	11.0	9.4	8.7	8.1	0.0		
Melaenornis	10.3	10.0	8.7	8.5	7.1	0.0	
Star. + Mock.	10.6	10.1	9.2	9.1	9.2	8.7	0.0

(*continued*)

TABLE 10. (*Continued*)

H. *Erithacus* and *Melaenornis* join at Δ 7.1 to form a new OTU (E. + M.), and the values of the two
rows are averaged.

B. + P. + D.	0.0					
Cinclus	10.9	0.0				
Turdus	10.4	9.2	0.0			
Myadestes	10.4	9.2	7.9	0.0		
E. + M.	10.6	9.7	8.7	8.3	0.0	
Star. + Mock.	10.6	10.1	9.2	9.1	9.0	0.0

I. The last merging of two genera into a single OTU involves *Turdus* and *Myadestes* which join at 7.9.
(This cluster is different from the final one obtained when all the data are used.)

B. + P. + D.	0.0				
Cinclus	10.9	0.0			
T. + M.	10.4	9.2	0.0		
E. + M.	10.6	9.7	8.5	0.0	
Star. + Mock.	10.6	10.1	9.2	9.0	0.0

(1986), Degens et al. (1986), Lausen (1987), Lausen and Degens (1986), Lausen and Vach
(1986), Ostermann and Degens (1984a,b; 1985), Vach and Degens (1986).

The average linkage method is most useful when the average rates of genome evolution
are uniform or nearly so. When distance measures have large stochastic errors, average linkage
may be superior to other distance matrix methods in determining the true tree when it is known,
as in computer simulation studies (Tateno et al. 1982; Nei et al. 1983; Sourdis and Krimbas,
1987). Nei (1987:295–296) provided an assessment of the statistical properties of the average
linkage method.

Fitch-Margoliash Method

Methods that do not assume equal rates of genetic change among lineages have some advantages over UPGMA and offer an objective method for checking the validity of corrections
applied to aberrant data. Advocates of each clustering method defend it against competing
procedures, often generating more heat than light for the solutions to systematic problems. The
situation was summarized by Felsenstein (1984:169): "The difficulty has been that the proponents of each methodology have been concerned more with developing their own methods and
discrediting the alternatives than with exploring the logical interrelations among the methods."

We have used the FITCH program in the PHYLIP (Version 3.2) package of phylogenetic inference programs (Felsenstein 1989). FITCH uses the algorithm of Fitch and Margoliash
(1967) for fitting trees to distance matrices and the least squares method of Cavalli-Sforza and
Edwards (1967). These methods find the tree that minimizes the sum of squares, where:

$$\text{Sum of squares} = \sum_i \sum_j = n_{ij}(D_{ij} - d_{ij})^2/D_{ij}^2$$

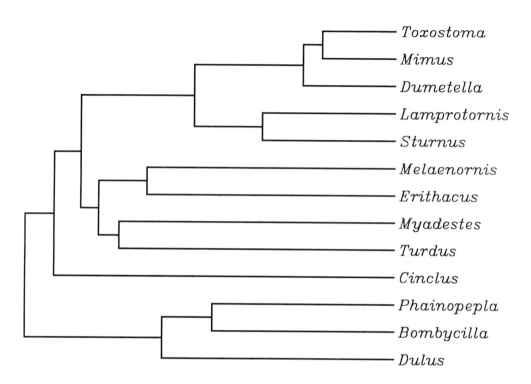

FIGURE 10. Average linkage (UPGMA) clustering of thirteen genera of Muscicapoidea. Data matrix in Table 10A.

D is the observed distance between the species i and j, d is the expected distance (the sum of the lengths of the segments on the tree from species i to species j), and n is the number of times each measurement has been replicated.

For the best tree they compute the percent standard deviation which is given by:

$$\%SD = \left(\left\{ 2 \sum_{ij} [(D_{ij} - d_{ij})/D_{ij}]^2 \right\} / [N(N - 1)] \right)^{0.5} \times 100$$

in which D and d are the observed and expected distances, as before, and N is the number of taxa used.

A summary of the operations abstracted from Nei (1987:298–299), follows: Clustering begins with three taxa. If the taxa are designated A, B, and C and a node is placed between A and B, then x is the distance from the node to A, y is the distance from the node to B, and z is the distance from the node to C. The estimated distances x, y, and z may be determined from measurements made among the taxa by the equations:

$$x = [d(A,B) + d(A,C) - d(B,C)]/2$$
$$y = [d(A,B) - d(A,C) + d(B,C)]/2$$
$$z = [-d(A,B) + d(A,C) + d(B,C)]/2$$

When there are more than three taxa, let A and B represent those having the smallest distance between them and let C represent a composite taxon consisting of all others except A and B. The distance (A,C) represents the average of all the distances from A to the other taxa except B, and the distance (B,C) represents the average distance from B to the other taxa except A.

A and B are then combined into one taxon and the distances from it to all the other taxa are recalculated. The procedure begins again by choosing the two taxa that show the smallest distance between them. (The combined taxon consisting of A and B does not necessarily have to be one of them.) The two closest taxa are designated A and B; the distances between them and all other taxa, designated again as C, are averaged; and branch lengths x, y, and z are calculated by the same expressions as above. The procedure is repeated until all taxa have been clustered.

The FITCH algorithm and its companion, KITSCH, which does assume uniform rates of genetic change, require two conditions to be met for maximum effectiveness (Felsenstein 1989, PHYLIP computer disk, DISTANCE.DOC file, p. 107 PHYLIP documentation): (1) Each distance is measured independently from the others: no datum contributes to more than one distance. (2) The distance between each pair of taxa is drawn from a distribution with an expectation that is the sum of values (in effect amounts of evolution) along the tree from one tip to the other. The variance of the distribution is proportional to a power p of the expectation.

Felsenstein notes: "DNA hybridization and immunological distances may be additive and independent if transformed properly and if the standards against which each value is measured are independent." We have not attempted a critical analysis of the extent to which the data presented in the matrices meet these criteria.

The FITCH and KITSCH programs provide several options. We have used the replicate option, which allows for varying numbers of measurements per cell, and the shuffle option, which varies the order of input of taxa. When available we have used complete data matrices; cells lacking actual data have been filled with the reciprocal value coded with $N = 1$.

Both FITCH and KITSCH produce trees that can be written to computer files and converted to plotfiles via the PLOTGRAM program, also available with PHYLIP 3.2. Before being run on PLOTGRAM, trees were edited to incorporate taxon names longer than the ten characters utilized by FITCH. Plotfiles of trees were plotted on a Hewlett Packard Laser Jet Plus printer via PrintAPlot 1.0 (Insight Development Corp.).

Figures 353–385 were derived from average linkage clustering done by hand, thus empty cells could be ignored and varying numbers of taxa and branches within principal groups could be used. The figures derived from UPGMA also contain many branches for which few measurements were made; thus complete matrices are not available, even among the species used as tracers. These diagrams are pictorial representations of the distances.

The branches to many of the higher groups (particularly among the non-passerines) have been corrected for branch-length differences. This involved taking the labeled taxa three at a time, clustering the two that were closest, and using the third as an out-group with which a relative rate test was performed. When branch-length differences were detected, other out-groups were used to perform additional relative rate tests. If a consistent absolute difference in branch length was obtained, the shorter branch length was corrected in the matrix by the appropriate amount and the data were reclustered (see Table 17).

Correction Factors for DNA Hybridization Data

The necessity for correcting any value of a DNA-DNA melting curve has been questioned and debated. The following is based on the discussion of this issue by Sibley et al. (1990).

The corrections for delta values and percent hybridization values that we have used were developed from years of experience in observing differences among data sets that should be identical. For example, the criteria for a good homoduplex melting curve are that it should be smoothly sigmoid in shape, have a $T_{50}H$ (and T_m) ca. 86°C, and a slowly rising foot region. For homoduplexes with a $T_{50}H$ below 84°C a correction may be required, or the entire set must be discarded. It is costly in time and money to produce data, and corrections are justified if the problem is understood. The corrections we have used are empirical, logically derived, and internally consistent. The conclusions based on the corrected data are not changed; only the level of significance may be higher than for uncorrected data. Corrections in the data compensate for errors made in the laboratory.

The reasons to correct the T_m or $T_{50}H$ of a DNA-DNA hybrid include (1) temperature overshoots during the thermal elution procedure, (2) variation in the average fragment length of tracer and/or driver DNAs, and (3) interexperiment variability, which may be caused by 1 and/or 2, or by other factors not well understood.

TEMPERATURE OVERSHOOTS

A temperature overshoot occurs when the temperature in the water bath goes above the set point for a given increment, e.g., if the correct temperature for an elution increment is 70.0°C but the temperature during elution is actually 70.3°C. An overshoot causes a peak followed by a depression in what should be a smooth frequency distribution of counts. Fig. 11 shows an extreme example. Plotting the data as cumulative distributions will smooth out the effects of small temperature overshoots, but not those of large ones.

Temperature overshoots melt some of the DNA duplexes that should dissociate at the next higher temperature increment and thus add their counts to the lower increment. Correspondingly fewer counts will elute at the next higher temperature. If the overshoot occurs away from the T_m of a hybrid, it may pose little or no problem, but if it occurs near the T_m (or $T_{50}H$), where the transition from double- to single-stranded DNA is most rapid, it can affect the calculation of $T_{50}H$. Obviously, the only error is in the assignment of counts to two adjacent increments, and the solution is to correct the counts by subtracting from the lower temperature and adding to the upper temperature. This is analogous to correcting a spelling error in the text.

For curves with substantial midrange temperature overshoots it is not always easy to compute a correct $T_{50}H$. Each curve in an experiment will be affected in the same way, so the calculation of the $T_{50}H$ can be done consistently. The curve of *Phaethon/Fregata* in Fig. 12 demonstrates some of the problems. From the line segments surrounding the 50th percentile, it can be seen that the choice of line segment as the basis for calculating the $T_{50}H$ will affect the result. If the $T_{50}H$ is calculated as the temperature at the 50th percentile and also extrapolated from the segment with the steepest slope, the values differ by about 0.2°C.

It is simple to correct the effects of a temperature overshoot when plotting melting curves; the irregularity can be judged by eye, and the percent counts in the two adjacent cells can be adjusted to yield a smooth curve. The relative positions of the curves are not changed, but the appearance of the curves is improved.

LINEAR CORRECTION

Changes in the behavior of the tracer DNA may be due to strand scission caused by the radiation emitted by the tracer nuclide. ^{125}I is known to damage DNA over relatively short periods of time. The first experiment carried out with a tracer is therefore likely to be the best, and later ones may show the effects of strand scission.

This problem was examined by setting up identical experiments on 1, 6, 10, and 14 days after the preparation of the tracer, as shown in Fig. 13. The homoduplex melting curve in the set that began incubation on the day after iodination has a sharp peak with a high melting temperature. As the tracer DNA was degraded over time, the sharpness of the homoduplex diminished and the peak became lower and broader. The $T_{50}H$ of the homoduplex was reduced as the shape of the curve changed, but the heteroduplexes were less affected. Thus, the $\Delta T_{50}Hs$ became smaller with time, necessitating their correction to the value obtained in the first experiment. Graphs of the heteroduplex curves can be superimposed, demonstrating that their $T_{50}Hs$ were unchanged. The correction procedure is to substitute the value of a good homoduplex for the faulty one and to calculate the delta values based on the substituted homoduplex. This procedure has also been used when the homoduplex failed to elute or was lost by accident, both rare events. At other times all hybrids in an experiment will be affected by the same amount (i.e., both homoduplexes and heteroduplexes are shifted equally toward a lower melting temperature); thus the delta values are unchanged.

Corrections for driver length in individual hybrids can be made if the data are available.

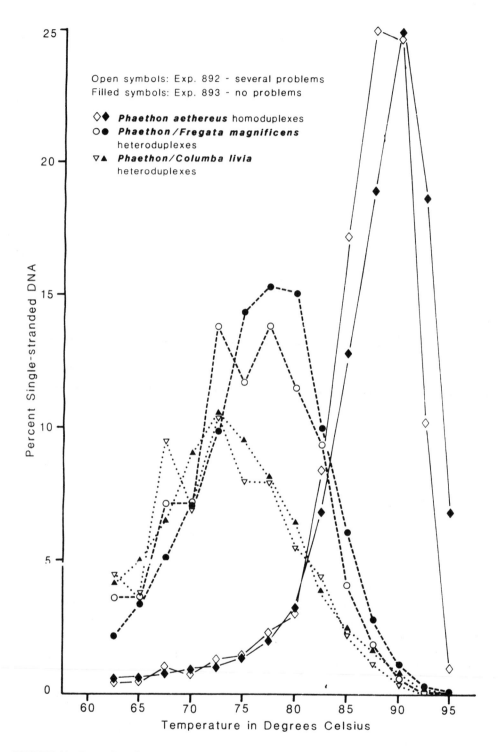

FIGURE 11. Examples of good and bad curves plotted as frequency distributions.

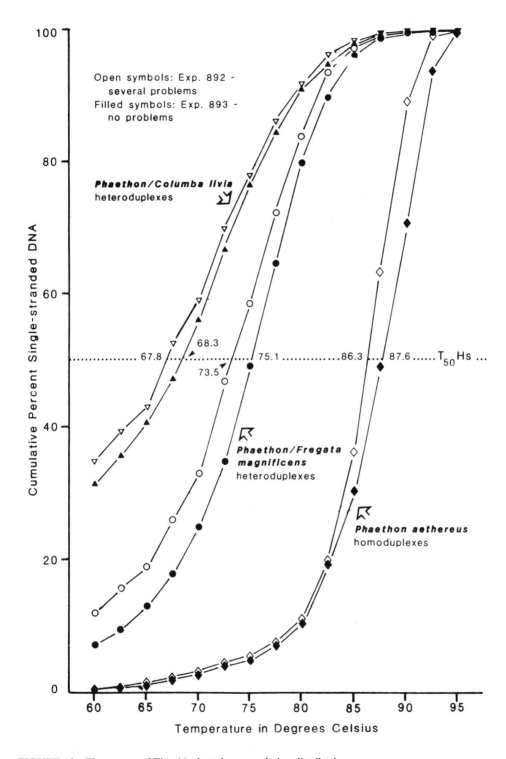

FIGURE 12. The curves of Fig. 11 plotted as cumulative distributions.

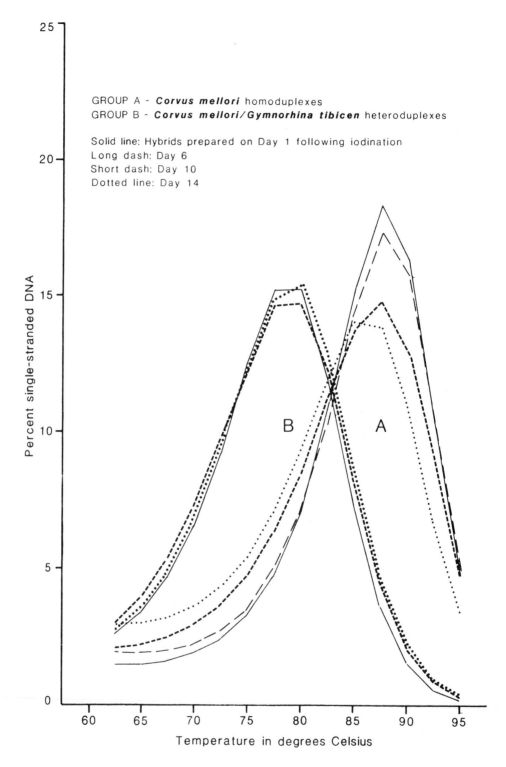

FIGURE 13. Effect of age of tracer on DNA-DNA hybrids. Note the progressive change in the curves of the homoduplex resulting in a decrease in the $T_{50}H$. The heteroduplex curves are not affected.

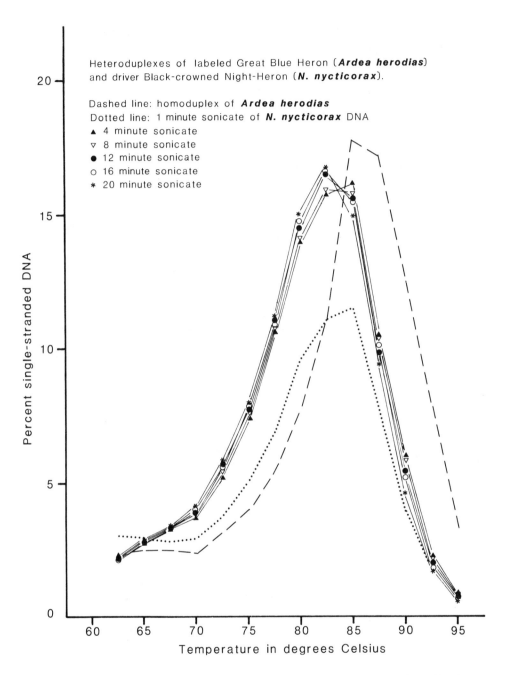

FIGURE 14. Effect of sonication time on driver DNA. Sonication times between 4 and 20 minutes produce smaller average fragment sizes and slightly lower melting temperatures.

Most DNA hybridization experiments have used a driver fragment length averaging 500 base pairs. If shorter fragments are used the T_m will be reduced, and a correction for their length can be made. The relationship is:

$$T_m \text{ reduction} = 500/\text{average driver length in bp}$$

The average driver length of fragments is determined by comparing their electrophoretic mobility with that of fragments of known length (i.e., phage or plasmid DNAs which have been digested with specific endonucleases, as discussed in chapter 5 under "Fragment Size").

Within reasonable limits, the length of sonication time has little effect on DNA hybrids (Fig. 14), and it can be precisely controlled. Most problems with the fragment length of tracers probably are due to strand scission during the iodination reaction. This is indicated by homoduplex T_ms lower than the optimum and by a rapidly rising foot of the cumulative melting curve. DNAs may also be damaged during field collection, shipping, or extraction.

TABLE 11. Reciprocal DNA-DNA Hybridization Distances

Radiolabeled species	Unlabeled species	$\Delta T_{50}H$
Paradisaea minor	*P. paradiseus*	1.5
Ptiloris paradiseus	*P. minor*	1.4
Chlamydera nuchalis	*P. violaceus*	2.7
Ptilonorhynchus violaceus	*C. nuchalis*	2.6
Daphoenositta chrysoptera	*P. pectoralis*	6.8
Pachycephala pectoralis	*D. chrysoptera*	6.9
Pachycephala pectoralis	*P. paradiseus*	7.3
Ptiloris paradiseus	*P. pectoralis*	7.2
Pachycephala pectoralis	*D. brunneopygia*	9.9
Drymodes brunneopygia	*P. simplex*	9.9
Malurus lamberti	*S. frontalis*	10.9
Sericornis frontalis	*M. lamberti*	10.7
Pachycephala pectoralis	*A. inornata*	11.7
Acanthiza chrysorrhoa	*P. pectoralis*	11.6
Daphoenositta chrysoptera	*A. carunculata*	11.9
Anthochaera carunculata	*D. chrysoptera*	11.7
Daphoenositta chrysoptera	*E. albifrons*	12.0
Ephthianura albifrons	*D. chrysoptera*	12.3
Malurus lamberti	*G. cyanoleuca*	12.8
Grallina cyanoleuca	*M. lamberti*	13.0
Malurus lamberti	*D. brunneopygia*	12.9
Drymodes brunneopygia	*M. lamberti*	13.0
Malurus lamberti	*P. pectoralis*	13.1
Pachycephala pectoralis	*M. lamberti*	12.8
Malurus lamberti	*D. chrysoptera*	13.5
Daphoenositta chrysoptera	*M. lamberti*	13.3
Malurus lamberti	*C. cruralis*	14.5
Cincloramphus cruralis	*M. lamberti*	14.7

Source: Sibley and Ahlquist 1983.

PROPORTIONAL CORRECTION

Proportional corrections are used to adjust differing $\Delta T_{50}H$ values between different experiments using the same tracer species. The causes of differences in what should be identical values are not obvious, but it is possible to determine which of several sets represents the best one and to correct the others in proportion to it.

If the $T_{50}H$ values of a good set are plotted against NPH for the same set the regression is linear, as would be expected by the way that $T_{50}H$ is calculated. For such sets the correlation coefficient (r) is typically above 0.95. Suboptimal sets either do not lie along the regression line or yield curvilinear distributions. Individual aberrant hybrids also may not lie close to the linear regression.

The correction is made by moving the aberrant point to the linear regression, determining the new NPH value, and calculating the new $T_{50}H$ value. This involves the scaling upward or downward of the cumulative distribution, but the shape of the cumulative curve is not

TABLE 12. Averages of Discrepancies in Reciprocal ΔT_m Values among some Herons and an Ibis Out-group[a]

Species	$\bar{X}$	N	SD	Range
Plegadis falcinellus (Glossy Ibis)	0.2	8	0.25	0.6
Botaurus lentiginosus (American Bittern)	0.2	12	0.14	0.4
Casmerodius a. egretta (Great Egret)	0.2	10	0.24	0.8
Egretta thula (Snowy Egret)	0.2	13	0.20	0.6
Ixobrychus exilis (Least Bittern)	0.2	11	0.26	0.9
Nyctanassa violacea (Yellow-crowned Night-Heron)	0.2	10	0.10	0.3
Nycticorax nycticorax (Black-crowned Night-Heron)	0.2	13	0.14	0.4
Tigrisoma lineatum (Rufescent Tiger-Heron)	0.2	12	0.15	0.6
Bubulcus ibis (Cattle Egret)	0.3	12	0.20	0.7
Butorides s. virescens (Green-backed Heron)	0.3	11	0.17	0.6
Ardea herodias (Great Blue Heron)	0.4	13	0.20	0.6
Cochlearius cochlearius (Boat-billed Heron)	0.4	7	0.21	0.5
Hydranassa caerulea (Little Blue Heron)	0.5	7	0.25	0.6
Syrigma sibilatrix (Whistling Heron)	0.6	9	0.19	0.6

[a]Data from Sheldon (1986).

changed. The amount of change in the $T_{50}H$ is not linear; it is related to the magnitude of the correction applied to the NPH, but it will not be the same among all hybrids being corrected because of the different shapes of individual curves. For outliers the proportional correction is similar to a fragment length correction, and it may improve the discrimination of entire experiments, but it does not alter the basic pattern of the data.

ERROR ESTIMATION

Various aspects of error measurement among DNA-DNA hybrids have been discussed by Sibley and Ahlquist (1983), Sibley et al. (1987), Ahlquist et al. (1987), Bledsoe (1987, 1988b), Sheldon (1987a,b), Bledsoe and Sheldon (1989), and Sheldon and Bledsoe (1989).

Examples of reciprocity are shown in Tables 11 and 12. Selected reciprocal comparisons involving passerines of the parvorder Corvida are given in Table 11. The range of reciprocal difference is 0.3°C. Sheldon's (1986) heron data (Table 12) have a somewhat higher range of reciprocal difference (up to 0.9°C), but the average is 0.2–0.6°C. Most other data are similar.

TABLE 13. DNA-DNA Hybridization Data for Comparisons between the Cape Weaver and Other Species of Birds[a]

Name	$\Delta T_{50}H$	ΔMode	ΔT_m	NPH
A. Cape Weaver (*Ploceus capensis*)	0.0	0.0	0.0	100
Village Weaver (*Ploceus cucullatus*)	0.9	0.6	0.7	96.7
Red-billed Quelea (*Quelea quelea*)	4.3	3.7	3.6	95.9
Red Bishop (*Euplectes orix*)	5.1	5.1	4.8	91.3
Thick-billed Weaver (*Amblyospiza albifrons*)	6.8	6.2	6.0	89.6
B. Red-winged Starling (*Onychognathus morio*)	10.2	8.6	8.3	81.3
Golden-crested Myna (*Ampeliceps coronatus*)	10.4	8.9	8.6	82.0
Common Starling (*Sturnus vulgaris*)	10.7	8.7	8.5	79.8
Singing Starling (*Aplonis cantoroides*)	10.7	9.5	9.6	81.3
Pied Starling (*Spreo bicolor*)	11.1	9.4	10.1	80.0
C. Common Crow (*Corvus brachyrhynchos*)	12.0	8.9	8.7	78.0
Mexican Jay (*Aphelocoma ultramarina*)	12.0	.1	9.0	75.1
Malaysian Treepie (*Dendrocitta occipitalis*)	12.2	9.6	9.2	74.8
Blue Jay (*Cyanocitta cristata*)	12.4	9.6	9.2	75.0
Black-billed Magpie (*Pica pica*)	12.5	9.6	9.8	75.1
D. Stout-billed Cinclodes (*Cinclodes excelsior*)	19.5	16.1	13.7	53.4
Black-tailed Leafscraper (*Sclerurus caudacutus*)	19.6	16.0	13.6	53.3
Striped Leafgleaner (*Hyloctistes subulatus*)	19.6	16.5	13.9	58.0
Pale-legged Hornero (*Furnarius leucopus*)	19.9	16.4	13.8	52.4
Chestnut-crowned Leafgleaner (*Automolus rufipileatus*)	20.2	16.3	13.7	51.7
E. Green Kingfisher (*Chloroceryle americana*)	27.9	21.3	15.3	36.5
Sacred Kingfisher (*Halcyon sancta*)	28.5	20.6	15.0	35.7
Hook-billed Kingfisher (*Melidora macrorhina*)	28.7	20.4	15.0	35.4
Common Paradise Kingfisher (*Tanysiptera galatea*)	28.8	19.7	15.2	34.6
Belted Kingfisher (*Ceryle alcyon*)	29.8	20.8	15.1	33.6

Source: Sibley and Ahlquist 1983.
[a]A = Weaverbirds, Ploceidae; B = Starlings, Sturnidae; C = Crows, etc., Corvidae; D = Ovenbirds, Furnaridae; E = Kingfishers, Alcedinidae.

TABLE 14. DNA-DNA Comparisons between the Yellow-rumped Thornbill and Other Passerine Taxa

Taxa	$\Delta T_{50}H$				ΔMode				ΔT_m				NPH			
	Range	x̄	SE	SD	Range	x̄	SE	SD	Range	x̄	SE	SD	Range	x̄	SE	SD
A. Ten identical DNA-DNA hybrids between the Yellow-rumped Thornbill (Acanthiza chrysorrhoa) and the Red Wattlebird (Anthochaera carunculata)	8.6–9.2 (0.6)	8.8	0.1	0.2	7.8–8.5 (0.7)	8.1	0.1	0.2	7.2–7.9 (0.7)	7.6	0.1	0.2	81.1–86.7 (5.6)	84.4	0.7	2.2
B. Nine DNA-DNA hybrids between the Yellow-rumped Thornbill and nine genera of honeyeaters (Meliphagidae)[a]	7.4–9.1 (1.7)	9.1	0.2	0.7	6.8–9.3 (2.9)	8.3	0.2	0.7	6.2–9.2 (3.0)	8.3	0.2	0.6	81.3–90.4 (9.1)	85.5	0.9	2.8
C. 19 DNA-DNA hybrids between the Yellow-rumped Thornbill and 19 genera of oscine passerines[b]	12.7–15.0 (2.3)	14.0	0.1	0.6	8.1–11.0 (2.9)	10.0	0.2	0.7	10.9–11.9 (1.0)	11.3	0.1	0.3	73.1–82.8 (9.7)	77.6	0.5	2.4

Source: Sibley and Ahlquist 1983.

[a]Prosthemadera, Acanthorhynchus, Conopophila, Plectorhyncha, Ramsayornis, Meliphaga, Certhionyx, Myzomela, Lichmera.

[b]Ficedula, Melaenornis, Parus, Stachyris, Turdoides, Pycnonotus, Thryothorus, Copsychus, Turdus, Sturnus, Toxostoma, Prunella, Motacilla, Anthreptes, Emberiza, Passer, Euplectes, Progne, Ammomanes.

TABLE 15. DNA-DNA Comparisons to Determine the Magnitude of Experimental Error in $T_{50}H$ Values

	N	Average $T_{50}H$ or $\Delta T_{50}H$	SE	SD	Range	Low value	High value
A. DNA-DNA hybrids composed of the same sample of *Turdus migratorius* DNA as driver, and the species below as tracers							
American Robin (*Turdus migratorius*)	11	88.5	0.2	0.6	1.7	87.6	89.3
Townsend's Solitaire (*Myadestes townsendi*)	8	7.9	0.2	0.5	1.1	7.3	8.4
Black-headed Bush-Shrike (*Laniarius barbarus*)	9	13.9	0.1	0.2	0.7	13.5	14.2
Chestnut-cr. Gnateater (*Conopophaga castaneiceps*)	9	20.2	0.1	0.3	0.8	19.9	20.7
B. DNA-DNA hybrids composed of driver DNAs from different individuals of *Turdus migratorius*, and the species below as tracers							
American Robin (*Turdus migratorius*)	13	87.1	0.2	0.6	2.1	86.3	88.4
Townsend's Solitaire (*Myadestes townsendi*)	11	9.1	0.2	0.7	2.4	8.0	10.4
Black-headed Bush-Shrike (*Laniarius barbarus*)	11	13.6	0.2	0.6	1.8	12.8	14.6
Chestnut-cr. Gnateater (*Conopophaga castaneiceps*)	11	21.0	0.3	0.9	3.5	19.1	22.6
C. DNA-DNA hybrids composed of driver DNAs from different species of the genus *Turdus* and tracers of the species listed below							
American Robin (*Turdus migratorius*)	22	1.1	0.2	0.8	2.8	0.0	2.8
Townsend's Solitaire (*Myadestes townsendi*)	20	9.1	0.2	0.7	2.1	8.1	10.2
Black-headed Bush-Shrike (*Laniarius barbarus*)	20	13.3	0.2	0.8	2.7	11.7	14.4
Chestnut-cr. Gnateater (*Conopophaga castaneiceps*)	20	20.6	0.2	0.9	3.3	18.9	22.2

Source: Sibley and Ahlquist 1983.

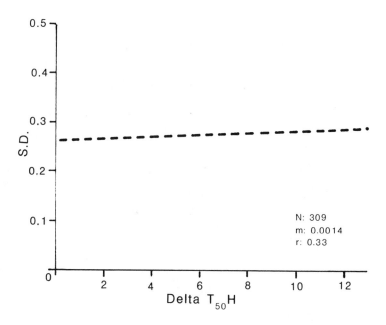

FIGURE 15. Plot of standard deviation (S.D.) versus delta $T_{50}H$. The dashed line represents a linear regression to 309 data points.

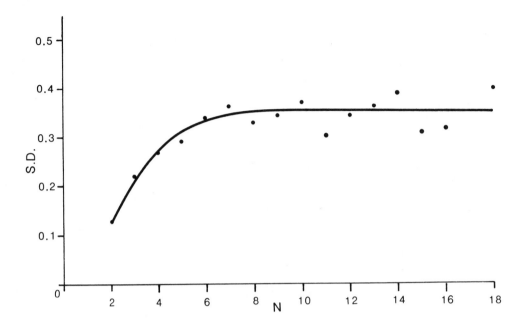

FIGURE 16. The same data as in Fig. 15 plotted as standard deviation (S.D.) versus N, the number of DNA comparisons in a set.

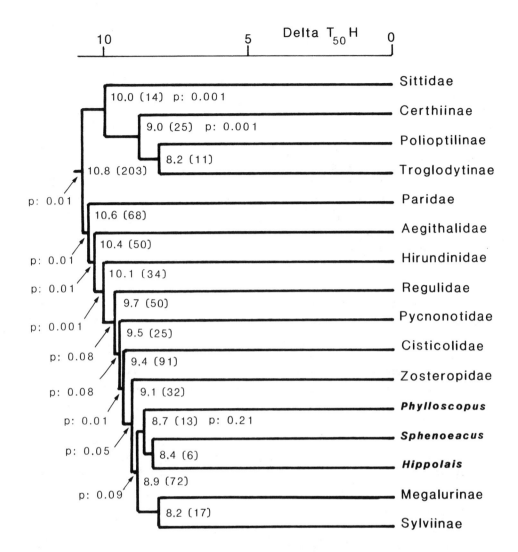

FIGURE 17. Relationships among members of the Sylvioidea determined by average linkage (UPGMA) clustering of DNA-DNA hybridization distances. Student's *t*-tests were used to test the significance of differences between a given node and the one having the next lower average delta $T_{50}H$ value. The probability *p* that the nodes are indistinguishable is given for each.

The data matrices accompanying the FITCH phylograms include a few examples of large reciprocal differences between cells involving a number of replicates. These examples of non-reciprocity are noted and commented on where they occur; they may influence tree construction. We do not know the reason for their occurrence, but experimental error is the probable culprit.

The magnitude of reciprocal differences usually can be controlled by a combination of careful preparation of single-copy DNA, sonication to produce fragments of uniform average length, and control of the conditions of thermal elution. The minimum average reciprocal difference that can be achieved between cells of a matrix seems to be ca. 0.2.

Data on DNA-DNA hybridization comparisons between various groups of birds are presented in Tables 13–15. Table 13 compares NPH, Δ mode, ΔT_m, and $\Delta T_{50}H$ for hybrids between a labeled Cape Weaver (*Ploceus capensis*) and five members each of starlings, corvines, furnariids, and kingfishers. For these same groups, respectively, the range in $\Delta T_{50}H$ is 0.9, 0.5, 0.7, and 1.8; thus a slight rise in range with a large increase in delta values is seen. Note also that for the comparisons to the kingfishers there is a range of only 2.9 in NPH.

Table 14 presents comparisons of hybrids between a labeled Yellow-rumped Thornbill (*Acanthiza chrysorrhoa*) and increasing numbers of species in different out-groups. Data are given from comparisons to 10 replicates of the same driver of the Red Wattlebird (*Anthochaera carunculata*), nine genera of honeyeaters (Meliphagidae), and 19 genera of oscine passerines. It is apparent that increasing the number of taxa compared increases the range and standard deviation of the $\Delta T_{50}H$ values. This is caused by variation in the preparation of samples and possibly by differences in each of the branch lengths in the case of the comparisons to the oscines.

It is apparent that the standard deviation (SD) and standard error of the mean rise slightly with an increase in the number of comparisons and with increasing $\Delta T_{50}H$ from the tracer species, but they do not rise rapidly. In fact, Figure 15 demonstrates that SD rises only slightly with $\Delta T_{50}H$ even for high delta values. Figure 16 shows that SD levels off at ca. 0.35 after the number of comparisons reaches five.

The data indicate that there is a lower limit to the error that is due to passing DNA duplexes over hydroxyapatite. The standard error of the mean, however, will continue to decrease with increasing N, so that it may be possible to separate nodes differing by only 0.1–0.2°C. That this can be done is shown in the phylogram of the various groups of the Sylvioidea (Fig. 17). The statistics at each node may be criticized as inappropriate, but essentially the same tree is derived from the FITCH algorithm. Thus, the trees are consistent under different forms of analysis and reasonable when considered in light of what we know about the groups of organisms that they depict. We view this as a trivial matter because it would make no difference in the classification based on these data if the series of closely stepped branches from $\Delta T_{50}H$ 8.9 to 10.6 were collapsed into a polychotomy at the average $\Delta T_{50}H$ of 9.7. The same groups would still be recognized as families under our system of defining categories.

CHAPTER TWELVE

Tempo of Evolution

How fast, as a matter of fact, do animals evolve in nature? That is the
fundamental observational problem of tempo in evolution. It is the first question
that the geneticist asks the paleontologist.

Simpson 1944:3

Change over time is inherent in the concept of organic evolution, hence the existence of a
rate, or rates, of evolution is a fundamental question. To Simpson (1944:xvii) the tempo of
evolution "has to do with evolutionary rates under natural conditions, the measurement and
interpretation of rates, their acceleration and deceleration, the conditions of exceptionally slow
or rapid evolution, and phenomena suggestive of inertia and momentum."

Simpson viewed evolution as proceeding at many different rates in different characters
of different organisms at different times, and the evidence of our eyes when we examine
morphological traits supports that view. Simpson proposed a "synthesis of paleontology and
genetics" which led him to define "Rate of evolution . . . as amount of genetic change
per . . . unit of absolute time" (1944:3). This definition is still valid, but for Simpson in 1944
it was "unusable in practice. Direct study of genetic change is impossible to the paleontologist.
It is, so far, possible only to a limited extent among living animals and those usually do not
change sufficiently in the time available to yield a reliable measure of rate. Even rough
estimation has some usefulness, but absolute time cannot yet be accurately measured for
paleontological materials, and it is desirable to examine relative as well as absolute time."

In the absence of methods to measure the rate of genetic change over long time spans,
Simpson provided a practical definition of "rate of evolution . . . as amount of morphological
change relative to a standard. It is assumed that phenotypic evolution implies genetic change
and that rates of evolution as here defined are similar to, although not identical with, rates of
genetic modification."

This definition has been widely accepted by evolutionary biologists, but only rarely is it
true. There is, of course, a relationship between genotype and phenotype, but the perceived
rate of morphological evolution is not highly correlated with the rate of genetic evolution (e.g.,
A. C. Wilson et al. 1977:616, Maxson 1984).

The Evolution of Proteins and the Molecular Evolutionary Clock

Techniques to determine the amino acid sequences of protein molecules were developed in the
1950s and by the early 1960s the sequences of the hemoglobins, cytochromes *c*, and other
proteins were known from several species. When Zuckerkandl and Pauling (1962, 1965), and
Margoliash (1963), compared the sequences of proteins from different species they noted that

the number of amino acid replacements was correlated with the absolute length of time since the different lineages had diverged from one another. They proposed that proteins evolve at constant rates and therefore might be used as a "molecular evolutionary clock" to date the divergence nodes in phylogenies reconstructed from protein sequences. A decade later, Zuckerkandl (1976:435) described the protein clock: "If we pool all changes in proteins that were accepted by evolution . . . we seem to witness that they conform roughly to the prediction of the existence of an approximate evolutionary clock."

This cautious definition, lacking any claim to precision for the protein clock, was prompted by the hostile reception accorded the idea when it was first proposed. To many biologists it seemed unreasonable that molecules should display regularity when it was obvious that morphological evolution was irregular and it was clear that the genotype determined the phenotype. However, as Zuckerkandl (1976:435) pointed out, "it was expected from the start . . . that the molecular clock should be, at best, only approximate. The question is: how approximate?" Fitch (1976) calculated the variation in the rates of seven proteins from 17 mammals as approximately twice that of radioactive decay. He described the protein clock as "erratic" and "sloppy," but if "averaged over enough events the variability tends to be washed out" (p. 175).

The next question is: how many proteins must be averaged to wash out the variability, i.e., to produce the same stable average for all sets of comparisons?

Each protein evolves at its own rate, and the rates for different proteins vary over several hundred-fold from the slowly evolving histones, H4 and H3, to the rapidly changing immunoglobulins, snake venom toxins, and fibrinopeptides (A. C. Wilson et al. 1977:610; Doolittle 1979:30). To obtain a stable average rate it would be necessary to compare the sequences of a considerable number of proteins whose individual rates reflect the frequency distribution of rates of the entire genome. This would involve an immense amount of work because the average protein of 300–400 amino acids is coded for by ca. 1000 bases, which is less than one-millionth of the nuclear DNA content of most eukaryotes.

Some data seem to support the existence of reasonably accurate protein clocks (e.g., Sarich and Wilson 1967a,b; Dickerson 1971; Wilson et al. 1977), but other studies do not. Romero-Herrera et al. (1979:767) reviewed the "thirteen year history of assessing evolution by amino acid analysis" and concluded that molecular clocks based on proteins are unreliable for estimating divergence dates. Similarly, Baba et al. (1982:24) reported that "accurate divergence dates" cannot be generated from amino acid data, and M. Goodman et al. (1982a:376) stated that "Individual proteins proved to be very poor evolutionary clocks because they evolved at markedly non-uniform rates."

Goodman et al. (1982b:167) suggested "that each kind of protein has a history of marked nonuniformity of evolutionary rate during different periods of descent," and Avise and Aquadro (1982) found at least a twenty-fold variation in protein clocks based on electrophoretic data.

Y. M. Lee et al. (1985) compared the amino acid sequences of the enzyme superoxide dismutase in man, horse, cow, *Drosophila melanogaster*, and yeast (*Saccharomyces cerevisiae*). They found that the rate of evolution of this protein is far from constant. The number of amino acid replacements per 100 residues per million years is 30.9 when the three mammals are compared to each other, 10.6 when *Drosophila* is compared to the three mammals, and 5.8 when the yeast enzyme is compared to the four animals. The first value is one of the fastest known for any protein, the second is similar to that of the globins, and the third is similar to the rates of some cytochromes and other slowly evolving proteins. They concluded that "using the primary structure of a single gene or protein to time evolutionary events or to reconstruct phylogenetic relationships is potentially fraught with error."

Thus, proteins are imperfect evolutionary clocks, at least in part because different proteins evolve at different rates and each protein reflects but a minuscule percentage of the total genetic information in the genome.

The Evolution of DNA

The fact that different proteins evolve at many different rates indicates that different genes also evolve at many different rates, and the range in the rates of nucleotide substitution must be at least as great as the range in the rates of amino acid replacement. We may therefore assume that a molecular clock based on the sequence of nucleotides in a single gene, or even in several genes, will suffer from the same problems that afflict protein clocks. As Friday (1981:13) noted, "phylogenetic conclusions derived from a study of nucleotide sequences will be subject to the same suspicions as those derived from amino acid sequences."

The solution is to use a method that compares all, or a large percentage, of the genomes of different taxa and to provide a measure of the average genealogical distance between them, because "a process averaged over a genome may be considerably better than a precise value from a single locus that could be unrepresentative of the genome" (Fitch 1976:163).

The discrepancy between the perceived variable rates of morphological (organismal) evolution and the evidence of more or less steady rates of protein and DNA evolution were surprises to molecular evolutionists who had expected Simpson's definition to be supported by the data of macromolecular evolution. To most traditional biologists the evidence of a constant rate of protein evolution was irrational and many of them rejected the idea as impossible nonsense. Some molecular data produced phylogenetic trees congruent with morphological evidence, but congruence in branching pattern does not require that rates of evolution be uniform or constant.

The Neutral Theory of Molecular Evolution

The controversies and misunderstandings were exacerbated in 1968 when Motoo Kimura proposed his "neutral theory" and argued that it explains the constant rate of molecular evolution. This was followed by the suggestion of King and Jukes (1969) that the neutral theory of Kimura was evidence of non-Darwinian evolution. Here was provocation indeed. Evolution without Darwin seemed to be evolution without natural selection, and that is biological heresy. The controversy intensified.

During the past 20 years the heat has cooled and light has entered the debate, but there remains a legacy of suspicion that there is something heterodox about the very idea of a constant rate of molecular evolution. It is important to understand that Kimura's theory supplements, not replaces, evolution by Darwinian natural selection. In fact, the mechanism that permits the accumulation of selectively neutral mutations must itself be a product of natural selection.

Kimura provided a synopsis (1983a) and a book (1983b) in an

attempt to convince the scientific world that the main cause of evolutionary change at the molecular level—changes in the genetic material itself—is random fixation of selectively neutral or nearly neutral mutants rather than positive Darwinian selection. This thesis, which I here call the neutral theory of molecular evolution, has caused a great deal of controversy since I proposed it in 1968 to explain some then new findings in evolution and variation at the molecular level. The controversy is not surprising, since evolutionary biology has been dominated for more than half a century by the Darwinian view that organisms become progressively adapted to their environments by accumulating beneficial mutants, and evolutionists naturally expected this principle to extend to the molecular level. The neutral theory is not antagonistic to the cherished view that evolution of form and function is guided by Darwinian selection, but it brings out another facet of the evolutionary process by emphasizing the much greater role of mutation pressure and random drift at the molecular level (1983b:ix).

The evidence that caused Kimura to develop his theory came from the stochastic theory of population genetics and from molecular genetics, especially from the large amount of intraspecific genetic variability revealed by electrophoretic comparisons of polymorphic proteins. Kimura supported his arguments with mathematical analyses, and these should be studied to obtain a complete understanding, but the following quotations from his book, and comments about them, may help to dispel the suspicion that there is something heretical about this important theory.

The neutral theory asserts that the great majority of evolutionary changes at the molecular level, as revealed by comparative studies of protein and DNA sequences, are caused not by Darwinian selection but by random drift of selectively neutral or nearly neutral mutants. The theory does not deny the role of natural selection in determining the course of adaptive evolution, but it assumes that only a minute fraction of DNA changes in evolution are adaptive in nature, while the great majority of phenotypically silent molecular substitutions exert no significant influence on survival and reproduction and drift randomly through the species.

The neutral theory also asserts that most of the intraspecific variability at the molecular level, such as is manifested by protein polymorphism, is essentially neutral, so that most polymorphic alleles are maintained in the species by mutational input and random extinction. In other words, the neutral theory regards protein and DNA polymorphisms as a transient phase of molecular evolution and rejects the notion that the majority of such polymorphisms are adaptive and maintained in the species by some form of balancing selection.

The word 'neutral' is not used in a strict, literal sense. The emphasis is not on neutrality *per se*, but on mutation and random drift as the main explanatory factors. The mutant genes that are important in molecular evolution and polymorphism are assumed to be nearly enough neutral for chance to play a major role. As the theory has developed, more attention has been given to selective molecular constraints, selection acting in indirect ways . . . and very weak negative selection acting on genes drifting to fixation. The theory does not, then, assume that selection plays no role; however, it does deny that any appreciable fraction of molecular change is due to positive selection or that molecular polymorphisms are determined by balanced selective forces. . . .

I want the reader to realize that 'neutral theory' is shorthand for 'the theory that at the molecular level evolutionary changes and polymorphisms are mainly due to mutations that are nearly enough neutral with respect to natural selection that their behavior and fate are mainly determined by mutation and random drift'. I also must emphasize that the theory does not deny the occurrence of deleterious mutations. On the contrary, selective constraints imposed by negative selection are a very important part of the neutralist explanation of some important features of molecular evolution (1983b:xi–xii).

Thus, Kimura assumes that few new mutations are immediately positive, that a somewhat larger number are deleterious, and that most are selectively neutral or nearly neutral. The positive ones will penetrate the population rapidly, the deleterious ones will be eliminated, and the neutrals will penetrate the population by random drift and either be lost by drift or become positively selected if changes in the sources of selection so dictate.

An important element in the development of Kimura's theory resulted from the application of electrophoretic methods which "suddenly disclosed, starting in 1966, a wealth of genetic variability showing high incidence of molecular polymorphism at a large fraction of loci in various organisms. According to Lewontin and Hubby (1966), the average per locus heterozygosity is about 12% and the proportion of polymorphism is 30% for 18 randomly chosen loci in *D. pseudoobscura*. A similar result was reported . . . in man. In these organisms, then, there must be thousands of loci where variants are segregating at high frequencies, and each individual may be heterozygous at hundreds or even thousands of loci. However, these polymorphisms were accompanied by no visible phenotypic effects and no obvious correlation with environmental conditions" (1983:27).

The existence of genetic polymorphisms is well established and accepted by all biologists. It is also clear that most polymorphisms are not expressed at the phenetic level. What then, is the function of the "hundreds or even thousands" of silent loci? We suggest that the system that permits the accumulation of neutral mutations came into existence because of the effects of natural selection. It seems likely that most Darwinians would have accepted his theory had Kimura made the point that the incorporation of neutral mutations into the genomes of all organisms provides the genetic variability that makes it possible for lineages to survive when the environment changes. Populations that have incorporated a large array of functionally equivalent alleles containing neutral mutations are likely to include individuals that are pre-adapted by their possession of the appropriate mutant genes to survive a selective bottleneck and those individuals survive the challenge. Thus, individuals are selected and their survival ensures the continuity of their lineage. Lineages that did not evolve this mechanism became extinct. Thus, the suggestion is that natural selection produced the mechanism for storing neutral mutations. The mechanism must have evolved early in the history of life; hence all living organisms are polymorphic. Thus, natural selection produced the system that permits the incorporation of neutral mutations and they are neutral only until they are selected by an environmental change. Few will ever become selectively positive, but the mechanism must allow for that low probability by producing and storing many mutant alleles. It seems inevitable that such a system would evolve. An analogy is that when the mortgage comes due there must be money in the bank to pay it because there is not enough time to go out and earn the money after the lender demands his payment; foreclosure is equivalent to extinction.

One of the important pieces of evidence in favor of the neutral theory is the well-established fact that less than 10% of the DNA in the genomes of living organisms codes for a detectable protein product; the other 90% or more may include the stored variability that is the money in the bank. The word "detectable" is an important element in this idea. Neutral alleles may produce a low level of product—a protein—which would provide the basis for a feedback system that could induce the amplification of such an allele if its product becomes more effective than that of the standard allele. Amplification is known to be induced by environmental challenges, and alleles such as the X and Y genes of ovalbumin are expressed at a much lower rate than is the primary ovalbumin gene (see chapter 3 and "Gene Amplification" in chapter 7).

It also makes sense that neutral mutations should have no phenotypic effect, but should be silent until selected by an environmental change; that they should penetrate a population by random drift unless they become positively selected; and that they should accumulate and be removed by chance. Natural selection cannot predict the future, but it permits organisms to profit from past experience. It cannot predict which mutants will be required for survival in the future, but it can produce a mechanism that increases the probability of survival by selecting lineages possessing the ability to incorporate a high level of genetic variability. In this, the neutral mutation system is like any other adaptation produced by natural selection.

One result of the neutral mutation system is that the rate of accession of neutral mutations determines the rate of molecular evolution, as Kimura (1983b:25) has emphasized: "The picture of evolutionary change that actually emerged from molecular studies . . . seemed to me quite incompatible with the expectations of neo-Darwinism. Among the salient features that were soon disclosed were the approximate uniformity of the rate of amino acid substitutions per year for each protein among diverse lineages, an apparent randomness in the pattern of substitutions, and a very high overall rate amounting to at least one mutant nucleotide substitution per genome every two years when extrapolated to the haploid amount of DNA in mammals."

Kimura (1983b:65–97) considered the rate of evolution at the molecular level: "It had long been a dream of population geneticists to find out at what rate genes are substituted in the species in the course of evolution. Such a rate should characterize the speed of evolution more unambiguously than any other measure of evolutionary rates based on phenotypes." Kimura quoted Simpson's definition that the ideal measurement of rate of evolution would be the genetic rate, and noted that this became feasible with the development of molecular genetics. Kimura reviewed several studies of proteins that demonstrate the principle that the number of amino acid substitutions is relative to time: "As compared with the evolution at the phenotypic level, molecular evolution has the remarkable feature that the rate of evolution is approximately constant (i.e. the same) throughout diverse lineages for a given protein" (p. 76). Kimura's calculations suggested that "the rate of molecular evolution in terms of mutant substitutions is constant per year, and, surprisingly, this does not seem to depend on such factors as generation time, living conditions, and the population size. . . . for selectively neutral mutants, the rate of evolution . . . is equal to the mutation rate per gamete, and it is independent of the population size. Thus the observed constancy can be explained most easily by assuming that the majority of amino acid substitutions is caused by random fixation of selectively neutral mutations, and that the rate of occurrence per gamete of neutral mutations is constant per year" (p. 81).

The idea of "constancy of the evolutionary rate is one of the most controversial subjects in molecular evolution, particularly when this is interpreted in the light of the neutral theory" (Kimura 1983b:82). Following this understatement, Kimura reviewed some of the criticisms based on protein comparisons and rejected them. With reference to nucleotide sequences he noted that "Already, it has become increasingly evident that the preponderance of synonymous and other silent base substitutions is a general but remarkable feature of molecular evolution and this is consistent with the neutral theory" (p. 90). This is followed by the examination of several examples which support Kimura's statement.

Kimura (1983b) defined five principles that distinguish molecular evolution from phenotypic evolution:

(i) For each protein [or gene], the rate of evolution in terms of amino acid [or nucleotide] substitutions is approximately constant per year per site for various lines, as long as the function and tertiary structure of the molecule remain essentially unaltered.

This is the rate-constancy hypothesis which Zuckerkandl and Pauling (1965) called the 'molecular evolutionary clock'. This is one of the most controversial subjects in molecular evolution. . . .

(ii) Functionally less important molecules or parts of molecules evolve (in terms of mutant substitutions) faster than more important ones. . . .

(iii) Those mutant substitutions that are less disruptive to the existing structure and function of a molecule (conservative substitutions) occur more frequently in evolution than more disruptive ones.

These two principles have very important bearings on the neutral theory of molecular evolution. . . . the probability of a mutation not being harmful and therefore selectively neutral is larger if the mutation occurs in a functionally less important molecule or part of a molecule, and thus has a higher chance of being fixed in the population by random genetic drift. This probability is also higher if the mutation is 'conservative', that is, if it has a less drastic effect. One of the most extreme situations is a synonymous substitution which occurs predominantly at the third codon position. . . .

(iv) Gene duplication must always precede the emergence of a gene having a new function.

The crucial point . . . is that the existence of two copies of the same gene enables one of the copies to accumulate mutations and to eventually emerge as a new gene, while the other copy retains the old function required by the species for survival through the transitional period. Shielded by the normal counterpart in the corresponding site of the duplicated DNA segment, mutations that would have been rejected before duplication can now accumulate, and through their accumulation, the stage is set for the emergence of a new gene. . . .

(v) Selective elimination of definitely deleterious mutants and random fixation of selectively neutral or very slightly deleterious mutants occur far more frequently in evolution than positive Darwinian selection of definitely advantageous mutants.

This is an extended form of the original neutral theory . . . which argues that very slightly deleterious mutations as well as selectively neutral mutations play an important role in molecular evolution. Adaptive changes due to positive Darwinian selection no doubt occur at the molecular level (and of course at the phenotypic level), but I believe that definitely advantageous mutant substitutions are a minority when compared with the relatively large number of 'non-Darwinian' type mutant substitutions, that is, random fixations of mutant alleles in the population through the process of random drift of gene frequency. This leads to an important principle for the neutral theory stating that 'the neutral mutants' are not the limit of selectively advantageous mutants but the limit of deleterious mutants when the effect of mutation on fitness becomes indefinitely small. This means that mutational pressure causes evolutionary change whenever the negative-selection barrier is lifted (pp. 98–113).

These principles are supported by examples, discussion, and mathematical analyses. Kimura notes criticisms of, and weaknesses in, the neutral theory, but his confidence in its underlying validity and his command of the field are clear. His last paragraph builds on Darwin's familiar last sentence in the *Origin of Species*, which begins, "There is grandeur in this view of life."

We now know that underneath this remarkable procession of life and indeed, deep down at the level of the genetic material, an enormous amount of evolutionary change has occurred, and is still occurring. What is remarkable, I think, is that the overwhelming majority of such changes are not caused by natural selection but by the random fixation of selectively neutral or nearly neutral mutants. Although such random processes are slow and insignificant for our ephemeral existence, in the span of geological times, they become colossal. In this way, the footprints of time are evident in all the genomes on the earth. This adds still more to the grandeur of our view of biological evolution (1983b:327).

Kimura's neutral theory is logical and it explains several aspects of molecular evolution, but it has not been accepted without question and doubt. J. H. Gillespie (1984a) challenged the neutral theory and proposed a model of molecular evolution by natural selection, the dynamics of which are determined by the nature of the mutational process of DNA. "This is due to the very low nucleotide mutation rate that effectively limits natural selection to those alleles that differ from the currently fixed allele by a single nucleotide. As a consequence . . . evolution should proceed in a series of bursts if natural selection is the main mechanism for the change. A typical burst of evolution is shown to involve about 1.5 to 2.5 allelic substitutions on average."

Gillespie (1984b) further examined the neutral allele theory and proposed a revision in the standard interpretation of the molecular clock. He made a statistical analysis of the amino acid sequences of five proteins (also used by Kimura 1983b) and concluded that "the apparent constancy of the rate of molecular evolution may be an artifact due to the very slow rate of evolution of individual amino acids. A statistical analysis of protein evolution using a stationary point process as the null hypothesis leads to the conclusion that molecular evolution is episodic, with short bursts of rapid evolution followed by long periods of slow evolution." Gillespie suggested that "the structure of DNA will cause evolution to proceed in a series of bursts, even if the changes in the environment proceed in a Poisson fashion."

This critique and alternative proposals pertain to proteins and the protein clocks, but do they also relate to the DNA clock which is the result of averaging over the genome? The answer, from Gillespie (pers. comm. Jan. 1986), was that "the episodic models have little relevance" to the DNA hybridization data because the "averaging property of hybridization" will conceal fluctuations (episodes) in the rates of individual genes.

Another explanation for the relative constancy of the rates of evolution of proteins is the Red Queen hypothesis of Van Valen (1973, 1974). This idea suggests that the complex interactions among organisms produce a relatively constant selection pressure on all species through time and therefore produces a constant rate of protein evolution. The Red Queen's ecological treadmill runs at a relatively constant rate because as one organism in a community incorporates a new mutation its selective relationships to other members of the community change and thus bring a new selective pressure to bear on them. Their responses, in turn, provide new selective pressures, and the selection pressure remains constant through time on all species. J. H. Gillespie (1984a:1127) suggests that "In such an interacting system a relatively minor forcing function, say climatic changes, may keep the system moving while the internal limitations [posed by the mutational structure of DNA] will keep it moving at a relatively constant rate." This mechanism may be important for the portion of the genome under strong selection, but it may have little effect on the non-coding sequences that determine the average rate of genomic evolution.

Hartl et al. (1985) based their support for Kimura's neutral theory on "considerations of general characteristics of metabolic enzymes. Among the class of gene products for which the considerations are valid, the rather surprising conclusion is that long-continued action of

Darwinian natural selection may, itself, result in a situation in which many mutations are selectively neutral or nearly neutral." Their argument is based on the fact that "Many enzymes in intermediary metabolism manifest saturation kinetics in which flux is a concave function of enzyme activity and often of the Michaelis-Menten form. . . . when natural selection favors increased enzyme activity . . . a point of diminishing returns will be attained in which any increase in flux results in a disproportionately small increase in fitness. Enzyme activity ultimately will reach a level at which the favorable effect of an increase in activity is of the order of $1/(4N_e)$ or smaller, where N_e is the effective population number. At this point, many mutations that result in small changes in activity will result in negligible changes in fitness and will be selectively nearly neutral. . . . this process is a mechanism whereby conditions for the occurrence of nearly neutral mutations and gene substitutions can be brought about by the long-continued action of natural selection."

Hartl and Dykhuizen (1985) reviewed the experimental findings of Hartl et al. (1985) and proposed that neutral alleles are the basis for preadaptation: "In a relatively constant environment, such alleles will originate, undergo random genetic drift, and ultimately become fixed or lost, solely as a result of chance because of their latent selection never having had the opportunity to be expressed. However, if the environment changes, then the latent selection of these formerly neutral allesles will be expressed, and the ultimate fate of the alleles will be determined by the action of natural selection."

This is essentially the same explanation as our "money in the bank" idea described above, except that we attribute the existence of the mechanism for storing selectively neutral alleles to the action of natural selection on lineages. Zuckerkandl et al. (1989, below) present another version of this concept.

Stebbins and Hartl (1988) suggested that "polymorphic alleles or new mutations can sometimes possess a latent potential to respond to selection in different environments, although the alleles may be functionally equivalent or disfavored under typical conditions." They proposed that anagenic advances "often come from capitalizing on preexisting latent selection potentials in the presence of novel ecological opportunity."

Dyson (1985:16–17) found Kimura's theory "helpful even though I do not accept it as dogma. In my opinion, Kimura has overstated his case, but his picture of evolution may sometimes be right. . . . In particular, I find it reasonable to suppose that genetic drift was dominant in the very earliest phase of biological evolution, before the mechanisms of heredity had become exact." Dyson described his concept of the rate of evolution during the origin of life and concluded that it was "an isolated event occurring on a rapid time scale. In this hypothetical context, it is consistent to examine the consequences of genetic drift acting alone. Darwinian selection will begin its work after the process of genetic drift has given it something to work on."

Easteal (1988) investigated the "molecular clock hypothesis by comparison of the rates of nucleotide substitution in globin genes of mice, cows and goats, humans, and rabbits, using the relative rate test." He concluded that his result provides "strong support for the neutral theory of molecular evolution and demonstrates that molecular evolutionary rate does not depend on generation time." Easteal noted that his conclusion is "discrepant with the conclusions of most other, recent, similar studies" which have suggested a correlation between the rate of accumulation of neutral mutations and generation time. The rates of single genes or proteins may be relatively independent of generation time, but our data indicate that average genomic rates are correlated with age at maturity.

Wolfe et al. (1989) presented evidence "for significant variation in mutation rate among regions in the mammalian genome" based on comparisons of rates for 14 genes that have been sequenced in both human and Old World monkey genomes. They proposed that the "differences arise because mutation patterns vary with the timing of replication of different chromosomal regions in the germline." Thus, "different mammalian genes do not have the same molecular clock."

As an explanation for the large number of *Alu* sequences and the general problem of the large percentage of non-coding DNA in eukaryotic genomes, Zuckerkandl et al. (1989) proposed that "continued insertion into the genome of functional *Alu* sequences is expected to compensate for the functional eclipse of older sequences attributable to structural adulteration and can be presumed to establish a renewable store of functional sequences [that] could be maintained at almost no selective cost. A strategy of maintaining function in multiple sequence copies with selection limited to a very few master (source) sequences may be resorted to also by other types of DNA sequences that are generated repeatedly during evolution and that are spread over many sectors of the genome."

This proposal is essentially the same as our "money in the bank" hypothesis presented above and both are compatible with the preadaptation hypothesis of Hartl et al. (1985). We emphasize the function of alternate alleles in relation to the survival of lineages that encounter new selective demands during environmental changes, Hartl et al. (1985) provide experimental evidence for preadaptation, and Zuckerkandl et al. (1989) direct attention to the "functional eclipse of older sequences" which would occur as the effectiveness of the protein product of the "master" or "source" gene is reduced by changes in the selective environment. In these hypotheses the switch to a selectively neutral allele already present in the genome increases the probability of survival for the lineage.

We conclude that there is no conflict between Darwinian selection and Kimura's neutral theory of molecular evolution. Natural selection explains the origin of the system that permits the accumulation of neutral mutations, and the polymorphic structure of genomes appears to be required for the long-term survival of lineages in an ever-changing world. Molecular clocks are corollaries of the neutral mutation theory, but their rates may be modified by demographic factors that determine the rate of accession and drift of selectively neutral, or near neutral, alleles. In the following chapter we consider the effects of generation time and age at first breeding on the average rate of genomic evolution.

CHAPTER THIRTEEN

Demographic Factors and Rates of DNA Evolution

Generation Time

The length of a generation is defined as the time required for a population to replace itself, weighted for age-specific contributions. To determine the generation time for a wild species requires a long-term study of marked individuals to obtain the primary demographic parameters of fecundity and mortality, including the age at first breeding, clutch size, survival of offspring and adults, number of broods, population size, and proportions of age classes. A "life table" summarizes the results (e.g., Cody 1971, Ricklefs 1972). Thus, the determination of a generation time is not simple and it is accurately known for few species of birds.

The effect of generation time on the average rate of genomic evolution has been debated since Laird et al. (1969), Kohne (1970) and Kohne et al. (1972) suggested that the generation length influences the rate of accumulation of mutations in DNA, hence the rate of genomic evolution. This suggestion was based on the observation that a correction for different generation times made certain of their data compatible, and they concluded that the rate of molecular evolution appears to be faster in species with short generation times. The evidence came from DNA-DNA hybridization comparisons between the single-copy DNAs of *Rattus* and *Mus*, which were assumed to have diverged about 10 million years ago (MYA) but which gave ΔT_m values ca. 15–20, much greater than expected if the rodents were evolving at the same average rate as primates and other large mammals. When the rat-mouse comparisons were corrected for generation time and compared with the delta values for such taxon pairs as cow-sheep, human-chimpanzee, and human-gibbon DNA hybrids, also corrected for generation time, a reasonably constant rate, expressed as nucleotide substitutions per generation, was obtained.

Laird et al. (1969) used DNA hybridization to compare the rates of genome evolution in several rodents and rabbits with those of artiodactyls (cow, sheep, pig). The divergence time for the *Mus-Rattus* divergence was estimated from fossils as 10 MYA, and the ΔT_m was 15.0. Thus, the rate for the mouse-rat lineages was ca. 1.5 ΔT_m per MY since the most recent common ancestor, or a constant of ΔT_m 1.0 = 0.67 MY. The cow-sheep divergence time was estimated at ca. 50 MYA and the ΔT_m was ca. 5.5, thus the artiodactyl rate is ca. 0.1 ΔT_m per

MY, giving a constant of Δ T$_m$ 1.0 = 9.1 MY. Laird et al. (1969) corrected their data by assuming that rodents have 2–3 generations per year and that artiodactyls have 0.3–0.5 generations per year. These corrections yield a constant of ca. 2.0 for both groups. If this is correct, rodents evolve ca. 14–15 times faster than artiodactyls.

The generation-time hypothesis was also supported by Kohne (1971), Kohne et al. (1972), and Hoyer et al. (1972). These studies used the DNAs of primates and rodents and led to the conclusion that the rate of nucleotide sequence change in primates is 10–20 times lower than in rodents, but when corrected for differences in generation times, the rodent and primate rates are essentially equal.

Kohne et al. (1972) assumed that the human-chimpanzee divergence occurred 15 MYA, human-gibbon 30 MYA, and human–Old World monkeys 45 MYA. The *Mus-Rattus* branch was assumed to have been 10 MYA. Again, when corrected for generation times, the rates for rodents and primates were close to equal. [We now know that the primate divergences were actually closer to 6–7 MYA for human-chimpanzee, 17–22 for human-gibbon, and 25–34 for human-Old World monkeys (Sibley and Ahlquist 1984a, 1987d).]

The divergence times used for some of these calculations are subject to doubt, but an effect of generation time on the rate of DNA evolution was widely accepted. It was opposed by Wilson and Sarich (1969), Sarich (1972), Sarich and Wilson (1973), Sarich and Cronin (1977), Wilson et al. (1977:592–595), Sibley and Ahlquist (1983), and Benveniste (1985).

Kimura (1983b:81, 246–248, 310) discussed the problem and, although favoring rate constancy per year, found reasons to suggest that generation time may have an effect on the rate. He noted: "The problem of rate-constancy in molecular evolution becomes much more complicated if . . . extended to include organisms having widely different generation spans such as *Drosophila*, mouse and man. Whether the rate-constancy rule is applicable to such a case is not absolutely certain, but it is likely that the rule holds approximately. This has been used . . . to criticize the neutral theory as follows: mutational studies suggest that the spontaneous mutation rate per generation, but not per year, appears to be roughly equal among animals whose generation spans are very different, and in view of the theorem $k = v$ for neutral mutations, we should expect, if the neutral theory is valid, that the evolutionary rate is constant per generation rather than per year, contrary to observations" (p. 310).

Although Benveniste (1985) could see no evidence of a generation time effect in certain DNA comparisons among primates, he cautioned that "the key parameter in generation time may be the number of cell replications per year in the germ line instead of gestation lengths. At this level the difference between hominoids and catarrhines [Old World monkeys] may be very small and may account for the apparent 'success' of the DNA hybridization rate tests. The rates of molecular evolution may also not always be constant."

Evidence of a generation-time effect was found by Wu and Li (1985), who compared the nucleotide sequences of eleven homologous genes from *Mus*, *Rattus*, and man with those of one or more other mammals (pig, cow, goat, dog) as reference species in relative rate tests. This procedure eliminated the problem of assumptions about divergence times. They found that the coding regions of the eleven genes from rodents (*Mus*, *Rattus*) evolve significantly faster than those of man and ascribed the difference to the shorter generation time, hence higher mutation rates, of the rodents. "The ratio of the number of nucleotide substitutions in the rodent lineage to that in the human lineage is 2.0 for synonymous substitutions and 1.3 for nonsynonymous substitutions. Rodents also evolve faster in the 5′ and 3′ untranslated regions of five different mRNAs; the ratios are 2.6 and 3.1 respectively." They noted that "This tendency is more consistent with the neutralist view of molecular evolution than with the selectionist view. A simple explanation for the higher rates in rodents is that rodents have shorter generation times and, thus, higher mutation rates" (p. 1741).

Wu and Li (1985:1744) commented:

An immediate question is why the difference in the synonymous rate between rodent and man is only 2-fold, not . . . as their difference in generation time, which is probably 100-fold. There are four possible reasons. First, mutation rate seems to depend more on the number of DNA replications or cell cycles per unit time in the germ line than on the number of generations per unit time. . . . It has been estimated that the number of cell cycles per year is only about 7.5 times higher in mouse than in man [Vogel et al. 1976]. Second, our estimates of the substitution rates refer to the average rates in each of the two lineages since their divergence. Third, there may be replication-independent mutations. . . . Fourth, the effective population size (N_e) in the rodent lineage has probably been larger than that in the human lineage. . . . As synonymous mutations are not completely free of selective constraints . . . an increase in N_e may reduce to some extent the synonymous rate because selection against slightly deleterious mutants is more effective in large populations. . . .

Since our results suggest the generation-time effect to be weak on nonsynonymous substitution, it is easy to explain why many studies based on protein sequence data and immunological data did not show the generation time effect [Wilson et al. 1977] because these studies essentially examined nonsynonymous substitutions. On the other hand, DNA hybridization studies often showed the generation-time effect [Laird et al. 1969, Kohne 1970], for these studies presumably examined the average of the genome, which would contain many weakly constrained regions such as synonymous sites and introns.

Our results raise cautions on the use of the molecular clock in the estimation of divergence time. The generation-time difference between rodent and man has only about a 2-fold effect on the synonymous rate because our study refers to the long-term average along each lineage. Actually, the average generation time of rodents since the time of the mouse-rat divergence is probably much shorter than the average mammalian generation time. Likewise, apes and man may have acquired their long generation times only in the relatively recent past. Therefore, an application of the average mammalian rate to either group may result in substantial over- and under-estimation of species divergence time. Of course, for organisms with similar generation times, synonymous substitution may still serve as a molecular clock. . . .

Although we propose the generation-time effect as a plausible explanation for the higher substitution rates in rodents than in man, we do not rule out other explanations, such as a less accurate DNA replication system and, thus, higher mutation rates in rodents.

Catzeflis et al. (1987) confirmed the observations of Wu and Li (1985), and others, that the rodents are evolving much faster than the hominoid primates and, presumably, than other large mammals with longer generation times. The average rate of DNA evolution in arvicoline (microtine) and murine rodents was calculated as $\Delta T_{50}H\ 1.0 = 0.40\,MY$, thus, ca. 10 times as fast as in most birds and the hominoid primates (Sibley and Ahlquist 1983, 1984a).

Sibley and Ahlquist (1983) compared the single-copy DNAs of long- and short-generation species of procellariid birds using a relative rate test in which a Ringed Plover (*Charadrius hiaticula*) was the reference taxon. The Waved (or Galapagos) Albatross (*Diomedea irrorata*) was considered to be the long-generation species, and three petrels, a shearwater, a prion, and a storm petrel were viewed as short-generation species. The range in $\Delta T_{50}H$ values was 11.7 to 12.0. A similar pattern was obtained when we used a Great Blue Heron (*Ardea herodias*) as the tracer taxon. We concluded that the generation time does not affect the average rate of DNA evolution.

We now know that this conclusion was wrong, and that birds with delayed maturity and long generation times incorporate base substitutions more slowly than species that begin to breed at early ages and have short generation times. The reason for our erroneous conclusion was that there are no significant differences in the ages at first breeding or generation times of the species we compared. The Galapagos (or Waved) Albatross is one of the smaller albatross species and it begins to breed when 4–6 years old (M. P. Harris 1969, 1973). Most smaller species of procellariids also begin to breed at about 4–6 years of age. For example, the Manx Shearwater (*P. puffinus*) first breeds at age 5 and the Sooty Shearwater (*P. griseus*) at about age 6. The Short-tailed Shearwater (*P. tenuirostris*) begins to breed at from 5–8 years of age with a mean at 6 years (various sources, summarized by Lack 1966:261 and 1968:281). Leach's Storm-Petrel (*Oceanodroma leucorhoa*) and the British Storm-Petrel (*Hydrobates pelagicus*) begin to breed at 4–5 years of age (Cramp and Simmons 1977:156), thus they do not differ greatly from other species of procellariids. The diving petrels (*Pelecanoides*) begin to breed at ca. 2 years and are short-lived compared to other procellariids (Croxall and Gaston 1988:1184–1185). Table 16 presents the ages at first breeding for some groups of birds.

We have found that the largest albatrosses, such as the Royal (*Diomedea epomophora*), consistently have shorter branch lengths in relative rate tests than do the smaller procellariids. Similarly, certain other, mostly large, non-passerine birds show the same phenomenon. Because our early studies were mainly with the passerines, most of which begin to breed at one year of age, we became convinced that all birds are evolving at the same average rate—the uniform average rate of some of our previous publications. This seems to be true for most passerines but not for all non-passerines.

We conclude that generation time does have an effect on the average rate of genomic evolution, and that this must be taken into account when calculating divergence times from DNA-DNA hybridization delta values. Fortunately, many of our avian comparisons require no correction because they have been based on the assumption of a uniform average rate for birds with a one-year generation time. For species with delayed maturity and long generation times, a correction must be made.

Age at First Breeding or First Reproduction

There is a fairly high correlation between generation time and the age at first breeding, often called the age at maturity or first reproduction. Ages at first breeding are known for many species of birds. Dr. B. G. Murray, Jr. (pers. comm.) calculated three examples based on long-term field studies, as follows.

The Northern Gannet (*Morus bassanus*) studied by Nelson (1966, 1978), begins to breed at ca. 5 years and has a generation time of 12.8 years; the ratio between these values is 2.6. The Prairie Warbler (*Dendroica discolor*; Nolan 1978) breeds at 1 year of age, has a generation time of 2.8 years, and the ratio therefore is 2.8. Females of the Florida Scrub Jay (*Aphelocoma caerulescens*; Woolfenden and Fitzpatrick 1984) begin to breed at an average age of 2.4 years, have a generation time of 5.8 years, and a ratio of 2.4.

Whether the ratio between age at first breeding and generation time is relatively constant for birds at between 2.0 and 3.0 is uncertain, but several other demographic parameters are also correlated, including longevity and clutch size. Thus, in general, birds that begin to breed at

TABLE 16. Ages at First Breeding in Birds. The ages are in years with averages or highest percentages in parentheses.

Taxon	Age Range (Average)	Reference
Struthio, Ostrich	2–5(3)	Lack 1968
Rhea, Rhea	1–2(2)	Sick 1964c
Casuarius, cassowary	2–3	Crome 1976
Dromaius, Emu	2–3	Davies 1976
Apteryx, kiwis	3–6(4)	Davies 1976
Tinamidae, tinamous, 3 spp.	1	Bump and Bump 1969
Cracidae, guans, etc.	1–2	Lack 1968
Megapodiidae (*Leipoa*)	2–4	Bellchamber 1916, Frith 1962
Phasianidae, pheasants	1	Cramp and Simmons 1980
Anseranas, Magpie Goose	(3)	Kear 1973
Cygnus, swans	2–4(3)	Cramp and Simmons 1977
Anser, *Branta*, geese	2–4(3)	Cramp and Simmons 1977
Anatidae, ducks	1–3(2)	Cramp and Simmons 1977
Turnix, buttonquail	5 mos. (captive)	Lack 1968
	4 mos. (captive)	Rutgers and Norris 1970
Picidae, woodpeckers	1	Cramp 1985
Upupa, hoopoe	1	Cramp 1985
Coracias, roller	1–2	Cramp 1985
Kingfishers	1	Cramp 1985
Meropidae, bee-eaters	1–2	Cramp 1985
Coliidae, mousebirds	1	Lack 1968
Cuculus, cuckoo	1–2	Cramp 1985
Psittacidae, parrots	1–4(2)	Lack 1968
Apus, swift	1–3(2)	Lack 1968
Strigiformes, owls	1–3(2)	Scherzinger 1975
Caprimulgidae, nightjars	1	Cramp 1985
Columbidae, pigeons, doves	1 or less	Cramp 1985
Otididae, bustards	1–4(2–3)	Cramp and Simmons 1980
Gruidae, cranes	3–7(4–5)	Johnsgard 1983
Fulica, coot	1–2	Cramp and Simmons 1980
Gallinula, moorhen	1	Cramp and Simmons 1980
Rallidae, rails	1	Cramp and Simmons 1980
Pterocles, sandgrouse	1	Cramp 1985
Scolopacidae, sandpipers	1–3(2)	Cramp and Simmons 1982
Jacanidae, jacanas	2	Lack 1968
Burhinidae, thickknees	(3)	Cramp and Simmons 1982
Charadriinae, plovers, etc.	1–4(2)	Cramp and Simmons 1982
Haematopus, oystercatchers	3–5(4)	Harris 1967
Stercorarius parasiticus	3–7(4.4)	O'Donald 1983
Stercorarius skua	4–9(7–8)	Cramp and Simmons 1982
Larini, large gulls	3–7(4)	Cramp and Simmons 1982
Larini, small gulls	2–4(3)	Cramp and Simmons 1982
Sternini, terns	2–5(3)	Cramp 1985
Alcinae, auks, puffins		
Fratercula arctica, puffin	3–8+(6.5)	Hudson 1985
Cepphus grylle, guillemot	2–8(5)	Hudson 1985
Alca torda, auk	4–5	Hudson 1985
Uria aalge, murre	4–6	Hudson 1985
Pandion, Osprey	3	Cramp and Simmons 1980
Aquila, eagles	3–5	Cramp and Simmons 1980
Accipitrinae, hawks	1–3(2)	Cramp and Simmons 1980

(*continued*)

TABLE 16. (*Continued*)

Taxon	Age Range (Average)	Reference
Old World vultures		
Aegypius monachus	5–6	Cramp and Simmons 1980
Aegypius tracheliotis	9	Mendelssohn and Leshem 1983
Neophron percnopterus	(5)	Cramp and Simmons 1980
Gypaetus barbatus	5–7	Mendelssohn and Leshem 1983
Haliaeetus albicilla, eagle	5–6	Cramp and Simmons 1980
Haliaeetus vocifer, eagle	5+	Brown 1980
Milvus migrans, kite	2	Cramp and Simmons 1980
Falconidae, falcons, 9 species	1–4(2)	Cramp and Simmons 1980 Cade 1982
Podicipedidae, grebes	1–2(2)	Cramp and Simmons 1977
Sulidae, boobies, gannets	3–5(4)	Nelson 1978
Phalacrocorax, cormorants	3–5(4)	Cramp and Simmons 1977
Ardeidae, herons	1–2	Cramp and Simmons 1977
Phoenicopteridae, flamingos	2–3	Cramp and Simmons 1977
Threskiornithidae, spoonbills	2–3	Allen 1942
Pelecaninae, pelicans	3–6(4)	Cramp and Simmons 1977
Ciconiinae, storks	2–7(4)	Cramp and Simmons 1977
Cathartinae, New World vultures	6–8, probably	
Vultur, Andean Condor	8, captive	Lint 1960
Gymnogyps, California Condor	6, captive	San Francisco Chronicle, Feb. 2, 1990
Fregata, frigatebirds	4	Cramp and Simmons 1977
Spheniscidae, penguins		
Megadyptes antipodes	2(51%), 3(45%)4	Richdale 1957
Eudyptes schlegeli	5–9+	Lack 1968
Pygoscelis adeliae	3–7(4)	Ainsley et al. 1983
Aptenodytes forsteri	4 (captive)	Rutgers and Norris 1970
Gaviidae, loons	2–3	Cramp and Simmons 1977
Procellariidae, tubenoses		
Fulmarus glacialis, fulmar	6–12(9)	Cramp and Simmons 1977
Puffinus puffinus, shearwater	3–8(5–6)	Cramp and Simmons 1977
Puffinus tenuirostris	6	Serventy 1956
Pelecanoides, diving petrels	2	Lack 1968
Hydrobates pelagicus	4–5	Cramp and Simmons 1977
Oceanodroma leucorhoa	4–6(5)	Cramp and Simmons 1977
Diomedea irrorata, albatross	4	Harris 1969, 1973
Diomedea nigripes	5	Lack 1968
Diomedea immutabilis	7	Lack 1968
Diomedea epomophora	8–11	Lack 1968
Diomedea exulans	9–11+	Lack 1968
Passeriformes		
Procnias, bellbirds	3	Snow 1982
Pipridae, manakins	1–2	Lack 1968
Menura, lyrebirds, females 2–3, males 5–7		Lill 1985 and pers. comm.
Bowerbirds, females 1–2 years, males 5–7		A. Lill, pers. comm.
Climacteris, treecreepers	1	R. Noske, pers. comm.
Malurus, fairywrens	1–3	Lack 1968
Corvinella, shrike	5+	Grimes 1980
Corcorax, Australian chough	2	Lack 1968
Corcorax, Australian chough	4	I. Rowley, pers. comm.

(*continued*)

TABLE 16. (*Continued*)

Taxon	Age Range (Average)	Reference
Struthidea, Apostlebird	4	G. Chapman, pers. comm.
Gymnorhina, Australian magpie	2	Lack 1968
Gymnorhina, Australian magpie	4	I. Rowley, pers. comm.
Corvus, rook, crow	2	Lack 1968
Aphelocoma, jay	1–3(2.4)	Woolfenden and Fitzpatrick 1984
Most small passerines	1, some 2	
Estrildine finches	less than 1	Lack 1968

Honeyeaters, fairywrens, monarchs, thornbills, and fantails breed by the end of their first year. Males of communal species may not breed until 2–3 years of age. R. Schodde, pers. comm.

age one year are short-lived, lay more than two eggs per clutch and more than one clutch per year, and have relatively low survival of eggs and young. Conversely, birds that delay first reproduction to four or more years of age tend to lay one or two eggs per clutch, breed only once per year or every other year, have high survival rates, and long lives. Many intermediate conditions are known that vary with latitude, method of feeding, nesting site conditions, and other factors.

In the absence of accurate values for generation times, we will use the average age at first breeding as an index to the relative accession rate of neutral mutations, hence to the relative rates of genomic evolution. In many of the non-passerine melting curves (Figs. 18–185) the evidence of different relative rates may be seen and these are noted in the discussions of the DNA hybridization evidence for each group.

Most of the species with delayed maturity are seabirds or large landbirds, including the tubenoses (procellariids), penguins, storks, New World vultures, large raptors, cranes, and bustards. The heteroduplex melting curves of these taxa tend to be closer to all homoduplex curves than taxa that begin to breed at age one year.

Experimental errors and variation among closely related species complicate the picture, but the trend is clear enough to support the hypothesis. Unfortunately, we did not detect the full extent of the evidence of this phenomenon until the laboratory at Yale was closed down in 1986, thus we lack the ideal combinations of taxa in single experiments.

The following statements summarize our current understanding of the relationship between generation time, as expressed by age at first breeding, and DNA hybridization data.

1. Most species of birds (probably up to 80%) begin to breed at the age of approximately one year. This includes most passerines, many small non-passerines, pigeons, rails, some waterfowl and galliforms. Most of these species probably have similar life tables and other aspects of population demographics which would give them approximately equal generation times, although this has not been determined. That these species have similar rates of genomic change is shown by the roughly equal branch lengths in the FITCH-derived dendrograms when compared to those of groups with widely differing generation times.

2. In most cases of significant branch-length shortening the species have delayed maturity, and the greater the branch-length shortening, the older the average age at first breeding.

This is most apparent in such groups as the tubenoses (procellariids), penguins, storks, New World vultures, large raptors, some shorebirds, bustards, and cranes. In most instances the absolute amount of branch-length shortening is consistent for a group. Table 17 shows that the albatrosses have shortened branch lengths relative to shearwaters by an average of 1.0°C (range 0.8–1.2°C) for a variety of tracers used in out-group comparisons. The values hold for tracers as close to tubenoses as penguins or as distant as a galliform at a Δ T$_{50}$H over 25°C. When other pairs of taxa are examined, similar consistent values are found. The largest branch-length differences we have found between sister taxa are between falcons and accipitrids (ca. 2.4°C) and between swifts and hummingbirds (ca. 2.2°C).

3. In the few cases in which species or groups begin breeding at less than one year of age (e.g., tinamous, estrildine finches, and possibly turnicids) branch lengths are longer than those of their near relatives.

4. Generation times are known for few species of birds and using the age at first breeding as a substitute for generation time is problematical. It also is difficult to assign a meaningful average age at first breeding to many groups because different species within the group may vary in the onset of breeding and the sexes, different individuals, or different populations within a species may vary in the age at which they begin to breed.

5. An important unknown is when delayed maturity began in the history of a lineage. For example, the large white-headed gulls (*Larus* spp.) may have evolved increasingly delayed

TABLE 17. Multiple Relative Rate Tests. The data show consistent variation in the Δ T$_{50}$H values between 14 tracer species and the driver DNAs of several species of albatrosses and shearwaters. The average branch length difference is 1.02 with a standard deviation of 0.15. The numbers in parentheses are replicate comparisons. Reciprocal comparisons have not been made in all cases, but the available data show approximately equal branch length differences.

Tracer	Drivers		Average Difference
	Albatrosses	Shearwaters	
Eudyptula minor, penguin	9.6 (8)	10.7 (13)	1.1
Gavia stellata, loon	8.0 (1)	8.8 (16)	0.8
Fregata magnificens, frigatebird	9.2 (2)	10.1 (7)	0.9
Scopus umbretta, Hamerkop	11.4 (2)	12.6 (2)	1.2
Gorsachius leuconotus, heron	10.1 (6)	11.0 (12)	0.9
Phaethon aethereus, tropicbird	10.8 (3)	12.0 (3)	1.2
Calidris minutilla, sandpiper	13.6 (5)	14.4 (5)	0.8
Dromas ardeola, Crab Plover	12.0	13.0	1.0
Pterocles bicinctus, sandgrouse	13.9	14.8	0.9
Aramus guarauna, Limpkin	10.2 (15)	11.1 (15)	0.9
Psophia crepitans, trumpeter	13.0 (6)	14.1 (6)	1.1
Porphyrio porphyrio, gallinule	17.4	18.6	1.2
Urocolius indicus, mousebird	20.1	21.3	1.2
Francolinus natalensis, francolin	27.0	28.1	1.1

maturity from 2–3 years to more than 4 years only since their probable speciation during the Pleistocene and, therefore, would be expected to show little effect of branch-length shortening compared to other gulls and terns with earlier ages at maturity. In the condors, storks, and cranes which probably have had a long evolutionary history, branch-length shortening due to delayed maturity may be expected to be more obvious. In both examples the expected is found, but this does not prove that the explanation is correct, only plausible.

6. It is possible that other factors may influence the average rate of genomic change among lineages (Britten 1986). For example, the number of divisions in the cell cycle or the efficiency of repair mechanisms may be important, but virtually nothing is known about such factors in birds.

7. Experimental errors of various types can influence the FITCH-derived trees. For example, some genera such as *Pterocles*, *Mionectes*, *Cinclus*, and *Sialia* have branch lengths longer than those of related taxa, but there seems to be nothing unusual about their generation times. This is expected to be more of a problem in those groups where only one or a few species were studied.

8. In our data there is considerable evidence suggesting a link between demographic factors and the average rate of genomic change, but the evidence is sometimes conflicting and always incomplete. For example, some of the sets of melting curves with ratite species as the tracers include representatives of groups with heteroduplex curves closer to the ratites than are those of the galliforms and anseriforms, but the average $\Delta T_{50}H$ distances indicated that the galliforms and anseriforms are closest to the ratites. Is this discrepancy due to experimental errors in the delta values, to different average rates among the taxa, or to something else? This situation seems to occur only when birds with delayed maturity are involved in the comparisons.

9. A search for correlations between life history traits and molecular evidence of evolutionary rates may be productive. There is an extensive literature on life history patterns, and studies such as those of Harvey and Zammuto (1985), Partridge and Harvey (1988), and Saether (1988) provide the demographic information for the development of appropriate experiments.

CHAPTER FOURTEEN

A Chronological Survey of the Classification of Birds

The non-passerine birds are discussed in the following pages. The history of passerine classification is treated under the Order Passeriformes: The Perching Birds.

The large anatomical differences among non-passerine groups have provided the bases for defining a large number of orders and families and for a wide variety of opinions concerning their relationships. The taxonomic literature pertaining to the non-passerines is large, and in this brief review we consider only the work of those systematists who treated the non-passerines more or less completely, or who influenced modern ideas about avian classification. The details of taxonomic proposals are noted in the accounts of orders and families. Additional comments on the classification of the passerines precede the treatment of the order Passeriformes.

The emphasis in this historical review is on the period since the publication of Darwin's *Origin of Species* (1859), but earlier authors who made a lasting impression on avian systematics are included. More complete accounts of these early ornithologists and their work may be found in the introduction to Newton's *A Dictionary of Birds* (1896) and in E. Stresemann's *Die Entwicklung der Ornithologie* (1951), and the English translation (1975) entitled *Ornithology from Aristotle to the Present*. O'Hara (1988) reviewed the diagrammatic classifications of birds published between 1819 and 1901.

The historical roots of systematic ornithology can be found in the writings of Aristotle, Pliny, Turner, and others (Newton 1896:Intro. 2–7), but the classification produced by Francis Willughby (1635–1672) and John Ray (1628–1705) had the most influence on later writers. Newton (1896:Intro. 7) considered their work to be "the foundation of modern Ornithology" and Zimmer (1926:677) called it "the cornerstone of modern systematic ornithology." The importance of the *Ornithologiae* (1676) of Willughby and Ray lies in its coverage of all birds known at the time and their arrangement into a logical, hierarchical classification. The main division was into "Land-fowl" and "Water-fowl," each of which was further subdivided on the basis of other characters. An English translation of the original Latin text was published in 1678.

The binomial system of nomenclature, developed by Carolus Linnaeus (1707–1778), was an important step in the development of systematic biology. In the tenth edition of his *Systema Naturae* (1758) Linnaeus consistently applied the binomial method for the first time, and this edition was later adopted as the basis for the priority of scientific names. To Linnaeus the world was the work of the Lord and classification the representation of the Plan of Creation. His logic was Aristotelian, but the convenience of his hierarchical system of categories, and an unambiguous binomialism, proved so useful that succeeding generations ignored his philosophy and embraced his methods.

For the most part, Linnaeus followed the Willughby-Ray classification of birds and, according to Newton (1896:Intro. 8), "where he departed from his model he seldom improved upon it." The Linnaean classification was based primarily on characters of the bill and feet; thus unrelated birds often were clustered together. For example, the "Ordo Accipitres" included vultures (*Vultur*), diurnal birds of prey (*Falco*), owls (*Strix*), and shrikes (*Lanius*). The classification of birds in the tenth edition (1758) was as follows. The genera and species of Linnaeus are identified by English names or modern genera:

Class Aves
  Order Accipitres: Vultures, Hawks, Owls, Shrikes, *Tyrannus*, Bulbuls, Waxwings
  Order Picae: Parrots, Toucans, Cuckoos, Woodpeckers, Corvines, Rollers, Orioles, Troupials, Grackles, Nuthatches, Bee-eaters, Hummingbirds, Hornbills, Anis, Mynas (*Gracula*), Birds of Paradise, Kingfishers, Todies, Hoopoes, Creepers
  Order Anseres: Ducks, Geese, Auks, Petrels, Albatrosses, Pelicans, Cormorants, Gannets, Tropicbirds, Loons, Grebes, Gulls, Terns, Skimmers
  Order Grallae: Flamingos, Spoonbills, Storks, Herons, Cranes, Ibises, Avocets, Sandpipers, Coots, Gallinules, Rails, Trumpeters, Bustards, Ratites
  Order Gallinae: Peafowl, Turkeys, Guans, Pheasants, Guineafowl, Grouse, Partridges, New World Quail, Old World Quail
  Order Passeres: Pigeons, Larks, Starlings, Dippers, Thrushes, Mockingbirds, Finches, Buntings, Wagtails, Flycatchers, Warblers, Wrens, Kinglets, Titmice, Manakins, Swallows, Swifts, Nightjars

Linnaeus provided a methodology and a format for all systematic biologists, and numerous classifications of birds based on the Linnaean model were proposed during the century between the tenth edition of the *Systema Naturae* (1758) and the *Origin of Species* (1859). The names of Brisson, Illiger, Merrem, Vieillot, Buffon, Latham, Pennant, Lesson, Cuvier, Temminck, L'Herminier, Wagler, Gervais, Brandt, Swainson, Cabanis, Newman, Bonaparte, Fitzinger, and others can be cited, but their classifications were based mainly on characters visible in museum skins, a procedure that was later derided as the "beak-foot-feather" method of avian systematics. Gadow (1893) and Newton (1896) reviewed these early classifications.

The search for a theoretical framework for classification led a few ornithologists of the early nineteenth century to embrace the mystical nonsense of the Quinarians, whose prophet was William S. MacLeay, an entomologist. Nicholas A. Vigors (1785–1840) and William Swainson (1789–1855) were the most prominent ornithologists to adopt and defend the Quinary System, but this excursion into self-delusion was discredited long before Darwin provided a solid basis for systematics. Newton (1896:Intro. 31–35) reviewed the Quinarians and their impact on avian systematics. Swainson (Newton 1896:33) presented the five propositions of the Quinarians:

I. That every natural series of beings, in its progress from a given point, either actually returns, or evinces a tendency to return, again to that point, thereby forming a circle.

II. The primary circular divisions of every group are three actually, or five apparently.

III. The contents of such a circular group are symbolically (or analogically) represented by the contents of all other circles in the animal kingdom.

IV. That these primary divisions of every group are characterized by definite peculiarities of form, structure and economy, which, under diversified modifications, are uniform throughout the animal kingdom, and are therefore to be regarded as the PRIMARY TYPES OF NATURE.

V. That the different ranks or degrees of circular groups exhibited in the animal kingdom are NINE in number, each being involved within the other.

Today it seems amazing that such ideas attracted protagonists, but the Quinarian theory persisted until about 1850 in England, although it had few adherents there and virtually none elsewhere. Newton (1896:34) suggested that the Quinarian System was attractive because "The purely artificial character of the System of Linnaeus and his successors had been perceived, and men were at a loss to find a substitute for it."

O'Hara (1988) discussed the Quinarian Period as extending from 1819 to 1840 and reproduced the diagram of five circles and sets of five groups and subgroups within each circle that represented the affinities among the orders and families of birds. The Quinarians differentiated between "affinity" (homology) and "analogy," although the application of these terms in relation to the five-circle structure of nature included additional dimensions. Strickland (1843) used the kingfishers to illustrate his attack on the Quinarians and to present his own "true method" to represent affinities. He proposed a "scale of degrees of generic affinity" and noted that affinity determines "the place of a species in the natural system," whereas analogy is "in no way involved in the natural system" (O'Hara 1988:2751). O'Hara also discussed the diagrammatic representations of Wallace, Garrod, Mitchell, and Sharpe.

One of the first to investigate new systematic characters in birds was Christian Ludwig Nitzsch (1782–1837), who made extensive studies of pterylography. Nitzsch did not live to complete his *System der Pterylographie* (1840), which was edited and published by C. C. L. Burmeister, who occasionally injected his own interpretations of the pterylographic patterns.

The systematic works of George Robert Gray (1808–1872) strongly influenced nineteenth-century ornithology, and some of his arrangements persist in classifications in use today. Gray took Cuvier's system as the basis for his *List of the Genera of Birds*, first published in 1840 and followed by several editions. *The Genera of Birds* (1844–49) was a three-volume work, and from 1869 to 1871 Gray published the three volumes of the *Hand-List of the Genera and Species of Birds*. Gray's classifications were based primarily on external characters in the beak-foot-feather tradition, but his works had a lasting influence by providing a guide for arranging museum collections and organizing faunal studies.

Spencer Fullerton Baird (1823–1887), the "Nestor of American Ornithologists" (Coues 1884) was the leader in North American ornithology during the mid–1800s. In 1858, with the assistance of John Cassin and George N. Lawrence, Baird published the report on the birds collected during the expeditions to determine "the most practicable and economic route for a railroad from the Mississippi River to the Pacific Ocean." Baird (1858:xiii) noted that "by the insertion of the . . . few species not noticed by the expeditions, this report becomes an exposition of the present state of our knowledge of the birds of North America, north of Mexico." In his Introductory Remarks (pp. 1–2) Baird recorded a brief history of avian systematics and the sources of his classification.

The classification of birds . . . has engaged the attention of a large number of naturalists, although until within a comparatively short time there has not been any very great difference in the systems adopted by the leading writers on general ornithology. The more commonly received basis has been the character of the bill and the shape and general structure of the feet, as expressed in the terms Raptores, Insessores, Scansores, Rasores, Cursores, Grallatores, and Natatores of most authors; the Insessores again divided into Fissirostres, Tenuirostres, Dentirostres, and Conirostres, and, according to some systems, including, also, the Scansores as a subdivision, instead of that group being of higher independent rank.

Within a few years, however, a great change has taken place in the methods of ornithological classification, and most continental authorities have abandoned the old arrangement of the non-rapacious land birds, as based on the shape and character of the bill, and substituted a much more natural system. The principal agents in this reform have been Nitzsch, Andreas Wagner, Sundevall, Keyserling and Blasius, J. Müller, Cabanis, Bonaparte, Reichenbach, Hartlaub, Burmeister, and several other systematic writers, all contributing more or less to the final result. The most important step was the discovery announced by Müller in reference to the presence or absence of certain peculiar vocal muscles, which proved the key-note to an entirely new arrangement. In addition to this there has been latterly taken into account the number of primary quills, (or quills of the first joint of the wing,) whether ten or nine, and if ten whether the first be about as long as the second, about half as long, or very rudimentary; also the character of the feet, whether the toes be three anterior and one posterior, or two anterior and two posterior, (and if so, whether the inner or the outer anterior toe be reversible,) or four more or less anterior. Particular reference is also made to the peculiarities of the scales on the legs, the position of the hind toe in relation to the plane of the others, the extent of feathering on the legs, the amount of webbing between the toes, the number of tail feathers, &c.

In the following report I have followed very closely the outlines given by Cabanis, in the "Ornithologische Notizen," . . . although obliged, in most cases, to construct the characters of many of the subdivisions for myself. In the discussion of the higher groups I have however derived invaluable assistance from the work of Burmeister. I have also made constant use of the diagnoses of Keyserling and Blasius, which are pre-eminent for acuteness and precision.

Baird diagnosed the orders of North American birds on the basis of the position of the hind toe, tarsal scutellation, syringeal structure, characters of bills and feet, and the number of rectrices and remiges. His classification follows:

Order I. Raptores
      Family Vulturidae: Vultures
        Subfamily Cathartinae: American Vultures
      Family Falconidae: Diurnal Birds of Prey (6 subfamilies)
      Family Strigidae: Nocturnal Birds of Prey (5 subfamilies)

Order II. Scansores
      Family Psittacidae: Parrots
      Family Trogonidae: Trogons
      Family Cuculidae: Cuckoos
      Family Picidae: Woodpeckers

Order III. Insessores
    Suborder A. Strisores
      Family Trochilidae: Hummingbirds
      Family Cypselidae: Swifts
      Family Caprimulgidae: Goatsuckers

Suborder B. Clamatores
    Family Alcedinidae: Kingfishers
    Family Prionitidae: Motmots
    Family Colopteridae: Suboscine Passerines
Suborder C. Oscines (See families under Passeriformes)

Order IV. Rasores
  Suborder A. Columbae
    Family Columbidae: Pigeons
  Suborder B. Gallinae
    Family Penelopidae: Guans, Chachalacas, Curassows
    Family Phasianidae: Pheasants, Turkeys
    Family Tetraonidae: Grouse.
    Family Perdicidae: Partridges, New World Quail

Order V. Grallatores
Suborder A. Herodiones
    Family Gruidae: Cranes
    Family Aramidae: Limpkin
    Family Ardeidae: Herons
    Family Tantalidae: Wood Storks, Ibises
    Family Plataleidae: Spoonbills
    Family Phoenicopteridae: Flamingos
  Suborder B. Grallae
   Tribe 1. Limicolae
    Family Charadriidae: Plovers, Surfbird
    Family Haematopodidae: Oystercatchers, Turnstones
    Family Recurvirostridae: Avocets, Stilts
    Family Phalaropidae: Phalaropes
    Family Scolopacidae: Snipe, Sandpipers, Curlews
   Tribe 2. Paludicolae
    Family Rallidae: Rails, Coots, Gallinules

Order VI. Natatores
  Suborder A. Anseres
    Family Anatidae: Swans, Geese, Ducks (6 subfamilies)
  Suborder B. Gaviae
   Tribe 1. Totipalmi
    Family Pelecanidae: Pelicans
    Family Sulidae: Gannets, Boobies
    Family Tachypetidae: Frigatebirds
    Family Phalacrocoracidae: Cormorants
    Family Plotidae: Anhingas
    Family Phaetontidae [sic]: Tropicbirds
   Tribe 2. Longipennes
    Family Procellaridae [sic]: Albatrosses, Shearwaters
    Family Laridae: Gulls, Terns, Jaegers, Skimmers
   Tribe 3. Brachypteri
    Family Colymbidae: Loons and Grebes
      Subfamily Colymbinae: Loons
      Subfamily Podicipinae: Grebes.
    Family Alcidae: Auks, Murres, Puffins

With the publication of Charles Darwin's *Origin of Species* in 1859 systematic biology was provided with a philosophical basis. The impact of natural selection on avian systematics was epitomized by Newton (1896:78–79):

Until about [1860] systematists, almost without exception, may be said to have been wandering with no definite purpose. No doubt they all agreed . . . that they were prosecuting a search for . . . the True System of Nature; but that was nearly the end of their agreement, for in what that True System consisted the opinions of scarcely any two would coincide, unless to own that it was some shadowy idea beyond the present power of mortals to . . . comprehend. The Quinarians, who boldly asserted that they had fathomed the mystery of Creation, had been shewn to be no wiser than other men, if indeed they had not utterly befooled themselves; for their theory at best could give no other explanation of things than that they were because they were. The conception of such a process as has now come to be called by the name of Evolution was certainly not novel; but except to two men the way in which that process was or could be possible had not been revealed. Here there is no need to enter into the details of the history of Evolutionary theories; but the annalist in every branch of Biology must record the eventful First of July 1858, when the now celebrated views of Darwin and Mr. Wallace were first laid before the scientific world, and must also notice the appearance towards the end of the following year of the former's Origin of Species, which has effected one of the greatest revolutions of thought in this or perhaps in any century. The majority of biologists who had schooled themselves on other principles were of course slow to embrace the new doctrine; but their hesitation was only the natural consequence of the caution which their scientific training enjoined. A few there were who felt as though scales had suddenly dropped from their eyes, when greeted by the idea conveyed in the now familiar phrase "Natural Selection"; but even those who had hitherto believed, and still continued to believe, in the sanctity of "Species" at once perceived that their life-long study had undergone a change, that their old position was seriously threatened by a perilous siege, and that to make it good they must find new means of defence. Many bravely maintained their posts, and for them not a word of blame ought to be expressed. Some few pretended, though the contrary was notorious, that they had always been on the side of the new philosophy, so far as they allowed it to be philosophy at all, and for them hardly a word of blame is too severe. Others after due deliberation, as became men who honestly desired the truth and nothing but the truth, yielded wholly or almost wholly to arguments which they gradually found to be irresistible. But, leaving generalities apart, and restricting ourselves to what is here our proper business, there was possibly no branch of Zoology in which so many of the best informed and consequently the most advanced of its workers sooner accepted the principles of Evolution than Ornithology, and of course the effect upon its study was very marked. New spirit was given to it. Ornithologists now felt they had something before them that was really worth investigating. Questions of Affinity, and the details of Geographical Distribution, were endowed with a real interest, in comparison with which any interest that had hitherto been taken was a trifling pastime. Classification assumed a wholly different aspect. It had up to this time been little more than the shuffling of cards, the ingenious arrangement of counters in a pretty pattern. Henceforward it was to be the serious study of the workings of Nature in producing the beings we see around us from beings more or less unlike them, that had existed in bygone ages and had been the parents of a varied and varying offspring—our fellow-creatures of today. Classification for the first time was something more than the expression of a fancy, not that it had not also its imaginative side. Men began to figure to themselves the original type of some well-marked genus or Family of Birds. They could even discern whole groups that now differed strangely in habits and appearance—their discernment aided, may be, by some isolated form which yet retained undeniable traces of a primitive structure. More dimly still visions of what the first Bird may have been like could be reasonably entertained; and, passing even to a higher antiquity, the Reptilian parent whence all Birds have sprung was brought within reach of man's consciousness. But relieved as it may be by reflexions of this kind—dreams some may perhaps still call them—the study of Ornithology has unquestionably become harder and more serious; and a corresponding change in the style of investigation, followed in the works that remain to be considered, will be immediately perceptible.

The pre-Darwinians had lacked a unifying concept, but after 1859 evolution by natural selection provided the stimulus for a rational search for evidence of common ancestry, and the recognition of the phenomenon of convergent evolution made superficial similarities suspect. Homology became the criterion for the validity of characters, and the skeleton, musculature, and other internal structures became the principal sources of genealogical evidence.

Ornithologists were quick to embrace Darwinism, perhaps because one of the most respected among them, Thomas Henry Huxley (1825–1895), was also the most eloquent advocate of Darwin's ideas. Huxley's impact on the classification of birds was enormous. As Gadow (1893:33, transl.) noted: "The serious search for anatomical characters, as a basis for the natural system so often aspired to, began with Huxley." Huxley's famous paper on the avian palate (1867) provided the first of what was to be a series of attempts by his successors to find characters indicative of the relationships among the higher avian categories.

"In 1867 Professor Huxley promulgated his celebrated 'Classification of Birds,' and this has been universally recognized as an epoch-making memoir in the history of Ornithology. . . . no sketch of the classificatory schemes of the Darwinian epoch would be complete without an epitome of Professor Huxley's Classification, the publication of which had immediate and far-reaching results. I have also incorporated the results of his later memoirs" (Sharpe 1891:4).

A synopsis of Huxley's classification, as presented by Sharpe, follows. The vernacular names have been added:

Order I. SAURURAE, Haeckel.
    Genus 1. *Archaeopteryx*

Order II. RATITAE, Merrem.
    1st Group. Genus 1. *Struthio*, Ostrich
    2nd Group. Genus 1. *Rhea*, Rheas
    3rd Group. Genus 1. *Casuarius*, Cassowaries
        Genus 2. *Dromaeus*, Emus
    4th Group. Genus 1. *Dinornis*, Moas
    5th Group. Genus 1. *Apteryx*, Kiwis

Order III. CARINATAE, Merrem.
    Suborder I. DROMAEOGNATHAE
        Family 1. Tinamidae: Tinamous
    Suborder II. SCHIZOGNATHAE
        Group 1. Charadriomorphae
            Family 1. Charadriidae: Plovers, etc.
                2. Scolopacidae: Sandpipers, etc.
        Group 2. Geranomorphae
            Family 1. Gruidae: Cranes, etc.
                Intermediate forms: *Psophia, Rhinochetus*.
            Family 2. Rallidae: Rails, etc.
                Intermediate forms: *Otis, Cariama*.
        Group 3. Cecomorphae
            Family 1. Laridae: Gulls, Terns
                2. Procellariidae: Albatrosses, Shearwaters, Petrels
                3. Colymbidae: Loons, Grebes
                4. Alcidae: Auks, Murres, Puffins
        Group 4. Spheniscomorphae: Penguins

Group 5. Alectoromorphae: Galliformes
Group 6. Turnicomorphae: *Turnix*
Group 7. Pteroclomorphae: Sandgrouse
Group 8. Heteromorphae: *Opisthocomus*. Hoatzin
Group 9. Peristeromorphae: Pigeons, Doves
Suborder III. DESMOGNATHAE
Group 1. Chenomorphae
Family 1. Anatidae: Ducks, Geese, Screamers
Group 2. Amphimorphae: Flamingos
(Genus *Phoenicopterus*)
Group 3. Pelargomorphae
Family 1. Ardeidae: Herons
2. Ciconiidae: Storks
3. Tantalidae: Wood Stork
Group 4. Dysporomorphae: Pelicans, Cormorants, etc.
(*Totipalmes*, Cuv.; *Steganopodes,* Cuv.)
Group 5. Aetomorphae: Hawks, Vultures, Owls
(*Raptores,* Cuv.)
Family 1. Strigidae: Owls
2. Cathartidae: New World Vultures
3. Gypaetidae: Old World Vultures
4. Gypogeranidae: Secretarybird
Group 6. Psittacomorphae: Parrots
Group 7. Coccygomorphae
Family 1. Coliidae: Colies or Mousebirds
2. Musophagidae: Turacos
3. Cuculidae: Cuckoos
4. Bucconidae: Puffbirds
5. Rhamphastidae: Toucans
6. Capitonidae: Barbets
7. Galbulidae: Jacamars
8. Alcedinidae: Kingfishers
9. Bucerotidae: Hornbills
10. Upupidae: Hoopoes
11. Meropidae: Bee-eaters
12. Momotidae. Motmots
13. Coraciidae: Rollers
14. Trogonidae: Trogons
Intermediate Group: Celeomorphae (Picidae) Woodpeckers
Suborder IV. AEGITHOGNATHAE
Group 1. Cypselomorphae
Family 1. Trochilidae: Hummingbirds
2. Cypselidae: Swifts
3. Caprimulgidae: Goatsuckers
Group 2. Coracomorphae: (Passeri). Passerines

Huxley's four "suborders" were based on his four types of the bony palate. See below for a review of the history of the use of palatal structure in avian classification.

From 1870 to 1900 the avian anatomists, primarily in England, Germany, and the United States, were active and productive. Numerous problems were solved and the fallacies of the beak-foot-feather approach were revealed. Collections were growing rapidly, and there was a sense of confidence that morphology held the keys to all the doors that must be opened to gain access to the evidence for the reconstruction of the phylogenies of all groups of organisms.

Carl Jacob Sundevall (1801–1875) was among the first to use myology in avian taxonomy (1851). He questioned Owen's suggestion that the ambiens muscle maintains a sleeping bird on its perch by producing a tension on the flexor muscles when the legs are folded. Sundevall also set off the Passeriformes (in which he included the hoopoes, *Upupa*) because they lack a vinculum between the deep flexor tendons of the toes. The vinculum in the broadbills was discovered by Garrod (1877b).

In spite of his anatomical studies Sundevall's classification (1872) was based primarily on external characters and was already an anachronism when published. As he recorded in the introduction, the 1872 version was "only a new edition, improved and corrected as time has passed on, of the one which I published in 1835" (1872, see 1889:1). Sundevall introduced several complex categorical names that were never adopted by others, although his classification influenced Sclater's (1880) arrangement and Sharpe (1877:2) used it, in part, as the basis for the classification in the *Catalogue of Birds in the British Museum*. The non-passerine groups of Sundevall's classification follow, with English names added:

Agmen I. PSILOPAEDES or GYMNOPAEDES (Hatched naked)
  Order I. Oscines [Passeriformes]
  Order II. Volucres "Picae of Linnaeus, for the most part."
    Series i. Zygodactylae
      Cohort 1. Psittaci (6 fam.): Parrots
      Cohort 2. Pici (6 fam.): Woodpeckers, Piculets, *Jynx*
      Cohort 3. Coccyges (12 fam.): Honeyguides, Barbets, Toucans, Jacamars, Puffbirds,
          Leptosomus, Cuckoos
    Series ii. Anisodactylae
      Cohort 4. Caenomorphae (4 fam.): Kingfishers, Turacos, Rollers
      Cohort 5. Ampligulares (4 fam.): Trogons, Nightjars, Swifts
      Cohort 6. Longilingues or Mellisugae (12 fam.): Hummingbirds
      Cohort 7. Syndactylae (4 fam.): Bee-eaters, Motmots, Hornbills
      Cohort 8. Peristeroideae (3 fam.): Pigeons, Doves

Agmen II. PTILOPAEDES (Most species hatched with thick down)
  Order III. Accipitres
      Cohort 1. Nyctharpages (4 fam.): Owls
      Cohort 2. Hemeroharpages (8 fam.): Hawks, Falcons, etc.
      Cohort 3. Saproharpages (2 fam.): Old World Vultures
      Cohort 4. Necroharpages (2 fam.): New World Vultures, Caracaras, Cariamas
  Order IV. Gallinae
      Cohort 1. Tetraomorphae (2 fam.): Sandgrouse, Grouse
      Cohort 2. Phasianomorphae (6 fam.): Pheasants, Quail, *Turnix*
      Cohort 3. Macronyches (2 fam.): Megapodes
      Cohort 4. Duodecimpennatae (2 fam.): Guans, Curassows
      Cohort 5. Struthioniformes (1 fam.): Tinamous
      Cohort 6. Subgrallatores (2 fam.): Seedsnipe, Sheathbills
  Order V. Grallatores
      Cohort 1. Herodii (1 fam.): Herons
      Cohort 2. Pelargi (4 fam.): Storks, Ibises, Hammerhead, Shoebill
      Cohort 3. Limicolae (2 fam.): Sandpipers, Avocets, Stilts

Cohort 4. Cursores (8 fam.): Plovers, Oystercatchers, Bustards, Thick-knees, Kagu, Plains-
    wanderer, Sunbittern, Cranes, Trumpeters, Jacanas, Rails, Sungrebes, Cariamas
Order VI. Natatores
    Cohort 1. Longipennes (3 fam.): Crab Plover, Terns, Gulls, Skimmers
    Cohort 2. Pygopodes (3 fam.): Auks, Loons, Grebes
    Cohort 3. Totipalmatae (1 fam.): Tropicbirds, Anhingas, Boobies, Cormorants, Frigatebirds,
    Pelicans
    Cohort 4. Tubinares (3 fam.): Tubenoses
    Cohort 5. Impennes (1 fam.): Penguins
    Cohort 6. Lamellirostres (2 fam.): Flamingos, Waterfowl
Order VII. Proceres
    Cohort 1. Proceres Veri (2 fam.): Ratites
    Cohort 2. Subnobiles (1 fam.): Kiwis

Sundevall's classification contained many erroneous associations, including parrots with woodpeckers, owls with hawks, sandgrouse with grouse, *Turnix* with galliforms, tinamous with galliforms, auks with loons and grebes, loons with grebes, and flamingos with waterfowl. As noted above, Sundevall's system was based on his 1835 version and was used by Sharpe (1872) as the basis for part of the classification in the *Catalogue of Birds*. Later authors copied from Sharpe, including Wetmore (1930) and Peters (1931). Thus, the source of some of the erroneous groupings in later arrangements may have been Sundevall's classification, which was based on those of Linnaeus and Cuvier (Sundevall 1872, see 1889:1–2) with modifications derived from the works of Nitzsch (1840), Keyserling and Blasius (1839), J. P. Müller (1845), Lilljeborg (1866), and others. Sundevall (1872, see 1889:8) noted the work of Huxley (1867) on the bony palate, but declined to "adopt Huxley's views in a general system of Ornithology."

William Kitchen Parker (1823–1890) was primarily interested in the structure and development of the avian skeleton. He did not develop complete classifications of birds, but his data were utilized by others and his papers included several oriented toward the relationships of higher categories. Newton (1896:Intro. 79) credited Parker with breaking "entirely fresh ground" in his anatomical studies, but Newton (p. 81) also criticized Parker for his frequent failure to interpret his observations in terms of phylogenetic relationships. Parker's prose was often turgid and elaborate to the point of being unintelligible, but his contributions are substantial once the language has been deciphered.

The contributions of Alfred Newton (1829–1907) were less those of a participant than of an observer and often acerbic critic. His historical critiques (1896:Intro.) provide valuable reviews of the work of his predecessors and contemporaries.

Alfred Henry Garrod (1846–1879) published his first ornithological paper in 1872 at the age of 26 and died of tuberculosis seven years later, aged 33. During this brief period, when he was Prosector to the Zoological Society of London, he published 38 papers on avian anatomy. His well-known work on the muscles of the thigh (1873d, 1874a) was the basis for the "pelvic muscle formula" that he and others used to define and diagnose orders and families of birds. Garrod also studied the nasal bones (1873a), the carotid arteries (1873b), and the deep plantar tendons (1875). In several papers he described the tracheal and syringeal structures in birds (see Forbes 1881d).

Garrod (1874a) based the two major groups in his classification primarily on the condition of the ambiens muscle. His subclass Homalogonatae included birds with an ambiens, the Anomalogonatae those lacking the ambiens. Exceptions had to be made for some storks that lack the ambiens, although most storks have it, and the herons lack it entirely. A synopsis of Garrod's classification follows:

Class AVES
  Subclass HOMALOGONATAE
    Order Galliformes
      Cohort Struthiones
        Family Struthionidae: Ostrich, Rheas
             Casuariidae: Cassowaries
             Apterygidae: Kiwis
             Tinamidae: Tinamous
      Cohort Gallinaceae
        Family Palamedeidae: Screamers
             Gallidae: Pheasants, Grouse, etc.
             Rallidae: Rails, etc.
             Otididae: Bustards
             Musophagidae: Turacos
             Cuculidae: Cuckoos
    Order Anseriformes
      Cohort Anseres
        Family Anatidae: Ducks, Geese, Swans
             Spheniscidae: Penguins
             Colymbidae: Loons
             Podicipidae: Grebes
      Cohort Nasutae
        Family Procellariidae: Albatrosses, Shearwaters
             Fulmaridae: Fulmars, Petrels
    Order Ciconiiformes
      Cohort Pelargi: Storks
      Cohort Cathartidae: New World Vultures
      Cohort Herodiones: Herons
      Cohort Steganopodes
        Family Phaethontidae: Tropicbirds
             Pelecanidae: Pelicans
             Phalacrocoracidae: Cormorants
             Fregatidae: Frigatebirds
      Cohort Accipitres
        Family Falconidae: Falcons, Hawks, Eagles
             Strigidae: Owls
    Order Charadriiformes
      Cohort Columbae
        Family Columbidae: Pigeons, Doves
             Pteroclidae: Sandgrouse
      Cohort Limicolae
        Family Charadriidae: Plovers, etc.
             Gruidae: Cranes
             Laridae: Gulls, Terns
             Alcidae: Auks, Murres, Puffins

Subclass ANOMALOGONATAE
  Order Piciformes
      Family Picariae: Woodpeckers, Toucans, Barbets
          Upupidae: Hoopoes
          Bucerotidae: Hornbills
          Alcedinidae: Kingfishers
  Order Passeriformes
      Family Passeres: Passerines
          Bucconidae (?): Puffbirds
          Trogonidae: Trogons
          Meropidae: Bee-eaters
          Galbulidae: Jacamars
          Caprimulgidae: Goatsuckers
          Steatornithidae: Oilbird
          Coraciidae: Rollers, Motmots, Todies
  Order Cypseliformes
      Family Macrochires: Swifts, Hummingbirds

Garrod's successor as Prosector to the Zoological Society of London was William Alexander Forbes (1855–1883), who died at 28 while on an expedition in Nigeria. Forbes was also prolific during his short life, producing several important papers on avian anatomy and classification.

Philip Lutley Sclater (1829–1913) was the author of 582 papers on birds, many of which dealt with avian systematics. He published a classification in 1880, based on the works of Huxley, Parker, Garrod, and Sundevall, somewhat modified by his own work.

A synopsis of Sclater's arrangement follows:

Class AVES
  Subclass CARINATAE
    Order PASSERES (See under the Passeriformes)
    Order PICARIAE
      Suborder Pici: Picidae
          Cypseli: Trochilidae, Cypselidae, Caprimulgidae
          Anisodactylae: Coliidae, Alcedinidae, Bucerotidae, Upupidae,
            Irrisoridae (Phoeniculidae), Meropidae, Momotidae, Todidae,
            Coraciidae, Leptosomidae, Podargidae, Steatornithidae
          Heterodactylae: Trogonidae
          Zygodactylae: Galbulidae, Bucconidae, Rhamphastidae, Capi-
            tonidae, Indicatoridae
          Coccyges: Cuculidae, Musophagidae
    Order PSITTACI: Cacatuidae, Stringopidae (Owl Parrot), Psittacidae
    Order STRIGES: Strigidae, Asionidae
    Order ACCIPITRES: Falconidae, Cathartidae, Serpentariidae
    Order STEGANOPODES: Fregatidae, Phaethontidae, Pelecanidae, Phalacrocoracidae,
          Plotidae (Anhingidae)
    Order HERODIONES: Ardeidae, Ciconiidae, Plataleidae
    Order ODONTOGLOSSAE: *Phoenicopterus*
    Order PALAMEDEAE: Palamedeidae (Anhimidae)
    Order ANSERES

Order COLUMBAE:
>> Columbae: Carpophagidae, Columbidae, Gouridae, Didunculidae
>> Didi: Dodo, Solitaire
Order PTEROCLETES: Pteroclidae
Order GALLINAE
>> Peristeropodes: Cracidae, Megapodiidae
>> Alectoropodes: Phasianidae, Tetraonidae
Order OPISTHOCOMI: Opisthocomidae
Order HEMIPODII: Hemipodiidae (Turnicidae)
Order FULICARIAE: Rallidae, Heliornithidae
Order ALECTORIDES: Aramidae, Eurypygidae, Gruidae, Psophiidae, Cariamidae,
>> Otidae
Order LIMICOLAE: Oedicnemidae (Burhinidae), Parridae, (Jacanidae),
>> Charadriidae, Chionididae, Thinocoridae, Scolopacidae
Order GAVIAE: Laridae
Order TUBINARES: Procellariidae
Order PYGOPODES: Colymbidae, Alcidae
Order IMPENNES: Spheniscidae
Order CRYPTURI: Tinamidae
Subclass RATITAE
Order APTERYGES
Order CASUARII
Order STRUTHIONES

Newton (1896:95) introduced his review of Sclater's classification by calling it "a laudable attempt at a general arrangement of Birds, trying to harmonize the views of ornithotomists with those taken by the ornithologists who study only the exterior; but, as he explained, his scheme is really that of Huxley reversed, with some slight modifications mostly consequent on the recent researches of Parker and Garrod, and . . . a few details derived from the author's own extensive knowledge of the Class."

Newton then dissected Sclater's effort in some detail, noting many points of uncertainty, and concluded that "As a whole it is impossible not to speak well of the scheme thus sketched out."

Elliott B. Coues (1842–1899) was one of the most gifted and prolific of American ornithologists of the latter half of the nineteenth century. His elegant prose and notorious personal life set him apart from his contemporaries and provide mostly unattainable goals for his successors. The editions of Coues's *Key to North American Birds* are among the classics of American ornithological literature. Coues was a disciple of Spencer Fullerton Baird, to whom he dedicated the editions of the *Key*. (Coues is pronounced "Cows," not "Coos.")

In *Birds of the Northwest* (1874), Coues presented a classification that shows the effects of the transition between the pre- and post-Darwinian periods. With reference to the classification of birds he wrote:

no leading ornithologists are as yet agreed in detail upon a system of classification; nor is there any probability that such agreement will soon be brought about. That we are, however, gradually approaching this desirable consummation, is shown by the very general acceptance of many groups established of late years upon investigation of structural characters which were long in receiving the attention their importance demanded, as well as in an equally general admission of a certain sequence of these groups. The questions which remain open have less concern with the definition of groups, excepting some of those among *Passeres*, than with their value in the taxonomic scale. It has become evident that certain old "orders" of birds cannot endure in the light of recent discoveries; and that the *Raptores*, which long headed the system, must give way to the more highly-organized Oscines. It is most probable . . . that those remarkable extinct forms, the *Archeopteryx* and *Ichthyornis*, represent one primary group of *Aves* (*Saururae*); that the struthious birds constitute another (*Ratitae*); and that all remaining birds compose a third (*Carinatae*). These divisions may be rated either as subclasses or as orders; to consider them as of only ordinal grade, would probably be to correlate them most nearly with the recognized orders of other classes of Vertebrates. Upon such basis the *Carinatae* are susceptible of division into a large number—some fifteen or more—of groups of approximately equivalent value, to be rated as suborders or super-families (pp. viii-ix).

The classification adopted by Coues (1874) had been used in the first edition of the *Key* in 1872. As noted above, he had reversed the order of groups, placing the Passeres first in the sequence, as follows:

Order Passeres: Perchers
   Suborder Oscines: Singing Birds
   (19 families. See under Passeriformes for details)
   Suborder Clamatores: Non-melodious Passeres
      Family Tyrannidae: American Flycatchers
Order Picariae: Picarian Birds
   Suborder Cypseli: Cypseliform Birds
      Family Caprimulgidae: Goatsuckers
      Family Cypselidae: Swifts
      Family Trochilidae: Hummingbirds
      Family Alcedinidae: Kingfishers
      Family Cuculidae: Cuckoos
      Family Picidae: Woodpeckers
      Family Aridae: Parroquets
Order Raptores: Birds of Prey
      Family Strigidae: Owls
      Family Falconidae: Diurnal Birds of Prey
      Family Cathartidae: American Vultures
Order Columbae: Pigeons &c.
      Family Columbidae: Pigeons
Order Gallinae: Gallinaceous Birds
      Family Meleagrididae: Turkeys
      Family Tetraonidae: The Grouse, &c.
         Subfamily Tetraoninae: Grouse
         Subfamily Odontophorinae: American Partridges
Order Grallatores: Wading Birds
   Suborder Limicolae: Shore Birds
      Family Charadriidae: Plover
         Subfamily Charadriinae: True Plover
      Family Recurvirostridae: Avocets
      Family Phalaropidae: Phalaropes
      Family Scolopacidae: Snipe, &c.
   Suborder Herodiones: Herons and Their Allies
      Family Tantalidae: Ibises, &c.
         Subfamily Tantalinae: Wood Ibises
         Subfamily Ibidinae: True Ibises

    Family Ardeidae: Herons
      Subfamily Ardeinae: True Herons
   Suborder Alectorides: Cranes, Rails, &c.
    Family Gruidae: Cranes
    Family Rallidae: Rails
Order Lamellirostres: Anserine Birds
Family Anatidae: Swan, Geese, and Ducks
   (5 subfamilies, with *Dendrocygna* in the Anserinae (geese)
Order Steganopodes: Totipalmate Birds
    Family Pelecanidae: Pelicans
    Family Phalacrocoracidae: Cormorants
Order Longipennes
    Family Procellaridae [sic]: Albatrosses, Shearwaters, Petrels
    Family Laridae: Gulls, Terns, Jaegers, Skimmers
     (4 subfamilies)
Order Pygopodes: Loons, Grebes, Auks
    Family Colymbidae: Loons
    Family Podicipidae: Grebes
    Family Alcidae: Auks, Murres, Puffins

    This sequence of groups, with the Passeres first, was used in the first edition of the American Ornithologists' Union checklist (1886), but reversed in the second edition (1895) and subsequent editions to the sixth (1983).

    Leonhard Hess Stejneger (1851–1943), later to turn to herpetology, began his career in ornithology in 1882. His classification (1885) was favorably reviewed by Newton (1896:Intro. 98–100) and apparently had some influence on his successors.

    Henry Seebohm (1832–1895) published a classification (1890a) that was dismissed as retrograde by Gadow (1893:55). Newton (1896:Intro. 103), in one of his most sharply worded critiques, accused Seebohm of plagiarism and incompetence: "The author's natural inability to express himself with precision, or to appreciate the value of differences, is everywhere apparent, even when exercising his wonted receptivity of the work of others, and especially of Dr. Stejneger and Prof. Fürbringer." This harsh opinion was tempered by the more charitable obituary by Sclater (1896:160), who described Seebohm as "kind-hearted and liberal . . . and will be greatly missed by a large circle of friends."

    Another prolific osteologist was Robert Wilson Shufeldt (1850–1934), who produced an astonishing array of descriptive papers between 1881 and 1923. Shufeldt seems often to have worked in a rather haphazard fashion, simply describing and comparing what he happened to have before him, but he placed on record an impressive number of observations over the more than forty-year span of his productive life.

    Richard Bowdler Sharpe (1847–1909) was not an anatomist and he made few contributions to the classification of the higher categories. His classification (1891) was based on the work of others and was the target of "much unfavorable criticism" (Allen 1910:128). Sharpe's great contribution was the 27 volumes of the *Catalogue of Birds in the British Museum*, published between 1874 and 1898. Sharpe himself wrote eleven volumes and parts of three others. He edited or assisted with the remainder. The authors and coverage of the volumes containing the non-passerines are as follows:

    Sharpe: Vol. 1, 1874, Falconiformes; Vol. 2, 1875, Strigiformes; Vol. 17, 1892,

Coraciiformes, Coliiformes; Vol. 23, 1894, Gruiformes (part); Vol. 24, 1896, Charadrii; Vol. 26, 1898, Ciconiiformes.

W. R. Ogilvie-Grant: Vol. 17, 1892, Bucerotidae, Trogonidae; Vol. 22, 1893, Galliformes; Vol. 26, 1898, Pelecaniformes, Gaviiformes, Podicipediformes, Alcidae, Sphenisciformes.

Osbert Salvin: Vol. 16, 1892, Upupidae, Phoeniculidae; Vol. 25, 1896, Procellariidae.

T. Salvadori: Vol. 20, 1891, Psittaciformes; Vol. 21, 1893, Columbiformes; Vol. 27, 1895, Anseriformes, Tinamiformes, Struthioniformes (all ratites).

Howard Saunders: Vol. 25, 1896, Laridae.

Ernst Hartert: Vol. 16, 1892, Apodiformes, Caprimulgiformes.

Edward Hargitt: Vol. 18, 1890, Picidae.

P. L. Sclater: Vol. 19, 1891, Ramphastidae, Galbulidae, Bucconidae.

G. E. Shelley: Vol. 19, 1891, Indicatoridae, Capitonidae, Cuculidae, Musophagidae.

The passerines were treated in volumes 3–15.

Peter Chalmers Mitchell (1864–1945) wrote several works on avian anatomy that affected the classification of birds. He published on the condition of the fifth secondary (quintocubitalism), the intestinal tract, the peroneal muscles, and the anatomy of several groups, including the gruiforms and the kingfishers.

Maximilian Fürbringer (1846–1920) is primarily known to ornithologists for his two large volumes on avian anatomy and classification (1888). It is quite possible that Fürbringer's work, in German and far too long for ready digestion, would have had little immediate effect on most English-speaking ornithologists had it not been for the ideal interpreter, the talented and bilingual Hans Gadow (1888). These two anatomists were to have a substantial impact on avian classification during the next century. The widely used classification of Wetmore (1930, 1960) was based mainly on those of Gadow and Fürbringer.

Fürbringer's classification (1888, 2:1565–1567) was republished by Gadow (1893:48–52). Gadow's version follows, somewhat rearranged and with vernacular names added. Fürbringer used five main higher categories: order, suborder, intermediate suborder, gentes (Gens), and family. Following is the arrangement of the extant groups.

Order Struthiornithes
    Suborder Struthioniformes
        Gens Struthiones
            Family Struthionidae: Ostriches
Order Rheornithes
    Suborder Rheiformes
        Gens Rheae
            Family Rheidae: Rheas
Order Hippolectryornithes
    Suborder Casuariiformes
        Gens Casuarii
            Family Dromaeidae: Emus
            Family Casuariidae: Cassowaries
    Suborder Palamedeiformes
        Gens Palamedeae
            Family Palamedeidae: Screamers (Anhimidae)

Order Pelargornithes
  Suborder Anseriformes
    Gens Anseres
      Family Anatidae: Ducks, Geese, Swans
  Suborder Podicipitiformes
    Gens Colymbo-Podicipites
      Family Colymbidae: Loons
      Family Podicipidae: Grebes
  Suborder Ciconiiformes
    Gens Phoenicopteri
      Family Phoenicopteridae: Flamingos
    Gens Pelargo-Herodii
      Family Plataleidae: Ibises, Spoonbills
      Family Ciconiidae: Storks
      Family Scopidae: Hammerhead (*Scopus*)
      Family Ardeidae: Herons, Egrets, etc.
      Family Balaenicipidae: Shoebill (*Balaeniceps*)
    Gens Accipitres
      Family Gypogeranidae: Secretary-bird
      Family Cathartidae: New World vultures
      Family Gypo-Falconidae: Hawks, Vultures, Falcons
    Gens Steganopodes
      Family Phaetontidae [sic]: Tropicbirds
      Family Phalacrocoracidae: Cormorants, Boobies
      Family Pelecanidae: Pelicans
      Family Fregatidae: Frigatebirds
  Int. Suborder Procellariiformes
    Gens Procellariae
      Family Procellariidae: Albatrosses, Petrels, etc.
  Int. Suborder Aptenodytiformes
    Gens Aptenodytes
      Family Aptenodytidae: Penguins
Order Charadriornithes
  Suborder Charadriiformes
    Gens Laro-Limicolae
      Family Charadriidae: Plovers, etc.
      Family Glareolidae: Coursers, Pratincoles
      Family Dromadidae: Crab Plover
      Family Chionididae: Sheathbills
      Family Laridae: Gulls, Terns
      Family Alcidae: Auks, Murres, Puffins
      Family Thinocoridae: Seedsnipe
    Gens Parrae
      Family Parridae: Jacanas
    Gens Otides
      Family Otididae: Bustards
  Int. Suborder Gruiformes
    Gens Eurypygae
      Family Eurypygidae: Sunbittern
      Family Rhinochetidae: Kagu
    Gens Grues
      Family Gruidae: Cranes

      Family Psophiidae: Trumpeters
      Family Cariamidae: Seriemas
    Int. Suborder Ralliformes
      Gens Fulicariae
        Family Heliornithidae: Sungrebes, Finfoots
        Family Rallidae, Rails: Coots
      Gens Hemipodii
        Family Mesitidae, Mesites
        Family Hemipodiidae: *Turnix*, *Pedionomus*
Order Alectorornithes
  Suborder Apterygiformes
    Gens Apteryges
      Family Apterygidae: Kiwis
  Suborder Crypturiformes
    Gens Crypturi
      Family Crypturidae: Tinamous
  Suborder Galliformes
    Gens Galli
      Family Megapodiidae: Megapodes
      Family Cracidae: Guans, Curassows
      Family Gallidae: Pheasants, Grouse, etc.
      Family Opisthocomidae: Hoatzin
Order Coracornithes
  Suborder Coccygiformes
    Gens Coccyges
      Family Musophagidae: Turacos
      Family Cuculidae: Cuckoos
    Gens Galbulae
      Family Bucconidae: Puffbirds
      Family Galbulidae: Jacamars
  Suborder Pico-Passeriformes
    Gens Pico-Passeres (Pici)
      Family Capitonidae: Barbets
      Family Rhamphastidae: Toucans
      Family Indicatoridae: Honeyguides
      Family Picidae: Woodpeckers
    Gens Pico-Passeres (Passeres)
      Family Pseudoscines: Suboscines
      Family Passeridae: Oscines
    Gens Macrochires
      Family Cypselidae: Swifts
      Family Trochilidae: Hummingbirds
    Gens Colii
      Family Coliidae: Colies
    Int. Gens Trogones
      Family Trogonidae: Trogons
  Suborder Halcyoniformes
    Gens Halcyones
      Family Halcyonidae: Halcyonid kingfishers
      Family Alcedinidae: Alcedinid kingfishers
    Gens Bucerotes
      Family Upupidae: Hoopoes

Family Bucerotidae: Hornbills
Gens Meropes
Family Meropidae: Bee-eaters
Int. Gens Todi
Family Momotidae: Motmots
Family Todidae: Todies
Suborder Coraciiformes
Gens Coraciae
Family Coraciidae: Rollers
Family Leptosomidae: Cuckoo-Rollers
Gens Caprimulgi
Family Caprimulgidae: Goatsuckers
Family Steatornithidae: Oilbird
Family Podargidae: Frogmouths
Gens Striges
Family Strigidae: Owls

Hans Friedrich Gadow (1855–1928) was born in Germany and studied anatomy under Haeckel and Gegenbaur. His first paper (1876) was on the intestinal tract of birds, a subject that interested him throughout his life. As a young man Gadow went to England to work with Sharpe on the *Catalogue of Birds*, of which he compiled volumes 8 and 9 on groups of passerines. He became a British citizen, married the daughter of the Professor of Physics at Cambridge, and spent the rest of his life as Curator of the Stricklandian Collections and Lecturer, later Reader, on the morphology of vertebrates at Cambridge University. He was the acknowledged authority on vertebrate anatomy in England.

Gadow (1892:229) introduced his classification by noting that by undertaking the continuation of the Aves part of Bronn's *Klassen und Ordnungen des Thier-Reichs*, he

pledged not only to a descriptive account of the anatomical structure of birds, but also a systematic treatment of this Class with its Orders.

The anatomical portion has been written with the view of abstracting therefrom a classification. In the meantime (after Huxley, Garrod, Forbes, Sclater, and Reichenow's systems) have appeared several other classifications: one each by Prof. Newton, Dr. Elliott Coues, Dr. Stejneger, Prof. Fuerbringer, Dr. R. B. Sharpe, and two or three by Mr. Seebohm. Some of these systems or classifications give no reasoning, and seem to be based upon either experience in ornithological matters or upon inclination—in other words, upon personal convictions. Fuerbringer's volumes of ponderous size have ushered in a new epoch in scientific ornithology. No praise can be high enough for this work, and no blame can be greater than that it is too long and far too cautiously expressed. For instance, the introduction of "intermediate" groups (be they suborders or gentes) cannot be accepted in a system which, if it is to be a working one, must appear in a fixed form. In several important points I do not agree with my friend; moreover, I was naturally anxious to see what my own resources would enable me to find out. This is my apology for the new classification which I propose in the following pages.

Gadow used Fürbringer's data, plus other sources and his own research, to develop a new classification (1892, 1893). Based on "about forty characters from various organic systems" (1892:230) Gadow's system became the principal basis for the classifications of birds in use in this century. Wetmore (1930) based his classification primarily on that of Gadow, and most of the classifications published since 1930 have been based on that of Wetmore, hence indirectly on the Fürbringer-Gadow arrangement. For example, Peters (1931:v) cited Wetmore (1930) as the basis for the classification employed in his *Check-list of Birds of the World*, and Mayr and Amadon (1951) noted that they had departed from Wetmore's arrangement only when changes were "clearly indicated by recent evidence."

Gadow's forty characters, and the method he used to develop his classification, are important for an understanding of the basis for the classifications in use since 1893. Fortunately, Gadow was explicit on both points. His "List of Characters employed in determination of the Affinities of various Groups of Birds" (1892:254–256) follows:

A. Development.
   Condition of young when hatched: whether nidifugous or nidicolous; whether naked or downy, or whether passing through a downy stage.
B. Integument.
   Structure and distribution of the first downs, and where distributed.
   Structure and distribution of the downs in the adult: whether absent, or present on pterylae or on apteria or on both.
   Lateral cervical pterylosis: whether solid or with apteria.
   Dorso-spinal pterylosis: whether solid or with apterium, and whether forked or not.
   Ventral pterylosis: extent of median apterium.
   Aftershaft: whether present, rudimentary, or absent.
   Number of primary remiges.
   Cubital or secondary remiges: whether quinto- or aquinto-cubital.
   Oil-gland: present or absent, nude or tufted.
   Rhamphotheca: whether simple or compound, *i.e.*, consisting of more than two pieces on the upper bill.
C. Skeleton.
   Palate: Schizo-desmognathous. Nares, whether pervious or impervious, *i.e.*, with or without a complete solid naso-ethmoidal septum.
   Basipterygoid processes: whether present, rudimentary, or absent; and their position.
   Temporal fossa: whether deep or shallow.
   Mandible: os angulare, whether truncated or produced; long and straight or recurved.
   Number of cervical vertebrae.
   Haemapophyses of cervical and of thoracic vertebrae: occurrence and shape.
   Spina externa and spina interna sterni: occurrence, size, and shape.
   Posterior margin of the sternum: shape of.
   Position of the basal ends of the coracoids: whether separate, touching, or overlapping.
   Procoracoid process: its size and the mode of its combination with acrocoracoid.
   Furcula: shape; presence or absence of hypocleidium and of interclavicular process.
   Groove on the humerus for the humero-coracoidal ligament: its occurrence and depth.
   Humerus: with or without ectepicondylar process.
   Tibia: with bony or only with ligamentous bridge, near its distal tibio-tarsal end, for the long extensor tendons of the toes; occurrence and position of an intercondylar tubercle, in vicinity of the bridge.
   Hypotarsus: formation with reference to the tendons of the long toe-muscles:—(1) simple, if having only one broad groove; (2) complex, if grooved and perforated; (3) deeply grooved and to what extent, although not perforated.
   Toes: number and position, and connexions.

D. Muscles.

Garrod's symbols of thigh muscles A B X Y,—used, however, in the negative sense.

Formation of the tendons of the m. flexor perforans digitorum: the number of modifications of which is 8 (I.–VIII.) according to the numbering Bronn's *Vögel*, p. 195, and Fuerbringer, p. 1587.

E. Syrinx.

Tracheal, broncho-tracheal, or bronchial. Number and mode of insertion of syringeal muscles.

F. Carotids.

If both right and left present, typical: or whether only left present, and the range of modifications.

G. Digestive organs.

Convolutions of the intestinal canal. Eight types, numbered I.–VIII., according to Bronn's *Vögel*, p. 708, and P.Z.S. 1889, pp. 303–316.

Caeca: whether functional or not.

Tongue: its shape.

Food.—Two principal divisions, *i.e.*, Phytophagous or Zoophagous, with occasional subdivisions such as Herbivorous, Frugivorous, Piscivorous, Insectivorous, etc.

List of Characters Employed occasionally.

Shape of bill.

Pattern of colour.

Number of rectrices; and mode of overlapping of wing-coverts, according to Goodchild (P.Z.S. 1886, pp. 184–203).

Vomer. Pneumatic foramen of humerus.

Supraorbital glands.

Crop.

Penis.

Certain wing-muscles according to Fuerbringer.

Mode of life: Aquatic, Terrestrial, Aerial, Diurnal, Nocturnal, Rapacious, etc.

Mode of nesting: breeding in holes.

Structure of eggs.

Geographical distribution.

It is not practical to undertake an analysis of all of Gadow's 40 characters, but there are six that represent a variety of anatomical systems, namely, palatal structure, pelvic musculature, deep plantar tendons, intestinal convolutions, carotid arteries, and the fifth secondary. Any other selection would serve as well to show the basis for Gadow's (hence Wetmore's) system, and to demonstrate that anatomical characters are subject to convergence and difficult to interpret as evidence for the reconstruction of phylogeny.

The power of tradition is so strong that proposals for changes in the classification of birds have little prospect of acceptance unless accompanied by overwhelming evidence that they represent a closer approach to a "natural" classification. To provide the sense of confidence that is required to surmount the hurdles of tradition and usage it is necessary to present new, convincing data and also to show that the evidence used by Gadow was not beyond question.

1. PALATAL STRUCTURE

Cornay (1847) had proposed a classification based on the palatal bones (Newton 1896:Intro.69–70), but it was Huxley (1867) who convinced ornithologists of their utility for classifying the higher categories. Huxley proposed four palatal types:

1. Dromaeognathous. Vomer broad posteriorly, interposed to prevent articulation of the basisphenoidal rostrum with pterygoids and palatines. The term "palaeognathous" is a synonym of "dromaeognathous."

2. Desmognathous. Vomer small or absent; maxillopalatines meet in mid-line; pterygoids and palatines articulate with the basisphenoidal rostrum.

3. Schizognathous. Vomer sometimes small, but present, usually terminating in a point anteriorly; maxillopalatines variable in size and shape, do not meet in mid-line with each other or with the vomer.

4. Aegithognathous. Vomer broad and truncate anteriorly; maxillopalatines do not join but do touch the basisphenoidal rostrum.

A fifth palatal type was suggested by W. K. Parker (1875b) for some Piciformes. This saurognathous palate has small maxillopalatines, hardly extending inward from the maxillae. Hence the skull is widely schizognathous.

The palatal types became the basis for the suborders in Huxley's classification. Within these groups Huxley arranged the families on finer distinctions of palatal morphology and other characters of the skull.

Newton (1868) moved quickly to counterattack with a critique that is a model of damning with great praise. He pointed out exceptions to Huxley's groupings and objected to the single-character nature of Huxley's classification. Huxley (1868) ably defended himself by showing that he used other than palatal characters and that single characters were often excellent guides to affinity. This skirmish ended in a draw but it was only the first battle in a long war.

Some years later Newton (1896:Intro.82–85) again reviewed Huxley's paper on the palate and again expressed his admiration for the author, but he attributed the acceptance of Huxley's proposals as much to the salesmanship of the author as to the power of his scientific discoveries: "That the palatal structure must be taken into consideration by taxonomers as affording hints of some utility there could no longer be a doubt; but the present writer is inclined to think that the characters drawn thence owe more of their worth to the extraordinary perspicuity with which they were presented by Huxley than to their own intrinsic value, and that if the same power had been employed to elucidate in the same way other parts of the skeleton—say the bones of the sternal apparatus or even of the pelvic girdle—either set could have been made to appear quite as instructive and perhaps more so. Adventitious value would therefore seem to have been acquired by the bones of the palate through the fact that so great a master of the art of exposition selected them as fitting examples upon which to exercise his skill" (pp. 84–85).

Beddard (1898a) reviewed the work of Huxley (1867) and of W. K. Parker (1875a,b) on the palate and added numerous observations from his own studies. He suggested that the desmognathous, schizognathous, and aegithognathous palate types intergrade into one another and that "neither are any of the subdivisions . . . really satisfactory from the classificatory point of view" (p. 140). Beddard found so many exceptions and intermediate conditions in palatal structure that he concluded: "It appears, therefore, undesirable to lay too much stress upon the modifications of the palate . . . as a basis of classification" (p. 150).

Pycraft (1900) proposed that the palate, rather than the sternum, should be the basis for the major subdivisions of birds. Under this arrangement the tinamous would be associated with the ratites as the Palaeognathae, the remaining carinate groups to be the Neognathae. Pycraft (1901:354) concluded that "the differences between the Palaeo- and Neognathine palate are those of degree and not of kind." His discussion and conclusions seem to add little to the general debate, but they further emphasize the lack of sharply definable palatal types and the existence of many intermediate conditions—in short, evidence that the palate, like all other structures, is adapted to the requirements of life in each case.

DeBeer (1937) pointed out that the saurognathous condition is not distinguishable from the schizognathous and that some neognathous forms are paleognathous during embryonic development. McDowell (1948) concluded that the paleognathous and neognathous palatal types are not distinctive, cannot be defined morphologically, and are actually composed of a heterogeneous assemblage of four distinct morphological conditions.

However, both Hofer (1945, 1955) and Simonetta (1960) considered the palaeognathous palate to be morphologically uniform although they were cautious about its taxonomic implications.

E. Stresemann (1951, see 1975:280) was pessimistic about further progress in the reconstruction of avian phylogeny and suggested that "In fact there has been a regression. Some structural similarities in higher groups, which were thought to be useful in reconstructing a genealogical tree, have proved to be convergences, after they had been functionally explained. Thus the types of skull formation, on which in 1867 Thomas Huxley had based his highly regarded ornithological systematics, were in 1947 [1949] shown by Helmut Hofer of Vienna to be due to the kinetics of the skull."

Bellairs and Jenkin (1960) reviewed the literature and pointed out the exceptions and the lack of sharp demarcations between the named palatal conditions, and Bellairs (1964:592) concluded that "while palatal characters may be of value as a guide to the systematics of the smaller groups, they do not in themselves provide a reliable basis for major classifications."

The most recent analysis is that of Bock (1963), who restudied the skulls of the ratites and tinamous and redefined the palaeognathous palate. He contended that this palatal type is real but that the definition is not simple, rather it depends on a complex configuration of several features, as follows: "(a) The vomer is relatively large, and articulates with the premaxillae and maxillo-palatines anteriorly and (except for the ostrich) with the pterygoids posteriorly; (b) the pterygoid prevents the palatine from articulating with the basisphenoid rostrum; (c) the palatine articulates with the pterygoid along a suture; (d) the basitemporal articulation is large, and is found near the posterior end of the pterygoid; (e) the articulation between the pterygoid and the quadrate is complex, and includes part of the orbital process of the quadrate; and (f) the paleognathous palate presents a general configuration similar in all birds possessing it, and sharply distinct from the condition found in all other birds" (p. 50).

Bock (1963) used this evidence to support his argument that the ratites, including the tinamous and kiwis, are monophyletic. The DNA-DNA data (Sibley and Ahlquist 1981a) show that the kiwis are most closely related to the cassowaries and emus and that the tinamous are the sister group of the ratites, thus supporting Bock's argument.

Burton (1984:405) noted that desmognathy "is found throughout the Coraciiformes, but within the Piciformes it is seen only in the Galbuloidea, the Ramphastidae, and, weakly developed, in some Capitonidae. The Ramphastidae, like the Bucerotidae [hornbills], have the anterior part of the palatines fused as well . . . presumably . . . a consequence of the evolution of massive bills in these two families. . . . The desmognathous forms include a large proportion of birds which feed on active, and often large animal prey, and it is possible that desmognathy provides some support against stresses incurred through killing and consuming such prey."

Thus, desmognathy, and perhaps other palatal conditions, may reflect adaptive responses as well as or instead of phylogeny.

2. PELVIC MUSCULATURE

Garrod (1873d, 1874a) proposed a classification based in part on the presence or absence of certain muscles of the thigh. In Garrod's scheme four muscles were designated by letter symbols, and a "pelvic muscle formula" could then be written to designate the presence or absence of these four muscles in any group of birds. The four muscles, their code letter symbols, and some synonyms (in parentheses) used by George and Berger (1966:233) are as follows:

A Femoro-caudal (Piriformis pars caudofemoralis)
B Accessory femoro-caudal (Piriformis pars iliofemoralis)
X Semitendinosus (Flexor cruris lateralis)
Y Accessory semitendinosus

In addition, the presence or absence of the ambiens was indicated by plus or minus signs. Thus a bird with all five of these muscles would be designated ABXY+ (or ABXY Am).

Garrod based his major subdivision of the class on the presence or absence of the ambiens. Those birds possessing it were designated "homalogonatous," those lacking the ambiens "anomalogonatous," and the two subclasses in his classification became the Homalogonatae and the Anomalogonatae. Garrod also believed that characters of pterylography, myology, oil-gland feathering, and caecal development were correlated with the ambiens. Such correlations seemed at first to be convincing (Forbes 1881d), but there were exceptions that had to be explained away. In some cases this led to associations that were disputed by other evidence. For example, the owls and goatsuckers lack the ambiens (anomalogonatous) but have the dorsal pterylosis pattern of the Homalogonatae. Additional difficulties were pointed out by Newton (1896:Intro. 92–93), who concluded that "common sense revolts at the acceptance of any scheme which involves so many manifest incongruities."

Beddard (1898a:95–97) showed that the ambiens is present in some storks and absent in others, but he noted the degrees of development of the ambiens in several groups and concluded that Garrod's two divisions based on the ambiens could be supported. Most of Beddard's argument rested on the work of Mitchell (1894), who described the relationships between the ambiens and the flexors of the leg. In some otherwise homalogonatous birds (e.g., *Nycticorax*) which lack an obvious ambiens, Mitchell found what he considered to be the rudiment of the ambiens, while in the unquestionably anomalogonatous genus *Corvus* no such rudiment could be located.

Gadow (1892, 1893) used Garrod's formula, but it is clear from his discussions (1891b:208; 1893:37) that he considered the formula to be of limited value. In his list of characters (1892:255) Gadow included Garrod's pelvic muscle symbols but noted that they were "used, however, in the negative sense." By this he seems to have meant that he used the muscle formula to distinguish between groups rather than to indicate affinities.

Hudson (1937:59–63) proposed that Garrod's formula be expanded by the addition of two muscles and a vinculum, as follows:

C M. ilio-trochantericus medius
D M. glutaeus medius et minimus
V Vinculum connecting the tendon of the flexor perforatus digiti III with that of the flexor perforans et perforatus digiti III

Hudson noted that in spite of the problems associated with using the myological formulae to indicate relationships they "can at least serve as aids in characterizing the higher groups of birds" (p. 62). Although Hudson considered the muscle formulae to be of limited value, he noted that an examination of the entire pelvic musculature could be informative. For example, the Fregatidae and Falconiformes have identical formulae using Hudson's expanded version of Garrod's formula, but these two groups show "radical disagreement" when the entire musculature of the pelvic limb is considered. On the other hand, the similar formulae of the Piciformes and Passeriformes are supported by the similarity in all the other pelvic muscles as well.

Berger (1959) proposed the addition of three more muscles to the Garrod-Hudson set of eight items. These were as follows:

E Iliacus
F Plantaris
G Popliteus

J. George and Berger (1966:233) reviewed the history of the pelvic muscle formulae and presented a table (pp. 234–236) of formulae for most groups of birds. They concluded: "It is obvious that a leg-muscle formula tells nothing about the relative development or peculiarities of structure of the muscles, nor does it reveal anything about the approximately 36 other muscles of the pelvic limb. For understanding functional anatomy as well as phylogenetic relations, a knowledge of the complete myology is essential (see the discussion in Newton and Gadow, 1893: pp. 603–604). It is obvious, as well, that myological data must be used in conjunction with other information, both anatomical and biological, in order to ascertain phylogenetic relationships. Muscle formulas may yet prove useful in technical diagnoses of families or other taxonomic categories, but how useful remains to be determined" (p. 236).

The complete set of letter abbreviations, standardized names (Baumel 1979), and synonyms is given in Table 18.

TABLE 18. The Pelvic Formula Muscles of Birds. From Baumel 1979 and Kurochkin 1968.

Letter Symbol	Standard Name	Synonyms
A	Caudofemoralis	Femoro-caudal; Piriformis, pars caudofemoralis
B	Iliofemoralis	Accessory femoro-caudal; Piriformis, pars iliofemoralis
C	Iliotrochantericus medius	Ilio-trochantericus
D	Iliofemoralis externus	Gluteus medius et maximus
E	Iliofemoralis internus	Iliacus
F	Plantaris	Plantaris
G	Popliteus	Popliteus
M	Fibularis [Peroneus] longus	(None)
N	Fibularis [Peroneus] brevis	(None)
X	Flexor cruris lateralis, pars pelvica	Semitendinosus; Flexor crurus lateralis
Y	Flexor cruris lateralis, pars accessoria	Accessory semitendinosus
Am	Ambiens	Ambiens
V	Vinculum tendinum flexorum (muscles same as opposite)	Vinculum connecting tendon of M. flexor perforatus digiti III to that of M. flexor perforans et digiti III

3. THE DEEP PLANTAR, OR DEEP FLEXOR, TENDONS

Sundevall (1835) was the first to utilize "the properties of the hind toe and of the wing-coverts, which are characteristic of the true Passeres" (1872, see 1889:4). He discovered that in the passerines and *Upupa* "the tendon of the *flexor longus hallucis* muscle is quite independent of that of the *flexor perforans digitorum*; whilst in other birds the former joins the latter, so preventing the two from being quite independent in their action" (Garrod 1875:340). The later discovery of a vinculum between the two tendons in the Eurylaimidae (Garrod 1877b) some-what modified this definition, but the disposition of the deep plantar tendons became an important character in classification when Garrod (1875) extended his observations to other groups of birds. He described the arrangement of these tendons in many species and found a vinculum between them in all except the passerines, *Upupa*, *Botaurus stellaris*, and *Ardea cinerea*.

Of particular interest was Garrod's discovery of two different arrangements of the deep plantar tendons in birds with zygodactyl feet. Furthermore, the two plantar tendon types were correlated with the presence or absence of the ambiens muscle, which was the basis for Garrod's two suborders. One can imagine Garrod's delight in finding these correlations, which led him to conclude that "these new observations are therefore strongly in favour of the naturalness of the classification proposed" (1875:347). Garrod had discovered that the parrots, cuckoos, and turacos have the ambiens (Homalogonatae) and also agree in the arrangement of their deep flexors, and that the anomalogonatous Picidae, Ramphastidae, Capitonidae, Bucconidae, and Galbulidae possess a different deep flexor pattern. Although Garrod's confidence in his two groups based on the ambiens was not shared by his successors, the groupings based on the deep plantar tendons have persisted in classifications to the present.

Gadow and Selenka (1891:195) described seven patterns of insertion of the deep plantar tendons and Gadow (1894:615–618) listed eight major types with several variants for a total of 15 patterns, and he also found a vinculum in *Upupa*.

Beddard (1898a:178, footnote) noted that the plantar vinculum is occasionally absent in the Green Broadbill (*Calyptomena viridis*), and Pycraft (1905b) considered the deep plantar tendons to be of doubtful taxonomic value in the classification of the broadbills.

Mitchell (1901c) examined the deep plantar tendons in 17 species of kingfishers and found 10 different variants. (See Coraciiformes in Accounts of the Groups for additional comments on this subject.)

W. DeW. Miller (1919) confirmed the findings of Garrod on the deep plantar tendons in the jacamars and puffbirds. Miller dissected additional species of several piciform families and found all to be "antiopelmous" (Gadow's Type VI) as Garrod had claimed. Miller also affirmed his belief in close relationships among the families possessing "antiopelmous, zygodactyle feet," noting: "As this character is not neutralized or overbalanced by any of equal or greater value we may regard these families as forming a natural group, an order or suborder" (p. 286).

The most recent review of the conditions of the deep plantar tendons is that of J. George and Berger (1966:447–449), who updated and annotated Gadow's eight major patterns as follows:

Type I. The flexor hallucis longus tendon inserts on the hallux; the flexor digitorum longus trifurcates, sending branches to digits II, III, and IV. The vinculum passes downward from the hallucis tendon and fuses with the flexor digitorum tendon; hence, the flexor hallucis longus muscle aids in flexing all of the toes. This pattern is found in many birds: for example, *Columba*, Ardeidae, Ciconiidae, Galliformes, many Gruiformes, Charadriiformes, Psittacidae, Musophagidae, Cuculidae, and Eurylaimidae. Hudson *et al.* (1959) reported considerable variation in the development of the vinculum among genera of galliform birds.

Type II. This type is like Type 1 except that most of the flexor hallucis longus tendon becomes the vinculum and fuses with the tendon of M. flexor digitorum longus. Only a small part of the hallucis tendon continues distad to insert on the hallux. This pattern is found in the Spheniscidae, *Apteryx*, Tinamidae, Pelecaniformes, Anhimidae, Anatidae (Gadow).

Type III. The two deep plantar tendons are "more or less fused throughout the greater extent" of the tarsometatarsus but the vinculum passes from the distal portion of the hallucis tendon to the branch of flexor digitorum longus which goes to digit II only. This pattern is found in *Sagittarius*, the Accipitridae, *Falco*, and *Polihierax* (Hudson 1948; Berger 1956).

Type IV. The entire tendon of M. flexor hallucis longus fuses with the tendon of M. flexor digitorum longus. The combined tendon trifurcates and sends branches to digits II, III, and IV; no branch is sent to the hallux. This pattern is found in tridactyl birds and those in which the hallux is small: for example, *Rhea*, *Casuarius*, *Dromaius*, *Gavia*, *Podiceps*, Procellariidae, *Phoenicopterus*, some Anhimidae, *Turnix*, and *Pterocles* (mostly after Gadow).

Type V. The entire tendon of M. flexor hallucis longus fuses with the tendon of M. flexor digitorum longus. The common tendon then gives rise to four branches, which supply all four toes (e.g., *Fregata*, Cathartidae, *Pandion*, *Chordeiles*, *Chaetura*, *Apus*, *Colius*, *Buceros*, *Aceros*). Neither Fisher (1946) nor Hudson (1948) found the elaborate branching to the toes in the Cathartidae described by Gadow. In *Coracias abyssinica* the tendon of flexor hallucis fuses with the lateral margin of the tendon of flexor digitorum in the distal fourth of the tarsometatarsus. The combined tendon then sends branches to all four toes, but there is no crossover of the tendons visible grossly; the tendon of M. flexor hallucis longus contributes to that part of the combined tendon that supplies digit IV and the hallux. An "exaggerated conditon" of this type is found in todies, motmots, bee-eaters, and some kingfishers, in which the tendon to the hallux arises a short distance superior to the fusion of the two deep plantar tendons (Gadow). Hudson (1937) describes a similar pattern in *Chen [Anser]* and *Mergus*.

Gadow described a third modification in the Trochilidae, in which the tendon of flexor hallucis longus supplies digits I and IV and the tendon of the flexor digitorum longus supplies digits II and III.

An apparently previously unrecorded pattern is found in *Chloroceryle americana*. The tendon of M. flexor digitorum longus supplies all four digits; the tendon bifurcates just inferior to the hypotarsus. The medial branch supplies the hallux; the larger lateral branch trifurcates at the level of metatarsal I and supplies digits II, III, and IV. M. flexor hallucis longus *does not send a branch to the hallux*. The tendon bifurcates and sends branches, which join similar branches of the digitorum tendon, to digits III and IV only.

Type VI. The tendon of M. flexor digitorum longus is reinforced by a vinculum and inserts on digit III only. The tendon of M. flexor hallucis longus sends a vinculum to the digitorum tendon and also sends branches to insert on the hallux and on digits II and IV. By means of the vinculum, therefore, the hallucis tendon acts on all four toes. This pattern is found in the Piciformes (Galbulidae, Bucconidae, Capitonidae, Indicatoridae, Ramphastidae, Picidae, Jyngidae). Berger found this configuration of tendons in *Indicator variegatus*.

Type VII. The deep plantar tendons are independent throughout; a vinculum is absent. The flexor hallucis tendon inserts on the hallux only. The flexor digitorum trifurcates and inserts on digits II, III, and IV. This pattern is characteristic of the Passeriformes (except the Eurylaimidae and *Philepitta*). Berger found this pattern in the cotinga, *Procnias mocino [nudicollis]*.

The questions are: (1) How consistent are these patterns of the deep plantar tendons within groups? (2) Are the deep plantars, as W. DeW. Miller (1919) claimed, indicative of natural groups?

At least two facts should be considered in evaluating the deep plantar tendon patterns. First, Gadow (1894: 618) noted that Types I, II, III, IV, and VII "are closely allied to each other; I. and IV. to be derived from II. and VII. from I., while III. is a comparatively primary condition; V,a shows a primitive stage, whence are developed in diverging directions V,b, V,c, V,d, VI. and VII. Any derivation of VI. from VIII. or *vice versa* is impossible; and the same applies to V,c and VI." Second, Mitchell (1901c) found an enormous amount of variation among the kingfishers.

The possible derivations noted by Gadow indicate that the condition in the Piciformes (Type VI) could have been derived from the pattern found in the Coraciiformes (Type Va,b), and the variation found in the kingfishers suggests that there is nothing highly restrictive about the adaptive potential of the deep flexor tendon patterns. Instead of viewing these patterns as diagnostic of the Piciformes, which is possibly an exercise in circular reasoning, it is at least equally valid to view them as merely another variable adaptive character that responds readily to the demands of natural selection. So viewed, it is possible to see the Type VI tendons of the jacamars and puffbirds as another variant of the many kingfisher patterns rather than as proof that the Galbulae are piciform. Also consistent with this view is the range of taxa that share little more than Type I, Type II, Type IV, or Type V patterns as noted above.

4. CONVOLUTIONS OF THE INTESTINAL TRACT

Several earlier workers published observations on the intestinal tract in birds (Beddard 1911:48), but it was Gadow (1879, 1889) who first developed a scheme for using the convolutional pattern of the small intestine as a taxonomic character. Gadow (1889) examined more than 300 species representing "nearly every principal family" (p. 304) and presented a set of diagrams illustrating the principal patterns. Two main types, orthocoelous and cyclocoelous, were identified. Of the orthocoelus condition Gadow noted four main variants and two additional subvariants. Brief descriptions of these coiling patterns follow.

A. Cyclocoelous. Some of the intestinal loops form a spiral. The terms "telogyrous" and "mesogyrous" were used to describe variants of the spiral pattern.

B. Orthocoelous. Intestine forms a number of loops that run parallel to one another in the long axis of the body.

1. Isocoelous. Second and subsequent loops closed and left-handed. Ascending branch of one loop runs side by side with descending branch of next loop.

2. Anticoelous. Second loop closed and left-handed, third loop closed and right-handed.

3. Plagiocoelous. At least second loop, which is generally open, doubled over in horseshoe shape.

4. Pericoelous. Second loop open, left-handed, and surrounding third loop, which is generally straight and closed. "This formation is of especial interest because it leads quite gradually to the" cyclocoelous pattern (Gadow 1889:305).

Two subvariants were named anti-pericoelous and iso-pericoelous.

Gadow described the intestinal convolutions in many groups and made comparisons among them. He noted several additional modifications of the named patterns and found that many of the similarities between groups "are perhaps merely coincidences, and in this case can have no taxonomic significance; but if these similarities coincide with those of several other organic characters, they are entitled to a higher rank as indicating not convergence but common descent of those birds in which they persistently occur" (1889:307).

Forbes (1880e) strongly disagreed with some of the assemblages proposed by Gadow (1879). Forbes noted that within the group with a mesogyrous pattern are the falconiform genera *Accipiter* and *Melierax*, the kingfisher *Halcyon*, and the flamingo *Phoenicopterus*. He wrote (1880e:236–237): "It seems to me that, as it is a well known fact that individuals of the same species vary, sometimes very greatly, in the length of their intestines, the stowing away of a greater or less amount of gut in a given space, the abdominal cavity, becomes simply a mechanical problem, and therefore there is less help in forming a sound view of the mutual affinities of birds to be derived from the facts in this direction described by Dr. Gadow than from many other points, more complicated, and therefore less easily altered, in the structure of birds."

Forbes's objection was valid, for it is possible to find both consistency and inconsistency in Gadow's data. Within the Charadriiformes Gadow (1889) noted that some sandpipers and plovers ("Limicolae") are pericoelous, others cyclocoelous. Some Laridae are pericoelous, others cyclocoelous; some Alcidae are amphicoelous, others cyclocoelous. Several types of convolutions occur within the diurnal raptors, the Procellariidae, and the herons, but the Passeriformes "are a very uniform group" (p. 315).

Gadow (1889) was aware of the relationship between food habits and the structure of the digestive tract, but he also thought that dietary modifications often affected the caeca, crop, and stomach rather than the pattern of intestinal coiling (e.g., p. 310). The similarities between parrots and hawks in coiling pattern (telogyrous), presence of a crop, and absence of functional caeca posed a problem Gadow could not explain, for he discounted a relationship between these two groups of birds (p. 313).

Gadow and Selenka (1891:707–709) described eight pattern types and listed the birds having each pattern. Some of the groups seem reasonable (e.g., rails, shorebirds, pigeons) but others (herons, hawks, parrots) do not.

Mitchell (1896) introduced his first long paper on the avian intestinal tract by stating that Gadow "has . . . proved the taxonomic value of the intestinal convolutions in birds" (p. 136). Mitchell included the mesenteries and veins in his study and began with the assumption that the simple condition in *Alligator* was the "ground-type." He then described the variations he found in birds.

Mitchell (1896) agreed and disagreed with Gadow on various points and concluded that "in these loopings of the gut in birds, there is an almost kaleidoscopic variety, and apparently these varieties are of systematic value; what are their utilities?" (p. 159). This rather cryptic remark apparently meant that Mitchell wasn't certain how to interpret the variation he had encountered.

Beddard (1898a:23–30) reviewed the papers by Gadow and Mitchell but did not present an opinion as to the taxonomic value of the intestinal convolutions. However, he did include data on intestinal patterns in his discussions of the groups of birds.

Mitchell (1901a) soon published an expanded study of the avian intestinal tract based on "many hundreds of birds, including a number of rare forms, and representing nearly all the important groups of birds" (p. 175). He took the condition in the Horned Screamer (*Anhima cornuta*) as his starting point because it seemed to him to represent the "primitive ancestral, or central condition, from which the conditions found in the other cases have diverged" (p. 178). Mitchell called this pattern archecentric and the modified conditions apocentric. He then introduced definitions of four "homoplastic modifications" of the gut and coined several other terms to describe other conditions and to organize a scheme to reconstruct the evolutionary pathways of the avian intestinal tract. These terms and Mitchell's arguments are largely irrelevant to the taxonomic evaluation of his data. Mitchell presented diagrams that summarized his ideas about the "relations of the intestinal tracts, and not necessarily the relations of the possessors of these tracts" (p. 270). He thus avoided a confrontation between his intestinal tract data and those from other sources.

It was Beddard (1911) who finally evaluated the intestinal tract patterns in taxonomic terms. He was critical of the methods of Gadow and Mitchell, noting that the latter over-simplified the actual variation "with the result that birds which are separated by marked characters are represented as being almost identical" (p. 49–50). Beddard described the intestinal tract in an additional number of species and came to the general conclusion that although the facts concerning the intestinal convolutions do not "permit of any complete scheme of classification" (p. 89) there are indications of relationship in some cases. Within some groups all species have a nearly identical intestinal pattern. Thus, all parrots are alike, as are the galliforms, diurnal raptors, and owls. However, the members of other groups diverge greatly from one another, as in the "Picopasseres, Limicolae, Grues, [and] Struthiones" (p. 93).

Beddard concluded that "certain classificatory results seem to follow from a comparison of the differences exhibited by the intestinal tract. Thus, the resemblance of both Cuculi and Musophagi to the Picopasseres, and the likeness between all the Accipitres (New World and Old World, nocturnal and diurnal) are remarkable. The close likeness between the Bustards and the Cariamidae is to be commented upon. The passerine character of the gut of *Turnix* and the possible likeness between *Crypturus* and *Rhea* seem also to be shown" (p. 89). Since several of these "classificatory results" can be shown to be wrong or doubtful, it seems reasonable to conclude that the taxonomic value of the intestinal convolutions is virtually nil.

5. THE CAROTID ARTERIES

Garrod (1873b) was the first to make extensive use of the arrangement of the carotid arteries as a taxonomic character. He examined 400 species representing some 300 genera and described four principal patterns:

1. Two carotids of equal size which run up the neck and enter the hypapophysial canal, running side by side but separate. Present in many groups of birds.

2. The left carotid only developed. In all Passeriformes and several other groups.

3. The right carotid artery present in its normal position in the hypapophysial canal but the left superficial in company with the left jugular vein and vagus nerve. Present in some parrots.

4. The two carotid arteries merge and a single artery runs in the hypapophysial canal to the head. Variation in the size of the two trunks. Of equal size in *Botaurus*, the right larger in *Phoenicopterus*, the left larger in *Cacatua*.

Garrod (1874c) found a fifth condition in a bustard (*Eupodotis*), in which only the right carotid is present. Garrod (1876a) and Ottley (1879) found that in the Ground Hornbill (*Bucorvus*) both carotids are reduced to fibrous cords, their vascular function having been assumed by other vessels.

Forbes (1881d:7) reviewed Garrod's work and concluded that "the disposition of the carotid arteries has not much significance amongst birds, there being many families in which, whilst the majority of the species have two, some have only one carotid." Forbes cited several such cases including *Tockus* and *Bucorvus* (hornbills) and *Apus* and *Cypseloides* (swifts). "In other cases" Forbes noted, "the characters of the carotids hold good through very large groups: thus no Passerine bird has ever yet been found with more than a left carotid, and no Pigeon, Duck, or Bird of Prey without two normally placed ones."

Forbes (1882e) found a modification in the Australian Logrunner *Orthonyx* (Corvoidea: Orthonychidae) in which the left carotid runs superficially rather than in the hypapophysial canal.

Beddard (1898a:54), after reviewing the work of Garrod, Forbes, and others, concluded that "these facts, striking though they are, are unfortunately of but little value in classification, or at least their value is not understood."

The next important studies of the carotid pattern were those of Glenny, who published a series of some 40 papers beginning in 1940. In 1955 he summarized this work and included a bibliography of his own papers. Glenny (1955:527) stated that "even Forbes and Beddard failed to interpret Garrod's studies satisfactorily" and expressed his belief that further extensive embryological studies will be necessary before the various patterns in adult birds can be interpreted.

Glenny described four major bicarotid patterns and six major unicarotid patterns, with additional modifications in each group. Using a coded system he set up a series of five bicarotid arrangements based on his 1955, 1957, 1965, and 1967 papers. Unless otherwise indicated the data are from the 1955 review.

Class A—Two Carotids

A-1. Bicarotidinae normales: the two dorsal carotids enter the hypapophysial canal and pass anteriorly to the head without fusing. This is the basic arrangement from which all others have been derived. It is found in some species in most orders of birds but exclusively only in the following groups (names from Wetmore 1960): Struthionidae, Casuariidae (Glenny 1965), Tinamiformes, Spheniscidae, Gaviidae, Anseriformes, Falconiformes, Columbiformes, and Strigiformes. The Casuariidae are mostly A-1, but some *Casuarius* are not; most Procellariidae are A-1, but a few are unicarotid; all Galliformes, except the Megapodiidae, and all Gruiformes, except the Heliornithidae, Turnicidae, and some Otididae, are A-1. The Charadriiformes, except for some alcids, and the Caprimulgiformes, except the Podargidae and Nyctibiidae, are A-1. Some parrots are A-1 (Glenny 1957).

A-2-d. Bicarotidinae abnormales: right vessel superficial. No examples.

A-2-s. Bicarotidinae abnormales: left vessel superficial. Uncommon, found in many parrots (Glenny 1957).

A-3. Bicarotidinae infranormales: both vessels superficial. Rare, known only in certain cuckoos (*Zanclostomus*, *Phaenicophaeus*. In *Rhamphococcyx* the left dorsal carotid serves as a reduced ascending esophageal artery; the right carotid is a small ligament. Coded by Glenny (1955:583) as A-3-s/A-4-d.

A-4. Ligamenti carotidinae normales (ligamenti ottleyi): both dorsal carotids atrophied. Function taken over by other vessels. Rare, known only in *Bucorvus* (Bucorvidae) and *Rhopodytes* (Cuculidae).

Class B—One Carotid

B-1. Conjuncto-carotidinae normales: single carotid in the hypapophysial canal, formed from two vessels of equal size. Found only in the herons, where it is quite inconsistent, even within genera and species; e.g., most *Ardea* are A-1, but *A. herodias treganzai* is B-1, while *A. h. herodias* is A-1. *Butorides virescens* is B-1, *B. sundevalli* is A-1; *Ixobrychus minutus* and *I. sinensis bryani* are A-1, but *I. s. sinensis* is B-1. Thus, carotids in the Ardeidae are variable.

B-2-d. Conjuncto-carotidinae abnormales: right side reduced. Like B-1, but the right carotid smaller than the left. Found in *Cacatua sulphurea* (Psittacidae) (Glenny 1957) and *Podargus ocellatus* (Podargidae). Other Podargidae are B-4-s and other *Cacatua* are B-3b-d.

B-2-s. Conjuncto-carotidinae abnormales: left side reduced. In some herons (*Ardeola speciosa*), some specimens of *Botaurus lentiginosus*, the flamingos, and perhaps in *Cacatua* (Glenny 1955:580). *Megapodius nicobariensis* is B-2-s; other megapodes are B-4-s or B-3b-d.

B-3a-d. Ligamentum carotidinae-conjuncti: partial lumen, ligament on right side. In a specimen of *Priocella antarctica* [*Fulmarus glacialoides*] (Procellariidae) and in a hornbill *Tockus* (Bucerotidae).

B-3a-s. Ligamentum carotidinae-conjuncti: partial lumen; ligament on left side. (No examples given by Glenny 1955.)

B-3b-d. Ligamentum carotidinae-conjuncti: entire, on right side. Found in pelicans, *Megapodius pritchardii* (but not other megapodes), *Chaetura vauxi*, *Chaetura cinereiventris*, and *Tachornis phoenicopia* (Apodidae), and in *Cacatua galerita*, *leadbeateri*, and *sanguinea* (Psittacidae). See *C. sulphurea*, above, under B-2-d. See Glenny 1957, for details.

B-3b-s. Ligamentum carotidinae-conjuncti: entire, on left side. No examples.

B-4-d. Dextro-carotidinae normales: right carotid alone enters hypapophysial canal. Found in *Eupodotis* (Otididae), but other bustards are A-1; also reported in the Brown-headed Barbet (*Megalaima zeylanica*), but other barbets are B-4-s.

B-4-s. Laevo-carotidinae normales: left carotid alone enters hypapophysial canal. This arrangement in many groups: rheas, kiwis (Glenny 1965), grebes, colies, trogons, Piciformes (except the Brown-headed Barbet, above, under B-4-d), Passeriformes (except *Orthonyx*, Orthonychidae, which is B-5-s), *Anhinga*, *Balaeniceps*, Turnicidae, Nyctibiidae, *Hemiprocne*, Trochilidae, Upupidae, Phoeniculidae (but other groups are B-2-s or B-3b-d). One specimen of *Casuarius* (Glenny 1955:553) was B-4-s, others were A-1. One *Pelecanoides garnoti* was B-4-s, others were A-1 (Glenny 1955:557); *Sula* is B-4-s, *Morus* is A-1 (Sulidae); *Fregata aquila* is A-1, *F. minor* is B-4-s (Glenny 1955:558); most Alcinae were A-1, but *Plautus alle* and five specimens of *Synthliboramphus antiquus* were B-4-s. Two specimens of *S. antiquus* and two of *S. wumizusume* were A-1 (Glenny 1955:576). Most bee-eaters (Meropidae) are B-4-s, but *Melittophagus* is A-1.

B-5-d. Dextro-carotidinae infranormales: right carotid is superficial, left is lacking. No examples.

B-5-s. Laevo-carotidinae infranormales: left carotid is superficial, right is lacking. Known only in *Orthonyx*.

B-6a-d. Ligamentum unicarotidinae (ligamentum ottleyi): entire, right side. No examples.

B-6a-s. Ligamentum unicarotidinae: entire, left side. No examples.

B-6b-d. Ligamentum unicarotidinae: incomplete or lacking, right side. No examples.

B-6b-s. Ligamentum unicarotidinae: incomplete or lacking, left side. No examples.

The B-6 series represents Glenny's assumption that if there is further atrophy of the unicarotid condition, other arteries will take over the function of the carotids.

It seems obvious that the numerous exceptions and special cases render the adult carotid artery patterns virtually useless as a basis for a general classification of the higher categories. Glenny is probably correct in his belief that only extensive embryological studies will clarify the situation. Certainly, the data available to Gadow in 1892 cannot be considered as reliable evidence for the reconstruction of avian phylogeny.

6. THE FIFTH SECONDARY

Gerbe (1877) first noticed that some birds apparently lack a fifth secondary, but it was Wray (1887) who brought the condition to the attention of taxonomists. The gap in the secondaries was detected because a greater covert is present between the fourth and sixth secondaries, but no secondary is present at the corresponding position. It was therefore assumed that the fifth secondary was missing. Birds lacking the fifth secondary were termed aquintocubital and birds having a fifth secondary were called quintocubital. Mitchell (1899) suggested the substitution of "diastataxic" and "eutaxic" for these conditions.

The taxonomic value of the presence or absence of the fifth secondary was quickly investigated and its significance debated. Various authors (e.g. Gadow 1888b; Sclater 1890; Goodchild 1886, 1891; Pycraft 1890, 1899c; Gadow and Selenka 1891; Degen 1894; Seebohm 1895; Mitchell 1899, 1901c; W. DeW. Miller 1915, 1924a; Steiner 1946, 1956, 1958) assembled data on the fifth secondary in many groups of birds.

W. DeW. Miller (1924a) and Steiner (1956, 1958) reviewed the earlier work, added to it, corrected several errors, and presented useful summaries on which the following lists are based.

A. All or Mostly Diastataxic
   Archaeornithes (*Archaeopteryx*)
   Casuariidae (Emu, Cassowaries)
   Gaviidae (Loons)
   Podicipedidae (Grebes)
   Spheniscidae (Penguins)
   Procellariidae (Petrels, Albatrosses)
   Pelecaninae (Pelicans)
   Phalacrocoracidae (Cormorants, except *Nannopterum*)
   Ardeidae (Herons)
   Ciconiinae (Storks)
   Phoenicopteridae (Flamingos)
   Anseriformes (Ducks, Geese, Screamers)
   Falconides (Hawks, Falcons)
   Gruidae (Cranes)
   Eurypygidae (Sunbitterns)
   Otididae (Bustards)
   Charadrii (Shorebirds, including *Pedionomus*) except *Philohela*
   Pteroclidae (Sandgrouse)
   Psittaciformes (Parrots)
   Strigi (Owls)
   Hemiprocnidae (Crested-swifts)
   Caprimulgi (Goatsuckers)
   Coraciidae (Rollers)
   Leptosomidae (Cuckoo-rollers)

B. Groups Containing Both Eutaxic and Diastataxic Forms
   Except for the Rallidae and Aramidae, the Gruiformes separate into eutaxic and diastataxic groups on family lines and are so listed above and below. The rails, pigeons, and kingfishers are especially complex, and some additional comments on these groups are presented below.

Megapodiidae (Megapodes). *Megapodius* and *Megacephalon* are diastataxic; *Leipoa* and *Alectura* are eutaxic.

Columbidae (Pigeons). See below.

Heliornithidae. Limpkins diastataxic; sungrebes eutaxic.

Rallidae (Rails). See below.

Charadrii (Shorebirds). Diastataxic, except *Philohela*.

Kingfishers. See below.

Apodidae (Swifts). "Chaeturinae" variable. "Micropodinae" eutaxic. See W. DeW. Miller (1924a:310).

Trochilidae (Hummingbirds). Diastataxic except *Glaucis hirsuta*, *Phaethornis guy*, and *Eutoxeres aquila*. The unique type specimen of *Eucephala caeruleo-lavata* Gould (*Cyanophaia caeruleolavata*) is eutaxic in one wing, diastataxic in the other (Miller 1924a:311). Peters (1945:48–49) thought this specimen to be "almost certainly" a hybrid.

Brachypteraciidae (Ground-rollers). See Steiner 1956:19.

C. All or Mostly Eutaxic

Ostrich and rheas

Tinamiformes (Tinamous)

Galliformes (Pheasants, Grouse, etc., except some megapodes)

Mesitornithidae (Roatelos, *Monias*)

Turnicidae (Bustardquails)

Psophiidae (Trumpeters)

Rhynochetidae (Kagu)

Cariamidae (Seriemas)

Cuculiformes, including *Opisthocomus* (Cuckoos)

Coliiformes (Colies)

Trogoniformes (Trogons)

Coraciiformes (most Kingfishers, Bee-eaters, Motmots, but not Rollers)

Piciformes (Woodpeckers, Barbets, Toucans, etc.)

Passeriformes (Perching Birds)

Rallidae. Most rails are diastataxic, but Miller (1924a:309) listed eight eutaxic species. In at least two genera, *Creciscus* (*Laterallus*) and *Sarothrura*, both conditions are found, and in some *Sarothrura* both conditions are present within a single species. Miller concluded that "the taxonomic value of this feature in *Sarothrura* is comparable to that of the relative development of the tenth primary in *Vireosylva* and *Lanivireo*" (p. 308).

Columbidae. Mitchell (1899) found that most pigeons are diastataxic, but he discovered seven eutaxic species. Bates (1918) added several more, and Miller (1924a:306–307) presented a list of 36 diastataxic and 20 eutaxic species. All of the eutaxic forms were members of the "Peristeridae," which included such genera as *Geopelia*, *Scardafella*, *Columbina*, *Chamaepelia*, *Claravis*, *Tympanistria*, *Turtur*, *Phaps*, *Ocyphaps*, *Gallicolumba*, and *Starnoenas*. Other genera of the "Peristeridae" were listed as diastataxic, including *Zenaida*, *Zenaidura*, *Streptopelia*, *Oena*, *Chalcophaps*, *Leptotila*, *Oreopeleia*, and *Caloenas*. All members of the "Treronidae" and "Columbidae" were found to be diastataxic. The complications extend beyond these bare lists. (See Miller 1924a:307 and Steiner 1956:14–15.)

The kingfishers include both conditions. Using names from Peters (1945), the following summarizes the findings of Mitchell (1901c): (1) Eutaxic species: *Halcyon pileata* (but with vestige of "old diastataxic condition"), *Halcyon coromanda rufa*, *Chloroceryle americana*, *C. inda*, *Cittura cyanotis* (including *C. c. sanghirensis*), *Alcedo meninting* (*A. asiatica*), *A. atthis* (including *A. a. ispida* and *A. a. bengalensis*), *Ceyx rufidorsa*. (2) Diastataxic species: *Dacelo novaeguineae*, *Halcyon chloris* (including *H. s. vagans*), *Ceryle maxima*, and *C. alcyon*.

Mitchell (1901c:102–103) observed that "the seventeen Kingfishers which I have examined thus show plainly that here, as in the Columbidae, the conditions known as eutaxy and diastataxy cannot be regarded as fundamental characters in any of the greater schemes of classification. Both conditions occur, scattered as it were indiscriminately within the confines of the group, and sometimes even within the confines of a genus. Nor are the two conditions absolutely marked off one from another, but lend themselves to an arrangement in a graded series, which suggests the production of one condition as a simple modification of the other."

By examining other characters Mitchell tried to show that the eutaxic pigeons (1899) and kingfishers (1901c) are the more specialized. The attempt fails because it depends on Mitchell's subjective definition of "primitive" and "specialized" in each example.

Pycraft (1899c:254) discussed diastataxy as a factor in classification and noted that a division of the Aves into two groups of eutaxic and diastataxic birds was impossible, but he thought that the condition of the fifth secondary could be used within groups. "The presence of diastataxy in a little coterie of forms, admittedly related, but hitherto indiscriminately mixed with eutaxic, will . . . justify our separating them . . . on the assumption . . . that they are . . . more closely related one to the other than to the neighbouring eutaxic forms." But the mixed groups made it necessary for Pycraft to propose a theory for which there was no evidence, let alone proof. He wrote: "The presence of discordant elements in the shape of eutaxic forms amongst our now diastataxic groups—such as the Kingfishers, Swifts, and Pigeons—must be attributed to reversion or secondary readjustment of the feathers resulting once more in eutaxy. This is not as convincing as it should be; but it demands less of us than the alternative hypothesis, that diastataxy has been independently acquired wherever it occurs" (p. 254).

Steiner (1918, 1946, 1956, 1958) worked out the embryological basis of diastataxy and provided the most likely explanation for the seemingly haphazard distribution of the condition of the fifth secondary. Steiner (1956) argued that diastataxy is the primitive condition and that eutaxy has been derived from it, independently, in various groups of birds. Steiner reinvestigated the condition in *Archaeopteryx* and, in opposition to DeBeer (1954), found it to be diastataxic. Steiner's (1956:5, transl.) description of the development of the secondaries in a diastataxic wing is as follows:

The earliest secondary feather germs appear on the ulnar margin of the forearm. They form as small round buds (papillae) and occur in two separate rows, one that begins proximally near the elbow and a second which is located distally and extends to the wrist. It is clear that there are two separate rows, the proximal extends above the distal and the distal row extends below the proximal to the elbow. This observation provides the explanation for the development of diastataxis; the secondaries which insert on the margin of the wing in Recent birds have developed from two separate rows of feathers situated on the forearm. The proximal half of the secondary series originated from the upper row, the distal half from the lower row. Accordingly, the secondary coverts are arranged in gradually rising transverse rows and are displaced along the forearm to the extent of one longitudinal series of feathers. The place of transition from the proximal portion of the row to the distal portion is at the fifth and sixth cross-rows respectively. Thus, here the feathers have intermediate positions and the fifth secondary does not develop. In eutaxic birds the feather germs also develop in two rows, one proximal, the other distal. The early stages are like those of the diastataxic wing but very soon the eutaxic wing begins to develop in a different fashion.

In the mixed groups (doves, kingfishers, etc.) Steiner found developmental stages intermediate between eutaxy and diastataxy. He concluded that a eutaxic wing is correlated with the need for a strong "rowing wing" as in tree-, brush-, and ground-dwelling birds or in marsh and water birds that must fly without a running start. Furthermore, in the embryos of ostriches and rheas (Steiner 1946), which are eutaxic, it is possible to see evidence of the earlier diastataxic condition. The diastataxic wing tends to be present in long-winged birds which do not live in dense vegetation or have to fly upward to escape predators.

Steiner (1956:14–16) concluded that the taxonomic significance of diastataxy is as a character that indicates the primitive species in the mixed groups where both conditions occur and that therefore can be important in understanding the phylogeny of such groups.

We conclude that the taxonomic value of diastataxy is limited. The wide occurrence of each condition in unrelated forms and the variation within closely related groups of species indicates, as Steiner noted, that it is adaptive and of taxonomic value only to bolster other evidence, and then only in special cases. As a character in higher-category classification it should be viewed with distrust.

We believe the point has been made. These six characters are all useful to some degree, but none is consistent. We are not the first to make this suggestion; the original authors were aware of the problems, but their successors have not always been as wary. All of Gadow's 40 characters can be shown to suffer from the same disabilities because all are adaptive and subject to convergence. They are not devoid of taxonomic information, but they must be interpreted with caution.

Does this caveat extend to all morphological characters? To the extent that all morphological characters are subject to convergence and misinterpretation, it must. Morphological structures contain similarities due to history (homology) and function (analogy), and only homologous similarities provide the evidence needed to reconstruct phylogeny. It is not always possible to separate the two.

Gadow's procedure was a kind of numerical taxonomy, but Gadow did attempt to weigh his characters. He described the "laborious process" involved in making the many comparisons among groups, noted the trogons and colies as "notoriously difficult forms," and established the endings for subfamilies (inae), families (idae), and orders (formes) (1892:235). He described his method as follows (1892:229):

The author of a new classification ought to state the reasons which have led him to the separation and grouping together of the birds known to him. This means not simply to enumerate the characters which he has employed, but also to say why and how he used them. Of course there are characters and characters. Some are probably of little value, and others are equivalent to half a dozen of them. Some are sure to break down unexpectedly somewhere, others run through many families and even orders; but the former characters are not necessarily bad and the latter are not necessarily good. The objection has frequently been made that we have no criterion to determine the value of characters in any given group, and that therefore any classification based upon any number of characters however large (but always arbitrary, since composed of non-equivalent units) must necessarily be artificial and therefore probably a failure.

This is quite true if we take all these characters, treat them as all alike, and by a simple process of plus or minus, i.e., present or absent, large or small, 1, 2, 3, 4, &c., produce a "Key," but certainly not a natural classification.

To avoid this evil, we have to *sift* or *weigh* the same characters every time anew and in different ways, whenever we inquire into the degree of affinity between two or more species, genera, families, or larger groups of creatures.

This I have tried to do in a manner hitherto not applied to birds; it may have been done by others, but they have not published any account of this process. Certainly it has not been applied throughout the whole Class of Birds.

I have selected about forty characters from various organ systems . . . preferring such characters which either can be expressed by a formula or by some other short symbol, or which, during the working out of the anatomical portion of Bronn's 'Aves,' have revealed themselves as of taxonomic value, and of which I have learnt to understand the correlation, determining causes, and range of modification. Other characters, perhaps too complicated, too variable, or last, but not least, too imperfectly known in many birds, are left out or reserved for occasional employment.

Of my 40 characters about half occur also in Fuerbringer's table, which contains 51 characters. A number of skeletal characters I have adopted from Mr. Lydekker's [1891] 'Catalogue of Fossil Birds,' after having convinced myself, from a study of that excellent book, of their taxonomic value. Certain others referring to the formation of the rhamphotheca, the structure and distribution of the down in the young and in the adult, the syringeal muscles, the intestinal convolutions, and the nares, have not hitherto been employed in the Class of Birds.

Groups of birds, arranged in *bona fide* families, sometimes only genera of doubtful affinity, were compared with each other—each family with every other family or group—and the number of characters in which they agree was noted down in a tabular form. Presumably families which agree in all 40 characters would be identical, but this has never happened. There are none which differ in less than about 6, and none which agree in less than 10 points. The latter may be due to their all being birds. It is not easy to imagine two birds which would differ in all the 40 characters.

In another table all the families were arranged in lines according to their numerical coincidences, and attempts were made to arrange and to combine these lines of supposed affinities in tree-like branches. These attempts are often successful, often disappointing. Of course this merely mathematical principle is scientifically faulty, because the characters are decidedly not all equivalent. It may happen that a great numerical agreement between two families rests upon unimportant characters only, and a small number of coincidences may be due to fundamentally valuable structures, and in either case the true affinities would be obscured. This it was necessary to inquire into. But at any rate I obtained many hints from this simple mode of calculation, indicating the direction which further inquiry should take.

The *Psittaci* may serve as an example of my mode of sifting characters.

According to the numerical agreement of the 40 characters employed generally, we have the following table:

Psittaci agree with Coccyges in 31 points, with Pici in about 29, with Coraciidae 25, Falconidae 25, Striges 22, Bucerotidae 22, Gallidae 21, against 19 points of difference.

A previous line of investigation had revealed the fact that the Coccyges [cuckoos] and Gallidae [galliforms] are intimately connected with each other through *Opisthocomus*. This knowledge obviated further inquiry as to the affinity between Psittaci and Gallidae.

At least one weakness in Gadow's method is revealed by the example of the Hoatzin (*Opisthocomus*). We have shown by protein (Sibley and Ahlquist 1973) and DNA comparisons (this volume) that the Hoatzin is a cuckoo and that the cuckoos are not closely related to the galliforms. It is also obvious that living taxa do not "connect" other living taxa.

Gadow presented all of his data for the comparisons between the parrots and other groups as an example of his method. He then presented his classification in which the characters of each group were listed under the name of the taxon. The result is impressive and it conveys a sense of careful and extensive comparisons based on a huge amount of work. Nothing as authoritative and complete had come before and the avian systematists of the following century based their classifications on that of Gadow; unless the evidence to the contrary was overwhelming, his conclusions were accepted.

In his 1893 treatise on the systematics of birds in Bronn's *Klassen und Ordnungen des Thier-Reichs*, Gadow reviewed many previous classifications, discussed each group of birds, and presented his classification (pp. 299–303). Gadow's arrangement, organized in the modern format, including vernacular names and omitting subfamilies and most extinct groups, follows:

Class Aves
  Subclass Archeornithes, *Archeopteryx*
  Subclass Neornithes
    Division 1. Ratitae: Ratites (Struthiones, Rheae, Casuarii, Apteryges)
    Division 2. Odontolcae: extinct toothed birds
    Division 3. Carinatae: Carinates

    Brigade 1.
      Legion 1. Colymbomorphae
        Order Colymbiformes
          Suborder Colymbi
            Family Colymbidae: Loons (Gaviidae)
          Suborder Podicipedes
            Family Podicipedidae: Grebes
        Order Sphenisciformes
          Suborder Sphenisci
            Family Spheniscidae: Penguins
        Order Procellariiformes
          Suborder Procellariae
            Family Procellariidae: Albatrosses, Petrels, etc.
      Legion 2. Pelargomorphae
        Order Ciconiiformes
          Suborder Steganopodes
            Family Phaethontidae: Tropicbirds
            Family Sulidae: Gannets, Boobies
            Family Phalacrocoracidae: Cormorants, Anhingas
            Family Fregatidae: Frigatebirds
            Family Pelecanidae: Pelicans
          Suborder Ardeae
            Family Ardeidae: Herons, Shoebill
            Family Scopidae: Hammerhead
          Suborder Ciconiae
            Family Ciconiidae: Storks
            Family Ibidae: Ibises, Spoonbills
          Suborder Phoenicopteri
            Family Phoenicopteridae: Flamingos
        Order Anseriformes
          Suborder Palamedeae
            Family Palamedeidae: Screamers
          Suborder Anseres
            Family Anseridae: Ducks, Geese, Swans

Order Falconiformes
    Suborder Cathartae
        Family Cathartidae: New World Vultures
    Suborder Accipitres
        Family Gypogeranidae: Secretarybird
        Family Vulturidae: Old World Vultures
        Family Falconidae: Eagles, Hawks, Kites, Falcons
        Family Pandionidae: Osprey
Brigade 2.
  Legion 1. Alectoromorphae
    Order Tinamiformes
      Suborder Tinami
        Family Tinamidae: Tinamous
    Order Galliformes
      Suborder Mesites
        Family Mesitidae: Mesites, Monias
      Suborder Turnices
        Family Turnicidae: Buttonquails
        Family Pedionomidae: Plains-wanderer
      Suborder Galli
        Family Megapodiidae: Megapodes
        Family Cracidae: Curassows, Guans, Chachalacas
      Suborder Opisthocomi
        Family Opisthocomidae: Hoatzin
    Order Gruiformes
        Family Rallidae: Rails, Gallinules, Coots
        Family Gruidae: Cranes, Limpkin, Trumpeters
        Family Dicholophidae: Seriemas
        Family Otididae: Bustards
        Family Rhinochetidae: Kagu
        Family Eurypygidae: Sunbittern
        Family Heliornithidae: Sungrebes
    Order Charadriiformes
      Suborder Limicolae
        Family Charadriidae: Plovers, Avocets, Stilts, Sandpipers
        Family Chionididae: Sheathbills
        Family Thinocoridae: Seedsnipe
        Family Glareolidae: Pratincoles, Crab Plover
        Family Oedicnemidae: Thick-knees
        Family Parridae: Jacanas
      Suborder Lari
        Family Laridae: Gulls, Jaegers, Skuas, Terns, Skimmers
        Family Alcidae: Auks, Murres, Puffins
      Suborder Pterocles
        Family Pteroclidae: Sandgrouse
      Suborder Columbae
        Family Columbidae: Pigeons, Doves
  Legion 2. Coraciomorphae
    Order Cuculiformes
      Suborder Cuculi
        Family Cuculidae: Cuckoos, Roadrunners, Coucals
        Family Musophagidae: Turacos

        Suborder Psittaci
           Family Trichoglossidae: Keas (*Nestor*), Lories, *Opopsitta*
           Family Psittacidae: Owl Parrot, Cockatoos, all other parrots
      Order Coraciiformes
        Suborder Coraciae
           Family Coraciidae: Rollers
           Family Momotidae: Motmots, Todies
           Family Alcedinidae: Kingfishers
           Family Meropidae: Bee-eaters
           Family Upupidae: Hoopoes, Hornbills
        Suborder Striges
           Family Strigidae: Owls
        Suborder Caprimulgi
           Family Steatornithidae: Oilbird
           Family Podargidae: Frogmouths, Owlet-frogmouths
           Family Caprimulgidae: Goatsuckers, Potoos
        Suborder Cypseli
           Family Cypselidae: Swifts
           Family Trochilidae: Hummingbirds
        Suborder Colii
           Family Coliidae: Mousebirds or Colies
        Suborder Trogones
           Family Trogonidae: Trogons
        Suborder Pici
           Family Galbulidae: Jacamars, Puffbirds
           Family Capitonidae: Barbets, Honeyguides
           Family Rhamphastidae: Toucans
           Family Picidae: Woodpeckers, Piculets, Wrynecks
      Order Passeriformes (See under Passeriformes, below)

Most of these groups and their names will be familiar to living ornithologists because Wetmore and others adopted Gadow's system with minor modifications. A comparison between Gadow's classification and that of Wetmore (e.g., 1960) reveals many similarities, and Wetmore (1930) acknowledged that his arrangement owed much to Gadow. Thus, Gadow's system has prevailed for nearly a century.

    The apparent success that Gadow had achieved may have been an important factor in the decline of interest in avian anatomy and higher-category systematics that characterized the next half century or more. The volumes of Fürbringer and Gadow seemed to leave little to be done by others interested in avian anatomy and classification, among whom was Frank Evers Beddard (1858–1925). In the preface to his book *The Structure and Classification of Birds* (1898a), Beddard wrote that

It was the intention of my predecessor in the office of Prosector to the Zoological Society, the late Professor Garrod, F.R.S., to write a treatise upon bird anatomy. This intention was so far realised that a nearly complete account of the anatomy of the fowl . . . was actually drawn up; . . . Professor Garrod's successor . . . the late Mr. W. A. Forbes, had every intention of finishing the work commenced; but unfortunately death took place before any actual additions had been made. . . . I have, on the kind encouragement of Mr. Sclater, determined to . . . carry out this plan of my two forerunners, and the present volume is the result.

    It must be admitted that a handbook upon bird anatomy was more wanted at the time that it was first conceived by Mr. Garrod than it is at the present day. Zoologists had then nothing of a general character save the incomplete fragment of Bronn's 'Thierreich' and the sections devoted to bird anatomy in such comprehensive works as those of Meckel and Cuvier. We now have two treatises of first-rate merit, that of Fürbringer and Dr. Gadow's completion of the section 'Aves' in Bronn's 'Thierreich'. . . . I commence with a general sketch of bird structure . . . avoiding histological detail and the elaborate description of anatomical facts which are not, in the present state of our knowledge, of great use in classification. . . . Dr. Gadow has also treated bird anatomy from this point of view; . . . I have felt it useless to attempt to vie with Professor Fürbringer's magnificent treatise upon birds. . . . I believe, however, that I have been able to note the principal facts in the anatomy of the different orders of birds, and that nothing of first-rate importance has been omitted.

Beddard's contributions began in 1884 when he succeeded Forbes, and continued until 1914. His volume on avian structure and classification was overshadowed by those of Fürbringer and Gadow, but it provided a summary for English-speaking anatomists and is still a useful reference. Many of the characters listed under the orders and families of birds in the present volume were taken from Beddard's book.

William Plane Pycraft (1868–1942) published a number of papers on avian morphology between 1890 and 1927, including several on pterylography and osteology, but most of his work was in relation to classification. From 1898 to 1933 Pycraft was in charge of the spirit and osteological collections of birds in the British Museum of Natural History.

Hubert Lyman Clark (1870–1947) wrote a series of papers on avian anatomy, especially on pterylosis, and published a classification of birds (1901b) based mainly on pterylography. Some of his proposed groupings make sense, but several cannot be supported by other evidence. For example, Clark placed the procellariiforms with the ducks, pelicans and auks, and considered the penguins to be unique and separate. He thought that the Hoatzin (*Opisthocomus*) is a falconiform, and placed the bustards near the herons and storks. It is hardly surprising that his classification was ignored.

Another attempt to use plumage characters was that of Asa Crawford Chandler (1891–1958), who published a study of the taxonomic significance of feather structure (1916). He examined feathers microscopically and made a number of taxonomic proposals, many of which are clearly invalid, but Chandler's illustrations provide useful information on feather structure.

Waldron DeWitt Miller (1879–1929) began his work on higher-category systematics with a revision of the kingfishers (1912), and gave particular attention during the next 14 years to pterylosis and foot structure. He was associated with Alexander Wetmore in the early stages of the development of the classification for the fourth edition of the American Ornithologists' Union Check-list of North American Birds (1931).

Percy Roycroft Lowe (1870–1948) began to publish on avian systematics in 1912 and was especially active during his tenure in charge of the Bird Room of the British Museum of Natural History from 1919 to 1935. Lowe's systematic works included anatomical studies of the shorebirds, as well as sometimes controversial papers on the ratites, penguins, galliforms, coraciiforms, and piciforms.

Since 1930 the most widely accepted classification of birds has been that developed by (Frank) Alexander Wetmore (1886–1978). Wetmore's interest in the subject seems to have begun in 1924, when he was appointed to a committee to prepare the fourth edition of the American Ornithologists' Union Check-List of North American Birds.

In November 1924, the annual meeting of the American Ornithologists' Union (A.O.U.) was held in Pittsburgh, Pennsylvania, and

the preparation of a fourth edition of the Check-List was authorized to be undertaken at once and Witmer Stone was appointed chairman . . . with power to appoint a Committee and subdivide the duties. He chose: Jonathan Dwight, Joseph Grinnell, Waldron deWitt Miller, Harry C. Oberholser, T. S. Palmer, Charles W. Richmond, and Alexander Wetmore as his associates. Two subcommittees were also appointed, one, consisting of Dr. Wetmore and Mr. Miller, being authorized to draw up a new scheme of classification . . . for use in the new edition. This classification down to families and subfamilies, was published in 'The Auk' for July 1926, pp. 337–346.

Before its work was completed the Committee suffered severely by the deaths of Dr. Dwight and Mr. Miller [in 1929], though fortunately not before Mr. Miller had finished his work on the classification and Dr. Dwight had given his advice and views on the general problems confronting the Committee (A.O.U. 1931:iv).

Wetmore and Miller (1926) reviewed the history of the classifications used in the earlier editions of the A.O.U. checklist (1886, 1895, 1910) and defined their procedure:

As relationships indicated in the old list are in a number of cases wholly erroneous it has perpetuated false ideas from generation to generation, obviously improper procedure. Change in the present accepted-order will no doubt occasion complaint but if we are to advance in our science we must assimilate modern ideas, otherwise our mechanism will assume the general utility of a stage coach in a time of automobiles and airships.

In preparing a revised classification we have taken Gadow's work as a basis and have incorporated in it various changes that have been made by later workers. In general we have accepted changes from the present order only when they appear to us definitely established on proper grounds. When doubt seems to attach to any suggestion we have followed the older classification. Our aim has been, so far as possible, to present established modern views in a conservative manner. In the few instances where we have not been in absolute agreement as to procedure the matters under dispute have been referred for decision to Dr. Stone as chairman of the committee as a whole.

In summary we propose to group North American birds in twenty orders, as against seventeen found in previous editions of the 'Check-List.' The sequence followed is one that seems best to illustrate the advance of the different groups from an evolutionary standpoint with due reference to specialization and adaptation for peculiar modes of life.

In studying the present arrangement it must be borne in mind always that the different groups do not represent milestones along a direct road leading from highest to lowest, but that they are the modern terminals of diverging lines of evolution connected by common ancestors in a past more or less remote. It is not difficult to place them on a plane surface where their relationship to one another may be presented in . . . two dimensions, but it is another thing entirely to range them in a single line. For the last there must be careful weighing of characters to determine those of basic value and an allocation of rank that will not clash with facts. The problems involved are often difficult and in some cases can only be settled arbitrarily.

This seems to be the only statement Wetmore ever made about his method and philosophy of classification. The 1926 classification listed 27 orders for the birds of the world, with separate orders for the five groups of ratites, including the tinamous, placed in the superorder Palaeognathae. The other orders, in the superorder Neognathae, were:

Order Sphenisciformes. Penguins
Order Gaviiformes. Loons
Order Colymbiformes. Grebes

Order Procellariiformes. Tube-nosed Swimmers
Order Pelecaniformes. Totipalmate Swimmers
Order Ciconiiformes. Herons, Storks, Ibises, etc.
Order Anseriformes. Screamers, Ducks, etc.
Order Falconiformes. Vultures, Hawks, Eagles, etc.
Order Galliformes. Gallinaceous Birds
Order Megalornithiformes. Cranes, Rails, Mesites, Turnices
Order Charadriiformes. Shore-birds, Gulls, Auks, etc.
Order Columbiformes. Pigeons, Doves, Sand Grouse
Order Psittaciformes. Parrots, Macaws, etc.
Order Cuculiformes. Cuckoos, Plantain-eaters, etc.
Order Strigiformes. Owls
Order Caprimulgiformes. Goatsuckers, etc.
Order Micropodiformes. Swifts and Hummingbirds
Order Coliiformes. Colies
Order Trogoniformes. Trogons
Order Coraciiformes. Kingfishers, Rollers and Hornbills
Order Piciformes. Woodpeckers and Jacamars
Order Passeriformes. Perching Birds

The fourth edition of the A.O.U. checklist (1931) followed the Wetmore and Miller arrangement with only a few changes, e.g., the Megalornithiformes became the Gruiformes. Wetmore was elected President of the A.O.U. in 1926 and continued his interest in the classification of the birds of the world.

In 1930 Wetmore published the first of five editions (1934, 1940, 1951, 1960) of his classification. He introduced it (1930:1) as follows:

Since preparing a classification of North American birds in collaboration with the late W. deW. Miller, of the American Museum of Natural History, for use in the fourth edition of the official Check-list of the American Ornithologists' Union, now in course of publication, the writer has continued investigations in this interesting subject, with the result that he here offers an arrangement of the known birds of the world, living and fossil, in accordance with his present understanding of their relationships. The work of Hans Gadow has been taken as a starting point, and such changes have been incorporated as seem justified from personal research or from the investigations of others. In general, only such variations from the current order have been accepted as seem to be firmly established. Where doubt seems to attach to any proposition, the older classification has been followed; so the following scheme presents a conservative arrangement so far as possible. The list is complete for all categories down to families. Attempt has been made to follow a definite terminology for the various groups, so that there may be no misunderstanding of their proper rank.

The 1930 version of Wetmore's classification shows the influence of Gadow on the non-passerines and of Sharpe's *Hand-List* and Ridgway's *Birds of North and Middle America* on the passerines. Wetmore made a few changes in the later editions, but they were mainly in the categorical levels assigned to various groups. For example, in the 1930 edition Wetmore included the order Sphenisciformes (penguins) in the superorder Neognathae, but in his later versions (1934, 1940, 1951, 1960) he assigned the Sphenisciformes to the monotypic super-order Impennes because of their anatomical and behavioral specializations (1960:2), although Gadow (1893) and others had concluded that the penguins are most closely related to the Procellariiformes. This demonstrates Wetmore's acceptance of the Darwinian philosophy that grades of morphological difference should be recognized by categorical ranks. The living non-passerine groups of Wetmore's 1960 classification follow:

Class Aves
  Subclass Neornithes: True Birds
    Superorder Impennes
      Order Sphenisciformes
          Family Spheniscidae: Penguins
    Superorder Neognathae: Typical Birds
      Order Struthioniformes
          Family Struthionidae: Ostriches
      Order Rheiformes
          Family Rheidae: Rheas
      Order Casuariiformes
          Family Casuariidae: Cassowaries
              Dromiceidae: Emus
      Order Apterygiformes
          Family Apterygidae: Kiwis
      Order Tinamiformes
          Family Tinamidae: Tinamous
      Order Gaviiformes
          Family Gaviidae: Loons
      Order Podicipediformes
          Family Podicipedidae: Grebes
      Order Procellariiformes
          Family Diomedeidae: Albatrosses
              Procellariidae: Shearwaters, Fulmars
              Hydrobatidae: Storm Petrels
              Pelecanoididae: Diving Petrels
      Order Pelecaniformes
        Suborder Phaethontes
          Family Phaethontidae: Tropicbirds
        Suborder Pelecani
          Superfamily Pelecanoidea
          Family Pelecanidae: Pelicans
          Superfamily Suloidea
          Family Sulidae: Boobies, Gannets
              Phalacrocoracidae: Cormorants
              Anhingidae: Snake-birds
        Suborder Fregatae
          Family Fregatidae: Frigate-birds
      Order Ciconiiformes
        Suborder Ardeae
          Family Ardeidae: Herons, Bitterns
              Cochleariidae: Boatbilled Herons
        Suborder Balaenicipites
          Family Balaenicipitidae: Whale-headed Storks
        Suborder Ciconiae
          Superfamily Scopoidea
          Family Scopidae: Hammerheads
          Superfamily Ciconioidea
          Family Ciconiidae: Storks, Jabirus

Superfamily Threskiornithoidea
Family Threskiornithidae: Ibises, Spoonbills
Suborder Phoenicopteri
Family Phoenicopteridae: Flamingos
Order Anseriformes
Suborder Anhimae
Family Anhimidae: Screamers
Suborder Anseres
Family Anatidae: Ducks, Geese, Swans
Order Falconiformes
Suborder Cathartae
Superfamily Cathartoidea
Family Cathartidae: New World Vultures
Suborder Falcones
Superfamily Sagittarioidea
Family Sagittariidae: Secretarybirds
Superfamily Falconoidea
Family Accipitridae: Hawks, Old World Vultures, Harriers
Pandionidae: Ospreys
Falconidae: Falcons, Caracaras
Order Galliformes
Suborder Galli
Superfamily Cracoidea
Family Megapodiidae: Megapodes
Cracidae: Curassows, Guans, Chachalacas
Superfamily Phasianoidea
Family Tetraonidae: Grouse
Phasianidae: Quails, Pheasants, Peacocks
Numididae: Guineafowl
Meleagrididae: Turkeys
Suborder Opisthocomi
Family Opisthocomidae: Hoatzins
Order Gruiformes
Suborder Mesitornithides
Family Mesitornithidae: Roatelos, *Monias*
Suborder Turnices
Family Turnicidae: Bustardquails
Pedionomidae: Plainwanderers
Suborder Grues
Superfamily Gruoidea
Family Gruidae: Cranes
Aramidae: Limpkins
Psophiidae: Trumpeters
Superfamily Ralloidea
Family Rallidae: Rails, Coots, Gallinules
Suborder Heliornithes
Family Heliornithidae: Sungrebes
Suborder Rhynocheti
Family Rhynochetidae: Kagus
Suborder Eurypygae
Family Eurypygidae: Sunbitterns

Suborder Cariamae
    Family Cariamidae: Seriemas
Order Charadriiformes
    Suborder Charadrii
        Superfamily Jacanoidea
            Family Jacanidae: Jacanas
        Superfamily Charadrioidea
            Family Rostratulidae: Painted Snipe
                Haematopodidae: Oystercatchers
                Charadriidae: Plovers, Turnstones, Surfbirds
                Scolopacidae: Snipe, Woodcock, Sandpipers
                Recurvirostridae: Avocets, Stilts
                Phalaropodidae: Phalaropes
        Superfamily Dromadoidea
            Family Dromadidae: Crabplovers
        Superfamily Burhinoidea
            Family Burhinidae: Thick-knees
        Superfamily Glareoloidea
            Family Glareolidae: Pratincoles, Coursers
        Superfamily Thinocoroidea
            Family Thinocoridae: Seedsnipe
        Superfamily Chionidoidea
            Family Chionididae: Sheathbills
    Suborder Lari
        Family Stercorariidae: Skuas, Jaegers
                Laridae: Gulls, Terns
                Rynchopidae: Skimmers
    Suborder Alcae
        Family Alcidae: Auks, Auklets, Murres
Order Columbiformes
    Suborder Pterocletes
        Family Pteroclidae: Sandgrouse
    Suborder Columbae
        Family Columbidae: Pigeons, Doves
Order Psittaciformes
        Family Psittacidae: Lories, Parrots, Macaws
Order Cuculiformes
    Suborder Musophagi
        Family Musophagidae: Plantain-eaters, Touracos
    Suborder Cuculi
        Family Cuculidae: Cuckoos, Roadrunners, Anis
Order Strigiformes
        Family Tytonidae: Barn Owls
                Strigidae: Typical Owls
Order Caprimulgiformes
    Suborder Steatornithes
        Family Steatornithidae: Oilbirds
    Suborder Caprimulgi
        Family Podargidae: Frogmouths
                Nyctibiidae: Potoos
                Aegothelidae: Owlet-frogmouths
                Caprimulgidae: Goatsuckers

Order Apodiformes
   Suborder Apodi
      Family Apodidae: Swifts
         Hemiprocnidae: Crested Swifts
   Suborder Trochili
      Family Trochilidae: Hummingbirds
Order Coliiformes
      Family Coliidae: Colies
Order Trogoniformes
      Family Trogonidae: Trogons
Order Coraciiformes
   Suborder Alcedines
     Superfamily Alcedinoidea
      Family Alcedinidae: Kingfishers
     Superfamily Todoidea
      Family Todidae: Todies
     Superfamily Momotoidea
      Family Momotidae: Motmots
   Suborder Meropes
      Family Meropidae: Bee-eaters
   Suborder Coracii
      Family Coraciidae: Rollers
         Brachypteraciidae: Groundrollers
         Leptosomatidae: Cuckoo-rollers
         Upupidae: Hoopoes
         Phoeniculidae: Woodhoopoes
   Suborder Bucerotes
      Family Bucerotidae: Hornbills
Order Piciformes
   Suborder Galbulae
     Superfamily Galbuloidea
      Family Galbulidae: Jacamars
         Bucconidae: Puffbirds
     Superfamily Capitonoidea
      Family Capitonidae: Barbets
         Indicatoridae: Honeyguides
     Superfamily Ramphastoidea
      Family Ramphastidae: Toucans
   Suborder Pici
      Family Picidae: Woodpeckers, Piculets
Order Passeriformes (See below under Passeriformes)

Wetmore's eclectic classification provided an organized arrangement for all groups of birds, including the oscine Passeriformes, which Gadow had viewed as morphologically uniform and had left in much the same condition proposed by Sundevall, Sharpe, and Sclater many years earlier. Wetmore's classification has been used to organize museum collections and as the basis for the arrangement of taxa in thousands of books.

James Lee Peters (1889–1952) was appointed to the A.O.U. Check-list Committee in 1929 to fill one of the vacancies created by the deaths of Miller and Dwight. At this time, Peters was already working on his magnum opus, the *Check-List of Birds of the World*, the first volume of which was published in 1931. Peters introduced volume 1:

It is now nearly thirty-two years since the first volume of Sharpe's *Handlist of the Genera and Species of Birds* made its appearance. The five volumes comprising that work have long been the one and only standard catalogue available to ornithologists, and it is a pity that Sharpe's work could not have remained so, but the rapidity of the increase of ornithological knowledge has made it clear for a number of years that a new work along the same, or perhaps slightly more elaborate, lines was needed.

The order of families and higher groups followed in this work is essentially the same as that proposed by Wetmore in the *Proceedings U.S. National Museum*, 76, Art. 24, 1930, pp. 1–8. The arrangement of the subfamilies and the sequence of genera and species have been compiled from many sources and from personal examination of material.

Thus, Wetmore's classification was adopted for the worldwide Peters' Check-list and was used for the first seven volumes (1931–1951) that were published before Peters' death in 1952. Volumes 1–6 contained the non-passerines, and volume 7 the passeriform suborder Eurylaimi (broadbills) and the superfamily Furnarioidea (ovenbirds, antbirds, etc.) of the suborder Tyranni. The remainder of the Passeriformes had been planned for volumes 8 to 15. Additional discussion of passerine classifications is presented under the Passeriformes.

One notably unsuccessful attempt to promote a different classification was that of René Verheyen (1907–1961), who wrote a series of papers between 1953 and 1961 in which he proposed radical new arrangements of many groups. Verheyen's method was to make a large number of measurements of skeletal elements and to subject the data to a kind of numerical analysis. In some cases he split morphologically uniform groups into many monotypic genera, and in others he proposed alliances between taxa that for years had been acknowledged to be only convergently similar. Although Verheyen's studies stirred controversy, his proposals were not accepted because he was unable to offer convincing evidence of the relationships he suggested and, in most cases, there is evidence contrary to his claims.

Stresemann (1959) castigated Verheyen and was pessimistic about the possibility of improvements in the systematics of higher categories: "As far as the problem of relationship of the orders of birds is concerned, so many distinguished investigators have labored in this field in vain, that little hope is left for spectacular breakthroughs."

Erwin Stresemann (1889–1972) began his long and distinguished career early in this century and he succeeded Anton Reichenow as head of the Bird Department in the Berlin (Humboldt) Museum in 1921. Stresemann's numerous publications are principally systematic, although most do not concern higher categories. Nöhring (1973) wrote a biography and obituary of Stresemann.

The classification followed by Stresemann (1934) in writing the Aves section of Kükenthal and Krumbach's *Handbuch der Zoologie* was based primarily on that of Fürbringer, somewhat modified by that of Gadow, but Stresemann declined to unite in a single order those groups that Gadow (1892) included in his Gruiformes. Similarly, Stresemann gave ordinal rank to most of the subgroups in Gadow's Coraciiformes. Gadow recognized 20 orders, but Stresemann divided the living birds into 48 orders in 1934 and 50 in 1959. Stresemann's classification of the living non-passerines follows. Where Stresemann did not designate families it is assumed that the order contains one family, and only the ordinal and vernacular names are given.

Class Aves
   Order Struthiones
      Family Struthionidae; Ostriches

Order Rheae
    Family Rheidae; Rheas
Order Casuarii
    Family Casuariidae; Cassowaries
    Family Dromaeidae; Emus
Order Apteryges
    Family Apterygidae; Kiwis
Order Crypturi
    Family Tinamidae; Tinamous
Order Galli
    Family Cracidae; Guans, Chachalacas, Curassows
    Family Megapodiidae; Megapodes
    Family Phasianidae; Pheasants, Guineafowl, Turkeys, Grouse, Quail
Order Opisthocomi
    Family Opisthocomidae; Hoatzin
Order Turnices
    Family Turnicidae; Bustardquails
    Family Pedionomidae; Plains-wanderer
Order Columbae; Pigeons, Doves
Order Pterocletes
    Family Pteroclidae; Sandgrouse
Order Ralli; Rails, Gallinules, Coots
Order Heliornithes; Sungrebes
Order Mesoenades; Mesites
Order Jacanae; Jacanas
Order Thinocori; Seedsnipe
Order Rhinocheti; Kagu
Order Eurypygae; Sunbittern
Order Cariamae
    Family Cariamidae; Seriemas
Order Psophiae; Trumpeters
Order Grues
    Family Gruidae; Cranes
    Family Aramidae; Limpkins
Order Otides; Bustards
Order Laro-Limicolae
    Family Burhinidae; Thick-knees
    Family Dromadidae; Crab Plover
    Family Glareolidae; Pratincoles, Coursers
    Family Chionididae; Sheathbills
    Family Charadriidae; Plovers, Sandpipers, Avocets, Phalaropes, etc.
    Family Laridae; Gulls, Jaegers, Terns, Skimmers
Order Alcae; Auks, Murres, Puffins
Order Colymbi; Loons
Order Podicipedes; Grebes
Order Sphenisci; Penguins
Order Tubinares; Albatrosses, Petrels, Shearwaters
Order Anseres; Ducks, Geese, Swans
Order Anhimae; Screamers
Order Steganopodes
    Family Phaethontidae; Tropicbirds
    Family Pelecanidae; Pelicans

Family Sulidae; Gannets, Boobies
Family Phalacrocoracidae; Cormorants, Anhingas
Family Fregatidae; Frigatebirds
Order Phoenicopteri; Flamingos
Order Gressores
Family Plegadidae; Ibises, Spoonbills
Family Ciconiidae; Storks
Family Balaenicipitidae; Shoebill
Family Scopidae; Hammerhead
Family Ardeidae; Herons
Order Accipitres
Family Cathartidae; New World Vultures
Family Sagittariidae; Secretarybird
Family Falconidae; Hawks, Eagles, Kites, Osprey, Falcons, etc.
Order Cuculi
Family Musophagidae; Turacos
Family Cuculidae; Cuckoos
Order Psittaci; Parrots
Order Striges; Owls
Order Caprimulgi
Family Caprimulgidae; Goatsuckers
Family Nyctibiidae; Potoos
Family Podargidae; Frogmouths
Family Aegothelidae; Owlet-frogmouths
Family Steatornithidae; Oilbird
Order Coraciae
Family Coraciidae; Rollers
Family Leptosomatidae; Cuckoo-rollers
Family Brachypteraciidae; Ground-rollers
Order Halcyones; Kingfishers
Order Meropes; Bee-eaters
Order Momoti; Motmots
Order Todi; Todies
Order Upupae
Family Upupidae; Hoopoes
Family Bucerotidae; Hornbills
Order Trogones; Trogons
Order Colii; Mousebirds
Order Macrochires
Family Micropodidae; Swifts
Family Trochilidae; Hummingbirds
Order Pici
Suborder Galbuloidea
Family Galbulidae; Jacamars
Family Bucconidae; Puffbirds
Suborder Picoidea
Family Rhamphastidae; Toucans
Family Indicatoridae; Honeyguides
Family Capitonidae; Barbets
Family Picidae; Woodpeckers, Wrynecks
Order Passeriformes (See under Passeriformes)

In his 1959 list "Suggested Avian Orders," Stresemann (1959:278) recognized two additional orders; the Musophagae (turacos) were separated from the Cuculi, and the Macrochires were split into the Apodes (swifts) and Trochili (hummingbirds). Stresemann (1959:270) noted that "all the avian systems presented in the standard works in this century are similar to each other, since they are all based on Fürbringer and Gadow. My system of 1934 does not differ in essence from those which Wetmore (1951) and Mayr and Amadon (1951) have recommended."

Stresemann (1959) reviewed and criticized the proposals made by various authors during the preceding 60 years; his essay should be read and reread by all avian taxonomists, especially by those who believe that traditional classifications must be right because they are familiar. Stresemann was especially critical of Verheyen, but he also questioned the proposals of Lowe, Beecher, Cottam, and others. Following a comparison between Wetmore's classification and those of Verheyen, Lowe, and others, Stresemann (1959:274) commented that

Even though this is only a small selection from recent proposals, I fear that readers are already confused. But they need not feel ashamed of their discomfort. In my opinion only few, if any, of these taxonomic variants will survive the struggle of existence. Most of them will be forgotten in a few years, even though they have been to a large part the result of laborious and conscientious investigations. They have however contributed to one important realization. They have made it apparent that the relationship of certain species or groups of species is far less unequivocably established than one would conclude from a study of currently adopted systems, the authors of which attempt to present a simplified phylogenetic tree of birds. This "attempt to reduce the number of the branches of the phylogenetic tree, to make the ornithic tree simpler, more a noble tree with fewer but more generous branches," as Friedmann (1955) has put it, may have didactic advantages, but does not give a realistic representation of the actual pattern of development. Fürbringer's (1888) attempt at phylogenetic tree construction conveys a more realistic view of actuality. It shows a tall trunk which after sending out a few side branches (the ratites or protocarinates), splits up completely into a dense bush of individual branches. These branches either diverge widely from each other, or else remain closely parallel for longer or shorter stretches. The main branches correspond to the 73 families or family groups accepted by Fürbringer. He attempted to combine these into Gentes, Subordines, Ordines and Subclasses, but emphasized that the difficulties and uncertainties grow with each higher category. Let me quote his own words: "At the present time only very little is completely certain, some is highly probable, the majority of the groupings are however probable only to a medium degree."

The degree of uncertainty has decreased remarkably little since the time when the great anatomist wrote these words—in spite of all the efforts of subsequent authors. The currently adopted systems have eliminated with good reason many of Fürbringer's hypothetical groupings, particularly his Subordines and Ordines, and retained only the Gentes of his system, for which they use the name orders. Wetmore has not been entirely consistent in this, because his orders correspond sometimes to Fürbringer's Subordines, sometimes to his Gentes, which leads to unharmonious results. No doubt Wetmore has been guided by didactic considerations—an endeavor to propose a system that would be convenient for teaching purposes. Lowe (1939) seemed to have had the same objective when he was loath to place the Apodes and the Trochili into two separate orders. This, he said, "is an easy way of getting out of a difficult situation, but it tells us nothing of their affinities. In effect, it merely tells us that the swifts are swifts and the hummingbirds are hummingbirdlike birds." For this reason Lowe decided to redefine the order Passeriformes and include in it as suborders the Passeres, Cypseli, Trochili and Pici. However this is a rather hypothetical grouping, which has not fully pleased anyone. Personally I prefer a system that is as realistic as possible, a system in which no room is given to phylogenetic speculations, and in which the gaps in our knowledge are frankly admitted. If one follows these guiding principles one is forced to recognize a greater number of the highest categories, that is orders, than accepted by Wetmore—indeed even more than I admitted in 1934. Combining swifts and hummingbirds in the order Macrochires and turacos and cuckoos in the order Cuculi, as I had done following Fürbringer, was insufficiently supported by the evidence and has since been heavily attacked. The new attacks against Wetmore's system are particularly directed against those places where the author adopted as an "order" one of Fürbringer's Subordines, that is a category of "medium probability" and gave it the same rank as one of Fürbringer's Gentes, that is a category of "high probability." It seems to me that the critics would have done a more useful job if they had been satisfied to leave isolated, as groups "incertae sedis," those elements from Wetmore's structure which they removed as incongruous. However, like Lowe, they thought that that would "tell us nothing of their affinities," and thus they have inserted these building stones in a different place, where they fit even less.

Stresemann then noted several proposals with approval, but even some of these (as we will demonstrate) have not proved to be correct. Stresemann's theme in his 1959 review was that the relationships among the higher categories of birds were largely unknown, and probably unknowable because the available sources of evidence had been exhausted and there were no additional sources to be explored. He did not foresee the developments in molecular evolution that were already in progress.

A Classification of Recent Birds by Ernst Mayr and Dean Amadon (1951) presents a somewhat different arrangement of groups, although the composition of most higher catego-ries is essentially the same as in the classifications of Wetmore and Stresemann. Mayr was a student of Stresemann, and the categorical names in the Mayr and Amadon classification reflect this association, although Stresemann tended to recognize more orders and families. Mayr and Amadon attempted

to arrive at a natural arrangement for each family or other unit. Two important aims . . . are to keep related groups as close together as possible and to put ancestral groups first, derived groups later. Specialization is often a clue to relationship and phylogenetic sequence, but de-specialization may occur and much phylogenetically meaningless specialization exists. The problem of the relationship of the avian orders is an old one and one that will probably never be solved satisfactorily. One point that is frequently overlooked is that all living birds are exceedingly specialized in different directions and that this specialization had its beginning in the remote past. The connections between the living orders is lost in antiquity, and their analysis is further obscured by much convergent evolution of habitus type. [An] example of convergence is that of the "Ratites," a group which consists of at least five unrelated groups of birds, which have become flightless secondarily and attained large size. In view of the frequency of convergence among birds, it seems mandatory that some of the other heterogeneous-appearing orders of birds . . . be reexamined to evaluate the authenticity of relationship of the included families and suborders.

Although the ratites were viewed as only convergently similar, their common ancestry was soon to be demonstrated by both morphological and molecular evidence.

Following is the Mayr and Amadon (1951) classification of the living non-passerines, with subfamilies omitted. The numbers of living species, as counted in 1951, follow the names of families.

Order Struthiones
   Family Struthionidae; Ostrich, 1
Order Apteryges; Moas (fossil) and Kiwis
   Family Apterygidae; Kiwis, 3

Order Casuarii
    Family Casuariidae; Cassowaries, 3
    Family Dromaeidae; Emus, 2
Order Rheae
    Family Rheidae; Rheas, 2
Order Crypturi (Tinamiformes)
    Family Tinamidae; Tinamous, 33
Order Sphenisci
    Family Spheniscidae; Penguins, 16
Order Tubinares (Procellariiformes)
    Family Diomedeidae; Albatrosses, 13
    Family Procellariidae; Storm Petrels, Shearwaters, 73
    Family Pelecanoididae; Diving Petrels, 4
Order Podicipedes (Colymbiformes)
    Family Podicipitidae; Grebes, 20
Order Gaviae
    Family Gaviidae; Loons, 4
Order Steganopodes (Pelecaniformes)
    Family Phaethontidae; Tropic Birds, 3
    Family Fregatidae, Frigate Birds, 5
    Family Phalacrocoracidae; Cormorants, Anhingas, 31
    Family Sulidae; Boobies, Gannets, 9
    Family Pelecanidae; Pelicans, 6
Order Falcones or Accipitres
    Family Accipitridae; Hawks, Eagles, etc., 205
    Family Falconidae; Falcons, etc., 58
    Family Pandionidae; Osprey, 1
    Family Cathartidae; New World Vultures, 6
    Family Sagittariidae; Secretary Bird, 1
Order Gressores (Ciconiiformes)
    Family Ardeidae; Herons, etc., 59
    Family Threskiornithidae; Ibises, etc., 28
    Family Ciconiidae; Storks, 17 (including *Balaeniceps*)
    Family Scopidae; Hammerhead, 1
Order Phoenicopteri
    Family Phoenicopteridae; Flamingos, 6
Order Anseres
    Family Anatidae; Swans, Geese, Ducks, 145
    Family Anhimidae; Screamers, 3
Order Galli
    Family Megapodiidae; Brush Turkeys, 10
    Family Cracidae; Guans, etc., 38
    Family Phasianidae; Pheasants, Quail, Guineafowl, Grouse, etc., 190
    Family Meleagrididae; Turkeys, 2
    Family Opisthocomidae; Hoatzin, 1
Order Cuculi
    Family Musophagidae; Turacos, 19
    Family Cuculidae; Cuckoos, 128
Order Grues
    Family Cariamidae; Seriamas, 2
    Family Psophiidae; Trumpeters, 3

Family Gruidae; Cranes, 14
Family Aramidae; Limpkin, 1
Family Eurypygidae; Sun Bittern, 1
Family Heliornithidae; Sun Grebes, 3
Family Rhynochetidae; Kagu, 1
Family Otididae; Bustards, 23
Family Rallidae; Rails, 132
Family Mesoenatidae; Roatelos, 3
Family Turnicidae; Button Quails, Plains Wanderer, 16
Order Laro-Limicolae (Charadriiformes)
Family Jacanidae; Jacanas, 7
Family Thinocoridae; Seed Snipe, 4
Family Chionididae; Sheath Bills, 2
Family Dromadidae; Crab Plover, 1
Family Burhinidae; Thick-knees, 9
Family Haematopodidae; Oystercatchers, 6
Family Charadriidae; Plovers, Sandpipers, Phalaropes, Avocets, etc., 152
Family Glareolidae; Pratincoles, Coursers, 16
Family Laridae; Jaegers, Skuas, Gulls, Terns, Skimmers, 89
Family Alcidae; Auks, etc., 22
Order Columbae
Family Pteroclidae; Sand Grouse, 16
Family Columbidae; Pigeons, 289
Family Raphidae; Dodos, 3
Order Psittaci
Family Psittacidae; Parrots, 316
Order Striges
Family Strigidae; Typical Owls, Barn Owls, 134
Order Caprimulgi
Family Aegothelidae; Owlet Frogmouths, 8
Family Podargidae; Frogmouths, 12
Family Caprimulgidae; Goatsuckers, etc., 67
Family Nyctibiidae; Potoos, 5
Family Steatornithidae; Oil Bird, 1
Order Trogones
Family Trogonidae; Trogons, 35
Order Coraciae
Family Coraciidae; Typical Rollers, Cuckoo Rollers, Ground Rollers, 17
Family Alcedinidae; Kingfishers, 87
Family Meropidae; Bee-eaters, 25
Family Momotidae; Motmots, 8
Family Todidae; Todies, 5
Family Upupidae; Typical Hoopoes, Tree Hoopoes, 7
Family Bucerotidae; Hornbills, 45
Order Colii
Family Coliidae; Mousebirds, 6
Order Macrochires (Apodiformes; Micropodiformes)
Family Apodidae; Swifts, Crested Swifts, 79
Family Trochilidae; Hummingbirds, 319
Order Pici
Family Bucconidae; Puffbirds, 32
Family Galbulidae; Jacamars, 14

Family Capitonidae; Barbets, 76
Family Picidae; Wrynecks, Piculets, Woodpeckers, 210
Family Ramphastidae; Toucans, 37
Family Indicatoridae; Honey Guides, 12
Order Passeres (See under Passeriformes)

Herbert Friedmann (1900–1987) spent most of his long career at the U.S. National Museum (now the National Museum of Natural History) and many of his publications dealt with the avian social parasites, cowbirds and cuckoos, and with avian systematics. In 1955 he discussed "recent revisions in classification" with reference to all taxonomic levels. He noted the tendency to "unite families where possible, to reduce the disproportionately large number of them and to bring the classification of birds more into harmony with that of other groups." His examples included the merging of "the Turdidae, Muscicapidae, and Sylviidae into one family; the proposed division of the Coerebidae, putting one part in the Parulidae and the other part in the Thraupidae;" and other suggestions. The two mentioned have turned out to be wrong, if our DNA-DNA hybridization evidence is to be believed. Some of the other examples given by Friedmann have also proved to be wrong, but the placement of the Wrentit (Chamaeidae) in the Timaliidae (by Delacour 1946) was correct. Friedmann compared the classifications of Mayr and Amadon (1951) and of Wetmore (1951), noting similarities and differences in the number of families and subfamilies, and the sequence of passerine families. The only comments about the non-passerines in Friedmann's essay concerned the merging of "the Anhingidae with the Phalacrocoracidae, the Tetraonidae and Numididae with the Phasianidae, the Phoeniculidae with the Upupidae, etc." We disagree with these proposals, except for that of including the Tetraonidae in the Phasianidae.

Robert W. Storer (1971) discussed the classification of birds, including reviews of several problem groups and the principles of classifying. He introduced his classification: "Like all classifications, the following one is to a large extent subjective." Its eclectic origin was specified by stating that he had incorporated what he felt were the "best features" of the arrangements of previous authors and the suggestions of specialists on various groups. The classification included fossil groups and, for Recent families, vernacular names, brief descriptions of geographical range, and numbers of genera and species. Storer's arrangement is similar to that of Wetmore (1960) in some aspects, but he placed the penguins in an order (Sphenisciformes) adjacent to the tubenoses (Procellariiformes), thus emphasizing the phylogenetic proximity of these two groups, and he separated the loons and the grebes with several other orders between them. Storer noted Ligon's (1967) conclusion that the New World vultures are most closely related to the storks, but declined to place them together because "there remain the problems of what to do with the ibises, spoonbills, hammerhead (*Scopus*), and whale-headed (*Balaeniceps*) 'stork,' which Ligon did not include in his discussion."

Walter J. Bock has published a series of systematic studies during the past thirty-five years, including a classification (1982) that owes much of its structure to those of Wetmore, and Mayr and Amadon. Bock's classification includes reviews of the characters of the groups and references to the literature. Bock placed the penguins in the superorder Impennes, as did Wetmore (1960), and noted that "This group is believed to be closely related to and descended from the Procellariiformes, but is separated as a superorder because of the extreme modifications for swimming and life in the cold southern oceans" (p. 967). This identifies Bock as a member of the evolutionary school of classification; indeed, he has been one of the most able proponents of this viewpoint (e.g., 1973).

"During the past 50 years of stagnation in the development of avian classification, new data has [sic] been acquired making a rearrangement of avian families possible, because the orders in the Fürbringer-Gadow-Wetmore tradition are more ecological than systematic groups." With this introduction, Mlíkovsky (1985) proposed a new classification with the hope that it would "stimulate new ornithosystematical research." This classification included fossil groups, which are omitted from the following synopsis.

Struthioniformes: Struthionidae, Rheidae, Casuariidae
Passerida (new subclass for the 1st branch of the Cenozoic radiation; type: Passer Linné 1758):
Alciformes: Stercorariidae, Rynchopidae, Alcidae.
Ardeiformes: Gaviidae, Phaethontidae, Ardeidae, Sulidae, Phalacrocoracidae, Anhingidae,
    Opisthocomidae.
Bucerotiformes: Upupidae, Phoeniculidae, Bucerotidae, Eurylaimidae, Philepittidae.
Ralliformes: Rallidae, Aramidae, Psophiidae, Gallinulidae, Heliornithidae, Rhynochetidae,
    Eurypygidae, Mesitornithidae, Turnicidae (incl. Pedionomidae), Cariamidae.
Accipitriformes: Cuculidae, Centropodidae, Accipitridae (incl. Pandionidae), Sagittariidae,
    Phasianidae, Cracidae, Megapodiidae.
Strigiformes: Strigidae, Leptosomatidae, Steatornithidae, Caprimulgidae (incl. Nyctibiidae),
    Podargidae (incl. Aegothelidae), Musophagidae (incl. Couidae), Falconidae.
Columbiformes: Halcyonidae, Todidae, Momotidae, Meropidae, Trogonidae, Columbidae.
Trochiliformes: Bucconidae, Galbulidae, Coraciidae, Apodidae, Trochilidae.
Tyranniformes: Tyrannidae (incl. Oxyruncidae), Querulidae (incl. Phytotomidae), Pipridae,
    Thamnophilidae (incl. Conopophagidae), Scytalopodidae, Furnariidae, Dendrocolaptidae.
Passeriformes: many families with less known relationships.
Ciconiida: (new subclass for the 2nd branch of the Cenozoic radiation; type Ciconia Brisson 1760).
Apterygiformes: Procellariidae, Hydrobatidae, Pelecanoididae, Spheniscidae, Apterygidae,
    Tinamidae, Podicipedidae, Dromadidae, Chionididae.
Ciconiiformes: Ciconiidae (incl. Balaenicipitidae), Pelecanidae, Fregatidae, Scopidae, Vulturidae
    [New World vultures], Charadriidae, Glareolidae, Pterocletidae, Laridae.
Anseriformes: Phoenicopteridae, Recurvirostridae, Haematopodidae, Burhinidae, Anseridae,
    Anhimidae, Otididae, Jacanidae, Rostratulidae, Gruidae.
Plataleiformes: Plataleidae, Scolopacidae (incl. Phalaropodidae. Piciformes: Pteroglossidae,
    Capitornidae, Indicatoridae, Picidae.
Aves inc. sedis: Hemiprocnidae, Thinocoridae.
Passerida inc. sedis: Acanthisittidae, Pittidae.
Ciconiida inc. sedis: Coliidae, Psittacidae.

In addition to evidence from other sources, Mlíkovsky based his classification on "A large amount of data . . . evaluated by means of new methods of biological systematics (developed by Mlíkovsky) which have been based especially on new achievements in mathematical logics." No comment.

There have been other classifications proposed during the past 50 years, but most reflect the concepts of avian phylogeny that were inherited from Huxley, Fürbringer, and Gadow and rendered into authoritarian tradition by Wetmore and Stresemann.

As "a first attempt at a phylogenetic classification of Recent birds" Cracraft (1981) proposed to apply the principles of classification enunciated by Willi Hennig (1966) to the analysis of morphological characters. Cracraft (1981:683) stated his

view that most avian orders (say, of Mayr and Amadon 1951, or of Wetmore 1960) are monophyletic, but that most hierarchical arrangements of taxa within orders are not. The reasons for this are not difficult to identify (Cracraft 1972, 1980): it has resulted from the attempts of avian systematists to cluster taxa on the basis of overall (or weighted) similarity and to bestow high rank on taxa that are morphologically divergent compared to their closest relatives. More specifically, systematists have not partitioned similarity into its primitive and derived components and clustered using only the latter. Because a distinction is not made between primitive and derived characters, the analysis of different anatomical systems frequently has produced conflicting opinions about relationships. Such conflicts are often so pronounced that some workers have viewed the situation as hopeless; Stresemann's (1959) rationalizations and classification are the epitome of this viewpoint, but evidence of it can be found in virtually every classification. A cladistic analysis can help resolve this conflict by showing that at least some of the confusion is the result of uniting taxa on the basis of primitive characters. . . . This is not to say, of course, that every cladistic analysis applied to the same group will always produce either identical results or a fully resolved phylogenetic hypothesis, but at least the reasons for any differences of opinion will be easy to identify.

Cracraft reviewed the principles of phylogenetic classification and introduced his classification

as a preliminary expression of ideas that will certainly be modified and improved with future work. No aspect of the classification is viewed as writ in stone.

I make no pretense about providing complete documentation for each . . . allocation, but . . . approach this problem from two standpoints. First, many of the reasons for these decisions are based on published or soon to be published studies. . . . Second, for . . . decisions . . . based on little evidence or [that] merely follow tradition, I have . . . made note of this. It is too early to document a complete phylogeny of birds, and thus I have tried to call attention to areas of controversy and . . . questions in need of more study. I have not consciously ignored contemporary opinions that are at variance with my views. I believe that this classification is as well documented, if not better, as any classification proposed in recent years.

The classification attempts to maintain traditional names and ranks . . . to the extent possible. Two problems within ornithology have been the tendency to conceptualize groups . . . as being "orders" or "families" and to assume that certain morphological or behavioral distinctions are worth ordinal or familial rank. This type of thinking has hurt avian systematics. . . . A final decision about the relative ranks of avian taxa will have to await the integration of avian phylogenetic results with those of the other vertebrates and an eventual classificatory scheme for all these taxa.

Because phylogenetic classifications embody more information . . . and are more complex than traditional classifications, it has been necessary to introduce additional levels (e.g., divisions, cohorts) not usually found in recent classifications. . . . these categorical levels, however, have been used in previous . . . classifications or are common in those of other vertebrates. . . . the introduction of these levels increases the information content of the classification.

Thus, unlike many previous classifiers, Cracraft presented his philosophy of classification and the basis for his arrangement. Cladistic principles are logical, but can they be used to derive the true, one and only, phylogeny from morphological characters? If so, the derivation of a classification that is isomorphic with that phylogeny is also possible. Cracraft's classification of the living non-passerines follows. The format has been slightly modified to conserve space, and vernacular names are added for convenience.

Class Aves
  Subclass Neornithes

  Division 1
    Cohort Gavio-impennes
      Order Sphenisciformes; Spheniscidae, Penguins
      Order Gaviiformes: Gaviidae, Loons
                        Podicipedidae, Grebes
    Cohort Stegano-tubinares
      Order Procellariiformes
        Suborder Diomedeae; Diomedeidae, Albatrosses
        Suborder Procellariae; Hydrobatidae, Storm Petrels
                              Procellariidae, Shearwaters, etc.
      Order Pelecaniformes
        Suborder Phaethontes, Phaethontidae, Tropicbirds
        Suborder Steganopodes
          Infraorder Fregatae; Fregatidae, Frigatebirds
          Infraorder Pelecani
            Superfam. Pelecanoidea; Pelecanidae, Pelicans
            Superfam. Suloidea; Sulidae, Boobies, Gannets
                              Phalacrocoracidae, Cormorants, Anhingas

  Division 2
    Order Palaeognathiformes
      Suborder Tinami; Tinamidae, Tinamous
      Suborder Ratiti
        Infraorder Apteryges: Dinornithidae, Moas
                            Apterygidae, Kiwis
        Infraorder Struthiones
          Superfam. Casuaroidea; Casuariidae, Cassowaries
                              Dromiceidae, Emus
          Superfam. Struthionoidea; Rheidae, Rheas
                              Struthionidae, Ostrich

  Division 3
    Order Ciconiiformes
      Suborder Ardeae; Ardeidae, Herons
                      Balaenicipitidae, Shoebill
      Suborder Ciconiae
        Infraorder Scopiae; Scopidae, Hammerhead
        Infraorder Ciconii
          Superfam. Threskiornithoidea; Threskiornithidae, Ibises, etc.
          Superfam. Ciconoidea; Ciconiidae, Storks
                              Phoenicopteridae, Flamingos
    Order Falconiformes
      Suborder Cathartae, Cathartidae, New World Vultures
      Suborder Accipitres
        Infraorder Sagittarii; Sagittariidae, Secretarybird
        Infraorder Falconi
          Superfam. Strigoidea, Strigidae, Owls
          Superfam. Falconoidea, Pandionidae, Osprey
                              Accipitridae, Accipitrinae, Hawks, Eagles
                              Falconinae, Falcons

Division 4
  Order Anseriformes; Anhimidae, Screamers
                            Anatidae, Ducks, Geese, Swans
  Order Galliformes
    Suborder Opisthocomi; Opisthocomidae, Hoatzin
    Suborder Galli
      Infraorder Megapodi; Megapodiidae, Megapodes
      Infraorder Phasiani
        Superfam. Cracoidea; Cracidae, Guans, etc.
        Superfam. Phasianoidea; Numididae, Guineafowl
                            Phasianidae, Pheasants, Quail, etc.

Division 5
  Order Gruiformes
        Mesitornithidae, Mesites, *incertae sedis*
        Otididae, Bustards, *incertae sedis*
        Turnicidae, Bustardquails, *incertae sedis*
    Suborder Grues
     Infrasuborder Grui; Gruidae, Cranes
     Infrasuborder Arames
      Infraorder Arami; Aramidae, Limpkin
      Infraorder Psophii
        Superfam. Psophioidea; Psophiidae, Trumpeters
                            Cariamidae, Seriemas
        Superfam. Rhynocheti; Rhynochetidae, Kagu
                            Eurypygidae, Sunbittern
    Suborder Ralli; Heliornithidae, Sungrebes
                            Rallidae, Rails, Gallinules, Coots
  Order Charadriiformes
    Suborder Alcae; Alcidae, Auks, Murres, Puffins
    Suborder Charadriomorpha
      Infraorder Dromae; Dromadidae, Crab Plover
      Infraorder Lari
        Superfam. Stercorarioidea; Stercorariidae, Jaegers, Skuas
        Superfam. Laroidea; Rynchopidae, Skimmers
                            Laridae, Gulls, Terns
      Infraorder Chionae; Chionididae, Sheathbills
                            Thinocoridae, Seedsnipe
      Infraorder Burhini; Burhinidae, Thick-knees
      Infraorder Charadrii
        Superfam. Haematopoidea; Haematopodidae, Oystercatchers
                            Recurvirostridae, Avocets, Stilts
        Superfam. Charadrioidea; Glareolidae, Coursers
                            Vanellidae, Lapwings
                            Charadriidae, Plovers
    Suborder Scolopaci
        Superfam. Jacanoidea; Jacanidae, Jacanas
                            Rostratulidae, Painted Snipe
        Superfam. Scolopacoidea; Scolopacidae, Sandpipers, etc.
  Order Columbiformes; Pteroclidae, Sandgrouse
                            Columbidae, Pigeons, Doves

Division 6
    Order Psittaciformes; Psittacidae, Parrots

Division 7
    Order Cuculiformes; Musophagidae, Turacos
                              Cuculidae, Cuckoos

Division 8
    Order Caprimulgiformes
        Suborder Podargi; Aegithelidae, Owlet-frogmouths
                      Podargidae, Frogmouths
        Suborder Caprimulgi
            Infraorder Steatornithes; Steatornithidae, Oilbird
            Infraorder Caprimulges; Nyctibiidae, Potoos
                          Caprimulgidae, Nightjars
    Order Apodiformes
        Suborder Trochili, Trochilidae, Hummingbirds
        Suborder Apodi, Hemiprocnidae, Crested Swifts
                    Apodidae, Typical Swifts

Division 9
    Order Piciformes
        Suborder Galbulae; Galbulidae, Jacamars
                    Bucconidae, Puffbirds
        Suborder Pici
            Superfam. Capitonoidea, Capitonidae, Barbets
                          Ramphastidae, Toucans
            Superfam. Picoidea; Indicatoridae, Honeyguides
                          Picidae, Woodpeckers
    Order Coliiformes; Coliidae, Colies
    Order Coraciiformes
        Suborder Alcedines
           Infraorder Alcedini
                Superfam. Alcedinoidea; Alcedinidae, Kingfishers
                            Meropidae, Bee-eaters
                Superfam. Momotoidea; Todidae, Todies
                          Momotidae, Motmots
           Infraorder Coracii
                Superfam. Leptosomatoidea; Leptosomatidae, Cuckoo-rollers
                Superfam. Coracioidea; Coraciidae, Rollers
                          Brachypteraciidae, Ground-rollers
           Infraorder Trogones; Trogonidae, Trogons
        Suborder Upupes; Upupidae, Hoopoes
                    Phoeniculidae, Wood Hoopoes
        Suborder Bucerotes, Bucerotidae, Hornbills
    Order Passeriformes (See under Passeriformes)

Whatever may be the virtues of cladistic analysis, Cracraft's classification indicates that it does not consistently separate homology from analogy, as indicated by his placing the loons and grebes together and the owls with the falconiforms. He referred to the fact that many nineteenth-century systematists associated the hawks and owls as part of the support for these conclusions; true, but others did not.

Cracraft's classification was vigorously attacked by Olson (1982), who summarized his critique: "Abstract.—A recently proposed 'phylogenetic' classification of birds (Cracraft 1981b) is not constructed according to cladistic principles and contains little information to support most of the taxa proposed in it. That which is presented is frequently misleading or erroneous. The nomenclature used is inconsistent and ungrammatical. In failing to provide synapomorphies to cluster taxa, in using data that are not presented in a primitive-derived sequence, in citing differences as evidence of nonrelationship, and using convergence to refute phylogenetic hypotheses, Cracraft commits the very methodological transgressions for which he has long criticized other systematists" (p. 733).

In his Conclusion Olson stated that

The one unequivocal message that has emerged from recent arguments is that not all systematists are willing to accept one and the same methodology. Mayr and others (see Mayr 1981 and references cited therein) have presented counterarguments and alternatives to cladistics, for example. Dissent could continue indefinitely without a consensus being reached. Overlooked in the tumult is the basic fact that advances in avian systematics are the result of hard, often tedious work, whether it entails breaking up rocks and grinding out fossils, dissecting tiny muscles for hours under a microscope, skinning birds and counting feathers in pterylae, or other laborious procedures. Only through the accumulation of more and more data in this manner will our understanding of avian evolution be promoted. Unfortunately, the era of Hennig, Popper, and Croizat, which has brought such controversy to systematics, has also created an environment in which unsubstantiated speculation is not only condoned but encouraged. Yet before we will ever have a phylogeny that reflects the probable evolutionary history of the Class Aves, someone will have to do the work upon which such a phylogeny must ultimately be based (p. 738).

It is obvious that a consensus about the phylogeny and classification of birds had not yet been achieved in 1982.

CHAPTER FIFTEEN

Principles and Methods of Classification

In regard to classification and all the endless disputes about the "Natural System," which no two authors define in the same way, I believe it ought, in accordance to my heterodox notions, to be simply genealogical. But as we have no written pedigrees you will, perhaps, say this will not help much; but I think it ultimately will, whenever heterodoxy becomes orthodoxy, for it will clear away an immense amount of rubbish about the value of characters, and will make the difference between analogy and homology clear. The time will come, I believe, though I shall not live to see it, when we shall have very fairly true genealogical trees of each great kingdom of Nature.

Charles Darwin 1857:104

Had Darwin left it at this the history of ideas about how to classify organisms might have been different, but he made a critical addition in the *Origin of Species* (1859:420): "But I must explain my meaning more fully. I believe that the *arrangement* of the groups within each class, in due subordination and relation to each other, must be strictly genealogical in order to be natural; but that the *amount* of difference in the several branches or groups, though allied in the same degree in blood to their common progenitor, may differ greatly, being due to the different degrees of modification which they have undergone; and this is expressed by the forms being ranked under different genera, families, sections, or orders."

The idea that classifications should express both "genealogy" (phylogeny) and degrees of morphological specialization became the basis for classifying and was virtually the only philosophy of classification until the late 1950s (e.g., Sokal and Michener 1958). More on this below.

The classifications of birds reviewed in this book support Raikow's (1985b:187) claim that "the higher-level classification of birds is in an unsatisfactory state." We also agree with Raikow (1985b:188) that "a classification should reveal the pattern of order that underlies the diversity among species and that the source of this diversity is the evolutionary history of the group." Many biologists will accept these statements, but there is substantial controversy about the relationship between the evidence of evolutionary history and the construction of a classification.

Today there are three schools of thought in systematics: the traditional or eclectic (evolutionary), the phenetic (numerical taxonomy), and the cladistic (phylogenetic). Numerical methods may also be used in cladistic analyses, thus another distinction is between numerical phenetics and numerical cladistics.

The adherents of the traditional, or so-called evolutionary, school accept the view expressed by Darwin (1859:420, quoted above) and advocate an eclectic selection of evidence as the basis for a classification that will express both the phylogeny (clades) and the degree of morphological specialization of lineages (grades). To achieve this goal it is assumed that "greater phenotypical similarity implies greater genetical similarity and hence closer relationship" (Bock 1973:377). This idea was proposed by Simpson (1944:3) as the practical solution to what he considered the ideal, namely, that the "Rate of evolution might most desirably be defined as amount of genetic change in a population per . . . unit of absolute time."

There is, of course, a relationship between phenotype and genotype, but morphological characters evolve at many different rates and the relationship between morphology and phylogeny is neither simple nor direct. To the human eye closely related taxa may look so different that they are judged to merit recognition as members of different higher categories, and distantly related but convergently similar species may be thought to be close relatives. With this method art replaces science and the subjective evaluations of the taxonomist are the only criteria for the erection of categories and their arrangement in a classification. Intuition is not a substitute for measurement, and the failures of the eclectic school litter the historical landscape of avian systematics.

Thus, the evolutionary systematists permit the recognition of groups that are not monophyletic, and they have not defined a set of objective, quantitative procedures to produce classifications (Sokal 1985:734). Hull (1970:49) argued that "decreasing the amount of art in taxonomy is desireable" and suggested that "the resistance to making taxonomic practice and procedures explicit seems to have stemmed from two sources: one, an obscurantist obsession with the ultimate mystery of the human intellect; the other, a concern over how much theoretical significance one must sacrifice in order to make biological classification explicit." Raikow (1985b:189) dismissed eclectic classifications as meaningless because they are inconsistent in the "methods by which taxa are recognized and ranked" and therefore ambiguous "about the information content of both taxa and categories." We agree with Hull and Raikow.

The pheneticists argue that organisms should be classified according to their "overall similarity," which is based on as many phenotypic characters as possible with each character being given equal weight (Sokal and Sneath 1973:5). The same characters are compared among taxa, which are then clustered in a hierarchical arrangement on the basis of shared similarities. "The goal of phenetic taxonomy is to arrange objects or operational taxonomic units (OTU's) in a stable and convenient classification. It is believed that basing classifications on similarity will result in such stability and convenience. The measurement of similarity is made on the basis of numerous, equally weighted characteristics. The degree of belonging to a class is based on its constituent properties. . . . a system of classification is the more natural the more propositions there are that can be made regarding its constituent classes, affinity in a polythetic taxon is based on the greatest number of shared character states. No single state is either essential to group membership or sufficient to make an organism a member of the group" (Sokal 1985:733).

Attempts to use morphological characters under this approach have had limited success as the basis for constructing classifications for essentially the same reasons that eclectic procedures have failed. Numerical taxonomists have had little effect on avian systematics, but they have made valuable contributions to the mathematical treatment of data analyzed by computer programs.

Sneath and Sokal (1973:73) equated "unit characters" with the bits of information theory and "tentatively" identified "taxonomic bits with the genetic code." They equated "taxonomic bits" with nucleotides by noting that "the number of bits in the genome ranges from around 10^4 for some viruses to around 10^{11} for many higher animals." Colless (1967:295) suggested that "the codon elements thus employed as attributes must, surely, be the ultimate approximation of our notion of 'unit attributes' . . . and the rationale provides a valuable illustration of the ultimate identity of phylogenetic and phenetic procedures."

The cladists, or phylogeneticists, attempt to express only the branching pattern of the phylogeny in their classifications. Most cladists use morphological characters analyzed by the methods proposed by Willi Hennig (1966) in which any character is partitioned into "primitive" and "derived" character states. Primitive character states are those present in all members of a group and, therefore, must represent the condition in the common ancestor of the group. Derived character states are those that have evolved from the primitive state, are shared by a more limited set of taxa, and therefore define related subsets of the total set. A clade is a monophyletic group clustered by shared derived characters (synapomorphy). A cladogram is a synapomorphy distribution diagram and takes the form of a nested arrangement of clades. A phylogenetic tree is a hypothesis of genealogical relationships based on a cladogram.

In a cladistic classification only monophyletic groups are recognized as taxa. A monophyletic group consists of an ancestral species (usually hypothetical) and all of its descendants, and "rank is determined by position in the cladogram so that the ranking pattern mirrors the pattern of nested clades on which it is based" (Raikow 1985b:189).

In any Linnaean classification, the taxa are arranged in a nested hierarchy of progressively more inclusive ranks or categories. In cladistic classifications, the pattern of cladistic relationships, usually taken to hypothesize genealogy, is the basis for ranking. The clades are recognized as taxa and their rank is determined by their position. More inclusive groups are ranked at higher category levels than less inclusive groups. In its simplest form, a cladistic classification places all sister taxa at the same rank. This is totally unambiguous; the classification exactly expresses the genealogy. This procedure has been criticized, however, because it produces classifications with so many ranks and taxa that they may become impractical. Various methods have therefore been devised to simplify cladistic classifications while retaining the essential feature of consistency. It is significant that one can always reconstruct the phylogeny from the classification (Raikow 1985b:195).

Willi Hennig, the patron saint of cladism, proposed that the age of origin should be the basis for the absolute ranking of categories. He wrote (1966:160) that it seems evident

that morphological divergence is not a suitable way of determining absolute rank order if all groups of the same rank are to be comparable in a theoretically incontestable way. But this does not mean that there is no way of achieving this goal. In the phylogenetic system there are actually groups that are unquestionably comparable ("equivalent") in an exactly determined sense, and in every case these must have the same absolute rank. These are the groups that stand in a sister-group relation to one another. . . . The most important reason why sister groups are comparable to such an unsurpassed degree is their origin from the same "root," in other words the fact that they began their development from the same initial conditions and passed through it from the same prerequisites. A part of these prerequisites is the simultaneity of their origin. . . . establishing the absolute rank of systematic categories according to age of origin would mean solving the problem of making directly recognizable—by their absolute rank—which groups are in a definite sense comparable. This measure is even a logical augmentation of the fundamental structural principle of the phylogenetic system. . . . this structural principle is based on the assumption that, in ordering monophyletic groups in the system according to relative rank, they are arranged according to their relative age of origin. Consequently it is logical to augment relative age of origin by a determination of absolute rank according to absolute age of origin. Obviously this kind of determination of the absolute rank of systematic categories can never lead to a breakdown of the basic structural principles of the phylogenetic system.

Hennig discussed several possible methods for determining the absolute ages of higher taxa, but in 1950, when the German edition of his book was published, there was "no single method with which the age of origin of systematic groups can be determined accurately and certainly. Even in the most favorable cases only minimal and maximal limits can be recognized. Consequently objections to determining the absolute rank of systematic groups on the basis of their age seem to be justified. The idea of determining the rank of a group by its age has hitherto been rarely expressed; it has always been rejected either by the author himself or by other critics" (Hennig 1966:182).

Most of Hennig's disciples have also rejected this principle, probably because, as Hennig noted, the absolute age of origin cannot be determined from morphology because of the different rates of evolution among morphological characters. DNA-DNA hybridization provides relative dates, and a few reasonably accurate absolute dates, for the origins of sister groups. We have based the categories in our classification on Hennig's principle with modifications for practicality. Raikow (1985b:196) agrees that our procedure is acceptable because it estimates "divergence by calibrating DNA hybridization measurements against dates based on geological events and the fossil record" and "meaningful because [it is] applied consistently throughout the analysis." We appreciate Raikow's comments, but it is clear that different rates of genomic evolution also pose problems for DNA comparisons.

Cladistic analysis may be the most effective procedure for the analysis of morphological characters, but the method has its problems and its critics. As Ghiselin (1984:219) noted:

Cladistic techniques often give ambiguous results. Different data imply different genealogies. Usually this is the result of parallel evolution—derived conditions have evolved more than once. As the cladists see it, the only permissible solution under such circumstances is to opt for the most 'parsimonious' tree, in the sense of the one that invokes the smallest number of changes. One cannot use one's understanding of the organisms to decide which changes have occurred more than once. This is called 'character weighting' and is not allowed. We are forbidden, for example, to say that a vestigial part represents the ancestral condition, or to consider what would be physiologically advantageous in a new environment. We are told that invoking multiple changes means an ad hoc hypothesis—even when we know that multiple changes have in fact occurred. Again the Popperian philosophy can be invoked against such views. Popper clearly distinguishes between ad hoc hypothesis, intended to preclude refutation, from auxiliary hypotheses, which enrich the system and narrow down the range of acceptable possibilities. There need be nothing ad hoc in phylogenetics about invoking stratigraphy, biogeography, genetics, embryology, or ecology. Popper calls not for naive parsimony, but for stringency.

Abbott et al. (1985:250) also commented on the problems of the cladist school and noted the schism between the classical and the pattern cladists:

The classical cladists (or Hennigian or evolutionary cladists) persist in interpreting cladograms in terms of possible phylogenies, the placing and sequences of fossils, the adaptive nature of synapomorphies and of biogeographic perspectives. The precision in cladist methodology is an enormous advance over narrative methods, but even so the method has, rightly, been criticized (Halstead 1982) for the apparent precision and respectability that a cladogram confers on what is really a speculation. Selecting synapomorphies, inferring polarity, and resolving conflicts are subjective, unreliable exercises, as Halstead demonstrates. We would also criticize the monothetic evolutionary model held by Hennig, although this has puzzlingly been dropped by some recent cladists. So, for instance, the presence of various chlorophylls might be proposed as a synapomorphy limiting several groups of green plants, even though there are substantial exceptions such as the lack of the chlorophylls in the parasitic angiosperm family Orobanchaceae.

By contrast the pattern cladists (or transformed cladists) offer cladism as the most effective hierarchical method of describing the variation pattern found among organisms. Synapomorphy is rephrased either as statements of homology (Patterson 1982), or as shared, less-generalized character states; and a cladogram is seen as representing the natural pattern or the classification, but not the phylogeny. They admit the uncertain tie between cladistic results and the true phylogeny. This view has much to commend it and . . . pattern cladism is increasingly being compared with phenetics in terms of precise information-preserving classification structures.

We see DNA hybridization as compatible with Hennigian principles but providing a source of evidence other than morphology for the reconstruction of phylogeny. Some cladists (for example, Robert Raikow) agree. Other cladists do not. Eldredge and Cracraft (1980:48) state that "Techniques such as DNA hybridization, starch-gel electrophoresis, or immunological reactions can be used to estimate the degree of genetic similarity among species. The methods of analysis adopted in these studies, although routinely used to produce branching diagrams depicting concepts of relationship, are qualitatively different [from cladistic analysis] . . . in that they make no attempt to distinguish between primitive and derived similarities. Instead, similarity (or dissimilarity) matrices are produced [which]. . . . are then analyzed by various clustering techniques to yield branching diagrams. This approach is analogous methodologically to the concept of general 'overall similarity' adopted by numerical taxonomy in that similarity is expressed as a numerical value in a data matrix, and then the latter is used to produce a branching diagram of some kind. . . . cladistic analysis . . . is theoretically and methodologically distinct from the techniques mentioned above."

Ghiselin (1984:220), a reasonably neutral, but critical, observer, commented:

The metaphysical dogma that systematics proceeds by correlating characters leads to legitimate empirical evidence being discarded because it does not fit in with methodological fiats. A good example is DNA hybridization, which theory suggests and experience has shown can be a very useful technique. Eldredge and Cracraft [1980:48] reject it, because it does not distinguish primitive characters from derived ones. As good Popperians we ought to refute something here. How does DNA hybridization work? It uses a mode of inference similar to that of isotopic dating, in which a substance changes from one kind to another, and the proportion of the two is a measure of time elapsed since the origin. In DNA the initial condition is that of the ancestral population, in which for practical purposes the homologous parts of the DNA are identical. After speciation, changes occur such that the proportion of non-identical homologues increases. The proportion of non-identical homologues is a function of the time that has elapsed since speciation, and the tendency to hybridize is a good index of it. The technique may, perhaps, measure absolute time, but relative time is enough to give branching sequences. The technique works. It works because, in spite of cladist animadversions, in phylogenetic research we need not merely put similar objects together. Any procedure that allows us to discriminate between lineages ought to be acceptable.

All this is symptomatic. Cladistic philosophy treats the universe as if it were something other than a whole. Every character is treated as if it lived in a little world all its own; this in spite of the fact that the existence of but one true phylogenetic tree for the whole of life is one of the basic premises. Whatever the merits of phylogenetic analysis, we also need synthesis. The various branches of knowledge must cohere and lend each other mutual support. In setting up an extreme dichotomy between pattern and process, we lose the advantage of what Hennig called 'reciprocal illumination'. Evolutionary biology without phylogenetics is like physics without astronomy. Phylogenetics without evolutionary biology is like astronomy without mechanics.

We agree with Ghiselin, but Eldredge and Cracraft also have a point, if not exactly the one they presented above. DNA hybridization distance values are analyzed in a matrix and the average measurements for each node are used to reconstruct the branching pattern of the phylogeny. The measures, however, are not of "overall similarity" but of median sequence divergence, which may be construed as an index to median similarity or dissimilarity. It seems reasonable to assume that a median distance measure, based on essentially the entire genome, is a better index to the properties of that genome than the relatively small number of morphological characters used in numerical taxonomy or cladistics, or the small number of proteins indexed by electrophoretic or immunological methods.

It is interesting that Eldredge and Cracraft (1980:48) accept amino acid sequences of proteins as valid data for cladistic analysis because they "can be evaluated in terms of primitive and derived similarities." A protein sequence indexes an average of about 1000 nucleotides, but avian DNA hybridization values are the averages of about a billion nucleotides—a million times as much information as in an average protein. Furthermore, it has become clear during the past few years that if the sequence of a large enough segment of DNA is determined it will give the same answer as DNA hybridization to questions of phylogenetic relationship (e.g., Britten 1986, Miyamoto et al. 1987, Goodman et al. 1990, Koop et al. 1989). To reject distance measures based on the entire genome in favor of the information in a minute product of that genome is to favor ideology over reason. This attitude has more to do with politics than with science.

Raikow (1985b:209–210) summarized his review of problems in avian classification:

To simplify greatly, the matter in contention seems to boil down to this: relationships between species may be expressed in terms of overall similarity or of genealogy. Whatever one's kind of data or method of analysis and however clearly or uncertainly that methodology is explained or understood, one is ultimately trying to express either a pattern of resemblances or one of descent. Given this, it might be expected that there would be two taxonomic schools, but there are instead three. One is the phenetic school, which uses the methods of numerical taxonomy to construct phenograms or patterns of similarity in morphological characters or biochemical substances. This school . . . has not been greatly active in ornithology. The second school is that of cladistics, which aims at reconstructing the pattern of phylogeny. The third school, eclectic or traditional taxonomy, is the approach that has been used for many years in ornithology and on which our standard classifications are mainly based; for this reason I have given it much attention. In this school, classification is based on a combination of similarity and genealogy.

Shall we then classify by similarity, by genealogy, or by a combination of the two? To put it another way, do we want our classifications to be maximally predictive of resemblance or of descent? Inasmuch as the pattern of avian diversity has its origin in evolutionary history, I agree with most avian systematists that purely phenetic classification is not the road to follow and I will say no more about numerical taxonomy. The real debate is between the cladistic and eclectic schools.

A classification is a statement about a hierarchical arrangement of subordinated groups. If those groups are generated by a single method, then there is no ambiguity about their meaning. This is the advantage of cladistic classification: it tells us with certainty what an author has decided about the pattern of genealogical descent uniting the species included.

The eclectic system, in contrast, has attempted to include both relationships of similarity and of descent within a single classification. Because the two give different patterns, they cannot be combined except by some arbitrary and subjective intermixture of the two. As a result, eclectic classifications are ambiguous in that we never know what kind of relationship is being hypothesized. This approach has fostered in avian systematics an atmosphere of authoritarianism that is contrary to the scientific ideal of inquiry and debate.

What then is our prospect for obtaining in the near future a satisfactory classification of birds? I believe that the prospect is good and that the desired goal will result from the application of cladistic classifying methods to the findings of both traditional (e.g., morphological) and new (e.g., DNA hybridization) data, and the fruitful comparison of their results. Cladistic classification is not without difficulties, however, and will ultimately be subject to the test of time and usage. Who would dare to predict what the seventh edition of the A.O.U checklist will look like? Not I.

We agree with Raikow, but we hope to see evidence in the next A.O.U checklist that at least some of our results have been accepted. David Hull (1988) describes and discusses the recent history of systematic biology, with emphasis on the competition and cooperation among and within the three schools.

CHAPTER SIXTEEN

Classification of Birds Based on DNA-DNA Hybridization

We believe that DNA hybridization provides data that are a valid basis for the reconstruction of phylogeny and we accept the view that classifications should be based only on the branching pattern of the phylogeny. Because avian genomes appear to evolve at about the same average rate when corrected for age at first breeding (or generation time), the $\Delta T_{50}H$ values are relative to time. Therefore, we adopt Hennig's (1966) proposals that categorical rank should be based on the time of origin and that sister groups should be assigned coordinate rank. The application of these principles should produce a classification that approaches the desirable goal of categorical equivalence. Hennig (1966:161–182) discussed the problems associated with determining the ages of origin of groups of organisms and concluded that the available methods were inadequate. The present methods still fall short of the ideal, but we have tried to incorporate the principle of categorical equivalence by assigning ranks on the basis of $\Delta T_{50}H$ values, as in Table 19. The delta values express degrees of genomic divergence, and since the average rate of divergence is relative to time, this procedure provides an approach to categorical equivalence based on time of origin. The evolution of different lineages at somewhat different average rates introduces an error of uncertain magnitude. Present evidence suggests that this is not a major problem for avian data.

The DNA-based phylogeny contains so many dichotomies, at many levels, that it is impractical to assign different categorical names to each level of branching, as proposed by Hennig (1966:154–160). Therefore, to obtain maximum isomorphy between phylogeny and classification, and to prevent the number of categorical ranks from becoming impractically large, we adopt the principles of "subordination and sequencing of units" proposed by Nelson (1973). The groups in the classification are subordinated according to their relative times of origin, and the groups assigned to the same categorical rank are listed in the sequence that reflects the age of the origin of their lineage; that is, the oldest branch within a group is listed first, the next oldest second, etc. This sometimes results in more than two adjacent lineages with the same rank. In such cases, the first one listed is the sister group of all the others, the second is the sister group of the remaining groups, etc.

TABLE 19. Categories, Endings of Categorical Names, and $\Delta T_{50}H$ Ranges for Each Categorical Rank.

Category	Ending	Delta $T_{50}H$ Range
Superclass	———	33–36
Class	———	31–33
Subclass	-ornithes	29–31
Infraclass	-aves	27–29
Parvclass	-ae	24.5–27
Superorder	-morphae	22–24.5
Order	-iformes	20–22
Suborder	-i	18–20
Infraorder	-ides	15.5–18
Parvorder	-ida	13–15.5
Superfamily	-oidea	11–13
Family	-idae	9–11
Subfamily	-inae	7–9
Tribe	-ini	4.5–7
Subtribe	-ina	2.2–4.5
Congeneric spp.	———	0–2.2

When the classification was first developed the categories were based on units of 10 million years and equated with $\Delta T_{50}H$ values on the basis of $\Delta T_{50}H$ $1.0 = 4.5$ million years. It is now clear that this calibration factor is not applicable to all birds but only to those that begin to breed at ca. 2–4 years of age. Species that mature earlier may evolve slightly faster and those that mature later evolve more slowly.

Although we have modified the basis for categorical rank from absolute time to $\Delta T_{50}H$ values, we have retained the $\Delta T_{50}H$ ranges originally assigned to the categories. We began by assigning ordinal rank to the Passeriformes. The $\Delta T_{50}H$ value for the passerine branch is 21.6, and the ordinal level became $\Delta T_{50}H$ 20.0–22.2. The other ranks were developed above and below this level. The application of this system requires four categories in addition to those traditionally used. These are infraclass and parvclass between class and order, and infraorder and parvorder between order and family. For consistency the endings of categories below class have been standardized, as in Table 19.

The sequence of categories in the classification is partly determined by the relationships among groups and partly by arbitrary decisions. There is no single correct sequence because the three-dimensional tree is constrained by a two-dimensional page. The branches sharing a common root may be rotated 180° on the common axis without changing the relationships among the groups, but this would change the sequence of the groups in the classification.

Some of the changes in the sequence of passerine groups are based on DNA hybridization evidence that revealed clusters of related taxa not previously recognized. For example, in Wetmore's (1960) classification the nectarivorous groups (honeyeaters, sunbirds, flowerpeckers, white-eyes) were placed in a consecutive series of families, implying a closer relationship to one another than to other groups. The DNA comparisons show that the honeyeaters are members of the Australo-Papuan endemic radiation (Corvida), the sunbirds and flowerpeckers are members of a passeroid radiation that includes the African sugarbirds and the Papuan melanocharitids, and the white-eyes are sylvioids. Other examples include the starling-mockingbird alliance, the relationships among the members of the Passeridae (sparrows, wagtails, accentors, weavers, waxbills), and the numerous effects of the discovery of the Australo-Papuan endemic radiation. There are fewer changes in the sequence of non-passerine groups, but the so-called higher non-passerines (woodpeckers, rollers, etc.) have become the lower non-passerines, and the allegedly primitive waterbirds (loons, grebes, tubenoses, etc.) have been moved to higher ground. These changes were not arbitrary; they were dictated by the data.

Sibley et al. (1988) expressed uncertainty about the position of the Turniciformes in their classification by placing the group in the limbo of *incertae sedis*. In captivity, *Turnix* species begin to breed at the age of three to five months, therefore it seemed possible that their average rate of genomic evolution is faster than that of their nearest living relatives. If so, the branch length we observe might be longer by an unknown factor and the correct position of the branch node may be elsewhere in the tree. However, in the wild it is likely that *Turnix* species do not begin to breed until older than five months, perhaps not until one year of age. If so, and hard data are lacking, the position of the Turniciformes in our classification may be appropriate. The melting curves in Fig. 41, in which *Turnix* is the tracer taxon, demonstrate the isolated position of the turnicids. We have, therefore, substituted the parvclass Turnicae for "Infraclass ?" preceding the order Turniciformes and deleted the "*inc. sedis*" following the order Turniciformes.

A second change in the Sibley et al. (1988) classification involves the relative positions of the parvclasses Ratitae and Galloanserae. The averages of large numbers of $\Delta T_{50}H$ values indicated that the branch between the Ratitae and the Galloanserae was at $\Delta T_{50}H$ 25.9 and that an older branch at 28.0 separated the Ratitae + Galloanserae (Eoaves) from the rest of the groups (Neoaves). All of these large delta values were calculated from extrapolated data representing the melting of the most conserved sequences, because none of the melting curves in this far-out region cross the 50% hybridization line within the domain of the curves. Recently, we produced melting curves of the data pertaining to these branches (Figs. 18–40) and some of them show that several groups (storks, ibises, flamingos, penguins, cathartine vultures, bustards) cluster as close to the ratites as do the galliforms and anseriforms, or slightly closer. We believe that this is caused by the effects of delayed maturity, hence slower genomic evolution (see chapter 13 and Table 16), but it will require additional DNA-DNA comparisons to increase confidence in this opinion. The melting curves indicate that the branch between the Ratitae and the Galloanserae is probably misplaced in the UPGMA tree (Sibley et al. 1988:Fig. 1); we have, therefore, changed the position of the infraclass Neoaves from just before the parvclass Picae to just before the parvclass Galloanserae.

The criteria for categories in Table 19 are useful as guidelines, but it has been necessary to be flexible because there are many more levels of branching in the DNA-based phylograms than there are categories in the classification. There are many places in our classification where a given taxon may be moved up or down in rank. Thus, only the dendrograms and the melting curves provide the pattern of branching inferred from the DNA comparisons; the classification reflects this pattern, but does not reproduce it in detail.

We have not used the subtribe category and seldom have suggested generic changes unless the DNA data support a proposal by a previous author. DNA hybridization data are available for most of the groups of living birds. Groups for which data are lacking are listed as *incertae sedis* and placed in their traditional positions or in one suggested by data from other sources. Our classification follows:

Class Aves
  [Subclass Archeornithes, *Archeopteryx*]
  Subclass Neornithes
    Infraclass Eoaves
      Parvclass Ratitae
        Order Struthioniformes
          Suborder Struthioni
            Infraorder Struthionides
              Family Struthionidae: Ostrich
            Infraorder Rheides
              Family Rheidae: Rheas
          Suborder Casuarii
            Family Casuariidae
              Tribe Casuariini: Cassowaries
              Tribe Dromaiini: Emus
            Family Apterygidae: Kiwis
        Order Tinamiformes
            Family Tinamidae: Tinamous
    Infraclass Neoaves
      Parvclass Galloanserae
        Superorder Gallomorphae
        Order Craciformes
          Suborder Craci
              Family Cracidae: Guans, Chachalacas, Curassows
          Suborder Megapodii
              Family Megapodiidae: Megapodes, Scrubfowl, Brush-turkeys
        Order Galliformes
          Parvorder Phasianida
            Superfamily Phasianoidea
              Family Phasianidae: Pheasants, Old World Quails, Grouse
            Superfamily Numidoidea
              Family Numididae: Guineafowl
          Parvorder Odontophorida
              Family Odontophoridae: New World Quails
        Superorder Anserimorphae
        Order Anseriformes
          Infraorder Anhimides
            Superfamily Anhimoidea
              Family Anhimidae: Screamers
            Superfamily Anseranatoidea
              Family Anseranatidae: Magpie Goose
          Infraorder Anserides
              Family Dendrocygnidae: Whistling-Ducks
              Family Anatidae
                Subfamily Oxyurinae: Stiff-tailed Ducks
                Subfamily Stictonettinae: *Stictonetta*

Subfamily Cygninae: Swans
Subfamily Anatinae
   Tribe Anserini: Geese
   Tribe Anatini: Typical Ducks
Parvclass Turnicae
  Order Turniciformes
      Family Turnicidae: Buttonquails (*Turnix, Ortyxelos*)
Parvclass Picae
  Order Piciformes
    Infraorder Picides
      Family Indicatoridae: Honeyguides
      Family Picidae: Woodpeckers, Wrynecks, Piculets
    Infraorder Ramphastides
     Superfamily Megalaimoidea
      Family Megalaimidae: Asian Barbets
     Superfamily Lybioidea
      Family Lybiidae: African Barbets
     Superfamily Ramphastoidea
      Family Ramphastidae
       Subfamily Capitoninae: New World Barbets
       Subfamily Ramphastinae: Toucans, Toucanets
Parvclass Coraciae
  Superorder Galbulimorphae
   Order Galbuliformes
    Infraorder Galbulides
      Family Galbulidae: Jacamars
    Infraorder Bucconides
      Family Bucconidae: Puffbirds
  Superorder Bucerotimorphae
   Order Bucerotiformes
      Family Bucerotidae: Typical Hornbills
      Family Bucorvidae: Ground-Hornbills
   Order Upupiformes
    Infraorder Upupides
      Family Upupidae: Hoopoes
    Infraorder Phoeniculides
      Family Phoeniculidae: Woodhoopoes
      Family Rhinopomastidae: Scimitar-bills
  Superorder Coraciimorphae
   Order Trogoniformes
      Family Trogonidae
       Subfamily Apaloderminae: African Trogons
       Subfamily Trogoninae
        Tribe Trogonini: New World Trogons
        Tribe Harpactini: Asian Trogons
   Order Coraciiformes
    Suborder Coracii
     Superfamily Coracioidea
      Family Coraciidae: Typical Rollers
      Family Brachypteraciidae: Ground-Rollers (*inc. sedis*)
     Superfamily Leptosomoidea

              Family Leptosomidae: Courol or Cuckoo-Roller
      Suborder Alcedini
        Infraorder Alcedinides
          Parvorder Momotida
            Family Momotidae: Motmots
          Parvorder Todida
            Family Todidae: Todies
          Parvorder Alcedinida
            Family Alcedinidae: Alcedinid Kingfishers
          Parvorder Cerylida
            Superfamily Dacelonoidea
              Family Dacelonidae: Dacelonid Kingfishers
            Superfamily Ceryloidea
              Family Cerylidae: Cerylid Kingfishers
        Infraorder Meropides
          Family Meropidae: Bee-eaters
  Parvclass Coliae
    Order Coliiformes
        Family Coliidae
          Subfamily Coliinae: Typical Mousebirds or Colies
          Subfamily Urocoliinae: Long-tailed Mousebirds
  Parvclass Passerae
   Superorder Cuculimorphae
    Order Cuculiformes
      Infraorder Cuculides
        Parvorder Cuculida
          Superfamily Cuculoidea
            Family Cuculidae: Old World Cuckoos
          Superfamily Centropodoidea
            Family Centropodidae: Coucals
        Parvorder Coccyzida
          Family Coccyzidae: American Cuckoos
      Infraorder Crotophagides
        Parvorder Opisthocomida
          Family Opisthocomidae: Hoatzin
        Parvorder Crotophagida
          Family Crotophagidae
            Tribe Crotophagini: Anis
            Tribe Guirini: Guira Cuckoo
        Parvorder Neomorphida
          Family Neomorphidae: Roadrunners, Ground-Cuckoos
   Superorder Psittacimorphae
    Order Psittaciformes
        Family Psittacidae: Parrots, Macaws, etc.
   Superorder Apodimorphae
    Order Apodiformes
        Family Apodidae: Typical Swifts
        Family Hemiprocnidae: Treeswifts or Crested Swifts
    Order Trochiliformes
        Family Trochilidae
          Subfamily Phaethornithinae: Hermits
          Subfamily Trochilinae: Typical Hummingbirds

Superorder Strigimorphae
  Order Musophagiformes
        Family Musophagidae
          Subfamily Musophaginae: Turacos
          Subfamily Criniferinae: Plantain-eaters, Go-away-birds
  Order Strigiformes
    Suborder Strigi
      Parvorder Tytonida
        Family Tytonidae: Barn-Owls, Grass-Owls
      Parvorder Strigida
        Family Strigidae: Typical Owls
    Suborder Aegotheli
        Family Aegothelidae: Owlet-Nightjars
    Suborder Caprimulgi
      Infraorder Podargides
        Family Podargidae: Australian Frogmouths
        Family Batrachostomidae: Asian Frogmouths
      Infraorder Caprimulgides
      Parvorder Steatornithida
        Superfamily Steatornithoidea
        Family Steatornithidae: Oilbird
        Superfamily Nyctibioidea
        Family Nyctibiidae: Potoos
      Parvorder Caprimulgida
        Superfamily Eurostopodoidea
        Family Eurostopodidae: Eared-Nightjars
        Superfamily Caprimulgoidea
        Family Caprimulgidae
          Subfamily Chordeilinae: Nighthawks
          Subfamily Caprimulginae: Nightjars, Whip-poor-wills
Superorder Passerimorphae
  Order Columbiformes
        Family Raphidae: Dodos, Solitaires
        Family Columbidae: Pigeons, Doves
  Order Gruiformes
    Suborder Grui
      Infraorder Eurypygides
        Family Eurypygidae: Sunbittern
      Infraorder Otidides
        Family Otididae: Bustards
      Infraorder Gruides
      Parvorder Gruida
        Superfamily Gruoidea
        Family Gruidae: Cranes
        Family Heliornithidae
          Tribe Aramini: Limpkin
          Tribe Heliornithini: New World Sungrebe (*Podica, Heliopais inc. sedis*)
        Superfamily Psophioidea
        Family Psophiidae: Trumpeters
      Parvorder Cariamida
        Family Cariamidae: Seriemas
        Family Rhynochetidae: Kagu

Suborder Ralli
    Family Rallidae: Rails, Gallinules, Coots
Suborder Mesitornithi *inc. sedis*
    Family Mesitornithidae: Mesites, Monias, Roatelos
Order Ciconiiformes
Suborder Charadrii
  Infraorder Pteroclides
    Family Pteroclidae: Sandgrouse
  Infraorder Charadriides
   Parvorder Scolopacida
    Superfamily Scolopacoidea
     Family Thinocoridae: Seedsnipe
     Family Pedionomidae: Plains-wanderer
     Family Scolopacidae
      Subfamily Scolopacinae: Woodcock, Snipe
      Subfamily Tringinae: Sandpipers, Curlews
    Superfamily Jacanoidea
     Family Rostratulidae: Painted-snipe
     Family Jacanidae: Jacanas, Lily-trotters
   Parvorder Charadriida
    Superfamily Chionidoidea
     Family Chionididae: Sheathbills
    Superfamily Charadrioidea
     Family Burhinidae: Thick-knees
     Family Charadriidae
      Subfamily Recurvirostrinae
       Tribe Haematopodini: Oystercatchers
       Tribe Recurvirostrini: Avocets, Stilts
      Subfamily Charadriinae: Plovers, Lapwings
    Superfamily Laroidea
     Family Glareolidae
      Subfamily Dromadinae: Crab Plover
      Subfamily Glareolinae: Coursers, Pratincoles
     Family Laridae
      Subfamily Larinae
       Tribe Stercorariini: Jaegers, Skuas
       Tribe Rynchopini: Skimmers
       Tribe Larini: Gulls
       Tribe Sternini: Terns
      Subfamily Alcinae: Auks, Murres, Puffins, Guillemots
Suborder Ciconii
  Infraorder Falconides
   Parvorder Accipitrida
    Family Accipitridae
     Subfamily Pandioninae: Osprey
     Subfamily Accipitrinae: Eagles, Old World Vultures, Hawks, Kites,
      Harriers
    Family Sagittariidae: Secretary-bird
   Parvorder Falconida
    Family Falconidae: Falcons, Caracaras
  Infraorder Ciconiides
   Parvorder Podicipedida

        Family Podicipedidae: Grebes
      Parvorder Phaethontida
        Family Phaethontidae: Tropicbirds
      Parvorder Sulida
       Superfamily Suloidea
        Family Sulidae: Boobies, Gannets
        Family Anhingidae: Anhingas, Darters
       Superfamily Phalacrocoracoidea
        Family Phalacrocoracidae: Cormorants, Shags
      Parvorder Ciconiida
       Superfamily Ardeoidea
        Family Ardeidae: Herons, Egrets, Bitterns
       Superfamily Scopoidea
        Family Scopidae: Hamerkop or Hammerhead
       Superfamily Phoenicopteroidea
        Family Phoenicopteridae: Flamingos
       Superfamily Threskiornithoidea
        Family Threskiornithidae: Ibises, Spoonbills
       Superfamily Pelecanoidea
        Family Pelecanidae
         Subfamily Balaenicipitinae: Shoebill
         Subfamily Pelecaninae: Pelicans
       Superfamily Ciconioidea
        Family Ciconiidae
         Subfamily Cathartinae: New World Vultures, Condors
         Subfamily Ciconiinae: Storks, Openbills, Adjutants, Jabiru
       Superfamily Procellarioidea
        Family Fregatidae: Frigatebirds
        Family Spheniscidae: Penguins
        Family Gaviidae: Loons or Divers
        Family Procellariidae
         Subfamily Hydrobatinae: Storm-Petrels
         Subfamily Procellariinae: Shearwaters, Petrels, Diving-Petrels
         Subfamily Diomedeinae: Albatrosses
Order Passeriformes
  Suborder Tyranni (Suboscines)
    Infraorder Acanthisittides
        Family Acanthisittidae: New Zealand Wrens
    Infraorder Eurylaimides
      Superfamily Pittoidea
        Family Pittidae: Pittas
      Superfamily Eurylaimoidea
        Family Eurylaimidae: Broadbills
        Family Philepittidae: Asities (*inc. sedis*)
    Infraorder Tyrannides
      Parvorder Tyrannida
        Family Tyrannidae
         Subfamily Pipromorphinae: Mionectine Flycatchers, *Corythopis*
         Subfamily Tyranninae: Tyrant Flycatchers
         Subfamily Tityrinae
          Tribe Schiffornithini: *Schiffornis*
          Tribe Tityrini: Tityras, Becards

Subfamily Cotinginae: Cotingas, Plantcutters, Sharpbill
Subfamily Piprinae: Manakins
Parvorder Thamnophilida
Family Thamnophilidae: Typical Antbirds
Parvorder Furnariida
Superfamily Furnarioidea
Family Furnariidae
Subfamily Furnariinae: Horneros, Ovenbirds, Spinetails, etc.
Subfamily Dendrocolaptinae: Woodcreepers, Scythebills
Superfamily Formicarioidea
Family Formicariidae: Ground Antbirds
Family Conopophagidae: Gnateaters
Family Rhinocryptidae: Tapaculos
Suborder Passeri (Oscines)
Parvorder Corvida
Superfamily Menuroidea
Family Climacteridae: Australo-Papuan Treecreepers
Family Menuridae
Subfamily Menurinae: Lyrebirds
Subfamily Atrichornithinae: Scrub-birds
Family Ptilonorhynchidae: Bowerbirds
Superfamily Meliphagoidea
Family Maluridae
Subfamily Malurinae
Tribe Malurini: Fairywrens
Tribe Stipiturini: Emuwrens
Subfamily Amytornithinae: Grasswrens
Family Meliphagidae: Honeyeaters, *Ephthianura*, *Ashbyia*
Family Pardalotidae
Subfamily Pardalotinae: Pardalotes
Subfamily Dasyornithinae: Bristlebirds
Subfamily Acanthizinae
Tribe Sericornithini: Scrub-wrens, Mouse-warblers, etc.
Tribe Acanthizini: Thornbills, Whitefaces, Gerygones, etc.
Superfamily Corvoidea
Family Eopsaltriidae: Australo-Papuan robins, *Drymodes*
Family Irenidae: Fairy-bluebirds, Leafbirds
Family Orthonychidae: Logrunner, Chowchilla
Family Pomatostomidae: Australo-Papuan babblers
Family Laniidae: True Shrikes (*Lanius, Corvinella, Eurocephalus*)
Family Vireonidae: Vireos, Greenlets, Peppershrikes, Shrike-Vireos
Family Corvidae
Subfamily Cinclosomatinae: Quail-thrushes, Whipbirds, Wedgebills
Subfamily Corcoracinae: White-winged Chough, Apostlebird
Subfamily Pachycephalinae
Tribe Neosittini: Sittellas
Tribe Mohouini: Whitehead, Yellowhead, Pipipi
Tribe Falcunculini: Shrike-tit, *Oreoica, Rhagologus*
Tribe Pachycephalini: Whistlers, Shrike-thrushes, Pitohuis
Subfamily Corvinae
Tribe Corvini: Crows, Ravens, Magpies, Jays, Nutcrackers, Choughs
Tribe Paradisaeini: Birds-of-Paradise, *Melampitta*

Tribe Artamini: Currawongs, Wood-swallows, *Peltops*, *Pityriasis*
Tribe Oriolini: Orioles, Cuckoo-shrikes
Subfamily Dicrurinae
Tribe Rhipidurini: Fantails
Tribe Dicrurini: Drongos
Tribe Monarchini: Monarchs, Magpie-larks
Subfamily Aegithininae: Ioras
Subfamily Malaconotinae
Tribe Malaconotini: Bushshrikes, Boubous, Tchagras, Gonoleks
Tribe Vangini: Helmetshrikes, Vangas, *Batis*, *Platysteira*
Family Callaeatidae: New Zealand wattlebirds (*inc. sedis*)
Parvorder *Incertae sedis*
Family Picathartidae: *Picathartes*, *Chaetops*
Parvorder Passerida
Superfamily Muscicapoidea
Family Bombycillidae
Tribe Dulini: Palmchat
Tribe Ptilogonatini: Silky-flycatchers
Tribe Bombycillini: Waxwings
Family Cinclidae: Dippers
Family Muscicapidae
Subfamily Turdinae: Thrushes, *Chlamydochaera*, *Brachypteryx*, *Alethe*
Subfamily Muscicapinae
Tribe Muscicapini: Old World Flycatchers
Tribe Saxicolini: Chats (*Erithacus*, *Oenanthe*, etc.)
Family Sturnidae
Tribe Sturnini: Starlings, Mynas, Oxpeckers
Tribe Mimini: Mockingbirds, Thrashers, American Catbirds
Superfamily Sylvioidea
Family Sittidae
Subfamily Sittinae: Nuthatches
Subfamily Tichodromadinae: Wallcreeper
Family Certhiidae
Subfamily Certhiinae
Tribe Certhiini: Tree-Creepers
Tribe Salpornithini: Spotted Creeper
Subfamily Troglodytinae: Wrens, *Donacobius*
Subfamily Polioptilinae: Gnatcatchers, Verdin, Gnatwrens
Family Paridae
Subfamily Remizinae: Penduline-Tits
Subfamily Parinae: Titmice, Chickadees
Family Aegithalidae: Long-tailed Tits, Bushtits, Pygmy Tit
Family Hirundinidae
Subfamily Pseudochelidoninae: River-Martins (*inc. sedis*)
Subfamily Hirundininae: Swallows, Martins
Family Regulidae: Kinglets, Firecrest, Goldcrests
Family Pycnonotidae: Bulbuls, Greenbuls
Family Hypocoliidae: Grey Hypocolius (*inc. sedis*)
Family Cisticolidae: African Warblers (*Cisticola*, *Prinia*, *Apalis*, etc.)
Family Zosteropidae: White-eyes
Family Sylviidae
Subfamily Acrocephalinae: Leaf-Warblers, Reed-Warblers, etc.

Subfamily Megalurinae: Grassbirds, Songlarks, Fernbird
Subfamily Garrulacinae: Laughingthrushes, Liocichlas
Subfamily Sylviinae
  Tribe Timaliini: Babblers, Minlas, Fulvettas, Yuhinas, Parrotbills
  Tribe Chamaeini: Wrentit
  Tribe Sylviini: Sylviine Warblers (*Sylvia* including *Parisoma*)
Superfamily Passeroidea
  Family Alaudidae: Larks
  Family Nectariniidae
    Subfamily Promeropinae: Sugarbirds
    Subfamily Nectariniinae
      Tribe Dicaeini: Flowerpeckers, Mistletoebird
      Tribe Nectariniini: Sunbirds, Spider-hunters
  Family Melanocharitidae
      Tribe Melanocharitini: Berrypeckers (*Melanocharis, Rhamphocaris*)
      Tribe Toxorhamphini: Longbills (*Toxorhamphus, Oedistoma*)
  Family Paramythiidae: Tit Berrypecker (*Paramythia*), Crested Berrypecker
    (*Oreocharis*)
  Family Passeridae
    Subfamily Passerinae: Sparrows, Rock Sparrows, Snowfinches
    Subfamily Motacillinae: Wagtails, Pipits, Longclaws
    Subfamily Prunellinae: Accentors
    Subfamily Ploceinae: Weavers, Malimbes, Fodys, Bishops, Widowbirds
    Subfamily Estrildinae
      Tribe Estrildini: Waxbills, Firefinches, Parrotfinches, Munias
      Tribe Viduini: Indigobirds, Whydahs
  Family Fringillidae
    Subfamily Peucedraminae: Olive Warbler
    Subfamily Fringillinae
      Tribe Fringillini: Chaffinches, Bramblings
      Tribe Carduelini: Goldfinches, Crossbills, Linnets, Bullfinches
      Tribe Drepanidini: Hawaiian Honeycreepers
    Subfamily Emberizinae
      Tribe Emberizini: Buntings, Longspurs, Towhees, American Sparrows
      Tribe Parulini: Wood Warblers, including *Zeledonia*
      Tribe Thraupini: Tanagers, Swallow-tanager, Neotropical
        Honeycreepers, Plushcap, Tanager-finches
      Tribe Cardinalini: Cardinals, Grosbeaks
      Tribe Icterini: Troupials, Meadowlarks, New World Blackbirds,
        Cowbirds, Oropendolas, Caciques, Bobolink

CHAPTER SEVENTEEN

Melting Curves and Dendrograms

The calculation of delta values and other properties of the data have been discussed in chapter 11. The following sections are the group accounts of each order and family of living birds. At the end of each group account is a section entitled "The DNA Hybridization Evidence" in which we discuss our interpretation of the data, including the melting curves produced from the counts of radioactivity using the computer program Microsoft EXCEL, the Fitch-Margoliash dendrograms produced by Felsenstein's PHYLIP computer program, and the average linkage (UPGMA) dendrograms. The melting curves are Figs. 18–324, the FITCH trees are Figs. 325–352, and the UPGMA trees are Figs. 353–385, at the back of the book.

Melting Curves

Melting curves depict the relationships between the homoduplex hybrid (tracer-tracer) and each of up to 11 (rarely 12) heteroduplex DNA-DNA hybrids (tracer-driver). All comparisons are between the homoduplex curve and the heteroduplex curves, not between heteroduplex curves. Heteroduplex curves equidistant from the homoduplex curve may be closely related to one another if they are on the same branch of the tree, but they may be on different branches and be equidistant from the homoduplex. The axes of the curves in the figures are the percent single-stranded DNA for the vertical (y) axis, and degrees Celsius for the horizontal (x) axis. These designations were omitted from the figures to save space on the printed pages. The quality of the curves varies; an excellent homoduplex curve has a slowly rising foot region from 60°C to ca. 80°C, then a smooth rise beginning at ca. 85°C, with a $T_{50}H$ (and T_m) of 86°C or higher. Examples of such curves are Fig. 52 (*Bucorvus*) and Figs. 91–94 (*Chaetura*), which have $T_{50}H$ values ca. 87°C. Most homoduplex curves are less than perfect, with more rapidly rising feet and $T_{50}H$ values from 82.5 to 85°C. However, only the relative positions of the curves are important when comparing curves, and the relative positions do not change regardless of the quality of the curves.

In the laboratory each experimental set included a homoduplex and 24 heteroduplexes; a

265

few sets of 12 were produced during the early years. The EXCEL program provides for the editing of the data in various ways but permits no more than 13 curves to be displayed at one time. This is not a handicap because if all 25 were to be placed in a single figure it would be impossible to distinguish among many of them. Several editing procedures were used to produce the figures.

1. Aberrant curves (e.g., tracer-driver combinations that did not reassociate or had other problems that made them useless) were deleted. This was not a significant problem.

2. The 13 or fewer (usually 12) curves to be used in a given figure were chosen by including at least one curve representing each major taxonomic group in the experiment. The closest and most distant curves relative to the homoduplex were usually included to provide perspective. For experiments that included several closely related species the curves of just these species were examined on the computer display and one or two were chosen to represent the group. Closely related species usually cluster together, and the choice was simple—we used those with the shortest English names so they would be more likely to fit the limited space at the top of the figure. If there was variation, one or two in the middle were chosen, rather than the extremes. When the heteroduplex curves of closely related taxa were not identical we assumed that the median curves were the best representatives of the group.

3. The 12 (or fewer) columns of data in the spreadsheet were arranged in order of increasing distance from the homoduplex, using the cut-and-paste function of EXCEL. This arranged the scientific names in the legend in the box in the same sequence as the curves. The actual sequence of the curves is often difficult to determine when all 12 are in place, but with EXCEL it is possible to delete individual curves from the display, gradually revealing the true sequence of the curves even when they are close together and not clearly separate in the figures. Thus, the sequence of scientific and English names in the figures is the sequence of the curves in the figures. If two or more are identical in position it is irrelevant which comes first.

4. Temperature overshoots (see chapter 11) produce small departures from the smooth sigmoid shape typical of cumulative curves without overshoots. These irregularities may be eliminated by subtracting one or two percentage points from the overshot value and adding an equal amount to the undershot value. This does not change the positions of the curves, but it makes them look better. Thus, the curves in the figures are smooth sigmoids, but about 20% have been corrected for this obvious laboratory error.

5. If the frequency distributions of the fragment sizes of all DNA hybrids in an experimental set are the same, the melting curves will be parallel to one another. Curves cross because they differ in the frequency distribution of their fragment sizes. For example, a heteroduplex with an excess of short-stranded fragments may cross another curve in the mid-range of the temperature scale. Variation in the distribution of fragment sizes was frequent in our past work and many curves cross, mainly in the low-temperature region of the foot. It was usually possible to determine the correct position of a given curve relative to the other curves because its position in the rapidly melting region between 85° and 90°C indicated its correct position in the series. If a curve was so aberrant that its position was uncertain, it was deleted. In some cases we have uncrossed curves using the editing facilities of EXCEL, but the relative positions of the curves have not been changed.

6. In a few cases the driver DNA of the homoduplex of an interesting experiment failed to reassociate sufficiently to produce a useful homoduplex curve. The condition of the hetero-

duplex curves indicated that the tracer was good. There are two ways to salvage this situation: (1) Change the count data to raise the percentage of hybridization of the homoduplex to an appropriate level by trial and error. (2) If there is a good heteroduplex that is closely related to the homoduplex, use its curve for the homoduplex curve, but use the original heteroduplex curves formed with the original tracer. This yields a normal set of curves that present the same view of the relationships that the original homoduplex curve would have if it had been good.

Of the 1069 experimental sets of birds, the data for 508 were transcribed into EXCEL and analyzed; melting curves of 306 of the 508 sets are presented in Figs. 18–324. There were 26,554 individual hybrids of avian taxa produced during the 11.5 years of the study; ca. 3366 (11 × 306) of these are in the figures. Did bias enter into the choices that had to be made? Perhaps, but our goal was to use the best curves in the sets that provided the maximum amount of information about the relationships among the higher categories; thus, many of the sets not used for the figures included only species closely related to the tracer and to one another. Others were not used because they were of low quality—for example, because of the effects of short-stranded tracers or low tracer-tracer reassociation. Many sets were identical or nearly so and would be redundant. The sets in the figures cover as much of the domain of avian relationships as our data permitted and space allowed. Any gaps are due to lack of DNAs or to lack of useful data. Perfection remains elusive.

7. Legends. The scientific names in the box to the right of the curves, and the English names at the top, are from Sibley and Monroe (1990). The spaces available for both sets of names are limited by EXCEL. Only 12 will usually fit in the box and only three lines of type are available at the top. If many of the English names were unusually long it was necessary to delete one or two of the curves; hence many figures contain fewer than 12 curves.

Dendrograms

The FITCH trees are based on the uncorrected $\Delta T_{50}H$ values and were produced by the PHYLIP program. Differences in branch lengths may indicate differences in average genomic rates, but they also include differences caused by experimental errors. Some of the matrices contain unequal reciprocals which may indicate differences in genome size but more likely are caused by experimental errors. In either case, they will affect branch lengths in the dendrograms.

A few dendrograms were produced by the KITSCH program, a modified Fitch-Margoliash algorithm that assumes equal rates of DNA evolution. KITSCH trees are accompanied by FITCH trees based on the same data matrix.

The data matrices give the average $\Delta T_{50}H$ value and the number of replicate measurements for each cell. The order of taxa in a matrix is the order in which the taxa were clustered to produce the dendrogram, unless otherwise indicated. Like other clustering algorithms, FITCH is sensitive to the sequence of data entry and may produce different trees from different entry sequences.

For each FITCH and KITSCH tree, the sum of least squares, average percent standard deviation, number of trees examined, branch lengths, and internodal distances are given. The sum of least squares and the average percent standard deviation are measures of the goodness-of-fit of the calculated branch lengths to the original data. In general, the smaller the sum of squares and the average percent deviation, the better the fit, but these values are relative to the

Part Two

Accounts of the Groups of Birds

The following sections present reviews of the characters, taxonomic histories, and classifications of previous authors and the results of our DNA-DNA comparisons. Each major group is introduced by the pertinent portion of our classification of birds, followed by a synopsis of some of the morphological characters that have been used as the basis for previous classifications. These characters were drawn from many sources, including Beddard (1898a), Fürbringer (1888), Gadow (1892, 1893), Glenny (e.g., 1942a, 1967), Hudson (e.g., 1937), Huxley (1867), D. W. Johnston (1988), Ridgway (e.g., 1901, 1914), Sharpe (volumes of the *Catalogue of Birds*), and Stresemann (1934).

The taxonomy follows Sibley and Monroe (1990), including the English names and the numbers of genera and species indicated for the higher categories—e.g., 1/1 for the Struthionidae means one genus and one species. Sibley and Monroe (1990) includes descriptions of geographic ranges for all species and comments about the taxonomic status of many.

The historical reviews of the classification of each group are intended to show the many opinions about avian relationships that have been proposed and the various sources of evidence on which those opinions have been based. The results of the DNA comparisons are presented in melting curves, dendrograms, and summaries at the end of each group account. We have included some estimates of the datings of divergence events, but these should be viewed as tentative; we do not claim that our calibrations are correct. We do believe that the branching patterns depicted in the dendrograms are closer to the true phylogeny than any that have been proposed in the past. However, the branch lengths may not reflect the relative rates of DNA evolution, as discussed above in chapter 13. Chapter 17, on melting curves and dendrograms, should be read before using the information under "The DNA Hybridization Evidence" at the end of each group account.

Ratites and Tinamous

Subclass Neornithes
  Infraclass Eoaves
    Parvclass Ratitae
      Order STRUTHIONIFORMES: Ratites
        Suborder Struthioni
          Infraorder Struthionides
            Family Struthionidae: Ostrich
          Infraorder Rheides
            Family Rheidae: Rheas
        Suborder Casuarii
          Family Casuariidae
            Tribe Casuariini: Cassowaries
            Tribe Dromaiini: Emus
          Family Apterygidae: Kiwis
      Order TINAMIFORMES
        Family Tinamidae: Tinamous

The living ratite birds are the Ostrich (*Struthio camelus*) of Africa and Arabia; the Greater Rhea (*Rhea americana*) and Lesser Rhea (*Rhea pennata*) of South America; the Emu (*Dromaius novaehollandiae*) of Australia; three species of cassowaries (*Casuarius*) of New Guinea, nearby islands, and northeastern Australia; and three species of kiwis (*Apteryx*) of New Zealand.

The extinct ratites include ca. 13 species of moas (Dinornithidae) of New Zealand (Cracraft 1976); eight mihirung birds (Dromornithidae) of Australia (P. Rich 1979); nine elephant birds (Aepyornithidae) of Africa, Madagascar, and Europe; and some 16 relatives of the living ratites known only as fossils. *Struthio* fossils are known from the Miocene, Pliocene, and Pleistocene of Mongolia, central and southern Asia, and the Near East (Mikhailov and Kurochkin 1988:108). *Gobipteryx minutus*, from the Upper Cretaceous of Mongolia, was described as a ratite by Elzanowski (1977). Brodkorb (1976) stated that *Gobipteryx* was a reptile, but its avian status has been defended by Elzanowski (Olson 1985:94), who rejects "any close relationship between *Gobipteryx* and the living paleognaths." Kurochkin (1988:108) notes that avian bone remains are known from 9 Lower and Upper Cretaceous localities of Mongolia and that many bird feather impressions were found in 10 Lower Cretaceous sites. Among them were the remains of *Ambiortus* and *Gobipteryx*. The Lower Cretaceous fossils are mainly those of paleognaths "which form the most ancient and archaic group of birds." Cracraft (1986) reviewed the Cretaceous taxa. Houde (1988) considers the early Tertiary Lithornithiformes to be a paraphyletic assemblage related to the ratites.

Thus, there are 10 living species, and probably more than 50 extinct species, of paleognathous birds. *Sylviornis neocaledoniae* (Poplin 1980) was described as a ratite, but Poplin et al. (1983) and Poplin and Mourer-Chauviré (1985) obtained additional material and concluded that it was a large, flightless megapode.

Order STRUTHIONIFORMES: Paleognathous (dromaeognathous) palate; flightless; wings reduced; no keel on sternum; coracoid fused with scapula; clavicles absent or reduced; pygostyle present in the Ostrich (DeBeer 1964:682, *contra* Gadow 1893:90); no pterylae, feathers distributed over body of adult, or with small apteria in some; no hamuli, barbs not connected; rhamphotheca compound, maxilla covered at base with a cere which envelopes the nasal grooves; eutaxic; penis present; nares impervious, holorhinal; caeca present; oil gland absent in adult Ostrich, rheas, cassowaries, and Emu but present (naked) in the chicks of rheas and emus. Present (naked or with minute feathers) in kiwis (D. W. Johnston 1988); proximal articulating head of quadrate single; nidifugous.

Family STRUTHIONIDAE: 1/1. The Ostrich occurs today only in Africa; formerly its range extended to Syria, Jordan, Iraq, and Saudi Arabia. The population of northeastern Africa (*S. c. molybdophanes*) may be a distinct species, but both races occur in northeastern Kenya. They are usually merged into a single species, but morphological differences and possible sympatry in the Tana River region of northeastern Kenya suggest that two species may be present. As for many such questions there is not necessarily a single, precise answer.

Pelvic muscles ABXY+; two toes (3 and 4); terminal phalanges shortened, with small nails; no clavicles; large procoracoid; maxillo-palatines articulating with vomer, which touches neither palatines nor pterygoids; pubes united in a symphysis; pygostyle present; two carotids; 20 cervical vertebrae; 16 primaries; 20 secondaries; 50–60 rectrices; no aftershaft; caeca large, with spiral valve; beak broad, short, and flat; external nares oval; no syrinx. The Ostrich is the largest living bird.

Family RHEIDAE: 1/2. South America. Pelvic muscles BXY+; three toes, no hallux; middle phalanges short; left carotid only; maxillo-palatines large, fenestrated, not touching vomer; palatines short, articulating with vomer; procoracoid process large; no aftershaft; 12 primaries; 16 secondaries; no rectrices; ventral apterium present; 17 cervical vertebrae; caeca large with vestiges of spiral valve; syrinx tracheobronchial with one pair of intrinsic muscles and modified tracheal and bronchial rings; only the male incubates.

Family CASUARIIDAE: 2/4. The three species of cassowaries (*Casuarius*) occur on New Guinea and adjacent islands, and in northeastern Australia. The Emu (*Dromaius novaehollandiae*) occurs over most of Australia. Pelvic muscles ABXY+ in *Casuarius*, BXY in *Dromaius*; three toes; middle phalanges short; vomer long, articulating with palatines and pterygoids; maxillo-palatines large, fused with vomer and premaxilla; procoracoid process small; clavicles rudimentary; aftershaft as long as main feather; small clavicles present; caeca reduced; two carotids but only the left goes to the head; no syrinx; wing feathers reduced to spines (rachis); no rectrices; 18–19 cervical vertebrae in *Casuarius*, 20 in *Dromaius*; no pubic symphysis; male incubates.

Family APTERYGIDAE: 1/3. New Zealand. Pelvic muscles ABXY+; 4 toes, hallux small and elevated; long, decurved beak, with nostrils opening at tip; olfactory sense functional; plumage lax, hairlike; no aftershaft; wings short, concealed in body plumage; no pubic symphysis; eyes reduced, pecten absent; mainly nocturnal habits; left carotid only; caeca long, slender; no syrinx but can vocalize; 3–4 primaries; 9 secondaries; no rectrices; 16 cervical vertebrae; small apteria present; one to three (rarely) large eggs; male incubates; young hatched active and fully feathered, soon leave burrow nest to follow adults.

The sister group of the Struthioniformes is the order TINAMIFORMES, the tinamous of the Neotropics. The 47 living species range from northeastern Mexico to Tierra del Fuego (Blake 1979). Four extinct species are known (Brodkorb 1963a).

Family TINAMIDAE: 9/47. Dromaeognathous; pelvic muscles ABXY+; two carotids; volant; carinate; short wings and tail; 3 or 4 toes; rhamphotheca complex; nostrils covered by a cere; pygostyle absent; skeleton pneumatic; flexor tendons Type 2; eutaxic; holorhinal (some schizorhinal), impervious nares; small oil gland; large caeca; tracheobronchial syrinx, muscles variable; large crop; aftershaft varies from large to rudimentary; dorsal powder downs in some species; 10 primaries; 13–16 secondaries; 8–12 small rectrices; 16–18 cervical vertebrae; sparse adult down; furcula U-shaped; eggs with porcelain-like shells, unicolored and intensely pigmented blue, green, beige, brown, etc.; male incubates; nidifugous.

The ratites and the tinamous will be discussed together because their taxonomic histories are intertwined, and because they are sister groups.

Historical Review of the Classification

Merrem (1813) was the first to place the large ratites apart from other birds because they lack a keel on the sternum. Lesson (1831) placed the large ratites and the kiwis in his "Oiseaux Anormaux," as opposed to the "Oiseaux Normaux," which included all other birds. Lesson placed *Apteryx* in the "Family Nullipennes" and the other ratites in the "Family Brevipennes"; the tinamous were put with the gallinaceous birds.

Darwin (1859:106, 226) believed that the ratites had evolved from flying ancestors through "disuse" of their wings and increasing use of their hind limbs, but Owen (1866:12), who was not a strict selectionist, characterized the "cursorial" birds by the "arrested development of the wings unfitting them for flight." Owen grouped the flightless birds together, but he thought that the Ostrich was allied to the bustards (Otididae) and that the kiwis and moas were closest to the megapodes (Megapodiidae).

Huxley (1867) described the dromaeognathous palate shared by the ratites and tinamous, but he emphasized skeletal differences among them and made five groups within the "Ratitae," one of his three major orders. He placed the tinamous in the order "Carinatae," following the "Ratitae." Huxley's palatal types have been an important factor in subsequent ideas about the relationships of the ratites.

Sundevall (1872, see 1889:248) placed the ratites in his "Order VII. PROCERES," which was divided into "Cohort 1. Proceres Veri," including "Fam. Struthioninae" for *Struthio* and *Rhea* and "Fam. Dromaeinae" for the Emu and cassowaries. "Cohort 2. Subnobiles" included the kiwis in the "Fam. Apteryginae." The tinamous were placed in "Order IV. GALLINAE, Cohort 5. Struthioniformes, Fam. Crypturinae" with the gallinaceous birds, sandgrouse, seedsnipe, and sheathbills (pp. 197–207). Sundevall noted that the tinamous resemble "the Ostriches in their entire aspect, and [have] the bones in the base of the skull formed as in those birds (*cf.* Huxley's Syst., supra p. 9, Dromaeognathae)" (p. 206).

The reference to "supra p. 9" is to a synopsis of Huxley's classification in the introduction to Sundevall's book. Thus, Sundevall was aware of Huxley's evidence, but chose to place the tinamous with the galliforms because of similarities of the bill, feet, and plumage, as indicated by the diagnosis of the "Gallinae" (p. 197).

Mivart (1877), who studied the axial skeleton, treated the ratites as a single family without speculating about their nearest relatives. He concluded that *Dromaius* and *Casuarius* are the most closely related genera, that *Apteryx* is next most closely related to them, and that *Struthio* and *Rhea* are more distant from the ratites of Australia and New Zealand. Mivart presented a diagram identical in topology to our tree based on DNA comparisons.

An osteological study convinced Seebohm (1888b) that the tinamous are allied to the galliforms, so he placed them in a suborder, Crypturi, next to his suborders Gallinae and Pterocletes (sandgrouse).

Gadow (1889) found the intestinal convolutions of the ratites to differ among the genera, agreeing only in having the second intestinal loop right-handed and the third left-handed. This arrangement also occurs in the tinamous, gallinaceous birds, the Hoatzin (*Opisthocomus*), and the cuckoos.

From a study of wing pterylosis, Wray (1887:350) concluded that the "wings of the Ratitae are of the same general plan as those of the Carinatae, presenting a modification of a more generalized type, which correlates with their bony structure." In another study of pterylosis, Goodchild (1891:324) noted that "the wing style of the tinamous (Crypturi) differs in no essential respect . . . from that of the Gallinae."

After 1867, some writers followed Huxley in treating the ratites as a single group, but others, including Fürbringer (1888, 1902), argued that the similarities among the ratites, including the palatal bones, were due to convergence and that each main group had evolved independently from unknown ancestors. However, Gadow (1893) provided additional evidence of the monophyly of the ratites, and Newton (1896:Intro. 108) attacked Fürbringer's argument for a multiple origin of the ratites, calling it "hardly convincing" and contending that "the characters possessed by all of them in common . . . point indubitably to a single or common descent."

Gadow (1893) placed the ratites in the "Unterclasse Neornithes" and "Division Neornithes Ratitae." In the "Ratitae" he divided the living ratites into four groups of unspecified categorical rank: "Struthiones, Rheae, Casuarii, Apteryges."

In the *Catalogue of Birds*, Salvadori (1895) placed the ratites in the "Subclass Ratitae" and recognized the same four subgroups as Gadow, but Salvadori designated them as orders: "Struthiones, Rheae, Casuarii, Apteryges."

Beddard (1898a) placed the ratites in his order "Struthiones" next to the order "Tinami." He found many points of agreement between these two groups, and some between the tinamous and the galliforms. Beddard disagreed with Fürbringer's wide separation of the ratite groups and cited several characters, including the palate, which he felt were evidence of a common ancestry. He commented that "there is no doubt that the various types of struthious birds do require separating into at least six families; but the likenesses among them appear to me to forbid any wider separation" (p. 494). The battle of monophyly versus polyphyly of the ratites had begun.

In the *Hand-List*, Sharpe (1899) divided living birds into the subclasses Ratitae and Carinatae, with the ratites, tinamous, and galliforms arranged as follows:

Sub-Class RATITAE
      Order Rheiformes
            Fam. Rheidae, *Rhea*
      Order Struthioniformes
            Fam. Struthionidae, *Struthio*
      Order Casuariiformes
            Fam. Dromaeidae, *Dromaeus*
            Fam. Casuariidae, *Casuarius, Hypselornis*
      Order Apterygiformes
            Fam. Apterygidae, *Apteryx*
Sub-Class CARINATAE
      Order Tinamiformes
            Fam. Tinamidae
      Order Galliformes

Pycraft (1900) included the ratites in his superorder Palaeognathae, based on a study of their skeletons, certain muscles, pterylosis, and reproductive systems. He considered his Palaeognathae to be "polyphyletic" and placed the rheas, tinamous, moas, and elephant birds in one subgroup, and the Emu and cassowaries close to one another with the Ostrich nearby. The kiwis were set apart, but viewed as closest to the moas. This arrangement presents an impossible pattern of branching and reveals a confused concept of phylogeny.

H. L. Clark (1901b) proposed a classification based on pterylosis, in which the ratites were separated as the subclass Ratitae, but placed together in a single "Struthioniform" order, defined as "Adult without apteria or oil-gland; plumage soft and lax, intermediate between down and contour-feathers."

The patterns of the intestinal convolutions were interpreted by Mitchell (1896a:141) as evidence that *Rhea* is intermediate between *Struthio* and *Dromaius*. Mitchell (1901a:216) found the pattern in the tinamous to differ from those of the ratites and galliforms, but to be similar to that of the bustards (Otididae).

Beddard (1910) disagreed with Mitchell. He concluded that the large ratites differ from one another in their intestinal coilings, but found similarities between rheas and tinamous. Beddard thought that the kiwis and the tinamous are similar to the galliforms in these characters, in spite of dietary differences between the kiwis and the galliforms.

L. Harrison (1916a,b) believed that the feather mites (Mallophaga) indicate that the kiwis are related to the rails and have nothing in common with the large ratites. He noted (1916b:259–60): "the Ostriches and Rheas would seem to have certainly originated from a common ancestral stock, from which I believe the Emeus also to have been derived, though the evidence here is not quite so convincing."

Based on detailed comparisons of feather structure, Chandler (1916) argued that the ratites, especially *Struthio*, were not derived from flying ancestors. As evidence, he cited the following "primitive characters": (1) absence of plumules, filoplumes, and aftershafts; (2) virtual absence of apteria; (3) similarity of teleoptiles to neossoptiles; (4) structure of barbules. He suggested that the Ostrich and rheas form one group, the Emu, cassowaries, and kiwis another.

Chandler thought that the lack of hooklets (hamuli) on the barbs of the feathers of the ratites, which are present in the tinamous and other flying birds, was sufficient to disprove a relationship between the two groups. Clearly, this is a derived condition related to the flightlessness of the ratites, not evidence of their relationships to other groups. Chandler (p. 342) also found the structure of the down in the tinamou genera *Calopezus* (*Eudromia*) and *Nothura* to be similar to that of the galliforms, which he interpreted as evidence of "unmistakeable relationship."

Wetmore (1930) placed the ratites and tinamous in the superorder "Palaegnathae," with each of the groups in a separate order. He used the same grouping in 1934 and 1940, but following McDowell's (1948) claim that the palaeognathous palate actually consists of four different morphological conditions, Wetmore combined the Palaeognathae and Neognathae in his 1951 and 1960 editions and included the orders of the ratites in the Neognathae. In the introductions to these two latter versions he noted: "For years I have felt that recognition of the Palaeognathae, as a separate group apart from other birds, on the basis of a supposed peculiarity in the palate, stood on flimsy ground. The studies of McDowell demonstrate that the structure of the palaeognathous palate, in which the palatine and pterygoid bones are articulated by a squamous suture, is variable from order to order, and in fact the details of this union differ considerably in the several groups. For example, McDowell points out that in *Dromiceius* the palatine and pterygoid are not in contact, while in a number of families placed in the Neognathae, as in the Anatidae . . . the two bones are in articulation. As there is no clear-cut separation, the former Palaeognathae must be combined with the Neognathae" (1960:4).

Stresemann (1934) followed Fürbringer by placing each of the ratite groups and the tinamous in separate orders, indicating his acceptance of their polyphyly. The similarities between the tinamous and galliforms were attributed to convergence.

In addition to the debate about the relationships among the ratite groups, there was also the question of whether the flightless groups had descended from flying or non-flying ancestors. Lowe believed that the ancestors of the ratites had been flightless and he defended this view in a series of papers (1928, 1930, 1935, 1942, 1944). Lowe proposed that the ratites had shared a common ancestry with the coelurosaurian reptiles such as *Struthiomimus* and *Ornitholestes*. He regarded *Archeopteryx* as an early offshoot in the reptilian radiation, not in the lineage of birds. The main points in his argument follow. The word "primitiveness" is as used by Lowe. 1. In all ratites: the primitiveness of the dromaeognathous palate, the musculature, and the plumage structure. 2. In *Struthio*: a. the absence of the rudimentary clavicle in the embryo; b. the persistence of skull sutures; c. the obtuse angle between coracoid and scapula; d. similarity of the manus to that of *Ornitholestes*.

Gregory (1935) and Murphy (1935) disagreed with Lowe's interpretations and in careful critiques they refuted the arguments in Lowe's earlier papers on the ratites. Brock (1937) studied the cartilaginous skull of the embryo Ostrich and found no evidence indicating that the Ostrich is an offshoot of the avian line before the evolution of flight. Steiner (1936) and Lutz

(1942) observed that the structure of the Emu embryo closely resembles that of carinate embryos, with the hallux opposed to the other digits. Because the first digit is lost in the adult, Lutz suggested that the ancestors of the Emu either lived in trees or had a greater development of the hind toe.

However, Friant (1945a,b; 1946; 1959), who also studied the skeleton, agreed with Lowe's conclusions concerning the "primitiveness" of the ratites.

Oliver (1945) studied ratite skeletons and found "some characters in the leg bones. . . . there are three types of inner condyles in the femora. *Apteryx* is like *Casuarius*; the moas are like *Aepyornis*; *Rhea* is like *Struthio*. In the tibia the cnemial crest is lowest in *Apteryx* and the moas. It is similar . . . in the Casuariidae and Aepyornithidae, but higher. In *Rhea* and *Struthio* the external cnemial crest is reduced. The metatarsus of *Apteryx* resembles that of the moas" (p. 73). Oliver (1945) concluded that the moas and kiwis are "primitive" and related, that the "cassowaries, emus, and Aepyornithidae form a midway group, while the rhea and ostrich are advanced types."

McDowell (1948) considered the palaeognathous palate (dromaeognathous of Huxley 1867) to be variable and impossible to define. He distinguished four types of the palaeognathous palate and recognized four corresponding orders: Tinamiformes (for the tinamous and rheas), Apterygiformes (kiwis, moas, and possibly elephant-birds), Casuariiformes, and Struthioniformes. McDowell's opinion had considerable impact, for example on Wetmore, as noted above, although Wetmore declined to merge the rheas and tinamous in a single order.

Howard (1950) reviewed the fossil evidence on the ratite problem and found it inconclusive for assessing their affinities, while Berlioz (1950) viewed the different ratite groups as families in his order Struthioniformes.

Mayr and Amadon (1951:4) noted that "the problem of ratite phylogeny continues to receive much attention. The present consensus is that the main groups of these birds are of independent origin. Stresemann's suggestion that the kiwis . . . be placed in the same order as the moas . . . is followed. McDowell (1948) may well be correct in believing the rheas to be allied to the tinamous, but we doubt whether they should be placed in the same order, pending further study." They questioned several fossil allocations and (pp. 32–33) recognized five orders for the ratites and tinamous at the beginning of their systematic list.

Thus, in 1951, the most influential classifications—those of Stresemann, Wetmore, and Mayr and Amadon—were supporting Fürbringer's argument for separate origins and convergent similarities among the ratites.

The significance of having morphologically similar parasites also produced contention. *Rhea* and *Struthio* have feather lice (Mallophaga) that are considered to be congeneric species of *Struthiolipeurus*, a genus found on no other birds (Rothschild and Clay 1952:145). The Ostrich and rheas also share what is considered to be the same species of tapeworm (Cestoda), *Houttuynia struthiocameli*, not found in other birds, and two species of mites (Acarina), *Paralges pachycnemis* and *Pterolichus bicaudatus*. Rothschild and Clay interpreted these parasites as evidence of a common ancestry for the Ostrich and rheas, but von Keler (1957) suggested that the feather lice may be similar because of convergence, since the hosts have similar feather structures. Clay (1950, 1957) found that the Mallophaga of tinamous resemble those of gallinaceous birds.

The structure of the Ostrich chondrocranium is like that of carinate birds (Frank 1954), and Webb (1957:145) concluded from a study of the ontogeny of cranial bones and nerves that the "Dromaeognathae" are not primitive but are "a neotenic offshoot of some ancestral bird." Webb derived the palatal structures of the other ratites from that of *Struthio* because, like carinate birds, it lacks a vomer-pterygoid connection. Hofer (1945, 1955) and Simonetta (1960) considered the ratite palate to be a uniform structure, but declined to express taxonomic opinions based on their data.

Starck (1955) and Lang (1956) studied the brain, palate, and pelvis, the development of the olfactory system, arrangement of the trigeminal muscles, and mode of reproduction, from which they concluded that the kiwis and moas are widely separated from the other ratites.

The controversy about independent origins for ratites and carinates was reopened by Holmgren (1955) and Glutz von Blotzheim (1958), who believed that carinate birds arose from "generalized" Jurassic coelurosaurs and that the ratites evolved from the larger Cretaceous coelurosaurs. In rebuttal, DeBeer (1956, 1964) cited the structure of the wing, presence of a pygostyle, and complexity of the ratite cerebellum as evidence that the ratites had evolved from flying avian ancestors. He interpreted the palate, condition of the plumage, and presence of skull sutures in adult ratites as neotenic structures associated with the loss of flight.

Eichler (1955) presented a phylogeny of the tinamous based on their Mallophaga, and proposed that the Tinamidae should be divided into three subfamilies. Dubinin (1958) summarized his own work and that of others on bird parasites, emphasized the monophyly of the large ratites, and supported a relationship between tinamous and galliforms.

The histology of the long bones of birds was studied by Zavattari and Cellini (1956), who found that the ratites (exemplified by *Struthio*, *Rhea*, *Casuarius*) have a complex Haversian canal system, superficially like that of mammals. Carinate birds have an irregular disposition of Haversian canals. Tinamous differ from both ratites and carinates, but were thought by these authors to be closer to the ratites. *Apteryx* was not examined.

Tyler and Simkiss (1959) found similar chemical compositions, pore shape, and other aspects of fine structure in the egg shells of kiwis and tinamous. Cassowary and Emu egg shells were similar, but the egg shells of the Ostrich and rheas differed from one another and were unlike those of the cassowaries and Emu.

Paper electrophoretic comparisons of the egg-white proteins indicated a relationship among *Casuarius*, *Dromaius*, and *Struthio*, but the evidence concerning *Rhea* was equivocal. The egg-white patterns of the tinamous were not especially similar to either the ratites or the galliforms (Sibley 1960).

Verheyen produced some of the more extreme opinions about the relationships among the ratites and between them and other groups of birds. Primarily from comparisons of skeletal characters, he concluded that the kiwis are distantly related to the penguins (1960h), that the rheas are the nearest relatives of the tinamous (1960g), and that the tinamous should be placed in the order Galliformes (1960a). The flavor of Verheyen's opinions may be sampled in the English summary of his paper (1960g) on the relationships of the rheas and tinamous:

In almost all ancient and recent bird catalogues we find the Rheas . . . lumped with the Ostriches . . . the Cassowaries . . . the Emus . . . and . . . the Kiwis . . . into the subclass Ratitae . . . in opposition to the Carinatae. This oversimplified classification, due to Merrem (1812) has been checked . . . by a large number of morphologists [etc.] . . . and although it is already firmly established that close relationship between the orders of Ratitae is pure fiction, only a very few research workers made a serious attempt to clarify the position of the different Ratitae with regard to the . . . Carinatae.

The lack of this kind of information was very harmful to progress . . . and to understand[ing] avian evolution; it is . . . responsible for the thousands . . . of pages treating the hypothetical interrelationships of the Ratitae which would never have been written if comparative anatomy . . . had been . . . encouraged and understood.

However for the majority of . . . ornithologists taxonomy is still cataloguing, without saying anything about the way in which their "natural" group has come into being and it is a pity that . . . students should keep on manipulating skins as if that were the chief aim of scientific ornithology. Some of the Ratitae have their relatives within the Carinatae. We know already that the Kiwis . . . are distantly related to the Penguins . . . and . . . we have produced evidence that the Rheas are the nearest relatives of the Neotropical Tinamous (Tinamidae-Galliformes).

Meise (1963) reviewed ratite and tinamou behavior patterns and concluded that the similarities indicate monophyly. He considered the behavioral differences among the ratites and tinamous to be no greater than among the Galliformes.

From a study of the bony palate, Bock (1963) also supported the monophyly of the ratites and tinamous. Contrary to McDowell (1948), Bock argued that the homology of the palaeognathous palate in ratites and tinamous is indicated by:

1. Relatively large vomer, articulating anteriorly with the premaxillae and maxillopalatines and posteriorly with the pterygoids, except in *Struthio*.
2. Pterygoid prevents the palatine from articulating with the basisphenoidal rostrum.
3. Palatine articulates with the pterygoid along a suture.
4. Basitemporal articulation is large, and near the posterior end of the pterygoid.
5. Pterygoid-quadrate articulation is complex, including part of the orbital process of the quadrate.

Wilson et al. (1964) and Kaplan (1965) reported that the palaeognathous birds they examined (*Struthio*, *Rhea*, a tinamou) possess lactate dehydrogenases (LDH) of a higher inactivation temperature and greater relative electrophoretic mobility than those of neognathous birds. Such characteristics were similar to those found in such reptiles as a caiman (*Caiman*), a monitor lizard (*Varanus*), and a rattlesnake (*Crotalus*). The properties of tinamou LDH correspond more closely to those of ratite LDH than to those of other groups of birds.

An immunoelectrophoretic study by H. Miller and Feeney (1964) found similarities among the egg-white proteins of the large ratites, and tinamou egg white reacted with anti-cassowary antiserum.

Glenny (1965) found the carotid artery pattern of a kiwi and a rhea to be the B-4-s, single carotid, type. The Ostrich and the Casuariidae have the double carotid (A-1) arrangement. Glenny interpreted these conditions as evidence of a close relationship among the Ostrich, cassowaries, and Emu, and for separate ancestries for the rheas and kiwis.

The ratites and tinamous share a conformation of the rhamphotheca not found in other birds. Parkes and Clark (1966) interpreted this "as an additional piece of evidence that resemblances among this group are to be attributed to monophyletic origin rather than to convergence."

Comparisons of the egg-white proteins, using several methods, caused Osuga and

Feeney (1968:560) to conclude that "close biochemical and immunochemical relationships were found among the ratites, and they appeared remotely related to the tinamou."

Gysels (1970) compared the electrophoretic patterns and immunodiffusion reactions of the eye lens proteins of tinamous with those of several ratites and other groups of birds. He concluded that the tinamous are closest to *Rhea*, but that *Rhea* is even closer to *Casuarius*, and that *Casuarius* is closest to the Galliformes.

Sibley and Frelin (1972) used isoelectric focusing in acrylamide gel to compare the egg-white proteins of the ratites and several species of tinamous. They also compared the tryptic peptides of the ovalbumins of these groups. They concluded that the large ratites are more closely related to one another than any one of them is to any other group, that the kiwis are not closely related to the large ratites or tinamous, and that the tinamous are not closely related to the ratites but may be distantly related to the Galliformes.

Sibley and Ahlquist (1972) reviewed the taxonomic history of the ratites and tinamous, and most of the preceding historical review is based on this earlier publication. We sought to answer two questions: 1. Have the flightless ratites evolved from flying ancestors? 2. What are the relationships of the large ratites to one another, to the kiwis and tinamous, and to other birds?

We summarized the previous evidence (1972:50) and suggested that it indicated that the ratites evolved from flying ancestors, and that "the relationship of the large ratites to one another is suggested by a considerable body of evidence . . . from morphological, parasitological, ethological, and biochemical studies. A relationship of the tinamous to the large ratites is suggested by the data on palate and rhamphothecal structures, but the pterylography and Mallophaga suggest an alliance with the gallinaceous birds. Other characters are equivocal. The affinities of *Apteryx*, in spite of all previous studies, are still an enigma."

From all available evidence, including electrophoretic comparisons of the egg-white proteins, we concluded (1972:52) that "Although we believe that the large ratites are monophyletic and should be united in a single order, we do not believe that the relationships of the kiwis and tinamous have yet been determined beyond question."

The amino acid compositions of the proteins of the eggshell membranes were examined by Krampitz et al. (1974). They found that Emu and cassowary proteins are most alike, that those of the Ostrich and Greater Rhea differ somewhat from one another and from those of the other ratites, and that the kiwi proteins differ from those of the other ratites. It should be noted that amino acid compositions indicate nothing about the sequence of the amino acids in the intact proteins, and such evidence is of limited value as an index to the genetic information content of protein molecules.

Further evidence linking ratites and tinamous has been found by Semba and Mathers (pers. comm.) in the "vaned" ocular pecten that occurs only in *Rhea*, *Struthio*, and tinamous. The kiwis have a unique conical pecten, and the Emu and cassowaries have a pleated pecten of the type found in virtually all other groups of birds. The conical pecten of the kiwis may have been derived from the pleated type, and its modified structure is probably related to the nocturnal habits of the kiwis and their reduced reliance on vision.

Cracraft (1974) conducted a cladistic analysis of the hind limb and pelvic skeletal characters of the ratites, including the extinct groups. He accepted the conclusions of Bock (1963a), Meise (1963), and Parkes and Clark (1966) that the ratites and tinamous form a monophyletic cluster. Cracraft considered the ratites and tinamous to be one another's closest relatives because they share "the following derived characters": the paleognathous palate, a unique rhamphothecal structure, a large ilioischiatic fenestra.

Cracraft's morphological study of the ratites was the first, on birds, to use the methodology of "phylogenetic systematics" based on the principles expounded by Hennig (1966). (See chapter 15.) The essence of this approach is the "character analysis of primitive-derived sequences" (Cracraft 1972, 1974). Cracraft (1972) was optimistic that "with careful analysis of characters [using] primitive-derived sequences . . . we will be able to resolve the phylogenetic relationships of avian families." Cracraft's study was, therefore, a test of the application of Hennigian principles. Cracraft's "theory of relationship" to be examined by his study was as follows: 1. The tinamous and ratites form a monophyletic group. 2. The tinamous and ratites are each other's closest relatives, i.e., they are "sister groups." 3. The emus and cassowaries are most closely related to the ostriches and rheas, and not to the moas and kiwis.

Cracraft (1974) used a set of 25 characters of the post-cranial skeleton, including grooves, condyles, fossae, trochleae, shafts, fenestrae, processes, sulci, foramina, and similar structures of the femur, tibiotarsus, tarsometatarsus, pelvis, sternum, and scapulo-coracoid, plus the "general proportions" of the wing skeleton.

Cracraft concluded that the "postcranial morphology shows a clear relationship of the emus and cassowaries to the ostriches and rheas, and not to the moas and kiwis." Cracraft (1981) proposed the following classification for the ratites and tinamous:

Division 2
  Order Palaeognathiformes
    Suborder Tinami
            Family Tinamidae, Tinamous
    Suborder Ratiti
      Infraorder Apteryges
            Family Dinornithidae, Moas
            Family Apterygidae, Kiwis
      Infraorder Struthiones
        Superfamily Casuarioidea
            Family Casuariidae, Cassowaries
            Family Dromiceidae, Emus
        Superfamily Struthionoidea
            Family Rheidae, Rheas
            Family Struthionidae, Ostriches

For some of his 25 characters Cracraft identified "evolutionary trends," using outline drawings to illustrate the differences he defined between some of the taxa. A. H. Bledsoe (pers. comm.) checked the characters used by Cracraft and found that he could not always discern the trends depicted by Cracraft, or that some other trend seemed equally probable. Cracraft considered *Struthio* to be the most "derived" and the tinamou to be the most "primitive" taxa; thus, his trends began with a tinamou (*Crypturellus*). Bledsoe found that if the tinamou was omitted from the analysis, the Ostrich was considered the out-group, and character polarity was then assigned according to the rules of Hennig (1966), he developed a phylogeny concordant with that of our DNA comparisons (Sibley and Ahlquist 1981a). In addition, use of a different set of skeletal characters would alter the phylogram. Thus, the out-group chosen and the characters used have major effects on the results. (See Bledsoe 1988a, below.)

A. J. Baker and C. McGowan (pers. comm.) also tried to reconstruct Cracraft's ratite phylogeny. After checking Cracraft's characters and examining a series of specimens, they found that some of the supposedly dichotomous character states were actually the extremes of a continuum. They used out-group comparisons to determine character-state polarity and found that Cracraft's assumption that "common equals primitive" was not always sustained. They also added new characters, and the results were vastly different from the phylogeny proposed by Cracraft. Baker and McGowan concluded that they were unable to substantiate Cracraft's hypothesis of ratite phylogeny.

Cracraft (1974:517) stated his belief that "there was little convergence [in the characters he studied and that the only] major morphological convergence occurred in the pelvis [in which] a lateromedial compression . . . probably evolved independently in the kiwis and in the superfamily Struthionoidea."

Cracraft's confidence in the absence of convergence in the leg bones of these large, cursorial species was surely misplaced. In fact, it seems probable that convergence accounts for at least some of the similarities that exist among the hind limbs of the large ratites and that these similarities caused Cracraft to consider the Emu and cassowaries to be more closely related to the Ostrich and rheas than to the kiwis. The DNA comparisons indicate that the kiwis are the closest living relatives of the Emu and cassowaries.

Gingerich (1976) objected to Cracraft's claim that the three "character states" used by Cracraft to support the monophyly of the ratites and tinamous are derived, and argued that all three could be primitive. Gingerich concluded that "Evidence that ratites are strictly mono-phyletic remains to be discovered and it is possible, even probable, that the groups of living ratites and tinamous are paraphyletic" (p. 32). Cracraft (1981) rebutted Gingerich's critique.

The debate about the interpretation of morphological characters may never be resolved, but the congruence of molecular data, behavioral traits, and many morphological characters provides ample evidence that the ratite-tinamou assemblage is monophyletic.

Prager et al. (1976) used the immunological method of micro-complement fixation to compare the transferrins of the ratites, tinamous, and representatives of the other traditional avian orders. They concluded that the ratites and tinamous constitute a monophyletic assem-blage and that the differences among the ratites are congruent with the timing of the breakup and drift of the southern continents.

Prager and Wilson (1980) summarized the results of several studies (Prager et al. 1976, Ho et al. 1976, Prager and Wilson 1976) using micro-complement fixation to compare the properties of several proteins representing many of the major groups of birds. They concluded that "there were at least two major phases in the history of birds: the first probably involving an early adaptive radiation of paleognathous birds [ratites and tinamous] with limited capacity for sustained flight and the second involving a later adaptive radiation of carinate birds."

De Boer (1980) reviewed several studies of the chromosome complements of the large ratites and added the results of his study of the karyotype of the Brown Kiwi (*Apteryx australis*). The chromosomes of the ratites are remarkably alike, but they differ from those of other groups of birds, thus supporting monophyly for the group. Within the ratites there are small but revealing differences. De Boer (1980) stated that "the kiwi chromosomes are indistinguishable from those of the emu and cassowary. The karyotype of the ostrich differs only in the possible absence of the secondary constriction in the sixth pair and the somewhat smaller short arm in the third pair. The rhea karyotypes differ only by the submedian position of the centromere in the elements of the fifth pair."

Thus, the Emu, a cassowary, and the Brown Kiwi have identical karyotypes which differ from those of the Ostrich and rheas, and the latter two differ from one another. Boer's interpretation of these observations was confused by his acceptance of Cracraft's phylogeny, but the karyotype evidence agrees perfectly with the phylogeny of the ratites based on the DNA hybridization data.

Stapel et al. (1984) compared the sequences of the 173 amino acids in the eye lens protein α-crystallin A in Ostrich, Greater Rhea, and Emu and in representatives of 13 other avian "orders." They concluded that the ratites "as a monophyletic assemblage, represent the first offshoot of the avian line." A tree constructed from the sequence data depicts the ratites "as the sister group of all other birds. The Galliformes and Anseriformes appear to be the next branch off from the main avian stem." This is congruent with our DNA hybridization evidence.

McGowan (1982) studied the wing musculature of the Brown Kiwi (*Apteryx australis*) and concluded that the ratites were derived from a primitive flying ancestor that had not evolved the advanced flight mechanism of the carinates. McGowan (1986) added support to this conclusion from a study of the wing musculature of the Weka (*Gallirallus australis*), a flightless rail of New Zealand.

McGowan (1984) examined the ontogeny of the tarsal region in birds and found two different conditions. Carinates have a pretibial bone which fuses with the calcaneum. The pretibial is absent in ratites and tinamous, which have an ascending process that fuses with the astragalus, as in theropod dinosaurs. "This implies that, since carinates possess the unique pretibial bone, they could not have given rise to the ratites, which are primitive for this feature."

Olson (1985) argued that "the great diversity in . . . morphology within the large ratites favors their having evolved their ratite grades of morphology independently of one another." Diversity alone is not evidence of polyphyly. To prove that the ratites are not monophyletic it is necessary to demonstrate that at least one of the ratites is more closely related to the members of some other group than to the other ratites. This has not been done.

Craw (1985) conducted a "panbiogeographic analysis" of the ratite birds and concluded that the "track for the ratites is oriented across the Atlantic [ostrich-rheas] and Indian [Australian–New Zealand ratites] Oceans" and that "the minimum distance criterion orients the track connecting the Australasian with the South American–African ratites across the Indian Ocean rather than the Pacific Ocean; a track orientation that is also supported by the presence on Madagascar of extinct ratite species belonging to the family Aepyornithidae [elephant birds]."

Houde (1986) suggested that "the ancestors of ostriches are . . . among a group of North American and European birds, the 'Lithornis-cohort', that had the potential of flight and from which the kiwis may have arisen separately." He speculated that the Ostrich arose from a European member of the Lithornis-cohort, and the rheas from a North American member of the Lithornis-cohort. Houde proposed that "kiwis could have evolved directly from a paleognath that flew to New Zealand and lost its power of flight independently of other ratite birds." This remarkable and improbable hypothesis is based on the retention by kiwis of "primitive characters that are uniquely derived in the *Lithornis*-cohort . . . suggesting a relatively close relationship." Houde used his hypothesis to challenge the Gondwana origin of the ratites and the calibration of our DNA hybridization data in absolute time based on the assumption that the split between the Ostrich and rhea lineages occurred ca. 80 MYA. Houde misread our paper on the hominoids (Sibley and Ahlquist 1984a) and stated that we had used the ratite-based calibration (Sibley and Ahlquist 1981a) to calibrate the dating of hominoid divergences. In fact, the two calibrations were independent. The hominoid calibration was based on the fossil evidence of the divergence of the Orangutan lineage (Pilbeam 1983, 1985) and the two calibrations were similar only by coincidence.

Houde's speculative proposals are certainly less probable than the theory of the Gondwana origin of the ratites. The evidence from morphology and molecules, described herein, indicates that the living ratites are monophyletic, that the Ostrich and rheas are sister lineages, and that the kiwis are most closely related to the Australo-Papuan ratites. To invalidate our DNA hybridization data a critic must prove that our delta values do not represent relative time, not merely that the absolute time calibration may be incorrect. We have repeatedly stated, in print, that all absolute time calibrations are "tentative and subject to correction." That is still true, but Houde's evidence has no bearing on the question because he has no proof that the *Lithornis*-cohort left any descendants, let alone that they were the ancestors of the Ostrich, rheas, and kiwis. It is obvious that DNA molecules had ancestors.

Houde (1988) published a more extensive treatment of the "Lithornithiformes" which he considers to be paraphyletic to the ratites. The three genera (*Pseudocrypturus, Lithornis,* and *Paracathartes*) are viewed as successively closer to the ratites.

Bledsoe (1988a) used numerical cladistic methods to reconstruct the phylogeny of the ratites, based on 83 characters of the post-cranial skeleton. He concluded that the Ostrich and rheas form the sister group of the extinct elephant-birds, that the cassowaries and Emu are the sister group of the kiwis, and that the Ostrich-rhea clade is the sister group of the cassowary-Emu-kiwi clade. The extinct moas were considered to be the sister group of the other ratites, and the tinamous are the sister group of the ratites. Bledsoe's cladistic analysis corroborated the initial assumption of ratite monophyly with a suite of seven uniquely derived character states of the living ratites, six of which are known to occur in the elephant-birds but five of which are not known in the moas, which lacked forelimb skeletal elements. Bledsoe concluded that his tree of the living ratites is congruent with evidence from DNA hybridization (Sibley and Ahlquist 1981a, 1987c) and protein transferrin comparisons (Prager et al. 1976).

Many morphological studies of the ratites were briefly reviewed above. These reviews demonstrate that adaptive evolution produces conflicting evidence in different organ systems and erases, or confuses, the phylogenetic trail as a function of time. Recently divergent forms, such as the Emu and cassowaries, are readily recognized as close relatives, but the descendants of more ancient dichotomies provide the basis for differing interpretations and the resulting disagreements. Even a group as small as the ratites has generated hundreds of publications without the development of a consensus about their phylogeny.

The DNA Hybridization Evidence (Figs. 18–24, 325–328, 353, 354, 357)

In an earlier study (1981a) we used Δ mode values and an incomplete set of $T_{50}H$ values to compare DNA-DNA hybrids among the ratites and a tinamou. Since 1981 we have made additional comparisons. Dates of divergences were based on the assumption that the Ostrich-rhea split occurred ca. 80 MYA, as discussed below. This calibration is tentative and subject to correction. Many of the dates seem too old in view of the known fossil evidence, but they may be regarded as relative dates and corrected when a better basis for the calibration is discovered. The $\Delta T_{50}H$ values are relative to absolute time, but the calibration of these values is difficult.

The average $\Delta T_{50}H$ for the ratite-tinamou divergence from the waterfowl-galliform clade was calculated as 25.9, and the divergence between these groups and the other groups of birds was found to be $\Delta T_{50}H$ 28.0. On this evidence we placed the galliforms and anseriforms on the same side of the oldest branch as the ratites and tinamous. However, the evidence from the melting curves (see below) casts doubt on this conclusion and we have revised the classification of Sibley et al. (1988) by leaving the ratites and tinamous in the Eoaves and transferring the Galloanserae to the Neoaves, which also includes all other groups of living birds.

The DNAs of the ratites have been compared with those of many other groups and the evidence indicates that the living ratites are monophyletic; that is, they are more closely related to one another than any one of them is to the members of any other group of living birds. The DNA comparisons indicate that the tinamous and ratites are sister groups that probably diverged in the mid-Cretaceous (Δ 21.8) (Fig. 357). The earliest dichotomy within the ratite cluster was ca. 80 MYA (Δ 17.9), which split the Ostrich-rhea clade from the cassowary-Emu-kiwi clade. The Ostrich-rhea split at Δ 17.1 (ca. 75–80 MYA) may have been a result of the opening of the Atlantic between Africa and South America. The New Zealand kiwi lineage diverged from the Australian cassowary-Emu lineage at Δ 9.5, and the branch between *Casuarius* and *Dromaius* was at Δ 5.0, possibly ca. 20–25 MYA, in the early Miocene. The three species of kiwis probably diverged since the late Miocene: *Apteryx oweni* at Δ 1.4, *A. haastii* at Δ 1.0, and the North and South island subspecies of *A. australis* at Δ 0.7.

The divergence between the *Struthio* and *Rhea* lineages at $\Delta T_{50}H$ 17.1 was used to calibrate the $\Delta T_{50}H$ scale against absolute time. We assumed that the Atlantic became impassable for the most recent common ancestor of the Ostrich and rheas about 80 MYA, thus giving a calibration constant of $\Delta T_{50}H$ 1.0 = 4.7 MY.

The significance of the divergence between the Ostrich-rhea clade and the Australian–New Zealand ratites at Δ 17.9 (ca. 80–81 MYA) is uncertain. It may be related to the separation between Africa and the Antarctic-Australian land mass, although that divergence may have been as early as 130 MYA, as some of the geological evidence suggests. South America and Australia were previously thought to have been in contact via Antarctica until ca. 70 MYA (through an archipelagic connection) and the ancestor of the Australian–New Zealand ratites was assumed to have come from South America via that route. However, Cande and Mutter (1982) concluded that Australia broke away from Antarctica ca. 90 MYA.

The divergence between the Australian Casuariidae and the New Zealand Apterygidae (Δ 9.5) may have occurred ca. 40–45 MYA, long after the opening of the Tasman Sea ca. 80 MYA. Although the Tasman Sea was, and is, wide and deep in the south, "between north-western New Zealand and northeastern Australia the sea was shallow and the Lord Howe Rise, the Norfolk Ridge and the Queensland Plateau may have supported emergent archipelagos long after the separation of the major land masses" (Sibley and Ahlquist 1981a:322). The collision between Australia and the Pacific plate, ca. 40–45 MYA, produced volcanic islands and island arcs whose remains are present today as guyots on the floor of the northern Tasman Sea. The common ancestor of the kiwis and the cassowaries could have taken thousands or millions of years to make the crossing, moving from one island to the next, without having to swim any great distances. Thus, there is nothing in the geological history of the region that precludes a divergence between the New Zealand and Australian ratites at ca. 40–45 MYA.

The tinamou-ratite divergence (Δ 21.5) may have occurred in the mid-Cretaceous, before the opening of the Atlantic. The DNAs of four species of tinamous were available and that of *Nothoprocta cinerascens* was used as a tracer. Two other species of the same genus are Δ 4.2 from *cinerascens*, but species of *Crypturellus* and *Eudromia* are Δ 11.4 from the tracer species. These values indicate that two superfamilies could be recognized. One would be the Tinamoidea, containing the family Tinamidae, but the genera to be included in the Tinamidae (except for *Tinamus*) are not obvious, and the names and contents of the other superfamily and family will require additional information. Therefore, we defer these proposals pending further study.

The melting curves (Figs. 18–24) depict the relationships of the ratites and tinamous. In Fig. 18 the Ostrich homoduplex is compared with the heteroduplex curves of three other ratites, a tinamou, a New World vulture (*Cathartes*), an ibis, a penguin, a bustard, a duck, a coot, and a galliform. The three ratites are closest to the Ostrich, but the vulture, ibis, and penguin are closer to the Ostrich than are the tinamou, duck, and galliform. This seems to contradict our classification that places the ratites closer to the galliforms and anseriforms than to any other groups of the Neoaves. We interpret this as evidence of the effect of delayed maturity in *Cathartes, Plegadis, Spheniscus,* and *Eupodotis. Mycteria*, in Fig. 21, also has delayed maturity, compared with the anseriforms (ca. 2 years) and galliforms (1 year). *Fulica* begins to breed at 1–2 years of age (Table 16).

In Figs. 18, 19, and 24, the kiwi and Emu and/or cassowary curves cluster tightly, indicating equal genetic distances from the Ostrich, *Rhea*, and tinamou. The Greater Rhea curve is more distant and in Fig. 19 (*Rhea*) the *Rhea-Struthio* curve is in the same relative position, showing the reciprocity between the two measurements. However, this does not necessarily mean that the Ostrich and rhea lineages diverged before either diverged from the Emu-cassowary-kiwi lineage. It may be evidence of different average genomic rates; that is, the rhea lineage may have been evolving more rapidly, thus accumulating more neutral mutations in the same length of time. This is suggested by Fig. 24 (*Nothoprocta*) in which the *Rhea* and *Struthio* curves are farther from the homoduplex than are those of *Apteryx* and *Dromaius*. However, in Figs. 20 (*Dromaius*) and 22 (*Casuarius*) the Ostrich and rhea curves are equidistant from that of the homoduplex. Thus, the relative positions of the Ostrich and rhea curves may reflect a slower average rate of evolution in the rhea lineage, but the same effect could be caused by variation in the behavior of the *Rhea* driver DNA in the different experiments, i.e., experimental error.

The FITCH tree (Fig. 325) shows the monophyly of the ratites and tinamous (*Nothoprocta*), but the position of the Ciconiiformes may reflect a slower rate of DNA evolution in these groups (shorebirds, storks, New World vultures, tubenoses, etc.), many of which do not begin to breed until 3–4 years old, compared with 2 years in anseriforms and 1 year in galliforms. The KITSCH tree for the same taxa (Fig. 326) clusters the Ciconiiformes with the Galliformes and Anseriformes, not with the tinamous and ratites. In the UPGMA tree (Fig. 357), the Anseriformes and Galliformes cluster with the ratites and tinamous; together they form an assemblage that is the sister group of all other living birds.

Thus, there are three possible trees suggested by the DNA hybridization data; the problem is to choose the one most likely to represent the branching pattern that occurred among these groups. In each lineage there are species with delayed maturity and, presumably, relatively slower rates of genomic evolution which produces short branches. The ratites are slowed relative to the tinamous (Fig. 325), the cracids and megapodes are slowed relative to the phasianids, and the screamers and Magpie Goose (*Anseranas*) are slowed relative to the anatids (Fig. 328). These differences are correlated with ages at maturity.

To reduce the effects of differences in average rates of DNA evolution, a small matrix consisting of data for species that begin to breed at one or two years of age was constructed. The Anatidae, Phasianidae, Tinamidae, and Rallidae were chosen. The Rallidae are members of the Gruiformes, but they represent the waterbird groups as well as would members of the Ciconiiformes, of which only the sandpipers (Scolopacidae) begin to breed at age one, and we have too few comparisons involving the sandpipers.

This simplified matrix of uncorrected $\Delta T_{50}H$ values was clustered using the FITCH and KITSCH routines (Fig. 327). In the FITCH tree the Phasianidae and Anatidae cluster closest together, as expected, with the Rallidae and Tinamidae as out-groups. The topology is similar to that of Fig. 325. The long branch to the Tinamidae may reflect their early maturity (Table 16). This tree is unrooted and an unequivocal root requires non-avian comparisons, which are lacking.

The KITSCH tree (Fig. 327), although not rooted, establishes the Tinamidae as the oldest lineage, with a goodness-of-fit value only slightly below that of the FITCH tree. Thus, it is similar to the KITSCH tree in Fig. 326, and if rooted arbitrarily at mid-span, it yields the same clades as the KITSCH tree.

This arrangement seems to be the best representation of all of the data, morphological and molecular. It recognizes the Galloanserae as the oldest clade in the Neoaves, and the ratites and tinamous as the sister group of all other living birds.

We conclude that the living ratites are monophyletic and that the tinamous are their nearest living relatives. It is clear that the Emu and cassowaries are the most closely related genera and that the kiwis are their next nearest relatives. The position of *Rhea* relative to *Struthio*, and to the kiwi-cassowary-Emu group, remains uncertain. The melting curves (Figs. 18–24) suggest that the Ostrich and rheas are ca. equidistant from the other ratites and may be members of the same clade, as indicated by the UPGMA tree (Fig. 357). Figs. 325 and 326 suggest that the rheas may be closer to the kiwi-cassowary-Emu clade than is the Ostrich. The differences among the clustering methods may be attributed to the non-reciprocity of the Ostrich-rhea comparisons (see Fig. 325) and to the branch-length shortening of the kiwi-cassowary-Emu clade relative to the Ostrich and rheas. These explanations may be correct, or they may be viewed as special pleading to explain away discrepancies. Perhaps they include some of each.

Gallinaceous Birds

Infraclass Neoaves
  Parvclass Galloanserae
    Superorder Gallomorphae
      Order CRACIFORMES
        Suborder Craci
            Family Cracidae: Guans, Chachalacas, Curassows
        Suborder Megapodii
            Family Megapodiidae: Megapodes, Scrubfowl, Brush-turkeys
      Order GALLIFORMES
        Parvorder Phasianida
          Superfamily Phasianoidea
            Family Phasianidae: Pheasants, Grouse, Old World Quail, etc.
          Superfamily Numidoidea
            Family Numididae: Guineafowl
        Parvorder Odontophorida
            Family Odontophoridae: New World Quails

One or more of the 283 species of gallomorphs occurs on all continents and many islands from the Arctic to the tips of the southern continents. They are absent from Polynesia, New Zealand, and the Antarctic. The cracids are confined to the Neotropics; the megapodes to Australasia, southeast Asia, the Philippines, and the islands of the southwest Pacific. The New World quails occur in the Americas, the guineafowl in Africa and Madagascar, the grouse in the Holarctic, turkeys in North America, and the partridges in Eurasia and Africa. The pheasants occur primarily in southeastern Asia, and the francolins in Africa and Asia. The Congo Peafowl (*Afropavo congensis*) is known only from the Ituri Forest of eastern Zaire.

Superorder GALLOMORPHAE: 75/283. The fowl-like birds; terrestrial or arboreal; 4-toed; schizognathous; (A)BCDXYV+ (Hudson 1937); two carotids (except in megapodes); sternum usually with two deep incisions on each side; quadrate bone double; intestinal convolutions Type V; flexor tendons Type 1; eutaxic (except megapodes); holorhinal, impervious nares; oil gland variable, sparsely to densely tufted or, rarely, naked, absent in some; tracheo-bronchial syrinx; aftershaft large; 10 primaries; 9–20 secondaries; 8–32 rectrices; 16 cervical vertebrae; crop large; gizzard muscular; down only on apteria; no true powder downs; true basipterygoid processes absent, secondary basipterygoid processes articulate with anterior ends of pterygoids; eggs usually white or monochrome, some spotted; nidifugous downy young in which remiges grow rapidly and which soon fly.

Order CRACIFORMES: 17/69. Family CRACIDAE: 11/50. Long-tailed, arboreal, Neotropical gallomorphs with hallux at same level as fore toes; toe nails curved; skeleton highly pneumatic; trachea of males usually coiled; sternal incisions shallower than in the Galliformes; biceps slip absent; small penis; aftershaft small; oil gland with short tuft or, rarely, naked; nest usually in a tree; two white eggs. 7 genera (Vuilleumier 1965); 11 genera (Vaurie 1968).

Family MEGAPODIIDAE: 6/19. Terrestrial; left carotid only; hallux on same level as fore toes; diastataxic; oil gland nude or with short tuft; eggs relatively large, not incubated by parents, but laid in warm sand, earth, decaying vegetation, or volcanically warmed soil; young hatched fully feathered and soon able to fly.

Order GALLIFORMES: 58/214. Family PHASIANIDAE: 45/177. The Phasianidae may be subdivided into several subfamilies and tribes but, until the DNA data are more extensive, we will recognize only the family and note the following subgroups without using categorical names.

Grouse and Turkeys: 8/19. Grouse 6/17. Turkeys 2/2. In the grouse the nostrils are covered by feathers; tarsus and toes often feathered, or toes laterally pectinate; tail molt centripetal; no tarsal spurs; no penis; aftershaft long; oil gland variable, usually bilobed, tufted, rarely absent, e.g., in *Argusianus*. Holarctic distribution. The turkeys are large grouse in which the males have colored, erectile caruncles; tail long; tarsal spurs in males.

Pheasants, Peafowl, Junglefowl: 16/50. Primarily terrestrial; hallux elevated; mandibular tomium not serrated; tail molt centripetal; 14–32 rectrices; most have tarsal spurs; other characters variable among the species.

Partridges, Francolins, Old World Quail: 20/106. Boundaries of this group unclear, but it includes *Perdix*, *Alectoris*, *Francolinus*, and *Coturnix* based on DNA hybridization evidence. Few species with tarsal spurs; tail molt centrifugal; 8–22 rectrices; usually monogamous; other characters variable.

Family NUMIDIDAE: 4/6. Upper part of head usually bare, often with a bony, erect, vertical "helmet," a bristly or curly crest, or an occipital feathered patch; second metacarpal without backward process; costal processes outwardly inclined; oil gland bilobed, tufted; full plumage of back has an arched contour; tail relatively small, drooping, 14–16 rectrices; plumage spotted or striped. Confined to Africa.

Family ODONTOPHORIDAE: 9/31. The New World quails usually have been viewed as a subfamily of the Phasianidae. They are small, compact galliforms, with a short, stout bill with a curved culmen and a serrated, or toothed, mandibular tomium; bare nostrils; hallux above level of other toes; none have tarsal spurs; rectrices 10–14, never acuminate; tail molt centrifugal; acrotarsium with a single row of broad, transverse, scutes; planta tarsi with two or more rows of long scutes but partly covered with small scales; oil gland bilobed, usually tufted, sometimes naked in some individuals; monogamous; lay 10–15 eggs, incubation 22–30 days; nest on ground.

The usual two questions; relationships within the order and to other orders, apply to the Craciformes and Galliformes. The DNA evidence indicates that the Anserimorphae is the sister group of the Gallomorphae. The divergence at $\Delta T_{50}H$ 22.9 was probably in the mid Cretaceous. The Galliformes and Craciformes diverged at Δ 21.6.

The Hoatzin (*Opisthocomus hoazin*) has often been placed in the Galliformes, but the DNA comparisons confirm earlier evidence from egg-white protein electrophoresis (Sibley and Ahlquist 1973) that the Hoatzin is a New World cuckoo, and its affinities will be treated under the Cuculiformes.

Historical Review of the Classification

The cracids and the typical galliforms usually have been placed in the same order, Galliformes, and will be treated together in the following review.

In his order Gallinae, Linnaeus (1758) included only species that are still recognized as gallomorphs. His genera of Gallinae were *Pavo, Meleagris, Crax, Phasianus*, and *Tetrao*.

In most of the early classifications the galliform groups were placed together, sometimes with the bustards, the ratites, tinamous, rails, pigeons, or the lyrebirds (*Menura*) in the same cluster or nearby. It is obvious that superficial similarities were the basis for such associations.

Lilljeborg (1866) included the Phasianidae, Tetraonidae (grouse), the tinamous, and the sandgrouse in his order "Gallinae." He placed the megapodes and cracids ("Penelopidae") in the order "Pullastrae," which included the pigeons and doves.

Huxley's (1867) order "Alectoromorphae" included the Turnicidae, Phasianidae, sandgrouse, megapodes, and cracids. He commented: "The Turnicidae approach the Charadriomorphae, the Pteroclidae [sandgrouse] the Peristeromorphae [pigeons]; while the Cracidae have relations with the birds of prey on one hand, and with *Palamedea* [screamers] and the other Chenomorphae [waterfowl] on the other" (p. 459). Huxley (1868) proposed the suborders "Peristeropodes," containing the Cracidae and Megapodiidae, and the "Alectoropodes," including the pheasants, turkeys, grouse, and guineafowl. In the Peristeropodes the hallux is at the same level as the front toes (incumbent); in the Alectoropodes it is raised above the level of the other toes.

Sclater and Salvin (1870) followed Huxley in subdividing the Cracidae into the Penelopinae and Cracinae on the basis of postacetabular characters, and they recognized a subfamily for the Horned Guan (*Oreophasis derbianus*).

In Sundevall's classification (1872, see 1889:197) the order Gallinae was organized as follows (vernacular names added):

Order Gallinae
  Cohort Tetraonomorphae
    Fam. Pteroclinae: Sandgrouse
    Fam. Tetraoninae: Grouse and Horned Guan (*Oreophasis*)
  Cohort Phasianomorphae
    Fam. Phasianinae: some pheasants, *Gallus*
    Fam. Pavoninae: Peafowl, some pheasants, turkeys
    Fam. Perdicinae: Guineafowl, Francolins, Partridges, Old World Quail, New World Quail
    Fam. Hemipodiinae: *Turnix*
  Cohort Macronyches

Fam. Catheturinae: Megapodes, except *Megapodius*
Fam. Megapodiinae: *Megapodius*
Cohort Duodecimpennatae
Fam. Cracinae: some guans, etc.
Fam. Penelopinae: some guans, etc.
Cohort Struthioniformes
Fam. Crypturinae: Tinamous
Cohort Subgrallatores
Fam. Thinocorinae: Seedsnipe
Fam. Chionidinae: Sheathbills

Garrod (1873d, 1874a) recognized only seven orders of birds, and his "Order Galliformes" included the Ostrich, rheas, cassowaries, kiwis, tinamous, screamers, rails, bustards, flamingos, turacos, cuckoos, and parrots! His "Cohort Gallinaceae" consisted of the above groups from the screamers to the cuckoos, inclusive. In 1879, Garrod examined the tracheal anatomy of many galliforms, but discovered little about their relationships. He thought that *Argusianus*, *Lophortyx*, and *Coturnix* belong in the Coturnicinae, and that *Phasianus*, *Lagopus*, *Perdix*, and possibly *Meleagris* form part of the Phasianinae. He considered *Numida* and *Gallus* difficult to classify and maintained the Cracidae as a separate family.

Sclater (1880b) divided his Gallinae into the Peristeropodes (Cracidae, Megapodiidae) and Alectoropodes (Phasianidae, Tetraonidae). Elliott (1885) followed the same arrangement. Reichenow (1882) included the Megapodiidae, Cracidae, Opisthocomidae (Hoatzin), Phasianidae, Perdicidae, and Tetraonidae in his order Rasores. He divided the Phasianidae into subfamilies for the peafowl and typical pheasants and recognized Old World and New World groups in his Perdicidae.

Galliform morphology was studied by Parker (1864, 1891b), the Cracidae by Gadow (1879), and Shufeldt described the skeletons of North American grouse (1881b), *Gallus* (1888c), and the turkeys (1914a).

The Gallinae of Seebohm (1888b) consisted of the suborders Crypturi (tinamous), Gallinae (galliforms), Pterocletes (sandgrouse), and Columbae (pigeons). The Phasianidae, Cracidae, and Megapodiidae were considered to be intermediate between the tinamous and sandgrouse. Seebohm (1890a) expanded this group to include the loons, grebes, rails, and shorebirds and called it the order Gallo-Grallae. In 1895 he renamed his earlier suborder Gallinae as the Galli, and placed it in the order Galliformes with the suborder Psophiae containing the Cariamidae, Psophiidae, Opisthocomidae, and Podicidae (sungrebes). The other families he had once considered to be close to the galliforms were assigned to the Charadriiformes, Gruiformes, and Turniciformes.

In his "Subordo Galliformes" Fürbringer (1888) placed the Megapodiidae, Cracidae, Gallidae, and Opisthocomidae. The adjacent groups were the Apterygiformes and Crypturiformes (tinamous) on one side, and the Columbiformes on the other.

Sharpe (1891) divided his Galliformes as follows:

Order GALLIFORMES
Suborder Megapodii. (Australasian and Indo-Malayan.)
Suborder Craces. (Neotropical.)
Suborder Phasiani.
Fam. Phasianidae. (Palaearctic and Indian.)
Fam. Tetraonidae. (Palaearctic and Nearctic.)

Fam. Perdicidae. (Cosmopolitan.) [including New World quails]
Fam. Numididae. (Ethiopian.)
Fam. Meleagridae. (Nearctic and Neotropical.)
Suborder Hemipodii. (Sub-temperate and Tropical portions of the Old World.)
    Fam. Turnicidae. [not including *Pedionomus*]
Suborder Pterocletes. (Sub-tropical portions of the Palaearctic Region, Indian Region, Ethiopian
    Region.)
Suborder Geophapes. (Australasian) [including only *Geophaps*!]

Gadow's (1892) Galliformes contained two suborders, Turnices (including *Pedionomus*) and Galli, the latter consisting of two families, Gallidae and Opisthocomidae. In 1893 his Galliformes included the suborders and families Mesites (Mesitidae), Turnices (Turnicidae, Pedionomidae), Galli (Megapodiidae, Cracidae, Gallidae), and Opisthocomi (Opisthocomidae). In both classifications Gadow placed the Galliformes between the tinamous and the gruiforms.

In volume 22 of the *Catalogue of Birds*, Ogilvie-Grant (1893) treated four orders: Pterocletes (sandgrouse), Gallinae (galliforms), Opisthocomi (Hoatzin), and Hemipodii (*Turnix* and *Pedionomus*). The Gallinae were subdivided as follows:

Order GALLINAE
Suborder Alectoropodes
    Fam. Tetraonidae: Grouse
    Fam. Phasianidae: Pheasants, Partridges, Francolins, Old World Quail, Guineafowl, New World
    Quail
Suborder Peristeropodes
    Fam. Megapodiidae: Megapodes
    Fam. Cracidae: Guans, Chachalacas, Curassows

The Gallinae of Ogilvie-Grant followed the classification of Sclater (1880b) and included the same species we recognize in our Galliformes. Ogilvie-Grant (1893:33) diagnosed the group as:

Maxillo-palatines not coalesced with one another or with the vomer; nasals holorhinal; true basipterygoid processes absent, but represented by sessile facets situated far forward on the sphenoidal rostrum.

    Episternal process of the sternum perforated to receive a process from the base of the coracoids; two deep notches on each side of the posterior margin of the sternum; external xiphoid processes bent outwards over the hinder ribs and with expanded extremities.

    Bill short and stout, the culmen arched and overhanging the mandible.

    Hallux always present, but varying in size and position.

    Oil-gland tufted, nude or absent. Well-developed after-shafts to the feathers of the body. Fifth secondary quill present.

    Nestling born covered with down and able to run a few hours after being hatched.

Many similarities in the arrangement of the secondary coverts of galliforms and tinamous were found by Goodchild (1886, 1891), who stated that the "wing style of the tinamous differs in no essential respect . . . from that of the Gallinae" or Hemipodii (1891:324). Clark (1898) found that the New World quails differ from the grouse in their pterylosis, and he (1901b) placed the tinamous as one of the groups in his "galliform birds." Dwight (1900) described the molts of the North American Tetraonidae, in which he included the New World quails as well as the grouse.

Beddard (1898a) reviewed the works of his predecessors and concluded that "the Galli seem to be . . . an ancient group of birds" with relationships to the tinamous and the Anseriformes.

In the *Hand-List* Sharpe (1899) departed from the arrangement used by Ogilvie-Grant (1893) in the *Catalogue of Birds*. Sharpe's order Galliformes followed the Tinamiformes and was followed by the Hemipodii (Turnicidae), the Pteroclidiformes (sandgrouse), and the Columbiformes (pigeons). Sharpe's Galliformes follows:

Order GALLIFORMES
    Suborder Megapodii
      Fam. Megapodiidae: Megapodes
    Suborder Craces
      Fam. Cracidae: Guans, etc.
    Suborder Phasiani
      Fam. Tetraonidae: Grouse
      Fam. Phasianidae: Pheasants, Francolins, Partridges, Old World Quail
      Fam. Numididae: Guineafowl
      Fam. Meleagridae: Turkeys
      Fam. Odontophoridae: New World Quail

This seems to be the first time the New World quails were placed in a separate family.

Beebe (1914) considered many different morphological characters as the basis for a classification, but used the sequence of the molting of rectrices as the primary basis for generic groupings. His Perdicinae (including *Ithaginis* and *Tragopan*) was characterized by a centrifugal tail molt, but most of the typical pheasants were found to have a centripetal molt. The peafowl (*Pavo*) were separated in the Pavoninae because their tail molt begins with the next to the outer rectrix and the outer pair molt just before the inner ones. In the peacock pheasants and argus pheasants (Beebe's Argusianinae) the tail molt begins with the third from the central pair and proceeds in both directions. Beebe (1918–22) monographed the pheasants.

Chandler (1916) found the galliforms to be similar to one another in feather structure, but he thought that the megapodes and cracids showed affinities to the cuckoos, and the phasianids to the pigeons. Chandler concluded that "unmistakeable relationship is also shown to the Tinami [tinamous], which, according to feather structure, should be considered as a specialized offshoot from a primitive gallinaceous stem" (p. 342). Chandler included the Turnicidae and *Pedionomus* in a suborder of his Galliformes. As for other groups, Chandler's taxonomic conclusions make little sense, and it seems clear that similar feather structure often reflects convergent adaptations, not phylogeny.

Miller (1924a) reviewed the condition of the fifth secondary and noted that the Galliformes are eutaxic except for some megapodes. *Leipoa* and *Alectura* are eutaxic, *Megapodius* and *Megacephalon* are diastataxic.

Stresemann (1934) followed Fürbringer (1888) by recognizing three families of galliforms. His Phasianidae was divided into the Numidinae, Meleagridinae, and Phasianinae. Peters (1931) separated the Cracidae and Megapodiidae in the superfamily Cracoidea, and placed the Tetraonidae, Phasianidae, Numididae, and Meleagrididae in the Phasianoidea.

Hachisuka (1938) classified the galliforms mainly on the color and shape of feathers, egg color, and geographical distribution. He recognized the Megapodiidae, Cracidae, Tetraonidae, and Phasianidae. He divided the Phasianidae into four subfamilies and 58 genera, nearly half of which were monotypic.

Lowe (1938) studied the Congo Peafowl (*Afropavo congensis*), but found that the "Phasianidae are osteologically so uniform . . . that it is difficult to find characters to distinguish the various groups" (p. 226). He tentatively concluded that *Afropavo* is an "unspecialized generalized or primitive peacock," closest to the "Pavoninae and Argusianinae."

Mayr and Amadon (1951) reduced the guineafowls and grouse to subfamilies in the Phasianidae, but Wetmore (1951, 1960) retained these groups as families, and recognized the suborder Opisthocomi for the Hoatzin. Delacour (1951a) divided the 49 species of pheasants into 16 genera. Storer (1960a) followed Wetmore's classification, but in 1971 he included the Opisthocomidae in the Cracoidea, and the turkeys and grouse in the Phasianidae.

Verheyen (1956d) considered the galliforms to be osteologically uniform, but he recognized the Megapodiidae, Cracidae, and Phasianidae, with several subfamilies and tribes in each. In his 1961 classification the Galliformes included the suborders Tinami, Opisthocomi, and Turnices.

A. P. Gray (1958), Peterle (1951), and Cockrum (1952) listed many interspecific hybrids between galliforms. Sibley (1957) pointed out that the numerous intergeneric and interfamilial hybrids are evidence of close relationships and that this emphasizes the taxonomic weakness of monotypic genera based solely on the secondary sexual characters of males.

Hybrids have been recorded among some genera of New World quail, including *Colinus*, *Lophortyx*, *Callipepla*, and *Oreortyx* (Bailey 1928, Compton 1932, McCabe 1954, Banks and Walker 1964, Johnsgard 1970, 1971) but hybridization between odontophorids and other galliforms has not been proved. Seth-Smith (1906) mentioned a supposed hybrid, *Lophortyx californicus* × *Ammoperdix heyi*, but gave no details. Considering the large genetic gap between the Odontophoridae and other galliforms revealed by the DNA comparisons it is improbable that any New World quail would be able to produce viable hybrids with members of other galliform groups. From a study of molt and pterylography Ohmart (1967) suggested the merger of *Lophortyx* and *Callipepla*, and Johnsgard (1970) recommended that *Callipepla* and *Lophortyx* be included in *Colinus*.

Sibley (1960) found that the egg-white protein patterns of the galliforms are similar to one another and suggested that only the Megapodiidae and Phasianidae should be recognized as families, with the other families in Peters' (1934) classification reduced to subfamilies in the Phasianidae. The DNA evidence shows that these suggestions were wrong.

Immunological comparisons of certain galliform proteins caused Mainardi (1958a, 1959, 1960b, 1963) and Mainardi and Taibel (1962) to conclude that *Phasianus*, *Meleagris*, and *Numida* are closely related and that even subfamily status for these three taxa is not warranted. Mainardi retained the Cracidae and Megapodiidae, but did not recognize the superfamily Cracoidea, and *Numida* was considered to be closest to the cracids. *Gallus* and *Coturnix*, although generally similar to the phasianids, were widely separated from each other and from other genera.

The appendicular musculature of the galliforms was examined by Hudson and his colleagues (Hudson et al. 1959, 1966, Hudson and Lanzillotti 1964) who measured and compared the dimensions of muscles. The Hoatzin (*Opisthocomus hoazin*) differed from all of the galliforms studied. Other conclusions were: "1. Place the Megapodiidae and Cracidae in the Cracoidea. 2. Separate the grouse as the family Tetraonidae on the basis of measurements, the absence of the adductor digiti II muscle, presence of a sesamoid bone in the extensor indicis longus, and the feathering of the tarsus. 3. Recognize the Numidinae, Meleagridinae, Pavoninae, Odontophorinae, and Phasianinae in the Phasianidae."

G. A. Clark (1960, 1964a,b) concluded from embryological evidence that the megapodes are specialized and probably evolved from a pheasant-like ancestor. Differences in feather structure at hatching caused Clark to conclude that megapodes and cracids are not closely related. Considering the different environments encountered by the hatchlings of the two groups it is not surprising that their natal plumages differ.

Holman (1961) compared the skeletons of living and fossil New World quails and concluded that they represent a separate family. On the basis of pelvic structure he recognized two groups within the Odontophoridae: (1) *Odontophorus, Dactylortyx, Cyrtonyx, Rhynchortyx*; (2) *Dendrortyx, Philortyx, Oreortyx, Colinus, Callipepla, Lophortyx*. Holman (1964) studied the osteology of the gallinaceous birds.

The agar gel electrophoretic patterns of the soluble proteins of the eye lens, and of several muscles, convinced Gysels and Rabaey (1962) that *Afropavo congensis* should be isolated in a monotypic subfamily, remotely allied to *Pavo*. Hulselmans (1962) reached a similar conclusion from a study of the hind limb musculature of *Afropavo*.

From a study of the skull Simonetta (1963) suggested a common origin for the Anseriformes and Galliformes.

Brodkorb (1964) summarized the data on fossil galliforms. The Megapodiidae are known only from the upper Pleistocene, and the earliest fossil assigned to the Cracidae is from the lower Eocene of Wyoming. The New World quails are known from the lower Oligocene, the Phasianinae from the upper Oligocene, grouse from the lower Miocene, and turkeys from the upper Pliocene.

Vuilleumier (1965) showed that the casques, wattles, and areas of naked skin in cracids are species-specific recognition signals, which had been used by taxonomists as generic characters. He reduced the number of cracid genera from eleven to seven and proposed that the Cracidae probably originated in the Tertiary in North America and radiated there before colonizing South America.

Vaurie (1964, 1965a–c, 1966a,b, 1967a–d, 1968) disagreed with Vuilleumier and restored the genera the latter had synonymized. Vaurie recognized three tribes in the Cracidae: Penelopini (*Ortalis, Penelope, Pipile, Aburria, Chamaepetes, Penelopina*), Oreophasini (*Oreophasis*), Cracini (*Nothocrax, Mitu, Pauxi, Crax*).

Stresemann and Stresemann (1966a) and E. Stresemann (1965, 1967) found a distinctive molt pattern in the Cracidae, and a centrifugal tail molt in the "Perdicinae" which included the New World quail genera *Lophortyx, Colinus,* and *Callipepla*. Short (1967) reviewed the evidence of relationships among the species of grouse and reduced the genera from the eleven of Peters (1934) to six. He concluded that the "Tetraoninae evolved along with turkeys (Meleagridinae) and New World quail (Odontophorinae) from early North American phasianid stock" (p. 34).

Arnheim and Wilson (1967) compared the lysozymes of several species of galliforms by microcomplement fixation. An antiserum against *Gallus* lysozyme was tested against the lysozymes of other species. *Alectoris, Francolinus,* and the New World quails reacted strongly to the anti-*Gallus* antiserum, but the pheasants, usually thought to be closely related to *Gallus*, reacted relatively weakly. To check this unexpected result Arnheim et al. (1969) compared the amino acid compositions and tryptic peptide maps of the lysozymes of the Bob-white (*Colinus virginianus*) and the Ring-necked Pheasant (*Phasianus colchicus*) with that of *Gallus*. Their results indicated that the lysozymes of *Colinus* and *Gallus* are most alike, probably differing by about two amino acid replacements, while the lysozymes of *Colinus* and *Phasianus* possibly differ by as many as seven amino acids. Antisera against the lysozymes of *Colinus* and *Phasianus* were used in microcomplement fixation tests and seemed to confirm that *Colinus* and *Gallus* are virtually identical and that *Phasianus* can be distinguished from both.

Immunological comparisons and peptide maps are indirect and incomplete methods for comparing proteins; in addition, a single protein represents but a tiny percentage of the information in the genome. Thus, the results summarized above cannot be assumed to reflect the true relationships among the taxa compared.

Somewhat more information is provided by the complete amino acid sequences of proteins, although one protein still represents only a minute fraction of the total genetic information.

The amino acid sequences of the lysozymes of *Gallus* (Canfield 1963a,b, Canfield and Anfinsen 1963), *Meleagris* (LaRue and Speck 1970), and *Coturnix* (Kaneda et al. 1969) have been determined. *Gallus* and *Meleagris* lysozymes differ by at least seven amino acids, *Gallus* and *Coturnix* by at least six, and *Meleagris* differs from *Coturnix* by ten. These data suggest a closer relationship between *Gallus* and *Coturnix* than between *Coturnix* and *Meleagris*.

Sibley and Ahlquist (1972) compared the electrophoretic patterns of the egg-white proteins of members of all of the major groups of galliforms. The patterns of all galliforms are similar and support the other evidence that the Galliformes, as usually constituted, is a monophyletic group. This does not include the Hoatzin, which is a New World cuckoo, not a galliform.

Johnsgard (1973) proposed a classification of the galliforms:

Order Galliformes
    Superfamily Cracoidea
        Family Megapodidae
        Family Cracidae
    Superfamily Phasianoidea
        Family Phasianidae
            Subfamily Meleagridinae
            Subfamily Tetraoninae
            Subfamily Odontophorinae
            Subfamily Phasianinae
                Tribe Perdicini
                Tribe Phasianini
            Subfamily Numidinae

Nolan et al. (1975) compared the immunological properties of certain proteins with other evidence of the relationships among *Gallus*, *Phasianus*, and *Meleagris*. They noted that ornithologists seem to agree that "the turkey shows less overall resemblance to the chicken than the pheasant does." Schnell and Wood (1976) made a numerical taxonomic analysis of the limb musculature data of Hudson et al. (1966), plus data from 51 skeletal dimensions. They concluded that the limb muscle characters "do not show any clearcut separation of one form from the other two and certainly do not suggest that *Meleagris* is substantially different from *Gallus* and *Phasianus*." The skeletal dimensions produced essentially the same conclusion.

From a comparison of lysozymes, Prager and Wilson (1976) concluded that the Cracidae are no more closely related to the galliforms than they are to certain anseriforms.

Crowe (1978) conducted a cladistic analysis of morphological characters of the four genera and six species of guineafowl. He suggested that the Numididae was derived from a francolin-like Asiatic phasianid ancestor. Crowe and Crowe (1985) made a cladistic analysis of skeletal and integumentary characters, plus a study of vocalizations, behavior, and ecology of 36 species of francolins. One of their conclusions was that the monophyly of *Francolinus* is not firmly established.

Poplin (1980) described a subfossil from New Caledonia as a possible ratite, which Poplin et al. (1983) and Poplin and Mourer-Chauviré (1985) have shown to be a large, flightless megapode.

Glaus et al. (1980) compared the mtDNAs of five species of galliform birds with the technique of restriction enzyme mapping. They found the Ring-necked Pheasant (*Phasianus colchicus*) to be most similar to the Japanese Quail (*C. coturnix*), differing in 0.35% of the restriction sites. The Turkey (*Meleagris gallopavo*) differed from the Japanese Quail in 0.3% of restriction sites and from the Ring-necked Pheasant in 0.47%, average = 0.43%. The Helmeted Guineafowl (*Numida meleagris*) differed from the above-named three species by an average of 0.46% of all sites, and the Domestic Fowl (*Gallus*) was most divergent at an average of 0.54% of all restriction sites. The authors declined to propose a phylogeny because they could not determine the actual sequence of divergences in the mtDNAs they compared.

Stock and Bunch (1982) compared the chromosome banding patterns of eight species of galliforms and defined two groups: (1) *Gallus*, *Numida*, *Coturnix*, and *Pavo*; (2) *Phasianus*, *Meleagris*, *Colinus*, and *Centrocercus*. They concluded that *Crax* is related to the other galliforms (*contra* Prager and Wilson 1976), and proposed that all galliforms should be united in one family.

Gutierrez et al. (1983) used starch gel electrophoresis to compare 27 presumptive genetic loci from 10 species of galliforms, including an Old World quail (*Coturnix*), a partridge (*Alectoris*), *Phasianus*, and six species of New World quail. They used a fossil odontophorid from the mid-Miocene to calibrate genetic distances and suggested that *Oreortyx* branched at ca. 12.6 MYA, *Colinus* at ca. 7 MYA, and that the *Callipepla-Lophortyx* branch occurred 2.8 MYA. The divergence between *Phasianus* and the New World quail was dated at 35 MYA, in the early Oligocene. If this is correct, a calibration of this same branch from our DNA comparisons ($\Delta T_{50}H$ 15.1) yields a calibration constant of $\Delta T_{50}H$ 1.0 = 2.3 MY. However, Prager and Wilson (1976) calculated this date as ca. 63 MYA, based on a transferrin immunological distance of 65. A 63 MYA divergence yields a calibration constant for our DNA comparisons of δ 1.0 = 4.2 MYA, thus close to the Ostrich-Rhea calibration factor of 4.7.

Helm-Bychowski and Wilson (1986) mapped 161 restriction sites in the nuclear DNA of seven species of galliforms. The mapped sites belong to three regions on different chromosomes, bear eight genes, and span 56 kb. The maps differed from one another at a minimum of 77 sites and nine length mutations. The authors calculated the amount of nucleotide sequence divergence represented by these changes and concluded that the Domestic Fowl (*G. gallus*) and Jungle Fowl (also *G. gallus*) are most closely related, followed by Chukar (or Rock) Partridge (*Alectoris graeca*), a group consisting of Turkey and Ring-necked Pheasant, then Peafowl (*Pavo cristatus*), and finally Helmeted Guineafowl (*Numida meleagris*).

Johnsgard (1986) monographed the pheasants. His dendrogram of the Galliformes (p. 7) reflects his 1973 classification, with the New World quail assigned to the Phasianidae.

The DNA Hybridization Evidence (Figs. 25–34, 325–328, 353, 354, 357)

The DNA comparisons show that the Gallomorphae and the Anserimorphae are sister groups that diverged from their common ancestor at Δ T$_{50}$H 22.9. The oldest branch within the Gallomorphae resulted in the divergence of the megapode-cracid lineage (Craciformes) from that leading to the Galliformes. This branching occurred at Δ 21.6. The divergence between the lineages that produced the infraorders Craci and Megapodii is at Δ 19.8. This is virtually the same delta value (19.7) we obtained between the passerine suborders Tyranni (suboscines) and Passeri (oscines) (Fig. 369).

The oldest branch within the Galliformes (Δ 15.1) split off the lineage of the New World quails (parvorder Odontophorida) from that of the parvorder Phasianida. The New World quails have sometimes been placed in their own family, but the size of this delta value was a surprise. Prager and Wilson (1976) estimated this divergence as 63 MYA, which yields a calibration constant from our DNA comparisons of Δ 1.0 = 4.2 MY. Gutierrez et al. (1983) suggested that this branch occurred ca. 35 MYA.

The next branch occurred at Δ 12.8 when the Numidoidea (guineafowls) diverged. This was followed by the divergence between the grouse and turkeys and the other phasianids at Δ 11.1.

We have not worked out the details within each of these groups, but it is apparent that the Galliformes are not as uniform genetically as they have seemed to be from morphological comparisons. Like the waterfowl, pigeons, parrots, and some other groups, they have retained a similar morphotype over a long time, while diverging substantially at the genetic level.

The melting curves (Figs. 25–34) support the Δ T$_{50}$H distance measures. Except for the Cracidae and the Megapodiidae, the gallomorphs begin to breed at one year of age, thus we may assume that the relative positions among the Galliformes are not affected by different ages at maturity. The possibly slower rates of the craciforms do not seem to present a problem. In Fig. 25 (*Gallus*) the sequence of taxa at increasing distances from the homoduplex is the same as in the UPGMA tree (Fig. 357). The relative positions of the guineafowl (*Numida*), New World quail (*Colinus*), the cracids (*Ortalis, Crax*), and the megapode (*Alectura*) are the same as in the dendrograms. In Fig. 26 (*Gallus*, same experiment as Fig. 25), the swan is closer to *Gallus* than is the stork, which is also a delayed-maturity species (Table 16). The positions of the turaco, moorhen, and Ostrich are evidence that the Galloanserae are members of the Neoaves, not the Eoaves. Fig. 27 (*Francolinus*) confirms the information in Figs. 25 and 26 concerning the relationships among the phasianids, the guineafowl (*Guttera*), and the New World quail (*Oreortyx, Colinus*). It is clear that the Old World quail (*Coturnix*) clusters with the pha-sianids, not with the New World quail.

Fig. 28 (*Francolinus*) also shows the relative distances among the cracids, megapodes, anseriforms, and ratites. The position of *Diomedea epomophora* (8–11 years at first breeding) at the same distance from *Francolinus* as *Anas* and *Branta* (2–3 years at maturity) shows the effect of the rate slowdown in the albatross lineage. The Ostrich and tinamou are at the greatest distance.

Fig. 29 (*Numida*) demonstrates the reciprocity between the guineafowl and the phasianids and odontophorids. Note that the phasianids are slightly closer to *Numida* than are the New World quail, just as in the UPGMA (Fig. 357) and FITCH (Fig. 328) trees. The positions of *Crax*, *Penelope*, and *Aepypodius* are also as in the dendrograms.

Fig. 30 (*Numida*) shows the effects of delayed maturity on *Grus* and *Ardeotis*, and the effect of early maturity on the two species of *Turnix*. The position of *Turnix* in the phylogeny is not clear, but it is apparent that the buttonquails are an isolated group with no close relatives.

Fig. 31 (*Numida*) includes several species with delayed maturity (albatross, stork, penguin, Old World vulture), and others that begin to breed at one or two years of age. To sort out the relationships of these groups it is necessary to examine other curve sets in which these are the tracer taxa.

Fig. 32 (*Numida*) identifies a number of groups that are not closely related to the galliforms. Note the position of the cuckoo (*Oxylophus*). In many of the curve sets, the cuckoos are among the most distant from various tracer taxa, indicating their ancient origin and long separation from other lineages.

Fig. 33 (*Callipepla*) provides conclusive evidence of the substantial genetic distance between the New World quail and the other groups of galliforms, including the turkeys and grouse.

Fig. 34 (*Penelope*) shows the large genetic distance between the cracids and other galliforms. The megapodes are not any closer than are the guineafowl and phasianids. Several delayed-breeding taxa (*Coragyps*, stork, bustard) provide additional interest and the Ostrich remains at the outer fringe.

Fig. 328, the FITCH tree, and Fig. 357, the UPGMA tree, show the same patterns as in the melting curves. *Anseranas* begins to breed at ca. 3 years, but there are no data for *Anhima*. The large distance between *Penelope* and *Alectura* in Fig. 34 is indicated in the FITCH tree. In the melting curves, the megapodes and cracids tend to be about equidistant from the phasianid, numidid, and odontophorid tracers, suggesting that the Craciformes have been evolving at about the same average rate. The cracids are always the closer of the two groups to the galliform tracers, indicating a more recent divergence, as indicated in the FITCH tree.

We conclude that the Craciformes and Galliformes are more closely related to one another than either is to any other group and that our classification is a fair reflection of the relationships among the Phasianidae, Numididae, and Odontophoridae. Of special interest is the evidence that the New World quail are not closely related to the Old World quail, and neither are they closely related to the turkeys or the grouse. The Odontophoridae must be the descendants of an early divergence in South America while that continent was isolated from North America.

Waterfowl:
Screamers, Ducks, Geese, and Swans

Superorder Anserimorphae
  Order ANSERIFORMES
    Infraorder Anhimides
      Superfamily Anhimoidea
        Family Anhimidae: Screamers
      Superfamily Anseranatoidea
        Family Anseranatidae: Magpie Goose
    Infraorder Anserides
      Family Dendrocygnidae: Whistling-Ducks
      Family Anatidae
        Subfamily Oxyurinae: Stiff-tailed Ducks
        Subfamily Stictonettinae: *Stictonetta*
        Subfamily Cygninae: Swans
        Subfamily Anatinae
          Tribe Anserini: Geese
          Tribe Anatini: Typical Ducks

Order ANSERIFORMES: 48/161. Desmognathous; two carotids; holorhinal, pervious nares; caeca large, except in *Mergus*; syrinx with two pairs of extrinsic muscles; 11 primaries, outer reduced; diastataxic; aftershaft small or absent; oil gland large, densely tufted, bilobed; sternum with one pair of incisions which may be closed at posterior margin; no spina interna; basipterygoid processes present, articulating with pterygoids far forward; eggs plain white or brownish; young nidifugous with thick down.

Family ANHIMIDAE: 2/3. The screamers occur in the lowlands of tropical and subtropical South America in marshes and other wet environments. They are the size of small turkeys with small heads, fowl-like bills, and loud voices.

Pelvic muscles A(B)XY+; no biceps slip; flexor tendons Type 4; tongue not fleshy; no apteria; 19–20 cervical vertebrae; no uncinate processes on ribs; rudimentary basal toe webs; long hallux at level of fore toes; tarsal scutes similar to those of geese, being small, 6-sided, reaching to above intertarsal joint; no copulatory organ; skeleton highly pneumatic including

301

toes and wing phalanges; subcutaneous spaces pneumatic (emphysematous); remiges not molted simultaneously; wings with two large bony spurs; herbivorous; nest of aquatic plants or sticks, near or over water; 4–7 eggs; young remain in or near nest until able to run.

Family ANSERANATIDAE: 1/1. *Anseranas semipalmata*, the Magpie Goose of northern Australia and southern New Guinea, is the only species. Feet semipalmate; hind toe long, on same level as anterior toes; plumage boldly pied; neck and legs long; bony protuberance on crown; flight feathers molted progressively, not simultaneously, so able to fly during wing molt. Both sexes incubate.

Family DENDROCYGNIDAE: 2/9. *Dendrocygna* differs from the Anatidae in being sexually monomorphic with long legs and necks; both sexes incubate; mutual preening; voice is a high-pitched whistle; dive for food. *Thalassornis leuconotus* has been thought to be related to the Oxyurinae.

Family ANATIDAE: 43/148. Pelvic muscles ABX+; biceps slip present; flexor tendons Type 2; apteria present; uncinate processes present; lamellate bill covered with thin skin and terminal nail; tongue fleshy and bordered with spiny processes; feet palmate, hallux set higher than front toes; penis present; remiges molted simultaneously; osseus tracheal bulla in most ducks; 16–25 cervical vertebrae.

The subfamily STICTONETTINAE is recognized in the classification because Madsen et al. (1988) found that the single-copy DNA of the Freckled Duck (*Stictonetta naevosa*) differs substantially from that of other anatids.

The principal systematic problems concerning the waterfowl are: (1) the relationships between the Anseriformes and other orders; (2) the relationships among the Anhimidae, the Anseranatidae, Dendrocygnidae, and the typical waterfowl (Anatidae); (3) the relationships among the genera of ducks, geese, and swans.

The flamingos, the gallinaceous birds, and the herons have been proposed most frequently as possible relatives of the Anseriformes.

Historical Review of the Classification

Nitzsch (1840) found that the pterylosis is the same in all ducks and geese, but that it differs from that of other groups. He placed the Anatidae between the procellariids and the pelecaniforms in a large assemblage of aquatic birds. The Anhimidae differ from the Anatidae in having the feathers evenly distributed over the body, i.e., they lack apteria.

It was Parker (1863) who first noted that the skull of the Northern Screamer (*Chauna chavaria*) is ducklike and that the sternum of the screamers is "thoroughly anserine." Parker considered the pelvis of the Spur-winged Goose (*Plectropterus gambensis*) to be "exactly intermediate" between that of a goose (e.g., *Anser*) and that of a screamer.

Primarily on the basis of skull characters, Huxley (1867) placed the waterfowl and screamers in his Chenomorphae, which he believed to be related to the flamingos and herons. He thought the screamers may be distantly allied to the Cracidae (chachalacas, guans).

Sundevall (1872, see 1889:223) placed the birds with "Toes webbed" in his "Order Natatores" within which, in "Cohort 6. Lamellirostres," were "Fam. Phoenicopterinae" for the flamingos, and "Fam. Anatinae" for the ducks, geese, and swans. The screamers were placed in the "Fam. Palamedeinae" of the adjacent "Order Grallatores," with the herons, storks, sandpipers, plovers, bustards, cranes, rails, and sungrebes. Sundevall called the screamers "A singular form of bird! Truly Grallatorial, but evidently widely separated from all the preceding." Following a description of their characters, he noted that "The birds here mentioned seem to differ equally from the rest of the Grallatores and all other birds. The bones situated at the base of the skull [palate] were found by Huxley to be formed like those of the Ducks, and he united the Screamers and the Ducks in one family. . . . This celebrated author observes, moreover, that a form even in external parts truly intermediate was to be found in *Choristopus* (Anseranas, Less.), and this is obviously correct. We can therefore have scarcely any doubt of the true affinity of these birds. *Palamedea*, however, differs greatly and in the whole of its external structure from the Duck form. We believe, therefore, that these birds, in an ordinary system, ought rather to be enumerated in different orders; but otherwise, in any system illustrating affinity based on a common origin" (pp. 223–224).

Once again, the dilemma: whether to classify on the basis of morphological similarities and differences or on the basis of phylogeny. Sundevall chose the former and placed the screamers and the waterfowl in separate orders, but acknowledged that Huxley was "obviously correct" in having determined their "true affinity." Sundevall identified his procedure as "an ordinary system," presumably contrasted with an extraordinary system that would be based on phylogeny alone.

Garrod (1873d, 1874a) thought that the screamers are related to the galliforms and the rails, and that the Anatidae are close to the penguins, loons, and grebes. In a study of the pterylosis, visceral anatomy, osteology, and myology of the screamers Garrod (1876b) found similarities to the ratites and herons.

Sclater and Salvin (1876) reviewed the New World waterfowl and divided the Anatidae into seven subfamilies, and Sclater (1880a) listed 176 "certainly known species of Anatidae."

Forbes (1882d) found the trachea of the Musk Duck (*Biziura lobata*) to be simple in structure like that of the stiff-tailed ducks (*Oxyura*).

The screamers have a horizontal fibrous septum passing across the abdominal cavity and covering the intestine, and a similar structure is found in the storks (Beddard 1886b). Beddard also described the subcutaneous air cells of the screamers, which he believed to be modified pre- and post-bronchial air sacs. He also pointed out that the bronchial air sacs of storks and flamingos are divided into several chambers.

Fürbringer (1888) placed the waterfowl in his order Pelargornithes, suborder Anseriformes, gens Anseres, family Anatidae. Other members of this order were the grebes, loons, flamingos, herons, storks, falconiforms, and pelecaniforms. The screamers were placed in the order Hippolectryornithes, suborder Palamedeiformes, gens Palamedeae, family Palamedeidae; other members of this order were the cassowaries, emus, and elephant birds. However, Fürbringer (1888:1568) noted that a linear listing does not express the genealogical relationships among groups and he presented an arrangement in which the Palamedeiformes were brought into the vicinity of the Anseriformes. Gadow (1888a:180), in his review of Fürbringer's volumes, interpreted Fürbringer's ideas about these groups, as follows:

Anseriformes.—Probably an old and small pre-Miocene group, which has marked its broader development more recently. . . . Amongst recent Lamellirostres, Mergus is the lowest, Cygnus the highest type; they are distantly allied to the Podicipitiformes [grebes].

Palamedeiformes show many connective points with the Anseres, Steganopodes [pelecaniforms], and Pelargo-Herodii [storks, herons], but their reception into the Pelargornithes is rendered impossible by various fundamental and primitive peculiarities. Through their intestines and pterylosis they somewhat resemble Rhea. Whether we place them nearer to the Anseres than to the Pelargi and Steganopodes depends upon the taxonomic value which we happen to attribute to their skeletal, muscular, intestinal, or external features.

Shufeldt (1888a) described the skeletons of several North American waterfowl; Beddard and Mitchell (1894) and Mitchell (1895) described the anatomy of the three species of screamers.

Sharpe (1891) included the Anseres and Palamedeae (Anhimae) as suborders in the Anseriformes, with the Anseres divided into four families: Cnemiornithidae (extinct, New Zealand); Anseranatidae (Magpie Goose); Plectropteridae; Anatidae. The Anatidae were divided into four subfamilies: Anserinae, Cygninae, Anatinae, Merginae. The flamingos (Phoenicopteriformes) were the adjacent, preceding order.

Gadow (1892) also placed the suborders Palamedeae and Anseres in the Anseriformes, which were characterized as follows:

ANSERIFORMES.
    Cosmopolitan. Aquatic. Nidifugous.
    Young downy.
    Neck long, without apteria.
    Aftershaft rudimentary.
    Oil-gland tufted. Aquinto-cubital.
    Rhamphotheca with ceroma; bill with lamellae. Nares pervious.
    Desmognathous. With basipterygoid processes.
    Angulare of mandible long and recurved.
    Coraco-humeral groove indistinct.
    No ectepicondylar process.
    Two pairs of pectoro-tracheal muscles. (*Unique*.)
    Intestinal convolutions of type III.
    Caeca functional.
    Penis large, spiral. (*Unique* among Carinatae.)
  I. Palamedeae.
    Neotropical.
    Basipterygoid articulation on middle of pterygoids.
    Hypotarsus simple.
    Ribs without uncinate processes. (*Unique*.)
  II. Anseres.
    Basipterygoid processes articulating with the palatine end of the pterygoids.
    Hypotarsus complex.
    Ribs with uncinate processes.

Gadow (1893) placed the Ciconiiformes, Anseriformes, and Falconiformes as the three orders in the legion Pelargomorphae. The Phoenicopteri were in the Ciconiiformes, adjacent to the Anseriformes. The lack of basipterygoid processes and possession of only one pair of sterno-tracheal muscles were cited by Gadow (pp. 131–132) as the characters separating the Ciconiiformes from the Anseriformes.

In the *Catalogue of Birds* Salvadori (1895) followed the classification proposed by Sclater and Salvin (1876) and Sclater (1880a). Salvadori's order Chenomorphae was divided into three suborders: Palamedeae (screamers), Phoenicopteri (flamingos), and Anseres (ducks, geese, swans). Each suborder contained one family; the 205 species of Anatidae were divided into 64 genera and eleven subfamilies.

From skeletal evidence Seebohm (1889) concluded that the Anseres are related to the flamingos, storks, and herons, and that the screamers are a link between the Anseres and Galliformes. In 1895, Seebohm proposed three families of Anseres: Anatidae (waterfowl), Palamedeidae (screamers), and Phoenicopteridae (flamingos).

Shufeldt (1901b) compared the skeletons of the Horned Screamer (*Anhima cornuta*), the Coscoroba Swan (*C. coscoroba*), and the Turkey (*Meleagris gallopavo*), and concluded that the screamer resembles the goose or the turkey in most characters. However, he also believed that the screamer was not closely related to either the goose or the turkey and agreed with Fürbringer (1888) that the screamers constitute a separate group. Shufeldt (p. 461) concluded that the screamers should be "placed near the Anseres" but "between the latter and the ostrich type of birds."

Pycraft (1906a) also examined skeletal elements and recommended that the stiff-tailed ducks (*Oxyura, Thalassornis, Biziura*) be merged with the diving ducks (Fuligulinae, or Aythyinae), and that *Histrionicus, Melanitta, Tachyeres*, and *Somateria* be placed in the Somateriinae.

A study that was to have a major influence on the development of research in animal behavior was published by Oskar Heinroth in 1911. His comparative studies of waterfowl courtship behavior as clues to relationships among species were the first to use behavior in systematics. The later studies by Konrad Lorenz (e.g., 1941) were based on Heinroth's methods and ideas.

Shufeldt (1914c) followed Salvadori (1895) for the species composition of eleven of twelve subfamilies, but placed the whistling-ducks in a separate subfamily, Dendrocygninae, on the basis of a morphological study.

The microscopic structure of feathers suggested to Chandler (1916) that the waterfowl are highly specialized, and that such genera as *Branta, Anser*, and *Cygnus* link the Anseriformes to the flamingos. Chandler was unable to link the screamers with any other group on the basis of feather structure.

Stresemann (1934) followed Fürbringer (1888) in his classification of the waterfowl, and Peters' (1931) classification shows the influence of Salvadori (1895). Peters split 167 species of anatids into 62 genera, of which 42 were monotypic. Generic splitting was carried to an extreme by von Boetticher (1940, 1942) who recognized 84 genera, 55 of them monotypic. Most of the genera were based primarily on the secondary sexual characters of the males.

Miller (1937) studied the skeletal and muscular adaptations of the Hawaiian Goose, or Nene (*Branta sandvicensis*), to life on the dry lava uplands of Hawaii. He concluded that this species is closely related to *Branta* and pointed out that *Chloephaga* differs from the anserines. On the basis of 115 characters he separated *Chen, Anser, Philacte, Nesochen* (the Nene), and *Branta. Nesochen* has been merged with *Branta* by most subsequent authors.

DeMay (1940) studied the subcutaneous air cells in the Northern Screamer (*Chauna chavaria*) and showed that the cervical air sacs are continuous with the air cells, which cover the main part of the body as well as the extremities. The bones are pneumatic, including the digits. In pelicans, boobies, gannets, and tropicbirds, which dive into the water from considerable heights, the subcutaneous air cells cushion the impact, but their function in screamers is unknown.

Based in part on earlier studies by Delacour (1936, 1938), Delacour and Mayr (1945, 1946) proposed a classification based on patterns of tarsal scutes, tracheal structure, plumage patterns of downy young, hybridization, and behavior. They recognized that interspecific hybrids are evidence of close relationship, and they argued against the recognition of mono-typic genera based on male secondary sexual characters. Their conclusions were similar to those of Heinroth (1911), but they considered more species. Their proposed classification follows:

Family Anatidae
  Subfamily Anserinae
    Tribe Anserini: *Branta, Anser, Cygnus, Coscoroba*
    Tribe Dendrocygnini: *Dendrocygna*
  Subfamily Anatinae
    Tribe Tadornini: *Lophonetta, Tadorna, Alopochen, Neochen, Cyanochen, Chloephaga, Cereopsis, Tachyeres*
    Tribe Anatini: *Anas, Hymenolaimus, Malacorhynchus, Rhodonessa, Stictonetta*
    Tribe Aythyini: *Netta, Aythya*
    Tribe Cairinini: *Amazonetta, Chenonetta, Aix, Nettapus, Sarkidiornis, Cairina, Plectropterus, Anseranas*
    Tribe Mergini: *Somateria, Melanitta, Histrionicus, Clangula, Bucephala, Mergus*
    Tribe Merganettini: *Merganetta*
    Tribe Oxyurini: *Oxyura, Biziura, Thalassornis, Heteronetta*

All anseriforms have two carotids (A–1 pattern) and there are no significant differences between the Anhimidae and Anatidae in the carotid arrangement (Glenny 1944b, 1955).

The morphology of the quadrate bone was the basis for Friant's (1947) conclusion that the Anhimae are the survivors of an ancient group that was the ancestor of flamingos and waterfowl.

Von Boetticher and Eichler (1951) based a classification of waterfowl on the distribution of certain genera of Mallophaga of the family Acidoproctidae. *Anseranas* is uniquely para-sitized by *Heteroproctus* and was placed in a monotypic family, Anseranatidae. The Ansereae and Cygneae are distinguished by being the hosts of the genus *Ornithobius*. *Acidoproctus* is found on the Tadorneae, Dendrocygneae, Hymenolaimeae, Aythyeae, and Cairineae, and no acidoproctids parasitize the Mergeae, Somatereae, or Anateae.

Timmerman (1963) made additional suggestions based on the *Ornithobius* complex of the mallophagan family Philopteridae. He found *Ornithobius* on geese and swans, *Both-riometopus* on screamers, and *Acidoproctus* on *Anseranas, Dendrocygna, Alopochen, Plectropterus, Netta,* and *Aythya.* Timmerman distinguished two groups of swans, one includ-ing *Cygnus olor, melanocoryphus,* and *atratus,* the other *C. cygnus, buccinator,* and *colum-bianus.* He thought that *Dendrocygna arborea* is more closely related to *D. autumnalis* than to *guttata. D. guttata* and *eytoni* seem to be closely allied to *D. arcuata* and *javanica,* but *bicolor* and *viduata* form a rather distinct species pair.

As a general observation: the attempts to base the classification of the host species of birds on the presumed relationships of their parasites have not been successful.

Mayr and Amadon (1951) suggested that "the waterfowl are a very distinct group but may be placed between the flamingos and gallinaceous birds. The two South American families Anhimidae (Anseres) and Cracidae (Galli) may be distantly related." They included the Anhimidae and Anatidae in their order Anseres and agreed with von Boetticher (1943a) that *Anseranas* deserves to be placed in a monotypic tribe.

Yamashina (1952) found the chromosomes of the waterfowl to be similar and he recognized a limited number of genera. The Mandarin Duck (*Aix galericulata*) has an unusual karyotype that differs from that of most ducks, including its close relative the Wood Duck (*Aix sponsa*). The Wood Duck has the normal anatine karyotype and has hybridized with other species of anatines, but hybrids involving the Mandarin Duck have been rare (Gray 1958), and it has been suggested that the chromosomal differences may prevent hybridization. Johnsgard (1968) reported apparently valid hybrids between the Mandarin Duck and both the Wood Duck and Laysan Mallard (*Anas platyrhynchos laysanensis*). These hybrids were probably infertile and the significance of the aberrant karyotype of the Mandarin remains unclear.

Delacour (1954) followed the classification of Delacour and Mayr (1945), but placed *Anseranas* in a separate subfamily and merged the Merganettini with the Anatini.

From his extensive measurements of bones, Verheyen (1953, 1955a,b) concluded that the Anseriformes are polyphyletic and he divided them into 16 families, seven of which were monotypic. He placed the screamers in their own order, Anhimiformes (1956g), and considered them most closely related to *Anseranas* and distantly allied to the Casuariidae. In 1961 Verheyen reduced most of his 16 families to subfamilies or tribes, but dismissed the numerous waterfowl hybrids by arguing that "evidence was accumulating that the inbreeding [hybridization] situation, in a group of more or less related species, is general and [like] any other organic feature, susceptible to vary in its numerous attributes from group to group" (p. 19). This epitomizes Verheyen's idiosyncratic view of the characters and evidence of systematic relationships. Sibley (1957, 1961) and Johnsgard (1960d) have discussed hybridization in birds, especially in the Anatidae. However variable, hybridization occurs only between closely related birds.

A serological study caused Cotter (1957) to conclude that *Aix* and *Cairina* are more closely related to one another than either is to *Anas*, thus supporting their association in the Cairinini.

Humphrey (1958) studied the trachea and tracheal bulla in *Melanitta*, *Clangula*, *Bucephala*, *Mergus*, and the eiders. He suggested that the eiders are closest to the Anatini and should be placed next to them in the Somateriini, and that *Lampronetta* should be merged with *Somateria*.

Comparisons of the electrophoretic patterns of the egg-white proteins of 56 species of Anatidae showed that "the Anatidae are a very closely related group" although *Anseranas* and *Dendrocygna* each has a distinctive pattern (Sibley 1960).

Wetmore (1930, 1960) and Storer (1960a, 1971) divided the Anseriformes into the suborders Anhimae and Anseres.

Evidence from cranial morphology and kinesis caused Simonetta (1963) to suggest a common origin for the waterfowl and galliforms.

From his extensive studies of waterfowl behavior, Johnsgard developed a number of ideas about relationships within the Anatidae (1960a–f; 1961a–f; 1962; 1963; 1964; 1965a,b; 1966a,b; 1967; 1968b). Those differing from the classification of Delacour and Mayr (1945) are:

Anseranas placed in a separate family.
Cereopsis moved from Tadornini to Anserini.
Stictonetta seems to have anserine affinities.
Tachyeres placed in a separate tribe.
Callonetta moved from Anatini to Cairinini.
Merganetta moved from Anatini to Aythyini.
Rhodonessa moved from Anatini to Aythyini.
Thalassornis moved from Oxyurini to Dendrocygnini.

Woolfenden (1961) compared the postcranial osteology of most genera of waterfowl and supported subordinal rank for the screamers. In the Anatidae he recognized the Anatinae and Anserinae and proposed the following changes from the classification of Delacour and Mayr (1945).

Anseranas in a separate family.
Stictonetta moved from Anatini to Dendrocygnini.
Cereopsis in a monotypic tribe.
Plectropterus moved from Cairinini to Tadornini.
Tachyeres moved from Tadornini to Anatini.
Cairinini merged with Anatini.
Merganetta in a separate tribe.
Rhodonessa moved from Anatini to Aythyini.

From their behavioral and ecological studies of *Anseranas*, Davies and Frith concluded that its unusual characteristics are adaptations to living in tropical swamps, and they found its behavior to be like that of the Anserini (Davies 1961, 1962a,b, 1963, Davies and Frith 1964, Frith and Davies 1961).

Frith (1964a,b) examined the behavior, plumage of the downy young, and tracheal anatomy of the Freckled Duck (*Stictonetta naevosa*), and concluded that it is not an anatine but may be closest to the swans.

The earliest fossil that seems to be an anseriform is *Eonessa* from the Eocene of Utah (Wetmore 1938, Brodkorb 1964). *Gallornis* (Lambrecht 1933), from the Lower Cretaceous of France, was thought to be anseriform, but Brodkorb (1963a,b) placed it in the suborder Phoenicopteri, which seems highly improbable.

Howard (1964a,b) reviewed the fossil Anseriformes and noted that by the Oligocene (ca. 25–38 MYA) the Anserinae and Anatinae are separable. *Branta* (Anserini) and *Anas* (Anatini) are Δ T$_{50}$H 6.7 apart; if we use the calibration constant of Δ 1.0 = 4.5 MY, the *Branta-Anas* divergence occurred at ca. 30 MYA. However, if the two groups could be distinguished from fossils in the Oligocene, the divergence must have been earlier. It is also possible that the fossils do not represent living *Branta* and *Anas*. These comments are tentative and subject to correction.

Many modern genera and several tribes were present by the Miocene (5–25 MYA), and about 10 Pliocene (2–5 MYA) species are indistinguishable from living species. Members of the Tadornini apparently occurred in North America during the Pleistocene (less than 2 MYA).

Tyler (1964) examined the structure and composition of egg shells. Based on a plot of total shell nitrogen versus shell thickness, Tyler suggested that *Anseranas* is distinct from other anseriforms; the Dendrocygnini can be separated from the Anserini, and the Tadornini are "almost but not quite separate from the Dendrocygnini, but clearly separate from the Anserini." *Plectropterus* was near *Anser*, the Oxyurini near the Dendrocygnini, and *Chauna* near *Branta*. When insoluble shell nitrogen was plotted against total shell nitrogen, most tribes were similar, but *Dendrocygna* was partially separated, with *Anseranas* and *Cereopsis* even more distant, and *Chauna* fell between *Dendrocygna* and *Cereopsis*. Thus, there are some suggestions of taxonomic interest in these comparisons, but they also present conflicts with more valid evidence of relationships.

Baker and Hanson (1966) compared the hemoglobins and serum proteins of eight species of *Anser* and three of *Branta* using starch gel electrophoresis. They found only minor variations, indicating the close relationships among the geese.

Sibley and Ahlquist (1972) compared the starch gel electrophoretic patterns of the egg-white proteins of *Chauna torquata* and 89 species of anatids with one another and with those of many other groups of birds. The anatid patterns were fairly uniform but *Dendrocygna* was distinctive; *Anseranas* was similar to other waterfowl. The *Chauna* pattern showed similarities to both waterfowl and herons, but was unlike both. "The patterns of the waterfowl resemble those of the gallinaceous birds in having a multiple ovalbumin and similar mobilities of the conalbumins, but there are many differences in detail between the patterns of the two groups. The patterns of the waterfowl are unlike those of other palmate, or totipalmate, swimming birds." Sibley and Ahlquist concluded that "the Anatidae form a closely related group of species" but that the egg-white protein comparisons "cannot be used to suggest relationships within the family. On the basis of previous studies, the egg-white patterns and the evidence from the tryptic patterns of ovalbumin and hemoglobin, the Anseriformes appear to be allied to the flamingos and to the ciconiiform birds more closely than to any other group." The DNA comparisons show this conclusion to be wrong.

Bottjer (1983) reviewed the history of anatid classification and conducted a serological study of the waterfowl using the techniques of immunoelectrophoresis and haemagglutination inhibition. He found the whistling-ducks to be distinctive, "not the sister-group to the Anserini" as proposed by Delacour and Mayr (1945) and Johnsgard (1968b). Bottjer's classification recognized the families Anhimidae, Anseranatidae, and Anatidae; in the Anatidae, the subfamilies Dendrocygninae, Anserinae, Oxyurinae, and Anatinae. His results show many congruencies with the DNA hybridization evidence.

Livesey (1986) made a cladistic analysis of 120 mostly skeletal, morphological characters of all Recent genera of the Anseriformes. He derived a phylogenetic tree from the data and proposed the following classification:

Order Anseriformes
  Suborder Anhimae
    Family Anhimidae
  Suborder Anseres
    Family Anseranatidae
    Family Anatidae
      Subfamily Dendrocygninae
      Subfamily Thalassorninae

Subfamily Anserinae
  Tribe Anserini
  Tribe Cygnini
Subfamily Stictonettinae
Subfamily Plectropterinae
Subfamily Tadorninae
  Tribe Sarkiornini
  Tribe Tadornini *sedis mutabilis*
    Subtribe Tadorneae
    Subtribe Malacorhyncheae
    Subtribe Chloephageae *sedis mutabilis*
    Subtribe Cyanocheneae
    Subtribe Merganetteae
Subfamily Anatinae
  [Tribe] "Anatini" *incertae sedis*
  Tribe Aythyini
  Tribe Mergini
  Tribe Oxyurini

Madsen et al. (1988) compared the single-copy DNAs of 13 species of anseriforms using DNA-DNA hybridization. Their results agreed well with traditional arrangements. Their tree differed from ours in placing *Anseranas* in the anatid clade, rather than as the sister group of the screamers. They suggested that "the tribes Anatini, Aythyini, Tadornini, Mergini, and Cairinini diverged more recently than the Anserini, Stictonettini, Oxyurini, Dendrocygnini, and Anseranatini." The Freckled Duck (*Stictonetta*) "is only distantly related to the other Anatidae." The stiff-tailed ducks (Oxyurini) are "remotely related to the other Anatidae" and the whistling ducks (Dendrocygnini) "form an isolated tribe with no close relationship to the swans and geese (subfamily Anserinae)." The screamers were found to be "distantly related to the Anatidae."

The DNA Hybridization Evidence (Figs. 35–40, 325–328, 353, 354, 357)

The Anserimorphae branched from the Gallomorphae at Δ T$_{50}$H 22.9, the divergence between the Anhimides and the Anserides occurred at Δ 16.1, and between the screamers (Anhimidae) and the Magpie Goose (Anseranatidae) at Δ 12.4. The whistling ducks (Dendrocygnidae) diverged from the Anatidae at Δ 9.8.

The branching pattern (Fig. 357) agrees well with that found by Madsen et al. (1988), except for the position of *Anseranas*, as noted above.

The melting curves in Fig. 35 (*Anas*) show the relative positions of the major groups to the Mallard, with the Ostrich and Greater Rhea as distant outgroups. In Fig. 36 (*Anas*) several taxa with delayed maturity (eagle, crane, bustard, New World vulture) are slightly closer to *Anas* than are taxa with earlier ages at first breeding (falcon, moorhen, doves). The differences are not significant and Fig. 36 indicates that the heteroduplex taxa are not closely related to the waterfowl.

In Fig. 37 (*Anas strepera*) the anseriform hybrids confirm the evidence in Fig. 35 and add several taxa. The positions of the curves of the flamingo and a megapode are equidistant from *Anas*. Flamingos often have been suggested as close relatives of the anseriforms, but there is nothing in our DNA hybridization data to support this idea. In Figs. 160–165 the flamingos are closer to the storks, ibises, and herons than to the waterfowl.

Fig. 38 (*Anhima*) shows that the Magpie Goose is closer to the screamers than are the members of the Anserides. Fig. 39 (*Chauna*) also shows the distant, but closest, relationship between the Anserides and the screamers. The ratites (*Rhea*) are in their usual distant position. The other heteroduplex taxa include several birds with delayed maturity (flamingo, stork, crane), but the others are mostly 2- or 3-year taxa and the small differences are not clearly due to this factor.

Fig. 40 (*Anseranas*) again shows that *Anseranas* and the screamers are closest relatives, although not closely related. The sequence of the outermost curves from *Mycteria* to *Gallus* may reflect the effects of ages at first breeding. *Mycteria*, the flamingo, cracid, and megapode are 2–4-year taxa; the heron and the Domestic Fowl are 1–2-year species. The difference is not great but may contribute to the relative positions of the curves.

The FITCH tree (Fig. 328) also shows the relative positions of *Anas*, *Anseranas*, and *Anhima*. In this tree, the galliforms and anseriforms are presented as closest relatives, and we believe this is correct, but other groups are not represented.

The UPGMA trees (Figs. 353, 354) place the Gallomorphae and Anserimorphae as sister groups. This agrees with the FITCH tree, and is indicated by the melting curves.

We conclude that the Gallomorphae and Anserimorphae are closest relatives, but that the divergence between them occurred in the late Cretaceous or early Tertiary. The data suggest that the differences in ages at first breeding among these taxa have had an effect on the relative rates of DNA evolution. The megapodes and cracids exhibit evidence of a slower rate relative to the phasianids, the waterfowl are slowed with respect to the galliforms, and *Anseranas* and the screamers have evolved more slowly than the typical ducks. The differences are not great enough to confuse the evidence of relationships and we believe that the branching pattern indicated in the UPGMA tree for the Gallomorphae and Anserimorphae is a reasonable representation of their relationships to one another.

Sibley et al. (1988) placed the parvclass Galloanserae with the Ratitae in the infraclass Eoaves. In view of the further analysis of the DNA hybridization data reported in this section, and in the sections on the Ratites and Tinamous and Gallinaceous Birds, we have moved the Galloanserae to the beginning of the infraclass Neoaves, as discussed in chapter 16.

Buttonquails or Hemipodes

Parvclass Turnicae
  Order TURNICIFORMES
    Family Turnicidae: Buttonquails

Order TURNICIFORMES, Family TURNICIDAE: 2/17. *Turnix* species are called button-quails; *Ortyxelos meiffrenii*, the Lark Buttonquail, is also called the Quail-plover or Lark-quail. These vernacular names reflect the external similarities between the turnicids and the true quail (*Coturnix*).

Species of *Turnix* occur in Southern Europe, Africa, Madagascar, Asia to the Philippines, Okinawa, Indonesia, New Guinea, Australia, New Britain, Solomon Islands, Bismarck Archipelago, and New Caledonia. *Ortyxelos* occurs in sub-Saharan Africa from Senegal and Ghana to southern Chad, southern Sudan, and southeastern Kenya.

The palate is aegithognathous, or nearly so; vomer broad and paired posteriorly; large basipterygoid processes originate from basisphenoidal rostrum; no hallux; one deep sternal incision each side; no crop; large gizzard and caeca; long aftershaft; 15 cervical vertebrae; 10 primaries; 12 short rectrices; tufted oil gland; only left carotid; eutaxic; podotheca with single anterior row of transverse scutes; syrinx tracheo-bronchial, tracheal rings cartilaginous; schizorhinal, pervious nares; female larger than male and more brightly colored; only females have specialized vocal organ and vocalize during breeding season; nest on ground; eggs 2–4, glossy, variously colored; only the male incubates and cares for nidifugous young; females probably polyandrous; young have two molts by the age of ca. 10 weeks.

In captivity *Turnix* has been recorded as breeding when only three to five months old (Bruning 1985; Table 16). The age of maturity in the wild seems to be unknown, but it is likely that it averages longer than in captivity. Alan Kemp (pers. comm.) notes that in southern Africa *Turnix* breeds only during the wet summer when soft grass seeds are available. Thus, they must be unable to breed before the age of one year in areas with pronounced wet and dry seasons. Where soft grass seeds are available at all times they may breed when less than one year of age. Sibley et al. (1988) speculated that early maturity may be correlated with a rapid average rate of genomic evolution and that the large genetic gap between the turnicids and other groups of birds may not indicate an ancient origin, but a rapid accession and drift of neutral mutations. See further comments below under "The DNA Hybridization Evidence."

The Turnicidae have usually been viewed as most closely related to the Plains-wanderer (*Pedionomus*) of Australia. In most classifications these two groups have been placed in the Galliformes or the Gruiformes. It is now clear that *Pedionomus* is a charadriiform while *Turnix* and *Ortyxelos* seem to be members of a lineage with no close living relatives.

Historical Review of the Classification

Superficially, the buttonquails look like small true quail and in many early classifications *Turnix* was placed with the galliforms (Illiger 1811, Vieillot 1816, Cuvier 1817, Temminck 1820). Gray (1844–49) placed *Turnix* with the grouse in the Tetraonidae. Huxley (1867) assigned *Turnix* to his "Group 6. Turnicomorphae" and suggested that it is related to the tinamous, the sandgrouse, and the plovers, with *Pedionomus* "being perhaps the connecting link between the latter and it." It is impossible to imagine the branching pattern of such a phylogeny.

Sundevall (1872, see 1889) placed *Turnix* in the "Gallinae." Parker (1875a:292) described the various modifications of the aegithognathous palate and defined the condition in the Turnicidae as: "a. *Incomplete.*—Aegithognathism occurs in the 'Turnicomorphae' (*Hemipodius*, *Turnix*). Here the vomerine cartilages (cartilages to which the symmetrical vomers are attached) . . . are very large, and incompletely ossified, and the broad *double* vomer has a 'septo-maxillary' at each angle; but these bones are only strongly *tied* to the 'alinasal' cartilage, and do not graft themselves upon it: their union is with the vomerine cartilage."

Parker (1875a:294–300) presented one of his rambling, turgid commentaries "On the Morphology of the Face in the 'Turnicomorphae'." He began by noting that he "can correct some things in which I was misled in my former paper ('On the Gallinaceous Birds', Trans. Zool. Soc. vol. v. p. 172)." (This paper was published in 1864 and actually entitled "On the osteology of gallinaceous birds and tinamous." See Parker 1864.) Parker (1864) had concluded that the "Turnicomorphae" are related to the galliforms. Selections from his 1875a essay may convey its flavor.

> If the palate of the young *Turnix* . . . be compared with that of the *Syrrhaptes* [sandgrouse], Grouse, Plover, and Pigeon, . . . it will be seen at a glance that these birds have much in common; they belong, evidently, to one morphological stratum, or nearly so. But the *Turnix* is the lowest of these types; and it would seem as if he and his compeers were the waifs and strays of a large and widely distributed group of birds only a little higher in the scale than the Tinamous.
>
> From such a group, largely extinct, the Sand-Grouse may have arisen; from such a stock the Plovers; and these old types may also be looked upon as zoologically paternal to several other modern families, the greatest of these being the Passerines. As to the relation of the Hemipods to existing types, I cannot do better than refer the reader to Professor Huxley's paper on the "Alectoromorphae" (Zool. Proc. 1868, pp. 302–304).
>
> There, however, no suspicion has been given as to the meaning of the broad "vomer" in relation to the passerines; it is merely compared to that of the Grouse—not of *Lagopus* [ptarmigan], but of *Tetrao urogallus* [Capercaillie]. . . . But even that vomer is a poor representative of that of the Hemipod, and for some years it has been a mystery to me because of its passerine form. . . .

The parasphenoidal bar . . . is rather massive in the young; but in the old [p. 295] Hemipod . . . it is much more like that of the Ostrich family; and this trabecular underbearer of the ethmoid . . . is swollen and spongy as in the "Ratitae."

The cranio-facial "hinge," however, is as perfect as in the Fowl; and the rest of the coalesced trabecular bar is unossified and forms the lower edge of a feeble septum nasi. . . . As in the Crow and many of the "Coracomorphae," the trabecular base of the septum is alate in its middle region. The praemaxilla . . . remains but little different from what is seen in the ripe chick of the Fowl . . . having a form common to Pigeons, Sandgrouse, and Hemipods (p. 295).

Parker proceeded in this style for several pages, seeming to ally *Turnix* with various groups, including tinamous, passerines, plovers, pigeons, and sandgrouse. On pages 299–300 he concluded:

Considered by itself, the Hemipode is a low type of the "Carinatae," more reptilian in some respects than the "Ratitae" down below it. But if it be looked at as a remnant of an ancient and almost extinct race, a race from which the most highly gifted and the most numerous of all the feathered tribes have probably sprung, then the interest increases ten-fold, and the morphologist will never rest until the relations of every branch of this simple stock are understood.

To this end a clear conception of what is *highest* in the facial morphology of birds is, before all things, necessary; and our Old-World Crows and Warblers will furnish us with "that which is most perfect in its own kind," and therefore fit to be "the measure of the rest."

These samples of Parker's prose may be amusing, but they do little to establish the affinities of the buttonquails. However, they may have influenced subsequent authors.

Apparently Stejneger (1885) was not influenced by Parker, for he included *Turnix sylvatica* in an illustration of several species of galliforms.

In his "Ordo Charadriornithes" Fürbringer (1888) placed the shorebirds, jacanas, thick-knees, bustards, Sunbittern, Kagu, *Aptornis*, cranes, trumpeters, seriemas, sungrebes, rails, mesites, and buttonquails. Thus, Fürbringer was the first to ally the buttonquails with the rails and mesites when he placed the "Hemipodiidae" in the "Intermediäre Subordo *Ralliformes*" with the Rallidae, Heliornithidae, and Mesitidae, and suggested that these groups are distantly related to the tinamous and kiwis through the "Hemipodiidae" (Turnicidae). Fürbringer's "Charadriornithes" included the same groups that Wetmore and Miller (1926) divided into their orders Charadriiformes and Megalornithiformes (Gruiformes). Thus, for these groups, it seems clear that Wetmore and Miller (1926) followed Fürbringer when they assembled their classification from various sources. Wetmore (1930, 1960) adopted the same arrangement.

Ogilvie-Grant (1889) reviewed the genus *Turnix* and recognized 22 species. He used the female plumages as the principal basis for separating species, but did not comment on the relationships of the buttonquails to other groups.

Gadow (1892, 1893) included the "Turnices" in his order Galliformes, which included *Pedionomus* and the Hoatzin (*Opisthocomus*), as well as the traditional galliform groups. Gadow thus returned to the galliform theory of the relationships of the Turnicidae, which Parker (1875a) had disavowed and which Fürbringer (1888) had not followed.

Gadow (1893:168) compared the characters of *Turnix* with those of the galliforms, sandgrouse, and rails. He concluded (p. 171) that the Turnices have some affinity to the Mesites and the "Rallo-Galli." He suggested that their next nearest relatives are the galliforms, and that a direct relationship to the tinamous ("Crypturi") is unlikely. He attributed the morphological similarities between *Turnix* and the tinamous to the effects of similar habits, i.e., to convergence. Gadow (1893:174) noted that separating the galliforms from the rails is difficult because the similarities in the arrangement of the intestines and the structures of the sternum and shoulder girdle may be due to their similar modes of life, i.e., to convergence. He concluded that a relationship exists between the galliforms and the rails, but that it is weaker than that of the galliforms to the Turnices and to the tinamous.

Gadow (1893:180) noted that Fürbringer (1888) proposed an entirely new classification when he assigned the Heliornithidae (sungrebes), Rallidae (rails), Mesitidae (mesites), and Hemipodiidae (*Turnix, Pedionomus*) to the Ralliformes, an intermediate suborder of his order "Charadriornithes." Gadow declined to follow Fürbringer in this arrangement; instead he placed the Turnicidae in the Galliformes with the mesites, megapodes, cracids, "Gallidae," and the Hoatzin (Opisthocomidae).

Gadow (1898:33) again included the "Hemipodii" in the Galliformes; thus he had not changed his mind since 1893.

In the *Catalogue of Birds* Ogilvie-Grant (1893) placed *Turnix* and *Pedionomus* in the "Order Hemipodii" following the galliforms ("Gallinae") and the Hoatzin ("Opisthocomi").

In the *Hand-List* Sharpe (1899) placed the Turnicidae, containing *Turnix* and *Pedionomus*, in the "Order Hemipodii" between the Galliformes and "Pteroclidiformes" (sandgrouse).

Beddard (1898a) placed the "Turnices" between the "Columbae" (pigeons) and "Pterocletes" (sandgrouse) on one side and the "Ralli" (rails) on the other. This reflected some pigeon-like characters Beddard noted (p. 321), and acknowledged a possible relationship to the rails, possibly due to Fürbringer's influence.

Beddard (1911) found the alimentary tract of the Turnicidae to be similar to that of the passerines, and unlike that of the galliforms. He described the anatomy of the "Hemipodes" based in part on Parker (1864, 1875a). Beddard noted that the "nostrils are pseudo-holorhinal, and, as in pigeons, there is a considerable alinasal ossification, reducing the long nares, which are perfectly pervious. As is also the case with the pigeons, the ectethmoids are large and solid, and have fused with the lacrymals." He dismissed a close relationship with the galliforms, but did not propose a relationship with any other group.

Lowe (1923:277) speculated that the Turnicidae, sandgrouse, and seedsnipe are the "blind-alley offshoots of an ancient generalized and basal group (now extinct), from which group sprang the now dominant Plovers, Pigeons, and Fowls."

As noted above, Wetmore and Miller (1926) placed the Turnices in the Megalornithiformes, which became the Gruiformes of Wetmore (1930). They noted (p. 338) that following the appearance of the first edition of the A.O.U. checklist in 1886 came "the work of Fuerbringer, in 1888, that of Sharpe in 1891, and that of Gadow in 1893, the first and last based upon profound anatomical studies that revealed relationships hitherto unsuspected which indicated radical changes in existing systems of classification." They also noted that they used "Gadow's work as a basis and have incorporated in it various changes that have been made by later workers." For the Turnicidae there is no explanation for the departure from Gadow's arrangement, but Wetmore and Miller apparently followed Fürbringer for the classification of the buttonquails.

Wetmore (1930, 1960), following Wetmore and Miller (1926), included the Turnicidae and Pedionomidae in the suborder Turnices of the Gruiformes, and Peters (1934) used the same arrangement. Ridgway and Friedmann (1941) included the Turnices in the Gruiformes, but noted that their aegithognathous palate differs from that of other members of the order.

Stresemann (1934) placed his "Ordnung der Aves: TURNICES" between the order "Opisthocomi" (Hoatzin), and the order "Columbae" (pigeons). Concerning their place in the system, Stresemann wrote (transl.): "The Turnices occupy a widely isolated position. The Galli are only superficially similar, [and] a connection with other orders, perhaps the Pterocletes [sandgrouse] or Thinocori [seedsnipe], is equally improbable." He must have had Lowe's (1923) wild speculation, quoted above, in mind.

Mayr and Amadon (1951) placed the Turnicidae (including *Pedionomus*) in their order Grues, thus following Fürbringer and/or Wetmore.

Verheyen (1958a) placed the Turniciformes between the Columbiformes and the Galliformes as "*le lien morphologique*" between the pigeons and the galliforms. In 1961, Verheyen allocated the Turnicidae and Pedionomidae to a suborder of the Galliformes.

The carotid pattern of *Turnix* is the B–4–s type, which is shared with *Podica*, *Heliornis*, and some bustards (Glenny 1967).

Bock and McEvey (1969a) found skeletal differences between *Turnix* and *Pedionomus* and supported their separation in two families. They also recognized *Ortyxelos* as distinct from *Turnix*.

Olson and Steadman (1981) presented morphological evidence that *Pedionomus* is a charadriiform, most closely related to the seedsnipe. The DNA evidence agrees.

In summary, the morphological evidence pertaining to the affinities of the Turnicidae must be described as conflicting and uncertain. The buttonquails differ from all other groups in several characters, and at least some of their similarities to other groups are due to convergence. Because Wetmore (1930, 1934, 1940, 1951, 1960), Peters (1934), and those who followed their classifications assigned the Turnicidae to the Gruiformes, a strong tradition was established. Whether the assignment of the Turnicidae to the Gruiformes is correct depends on the validity of the work of Fürbringer (1888), whose opinion was adopted by Wetmore and Miller in 1926, although it was rejected by Gadow (1893) and other contemporaries of Fürbringer. Tradition is a strong force in systematics, but it does not supersede evidence from sources that reflect phylogenetic relationships.

The DNA Hybridization Evidence (Figs. 41, 353, 354, 358)

In Fig. 41 (*Turnix*) a diverse set of taxa, including five genera of the Gruiformes, are about equally distant from *Turnix sylvatica*. In Fig. 30 (*Numida*) the two species of *Turnix* are the most distant among representatives of the galliforms, anseriforms, gruiforms, and ratites. In Figs. 112, 116, 120, and 121, *Turnix* is compared with four genera of gruiforms. In these melting curves, *Turnix* is the most distant from the tracer taxon. Most of the driver species in these four sets are gruiforms, but *Pedionomus* is in all four, and *Rostratula* is in Fig. 120. Thus, the curves of these two charadriiform genera are closer to the gruiform homoduplexes than are the *Turnix* curves. Note that the *Turnix* curves in Figs. 112, 116, 120, and 121 intersect the vertical axis (% single-stranded DNA) from ca. 55% to 70%, but in Fig. 30 the *Turnix* curves intersect the vertical axis ca. 85–90%. These observations suggest that *Turnix* is more closely related to the gruiforms than to the galliforms.

The positions of the two charadriiform genera (*Pedionomus*, *Rostratula*) that are closer to the gruiform tracers than is *Turnix* may be explained by differences in rates of genomic evolution. It seems reasonably certain that *Turnix* begins to breed at an early age, possibly less than one year. From this we may assume that it has a faster rate than most of the gruiforms, with the possible exception of the rails (Table 16). Most charadriiforms begin to breed at more than one year of age. Thus, we may speculate that the relative position of *Turnix* is due to its own faster-than-average rate of DNA evolution, added to the relatively slower rates of most gruiforms and charadriiforms. The additive effect is to increase the distance between *Turnix* and all other taxa, but to increase it most to those taxa that are, like the galliforms, distant phylogenetically and begin to breed at one year of age. We might conclude from this that *Turnix* is indeed most closely related to the gruiforms; that is, that it diverged more recently from the gruiform lineage than from some other lineage. However, we have no simple way to apply a correction factor for the effects of different average genomic rates, and we lack information on the ages at first breeding for many groups.

Thus, *Turnix* poses a special problem, as noted by Sibley et al. (1988):

The 27 delta $T_{50}H$ values between *Turnix* and other taxa are large, ranging from 22.7 to the pectoral sandpiper (*Calidris melanotos*) to 29.8 to the ostrich (*Struthio camelus*); average = 27.0. The range of 7.1 is unusually large. The smaller delta values are between *Turnix* and members of the Gruiformes and Charadriides; the larger delta values are between *Turnix* and the ratites, tinamous, galliforms and anseriforms. Members of several other non-passerine groups produced delta values between the extremes. Thus, *Turnix* seems to have no close living relatives, but *Turnix* species begin to breed at the age of three to five months (Bruning 1985), therefore it is possible that their average rate of genomic evolution is faster than the rate(s) among their nearest relatives. If so, the branch length we observe may be longer by an unknown factor and the correct position of the branch node may be elsewhere in the tree, possibly among the gruiforms where the Turnicidae have often been assigned. The problem is not insoluble, but will require additional comparisons and, perhaps, the development of a correction for different ages at first breeding. For now we leave the Turnicidae in the position indicated . . . but designate the group as *incertae sedis*.

Does the *Turnix* problem cast doubt on the positions of all taxa in the tree? We think not, because nearly all other groups consist of many species and several levels of branchings, but the members cluster in spite of somewhat different ages at maturity. For example, members of the Procellariidae range in age at first breeding from ca. 3–4 years (storm petrels) to more than 10 years (large albatrosses). Differences in branch lengths are revealed by relative rate tests, but all procellariids are closer to one another than to any outside group. Similarly, the estrildine finches begin to breed when less than one year of age, but they cluster with the other members of the Passeridae and are closest to the viduines, as expected.

If the age at first breeding in the wild is only three to five months, as it is in captivity (Bruning 1985; Table 16), the above speculation may be correct. However, it is likely that *Turnix* does not begin to breed until older than five months in the wild. In general, well-fed captive birds tend to breed earlier than the same species in the wild. For example, a captive Stephanie's Astrapia (*Astrapia stephaniae*, a bird-of-paradise) laid three eggs at the age of 5–6 months (Bishop and Frith 1979). There seem to be no records of age at first breeding in wild birds-of-paradise, but it is unlikely that they begin before ca. one year.

Thus, it is possible that the species of *Turnix* are actually as isolated as their positions in Figs. 41 and 353 suggest. We conclude that this problem remains unsolved, but that the Turnicidae are as likely to be members of the Gruiformes as of any other higher category. They may also represent a distinct and isolated group, as indicated in our classification.

Woodpeckers, Honeyguides, Barbets, Toucans, Jacamars, and Puffbirds

Parvclass Picae
    Order PICIFORMES
        Infraorder Picides
            Family Indicatoridae: Honeyguides
            Family Picidae: Woodpeckers, Wrynecks, Piculets
        Infraorder Ramphastides
          Superfamily Megalaimoidea
            Family Megalaimidae: Asian Barbets
          Superfamily Lybioidea
            Family Lybiidae: African Barbets
          Superfamily Ramphastoidea
            Family Ramphastidae
                Subfamily Capitoninae: New World Barbets
                Subfamily Ramphastinae: Toucans, Toucanets
Parvclass Coraciae
    Superorder Galbulimorphae
    Order GALBULIFORMES
        Infraorder Galbulides
            Family Galbulidae: Jacamars
        Infraorder Bucconides
            Family Bucconidae: Puffbirds

The Piciformes and Galbuliformes are not closely related, but they have been placed together in most classifications. For convenience, their taxonomic histories will be discussed together.

The Piciformes and Galbuliformes have been thought to be closely allied because they share the following characters: zygodactyl feet, with Type 6 flexor tendons (vinculum present but flexor digitorum supplies only digit 3, other toes supplied by trifurcate flexor hallucis); holorhinal, impervious nares; no basipterygoid processes; pelvic muscles AXY or AX; 14 cervical vertebrae; all thoracic vertebrae free; 5 complete ribs; metasternum with two pairs of notches (closed in some Picidae); long deltoid muscle covers nearly entire humerus; eutaxic; syrinx tracheo-bronchial; no adult downs; eggs white; nest in holes; young naked at hatching.

Order PICIFORMES: 51/355. Desmognathous (toucans, some barbets), saurognathous (woodpeckers), or aegithognathous; oil gland variable: absent or widely bilobed, naked or tufted in Picidae, indistinctly bilobed and tufted in Indicatoridae, bilobed and naked or tufted in toucans and barbets; no caeca; single, left carotid; no hypocleideum, furcula incomplete.

Family INDICATORIDAE: 4/17. The honeyguides occur in Africa, the mountains of India, and southeastern Asia in Malaysia, Sumatra, and Borneo. The nostrils are in the center of a large nasal fossa; only 9 primaries; the skin is thick (presumably as a defense against bee stings); some species "guide" to beehives and feed on beeswax; brood parasites, often on barbets.

Family PICIDAE: 28/215. The woodpeckers occur in the Americas, Africa, Eurasia, and southern Asia east to the Philippines, Celebes, the Andaman Islands, Taiwan, and Okinawa. They are absent from Madagascar, New Guinea, Australia, and most islands (Short 1982). The wrynecks (*Jynx*) occur in Europe, Asia, and Africa, and the piculets (*Picumnus*, *Sasia*) occur in the Neotropics, southern Asia, and Africa (Nigeria and Zaire).

Family MEGALAIMIDAE: 3/26. The Asian barbets occur in the tropics of eastern Asia. The inclusion of *Calorhamphus* and *Psilopogon* in this family is tentative; we have compared only the DNA of *Megalaima*.

Family LYBIIDAE: 7/42. The African barbets occur in the wooded areas of Africa south of the Sahara. The Old World barbets (Megalaimidae and Lybiidae) have stout, subconical bills, with numerous, long, rictal bristles.

Family RAMPHASTIDAE, Subfamily CAPITONINAE: 3/14. The New World barbets range from Costa Rica to Bolivia and Brazil. They tend to have fewer and shorter rictal bristles than do the Old World barbets. The cross-sectional shape of the bill in the New World barbets is like that of the toucans, and differs from that of the Old World barbets.

It was a surprise to discover that the New World barbets are more closely related to the toucans than to the Old World barbets. However, the Toucan Barbet (*Semnornis ramphastinus*) and the toucanets (*Aulacorhynchus*) are morphologically intermediate in many ways between the toucans and the capitonines. The toucans are specialized New World barbets.

Family RAMPHASTIDAE, Subfamily RAMPHASTINAE: 6/41. The toucans occur in forests of the Neotropics from Mexico to Peru, Brazil, and northeastern Argentina. The large, brightly colored bill is extremely light; the interior is a network of bony fibers. The pelvic muscle formula is AXY; vomer truncate; clavicles separate; tongue long, narrow, thin, with lateral notches.

Order GALBULIFORMES: 15/51. Desmognathous; tongue normal, long and thin; two carotids; oil gland naked, bilobed; complete furcula with hypocleideum; caeca long, globose; no ectepicondyloid process on humerus; wing coverts non-oscinine, i.e., proximally overlapping middle covert row absent or imperfectly developed; aftershaft vestigial (Bucconidae) or reduced (Galbulidae) (Sibley 1956); 10 primaries; 10–12 secondaries; 12 rectrices.

Family GALBULIDAE: 5/18. The jacamars range from southern Mexico to northern Argentina in tropical and subtropical forest. The bills of jacamars are long and pointed and the gonys is carinate; no vomer; tarsi smooth behind; plumage in most species is metallic green.

Family BUCCONIDAE: 10/33. The puffbirds range from southern Mexico to northern Argentina in tropical forest. The bill is pointed, anteriorly compressed with the tip decurved, often uncinate; gonys rounded; vomer present; tarsi scutellate behind; plumage full, lax, dull-colored.

Historical Review of the Classification

Under various names and with varying content, the piciform birds were usually grouped together in most of the early classifications. The order Picae of Linnaeus (1758) included *Ramphastos*, *Jynx*, and *Picus*, as well as the parrots, hornbills, cuckoos, kingfishers, and several other groups. In his Scansores Illiger (1811) placed the parrots, cuckoos, trogons, puffbirds, jacamars, toucans, and woodpeckers. The tribe Zygodactyli of Vieillot (1816) contained the cuckoos, woodpeckers, and parrots. Thus, from the earliest classifications, foot structure was used as the basis for defining taxa, and the yoke-toed (zygodactyl) birds were assumed to be closely related.

Nitzsch (1840) based his classification partly on pterylosis and his order Picariae included several subgroups, among them the Todidae (rollers, motmots, todies, jacamars), Cuculinae (cuckoos, honeyguides, trogons), and Picinae (puffbirds, barbets, toucans, woodpeckers).

Gray (1844–49) distributed the piciforms between two orders, but Lilljeborg (1866), who depended mainly on beak and foot characters, placed all of the zygodactyl birds together, as had Vieillot (1816).

Huxley (1867) recognized that the palate of woodpeckers is intermediate between desmognathous and aegithognathous, a condition that Parker (1875b) called saurognathous. Huxley placed the jacamars, toucans, puffbirds, and barbets with the cuculiforms in his Coccygomorphae. He erected the Celeomorphae for the woodpeckers, which he thought to be intermediate between the Coccygomorphae and the Aegithomorphae (swifts, goatsuckers, passerines).

Sclater (1870) was the first to dissect a specimen of a honeyguide (*Indicator*), which had been placed with the cuckoos by previous authors. He was aware of Blyth's (1842) opinion that honeyguides are related to woodpeckers, and he examined the tongue, sternum, pectoral girdle, skull, pterylosis, and digestive tract of the honeyguide. He concluded that it is not a member of either the Cuculidae or Picidae but should be separated in its own family, "best placed in the second section of the Coccygomorphae, as arranged by Prof. Huxley . . . next to the Capitonidae" (p. 180). This placed the Indicatoridae in the position they have since occupied in most classifications, for example, Wetmore (1960).

Marshall and Marshall (1871) defined an order (Fissirostres, containing the goatsuckers, trogons, and puffbirds) for arboreal birds that use their wings in pursuit of food and whose feet are adapted only for perching. Their order Scansores was composed of arboreal birds that use their feet in pursuit of food and in which the outer toe is "versatile" or "turned completely backwards." This included the toucans, barbets, cuckoos, and turacos. They suggested that the nearest relatives of the barbets are the toucans and honeyguides, and that the barbets approach the woodpeckers (e.g., *Picumnus*) through *Barbatula* (*Pogoniulus*) and the cuckoos through *Trachyphonus*.

In his "Volucres Zygodactylae" Sundevall (1872, see 1889) placed the parrots in "Cohort 1. Psittaci." "Cohort 2. Pici" included the woodpeckers, piculets, and wrynecks.

"Cohort 3. Coccyges" contained the honeyguides, barbets, toucans, jacamars, puffbirds, and the Cuckoo-Roller (*Leptosomus*). Bills, feet, and feathers were the principal defining characters.

In Garrod's (1873d, 1874a) system the Piciformes included the Picidae, Ramphastidae, and Capitonidae, but the Bucconidae and Galbulidae were assigned to the Passeriformes.

Parker (1875b) studied the skull in woodpeckers and wrynecks and commented on their palatal types. He noted (p. 2) Huxley's (1867) description of the palate and proposed that the group be called the Saurognathae because their palates are like those of "early embryos of the Passerinae . . . their palatal region arrested at a most simple and Lacertian stage." Parker concluded: "The 'Celeomorphae' of Huxley form a . . . natural and well-defined group . . . equal, zoologically, to the Pigeons or the Parrots" (p. 20). The palate of *Picumnus* agrees "with that of the last of the Rhynochosaurian Lizards (namely *Hatteria*). . . . In the low South-American Passerinae, the 'Formicariidae' and the 'Cotingidae,' the essentially Reptilian face shows itself most clearly." The principal character of "the 'Celeomorphae' is the want of fusion of the parts of the palate at the mid line."

The anatomy of a honeyguide (*Indicator*) was also studied by Garrod (1878d), who noted the earlier work of Blyth (1840, 1842), Sclater (1870), and Blanford (1870), all of whom had considered the honeyguides to be piciforms, not cuculiforms. Garrod reaffirmed his confidence in the correlation between the condition of the dorsal pteryla and the presence (homalogonatous) or absence (anomalogonatous) of the ambiens muscle: "When the dorsal tract develops a fork *between* the shoulder-blades a bird is homalogonatous; when the tract runs on unenlarged to near the lower ends of the scapulae, then it is anomalogonatous. Again, among the Anomalogonatae, when the pectoral tract bifurcates into an outer and an inner branch just after commencing on the chest, then the bird is one of the Piciforms, and has a tufted oil-gland; when the pectoral tract does not bifurcate at all, or only at the lower end of its pectoral portion but is only increased in breadth instead, then the bird is Passeriform, and has a naked oil-gland. Exceptions to these rules scarcely exist" (p. 931).

By these criteria, *Indicator* was declared to be piciform, not cuculiform. Garrod also noted that the palate is "but little different from that of the Capitonidae." The feather tracts of *Indicator* are similar to those of the Picidae, Capitonidae, and Ramphastidae, and its soft-part anatomy, carotids, deep plantar tendons, pelvic muscles, and other characters are also similar to their conditions in these families and differ from those of the cuckoos. Garrod (p. 935) proposed that the suborder Pici should contain two families, Picidae and Capitonidae, the latter to include the Indicatorinae, Capitoninae, and Ramphastinae.

The Picariae of Sclater (1880b) encompassed the same birds that Wetmore (1960) placed in seven orders: Cuculiformes, Apodiformes, Caprimulgiformes, Coliiformes, Trogoniformes, Coraciiformes, and Piciformes. The Pici (woodpeckers) were placed some distance from the the Zygodactylae (jacamars, puffbirds, toucans, barbets, honeyguides). In a monograph of the jacamars and puffbirds Sclater (1882) expressed his conviction that these two groups are more closely related to each other than either is to any other group. In his introduction, Sclater quoted Forbes as believing that the jacamars and puffbirds are closely related to the bee-eaters, rollers, and *Leptosomus*.

Forbes (1882a) found a long "intestiniform" gall bladder in several species of toucans and barbets, similar to that of woodpeckers. The condition in *Indicator* was unknown to

Forbes. He also noted the exceptionally large deltoid muscle in the Picidae, *Indicator*, toucans, and barbets (also in the passerines, some pigeons, and the seriemas, *Cariama*). A sesamoid bone, the scapula accessoria, was noted in the Pici and passerines. Forbes concluded (p. 96) that these additional points of resemblance between woodpeckers and barbets made their relationship "even more certain than before." The cranial differences between the two groups indicated to him that the structure of the skull is not "a certain, or even sufficient, index to their systematic classification."

Stejneger (1885) also used an order Picariae to include the same taxa as in Sclater's (1880b) Picariae, with the Piciformes of later authors (e.g., Wetmore 1960) in the superfamily Picoideae.

Fürbringer (1888) included the "higher" non-passerines and passerines in his order Coracornithes, with the barbets, toucans, honeyguides, woodpeckers, passerines, hummingbirds, swifts, colies, and trogons in the suborder Pico-Passeriformes. The jacamars and puffbirds were placed in an intermediate gens between the Coccygiformes (turacos, cuckoos) and the Capitonidae (barbets). Thus, the piciforms and galbuliforms were close together and the sequence of taxa was similar to that used in later classifications.

Shufeldt (1888e) described the pterylosis of several woodpeckers and figured the feather tracts of three North American species. Shufeldt (1891d) doubted the interpretations of the palatal structure of woodpeckers proposed by Huxley, Parker, and Garrod. He opposed the idea that the saurognathous type was essentially a reptilian pattern and insisted that specialization could account for some of the characters and the errors of his predecessors for others. He summarized the "chief osteological characters of the North-American Pici" (p. 126) and "the probable position of the Pici in the System" (p. 128). He believed that the woodpeckers are more nearly allied to the passerines than to any other living group. This erroneous idea has survived to the present.

Volumes 16 (Salvin and Hartert 1892), 17 (Sharpe and Ogilvie-Grant 1892), 18 (Hargitt 1890), and 19 (Sclater and Shelley 1891) of the *Catalogue of Birds* were published out of chronological order, but the classification had been determined in advance. As recorded (Salvin and Hartert 1892:1), the classification of the "Order Picariae" followed that of Sclater (1880b) "in reviving the term 'Picariae' for the next order, which would comprise the *Cypseli* (*Macrochires*), *Anisodactyli*, *Heterodactyli*, *Scansores*, and *Coccyges*, although we are not aware that the order with these wide limits has been or can be diagnosed." Within this assemblage the piciforms and galbuliforms were placed in the suborder Scansores:

Order Picariae
  Suborder Scansores
    Family Picidae
      Subfamily Picinae, Woodpeckers
      Subfamily Picumninae, Piculets
      Subfamily Iynginae [sic], Wrynecks
    Family Indicatoridae, Honeyguides
    Family Capitonidae, Barbets
    Family Ramphastidae, Toucans
    Family Galbulidae
      Subfamily Galbulinae, Jacamars
      Subfamily Jacameropinae, *Jacamerops*
    Family Bucconidae, Puffbirds

The Galbulidae and Bucconidae were set apart from the other families by the possession of "Oil-gland nude; caeca developed" (Hargitt 1890:1).

Within his large pico-passerine order Seebohm (1890b) placed the piciforms in the suborder Scansores, based mainly on the condition of the deep plantar tendons. He noted similarities among the Scansores, trogons, hoopoes, and passerines. In 1895 Seebohm returned to a more conventional arrangement by recognizing an order Piciformes for the usual groups, but he merged the Bucconidae into the Galbulidae and the Indicatoridae into the Capitonidae, thus following Gadow (1893).

Sharpe (1891) placed the toucans, barbets, and honeyguides in his order Scansores, and the woodpeckers, jacamars, and puffbirds in the Piciformes. These two orders were listed between the parrots (Psittaciformes) and the passerines. Sharpe believed that the parrots have no close relatives, but that they combine "certain Accipitrine characters" with "a zygodactyle foot like so many members of the Picarian assemblage." He also noted that the development of feathers in nestling parrots is "in true Picarian fashion. . . . the new feathers are enclosed in the sheath till they attain almost their normal length; and in this respect the parrots resemble Kingfishers and other Picarian birds. The mode of nesting, too, is Picarian. . . . the Picariae have one feature in common which is characteristic of nearly the whole Order . . . they lay white eggs . . . in the hole of a tree or a bank . . . often tunnelled by the birds themselves. The principal exceptions . . . are the Coccyges [cuckoos, turacos] . . . which . . . though zygodactyle . . . have little to do with the other so-called *Picariae*, and in many respects exhibit Galline affinities. The *Caprimulgi* also are an exception to the Picarian rule as regards the colour of their eggs."

The Passeriformes of Gadow (1892) contained two suborders, Pici and Passeres. The Pici included the same groups as in Wetmore's (1960) Piciformes. Gadow (p. 234) found that of his 40 characters, 29 were held in common between the Pici and Psittaci, but he thought that the 11 differences were more important than the 29 similarities. He concluded that "the Pici are an offshoot" of the Coraciiformes and that "the resemblances between the Pici and Psittaci have therefore chiefly to be looked upon as convergent analogies." In 1893 Gadow transferred the piciforms from the Passeriformes and placed them in his large order Coraciiformes. He believed that the nearest relatives of the Pici are the bee-eaters and kingfishers.

Beddard (1896b) called attention to certain errors in Nitzsch's (1840) drawings of feather tracts in the barbets and toucans and, from his own work, concluded that these two groups are similar to one another and to the woodpeckers in their pterylography. He also commented on variations in the barbets associated with generic limits, and on differences between New World and Old World forms.

Beddard (1898a:183) defined his "Pici" as "Feet zygodactyle; aftershaft small or rudimentary; oil gland tufted. Muscle formula of leg, AXY (AX); Gall bladder elongated. Skull without basipterygoid processes." In the Pici he included the Picidae (woodpeckers); the Bucconidae, "a South American family of zygodactyle birds whose anatomy is . . . little known . . . only provisionally that I place them in the present position" (p. 188); the Ramphastidae (toucans); and the Capitonidae (barbets and honeyguides). The jacamars (Galbulidae) were placed in the "Coraciae" with the todies, motmots, hornbills, etc. (p. 213).

In the *Hand-List* Sharpe (1900) used the following classification:

Order Scansores
  Suborder Indicatores

> Family Indicatoridae, Honeyguides
> Suborder Capitones
>   Family Capitonidae, Barbets
> Suborder Rhamphastides
>   Family Rhamphastidae, Toucans
> Order Piciformes
> Suborder Galbulae
>   Family Galbulidae
>   Subfamily Galbulinae, Jacamars, 5 genera
>   Subfamily Jacameropinae, *Jacamerops*
> Suborder Buccones
>   Family Bucconidae, Puffbirds
> Suborder Pici
>   Family Picidae
>   Subfamily Picinae, Woodpeckers
>   Subfamily Picumninae, Piculets
>   Subfamily Iynginae [sic], Wrynecks

Shufeldt (1904b) recognized the adjacent supersuborders Picariformes (barbets, toucans, honeyguides) and Piciformes (woodpeckers). The jacamars and puffbirds were assigned to the "Jacamariformes," placed between the hummingbirds and trogons in his linear sequence. He did not provide evidence for these proposals.

According to Chandler (1916) the barbets, toucans, and woodpeckers share characters of their contour feathers that are intermediate between those of the coraciiforms and passeriforms. He thought that the Great Jacamar (*Jacamerops aurea*) is most like *Coracias* (rollers), but in the puffbird genus *Malacoptila* the barbules are of "typical passerine type." He considered the down feathers of the jacamars and puffbirds to be most like those of the rollers, and that those of the barbets, toucans, and woodpeckers resemble those of the passerines. Chandler concluded that "the Trochilidae and the suborder Pici, with the exception of the Galbulidae, show such striking likenesses to the Passeriformes that it is difficult to deny their closer alliance to that group than to the Coraciiformes" (p. 379). Here, again, is the claim that the piciforms and passeriforms are closely related.

W. DeW. Miller (1919) confirmed Garrod's (1875) observations on the deep plantar tendons in the piciforms. He found that the puffbirds and jacamars have the antiopelmous arrangement (Garrod's Type 6), as do the woodpeckers, toucans, and barbets. Miller cited Stejneger's statement that the honeyguides are antiopelmous, although Miller did not know Stejneger's source, which was, presumably, Garrod (1878d, see above). Miller assumed that the wrynecks and piculets are also antiopelmous and, therefore, concluded that the birds having zygodactyl, antiopelmous feet form "a natural group, an order or suborder." In addition, these birds lack the ambiens. The other zygodactyl groups, the parrots and cuckoos, have desmopelmous tendons (Garrod's Type 1) and an ambiens muscle.

Stresemann (1934) included the usual groups in his order Pici and believed them to be most closely related to the "primitive" passerines, thus reinforcing the traditional association.

The pterylography of 23 species or subspecies of North American woodpeckers was studied by Burt (1929), who determined that they are essentially uniform. Only the sapsuckers (*Sphyrapicus*) were separable from the other nine genera examined.

In his study of the adaptive modifications of woodpeckers Burt (1930) reported correlations between morphological characters and behavior. He proposed a division of the Picidae into two groups "according to whether or not the accessory semitendinosus muscle is present" and "by the type of skull, that is, whether the frontals are folded or not." One group includes "*Picoides, Dryobates, Xenopicus,* and *Sphyrapicus.* The other . . . less specialized for arboreal life . . . [is] represented . . . by *Ceophloeus, Centurus, Balanosphyra, Melanerpes, Asyndesmus,* and *Colaptes*" (p. 522).

The sclerotic plates in the eyes of woodpeckers are most similar in number and arrangement to those of rollers, kingfishers, and the Hoopoe. They differ slightly from those in *Cuculus,* some parrots, and many passerines (Lemmrich 1931).

The functional anatomy of the foot of birds with pamprodactyl, heterodactyl, and zygodactyl feet was studied by G. Steinbacher (1935), who examined members of all piciform groups but did not compare them with the coraciiforms, except *Leptosomus.* He found four types of zygodactyl feet, characterized by the Cuculoidea, the Galbuloidea, the Picoidea, and the Psittaci (p. 277). He considered the cuckoo type to be the most primitive and the woodpecker the most specialized. The foot in the Galbuloidea was thought to be intermediate between the cuculine and picine structures. Steinbacher concluded that the differences among the foot types cannot be explained on purely functional grounds and, therefore, that they are of great value in systematics.

Krassowsky (1936) examined the function of the palate and other skull features in woodpeckers, but was not concerned with their relationships.

J. Steinbacher (1937) studied the skeleton, musculature, digestive system, syrinx, pterylography, and molt in the jacamars and puffbirds. He compared them with the Picidae, Capitonidae, Ramphastidae, and Coraciidae, but not with kingfishers or bee-eaters. He concluded that the Galbulidae and Bucconidae are closely related to one another and to the Picidae and Capitonidae.

The Capitonidae are "zygodactylous perching birds with ten tail feathers" (Ripley 1945:542). After reviewing several previous classifications, Ripley observed that "the members of the Galbulae hardly deserve family rank." He proposed "two families for the suborder as follows: superfamily Galbuloidea; families Galbulidae and Bucconidae; the latter to contain three subfamilies, Bucconinae, Capitoninae and Indicatorinae" (p. 543). He recognized 9 genera and 66 species of barbets in 1945, but changed the number of species to 71 in 1946.

Lowe (1946) discovered an error in Garrod's (1878d) description and figure of the palate of *Indicator* and noted "that *Indicator,* as regards its vomer, is a good way in advance of *Picus,* and other . . . Woodpeckers, on its way to become what we now think of as a Passerine vomer" (p. 106). Lowe described the palate in the woodpeckers and stated that *Indicator* and the Picidae exhibit a "very close similarity" in this region. He emphasized the similarities between the Pici and the Passeres and thought that the two groups should be treated as suborders of the Passeriformes. His proposed classification assigned the Picidae, Indicatoridae, Capitonidae, and Ramphastidae to the suborder Pici. The hoopoes were thought to be close to the Pici but, in his "final conclusion" (p. 113) Lowe did not include them in that suborder.

The mallophagan fauna of the Piciformes has affinities to that of the passerines (Clay 1950). Mallophaga from the jacamars and puffbirds were not examined.

"The presence, reduction, or absence of one toe is of no very great importance as to the relationships of birds otherwise closely allied" (Delacour 1951b:49). Delacour recommended that the three-toed and four-toed woodpeckers should be placed in the same genus when other evidence indicates close relationship.

Beecher (1953a) studied the jaw muscles, tongue, horny palate, ectethmoid plate, plumage, and several other characters of the piciforms. He concluded that the barbets, jacamars, puffbirds, toucans, woodpeckers, and honeyguides form a natural unit. The honeyguides differ most, but Beecher ascribed the differences to specializations associated with their wax-eating (cerophagy) and brood parasitic habits. The skulls of jacamars "suggest their close alliance with the barbets" (p. 293).

Verheyen (1955c, 1961) reviewed the characters of the piciforms and added data from his own studies consisting mainly of skeletal measurements. He thought that the conclusions of Stresemann (1934) and of J. Steinbacher (1937) were correct and proposed the following classification:

Order Piciformes
  Suborder Galbuloidea
    Family Bucconidae
    Family Galbulidae
  Suborder Picoidea
    Family Ramphastidae
    Family Capitonidae
    Family Picidae (Picumninae, Picinae, Jynginae)
    Family Indicatoridae

Sibley (1956) confirmed the presence of an aftershaft in the jacamars and of a group of homologous barbs in the puffbirds, including *Malacoptila*. He concluded that the Bucconidae should be diagnosed as possessing an aftershaft, although it is vestigial in comparison with that of the Galbulidae.

Bock (in Bock and Miller 1959) analyzed the functional and morphological characteristics of the feet in certain groups. He proposed that the zygodactyl foot in the truly scansorial woodpeckers should be termed "ectropodactyl" because "toes two and three point forward, the fourth toe is thrust out to the . . . side at right angles . . . and the hallux usually . . . is functionless" (pp. 42–43). Bock argued that the zygodactyl foot is a perching adaptation, not a climbing adaptation, and that the same is true of the anisodactyl, syndactyl, and heterodactyl arrangements. These different patterns merely represent different ways to accomplish the same function. Bock agreed with G. Steinbacher (1935) that the differences among the foot types are phylogenetic rather than functional: "The several perching- or climbing-foot types evolved because of functional demands, but the morphological differences between the types of perching feet or between those of climbing feet are the result of the different ways that birds happened to adapt to these functional demands (multiple pathways) and cannot be explained on functional grounds" (p. 41). However, Bock disagreed with Steinbacher on the taxonomic value of foot types. He concluded (p. 42) that "although the morphological differences between the foot types serving one particular function (i.e., perching or climbing) cannot be explained on functional grounds and although the divergence between these birds may have occurred at the time the orders of birds evolved, the foot types are too rigidly tied to their function to provide reliable taxonomic characters."

Bock wrote that "there is little doubt that the Pici, the Psittaci, and the Cuculidae have all acquired their zygodactyl foot independently of one another" (p. 30). If this and his other conclusions are correct it also seems possible that the zygodactyl foot is a doubtful basis for the definition of the Piciformes. It seems especially appropriate to question the alliance of the jacamars and puffbirds (our Galbuliformes) to the Piciformes because the two groups have little in common other than their zygodactyl feet.

Goodwin (1964) reviewed the systematics of the barbets and agreed in most respects with Ripley (1945, 1946). He did not comment on the relationships to other groups.

Haffer (1968) reported similarities in the pattern of the wing and tail molt in jacamars and puffbirds, and supported their inclusion in the suborder Galbuloidea. Of the piciform groups the barbets most closely resemble the galbuliforms in their molt pattern.

Cottrell (1968) reviewed the genera of puffbirds and recommended the recognition of *Bucco*, *Malacoptila*, *Micromonacha*, *Nonnula*, *Hapaloptila*, *Monasa*, and *Chelidoptera*.

Zusi and Marshall (1970) examined the pterylosis, tongue, hyoid apparatus, and skull of several woodpeckers, including the Rufous-bellied Woodpecker (*Hypopicus hyperythrus*) of Asia. They concluded that *Hypopicus* is a *Dendrocopos*, although it apparently feeds in part like the sapsuckers (*Sphyrapicus*) and has a tongue "hair-tufted like a brush."

From a study of the ecology and behavior of Lewis' Woodpecker (*Asyndesmus lewis*) C. E. Bock (1970) concluded that this somewhat aberrant species is related to *Melanerpes*, especially to the Red-headed Woodpecker (*Melanerpes erythrocephalus*).

Short (1970) suggested, from plumage patterns and other aspects of morphology, that the African woodpecker genera *Campethera*, *Geocolaptes*, and *Dendropicos* are closely related to certain New World forms, e.g., *Colaptes*, *Veniliornis*, and *Piculus*.

Sibley and Ahlquist (1972) compared the starch gel electrophoretic patterns of the egg-white proteins of at least one species in each group of the "Piciformes," except the toucans. The patterns of barbets and woodpeckers were much alike, and those of puffbirds and jacamars showed "many similarities" to one another, but differed from those of the woodpeckers "in all aspects." The pattern of "*Indicator* differs from those of the other Piciformes" and there were no consistent similarities between the patterns of the piciforms and those of other groups. We concluded that the "barbets and woodpeckers seem to be closely allied" but that our evidence did not "support a close relationship between the honeyguides and the barbets." Also, "The Galbulidae, and perhaps the Bucconidae . . . may not be piciform. They may be closely allied to the Alcedinidae."

Jeikowski (1974) examined 305 wings of 32 species of the kingfisher genus *Halcyon* to study the transition between the two types of secondary pterylosis: eutaxy and diastataxy. He found it possible to reconstruct the process of transition by using the individual variation in *Halcyon monacha* and *H. princeps*. The process involves developmental shifts in the positions of the fifth secondary and its coverts. Both eutaxic and diastataxic individuals are found in the same species and the two wings of some individual birds may differ in the stage of the transitory process. Jeikowski concluded: "The mechanism responsible for the process of transformation remains entirely obscure. No external structural characteristics in *Halcyon* could be found to be correlated with diastataxy. The main result is: Regarding eutaxy as primordial it would be impossible to explain the dorsal transitory stages in *Halcyon*. On the contrary, eutaxy must be derived from diastataxy, the latter being the primary condition" (p.

179). Whatever may be the process, the condition of the fifth secondary is a doubtful basis for classification.

Feduccia and Martin (1976) reviewed the Eocene zygodactyl birds of North America and proposed that four extinct genera be placed in their new family, Primobucconidae, "affiliated with the Bucconidae." They suggested that "Primobucconids appear to have been the dominant small perching birds of the Eocene of North America" (p. 101). They speculated that "The order Piciformes probably arose in the New World and its forms occupied the 'perching' arboreal adaptive zone in the early Tertiary of North America when tropical and subtropical climates predominated. Later, the order spread to the Old World where the Miocene Zygodactylidae and the modern families Picidae, Capitonidae, and Indicatoridae are represented. . . . it was probably not until the mid-Tertiary that the passerines took over in North America as the predominant 'perching' group" (p. 110).

Swierczewski and Raikow (1981) made a cladistic analysis of the hind limb muscles of the traditional piciforms and proposed that the order Piciformes is monophyletic and composed of two branches: suborder Galbulae (Bucconidae, Galbulidae) and suborder Pici, which is further subdivided into two ` groups, (Capitonidae, Ramphastidae) and (Indicatoridae, Picidae). This arrangement of the Pici is generally congruent with the DNA hybridization evidence, although differing in several details.

Simpson and Cracraft (1981) made a cladistic analysis of several skeletal characters and agreed with the phylogeny of Swierczewski and Raikow (1981). Simpson and Cracraft hypothesized "that the piciforms constitute a monophyletic group on the basis of possessing a unique flexor tendon pattern of the hindlimb, a M. flexor hallucis longus with three heads of origin, zygodactyly, and a well-developed sehnenhalter [accessory articulating process, or tendonal groove] on the outer (IV) trochlea of the tarsometatarsus." They proposed the following classification (p. 493):

Order Piciformes
    Suborder Galbulae
        Family Bucconidae
        Family Galbulidae
    Suborder Pici
        Superfamily Ramphastoidea
        Family Capitonidae
        Family Ramphastidae
        Superfamily Picoidea
        Family Indicatoridae
        Family Picidae

Simpson and Cracraft (1981:491) questioned the monophyly of the Primobucconidae (Feduccia and Martin 1976) and the assignment of some of the fossil taxa to the Piciformes. They also doubted the inclusion of *Zygodactylus* in the Galbulae, and suggested placing "the Zygodactylidae as a basal member of the Pici."

Cracraft (1981) cited the studies of Swierczewski and Raikow and of Simpson and Cracraft in support of his "highly corroborated hypothesis of relationships" within the Piciformes.

Olson (1983) rebutted the arguments of Swierczewski and Raikow (1981) and of Simpson and Cracraft (1981) and argued for a polyphyletic origin for the traditional Piciformes. He claimed that "The structure of the zygodactyl foot in the Galbulae is very distinct from that in the Pici, and no unique shared derived characters of the tarsometatarsus have been demonstrated for these two taxa. The supposedly three-headed origin of M. flexor hallucis longus shared by the Galbulae and Pici is doubtfully homologous between the two groups, leaving only the Type VI deep flexor tendons as defining the order Piciformes. This condition is probably a convergent similarity. Evidence is presented supporting a close relationship between the Galbulae and the suborder Coracii and between the Pici and the Passeriformes. There are fewer character conflicts with this hypothesis than with the hypothesis that the Piciformes are monophyletic."

Olson (1983:130) presented his evidence in support of his belief that the Galbulae are "closely related to the rollers, or Coracii of Maurer and Raikow (1981), which includes the Coraciidae, Brachypteraciidae, and Leptosomidae. The Pici, on the other hand, I believe are more closely related to the Passeriformes. These observations are preliminary."

Raikow and Cracraft (1983) rejected Olson's hypothesis and reaffirmed their belief that "a monophyletic origin of the Piciformes remains the hypothesis of choice."

Short (1982) reviewed the biology, structure, behavior, zoogeography, systematics, and species of the Picidae of the world. He recognized "27 genera and 198 species, the latter representing 150 biogeographic species (which are superspecies plus those species that are not members of superspecies). The 32 superspecies that are treated contain 81 species. Thus nearly 41 percent of the 198 species are allospecies . . . of superspecies." Short synonymized 12 of the genera recognized by Peters (1948) and reduced 28 of the species of Peters to subspecies or synonyms. Short recognized 12 taxa (genera or species) not so treated by Peters. Short's classification of the Picidae follows (English names and genera added):

Jynginae, Wrynecks (*Jynx*)
Picumninae
  Picumnini, Piculets (*Picumnus, Sasia*)
  Nesoctitini, Antillean Piculet (*Nesoctites*)
Picinae, Woodpeckers
  Melanerpini (*Melanerpes, Sphyripicus, Xiphidiopicus*)
  Campetherini (*Campethera, Geocolaptes, Dendropicos, Picoides* including *Dendrocopos*)
  Colaptini (*Veniliornis, Piculus, Colaptes, Celeus*)
  Campephilini (*Dryocopus, Campephilus*)
  Picini (*Picus, ·Dinopium, Chrysocolaptes, Gecinulus, Sapheopipo, Blythipicus, Reinwardtipicus*)
  Meiglyptini (*Meiglyptes, Hemicircus, Mulleripicus*)

Buchholz (1986) described a fossil cavity and entrance hole preserved in a piece of petrified wood from the Eocene of Arizona which "even in details . . . is very close to recent cavities produced by representatives of the genus *Picoides*. It is . . . concluded that woodpeckers . . . must be at least of Eocene age." This places woodpeckers in the record ca. 40–50 MYA, although fossil bones of woodpeckers are known only back to the Miocene, less than 25 MYA. Of course, there is nothing in this fossil cavity that proves it was made by an ancestor of the Picidae; there may have been another lineage, now extinct, that made similar nesting cavities. However, if our dating calibration of $\Delta T_{50}H$ 1 = ca. 4–5 million years is correct for woodpeckers, their lineage may have branched from their closest living relatives more than 50 MYA. It is probable that this calibration does not apply to woodpeckers which begin to breed at age one year, but if the calibration is ca. Δ 1 = 2 million years, the piciform branch in our

UPGMA tree at Δ T$_{50}$H 26.3 would have been ca. 53 MYA. Speculation is cheap; facts are rare and costly.

Kitto and Wilson (1966) found that woodpeckers have an unusual soluble malate dehydrogenase (S-MDH) electrophoretic pattern which differs from that of other groups of birds. Avise and Aquadro (1987) showed that the woodpecker S-MDH pattern of three intensely staining bands also occurs in honeyguides, barbets, and toucans, in contrast to the typical avian pattern of "an intense major band with one or two much lighter anodic subbands." S-MDH has been assayed in 26 of the 27 orders recognized by Wetmore (1960) and in 16 of the passerine groups traditionally recognized as families. Except for the groups noted above all have the typical S-MDH pattern, including the jacamars, puffbirds, rollers, kingfishers, hornbills, motmots, wood-hoopoes, hoopoes, trogons, and colies. Avise and Aquadro concluded that the S-MDH evidence supports the arrangement proposed by Sibley and Ahlquist (1986).

S. M. Lanyon and Zink (1987) used starch-gel electrophoresis to compare 20 protein-coding loci among 14 genera of New World piciforms, 12 genera of galbuliforms, and *Momotus*. Their results were congruent with the DNA hybridization data in that the New World barbets and toucans form a clade that is the sister group of the woodpeckers, the jacamars and puffbirds form a clade that is the sister group of *Momotus*, and the jacamar-puffbird-*Momotus* clade is the sister group of the woodpecker-barbet-toucan clade.

The phylogenetic relationships of the barbets and toucans based on morphology, with comparisons to DNA-DNA hybridization, were examined by Prum (1988). Prum made a cladistic analysis of 32 morphological characters from the literature plus independent osteological characters. Although critical of our data, Prum concluded that his results were congruent with ours in most respects, noting that "The degree of congruence between morphology and the . . . DNA-DNA phylogeny of the ramphastoids is certainly among the greatest yet identified . . . for any avian group" (p. 336). Prum's classification places the toucans and barbets in the Ramphastidae and recognizes six subfamilies of barbets. *Trachyphonus*, *Calorhamphus*, and *Semnornis* are placed in monotypic subfamilies, and the toucans in the Ramphastinae. *Trachyphonus* is regarded as the sister group of the other ramphastids, and the Toucan Barbet (*Semnornis*) as the sister group of the toucans.

The DNA Hybridization Evidence (Figs. 42–50, 329–332, 353, 354, 358)

The Piciformes have long been thought to be one of the groups of "higher" non-passerines and it has often been suggested that they are related to the Passeriformes. It is surprising, therefore, to find that the DNA data indicate that the Piciformes are the descendants of what may be one of the oldest lineages in the avian tree and that they are far from the passerine stem. This is congruent with the record of the fossil woodpecker nest from the Eocene, noted above (Buchholz 1986).

The piciform lineage (parvclass Picae) branched from the coraciiform lineage (parvclass Coraciae) at Δ T$_{50}$H 26.3, and these diverged from the Turnices at Δ 27. It seems likely that these branches occurred in the upper Cretaceous.

The piciforms split into the barbet-toucan clade and the woodpecker-honeyguide clade at Δ 16.5. The honeyguides and woodpeckers diverged at Δ 11.0 (Fig. 358).

The barbets split into an Asian lineage and an African–New World lineage at Δ 12.8, and the New World barbet-toucan clade branched from the African barbets at Δ 11.5. The toucans and New World barbets diverged at Δ 6.1 and the New World barbet cluster retained the barbet morphology. However, such species as the Toucan Barbet (*Semnornis ramphastinus*) and the toucanets (*Aulacorhynchus*) are morphologically intermediate. For example, Burton (1984) concluded from a study of the head region that "It seems reasonable simply to regard toucans as a specialized group of barbets that have arisen and radiated in South America," and Short (1985) stated that "Toucans effectively are large, specialized, tooth-billed barbets." These authors were unable to detect that the toucans and New World barbets are more closely related to one another than the New World barbets are to the Old World barbets.

The melting curves provide a relatively uncomplicated picture of the relationships among the subunits of the Picae, perhaps because there are no significant differences in rates of DNA evolution along any of the branches. Figs. 42 and 43 (*Picoides*, same experiment) show the relationships between the woodpecker tracer and several other groups including barbets, jacamars, puffbirds, rollers, kingfishers, motmots, bee-eaters, hornbills, swifts, hummingbirds, mousebirds, cuckoos, passerines, and a hoopoe. It is clear that the passerines are not the closest relatives of the woodpeckers and that the woodpeckers are about equidistant from most of the groups listed.

Fig. 44 (*Indicator*) shows that the woodpeckers are closer to the honeyguides than are the barbets and toucans. There may, or may not, be any significance to the slightly closer position of the toucan and New World barbet curves to the tracer, compared with the curves of the Old World barbets. This might be caused by a small rate difference, or by experimental differences.

Fig. 45 (*Megalaima*) includes about the same taxa as in Fig. 44, from the viewpoint of an Asian barbet. The other barbets and toucans are slightly closer to *Megalaima* than are the honeyguide and the woodpecker.

Fig. 46 (*Pteroglossus*) views the piciform world from the toucan position. Other toucans and the New World barbets cluster closest to *Pteroglossus*, the African barbets (*Lybius, Tricholaema*) are next in line, the Asian barbet (*Megalaima*) is next, and the honeyguide and woodpecker are most distant. This set of curves tells the story of the toucan-New World barbet alliance. The distances are so great and the experiment was of such high quality that there can be no doubt about the close relationship between the Ramphastinae and Capitoninae. Toucans are New World barbets with big bills. The evolution of the large bills has been accompanied by other adaptive adjustments, including nesting in natural tree cavities or old woodpecker holes because they are unable to dig their own nest cavities (Skutch 1985).

Figs. 47–49 (*Galbula*) show that the jacamars are closest to the puffbirds, but the divergence between them was not recent. The $\Delta T_{50}H$ value of the branch is 17.5, and this large distance is indicated by the relative positions of the melting curves in Figs. 47–50. These four figures include representatives of many other non-passerine groups and show that the jacamars and puffbirds have no close living relatives, but are closest to one another. The large distances among the genera of puffbirds in Fig. 50 attests to their long evolutionary history. There is no evidence in the melting curves for a close relationship between the Piciformes and Galbuliformes. Several groups appear to be closer to the Galbuliformes than the Piciformes, and our classification reflects this evidence.

Fig. 329, the FITCH tree, suggests that the galbuliforms, trogons, and rollers may have

Hornbills, Hoopoes, Trogons, Rollers, Motmots, Todies, Kingfishers, and Bee-eaters

Parvclass Coraciae
  Superorder Bucerotimorphae
    Order BUCEROTIFORMES
        Family Bucerotidae: Typical Hornbills
        Family Bucorvidae: Ground-Hornbills
    Order UPUPIFORMES
      Infraorder Upupides
        Family Upupidae: Hoopoes
      Infraorder Phoeniculides
        Family Phoeniculidae: Woodhoopoes
        Family Rhinopomastidae: Scimitar-bills
  Superorder Coraciimorphae
    Order TROGONIFORMES
        Family Trogonidae
          Subfamily Apaloderminae: African Trogons
          Subfamily Trogoninae
            Tribe Trogonini: New World Trogons
            Tribe Harpactini: Asian Trogons
    Order CORACIIFORMES
      Suborder Coracii
        Superfamily Coracioidea
        Family Coraciidae: Typical Rollers
        Family Brachypteraciidae: Ground-Rollers (*inc. sedis*)
        Superfamily Leptosomoidea
        Family Leptosomidae: Courol or Cuckoo-Roller
      Suborder Alcedini
       Infraorder Alcedinides
        Parvorder Momotida
          Family Momotidae: Motmots
        Parvorder Todida
          Family Todidae: Todies
        Parvorder Alcedinida

Family Alcedinidae: Alcedinid Kingfishers
Parvorder Cerylida
Superfamily Dacelonoidea
Family Dacelonidae: Dacelonid Kingfishers
Superfamily Ceryloidea
Family Cerylidae: Cerylid Kingfishers
Infraorder Meropides
Family Meropidae: Bee-eaters

Our Bucerotimorphae and Coraciimorphae include the same groups that Wetmore (1960) placed in his Coraciiformes plus Trogoniformes. This section includes the hornbills, hoopoes, rollers, motmots, todies, kingfishers, and bee-eaters. The trogons are treated in the following section.

Few groups of birds are as morphologically heterogeneous as the members of the Bucerotiformes and Coraciiformes. It is difficult to find many characters that apply to all of them, but they have been placed together, or close to one another, in most classifications. Except in the trogons the palate is desmognathous. The pelvic muscle formula is AXY (Garrod 1873d) except in the Alcedinidae, in which it is AX. The feet vary but usually have three toes directed forward and a hallux. The kingfisher genera *Ceyx* and *Alcedo* include species in which the second toe is vestigial or absent. Basipterygoid processes absent or rudimentary; hypotarsus complex; syrinx tracheo-bronchial or, in *Leptosomus*, bronchial. Nest in holes; young nidicolous; gymnopaedic (except *Upupa*). The trogons differ in several of these characters.

Family BUCEROTIDAE: 8/54. Family BUCORVIDAE: 1/2. Bucerotid hornbills occur in Africa, India, Philippines, Celebes, Malaysia, Indonesia, New Guinea, Bismarck Archipelago, and the Solomon Islands. The Ground-Hornbills (*Bucorvus*) occur over most of sub-Saharan Africa. In all hornbills the bill is large, often with a casque composed of cancellous bone (except *Rhinoplax*, wherein solid), a distinct area on the skull supports special tissue for growing the keratin sheath of the bill; holorhinal, impervious nares; tongue short, barbed at base; basipterygoid processes present but not reaching pterygoid; atlas and axis fused; 14 cervical vertebrae in Bucerotidae, 15 in Bucorvidae; 8 complete ribs; 2nd and 4th toes joined (syndactyl) to 3rd; long, flattened "eyelashes" on upper eyelid; syrinx tracheo-bronchial with one pair of syringeal muscles; subcutaneous pneumaticity highly developed and appendicular skeleton pneumatic to the terminal phalanges but not the dorsal vertebrae, ribs, sternum, scapula or furcula; cervicocephalic and pulmonary air-sac systems joined; oil gland tufted, distinctly bilobed; no caeca; median division of kidney lacking; no aftershaft; no down; eutaxic; 11 primaries according to Gadow (1892), 10 *fide* W. DeW. Miller (1924a) and Sanft (1960); 10 rectrices; carotids in *Bucorvus* replaced by fibrous cords and carotid function assumed by other vessels, not homologous to the carotids in other birds; only left carotid in other genera; plumages have only melanins, lack colored pigments; bill, casque, bare facial skin, feet, and eyes variously and brightly colored; eggs oval, with pitted shell; brood patch feathered; except in *Bucorvus*, the female incubates and broods the young in a nest hole that is walled in with mud by the male, who feeds the female and young through a narrow opening.

Family UPUPIDAE: 1/2. The hoopoes (*Upupa epops* and *U. africana*) are sometimes considered races of a single species. Hoopoes occur in Europe, Asia, Malaysia, Africa, and Madagascar. They have a short, slender tarsus with scutes before and behind; 2nd toe free from 3rd; no caeca; 10 primaries; 10 rectrices; bill long, slender, curved; tongue short, without basal barbs; oil gland tufted, distinctly bilobed; aftershaft absent or rudimentary; flexor tendons Type 7; nostrils "pseudo-holorhinal" (Beddard 1898a:223), impervious; 14 cervical vertebrae; left carotid; no vomer; erectile crest; no metallic gloss to feathers; no colored plumage pigments; oil gland of brooding female emits a foul-smelling blackish-brown oil that can be sprayed in defense; eggs oval with pitted shell; nestling with thick down.

Family PHOENICULIDAE: 1/5. The species of *Phoeniculus* are confined to Africa. The woodhoopoes share some characters with *Upupa*, but the nostrils are elongate and operculate; tail long, graduated; no crest; metallic plumage colors; oil gland small, tufted, single-lobed; brooding female produces a foul-smelling oil-gland secretion as in *Upupa*.

Family RHINOPOMASTIDAE: 1/3. The species of *Rhinopomastus* are confined to Africa. The anatomy of the scimitar-bills is not well known, but they apparently share many characters with the woodhoopoes. Bill strongly decurved; skull less robust than in *Phoeniculus*; oil gland as in *Phoeniculus*.

Family TROGONIDAE: 6/39. See following section.

Family CORACIIDAE: 2/12. Typical rollers occur in Africa; southern Europe; Arabia; central, southern, and eastern Asia; Korea; Indonesia; Australia; New Guinea; Bismarck Archipelago; and the Feni Islands in the northern Solomons. Bill medium length, stout, with terminal hook; vomer narrow; long, anterior, tarsal scutes; nares holorhinal, impervious; two carotids; long caeca; diastataxic; aftershaft present; oil gland naked, flattened, indistinctly bilobed.

Family BRACHYPTERACIIDAE: 3/5. The ground-rollers are confined to Madagascar. We lack DNA of this group. Large, ground-dwellers; nails of 1st and 4th toes turned outward, those of 2nd and 3rd toes are turned inward. Relationships uncertain, may be a subfamily of the Coraciidae; oil gland as in Coraciidae.

Family LEPTOSOMIDAE: 1/1. The Cuckoo-Roller, or Courol, occurs on Madagascar, Grand Comoro, Mayotte, and Anjouan islands. Short-legged, insectivorous, tree-dwellers; bronchial syrinx; slit-like nostrils; powder downs in two patches in the lumbar region, between dorsal and femoral feather tracts (Sclater 1865b:682); oil gland naked, indistinctly bilobed; 10 primaries; 12 secondaries; 12 rectrices; large aftershaft on body feathers; widely spread 4th toe; sexually dimorphic.

Family MOMOTIDAE: 6/9. The motmots occur in the neotropics from Mexico to northern Argentina. Tomia of maxilla and mandible serrate; no caeca; small vomer; oil gland flattened, distinctly bilobed, naked or minutely tufted; small aftershaft; 11 primaries; eutaxic; 10 rectrices, 12 in *Momotus*, middle pair longest and spatulate-tipped in many species; no down in adults; at least two metasternal notches closed. Nest in hole in earthen bank or, rarely, level ground; 2–4 white eggs; nidicolous, naked young.

Family TODIDAE: 1/5. Todies occur on the Caribbean islands of Cuba, Hispaniola, Jamaica, and Puerto Rico. Small birds with bright green dorsum, red throat; long, flat bill, tomia finely serrate; tongue long; caeca with expanded ends; oil gland indistinctly bilobed, tufted; eutaxic; 10 primaries. Nest in burrow in bank; 2–3 white eggs; nidicolous, naked young.

The kingfishers have pelvic muscle formula AX; no vomer; no caeca; no aftershaft; usually 11 primaries, 10 in *Alcedo*; 12 rectrices except *Tanysiptera* with 10; two carotids; oil gland bilobed and tufted except naked in *Tanysiptera*; nestlings look spiny because the developing feathers retain their sheaths. The following three families of kingfishers have often been recognized as subfamilies, e.g., Peters (1945).

Family ALCEDINIDAE: 3/24. The alcedinid kingfishers occur in Africa, Madagascar, Europe, Asia, Indonesia, New Guinea, Solomon Islands, and northern Australia. The included genera are *Alcedo*, *Ceyx*, and *Ispidina*.

Family DACELONIDAE: 12/61. The dacelonid kingfishers occur in Africa, Yemen, India, Sri Lanka, southern China, Philippines, southeast Asia, Indonesia, New Guinea, Australia, New Zealand, and southwest Pacific islands including Samoa, Tahiti, Marquesas. The genera of dacelonids are *Lacedo*, *Dacelo*, *Clytoceyx*, *Melidora*, *Todirhamphus*, *Syma*, *Cittura*, *Pelargopsis*, *Halcyon*, *Caridonax*, *Actenoides*, and *Tanysiptera*.

Family CERYLIDAE: 3/9. The cerylid kingfishers consist of the genera *Ceryle*, *Megaceryle*, and *Chloroceryle*. *Chloroceryle* (4 species), *Megaceryle alcyon*, and *M. torquata* occur in the New World; *Ceryle lugubris*, *maxima*, and *rudis* occur in southern and eastern Asia or Africa.

Family MEROPIDAE: 3/26. Bee-eaters occur in Africa and from southern Europe (Spain, France, Italy, Rumania) across southern Eurasia to the Philippines, Australasia, and Indonesia. Syndactyl; holorhinal; 14 cervical vertebrae; 4 pairs of complete ribs; left carotid only, except *Nyctiornis* with two; two lateral sternal notches; 10–11 primaries; 12 rectrices; eutaxic; small aftershaft; long caeca; bill long; oil gland indistinctly bilobed, naked; plumage colorful, sexes alike; nest in hole in bank or level ground; nidicolous, naked young, develop "spiny" feathers as do kingfishers.

Historical Review of the Classification

Linnaeus (1758) placed the coraciiforms he knew about in his order Picae, although not together. *Upupa* was with *Certhia* because of their long, slender bills, and *Coracias* was next to the starlings and *Oriolus*. However, *Buceros*, *Alcedo*, *Merops*, and *Todus* were allied as having Pedibus gressoriis; thus the similar foot structure formed an early basis for the group.

In the order "Ambulatores" of his bill-foot classification, Illiger (1811) placed the kingfishers and bee-eaters in the "Angulirostres," the Eurasian Hoopoe with the Wallcreeper (*Tichodroma*) and the sunbirds in the "Tenuirostres," the hornbills in the "Dentirostres," and *Coracias* with *Corvus*, *Paradisaea*, and others, also in the Dentirostres.

Temminck (1820–40) adopted a scheme similar to that of Illiger, and L'Herminier (1827) listed the rollers, bee-eaters, kingfishers, hornbills, and hoopoes in sequence following the toucans and woodpeckers.

Nitzsch (1840) included the coraciiforms in his order Picariae. His Todidae included the rollers, motmots, todies, and jacamars, followed by the Cuculinae (cuckoos, honeyguides, trogons), the Picinae (puffbirds, barbets, toucans, woodpeckers), Psittacinae (parrots), Lipoglossae (hornbills, hoopoes, kingfishers), and the Amphibolae (turacos, mousebirds, Hoatzin). Thus, the tendency to associate these taxa began early, although they were divided in various ways and mixed with the piciforms and other groups.

Gray (1844–49) grouped the rollers, todies, motmots, kingfishers, and bee-eaters with the broadbills, trogons, puffbirds, and jacamars; *Upupa* with the curve-billed birds of paradise *Epimachus* (sicklebills), and the hornbills with the Hoatzin, turacos, and colies.

Todus was assigned to the Tyrannidae by Cabanis (1847), but the rollers, hoopoes, bee-eaters, kingfishers, and hornbills (plus the broadbills and frogmouths) were included in his Coraciidae.

In his review of the woodhoopoes (*Phoeniculus*), Strickland (1843) concluded that *Irrisor* was the correct generic name, and it was used in many subsequent publications. He compared the woodhoopoes with *Upupa* (beaks, feet, plumage) and concluded that the two genera are related and should be assigned to two subfamilies in the Upupidae. He "conjectured that the Upupidae are allied in one direction by means of *Epimachus* or *Astrapia* to the Paradiseidae, and in another by *Merops* to the Alcedinidae. . . . in a third direction they are perhaps connected through *Lamprotornis* with the Corvidae" (p. 243). It would be difficult to condense more nonsense into this many words; obviously Strickland was looking at superficial similarities from a pre-Darwinian viewpoint. However, by allying the starling *Lamprotornis* with the Corvidae, Strickland may have contributed to the traditional association between the starlings and the corvines.

Sclater (1865b) reviewed what was known about *Leptosomus* and described its pterylosis, skeleton, tongue, and feet. He noted the unusual slit-like nostrils, which are shaped like those of *Eurystomus* but which, in *Leptosomus*, are located near the tip of the bill, not at the base. He noted the other features listed above, including the unusual powder downs on each side of the rump. He found the sternum not especially similar to that of *Coracias* but neither is it "in any respect more like that of the Cuculidae" (p. 161). The feet differ from those of cuckoos, puffbirds, and other zygodactyl groups although the fourth toe tends to extend "laterally, rather more behind than in front." He recommended that *Leptosomus* be removed from the Cuculidae and placed near the Coraciidae in its own family, and thought that *Brachypteracias* "may be the missing link which connects *Leptosomus* with the Coraciidae" (p. 163).

In his "Coccygomorphae" Huxley (1867) included, in sequence, the Coliidae, Musophagidae, Cuculidae, Bucconidae, Ramphastidae, Capitonidae, Galbulidae, Alcedinidae, Bucerotidae, Upupidae, Meropidae, Momotidae, Coraciidae, and Trogonidae.

Carus (1868) departed little from Huxley's arrangement but Sundevall (1872, see 1889) distributed the members of Huxley's Coccygomorphae between two orders and among several cohorts.

Garrod (1874a) included the hoopoes, hornbills, and kingfishers in the Piciformes, and the bee-eaters, rollers, motmots, and todies in the Passeriformes.

Cunningham (1870) compared the neck muscles, viscera, oil gland, tongue, and orbital region of the skull in three kingfishers, *Ceryle torquata*, *Dacelo gigas*, and *Alcedo atthis*. In most of the characters the three differed; *Ceryle* and *Alcedo* were alike in their tongues and shape of the lachrymal bone.

In his monograph of the kingfishers Sharpe (1868–71) suggested that the Alcedinidae are related to the Todidae through *Myioceyx*, to the Bucerotidae via *Dacelo* and *Melidora*, and to the Meropidae through *Tanysiptera*. This is another example of muddled thinking about the significance of morphological similarities as indices to relationships.

According to Sclater (1872), *Todus* is closest to the small Tody-Motmot (*Hylomanes momotula*), and also closely allied to the kingfishers. Here, again, is an example of naming a single species in one clade as the closest relative of the members of another clade.

From skeletal evidence Murie (1872b) considered the motmots to be closely related to the todies, next most closely related to the kingfishers, and less closely related to the rollers. He believed the todies to be closest to the motmots, next to the kingfishers, then the rollers, and, finally, the bee-eaters. Murie (1972c) recommended that the Todidae be placed next to the Momotidae and Alcedinidae. Although *Todus* has a desmognathous palate Murie thought that it has many passerine features in its skeleton.

According to Murie (1873:181) it was Gould who "originally suggested the relationship of the Hoopoes to the Hornbills, an idea which took root and fructified under its foster-parent, Mr. Blyth." Murie added "additional data, structural and otherwise" (p. 191) on this question and examined the pterylosis and other characters of the hoopoes, woodhoopoes, scimitar-bills, and various other taxa that had been considered as possible relatives. Murie dismissed Sundevall's alliance of the hoopoes with the larks, and other proposals relating hoopoes to creepers (*Certhia*), sunbirds, starlings, crows, and birds of paradise. Nor did he find evidence for a relationship between hoopoes and bee-eaters, kingfishers, rollers, and motmots, although "*Merops* and *Alcedo* offer more than a passing likeness" (p. 205). Murie concluded that the hoopoes are most closely related to the hornbills and that the small hornbills (e.g., *Tockus*) show the greatest resemblances to the hoopoes. He suggested that the Tertiary fossil "*Cryptornis antiquus* (Gervais) . . . discovered in the gypsum near Paris" (p. 206) is the possible link between *Upupa* and the hornbills. Murie agreed with "Strickland's juxtaposition of *Upupa* and *Irrisor*" (*Phoeniculus*) and stated that "the Irrisoridae contain two . . . genera, *Irrisor* and *Rhinopomastus*" (p. 207).

In the ground-hornbills (*Bucorvus*) the carotids are reduced to fibrous imperforate cords, and their function as blood vessels has been assumed by the enlarged "comes nervi vagi" (Garrod 1876a, Ottley 1879).

Garrod (1878a) placed the motmots in his order Piciformes, which included the hornbills, kingfishers, todies, and barbets, as well as the woodpeckers. In this assemblage he believed that the todies are closest to the motmots, basing his arrangement on the lack of colic caeca in the motmots (except *Momotus*), which also have a tufted oil gland—characters that separate them from the rollers, which Garrod placed in the Passeriformes.

The coraciiforms were grouped with the colies, *Podargus*, and *Steatornis* in Sclater's (1880b) suborder Anisodactylae of his order Picariae. In Stejneger's (1885) classification the Picariae contained eight superfamilies. The superfamily Coracoideae included the nightjars, rollers, and *Leptosomus*; the Colioideae contained the colies; the Alcedinoideae was composed of the bee-eaters, todies, motmots, kingfishers, and hornbills, and the Upupoideae the hoopoes and woodhoopoes.

Forbes (1880d) dissected the Courol (*Leptosomus*) and compared its structure with those of many other groups. The foot and deep flexor tendons are like those of *Coracias*, not as in the cuckoos, parrots, or piciforms. *Leptosomus* also agreed with the rollers in pterylosis, lack of an ambiens, and other characters. However, *Leptosomus* differs from *Coracias* in syringeal structure and the presence of powder downs. Forbes concluded that the Courol is closest to the typical rollers.

Forbes (1882c) dissected several specimens of *Todus* and examined the usual characters. He corrected several of the observations of Nitzsch and Murie, and listed 18 differences between todies and motmots. He disagreed with "the proposition that the Todies are more closely related to the Motmots than to any other group" (p. 449) and concluded "that *Todus* is a much isolated form, with affinities to both the Passeriformes and Piciformes of Garrod" and that it should be placed in "a group *Todiformes*, equivalent to Passer-, Pici-, and Cypseliformes, for the sole reception of the genus *Todus*." Although specialized, this genus "represents more nearly than other existing forms the common stock from which all the living groups of Anomalogonatous birds have been derived" (p. 450). This seems like a heavy burden for a small bird restricted to a few islands in the West Indies.

Shufeldt (1884) described the skeleton of the Belted Kingfisher (*Megaceryle alcyon*) of North America and reviewed the classification of the "order Picariae," which he considered to be an unnatural group.

"The Bee-eaters must certainly be ranged next to the Rollers, to which they are very closely allied, and they are also nearly allied to the Jacamars, as also, but in a less degree, to the Kingfishers, Motmots, Hoopers [sic], and Hornbills" (Dresser 1884–86:xi). In support of this opinion Dresser quoted from Beddard's notes on pterylography, osteology, and myology. In 1893 Dresser restated his view that the rollers are allied to the bee-eaters and jacamars, again quoting from Beddard's notes on anatomy.

Fürbringer's order "Coracornithes" (1888) contained four suborders. In the suborder Halcyoniformes were the kingfishers, hoopoes, hornbills, and bee-eaters. The motmots and todies were in an intermediate gens, Todi, and the Coraciiformes contained the rollers, *Leptosomus*, caprimulgiforms, and owls. The Coccygiformes included the cuckoos and turacos, and the piciforms, passerines, swifts, hummingbirds, colies and trogons were placed in the Pico-Passeriformes.

The viscera, syringes, and muscles of several hornbills were examined by Beddard (1889c). He stated that the only birds to which the hornbills "might be supposed to be allied . . . are the Colies and Caprimulgidae; the presence of the ligament uniting the biceps to the tensor patagii in *Bucorvus* is no doubt the representative of the muscular slip existing in the former groups. . . . *Podargus* has the same great development of muscular fibres in the horizontal septum attached to the gizzard that has been recorded above in the Hornbills" (p. 593).

Seebohm's (1890a–c) classification contained much nonsense due to his attempt to adhere to an arbitrary set of defining characters. The hoopoes were placed in the order Pico-Passeres while the kingfishers, rollers, hornbills, etc., were allied with the goatsuckers and swifts in the Picariae. The New World vultures were assigned to the subclass Coraciiformes, next to the Bucerotes, because of the arrangment of the flexor tendons! In 1895 Seebohm excluded the cathartine vultures from his Coraciiformes and transferred the hoopoes to the Cuculiformes.

Sclater (1890) noted the eutaxic wing in the "Anisodactylous Picarians" and listed *Colius, Buceros, Upupa, Merops, Todus, Podargus, Steatornis*, and *Coracias* as being quintocubital (eutaxic). However, he found "a singular anomaly . . . in the Alcedinidae" in which the fifth secondary is "*present* in *Alcedo ispida, Cittura sanguirensis*, and *Ceryle americana*, but *absent* in *Halcyon vagans* and *H. chloris*. What is still more remarkable, it seems to be absent in *Ceryle alcyon*, though it is certainly present in a specimen of *C. americana* now before me" (p. 80). Thus, a character that had been thought to be consistent within major groups proved to be variable within a genus.

The Coraciiformes of Sharpe (1891) was a large assemblage that contained the usual groups plus the caprimulgiforms, swifts, hummingbirds, and colies. In his classification the suborder Leptosomati was next to the Podargi, followed by the Coraciae, Halcyones, Bucerotes, Upupae, Meropes, Momoti, and Todi.

Gadow's (1892) Coraciiformes included the owls, goatsuckers, swifts, hummingbirds, colies, trogons, rollers, motmots, kingfishers, bee-eaters, hoopoes, and hornbills. His 1893 arrangement was essentially the same, but it included the Pici as an additional suborder of the Coraciiformes. In the 1892 list the Pici were in the Passeriformes.

In the *Catalogue of Birds*, volumes 16 (Salvin and Hartert 1892), 17 (Sharpe and Ogilvie-Grant 1892), 18 (Hargitt 1890), and 19 (Sclater and Shelley 1891) contained the numerous subdivisions of the "Order Picariae." Volumes 16 and 17 included the Bucerotiformes and Coraciiformes of our classification.

According to the introductory comments on page 1 of volume 16, the classification adopted for the "Picariae" in the *Catalogue* was based on that of Sclater (1880b) which was viewed as an improvement on that of Garrod (1874a). The subdivisions were those defined by Seebohm (1890a). The writers (presumably Salvin and Hartert) commented: "We . . . follow Mr. Sclater . . . in reviving the term 'Picariae' for the next order, which would comprise the *Cypseli* (*Macrochires*), *Anisodactyli*, *Heterodactyli*, *Scansores*, and *Coccyges*, although we are not aware that the order with these wide limits has been or can be diagnosed. To Mr. Seebohm . . . we are much indebted for . . . defining the divisions in the following scheme. The adoption of an 'order of Picarians' is, at best, a provisional measure, and if this 'order' be thought to be inadmissible, then the divisions proposed by Mr. Seebohm would have to rank as separate orders, and might be arranged in a sequence more in conformity with what are, at present, considered their natural affinities."

The resulting classification follows:

Order Picariae
  (Anisodactyli and Pamprodactyli)
  Suborder Upupae
    Family Upupidae: Hoopoes
    Family Irrisoridae: Woodhoopoes, Scimitar-bills
  Suborder Trochili: Hummingbirds
  Suborder Coraciae
    Family Cypselidae: Swifts
    Family Caprimulgidae: Goatsuckers
    Family Podargidae: Frogmouths
    Family Steatornithidae: Oilbird
    Family Leptosomatidae: Cuckoo-Roller or Courol
    Family Coraciidae: Ground-Rollers, Rollers
    Family Meropidae: Bee-eaters
  Suborder Halcyones
    Family Alcedinidae: Kingfishers
    Family Momotidae: Motmots
    Family Todidae: Todies
    Family Coliidae: Colies
  Suborder Bucerotes
    Family Bucerotidae: Hornbills
  (Heterodactyli)
  Suborder Trogones
    Family Trogonidae: Trogons
  (Zygodactyli)

Suborder Scansores: Woodpeckers, Honeyguides, Barbets, Toucans, Jacamars, Puffbirds
Suborder Coccyges: Cuckoos, Turacos

There was no morphological diagnosis of the Picariae, but the three major subgroups were based on the arrangement of the toes (Anisodactyli and Pamprodactyli; Heterodactyli; Zygodactyli), and the suborders on the flexor tendons, palate, pterylosis, and ambiens. The association of these groups became a feature of most subsequent classifications, although the categorical names and ranks were often changed.

In the kingfishers, Beddard (1896c) examined the pterylosis, wing tendons, expansor secundariorum, fifth secondary, tensor patagii brevis, biventer link of the cervical musculature, and condition of the oil gland. He noted that "The family Alcedinidae shows more structural variation . . . than any other family of Picarian Birds" and that this diversity precluded the "subdivision of the family, at least without further facts." However, in all species he examined, the pelvic muscle formula was AX and the syrinx was tracheo-bronchial, but the condition of the fifth secondary was variable and he noted "the somewhat disappointing fact that no particular results seem to be obtainable from a comparison of the quintocubital with the aquintocubital genera" (p. 606).

Beddard (1898a) included the hornbills, hoopoes, and scimitar-bills in his Bucerotes. In the Coraciae he placed the rollers, Cuckoo-Roller, bee-eaters, motmots, todies, and jacamars. The kingfishers were assigned to the Alcedines, between the Pici and the Colii. Thus, the jacamars (Galbulidae) were placed with the coraciiforms while the puffbirds (Bucconidae) were allied with the Pici. "The *skull* of the Galbulidae is very like that of the Bucconidae" (p. 214).

Beddard (1901b) studied the skeleton of the ground-hornbills (*Bucorvus*) and compared it with those of other hornbills, but he did not comment concerning the relationships of the Bucerotidae.

The anatomy of the kingfishers, including the presence (eutaxy) or absence (diastataxy) of the fifth secondary, was studied by Mitchell (1901c). In the 17 species he examined some were eutaxic, some diastataxic, some intermediate. He concluded that these conditions, "as in the Columbidae . . . cannot be regarded as fundamental characters in . . . classification. Both conditions occur, scattered as it were indiscriminately within the confines of the group, and sometimes even within . . . a genus" (p. 102). Mitchell also examined the myology of several kingfishers, seeking correlations between the condition of the fifth secondary and variations in musculature. In the arrangement of the deep flexor tendons there are at least 10 variations. He found correlations between the tendon patterns and the condition of the fifth secondary in a general way that he thought were due to "changes which may be summed up as specialization. There is no *rigid* correlation between the degrees of specialization of different organs in the same species . . . but there is a general correlation, so that if any species be far advanced in one organ it is more likely to be far advanced in other organs" (p. 121). Regardless of the validity of Mitchell's explanation, it seems clear that the condition of the fifth secondary is not a firm basis for the classification of the higher categories.

Fürbringer (1902) modified his earlier (1888) classification of the "order Coracornithes" by recognizing three suborders: Coccygiformes (turacos, cuckoos), Pico-Passeriformes (piciforms, passerines, swifts, hummingbirds, colies, trogons), and Coraciiformes (coraciiforms, caprimulgiforms, owls).

Shufeldt (1903b) reviewed the classification of the kingfishers and compared their skeleton with those of other groups. He thought that the kingfishers "are most nearly related to the Galbulidae" (p. 722) but he also found resemblances to the Roadrunner (*Geococcyx californianus*: Cuculiformes) and to the bee-eaters (Meropidae: Coraciiformes). Shufeldt (1904b) erected the supersuborders Coraciiformes (Cuckoo-Roller, rollers) and Halcyoniformes (other coraciiforms), but did not comment on their relationships to other groups.

Knowlton (1909) recognized a cumbersome assemblage as his "Coraciiformes," including the traditional coraciiforms, plus the owls, goatsuckers, swifts, hummingbirds, colies, trogons, and piciforms.

Chandler (1916) accepted Knowlton's (1909) Coraciiformes, but he was perplexed in assessing relationships among the included groups on the basis of feather structure. He found that the remiges of *Coracias*, *Momotus*, and *Merops* are similar to one another, but those of the kingfishers differ from them. *Upupa* and *Irrisor* (*Phoeniculus*) were similar and could be distinguished from the other coraciiforms. Similarly, the hornbills were similar to one another and differed from other groups. The down feathers of rollers, bee-eaters, motmots, and woodhoopoes were similar. The down of kingfishers differed somewhat, but the downy barbules of the hornbills have a "peculiar and unusual appearance." Chandler did not speculate on the relationships among the coraciiform groups but merely concluded that "the Coraciidae and near allies, the Striges, Caprimulgi, Bucerotidae and Cypselidae [swifts], have types of feathers which are to be regarded as independent offshoots from the main line of evolution" (p. 378). Freely translated, this seems to mean that feather structure is useless for assessing higher category relationships.

The purposes of W. DeW. Miller's (1912) study of the kingfishers were "to establish the proper subfamily divisions of the Alcedinidae" and to determine "the characters and relationships of the three genera currently united under *Ceryle*" (p. 239). He examined skins and skeletons and reviewed the proposed classifications of the group. He advocated splitting *Ceryle* into *Ceryle*, *Megaceryle*, and *Chloroceryle*, and the recognition of three subfamilies, Cerylinae, Alcedininae, and Dacelinae. Miller (1915) found the rollers (*Coracias*, *Eurystomus*) to be diastataxic, not eutaxic, as had been stated by Gadow and Beddard. He noted that the ground-roller "*Corapitta*" (*Atelornis*) *pittoides* is "apparently eutaxic" and that "*Leptosoma* has not been investigated" (p. 131).

Miller (1920) reviewed the nomenclature and characters of the ceryline kingfishers and again recommended the recognition of three genera. He examined the deep plantar tendons in several species and found points of agreement and disagreement with Mitchell (1901c). Miller used the condition of the fifth secondary as a major character in his key to the genera of Cerylinae, with *Megaceryle* and *Ceryle* being diastataxic and *Chloroceryle* eutaxic. Miller (1924a) recorded the kingfishers as one of the groups with both eutaxic and diastataxic species; the rollers (including ground-rollers and the Cuckoo-Roller) as diastataxic; and the bee-eaters, motmots, todies, hornbills, and hoopoes as eutaxic.

Miller (1924a) found only 10 primaries (and no remicle) in the hornbills although Gadow (1892:252) had reported 11. The remicle is present in the kingfishers, but the covert of the 11th primary has been lost. The kingfishers, rollers, and motmots have 10 primaries plus the remicle; in the Meropidae Miller noted "11th very vestigial; 10 in Meropinae." The todies, hornbills, and hoopoes have 10 functional primaries and no remicle. The motmots, "except

Momotus, have normally but ten rectrices. Several exceptions, however, have been noted and evidently the number of tail-feathers in some of the genera at least is an unstable character. The exceptional specimen of *Baryphthengus ruficapillus* had six rectrices on one side of the tail (the other side being imperfect). A skin of *B. (Urospatha) martii semirufa* has six rectrices on one side, five on the other . . . twenty-two have ten rectrices, one has eleven . . . and one has twelve" (pp. 319–320).

Miller (1924b) found an aftershaft in some kingfishers, none in others, and absent in *Upupa* but present in *Phoeniculus*. It is also absent in the hornbills but present in the coraciiforms. The presence of an aftershaft is "unquestionably a primitive character" and its reduction or loss is a sign of specialization, according to Miller.

Friedmann (1930) called attention to the variations in the caudal molt of certain coraciiforms, colies, and piciforms. The kingfishers apparently have a centrifugal tail molt. The Phoeniculidae seem to have the condition reported in woodpeckers, i.e., the "tail molt is centrifugal beginning with the next to the middle pair and proceeding outward, the middle pair being shed after the fourth pair" (p. 4). In the one bee-eater examined the tail molt was irregular and in hornbills the females drop all of the rectrices simultaneously while confined in the nest chamber. In male hornbills of some species the tail molt is regularly centrifugal, in others somewhat irregularly so. As noted by Wetmore (1914), the tail molt in the Helmeted Hornbill (*Buceros vigil*) is exceptional in that only one feather of the central pair is developed at one time.

Lemmrich (1931) found essentially identical arrangements and numbers of sclerotic eye ring plates in *Coracias, Alcedo, Upupa, Picus,* and *Dendrocopos. Cuculus* and *Psittacus* differ but slightly from the coraciiforms and piciforms in this character.

E. Stresemann (1934, 1959) divided the Coraciiformes of Wetmore (1960) into six orders: Coraciae, Halcyones, Meropes, Momoti, Todi, Upupae followed by the Trogones. Although Stresemann made six orders of the coraciiforms, his comments indicate that he considered them related to one another:

> Order Coraciae (Rollers): "Fürbringer was inclined to unite the Coraciae and Caprimulgi; other authors, perhaps more correctly, place the Halcyones as the closest relatives."
>
> Order Halcyones (Kingfishers): "Obviously most nearly related to the Meropes, Coraciae and Momoti."
>
> Order Meropes (Bee-eaters): "Probably related to the Coraciae and Halcyones, perhaps also allied to the Upupae."
>
> Order Momoti (Motmots): "Closest relatives are the Halcyones, Coraciae and Todi."
>
> Order Todi (Todies): "Equally related to the Halcyones and Momoti."
>
> Order Upupae (Hoopoes, Woodhoopoes, Hornbills): "Fürbringer maintained the Meropes and Halcyones as the nearest relatives of the Upupae and also it seemed to him that there is a relationship with the Passeres" (transl.).

Lowe (1946:119) listed 22 characters of the Eurasian Hoopoe (*Upupa epops*) and noted that it is "in some respects, especially as regards the palatal region . . . characteristically Coraciiform; in others typically Passerine and in other Picine. . . . In the Coraciiforms the presence of an Expansor secundariorum muscle is invariable. It is absent in *Upupa* and there are other characters which point to the Pici and Passeres." Lowe tentatively placed the Pici as a suborder of the Passeriformes to include the Picidae, Indicatoridae, Capitonidae, Ramphastidae, and Upupidae.

Lowe (1948:572) disagreed with Sclater's (1924) definition of the Coraciiformes. "The Coraciiformes have for many years been loaded with a heterogeneous collection of forms which custom has blindly accepted." He objected primarily to the inclusion of "the Swifts and Humming Birds, to say nothing of the Colies and the Hoopoes." Lowe was willing to admit the rollers (*Coracias*) and "the following outlying genera, viz. *Eurystomus*, *Brachypteracias*, *Uratelornis*, *Atelornis*, *Geobiastes*, and *Leptosomus*" and possibly the Alcedinidae, Meropidae, and Momotidae, but "it is certain that the Striges, the Bucerotidae, the Upupidae . . . the Cypseli, the Coliidae . . . and the Trogonidae . . . cannot be so included" (p. 574). Lowe advocated a separate order for the hornbills because of "the peculiar structure of the bill and the universal form of the latissimus dorsi muscle" as well as several additional characters which "prove their complete isolation from the Coraciiformes" (p. 578). The hoopoes are "nearly Passerine, and in any case cannot be associated with the Coraciiformes" (p. 580). Lowe agreed with Forbes (1882b) that *Todus* is an isolated form "with affinities to both the Passeriformes and Piciformes of Garrod" and he proposed the establishment of "a group Todiformes equivalent to Passeri, Pici and Cypseliformes for the sole reception of the genus *Todus*, which is Forbes' summing-up, and with which I agree" (p. 582). Thus, the Coraciiformes according to Lowe (1948) would include only the Coraciidae, Brachypteraciidae, Leptosomidae, and, possibly, the Alcedinidae, Meropidae, and Momotidae.

Clay (1950) noted that the motmots, bee-eaters, rollers, and hoopoes are parasitized by some mallophagan genera which are shared with, or related to, those of the passerines. The rollers and bee-eaters share members of the genus *Meromenopon*, and *Hopkinsiella*, which is found on the Phoeniculidae, seems to be related to *Upupicola* of the Upupidae. The mallophaga of the kingfishers and hornbills are unlike those of other groups.

Delacour (1951b) advised that "the number of toes be disregarded" as the basis for the classification of the small kingfishers, and that the species be assigned to *Alcedo* and *Ceyx* according to habitat, coloration, and other characters.

Verheyen (1955d) examined the skeletons and other characters of the coraciiforms and presented a new classification. His order Upupiformes included the hoopoes, wood-hoopoes, scimitarbills, and hornbills, and his Coraciiformes the rollers, bee-eaters, motmots, kingfishers, and todies. In 1961 Verheyen reduced these orders to suborders and expanded his Coraciiformes to include the suborders Trochili, Apodi, and Trogones.

The paper electrophoretic patterns of the egg-white proteins of the bee-eaters, motmots, and kingfishers are much alike, but they differ from the roller genus *Eurystomus*, which has a pattern similar to that of the parrot *Psephotus varius*. This similarity was ascribed to coincidence, not close relationship (Sibley 1960:243).

Sanft (1960) reviewed the characters of the hornbills and described the species and subspecies.

Manger Cats-Kuenen (1961) studied the bill and casque of the Helmeted Hornbill (*Rhinoplax* [*Buceros*] *vigil*) and other hornbills. The functions of the casque were suggested to be a signal character "to overawe assailants and congeners," and "the larger casques probably serve as a soundboard" (p. 46). In *Rhinoplax* "the heavily reinforced casque with its thick rostral horn layer . . . will be able, like the heavy head of a hammer, to add force to the blows of the smaller, short, straight and less imposing bill. The casque itself, built to intercept blows, will have been modified to serve . . . as a hammer in the acquisition of food, as a shield for the defense against enemies . . . and as a 'trowel' for building the wall of the nest" (p. 46).

V. Stresemann and Stresemann (1961b) separated the Alcedinidae into three subfamilies on the basis of the molt pattern of the primaries. The Daceloninae (including *Pelargopsis*) follow the descending mode, beginning with the first primary. A descending pattern is also found in the Alcedininae, but the molt begins at two foci, represented by primaries one and seven. In the Cerylinae the primary molt is somewhat irregular and never follows the descending pattern. These three groups "agree exactly with the three subfamilies . . . as classified in 1912 by W. DeW. Miller, who based his arguments on morphological evidence" (p. 445). The Stresemanns also presented a historical review of the classification of the kingfishers.

Forbes-Watson (1967) reported the first known nest of the Cuckoo-Roller (*Leptosomus discolor*), which he discovered on Mayotte Island in the Comoros. He described the nest, young, food, and behavior and suggested (p. 430) that the Leptosomidae "would not seem to be particularly closely-related to the Coraciidae." The remnants of copious white down on the young Cuckoo-Rollers suggested a possible relationship to the Upupidae, which is the only family that "has down, and that is scanty. . . . The tinted, not pure white, eggs and smelly nest also remind one of the Upupidae and also of the Phoeniculidae."

Fry (1969) reported on a four-year field study of 12 African bee-eaters and a review of museum specimens of all 24 species of the group. He merged *Aerops*, *Melittophagus*, *Bombylonax*, and *Dicrocercus* into *Merops*, which then includes 21 species. He retained *Meropogon* for *forsteni* and *Nyctyornis* for *amictus* and *athertoni*. Fry speculated that the Meropidae "probably originated in southeast Asian forest and spread through former forest to Africa." He did not comment on the relationships of the bee-eaters to other groups.

Cracraft (1971) reviewed the classification of the rollers and presented comparisons of skeletal elements. He proposed a classification of the suborder Coracii, as follows:

Suborder Coracii
  Superfamily Coracioidea
    Family Coraciidae, Rollers
    Family Brachypteraciidae, Ground-Rollers
  Superfamily Leptosomatoidea
    Family Leptosomatidae, Cuckoo-Roller or Courol

Sibley and Ahlquist (1972) compared the starch gel electrophoretic patterns of the egg-white proteins of members of most of the coraciiform groups. We interpreted the patterns as evidence of a "distinct, but rather distant, alliance among the Alcedinidae, Todidae, Momotidae, and Meropidae." The todies were suggested as "more closely related to the kingfishers than . . . to the motmots." Other possible relationships were uncertain, but the heterogeneity of the anatomical characters of members of the group "is matched by the variation in their egg white protein patterns."

Feduccia (1974, 1975a–c, 1976, 1977) described the structure of the stapes in representatives of nearly all living families of birds. Most birds have a primitive form of the stapes in which the footplate is flat and the shaft is a straight bony rod emanating from the center of the footplate. The hornbills and rollers, including the Cuckoo-Roller and ground-rollers, have the primitive form, but Feduccia found a unique anvil form of the stapes in the hoopoes and woodhoopoes (1975c). Another derived morphology occurs in the bee-eaters, kingfishers, motmots, todies, and trogons. In these, "a large, hollow, bulbous basal and footplate area exhibits a large fenestra (or excavation) only on one side (the posterior aspect). The fenestra . . . leads to a large hollow fossa; the stapedial shaft is shifted to the periphery of the footplate, thus producing a different lever system" (1977:21). Feduccia proposed the following classification (1977:30):

Order Piciformes, woodpeckers and allies
Order Coraciiformes, rollers, ground-rollers, and cuckoo-rollers
Order Upupiformes, hoopoes and woodhoopoes
Order Bucerotiformes, hornbills
Order Alcediniformes
   Superfamily Meropoidea
     Family Meropidae, bee-eaters
   Superfamily Alcedinoidea
     Family Alcedinidae, kingfishers
     Family Momotidae, motmots
     Family Todidae, todies
   Superfamily Trogonoidea
     Family Trogonidae, trogons
Order Tyranniformes, suboscine or tyranniform birds
Order Passeriformes, oscines or passeriform birds

Feduccia (1979) retracted part of his 1977 arrangement because scanning electron microscopy revealed "the manifest differences between suboscines and the alcediniform coraciiforms" in the form of the stapes. His new conclusion was "that the suboscine and alcediniform stapes evolved independently, and that the suboscines are more closely related to the oscines than to the alcediniforms."

Brodkorb (1976) described *Alexornis antecedens* from the Upper Cretaceous of Baja California, Mexico, as the type of a "new family Alexornithidae, and a new order Alexornithiformes, thought to be ancestral to the Tertiary and Recent orders Coraciiformes and Piciformes. . . . *Alexornis* is the only certain land bird known from the Cretaceous." Olson (1976) described "a new genus and species of tody, *Palaeotodus emryi* . . . from the 'middle' Oligocene . . . of Wyoming, providing the first record of the modern family Todidae outside the West Indies. . . . The Todidae and Momotidae appear to be more closely related to each other than either is to any other family of Coraciiformes. The Momotidae were evidently derived from the Old World. The Todidae appear to have been derived from a momotid-like ancestor in the Oligocene or earlier. . . . The Coraciiformes appear to have been one of the prevalent groups of small land birds in the Oligocene."

Kemp (1979) reviewed the biology and radiation of the hornbills, and Kemp and Crowe (1985) presented a phylogenetic (cladistic) analysis of the Bucerotidae, with comments on the systematics and zoogeography of the Afrotropical species and subspecies. A new species, *Tockus leucomelas*, was separated from its close relative, *Tockus flavirostris*. A modified classification was developed from the cladogram of their phylogenetic analysis.

Fry (1980) concluded from a study of the plumages, geographic distribution, and anatomical and biological characters that the kingfishers "arose in Malesia, and that the 18 Afrotropical kingfishers are the product of 8–11 separate invasions from Malesia, one via America."

Maurer and Raikow (1981) compared the limb musculature among members of the coraciomorph groups, made a cladistic analysis of their data, and developed the following classification based on "limb muscle synapomorphies":

Order Coraciiformes
  Suborder Coracii
       Family Coraciidae, typical rollers
       Family Brachypteraciidae, ground-rollers
       Family Leptosomidae, Cuckoo-Roller
  Suborder Alcedines
   Infraorder Bucerotomorphae
       Family Bucerotidae
         Subfamily Bucorvinae, ground-hornbills
         Subfamily Bucerotinae, typical hornbills
   Infraorder Alcedinomorphae
    Subinfraorder Upupides
       Family Phoeniculidae, woodhoopoes, scimitar-bills
       Family Upupidae, Hoopoe
    Subinfraorder Alcedinides
       Family Trogonidae (*incertae sedis*), trogons
      Superfamily Momotoidea
       Family Todidae, todies
       Family Momotidae, motmots
      Superfamily Alcedinoidea
       Family Meropidae, bee-eaters
       Family Alcedinidae
         Subfamily Daceloninae, forest kingfishers
         Subfamily Alcedininae, fishing kingfishers
           Tribe Alcedinini
           Tribe Cerylini

This classification is congruent with our DNA-based arrangement in that: (1) the hornbills and hoopoes are allied; (2) the trogons are recognized as relatives of the coraciiforms; (3) the todies, motmots, bee-eaters, and kingfishers are allied. The principal discrepancy is in the primary division within the two classifications. In the DNA-based phylogeny the primary dichotomy separates the hornbill-hoopoe clade (Bucerotimorphae) from the trogon, roller, bee-eater, motmot, tody, kingfisher, clade (Coraciimorphae). Maurer and Raikow made their primary division between the rollers (Coracii) and all others (Alcedines). This produces other discrepancies, but perhaps the surprising aspect is not that the DNA and myological data produce somewhat different classifications but that they agree as well as they do.

Cracraft (1981) "tentatively" accepted "the hypothesis of coraciiform monophyly" and adopted "a somewhat conservative, noncommittal approach." He included the kingfishers, bee-eaters, motmots, and todies in his Alcedini, but assigned the trogons to a separate infraorder within the Alcedines. He hypothesized "that the Coracii are related to the Alcedini" and placed the "Leptosomatidae within the Coracii" after expressing doubts about the affinities of *Leptosomus* as treated in his 1971 paper. Cracraft thought that "the hoopoes and woodhoopoes are clearly closely related" and that the hornbills "almost certainly are related to the other coraciiforms . . . and possibly represent an early lineage. He placed them in "their own suborder to signal the uncertainty of their exact relationships within the order."

Burton (1984) studied the anatomy and evolution of the feeding apparatus in the Coraciiformes and Upupiformes. He described the anatomy of the jaws, tongue, and neck, and correlated the structure with feeding and other aspects of behavior. Based solely on the results of his study he proposed a phylogeny and the following classification (p. 438):

Order CORACIIFORMES
    Suborder Alcedines
        Family Meropidae, bee-eaters
        Family Alcedinidae, kingfishers
        Family Todidae, todies
        Family Momotidae, motmots
    Suborder Coracii
        Superfamily Galbuloidea
            Family Galbulidae, jacamars
            Family Bucconidae, puffbirds
        Superfamily Coracoidea
            Family Leptosomatidae, cuckoo-rollers
            Family Coraciidae, rollers
            Family Brachypteraciidae, ground-rollers
Order UPUPIFORMES
    Superfamily Bucerotidea [Bucerotoidea]
        Family Bucerotidae, hornbills
    Superfamily Upupoidea
        Family Upupidae, hoopoes
        Family Phoeniculidae, woodhoopoes

Burton's phylogeny and classification agree in some respects with those based on the DNA comparisons. For example, the jacamars and puffbirds are included in the same higher category as the rollers, rather than with the piciforms as in many traditional classifications.

Fry (1984) recognized three genera and 24 species of bee-eaters, with 21 species in *Merops*. The book includes accounts of each species including plumage descriptions, life history information, and detailed distributions.

The DNA Hybridization Evidence (Figs. 51–71, 329–332, 353, 354, 358–360)

The Bucerotimorphae and Coraciimorphae diverged at Δ T$_{50}$H 23.4 in the UPGMA tree (Fig. 353). The hornbills (Bucerotimorphae) and hoopoes (Upupiformes) diverged at Δ 20.8.

The DNA evidence agrees with previous ideas about the relationships among the three genera of hoopoes: *Upupa* on one branch, *Phoeniculus* and *Rhinopomastus* on the other. The Upupides and Phoeniculides diverged at Δ 17.0. The Phoeniculidae and Rhinopomastidae branched at Δ 10.2 (Fig. 354).

The ground-hornbills, *Bucorvus*, branched from the typical hornbills at Δ 9.2; we recognize the Bucorvidae and Bucerotidae. In the latter, *Anorrhinus* is the only identified member of a clade that branched at Δ 8.7. The coraciimorphs divided into the Trogoniformes and Coraciiformes at Δ 22.1, and the living trogons split into an African clade (Apaloderminae) and an Asian-American clade (Trogoninae) at Δ 7.4 (Fig. 359).

The Coraciiformes defined by the DNA data consists of essentially the same groups that compose the Coraciiformes of most traditional classifications. The subdivision of the kingfishers into three groups has been proposed several times in the past on the basis of morphological characters.

Thus, the DNA evidence is congruent with most of the morphological evidence of the relationships among the bucerotimorph and coraciimorph taxa, although the categorical assignments differ because different criteria have been used for their definition.

Some of the melting curves do not seem to agree with the UPGMA tree. Fig. 51 (*Buceros*) includes four genera of hornbills, a roller, a bee-eater, a kingfisher, a tody, a scimitar-bill, and a hoopoe. The relative positions of the curves show that the closest taxa to the hornbill are rollers, bee-eaters, and kingfishers, while the two upupiforms (*Rhinopomastus*, *Upupa*) are considerably farther out. The same situation occurs in Fig. 52 (*Bucorvus*). In Figs. 61 (*Coracias*), 64 (*Momotus*), 66 (*Todus*), and 67 (*Megaceryle*), the upupiform genera are the farthest from the tracer. In these six figures there are heteroduplexes representing groups in the parvclass Coraciae.

Figs. 54 and 55 (*Phoeniculus*) include representatives of many avian orders and families, including a hornbill and a trogon. In these two sets the heteroduplex curves cluster between ca. 45% and 58% on the single-stranded DNA scale, and except for the other upupiforms, the closest taxon to *Phoeniculus* is the hornbill, *Tockus*.

The FITCH trees (Figs. 330–332) provide additional information and questions. In Fig. 330 the branch lengths among the four genera of hornbills are virtually identical, and so are the branches to *Phoeniculus* and *Upupa* from their common node. This indicates that rates among the four hornbills, and between the two hoopoes, have been approximately equal. However, there is an obvious difference between the branch lengths to the hornbills and hoopoes from their common node. The branch to the hornbills is ca. 9.8 units long, that to the hoopoes ca. 12 units, a difference of about 20%. This may be caused by different ages at first breeding. We know that *Upupa* begins to breed at age one, but we have no records of age at maturity in hornbills (Table 16).

Fig. 331 includes genera representing the hornbills, rollers, kingfishers, motmots, todies, bee-eaters, and hoopoes. The FITCH tree does not match the UPGMA tree in some parts, although the kingfishers, motmots, and todies form a cluster as they do in the UPGMA tree. However, the roller (*Coracias*) is closer to this cluster than is the bee-eater (*Merops*), which is part of the kingfisher etc. cluster in the UPGMA tree. The positions of *Buceros* and *Phoeniculus* reflect the melting curves but not the UPGMA tree.

Fig. 332 examines a larger domain, including woodpeckers, trogons, jacamars, and puffbirds, in addition to the taxa in Fig. 331. The positions of the Picae, Galbulides, Bucconides, Alcedinida, Momotida, Todida, Coracii, Upupiformes, and Bucerotiformes agree quite well with the UPGMA tree and the melting curves. The bee-eaters (Meropides) are in the same relative position as in Fig. 331, which may indicate that they belong there, but the position of the trogons does not agree with the UPGMA tree, although they are on a long branch from other taxa in both trees. We discuss the trogons in a following section.

Fig. 53 (*Tockus*) shows the cluster of 11 species of hornbills, with *Bucorvus* (Bucorvidae) on their outer fringe.

Fig. 60 (*Coracias*) shows a large distance between rollers and the kingfishers, bee-eaters, motmots, hornbills, trogons, and mousebirds (*Urocolius*). In other sets of curves the mousebirds are in the same relative position to various tracers.

Fig. 62 (*Coracias*) includes an assortment of non-passerines and two passerines. All these taxa are more distant from *Coracias* than are some of those in Fig. 60.

Fig. 63 (*Coracias*) adds comparisons between *Coracias* and the piciforms and galbuliforms. The jacamars and puffbirds are closer to *Coracias* than are the piciforms, but both groups are quite distant from the roller tracer.

Fig. 65 (*Momotus*) shows the kingfisher (*Halcyon*) closer to *Momotus* than is *Todus*; this is also indicated in the FITCH tree in Fig. 331. In the UPGMA tree (Fig. 354) the Todidae and Alcedinidae are equidistant from the Momotidae at Δ 17.7, the average of 30 delta values. The trogon (*Harpactes*) and the puffbird (*Bucco*) are about equidistant from *Momotus* in Fig. 65, and this is also true in the FITCH tree. In the UPGMA tree, the trogons, puffbirds, and motmots are distant from one another, but the trogons are somewhat closer to the motmots than are the puffbirds. Rate differences and experimental errors can account for such discrepancies which, in the total picture, become trivial.

Fig. 68 (*Megaceryle*) clearly shows the three groups of kingfishers. It is surprising to find such large gaps between birds that are so similar in external appearance, but the same groups have been identified in the past from morphological characters.

Fig. 69 (*Alcedo*) shows the separation between the Alcedinida and the Cerylida. The tight clustering of the Dacelonoidea and the Ceryloidea indicates that the rates of DNA evolution have been about the same along both branches. This is also indicated by the nearly equal lengths of the branches in the FITCH tree, Fig. 331. The same relationships are shown in the UPGMA tree (Fig. 360).

Fig. 70 (*Merops*) shows the roller (*Eurystomus*) closer to *Merops* than is the motmot, kingfisher, and the other taxa. The trogon (*Apaloderma*) is more distant from *Merops* than are the jacamar and hornbill, but the differences are small and may not be significant. The position of *Leptosomus* compared with that of *Eurystomus* is interesting, but its significance is unknown.

Fig. 71 (*Merops*) adds more taxa to the comparisons with *Merops*, all quite distant from it. The piciforms (*Indicator*, *Lybius*) are the most distant.

What can we conclude from these conflicting data? It seems clear that the Galbuliformes, Bucerotiformes, Upupiformes, Trogoniformes, and Coraciiformes are more closely related to one another than any of them is to other non-passerine groups, but that there are wide phylogenetic gaps between these groups. The hoopoes appear to be evolving more rapidly than some of the others, which may account for their consistent position at the outer fringe of several sets of melting curves. These lineages are among the oldest of the non-passerine groups so it should not be surprising if their exact branching pattern is difficult to discern. Our proposed classification reflects most of what we see in the curves and FITCH trees, and the discrepancies are not large. The position of the todies is uncertain, but they are obviously closest to the kingfishers and motmots.

Trogons

Superorder Coraciimorphae
  Order TROGONIFORMES
    Family Trogonidae
      Subfamily Apaloderminae: African Trogons
      Subfamily Trogoninae
        Tribe Trogonini: New World Trogons
        Tribe Harpactini: Asian Trogons

Peters (1945) recognized 34 species of trogons in eight genera: *Trogon* (14 species), *Pharomachrus* (3), *Euptilotis* (1), *Priotelus* (1), and *Temnotrogon* (1) occur in the Neotropics from southern Arizona to northern Argentina, Cuba, Hispaniola, and Trinidad. *Apaloderma* (2) and *Heterotrogon* (1) occur in forested areas of Africa from the tropics to the Cape Region of South Africa, and *Harpactes* (11) occurs from India and Ceylon to southeastern China, Indonesia, Borneo, and the Philippines.

Sibley and Monroe (1990) include *Heterotrogon* in *Apaloderma*, *Temnotrogon* in *Trogon*, and recognize five more species, thus six genera and 39 species.

Trogons are among the most colorful birds; males are red, pink, orange, or yellow below, with a long, graduated tail that is usually black and white. The upperparts of the males of the American and African species are metallic green, but in all but one of the Asian species the dorsum is brown. Female plumages are mostly brownish and lack metallic colors.

Family TROGONIDAE: 6/39. Trogons have unique heterodactyl feet in which digits 1 and 2 are directed backward, 3 and 4 forward and united for their basal half; unique flexor tendons (Gadow's Type 8); a schizognathous palate (Forbes 1881c); holorhinal, impervious nostrils; basipterygoid processes; a large vomer; two deep sternal notches on each side; large aftershaft; only left carotid; pelvic muscle formula AX; short, rounded, eutaxic wing; 10 primaries; 11–12 secondaries (Clark 1918); 12 rectrices; oil gland naked, indistinctly bilobed; large caeca; tracheo-bronchial syrinx; thin, delicate skin; easily detached dense plumage; bill short, broad basally; culmen curved and uncinate; maxillary tomium usually serrate; tongue short and triangular or (*Priotelus*) fairly long with a bifurcate tip (Clark 1918); nidicolous young, naked at hatching (gymnopaedic); nest in holes; white eggs.

Many groups have been suggested as the nearest relatives of the trogons, but the morphological evidence is conflicting and the trogons usually have been placed in a separate order near the coraciiforms.

Historical Review of the Classification

The trogons have been placed in the vicinity of the cuckoos, colies, parrots, toucans, puffbirds, jacamars, and rollers from the earliest classifications to the present. For example, they appear among these groups in Brisson (1760), Illiger (1811), Merrem (1813), L'Herminier (1827), Wagler (1827), Nitzsch (1840), Gray (1844–49), Cabanis (1847), and Lilljeborg (1866).

Huxley (1867) had only a damaged specimen of *Trogon* and he thought that the palate was desmognathous, hence he placed the trogons in his Coccygomorphae with the colies, cuckoos, kingfishers, rollers, and several other groups. He also believed that the trogons are closely allied to the goatsuckers because *Trogon* "possesses basipterygoid processes, in which respect it resembles *Caprimulgus*." Forbes (1881c) showed that the trogon palate is actually schizognathous; if Huxley's material had been better he probably would have placed the trogons in his suborder Schizognathae, near the pigeons.

The toe structure and wide gape of the trogons caused Sundevall (1872, see 1889) to place them near the turacos, colies, rollers, goatsuckers, and swifts.

The trogons lack the ambiens muscle so Garrod (1874a) placed them in his Anomalogonatae. Because they have a nude oil gland and intestinal caeca he assigned them to his order Passeriformes between the puffbirds and the bee-eaters; in the same group were the passerines, goatsuckers, rollers, and motmots.

Garrod (1875:345) described the deep plantar tendons of *Trogon massena* and *Pharomachrus mocino*: "In these birds the tendon of the *flexor longus hallucis* is situated, as it ought to be, external to the *flexor perforans digitorum*; it also crossed it superficially, opposite about the middle of the tarso-metatarse [sic], sending down a slender vinculum in the normal manner. The peculiarity is in the ultimate destination of the tendons, the *flexor longus hallucis* and the *flexor perforans digitorum* each dividing into two near the metatarso-phalangeal articulation, the two portions of the former tendon running to the hallux and digit 2, the two of the latter to digits 3 and 4. . . . This arrangement is not found in any other group of birds, as far as my experience goes."

Sclater (1880b) used foot structure as the basis for some of his categories. The unique feet of the trogons prompted him to place them in the suborder Heterodactylae, order Picariae, between the suborders Anisodactylae (colies, coraciiforms, caprimulgiforms) and Zygodactylae (jacamars, toucans, puffbirds, barbets, honeyguides). Reichenow (1882) placed the trogons between the puffbirds and jacamars in his order Scansores.

Forbes (1881c) found the trogon palate to be schizognathous, not desmognathous as Huxley (1867) had thought. Forbes noted that "if Huxley's group 'Coccygomorphae' were retained" the trogons would have to be moved "to some other position, presumably in his suborder 'Schizognathae.' But . . . as we now know from Prof. Garrod's investigations, the so-called Coccygomorphae are an artificial group, made up of at least three very distinct series of birds. Furthermore, the fact that the Trogons are schizognathous, whereas their near allies, such as the Bucconidae, Galbulidae, Coraciidae, *Podargus*, &c., are desmognathous, shows that the structure of the palate has not that unique and peculiar significance that has been claimed for it in the classification of birds" (p. 837).

Stejneger (1885) placed the trogons in his order Picariae as a superfamily between the Picoideae (piciforms) and Micropodoideae (swifts, hummingbirds). This treatment was tentative, as indicated by his statement that "the trogons are rather peculiar, showing no special relationship to any other group of the present order, a circumstance which explains the fact that by the different systematists they have been associated with nearly all the groups of the Picariae" (p. 433).

Fürbringer (1888) thought the trogons were intermediate between the Coraciiformes and Pico-Passeriformes. Among the former he noted resemblances to the Caprimulgidae, Coraciidae, and Todidae, but he was more impressed by the similarities to the latter and placed the Trogones after the Colii in the suborder Pico-Passeriformes, order Coracornithes, which also included the hummingbirds, swifts, passerines, and piciforms.

Shufeldt (1889e) found no evidence of a close relationship between trogons and hummingbirds or goatsuckers, and suggested that the trogons might have been derived from the cuckoos rather than from "any other with which I am acquainted" (p. 387).

The intestinal coiling patterns caused Gadow (1889:315) to conclude that "the Trogonidae stand on a lower level than the Cypselidae, Trochilidae, and Coliidae, on the same level as the Caprimulgidae and Coraciidae, and connect them all to one another." He noted that the trogons have well-developed caeca similar to those of the rollers, goatsuckers, and owls.

It is impossible to visualize a phylogeny from the relationships described by Gadow in the foregoing quotation. In addition, it is apparent that caecal development is related to food habits, and has virtually no value as an index to the relationships among major groups of birds.

Seebohm's (1890a) classification was an anachronistic mixture of past arrangements, with the trogons placed between the hoopoes and the pigeons. This alliance apparently was based on the schizognathous palate, in spite of Forbes's (1881c) critique. Seebohm (1890b) treated the trogons as the suborder Heterodactyli of his order Pico-Passeres, based on the unique toe arrangement and the correlated pattern of the plantar tendons. He also noted that "they combine the cranial characters of *Caprimulgus* with the pterylosis of *Motacilla* [wagtails], and the thigh-muscles and sternum of *Alcedo* [kingfishers]. They are schizognathous and holorhinal; and they are the only birds of the Order of Pico-Passeres which permanently retain their basipterygoid processes" (p. 37). In 1895 Seebohm retained the trogons as an order between his Coraciiformes and Piciformes.

Sharpe (1891) believed the trogons to be the "most isolated" of the pico-passerine birds and he placed them in the order Trogones between the Coraciiformes and the Coccyges.

Gadow (1892) inserted the suborder Trogones between the Colii and Coraciae in his order Coraciiformes. The owls, swifts, hummingbirds, goatsuckers, and coraciiforms were placed in the same order. Gadow (1893) felt that the trogons branched off among ancestral coraciiform birds near the divergence between the Coraciae and the Striges-Caprimulgi. In his sequence (p. 301) of taxa he listed the Trogones between the Colii and Pici, the Galbulidae being the adjacent family on the piciform side.

In the *Catalogue of Birds* the large order Picariae included the suborder Trogones between the Bucerotes and Scansores (piciforms) (Ogilvie-Grant 1892, Hargitt 1890).

Beddard (1898a) reviewed the anatomical characters of the trogons and noted that "the very powerful tensor brevis muscle" is similar in certain ways to that of the passerines and that there are also resemblances to the Pici. He placed the Trogones between the Colii and the Coraciae.

In the *Hand-List* Sharpe (1900) placed the order Trogones between the suborder Colii of the order Coraciiformes and the order Coccyges.

According to Mitchell (1901a:257) the arrangement of the intestines in trogons was derived from a basic "coraciiform-cuculiform metacentre. . . . The Meropidae [bee-eaters], Momotidae, and the Trogones all retain the metacentric position with extremely little alteration."

Shufeldt (1904b) placed his "supersuborder Trogoniformes" between the Jacamariformes and the Coccygiformes, but did not comment on their resemblances to other groups. Reichenow (1913, 1914) placed the Trogonidae next to the Coliidae in his order Scansores, which also included the Piciformes and Cuculiformes.

Chandler (1916) noted that the remiges of the Cuban Trogon (*Priotelus temnurus*) seem much like those of *Coracias*, but that the down feathers of the trogons are most similar to those of hummingbirds. He made no proposals concerning trogon affinities.

Clark (1918) examined the pterylosis and other characters of the Cuban Trogon (*Priotelus*). He offered no conclusions but noted that the "spinal tract is quite passerine and those of the ventral surface are nearly as much so . . . [but, the] tracts of the head are entirely separated from those of the lower neck and throat, to a degree and in a manner which I have never seen in any other birds. . . . The secondaries are eleven or twelve in number but one or two of those at the elbow are very small and in examination of a skin, there would seem to be but ten; Nitzsch says there are eight to ten secondaries in the trogons" (pp. 286–287).

Clark also found that the tail coverts in *Priotelus* have "the usual passerine arrangement" (p. 288). He confirmed that the palate is schizognathous and found the tongue to be fairly long and with a bifurcate tip, thus differing from the short, triangular tongues of other trogons. Clark observed that the large gizzard in his specimen was full of fruits and that the caeca were "relatively very long, much longer than in the species of *Trogon* and *Pharomachrus* examined by Garrod" (p. 289).

E. Stresemann (1934) placed the order Trogones between the orders Upupae (hoopoes, hornbills) and Colii (colies), and Wetmore (1930, 1960) placed the Trogoniformes between the Coliiformes and the Coraciiformes.

Glenny (1943a, 1945c) examined the main arteries near the heart in 13 species of American and African trogons. All have only the left carotid and exhibit "a high degree of uniformity in the arterial arrangement-pattern . . . in contrast to the . . . pattern-variations observed in the Coraciiformes and Piciformes" (1945c:409).

Lowe (1948) questioned W. L. Sclater's (1924) inclusion of the trogons in the Coraciiformes because trogons are schizognathous and the rollers and other coraciiforms are desmognathous. Lowe also stressed the different form of the ectethmoid in the two groups and the two carotids in *Coracias* versus the single left carotid in the trogons.

Dorst (1950) described the microscopic structure of the feathers in several genera of trogons and noted adaptive differences with hummingbird feathers. Pinto (1950) reviewed some of the characters of trogons but added nothing to the solution of the question of their relationships to other groups. Clay (1950) found the Mallophaga of the trogons to be similar to those of the passerines.

Mayr and Amadon (1951), without comment, listed the order Trogones between the Caprimulgi and the Coraciae.

Verheyen (1956a) reviewed the morphological characters of the trogons and concluded that they share the most similarities with the Caprimulgi and next with the owls. He put the trogons in his order Caprimulgiformes between the Caprimulgi and the Steatornithes (Oilbird). Verheyen (1960c) proposed an arrangement based, in part, on the number of vertebrae in the six regions of the vertebral column and again considered the trogons to be caprimulgiforms. In 1961 he gave the trogons subordinal rank in his Coraciiformes, next to the swifts.

Sibley (1960) found the electrophoretic pattern of the egg-white proteins of *Apaloderma narina* to be short and relatively simple, thus similar to those of the passerines. Otherwise there was "little in the egg-white profile to suggest relationships."

Durrer and Villiger (1966) examined the fine structure of the iridescent feathers of five genera of trogons by electron microscopy. They found four different structures within the trogons and essentially identical structural patterns in the iridescent feathers of hummingbirds, jacamars, a starling (*Lamprotornis*), and a pheasant (*Lophophorus*). These are clearly convergent similarities, not clues to common ancestry.

Sibley and Ahlquist (1972) compared the electrophoretic pattern of the egg-white proteins of *Apaloderma narina* with those of many other groups of birds. Some similarities were noted with coraciiforms, swifts, colies, passerines, and cuckoos; the trogon patterns were quite different from those of the Caprimulgiformes and Piciformes. We concluded that "The affinities of the trogons remain obscure, but . . . the Coraciiformes should receive close scrutiny in seeking evidence of relationship."

Maurer and Raikow (1981) made a cladistic analysis of the variations in the limb muscles of the coraciiforms and concluded that "The present study supports the inclusion of the Trogonidae in the Coraciiformes, specifically within the subinfraorder Alcedinides, thus allying the trogons most closely with the assemblage of todies, motmots, bee-eaters, and kingfishers. Uncertainties in the data, however, preclude a more accurate placement of this family relative to the others, so it is listed as *incertae sedis* within the Alcedinides" (p. 418).

The DNA Hybridization Evidence (Figs. 56–59, 332, 353, 354, 359)

The trogons branched from the Coraciiformes at $\Delta T_{50}H$ 22.1 in the UPGMA tree (Fig. 354).

In Figs. 56–58, the Narina Trogon (*Apaloderma narina*) is the tracer taxon. The same tracer preparation was used in these experiments, which were done within the space of a few days, thus they are comparable with one another. The Narina Trogon was compared with species representing many non-passerine groups and two passerines (*Pachyramphus*, *Meliphaga*, Fig. 57). In Fig. 56 a New World trogon (*Trogon*) and an Asian trogon (*Harpactes*) are equidistant from *Apaloderma*. The next closest taxa are two turacos (*Crinifer*, *Tauraco*), then a kingfisher, jacamar, mousebird, jacamar, mousebird, and two puffbirds. We may assume that those beyond the kingfisher are equidistant from *Apaloderma*.

Fig. 57 poses a problem. The closest taxa to *Apaloderma* are two owls and two nightjars. These four curves intersect the vertical axis between 35% and 45% single-stranded DNA, whereas the turaco heteroduplexes in Fig. 56 intersect at ca. 42%. Is it possible that trogons are more closely related to owls than to turacos or kingfishers? Or is this the result of different rates of DNA evolution? Owls begin to breed at 1–3 years of age and nightjars at one year (Table

16), so they should not be among the slow taxa. We have no data on age at maturity for turacos or trogons. At this point we have no reason to assume that the owls, nightjars, or turacos are more closely related to trogons than the groups with which they have long been associated, but this possibility must be considered. The owls cluster quite close to other taxa with which they have not been associated in the past, e.g. Fig. 77 (*Cuculus*) and Fig. 111 (*Zenaida*). In Fig. 87 (*Ara*) nightjars are close to the homoduplex; in Fig. 103 (*Strix*) a turaco curve intersects the % single-stranded axis at 30%. Thus, either the owls, and perhaps the turacos, are slowly evolving lineages or we are seeing evidence of previously unsuspected affinities. For the present we can only present a trogon-owl-nightjar-turaco relationship as an interesting hypothesis to be investigated in the future.

In Fig. 58 (*Apaloderma*) the closest heteroduplex is that of a pigeon (*Treron*), which is at the same distance as several cuckoos, including *Opisthocomus*, *Guira*, and *Crotophaga*. These intersect the vertical scale at 45% to 60%.

Fig. 59 (*Harpactes*) had a poor tracer, but it was compared with species representing many non-passerine groups and, as in Fig. 57, an owl and a nightjar were the closest taxa to the homoduplex. The other taxa in Fig. 59 were a roller, hornbill, kingfisher, pigeon, and puffbird. Also in this experiment, but not illustrated, were the following taxa which were more distant from *Apaloderma* than the puffbird: cuckoo, bee-eater, woodpecker, parrot, hummingbird, swift, mousebird, hoopoe, and motmot.

The trogons are included in FITCH trees in Figs. 329 and 332. In Fig. 329 *Apaloderma* is at the end of the longest branch in the tree, ca. 21 units from *Coracias*, 24 from *Galbula* and *Malacoptila*, and 25 to 30 units from the Piciformes.

In Fig. 332, the Trogoniformes are 21 to 22 units from the Coracii and Todida; 23 units from the Bucerotiformes, Alcedinida, Momotida, and Meropides; and ca. 25 units from the Galbuliformes and the Picae. All of these distances are long, but so are the distances among some of the other groups. For example, from the Picae to the Galbuliformes is 27.6 units. The shortest distances are the 17.4 between the Todida and the Coracii, and the ca. 18 units between the Alcedinida and the Momotida.

We conclude that the trogons have no close living relatives and, unless they are more closely related to owls, nightjars, or turacos, they are members of the cluster that includes the rollers, todies, hornbills, kingfishers, motmots, and bee-eaters.

Mousebirds or Colies

Parvclass Coliae
Order COLIIFORMES
Family Coliidae
Subfamily Coliinae: Typical Mousebirds
Subfamily Urocoliinae: Long-tailed Mousebirds

The colies or mousebirds of Africa are a strange and interesting group of six species, remarkable for many peculiarities of habit and structure that set them well apart from all other birds. Generally drab in colouring, they are characterized by their long stiff tails and pronounced crests, and all are of a similar shape and size. Together their ranges cover virtually all of unforested Africa south of the Sahara, and in some habitats the birds are very common. . . .

In behaviour and ecology the colies . . . are gregarious, living in small parties the year around, even while breeding . . . and they feed in similar ways. They are . . . frugivorous, but . . . not exclusively so, eating much foliage and . . . nectar of flowers (Rowan 1967:64).

Schifter (1985) reviewed the systematics and distribution of the colies. Prinzinger and Prinzinger (1985) observed *Colius striatus* feeding on meat intended to attract wild carnivores at a tourist resort in Kenya.

Order COLIIFORMES, Family COLIIDAE: 2/6. *Colius*, 4 species; *Urocolius*, 2 species. The palate is "indirectly desmognathous" and the vomer is "reduced to the merest vestige" (Pycraft 1907a:253). First and fourth toes reversible, i.e., they can face either forward or backward to whatever position is most effective for the object being grasped; thus, the foot is pamprodactyl; pygostyle with two sets of lateral processes, a small and narrow anterior pair and a broad-based, wing-like, enlarged, posterior pair; nares holorhinal, impervious; pelvic muscle formula AXY; no basipterygoid processes; 13 cervical vertebrae; metasternum with two deep notches on each side; furcula with hypocleideum; only left carotid; latissimus dorsi metapatagialis absent; syrinx tracheo-bronchial; no caeca; thick skin; large aftershaft; no down feathers; plumage soft and hair-like; 10 primaries; 10 secondaries; eutaxic; oil gland tufted, distinctly bilobed; molt of primaries and secondaries usually irregular, sometimes regular; tail molt irregular and centripetal; 10 rectrices (from Murie 1872a, Garrod 1876e, Beddard 1898a, Pycraft 1907a, Rowan 1967, Berman and Raikow 1982, Rich and Haarhoff 1985, D. W. Johnston 1988).

According to Gadow (1892) the flexor tendons are Type 5, but Pycraft (1907a:237–238) disputed this and described a unique arrangement in the colies which he believed was derived from the same type found in swifts and hummingbirds.

Thus, the colies possess a unique combination of characters, and their relationships to other groups have been uncertain.

Historical Review of the Classification

In some of the earlier classifications the colies were allied with the passerines (Brisson 1760, Illiger 1811). Nitzsch (1840) placed the colies with the turacos and Hoatzin in his Amphibolae, and Cabanis (1847) used the same arrangement. The desmognathous palate led Huxley (1867) to place *Colius* in his Coccygomorphae, next to the Musophagidae.

Skeletal characters caused Murie (1872a) to advocate ordinal rank for *Colius*; he was convinced that it is neither a passerine nor a parrot, and not close to the woodpeckers or the Hoatzin. He found evidence of an alliance with the rollers and turacos, but was not convinced of their value. He summmarized his study as follows:

The facts are these: if we take one set of regional characters—the feet, the head, the breast bones, the pelvis, and so on—we can place it in as many different groups; we can even trace Raptorial kin; so that it is hard to say where *Colius* could not be wedged in, and plausibly too. Not only is it entitled to be considered aberrant, but to afford the strongest proof of the interlinking of type—not in the chain-series so often advocated, but, like the Isle of Man tripodal coat-of-arms, kicking its legs about, and whichever alighting upon, there it stands.

But if, in the true spirit of ornithology, we take the bird in its completeness, it will be allowed it does not so closely resemble any acknowledged individual group as to come under its definition.

Without advocating its proper place, I propose equally to exclude it from the old Fissirostral and Scansorial, and the Passerine groups, the recent Coccygomorphae and Coracomorphae. It, as I conceive, is equally with the Woodpeckers and Goatsuckers, Celeomorphae and Cypselomorphae, annectant betwixt the Coccygomorphae and Coracomorphae (pp. 277–278).

Like so many others, the branching pattern of Murie's tree cannot be visualized; it was a tree of similarities, not of dichotomous branchings, but it expressed the confusion and frustration engendered by the mosaic of characters of the colies. However, Murie's placement "annectant betwixt the Coccygomorphae and Coracomorphae" was a good description of the position of the colies in our classification (Sibley et al. 1988:416).

Sundevall (1872, see 1889:158) placed the colies with the turacos and rollers in the "Coenomorphae," based on the arrangement of the toes and structure of the feet and bill.

Garrod (1876e) found that the sternum of *Colius* resembles that of the barbets and that, like the swifts, the colies have a "tough skin." The left carotid and pelvic muscle formula (AXY) are the same as in most piciforms and passerines. Garrod thought that the plantar tendons were as in the kingfishers, but Pycraft (1907a) disagreed, and the great variation in these tendons casts doubt on their significance for taxonomy. Garrod concluded that the colies are allied on the one hand to the woodpeckers, barbets, and toucans, and on the other to the kingfishers and hornbills. He placed the Coliidae in the Piciformes, which he defined as birds lacking the ambiens muscle and caeca, and having a tufted oil gland.

Sclater (1880b) assigned the Coliidae to his suborder Anisodactylae, which included the coraciiforms, *Podargus*, and *Steatornis*. Reichenow (1882) inserted the Coliidae between the Musophagidae (turacos) and Crotophagidae (anis, *Guira*) in his order Scansores.

Stejneger (1885) reviewed various opinions about the colies, but offered no new ideas. He placed the colies in a superfamily between the Coracioideae (rollers, nightjars) and the Alcedinoideae (most coraciiforms) in his order Picariae.

The Macrochires (swifts, hummingbirds) and Pico-Passeres, according to Fürbringer (1888), are the nearest relatives of the colies, and he found several characters to support this opinion. In his classification he placed the "Gens Colii" between the Macrochires and Trogones in the order "Coracornithes," which also included the passerines, piciforms, and cuculiforms. He thought that any similarities to the turacos are due to superficial analogies, and that a relationship to the swifts may be the most likely possibility.

Gadow (1889) found the intestinal convolutions of the colies to be "isocoelous" and he placed them nearest the turacos and trogons.

The suborder Halcyones of Seebohm's (1890c) order Picariae contained the Todidae, Momotidae, Coliidae, and Alcedinidae. In 1895, Seebohm renamed this assemblage as the suborder Picariae, and added to it the Cypselidae (swifts), Coraciidae (rollers), and Bucerotidae (hornbills).

Sharpe (1891) placed the colies in the suborder Colii of the order Coraciiformes, which included the caprimulgiforms, rollers, kingfishers, hornbills, hoopoes, bee-eaters, motmots, todies, swifts, and hummingbirds. The trogons (order Trogones) followed. Sharpe noted: "The Trogons . . . and the *Colii* are two somewhat separate groups, the former being perhaps the most isolated of any of the Pico-Passeres, while the Colies must also stand alone, a little group, between the *Cypseli* and the larger group of *Halcyones* &c., but without any very near relations" (p. 66).

In the *Catalogue of Birds* Sharpe (1892) modified his classification of the colies by including the Coliidae in the suborder Coracii of the order Picariae. The Coracii consisted of the same groups he placed in his Coraciiformes in 1891, except that the hornbills, hoopoes, and hummingbirds were given their own suborders. In the *Hand-List* (1900) Sharpe again changed the classification; the Coraciiformes consisted of the same groups as in his 1891 version, with the suborder Colii at the end, followed by the order Trogones.

Gadow (1892) compared the colies with other groups using his 40 or more characters, and noted: "Notoriously difficult forms, as, for instance, Trogons and Colies, naturally caused more trouble than others, since the number of comparisons had to be increased" (p. 235). He ranked the Colii as a suborder between the Macrochires (nightjars, swifts, hummingbirds) and the Trogones in the order Coraciiformes, which also included the owls and typical coraciiforms. In his discussion of the colies Gadow (1893:252–254) commented (transl.):

1. The colies have typically coraciiform intestinal coiling and flexor tendons.
2. The colies are related to the trogons, but even more closely related to the goatsuckers, hummingbirds, and swifts, especially with the swifts and the African caprimulgids.
3. The pterylosis of the colies is very similar to that of the swifts and hummingbirds.
4. The palate of the colies is "directly desmognathous" as in most "Coraciae." The palatal differences

between colies and goatsuckers are not important since both schizognathy and desmognathy occur in the caprimulgiforms.

5. The condition of the spina externa of the sternum indicates that the colies are related to the coraciiforms rather than to the goatsuckers and swifts.

6. The small procoracoid is like that of *Trogon*, but that of the motmots, passerines, and swifts is also smaller than that of most coraciiforms.

7. The deep, doubly cleft sternum, is relatively primitive and stands at the same level as that of the trogons. The solider sternum of goatsuckers and swifts is reflected in their better flying abilities.

Gadow's conclusions (1893:254) were that the colies differ in many ways from the goatsuckers and swifts but are nevertheless related most closely to them, especially to the swifts. He also considered the trogons to be members of this group.

Beddard (1898a) listed the Colii between the Alcedines and Trogones without comment concerning their relationships.

Mitchell (1901a:251) found the intestinal tract of *Colius* to be "relatively shorter and wider than in another bird . . . examined, and this modification, no doubt due to small size and frugivorous habit, has obliterated practically the underlying morphological form." He derived the intestinal tract arrangements of the colies, swifts, and hummingbirds from that of the Caprimulgidae.

In Shufeldt's (1904b) classification the colies were placed in a supersuborder between the cuckoos and the piciforms.

Pycraft (1907a) was able "to add some new facts, as well as to correct . . . errors of interpretation" made by his predecessors (p. 229). His conclusions may be summarized:

1. The pterylosis of colies and swifts show "a remarkable and significant likeness" (p. 249).

2. Down feathers are lacking and the oil gland is tufted.

3. The rhamphotheca is finch-like in shape with the tomium entire; nostrils circular with a slightly swollen rim and placed close to feathers of the lores.

4. The acrotarsium is covered by five large scutes which do not meet behind.

5. The hallux in wet-preserved specimens occurs in the normal posterior position but can easily be moved to the pamprodactyl position.

6. Nestling downs vestigial, represented by a few minute rami on the tips of the contour feathers.

7. Garrod (1876e) and Gadow (1895) were mistaken concerning the arrangement of the plantar, or deep flexor, tendons in the colies. Garrod thought these tendons were like those of the kingfishers, rollers, bee-eaters, and goatsuckers, and Gadow identified them as Type 5, as in hornbills and swifts. The true condition, according to Pycraft (1907a:237–238), is: "The *flexor longus hallucis* never completely fuses with the deeper tendon: the line of junction is always visible. Further, this tendon, the *fl. long. perf. digit.* splits up into two, one branch going to the hallux and one to D. II . . . while the *flex. perf. digit.* splits up to serve D.III.IV. This arrangement so far appears to be unique; yet it has probably been derived from an earlier and more primitive condition, shared in common with the Swifts and Hummingbirds . . . [but] in the Swifts, as in the Colies . . . the two tendons . . . still shew traces of their originally separate condition."

8. "Besides the Hornbills and the Macrochires, the Colies are . . . the only flying-birds in which the *latissimus dorsi metapatagialis* is absent" (p. 239).

9. The syrinx is tracheo-bronchial.

10. The intestinal tract is uniquely short and wide, lacks caeca, and agrees with that of the swifts in being a modification of the "archecentric" caprimulgid type (Mitchell 1901a).

11. The skeleton presents "many peculiarities which . . . make this group appear more isolated than is really the case; and this is especially true of the skull" (p. 240).

12. The sternum of the colies resembles that of the barbets but they differ in the structure of the keel (pp. 246–247).

13. The condyles of the tarso-metatarsus in the colies differ from those in swifts, "a fact which is all the more peculiar since both are pamprodactylous" (p. 248).

Pycraft (p. 253) summarized the comparisons and explained, or explained away, the differences between colies and swifts. He decided that "inasmuch as the Colies are undoubtedly related to the *Cypseli*, they are also related, though more remotely, to the *Caprimulgi*, since this last group represents the stock from which the two former have descended."

E. Stresemann (1934) thought the colies form an isolated group, and he declined to speculate about their affinities. He placed the Coliiformes between the Trogones and the Macrochires.

Lowe (1948) objected to W. L. Sclater's (1924) inclusion of the colies in the "Coraciiformes" and reviewed the condition of the patagial muscles and the ectethmoid, in both of which the colies differ from "the Coraciiformes proper." Lowe (p. 51) repeated Garrod's error concerning the lack of an ossified vomer in the colies; both Pycraft (1907a) and Schoonees (1963) found a vomer. Lowe did not express a preference for the taxonomic treatment of the colies, except to advocate their removal from the Coraciiformes.

Clay (1950) found the Mallophaga uninformative concerning the relationships of the colies.

Verheyen (1956e, 1961) concluded that the honeyguides (Indicatoridae) are the closest relatives of the colies and, to a lesser extent, the cuckoos. He noted similarities between colies and honeyguides in the sternum, furcula, coracoid, pelvis, atlas, and the "*composition numerique du rachis*" (p. 6). He also found differences and concluded that the separation of the colies and honeyguides was very ancient and that the colies should occupy their own order, Coliiformes.

Verheyen (1956e) recognized the subfamilies Coliinae and Urocoliinae, and Pocock (1966) assembled skeletal and behavioral evidence of the substantial differences between the four species of *Colius* and the two species of *Urocolius*.

Sibley (1960) found the paper electrophoretic pattern of the egg-white proteins of *Colius* to be "highly distinctive" and unlike that of any other group.

Starck (1960) described the structure of the basitemporal articulation in *Colius*, but made no useful taxonomic comparisons.

The cranial morphology of *Colius* was studied by Schoonees (1963) to determine "to which group and variety" of palatal type "as defined . . . by Huxley and Parker, this group belongs." He reviewed the studies of Huxley (1867), Murie (1872a), Garrod (1876e) and Pycraft (1907a) and noted discrepancies between them and his own findings. He confirmed the presence of a small vomer and that the palate is indirectly desmognathous in at least one specimen of *C. colius*. This verified Pycraft's (1907a) description of the palate in "*C. capensis*."

According to Schifter (1967) the embryology and development of *Colius* are similar to those of the woodpeckers and cuckoos, but the differences are so great that he decided the colies should be separated in their own order.

Berman and Raikow (1982) suggested a relationship between colies and parrots, based on hind limb musculature. The two groups are similar in the way they use their feet in climbing but the hind limb muscles may be convergently similar, or the similarities may be retained primitive characters (symplesiomorphies).

Rich and Haarhoff (1985) described an early Miocene fossil (*Colius hendeyi)* from South Africa and reviewed the osteology of the colies. They noted the "strikingly enlarged and broadened pygostyle" which is "unique . . . in having two sets of lateral processes, a small and narrow anterior pair and a broad-based, wing-like, enlarged, posterior pair; pygostyle extremely elongate." Other skeletal elements were also found to differ from those of all other groups of birds. The distinction between *Colius* and *Urocolius* is reflected in skeletal differences.

Schifter (1985) briefly reviewed the higher category relationships of the colies and presented a detailed study of their generic and specific relationships, distribution, geographic variation, ecology, and behavior. He supported the recognition of two genera and six species.

The DNA Hybridization Evidence (Figs. 72–75, 333, 334, 353, 355, 360)

The tracer DNAs of *Urocolius indicus* and *Colius striatus* were compared with driver DNAs of one another and with that of *U. macrourus*. The two genera are recognized because their lineages diverged at Δ 9.1. We place them in separate subfamilies, Urocoliinae and Coliinae, in the Coliidae. The Coliinae also includes *C. colius, castanotus,* and *leucocephalus.*

The colies diverged from their nearest living relatives at Δ T$_{50}$H 24.5, so we place the Coliiformes in the monotypic parvclass Coliae. We have made 132 DNA-DNA hybrid comparisons between *U. indicus* and pigeons, trogons, rollers, kingfishers, bee-eaters, motmots, hornbills, hoopoes, swifts, hummingbirds, jacamars, puffbirds, honeyguides, barbets, toucans, woodpeckers, and nearly every other group of birds, including waterbirds, hawks, galliforms, and passerines. All of these hybrids have delta values larger than 22.2; the average is 24.5 (Fig. 355).

Figs. 72–75 (*Urocolius*) include comparisons between *Urocolius indicus* and species representing many non-passerine groups. The two groups that are closest to *Urocolius* are the owls, nightjars, and turacos in Fig. 72, and the Kerguelen Petrel (*Lugensa)* in Fig. 75. These taxa intersect the vertical axis at or below the 50% level. We consider these groups to be among those with relatively slow average rates of DNA evolution and, therefore, their positions do not indicate that they are more closely related to the colies than any other group. In fact, their positions relative to *Urocolius* may be taken as evidence that they are among the groups with delayed maturity. This is known to be true for *Lugensa.* The owls begin to breed at an average age of two years and, according to available information (Table 16), the nightjars are mature at age one. We found no records of age at first breeding for the turacos, but, based on the tendency of DNA-DNA heteroduplexes to form melting curves that are among the closest to homoduplex curves representing several different groups, we suggest that the turacos are also among the groups with delayed maturity.

The isolated position of the colies is also indicated by the distances in the FITCH trees,

Figs. 333 and 334. In Fig. 333 *Colius* is 29.7 distance units from *Coccyzus*, and 23.9 units from *Tauraco*. The distances to the other cuckoos are between these extremes. In Fig. 334 *Colius* is 22.5 units from *Strix*, 23.0 from *Caprimulgus*, 25.5 from *Chaetura*, and 29.8 from *Amazilia*. We believe that the relatively short branch to *Strix* reflects the delayed maturity of the owls, not evidence that the mousebirds branched more recently from the owls than from the nightjars, swifts, or hummingbirds.

We conclude that the DNA hybridization data confirm the conclusions of many previous authors that the mousebirds, or colies, have no close living relatives, that they are the only survivors of an ancient divergence. Their closest living relatives are probably the terrestrial non-passerines of the superorders Bucerotimorphae, Coraciimorphae, and Cuculimorphae in our classification. We do not believe that the owls or procellariids are among their closest living relatives; the turacos might be, but the evidence is equivocal.

Cuckoos, Hoatzin, and Turacos

Parvclass Passerae
  Superorder Cuculimorphae
    Order CUCULIFORMES
      Infraorder Cuculides
        Parvorder Cuculida
          Superfamily Cuculoidea
            Family Cuculidae: Old World Cuckoos
          Superfamily Centropodoidea
            Family Centropodidae: Coucals
        Parvorder Coccyzida
          Family Coccyzidae: American Cuckoos
      Infraorder Crotophagides
        Parvorder Opisthocomida
          Family Opisthocomidae: Hoatzin
        Parvorder Crotophagida
          Family Crotophagidae
            Tribe Crotophagini: Anis
            Tribe Guirini: Guira Cuckoo
        Parvorder Neomorphida
          Family Neomorphidae: Roadrunners, Ground Cuckoos

  Superorder Strigimorphae
    Order MUSOPHAGIFORMES
        Family Musophagidae
          Subfamily Musophaginae: Turacos
          Subfamily Criniferinae: Plantain-eaters, Go-away-birds

The 143 species of cuckoos are divided among 30 genera; they occur on all continents and many islands. There are 23 species of turacos in five genera, confined to sub-Saharan Africa.

The DNA comparisons show that the cuckoos and turacos are not one another's closest living relatives, but they have been thought to be so by many authors and their taxonomic histories are intertwined; hence we will treat them together for convenience. The Hoatzin

(*Opisthocomus hoazin*) often has been placed in or near the Galliformes, or as a link between galliforms and cuckoos. There is ample evidence that it is a cuckoo and its taxonomic history is reviewed in a following section.

The Cuculiformes have been recognized as a diverse assemblage, even without the turacos. The DNA evidence confirms their diversity, as indicated by the classification above.

Order CUCULIFORMES: 30/143. Desmognathous; foot zygodactyl with the fourth toe permanently reversed; flexor tendons Type 1; pelvic muscles AFGXY+, ABFGXY+, ABEFGXY+; holorhinal, impervious nares; no basipterygoid processes; no cere; rostrum immovable; podotheca scutellate; expansor secundariorum "cuculine"; two bony canals in hypotarsus; 10 primaries; 9–13 secondaries; eutaxic; 8 rectrices in Crotophagidae, 10 in others; syrinx bronchial or tracheo-bronchial; two carotids; down on apteria only; 14 cervical vertebrae; 17–18 presacral vertebrae, 4 dorsal vertebrae; perforated atlas; furcula present; no bony canal formed by coracoid; oil gland bilobed and naked in Cuculides, Crotophagidae and Neomorphidae, with small tuft or naked in Opisthocomidae; aftershaft absent or small; "eyelashes" present; small vomer present; caeca present; 4 ribs reach sternum.

Order MUSOPHAGIFORMES: 5/23. Desmognathous; semi-zygodactyl foot with fourth toe reversible, not permanently directed backwards; flexor tendons Type 1; pelvic muscles ABDFGXY+; holorhinal, impervious nares; podotheca scutellate; expansor secundariorum "ciconiine"; one bony canal in hypotarsus; 15 cervical vertebrae; 19 presacral vertebrae; 5 dorsal vertebrae; notched atlas; no furcula; bony canal formed by dorsal processes of coracoid; oil gland bilobed, tufted; aftershaft present; eyelashes absent; no vomer; no caeca; 5 ribs reach sternum; unique green pigment turacin in feathers.

Historical Review of the Classification

The cuckoos and turacos were associated in some of the earliest classifications, including that of Linnaeus (1758:111). In his order Picae, genus *Cuculus*, Linnaeus included several cuckoos and a turaco. The species that Linnaeus called "*Cuculus persa*" is the Guinea Turaco (*Tauraco persa*). The turaco was placed in the list between *canorus*, the European Cuckoo, and *vetula*, the Lizard-Cuckoo (*Saurothera*) that occurs on several Caribbean islands.

In early classifications the cuckoos were also associated with other groups, some of which are still thought to be related to them. For example, Merrem (1813) included *Cuculus*, *Trogon*, *Bucco* (puffbirds), and *Crotophaga* in his Coccyges. Nearby, in the Levirostres, were *Ramphastos* (toucans), the Channel-billed Cuckoo (*Scythrops*), and *Psittacus* (African Grey Parrot).

In his order Picariae, Nitzsch (1840) included the cuckoos, swifts, woodpeckers, parrots, turacos, colies, the Hoatzin, goatsuckers, todies, hornbills, hoopoes, and kingfishers. One of his main divisions was the Cuculinae, which included the cuckoos plus *Leptosomus* (Cuckoo-Roller), *Indicator* (honeyguides), and the trogons. Nitzsch noted, however, that this group has "no definite pterylographic character; the only character that appears to occur in all of them is the nakedness of the tip of the oil-gland, which is not furnished with a circlet of feathers" (p. 90, Sclater's translation). Citing the possession of an aftershaft, 10 rectrices, and the tufted oil gland, Nitzsch placed the turacos in his Amphibolae, which included *Opisthocomus* and *Colius*.

Gray (1844–49) included the Musophagidae with the passerine birds near the colies,

Hoatzin, and hornbills. He placed the cuckoos in his order Scansores, which contained all zygodactyl birds. Lilljeborg (1866) defined an order Zygodactyli, containing parrots, piciforms, turacos, colies, cuckoos, and honeyguides.

In Huxley's (1867, 1868) classification, based on the palate, the Coccygomorphae included four groups: (1) Coliidae; (2) Musophagidae, Cuculidae, Bucconidae, Ramphastidae, Capitonidae, Galbulidae; (3) Alcedinidae, Bucerotidae, Upupidae, Meropidae, Momotidae, Coraciidae; (4) Trogonidae. The Psittacomorphae (parrots) and the Heteromorphae (only *Opisthocomus*, the Hoatzin) were adjacent to the Coccygomorphae.

Thus, the tradition for the association of these groups was established more than a century ago, based primarily on the zygodactyl arrangement of the toes.

Sundevall's (1872, see 1889) order Volucres, based on foot and feather characters, included parrots, woodpeckers, cuckoos, and several other groups. "Cohort 3. Coccyges" contained honeyguides, barbets, toucans, jacamars, puffbirds, Cuckoo-roller, and cuckoos. In "Cohort 4. Coenomorphae" he placed the turacos, colies, and rollers.

Garrod (1873d, 1874a) divided the Aves into those with and those without the ambiens muscle. In his Homalogonatae (with an ambiens) were the Musophagidae, Cuculidae, and Psittaci, with the galliforms nearby. The Anomalogonatae included all the other groups mentioned above in Huxley's classification.

Sclater (1880b) disagreed with Garrod's allocation of the cuculiforms. He admitted that they show "much affinity" with the galliforms but believed that they belong among the Picariae as defined by Nitzsch (1840). He placed the Cuculidae and Musophagidae in a suborder Coccyges in his order Picariae. The order Scansores of Reichenow (1882) included piciforms, colies, turacos, crotophagid cuckoos, and cuculid cuckoos. Stejneger (1885) included an order Picariae, roughly equivalent to that of Nitzsch, and placed the Cuculidae and Musophagidae in the superfamily Cuculoideae.

Beddard (1885) reviewed the characters of the cuckoos and proposed a division of the Cuculidae into the Cuculinae, Phoenicophainae, and Centropodinae (coucals).

Shufeldt (1885a, 1886a–c) described the anatomy of the Greater Roadrunner (*Geococcyx californianus*) and reviewed the characters of the cuckoos. He proposed that the North American Cuculidae should be placed in the Crotophaginae, Centropodinae (roadrunners), and Cuculinae (*Coccyzus*). He thought it possible that *Geococcyx* might be related to such birds as the Australian Kookaburra (*Dacelo gigas*, a kingfisher) or to the jacamars (Galbulidae).

In a monograph of the turacos Schalow (1886) reviewed the classifications of previous authors. He noted that the turacos were placed with the cuckoos in some of the earliest classifications but that many other groups have also been proposed as their allies, including pigeons, galliforms, woodpeckers, trogons, puffbirds, parrots, colies, rollers, Hoatzin, and even certain passerines. Schalow thought that the turacos are related to the colies.

Fürbringer (1888) combined the Cuculidae and Musophagidae in a suborder, Coccygiformes, considered them to be an outlying group of his order Coracornithes, and thought their nearest relatives are the jacamars and puffbirds which link the cuculiform birds to the "Pico-Passeres."

Seebohm (1890a) included the Cuculi and Musophagi in his order Coccyges and placed it near the orders Columbae (pigeons) and Pico-Passeres. In 1895 he defined an order Cuculiformes on the basis of the deep plantar tendons, presence of the fifth secondary (eutaxic), desmognathous palate, altricial young, and arrangement of the spinal pteryla. This order, containing the Cuculi (cuckoos, turacos) and Upupae (hoopoes), was part of his subclass Aegithomorphae, which included the Passeriformes, Turniciformes, and Galliformes. A more polyphyletic group is difficult to imagine.

Goodchild (1891) thought that the arrangement of the secondary coverts indicated that "the normal cuckoos . . . are intermediate between the Picarian birds and the Pigeons, while the Ground Cuckoos approach the Peristeropods [cracids, megapodes] and the Gouridae [crowned pigeons]" (p. 327).

In the *Catalogue of Birds* Shelley (1891) included the Cuculidae and Musophagidae in the Coccyges, one of several suborders in the large order Picariae. The Cuculidae were divided into six subfamilies.

Sharpe (1891) included the suborders Musophagi and Cuculi in his order Coccyges, placed between the Trogones and Psittaciformes. He commented that nearly all of "the Picariae have one feature in common . . . they lay white eggs . . . in the hole of a tree or a bank. . . . The principal exceptions to this rule are the *Coccyges . . .* which are either parasitic, or build open nests of rough construction, and lay eggs, sometimes of varied colours, and sometimes white. These birds, however, though zygodactyle, possess other characters which seem to show that at the present day, at least, they have little to do with the other so-called *Picariae*, and in many respects exhibit Galline affinities" (p. 65).

In his diagram of relationships the Cuculi and Musophagi are approximately equidistant from the Columbae and Colii (Sharpe 1891, pl. 9).

Gadow (1892) found that the parrots agree with the cuckoos in 31 of his 40 characters and that (p. 231) "the Coccyges and Gallidae are intimately connected with each other through *Opisthocomus.*" The Psittaci were found to agree with the Pici in 29 points, with the Coraciidae and Falconidae in 25, and with the owls in 22. He concluded: "The Psittaci are much more nearly allied to the Coccyges than to the Falconidae, and of the Coccyges the Musophagidae are nearer than the Cuculidae" (p. 232). The Cuculiformes were also thought to be linked to the Coraciiformes. In a "Final Conclusion," Gadow recorded his belief in a "close affinity between the Psittaci and Coraciidae, but less intimate than with the Coccyges . . . [which] are, however, closely related to the Coraciidae, and are (as indicated by the *Opisthocomus*-Gallidae connexion) the lowest of the three groups of Psittaci, Coraciidae, and Coccyges" (pp. 234–235). Gadow placed the cuckoos, turacos, and parrots in his order Cuculiformes next to his Coraciiformes, which included the owls, nightjars, swifts, hummingbirds, colies, trogons, rollers, motmots, kingfishers, bee-eaters, hoopoes, hornbills, and woodhoopoes. He used essentially the same arrangement in 1893.

Beddard (1898a) treated the Cuculi and Musophagi as adjacent groups, tabulated differences between them, and noted that "the skull of *Corythaix* [a turaco] is barely desmognathous, and by no . . . means especially like that of a cuckoo" (p. 284). Beddard considered "the question of the affinities of the cuckoos to be a difficult one. By Gadow they are placed nearest the Musophagi and next nearest to the Psittaci. Fürbringer's views do not greatly differ. There seems to be no doubt that these birds are an archaic group not far from the point where the Anomalogonatae and Homalogonatae of Garrod diverge. They are, like the Musophagi, quintocubital; their intestines are simple; and they have the complete muscle formula (B being in some forms absent). These characters are found in others among the more primitive of the higher birds" (p. 281).

Beddard thought that the cuckoos show similarities to the "Pico-Passeres . . . in the structure of the foot . . . the tendons of the patagium . . . the marked resemblance in the syrinx to . . . Caprimulgi, and in a less degree to the Striges" (p. 281). He also investigated the anatomy of the Channel-billed Cuckoo (*Scythrops*) (1898b), a ground-cuckoo (*Carpococcyx*) (1901a), a hawk-cuckoo (*Hierococcyx* = *Cuculus*), and allied forms (1902b).

In the *Hand-List* Sharpe (1900) placed the Musophagi and Cuculi in the order Coccyges, listed between the Trogones and Scansores (honeyguides, barbets, toucans).

The intestinal coiling pattern of the Cuculi is derived from a "coraciiform-cuculiform metacentre," according to Mitchell (1901a). He found a similar pattern in several genera of cuckoos but ascribed the differences in the tract of the turacos to their frugivorous diet.

Shufeldt (1901g) reviewed the osteology of the cuckoos and concluded that their affinities are with "the Musophagidae, Bucconidae, Galbulidae, Meropidae, Momotidae, Bucerotidae, Upupidae, Todidae, Coraciidae, Rhamphastidae, Capitonidae and perhaps some few others" (p. 47). He considered the cuckoos to be "quite remote" from "the Caprimulgi, the Cypseli, the Trogones, the Trochili and the Pici." He declined to follow Garrod in placing "the Cuculidae and Musophagidae together in with the Gallinaceous birds!" (p. 48). Shufeldt (1904b) made the Cuculi and Musophagi suborders in the order Cuculiformes. In 1909, in a study of the skeleton of *Clamator glandarius*, he used the same classification.

Pycraft (1903c) believed that cuckoos and turacos have similar skeletons. He also thought that skull characters indicate a relationship between cuckoos and some rollers and puffbirds, and through the Musophagidae to the Hoatzin.

Chandler (1916) was convinced that feather structure showed cuckoos and parrots to be "undoubtedly related," and he followed Knowlton (1909) by placing them in one order. Chandler also believed that "the Cuculiformes are very closely related to the Coraciiformes, and should probably be considered as nearly allied to the immediate forerunners of this group. The question of their descent is likewise easy, the only lower groups to which they show affinity being the peristeropode Galli and the Columbae; in general form of pennaceous barbules they are nearer to the former, but in the structure of the down and in some details of the structure of the pennaceous barbules, e.g., the prongs on the hooklets, they show affiliation to the latter. The Cuculi, especially the Musophagidae, come nearer the gallinaceous and columbid birds, while the parrots are nearer the Coraciiformes in the structure of their feathers" (p. 367).

E. Stresemann (1934) assigned the cuckoos and turacos to his order Cuculi. He considered the Hoatzin to be closely allied to the galliforms and to resemble the turacos only by convergence (p. 818). However, in 1965, he changed his mind when he discovered important differences between the molt patterns of the Hoatzin and the galliforms.

Moreau (1938) described various aspects of the biology of *Turacus* (*Tauraco*) *fischeri*, and the structure of the musophagid foot which he described "as having a fourth (outside) toe that can be brought back to form an angle of about seventy degrees with the first toe, and forward until it almost touches the third toe, but normally is held at right angles to the main axis of the foot" (pp. 668–669). This condition of "semi-zygodactyly" thus differs from the truly zygodactyl foot of the cuckoos in which the fourth toe is permanently reversed.

The genus *Coua*, a group of 10 species of non-parasitic cuckoos endemic to Madagascar, was studied by Rand (1936), Milon (1952), and Appert (1970, 1980). *Coua* is sometimes given subfamily rank (Couinae) (e.g., Thomson 1964) or included in the

Centropodinae with the coucals. Superficially at least, the couas resemble *Centropus* and the turacos (Moreau 1964), but their relationships to other cuckoos are uncertain.

Peters' (1940) classification of the cuckoos was much like that of Shelley (1891). Peters transferred *Tapera* and *Morococcyx* to the Neomorphinae and erected a subfamily for *Coua*.

Lowe (1943) found large differences between the cuckoos and turacos in pterylosis, osteology, and myology and recommended their placement in separate orders. He also contrasted their coloration, color patterns, and food habits.

The Mallophaga of the turacos are more like those of the galliforms than those of cuckoos (Clay 1947). Clay also reported that the Mallophaga of the Hoatzin show no obvious relationships to those of either the turacos or galliforms.

Hopkins (1949) suggested that the similarities between the Mallophaga of turacos and galliforms might be due to accidental transfer rather than common ancestry of the hosts.

Mayr and Amadon (1951:8) epitomized the uncertainty about the relationships of cuckoos and turacos by noting the "difference of opinion, first as to whether or not the turacos (Musophagidae) should be associated with the Galli, and second whether or not the cuckoos (Cuculidae) are related to the turacos." They thought "it best to place the turacos tentatively near the Galli" but also that "it is entirely possible that the Musophagidae are somewhat primitive relatives of the Cuculidae, so we tentatively follow convention in associating the two families in the same order." Conclusion: When in doubt, follow tradition.

The morphology of the hind limb in *Coccyzus*, *Crotophaga*, and *Geococcyx* was described by Berger (1952). He did not speculate on ordinal or familial relationships but did recommend that *Coccyzus* be placed in a separate subfamily because its pelvic muscle formula (AXY+) differs from that of the other genera in the Phaenicophaeinae (ABXY+).

Berger (1953a) found the pterylosis of *Coua caerulea* to be most similar to those of the New World genera *Geococcyx*, *Crotophaga*, and *Guira*. He also found (1953b) the appendicular anatomy of *Coua* to be similar to that of *Geococcyx*. Berger (1954) examined the wing musculature of the American genera *Coccyzus*, *Crotophaga*, and *Geococcyx* and concluded that the differences among them could be adaptations related to their flight patterns. He suggested that the "differences in flight pattern . . . may best be explained in terms of a progressive reduction in relative wing area and a progressive increase in body size from *Coccyzus* to *Geococcyx*."

Berger (1955) studied the anatomy of the glossy cuckoos and recommended that *Lampromorpha* and *Chalcites* be included in *Chrysococcyx*. In 1960 Berger compared the myology, pterylosis, and syringeal anatomy of the cuckoos and turacos and concluded that the turacos should be placed in a separate order, the Musophagiformes. He reviewed previous classifications of the cuckoos, pointed out the great anatomical diversity among the genera, and decided that Peters' (1940) classification is unsatisfactory.

Verheyen (1956b,c) reviewed the anatomical evidence, added data from a primarily osteological study, and concluded that the resemblances between cuckoos and turacos are due to convergence. He believed that the turacos are related to the galliforms, and that the cuckoos are closest to the woodpeckers and colies. He divided the Cuculiformes into the suborders Centropodes and Cuculi, and proposed that the Musophagiformes, with suborders Musophagi and Opisthocomi (Hoatzin), be placed next to the Galliformes.

Moreau (1958) reviewed the taxonomy of the Musophagidae and recognized 18 species in five genera. He discussed some of the opinions about the relationships of the turacos and suggested that comparisons between turacos and coucals (*Centropus*) might be "particularly relevant" in determining the affinities of the turacos. Moreau (1964) again reviewed the turacos and noted that they "have been associated . . . with either the Galliformes or the Cuculiformes, and have also been exalted to a distinct order, the Musophagiformes (Musophagae of Stresemann)" (p. 842).

Sibley (1960) found the electrophoretic patterns of the egg-white proteins of the turacos to be unlike those of galliforms. The pattern of *Tauraco corythaix* was similar to that of *Cacomantis merulinus* and that of *Crinifer concolor* resembled that of *Centropus benghalensis*. Sibley stated that "it seems apparent that the coucals . . . are indeed the link between typical cuckoos and turacos" (p. 243). This statement was nonsense, regardless of similarities between the protein patterns. A living group cannot be a link between two other living groups.

V. Stresemann and Stresemann (1961a) determined the primary molt sequence in most of the genera of cuckoos. The primaries molt in the unusual "transilient" mode in which the molt "proceeds by forward or backward leaps across one or more adjoining quills" (p. 330). The variations in molt patterns were considered to be "an important criterion of affinity" within the cuckoos, and generic groupings were proposed.

The Stresemanns (1966) found that the primary molt in the turacos and the kingfisher genus *Chloroceryle* occurs in two "action groups"—an outer and an inner. The molt sequence is "descendant" but is usually disturbed by transilience as in the cuckoos. In 1969 they described the molts in *Clamator* and found that its primary molt differs from that of *Cuculus*. They concluded that "this confirms the isolated position of *Clamator*."

Sibley and Ahlquist (1972) compared the electrophoretic patterns of the egg-white proteins of cuckoos, turacos, and other non-passerine taxa and concluded that "the Cuculi and Musophagi are related and should be placed in the same order." We declined to speculate about "the nearest allies of the Cuculiformes" and noted the anatomical and biochemical heterogeneity of the cuckoos.

R. F. Baird and P. V. Rich (pers. comm.) have a fossil "cuculid from the Paleocene of Brazil" which indicates that cuckoos were in South America at least 60 MYA.

In summary: Most authors have thought that the cuckoos and turacos are related, but their decisions were often influenced by tradition rather than by convincing evidence of homologous shared derived characters. A relationship between turacos and galliforms has frequently been proposed, usually because the Hoatzin (*Opisthocomus*) was considered to be the link. This is clearly not true; the Hoatzin is a cuckoo. The cuckoos have also been thought to be allied to the parrots, some piciforms, or some coraciiforms, but these proposals have gained little support.

The DNA Hybridization Evidence (Figs. 76–84, 333, 353, 355, 360)

The DNA comparisons show that the cuckoos have no close living relatives, but are the sister group of a large assemblage that includes more than half of the groups of living birds. The divergence between the Cuculimorphae and their sister group at $\Delta T_{50}H$ 23.7 probably occurred in the Cretaceous. This ancient branching helps to account for the extensive morphological and genetic differences between the cuckoos and other groups, and within the Cuculiformes.

It seems unlikely that the turacos (Musophagiformes) are closely related to the cuckoos; the turaco lineage diverged from the cuckoo lineage at Δ 23.7. The relationships of the turacos are discussed further under the Owls ("The DNA Hybridization Evidence"). See Figs. 100, 101.

The diversity within the Cuculiformes is not completely revealed by our data because we lack the DNAs of many genera. However, even these limited comparisons support Berger's (1960) conclusion that the group is diverse and that the classification of Peters (1940) does not express that diversity.

Fig. 76 (*Cuculus*) demonstrates the great diversity among the cuckoos, and the clusters relative to *Cuculus*.

Fig. 77 (*Cuculus*) includes heteroduplex curves of owls, Oilbird, pigeons, parrots, and a mousebird. The relative position of the owls (*Otus*, *Tyto*) and the nightjars again raises the question of rates of evolution and ages at maturity, as for the trogons and mousebirds.

Fig. 78 (*Cuculus*) includes additional groups, all quite distant from *Cuculus*, but with the *Turaco* curve closest to the homoduplex. Here again is the question of whether the position of the turaco curve indicates closer relationship to the cuckoos or a slower rate of DNA evolution. Because the turacos, owls, tubenoses, and several other groups produce melting curves that are among the closest to tracer-tracer curves of various taxa, we believe that the reasonable explanation is rate slowdown. For most of the taxa that behave in this manner we know that they do not begin to breed until more than one or two years of age, but we have no age at maturity data for the turacos.

Fig. 79 (*Opisthocomus*). In this experiment the tracer had a low percentage of reassociation, apparently because the Hoatzin driver DNA was faulty. The heteroduplex curves were normal. The percentage of hybridization of the homoduplex was corrected to produce a better-looking curve, but the heteroduplex curves were not corrected. Note that *Guira* is closest to *Opisthocomus*, the other cuckoos are next in the sequence, and the galliforms are most distant. This is evidence that the Hoatzin is more closely related to the cuckoos than to the galliforms.

Fig. 80 (*Crotophaga*) shows that *Guira* is closest to the anis, and that the roadrunners and other New World cuckoos are quite distant from the anis and *Guira*. The position of the *Turaco* curve may indicate that the turacos are related to the cuckoos, or that the turacos have a slower rate of DNA evolution. We cannot choose between these possibilities on present evidence.

Fig. 81 (*Crotophaga*) includes the Channel-billed Cuckoo (*Scythrops*), which is quite distant from the ani tracer, with a turaco next in the sequence, followed by a roller, trogon, kingfisher, motmot, jacamar, mousebird, woodpecker, and toucan. Again, the question of the significance of the position of the turaco curve: if the turacos did not occupy a similar position relative to other tracers (e.g. trogon, mousebird), we would accept the turaco curve as evidence that the turacos are the next closest relatives of the cuckoos. For the present, it is better to continue to question the significance of the turaco curves, as noted above; and see the following Fig. 82.

Fig. 82 (*Crotophaga*) lends credence to the view that the turacos are among the groups with delayed maturity and relatively slow rates of DNA evolution. Note that the closest curves to the homoduplex beyond *Guira* are a plover, a hawk, and a turaco. If we take these curves as direct evidence of relationships we must accept the plover and hawk as closer relatives of the cuckoos than are the turacos. However, the plovers and hawks begin to breed at an average age of two years, and we suggest that the curves reflect a rate slowdown in these groups. The position of the *Tauraco* curve suggests, again, that the turacos do not begin to breed until more than one year of age.

Fig. 83 (*Crotophaga*) includes another turaco (*Crinifer*), a caprimulgiform (*Steatornis*), and two owls. These curves intersect the vertical axis at ca. 40% to 45%, which is at the outer fringe of the positions of cuckoo heteroduplexes in some of the sets above. Previous comments about owls and turacos apply to this set.

Fig. 84 (*Geococcyx*) indicates that *Crotophaga* and *Guira* are closer to the roadrunners than are the other cuckoos in this set. Of special interest is the position of the turaco (*Corythaix-oides*), between the Jamaican Lizard-Cuckoo and the Dwarf Cuckoo. This provides additional evidence that the turacos have a slow rate of DNA evolution; they may also be the next closest relatives of the cuckoos. Another interesting aspect of these curves is the evidence that the New World cuckoos form three clusters: roadrunners and ground-cuckoos, anis and the Guira Cuckoo, and the American Cuckoos (*Coccyzus*, *Piaya*, *Saurothera*).

The FITCH tree (Fig. 333) clusters the roadrunner (*Geococcyx*) with the ani (*Crotophaga*), but the Old World *Cuculus* clusters with the American cuckoo (*Coccyzus*) as in Fig. 360. The turaco is 22.2 distance units from *Cuculus*; *Colius* is 27.3 units from *Cuculus*.

We conclude that the cuckoos are an ancient lineage with substantial genetic diversity among the living groups. Their next nearest living relatives are uncertain. The turacos may be their nearest relatives, but the evidence is not convincing because the effect of a slow DNA rate of evolution in the turacos may account for the relative positions of the turaco curves in some of the sets of melting curves. For the same reason we doubt that the owls and nightjars are especially close to the cuckoos. It is likely that the divergence of the cuckoo lineage was so long ago that the idea of close living relatives is irrelevant. The cuckoos are about equally diverged from many of the non-passerine groups.

The Hoatzin

Order CUCULIFORMES
   Infraorder Crotophagides
      Parvorder Opisthocomida
         Family Opisthocomidae: *Opisthocomus hoazin*, Hoatzin

The Hoatzin has been a taxonomic puzzle since its discovery over 200 years ago. It is a slender bird, about 65 cm long, brownish in color with lighter streaks and buffy tips to the tail feathers. The small head bears a ragged, bristly crest of reddish-brown feathers, and the bare skin of the face is bright blue. It has often been thought to resemble a chachalaca (*Ortalis*: Cracidae) but it is actually more similar to the Guira Cuckoo (*G. guira*) in color and pattern, although much larger. The Hoatzin is specialized in several ways and its structural peculiarities have made it difficult to prove an alliance to other avian groups.

The Hoatzin lives in the flooded forests and riparian growth along the rivers and streams of northern South America in the Guianas, Venezuela, and the basins of the Orinoco and Amazon rivers in Brazil, eastern Colombia, eastern Ecuador, and Bolivia. It feeds primarily on the leaves, flowers, and fruits of marsh plants, including *Montrichardia* (Araceae), the arboreal White Mangrove (*Avicennia*), and species of Rutaceae, Fabaceae, and several other plant families. Strahl (1985) recorded more than 40 species in over 20 families of plants in the diet of the birds he observed in Venezuela. Grimmer (1962) and Strahl (1985) found them feeding only on plants; others have recorded fish and crabs in their diet. Grajal et al. (1989) recorded 52 species of plants in 25 families, but 90% of the diet is composed of 17 plant species. The birds prefer new growth with a high water content.

The Hoatzin has a large, muscular crop with a deeply ridged interior lining. Grajal et al. (1989) found that active foregut fermentation of the fibrous plant matter takes place in the crop and that the ridged lining increases the absorptive area. This is the only known case of foregut microbial fermentation in birds, although the same process is found in mammals, such as the ruminant ungulates, colobine monkeys, sloths, and macropodid marsupials. The lower esophagus of the Hoatzin is greatly sacculated, which delays the passage rate of particles to the lower gut. Additional fermentation occurs in the paired caeca.

The sternum and pectoral girdle are modified to accommodate the crop. There is a large callosity on the ventral apterium in the breast region where the heavy, filled crop is often rested on a branch when the bird is perched.

Hoatzins form large flocks when not breeding, but with the first rains the flocks break up into smaller nesting groups of two to seven birds. Breeding groups are usually composed of a breeding adult pair and a variable number (0–5) of helpers at the nest, usually offspring of the previous year. Like the anis (*Crotophaga*) and the Guira Cuckoo, the Hoatzin forms a communal nesting association (Young 1929; Chapman 1938; Skutch 1935, 1966; D. E. Davis 1940a,b; Grimmer 1962; Strahl 1985).

The members of a nesting group build a single, flat nest of loosely entwined dry twigs in branches overhanging the water. Mating seems to be indiscriminate, possibly polygamous, and all members of the group incubate the eggs and care for the young. The two to five eggs are buffy with pink, brown, or bluish spots, and they hatch after ca. 28 days of incubation. The young have two claws on the digits of the wings with which they grasp branches when climbing near the nest before they can fly. The claws are lost before maturity, but the adults also use their wings for support when moving through the branches. The birds are rather clumsy in moving through the vegetation and they fly poorly, but both young and adults swim well. When alarmed the young birds may drop into the water and hide until the danger is past, then climb back to the nest. The young have two successive coats of down and are fed on plant material from the crops of the adults (Grimmer 1962, Sick 1964a). Other accounts of the natural history include those of Beebe (1909) Young (1929), Quelch (1890), Goeldi (1896), Chubb (1916), and Strahl (1985).

The young of the Groove-billed Ani (*Crotophaga sulcirostris*) and the Smooth-billed Ani (*C. ani*) also use their beak, feet, and wings in clambering about near the nest. When frightened, a flightless ani youngster either moves away through the branches or drops to the ground and hides in the vegetation, later returning to the nest (Skutch 1959, 1966). Beebe (1909) also commented on the behavioral similarities between the Hoatzin and the anis.

Family OPISTHOCOMIDAE: 1/1. *Opisthocomus hoazin*. Schizognathous; ABXY+; aftershaft present; oil gland feathered; 10 rectrices; sternum deeply incised in front to allow space for the crop; spina externa ankylosed with furcula; most other characters as in other cuculiforms.

Historical Review of the Classification

The Hoatzin was described by P. L. S. Müller in 1776 as *Phasianus hoazin*; thus, a relationship to the galliforms was suggested at the earliest possible time. Illiger (1811) was among those who placed the Hoatzin with the galliforms.

Nitzsch (1840) described the pterylosis and placed the Hoatzin with the colies and turacos in his family Amphibolae. Gray (1844–49) included the Hoatzin, colies, turacos, and hornbills in the tribe Conirostres of his order Passeres.

Huxley (1867) had only an incomplete skull and the feet of a Hoatzin for study. He found that the slender vomer bifurcates anteriorly unlike that in other birds, and that the tarsus is like that of the galliforms. He assigned *Opisthocomus* to a "special division" of his Schizognathae. Huxley (1868) soon made a complete study of the skeleton and decided that in most characters the Hoatzin is like the galliforms and columbiforms. The characters that differ from those of the latter two groups are either unique to the Hoatzin or similar to those of the turacos. Huxley thought that the Hoatzin is a highly modified form derived from a "Gallo-columbine" stock. He placed it in his suborder Schizognathae in a monotypic group, the Heteromorphae, placed between the sandgrouse (Pteroclomorphae) and the pigeons (Peristeromorphae). The cuckoos were far away in the suborder Desmognathae, group Coccygomorphae, family Cuculidae, between the turacos and puffbirds.

Sundevall (1872, see 1889:253) commented on *Opisthocomus* as one of "certain genera of doubtful position in the present system." He compared some of its characters with the megapodes, lyrebirds (*Menura*), guans (Cracidae), and the oscine passerines, and concluded: "All these points considered, *Opisthocomus* . . . can scarcely be placed in any other position than the last in the first order, after *Menura*, but in an Appendix, or, if it is preferred, in the place of a sixth Cohort, with the name Heteromorphae of Huxley, which cohort is distinguished from all the others of the first order by the following characters:—tarsus scaled in front; behind (on the sole) very numerously covered with diamond-shaped scales; the plumage hard and rather rigid."

Sundevall's "first order" was the Oscines and the fifth "Cohort" included mostly New World suboscine taxa, plus *Menura*. The cuckoos were in "Order II. Volucres."

The pelvic muscle formula of the Hoatzin, the anis, and the galliforms is ABXY+ (Garrod 1879a, Beddard 1898a:285). Garrod (1879a) noted other similarities to galliforms and cuckoos and concluded that the Hoatzin is an intermediate form which helps to ally the cuckoos and turacos to the galliforms.

Sclater (1880b) assigned *Opisthocomus* to a monotypic order which he thought to be most closely allied to the guans and chachalacas (Cracidae) but also distantly related to the cuckoos and turacos. Reichenow (1882) recognized the Opisthocomidae in his order Rasores (Galliformes). Elliott (1885) was reluctant to specify the nearest allies of the Hoatzin, and placed it in a monotypic order next to his Gallinae.

The myology of the Hoatzin was considered similar to those of the Barn Owl (*Tyto*) and the Wood Pigeon (*Columba palumbus*) by Perrin (1875). He made no comparisons to galliforms or cuckoos, so his conclusions are meaningless. Goodchild (1886) found the arrangement of the wing coverts of the Hoatzin to be most like that of cuckoos.

Seebohm (1888b) listed six skeletal characters in which the Hoatzin differs from the galliforms and agrees with the bustards. This caused him to place *Opisthocomus* in his suborder Grallae, with the gruiforms. A few years later, Seebohm (1895:27) viewed the Hoatzin as "in some respects the most aberrant of birds" and included it with the trumpeters (*Psophia*) and the sungrebes in his suborder Psophiae of the Galliformes.

Fürbringer (1888) argued for a close relationship between the Hoatzin and the galliforms. He recognized the Opisthocomidae and Gallidae in his suborder Galliformes, and believed that the next nearest relatives of the Hoatzin were the pigeons. He accepted a fairly distant alliance between *Opisthocomus* and the Rallidae and an even more remote relationship to the tinamous. Gadow (1888a:180), in his review of Fürbringer's *opus magnum*, recorded Fürbringer's opinion: "Closely allied to the Galli is Opisthocomus, an old type now dying out;

the last solitary species has reached a high degree of one-sided specialization, which elevates this bird above its nearest allies to the level of low arboreal birds." This cryptic comment seems meaningless, but Fürbringer's opinions carried as much weight as his ponderous volumes and served to mislead his successors about as often as they enlightened them.

Gadow (1889, 1892, 1893) found that *Opisthocomus* resembles the Galliformes and Cuculiformes in the following characters:

Galliformes—Precocial young; fusion of thoracic vertebrae; structure of syrinx, palate, and feet; large crop.

Cuculiformes—Deep temporal fossae, short mandibular processes, no basipterygoid processes, internal spine of sternum, structure of metasternum, large coracoid, spotted eggs, ten rectrices.

In the following characters *Opisthocomus* differs from both the Galliformes and Cuculiformes: Lack of apteria on sides of neck, number of cervical vertebrae, small thoracic haemapophyses, shape of liver, modification of the crop as a digestive organ, distribution of down on the adult.

Gadow (1892:231) believed that "the Coccyges and Gallidae are intimately connected with each other through *Opisthocomus*." He thought that the turacos were a cuculiform group most like the Hoatzin, but he placed the Opisthocomi as a suborder of the Galliformes in his classification (1893:300). This arrangement was adopted by Wetmore (1930) and E. Stresemann (1934). Gadow considered *Opisthocomus* intermediate between the Galliformes and Cuculiformes and found more resemblances to the Musophagidae than to the Cuculidae.

This is another example of the idea that living taxa can be the links, or connections, between other living taxa. This misconception survives to the present, in spite of its lack of phyletic logic. It is the result of confusing similarity with relationship—analogy with homology.

In his classification Sharpe (1891) placed the Opisthocomiformes between the Columbiformes and Ralliformes (rails, sungrebes). In his diagram of presumed relationships the Rallidae and Cracidae are closest to the Hoatzin, with the sandgrouse and pigeons more distant.

With typical prolixity Parker (1891a) discussed the embryology and anatomy of the Hoatzin. He emphasized the "primitive" characters of *Opisthocomus* and apparently thought it was at the base of the "Alectoromorphae," a group consisting of the pheasants, quail, sandgrouse, and pigeons. Parker was obviously baffled in trying to interpret the characters of the Hoatzin.

Pycraft (1895) corrected errors about the pterylosis of the Hoatzin in the papers of previous authors. He found a "striking general resemblance" in pterylosis among the Hoatzin, turacos, and coucals (*Centropus*), but "it is not improbable that the life-history of *Opisthocomus* is a survival of what was at one time shared by the Galli, since in nestlings of Cracidae and Gallidae the wing exhibits precisely the same phenomena as . . . noticed in *Opisthocomus*" (p. 362). However, Pycraft declined to comment on the relationships of the Hoatzin.

Beddard (1889a) described the embryonic wing of the Hoatzin and the syrinx and pterylosis of the young and adult. In his book (1898a) he stated that "There is no doubt that . . . the hoatzin . . . forms a well-marked group of birds" (p. 285). He reviewed previous papers on the Hoatzin, described its anatomy, and mentioned comparisons with several other groups. Although he did not comment on the relationships of the Hoatzin, he placed the Opisthocomi between the Musophagi and the Galli.

Mitchell (1896b, 1901a) examined the intestinal tract of the Hoatzin and, like Garrod (1879a), observed similarities between it and the cuckoos. However, he thought the Hoatzin was most similar to the sandgrouse and pigeons. He was impressed by what he considered important differences between the Hoatzin and the galliforms and cuckoos (1901a:221).

Shufeldt (1904b) placed the Hoatzin in a suborder in his Galliformes, which also included suborders for the tinamous and hemipodes. In his list, *Opisthocomus* precedes the sandgrouse and pigeons. He (1918a) described the skeleton and other aspects of the anatomy of a young Hoatzin, but did not compare it with other groups and did not comment on its relationships.

In British Guiana and Venezuela Beebe (1909) observed some aspects of the behavior of the Hoatzin. He described the use of the wing by adults in climbing, and correlated the weak flight with the large crop and correlated reduction in the size of the sternum. He was impressed by the behavioral similarities between the Hoatzin and the anis (*Crotophaga*).

Banzhaf (1929) studied the wing of the Hoatzin and concluded that the skeleton, musculature, and innervation of the distal part of the wing are most like those of the pigeons, but that the pectoral region and proximal section of the wing resemble those of the Galliformes. He thought that *Opisthocomus* is less closely related to the galliforms than had Fürbringer and others. He made comparisons with some other groups, but not with cuckoos; thus his conclusions are meaningless.

Böker (1929) thought that the Hoatzin might have evolved its peculiar flight and strong wing and tail feathers from a South American cuculiform ancestor with a gliding or fluttering flight. To determine how this may have occurred, he examined the Owl Parrot (*Strigops*), which also has a large crop and reduced sternum and pectoral musculature. Although he concluded that *Strigops* is a modified parrot (which was not in doubt) he could not determine the ancestry of the Hoatzin.

Stresemann (1934) placed *Opisthocomus* in its own order but, following Fürbringer, stated that it is closely related to the galliforms. He attributed turaco similarities to convergence. Wetmore (1930, 1960), Peters (1934), Mayr and Amadon (1951), and Storer (1960a) placed the Hoatzin in a monotypic suborder in the Galliformes.

Faith had replaced reason. The erroneous tradition begun by Müller in 1776, and sanctified by the authoritarian blessings of Huxley, Fürbringer, and Gadow, had become the gospel.

Lemmrich (1931) found that the 10 species of galliforms he studied had 13–15 bony plates in the sclerotic ring of the eye, but that the Hoatzin has 12. He noted that the difference is "very remarkable" (transl.) because there tends to be little variation within a related group. There are few birds with 12 plates but they include the cuckoos and parrots.

De Queiroz and Good (1988) examined the pattern of scleral ring overlap in *Opisthocomus*, galliforms, cuculiforms, and other birds to determine the pattern in the Hoatzin and "its bearing on the phylogenetic relationships of this taxon." Their results were equivocal, but they concluded that if it is assumed that the Hoatzin is either galliform or cuculiform, the "scleral ring morphology suggests a closer relationship to Cuculiformes" than to Galliformes.

The Hoatzin is parasitized by five genera of feather lice, of which four are not found on other birds and the fifth is widespread. According to Clay (1950), the distribution of Mallophaga suggests an "isolated position" for *Opisthocomus*.

Howard (1950) thought that the fossil *Filholornis* from the upper Eocene or lower Oligocene of France was allied to the cracids and the Hoatzin. Brodkorb (1964) proposed a new subfamily for *Filholornis* in the Cracidae. A. H. Miller (1953) described *Hoazinoides magdalenae* from the late Miocene of Colombia on the basis of the posterior portion of a skull. He regarded this species as a primitive member of the Opisthocomidae and interpreted its characters as indicating a relationship to the Cracidae. Brodkorb (1964) accepted Miller's opinion and placed the Opisthocomidae next to the Cracidae.

The skull musculature and its innervation in the Hoatzin were compared with galliforms, turacos, and pigeons by Barnikol (1953). He found similarities between the Hoatzin and the turacos but concluded that the Hoatzin is an isolated species with no close ties to any of these groups. Of 40 anatomical characters of the Hoatzin he found 8 shared with galliforms, 9 with pigeons, and 13 with turacos. Again, no comparisons were made with cuckoos.

It is not surprising that Parsons (1954) found the early embryo of the Hoatzin to be similar to that of the Domestic Fowl (*G. gallus*), but in the absence of comparisons with other groups this conclusion is useless as an index to relationships.

Verheyen (1956c) found that of 66 skeletal characters of the Hoatzin, 50 were shared with the turacos. This led him to combine the two groups in his order Musophagiformes, which he believed to be allied to the Anhimiformes (screamers) and Galliformes. Later (1961), "owing to new information," he placed *Opisthocomus* in a suborder of his Galliformes next to the Cracidae.

Hudson et al. (1959:Table 3) listed 13 aspects of the hind limb musculature in which the Hoatzin differs from galliforms. Hudson and Lanzilloti (1964:110) enumerated 21 "important ways" in which the pectoral musculature of *Opisthocomus* is unlike that of galliforms and concluded that "*Opisthocomus* has either been erroneously associated with the Galliformes, or has diverged so far from the original ancestral condition, that there is little or no justification for retaining it in the order" (p. 111).

E. Stresemann (1965) and Stresemann and Stresemann (1966a) discovered that the feathers and molting patterns of the Hoatzin differ from the galliforms in four aspects:

1. Flight feathers are lacking in the nestling plumage.
2. The first flight feathers grow nearly to the size of those of the adults and are not molted before the bird has matured.
3. Both outer secondaries are not shorter than the adjacent ones and all develop at the same time.
4. The primaries are not replaced in the sequence found in the galliforms but in a continuous stepwise process.

These differences plus those from anatomy prompted Stresemann (1965:64) to conclude: "Wenn *Opisthocomus* mit den Hühnervögeln verwandt ist, dann nur durch Adam und Eva." (If *Opisthocomus* is related to the galliforms, it is only through Adam and Eve.) Reason was beginning to supplant tradition.

Sibley and Ahlquist (1972) compared the starch gel electrophoretic patterns of the egg-white proteins of the Hoatzin with those of all pertinent groups. We concluded that "*Opisthocomus* is not closely related to the gallinaceous birds and neither is it close to the turacos (Musophagidae). We suggest instead that it is most closely allied to the neotropical Crotophaginae."

In 1973 Sibley and Ahlquist reviewed the Hoatzin problem and added comparisons of the egg-white proteins produced by the electrophoretic technique of isoelectric focusing in acrylamide gel. We concluded that "all evidence has been found to be consistent with an assignment to the subfamily Crotophaginae of the Cuculidae. There is no substance to the long-accepted alliance to the Galliformes and the relationship to the Musophagidae is simply that of the two families within the Cuculiformes."

In spite of the extensive morphological evidence to the contrary, Cracraft (1981) assigned the Hoatzin to the Galliformes. He cited Brush (1979) who found "no clear-cut similarities" between the electrophoretic patterns of the Hoatzin and cuckoos. Cracraft noted that "*Opisthocomus* might be related to cuckoos, but I find very little evidence to support it" and claimed that "the osteology of *Opisthocomus* is much more like galliforms than cuculiforms." He concluded that the systematic position of the Hoatzin "needs further analysis, and until that time I tentatively retain the family in the Galliformes."

The DNA Hybridization Evidence (Figs. 79, 360)

The DNA hybrids between *Opisthocomus* and other taxa indicate that the Hoatzin is a Neotropical cuckoo most closely related to *Geococcyx*, *Crotophaga*, and *Guira*. The divergence between the Hoatzin lineage and that of the roadrunners, anis, and the Guira Cuckoo was at $\Delta T_{50}H$ 16.4 (Fig. 360). Sibley et al. (1988) placed the Hoatzin in the monotypic parvorder Opisthocomida of the infraorder Crotophagides. The Crotophagides branched from the Cuculides at Δ 17.6. This divergence may have been a result of the opening of the Atlantic Ocean between Africa and South America. The delta value of 17.6 is close to that of 17.1 between the Ostrich and rheas.

Fig. 79 (*Opisthocomus*) shows that the Hoatzin is more closely related to the cuckoos than to the galliforms. The Cuculimorphae branched from a large assemblage of non-passerine groups at $\Delta T_{50}H$ 23.7.

The relationships of the cuckoos, including the Hoatzin, have been discussed above under the Cuckoos, Hoatzin, and Turacos.

We conclude that the Hoatzin is a highly modified cuckoo, most closely related to the Guira Cuckoo, the anis (*Crotophaga*), and the roadrunners (Neomorphidae).

Parrots

Superorder Psittacimorphae
  Order PSITTACIFORMES
    Family Psittacidae: Parrots, Macaws, Cockatoos, Lories

Family PSITTACIDAE: 80/358 (81/332 Forshaw 1973). Parrots are mainly tropical; a few species occur in temperate regions. They occur on all continents and many islands.

The parrots are defined by their distinctive, stout, hooked bill with a prominent cere, zygodactyl feet, and sparse, hard plumage. There has been little doubt about which birds are, and are not, parrots.

The palate is desmognathous; rostrum movable by a hinge-like articulation with the skull; feet prehensile, zygodactyl; nares holorhinal, impervious; expansor secundariorum absent; carotids usually two, but variable (only left in *Cacatua*); flexor tendons Type 1; pelvic muscles AXY+; sternum fenestrated or indented; diastataxic; no caeca; oil gland tufted or absent; furcula weak, absent in some; syrinx with three pairs of intrinsic muscles; 13–15 cervical vertebrae, usually 14; 10 primaries; 10–14 secondaries; usually 12 rectrices (14 in *Oreopsittacus*); aftershaft present; tarsus with small granular scales or papillae; orbital ring usually complete; crop present; nest in holes; eggs white; nidicolous; down over entire body; powder downs present, especially developed in uropygial region; young ptilopaedic.

Because they seem to lack close living relatives their nearest allies have been difficult to identify and several groups have been proposed. The strong, hooked bill has caused some systematists to associate the parrots with the hawks and owls. The zygodactyl foot is shared with the piciforms and cuckoos, but the parrots and cuckoos have Type 1 flexor tendons, while the piciforms have Gadow's Type 6. The parrots and cuckoos have desmognathous palates, similar pelvic muscle formulas, and similar nares, and they share several other characters, but these are all primitive characters shared with other groups as well. Parrots and cuckoos differ in bill structure, tarsal scutellation, presence (cuckoos) or absence (parrots) of the expansor secundariorum, eutaxy (cuckoos) and diastataxy (parrots), nestlings naked (cuckoos) or downy (parrots), caeca large (cuckoos) or absent (parrots), and in several other characters.

The parrots and pigeons also share some characters, but they differ in so many ways that a close relationship cannot be supported.

Historical Review of the Classification

Linnaeus (1758:96) placed the parrots in the genus *Psittacus* of his order Picae, with the toucans, hornbills, cuckoos, corvines, rollers, orioles, jacamars, starlings, birds of paradise, woodpeckers, hummingbirds, and several other taxa. The birds of prey were in the order Accipitres. Some early classifications (Moehring 1752, Bonaparte 1853, Fitzinger 1856) associated parrots and raptors because of the bill; others assigned the parrots a place near the toucans, woodpeckers, and cuckoos because of the zygodactyl feet (e.g., Brisson 1760, Illiger 1811, Merrem 1813, Vieillot 1816, Temminck 1820, Cabanis 1847).

Nitzsch (1840) placed the parrots in his order of "picarian" birds between the Picinae (woodpeckers) and Lipoglossae (hornbills, hoopoes, kingfishers). He found much variation among parrots in the feather tracts, number of rectrices, and other plumage characters. Gray (1844–49) recognized the Psittacidae, Cacatuidae, and Strigopidae for the parrots and placed them in his order Scansores with the piciforms and cuckoos. Similarly, Lilljeborg (1866) included the Psittacidae in his order Zygodactyli.

Huxley's (1867) "Group Psittacomorphae" was placed between the birds of prey (Aetomorphae) and the Coccygomorphae, the latter composed of 14 families including colies, cuckoos, rollers, trogons, and hornbills.

Finsch (1867) produced the first important monograph of the parrots. He thought them similar to the toucans and cuckoos. On the basis of external characters and the structure of the tongue he divided the Psittacidae into five subfamilies.

Sundevall (1872, see 1889) included the parrots in his order "Volucres," defined on foot and feather characters and noted as nearly the same as "the Picae of Linnaeus." Also in the Volucres were the woodpeckers (Pici), barbets, honeyguides, toucans, jacamars, puffbirds, rollers, cuckoos, turacos, colies, trogons, goatsuckers, swifts, hummingbirds, bee-eaters, kingfishers, hornbills, and pigeons (Coccyges).

Garrod (1872b) found the tongue of the Kea (*Nestor notabilis*) to be like that of the Owl Parrot (*Strigops*), hence *Nestor* is a "typical parrot," not a "trichoglossine" (brush-tongued) parrot.

In Garrod's (1874a) system, based on the oil gland, furcula, carotids, and pelvic musculature, the birds with an ambiens were assigned to the subclass Homalogonatae, those lacking it to the Anomalogonatae. Thus, the cuckoos, parrots, and pigeons were members of the former subclass, the piciforms of the latter. The cuckoos and parrots were placed in the Galliformes in adjacent suborders—another example of nonsense resulting from reliance on a single, minor character.

Garrod (1874d) proposed a classification of the suborder Psittaci, which, as modified by Beddard (1898a:269), follows:

Sub-Order Psittaci:—
    Fam. I. Palaeornithidae. Two carotids. Ambiens absent. Oil gland present.
        Subf.(1.) Palaeornithinae. [11 genera]
        Subf.(2.) Cacatuinae. Orbital ring complete. [cockatoos]

Subf.(3.) Stringopinae. Furcula lost. [5 genera]
Fam. II. Psittacidae. Left carotid superficial.
Div. a. Ambiens present.
Subf.(4.) Arinae. [7 genera]
Div. b. Ambiens absent.
Subf.(5.) Pyrrhurinae. [4 genera]
Subf.(6.) Platycercinae. Furcula lost. [4 genera]
Subf.(7.) Chrysotinae. Oil gland lost. [3 genera]

This outline indicates some of the variation within the parrots, and Beddard (1898a:268–269) presented a table showing the condition of the oil gland, ambiens, humeral head of the anconaeus, carotids, and furcula in 48 genera of parrots.

Forbes (1879) cited characters of pterylosis, the superficial left carotid, beak, nostrils, cere, skull, and pelvis to support a relationship among *Lathamus*, *Psephotus*, and *Platycercus*. He did not believe that *Lathamus* is close to *Trichoglossus* and argued that "the abnormal tufted tongue, the retention of the furcula, and the sharp pointed wings may be regarded as adaptations to its tree- and flower-dwelling modes of life" (p. 174). Forbes (1880a) reported on the pterylosis and anatomy of the pigmy parrots, *Nasiterna* (*Micropsitta*), and concluded that their closest relatives are most likely *Cyclopsittacus* (*Opopsitta*) and *Psittacella*. He also thought that *Micropsitta* is related to the ground parrots (*Pezoporus*, *Geopsittacus*) and more distantly to *Agapornis* and *Psittinus*.

Concerning the Psittaci, Sclater (1880b:403) commented: "The affinities of this ancient group to other orders appear to be somewhat remote, but their most natural position seems to be between the Picariae and the Accipitres." He followed Garrod (1874d) for the division of the parrots into families.

Reichenow (1881) thought that the parrots are closely related to the birds of prey. He divided the parrots into nine families. Kingsley (1885) placed his order Psittaci between the Accipitres and the Picariae, which included the cuckoos, goatsuckers, colies, rollers, and other taxa. His classification essentially followed that of Reichenow (1881).

Fürbringer (1888) recognized only a single family in the Psittaciformes and supported the idea that the pigeons are their nearest relatives. He also believed that the parrots are more distantly allied to the Galliformes and to the Coracornithes, a large assemblage composed of the cuckoos, rollers, colies, owls, goatsuckers, trogons, swifts, hummingbirds, woodpeckers, and passerines. In 1889 Fürbringer showed that the peculiarities of the Owl Parrot (*Strigops*) of New Zealand are correlated with its flightless, terrestrial, way of life.

Seebohm (1890a) placed the Psittaci in his subclass Falconiformes, next to the birds of prey. In 1895 he cited the diastataxic wing of the parrots as precluding an alliance with the cuckoos, and the pterylosis and cere as evidence of a relationship to the raptors.

Goodchild (1886, 1891) found that parrots have an arrangement of the secondary coverts similar to that of hawks and owls, a pattern also shared with the herons and cormorants.

Sharpe (1891) placed the Psittaciformes between the Coccyges (turacos, cuckoos) and the Scansores (toucans, barbets, honeyguides), and divided the parrots among six families, following Salvadori (1891). Sharpe commented that "the Parrots, however, do not appear to have any very close allies. In the character of the nestling they are not in the least Accipitrine, and the development of their feathers is carried on in true Picarian fashion—that is to say, that the new feathers are enclosed in the sheath till they attain almost their normal length; and in this respect the Parrots resemble Kingfishers and other Picarian birds. The mode of nesting, too, is Picarian" (p. 65).

In the *Catalogue of Birds* Salvadori (1891) acknowledged his debt to Sundevall, Reichenow, and Finsch as the sources of his classification, but had to "confess" that his arrangement did "not bring us nearer to an understanding of the mutual or phylogenetic relations of the different families" (p. viii). On the basis of characters of the bill, tongue, sternum, and orbital ring, Salvadori divided the Order Psittaci into the Nestoridae, Loriidae, Cyclopsittacidae, Cacatuidae, Psittacidae, and Stringopidae.

Gadow (1892) selected 40 characters "from various organic systems" and used the parrots as an example of his method "of sifting characters" for comparisons among avian groups. He found that the "Psittaci agree with Coccyges in 31 points, with Pici in about 29, with Coraciidae 25, Falconidae 25, Striges 22, Bucerotidae 22, Gallidae 21" (p. 231). He concluded that "the Psittaci are much more nearly allied to the Coccyges than to the Falconidae, and of the Coccyges the Musophagidae [turacos] are nearer than the Cuculidae [cuckoos] because of the vegetable food, ventral pterylosis, presence of an aftershaft, tufted oil-gland, absence of a vomer, truncated mandible, and absence of caeca" (p. 232). His comparison between parrots and owls convinced him that they are "far from each other" and that "the resemblances between the Pici and Psittaci have . . . to be looked upon as convergent analogies" (p. 234). His "Final Conclusion" (1892:234–235) was that

The sifting of all these characters shows an undoubtedly close affinity between the Psittaci and Coraciidae, but less intimate than with the Coccyges. The latter are, however, closely related to the Coraciidae, and are (as indicated by the *Opisthocomus*-Gallidae connexion) the lowest of the three groups of Psittaci, Coraciidae, and Coccyges. Cuculidae, as well as Coraciidae, are zoophagous, chiefly insectivorous. The Striges, as a lateral branch of the lower Coraciine stock, explain the considerable number of characters which connect the Striges with the Coccyges, 28 against 12, and with the Psittaci, 22 against 18. In our hypothetical tree the Psittaci would combine with the Coccyges into one bigger branch—Cuculiformes; the Psittacine twig to stand between that of the Musophagidae and looking towards the branch of the Striges, which again come out of the bigger branch of the Coraciiformes. This big branch and that of the Cuculiformes would ultimately combine into a still bigger branch; below this bifurcation would come off *Opisthocomus* and lower still that of the Gallidae. Thus the Psittaci permit us a glimpse at a large part of the Avine tree, namely at that big branch which downwards points towards the Galliformes and towards the Gallo-Ralline and Rallo-Limicoline region of the tree, while the same branch upwards ends not only in all the so-called Picariae but also in the Pico-Passeres.

Gadow (1892:247–249) translated this verbal dendrogram into a classification (vernacular names added):

Order Columbiformes: Pigeons, Doves
Order Cuculiformes
    Suborder Coccyges: Cuculidae, Musophagidae
    Suborder Psittaci: Psittacidae
Order Coraciiformes
    Suborder Striges: Owls
    Suborder Macrochires: Goatsuckers
    Suborder Colii: Colies
    Suborder Trogones: Trogons
    Suborder Coracii: Rollers, etc.

Gadow's assumption that the Hoatzin (*Opisthocomus*) linked the Coccyges to the galliforms was false; the Hoatzin is a New World cuckoo, as indicated by the egg-white proteins (Sibley and Ahlquist 1973) and confirmed by DNA comparisons (see Hoatzin).

Gadow (1893) divided the parrots into the Trichoglossidae and Psittacidae, on the basis of the presence or absence of horny fibers on the tongue, the condition of the orbital ring, and the direction of the grooves on the maxilla. He also modified the sequence of the groups in his classification by moving the Coraciae above the Striges (p. 301).

Beddard and Parsons (1893) found two main types of syringes in the parrots. In one group the semirings of the bronchi are straight but weak and cartilaginous, and separated by a membrane. The cockatoos and the Owl Parrot (*Strigops*) share this condition. In the other group the bronchial semirings are concave upwards, ossified, and frequently fused together. Genera of the Americas (*Amazona, Pionus*), Africa (*Psittacus, Poicephalus*), and Australasia (*Trichoglossus, Lorius, Eos, Tanygnathus, Polytelis, Platycercus*) share this condition. The syrinx and wing myology convinced Beddard and Parsons that the Owl Parrot is closely related to *Nestor* (Kea, Kaka) and the cockatoo genus *Calyptorhynchus*. They also thought that the cockatoos may be related to the Neotropical macaws (*Ara*).

Mivart (1895) described the hyoids of several parrot genera and (1896b) published a monograph of the lories ("Loriidae").

Beddard (1898a) reviewed the characters of the parrots and the classifications of Garrod, Gadow, Fürbringer, and others. He approved of Garrod's (1874d) arrangement and presented it (pp. 269–270), as noted above. Beddard (pp. 271–272) commented:

The determination of the affinities of the parrots to other groups of birds is one of the hardest problems in ornithology. They have been likened to the Accipitres (mainly, perhaps, on account of the hooked beak and its cere), and to the gallinaceous birds, in the neighbourhood of which they were placed by Garrod. It seems to me that the parrots, like the cuckoos, are a group of birds which are on the borderland between the Anomalogonatae and the higher birds. It is remarkable what a number of points there are in which they show resemblances to the Passeres—the complicated musculature of the syrinx, the absence of biceps slip and expansor secundariorum, the presence of a cucullaris propatagialis, found in the Passeres and in the somewhat passeriform *Upupa* and Pici, the small number of cervical vertebrae, the total want of caeca, allying them not certainly to the Passeres but again to the Pici and many Anomalogonatae, the reduced clavicles of some genera. Zygodactyle feet, moreover, are not found among the higher birds except in the Cuculi and the Musophagi, which are, similarly to the parrots, on the border line between the Anomalogonatae and higher birds. It is noteworthy also that of the Anomalogonatae which present a catapophysial canal (found . . . in one parrot) it is the Pici and the passerine alone. But while it is not so difficult to point out likenesses to the Anomalogonatae it is much harder to indicate resemblances to any of the higher groups of birds. . . . in my opinion . . . they must have emerged from a low anomalogonatous stock at a time not far removed from that at which the Cuculi and Musophagi also emerged, but that there is not a common starting point for all three groups.

It is difficult to discern any logic in the last sentence, but the entire statement is a good example of the kind of discussion that pervaded avian systematics at the end of the nineteenth century. Primitive characters were used as evidence of relationship, concepts of higher and lower groups were fashionable, morphological similarities ("likenesses" or "resemblances") were the only sources of evidence, and the notion that groups that possess characters shared with two other groups must lie in a borderland seemed reasonable. The tree-like structure of phylogeny was accepted, but its logical consequences frequently were ignored or misunderstood.

Thompson (1899) criticized Garrod's (1874d) classification of the parrots, pointing out that the use of a few unsatisfactory characters had led to an unnatural arrangement. Thompson examined the orbital ring, hyoid structure, osteology of the tympanic region, and the quadrate. From these he suggested that *Nestor* and *Strigops* belong in monotypic families, and he commented on the relationships of Australian parrots. He neither proposed a classification nor speculated about the nearest relatives of the parrots. He remarked that "To discover anatomical characters such as might yield . . . a natural classification of the Parrots has been the desire of many ornithologists, but the search has availed little."

In the *Hand-List* Sharpe (1900) used "Psittaciformes" as the ordinal name, but followed the division into six families that Salvadori (1891) had used in the *Catalogue* (see above).

According to Clark (1901b) the parrots and birds of prey (including owls) have a "falconiform" type of pterylosis, but the cuckoos and coraciiforms have the "passeriform" type.

Mitchell (1901a) found little variation in the intestinal convolutions in 10 genera of parrots. Although uncertain, he thought that the parrot gut could best be derived from the coraciiform type. Beddard (1911) examined the intestines of additional parrots but concluded nothing about their affinities.

Shufeldt (1902b) added some data to his 1886 paper, and suggested that parrots may be related to the owls, but was skeptical about a relationship to the falconiforms. He recommended a separate family for *Strigops* because of the reduced forelimb and carina associated with flightlessness.

Mudge (1902) proposed a classification based on tongue musculature and hyoid structure; a summary follows:

Family Loriidae
    Subfamily Eosinae, *Eos*
    Subfamily Loriinae, *Lorius*, *Vini*
Family Nestoridae, *Nestor*
Family Psittacidae
  Group 1
    Subfamily Psittaculinae, 5 genera
    Subfamily Pyrrhurinae, 2 genera
  Group 2
    Subfamily Bolborhynchinae, 5 genera
    Subfamily Tanygnathinae, 5 genera
    Subfamily Conurinae, 4 genera
    Subfamily Psittacinae, 2 genera
    Subfamily Eclectinae, 2 genera
    Subfamily Chrysotinae, 3 genera
    Subfamily Cacatuinae, 6 genera, including *Strigops*

Chandler (1916) believed their feather structure allied the parrots and cuckoos and that they should be placed in the same order. He also thought the parrots are related to the coraciiforms, in which he included the owls, goatsuckers, trogons, swifts, and piciforms.

From the skeleton of a Kea (*Nestor notabilis*) Shufeldt (1918b) considered it to be "an established fact" that a family Nestoridae should be recognized because of its distinctive morphology.

Wetmore (1930) recognized the Loriidae (lories) and Psittacidae (parrots, macaws) in the Psittaciformes, placed between the Cuculiformes and Strigiformes. In later versions (1951, 1960) he placed all parrots in the Psittacidae and inserted the Psittaciformes between the Columbiformes and Cuculiformes.

E. Stresemann (1934) was unable to suggest any group as the nearest relative of the parrots.

Peters (1937) recognized only the family Psittacidae in the Psittaciformes, but his subfamilies were based on the families of Salvadori (1891) and Sharpe (1900): Strigopinae (*Strigops*), Nestorinae (*Nestor*), Loriinae (lories of Australia, New Guinea), Micropsittinae (*Micropsitta*), Kakatoeinae (cockatoos), and Psittacinae (remaining genera).

Von Boetticher (1943b) made several suggestions concerning the allocation of parrot genera and (1964) developed a classification of the Psittacidae with the following subfamilies and tribes: Nestorinae, Psittrichasinae, Kakatoeinae, Micropsittinae, Trichoglossinae (tribes Psitticulirostrini, Trichoglossini), Strigopinae, Psittacinae (tribes Platycercini, Loriini, Loriculini, Psittacini, Araini). Kuroda (1967) used von Boetticher's system in his monograph of the parrots.

Mayr and Amadon (1951) placed the Order Psittaci between the orders Columbae and Striges, and commented: "The Psittaci are a strongly differentiated group. Resemblance to the Accipitres is probably mere convergence, and relationship to the Cuculi, championed by Gadow, must be rather distant at best. McDowell found similarities between the humeri of parrots and those of pigeons" (p. 9).

Glenny (1951, 1957) proposed a classification, based on the arrangement of the carotid arteries, in which he recognized nine subfamilies: Strigopinae, Loriinae, Micropsittinae, Psittinae, Kakatoeinae, Nestorinae, Lathaminae, Palaeopsittacinae, Neopsittacinae.

Verheyen (1956f) found skeletal similarities among the parrots, pigeons, and cuckoos. He recognized five families of parrots, with their subfamilies, as follows: Strigopidae, Kakatoeidae, Psittacidae (Amazoninae, Arinae, Psittaculinae, Psittacinae), Platycercidae (Nymphicinae, Nestorinae, Polytelinae, Platycercinae, Lathaminae), Trichoglossidae (Trichoglossinae, Loriculinae, Micropsittinae). In his 1961 classification Verheyen placed the Psittaciformes between the Columbiformes and Coraciiformes, and noted that the parrots seem to be distantly related to the Falconiformes and Cuculiformes.

Sibley (1960) compared the egg-white proteins of 10 species of parrots using paper electrophoresis. The six genera differed from one another and Sibley suggested that the diversity might indicate that large genetic gaps have evolved between the various groups of parrots, although they have all retained the characteristic beak, foot, and feather structures. That closely related parrots do have similar egg-white proteins was shown by the common pattern in five species of *Agapornis*.

Mainardi (1962b) also found unusual diversity in the parrots in his study of red cell antigens, and Gysels (1964b) reported a high degree of heterogeneity in the eye lens and muscle proteins. Gysels also noted that the mobilities of the "typical song bird component" and of the muscle protein "myogen" in *Agapornis* were the same as those of *Falco* and differed from those of other parrots. He suggested that his results might reopen the question of a relationship between parrots and birds of prey.

Brereton and Immelmann (1962) examined head-scratching behavior in parrots and suggested that the Strigopinae, Nestorinae, Loriinae, and Kakatoeinae are distinct groups. However, the Psittacinae were heterogeneous for this behavior. Brereton (1963) proposed a classification based on 12 characters in addition to the head-scratching method, namely: development of the temporal and postsquamosal fossae; presence or absence of the ambiens, furcula, and oil gland; carotid artery pattern; wing shape; hyoid structure; shape of auditory meatus; ossification of the orbital ring; tail length, and geographic distribution. A summary follows:

Order Psittaciformes
    Superfamily Cacatuoidea
        Family Cacatuidae, *Strigops* and cockatoos
        Family Palaeornithidae, 6 Australasian genera
        Family Amazonidae, 10 New World genera
        Family Psittacidae, 3 African, 1 New Guinea, 1 Fiji
    Superfamily Platycercoidea
        Family Nestoridae, *Nestor*
        Family Loriidae, Australasian lories
        Family Micropsittidae, *Loriculus, Micropsitta, Agapornis*
        Family Alisteridae, 4 Australian genera
        Family Pezoporidae, 3 Australian genera
        Family Platycercidae, 7 Australian, S.W. Pacific genera
        Family Forpidae, 4 Neotropical genera

Sibley and Ahlquist (1972) reviewed the taxonomic history of the parrots and noted that the Cuculidae "have been most often suggested as the nearest relatives of the parrots." The piciforms, columbiforms, falconiforms, strigiforms, and coraciiforms have also been proposed as parrot allies. The similarities between parrots and birds of prey were considered to be due to convergence. We compared the electrophoretic patterns of the egg-white proteins of 36 species of parrots with those of other groups of birds, and suggested that "their nearest allies seem to be the pigeons" and that the two orders "be united in a single superorder." The DNA data do not support this proposal.

Holyoak (1973) reviewed the taxonomic histories and specimens of the Nestorinae, Loriinae, and Platycercinae, and concluded that these groups form a monophyletic cluster. He thought that the Neotropical genera *Forpus, Amoropsittaca, Psilopsiagon*, and *Bolborhynchus* are more closely related to other New World parrots

than to any member of this Old World group. . . . the Loriinae appear to have arisen from a platycercine-like . . . stock, with the fig-parrots *Psittaculirostris* showing intermediate characters. Because of the marked gap between the fig-parrots and other groups . . . it is proposed that they be placed in a separate subfamily (Psittaculirostrinae). The Nestorinae may have evolved from an early lory-like stock.

    Melopsittacus and *Pezoporus* are . . . related to the Platycercinae. . . . *Lathamus* ought . . . to be retained in the Loriinae. . . . *Eunymphicus* is merged with *Cyanoramphus* because of similarities in . . . skull, pattern of plumage, coloration, distribution and calls. . . . *Bernardius* is kept separate from *Platycercus* (p. 157).

Forshaw (1969) recognized the Loriidae, Cacatuidae, and Psittacidae for Australian parrots. In his monograph of the parrots of the world (1973) Forshaw used the following classification:

Order Psittaciformes
    Family Loriidae: Lories and Lorikeets; Pacific distribution
    Family Cacatuidae
        Subfamily Cacatuinae: Cockatoos; Australia, New Guinea
        Subfamily Nymphicinae: *Nymphicus*; Australia
    Family Psittacidae
        Subfamily Nestorinae: *Nestor*; New Zealand
        Subfamily Micropsittinae: *Micropsitta*; S.W. Pacific
        Subfamily Psittacinae: Parrots and Parakeets; Africa, Australasia, South America
        Subfamily Strigopinae: *Strigops*; New Zealand

Smith (1975) reviewed the history of the classification of the parrots and presented the results of his dissections of 126 species in 51 genera and comparisons of external morphology and behavior for essentially all species. He found a strong correlation between geographical distribution and the groups he recognized as tribes. His classification follows:

Order Psitticiformes
    Family Psittidae
        Subfamily Platycercinae
            Tribe Platycercini, Australia, New Zealand, etc.
            Tribe Cacatuini, Australasia to Philippines
            Tribe Nestorini, New Zealand
            Tribe Strigopini, New Zealand
        Subfamily Loriinae
            Tribe Loriini, Australasia to Philippines
            Tribe Psittrichasini, *Psittrichas*, New Guinea
            Tribe Psittaculini, Old World tropics, Africa to Fiji
            Tribe Micropsittini, New Guinea, S.W. Pacific islands
            Tribe Psittaculirostrini, New Guinea, tropical Australia
        Subfamily Arinae
            Tribe Arini, New World parrots
        Subfamily Psittacinae
            Tribe Psittacini, large African parrots, 3 genera

The DNA data also suggest a division of the parrots into geographically delineated groups, but we lack the DNAs of so many genera that we are reluctant to attempt a subdivision of the Psittacidae at this time.

Homberger (1980) studied the feeding and drinking methods and the morphology of the bill, tongue, and mouth cavity in 92 species of Old World, Australian, and Pacific island parrots. New World parrots were not included. Homberger recognized the order Psittaci with one family, Psittacidae, and five subfamilies: Cacatuinae, Loriinae, Psittacinae, Psittrichadinae, and Loriculinae. The Psittacinae was divided into the tribes Platycercini, Psittaculini, and Psittacini.

Four drinking methods were correlated with the Cacatuinae, Loriinae, Psittacinae, and Psittrichadinae plus Loriculinae. Feeding methods were also correlated with taxonomic groups. On the basis of bill-tongue morphology and drinking method, the Cockatiel,

Nymphicus (*Leptolophus*), belongs in the Cacatuinae, and *Lathamus* is a member of the Platycercinae. *Prosopeia* was placed in the Platycercini; *Alisterus*, *Aprosmictus*, and *Polytelis* in the Psittaculini. Because *Psittrichas* differs from all other parrots in bill and tongue morphology, and feeding and drinking behavior, it was placed in a monotypic subfamily. Similarly, *Loriculus* was placed in a monotypic subfamily because of distinctive morphological and behavioral features. Thus, the resulting classification is based, at least in part, on specialized features of structure and behavior rather than phylogeny.

Guntert (1981) examined the digestive tracts of more than 500 specimens representing 134 parrot species. The gross morphology was studied, and the histology was examined by scanning electron microscopy. The structures of the esophagus, proventriculus, gizzard, and intestine were viewed as adaptations to different diets, feeding methods, and life histories. The results suggest that the ancestors of living parrots were forest-dwelling birds with an unspecialized granivorous diet. *Nestor*, *Psittrichas*, and the Loriinae, often assumed to be primitive forms, proved to be the most specialized (i.e., derived) in their digestive tract morphology. Two main trends were most successful in Old World parrots: 1. Nectar feeding evolved independently at least four times, in the Loriinae, in *Loriculus*, in *Lathamus discolor*, and possibly in the *Opopsitta* group. 2. Colonization of open grassland or deserts, combined with improved locomotor activity, led to an almost exclusive granivory, the correlated evolution of a more effective intestinal surface pattern, and a shorter gut length. A long intestine is often combined with less differentiated proventricular glands and is supposed to be primitive among parrots.

Ovenden et al. (1987) used six restriction endonucleases to digest the mtDNAs of 26 individuals of six species of *Platycercus*. They found evidence of three groups within the genus, characterized by the species *eximius*, *elegans*, and *icterotis*.

The DNA Hybridization Evidence (Figs. 85–89; 353, 355, 361)

The DNA data are congruent with other evidence that the parrots are the descendants of an ancient lineage. The branch from other living groups was at Δ 23.1 (Fig. 361). It seems obvious that morphological similarities to the birds of prey are due to convergence or to the retention of primitive characters.

The DNA data are limited, but they suggest that the parrots of Australasia, Africa, and the Americas form three subgroups. Until many more species have been compared we cannot be sure that taxonomic subdivisions are correlated with these three geographic regions. Therefore, we recognize only the family Psittacidae, but note the divergence at Δ 9.2 between the Australian taxa and those of Africa and South America. The African genus *Poicephalus* diverged from the New World genera at Δ 6.8.

Fig. 85 (*Ara*) shows that the parrots are not especially close to the pigeons, and Fig. 86 (*Ara*) indicates that the birds of prey are no closer to the parrots than are the pigeons. Fig. 86 includes several hawks and owls with delayed maturity, which cluster closer to *Ara* than the two falcons (*Falco*, *Microhierax*) which begin to breed at an average age of two years.

Fig. 87 (*Ara*) includes nightjars, turacos, swifts, cuckoos, and hummingbirds. The nightjars and turacos are slightly closer to *Ara* than are the swifts and cuckoos, with the hummingbirds farthest out. We suspect that these small differences reflect different average rates of genomic evolution rather than real differences in divergence times, but the data are not available to prove or disprove either hypothesis. It is possible to say that there is no evidence that the cuckoos are the group most closely related to the parrots.

Fig. 88 (*Ara*) includes four species of New World vultures, which are one of the groups with long-delayed maturity. That they cluster much closer to *Ara* than do the motmot, trogon, hornbill, mousebird, and toucan may reflect the differences in rates of DNA evolution rather than degrees of genetic relationship.

Note that in Figs. 85 to 88 there are no heteroduplex curves that intersect the percent single-stranded axis at less than 40%, and these taxa include pigeons, hawks, owls, nightjars, turacos, and New World vultures. Of these groups, the pigeons begin to breed at the age of one year or less; the others are known or suspected to be groups with delayed breeding. The nightjars are recorded as one-year breeders in Table 16, but the behavior of their DNAs in several experiments raises the suspicion that this may not be correct.

Fig. 89 (*Cacatua*) shows that the Australo-Papuan cockatoos are about equally distant from South American (*Brotogeris*, *Amazona*) and African (*Poicephalus*) parrots. Note that *Falco* and *Tyto*, both averaging two years at first breeding, are equidistant from *Cacatua*.

We conclude that the parrots have no close living relatives. Like the buttonquails, trogons, and mousebirds, they are the descendants of an ancient lineage. Our data are insufficient to propose subdivisions in the Psittacidae, but it seems likely that such subunits exist, possibly correlated with the African, New World, and Australasian regions.

Swifts and Hummingbirds

Superorder Apodimorphae
  Order APODIFORMES
    Family Apodidae: Typical Swifts
    Family Hemiprocnidae: Treeswifts or Crested Swifts
  Order TROCHILIFORMES
    Family Trochilidae
      Subfamily Phaethornithinae: Hermits
      Subfamily Trochilinae: Typical Hummingbirds

The swifts and hummingbirds have been associated in most of the classifications of the past 150 years. Although the DNA evidence places them in separate orders they are one another's closest living relatives, and we will discuss them together.

The 97 species of typical swifts occur widely in the tropical and temperate regions of the world where aerial insects are abundant. The four species of treeswifts (*Hemiprocne*) occur in southeast Asia, the Philippines, Indonesia, New Guinea, the Bismarck Archipelago, and the Solomon Islands.

The 319 species of hummingbirds are divided into 109 genera. Hummingbirds occur from Alaska (in summer) to Tierra del Fuego.

Superorder APODIMORPHAE: 128/422. The swifts and hummingbirds are small to extremely small birds with a pelvic muscle formula of A; a short humerus and long manus; 10 primaries, the outer the longest; 6–11 short secondaries; 10 rectrices; holorhinal, impervious nares; no basipterygoid processes; metasternum entire; furcula U-shaped with a short hypocleideum; left carotid (except *Cypseloides*, which has two); caeca usually absent; hypotarsus simple; aftershaft present; flexor tendons Type 5; nidicolous and gymnopaedic; white eggs.

Order APODIFORMES: 19/103. Aegithognathous with 6–7 pairs of ribs; deeply cleft gape; bill broad and short; tibial bridge present; nostrils open vertically; no operculum; tongue short, triangular, not extensile; secondaries 8–11; alular feathers 2–3; aftershaft large; syrinx tracheo-bronchial with sterno-trachealis muscle and one pair of intrinsic muscles; large salivary glands which increase in size during reproductive period when saliva is used in nest construction; no crop; no caeca; gall bladder present; oil gland naked, indistinctly bilobed; down only on apteria; eutaxic (except *Hemiprocne, Streptoprocne, Cypseloides*); all except *Hemiprocne* with a claw on the manus; 13 cervical vertebrae (14 in *Chaetura*).

Family APODIDAE: 18/99. No crests; flanks without a patch of downy or silky feathers; plumage hard; claw on manus; hallux varies in direction but not directed as strongly posteriad as in *Hemiprocne*.

Family HEMIPROCNIDAE: 1/4. Large apodiforms with crested heads or with plumes; flanks with patch of downy or silky feathers; general plumage soft; no claw on manus; hallux directed backwards, not reversible.

Order TROCHILIFORMES: 109/319. Schizognathous, anisodactyl, with 8 pairs of ribs; bill long and slender, gape not deeply cleft; tongue extensile, adapted for nectar-feeding; tibial bridge absent; nostrils lateral, broadly operculate; secondaries 6–7; alular feathers 0–1; aftershaft small or absent; 14–15 cervical vertebrae; syrinx with two pairs of special extrinsic muscles; no sterno-tracheal muscles; caeca rudimentary or absent; no gall bladder; oil gland naked, distinctly bilobed with lobes greatly separated; most diastataxic, some eutaxic; no claw on manus; nestling with spherical crop; two white eggs.

Historical Review of the Classification

In many of the earlier classifications the swifts and swallows were placed together, usually well separated from the hummingbirds, which were often associated with other slender-billed taxa, such as *Certhia, Nectarinia*, or even *Upupa*. In his genus *Trochilus*, Linnaeus (1758) included the hummingbirds and some slender-billed sunbirds; the swifts and swallows were in *Hirundo*. Similar associations may be found in the classifications of Brisson (1760), Illiger (1811), Merrem (1813), and Temminck (1820). However, L'Herminier (1827) examined the structure of the sternum and shoulder girdle and suggested a possible alliance between swifts and hummingbirds. Berthold (1831) studied the sternum of some 130 species and saw the similarities noted by L'Herminier, but concluded that the sternum is an unreliable source of evidence for classification, rather than that swallows are passerines and swifts are related to hummingbirds.

Nitzsch (1840) placed the swifts and hummingbirds together in the Macrochires, near the goatsuckers. In Gray's (1844–49, 1869–71) classifications the swifts were placed near the swallows and goatsuckers, and the hummingbirds with the Neotropical honeycreepers (Coerebini) and Australasian honeyeaters (Meliphagidae).

It was J. P. Müller's (1845) study of the syrinx that provided the basis for the separation of the swifts from the swallows and allied them to the goatsuckers.

Cabanis (1847), who based his classification primarily on the number of flight feathers and the tarsal envelope (podotheca), recognized the swallows as oscines (after Müller 1845) and placed the swifts, hummingbirds, and goatsuckers together in his Macrochires.

Wallace (1863) also believed that the hummingbirds are related to the swifts, not to the passerine sunbirds, which they resemble superficially, at least as museum specimens.

Sclater (1865a) studied the sternum and foot structure in swifts and proposed their division into the subfamilies Cypselinae and Chaeturinae. He was confident that "the Swifts have no relationship whatever with the Swallows" (p. 593).

The Cypselomorphae of Huxley (1867) contained the Trochilidae, Cypselidae, and Caprimulgidae, but Huxley believed that the swifts are "very closely related" to the swallows. Huxley considered the palates of these groups to be aegithognathous, but W. K. Parker (1875a) found that the palates of nightjars and hummingbirds are schizognathous. Parker believed that the swifts and hummingbirds are not closely related and that the swifts have indirect ties to the passerines, particularly to the swallows.

Sundevall (1872, see 1889) associated the swifts with the goatsuckers and trogons in the "Cohort Ampligulares," because they have wide mouths, and placed the hummingbirds in the adjacent "Cohort Longilingues," because of their slender, extensile tongues. He divided the hummingbirds into 12 families.

In Garrod's (1874a) classification based on the pelvic musculature, the swifts (Cypselinae) and hummingbirds (Trochilinae) are the only subfamilies in his family Macrochires, order Cypseliformes. Garrod thought that the differences between swifts and hummingbirds "are only of subfamily importance. The formula is A; the tensor patagii brevis and the pterylosis are characteristic, as is the sternum; and there is only a left carotid (except in *Cypseloides*)" (p. 123). Garrod (1877d) cited evidence from pterylography, the sternum, syrinx, intestinal coiling, deep plantar tendons, number of rectrices, and the insertion of the patagial muscles to support his contention that swifts are not closely allied to swallows. In all of these characters swifts resemble hummingbirds.

Sclater (1880b) associated the Trochilidae, Cypselidae, and Caprimulgidae in the suborder Cypseli, and Reichenow (1882) followed the same arrangement, but called the group the order Strisores.

Stejneger (1885:437) reviewed the differences between swifts and swallows:

Externally they may be easily distinguished; the swifts by having ten primaries, not more than seven secondaries, and only ten tail-feathers, while the swallows have but nine primaries, at least nine secondaries, and twelve tail-feathers. The swifts have also the dorsal tract bifurcate between the shoulders, while in the swallows it is simple. Internally they differ in a great number of points, but we shall only mention that the swifts have a pointed manubrial process and no posterior notches to the sternum, while the swallows have the manubrium bifurcate, and the posterior border deeply two-notched; the former have a myological formula A, the latter AXY; the former are synpelmous, the latter are schizopelmous; the former have a peculiar arrangement of the tensor patagii brevis, the latter have the general arrangement of the Passeres; . . . the former have a simple syrinx without intrinsic muscles, the latter have a very specialized syrinx; the former are without caeca, the swallows possess them, etc., the total effect being that the swifts are Picarians, and the swallows are Passeres.

Stejneger also enumerated the agreements between swifts and hummingbirds and placed them in the superfamily Micropodoideae in the order Picariae, after the trogons and at the end of his sequence of non-passerines.

Shufeldt (1885b) examined the skeletons of hummingbirds, swifts, and goatsuckers. Apparently he was either ignorant of or disagreed with Stejneger's evidence, for he concluded that "The Swifts are essentially modified Swallows, and, as the family Cypselidae, they belong, in the order Passeres, next to that group" (p. 914). Shufeldt (1886d:503) must have known about Stejneger's (1885) list of characters when he noted that "the humerus is highly pneumatic in *Trochilus*, which . . . is not the case among the Cypselidae, these latter agreeing with the Swallows . . . in having non-pneumatic humeri."

Lucas (1886) disagreed with those advocating the alliance of swifts and swallows (namely, Sharpe, Parker, Shufeldt) and supported "Huxley's union of Hummingbirds and Swifts" (p. 444). Lucas compared the skulls and other skeletal elements of a swift, a hummingbird, and a swallow and concluded that the skull of the swifts indicates "affinities not only with the Passeres but with the Hummingbirds and Goatsuckers" and that "the remaining portions of the skeleton . . . point to the relationship of *Chaetura* with *Trochilus*, while between these birds and the Passeres stand the Goatsuckers" (p. 451). Thus, there were at least three concepts of the relationships among these groups.

In his usual turgid prose Parker (1889c:2) disagreed with Sclater (1865a) and Garrod (1877d), and agreed with Shufeldt (1885b) that the "Swallow and the Swift are near akin," basing his opinion on palatal similarities, proportions of the wing bones, and other skeletal characters.

Goodchild's studies of the wing coverts (1886, 1891) convinced him that swifts and hummingbirds are closely allied. He demonstrated that they are unlike passerines, but was unable to suggest their nearest relatives.

Fürbringer (1888) accepted a close relationship between swifts and hummingbirds and placed them in his "Gens Macrochires." He believed that they and the mousebirds are closely related to a pico-passerine assemblage.

Shufeldt (1889e) reviewed the evidence on the "Macrochires" and added the results of a study of the anatomy of the Cedar Waxwing (*Bombycilla cedrorum*), two New World trogons, four species of caprimulgids, two swifts, seven hummingbirds, and six swallows. The Cedar Waxwing was used as the prototype of "a suitable and average Oscinine bird" for the comparisons with the other taxa (p. 387). Shufeldt concluded:

1. *Trogon* shows no evidence of close relationship to the Trochili or to the Caprimulgi.

2. The Caprimulgi are most closely related to the owls and "have no special affinity with the Cypseli, much less to the Trochili" (p. 388).

3. The swallows "possess . . . the . . . characters of the . . . Passerine stock. . . . They are true Passeres considerably modified . . . [by] the adoption of new habits." (pp. 388–389).

4. "Our modern Swifts were differentiated from the early Hirundine [swallow] stock" (p. 390).

5. Swifts differ from hummingbirds in their habits, nidification, feeding behavior, external characters and body form, pterylosis, skull and body skeleton, wing structure, pelvic structure, respiratory system, visceral anatomy, and digestive system.

6. Swifts and hummingbirds are unrelated to one another and the two groups should be placed in separate orders. The Cypseli "would be found just outside the enormous Passerine circle, but tangent to a point in its periphery opposite the Swallows." The Trochili belong in a separate order and the similarities between swifts and hummingbirds are superficial because "truly related organizations *never* exhibit such an array of inharmoniously associated sets of morphological characters" (p. 391).

Lucas (1889) reviewed certain skeletal elements of the swifts, including "*Dendrochelidon*" (*Hemiprocne*), and proposed a division of the superfamily Micropodoidea into the Micropodidae for the typical swifts and the Dendrochelidonidae for the crested-swifts. He thought that "in some points" the crested-swifts "incline towards the Goatsuckers" (p. 12).

Seebohm (1890a,c) agreed with Shufeldt (1885b, 1889e) that swifts and hummingbirds are not closely allied. He cited the structure of the deep plantar tendons as evidence for making the Trochili a suborder of the Pico-Passeres, next to the broadbills (Eurylaimi). In his system the swifts were placed next to the caprimulgiforms in the suborder Coraciae of the subclass Coraciiformes. In 1895 Seebohm maintained the Trochili as a suborder of the Passeriformes, but arranged the swifts, mousebirds, and coraciiforms in the suborder Picariae of the Coraciiformes.

Sharpe (1891) listed the suborders Caprimulgi, Cypseli, Trochili, and Colii in series in his order Coraciiformes, with the Trogones following. He used the same arrangement in the *Hand-List* (1900).

In a monograph of the hummingbirds Ridgway (1892:290) wrote: "The Humming Birds and Swifts . . . agree in numerous anatomical characters, and there can be no doubt that they are more closely related to each other than are either to any other group of birds. In fact, except in the shape of the bill and the structure of the bones of the face [palate], the Humming Birds and Swifts present no definite differences of osteological structure."

In volume 16 of the *Catalogue of Birds* Salvin was the author of the Upupae and Trochili, and Hartert of the Cypselidae, Caprimulgidae, Podargidae, and Steatornithidae. (Their classification is presented under the Caprimulgi.) These groups were placed in the order Picariae, with the hummingbirds in the suborder Trochili and the swifts in the suborder Coraciae, with the goatsuckers.

Gadow's (1892) classification was similar to that of Sharpe (1891). It included an order Coraciiformes with suborders Striges (owls), Macrochires (goatsuckers, swifts, hummingbirds), Colii (colies), Trogones (trogons), and Coraciae (rollers, motmots, kingfishers, bee-eaters, hoopoes, hornbills). This same sequence of groups was followed by Wetmore (1930, 1960).

In 1893 Gadow gave the Caprimulgi ordinal rank, but he believed them to be closely related to the swifts and hummingbirds (Cypseli). He also thought that the colies are somewhat more distant allies of the Cypseli.

Lucas (1895b) corrected Gadow's (1894:617) diagram of the deep plantar tendons of hummingbirds. Gadow (1895) agreed, added further corrections, and noted that the actual arrangement in the hummingbirds indicates the "last remnants of a regular four-split condition of the tendon" of the flexor longus hallucis and that this shows that hummingbirds are "still nearer related to the Cypseli" than previously demonstrated.

Lucas (1895c) also examined the deep flexor tendons of a crested-swift, *Macropteryx* (*Hemiprocne*), and found them to differ from those of the typical swifts. In the crested-swifts the flexor hallucis gives off a branch to the hallux and then continues "to blend, not with the undivided tendon of the flexor communis, but with that branch of it which goes to supply the fourth digit." This arrangement "does not agree with any of the seven modifications of . . . these tendons . . . figured by Garrod. But it is . . . like . . . *Scopus umbretta* [Hamerkop] figured by Beddard (P.Z.S. 1891, p. 18, fig. 46)" (p. 300).

"There are still to be found among living systematic ornithologists some who contend that the Humming-birds (*Trochili*) are more or less nearly related to the Swifts (*Cypseli*)" wrote Shufeldt (1893b). He then belabored Coues and Ridgway for "keeping alive the false idea that Swifts and Humming-birds" are related to one another. On Shufeldt's side of the argument were Parker and Huxley. These three believed that the swifts are related to the swallows and that the affinities of the hummingbirds were simply not known. Shufeldt listed 61 differences between swifts and hummingbirds, accompanied by scathing comments directed at his opponents. He summarized his polemic by submitting the "61 important structural differences . . . to the thoughtful systematist . . . confident . . . that after their weight has been duly appreciated there will no longer be any doubt . . . that not only is a typical Swift a widely different kind of bird from a Humming-bird, but that . . . the Swifts are but greatly modified Swallows" (p. 100).

Despite his confidence in his "61 differences," Shufeldt's crusade against the infidels was not yet over, for H. L. Clark (1902a) reopened the question of hummingbird-swift relationships. Clark's discussion was based only on pterylosis and he concluded that the two groups are so similar that they are probably related. Shufeldt's acerbic reply (1902c), published only two months later, quickly dismissed Clark's question, data, and arguments as incompetent or irrelevant. In his final sentence (p. 48) Shufeldt agreed with Clark's (1901a) opinion concerning the relationship between owls and goatsuckers "but one must get the ancient picarian bee completely out of one's anatomical thinking-cap before cypseline-trochiline comparisons can be made without bias and without prejudice."

Clark (1902b) published a brief reply to Shufeldt's attack, but waited four years until he had assembled a larger supply of pterylographic ammunition before returning to the battle. Clark's (1906) study of the feather tracts of swifts and hummingbirds reviewed the debate with Shufeldt and called attention to errors in Nitzsch's figures that Shufeldt had used to bolster his own arguments. Clark presented data on the pterylosis of 10 species of swifts and 21 species of hummingbirds, 17 of which he had studied personally. He concluded that the pterylosis of swifts and hummingbirds is sufficiently similar "to give support to the view that they have a common ancestry" (p. 89). On the contrary, "the pterylosis of the Caprimulgi" is not "sufficiently similar to that of swifts or hummingbirds" to indicate common ancestry (p. 90). Apparently Clark won the war, for neither he nor Shufeldt seems to have published more on this subject.

The alliance of the swifts and hummingbirds in the "Macrochires" was accepted by Beddard (1898a). He reviewed the arguments and noted that although Shufeldt (1885b, 1886d) "is disinclined to allow a very near affinity between the birds, it is undeniable that there are some resemblances" (p. 229).

Lucas (1895a) found that the name *Dendrochelidon* is preoccupied by *Macropteryx* for the crested-swifts (*Hemiprocne*) and, with a notice of the nomenclatural change, noted that the deep plantar tendons of crested-swifts resemble those of hummingbirds. He concluded that the differences between the crested-swifts and typical swifts "are greater than those . . . between any two families of Passeres" (p. 157).

In a report on the myology of the White-collared Swift, "*Hemiprocne*" (*Streptoprocne zonaris*), Lucas (1899) pointed out that the peroneus longus, a muscle found in passerines, is absent in *Streptoprocne*. Furthermore, the deep plantar tendons in the White-collared Swift differ from those of other swifts in that "while the muscle which ordinarily works the front toes, the flexor perforans, is present it has no separate tendon, but is attached to the muscle of the first digit, *flexor longus hallucis*. . . . below this single tendon sends off four slips, one to each digit, thus presenting the simplest condition possible and literally realizing Gadow's statement that the *flexor longus hallucis* is really a common flexor of all digits" (p. 78).

Mitchell (1896a, 1901a) found that swifts and hummingbirds have nearly identical intestinal tracts. He found several differences between them and the passerines and concluded that "the conformation of the Cypseli and Colii may also be an apocentric derivative of the Caprimulgid form, the apocentricity in both consisting of an immense reduction in the length of the whole gut, with degeneration of the caeca so that no vestige of them is left, and with obliteration of the loops in Meckel's tract" (p. 256).

From a study of wing structure, including muscle innervation, Buri (1900) concluded that swifts and hummingbirds are closely related. He thought that the colies are the next nearest relatives of swifts, and that the Caprimulgi are more distant.

Thompson (1901) described the pterylosis of the Giant Hummingbird (*Patagona gigas*) and compared it to those of the Long-tailed Nightjar (*Caprimulgus macrurus*) and the White-rumped Swiftlet (*Collocalia spodiopygius*). He wrote: "I am inclined to think that the facts of pterylosis, so far as they go, tend to justify the association of the Humming-birds with the Goatsuckers and Swifts, and, if anything, to bring them somewhat nearer to the [goatsuckers]. But I . . . confess that the evidence is confused and the judgment far from clear. There are many resemblances and many differences, and we are not yet in a position to decide what proportion of weight several characters deserve" (p. 324).

"If one will compare a plucked Swift and Swallow . . . it will at once appear that . . . the pterylosis is strikingly different" (Clark 1901b:372–373). Clark considered the pteryloses of the Cuculiformes, Coraciiformes, and Passeriformes to be similar, and he noted that "Nitzsch's . . . figures are often faulty, and . . . the relationship between the Goatsuckers and Swifts . . . [is] not borne out by examination of better material" (p. 381).

Fürbringer (1902) placed the swifts and hummingbirds in adjacent families in his "Gens Macrochires," between the Passeres and the Colii. He observed (p. 704) that Shufeldt's (1893b) list of 61 differences between swifts and hummingbirds could easily be increased but that their quality would not be improved sufficiently to provide a basis for the wide separation of the two groups.

Without comment Shufeldt (1904b) assigned the swifts and hummingbirds to separate orders, with the Trochiliformes between the Todidae of his Halcyoniformes and the Bucconidae (puffbirds) of his Jacamariformes; the Cypseliformes were placed between his Piciformes (only woodpeckers) and Eurylaemiformes (broadbills).

The problem of generic limits in the hummingbirds was addressed by Taylor (1909), who noted that many genera are based on the same characters used to define species. Taylor advocated the placement of hybridizing species in the same genus. Ridgway (1909) disagreed, but Taylor's opinion was in accord with those of Sibley (1957), Banks and Johnson (1961), Short and Phillips (1966), and Lynch and Ames (1970).

Chandler (1916) described the fine structure of the feathers of swifts and hummingbirds and suggested that the Trochilidae are closely related to the passerines. In his "phylogenetic tree" (p. 391) he placed the swifts with the caprimulgiforms.

E. Stresemann (1934) included the swifts and hummingbirds in the same order, but did not suggest ties to other groups.

Lowe (1939b) took issue with Parker (1875a), Beddard (1898a), and others who had defined the hummingbird palate as schizognathous. Lowe argued that the trochilid palate represents a low degree of aegithognathism and redefined the order Passeriformes to include the swifts, hummingbirds, and Pici. Although he placed the swifts and hummingbirds in separate suborders, he believed them to be closely allied: "It seems to me almost unbelievable that their likeness could be due to convergence in two unrelated groups. The similarities exhibited are altogether too many, too exact, and too universal, affecting as they do a complete system of muscles, nearly all of them highly specialized, and in addition an osteological and intestinal system" (p. 327). Lowe believed that the swifts and hummingbirds had evolved from the "generalized trunk" of the passerine tree.

Wetmore (1947) reviewed the nomenclatural history of the generic names *Micropus* and *Apus* and provided the basis for the recognition of *Apus* Scopoli as the type genus of the swifts.

The Mallophaga are uninformative concerning the relationships of the swifts, but those of hummingbirds are also found on passerines (Clay 1950).

Lack (1956a) reviewed the 10 species of *Apus* and (1956b) the genera and nesting habits of all swifts. He recognized eight genera in the Apodidae, plus three species of *Hemiprocne* in the Hemiprocnidae.

The paper electrophoretic patterns of the egg-white proteins of swifts and hummingbirds suggested a relationship between them, and possibly between them and the passerines (Sibley 1960).

Wetmore (1960) included the swifts (Apodi) and hummingbirds (Trochili) as suborders in his Apodiformes, placed between the Caprimulgiformes and Coliiformes. He favored family status for the crested-swifts because: "The skull in the Hemiprocnidae is quite distinct in the general form of the cranium and in the development of the nasals, vomer, and palatines. The hypotarsus has a tendinal foramen (like that found in hummingbirds), and the plantar tendons have the flexor longus hallucis connected with the branch of the flexor perforans digitorum, which extends to the fourth digit. Coupled with this there may be noted the curious nest, which, fastened to the side of a branch, is barely large enough to contain one egg, and the further fact that these birds perch regularly on branches and twigs in trees."

The classification of the subfamily Chaeturinae was reviewed by Orr (1963), who questioned Lack's (1956b) classification, but did not comment on higher category relationships.

Verheyen (1956h), again deluded by convergence, assigned the hummingbirds to his order Upupiformes near the wood-hoopoes (*Phoeniculus*). The swifts were placed in the Apodiformes, near the Caprimulgiformes. In 1961 Verheyen placed the swifts and hummingbirds in adjacent suborders in his Coraciiformes, near the Upupae and Trogones.

Kitto and Wilson (1966) found that swifts and hummingbirds share a unique form of the enzyme malate dehydrogenase.

Cohn (1968) attributed the skeletal similarities between swifts and hummingbirds to convergence. In a study of flight mechanisms she concluded that to derive hummingbirds from a swift-like ancestor would require at least ten reversals of evolutionary trends. She believed that the hummingbirds may be closest to the stem of a pico-passerine assemblage leading to the New World suboscines but did not suggest the nearest allies of the swifts.

Brooke (1970) was unsure "whether the Apodi are an order or a suborder and, if the latter, of which order." He observed that Lowe's (1939b) "view that they are aberrant passerines has not found favour, and opinion is swinging away from the view that they are related to the Trochili (e.g., Cohn, 1968)" (p. 13). Brooke "noted a resurgence of the view that they are related to the Caprimulgi (Dr. C. T. Collins and Dr. P. Brodkorb, pers. comm.) but . . . we have not yet got the evidence to state this. They can stand as a separate order but this does not answer the question of their affinities" (p. 13). Brooke maintained the families Apodidae and Hemiprocnidae and two subfamilies, Cypseloidinae and Apodinae, in the Apodidae. The Apodinae were further divided into three tribes. He recognized 83 species of swifts in 19 genera, including *Hemiprocne*.

Among the differences between the Cypseloidinae and Apodinae given by Brooke (1970:23) were the number of peaks in the electrophoretic patterns of the egg-white proteins (Sibley 1960). Brooke is correct about the apparent differences, but there is no certainty that they are correlated with the two subfamilies because only one cypseloidine species was available.

A modified splenius capitis muscle occurs in swifts and hummingbirds, and in a less developed form in the Aegothelidae (owlet-frogmouths) (Burton 1971). Burton suggested that this modification may in some way be useful in aerial feeding by swifts, but its occurrence in swifts and hummingbirds, with their different feeding habits, seems more likely to indicate common ancestry. Other aerial feeders, such as pratincoles, bee-eaters, jacamars, tyrant flycatchers, and Old World flycatchers do not have the modified muscle.

Sibley and Ahlquist (1972) compared the electrophoretic patterns of 13 species of swifts, one crested-swift, and 16 hummingbirds. We concluded that these data did not clarify the degree of relationship between swifts and hummingbirds, or between either of them and other groups. The swift patterns resembled those of the colies, but "the significance of this similarity is unknown." It could be due to electrophoretic coincidence, as well as to common ancestry.

Cracraft (1981) thought that the "osteology of swifts and hummingbirds offers strong support for a sister-group relationship" and placed them in his Apodiformes. He also argued that the Caprimulgiformes and Apodiformes form "a monophyletic lineage" and "are each other's closest relative." He included the two orders in his "Division 8." Olson (1982) criticized this arrangement because Cracraft "does not present any synapomorphies that are common to all members of this division and that would define it as monophyletic."

The DNA Hybridization Evidence (Figs. 90–99, 334, 353, 355, 361)

The corrected $\Delta T_{50}H$ values support a sister-group relationship between swifts and hummingbirds, but the divergence was at $\Delta T_{50}H$ 21.3 (Fig. 361).

In the Apodiformes we recognize the Apodidae and Hemiprocnidae (Δ 9.5). Three subfamilies might be recognized in the Apodidae, but we lack the DNAs of many genera.

In the Trochiliformes we recognize two subfamilies, which separate the dimorphic species from the sexually monomorphic hermits.

The swifts and hummingbirds may have shared a common ancestor with the goatsuckers and owls at $\Delta T_{50}H$ 21.9, thus some of the morphological characters shared by swifts and goatsuckers may be retained primitive states.

In Fig. 90 (*Apus*) the closest curves to the homoduplex are those of other swifts, followed by a nightjar, roller, and hummingbird. Once again, a nightjar is close to a homoduplex, but in this case it belongs to one of the groups often considered to be related to the tracer taxon. This raises a question but does not answer it. Rollers have not been seriously considered as close relatives of swifts and they mature at 1 to 2 years, about the same as hummingbirds.

Figs. 91–94 (*Chaetura*) used the same excellent tracer preparation; note the high $T_{50}H$ and flat foot of the homoduplex. In Fig. 91 the seven species of swifts are closest to the homoduplex, with the curve of *Hemiprocne* at the greatest distance from *Chaetura*. The curves of the three nightjars and two hummingbirds intersect the vertical axis at ca. 30%, with the nightjars closer to the tracer than are the hummingbirds. The difference is small and may be due to rate differences.

Fig. 92 includes a hummingbird as the closest out-group taxon to *Chaetura*, followed by a pigeon, parrot, mousebird, three passerines, and two piciforms. These are probably birds that begin to breed at one to two years of age, and their relative positions may reflect time since divergence from a common ancestor with the swifts.

Fig. 93 presents some intriguing melting curves, compared with those in Figs. 91 and 92. The closest out-groups are an ibis, condor, stork, crane, and booby. These birds have delayed maturity and none is a logical candidate for the closest living relative of the swifts. Their melting curves intersect the percent single-stranded axis at or below 30%, while that of the hummingbird in Fig. 92 intersects the vertical axis at ca. 36%. This seems to be another example of the effect of delayed maturity on the rate of DNA evolution.

Fig. 94 provides more evidence of the correlation between delayed maturity and the rate of genomic evolution. The closest out-group to *Chaetura* is an albatross, followed by a hawk, loon, two owls, a nightjar, another owl, a grebe, and another nightjar. The correlation with delayed breeding is not perfect, but in virtually all experiments that include an albatross it is the closest, or one of the closest, taxa to the homoduplex, regardless of the obvious relationships of the tracer taxon.

Figs. 95–99 (*Amazilia*) present comparisons between a hummingbird and other groups. Fig. 95 includes only hummingbirds. The "Typical Hummingbirds" cluster closest to *Amazilia*, with the three hermits farthest out. This supports a long-recognized relationship.

Fig. 96 includes three additional species of hummingbirds, three swifts, and three caprimulgiforms. Thus, the swifts are closer to the hummingbird tracer than are the nightjars. The *Hemiprocne* curve intersects the vertical axis at ca. 45%. In Fig. 97, the *Hemiprocne* curve intersects the vertical axis at ca. 40%, another swift is next in line, followed by pigeons, parrots, a passerine, mousebird, another passerine, and two piciforms.

Fig. 98 offers more evidence of the effect of delayed first breeding. An albatross curve intersects the vertical axis at the same percentage single-stranded DNA as the swift in Fig. 97, followed by a frigatebird, loon, hawk, owl, etc. Fig. 99 presents a similar situation, with the California Condor curve beginning at ca. 44%, the stork next at ca. 46%, followed by a crane, a gull, sandpiper, turaco, cormorant, and two cuckoos ca. 60%. These curves do not provide a solution to the question of the closest relative of the hummingbirds, but they show that we cannot assume a simple relationship between DNA distance values and times of divergence.

In the FITCH tree (Fig. 334), *Amazilia* is 21.3 distance units from *Chaetura*, 22.7 units from *Strix*, and 24 units from *Caprimulgus*. In several FITCH analyses the swifts and hummingbirds cluster with each other despite the large difference in their branch lengths. The branch length difference between the two groups averages 4.4 distance units, one of the largest differences we have found between allied groups.

We conclude that the swifts and hummingbirds diverged more recently from one another than either diverged from any other lineage. The divergence was ancient, possibly in the late Cretaceous, but the morphological evidence and DNA comparisons support this conclusion better than any of the alternatives.

Owls

Superorder Strigimorphae
  Order STRIGIFORMES
    Suborder Strigi
      Parvorder Tytonida
        Family Tytonidae: Barn-Owls, Grass-Owls, Bay-Owls
      Parvorder Strigida
        Family Strigidae: Typical Owls

We place the owls and nightjars in the same order because the DNA evidence so indicates. The owls (Strigi) are treated in this section; the owlet-nightjars (Aegotheli), frogmouths, Oilbird, potoos, eared-nightjars, nighthawks, and nightjars (Caprimulgi) in the following section.

From the earliest times the owls have been recognized as a relatively homogeneous, well-delineated group. The raptorial adaptations of the feet and bill, soft plumage, and mainly nocturnal habits set them apart from other birds, but their nearest relatives have been difficult to identify with confidence. The diurnal birds of prey and the goatsuckers have been suggested most frequently but the morphological evidence has not provided a clear choice between these alternatives.

Suborder STRIGI: 25/178. The palate of owls is "schizognathous, with desmognathous tendency" (Gadow 1892:249) or "desmognathous" (Beddard 1898a:244); pelvic muscle formula AD (Hudson 1937); two carotids; coracoids connected; basipterygoid processes functional; flexor tendons Type 1; hypotarsus simple; syrinx bronchial with one pair of muscles; nares holorhinal, impervious; primaries 11; secondaries 12–18, diastataxic; rectrices 10–13, usually 12; caeca large, long, with expanded ends; tongue fleshy; no crop; oil gland naked or minutely tufted; no biceps slip or expansor secundariorum; 14 cervical vertebrae; outer toe reversible; eyes directed forward and encircled by a facial disk of feathers; nostrils hidden by stiff bristles; eggs white; young ptilopaedic; nidicolous.

Family TYTONIDAE: 2/17. Inner toe as long as middle toe, claw of middle toe pectinate; tail emarginate; sternum without manubrium; metasternum entire or with one notch each side; furcula ankylosed to carina; skull long and narrow; facial disk heart-shaped; legs long with feathers on posterior side of tarsus pointing upward; small aftershaft present; no primaries emarginate; no bony ring on tarsometatarsus.

Family STRIGIDAE: 23/161. Inner toe shorter than middle toe; claw of middle toe not pectinate; tail rounded; manubrium present; metasternum deeply 2-notched each side; furcula free from carina; skull relatively broad; facial disk more or less circular; feathers of tarsus point forward; no aftershaft; one to six primaries with inner web emarginate; tarsometatarsus with bony ring on ventral surface of proximal end.

The Strigidae and Tytonidae differ in additional characters (Ridgway 1914:598; Sibley and Ahlquist 1972:184).

There are 14 species of *Tyto*, and members of this genus occur worldwide in the tropics and temperate regions, except Hawaii and New Zealand. The bay-owls (*Phodilus*) are sometimes included in the Tytonidae, as here, but their affinities are still uncertain. The Oriental Bay-Owl (*P. badius*) occurs in southeast Asia, Malaysia, and Ceylon; the Congo Bay-Owl (*P. prigoginei*) is known only from the type specimen from Kivu Province, eastern Zaire.

The strigids range over the world, including the subpolar latitudes.

A confusing nomenclatural problem concerns the application of the generic name *Strix*, in which Linnaeus (1758) placed all the owls known to him, including species later assigned to *Bubo*, *Otus*, *Tyto* ("*Strix aluco*"), and others. Prior to 1910 the barn-owls (*Tyto*) were placed in either *Strix* or *Aluco* (see Allen 1908). Newton (1876) and Coues (1900) also discussed the problem. Mathews (1910:500) resolved the controversy by calling attention to the availability of *Tyto* Billberg (1828) for the barn and grass owls. The problem involves two generic names and two family names. Before 1910 the Barn Owl (*Tyto alba*) was usually called *Strix flammea*. Thus, the barn-owls were the Strigidae and the typical owls were usually placed in the Bubonidae or Asionidae. The generic names *Hybris* and *Aluco* also were applied to the barn-owls, and the family Aluconidae was often used. To avoid confusion in the following reviews we have indicated the currently used synonyms.

Historical Review of the Classification

Linnaeus (1758:86) began his Aves with the Accipitres, in which *Strix* was the third genus (p. 92), after *Vultur* and *Falco*. Most of the other early writers followed this arrangement by including the vultures, hawks, and owls in the same group at the beginning of their sequence of taxa. L'Herminier (1827), who based his system on the structure of the sternum and shoulder girdle, was the first to place the owls in a separate group from the falconiforms.

Nitzsch (1840) described the pterylography of several owls and divided them into two groups, one containing *Hybris* (*Tyto*) and *Photodilus* (*Phodilus*), the other including all other owls. Thus, the separation of the barn-owls and bay-owls from the typical owls began at an early date. Nitzsch regarded the owls as close allies of the falconiforms, although he noted several differences in pterylosis. He found that the ventral tract in the Barn Owl is like that of the Turkey Vulture (*Cathartes*), except that the contour feathers are more numerous and closer together.

Kaup published a series of papers on owls, culminating in a monograph (1859) in which he "reduced the three subfamilies of Bonaparte, the four of G. R. Gray, and the five of J.

Cassin into two natural subfamilies of Day and Night Owls, and . . . degraded to the rank of subgenera eleven genera" (p. 258). Kaup relied mainly on external characters but he examined the skulls of all available genera. He did not comment on the relationships of owls to other groups, and his "natural subfamilies" did not agree with those of other authors; in one (Striginae) he placed *Scops*, *Otus*, *Bubo*, and *Strix* (*Tyto*), in the other (Syrniinae) the remaining genera. Coues (1879:746) denounced Kaup as having "coined many new generic names . . . several of which have proven available; but his work cannot be considered of great merit or utility, and would be scarcely remembered were it not for the new genera proposed. His classification is hopelessly vitiated by his 'quinarian' freaks, and his way of working out species has the reverse of felicitous result. I should not be disposed to take issue with any one who might go so far as to consider the author in mention a magnificent failure."

Schlegel (1862) divided the owls into those with ear-tufts, the Oti, and those without, the Striges. This character was used in many subsequent classifications before 1900.

Lilljeborg (1866) placed the Strigidae in his order Accipitres and, based on the facial disk, recognized the Surnini, Strigini, and Hybridinae (*Tyto*).

Milne-Edwards (1867–71) supported Nitzsch's separation of the barn-owls from the typical owls and (1878c) considered *Phodilus* intermediate between the two groups.

Huxley (1867) thought that the owls differ from the other birds of prey "in most important particulars," yet he placed the owls, vultures, hawks, and falcons in his Aetomorphae, which he called "an eminently natural assemblage" (p. 462).

To Sundevall (1872, see 1889) the owls were members of the "Ptilopaedes" because the young are covered with thick down, and of the order Accipitres because they have raptorial bills and feet. The owls were placed in his "Cohort Nyctharpages" and divided into two series. In the first the "Fam. Glaucinae" included the barn-owls, "*Glaux*" (*Tyto*), and *Phodilus*. (Thus, *Glaux* is another synonym for the barn-owls and grass-owls.) The "Fam. Ululinae" included owls with the "facial border formed of oblong feathers, simply curved. Ear-orifice varying in shape. Bill . . . thick, curved from the base. The second primary, or more, externally sinuated towards the tip." This provides the flavor of Sundevall's characters, and the genera included in the Ululinae are known today as *Rhinoptynx*, *Asio*, and *Surnia*. In his "Second Series" the "Fam. Buboninae" ("Feathery horns are present, generally long; in the first two genera very short") included *Nyctea*, *Scotopelia*, *Ketupa*, *Bubo*, *Scops* (*Otus*), and in the "Fam. Noctuinae" ("No feathery horns") *Athene*, *Glaucidium*, *Ninox*, and others. The following "Cohort Hemeroharpages" contained the falconiforms.

Garrod (1873d, 1874a) found that the diurnal birds of prey have an ambiens muscle, but that owls do not. Although he based his main division of the Aves on the presence or absence of the ambiens, he included the Strigidae with the Falconidae in his "Cohort Accipitres," order Ciconiiformes, subclass Homalogonatae. He stated that the Strigidae are one of "those homalogonatous divisions" that "do not possess the ambiens muscle in any of their genera" (1874a:116). Thus, Garrod had to violate his belief in the importance of the ambiens to include the raptorial birds in the same cohort.

In the *Catalogue of Birds* Sharpe (1875a) placed the suborder Striges in the order Falconiformes with the diurnal birds of prey and based his classification of the owls on the structures of the feet, facial disk, and sternum. Sharpe divided the Striges into the Bubonidae (typical owls) and the Strigidae (barn and grass owls). The family Bubonidae was divided into the Buboninae and Syrniinae according to the structures of the facial disk and external ear.

Sclater (1879) insisted that the Barn Owl, *Strix flammea* (*Tyto alba*), should be the type of the Linnaean genus *Strix* and that its family should be the Strigidae, separated from other owls on characters of the furcula and sternum. The family name of the typical owls, in Sclater's opinion, should be the Asionidae, with the Long-eared Owl (*Asio otus*) as the type. Using characters of the ear opening, digital feathering, and feather "horns," he divided the Asionidae into the Asioninae, Syrniinae, Buboninae, Atheninae, and Nycteinae. In 1880 Sclater elevated the owls to ordinal rank and placed them next to the Accipitres. He suggested that the Osprey (*Pandion*) might be intermediate between the two groups because it lacks an aftershaft, as do the owls. A rudimentary aftershaft is present in *Tyto*.

Reichenow (1882) remained convinced of a close relationship between hawks and owls and included the owls in his order Raptatores. Shufeldt reported on the skeleton (1881a) and soft anatomy (1889d) of the Burrowing Owl (*Speotyto cunicularia*), but provided no evidence concerning the relationships between owls and other groups.

Barrows (1885) recognized two families of owls in the order Accipitres. He noted many differences between owls and diurnal raptors and attributed similarities between owls and the Osprey to coincidence.

Goodchild (1886, 1891) defined an "accipitrine style" of the secondary coverts shared by owls, parrots, most falconiforms, herons, and cormorants.

Fürbringer (1888) did not believe that the similarities between hawks and owls were proof of relationship. He found resemblances among owls, caprimulgiforms, rollers, and *Leptosomus*, and included these groups in his Coraciiformes. In his review of Fürbringer's work, Gadow (1888a:180) reported Fürbringer's belief that "The *Coraciiformes* are relatively least removed from the Charadriiformes. The Coraciae represent the lowest group of arboreal birds, and are related to the Caprimulgi, more remotely to the Owls, Trogons, and Bee-eaters. The Caprimulgi include . . . the Podargidae and Steatornithidae, whilst their apparent similarity with the Cypseli rests chiefly upon secondary analogies. The same applies to the Striges with reference to the Accipitres. Owls have so many important points in common with the Coraciae (Leptosomus), and especially with the Podargidae, that they have to be looked upon as Raptorial Coraciiformes or 'Podargoharpages'."

Fürbringer's Coraciiformes was a suborder in his "Order Coracornithes," a group that included the kingfishers, hornbills, hoopoes, bee-eaters, todies, rollers, caprimulgiforms, and owls.

Beddard (1888b) reviewed the characters separating the barn-owls and typical owls. He listed seven "osteological characters of the genus *Strix* [*Tyto*] . . . which apparently distinguish it from all others" (p. 340). Beddard also found support for the "division of the Striges into two families" (p. 341) in the structure of the tensor patagial muscles and, to some extent, in the syrinx. However, he admitted that the syringeal differences alone would not justify two families (p. 344) and that there is "a graded series . . . leading from *Strix* to *Scops*."

Beddard (1890c) weighed the evidence concerning the position of the Oriental Bay-Owl (*Phodilus badius*), added data from skeletal and soft anatomy, and suggested that *Phodilus* is more closely related to the typical owls than to the barn-owls. He noted that *Phodilus* "does present certain points of resemblance to *Strix* [*Tyto*]" but that "the structure of *Photodilus* [*Phodilus*] does not necessitate . . . a separate family . . . or the amalgamation of two generally recognized families into one" (p. 304).

Seebohm (1890a, 1895) placed the owls in the Falconiformes, but expressed his doubts

(1895:14–15): "It is very curious how many characters the Striges have in common with the Caprimulgi. In both these suborders the oil-gland is nude, and the down in adult birds is restricted to the feather-tracts, and in neither of them is the ambiens muscle present. None of these characters can be regarded as of much taxonomic value; in many other groups instances are to be found of the independent acquirement or loss of all of them. The similarity of the syrinx in the Striges and Caprimulgi is more important, but appears to me to be far outweighed by the presence of the cere in the Psittaci, Striges, and Accipitres, and the abnormal plantar tendons in the Caprimulgi."

Sharpe (1891:63) maintained "that the Ospreys are not Eagles at all, but represent an intermediate group between *Accipitres* and the *Striges*. Their skeleton is . . . Owl-like, and they have other characters in which they resemble the *Striges*. . . . Leading from the *Pandiones* we should next come across the *Striges*, but at a far distance . . . for the Owls form a well-marked group by themselves." He discounted a close relationship between owls and goatsuckers: "It was an old fancy that, because of a certain similarity in the style of plumage and because also of their crepuscular habits, the *Caprimulgi* and the *Striges* were nearly allied; and though this idea is now scouted, it would seem that the nearest approach to the *Striges* . . . will be found in the *Steatornithes* [Oilbird]; the *Podargi* [frogmouths] and, at a distance, the *Caprimulgi*, whence we should pass to the *Cypseli* [swifts] in one direction" (p. 65).

In his classification Sharpe (1891:78–79) placed the owls in the order Accipitriformes as the suborder Striges, following the suborder Pandiones (Osprey). The following order Coraciiformes began with the suborders Steatornithes and Podargi, but the suborder Caprimulgi was placed some distance below in the list, between the Todi and the Cypseli. Thus, Sharpe did not associate the Oilbird and the frogmouths with the potoos and caprimulgids, and viewed the owls as most closely related to the Osprey.

Gadow (1892) included the Striges in his order Coraciiformes next to the Macrochires (goatsuckers, swifts, hummingbirds). He found that the owls agreed with the parrots in 22 of his 40 characters and with the cuckoos in 28 (p. 235). In 1893 he made further comparisons between owls and other groups but, like Fürbringer, he did not support a close relationship between owls and hawks. He concluded: "The nearest relatives of the owls are the Caprimulgi, especially *Podargus* and also *Steatornis*, in spite of its frugivorous habits; then follow the Coraciae, and finally the Cuculi" (p. 240, transl.).

In most classifications prior to those of Fürbringer and Gadow, the owls had been placed with or near the falconiforms. Beddard (1898a) accepted the close relationship of owls and caprimulgiforms:

This conclusion, which is in harmony with much recent opinion, is curious in view of the external likenesses which bind together the two groups . . . likenesses which might fairly be put down to similarity of habit. These superficial resemblances are, however, enforced by more deep-lying structural similarities. Mitchell has found that . . . the Caprimulgi "come nearest to the owls" in the primitive character of the gut, while the caeca, swollen at the ends, are alike in both. The owls too are nearly the only other Coraciiform birds besides the Caprimulgi which have well-developed basipterygoid processes. . . .

The owls, formerly associated with the Accipitres and termed 'Accipitres nocturnae,' or 'Nyctharpages,' are now generally placed by themselves away from the hawks and in the neighbourhood of some of the birds comprised under the term 'picarian'. . . . The resemblances to the hawks are really only in habits and in beak and claw (pp. 243–244).

Beddard discussed the characters of the owls and noted that Gadow "has ingeniously pointed out that it is impossible to imagine that the Striges have been derived from the Accipitres, since, although without an ambiens, they have much the same structure of foot as the Accipitres *with* an ambiens. Hence it is difficult to believe that they would have lost it; he concludes that they are derived from some bird without an ambiens, and the failure of Mitchell to find the last trace of the missing ambiens—obvious in some birds which are clearly the descendants of birds with an ambiens—still further supports that way of looking at the matter" (p. 252).

The influence of Fürbringer, Gadow, and Beddard is indicated by the virtually universal acceptance of an owl-goatsucker alliance after 1890. An apparently correct authoritarian tradition had supplanted an erroneous one.

Clark (1894) studied the pterylosis of owls and goatsuckers, noted that owls have 11 primaries while goatsuckers have 10, and concluded "that the Caprimulgi are related to the Striges, and not very distantly either—probably a branch from the early part of the Strigine stem" (p. 572). He reviewed the opposing opinions of Garrod (1873d), Parker (1889b), and Sharpe (1891); noted that his study had revealed "some surprising similarities" between owls and caprimulgiforms; then retreated to a neutral position by stating that "perhaps, however, it is only an extraordinary case of what may be called 'analogous variation'" (p. 572).

Pycraft (1898a) wrote on the pterylography and (1903b) osteology of owls. He confirmed the main conclusions of Nitzsch (1840) except that he found "numerous small but very real differences by which not only genera but even species may be distinguished" from their pterylosis. He was critical of Kaup (1859), but favorably inclined toward Nitzsch, Newton (1871–74), Sharpe (1875a), and Gadow (1893). Pycraft's study of owl pterylosis did not produce "any very startling results" (p. 263), but he proposed a classification with the typical owls in the Asionidae and the barn-owls in the Strigidae. He evaluated the pterylographic evidence for relationships between owls and other groups and found points favoring alliances to the falconiforms and caprimulgiforms—once again, the safety of the middle ground, free of both controversy and contribution.

Sharpe (1899) placed the Strigiformes at the end of volume 1 of the *Hand-List*, following the suborder Pandiones of the Accipitriformes, thus expressing his belief in an affinity between the Osprey and the owls. The first group in volume 2 of the *Hand-List* (Sharpe 1900) was the Psittaciformes.

Mitchell (1901a) thought that the pattern of intestinal coiling in the owls is little modified from that of a "coraciiform-cuculiform metacentre." Beddard (1911) disagreed with Mitchell and with Gadow (1889), and stated: "The older opinion as to the Owls, that which placed them close to the Accipitres and not in the neighborhood of various Picarian genera, is most certainly justified by the close similarities in the mode of arrangement of the intestinal loops. At the same time, it is also easy to distinguish these two groups by the small but constant characters afforded by the ileo-duodenal ligament" (p. 90).

Pycraft (1903a) studied the pterylosis of the Oriental Bay-Owl (*Phodilus badius*) and concluded that it is a member of "the subfamily Asioninae, among which it stands as a somewhat aberrant genus with leanings towards *Asio*" (p. 46). He also found that the form of the external ear in *Phodilus* is unlike that of any other owl but "more nearly like that of *Asio* than . . . of any other genus." In a footnote (p. 46) Pycraft wrote: "there is nothing . . . in the pterylosis of this bird which . . . resembles that of *Strix* [*Tyto*]. Nitzsch, as Beddard has pointed out, seems to have imagined that a resemblance of the kind existed." Finally, Pycraft stated that *Phodilus* "is not a near ally of *Strix* [*Tyto*], as has been contended on more than one occasion" (p. 47). The "remarkable character" of the external ear of *Phodilus* caused Pycraft (1903a:47–48) to revise his 1898 classification of the Asionidae by placing *Asio, Syrnium, Photodilus, Bubo, Scops, Ninox,* and *Sceloglaux* in the subfamily Asioninae.

In Shufeldt's (1904b) classification the "supersuborder Strigiformes" contained the Bubonidae (typical owls) and the Strigidae (barn-owls). The Strigiformes were placed between the parrots and the caprimulgiforms.

From feather structure, Chandler (1916:372) concluded: "Although in the great length of the pennula and resulting softness of the plumage the Caprimulgi resemble the Striges, the details of structure, in so far as they differ in these suborders from that of the typical Coraciiformes, are not the same, and it is only reasonable to suppose that the similarities are due to parallel evolution and there is no closer relationship shown between these two groups than between either of them and other coraciiform groups."

E. Stresemann (1934) gave the barn-owls subfamily status in the Strigidae. He did not believe in a close relationship between owls and hawks and thought that the nearest relatives of the owls are probably the nightjars (Aegotheli, Caprimulgi).

Hudson (1937) found differences between the pelvic muscles of owls (*Bubo, Otus*) and those of a caprimulgid (*Chordeiles*) but he did not examine other Caprimulgi to determine the extent of variation.

Glenny (1943b) confirmed Garrod's (1873b) discovery that there are two carotids in the Barn Owl (*Tyto alba*) and found the same condition in seven North American strigids. Two carotids also occur in the falconiforms, caprimulgids, and *Steatornis*.

The owls are parasitized by two genera of Mallophaga, "the affinities of one (*Strigiphilus*) are unknown, the other (*Kurodia*) is found elsewhere only on the Falconiformes" (Clay 1950:44).

Mayr and Amadon (1951) placed their order Striges between the Psittaci and Caprimulgi and noted that "there are strong reasons to believe" the owls and goatsuckers to be related, "but the resemblance of goatsuckers to swifts is evidently superficial" (p. 9).

Verheyen (1956a, 1961) divided the Strigiformes into the usual two families, Tytonidae and Strigidae, with the latter composed of the Asioninae, Phodilinae, and Striginae. He noted that *Tyto* has been separated from the other owls by many characters, to which he added the weakly developed hyoid, the long, thin, mandibular rami, and the short internal process of the mandibular articulation. Verheyen placed *Steatornis* in his Caprimulgiformes but considered it intermediate between them and the owls.

In 1930 Wetmore placed the Strigiformes between the Psittaciformes and Caprimulgiformes, in 1960 between the Cuculiformes and Caprimulgiformes.

Sibley (1960) found that the paper electrophoretic patterns of the egg-white proteins support a relationship between the owls and caprimulgiforms, and noted that "The egg-white profile of *Tyto* . . . is distinctive but clearly similar to the other genera and neither supports nor refutes the separation of the two families."

Mees (1964) revised the taxonomy of Australian owls and kept the Tytonidae and Strigidae because there "does not seem to be any advantage in grading down the two families" to subfamilies.

From comparisons of the syringes of *Tyto*, *Phodilus*, and several strigid genera, A.H. Miller (1965) concluded "that *Phodilus* has more points of resemblance to the Strigidae than to *Tyto* although there are some departures from the Strigidae which are suggestive of *Tyto*. *Phodilus* is not, however, clearly intermediate between them" (p. 538).

Marshall (1966) assembled data on the skeleton, syrinx, voice, facial disk, ecto-parasites, and behavior of *Phodilus*. He stated that the Oriental Bay-Owl (*P. badius*) shows "departures from Strigidae, even greater removal from Tytonidae, and nothing clearly inter-mediate" and recommended "placing *Phodilus* in its own family, the Phodilidae" (p. 238). He also concluded that *Otus scops* and *O. flammeolus* are separate species because their voices are so different that "they cannot be in the same species" (p. 240). Marshall (1967) relied primarily on personal field observations and vocalizations of the screech owls (*Otus*) in a study of their species limits in North and Middle America, but did not consider higher category problems.

Bock and McEvey (1969b) reported on the os prominens, a large, hook-shaped ses-amoid bone in the tendon of the M. tensor patagii longus of the Strigidae. This bone is not found in *Tyto*, but is present in many hawks. The shape of the os prominens, and the relation-ships of the tendons and ligaments to it, differ in owls and hawks, so Bock and McEvey concluded that the structure does not indicate affinity between owls and hawks. They also discussed the osseous arch on the radius that serves as the attachment for Mm. pronator profundus and extensor indicus. They found the arch in the strigids and in *Tyto*. Because it is apparently unique to owls, Bock and McEvey felt that it indicates that *Tyto* is closely related to the other owls.

Flieg (1971) reported a captive hybrid between a male Barn Owl and a female Striped Owl (*Rhinoptynx clamator*). The female laid four eggs; two of them were fertile and develop-ment proceeded to the fifteenth day. Flieg observed that "Since the two families of Strigi-formes are thought to be taxonomically distinct, this record of hybridization may be of some value."

From comparisons of the electrophoretic patterns of the egg-white proteins, Sibley and Ahlquist (1972) concluded that *Tyto* is closely related to the other owls and should be placed in a tribe of the Strigidae. We thought that the evidence indicated that the caprimulgiforms "seem to be the closest relatives of the owls" but that the degrees of relationship of the owls to the falcons and caprimulgiforms "are yet to be determined."

Cracraft (1981) resurrected the long-moribund idea that the "Owls can be included in the Falconi, because they possess a derived tarsometatarsal and pelvic morphology shared with pandionids and accipitrids (including falcons); the Falconi (including owls) also have a unique pelvic myological pattern in that they have lost the piriformis pars iliofemoralis, the flexor cruris lateralis (semitendinosus) and accessory semitendinosus, and the vinculum connecting the flexors of digit III. . . . I have been unable to find evidence for a relationship between owls and any other group of nonpasserines. Caprimulgiforms are most often mentioned, but the morphological organization of caprimulgiforms is clearly similar to apodiforms and not to strigids. What is not often realized by contemporary ornithologists is that numerous 19th century workers saw the many similarities of hawks and owls as evidence of close relationship; it was 20th century systematists who overemphasized differences and concluded convergence."

Olson (1982) vigorously criticized Cracraft's "Division 3" as a category that "includes the Ciconiiformes and the Falconiformes, the latter including the Strigiformes. One will search in vain for a single synapomorphy that will define a group that contains both flamingos and owls as monophyletic within the Class Aves."

Amadon and Bull (1988) presented an annotated list of the species of living owls, within which Marshall and King reviewed the genus *Otus*. The classification followed the traditional arrangement with all species in the Strigiformes and Strigidae, and the strigids divided into Tytoninae (Barn Owls, Bay Owls), and Striginae (Typical Owls). They recognized 11 species of *Tyto*, two species of *Phodilus*, 51 of *Otus*, 17 of *Bubo*, 13 of *Strix*, 15 of *Glaucidium*, 16 of *Ninox*, and six of *Asio*, plus smaller numbers of species in the other genera, for a total of 162, vs 178 recognized by Sibley and Monroe (1990).

The DNA Hybridization Evidence (Figs. 102–103, 334, 353, 355, 362)

The corrected Δ T$_{50}$H values in Fig. 362 suggest that the owls and nightjars diverged from a common ancestor at Δ T$_{50}$H 19.1. They shared a common ancestor with the turacos at Δ 20.4, and with the hummingbirds and swifts at Δ 21.9.

Fig. 362 shows the branching pattern of the owls, with the branch between the barn owls and typical owls at Δ 13.6. It seems surprising that the hybrid eggs between *Tyto* and *Rhinoptynx* reported by Flieg (1971) were fertile and developed for 15 days.

The comparison between the DNAs of *Strix nebulosa* and *Ciccaba virgata* (Δ 1.2) suggest that *Ciccaba* may be merged with *Strix*. *Strix varia* is Δ 1.5 from *nebulosa*, and *S. leptogrammica* is Δ 2.0 from *nebulosa*. *Bubo* and *Nyctea* could be merged on the basis of their delta value of 1.9.

We lack the DNAs of many genera, thus we cannot be certain of the division of the Strigidae into subfamilies. Although *Speotyto* qualifies as the type of a subfamily at Δ 7.9 we prefer to recognize only the family Strigidae at this time.

The DNA hybridization data suggest that the turacos (Musophagiformes) may be more closely related to the owls than to any other living group. This may be an effect of relative rates of genomic evolution, but we lack evidence to prove or disprove this possibility. Evidence linking the turacos to the cuckoos is not convincing; we present the available evidence without advocating an answer to this question.

In Fig. 100 (*Tauraco*) the owls (*Bubo*, *Otus*) are the closest taxa to the homoduplex, with the nightjars next, followed by two pigeons, two parrots, a cuckoo, and two passerines. The owls intersect the vertical axis at ca. 33% to 35%. In Fig. 101 (*Tauraco*) several other non-passerine groups are represented; their melting curves are farther from the homoduplex than are those of the owls. If the relative positions of these curves are not significantly affected by different rates of DNA evolution, a relationship between owls and turacos may be real; but the distance between the groups is large and the relationship is not close.

Fig. 102 (*Strix*) presents the melting curves of 10 species of owls compared with the *Strix nebulosa* homoduplex. The cluster of species from *Lophostrix* to *Asio* includes typical strigine species. The gap between them and the *Glaucidium-Speotyto* pair suggest that the pygmy owls and Burrowing Owl form a separate cluster. The distant position of the two species of *Tyto* confirms other evidence that the barn and grass owls are not closely related to the strigids.

Fig. 103 (*Strix*) indicates the inclusion of *Ciccaba* in *Strix*, by the combination *Strix virgata*. The position of the curve of *Tauraco* may indicate a close relationship between owls and turacos, or may be influenced by a slow rate of DNA evolution in the turacos. We have no data on the age at first breeding of the turacos. The genera of Aegotheli and Caprimulgi vary in their intersection with the vertical axis from ca. 35% to 56%. Figs. 104 to 109 show the relationships among these groups and with the owls. The relationships are complex and unclear, in part because different rates of DNA evolution may be present. It does seem likely that the owls and the several groups of nightjars, frogmouths, potoos, etc. are more closely related to one another than to any other group.

In the FITCH tree, Fig. 334, *Strix* is 16.7 distance units from *Caprimulgus*, 17.1 units from *Podargus*, 17.4 from *Aegotheles*, 18.4 from *Chaetura*, and 22.7 from *Amazilia*. The short branch to *Strix* suggests a rate slowdown in the strigids which begin to breed at ca. two years of age; the caprimulgids begin at age one, as do *Colius* and *Amazilia*. Some of these differences in branch lengths may also be due to experimental errors, thus we note these differences, but small differences in ages at first breeding are unlikely to be important.

We conclude that the owls and nightjars are near relatives and there seems to be a real but distant relationship between them and the swifts and hummingbirds (Fig. 353). The clustering of the mousebirds with the nightjars in Fig. 334 may be a result of the particular set of taxa in the analysis, or it may indicate a fairly close relationship not revealed in the UPGMA tree. The owls are not closely related to the hawks and a distant relationship between the Musophagiformes and Strigiformes is possible but unclear.

Owlet-Nightjars, Frogmouths, Oilbird, Potoos, Eared-Nightjars, Nighthawks, and Nightjars

Order STRIGIFORMES
  Suborder Aegotheli
          Family Aegothelidae: Owlet-Nightjars
  Suborder Caprimulgi
    Infraorder Podargides
          Family Podargidae: Australian Frogmouths
          Family Batrachostomidae: Asian Frogmouths
    Infraorder Caprimulgides
      Parvorder Steatornithida
        Superfamily Steatornithoidea
          Family Steatornithidae: Oilbird
        Superfamily Nyctibioidea
          Family Nyctibiidae: Potoos
      Parvorder Caprimulgida
        Superfamily Eurostopodoidea
          Family Eurostopodidae: Eared-Nightjars
        Superfamily Caprimulgoidea
          Family Caprimulgidae
            Subfamily Chordeilinae: Nighthawks
            Subfamily Caprimulginae: Nightjars, Whip-poor-wills

The Aegotheli and Caprimulgi are specialized for crepuscular or nocturnal activity and many of them feed on flying insects. Whether by convergence or common ancestry they combine some of the morphological characters of owls and swifts and have often been associated with one or both of these groups. The DNA evidence reveals a phylogeny that is reflected by the classification given above.

The palate is schizognathous in the Caprimulgidae (except *Chordeiles*) and Nyctibiidae, desmognathous in *Chordeiles*, *Steatornis*, Podargidae, and Aegothelidae; pelvic muscle formula AXY or, in *Steatornis*, XY; two carotids in caprimulgids, only the left in podargids and *Nyctibius*; coracoids separated; basipterygoid processes small (absent in Podargidae and

Aegothelidae); flexor tendons Type 5a; feet anisodactyl, synpelmous; hypotarsus complex; syrinx bronchial or tracheo-bronchial; nares holorhinal, impervious; aftershaft small; primaries 10; secondaries 11–13; diastataxic; rectrices 10; adult downs restricted to apteria; powder downs only in *Nyctibius* and Podargidae; cervical vertebrae 13–15; oil gland variable, small and nude in most species, absent in *Podargus*; caeca large, absent in *Aegotheles*; intestinal convolutions Type 6; young ptilopaedic, nidicolous.

Family AEGOTHELIDAE: 1/8. Australia, New Guinea, New Caledonia, Halmajera, Batjan. 5 phalanges in outer toe; middle toe not pectinate; nostrils near tip of bill, obvious and open; no powder downs; no caeca; metasternum with 2 notches each side; feed on flying insects and ground-dwelling invertebrates; roost and nest in hollow trees, 3–4 white or spotted eggs, some line nest with green leaves; perch crosswise on branches.

Family PODARGIDAE: 1/3. Australia, New Guinea and adjacent islands (Trobriand, Fergusson, Goodenough), Solomon Islands.

Family BATRACHOSTOMIDAE: 1/11. Indonesia (Java, Sumatra, Borneo), Southeast Asia (Malaysia, Sabah, Indochina, Thailand, Burma), India, Sri Lanka, Philippines.

The frogmouths (Podargidae, Batrachostomidae) have 5 phalanges in the outer toe; middle toe not pectinate; fourth toe reversible; metasternum with 2 notches each side; bill heavy, wide, triangular, hooked; nostrils slit-like, near base of bill, protected by an operculum, overhung by feathers; large powder down patches on each side of rump; feed on the ground or in trees, do not "hawk" for insects; nest of twigs and feathers with lichens, mosses, etc.; 1–2 white eggs.

Family STEATORNITHIDAE: 1/1. Trinidad, Guianas, Venezuela to Ecuador and Peru. Frugivorous (oil palm fruits); bill hard, strong, owl-like with a subterminal tooth; rostrum movably articulated with the skull; long rictal bristles; 15 cervical vertebrae; bronchial syrinx; roost and nest colonially in caves; echolocate by audible clicks; nest of palm seeds and droppings; 2–4 white eggs.

Family NYCTIBIIDAE: 1/7. Southern Mexico to Brazil; Jamaica and Hispaniola. 4th toe with 5 phalanges; hallux with 3 phalanges; metasternum with two notches each side; middle toe not pectinate; iris yellow or orange; tarsus short; large powder down patches on sides and breast; maxilla with subterminal tooth; no rictal bristles; perch upright; a single spotted egg laid atop a broken tree stub.

Family EUROSTOPODIDAE: 1/7. Australia, New Guinea, Solomon Islands, New Caledonia, Celebes, Borneo, Sumatra, southeast Asia, northeastern and southern India (Kerala), East Pakistan, southwestern China, Philippines (Luzon, Mindoro, Mindanao). The Eared-Nightjars are like the caprimulgids in most characters, but they tend to be larger and darker in color, lack long rictal bristles, and have long, erectile tufts of feathers behind the ear coverts. One egg, laid on the ground.

Family CAPRIMULGIDAE: 14/76. Worldwide in tropical and temperate regions. 4th toe with 4 phalanges; hallux with 2 phalanges; metasternum with one notch on each side; claw of middle toe pectinate; feet weak, toes not expanded basally; bill small and weak, gape deeply cleft; large rictal bristles; no powder downs; two eggs laid on the ground, no nest.

From these descriptions of structure and habits it is obvious that the Aegotheli and Caprimulgi include a varied group of taxa. They have been viewed as most closely related to the owls, swifts, trogons, and several other groups. Their relationships to one another have been obscured by their specializations of structure and various classifications have been proposed, although they usually have been placed in the same order.

Historical Review of the Classification

Moehring (1752) may have been the first to place the nightjars and the owls together. His Accipitres included *Strix, Caprimulgus, Psittacus, Falco, Aquila,* and *Vultur.* However, in most of the early classifications the nightjars were associated with the swifts and the swifts were thought to be allied to the swallows. Linnaeus (1758) included the swallows and swifts in his order Passeres, genus *Hirundo,* followed by *Caprimulgus.* Similar arrangements were used by Brisson (1760), Illiger (1811), Merrem (1813), Temminck (1820), L'Herminier (1827), Wagler (1827), Gray (1840), Cabanis (1847), Fitzinger (1856–65), and Carus (1868–75).

Nitzsch (1840) recognized that the owls and nightjars may be related, but the nightjars were associated with the swifts, rollers, cuckoos, etc. in his classification. Lilljeborg (1866) placed the Caprimulgidae between the owls and swifts.

Sclater (1866a,b) based a subdivision of the nightjars on characters of the sternum, phalanges, and bill. He divided the Caprimulgidae into the Steatornithinae, Podarginae (*Podargus, Batrachostomus, Nyctibius, Aegotheles*), and Caprimulginae (typical nightjars).

In Huxley's (1867) classification the Caprimulgidae, Cypselidae (swifts), and Trochilidae (hummingbirds) comprised his "Group Cypselomorphae." He thought that *Aegotheles* is most like the swifts, that *Caprimulgus* resembles the trogons, and that *Podargus* is distantly related to the owls. He considered the Cypselomorphae to be close to the passerines and included both groups in his suborder Aegithognathae.

Sundevall (1872, see 1889) based his "Order Volucres" on the "Picae" of Linnaeus, and defined it by foot and feather characters. In "Cohort 5. Ampligulares (or Gapers)," he placed the families Trogoninae, Podarginae (including *Steatornis, Nyctibius, Aegotheles, Podargus*), Caprimulginae (other nightjars, plus the pratincole genus *Glareola*), and Cypselinae (swifts).

Garrod (1873c) found that *Steatornis* resembles the owls in its pterylosis, and agrees with the owls, caprimulgids, rollers, motmots, and jacamars in having two carotids, well-developed caeca, a nude oil gland, and in lacking the ambiens. Garrod retained *Steatornis* in a monotypic family but did not speculate about its nearest relatives.

In Garrod's system (1874a:117–118) the nightjars and the Oilbird were associated with the passerines, trogons, puffbirds, jacamars, bee-eaters, rollers, motmots, and todies in the order Passeriformes, subclass Anomalogonatae. The swifts and hummingbirds were in the adjacent order Cypseliformes, and the owls were next to the Falconidae in the "Cohort Accipitres" of the order Ciconiiformes, subclass Homalogonatae. Garrod placed the owls among the "homalogonatous" birds although, like the nightjars, they lack the ambiens.

Sclater (1880b) followed Huxley (1867) and associated the nightjars with the swifts and hummingbirds, and the owls with the falconiforms. Reichenow (1882) did much the same.

Newton (1884) separated the owls from the falconiforms and placed them near *Steatornis* "which, long confounded with the Caprimulgidae . . . at last . . . recognized as an independent form, and one cannot but think that it has branched off from a common ancestor with the owls. The Goatsuckers may have done the like, for there is really not much to ally them to the Swifts and Humming-birds . . . as has often been recommended" (p. 47). In a footnote (p.

47) Newton remarked on the "resemblance in colouration between Goatsuckers and Owls" and recommended that it "be wholly disregarded."

Although he emphasized the palatal differences among *Steatornis*, *Podargus*, and *Caprimulgus*, Stejneger (1885) believed them to be closely related. He erected the superfamily Coracioideae in his order Picariae for the Steatornithidae, Podargidae, Caprimulgidae (including *Nyctibius*), Leptosomidae, and Coraciidae. To Stejneger the palate of *Caprimulgus* was similar to that of the passerines, and several characters of *Steatornis* suggested an alliance to the owls.

Shufeldt (1885b) compared the skeletons of hummingbirds, nightjars, and swifts and concluded that *Nyctibius* and *Steatornis* are closely related to the owls, but that the swifts are closer to the swallows and unrelated to the nightjars.

Beddard (1886a) examined the anatomy of several Caprimulgi and concluded "that *Steatornis* is a peculiar type of Goatsucker and needs a special subfamily to itself. . . . A second subfamily will include *Podargus* and *Batrachostomus*, while *Aegotheles* ought perhaps to be" in a third subfamily. A fourth subfamily was proposed for *Caprimulgus*, *Chordeiles*, and *Nyctidromus*. Beddard noted that his study supported the classification proposed by Sclater (1866a).

Goodchild used the arrangement of the secondary coverts to suggest relationships. In 1886 he stated that the pattern of these coverts in the Caprimulgi does not resemble that of the swifts and hummingbirds, but is more like that of woodpeckers, and that the pattern of *Steatornis* is most like that of cuckoos. In 1891 he defined a "cuculine style" of the secondary coverts, which he believed to be a modification of the passerine condition, and to be shared by the cuckoos, nightjars, Oilbird, and frogmouths.

Fürbringer (1888) placed the owls and nightjars next to one another in his "suborder Coraciiformes" of the "Order Coracornithes." He attributed the similarities between swifts and nightjars to convergence.

From his study of the intestinal convolutions Gadow (1889) concluded that the affinities of the owls "rest with the Coraciidae and Caprimulgidae combined" and that "the Caprimulgidae, Cypselidae [swifts], and Trochilidae [hummingbirds] agree very much with each other. . . . The Cypselidae and Caprimulgidae are somewhat more closely related to each other, and the latter (including *Podargus*) turn towards the Owls." He thought that the trogons are part of this assemblage and especially close to the nightjars and rollers because they too are "isocoelous" and have large caeca "like the Coraciidae, Caprimulgidae and Striges" (p. 315).

In his subclass Coraciiformes, Seebohm (1890c:203) diagnosed the "Order Picariae" as follows: "Hallux always present, and connected with the *flexor perforans digitorum*, and not with the *flexor longus hallucis*: no ambiens muscle." In this group he recognized a suborder Coraciae, containing the Cypselidae, Caprimulgidae, Steatornithidae, Podargidae, Leptosomidae, Coraciidae, and Meropidae. In 1895 Seebohm gave the Caprimulgi subordinal rank in his order Coraciiformes next to the suborder Picariae, which included the Coraciiformes of recent authors, plus the colies and swifts.

Sharpe (1891) included the nightjars in his large order Coraciiformes and made suborders of the Steatornithes, Podargi, and Caprimulgi. He separated the Caprimulgi from the first two by several intervening groups, and placed them next to the swifts and hummingbirds. He noted that "It was an old fancy that . . . the *Caprimulgi* and the *Striges* were nearly allied"

(p. 65) but that this idea was no longer accepted and that the Steatornithes are the closest relatives of the owls.

In the *Catalogue of Birds* Hartert (1892) used the following classification:

Order Picariae
  Suborder Upupae: Hoopoes
  Suborder Trochili: Hummingbirds
  Suborder Coraciae
    Family Cypselidae: Swifts
    Family Caprimulgidae
      Subfamily Caprimulginae: Goatsuckers, Nightjars
      Subfamily Nyctibiinae: Potoos
    Family Podargidae
      Subfamily Podarginae: Frogmouths
      Subfamily Aegothelinae: Owlet-frogmouths
    Family Steatornithidae: Oilbird

Gadow (1892) proposed the following arrangement:

Order Coraciiformes
  Suborder Striges
    Family Strigidae: Owls
  Suborder Macrochires
    Family Caprimulgidae: Goatsuckers
    Family Cypselidae: Swifts
    Family Trochilidae: Hummingbirds
  Suborder Colii: Colies
  Suborder Trogones: Trogons
  Suborder Coraciae: Rollers, Motmots, Kingfishers, etc.

In 1893 Gadow elevated the Caprimulgi to subordinal rank in his Coraciiformes and suggested that, other than the owls, their nearest relatives were first the Coraciae, then the swifts. Wetmore (1930) adopted essentially the same arrangement.

Pycraft (1898a:268) considered Garrod's (1873c) conclusion that the pterylosis of *Steatornis* "resembles the Strigidae much more than any of the allied families" to be an overstatement.

Beddard (1898a:235) thought the nightjars have a "highly characteristic" syrinx and stated that: "Like the nearly related (?) cuckoos, we have both the tracheo-bronchial and the purely bronchial syrinx. Indeed, the stages are almost identical in the two groups. *Cuculus* and *Caprimulgus* correspond with a tracheo-bronchial syrinx; then we have *Centropus* and *Podargus*, and finally the culmination in *Crotophaga* and *Steatornis* of a syrinx furnished with a membrana tympaniformis, which does not commence until many rings below the bifurcation of the tube, the intrinsic muscles being attached to the first ring which borders upon it."

Beddard realized that the syringes of the nightjars also resemble those of owls and, in 1898, he believed the owls and nightjars to be the closest relatives. He was especially impressed by the similar intestinal tracts in the two groups. Mitchell (1901a) defined the intestinal pattern of the nightjars as archecentric (generalized) and thought those of the rollers, colies, swifts, hummingbirds, and passerines could have been derived from it. By 1911 Beddard no longer seemed to regard the similarities between the intestinal tracts of owls and nightjars as significant and he found more resemblances between the owls and hawks.

In the *Hand-List* Sharpe (1900) used the following sequence:

Order Coraciiformes
  Suborder Steatornithes
    Family Steatornithidae: Oilbird
  Suborder Podargi
    Family Podargidae
      Subfamily Podarginae: Frogmouths
      Subfamily Aegothelinae: Owlet-Nightjars
  Suborder Leptosomati: *Leptosomus*, the Cuckoo-Roller or Courol
  Suborder Coraciae: Rollers
  Suborder Halcyones: Kingfishers
  Suborder Bucerotes: Hornbills
  Suborder Upupae: Hoopoes
  Suborder Meropes: Bee-eaters
  Suborder Momoti: Motmots
  Suborder Todi: Todies
  Suborder Caprimulgi
    Family Caprimulgidae
      Subfamily Nyctibiinae: Potoos
      Subfamily Caprimulginae: Nightjars
  Suborder Cypseli: Swifts
  Suborder Trochili: Hummingbirds
  Suborder Colii: Colies or Mousebirds
Order Trogones: Trogons

This arrangement, with the Oilbird and the frogmouths separated from the other caprimulgiforms by rollers, kingfishers, etc., is the same as that proposed by Sharpe in 1891. He justified it by arguing that the Oilbird and frogmouths are related to the owls, and the other nightjars are related to the swifts. The "peculiar Leptosomati of Madagascar" (1891:65) were viewed as the connection between the Oilbird-frogmouth group and the rollers (Coraciae).

Clark (1901a) described the pterylosis of *Podargus* and reviewed those of other nightjars. He disagreed with Nitzsch (1840), who had said that the pterylosis of *Podargus* is like that of *Caprimulgus*. According to Clark, "the pterylosis of *Podargus* is very distinctive" and intermediate between those of caprimulgids and owls. He concluded that "the accumulated evidence thus confirms the view that Goatsuckers and Owls are near relatives" (p. 170). Clark also disputed Nitzsch's description of the pterylosis of the swifts and concluded that the swifts and nightjars are "strikingly different" in their pterylosis and that there seem "to be no connecting links" between them.

Chandler (1916) noted several similarities in feather structure between nightjars and owls, but he believed that the softness of the contour feathers in the two groups is due to convergence. Although he regarded both groups as members of the expanded Coraciiformes, he did not think they are closely related.

Wetmore (1918) dissected a specimen of *Nyctibius griseus* and reviewed the characters of the other caprimulgiform groups. He agreed with Gadow (1893) that "the Nyctibiidae seem to form an intermediate group" between the Podargidae and the Caprimulgidae and that the Aegothelidae "serves to narrow the gap still more." Wetmore proposed "that the suborder Nycticoraciae of the Order Coraciiformes may be divided into two superfamilies, the Steatornithoidae with the single genus *Steatornis* and the Caprimulgoidae with the families Podargidae, Nyctibiidae, Aegothelidae, and Caprimulgidae" (p. 586).

W. DeW. Miller (1924a) determined the condition of the vestigial 11th primary, or remicle, in various groups of birds. In owls and *Podargus* the remicle is normally present. In swifts, and usually in caprimulgids, there is only a single small feather, presumably the 11th lower covert, on the outer side of the 10th primary. Miller noted: "However, in the Australian nightjar, *Eurostopodus mystacalis* . . . both the covert and remicle are present. . . . Thus the nightjars are moved a trifle nearer the owls and farther from the swifts" (p. 315).

E. Streseman (1934) considered the nearest relatives of the Caprimulgi to be the owls.

Hudson (1937:77) concluded that a "study of the musculature of the pelvic limb in a goat-sucker (*Chordeiles*) and in certain owls *Bubo* and *Otus*), fails to disclose any unusual similarity. The formulae are very different (AXY for *Chordeiles* and AD for the owls) and there are numerous other striking differences in the pelvic musculature." The pelvic muscle formula of the Caprimulgidae differs from those of the swifts (A) and cuckoos (AXY+).

Glenny (1953b) observed that *Steatornis* and the caprimulgids have two carotids, but the Podargidae and *Nyctibius* have only the left, thus confirming Garrod (1873c) and Wetmore (1918).

Verheyen (1956a) analyzed a long list of anatomical characters in a study of the owls, trogons, and nightjars. He concluded that these groups are related to one another and he proposed a classification in which the order Caprimulgiformes contains the suborders Podargi, Caprimulgi, Trogones, and Steatornithes. The owls are in the adjacent order Strigiformes. In 1961 Verheyen moved the trogons to the Coraciiformes.

Sibley (1960) found similarities between the electrophoretic patterns of the egg-white proteins of owls and nightjars, and noted that "*Steatornis* is clearly caprimulgiform." There was "nothing in the egg-white protein patterns to support the suggestion that nightjars are related to the swifts," to the trogons, or to the Coraciiformes.

Snow (1961, 1962) studied the ecology and behavior of the Oilbird in Trinidad, reviewed the literature on the species, and concluded (1961:27–28) "that *Steatornis* is almost certainly closer to the caprimulgiform birds than to any other group, but even to them the relationship is very distant, while in certain characters they resemble the owls, perhaps due to convergence."

Sibley and Ahlquist (1972) concluded that "The Caprimulgidae, Nyctibiidae, and Steatornithidae are closely allied. The Podargidae and Aegothelidae seem closely related and, although caprimulgiform, comprise an outlying group. The nearest allies of the Caprimulgiformes are the Strigiformes."

Cracraft (1981) assigned the owls to the Falconiformes and decided that the nightjars are closest to the swifts. He found morphological evidence of "two well-defined lineages: aegothelids and podargids on the one hand, and caprimulgids and nyctibiids on the other."

The DNA Hybridization Evidence (Figs. 104–109, 334, 353, 355, 362)

The Strigi and the Caprimulgi diverged at $\Delta T_{50}H$ 19.1 (Fig. 362). The owls, not the swifts, are the closest living relatives of the nightjars. The DNA comparisons also reveal that the subgroups of the Caprimulgi are far more divergent from one another than most classifications have suggested. The generally similar plumage colors and patterns, evolved as concealing coloration, have probably influenced the opinions of many systematists.

The owlet-nightjars usually have been thought to be allied to the frogmouths, perhaps because both groups occur in the same geographical areas, but the DNA data show that the Aegotheli is the sister group of the Caprimulgi and that the two suborders diverged at Δ 18.8. Thus, the Aegotheli branched from the Caprimulgi soon after their common ancestor had diverged from the Strigi.

The frogmouths (Podargides) branched from the other Caprimulgi at Δ 17.9. The two genera of frogmouths, *Podargus* and *Batrachostomus*, diverged at Δ 10.3, which makes it necessary to place them in separate families in our system of assigning categories.

The potoos (*Nyctibius*) and the Oilbird (*Steatornis*) branched from the other Caprimulgides at Δ 16.9, and from one another at Δ 15.8. We assign them to separate superfamilies in the parvorder Steatornithida.

The eared-nightjars (*Eurostopodus*) usually have been placed in the Caprimulgidae, but the DNA comparisons indicate that they branched from the caprimulgids at Δ 12.3. We therefore assign them to a separate superfamily, Eurostopodoidea, the sister group of the Caprimulgoidea.

Within the Caprimulgidae, the DNA comparisons reveal large Δ $T_{50}H$ values between taxa that have been thought to be closely related. Thus, the subfamilial and generic allocations need some revision. The type species of *Caprimulgus* is *europaeus* (Linnaeus 1758:193), which is Δ 7.8 from *vociferus* in Fig. 362. This distance is within the subfamily level in our classification, hence these two species could be placed in separate genera and assigned to separate subfamilies. The values in Fig. 362 indicate that the generic status of other species of *Caprimulgus*, *Nyctidromus*, *Podager*, and *Phalaenoptilus* should also be reviewed. We cannot solve these problems with the present data, but the generic name *Antrostomus* is available for *vociferus* and *carolinensis*. Clearly, the caprimulgids have a large amount of genetic diversity concealed by a conserved external appearance.

The melting curves in Fig. 104 (*Aegotheles*) show the wide separation between the owlet-nightjars and the members of the Caprimulgi. The frogmouths are the most distant, rather than closely related to the owlet-nightjars, as suggested in the past.

Fig. 105 (*Podargus*) shows that the two frogmouth genera, *Podargus* and *Batrachostomus*, are not closely related, although they are closer to one another than to the other groups of the Caprimulgi. Note the position of the *Tauraco* curve, with that of *Aegotheles* slightly more distant from the homoduplex.

Fig. 106 (*Steatornis*) indicates the relatively isolated position of the Oilbird, and suggests that the potoos (*Nyctibius*) are its closest relatives. The curve of the Burrowing Owl clusters with those of the Caprimulgides and is about the same distance from *Steatornis* as that of *Aegotheles*. The curves of the swift, pigeon, cuckoo, and Song Sparrow are progressively more distant from that of the Oilbird.

Fig. 107 (*Chordeiles*) shows that *Nyctidromus* and *Caprimulgus* are closely related to the nighthawks, and that the potoos (*Nyctibius*) may be next most distant. The Barn Owl, Oilbird, turaco, Burrowing Owl, frogmouth, and owlet-nightjar are about equidistant from *Chordeiles*; the pigeon and swift are more distant.

Fig. 108 (*Caprimulgus*) includes several species of caprimulgids. The relative positions of *Nyctidromus* and three species of *Caprimulgus* suggest that some generic revision may be indicated. *Eurostopodus* is shown to be quite distant from the nighthawks and nightjars, hence we assigned it to a separate superfamily. The potoo, Oilbird, and frogmouth are distant from *Caprimulgus*.

Fig. 109 (*Caprimulgus*) suggests that the Caprimulgida are as closely related to owls as to potoos, Oilbird, and frogmouths. We think this is an effect of the rate slowdown in the owls, although the large genetic distances among the groups of the Caprimulgi contribute to the effect. We do not regard this as proof that the Oilbird, potoos, and frogmouths are more closely related to the owls than to the Caprimulgides, but that all of these groups are related and that rate differences complicate the interpretation of the melting curves.

The FITCH tree (Fig. 334) shows the short branch to *Strix*. Owls begin to breed at ca. two years of age; caprimulgids at one year. *Strix* is ca. 16.8 distance units from *Caprimulgus* and *Chordeiles,* and ca. 17.4 units from *Aegotheles*, *Podargus*, and *Steatornis*. These small differences are probably not significant in view of possible rate differences and experimental errors. *Strix* is 18.8 units from *Chaetura*, which may be significant.

We conclude that the Strigi, Aegotheli, and Caprimulgi are more closely related to one another than any of them is to another group. It seems probable that the swifts and hummingbirds are the next nearest relatives of the strigiforms (owls, nightjars). Rate differences complicate the interpretation of the DNA hybridization data, but the owls, caprimulgiforms, swifts, and hummingbirds form a monophyletic assemblage. The relationship of the turacos (Musophagiformes) and mousebirds (Coliiformes) to any or all of these groups is equivocal.

Pigeons and Doves

Superorder Passerimorphae
  Order COLUMBIFORMES
    Family Raphidae: Dodos, Solitaires. Extinct
    Family Columbidae: Pigeons, Doves

The pigeons and doves constitute a monophyletic group, although there is a moderately high degree of adaptive diversity within the order. The columbids are easily distinguished from other groups, but their nearest relatives have been uncertain. The sandgrouse (Pteroclidae) have been thought to be related to the Columbidae by many authors and the taxonomic history of this problem is reviewed under the Charadrii. The parrots, galliforms, and shorebirds most frequently have been proposed as the closest relatives of the pigeons and doves.

Family COLUMBIDAE: 40/310. Pigeons and doves occur on all continents and many islands. The extinct members of the Raphidae occurred on the Mascarene Islands in the Indian Ocean: the Dodo (*Raphus cucullatus*) on Mauritius and the Solitaire (*Pezophaps solitaria*) on Rodriguez. Another species probably occurred on Reunion, but the evidence is uncertain (Cheke 1985).

In the Columbidae the palate is schizognathous; pelvic muscle formula A(B)XY+; intestinal caeca small or absent; syrinx with asymmetrical extrinsic muscles; schizorhinal, impervious nares, with a fleshy cere over the slit-like nostrils; two carotids; hallux incumbent; flexor tendons Type 1; tarsi covered laterally and behind with hexagonal scales; thick plumage, feathers set loosely in the skin; diastataxic; 11 primaries; 12–20 rectrices; aftershaft small or absent; caeca small, not functional; well-developed bi-lobed crop; produce "pigeon milk" from crop lining for feeding young; oil gland naked or absent; nidicolous young hatched blind and without true down; nest of simple structure, composed of twigs, in tree or on ground; usually two white eggs per clutch, one in some species; drink by sucking or pumping.

Historical Review of the Classification

Linnaeus (1758) placed *Columba* in the "Passeres," but the 22 species he listed are still recognized as members of the Columbiformes. Many early authors placed the pigeons with, or near, the galliforms; for example, Nitzsch (1840) placed the "Columbinae" next to the "Gallinae." Huxley (1867) included the pigeons in the "Peristeromorphae," suborder "Schizognathae," and Sundevall (1872, see 1889) placed the "Cohort Peristeroideae" in his "Ordo Volucres, Series Anisodactyli" which also included the turacos, colies, trogons, nightjars, swifts, bee-eaters, motmots, kingfishers, and hornbills. This heterogeneous assemblage was based on the arrangement of the toes, with exceptions to the rule: "The fourth toe directed forwards. The toes, therefore, are generally three in front and one behind."

Garrod (1874b) used the size of the caeca, presence of the ambiens muscle, oil gland, gall bladder, and tarsal scutellation to classify the pigeons. His arrangement (generic names added) was as follows:

Family Columbidae
  Subfamily Columbinae: (*Columba, Streptopelia, Macropygia*)
  Subfamily Phapinae: (*Columbigallina, Metriopelia, Zenaida, Zenaidura, Caloenas, Turtur,*
    Ocyphaps, Phaps, Leucosarcia, Ducula, Didunculus, Lopholaemus)
  Subfamily Treroninae: (*Gallicolumba, Starnoenas, Geopelia, Treron, Ptilinopus, Goura*)

The Columbae of Sclater (1880b) included the pigeons and sandgrouse and he recognized four families of pigeons: Carpophagidae (fruit pigeons), Gouridae (*Goura*), Didunculidae (*Didunculus*), and Columbidae. Reichenow's (1913–14) arrangement of the pigeons was similar to that of Sclater, but he also recognized a family Geotrygonidae for most of the ground-dwelling species.

Elliot (1885) treated the pigeons as the order Columbae, placed between the sandgrouse and the falconiforms (Accipitres) and arranged in five families: Didiidae (Dodo and Solitaire), Didunculidae, Gouridae, Columbidae, and Carpophagidae.

Goodchild (1886) commented on similarities between plovers and pigeons in the arrangement of their secondary coverts, and noted that the sandgrouse differ, although later (1891) he reversed himself and concluded that the wing coverts are not significantly different between pigeons and sandgrouse. He found similarities between *Goura* and the Cracidae and Megapodiidae.

Fürbringer (1888) placed the Columbiformes between the Charadriiformes and Galliformes and also believed that they are allied to the parrots.

Seebohm (1888b) regarded the pigeons as "the tree-perching contingent" of the shorebirds.

In Sharpe's (1891) classification the Columbiformes were placed between the Galliformes and Opisthocomiformes (Hoatzin).

Shufeldt (1891a,e) thought that *Zenaida* and *Columba* are closely related and that *Starnoenas* should be placed in its own subfamily. Later (1901f) he divided his superfamily Columboidea into the Gouridae, Carpophagidae, and Columbidae.

Gadow (1893) divided the Columbidae into five subfamilies: Didunculinae, Treroninae, Caloenadinae, Columbinae, and Gourinae.

In the *Catalogue of Birds* Salvadori (1893) thought that "the safest and most natural mode of arranging them is offered by their external characters, and I propose a system which is not very different from those propounded in 1872 by Sundevall . . . and in 1880 by Sclater." Salvadori's classification follows:

Order Columbae
  Suborder Columbae [sic]
    Fam. Treronidae
      Subfam. Treroninae
      Subfam. Ptilopodinae
      Subfam. Carpophaginae
    Fam. Columbidae
      Subfam. Columbinae
      Subfam. Macropygiinae
      Subfam. Ectopistinae
    Fam. Peristeridae
      Subfam. Zenaidinae
      Subfam. Turturinae
      Subfam. Geopeliinae
      Subfam. Peristerinae
      Subfam. Phabinae
      Subfam. Geotrygoninae
      Subfam. Caloenadinae
    Fam. Gouridae
    Fam. Didunculidae
  Suborder Didi
    Fam. Dididae (extinct Dodo, Solitaire)

In the *Hand-List* Sharpe (1899) placed the Columbiformes between the sandgrouse (Pteroclidiformes) and the Opisthocomiformes and followed Salvadori's arrangement of families and subfamilies.

R. Martin (1904) studied the skeletons of 70 species of pigeons representing the principal groups, discussed the phylogeny of the Columbiformes, and proposed the following classification:

Order Columbiformes
  Suborder Didi
    Family Dididae: Dodo
    Family Pezophabidae: Solitaire
  Suborder Columbae
    Family Columbidae: Columbinae, Caloenadinae
    Family Peristeridae: Peristerinae, Phabinae, Ptilopodinae
    Family Treronidae: Treroninae
    Family Carpophagidae: Carpophaginae, Gourinae, Otidiphabinae
    Family Didunculidae: Didunculinae

Dubois (1902–04) recognized five families:

Treronidae: Treroninae, Ptilopodinae, Carpophaginae
Columbidae: Columbinae, Macropygiinae
Peristeridae: Zenaidinae, Turturinae, Geopeliinae, Chamaepeliinae, Phabinae, Geotryginae
Gouridae
Didunculidae

The Columbiformes of Wetmore (1930, 1960) and of Peters (1937) included the sand-grouse and pigeons as two suborders, and the Columbidae for all the pigeons. Peters recognized four subfamilies: Treroninae, Columbinae, Gourinae, and Didunculinae.

Irwin and his colleagues presented the results of their studies on the antigenic properties of the red blood cells in several species of columbids. Irwin (1932) found that two thirds of the antigenic specificities of *Streptopelia chinensis* are not present in the red cells of *S. risoria*, and that only one sixth of the antigenic specificities of *risoria* cells were not also shared with *chinensis*. Cumley and Cole (1942) and Cumley and Irwin (1944) found a correlation between the geographic distribution of the species of *Columba* and their red cell antigens. One series of antigens was specific to the Old World species, another to New World species. Only a few were common to one or two species of both hemispheres. A more complete list of the publications of Irwin, Cole, Cumley, et al. is presented by Sibley and Ahlquist (1972:152), and a detailed analysis by Sibley et al. (1974:110–115).

Mayr and Amadon (1951) placed their Columbae "near the Laro-Limicolae" and noted that "McDowell has found similarities between the humeri of parrots and those of pigeons" (p. 9).

Based on size and color pattern, Cain (1954) proposed subdivisions of *Ptilinopus*, and Husain (1958) revised *Treron* on the basis of color.

Verheyen (1957a) divided the Columbidae of Peters (1937) into three families—Caloenadidae, Duculidae, and Columbidae—and recognized 68 genera and numerous subfamilies and tribes.

Using external features, color pattern, and behavior, Goodwin (1958) merged *Zenaidura*, *Melopelia*, and *Nesopelia* into *Zenaida*, and *Osculatia* into *Geotrygon*. He believed *Starnoenas* is closely related to *Geotrygon* and that the American ground doves are more closely related to *Zenaida* than to Old World *Gallicolumba*. He also (1959a) lumped *Columbigallina*, *Eupelia*, and *Oxypelia* with *Columbina*, and *Leptophaps* and *Gymnopelia* with *Metriopelia*. Goodwin was unable to separate Old and New World species of *Columba* and he revised *Ducula* (1960), which he considered closely allied to *Ptilinopus*.

Sibley (1960) compared the paper electrophoretic patterns of the egg-white proteins of 31 species of columbids and found no evidence of relationships to other orders. The New World and Old World species of *Columba* had different patterns.

Harrison (1960) suggested that the chestnut coloration of the primaries in certain species of doves indicates relationship. He proposed that Salvadori's (1893) classification, which placed the bronze-winged doves in the Peristeridae, is a better indication of their relationships than that of Peters (1937).

From morphological and behavioral evidence Johnston (1961) merged *Columbigallina*, *Scardafella*, and *Eupelia* into *Columbina*. In 1962 he used the condition of the tenth primary, the angle of the skull at the frontal hinge, and other characters to divide the *Columba* of Peters (1937) into three genera: *Columba* for the Old World species plus the New World *fasciata*, *araucana*, and *caribaea*; *Oenoenas* for New World *subvinacea*, *plumbea*, *nigrirostris*, and *goodsoni*; *Patagioenas* for the remaining New World species.

Goodwin (1965) observed that estrildine finches sometimes drink by pumping in the manner of pigeons, and that species of *Streptopelia* vary their drinking method depending on the degree of thirst and cleanliness of the water. Goodwin concluded: "I think that the difference between the sucking drinking of pigeons and some others and the 'scooping up' method may not be so definite as has been implied. It seems to me probable that many birds that drink 'normally' suck as their bills go into the water and do not rely solely on scooping and gravity as sometimes appears. In some instances differences of drinking behavior have reference to different circumstances and may not therefore be a specific character when seen in two different species" (p. 77).

Goodwin (1967, 1983) proposed relationships among columbids based on behavior and plumage patterns. From his linear sequence of taxa and dendrograms the following groups can be identified. The genera in parentheses are those presumed to be most closely allied:

1. *Columba, Streptopelia, Aplopelia*

2. *Macropygia, Reinwardtoena, Turacoena*

3. (*Turtur, Oena*), *Chalcophaps, Henicophaps*, (*Phaps, Ocyphaps, Petrophassa*), *Leucosarcia, Geopelia*

4. *Zenaida* (*Columbina, Claravis, Metriopelia, Scardafella, Uropelia*), *Leptoptila*, (*Geotrygon, Starnoenas*)

5. A loose assemblage of distinctive genera: *Caloenas, Trugon, Microgoura, Otidiphaps, Goura, Didunculus*

6. *Phapitreron, Treron*, (*Ptilinopus, Drepanoptila, Ducula, Alectroenas*), (*Hemiphaga, Lopholaimus*), *Cryptophaps, Gymnophaps.*

Corbin (1967, 1968) compared the tryptic peptides of the ovalbumins of 18 species of columbids and suggested that "the Old and New World species-groups of *Columba* appear to have evolved from a common ancestor followed by speciation in the Eastern and Western hemispheres. Since the ovalbumins of some *Columba* species in each hemisphere are most similar to ovalbumins of *Columba* species in the other hemisphere, these data do not support the division of *Columba* into two or more genera" (1968:10–11). *Leptoptila* and *Streptopelia* were most similar to *Columba* and, within *Columba, fasciata* was most similar to other American species, especially to *flavirostris*. The Old World species *C. palumbus* was found to have an ovalbumin more similar to that of the New World species *cayennensis* than to those of other Old World species. Data from other sources however, indicate a close relationship among the Old World species *palumbus, oenas, guinea,* and *livia.*

Sibley and Ahlquist (1972) compared the electrophoretic patterns of the egg-white proteins of 55 species of columbids and found them similar to one another, but readily distinguishable from those of other groups. The shorebirds and parrots were suggested as possible relatives, but no evidence of a galliform alliance was observed. Within the Columbidae *Treron* and *Ducula* have similar patterns, as also do the New World ground doves and *Zenaida, Metriopelia,* and possibly *Leptoptila.*

Cracraft (1981) included the Gruiformes, Charadriiformes, and Columbiformes in his "Division 5" and concluded that "A cladistic interpretation of the available evidence suggests that pteroclids are the sister-group of columbids. The charadriiform characters of sandgrouse and pigeons can be interpreted to mean either (1) that the columbiforms are the sister-group of the charadriiforms or (2) that they are the sister-group of a portion of the charadriiforms. . . . In my opinion these alternatives have not yet received a satisfactory evaluation."

Olson (1982:734) commented on Cracraft's Division 5: "Once again, no synapomorphies are advanced in support of monophyly of this group."

The DNA Hybridization Evidence (Figs. 110–111, 353, 355, 362)

The Columbiformes is the sister group of a large assemblage, including the cranes, rails, shorebirds, birds of prey, herons, pelicans, and tubenoses. The branch between the pigeon lineage and the common ancestor of these groups occurred at Δ T$_{50}$H 20.8. The Passeriformes diverged from a common ancestry with the Columbiformes at Δ 21.6.

The DNA data show that the sandgrouse (Pteroclides) are the sister group of the shorebirds (Charadriides); they are discussed under the Charadrii.

The comparisons diagrammed in Fig. 362 suggest that the New World genera *Claravis*, *Columbina*, and *Scardafella* may form a cluster that could be recognized as a subfamily. *Phaps* and *Chalcophaps* might also be members of a subfamily. *Columba livia* and *Streptopelia* are closely related, and the New World genera *Zenaida*, *Geotrygon*, and *Leptotila* form a cluster. These observations suggest that a more extensive study of the pigeons may reveal additional intrafamilial clusters; for now we recognize only the family Columbidae without subdivisions.

Fig. 110 (*Zenaida*) shows the wide gap between the pigeons and the shorebirds (Charadrii), including the sandgrouse (*Pterocles*). These data should help to settle the debate about whether the sandgrouse are more closely related to the pigeons or the shorebirds. Figs. 123 and 124 (*Pterocles*) contain additional evidence.

Fig. 111 (*Zenaida*) compares the pigeons against owls, a nighthawk, swifts, mousebird, and a hummingbird. The position of the *Otus* heteroduplex curve is about the same as that of *Vanellus* in Fig. 110.

We conclude that the Columbiformes have no close living relatives, and that the sandgrouse are not closely related to the pigeons.

Cranes, Sunbittern, Bustards, Limpkin, Sungrebes, Trumpeters, Seriemas, Kagu, Rails, and Mesites

Order GRUIFORMES
  Suborder Grui
    Infraorder Eurypygides
        Family Eurypygidae: Sunbittern
    Infraorder Otidides
        Family Otididae: Bustards
    Infraorder Gruides
      Parvorder Gruida
        Superfamily Gruoidea
        Family Gruidae
          Subfamily Balearicinae: Crowned-Cranes
          Subfamily Gruinae: Gruine Cranes
        Family Heliornithidae
            Tribe Aramini: Limpkin
            Tribe Heliornithini: New World Sungrebe (Genera *inc. sedis*: *Podica, Heliopais*)
        Superfamily Psophioidea
        Family Psophiidae: Trumpeters
      Parvorder Cariamida
        Family Cariamidae: Seriemas
        Family Rhynochetidae: Kagu
  Suborder Ralli
        Family Rallidae: Rails, Gallinules, Coots
  Suborder Mesitornithi *inc. sedis*
        Family Mesitornithidae: Mesites, Monias, Roatelos

The boundaries of the order Gruiformes and the relationships of the subgroups, present many problems. The groups listed above are morphologically diverse but the DNA comparisons indicate that these groups, with the possible exception of those identified as *inc. sedis*, are more closely related to one another than to the members of any other order. We lack the DNAs of the mesitornithids and of *Podica* (African Finfoot) and *Heliopais* (Asian Finfoot).

The close relationship between *Aramus* and *Heliornis* was a surprise. It will be of special

427

interest to compare the DNAs of the African Finfoot (*Podica*) and the Asian Finfoot (*Heliopais*) with those of *Heliornis*, *Aramus*, *Grus*, and other taxa.

The Plains-wanderer (*Pedionomus torquatus*) of Australia has been identified as a member of the Charadriiformes (Olson and Steadman 1981, Sibley and Ahlquist 1985c), and the buttonquails (*Turnix*, *Ortyxelos*) are placed in a separate order Turniciformes.

Order GRUIFORMES: 53/196. Paludicoline, aquatic, or terrestrial birds with anterior toes free or incompletely webbed; basal ends of coracoids separated; spina interna muscle absent (except in Mesitornithidae); no crop; schizognathous, or with tendency toward desmognathy in Cariamidae and Rhynochetidae; pericoelous, or modified pericoelous intestinal coiling, except plagiocoelous in Mesitornithidae; basipterygoid processes absent, except in some cranes and the Houbara Bustard (*Chlamydotis undulata*); carotid arteries Type A-1 of Glenny, except B-4-s in Heliornithidae and *Tetrax*, and B-4-d in *Eupodotis*; flexor tendons Type 1, except Type 2 in Heliornithidae and Type 4 in Cariamidae; nares pervious, except in *Rhynochetos* wherein impervious; primaries 10 or 11, or rarely 8 or 9 in some rails; rectrices 12, except 16 in Mesitornithidae, 18 in Heliornithidae, 16–20 in Otididae; aftershaft present, except in *Heliornis* and *Heliopais* (present in *Podica*); powder downs absent, except 5 pairs in Mesitornithidae, and diffuse in *Rhynochetos* and *Eurypyga*; supraorbital furrows absent, except in Gruidae and some Rallidae; oil gland absent, naked, or sparsely to densely tufted.

Family EURYPYGIDAE: 1/1. Tropical swamps and mountain streams from southern Mexico to Brazil. Thin-necked; fan-tailed; semiarboreal; one pair of uropygial powder-down patches; ABXY+; small aftershaft; schizorhinal; no occipital foramina; sternum with one notch each side; caeca short; oil gland indistinctly bilobed, tufted; diastataxic; hallux incumbent; nest is a platform of mud and leaves saddled on a branch, near water; 1–3 eggs; young nidicolous. Riggs (1948) reviewed the literature on *Eurypyga*. Lyon and Fogden (1989) described the breeding behavior.

Family OTIDIDAE: 6/25. Southern Europe, Africa, Asia, Australia, southern New Guinea. Medium- to large-sized; primarily terrestrial in open plains and semi-deserts; no hallux; BXY+; no basipterygoid processes or occipital fontanelles; holorhinal; sternum with two notches each side; caeca large, with villi in upper third; rudimentary penis; large aftershaft with the downy base rose-red; rosy underdown restricted to apteria; diastataxic; tarsal scutes 6-sided; oil gland absent.

Family GRUIDAE: 2/15. Large, long-legged, long-necked marsh-dwellers with small, elevated hallux; pelvic muscles ABDXY+, ABXY+, BXY+ (*Balearica*), or XY+ (*Grus leucogeranus*); sternum entire; schizorhinal nares; diastataxic; caeca opposite one another; femorocaudal muscle present; oil gland large, bilobed, tufted.

Subfamily BALEARICINAE: 1/2. Africa.

Subfamily GRUINAE: 1/13. Holarctic, Africa, Australia.

Family HELIORNITHIDAE, Tribe ARAMINI: 1/1. Southeastern United States, Mexico, Caribbean islands, and South America to Argentina. Medium-sized, long-necked, long-legged, with large, incumbent hallux; bill long; femorocaudal muscle absent; caeca lateral and close together; diastataxic; BXY+; sternum entire; schizorhinal; occipital foramina present; oil gland bilobed, tufted.

Tribe HELIORNITHINI: 3/3. Southern Mexico to Argentina. Aquatic; small, with rail-like bill; toes lobed or scalloped and partly webbed; ABX+; hallux incumbent; holorhinal;

diastataxic; tibia mostly or completely feathered; neck long and slender; tail rounded with soft rectrices (not stiffened as in *Heliopais* and *Podica*); furcula ankylosed to sternum; no aftershaft; oil gland bilobed, tufted; hatchling naked and blind (altricial); adult male with marsupial-like pockets of skin on the flanks below the wings, in each of which a hatchling can be carried (Alvarez del Toro 1971, Brooke 1984).

The relationships of the African Finfoot (*Podica*) and the Asian Masked Finfoot (*Heliopais*) are uncertain. These genera differ from *Heliornis* in having stiffened rectrices and precocial young. The African and Asian species may be more closely related to one another than either is to *Heliornis*. Brooke (1984) reviewed the evidence and suggested that *Podica* and *Heliopais* be placed in a separate subfamily from that including *Heliornis*.

Family PSOPHIIDAE: 1/3. Northern South America. Medium-sized; short-billed; no occipital foramina; BXY+; sternum entire; holorhinal; eutaxic; upper margin of orbit bordered by five small bones; oil gland indistinctly bilobed, sparse, short tuft.

Family CARIAMIDAE: 2/2. Central South America in Brazil, Paraguay, and Argentina. Medium-sized; long necks and legs; bushy crests; omnivorous, predatory; BXY in *Cariama*, XY+ and BXY+ in *Chunga*; one sternal notch; small, elevated hallux; holorhinal; eutaxic; long caeca; aftershaft present; nail of second toe talon-like; no biceps slip or occipital fontanelles; oil gland single-lobed, naked.

Family RHYNOCHETIDAE: 1/1. New Caledonia. Medium-sized; short neck, long legs; bushy crest; ABXY+ (AXY+?); sternum entire; hallux present; large aftershaft; schizorhinal; eutaxic; short caeca; powder downs occur in scattered groups; large nasal operculum; no occipital foramina; oil gland single-lobed, naked.

Family RALLIDAE: 34/142. Worldwide in temperate and tropical areas. Small to medium-sized; paludicoline or aquatic; body compressed; toes long; wings short, rounded; ABDXY+; one sternal notch each side; large hallux, slightly raised; holorhinal (except *Nesolimnas*); most with nares pervious, but some impervious (e.g., *Rallicula*); diastataxic in most, eutaxic in *Himantornis*, *Amaurolimnas*; no basipterygoid processes; caeca long; no supraorbital furrows; no occipital foramina; biceps slip small, but usually present; oil gland bilobed, tufted in most species, naked in some individuals; nest on ground; eggs 6–12, variously colored and marked with spots and blotches; nestling down black or dark brown; nidifugous; males larger than females, but seldom differ in coloration, except in *Sarothrura*.

Family MESITORNITHIDAE: 2/3. Confined to Madagascar. Size of large thrushes; long, full tails; short wings; terrestrial; ABXY+; one sternal notch each side; hallux elevated; schizorhinal; eutaxic; five pairs of powder downs; flexor tendons Type 1; spina interna muscle present; no crop; caeca long; syrinx tracheo-bronchial; no aftershaft; oil gland absent; nest a thin platform of small twigs lined with leaves and fibers placed in small trees or bushes close to the ground; eggs usually single, more than one egg per nest may indicate two females laying in the same nest; eggs whitish or light yellow-brown with brown spots near one end; both sexes incubate and feed the young; nidifugous, downy young. Relationships uncertain. No DNA available.

Appert (1985) observed the three species in the wild. All are woodland birds living in groups on leaf-littered ground and foraging in and under the dead leaves. *Monias* also occurs in arid regions if leaf litter is present. They seldom fly, usually walk, but may run rapidly in a plover-like manner. When alarmed *Monias* may freeze or fly to a branch and remain motionless. They roost in groups in trees. Voices are loud and *Monias* may duet or call in chorus. "The systematic position of this very isolated group of birds is still uncertain and it is not yet possible to prove any special relationship to any other group" (Appert 1985:53).

Historical Review of the Classification

In early classifications the presently recognized members of the Gruiformes were assigned to various higher categories. For example, Linnaeus (1758) placed *Otis* with the ratites and the same or a similar arrangement was followed by Illiger (1811), Vieillot (1816), Cuvier (1817), and Temminck (1820). The same authors thought the cranes were related to herons and that *Turnix* was a galliform. Illiger (1811) proposed an alliance among *Fulica*, *Podica*, and *Phalaropus* (all have lobed toes), and Temminck (1820) placed these three genera in the same order. It is obvious that these arrangements were based on convergent similarities, but they established some of the traditional groupings.

Other pre-Darwinians were more successful in discerning evidence of common ancestry. Merrem (1813) associated *Rallus* and *Fulica*, and *Grus* and *Psophia*, although they were placed in different higher taxa, and *Otis* was placed elsewhere. L'Herminier (1827) used the sternum and shoulder girdle skeleton as the basis for his classification and concluded that cranes and rails are related but that neither group is close to the herons. Lesson (1831) placed *Otis* near *Psophia*, and W. Martin (1836) found *Cariama* crane-like and noted similarities to *Psophia* in its visceral anatomy.

The Alectorides of Nitzsch (1840) contained the screamers *Palamedea* (*Anhima*), *Otis*, *Dicholophus* (*Cariama*), *Psophia*, and *Grus*, in which only the screamers are not gruiforms. He found that the pterylosis of *Aramus* differs little from that of *Psophia* and *Grus*, but because of the rail-like bill and feet he placed *Aramus* in his Fulicariae with rails, jacanas, and *Heliornis*. *Eurypyga* was placed with the herons.

The Fulicariae of Giebel (1861) also included *Heliornis*, but Schlegel (1867) united *Heliornis* with the penguins (*Spheniscus*), auks (*Alca*), grebes, and loons in his Urinatores.

Gray (1844–49) made the bustards a subfamily of the Struthionidae (Ostrich), and thought that *Psophia* and the cranes were related to the herons. He put the Rallidae next to the phalaropes and gallinules, and the sungrebes near the jacanas and screamers.

Verreaux and Des Murs (1860) were impressed with the heron-like plumage and color pattern of the Kagu (*Rhynochetos*). Bartlett (1861) placed *Eurypyga* with *Balaeniceps* and *Cochlearius* in the Ardeidae because they have powder downs. He (1862) found resemblances between the Kagu and the Sunbittern in wing and tail markings and in the way they spread their wings during display. He noted (1866) that the eggs of the Kagu are blotched like those of the Sunbittern and the cranes, not plain like those of herons.

"Group 2. Geranomorphae" of Huxley (1867) included the cranes, trumpeters, Kagu, rails, bustards, and seriemas but not *Turnix*, which was isolated in its own "Group 6. Turnicomorphae." Huxley thought that the bustards connect the cranes with the plovers, while the seriemas are distantly allied to the diurnal birds of prey (Falconiformes).

From skeletal comparisons Parker (1868:158) decided that "the bustards are gigantic plovers." Murie (1871) concluded from a study of myology and osteology that *Rhynochetos* is closer to *Eurypyga* than either is to *Cochlearius*.

Sundevall (1872, see 1889) defined his "Order V. Grallatores" as having "The feet long, with the tibiae bare at the tip; the toes cleft" and included within it the herons, storks, ibises, shorebirds, bustards, Kagu, *Pedionomus*, *Eurypyga*, cranes, trumpeters, rails, jacanas, Limpkin, *Heliornis*, *Podica*, and screamers. The seriemas were included with the caracaras ("Polyborinae") in the "Accipitres," *Mesitornis* was assigned to the oscine passerines, and *Turnix* to the "Gallinae."

Garrod (1873d, 1874a) found the pelvic musculature of the rails and bustards to be alike, but he included *Burhinus* (thick-knees), *Sagittarius* (Secretarybird), *Cariama*, flamingos, and bustards in his Otididae. These groups were placed in the "Gallinaceae" with the screamers, galliforms, turacos, and cuckoos, but the cranes were placed between the plovers and gulls in the order Charadriiformes. Garrod (1876c:275) thought that *Aramus* "is most intimately related to *Grus*, which, with it, is not distant from *Ibis*, *Platalea* [spoonbills], and *Eurypyga*."

Bartlett (1877) thought that the Mesitornithidae were similar to the Eurypygidae. Milne-Edwards (1878a,b) found resemblances between the skeletons of the mesitornithids, the rails, and the Sunbittern, but Forbes (1882b) thought the mesitornithids were most like the Sunbittern and Kagu and not close to the rails.

Stejneger (1885:122) believed that the Psophiidae are "evidently related to the kagu and seriema, and likewise in their structure exhibiting characters to a certain degree uniting rails and cranes." Stejneger declared that *Aramus* is "completely intermediate between cranes and rails, making their separation into different sub-orders indefensible" (p. 127).

Goodchild (1886) found the arrangement of the secondary coverts in *Cariama* to be like that of the bustards and different from that in the Secretarybird. This arrangement is also shared by the Burhinidae, Charadriidae, Scolopacidae, Gaviidae, Alcinae, and Gruidae (1891).

According to Fürbringer (1888) the Gruiformes are connected with the Charadriiformes by *Eurypyga*, and with the rails by *Aramus*. He believed that *Cariama* is a highly specialized gruiform, only convergently similar to the falconiforms, and that the rails, *Heliornis*, mesites, and *Turnix* ("Ralliformes") are distantly related to the tinamous and kiwis, through the "Hemipodiidae" (Turnicidae).

Beddard (1890a) contended that *Psophia* and *Cariama* share the largest number of characters, and that the next closest ally of *Psophia* is *Burhinus* (thick-knees, Charadriiformes), followed by the Gruidae. Beddard (1890b, 1893) also studied the anatomy of the Heliornithidae and found that their myology is like that of loons and grebes, although their skeletons resemble those of rails. "The Heliornithidae form a distinct family which has traversed for a certain distance the branch leading from the Rails to the Colymbidae [loons] and has then diverged rather widely in a direction of its own" (1890b:442)—here again, the expression of a confused understanding of how evolution operates. The foregoing quotation seems to describe what Beddard saw in the morphological characters of these taxa, but the result cannot be represented by a dendrogram.

Sharpe (1891) decided that *Aramus* is intermediate between the cranes and rails, and that the trumpeters are the "most Galline of all the Crane-like birds" (p. 63). Like Huxley (1867), Sharpe thought the cariamas are a link between cranes and falconiforms.

Gadow (1892) included the "Turnices" in his order Galliformes, and encountered difficulties in diagnosing the Gruiformes. In a footnote referring to the Gruiformes he wrote: "Owing to the existence of such peculiarly specialized forms as *Eurypyga*, *Rhinochetus*,

Podica, Dicholophus, and *Otis* (all of which are most intimately related to the bulk of the Grues and Ralli), it is not possible to admit some important characters into the diagnosis of the Gruiformes. They all are absolutely *nidifugous* with the exception of *Eurypyga* and *Heliornis* (the young of *Rhinochetus* are unknown). They are typically *schizognathous*, except *Rhinochetus* and *Dicholophus*. They have a *tufted oil-gland* except *Rhinochetus, Eurypyga, Dicholophus*, and *Otis*. They have lateral *cervical apteria* except *Eurypyga, Dicholophus*, and *Otis*. Their *feet* are those of Waders, except the tridactyle cursorial *Otis. Rhinochetus* alone has impervious *nares*" (p. 244).

Gadow (1892:244–246) diagnosed the gruiform groups:

GRUIFORMES
  Cosmopolitan. Aquatic or paludic [marsh-dwelling].
  Angulare mandibulae truncated. Rhamphotheca simple.
  No basipterygoid processes.
  No ectepicondylar process.
  Flexors of type I. or IV.
  Peri-orthocoelous, type I. [intestinal convolutions].
I. Eurypygae.
  Neotropical.
  With powder-down patches. (*Unique* among Gruiformes.)
  Oil-gland nude. Schizorhinal.
1. Eurypygidae [Sunbittern].
  Aquinto-cubital. No lateral cervical apteria.
  Schizognathous. Nares pervious.
  18 cervical vertebrae.
  Sternum with one pair of notches.
  Nidicolous.
2. Rhinochetidae [Kagu].
  New Caledonia.
  Quinto-cubital. Lateral cervical apteria.
  Desmognathous. Nares impervious.
  16 cervical vertebrae.
  Sternum solid.
  Hypotarsus with high ridges.
3. Mesitidae [Roatelos, Mesites].
  Madagascar.
  Cubital. Lateral cervical apteria.
  Schizognathous. Nares pervious.
  Sternum with long simple posterior lateral processes. Clavicles rudimentary.
  17 cervical vertebrae.
  Spina interna alone developed. (*Unique* among Gruiformes.)
II. Ralli.
  Aquinto-cubital. With lateral cervical apteria.
  Oil-gland tufted.
  Schizognathous. Holorhinal.
  14 or 15 cervical vertebrae.
  Sternum with long simple posterior lateral processes.
  Hypotarsus without canals but with high ridges.
III. Grues.
  With lateral cervical apteria.

Oil-gland nude.
Schizognathous.
17–20 cervical vertebrae.
Sternum solid.
Hypotarsus complex.
IV. Dicholophi [Seriemas, *Cariama*].
Neotropical.
No cervical apteria.
Oil-gland nude.
Schizognathous. Holorhinal.
14 or 15 cervical vertebrae.
Sternum with two posterior notches.
Hypotarsus simple.
V. Otides [Bustards].
No cervical apteria. Downs of adults only on apteria. (*Unique* among Gruiformes.)
Schizognathous. Holorhinal.
Sternum with four posterior notches.
Hypotarsus complex. Hallux absent; feet *cursorial*.

In his 1893 classification, Gadow transferred the Mesitidae to the Galliformes, with the Turnicidae, Pedionomidae, galliforms, and the Hoatzin (*Opisthocomus*). The latter we now know to be a New World cuckoo, *Pedionomus* is a charadriiform, and the Turnicidae are the descendants of an ancient, monotypic lineage (see Turniciformes).

Gadow (1893) felt that *Aramus* and *Psophia* deserve only subfamily rank in the Gruidae and that the nearest relative of *Cariama* (*Dicholophus*) is *Psophia*, followed by *Rhynochetos* and *Eurypyga*. In his opinion the bustards, although gruiforms, stand alone with no obvious close relatives; their similarities to the thick-knees (Burhinidae) were attributed to convergence. The DNA evidence supports some of these opinions and opposes others.

In the *Catalogue of Birds* Sharpe (1894) divided the gruiforms into two orders: the Fulicariae contained the Rallidae and Heliornithidae, the Alectorides included the Aramidae, Eurypygidae, Mesitidae, Rhinochetidae, Gruidae, Psophiidae, and Otididae. Sharpe noted that "the Order *Fulicariae*, as limited by Dr. Sclater in his well-known arrangement of the Class 'Aves,' is hereby recognized. . . . In my own arrangement of 1891, I placed the *Ralliformes* at some little distance from the groups which are usually considered to be their nearest allies; and, in fact, I still look upon the Rails as a very peculiar and isolated group of birds, so that it does not matter whether they be called *Fulicariae* or *Ralliformes*, so long as they are not mixed up too closely with the Cranes and their allies" (1891:1).

Beddard (1898a) was impressed by the similarities between Gruiformes and Charadriiformes: "The very difficulty of finding any characters, greatly noteworthy, in which the groups in question [Limicolae, Grues, Otides, Ralli] vary is an index of how closely allied all four are. There can, to my mind, be no doubt of their common origin. The Limicolae on the whole come nearest to the Grues, and especially to the true cranes" (p. 358).

In the *Hand-List* Sharpe (1899) again changed his mind. In his "Order VII. Ralliformes" he put the Rallidae and Heliornithidae, followed by separate orders for the grebes, loons, penguins, tubenoses, auks, gulls (etc.), and Charadriiformes. The bustards were placed in the Charadriiformes as the suborder Otides, and the Gruiformes, which followed, included the suborders Grues, Arami, Rhinochetes, Mesoenatides, Eurypygae, Psophiae, and Dicholophi (seriemas). Thus, Sharpe expressed his conviction that the rails and sungrebes should not be "mixed up too closely with the Cranes and their allies."

Mitchell (1901a) found that the gruiform families, except the Turnicidae and Mesitornithidae, have a pattern of intestinal coiling like that of the Charadriiformes. He also suggested that the Rallidae, Aramidae, Gruidae, Otididae, and Eurypygidae have more primitive characters of the alimentary tract than do the Psophiidae, Cariamidae, Rhynochetidae, and Heliornithidae.

From skeletal characters Shufeldt (1894b) concluded that *Aramus* is intermediate between cranes and rails and he placed the three groups in the same superfamily. Based on similar evidence Beddard (1902a) argued that *Aramus* should be placed in the same subfamily as the cranes. Shufeldt (1904b, 1915a) disagreed with Beddard and placed *Aramus*, the Rallidae, and the Heliornithidae in his supersuborder Ralliformes. Mitchell (1915) noted several skull characters of *Aramus* that are "exceedingly like those of cranes," and Shufeldt (1915b) also changed his opinion and ranked *Aramus*, the cranes, and the trumpeters as separate families in his Gruoidea.

This debate about the affinities of the Limpkin demonstrates the difficulties involved in assigning categorical rank on the basis of subjective evaluations of degrees of morphological difference, as well as of determining degrees of relationship. The DNA evidence indicates that *Aramus* is closely related to *Heliornis*, but this alliance seems never to have been suggested from morphological characters.

Beddard (1911) noted that the intestinal coilings of certain bustards are nearly identical to those of the Black-legged Seriema (*Chunga burmeisteri*), but that neither group has a pattern that is especially similar to that of the cranes.

L. Harrison (1915) found similarities between the Mallophaga of rails and those of kiwis (*Apteryx*), a discovery that provides no support for the idea that parasites reflect the relationships of their hosts.

Chandler (1916) thought the feather structure of the Rallidae indicated "striking affinity" to the Charadriiformes, and that the cranes agree in some ways with the storks and in others with the shorebirds. He found *Aramus* to be intermediate between cranes and rails in the structure of the breast feathers, but its back feathers resemble those of the Cracidae and Megapodiidae. Chandler reasoned that the Gruidae, Aramidae, and Rallidae evolved from the stem leading to the Charadriiformes. *Psophia* and *Otis* share features with the galliforms, and Chandler thought them to be early offshoots of a line ancestral to the Galliformes and Columbiformes. *Eurypyga* and, to a lesser degree, *Cariama*, resemble the herons in some aspects of their feather structure, and are "almost certainly of ardeid derivation" (p. 354). It seems clear that feather structure is a flimsy basis for speculations about phylogeny.

Lowe (1924a:1151) studied the osteology, myology, and pterylosis of *Mesitornis*, "a primitive form of arboreal rail," and concluded that the Mesitornithidae should be placed in a separate order. Lowe (1931a) examined the evidence for relationships among the Gruiformes and Charadriiformes and, on the basis of a "less specialized" structure of the contour feathers, recognized the order Ralliformes for the Rallidae and Heliornithidae, thus agreeing with Sharpe (1899). Of the other gruiform groups he observed: "They seem to me to be neither distinct enough from the Charadriiformes, nor to agree enough among themselves in any outstanding character or characters, to justify their separation as an isolated order" (p. 496).

After emphasizing the similarities among these groups in myology, intestinal tract morphology, and pterylosis, Lowe pointed out 11 skeletal differences, none of which, however, "differs to such a degree that it ought to stand in rank as an ordinal character" (p. 501). Thus, he combined gruiforms and charadriiforms into his order "Telmatomorphae," defined by the following characters:

1. Dorsal feather tract forked and separated into dorsal and posterior portions.
2. Vomer anchored posteriorly to ethmo-palatine laminae.
3. Oil gland tufted.
4. Characteristic downs of chicks (to exclude Columbiformes).
5. Barbules of basal third of contour feathers with plumaceous structure at the proximal end.
6. Caeca well developed.
7. Diastataxic.
8. Palatines with internal laminae present.
9. Nostrils not tubular (to exclude Procellariidae).
10. Recurrent slip to tensor patagii longus muscle.

Lowe left the Cariamidae in an uncertain position because of their desmognathous palate. The "Turnicomorphs" and *Mesites* (*Mesitornis*) are excluded from Lowe's Telmatomorphae by his list of defining characters; apparently he thought that they should constitute separate orders.

E. Stresemann (1934) recognized 10 orders for 12 gruiform families and interposed other groups among them in his linear sequence. He based his classification on those of Fürbringer (1888) and Gadow (1892), but he declined to unite in a single order the groups that Gadow had placed in his Gruiformes. Stresemann presented a strong argument, but if the DNA evidence has revealed the true phylogeny, Gadow was more nearly correct than was Stresemann.

Wetmore (1930, 1960) recognized eight suborders for the living members of his Gruiformes. In the suborder Grues he placed the Gruidae, Aramidae, and Psophiidae, and in the Turnices the Turnicidae and Pedionomidae. The other suborders were monotypic. Peters (1934) followed Wetmore's arrangement.

Ridgway and Friedmann (1941:2–3) defined the Gruiformes and listed the morphological characters of each subgroup, noting the many exceptions and special cases among the suborders and families:

The above characters are common to a large group of mostly more or less aquatic birds that are related on the one hand to the Charadriiformes and on the other to the Galliformes, occupying, in fact, a position somewhat intermediate between these two. It is not, however, a homogeneous group, and it is doubtful whether the Cariamae and Heliornithes, at least, should not be excluded.

The Gruiformes, as here defined, agree with both the Charadriiformes and Galliformes in . . . the following characters:

(1) Schizognathous palate (desmognathous, however, in Cariamae and aegithognathous in Turnices).

(2) Double head to quadrate bone.

(3) Union of distal ends of ilium and ischium.

(4) Absence of slip to accessory femorocaudal muscles.

They agree with the Charadriiformes, but differ from the Galliformes, in the following:

(1) Basal ends of coracoids separated or merely touch each other.
(2) Absence of spina interna sterni muscle.
(3) Intestinal convolutions of Type I (instead of Type V).
From the Charadriiformes the Gruiformes differ in
(1) Heterocoelous (instead of opisthocoelous) dorsal vertebrae.
(2) Absence of basipterygoid processes.

The fossil evidence caused Howard (1950) to agree with Lowe (1931a) on the common ancestry of the Gruiformes and Charadriiformes. She emphasized that no gruiform or charadriiform groups can be recognized until the Eocene.

Hopkins (1942) decided that the Mallophaga show that the bustards "do not belong to the Gruiformes" (p. 104) and that he "would not be surprised" if the bustards should prove to be related to the Galliformes. He discounted even a distant relationship between bustards and charadriiforms. The DNA evidence shows that the bustards are members of the Gruiformes, and that the Galliformes are distant from all members of the group. Once again, the parasites fail as indicators of host relationships.

Mallophaga found on gruiforms were also studied by Clay (1950, 1953). Of five genera from rails, three are also found on *Aramus* and two on *Psophia*. Some of the ralline feather mites have also been reported from sungrebes and the Kagu, but four genera from cranes are shared by none of these groups. One mallophagan genus found on bustards appears to have close relatives on galliforms and sandpipers. The mallophagans parasitizing the Mesitornithidae and Turnicidae are related, but those of *Eurypyga* are uninformative. Two genera found on seriemas also occur on tinamous, a clear case of secondary infestation.

Verheyen (1957b–d, 1958a) concluded from skeletal measurements that the Gruiformes of Peters (1934) is an artificial assemblage and proposed four separate orders:

1. Ralliformes, with suborders Otides, Psophiae, Grues (Gruidae, Aramidae), and Ralli (Rallidae, Heliornithidae).

2. Cariamiformes (Cariamidae and *Sagittarius*).

3. Jacaniformes (Rhynochetidae, Eurypygidae, Jacanidae).

4. Turniciformes, with suborders Mesoenatides, Turnices (Turnicidae, Pedionomidae), Pterocletes (Thinocorythidae [seedsnipe], Pteroclididae).

Verheyen (1959d) included the grebes in his Ralliformes because of similarities between grebes and sungrebes. In his final classification (1961) he made other changes; the Ralliformes included only the Rallidae and Heliornithidae and he split his order Turniciformes by making the Mesoenatides a suborder of the Jacaniformes. He allocated the Turnicidae and Pedionomidae to a suborder of the Galliformes and transferred *Sagittarius* from the Cariamiformes to the Falconiformes. In this arrangement Verheyen assembled the Struthioniformes, Galliformes, Gruiformes, and Cariamiformes in the superorder Chamaeornithes, with the Jacaniformes and Ralliformes as members of the superorder Limnornithes. There is little in any of these decisions to foster faith in Verheyen's methods.

The paper electrophoretic pattern of the egg-white proteins of *Aramus* seemed more similar to those of rails than to those of cranes; the pattern of *Psophia* proteins seemed intermediate between those of rails and cranes, and there were some resemblances between the patterns of rails and those of charadriiforms and galliforms (Sibley 1960). The DNA evidence shows the fallacies in these suggestions and the limitations of the electrophoretic method used.

The starch gel electrophoretic patterns of the egg-white proteins of the gruiforms were studied by Hendrickson (1969), who found the pattern of *Aramus* to be intermediate between cranes and rails, and the patterns of *Turnix*, *Heliopais*, *Psophia*, and *Eurypyga* to be most like those of rails. The patterns of the Kagu, cariamids, and bustards differed from those of rails and from one another. Here again, the DNA evidence does not support the opinions based on the electrophoretic patterns.

Sibley and Ahlquist (1972) compared the egg-white proteins of members of most of the gruiform groups and concluded that the "patterns of the Rallidae, Aramidae, Gruidae, Heliornithidae, Psophiidae, Turnicidae and Eurypygidae are similar enough to suggest a relationship among these groups. The pattern of *Aramus* is more like those of rails than those of cranes, but since this single sample was partially denatured, the similarity is of little value in assessing relationships. The . . . Cariamidae may or may not fall within this group. The patterns of the bustards are not like those of the rail-crane group nor are they like those of the Burhinidae." Our other conclusions were equally doubtful. We now consider the electrophoretic patterns of proteins to be of limited value as evidence of higher category relationships, although they do reflect some of the older branchings in the phylogeny.

The arteries in the neck and thorax of the sungrebes were studied by Glenny (1967). *Podica* and *Heliornis* have the B–4-s carotid pattern, which is shared with *Turnix* and some bustards. Other gruiforms have the A–1 carotid arrangement.

Keith et al. (1970) considered the African flufftails (*Sarothrura*) to be "a distinctive, compact group of small Rallidae . . . which seem to have no particularly close relatives."

Olson (1973) reviewed and revised the classification of the rails. He viewed *Sarothrura* as "closely related to *Rallicula* and possibly to *Coturnicops* and *Micropygia* as well" (p. 392). We lack the DNAs of these two genera and cannot comment on this proposal. Olson (1973) also concluded that the Takahe (*Notornis mantelli*) of New Zealand is not generically separable from *Porphyrio*. The DNA comparisons support Olson's proposal; the divergence between *P. porphyrio* and *Notornis* was at Δ T$_{50}$H 0.3, thus probably less than 2 MYA.

Cracraft (1973, 1981, 1982) presented his hypotheses of gruiform relationships based on cladistic analyses of skeletal characters in fossil and living taxa. He proposed (1982) a "phylogenetic hypothesis" for the suborder Grues consisting of six branches in order of decreasing degrees of divergence: (1) cranes (Gruidae); (2) limpkins (Aramidae); (3) trumpeters (Psophiidae), seriemas (Cariamidae), and the extinct phorusrhacids; (4) Sunbittern (Eurypygidae); (5) the extinct genus *Aptornis* of New Zealand; (6) Kagu (Rhynochetidae). Cracraft (1981) placed the Heliornithidae and Rallidae in the suborder Ralli, and gave *incertae sedis* status to the Mesitornithidae, Otididae, and Turnicidae.

Olson and Steadman (1981) presented morphological evidence that *Pedionomus* is a charadriiform, most closely related to the seedsnipe (Thinocoridae) of South America, and recommended that "the Pedionomidae should be placed in the order Charadriiformes, immediately preceding the Thinocoridae." The DNA evidence also indicates that *Pedionomus* is related to the seedsnipe, not to the buttonquails (Turnicidae).

The DNA Hybridization Evidence (Figs. 112–122, 335, 336, 353, 356, 363)

The suborders Grui and Ralli diverged at Δ T$_{50}$H 19.1. The oldest branch in the Grui (Δ 17.5) produced the lineages of the infraorders Eurypygides and Otidides plus Gruides. The next dichotomy (16.9) produced the lineages leading to the infraorders Otidides and Gruides. Within the Gruides, the parvorder Gruida (cranes, Limpkin, sungrebes, trumpeters) branched from the Cariamida (seriemas, Kagu) at Δ 15.0. The Gruoidea (cranes, Limpkin, sungrebes) and the Psophioidea (trumpeters) diverged at Δ 12.7. The crane lineage (Gruidae) branched from the Heliornithidae (*Aramus, Heliornis*) at Δ 9.2 (Fig. 363).

The New World genera *Aramus* and *Heliornis* proved to be more closely related (Δ 4.5) than had been suspected. We lack the DNAs of the African Finfoot (*Podica senegalensis*) and the Masked Finfoot (*Heliopais personata*) of Asia.

Peters (1934) recognized the bustard genera *Lissotis, Lophotis*, and *Afrotis* for species that White (1965) included in *Eupodotis*. The DNA comparisons between *Eupodotis vigorsii* and *Eupodotis* (*Lissotis*) *melanogaster* (Δ 4.8), *Eupodotis* (*Lophotis*) *ruficrista* (4.2), and *Eupodotis* (*Afrotis*) *afra* (3.6) support Peters' treatment. By our criteria, these species, plus *Ardeotis kori* (*Otis kori* in White 1965) may be included in the same tribe, and the five genera may be recognized. However, we lack species representing several other genera of bustards and comparisons with their DNAs may alter this arrangement. This corrects the statement by Sibley and Ahlquist (1985c:121). Sibley and Monroe (1990) include *ruficrista, afra, vigorsii*, and *melanogaster* in *Eupodotis*.

The Ralli form a distinct cluster apart from the cranes and their allies. Sibley and Ahlquist (1985c) recognized the African flufftails (*Sarothrura*) as a separate family and that may be correct. However, we prefer to wait until additional material becomes available before confirming this arrangement. For now we recognize only the Rallidae for the rails, gallinules, and coots. The DNAs currently available are too limited to provide a basis for further subdivision. It is clear that the genetic distances within the group have a substantial range, indicating a long history.

As noted above, the DNA evidence supports the suggestion by Olson (1973) that the New Zealand Takahe (*Notornis mantelli*) is congeneric with *Porphyrio*.

Fig. 112 (*Eurypyga*) indicates that the Sunbittern is distant from the other gruiform groups. The position of the *Grus* heteroduplex curve closest to the homoduplex curve may, in part, be due to the 4–5 year average age at maturity in the cranes. The Takahe and Plainswanderer are at predictable relative distances. The *Turnix* curve is closer to the gruiforms than might have been expected considering the relative position of *Turnix* in Fig. 30, and the positions of *Cariama, Ardeotis, Aramus*, and *Grus* in Fig. 41. Whatever may be the reason for the position of *Turnix* in Fig. 112, it is outside the domain of the gruiform taxa.

Fig. 113 (*Eupodotis*) shows the clustering of the gruiform taxa at distances less than those to the rails (*Amaurornis, Fulica*). Note that *Eurypyga* is the gruiform taxon farthest from *Eupodotis*. The Sunbittern is in this same position relative to all gruiforms with which it has been compared.

Fig. 114 (*Eupodotis*) shows the effect of rate slowdowns correlated with ages at first breeding. The bustards have delayed maturity (2–3 years average), as do the storks, loons, and boobies. *Mycteria, Gavia*, and *Morus* cluster close to many tracer taxa which clearly are not their closest relatives. Note that *Eurypyga* is out beyond the heron, tropicbird, grebe, and cormorant, with the coot still farther out. The coots and rails begin to breed at 1–2 years (Table 16). Thus, the relative positions in Fig. 114 are difficult to interpret, but we believe that the differences in average genomic rates correlated with ages at first breeding account for such situations.

Fig. 115 (*Eupodotis*) provides additional examples of the effects of rate slowdowns. The *Spheniscus* and *Gavia* curves are closer to the bustard tracer than are those of *Aramus*, *Grus*, *Cariama*, *Heliornis*, and *Psophia*, probably because of the relatively slow rates of DNA evolution in the penguins and loons. Again, *Eurypyga* is the most distant of the gruiform taxa.

Fig. 116 (*Grus*) has a tracer of marginal quality, but the sequence of the curves should not be affected. The most interesting aspect of these curves may be the positions of the Limpkin and the Sungrebe, both quite close to *Grus*, with other gruiform taxa at greater distances. *Rallus* is closer to *Grus* than are *Eurypyga* and *Rhynochetos*, but *Turnix* is the farthest out. The Kagu material was of poor quality so we cannot place much confidence in its position.

In this set the effect of different rates and possibly experimental error combine to produce a complex and confusing picture. We may be accused of using these reasons to explain, or explain away, any situation that does not fit with preconceived ideas about the relationships of these groups. Perhaps, but the consistent behavior of certain taxa that always cluster close to any homoduplex must be explained. Doubters may become believers when they see Fig. 118.

Fig. 117 (*Aramus*) shows the relatively close relationship between the Limpkin and the Sungrebe, an unexpected alliance. The positions of the other taxa in Fig. 117 are about as expected from the evidence in other sets.

Fig. 118 (*Aramus*) provides strong evidence that there are different rates of DNA evolution correlated with age at first breeding. The albatrosses and shearwaters have ages at maturity of more than four years, ibises ca. 2–3 years, and large gulls ca. 4 years. The bustards mature at 2–3 years, rails at one year, and nothing is known about the age of maturity in *Pedionomus*. Unless we assume that the correlation is real and that it has the stated effect, there is no rational way to explain the relative positions of the curves in Fig. 118; unless, of course, one is willing to accept the notion that albatrosses and shearwaters are more closely related to the Limpkin than are bustards and rails. In other sets, the tubenoses will occupy the same relative positions vis-à-vis various tracer species.

Fig. 119 (*Heliornis*) shows the relationship between *Heliornis* and *Aramus*, the reciprocal of Fig. 117. The other taxa are in predictable positions except for *Rallus*, which is closer to *Heliornis* than is *Eupodotis*. This seems anomalous and we have no explanation.

Fig. 120 (*Psophia*) has *Grus* closest to the homoduplex. This may be correct, but it may, in part, reflect the delayed maturity of the cranes. Since we have no age-at-maturity data for *Psophia* and some of the other gruiform taxa, it is not profitable to speculate further. Again, *Eurypyga* is the outermost gruiform, slightly beyond the rail, *Amaurornis*. *Turnix* is far more distant from *Psophia* than are the charadriiforms, *Rostratula* and *Pedionomus*.

Fig. 121 (*Cariama*) again has the cranes (*Grus*, *Balearica*) closest to the homoduplex; again, this may, in part, reflect delayed maturity in the cranes. *Eurypyga* is the outermost gruiform, the charadriiform *Pedionomus* and the rail *Gallinula* are next, and *Turnix* again denies any close alliance with the gruiforms.

Fig. 122 (*Porphyrio*) presents a ralliform viewpoint, but without any gruiforms among the heteroduplexes. The three galliforms (*Crax*, *Aepypodius*, *Numida*) are about the same distance from *Porphyrio* as *Turnix* is from *Psophia* in Fig. 120.

The FITCH tree of Fig. 335 shows the short branch to *Grus* and the long branch to *Porphyrio* that are apparent in the melting curves. The *Grus-Aramus-Heliornis* relationship is of special interest; from *Aramus* to *Heliornis* is 2.1 distance units, *Aramus* to *Grus* is 6.5 units, and *Heliornis* to *Grus* is 8.6 units. From *Grus* to *Eurypyga* is 15.8 units, *Grus* to *Porphyrio* is 16.9 units, *Grus* to *Eupodotis* is 15.9 units. The longest distance is from *Porphyrio* to *Eupodotis*, which is 22.0 units. From *Porphyrio* to *Aramus* it is 16.4 units, thus a difference of 5.6 units between the longest and shortest spans of the tree with respect to *Porphyrio*. To reveal the effects of shortened branches it is necessary to eliminate the autocorrelated portions of the pathways by measuring from the base of the tree. The distance from the base to *Porphyrio* is 11.5 units and to *Aramus* it is 4.9 units. The difference of 6.6 units represents the slowdown in the pathway to *Aramus* compared with that to *Porphyrio*. Thus, there has been about 2.3 times more change along the *Porphyrio* pathway than along the *Aramus* pathway.

Fig. 336 is a KITSCH tree of the gruiforms that agrees with the average linkage tree in Fig. 363 and has essentially the same topology as the FITCH tree.

We conclude that the Gruiformes is a monophyletic taxon composed of highly divergent subunits. The buttonquails (Turnicidae), often placed with the gruiforms, are not closely related to them. *Pedionomus*, long placed with the Turnicidae in the Gruiformes, is a charadriiform related to the seedsnipe. The relatively slower rate of DNA evolution in the cranes with their 4–5 year average age at first breeding is apparent in the FITCH tree. The distances between *Grus* and the other taxa are shorter than they would be if all gruiform lineages had been evolving at the same average rate. We note that the FITCH tree clusters *Eurypyga*, *Cariama*, and *Eupodotis* as a unit, whereas the KITSCH and UPGMA trees do not. Whether these taxa form a real assemblage or an artifact caused by the small number of comparisons is unknown.

Sandgrouse and Shorebirds: Sandpipers, Plovers, Gulls, etc.

Tribe Rynchopini: Skimmers
Tribe Larini: Gulls
Tribe Sternini: Terns
Subfamily Alcinae: Auks, Murres, Puffins, Guillemots

The Charadrii, with 85 genera and 366 species, is one of the largest avian suborders. Adaptive radiation has produced the xerophilous sandgrouse, limicoline plovers and sandpipers, aerial-littoral gulls and terns, and the foot-propelled diving auks. Excepting the sandgrouse and the Plains-wanderer, these groups are the Charadriiformes, or shorebirds, of most recent classifications, and the Limicolae of earlier arrangements.

Among the many questions that have been asked about the relationships between the Charadrii and other groups, and among the charadriine taxa, are the following:

1. Are the jacanas most closely related to the painted-snipe and other shorebirds, or to the rails, with which they share some similarities?

2. Are the auks, murres, and puffins members of the Charadrii, or do their morphological similarities to the diving-petrels and penguins indicate a common ancestry with those groups?

3. Are the seedsnipe members of the Charadrii, or are they allied to the galliforms, the Turnicidae, or the sandgrouse, which share similar adaptive traits?

4. Are the pratincoles and coursers related to the gulls or to the plovers?

5. What are the relationships of the Crab Plover and the sheathbills?

6. Are the thick-knees related to the plovers, or might they be closer to the bustards?

7. What are the relationships of the sandgrouse?

8. What is the sister group of the Charadrii?

Suborder CHARADRII: 85/366. Limicoline, pratincoline, aquatic, or terrestrial birds with schizognathous palates (except Thinocoridae); diastataxic; 10 primaries; 11 secondaries; aftershaft present; two carotids (A–1 of Glenny 1955); caeca present; oil gland bilobed and tufted, except in the Pteroclidae in which the oil gland is naked; nidifugous, down-covered young. Other characters variable.

Family PTEROCLIDAE: 2/16. The sandgrouse occur in Africa, Madagascar, southern Europe, and Asia in arid or semi-arid regions. Pelvic muscle formula ABXY+; flexor tendons Type 4; holorhinal nares; long caeca; symmetrical extrinsic syringeal muscles; bill short, quail-like, without operculum; tarsus short, feathered; toes wide and short, the soles covered with small scutes; hallux small and elevated in *Pterocles*, absent in *Syrrhaptes*; biceps slip and expansor secundariorum present; 11 primaries, outer reduced; 17–18 secondaries; 14–18 rectrices; small aftershaft; naked oil gland; large, single-lobed crop; pneumatic skeleton; apteria with small amount of down; nidifugous, downy young.

Family THINOCORIDAE: 2/4. The seedsnipe occur in the Andes from Ecuador to southern Chile and Argentina, and in Tierra del Fuego. Aegithognathous; ABXY+; short legs and bills; holorhinal, impervious nares; basisphenoidal rostrum thick and long; vomer broad and forked posteriorly; no basipterygoid processes or occipital fontanelles; hallux present; a crop, gizzard, and long caeca; apteria with thick black down; nostrils operculate; 12 or 14 rectrices; coracoids not overlapping.

Family PEDIONOMIDAE: 1/1. *Pedionomus torquatus*, the Plains-wanderer of interior southeastern Australia, was long thought to be related to *Turnix*, but differs in having a hallux and in other characters. Olson and Steadman (1981) reviewed the taxonomic history and morphology of the Plains-wanderer and found evidence of its relationship to the charadriiforms in general and to the seedsnipe in particular. DNA comparisons agree.

The original habitat of the Plains-wanderer was flat, grassy plains. Today it is found mainly in sheep paddocks where it is active at night, usually solitary, and reluctant to fly. Female larger and more colorful than male; nest a scrape lined with grass, usually at the base of a bush or grass clump; eggs 4, pyriform, greenish with darker blotches; downy young light below, darker above with diffuse blackish spots.

Family SCOLOPACIDAE: 21/88. Worldwide. Bill variable, with sensory pits near tip, not swollen distally; nasal fossae narrow and pointed anteriorly; tarsus usually transversely scutellate front and back (except in curlews); toes with lateral membrane; hallux present (except *Crocethia*); ventral plumage sparse.

Family ROSTRATULIDAE: 1/2. One species of painted-snipe occurs in Africa, southern Asia, and Australia; the other in central South America. A crop-like enlargement of the esophagus; 14 rectrices; females larger and more colorful than males; males incubate and care for young.

Family JACANIDAE: 6/8. Tropics and subtropics of Africa, Asia, Australia, New Guinea, and Mexico to Argentina. ABXY+; no occipital foramina or supraorbital grooves; coracoids overlapping; toes and claws elongate; 10 rectrices; small caeca; schizorhinal; metacarpal spur present.

Family CHIONIDIDAE: 1/2. Sheathbills occur on Antarctic and subarctic islands and the southern tip of South America. Medium-sized; a saddle-shaped horny sheath encircles the base of the maxilla; ABXY+; nares holorhinal, pervious; no basipterygoid processes or occipital fontanelles; large supraorbital glands; 15 cervical vertebrae; long caeca; strong, thick, white plumage; 12 rectrices; no webs between toes; tarsus reticulate; carpal spur present.

Family BURHINIDAE: 1/9. Europe, Africa, Asia, Australia, and Neotropics. Medium-sized; holorhinal, pervious nares; no basipterygoid processes or occipital fontanelles; large eyes; 16 cervical vertebrae; no hallux; supraorbital glands present; coracoids overlap; nocturnal or crepuscular habits.

Family CHARADRIIDAE: 16/89. Worldwide.

Subfamily RECURVIROSTRINAE: 5/22.

Tribe HAEMATOPODINI: 1/11. Worldwide. Bill long, compressed, with chisel-like tip; ABXY+; legs stout; tarsus covered with small hexagonal scales; no hallux; toe webs reduced; transverse scutella only on distal half of short, thick toes; large supraorbital grooves.

Tribe RECURVIROSTRINI: 4/11. Virtually worldwide in temperate and tropical regions. Long-legged, long-necked, long-billed; tarsus reticulate; toes webbed to various degrees; hallux small or absent; ventral plumage dense.

Subfamily CHARADRIINAE: 11/67. Worldwide. Bill shorter than tarsus, tip inflated; hallux small or absent.

Family GLAREOLIDAE: 6/18.

Subfamily GLAREOLINAE: 5/17. Africa, southern Europe, Asia, Australia. Holorhinal (*Pluvianus*) or schizorhinal impervious nares with oblong nostrils; culmen curved; 15 cervical vertebrae; tarsus transversely scutellate fore and aft; ABXY+; no basipterygoid processes or occipital fontanelles; middle toe usually pectinate; usually in open country, often arid.

Subfamily DROMADINAE: 1/1. The Crab Plover occurs on the coasts and islands of the Indian Ocean, Red Sea, and Persian Gulf to India and Madagascar. Medium-sized; strong, compressed, ungrooved bill longer than head; nostrils basal, oval, schizorhinal; no basipterygoid processes or occipital fontanelles; hallux present; toes long, webbed, middle claw dilated on inner side and notched; plumage black and white.

Family LARIDAE: 28/129.

Subfamily LARINAE: 16/106. Worldwide.

Tribe STERCORARIINI: 2/8. Seacoasts of all continents, at least in winter. Cere present; rhamphotheca complex; caeca large; coracoids not overlapping; sternum with one notch each side; claws large, strongly hooked; bill gull-like, with hooked tip; AXY+.

Tribe RYNCHOPINI: 1/3. East coast of North America, coasts of South America, coasts and rivers of Africa, and larger rivers of India, Burma, southeast Asia. ABXY+; no biceps slip; bill specialized for skimming, the mandible longer than maxilla, both compressed to thin blades; caeca small; pupil of eye slit-like; wings long, pointed.

Tribe LARINI: 6/50. Worldwide. Small caeca; coracoids in contact; sternum with two notches each side; claws not hooked; plumage usually black and white, or gray; AXY+; expansor secundariorum present; tail usually truncate, rarely forked; culmen decurved terminally; maxilla overhangs mandible at the tip; no cere.

Tribe STERNINI: 7/45. Worldwide. ABXY+ (except *Gygis* with AXY+); expansor secundariorum absent (except in *Anous*); tail usually forked; bill straight, culmen not decurved and not overhanging mandible.

Subfamily ALCINAE: 12/23. Northern hemisphere, mainly Arctic seas and coasts. Short-winged, foot-propelled divers with palmate feet; bill variable in shape but laterally compressed, rhamphotheca complex and deciduous in many species; space between supraorbital grooves compressed into a ridge; no hallux; A(B)X; basipterygoid processes absent; occipital fontanelles present; sternum long, narrow, extending posteriorly beyond postero-lateral processes.

Historical Review of the Classification

Linnaeus (1758) placed the web-footed Charadrii in his order Anseres with the ducks, tubenoses, pelicans, loons, and grebes. The sandpipers, avocets, oystercatchers, and plovers were placed in the Grallae, with the storks, herons, rails, bustards, and the Ostrich.

This pattern was followed by many of his successors so that in most of the classifications proposed before 1867 the gulls were placed with the other web-footed birds, such as the shearwaters, loons, ducks, or pelicans; the auks were often associated with the penguins, and the plovers and sandpipers were usually grouped with the rails, bustards, or herons. Even Nitzsch (1840), whose pterylographic evidence provided valid clues in some cases, placed the auks with the penguins and the gulls with the tubenoses. However, he noted that the pterylosis of the gulls is similar to that of the sandpipers.

The true relationships among the charadriiform groups began to be delineated in 1867 when Huxley defined the palatal types and placed the schizognathous birds together. His suborder Schizognathae was organized as follows:

Order III. CARINATAE, Merrem.
  Suborder II. SCHIZOGNATHAE.

Group 1. Charadriomorphae.
   Family 1. Charadriidae.
   Family 2. Scolopacidae.
Group 2. Geranomorphae.
   Family 1. Gruidae.
   Family 2. Rallidae. (rails, bustards, seriemas)
Group 3. Cecomorphae.
   Family 1. Laridae.
   Family 2. Procellariidae.
   Family 3. Colymbidae. (loons)
   Family 4. Alcidae.
Group 4. Spheniscomorphae. (penguins)

Thus, although some of the charadriiforms were brought together, the power of traditional groupings is also evident in the position of the Geranomorphae, the association of the Laridae with the Procellariidae and loons, and of the Alcidae in the same order as the penguins. However, it was an improvement over previous arrangements because the auks and gulls were brought together for the first time and the auks and penguins were placed in separate groups.

During this period the traditional assemblages were still being defended; for example, Coues (1868) placed the penguins, auks, loons, and grebes in his order Pygopodes and stated his firm belief that "the position occupied by the Auks in this order is so evident as not to admit of question."

Sundevall (1872, see 1889:225) placed the web-footed charadriiforms in his order Natatores and the waders, such as plovers and sandpipers, in the order Grallatores, with the herons, storks, bustards, and rails.

Garrod (1873d, 1874a) included nearly all the schizorhinal birds in his Charadriiformes, which he divided into two cohorts, the Columbae (pigeons and sandgrouse), and the Limicolae. The Limicolae were further divided into the families Charadriidae (plovers, pratincoles, oystercatchers, stilts, jacanas), Gruidae (cranes, etc.), Laridae, and Alcidae. The thickknees (*Burhinus*) were placed with the bustards in the Galliformes, which also included the ratites, galliforms, rails, and cuckoos. Garrod (1877a) studied the anatomy of the seedsnipe, confirmed that their pterylosis is charadriiform, and pointed out several differences between the seedsnipe and the Turnicidae. He thought the closest allies of the seedsnipe are the coursers and pratincoles (Glareolinae) and, as evidence, cited the absence of an articulation of the pterygoid to the basisphenoidal rostrum, the absence of supraoccipital foramina, and similarities in palatal structure and myology. Garrod also noted the variation in the shape of the vomer in shorebirds. Most members of the group have a schizognathous palate in which the vomer is pointed anteriorly, but in the seedsnipe the vomer is broad anteriorly and, therefore, aegithognathous.

Sclater (1880b), who mainly followed Huxley's scheme, came close to the arrangement of Wetmore (1960), except that he placed the Alcidae with the loons and grebes in the Pygopodes. However, the other charadriiforms were in adjacent orders; the Laridae in the Gaviae, and the other groups, including the thick-knees, in the Limicolae. The bustards were allied with the other gruiforms and the penguins were separated as the order Impennes.

The controversy about the relationships of the jacanas was reviewed by Forbes (1881a), who presented new anatomical evidence. He noted that the "Parridae [Jacanidae] form a well-marked family" in his "Pluviales," with their closest relatives possibly being the Charadriidae, "from which they are easily distinguishable by the absence of supraorbital glands and occipital foramina, by their enormously elongated toes, by the number of rectrices, and other points" (p. 647). The absence of supraorbital glands is correlated with life in fresh water; these glands remove excess salt from the blood of birds that drink salt water and they will increase in size in relation to the salt content.

Stejneger (1885) noted that the Chionididae and Thinocoridae share (1) schizorhinal nares, (2) supraorbital impressions, (3) pelvic muscle formula of Garrod ABXY+, (4) two carotids, (5) vomer broad and rounded in front, (6) absence of occipital foramina and basipterygoid processes. Stejneger also observed that in the palate of the thinocorids the vomer is connected to the nasal cartilages "in a manner recalling that of the Aegithognathae." An aegithognathous palate, or a tendency towards it, is also present in *Turnix*, the swifts, honeyguides, some barbets, and the passerines. Stejneger placed the auks and gulls together, but allied them to the loons, sungrebes, and procellariids in the order Cecomorphae. The other charadriiforms were placed in the order Grallae.

Seebohm (1888a) monographed the Charadriidae, one of the eight families in his suborder Limicolae of the Charadriiformes. Concerning the allies of the Limicolae, he wrote: "The Pteroclidae form a stepping stone to the Pigeons, the Turnicidae and Thinocoridae to the Game Birds, the Dromadidae to both the Gulls and the more distant Herons, whilst the Chionidae form a second link to the gulls, the Parridae [jacanas] to the Rails, and the Otididae to the Cranes" (p. 5). Seebohm's Charadriidae included the plovers, sandpipers, thick-knees, pratincoles, stilts, and avocets. Seebohm (1888b), "by the aid of osteological characters alone," diagnosed a series of suborders "of the great Gallino-Gralline Group of Birds." In his "Gavio-Limicolae" he included the Laridae, *Dromas*, *Chionis*, seedsnipe, auks, plovers, sandpipers, pratincoles, and thick-knees. Thus, the group included most or all (jacanas not mentioned) of Wetmore's (1960) Charadriiformes. [Note: the words "Gavio," "Gaviae," etc., of this period refer to the gulls and their allies, not to the loons (*Gavia*), which were then placed in the genus *Colymbus*.]

Seebohm (1890a) recognized the suborders Gaviae (gulls and auks) and Limicolae for the charadriiforms. These suborders formed part of his order Gallo-Grallae, a large assemblage also containing the gruiforms, galliforms, loons, grebes, and tinamous. In his 1895 classification, Seebohm's Charadriiformes was composed of the suborders Gaviae, Limicolae, Grues, Pterocles, and Columbae. In the Limicolae he recognized the Charadriidae and Parridae (jacanas), and in the Gaviae the seedsnipe, sheathbills, and pratincoles were included in the Cursoridae.

Thus, within about seven years, Seebohm revised his concept of the boundaries and relationships of the Charadriiformes several times. The above quotation (1888a:5) concerning the allies of the Limicolae is a model of confusion and nonsense; it is impossible to imagine a phylogeny with the topology described by Seebohm in that sentence. Apparently he was thinking only of morphological similarities, not of a branching pattern. Members of the same order, the Charadriiformes, are described as stepping stones and links to various other orders, a logical and evolutionary impossibility. This confusion has persisted and it is possible to find similar statements in recent publications.

The osteology of the Surfbird (*Aphriza virgata*) was studied by Shufeldt (1888d), who concluded that it is more closely related to the plovers than to the sandpipers. He proposed monotypic families for *Aphriza* and for the turnstones, *Arenaria*.

In his suborder Charadriiformes, Fürbringer (1888) included the same groups of shorebirds usually recognized in recent classifications (e.g., Wetmore 1960), plus the bustards, which he bracketed with the thick-knees as the "Gens Otides." The sandgrouse were a gens in the "Intermediate Suborder Columbiformes," thus allied to the pigeons. Fürbringer (*fide* Gadow 1888a:180) thought, correctly, that the "Alcidae are closely allied to the Laridae." However, Fürbringer also revealed the seemingly universal confusion about phylogeny: "There can be but little doubt that the oldest *Charadriiformes* were gralline [cranes, rails, herons, etc.], so that the [bustards], with [thick-knees, jacanas, seedsnipe], stand nearer the common stock than the more specialized aquatic members. The *Gruiformes* are connected with the Charadriiformes by Eurypyga, with the Ralliformes by Aramus." This translated quotation by Gadow reveals that Fürbringer was as confused about phylogeny as Seebohm, but Fürbringer was far more successful in the composition of his Charadriiformes.

In the intestinal convolutions Gadow (1889) found similarities among the plovers and sandpipers ("Limicolae"), the gulls, and the pigeons. The rails and auks were similar to these groups, but also showed differences.

Shufeldt (1891c) examined the skeleton of *Chionis* and (1893a) reviewed the opinions about the relationships of the sheathbills (Chionididae). He proposed a suborder Chionides to "stand between my suborder Longipennes [Procellariidae] and the suborder Limicolae." He thought that the Crab Plover (*Dromas*) and the seedsnipe (Thinocoridae) might be included in his Chionides.

Sharpe (1891) arranged the charadriiforms in three orders: (1) Alciformes (Alcidae), (2) Lariformes (Stercorariidae, Laridae), (3) Charadriiformes (Dromadidae, Chionididae, Attagidae and Thinocoridae [seedsnipe], Haematopodidae, Charadriidae, Scolopacidae, Glareolidae and Cursoriidae [pratincoles, coursers], Parridae [jacanas], Oedicnemidae [thick-knees], and Otididae [bustards]). He did not "agree with placing the Auks with the Lari" and, although admitting that the two groups are related, considered the Alcidae to be "the nearest . . . to the outlying Tubinares" (p. 61). He admitted "the close affinity of the Charadrii and Lari" (p. 62) and noted that the jacanas combine charadriine and ralline characters. The bustards (Otididae) were included in his Charadriiformes because of their morphological similarities to the thick-knees.

In these quotes from Sharpe we see again the confusion caused by trying to express, in a classification, the morphological similarities due to convergence and those due to common ancestry.

Gadow (1892) proposed the following classification (English names added):

Order CHARADRIIFORMES
  Suborder Limicolae
    Family Chionididae: Sheathbills
    Family Charadriidae
      Subfamily Charadriinae: Plovers, etc.
      Subfamily Scolopacinae: Sandpipers, etc.
    Family Glareolidae: Pratincoles, Coursers
    Family Thinocoridae: Seedsnipe
    Family Oedicnemidae [Burhinidae]: Thick-knees

Family Parridae [Jacanidae]: Jacanas
Suborder Gaviae
Family Alcidae: Auks, Murres, Puffins
Family Laridae: Gulls, Terns

Gadow's classification was based on "about 40 characters from various organic systems." As a successful example of his method he noted that "Pteroclidae agree with Limicolae and with Columbae in about 29 points, with Alcae and with Gallidae in 24, with Ralli in 21, with Lari only in 18.—Again, Lari agree with Alcae and with Limicolae in 33 or 34; Limicolae agree with Alcae, Lari, and Ralli each in 33, with Pterocles and Columbae in 30 or 31, with Gallidae in 26. Combination of these lines shows that Lari and Pterocles are widely divergent from each other, while they each separately agree closely with the Limicolae; in other words, Lari and Pterocles are specialized in two different directions as terminal divergent branches of one common Limicoline stock" (1892:230, footnote). In this statement we see some of the basis for the long debate about whether the sandgrouse are more closely related to pigeons or to shorebirds.

Gadow placed the bustards in his Gruiformes and thus separated them from the thick-knees. In his 1893 classification, Gadow changed the Gaviae to the Lari, and included the suborders Pterocles (sandgrouse) and Columbae (pigeons, doves) in his Charadriiformes.

In the *Catalogue of Birds* Sharpe (1896) classified the shorebirds as follows (vernacular names added):

Order LIMICOLAE
Fam. Oedicnemidae [Burhinidae]: Thick-knees, Stone-curlews
Fam. Cursoriidae: *Dromas*, *Ortyxelos*, Pratincoles, Coursers
Fam. Parridae [Jacanidae]: Jacanas
Fam. Charadriidae
    Subfam. Arenariinae: Turnstones
    Subfam. Haematopodinae: Oystercatchers
    Subfam. Lobivanellinae: Wattled Plovers
    Subfam. Charadriinae: Plovers, Lapwings
    Subfam. Peltohyatinae: *Peltohyas*, Australian Dotterel
    Subfam. Himantopodinae: Stilts, Avocets
    Subfam. Ibidorhynchinae: Ibis-bill
    Subfam. Totaninae (toes webbed): Curlews, Godwits, etc.
    Subfam. Scolopacinae (toes not webbed): Sandpipers, etc.
    Subfam. Phalaropinae: Phalaropes
Fam. Chionididae: Sheathbills
Fam. Thinocorythidae: Seedsnipe

In the *Hand-List* Sharpe (1899) modified the classification:

Order CHARADRIIFORMES
Suborder Chionides
    Fam. Chionididae: Sheathbills
Suborder Attagides
    Fam. Thinocorythidae: Seedsnipe
Suborder Charadrii
    Fam. Charadriidae
        (Subfamilies as in the *Catalogue of Birds*, above)

Suborder Parrae
  Fam. Parridae: Jacanas
Suborder Cursorii
  Fam. Cursoriidae: *Ortyxelos, Pluvianus, Cursorius, Rhinoptilus*
  Fam. Glareolidae: Pratincoles
  Fam. Dromadidae: Crab Plover
Suborder Oedicnemi
  Fam. Oedicnemidae: Thick-knees, Stone-curlews
Suborder Otides
  Fam. Otididae: Bustards

The Laridae of Beddard (1896a) included the subfamilies Sterninae, Rynchopinae, Larinae, and Stercorariinae. *Rynchops* differs from the other larids in its pelvic muscle formula and in lacking the biceps slip; it agrees with the gulls and terns in having small caeca, and with the terns and jaegers in having an expansor secundariorum. Beddard (1898a) divided the shorebirds into two orders: Limicolae and Alcae. He also recognized the order Otides for the bustards and commented on their similarities to the gruiforms and charadriiforms, especially to the thick-knees (Burhinidae).

Beddard (1901c) studied the painted-snipe (Rostratulidae), compared them with *Gallinago, Scolopax,* and other charadriiforms, and concluded that they are not closely related to the Scolopacidae. He agreed "to some extent with Dr. Fürbringer's opinion that an alliance with the Parridae [Jacanidae] is not at all unreasonable" (p. 587). The DNA comparisons support this alliance.

P. C. Mitchell (1896a, 1901a) found a similar pattern of intestinal coiling in the charadriiforms, gruiforms, and Turnicidae. Other groups in his "Alectoromorphine Legion" were the Tinamidae, Columbidae, Pteroclidae, *Opisthocomus,* and the Galliformes. Beddard (1910) criticized Mitchell's conclusions based on the intestinal tract and, from his own studies, presented opposing views. Beddard commented:

1. "Among the Limicolae, with which . . . the Gulls and Terns . . . are to be placed, there are several variations" (p. 74).

2. The Alcidae are unlike the gulls and should be treated as "a distinct assemblage or . . . associated with the Grebes and Divers" (p. 78).

3. The condition in the alcid *Fratercula* was also considered to be similar to that in an "abnormal" specimen of the pheasant "*Euplocamus nycthemerus*" [*Lophura nycthemera*].

4. The "Ralli are a . . . circumscribed group . . . which bear only a general resemblance to other groups and . . . to no group in particular" (p. 90).

5. It "is by no means possible to distinguish . . . the intestinal tract of a Grebe or Tern from that of Owls . . . or large Passerine birds . . . while the Gulls and Terns . . . offer resemblances to . . . the other Limicoline birds" (p. 90).

The disagreements between Mitchell and Beddard discredit the taxonomic value of the intestinal coiling patterns, which are as likely to be related to convergence as to common ancestry.

From skeletal comparisons Shufeldt (1903a) proposed the supersuborder Lariformes for the skimmers, jaegers, gulls, terns, auks, and sheathbills, and the supersuborder Charadriiformes for the other charadriiforms. Shufeldt included the bustards with the thick-knees in his superfamily Otidoidea, and agreed with Forbes (1881a) that the jacanas are charadriiform, not gruiform. The same classification was used in Shufeldt's (1904b) arrangement of families and higher groups.

Mitchell (1905) studied the myology and wing pterylosis and repeated some of his earlier observations on intestinal coiling. His suborder Limicolae included the Charadriidae (including the Scolopacinae), Chionidae, Glareolidae, Thinocoridae, Oedicnemidae, and Parridae. He concluded: "With the exception of *Oedicnemus*, the Limicoline birds . . . show a definite and coherent series of modifications. The group is moving, or has moved, along the same anatomical lines. The limits of its variations overlap in a special way the variations displayed by the Gulls, and in a general way those exhibited by Gruiform birds" (p. 169). This murky passage seems to mean that Mitchell saw evidence of relationship between the Limicolae and the gulls, and a somewhat more distant alliance to the gruiforms.

To Chandler (1916:358), the "unquestionable likeness of the structure of feathers in the Alcidae to that in the Colymbiformes [loons, grebes] very strongly suggests the close relationships between them. The relation of the Laridae to the Alcidae, and of the Limicolae to the Laridae, is just as plainly indicated. . . . Relationship to the Gruidae is also suggested and it is probable that the latter represent an early offshoot from the limicoline stem." Chandler also thought that the feather structure of the coursers (*Cursorius*) indicated a close relationship to the herons.

Mathews and Iredale (1921) were impressed by the general similarity of the seedsnipe to galliforms and placed them in their order Galli. Without explanation they stated: "The internal characters cited in favour of a Charadriiform alliance were obviously misunderstood" (p. 217).

In 1914 Percy Lowe began a long series of papers on the relationships of the charadriiforms. He observed that the color patterns of adult plovers of the genus *Charadrius* are more similar than the sizes and shapes of their bills, and that the downy young have a uniform color pattern that would be useful in assessing generic relationships. From the simple color pattern, and the wide geographic distribution of *Charadrius*, Lowe suggested that all other plovers were derived from the ringed-plover group and he provided additional examples (1915a) to support this idea. In the sandpipers he separated the Eroliinae and Tringinae on the color pattern of the downy young, and concluded that the Ruff (*Philomachus pugnax*) and snipe (*Gallinago*) are eroliine, but that the phalaropes are tringine. Lowe believed that the mutations producing a certain type of color pattern are selectively neutral and he doubted that variations in the intensity of pigmentation have a genetic basis. It is now clear that the breast and head markings of the ringed plovers create a disruptive pattern that tends to conceal a bird sitting on a nest, and the variations among species presumably function as species-specific signals.

Lowe (1915b) presented osteological evidence to support his interpretion of the downy plumages. He was able to separate the Eroliinae and Tringinae on several palatal characters, the premaxilla, lachrymals, the angle formed by a line along the culmen and another along the basisphenoidal rostrum, plus other aspects of the skull. In these characters *Philomachus*, as well as *Ereunetes* and *Micropalama*, agree with the Eroliinae, not with the Tringinae.

According to Lowe (1915c) the skeleton of the Chatham Snipe (*Coenocorypha pusilla*) resembles that of a woodcock (*Scolopax*) more than that of a true snipe (*Gallinago*). He regarded *Coenocorypha* as a relict form that once had a wider distribution and may have been part of a group ancestral to the Scolopacinae.

Lowe next (1916a,b) examined the pterylosis and the skeleton, mainly the skull, of adults and embryos of the sheathbills (*Chionis*). He found little to suggest an alliance between sheathbills and either galliforms or columbiforms, but decided that *Chionis* shared more characters with plover-like forms, especially the oystercatchers, than with gull-like birds such as the jaegers. He believed that the sheathbills are specialized charadriiforms and noted that "It is probably nearer the truth to suppose that the Sheath-bills were differentiated as an offshoot from the main charadriiform stem before that stem had split into the charadriine and scolopacine branches, and that that offshoot was given off prior to the differentiation of the Skuas and Gulls; or, as an alternative speculation, that the main charadriiform stem split into a limicoline and a laro-limicoline branch—such groups as the Sheath-bills, Crab-Plover, Pratincoles, Skuas, Gulls, Terns, and Auks arising from the latter by various states of specialization" (1916a:152).

A study of the pterylosis and skeleton of the Crab Plover (1916b) did not clarify the relationships of *Dromas*, and Lowe was able to suggest only that, like a gull, it is probably a "specialized plover." He placed *Dromas* in a separate group in the Charadriiformes.

In 1922 Lowe returned to a consideration of the color and color patterns in plovers. He suggested that the light dorsal coloration, as in the Kentish Plover (*Charadrius alexandrinus*), is a primitive condition, and he found that the plovers varied in the development of the supraorbital furrows for the nasal gland and argued that this is correlated with the color of the back. Thus, in Lowe's opinion, an advanced charadriid would be one with a dark back and relatively extensive ossification in the supraorbital ridges. On the basis of these characters, he divided the plovers into four subfamilies and presented a provisional classification of the Charadriiformes divided into three suborders. The suborder Limicolae contained the Scolopacidae (including the phalaropes), and Charadriidae (including the oystercatchers, jacanas, and painted-snipe). The Lari-Limicolae included the Glareolidae, Dromadidae, Chionididae, gulls, and auks. The Burhinidae was the only family in the Oti-Limicolae. Lowe was uncertain of the relationship between the thick-knees and the bustards and he excluded the seedsnipe from his Charadriiformes.

Lowe (1923) thought that the seedsnipe may represent a basal group of the Charadriiformes or "that they, together with the families Turnicidae and Pteroclididae, should be regarded as the still-surviving blind-alley offshoots or relics of an ancient generalised and basal group (now extinct), from which group sprang the Schizomorphs or the now dominant Pigeons, Plovers, and Fowls" (p. 277).

Lowe (1925b) presented evidence from pterylosis and pelvic structure in support of an alliance of the Jacanidae to the Rallidae, and not to the Charadriidae, as he had proposed in 1922. Lowe also discovered that the Charadriiformes differ from the Gruiformes in the morphology of the quadrate-tympanic articulation; in this the jacanas are gruiform. The apparent value of this character led to an examination of other groups (Lowe 1926). When he inspected the quadrate of the seedsnipe, he modified his previous opinion (1923) of their relationships and proclaimed the Thinocoridae to be "undoubtedly" charadriiform. Similarly, he concluded that the quadrate of *Chionis* "is absolutely typical of the pluvialine as opposed to the larine division of the Charadriiformes" (1926:185). He also suggested that the Surfbird (*Aphriza virgata*) and the Willet (*Catoptrophorus*) are closely related to the sandpipers and not to the plovers as he had believed (1922:492, 1925b:147).

A study of the anatomy of the Tuamotu Sandpiper (*Prosobonia cancellata*) led Lowe (1927) to conclude that this species is a "generalised Scolopacine type . . . in which a tendency to specialize in the direction of the Curlew group had early occurred" (p. 116).

In 1931 Lowe published two long papers as the culmination of his work on the Charadriiformes. In the first (1931a) he presented data from anatomy, pterylosis, and downy plumage patterns, and concluded that

1. The painted snipe should be referred to a family, Rostratulidae, in the Limicolae.
2. The rails should be removed from the Gruiformes and treated as a separate order, Ralliformes, including the Rallidae and Heliornithidae (sungrebes).
3. The gruiforms (Gruidae, Psophiidae, Aramidae, Rhynochetidae, Eurypygidae, Otididae, Burhinidae, Jacanidae and, perhaps, the Cariamidae) should be combined with the charadriiforms as a suborder Grues in the order Telmatomorphae.
4. The Telmatomorphae also includes the suborders Limicolae (Rostratulidae, Charadriidae, Scolopacidae) and Laro-Limicolae (Thinocoridae, Glareolidae, Chionididae, Dromadidae, Laridae).

Lowe (p. 532) noted that "one of the most striking facts that has emerged from my anatomical studies is the decidedly gruine character of the Burhinidae, so that one has . . . been led to wonder why they have so persistently been referred to the Limicolae—and this also applies to the Jacanidae; while . . . the Rostratulidae . . . represent an ancient group with leanings towards the Gruae, yet . . . more limicoline than gruine."

Lowe (1931b) made further changes; the Thinocoridae were removed from the Laro-Limicolae and placed in a special suborder, Grui-Limicolae; the skuas, gulls, and auks were removed from the Laro-Limicolae to a new suborder, Lari. Lowe's "final classification of the telmatomorphine suborders" was as follows:

Grues: as listed above (3)
Grui-Limicolae: Thinocoridae
Limicolae: Rostratulidae, Charadriidae, Scolopacidae
Laro-Limicolae: Glareolidae, Dromadidae, Chionididae
Lari: Stercorariidae, Laridae, Alcidae

Lowe supported his conclusions with anatomical data and included discussions of the seedsnipe, various limicoline genera, the painted-snipe, the sheathbills, Crab Plover, Glareolidae, and others.

Lowe's last paper on the shorebirds primarily concerned correlations between plumage color and color pattern, and the development of the supraorbital, or nasal, glands in the plovers. He noted that there tend to be pairs of species in which one has a pale ("adumbrated") plumage and deep supraorbital grooves, and the other species has more intense plumage colors and color pattern and shallow supraorbital grooves. Lowe was aware of the correlation between the size of the nasal gland and salt versus fresh water, but felt that this did not completely explain the situations he had found. However, Bock (1958) criticized Lowe's interpretations and concluded that the size of the nasal gland has no taxonomic value (see below).

Dwight (1925) studied the molts and plumages of the gulls and developed a classification based on external characters in which 44 species were divided into nine genera. Sibley and Monroe (1990) recognize six genera and 50 species.

E. Stresemann (1934) divided the charadriiforms among four orders: the Alcae were placed next to the Laro-Limicolae because he considered the auks to be most closely allied to the gulls. He believed that the Jacanae are related to the Ralli and to the Laro-Limicolae, that the Thinocori are allied to the Grues and the Laro-Limicolae, but closest to the latter. He also suggested that the bustards may be distantly related to the Laro-Limicolae.

The literature of the Charadriiformes from 1894 to 1928 was reviewed by G. Carmichael Low (1931) and his classification included the suborders Oti-Limicolae (bustards, thick-knees), Limicolae (plovers, sandpipers, etc.), and Laro-Limicolae (*Dromas*, *Chionis*, Glareolidae, Thinocoridae, gulls, etc.).

Von Boetticher (1934) divided the Charadriiformes into the suborders Pteroclites (sand-grouse), Burhini (bustards, thick-knees, Crab Plover), Thinocori (seedsnipe, sheathbills), and Laro-Limicolae (Glareolidae, Cursoriidae, Laridae, Alcidae, Charadriidae).

Hudson (1937) compared the pelvic muscles in one or more species representing 16 of the 20 orders of North American birds, including two scolopacids (*Totanus*), a gull, and an auk (*Uria*). He found a rudimentary ambiens muscle in *Uria* although the alcines "are generally stated to lack this muscle." Hudson noted that Gadow (1891c) had recorded the ambiens in *Uria* "but this apparently has escaped the notice of taxonomists" (p. 77). Using his "amplified" formula, Hudson determined the pelvic muscle formulas of *Totanus* = ADXY Am V, *Larus* = ACDXY Am V, *Uria* = ABDX Am. He also reported on the deep flexor tendons and other aspects of the myology of the hind limb.

A. H. Miller and Sibley (1941) described *Gaviota niobrara* from the upper Miocene of Nebraska, based on the distal quarter of a humerus. Although clearly that of a gull, the bone showed some similarities to the Scolopacidae, for example, *Numenius*, and led the authors to suggest that the two groups may have been more closely related in the Miocene. This is obviously true, but the divergence between the Scolopacida and the Charadriida at $\Delta T_{50}H$ 15.6 probably occurred at least 50 MYA, in the Eocene.

The structure of the hind limb in the auks (Alcinae) was studied by Storer (1945a), who noted that his proposed arrangement of the genera agreed with that of Dawson (1920), based on eggshell characters. Storer proposed "seven groups of suprageneric rank" for 14 genera and (1945b) concluded that *Endomychura* is closer to *Synthliboramphus* than to *Brachyrhamphus*. From the external morphology and behavior of *Cepphus* and *Uria*, Storer (1952) concluded that unlike most alcines, *Uria* probably originated in the Atlantic and that *Cepphus* is closer to the ancestral stock than is *Uria*. Since both are living, they must be equidistant from the ancestral stock.

From the fossil record, Howard (1950) suggested that the shorebirds and gruiforms may have shared a common ancestry, noting that *Rhynchaeites* from the middle Eocene of Germany combines characters of shorebirds and rails. She pointed out that the allocation of many fossils is open to question because most of the extant groups are not readily distinguished from unassociated skeletal elements.

In the order Laro-Limicolae Mayr and Amadon (1951) recognized the families Jac-anidae, Thinocoridae, Chionididae, Dromadidae, Burhinidae, Haematopodidae, Charadriidae, Glareolidae, Laridae, and Alcidae. Most of these were not subdivided, but the Charadriidae included the subfamilies Charadriinae, Scolopacinae, Phalaropinae, Recur-virostrinae, and Rostratulinae. The Laridae included the Stercorariinae, Larinae, Sterninae, and Rynchopinae. The authors commented: "This diversified order may be connected with the Grues through one or all of the Burhinidae, Jacanidae, and Thinocoridae" (p. 8).

Von Boetticher (1954) criticized Peters (1934) for his recognition of 19 genera for the lapwing plovers and proposed that the 25 species be placed in four genera.

Hanke and Niethammer (1955) compared the esophageal structure of *Thinocorus* with that of *Pterocles* and several shorebirds and agreed that the seedsnipe are charadriiforms.

Larson (1955, 1957) analyzed the differentiation among the Palearctic Charadrii during the Tertiary, with special reference to the Pleistocene and the species relationships among plovers and sandpipers.

Verheyen (1957d) proposed an order, Jacaniformes, to contain the Eurypygidae (Sun-bittern), Rhynochetidae (Kagu), and Jacanidae (jacanas). He believed these groups are as close to the "Ralliformes" as to the Charadriiformes and should, therefore, be placed between them. Verheyen (1958d) proposed a classification in which the Charadriiformes included the Chionidae, Haematopodidae, Charadriidae, Scolopacidae, Tringidae, Rostratulidae, Glareolidae, Dromadidae, and Burhinidae. He considered this group to be related "on one hand to the Columbiformes and the Turniciformes and on the other to the Lariformes, the Jacaniformes and the Ralliformes" (p. 31, transl.).

Verheyen (1958b) proposed that the order "Alciformes" be recognized to include the diving-petrels and the auks. He suggested that the Alciformes is allied to the "Lariformes, to the Procellariiformes and to the Sphenisciformes" (transl.). He believed that the "Lariformes and the Procellariiformes on one side, the Sphenisciformes and the Alciformes on the other, have not acquired a similar appearance due to the phenomenon of convergence but rather from the effects of a paramorphogenic evolution" (p. 14, transl.). Verheyen placed the gulls and their allies in the Lariformes next to the Charadriiformes:

Order Lariformes
   Suborder Rynchopi: Family Rynchopidae, Skimmers
   Suborder Lari: Family Laridae (Larinae, Sterninae, Gyginae)
                 Family Stercorariidae (Stercorariinae, Anoinae)

Verheyen used his concept of paramorphogenesis to explain his ideas about relation-ships, but it is apparent that he was deluded by convergence and the simplistic idea that similarity in skeletal elements is a direct index to classification.

Timmerman (1957a,b) used the mallophagan parasites to suggest host relationships among the shorebirds. He concluded:

1. The gulls and waders (sandpipers, plovers, etc.) are more closely related to each other than either is to the auks, thus two suborders, not three, best represent the relationships.

2. *Rynchops* is most closely related to the terns.

3. *Arenaria* is a scolopacid, not a charadriid.

4. *Limnodromus* and *Limosa* are closely related to one another and belong in the Eroliinae (Calidrinae), not the Scolopacinae or Tringinae.

The DNA comparisons show that the plovers, gulls, and auks are more closely related to one another than to the sandpipers, thus opposing Timmerman's first item in the foregoing list. We have found no reason to believe that the relationships of parasites provide a consistent index to the relationships of the hosts.

Timmerman (1959, 1962, 1965) defended his proposal that the nearest relatives of the charadriiforms are the tubenoses (Procellariidae). Bock (1958) studied the skull of the plovers and reviewed the genera based on various characters. He concluded that the condition of the hind toe, wattles, and wing spur are of little or no taxonomic value, and that color and pattern must be used with caution. He was unable to find body skeleton characters "useful in understanding relationships within the plovers" (p. 54), and showed that the "degree of ossification of the supraorbital rims is strongly correlated with the size of the nasal glands and hence with the salinity of the water, and is of no taxonomic value" (p. 90). Lowe's interpretations of skull morphology and color patterns were criticized as "at variance with many of the observed facts and with many of the ideas and principles of evolution and classification" (p. 90). Bock proposed a classification of the plovers in which the Charadriinae includes the Vanellinae of Peters (1934); the 61 species and 32 genera recognized by Peters were reduced to 56 species in 6 genera, and *Arenaria* and *Aphriza* were considered to be scolopacids.

Bock (1964) concluded that the Australian or Inland Dotterel (*Peltohyas australis*) is a plover, not a courser. This was disputed by Jehl (1968a), who placed *Peltohyas* in the Cursoriinae.

Storer (1960b) reviewed the evolutionary history of the diving birds and reaffirmed his belief in two major lineages containing convergently similar species, namely, a penguin-procellariid group and a shorebird-gull-auk (charadriiform) group. He suggested that the loons (*Gavia*) were derived from the common ancestor of the charadriiform lineage, with the fossil *Colymboides* a possible link.

The behavior of gulls was studied by Moynihan (1955, 1956, 1958a,b, 1959a, 1962), who revised the Laridae (1959b) based on his observations and those of others, especially Tinbergen (1959). Moynihan's classification of the Laridae:

Family Laridae
  Subfamily Stercorariinae: Jaegers, Skuas
  Subfamily Larinae
    Tribe Larini: *Larus* (incl. *Gabianus*, *Pagophila*, *Rissa*, *Rhodostethia*, *Creagrus*, *Xema*)
    Tribe Rynchopini: Skimmers
    Tribe Sternini: *Anous* (incl. *Procelsterna*, *Gygis*), *Larosterna*, *Sterna* (incl. *Chlidonias*,
      Phaetusa, *Gelochelidon*, *Hydroprogne*, *Thalasseus*)

Wetmore (1960) divided the Charadriiformes into three suborders: Alcae (auks, murres, puffins), Lari (gulls, terns, jaegers, skimmers), and Charadrii (plovers, sandpipers, etc.). He disputed Moynihan's inclusion of *Rynchops* in the Laridae and argued that the skimmers deserve family rank:

The bill, compressed to knifelike form, with great elongation of the ramphotheca of the lower jaw, is unique, and the method of feeding, where the lower mandible cuts the water surface with the bird in flight, is equally strange. The structural modifications in the form of the skull from that found in skuas, gulls, and terns also are too extensive to be ignored. The elongated blade of the lower mandible anterior to the symphysis of the rami is intriguing but less important than the profound changes found elsewhere. The palatine bones are greatly expanded, the orbital process of the quadrate is reduced, the frontal area is inflated and produced posteriorly, with the compression of the lachrymal, and consequent reduction in size of the cavity for the eye, to enumerate the most outstanding differences in the osteology. Externally, the pupil of the eye is a vertical slit similar to that of a cat, and thus unlike that of any other group of birds. . . . Other peculiarities have been described in the musculature. The sum of these characters justifies treatment of the Rynchopidae as a distinct family in their suborder (p. 13).

This quotation epitomizes Wetmore's philosophy of classification. His argument is based on differences; similarities of skimmers to gulls or terns are not mentioned, and the idea of phylogeny does not appear, even by implication. Morphological specializations (grades) are the basis for the recognition of categorical rank, not the clades of the phylogeny.

Zusi (1962) studied the anatomical adaptations for feeding in the head and neck of the Black Skimmer (*Rynchops nigra*). He noted similarities to the terns, but did not propose taxonomic conclusions. He wrote: "The skimmers seem to embody a mixture of gull-like and tern-like characteristics, on which is superimposed a highly developed adaptive complex associated with feeding. This complex involves anatomy and behavior. It is probable that many morphological features of the entire body have been altered during the evolution of the unique feeding method, and that many behavior patterns, other than skimming, have been secondarily affected" (p. 96).

This statement contrasts with that of Wetmore (above) in noting similarities to gulls and terns, while describing the specializations associated with the unusual feeding method. Zusi wisely left open the question of phylogenetic relationships because morphology has no inherent time dimension, and differences do not constitute valid evidence of relationships.

Sibley (1960) compared the paper electrophoretic patterns of the egg-white proteins of 11 of the 16 charadriiform families recognized by Wetmore (1960). "A readily detectable pattern" was observed, with minor variations. The pattern of *Rostratula* egg white differed from those of other shorebirds, and the patterns of the loons and some rails were most similar to those of the charadriiforms.

E. Stresemann (1959) contended that there was no convincing evidence for the affinities of several shorebird groups and he supported the same four orders he had recognized in 1934. He placed the Jacanae and Thinocori within the gruiform groups, and the Laro-Limicolae and Alcae between the gruiforms and the loons (Gaviae). The DNA comparisons, and other evidence, show that this was a mistake; the charadriiform groups are monophyletic relative to the gruiforms.

Stresemann and Stresemann (1966a) found that the molt of the primaries in the Thinocoridae begins in an ascending fashion with primary 10, but after the eighth or seventh primary is dropped, the replacement proceeds irregularly. This pattern differs from that of other shorebirds in which the primary molt is regularly ascending, but other aspects of the molt, the form of the wing, and the number of secondaries and rectrices are the same. The Stresemanns (p. 222) concluded that the seedsnipe are related to the charadriiforms, not the gruiforms.

Verheyen's (1961) classification of the charadriiforms again illustrates the failure of his methods to distinguish between similarities due to convergence and those reflecting common ancestry:

Superorder Hygrornithes
    Order Spenisciformes: Penguins
    Order Procellariiformes: Shearwaters, Albatrosses, etc.
    Order Alciformes: Diving-Petrels, Auks, Loons
Superorder Limnornithes
    Order Pelecaniformes: Darters, Cormorants, Boobies, Pelicans
    Order Lariformes: Frigatebirds, Tropicbirds, Skimmers, Gulls, Jaegers

Order Charadriiformes: Sheathbills, Plovers, Sandpipers, Coursers, Crab Plover, Thick-knees, Painted-snipe
Order Jacaniformes: Mesites, Kagu, Sunbittern, Jacanas

Using phase-contrast microscopy, McFarlane (1963) examined avian sperm morphology. Like those of many other non-passerines, the Charadriinae, Recurvirostrini, Larinae, and Alcinae have cylindrical sperm, but those of the Scolopacidae have a spiral shape. The only other birds with spiral-shaped sperm are the passerines. McFarlane suggested that spiralization may be a recent evolutionary trend, that the Scolopacidae may have had a more recent origin than other charadriiforms, and that the similarity to passerine sperm may be due to convergence.

Regardless of the validity of McFarlane's suggestion, the difference between the spermatozoa of the Scolopacida and the Charadriida is congruent with the DNA evidence of an ancient divergence between the two groups. It will be of interest to test this hypothesis by examining the sperm of other members of the two suborders.

The erythropoiesis in the yolk sac, liver, spleen, and bone marrow from the tenth embryonic day to the first post-embryonic day was studied by Schmekel (1962, 1963). *Vanellus*, *Larus*, and *Uria* showed erythropoiesis in the yolk sac up to the twentieth embryonic day, or longer. The onset of hematopoiesis in the marrow did not depend on the date of hatching and superseded erythropoiesis in the yolk sac. The three genera are similar to one another in all these processes and differ from all others examined. Schmekel took this as evidence of a close relationship among plovers, gulls, and auks.

Perkins (1964) found the electrophoretic patterns of the hemoglobins and serum proteins of seven species of *Larus* to be identical, or nearly so, and he was unable to separate the species on this basis.

Gysels (1964a) and Gysels and Rabaey (1964) examined the eye lens and muscle proteins of the Razorbill (*Alca torda*), the Common Murre (*Uria aalge*), and the Atlantic Puffin (*Fratercula arctica*) by zone electrophoresis and immunoelectrophoresis in agar gel. They concluded that their electrophoretic evidence, and the absence of glycogen in the lens, indicated a close relationship between *Uria* and the penguins. They also concluded that *Alca* and *Fratercula* differ from the charadriiforms, from *Uria*, and from each other in these attributes. Sibley and Brush (1967) doubted the value of electrophoretic comparisons of lenticular proteins in systematics, and noted that the published figures in Gysels and Rabaey (1964) are difficult to evaluate. The origins are not properly aligned and the diffuse bands in their patterns may indicate that the proteins were denatured. Gysels and Rabaey tested the lens proteins for reactivity with antisera against lenses of Domestic Fowl (*Gallus gallus*) and European Starling (*Sturnus vulgaris*). It is doubtful that immunological comparisons between such widely diverged taxa are valid. To eliminate spurious cross-reactions, antisera to all species involved should be tested and reciprocal tests should be made. There is ample independent evidence of the monophyly of the auks, murres, and puffins and to suggest their fragmentation into two or three groups on such flimsy evidence is unwarranted.

Holmes and Pitelka (1964) compared various behavioral characters of the Curlew Sandpiper (*Calidris ferruginea*) with those of other shorebirds and concluded that it seems to bridge the gap between the Pectoral Sandpiper (*C. melanotos*) and the more typical members of the genus, sometimes placed in *Erolia*.

From immunological comparisons of the serum proteins of the Alcinae, Averkina et al. (1965) concluded that *Uria* and *Cepphus* are most closely related. *Alca* is next closest to them and *Fratercula* is more distant. They were unable to distinguish between subspecies of *Uria aalge* and *U. lomvia*.

Judin (1965) proposed a classification of the shorebirds based on anatomy, including jaw musculature and the propatagial tendons. He allocated the Gruiformes, Charadriiformes, and Columbiformes to a superorder, Charadriornithes. In the Charadriiformes he recognized three suborders: Jacanae (jacanas), Limicolae (painted-snipe, plovers, sandpipers), and Laro-Limicolae (Glareolidae, Pluvianidae, Chionidae, Thinocoridae, Dromadidae, Stercorariidae, Laridae, Alcidae).

Brown et al. (1967) found Sabine's Gull (*Xema sabini*) to be similar to other gulls in its breeding behavior, yet different enough to set it apart. They believed that some of the behavior of this species may be related to its habit of breeding in small, loose groups on the flat tundra during the short Arctic summer. They thought that Sabine's Gull is most closely related to Franklin's Gull (*L. pipixcan*), and noted similarities to the Swallow-tailed Gull (*L. furcatus*). Rylander (1968) used starch gel electrophoresis to compare the serum proteins of four *Calidris* sandpipers. He found much intraspecific variation and could not distinguish among species.

Jehl (1968a) found the color patterns of the downy young to be suggestive of relationships among genera, tribes, and families. His conclusions were:

1. The Rostratulidae are most closely related to the Jacanidae, but these two groups are not closely allied to other shorebirds.
2. The Burhinidae are allied to the Haematopodidae and the Recurvirostridae.
3. There is no evidence to link *Ibidorhyncha* most closely to the Recurvirostridae.
4. The Glareolidae are closely allied to the Charadriidae. *Peltohyas* is a courser; *Rhinoptilus* may not be a natural taxon.
5. The Charadriidae are related to the Recurvirostridae and Haematopodidae. *Phegornis* is a plover.
6. The Scolopacidae, which do not seem to be closely allied to the Charadriidae, comprise six families (p. 44).

Jehl's "tentative phylogeny" (p. 42) agrees with our DNA-based phylogeny except for the position of the Thinocoridae, which Jehl placed in the plover-gull clade next to *Chionis*, and which the DNA evidence shows to be a member of the Scolopacides. However, Jehl noted that "Relationships of the Thinocoridae cannot be inferred from the plumages of their chicks" (p. 40) and he cited Lowe (1931a), who described the downy young of *Thinocorus* as "calidrine-like." In most of the charadriiform groups the downy young plumages reflect the relationships revealed by the DNA comparisons. For example, the chicks of avocets, stilts, oystercatchers, and thick-knees are strikingly similar to one another, and they share some pattern markings with the plovers.

Sibley et al. (1968) reviewed the opinions concerning the relationships of the seedsnipe and compared the electrophoretic patterns of their hemoglobins and egg-white proteins with those of other groups. They concluded that the evidence indicated that the seedsnipe are charadriiforms, but could not decide to which shorebird group they are most closely related.

From an analysis of the structure of the bill and tongue Bedard (1969) defined three stages in the adaptive radiation of the Alcinae. Unlike Storer (1945b), he considered *Endo-*

mychura and the other small plankton feeders to be specialized. An opposite trend is found in the primarily fish-eating forms like *Uria* and *Alca*. The puffins (*Fratercula, Lunda, Cerorhinca*) and an auklet (*Cyclorrhynchus*) feed on both fish and plankton and have intermediate adaptations.

Hudson et al. (1969) compared 56 characters of the pectoral musculature, and 52 of the pelvic musculature, among several species of Laridae (gulls, terns, auks, etc.). They considered the skuas to be more specialized in leg musculature and the gulls more specialized in wing musculature. They recognized the subfamilies Stercorariinae, Larinae, and Sterninae in the Laridae, but believed that *Rynchops* has enough differences in its musculature to warrant family status. They also concluded that the auks (Alcinae) should be placed in a separate suborder, and regarded *Alca* and *Uria* as more specialized than the puffins.

Schnell (1970a,b), in a numerical taxonomic study of the "suborder Lari" (our Laridae), compared 51 skeletal characters among 93 species of jaegers, skuas, gulls, terns, and skimmers. He used multivariate statistical techniques and generated phenograms by treating his data in various ways. In most characters *Rynchops* seemed most like the terns and the differences between jaegers and gulls were greater than those between gulls and terns. In most cases Schnell was unable to obtain clusters of species within the gulls or terns and he was impressed by the uniformity of both groups.

Ahlquist (1974a,b) compared the egg-white proteins of 130 species of shorebirds using isoelectric focusing in acrylamide gels, and peptide maps of the ovalbumins of 80 species representing all the traditional groups except the Dromadinae. In general the trees generated from the peptide data are topologically similar to those obtained from DNA-DNA hybridization data, but they differ in detail. In hindsight such discrepancies can be understood as problems in determining peptide homologies and quantifying differences or in constructing and rooting the phylograms. The principal similarities in the conclusions reached in the DNA comparisons and peptide studies are (1) separation of the shorebirds into a sandpiper lineage and a gull-auk-plover lineage, (2) inclusion of the jacanas, seedsnipe, and painted-snipe with the sandpipers, (3) close relationship of auks to gulls, terns, etc., (4) the jaegers as the sister group of the gulls, terns, and skimmers. The principal differences are (1) glareolids clustered with plovers, not with gulls and terns, (2) oystercatchers, avocets, and stilts not closely related, (3) the curlews (*Numenius*) cluster with the recurvirostrids.

Strauch (1978) reported on his extensive study of the shorebirds based on 70 mainly skeletal characters analyzed by character compatibility methods. He concluded that the Charadriiformes should be divided into three suborders: Scolopaci, Charadrii, and Alcae. Strauch's Scolopaci includes the same groups as our Scolopacida based on DNA comparisons, except that we also include *Pedionomus*, which Strauch did not examine. The Charadrii of Strauch (our Charadriida) places the skuas, gulls, terns, and skimmers on one branch, and five lineages on a second branch: (1) *Dromas*, (2) *Pluvianellus, Chionis*, (3) *Pluvianus, Burhinus*, (4) Glareolidae, (5) plovers, lapwings, oystercatchers, avocets, stilts. Although Strauch's branching patterns are not strictly dichotomous, these groups agree with our Figs. 364 and 365, except that we found the auks (Alcinae) to be the sister group of the Larinae. Strauch (1978:329) placed the auks in his third suborder, Alcae, as a branch from the node between his Scolopaci and Charadrii, thus his three main groups form a trichotomy. He found that "None of the characters used in this study indicate that the Lari and alcids form a monophyletic line which excludes other charadriiforms. . . . The alcids are thus best considered distinct from the Lari unless new evidence indicates otherwise."

Except for the position of the auks, murres, and puffins (Strauch's Alcae is our Alcinae), the congruence between Strauch's phylogeny and the DNA-based phylogeny is excellent. It is likely that the reason Strauch's method did not cluster the auks with the other Laridae is that their skeletons are so highly modified in relation to their adaptations as foot-propelled divers.

This provides another example of the difficulties involved in basing a classification on morphological characters. As long as all members of a large group are adapted to essentially the same ecological niche they will cluster together by any method of comparison, but when one lineage has become specialized, for example in its feeding structures, it becomes difficult to evaluate its taxonomic relationships to other groups. The common result is to isolate such groups in higher taxa, thus concealing their phylogenetic affinities.

Strauch (1985) made "an estimate of the phylogeny of 22 extant and 1 extinct species of the Alcidae . . . from compatibility analyses of 33 cladistic characters of the skeleton, integument, and natural history." He recommended several changes in generic assignments and recognized ten genera, but stated that he favored a reduction in "the number of genera . . . to about six; however, a more conservative approach may be necessary to promote the acceptance of new ideas" (p. 537). Strauch presented a cladogram (p. 536) of his arrangement of the Alcidae in which the puffins are the sister group of the other alcids and four other clusters are represented by successive dichotomies. These relationships are reflected in his classification by listing the tribe Fraterculini first in the sequence of five tribes, with the other four tribes (Aethiini, Brachyramphini, Cepphini, Alcini) in the sequence of their branchings. Strauch justified this arrangement by a statement of preference for "the phyletic sequencing scheme (Eldredge and Cracraft 1980), in which taxa in a sequence are assigned the same rank."

Randi and Spina (1987) reviewed the systematics of the gulls and terns and added the results of an electrophoretic study of the blood proteins of the Italian species. Blood samples from five species of terns and five species of gulls that breed in Italy were compared at the levels of populations and species. Terns and gulls were clearly distinguished. *Larus audouinii* was the most differentiated species and *L. argentatus* was intermediate between *audouinii* and the members of the black-headed group, *melanocephalus, ridibundus,* and *genei.* The terns formed two groups: *Sterna albifrons* and *S. sandvicensis* clustered together, with *S. hirundo, Gelochelidon nilotica,* and *Chlidonias hybrida* forming a separate group. The authors suggested the inclusion of *Gelochelidon* in *Sterna* and expressed uncertainty about the status of *Chlidonias.*

Hackett (1989) used sequential starch gel electrophoresis to compare 19 enzymes representing 23 genetic loci in 15 species of terns, three gulls, two jaegers, and the Black Skimmer, with a plover, a dove, and a petrel used as out-groups. She concluded that "The merger of the genera *Thalasseus, Hydroprogne,* and *Gelochelidon* into *Sterna* by the AOU (1983) is justified" but that, *contra* the AOU (1983), her data support family rank for the gulls and terns (Laridae), the jaegers (Stercorariidae), and skimmers (Rynchopidae) as in the "classifications of Wetmore (1960) and Peters (1934)."

Dittmann et al. (1989) used starch gel electrophoresis to compare 26 tissue proteins in the three species of phalaropes and representatives of several other charadriiform genera. They concluded that Wilson's Phalarope (*Phalaropus tricolor*) is more closely related to the Red

Knot (*Calidris canutus*) and some other genera of sandpipers than to the other two species of *Phalaropus*.

The DNA Hybridization Evidence (Figs. 123–138, 337, 356, 363–365)

The DNA comparisons indicate that the sandgrouse lineage (Pteroclides) and the shorebird clade (Charadriides) last shared a common ancestor at Δ T$_{50}$H 17.1 (Fig. 363).

The sandpipers and allies (Scolopacida) branched from the plovers, gulls, etc. (Charadriida) at Δ 15.6. Within the Scolopacida a divergence at Δ 14.1 produced the Scolopacoidea (sandpipers, seedsnipe, Plains-wanderer) and the Jacanoidea (jacanas and painted-snipe). The Scolopacoidea split at Δ 13.3 into the Thinocoridae and Pedionomidae on one branch and the Scolopacidae on the other. The branch between the seedsnipe and the Plains-wanderer lineages occurred at Δ 10.8. Sibley et al. (1988) divide the Scolopacidae into the subfamilies Scolopacinae and Tringinae at Δ 7.6 (Fig. 364).

The Charadriida split into the Chionidoidea (sheathbills) plus Charadrioidea (thick-knees, oystercatchers, avocets, stilts, plovers) and the Laroidea (pratincoles, Crab Plover, jaegers, skimmers, gulls, terns, auks) at Δ 12.8. The Chionidoidea and Charadrioidea diverged at Δ 11.5, and the Charadrioidea split into the Burhinidae and Charadriidae at Δ 10.8. The Recurvirostrinae and the Charadriinae diverged at Δ 7.7. We recognize the tribes Recurvirostrini and Haematopodini because all of the constituent genera are represented in our data, but defer the subdivision of the Charadriinae until more taxa can be compared (Fig. 364).

In the Laroidea we recognize the Glareolidae and the Laridae which diverged at Δ 8.1, thus these two groups could be included in the same family under our criteria. The Glareolidae is divided into the Dromadinae, containing only the Crab Plover (*Dromas ardeola*), and the Glareolinae, including the pratincoles and coursers (Fig. 365).

The Laridae includes the Larinae and the Alcinae which diverged at Δ 6.1. The Larinae is divided into four tribes: Stercorariini (jaegers), Rynchopini (skimmers), Larini (gulls), and Sternini (terns). It may be possible to subdivide the Alcinae, but we lack the DNAs of several genera (Fig. 365).

Thus, the DNA comparisons confirm the inclusion of the same groups recognized by morphological characters as members of the charadriiform clade. The division into the Scolopacida and Charadriida is congruent with morphology, as are the subdivisions within each parvorder.

Fig. 123 (*Pterocles*) shows that the sandgrouse are more closely related to the charadriiforms than to the columbiforms. Fig. 124 (*Pterocles*) again shows the effect of delayed maturity on the rate of genomic evolution. The heteroduplex curves of the penguin, Turkey Vulture, stork, and hawk are closer to the *Pterocles* homoduplex than are the curves of the charadriiforms (stilt, plover, gull). Sandgrouse begin to breed at age one year. A discussion of the taxonomic history of the sandgrouse is presented in the following section.

Fig. 125 (*Thinocorus*) shows the relationship between the seedsnipe and the Plains-wanderer. Fig. 126 (*Pedionomus*) shows the reciprocal relationship between the Plains-wanderer and the seedsnipe. Note that although the two genera of seedsnipe are widely separated in Fig. 125, they are equidistant from *Pedionomus* in Fig. 126, indicating equal rates of DNA evolution along the two lineages.

Fig. 127 (*Calidris*) includes only charadriiform taxa. The clustering of species representing most of the major subgroups of the Charadrii indicates that all are roughly equidistant from the tringine sandpipers, although on at least four different branches. The position of *Burhinus* closest to *Calidris* may be due to the slower rate of genomic evolution in the thick-knees which begin to breed at age three (Table 16).

Fig. 128 (*Rostratula*) shows the substantial distances between the painted-snipe and the jacanas, sandpipers, Plains-wanderer, seedsnipe, and the true snipe (*Gallinago*).

Fig. 129 (*Irediparra*) supports the recognition of the three genera of jacanas, and shows the rather large distances between the jacanas and other groups of shorebirds.

Fig. 130 (*Haematopus*) shows the close relationship between the oystercatchers and the avocets, stilts, and plovers. The thick-knees are next, and the coursers and seedsnipe more distant.

Fig. 131 (*Cladorhynchus*) shows the close relationship between the stilts and oyster-catchers, with the plovers next, and the Crab Plover, curlew, and coursers more distant.

Fig. 132 (*Charadrius*) shows the close relationship between the plovers and the oyster-catchers and avocets, with the thick-knees next, then the murre, Crab Plover, gull, sheathbill, pratincole, sandpiper, and painted-snipe.

Fig. 133 (*Charadrius*) includes six members of the Charadriida (*Recurvirostra* to *Stiltia*), and four of the Scolopacida (*Steganopus* to *Attagis*), in sequence.

Fig. 134 (*Vanellus*) includes only members of the Charadrioidea and Laroidea. From this set, and several of those above, it is clear that the oystercatchers, avocets, and stilts are most closely related to the plovers and to one another.

Fig. 135 (*Vanellus*) includes only members of the Charadriida, showing the relative distances from the lapwing plover to *Charadrius*, two stilts, avocet, Crab Plover, and a sheathbill.

Fig. 136 (*Dromas*) shows that the Crab Plover is closest to the pratincoles, next to the gulls and auks, then the avocets, thick-knees, oystercatchers, stilts, plovers, and sheathbills.

Fig. 137 (*Glareola*) shows the close relationship between the pratincoles and the Crab Plover, with the Crab Plover as close to *Glareola* as are the two coursers, *Rhinoptilus* and *Cursorius*. The other taxa, except *Pterocles*, are members of the Charadriida.

Fig. 138 (*Sterna*) shows the close relationships among the terns, gulls, jaegers, auks, and Crab Plover (Laroidea), with the members of the Charadrioidea, Scolopacoidea, and Chionidoidea farther out.

Fig. 337, the FITCH tree, agrees well with the UPGMA tree and with the melting curves. The Scolopacida (*Calidris, Rostratula, Irediparra, Pedionomus, Thinocorus, Gallinago*) have longer branches than the Charadriida (*Chionis* to *Dromas*), possibly because the members of the Charadriida do not begin to breed until ca. 2–4 years, while the Scolopacida tend to begin at 1–2 years. This seems like a small difference to be noticeable, but the average branch length from the divergence between the two parvorders is 6.2 distance units for the Charadriida and 10.7 units for the Scolopacida.

We conclude that the infraorder Pteroclides (sandgrouse) is the sister group of the infraorder Charadriides (shorebirds), and that the Charadriides are divisible into two parvorders, Scolopacida and Charadriida, as in our classification. There is evidence that the Scolopacida are evolving more rapidly than the Charadriida and that the difference is correlated with the average ages at first breeding for the taxa for which ages at maturity are known.

Sandgrouse

Suborder Charadrii
 Infraorder Pteroclides
  Family Pteroclidae: Sandgrouse

Family PTEROCLIDAE: 2/16. The sandgrouse inhabit dry, open country, often in deserts or semi-deserts. The two species of *Syrrhaptes* occur in the steppes of central Asia, and the 14 species of *Pterocles* are found mainly in Africa, with representatives extending to southwestern, southern, and central Asia, India, southern Russia, Spain, southern France, and the Canary Islands.

The identity of the closest relatives of the sandgrouse is one of the most debated questions in avian systematics. They share several characters with the pigeons and doves (Columbiformes), but they also differ from them in many ways. They also resemble some of the shorebirds and some of the galliforms. Many of the characters of the sandgrouse are adaptations to an arid environment and such specializations obscure morphological comparisons with other groups. This debate involves the usual puzzle of the interpretation of the phylogenetic meaning of structural characters, i.e., of convergence versus common ancestry. In addition, certain behavioral patterns have been invoked as evidence of relationships.

Historical Review of the Classification

During much of their taxonomic history the sandgrouse have been thought to be most closely related to the pigeons and doves, but the plovers and galliforms frequently have been cited as their nearest relatives. In this review we note some of the past opinions; for further information see the Columbiformes, Galliformes, and Charadriiformes.

Nitzsch (1840) found pterylographic similarities between pigeons and sandgrouse and included them in his Columbinae, one of his eight principal divisions. Gray (1844–49) was impressed with the external similarities between sandgrouse and some galliforms and he placed the Pteroclididae in his order Gallinae. Bonaparte (1853) included *Pterocles*, the seedsnipe, and the tinamous in his Perdices.

Lilljeborg (1866) united the sandgrouse, seedsnipe, and sheathbills in the family Pteroclidae of his order Gallinae, which also included the tinamous, grouse, and pheasants.

W. K. Parker's thoughts about the sandgrouse were typically ambiguous: "The Sand-Grouse . . . although lower than the Grouse in many respects, being but little removed from the struthious type, yet are related, and that intimately to the Plovers and the Pigeons" (1864:237).

Huxley (1867) noted that *Pterocles*, the pheasants, and the Turnicidae agree in having similar basipterygoid processes, long and slender anterior processes of the palatines, small maxillopalatines, and imperfectly developed vomers. He included the sandgrouse in his Alectoromorphae (galliforms, *Turnix*, sandgrouse) and thought that they connected the galliforms to the pigeons. Huxley (1868) altered his opinion about the sandgrouse and added to the list of their anatomical similarities to the pigeons and galliforms:

In almost all those respects in which the Grouse differ from the Fowls they approach the Pigeons; and an absolute transition between these groups is effected by the *Pteroclidae*, whose popular name of 'Sand-Grouse' might fitly be exchanged for that of 'Pigeon-Grouse.'

1. I find the vertebrae in the cervical, dorsal, lumbar, and sacral regions to have the same number in *Pterocles* and *Syrrhaptes* as in the *Alectoromorphae*; and ankylosis takes place in the same manner. . . .

2. In the skull, the palatines, the maxillo-palatines, and the mandibles resemble the corresponding parts in the *Alectoromorphae*; the pterygoid and the basipterygoid processes, on the other hand, are like those of the *Peristeromorphae* [pigeons].

3. The sternum and furcula, as well as the coracoid . . . are completely Peristeromorphic; and so is the whole forelimb.

4. The pelvis has resemblances both to that of the Grouse and that of the Pigeons, but has some peculiarities of its own.

5. The foot contrasts strongly with that of the Pigeons in its extreme brevity of the tarsometatarsus and toes, and in the reduction of the hallux, but may be regarded as an exaggeration of that of the Grouse. . . .

Thus the *Pteroclidae* are completely intermediate between the *Alectoromorphae* and the *Peristeromorphae*. They cannot be included within either of the groups without destroying its definition, while they are perfectly definable in themselves. Hence, I think, the only adviseable course is to make them into a group by themselves, of equal value with the other two, under the head of *Pteroclomorphae* (p. 302).

Huxley's "only adviseable course" solved nothing but probably helped to fuel the long debate about the relationships of the sandgrouse.

Sundevall (1872, see 1889) placed the "Fam. Pteroclinae" in his "Order Gallinae" with the galliforms, tinamous, seedsnipe, and sheathbills. Sundevall apparently considered the true grouse to be the closest relatives of the sandgrouse, for he placed the Tetraoninae with the Pteroclinae in the "Cohort Tetraonomorphae."

Garrod (1874b) found the skull of *Pterocles* to be like "that of a Pigeon modified by the effects of a Grouse-like life" (p. 254). The shape of the head of the humerus, the sternum, the obturator internus muscle, and characters of the pelvis and the pectoral musculature also suggested to Garrod that the sandgrouse are related to the pigeons. He emphasized that in all these characters, *Pterocles* differs from the galliforms and he placed the Pteroclidae in his "Columbae" with the pigeons.

Elliot (1878:234) stated: "The natural position of the Pteroclidae . . . in the Class Aves, is between the Columbidae . . . on the one hand, and the Tetraonine series of Gallinaceous birds . . . on the other." He found that "in some of their characters they are also pluvialine, and their flight is especially Plover-like." (p. 235). Elliot also made the erroneous claim that the sandgrouse drink by sucking or pumping as do pigeons, thereby starting another prolonged debate.

The Columbae of Sclater (1880b) included the pigeons and sandgrouse and he saw similarities between the sandgrouse and the galliforms, especially the grouse. Reichenow (1882) erected a suborder Deserticolae for the seedsnipe, turnicids, and sandgrouse.

Gadow (1882) studied the pterylosis, osteology, myology, visceral anatomy, and natural history of the sandgrouse. He called attention to Elliot's apparent error concerning their drinking behavior: "The Sand-Grouse differ greatly from the Pigeons in their mode of drinking. It is well known that the latter, during the act of drinking, dip their bills into the water as far as the cleft of the mouth, and then suck the water in without raising their head till they have finished drinking. *Pterocles* and *Syrrhaptes*, on the other hand, drink as Fowls and other birds do, by taking up water mouthful by mouthful and letting it run down the throat" (p. 329). Gadow concluded: "No doubt Sand-Grouse are more nearly allied to the Rasores [galliforms] than the pigeons are. Consequently we must seek for their root between the Rasorial and Columbine branch. . . . Again, the Sand-Grouse are more clearly allied to the pigeons than to the Plovers; thus their branch must be put nearer to the Columbine branch than to that of the Plovers" (p. 331).

Elliot (1885:235) summarized the evidence as he saw it:

The sand-grouse . . . are now elevated to a distinct order, lying between the Alectoromorphae [galliforms] . . . and the Peristeromorphae [pigeons]. . . . They resemble the first of these great groups in their skull, palatines, maxillopalatines, and bill; and the second in their pterygoid and basipterygoid processes, sternum, furcula, coracoid, and fore-limbs. The foot with its short hallux, entirely wanting in *Syrrhaptes*, and the short tarso-metatarsus, are very unlike a pigeon's. The vocal organs are pigeon-like; the trachea is cartilaginous, with a pair of laryngeal muscles at its bifurcation; but the crop, gizzard, gall bladder, and small intestines are those of gallinaceous birds. The caeca coli are voluminous, and have twelve continuous longitudinal folds in their mucous membrane. The pterylosis differs somewhat from that of a pigeon. The lateral neck-spaces reach only to the beginning of the neck; the superior wing-space is absent; the lumbar tracts coalesce with the posterior part of the dorsal tract, and the latter joins the plumage of the tibia. The sand-grouse possess an aftershaft on the contour feathers, thus differing from the pigeons, and, unlike the gallinaceous birds, have a naked oil-gland. In some characters these birds are plover-like, but they drink like a pigeon, thrusting the bill up to the nostril into the water, and retaining it there until the thirst is satisfied.

Goodchild (1886) commented on similarities between plovers and pigeons in the arrangement of their secondary coverts and noted that the sandgrouse differ from the pigeons in this character. In 1891, in apparent opposition to his earlier opinion, he concluded: "I do not see anything whatever in the style of the wing coverts in this group to warrant its being separated far from the true pigeons" (p. 328).

Fürbringer (1888) included the pigeons and sandgrouse in his Intermediate Suborder Columbiformes. He believed that the Columbiformes stand between the Charadriiformes and the Galliformes, and that they are also allied to the parrots.

Seebohm (1888b) was convinced that the sandgrouse are intermediate between pigeons and galliforms. He retained them in a separate order but, later (1890a), included them in his

Columbae. By 1895, Seebohm doubted a sandgrouse-galliform relationship and suggested that the sandgrouse linked the pigeons with the charadriiforms. He viewed the pigeons as "the tree-perching contingent of the Charadriiformes."

Sharpe (1891) included the suborder Pterocletes as one of the six suborders in his order Galliformes.

Shufeldt (1891a,e) considered the sandgrouse to be osteologically intermediate between pigeons and grouse, but noted that "the plovers are not distant in another direction, and *Tinamus* and *Hemipodius* [*Turnix*] have also distant claims to kinship" (p. 508).

In the skulls of the sandgrouse Shufeldt (1901a) found similarities to the pigeons and galliforms and suggested that the sandgrouse be treated as a suborder between the two groups. In 1904 he placed the sandgrouse in the supersuborder Pteroclidiformes between the Galliformes and Columbiformes.

In the introduction to volume 22 of the *Catalogue of Birds*, Ogilvie-Grant (1893) stated his conviction that "The *Pterocletes* or Pigeon-Grouse form a small but well-marked group containing only 3 genera and 17 species, and appear to have been quite satisfactorily placed in a separate order between the *Columbae* or Pigeons and the *Gallinae* or True Game Birds, for they combine many characters found in both of these orders."

Gadow (1892) placed the suborders Pterocles and Columbae in his Columbiformes, but in 1893 he included the Limicolae, Lari, Pterocles, and Columbae in the Charadriiformes. Although Gadow (1893) obviously believed that the closest relatives of the sandgrouse are the pigeons, he also believed that the sandgrouse are related to the shorebirds. He concluded: "The Pteroclidae may be called 'steppe pigeons.' Their ancestors were the generalized shorebirds; their next nearest relatives, but not their direct ancestors, are the pigeons. The links with the gallinaceous birds seem to be based on analogy, or they go so far back that they cannot be regarded as conclusive proof of relationship. It is not possible, however, to derive the Pteroclidae from some extant families of shorebirds. The crop and caeca are developed as in the Thinocoridae. As in many pigeons, the intestinal coiling, the presence of an internal spine on the sternum, and the impervious nares guarantee to the sandgrouse a rank equivalent to that of the Limicolae. In the same way, the caeca and some aspects of the intestinal coiling, the syrinx, and the eggs make them more distant from the Columbae" (p. 209, transl.).

Meade-Waldo (1896, 1897, 1906, 1922) was apparently the first to report the unusual method by which adult sandgrouse transport water to their young by saturating their ventral feathers and flying back to the nest where the youngsters suck the water from the feathers. His observations on captive and wild *Pterocles* of several species were disbelieved and only recently confirmed (see below).

Beddard (1898a:318) took issue with Huxley's interpretation of the anatomical evidence:

The at least 'pseudo-holorhinal' nostrils have their counterpart among the Limicolae, in *Thinocorus*, and in some others. The solid ectethmoids too are also seen in that group, while Garrod's remark that the Alcae have a humerus like that of the Columbae and *Pterocles* is suggestive in the light of the unquestion-able likeness of the Alcae for the Limicolae, though the actual weight of this character may be thought by some to be discounted by the fact that it is met with in the Psittaci.

Moreover *Otis* [bustards], which is to be placed somewhere near the Limicolae, has the gal-linaceous union between the squamosal and the post-frontal process, to which I have referred as possibly affining the Pterocletes to the Galli. Other characters too, which appear at first sight to be arguments in favour of the position taken up by Huxley, may be interpreted fairly as marks of affinity with the Limicolae (and their immediate allies). Such are, for example, the long caeca (with folds in the bustards), the crop (present in *Thinocorus*) [seedsnipe], the gall bladder, &c.

It is at any rate clear that the Pterocletes occupy a lower place than the Columbae—that *they* have given rise to the Columbae, and not *vice versa*. The justice of this view is shown by the long caeca, the existence of an aftershaft, the complete muscle formula of the leg, and by a few other equally unmistakable characters. . . . It seems reasonable to look upon the Pterocletes as not far from the stock which produced the Limicolae, which itself was possibly not far again from the primitive gallinaceous stock.

In the *Hand-List* Sharpe (1899) made the Pteroclidiformes an order placed between the order Hemipodii (*Turnix, Pedionomus*) and the order Columbiformes.

Mitchell (1901a) noted that the intestinal tracts of *Pterocles* and the pigeons are "extremely similar, and there is no indication of any affinity with the conformations exhibited in the other Charadriiformes or Gruiformes" (p. 240).

Chandler (1916:362) concluded that "The Pteroclo-columbae, according to their feather structure, show more similarities to the gallinaceous birds than to any other group. . . . The relation of the Pteroclo-columbae to the Laro-limicolae, if there *is* any close relationship, is not shown at all in the structure of the feathers. The Pterocles show a number of differences from the Columbae . . . which are probably specializations of their own, and do not show closer approximation to any other group."

Bowen (1927) revised the genera of sandgrouse based on the time at which they drink at water holes. He found that some species drink early in the morning and late in the afternoon, while others are crepuscular, and felt that this was a better index to generic limits than other characters.

Waterston (1928) compared the Mallophaga of the sandgrouse with those of pigeons and galliforms: "*Syrrhaptoecus* has not, in my opinion, any close affinities with any of the Philopteridae found on Pigeons . . . though the latter family also, judged by its parasites, is related only to the galline group. Sand-Grouse and Pigeons must stand apart within this complex, and the position of the first-named would appear to be between the Grouse and the Pheasants."

Clay (1950) considered the Mallophaga to be uninformative on the affinities of the sandgrouse. In her opinion, *Neomenopon* has no obvious relationship with other feather lice, and *Syrrhaptoecus* is a member of the widespread Degeeriellinae.

E. Stresemann (1934) placed the sandgrouse and pigeons in separate, but adjacent, orders. On the basis of the skull, pelvis, and musculature he considered the two groups to be allied. He repeated the assertion that sandgrouse drink like pigeons.

Peters (1937) and Wetmore (1930, 1960) placed the sandgrouse as a suborder of the Columbiformes. Mayr and Amadon (1951) placed the Pteroclidae in the order Columbae and noted: "The Columbae may be tentatively placed near the Laro-Limicolae, but certain resemblances between pigeons and game birds may eventually prove to be of significance. It is unlikely that the sand grouse (Pteroclidae) are grouse-like except in superficial adaptions" (p. 9).

Verheyen (1958a) found the sandgrouse to be unlike the pigeons and he placed them in the order Turniciformes with the Mesitornithidae, Turnicidae, Pedionomidae, and Thinocoridae. In 1961 Verheyen broke up his "transitorial" order Turniciformes because "the position-principal includes ideas with reference to relationships" (p. 21). He considered the

Pteroclidae and Thinocoridae to be related by "paramorphogenesis" and included them in separate suborders of his Columbiformes.

Hüe and Etchécopar (1957) discussed the systematics and natural history of the sandgrouse and placed them in the Columbiformes.

Wickler (1961) noted that the sandgrouse, by making repeated sucks and raising the head after each, drink differently from pigeons. However, Meinertzhagen (1964) repeated the claim that sandgrouse drink like pigeons. He also noted: "It has been suggested that water is also carried to young in the abdominal feathers, but this is not so" (p. 712). Goodwin (1965) disagreed with Meinertzhagen and reported his own observations on captive sandgrouse which indicate that they do not drink like pigeons. Goodwin claimed that "there is no reason for anyone to suppose that their drinking methods indicate any close relationship between sandgrouse and pigeons. . . . I have long thought sandgrouse are probably most closely related to the true plovers to which, in spite of the differences involved in their adaptation to living in arid regions and feeding on seeds, they show many similarities, especially of behaviour" (p. 76).

Observations by Cade et al. (1966) on two species of *Pterocles* and several pigeons at African water holes revealed differences in drinking behavior. The sandgrouse drink for 5–10 seconds, then raise the head to swallow, repeating the sequence several times. The pigeons immerse their beaks and drink by pumping. Cade and Greenwald (1966) reported that the mousebirds (*Colius*) also drink by pumping.

Cade and Maclean (1967) observed and filmed adult male sandgrouse transporting water to their young on their ventral feathers. They also described the structure of these specialized feathers which permits them to retain more water than those of other birds. Their observations were confirmed by George (1969, 1970) on other species of *Pterocles*, making a total of at least four species in which water transport has been observed.

Maclean (1967) assembled behavioral and other evidence in support of an alliance between sandgrouse and charadriiforms. He compared the electrophoretic patterns of the egg-white proteins of *Pterocles* with those of several shorebirds and doves. The patterns of the sandgrouse resembled those of the charadriiforms more than those of the columbiforms and Maclean suggested that the sandgrouse be included in the Charadriiformes as a suborder next to the Charadrii.

Stegmann (1968, 1969) disagreed with Maclean and reasserted his belief that the sandgrouse are closely related to pigeons. Citing his papers (1957a,b; 1958; 1959) on the anatomy of sandgrouse and pigeons, Stegmann assembled morphological data on the skull, limbs, and vertebral column to support his position. He regarded the sandgrouse as more advanced in some respects than pigeons and argued that they are secondarily terrestrial. He viewed the "Pteroclo-Columbae" as an ancient group and believed that the Charadriiformes and Galliformes are groups of more recent derivation which have evolved convergent similarities to the sandgrouse.

Maclean (1969a) responded, claiming that Stegmann had ignored all evidence other than morphology. Maclean agreed that the sandgrouse and pigeons are structurally similar in many respects, but he disagreed with Stegmann's assertion that the sandgrouse wing is a modified dove wing: "Since it is not disputed that sandgrouse and doves probably have a charadriiform ancestor and since the sandgrouse wing is essentially charadriiform in shape, I fail to see the necessity to derive it from a dove wing. It is both more logical and much easier to derive the sandgrouse wing directly from a charadriiform wing instead of deriving so similar a structure from the very different dove wing" (p. 105).

Maclean uncovered a more fundamental error in Stegmann's insistence that the sandgrouse are secondarily terrestrial:

On the subject of the precocity of the young, it is my opinion that the redevelopment of so highly precocial a chick from one as highly altricial as that of doves is most unlikely. That the sandgrouse should have redeveloped so many charadriine behaviour patterns associated with ground nesting (egg coloration, clutch size, side-throwing, bobbing, chick type, nest scrape) after having been arboreal, as suggested by Dr. Stegmann, is asking too much of evolutionary processes and goes against the basic tenet that a feature once lost is seldom, if ever, re-acquired.

There is nothing at all in the make-up of any sandgrouse to indicate an arboreal ancestry; on the contrary, the indications are that the doves also had a terrestrial ancestor, since so many of them, however arboreal their nesting habits, still feed on the ground. Those doves that nest on the ground are almost certainly secondarily terrestrial nesters, but they show no trend whatever toward the sandgrouse condition. Most of the ground nesting doves still build nests; if they do not, they make no nest scrape and do not side-throw in the charadriine way. No ground nesting dove shows any tendency toward cryptic egg coloration or toward precocial young (p. 106).

However, the debate was not over; in a review of Maclean's (1969b) paper on the seedsnipe, Olson (1970) expressed his opinion about the sandgrouse: "Even the most perfunctory comparison of the skeletons of pteroclids will disclose that, element for element, they are scarcely distinguishable from columbids and that both differ significantly from any Charadriiform type, including the Thinocoridae. A number of characters linking the doves and sandgrouse have been noted by several early authors. It is inconceivable that this multitude of characters is attributable to convergence."

Von Frisch (1969, 1970) reported on observations of *Pterocles alchata* in southern France. He presented several behavioral similarities to shorebirds, but found little evidence of water transport to the young, possibly because water is relatively abundant in the area. Timmermann (1969) reviewed the evidence from the Mallophaga and concluded that the feather lice do not indicate a close relationship between sandgrouse and either pigeons or shorebirds. He thought he detected a distant alliance between sandgrouse and galliforms, but that any connection between shorebirds and sandgrouse could only have existed before the birds acquired their mallophagan parasites.

Ahlquist (1974a) compared the tryptic peptide map of the ovalbumin of the Pin-tailed Sandgrouse (*Pterocles alchata*) to those of a Wood Pigeon (*Columba palumbus*) and several shorebirds. The sandgrouse ovalbumin has 20 of 29 peptides homologous to those of shorebirds, of which 10–12 are identical in their mapping characteristics. Thirteen of 27 peptides are homologous with 10 identical between the sandgrouse and the pigeon. Although Ahlquist was reluctant to draw conclusions from these data because of the small number of comparisons, they indicate that the sandgrouse are closest to the shorebirds, concordant with the DNA comparisons. Additional ovalbumin tryptic maps were made for other members of our order Ciconiiformes, including *Gavia*, *Puffinus*, *Phaethon*, and *Podiceps*. The maps of these genera, and of the shorebirds and sandgrouse, were more similar to one another than to those of such non-ciconiiform taxa as *Anas*, *Ardeotis*, *Gallus*, and *Rallus*.

Fjeldså (1976) made a cladistic study of the sandgrouse and compared their morphology and behavior with those of charadriiforms and columbiforms. He concluded that the sandgrouse and pigeons evolved from a charadriiform ancestor, that the coursers and pratincoles (Glareolinae) "are their closest known precursors" (p. 235), and that coursers, sandgrouse, and doves "form a 'sister group' to the Charadrii" (p. 229).

The DNA Hybridization Evidence (Figs. 123–124, 337, 356, 363)

The DNA comparisons indicate that the oldest dichotomy in the Charadrii, at $\Delta T_{50}H$ 17.1, was the divergence between the two principal clades, the infraorders Pteroclides and Charadriides (Figs. 356, 363). This is a modification of the arrangement in Sibley and Ahlquist (1985c).

The Columbiformes branched earlier (Δ 20.8; Fig. 353) from the clade that includes the sandgrouse and shorebirds. Thus, the DNA evidence supports the other evidence that the sandgrouse are more closely related to the shorebirds than to the pigeons. The ancient divergences have provided ample time for the evolution of the convergent similarities and large differences that have formed the basis for the long controversy.

Figs. 123 and 124 have been discussed above under the Sandgrouse and Shorebirds. The FITCH tree, Fig. 337, includes *Pterocles* at 10.8 distance units from the root of the Charadriides.

We conclude that the sandgrouse are the sister group of the shorebirds (Charadriides) and that similarities to the pigeons are due to convergence or retained primitive characters.

Diurnal Birds of Prey: Hawks, Eagles, Old World Vultures, Harriers, Kites, Falcons and Caracaras, New World Vultures or Condors

Order CICONIIFORMES
  Suborder Ciconii
    Infraorder Falconides
      Parvorder Accipitrida
        Family Accipitridae
          Subfamily Pandioninae: Osprey
          Subfamily Accipitrinae: Hawks, Eagles, Old World Vultures
        Family Sagittariidae: Secretary-bird
      Parvorder Falconida
        Family Falconidae: Falcons, Caracaras
    Infraorder Ciconiides
      Parvorder Ciconiida
        Superfamily Ciconioidea
        Family Ciconiidae
          Subfamily Cathartinae: New World Vultures or Condors
          Subfamily Ciconiinae: Storks, Openbills, Adjutants, Jabiru

The diurnal birds of prey include raptors and carrion eaters. The raptorial species have talons and hooked bills; the carrion eaters tend to have bare heads and long necks. Specialized forms have modified bills and feet adapted for particular kinds of prey. Classifications have tended to be based on bills and feet, hence the members of this group have been placed together from the earliest times. The Falconides, as defined by the DNA comparisons, includes only the hawks, eagles, kites, harriers, Old World vultures, Osprey, Secretary-bird, falcons, and caracaras. It does not include the New World vultures, which are related to the storks, nor the owls, which are related to the caprimulgiforms. Our infraorder Falconides is equivalent to the traditional order Falconiformes, minus the New World vultures.

Infraorder FALCONIDES: 76/304. The Falconides have a desmognathous palate that approaches schizognathy; pelvic muscle formula A+, except *Sagittarius*, which has BXY+; basipterygoid processes in *Sagittarius*, absent in others; flexor tendons Type 3; two carotids; diastataxic wing; holorhinal, impervious nostrils; oil gland variable, bilobed, tufted except in

Microhierax; caeca small; syrinx tracheo-bronchial; aftershaft; usually 10 primaries, rarely 9; 11–26 secondaries; usually 12 rectrices, 14 in *Neophron*; cervical vertebrae usually 14, 15 in *Pandion* and Falconidae, 17 in *Pseudogyps* and *Gyps*; underdown present; usually a crop; small gizzard; male usually smaller than or same size as female; nidicolous; eggs white, spotted reddish, or unspotted; nestlings have two down plumages.

Parvorder ACCIPITRIDA: 66/241. Palate indirectly desmognathous (maxillo-palatines united only through junction with internasal septum), or schizognathous in *Elanus*; vomer without oval swelling and not touching the maxillo-palatines; palatal surface of maxilla without median ridge; no mandibular fossa; small procoracoid process not reaching furcula (furcula ankylosed to crista sterni in *Sagittarius*); no spina interna on sternum; syrinx with minute external tympaniform membrane and intrinsic muscles inserted on one of first three bronchial rings; eggs white or blotched brown, tinted green internally.

Parvorder FALCONIDA: 10/63. Palate directly desmognathous (maxillo-palatine processes united directly); vomer ends anteriorly in an oval swelling touching the maxillo-palatine processes; palatal surface of maxilla with longitudinal ridge; procoracoid process large and articulating with furcula; mandibular process present; spina externa and interna present; syrinx with large external tympaniform membrane on which the intrinsic muscles insert; eggs blotched and spotted reddish brown, not green internally.

Morphological characters and the DNA comparisons have shown that the New World vultures, or condors, are the sister group of the storks, and we have assigned the condors to the subfamily Cathartinae of the Ciconiidae, order Ciconiiformes. They are discussed under that heading. Because the Cathartinae usually have been included in the Falconiformes, their characters (based mainly on Friedmann 1950:3–9) and their taxonomic history are presented here.

Family CICONIIDAE, Subfamily CATHARTINAE: 5/7. Vulturine storks or condors, resembling the true vultures of the Old World but differing from these, as well as from all other falconiforms (our Falconides), as follows:

Nares holorhinal, pervious, elongated longitudinally; maxillo-palatines widely separated but bridged by a process from each meeting and co-ossifying with the median portion of the nasal septum; hallux relatively small, elevated, nonfunctional, connected with the flexor perforans digitorum (the latter also connected with the second and third digits), the flexor longis hallucis leading to the third and fourth digits, sometimes to the second, third, and fourth digits but never to the hallux; a distinct web or membrane between the basal phalanges of the second and third (inner and middle) toes; no intrinsic syringeal muscles; ambiens, semitendinosus, and accessory semitendinosus muscles present; oil gland nude; pelvic muscle formula AXY+ or XY+.

Palate indirectly desmognathous, the maxillo-palatines widely separated (but bridged as described above) and having the form of scroll-like plates; anterior palatine vacuity large; basipterygoid processes present, articulating with middle of pterygoids; large olfactory chamber; no trace of internasal septum; lachrymals fused with frontals, and without free posterior longitudinal spurs; no vomer; metasternum with two pairs of notches, the outer pair sometimes closed to form fenestrae; keel of sternum very deep; spina interna and externa absent; deep plantar tendons of Type V; index digit of wing with an external claw; tendons of patagium ciconiine; pectoralis primus (major) muscle divided into two parts; two carotids; gall bladder;

well-developed crop; tongue large and fleshy, with denticulations along its upturned lateral margins; stomach not a gizzard; diastataxic wing; contour feathers without aftershafts; eggs 1 or 2, deposited on bare earth, rock, or wood, usually in cavities; eggshells with yellow or greenish-yellow translucence.

D. W. Johnston (1988:210) described the oil gland as "Indistinctly bilobed, round papilla, naked, two separate, distinct orifices . . . differ markedly from the heavily tufted glands of the Ciconiidae, to which cathartids might otherwise be related (Ligon 1967)." This seems to assume that the oil gland has important systematic properties.

Historical Review of the Classification

The New World vultures usually have been included in the traditional order Falconiformes with the Old World vultures, hawks, eagles, etc., and their taxonomic histories are intertwined. Both groups will be reviewed in this section.

Linnaeus (1758) made the Accipitres his first order of birds; it included the genera *Vultur*, *Falco*, *Strix*, and *Lanius*, and contained the hawks, eagles, kites, vultures, falcons, owls, shrikes, tyrant flycatchers, cotingas, bulbuls, and waxwings.

The obvious nonraptors were soon excluded, leaving only the owls, hawks, and vultures in the "Raptatores" of Illiger (1811) and the "Rapaces" of Merrem (1813) and Temminck (1820).

The convergent similarities between owls and falconiforms caused them to be placed together in many later classifications, and this treatment was recently revived by Cracraft (1981).

Nitzsch (1840) made the raptors one of his eight divisions, the "Raubvögel," or Accipitrinae, which contained the diurnal raptors, Old World vultures, New World vultures, and owls. Nitzsch discovered that the four groups differed in their pteryloses. Gray (1844–49) placed the birds of prey in a single group at the beginning of his sequence.

The Aetomorphae of Huxley (1867) included all the raptors, although he conceded that they varied widely in many ways. He recognized four groups: Strigidae (owls), Cathartidae (New World vultures), Gypaetidae (hawks, eagles, falcons, Old World vultures), and Gypogeranidae (Secretary-bird). He placed the Aetomorphae between the pelecaniforms and parrots.

Sundevall (1872, see 1889) classified the raptors as follows:

AGMEN II.
  Ptilopaedes. With the young covered with thick down before the development of feathers.
    Order Accipitres (based on raptorial bill and feet)
      Cohort Nyctharpages: Owls. 4 families
      Cohort Hemeroharpages: Hawks, Falcons, Kites, Osprey. 8 families
      Cohort Saproharpages: Old World Vultures. 2 families
      Cohort Necroharpages: New World Vultures, Caracaras, Seriemas. 2 families

Sharpe (1874) divided his Accipitres into two suborders, Falcones and Pandiones, the latter for the Osprey. In the Falcones he recognized the Vulturidae for all the vultures, and the Falconidae for the falcons. He included *Sagittarius* and *Cariama*, as well as the caracaras, in the subfamily Polyborinae of the Falconidae.

The Falconidae, Cathartidae, and Sagittariidae were "impossible to unite in any intimate way," according to Garrod (1873d, 1874a). He thought the Cathartidae belong between the Pelargi (storks) and Herodiones (herons), thus he expressed the evidence of the relationship between the New World vultures and the storks. In his classification the order Ciconiiformes was arranged as follows:

Order Ciconiiformes
  Cohort Pelargi: Storks
  Cohort Cathartidae: New World vultures
  Cohort Herodiones: Herons, etc.
  Cohort Steganopodes: Totipalmate swimmers (pelecaniforms)
  Cohort Accipitres
    Family Falconidae: Hawks, Falcons, etc.
    Family Strigidae: Owls

Garrod placed *Sagittarius* and *Cariama* with the bustards and the flamingos in the Otididae of his order Galliformes!

Ridgway (1875) divided the Falconidae into two subfamilies with subgroups, as follows: Falconinae (Falcones, Polybori, Micrastures, Herpetotheres, Pandiones), and Buteoninae (Pernes, Buteones).

Sclater (1880b) placed his Striges and Accipitres in adjacent orders and divided the latter into the Falconidae, Cathartidae, and Serpentariidae. Reichenow's (1882) order Raptatores included the Vulturidae (all vultures), Falconidae, and Strigidae. Barrows (1885) used a similar arrangement; his Accipitres included the Gypogeranidae (Secretary-bird), Cathartidae, Falconidae (including Old World vultures and Osprey), and the Strigidae.

Goodchild (1886, 1891) found a similar arrangement of the secondary coverts, the "accipitrine style," in the parrots, owls, falconiforms (except *Pernis*, *Pandion*, *Sagittarius*), waterfowl, herons, and cormorants. In this character the New World vultures are most like the Marabou Stork, pelicans, frigatebirds, boobies, anhingas, and procellariids. This character is clearly useless for determining the relationships of these groups.

Fürbringer (1888) included the Gypogeranidae (*Sagittarius*), Cathartidae, and Gypo-Falconidae in his "Gens Accipitres." He placed the Accipitres between the ciconiiforms and pelecaniforms in his suborder Ciconiiformes. According to Gadow (1888a:179): "Fuerbringer holds that the Cathartidae are a very old and now declining Raptorial family, and that they have many structural points in common with the Ciconiidae, whilst the Gypo-falconidae exhibit genetic relations with the Steganopodes (Fregata) and with the Ardeidae. Gypogeranus had formerly (Miocene of France) a much wider distribution than now, and it is the last remnant of a group which branched off from the common Accipitrine Stork [Stock?] before the division into Cathartidae and Gypofalconidae took place."

Sharpe (1891) placed the Cathartidiformes between the Pelecaniformes and Accipitriformes, and included the Striges in the latter. The storks were distant from the cathartines.

Gadow (1892) divided his Falconiformes into the Cathartae and Accipitres following the Pelargi of the Ciconiiformes. In 1893 he inserted the Anseriformes between the Ciconiiformes and the Falconiformes, but separated the New World vultures (Cathartae) from the Old World vultures and other diurnal raptors (Accipitres).

Shufeldt (1883b) studied the skeletons of the cathartines and (1889a) of the Northern Harrier (*Circus cyaneus*). From skeletal characters he separated the American kites as the Elanidae (1891b). In his classification (1904b) he divided his "supersuborder Accipitriformes" into the Falconoidea (including five families of diurnal raptors) and the Cathartoidea, containing the cathartines. In 1909 he suggested that alliances between the raptors and some or all of the pelecaniforms, ciconiiforms, parrots, and *Cariama* were possible. He described the osteology of the Great Philippine Eagle (*Pithecophaga jefferyi*), concluding that it is most closely related to the South American Harpy Eagle (*Harpia harpyja*). Later (1922) he examined the skeleton of the Wedge-tailed Eagle (*Aquila audax*) of Australia.

Seebohm (1890a) established a subclass Falconiformes for the orders Raptores and Psittaci. The Raptores was divided into the suborders Serpentarii, Accipitres, and Striges. On the basis of the deep plantar tendon arrangement he placed the Cathartidae in his subclass Coraciiformes which also contained the goatsuckers, colies, swifts, and the typical coraciiform groups. He noted that in this cluster, the hallux is always present and receives its tendon from the flexor perforans digitorum, not from the flexor hallucis longus. This is another example of the nonsense that emerges from dependence on a single character. In 1895 Seebohm expressed less confidence in his allocation of the cathartines, but kept them as a separate order in his subclass Falconiformes, which also included the parrots, hawks, and owls.

Beddard (1898a) included the Cathartidae in his Accipitres and discussed their characters in comparison with those of the other members of the group. He identified eight characters in which the New World vultures differ from some or all of the falconiforms, namely, aftershaft, oil gland, pelvic muscle formula, accessory semimembranosus, caeca, syrinx, basioccipital processes, and type of desmognathous palate. He commented:

It is clear from the few characters—the principal ones, however . . . that the Cathartidae are more aberrant (considering the Falconidae to be the typical birds of prey) than are the Serpentariidae; for the Cathartidae diverge in all eight characters from the Falconidae, while the secretary vulture only diverges in three. What reason is there, it might be asked, to retain the American vultures within this order at all, particularly if the owls are to be—as I think they should—excluded? The only group which has the distinctive characters of the Cathartidae (besides, of course, the present group) is that of the Herodiones. There only do we find birds with ambiens and expansor secundariorum, without biceps slip, holorhinal, and with rudimentary or absent caeca. The Steganopodes also are not far off. It really comes to the beak and claws, the ceroma, and to the presence of various structures (e.g. the peculiar palate, the basipterygoid processes) which forbid their association with the Herodiones. The several groups are not far off, but on the whole the American vultures are more like the remaining birds of prey than like the stork tribe (p. 485).

Thus, after attempting to interpret several characters of uncertain significance, Beddard sought the safety of tradition; the beak-foot classification was still in vogue at the turn of the century, and parts of it persist to the present day.

Sushkin (1899a, 1900a,b, 1905) studied the skeletons of the raptors and recognized the Aquilidae and Falconidae in the suborder Accipitres. He excluded *Sagittarius* and *Pandion* from the Accipitres, but found similarities between the Accipitres and the kites (*Pernis, Aviceda, Elanoides, Leptodon*).

Pycraft (1902) also examined falconiform osteology and divided the order into the suborders Serpentarii, Cathartae, and Accipitres, the latter containing the Falconidae and Buteonidae. He believed that the cathartines are the most primitive members of the order and that the falconiforms share more characters with the gruiforms than with the ciconiiforms. He commented: "On osteological grounds . . . it is doubtful whether the Striges would ever have been separated from the Accipitres" (p. 314), but on the basis of the soft anatomy he thought they belong among the "picarian" birds.

In the patterns of intestinal coiling Mitchell (1901a) saw few similarities between cathartines and ciconiiforms, and nothing to suggest an alliance between *Sagittarius* and *Cariama*. Beddard (1911) noted that the falconiforms and owls share several characteristics of the alimentary tract not found in other birds. Convergence between these carnivorous groups is highly probable.

Reichenow (1913–14) was convinced of a hawk-owl relationship and placed them as suborders in his order Raptatores. Chandler (1916), however, found little in feather structure to support an owl-hawk alliance. He thought that the cathartines show an "astonishing likeness" to *Anhinga* in the nature of the distal barbules of the inner vane, and that the feather structure of *Sagittarius* is more like that of the Accipitridae than that of the New World vultures. Chandler concluded that the falconiforms were most likely derived from pelecaniform ancestors.

In 1924 Swann began the publication of a monograph on the birds of prey. After Swann's death in 1926, Wetmore assumed responsibility for the remaining parts, the last of which was published in 1945. In his order Accipitres Swann recognized the families Cathartidae, Aegypiidae (Old World vultures), Sagittariidae, and Falconidae. He placed *Pandion* in a subfamily next to the falcons.

The Accipitres of Stresemann (1934) contained the Cathartidae, Sagittariidae, and Falconidae. He placed *Pandion* in the Aquilinae of the Falconidae.

Wetmore (1930) divided his Falconiformes into the suborders Cathartae (Cathartidae) and Falcones (Sagittariidae, Accipitridae, Falconidae). In the 1960 version of his classification, Wetmore divided the Falcones into the Sagittarioidea (Sagittariidae) and the Falconoidea (Accipitridae, Pandionidae, Falconidae). Peters (1931) followed the same arrangement, but included *Pandion* in the Accipitridae.

Compton (1938) defined three patterns of pterylosis in the Falconiformes; accipitrid, falconid, and cathartid. In its pterylosis and flexor tendon arrangement, *Pandion* resembles the cathartines and Compton concluded that the Pandionidae should be placed in the suborder Cathartae. He also thought that *Sagittarius* is more closely related to the accipitrids than to the other falconiforms.

Miller and Fisher (1938) described the pterylosis of the California Condor (*Gymnogyps californianus*), and Fisher (1939, 1942, 1943, 1944, 1946, 1947) studied the pterylosis, osteology, and myology of the New World vultures. Fisher thought that *Coragyps* and *Cathartes* are more closely related to one another than either is to *Sarcorhamphus*, *Gymnogyps*, and *Vultur*. He found (1946) that the complete pelvic muscle formula for *Cathartes* and *Coragyps* is ACDXY+V, and CDXY+V for the other three genera.

Hudson (1948) compared the pelvic musculatures of *Cathartes*, *Coragyps*, *Sagittarius*, *Pandion*, four genera of accipitrids (*Accipiter*, *Buteo*, *Aquila*, *Circus*) and three falcons (*Falco*). He confirmed the formulas for the cathartines reported by Fisher (1946) and noted that they differ from that of *Sagittarius*, which is BDXY+V, and from that of the other falconiforms: AD+. Hudson also discovered many other points in which the Cathartinae and *Sagittarius* differ from one another and from other falconiforms. He wrote (1948:127): "It appears quite possible that the American vultures, secretary bird and the hawk and falcon tribe represent three entirely different lines of avian evolution and are no more closely related to each other than to the owls. . . . If these three lines were derived from a common source subsequent adaptive radiation has greatly obscured the original similarity of muscle pattern in the pelvic limb. I strongly suspect that the 'hawkish' appearance of *Sagittarius* has been developed through convergent evolution."

Hudson considered *Pandion* to be a "somewhat aberrant offshoot" of the hawk-falcon group and placed it in a separate suborder of the Falconiformes.

Berlioz (1950) implied a falconiform-strigiform relationship by placing the two orders next to one another. Howard (1950) found that the cathartines, secretary-birds, and typical hawks could be distinguished in Eocene fossils and noted that a cathartine vulture (*Plesiocathartes*) had been identified in the Eocene of France. Friedmann (1950) described the cathartines and commented: "The removal of the American vultures from very close association with the true so-called birds of prey (suborder Falcones) has been justified by the investigations of the best anatomists and systematists. . . . It is sufficient to say that the external resemblance between them and the Old World, or true, vultures . . . is merely a superficial one. . . . The exact relationships of the Cathartae are, however, somewhat complex. It has been fairly clearly demonstrated that they are not very distantly related to the Ciconiiformes, Pelecaniformes, and Procellariiformes. One authority has even placed them in the Coraciiformes . . . on account of the similarity in the arrangement of the plantar tendons . . . as in the . . . [hornbills, kingfishers, and rollers] being thus very different from that seen in the Falcones" (p. 5).

Mayr and Amadon (1951) were skeptical about the allocation of *Plesiocathartes*. They noted that

The American vultures are very distinct and may not be related to the other Falcones. Perhaps they are representatives of some ancient American radiation which may even include some or all of such families as the Anhimidae, Cracidae, and Tinamidae (McDowell, verbal communication). The occurrence of a cathartid, *Plesiocathartes*, in the upper Eocene of France requires confirmation, in the opinion of Dr. A. Wetmore who has examined the specimens (verbal communication).

The African secretary bird, *Sagittarius*, resembles the gruiform Cariamidae of South America. Some would transfer the Sagittariidae to the Grues, others the Cariamidae to the Accipitres. Actually, the resemblance may be parallelism. Still, *Sagittarius* may not belong to the Accipitres.

Certain similarities in the pterylography and in the plantar tendons of the Pandionidae and Cathartidae (Compton, 1938) are apparently of no phylogenetic significance (Hudson, 1948) (p. 6).

If the Mallophaga are to be believed, the traditional order Falconiformes is monophyletic. Clay (1950, 1951, 1957) reported that the distinctive and specialized mallophagan genus *Falcolipeurus* is found only on *Sagittarius*, cathartines, and the larger accipitrids. *Laemobothrion* is found on several groups of birds including falconiforms, and *Cuculiphilus* parasitizes *Gyps*, *Pseudogyps*, and the cathartines, as well as the cuckoos. *Kurodia* is found only on falconiforms and owls. Von Boetticher and Eichler (1954) supported Clay and believed that all falconiforms, except the New World vultures and *Sagittarius*, should be placed in the Falconidae.

Barnikol (1951, 1953, 1954), Starck and Barnikol (1954), and Starck (1959) found that the jaw muscles innervated by the trigeminus nerve are similar in falcons and owls and differ in other diurnal birds of prey. For example, *Falco tinnunculus* and *Strix aluco* have almost identical muscle proportions although they differ in external appearance and various measurements of the skull, brain, and eyes. These authors were cautious and did not ascribe excessive importance to their findings. Jollie (1953) agreed with Barnikol and Starck and placed the falcons in a separate order next to a combined caprimulgiform-strigiform group. Jollie thought that the New World vultures are best considered as a suborder in a procellariiform-pelecaniform assemblage, and that *Sagittarius* is most closely related to *Cariama*. Voipio (1955) accepted these proposals and declared the Falconiformes to be polyphyletic.

The Pearl Kite (*Gampsonyx swainsonii*) resembles a small falcon and had been placed in the Falconidae by Peters (1931) and Hellmayr and Conover (1949). Plotnick (1956) examined the bill, nostrils, and scutellation of the tarsus and toes and concluded that *Gampsonyx* is not a falcon, but is related to the kites (e.g., *Elanus*).

Clay (1958) found that *Gampsonyx*, unlike any falcon, is parasitized by a species of the mallophagan *Degeeriella*, of the same species-group found on *Elanus*. V. Stresemann (1959) found that *Gampsonyx* molts its primaries in the descending manner from the first to the tenth as do members of the Accipitridae. She agreed that its nearest relatives are the kites. Finally, Brodkorb (1960) pointed out that the skeleton of *Gampsonyx* is like that of accipitrids, not falconids, and thus corroborated the earlier opinions of Sushkin (1905) and Friedmann (1950), who, also on the basis of osteology, had placed *Gampsonyx* near the kites.

The molt patterns of the Falconiformes have been studied by Mebs (1960), Piechocki (1955, 1956, 1963a,b), Sutter (1956), V. Stresemann (1958, 1959), V. Stresemann and Stresemann (1960), and E. Stresemann and Stresemann (1966a). In falcons the primary molt begins with primary 4 and proceeds in both directions; the secondaries are molted from two foci. The outer focus is usually at secondary 5, from which the molt wave proceeds in both directions. Another molt wave begins with the innermost secondary and proceeds outward. In falcons the tail molt is centrifugal (i.e., inner to outer rectrices) except that the outermost (6th) rectrix is usually lost before 1 or 2. In *Falco peregrinus* the sequence is 1–2–6–3–4–5. The tail molt in *Falco vespertinus* seems to be irregular.

In the Accipitridae the primary molt begins with 1 and moves outward to 10. This pattern has been found in *Circus*, *Gypohierax*, *Geranospiza*, *Accipiter*, *Kaupifalco*, *Butaster*, and in the kites and the Honey Buzzard (*Pernis*). There are usually three secondary molt foci in the Accipitridae. In *Circus macrourus*, for example, the molt waves begin from secondaries 1, 5, and 8 or 9. The Stresemanns (1966a:334) reported that the tail molt of accipitrids is irregular with a tendency toward a transilient mode, for example, rectrices 1-6-4-2-3-5 or 6-1-4-5-3-2.

Verheyen (1957c) excluded *Sagittarius* from the Falconiformes and placed it and the Cariamidae in his order "Cariamiformes." He retained this arrangement in his classification of the remaining falconiforms (1959b), but later (1961) restored *Sagittarius* to the Falconiformes. Verheyen concluded that the diurnal birds of prey are allied on one hand with the cuckoos and on the other with a pigeon-parrot group. His classification (1961) follows:

Order Falconiformes
    Suborder Sagittarii: Sagittariidae; Secretary-bird
    Suborder Cathartes: Cathartidae; New World Vultures

Suborder Falcones: Polyboridae, Falconidae; Caracaras, Falcons
Suborder Pandiones: Pandionidae; Osprey
Suborder Accipitres: Buteonidae, Aegypiidae, Elanidae, Pernidae; Hawks, Old World Vultures,
Kites, Honey-Buzzards

The electrophoretic patterns of the egg-white proteins of *Coragyps* and *Cathartes* are much like that of the Wood Stork (*Mycteria americana*), but also similar to those of the falconiforms (Sibley 1960). There is nothing in these patterns on which to base an opinion about the relationships of these groups.

May (1962) compared the cranial structure of the embryonic Tawny Owl (*Strix aluco*) with that of the Eurasian Kestrel (*Falco tinnunculus*). There were similarities, but other species were not examined so the results are meaningless for present purposes.

Peakall (1963) compared the amino acid compositions of the ovalbumins of several birds. Three species of accipitrids were compared with *Cathartes* and *Coragyps*; the differences supported the conclusion that the New World vultures are not closely related to the typical falconiforms.

Ligon (1967:1) introduced his study of the relationships of the New World vultures, as follows: "The phylogenetic affinities of the New World vultures, Family Cathartidae, have been questioned for many years. Upon examination of many anatomical and other characters of this and other groups, I have concluded that the Cathartidae are not at all closely related to the remainder of the Falconiformes, that they share a great many features with the storks, Ciconiidae, and that the storks and herons are dissimilar. None of these conclusions is original (Garrod, 1873; Friedmann, 1950:5; Jollie, 1953; Cottam, 1957:54)."

Ligon (1967) re-examined various characters of the New World vultures and added new data from his own study. He compared characters of the skull, sternum, pelvic girdle, furculum, coracoid, cervical vertebrae, humerus, carpometacarpus, femur, tibiotarsus, tarsometatarsus; pectoral, wing, and thigh muscles; nestling plumages; syrinx; pterylosis; deep plantar tendons; external morphology; and several other characters of less importance. In his discussion Ligon commented:

The groups here considered may represent some of the more striking examples of convergence to be found in the class Aves. The two orders involved [Falconiformes, Ciconiiformes] are quite likely polyphyletic, each perhaps being composed of three or four groups. . . .

The major pieces of osteological evidence indicating a relationship between storks and [New World] vultures include characters of the skull, humerus, carpometacarpus, femur, tibiotarsus, and tarsometatarsus. The primary non-bone characters further indicating this relationship are: tendons of the patagium, thigh muscle formulae, nestling plumage, poor development or absence of a syrinx, and absence of intrinsic syringeal muscles. The extreme anatomical dissimilarities of herons and storks, and of vultures and accipitrids force one to conclude either that anatomy does not reflect phylogeny or that these members of the orders Ciconiiformes and Falconiformes are not at all closely related. Most of these differences have been known for many years, but their significance has not been faced and the problem has been resolved by placing these convergent but basically very different groups in different suborders within the same order. Both the statements of Beddard (1898) and Jollie (1953) . . . demonstrate the overriding effect that external and superficial appearances have had on higher bird classification. Cottam's (1957) proposal that *Balaeniceps* is allied to the pelecaniforms rather than to the Ciconiiformes is an example of a recent attempt to rectify this situation" (p. 22).

Ligon concluded that "the following taxonomic arrangement more accurately expresses the relationships of the groups here considered than those in general use today" (p. 23).

Order Ardeiformes
  Suborder Ardeae
    Family Ardeidae
Order Ciconiiformes
  Suborder Ciconiae
    Family Ciconiidae
  Suborder Sarcoramphi
    Family Vulturidae (New World vultures)
Order Accipitriformes
  Suborder Accipitres
    Family Accipitridae

Ligon summarized his conclusions, including the following: "The many and often striking anatomical similarities of the New World vultures and storks, coupled with other lines of evidence, indicate that they are more recently derived from a common ancestor than are vultures and accipitrids, or storks and herons. Extreme cases of convergence are indicated by the superficial similarity, especially in proportions, of the herons and storks, and of Old and New World vultures. . . . anatomical investigations do not support these apparent similarities."

The DNA comparisons support Ligon's conclusions.

Histological studies of the egg shells (Tyler 1966) have revealed few differences among the falconiforms, except that some species have shells with vacuoles or spaces in the outer layers. Shell vacuoles are present in *Accipiter, Buteo, Aquila, Pernis, Milvus, Haliaeetus, Gyps, Sarcogyps,* and *Pandion,* but absent in the Cathartinae, Falconidae, and *Sagittarius,* and possibly lacking in *Gypaetus barbatus* and *Neophron percnopterus.* The shells with vacuoles have an unetched outer layer with spaces between and within the crystals. The Falconidae differ from the Accipitridae in the ratio between total nitrogen and soluble nitrogen of the shell, but *Pernis* and *Pandion* are intermediate. Otherwise *Pandion* is like the accipitrids.

Brown and Amadon (1968) noted that "the falcons (or at least . . . *Falco*) differ from Accipitridae and agree with Strigidae, owls, in the following ways: absence of nest building instinct (in all but caracaras); killing of prey by biting and severing neck vertebrae, holding of food in one claw, hissing by young to show fear or threat and some movements of curiosity, e.g., head bobbing" (p. 24).

Brown and Amadon suggested many possible relationships within the order and used the following classification, with comments. Genera in parentheses were thought to be most closely related:

Order Falconiformes
  Suborder Cathartae
    Family Cathartidae, New World Vultures. 5 genera. Relationships to other groups unclear.
  Suborder Accipitres
    Family Pandionidae, Osprey. Possible affinity to kites
    Family Accipitridae
     Kites: (*Aviceda, Leptodon, Chondrohierax, Pernis, Henicopternis, Elanoides,*

Machaerhamphus); (*Gampsonyx, Elanus, Chelictinia*); (*Rostrhamus, Harpagus, Ictinia, Lophoictinia, Hamirostra, Milvus, Haliastur*).

Fish eagles: *Haliaeetus, Ichthyophaga*; (possible alliance to kites).

Old World vultures: *Gypohierax, Neophron, Gypaetus, Necrosyrtes, Gyps, Torgos, Sarcogyps, Aegypius, Trigonoceps*; (possible alliance to fish eagles).

Snake eagles: *Circaetus, Terathopius, Spilornis, Dryotriorchis, Eutriorchis*; (may have evolved from kites).

Harrier hawks, crane hawks, harriers: *Polyboroides, Geranospiza, Circus*; (linked to snake eagles via *Polyboroides*).

Sparrow hawks and goshawks: *Melierax, Megatriorchis, Erythrotriorchis, Accipiter, Urotriorchis*; (may be allied to harriers and to *Buteo*).

Sub-buteonines: *Butaster, Kaupifalco, Leucopternis, Buteogallus, Harpyhaliaetus, Heterospizias, Busarellus, Geranoaetus, Parabuteo*.

Buteos: *Buteo*.

Harpy eagles: *Morphnus, Harpia, Harpyopsis, Pithecophaga*.

Booted eagles: *Ictinaetus, Aquila, Hieraaetus, Spizaetus, Stephanoetus, Oroaetus, Polemaetus*.

Family Sagittariidae

Sagittarius; (possibly related to the eagles).

Suborder Falcones

Family Falconidae

Aberrant Neotropical genera: (*Milvago, Phalcobaenus, Polyborus, Daptrius*); *Herpetotheres*; *Micrastur*; (may be allied to typical falcons).

Falconets and falcons: *Spiziapteryx, Polihierax, Microhierax, Falco*.

Jollie (1976, 1977a–c) reviewed previous morphological studies and presented his comparisons of osteology, myology, and ptilosis with additional data from other organ systems and external anatomy. The following points summarize his conclusions (1977a:124–128):

1. The types included in the traditional order Falconiformes "are so dissimilar that their inclusion in a single order is undesirable."

2. The cathartid type "is the most distinct of the falconiforms. Its uniqueness . . . reflects a different heritage . . . which appears to be shared . . . with the procellariiforms, pelecaniforms, ciconiiforms, and charadriiforms. . . . it should be considered an independent order. . . . The suggestion by Ligon (1967) that the cathartids are a suborder of the ciconiiforms is rejected."

3. The sagittariid type shows "little agreement" with the cathartid type. It is "likely that they are separate evolutionary lines which have retained some features in common with other, equally distinct and separate lines such as the procellariiforms, ciconiiforms, pelecaniforms, stercorariids, and possibly gulls."

Sagittarius may or may not be related to the accipitrids and the differences suggest "that divergence occurred at such an early stage, that ordinal separation better expresses what must otherwise be anatomically meaningless."

4. The accipitrid type may have come "from a cursorial, vulturine type which was contemporaneous with a second type that eventually gave rise to the cathartiform, procellariiform, pelecaniform, ciconiiform, sagittariiform, spheneisciform, and charadriiform arrays. This ancestral type dates back at least to the Cretaceous."

5. The falconid type is not related to the accipitrid type. Osteological similarities, especially in the pectoral girdle, indicate a common origin for falconids and the "owls, parrots, cuckoos, and plantain eaters."

In his "Summary and Conclusions" Jollie stated: "The order Falconiformes . . . [was] examined . . . in terms of its [morphological] features. Comparisons are examined in terms of . . . similarities or lack of similarity. The evolutionary trends . . . are considered along with the idea of each species being a mosaic of features. The conclusion . . . [is] that the falconiforms is an artificial aggregation of species of four orders: Sagittariiformes, Cathartiformes, Accipitriformes, and Falconiformes. These orders are separated by morphological gaps as large as, or larger than, those separating many other orders. Whereas some of the present orders of birds can confidently be associated into even larger categories, the Accipitriformes stand alone as the earliest cursorial, scavenger-predatory line of birds. The Sagittariiformes and Cathartiformes appear to be natural parts of a vast array of birds of aquatic or shore habitats whereas the Falconiformes (*sensu stricto*) belong with an arboreal array."

Amadon (1977) discussed the taxonomy of the vultures and recommended that the Cathartae be maintained as a suborder of the Falconiformes, although whether the "cathartid vultures . . . belong in the order Falconiformes is uncertain." He noted that Brodkorb's use of Vulturidae instead of Cathartidae for the New World vultures is not required by the Rules of Nomenclature.

E. Stresemann and Amadon (1979) reviewed the falconiforms and provided the information for the first volume of the second edition of the *Check-list of Birds of the World*. Stresemann had died in 1972 and Amadon revised an earlier version of the manuscript by Stresemann. In a foreword, Amadon noted that "The suborder Cathartae may not belong in the Falconiformes, but again it may, and it is best left there. The suborder Sagittarii, too, may not belong in this order. If it does, it is presumably allied to the Accipitres, not the Falcones" (p. 272). Their classification follows:

Order Falconiformes
  Suborder Cathartae
    Family Cathartidae: New World Vultures
  Suborder Accipitres
    Family Accipitridae
      Subfamily Pandioninae: Ospreys
      Subfamily Accipitrinae: Hawks and Eagles
  Suborder Sagittarii
    Family Sagittariidae: Secretary-birds
  Suborder Falcones
    Family Falconidae
      Subfamily Polyborinae: Caracaras
      Subfamily Falconinae: Falcons

König (1982) reviewed the evidence pertaining to the relationships of the New World vultures and compared them with other avian groups, especially the storks and Old World vultures. His English summary stated that "The taxonomic status of the Cathartidae is uncertain. Comparative studies concerning anatomy, morphology and ethology stressed the hypothesis, that the New World vultures have to be considered as convergent developments to the Old

World vultures, who are not related to them. Systematically the Cathartidae should be classified as Ciconiiformes and not as Falconiformes."

The A.O.U. checklist committee (1983) "with a few exceptions" followed the traditional arrangement of Stresemann and Amadon (above), and noted: "That the diurnal birds of prey form a natural group has been questioned. The Cathartidae share several characters with the Ciconiidae (Ligon, 1967 . . .). Other authors consider the Accipitridae and Falconidae to be convergent" (p. 98). The A.O.U checklist classification of 1983 follows:

Order Falconiformes: Diurnal Birds of Prey
  Suborder Cathartae: American Vultures
    Superfamily Cathartoidea: American Vultures
      Family Cathartidae: American Vultures
  Suborder Accipitres: Secretarybirds, Kites, Eagles, Hawks and Allies
    Superfamily Accipitroidea: Kites, Eagles, Hawks and Allies
      Family Accipitridae: Kites, Eagles, Hawks and Allies
        Subfamily Pandioninae: Ospreys
        Subfamily Accipitrinae: Kites, Eagles, Hawks and Allies
  Suborder Falcones: Caracaras and Falcons
    Family Falconidae: Caracaras and Falcons
      Tribe Polyborini: Caracaras
      Tribe Herpetotherini: Laughing Falcons
      Tribe Micrasturini: Forest-Falcons
      Tribe Falconini: True Falcons

Cracraft (1981) proposed a "phylogenetic" classification of birds in which "Division 3" was composed of the "Orders Ciconiiformes, Falconiformes." He noted: "The placement of such disparate orders in the same Division may seem unwarranted, and, admittedly, there is no clear evidence for this. . . . Their placement in Division 3 is tentative and boldly hypothetical."

Cracraft included the owls with the falconiforms because "it is apparent that many 19th century avian morphologists and systematists were correct in assigning strigids to this order; the similarities between some falconiforms and owls are interpretable not as convergences but as shared derived characters." He placed the owls in the infraorder "Falconi, because they possess a derived tarsometatarsus and pelvic morphology shared with pandionids and accipitrids (including falcons); the Falconi (including owls) also have a unique pelvic myological pattern in that they have lost the piriformis pars iliofemoralis, the flexor cruris lateralis (semitendinosus) and accessory semitendinosus, and the vinculum connecting the flexors of digit III."

Cracraft dismissed the caprimulgiforms as owl relatives because their "morphological organization" is "clearly similar to apodiforms and not strigids." Cracraft's Falconiformes follows:

Order Falconiformes
  Suborder Cathartae
      Family Cathartidae
  Suborder Accipitres
    Infraorder Sagittarii
      Family Sagittariidae

Infraorder Falconi
    Superfamily Strigoidea
        Family Strigidae (including *Tyto*)
    Superfamily Falconoidea
        Family Pandionidae
        Family Accipitridae
    Subfamily Accipitrinae
    Subfamily Falconinae

Amadon and Bull (1988) presented an "annotated list of species" with the living groups arranged as follows:

Order Falconiformes
    Suborder Cathartae
        Family Cathartidae, Cathartid Vultures
    Suborder Accipitres
        Family Accipitridae
            Subfamily Pandioninae, Ospreys
            Subfamily Accipitrinae, Hawks, Kites, Eagles
    Suborder Sagittarii
        Family Sagittariidae, Secretarybirds
    Suborder Falconae
        Family Falconidae
            Subfamily Polyborinae, Caracaras, Laughing Falcons, Forest Falcons
            Subfamily Falconinae, Falcons and Falconets

Amadon and Bull (1988:297) noted: "Though similar to the Old World, or accipitrid, vultures in habits, the Cathartae have many anatomical and behavioral peculiarities. They may be more closely allied to the storks (Ciconiidae), unlikely as that seems, than to other hawk-like birds of prey. Still, everything considered, it is best to leave them in the Falconiformes for now."

How long is "for now"? It has been more than a century since Garrod (1873d, 1874a) called attention to the similarities between storks and New World vultures, and over 20 years since Ligon's (1967) study.

It is obvious that the classification of the birds of prey has not achieved a consensus. The various interpretations of the taxonomic value of morphological characters are apparent and the disparity in the opinions about relationships is evidence of the improbability of arriving at a stable classification based on anatomical characters.

The DNA Hybridization Evidence (Figs. 139–145, 338, 353, 356, 365)

The DNA data present a remarkably simple pattern for the relationships of the diurnal birds of prey. It seems clear that the New World vultures (Cathartinae) are more closely related to the storks than to the diurnal birds of prey (Falconides). It is equally clear that the Falconides and owls (Strigi) are not closely related to one another. These conclusions are congruent with substantial morphological evidence.

The infraorder Falconides includes only the typical hawks, eagles, harriers, kites, honey-buzzards, Old World vultures, Secretary-bird, Osprey, falcons, and caracaras.

The Accipitrida and Falconida diverged at Δ T$_{50}$H 15.2. The Falconides branched from their common ancestor with the grebes, herons, pelicans, tubenoses, etc. at Δ 16.4 (Fig. 356).

The branch that produced *Sagittarius* diverged from the accipitrid lineage at Δ 10.4 (Fig. 365). We recognize the Sagittariidae for the Secretary-bird. A fossil from France assigned to the Sagittariidae is from the "Upper Eocene or Lower Oligocene" (Brodkorb 1964), thus ca. 30–40 MYA. If we use the calibration factor of Δ 1.0 = 4.5 MY, the divergence between the Sagittariidae and Accipitridae occurred ca. 47 MYA (4.5 $\times$ 10.4). This is a reasonable divergence date if the fossil was correctly identified.

The Osprey lineage branched from the other accipitrids at Δ 7.8. We recognize the subfamily Pandioninae.

The Old World vultures apparently form a clade that branched from the typical accipitrines at Δ 5.2. These two groups could be recognized as tribes, but we lack the DNAs of many genera and defer further subdivision until more taxa can be compared. The Old World vultures are carrion-eating eagles.

The Falconida could be subdivided; the *Micrastur* lineage branched at Δ 9.6, and the *Herpetotheres* lineage branched at Δ 9.2 from the falconids. These values meet the criteria for the recognition of two families, but we prefer to wait until more taxa can be compared.

The true falcons (*Falco*, *Microhierax*) and the caracaras (*Polyborus*, *Phalcobaenus*, *Milvago*, *Daptrius*) diverged at Δ 7.8. These genera provide enough evidence to support the recognition of the subfamilies Polyborinae and Falconinae (Fig. 365).

Most of the birds of prey do not begin to breed until more than one year of age. The Old World vultures delay breeding until they are more than four years old. The New World vultures do not begin to breed until several years old. Lint (1960) recorded a captive Andean Condor that first bred at the age of eight years. An article in the *San Francisco Chronicle* for February 2, 1990, noted that a captive six-year-old female California Condor in the San Diego Wild Animal Park laid a fertile egg on January 24, 1990. The same bird produced an infertile egg in 1989.

Judging from the melting curves, we suspect that all of the cathartines are delayed breeders, probably beginning at 6–8 years. The falcons have an average age at maturity of two years (Table 16). This range in the ages at maturity complicates the interpretation of the melting curves.

Fig. 139 (*Buteo*) shows the close relationship between the broad-winged buteos and the accipitrines. *Pandion* is only moderately distant from *Buteo*, and *Sagittarius* is somewhat more distant. The curves of the New World vultures (*Cathartes*, *Coragyps*) are at the same position as that of the Secretary-bird. We found no record of the age at first breeding in *Sagittarius*, so it is impossible to be certain about the significance of this situation. *Sagittarius* is a large raptor, so it is likely that it has delayed maturity. As will become apparent, this kind of problem is present in most of the sets of melting curves pertaining to the raptors.

Fig. 140 (*Buteo*) is from the same experiment as Fig. 139 and it includes some of the same curves, plus others not in Fig. 139. In Fig. 140, a shearwater (*Puffinus*), a crane (*Balearica*), and a large owl (*Bubo*) are equidistant from the homoduplex. These three groups have delayed maturity. The falcon (average two years at maturity) is farther from *Buteo* than any species in this set except the macaw. If these curves are interpreted as if their positions are directly proportional to the genetic distances from *Buteo* we would have a strange tree indeed.

Fig. 141 (*Circus*) includes melting curves between an accipitrine (*Circus*), another accipitrine (*Accipiter*), the Old World vultures (*Gyps, Neophron, Gypaetus*), the New World vultures (*Coragyps, Sarcoramphus*), and the falcons (*Herpetotheres* to *Falco*). If these curves are taken as directly related to times of divergence they would indicate that the New World vultures diverged more recently from the accipitrines than did the falcons. However, the New World vultures begin to breed at ca. 7 years of age, the falcons at ca. 2 years. Granted the uncertainties about all factors affecting the relative positions of the melting curves, we consider it most likely that the position of the New World vulture curves is closer to the homoduplex than those of the falcons because of their slower average rate of DNA evolution. An argument can be made that this reflects genetic difference and should be the basis for constructing the dendrogram, but the phylogeny should represent the branching pattern. This may be a dilemma without a simple solution, but for the moment we will call attention to these problems without claiming to solve them.

Fig. 142 (*Circus*) provides more puzzles. Three owls (*Ninox, Bubo, Tyto*) are slightly closer to the homoduplex than is *Falco*, and owls and falcons begin to breed at ca. 2 years of age. The position of the Andean Condor curve, a bird that begins to breed at 6 to 8 years of age, is no longer surprising, but how do we interpret the owl-falcon curves?

Fig. 143 (*Gypaetus*) offers more problems. It is logical to find the Old World vultures (*Torgos, Sarcogyps*), an eagle, and a *Buteo* closest to the Lammergeier, but next in the sequence are two New World vultures (*Vultur, Sarcoramphus*), then a stork at the same distance as the Secretary-bird, followed by another stork, a caracara (falconid), and a falcon. Both groups of vultures and the storks are known to have delayed maturity and when the tracer is one of them the branch-shortening effect is amplified. The *Falco* is one of the smallest species and probably begins to breed at one year of age. Thus, the positions of these curves are probably due as much to the different rates of DNA evolution as they are to times of divergence.

Fig. 144 (*Falco*) looks at these groups from the viewpoint of a small falcon that probably begins to breed at one year of age. Other falconids (falcons and a caracara) are closest to the homoduplex, as expected. The New World vulture (*Vultur*), Old World vulture (*Gypaetus*), Osprey, eagle, and accipitrine kite (*Gampsonyx*) cluster quite closely together relative to *Falco*. With the possible exception of *Gampsonyx*, these species have ages at maturity from ca. 3 to 7 years.

Fig. 145 (*Daptrius*). *Daptrius*, a caracara, is compared with two caracaras, four falcons, an Old World vulture, two eagles, and the Osprey. The relative distances are about as expected and show the separation of the Falconida from the Accipitrida. The effects of different ages at maturity among these taxa are not obvious.

The FITCH tree (Fig. 338) reflects the evidence in the melting curves. *Falco* and *Daptrius* have the longest branches; *Cathartes* and *Ciconia*, both with delayed maturity, the shortest; *Circus, Buteo,* and *Gypaetus* form a clade. *Gypaetus* has a short branch in relation to *Circus* and *Buteo*, but still clusters with them. *Gypaetus* begins to breed at 5–7 years of age. The position of *Strix* as the sister group of *Cathartes* is deceptive; the distance from *Cathartes* to *Strix* is 9.6 units, but it is only 8.5 units from *Cathartes* to *Ciconia*. The positions of *Cathartes* and *Strix* on the same branch are probably the result of including two taxa with delayed maturity and no close relatives, not evidence of close relationship between owls and New

World vultures. The reason that *Ciconia* did not cluster closest to *Cathartes* may be related to the way the Fitch-Margoliash algorithm searches for the best fit by testing all possible arrangements among the available distances.

Fig. 339 shows that the New World vultures are closely related to one another and that all have short branches, with the two condors (*Gymnogyps, Vultur*) having the shortest. As noted above, *Vultur* begins to breed at ca. 8 years in captivity and a captive female *Gymnogyps* laid a fertile egg when 6 years old. Judging from the branch lengths in Fig. 339 it seems likely that the other New World vultures are also 6–8 years old at maturity. In Fig. 339 the stork (*Mycteria*) is closest to the vultures, but it too is a delayed breeder. The branch lengths to the New World vultures, stork, and ibis (*Threskiornis*) are about equal from their common node. In many sets of melting curves we have seen evidence that ibises, as well as storks, have relatively short branch lengths; records for ibises indicate that they begin to breed at 2 to 3 years of age (Table 16).

We conclude that the effects of different ages at first breeding produce problems in the interpretation of melting curves and dendrograms. The large birds of prey and the New World vultures are among the groups with the greatest ages at maturity. In spite of the problems, we also conclude that the New World vultures are more closely related to the storks than to the Accipitrida or the Falconida; that is, the storks and New World vultures shared a common ancestor more recently than either did with any other living group.

Grebes

Order CICONIIFORMES
  Suborder Ciconii
    Infraorder Ciconiides
      Parvorder Podicipedida
        Family PODICIPEDIDAE: Grebes

There are 21 living species of grebes divided among six genera. Storer (1979:140–155) recognized 20 species, but we recognize the Western Grebe (*Aechmophorus occidentalis*) and Clark's Grebe (*A. clarkii*) as separate species (A.O.U. 1985, Ahlquist et al. 1987). Grebes occur on all continents and on many islands, including Madagascar and New Zealand.

    Family PODICIPEDIDAE: 6/21. Medium-sized aquatic birds with the legs set far back; tarsus compressed laterally; toes with wide lateral lobes, the lobes broader on the inner side and united basally; claws broad and flat; hallux elevated; patella large. Schizognathous; pelvic muscles BCX; flexor tendons Types 2 and 4; single left carotid; diastataxic; holorhinal, pervious nares; oil gland tufted, bilobed; caeca short; sternum with one pair of incisions; tracheo-bronchial syrinx with asymmetrical extrinsic muscles; plumage soft; tongue small; 12 primaries, outermost minute; 15–21 secondaries; vestigial rectrices; 17–21 cervical vertebrae; mature down over all of body; nestling down striped, one coat; nidifugous; eggs 2–8, white, bluish, or greenish with chalky surface.

Historical Review of the Classification

Most taxonomists have assumed that the grebes and loons (Gaviidae) are closely related and their taxonomic histories have been intertwined from the earliest times to the present. For convenience we have discussed them together under the Family Gaviidae; the following comments are in addition to that discussion.

    Storer (1963a,b; 1967a,b; 1969) studied the behavior of grebes to clarify the relationships within the group. Zusi and Storer (1969) examined the osteology and myology of the

488

head and neck in *Podilymbus*, and Mayr (1945), Storer (1967a), and Niethammer (1964) compared the plumage patterns of the downy young in some species. The conclusions from these different sources of evidence are concordant and Storer (1967a) divided the grebes into three groups: (1) *Podiceps* and *Aechmophorus*, (2) *Rollandia*, (3) *Tachybaptus*. Storer (1979) recognized the following genera and species: *Rollandia* (*rolland, microptera*); *Tachybaptus* (*novaehollandiae, ruficollis, rufolavatus, pelzelnii, dominicus*); *Podilymbus* (*podiceps, gigas*); *Poliocephalus* (*poliocephalus, rufopectus*); *Podiceps* (*major, auritus, grisegena, cristatus, nigricollis, occipitalis, taczanowskii, gallardoi*); *Aechmophorus* (*occidentalis*).

In 1858, Lawrence described two species of large grebes from the western United States, the Western Grebe (*Aechmophorus occidentalis*) and Clark's Grebe (*Aechmophorus clarkii*). They were alike in plumage coloration and other characters, but differed in the shape and coloration of the bill and the extent of white on the head. The similarities were sufficient to convince later authors (e.g., Coues 1892) that the two forms were not separate species but varieties of a single species. Later they came to be regarded as color phases or "morphs." Storer (1965) reported evidence of assortative mating by sympatric populations in Utah, which was confirmed by Ratti (1979) and Nuechterlein (1981a,b). From these data it seemed possible that the two morphs might be separate species. Storer and Nuechterlein (1985) reviewed the plumage and morphological characters of the two types and decided "to recognize the two phases as species if and when the color phases in the Mexican population are shown to be reproductively isolated from each other" (p. 118).

A DNA-DNA hybridization comparison of the two forms revealed an average $\Delta T_{50}H$ of 0.5 between them, and the difference was statistically significant (Ahlquist et al. 1987). Occasional hybridization does not prove that two forms are, or are not, conspecific; the critical factor is whether the hybrids are selected against. The evidence is equivocal, but we favor their recognition as species, while agreeing with Storer and Nuechterlein (1985:118) that "it is the situation, not the nomenclature . . . that is of prime . . . interest."

The DNA Hybridization Evidence (Figs. 146–148, 180, 356, 366)

The grebe lineage branched from a common ancestor shared with the tropicbirds, cormorants, herons, and other members of the infraorder Ciconiides, at $\Delta T_{50}H$ 14.9. Thus, the Podicipedida is the sister group of the groups that branched later than Δ 14.9 in the infraorder Ciconiides. The Ciconiides shared a common ancestor with the infraorder Falconides at Δ 16.4 (Fig. 356).

Fig. 146 (*Aechmophorus*) shows that the loon (*Gavia*) is no closer to the homoduplex than is the penguin. The albatross is slightly more distant. From several experiments it has been obvious that penguins and albatrosses are among the groups with delayed maturity and relatively slow average rates of DNA evolution, which produces relatively short branches in FITCH trees and melting curves that are relatively close to the homoduplex curve. Thus, we should not be surprised to find the penguin and albatross curves among those closest to virtually any homoduplex. In Fig. 146, the loon curve clusters with these taxa and loons are known to begin to breed at ca. 2–3 years of age (Table 16). *Diomedea immutabilis* breeds first at ca. 7 years of age. There are no data for *Spheniscus demersus*, but it probably matures at ca. 3 years, about the same as the loons. From these facts and speculations it seems likely that the curves of the

The Totipalmate Swimmers:
Traditional Order Pelecaniformes

> Though this group shows much divergency of structure, its naturalness can
> hardly be doubted.
>
> *Beddard 1898a:402*

The traditional order Pelecaniformes is composed of birds with all four toes connected by a web, the totipalmate birds, namely, pelicans, boobies, gannets, cormorants, anhingas, frigatebirds, and tropicbirds. All but the tropicbirds have an obvious gular pouch; in the tropicbirds the throat region is covered by feathers and it is debatable whether a true gular pouch can be defined. In the frigatebirds the gular pouch is inflatable and used in display. The combination of totipalmate feet and gular pouch has seemed so unlikely to occur in unrelated birds that the monophyly of the group has been accepted by most systematists since Linnaeus (1758) placed these taxa together in his order Anseres as the genera *Pelecanus* and *Phaethon*. However, they vary in pelvic musculature, carotid artery arrangement, and several other characters. The desmognathous palate (schizognathous in *Phaethon*) is shared with the storks, herons, waterfowl, falconiforms, and cariamas. The pelecaniforms also differ in other characters and such diversity raises the question of possible polyphyly. The totipalmate foot defines the traditional Pelecaniformes, but the totipalmate condition may have evolved more than once, as did the palmate condition, or the totipalmate foot may be a retained primitive state.

The DNA hybridization evidence suggests a phylogeny for the totipalmate birds that will be rejected by some ornithologists and greeted with surprise by all. The DNA comparisons indicate that *Pelecanus* is the sister group of the Shoebill (*Balaeniceps rex*), and that the frigatebirds are members of the Procellarioidea, which also includes the albatrosses, petrels, penguins, and loons. The tropicbirds seem to be the descendants of an ancient divergence that makes them the sister group of a large assemblage of aquatic birds, including the other totipalmate taxa.

The effects of delayed maturity on the average rate of genomic evolution in these groups is uncertain, but some of the proposed relationships may be the result of this phenomenon. The evidence is discussed and evaluated below.

The DNA-based classification of the groups that include the traditional Pelecaniformes follows:

Order CICONIIFORMES
  Suborder Ciconii
    Infraorder Ciconiides
      Parvorder Podicipedida: Grebes
      Parvorder Phaethontida
        Family Phaethontidae: Tropicbirds
      Parvorder Sulida
        Superfamily Suloidea
          Family Sulidae: Boobies, Gannets
          Family Anhingidae: Anhingas, Darters
        Superfamily Phalacrocoracoidea
          Family Phalacrocoracidae: Cormorants, Shags
      Parvorder Ciconiida
        Superfamily Ardeoidea: Herons
        Superfamily Scopoidea: Hamerkop or Hammerhead
        Superfamily Phoenicopteroidea: Flamingos
        Superfamily Threskiornithoidea: Ibises
        Superfamily Pelecanoidea: Pelicans, Shoebill
          Family Pelecanidae
            Subfamily Balaenicipitinae: Shoebill
            Subfamily Pelecaninae: Pelicans
        Superfamily Ciconioidea: New World Vultures, Storks
        Superfamily Procellarioidea
          Family Fregatidae: Frigatebirds
          Family Spheniscidae: Penguins
          Family Gaviidae: Loons or Divers
          Family Procellariidae: Petrels, Albatrosses, etc.

The members of this classification are discussed under their respective superfamilies and in the following section.

The assemblage of totipalmate birds, the traditional order Pelecaniformes, was accepted in virtually all classifications from that of Linnaeus (1758) until the most recent, e.g., Dorst and Mougin (1979), the A.O.U. checklist (1983), and Cracraft (1985). The taxonomic history of this group records the evidence and arguments used by our predecessors.

A traditional classification of the totipalmate birds, as given in the *A.O.U. Check-list of North American Birds* (1983), follows:

Order Pelecaniformes: Totipalmate Swimmers
  Suborder Phaethontes: Tropicbirds
    Family Phaethontidae: Tropicbirds
  Suborder Pelecani: Boobies, Pelicans, Cormorants, Darters
    Family Sulidae: Boobies and Gannets
    Family Pelecanidae: Pelicans
    Family Phalacrocoracidae: Cormorants
    Family Anhingidae: Darters
  Suborder Fregatae: Frigatebirds
    Family Fregatidae: Frigatebirds

These groups share the totipalmate foot with the hallux turned forward and connected by a web to digit II. Other shared characters are the absence of an incubation patch (Howell and Bartholomew 1962, 1969; T. R. Howell, pers. comm.) and the location of the salt-excreting gland within the orbit, instead of in a supraorbital groove (Olson 1977). No other living birds have totipalmate feet and no other seabirds or waterbirds are known to lack an incubation patch. The condition of the incubation patch in *Anhinga* seems to be unknown. The intraorbital salt-excreting gland apparently is confined to these groups. In most of the species the furcula is ankylosed to the sternum. Other characters are:

Palate desmognathous, except schizognathous in *Phaethon*; pelvic muscles AXY in *Phaethon* (ambiens variable? Beddard 1898a:405), AX+ or ABX+ in *Phalacrocorax*, AX+ in *Anhinga* and *Sula*, AX in *Pelecanus*, A+ in *Fregata*; flexor tendons Type 2; carotids paired in *Phaethon*, *Fregata*, *Phalacrocorax*, single left in *Anhinga* and *Pelecanus*, paired or single left in *Sula*. Nares impervious, except *Phaethon*; oil gland tufted, bilobed; caeca small; syrinx tracheo-bronchial but variable; aftershaft rudimentary or absent; primaries 11, outermost usually minute; secondaries 16 in *Anhinga*, 17–19 in *Phaethon*, 15–21 in *Phalacrocorax*, 28 in *Sula*, 29 in *Pelecanus*; rectrices 12 in *Anhinga*, *Phaethon*, *Fregata*, 12–14 in *Phalacrocorax*, up to 16 in *Sula*, 20–24 in *Pelecanus*. Cervical vertebrae 14–15 in *Phaethon* and *Fregata*, 17 in *Pelecanus*, 18 in *Sula*, 20 in *Phalacrocorax*, 19–20 in *Anhinga*. Young nidicolous, hatched blind and (nearly) naked, except in *Phaethon* in which the young are covered with fine, long down at hatching.

From a total of 52 skeletal and behavioral characters analyzed, Cracraft (1985) identified "12 postulated synapomorphies" supporting the monophyly of the traditional Pelecaniformes, not including the lack of an incubation patch or the intraorbital salt gland. Thus, there may be at least 14 shared, derived characters that define the monophyly of the Pelecaniformes. However, a gular pouch may not be present in the tropicbirds, and the method of feeding by nestling tropicbirds is debatable. Van Tets (1965) reported that young tropicbirds feed from the gullet of the adult, but T. R. Howell (pers. comm.) has observed adults regurgitating into the throat of the young. In other pelecaniforms the young feed from the gullet of the adult.

Family PHAETHONTIDAE: 1/3. Gular pouch absent or reduced, throat covered by plumage; beak acuminate, slightly curved, mandibles serrate; central rectrices elongate; nostrils pervious, open in a slit-like aperture; palatines completely separate; vomer present; a deep nasal hinge; free end of clavicle not faceted for articulation with acrocoracoid. Skin with air cells (emphysematous). Small feet and short legs cannot support the body on land. A single egg; nest a scrape in sand or earth, often in shaded cavities, under overhanging rocks, or on cliffs; solitary or in loose colonies (Howell and Bartholomew 1962, 1969; Stonehouse 1985).

Family SULIDAE: 3/9. Gular pouch small; beak stout, straight, pointed, not hooked; linear groove on each side of culmen; nostrils completely closed in adults; palatines fused in midline with slight median keel; well-marked nasal hinge; anterior portion of sternum extended forward beyond anterior lateral process of sternum; mandibles serrate; claw of middle toe broad and pectinate.

Family ANHINGIDAE: 1/4. Moderately large gular pouch; slender, straight, pointed beak, mandibles serrate; no lateral groove on beak; nostrils rudimentary; neck long, slender, with articular surfaces of 8th and 9th cervical vertebrae modified to form S-shaped curve with angle at 8th vertebra; M. longus colli anticus inserts on 8th vertebra and, in contraction, acts to thrust neck and head forward during spearing action for impaling fish; temporal muscles meet behind skull along a median fibrous raphe which is ossified into a small bony style in *A. anhinga*; outer webs of central rectrices with transverse corrugations.

Family PHALACROCORACIDAE: 1/38 (9/37, Siegel-Causey 1988). Moderately large gular pouch; bill laterally compressed, hooked; nostrils almost closed; furcula not fused to carina sterni; temporal muscles extend beyond the skull and separated by a bony style; skin not emphysematous; no aftershaft.

Family PELECANIDAE, Subfamily PELECANINAE: 1/8. Large gular pouch; long beak with mandibular rami distensible; bill hooked at tip; palatines fused in midline, with median keel; furcula fused with the carina sterni; tarsi compressed, reticulate scutellation. Skin with air cells (emphysematous). See also under Herons, Hamerkop, etc. in the Pelecanoidea.

Family FREGATIDAE: 1/5. Large throat pouch that can be inflated from anterior air sacs by breeding males and used in display, uncertainly homologous with gular pouches of pelicans, cormorants, anhingas, and sulids; beak long, hooked, with deep lateral grooves; nostrils linear, closed or nearly closed, in grooves at base of bill; toe webs reduced to basal portions of toes; nails long, claw-like; middle toe pectinate on inner margin; tarsi short, feathered; palatines fused at posterior end only; a large vomer; no nasal hinge; sternum broader than long; furcula fused dorsally with head of coracoid, ventrally with carina sterni. See also under Albatrosses, Petrels, Shearwaters, etc. in the Procellarioidea.

Historical Review of the Classification

Nitzsch (1840:148) found the totipalmate birds to have "a very persistent type of pterylosis . . . [that] presents no generic differences, except, perhaps, a variation in the density of the plumage, which appears to be dependent on the climates in which the birds live." He found that *Pelecanus* somewhat resembles the Anseriformes in its pterylosis, and that *Anhinga*, with its small apteria, approaches the condition in the penguins.

Huxley (1867) believed that the totipalmate birds form a natural assemblage. He placed the pelicans as one of the groups in his Dysporomorphae, based on the development of the inferior edge of the interorbital septum and enlargment of an ascending process of the palatines. The remaining genera composed a second group, which lack these features.

Sundevall (1872, see 1889) placed his "Cohort Totipalmatae" in his "Order Natatores" with the other web-footed birds and commented that "This cohort is a very natural one, and is scarcely divisible into families. Therefore—A single family, Pelecaninae [sic], contains all the genera here mentioned, all being in the highest degree natural and very distinct."

Differences in the pelvic musculature were reported by Garrod (1873d, 1874a). He suggested that *Sula*, *Phalacrocorax*, and *Anhinga* form one family, and that each of the other genera (*Pelecanus*, *Fregata*, *Phaethon*) should be placed in separate families. He saw similarities between *Phaethon* and the ciconiiforms, and between *Fregata* and the falconiforms. He described the anatomy of *Anhinga*, including the modified cervical vertebrae associated with fish-spearing behavior (1876d, 1878c).

Garrod (1874a) departed from the traditional arrangements and placed the New World vultures (Cathartidae) between the storks (Pelargi) and herons (Herodiones), followed by the Steganopodes (totipalmate birds) and the Accipitres (hawks, falcons, owls). These groups were the members of his order Ciconiiformes.

From the postcranial skeleton Mivart (1878) concluded that *Pelecanus*, *Sula*, *Phalacrocorax*, and *Anhinga* form a natural group. He was unable to find characters uniting

Phaethon and *Fregata* with the other four genera, although the two groups were similar in the number and shape of the vertebrae and in pelvic characters. He did not speculate about the relationships of *Fregata* and *Phaethon*.

Sclater (1880b) recognized five families for the totipalmate birds in his order Steganopodes, placed between the Accipitres and Herodiones (herons, storks), thus following Garrod.

Stejneger (1885:180) did not accept Mivart's (1878) conclusions: "Mivart has shown that the four supergenera . . . [*Pelecanus, Sula, Phalacrocorax, Anhinga*] are more intimately related *inter se* than to the two other ones [*Phaethon, Fregata*]. These two, on the other hand, chiefly agree to differ from the former four in negative points, and hence their exclusion from these does not indicate any particular mutual intimacy. On the contrary, the tropic-birds and the frigate-birds are as different between themselves as each of them is from the rest."

Stejneger declined to split the order and erected the superfamilies Pelecanoideae, Fregatoideae, and Phaethontoideae to emphasize the differences among the groups. He contended that this order is "unquestionably nearly related to the Herodii" (p. 179).

Gadow (1889) found evidence in the intestinal convolutions to link the pelecaniforms to the ciconiiforms and also to the procellariiforms. He concluded (1893) that the Pelecaniformes are allied to the Ciconiiformes through the storks and to the falconiforms through the New World vultures.

From osteological comparisons Shufeldt (1883a, 1888b, 1894a, 1902a) decided that the totipalmate birds form a natural group and he recognized the suborders Pelecanoidea, Phaethontoidea, and Fregatoidea. He noted similarities between *Phaethon* and *Puffinus*, and *Phaethon* and the gulls. He thought that *Fregata* is similar to *Phaethon* in pelvic characters and that its skull is like that of the albatrosses.

Fürbringer (1888) placed the totipalmate birds in his suborder Ciconiiformes, which also included the flamingos, herons, storks, and falconiforms. He thought that the Cathartidae is an old and declining raptorial family and that the "Steganopodes" (totipalmate birds) are related to the diurnal birds of prey and also to the storks and herons.

Seebohm (1889, 1890a, 1895) divided his Steganopodes into five families, with *Anhinga* in the Phalacrocoracidae. He thought that the cormorants, anhingas, and boobies are the most closely related and that the nearest allies of the totipalmate birds are the herons and storks.

Sharpe (1891) divided his Pelecaniformes into five suborders and thought them to be allied to the falconiforms via *Fregata*. He also suggested a relationship to the Anseriformes.

Beddard (1898a) thought that the closest relatives of the "Steganopodes" are the procellariids, based on skeletal similarities between *Fregata* and *Diomedea*, especially the os uncinatum which "connects the lacrymal with the palatine. . . . The palate of *Diomedea* is remarkably like that of *Fregata*." He also believed that the herons and totipalmate birds are related because they share holorhinal nostrils, a small gizzard, large proventriculus, a double pectoralis primus muscle, and short colic caeca (p. 417).

In the *Catalogue of Birds* Sharpe and Ogilvie-Grant (1898) placed the "Order Steganopodes" between the Herodiones and the Pygopodes (loons, grebes). The usual five groups were recognized as families, united by the totipalmate foot. In the *Hand-List* Sharpe (1899) placed the totipalmate birds in the "Order Pelecaniformes" and recognized a sixth family, Plotidae, for the anhingas. He placed the Pelecaniformes between the extinct Ichthyor-nithiformes and the Cathartidiformes (New World vultures).

From their intestinal convolutions Mitchell (1901a) thought the pelecaniforms formed a central group, the "steganopod metacentre," from which could be derived the patterns of the procellariiforms, herons, storks, and falconiforms. He noted that the phylogeny of the intestinal tract did not necessarily reflect that of the groups of birds.

Pycraft (1898b) defended the uniformity of the "Steganopodes" on the basis of skeletal evidence and (1907a:24) suggested that the pelecaniforms are the "common ancestral stock from which have descended the Sphenisci, Colymbi, and Tubinares, on the one hand, and the Ciconiae, Accipitres, and Anseres on the other." As some of his evidence he cited "the nature of the relations between the squamosal and parietal before their fusion, and the nature of the palate at the same period."

Concerning feather structure Chandler (1916) wrote: "The Steganopodes are a group of birds in which primitive characters are curiously combined with specialized characters, the result being a rather heterogeneous aggregation of more or less related forms which are specialized along different lines. They seem to fall into three well-defined groups as follows: (1) *Phalacrocorax, Fregata, Sula, Pelecanus*; (2) *Plotus* [*Anhinga*]; and (3) *Phaethon*." Chandler thought the first group was the least specialized and had ties with the procellariiforms and ciconiiforms. In the feathers of *Anhinga* he saw "striking similarity" to those of the Cathartidae and concluded that the New World vultures had been derived from a pelecaniform ancestor. In Chandler's opinion *Phaethon* is not allied to the other totipalmate birds and should be considered an "aberrant larid form."

Mathews and Iredale (1921) emphasized the differences between the tropicbirds and the other pelecaniforms and placed *Phaethon* in the suborder Phaethontiformes of their order Lari. Lowe (1926) disagreed and presented evidence, mainly from the structure of the quadrate, that *Phaethon* is allied to the other totipalmate birds.

E. Stresemann (1934) thought that the nearest relatives of the pelecaniforms are uncertain, but that a distant affinity to the ciconiiforms and falconiforms was possible; he placed the cormorants and anhingas in separate subfamilies in the Phalacrocoracidae.

In spite of their diversity, Lanham (1947) concluded that the totipalmate birds form a natural order and assigned *Phaethon* and *Fregata* to separate suborders and the other genera to the suborder Pelecani. *Sula, Phalacrocorax,* and *Anhinga* were placed in the superfamily Sulides and the pelicans in the Pelecanides. Lanham noted a number of primitive characters shared by the tropicbirds, frigatebirds, and tubenoses, and suggested that the nearest relatives of the pelecaniforms are the procellariiforms.

Howard (1950) thought that the Upper Cretaceous *Eolopteryx* and the Eocene *Eostega* were possibly ancestral to the cormorants and boobies, and that the Eocene *Prophaethon* was a link between the cormorant-booby stem and the tropicbirds. The Miocene *Cyphornis* was thought to be similar to the cormorants, boobies, anhingas, and pelicans. Brodkorb (1963a) placed *Eolopteryx* and *Eostega* in the Sulidae.

Mayr and Amadon (1951) suggested that "*Phaethon* is certainly further removed from *Pelecanus* and its allies than is *Fregata*." They placed the Anhinginae in the Phalacrocoracidae.

The Pelecaniformes of Verheyen (1960b,c, 1961) included the suborders Pelecani,

Sulae, and Anhingae (anhingas, cormorants). He placed the frigatebirds and tropicbirds in suborders in his order Lariformes, which also included the suborder Lari (gulls, terns, jaegers, skimmers). His superorder Limnornithes included the Pelecaniformes, Lariformes, and Charadriiformes and he supported a relationship between the tropicbirds and the tubenoses.

The young of *Phaethon* are covered with long down and the adults have a series of air cells under the skin of the anterior portion of the body as in the Brown Pelican (*P. occiden- talis*), which also plunge-dives (Wetmore 1960). The young of *Fregata* are nearly naked at hatching and the adults lack subdermal air cells and do not plunge-dive. Also, the plumage of the frigatebirds is not waterproof. Some of these differences, and others of the internal anatomy, provided Wetmore with the basis for assigning the tropicbirds and frigatebirds to separate suborders, placed on either side of the suborder Pelecani, which contained the other totipalmate genera. The Anhingidae was recognized because of "a peculiar conformation of the cervical vertebrae through which the beak becomes a triggered spear in feeding. . . . The stomach also is unusual in possessing a curious pyloric lobe, lined with a mat of hair-like processes. And there is only one carotid artery while in cormorants there are two" (1960:7–8). Here again, differences were used as the basis for the recognition of higher categories.

Sibley (1960) found "marked dissimilarities" among the electrophoretic patterns of the egg-white proteins of the pelecaniforms. Those of *Phaethon* and *Fregata* were similar to one another and the similarity was assumed to be the result of relationship. Cormorants and anhingas had nearly identical patterns, but those of different species of *Sula* differed considerably from one another. Sibley concluded that the Pelecaniformes may be polyphyletic but "further evidence on this question is needed" (p. 231).

Cranial kinesis and morphology provided Simonetta (1963) with evidence of the polyphyly of the totipalmate birds. He thought *Fregata* is related to the tubenoses, but that *Phaethon* is an isolated genus of uncertain affinities.

Van Tets (1965) observed the social communication behavior of 15 pelecaniform species and compared them with those of other groups. He thought his evidence supported Lanham's (1947) arrangement and he found differences between gannets and boobies that he used to separate *Morus* (gannets) from *Sula*. He noted: "The close affinities of the Pelecaniformes to Procellariiformes and the Ciconiiformes are indicated by the mutual displaying of members of a pair facing each other on the nest as occurs not only in the gannets and in a modified form in the frigatebirds but also in the albatrosses, fulmars, and storks. A further resemblance can be noted . . . between the Rattling of the frigate birds and the Clappering displays of albatrosses and storks, between the Stretch display of herons and the Sky-pointing of boobies and the Wing-waving of the Little Pied Cormorant [*Phalacrocorax melanoleucus*], and between the Snap display of herons and the Snap-bowing of the Anhinga and the Gape-bowing of the Little Pied Cormorant. How many of these similarities are due to either homology or analogy still remains to be determined."

Meyerriecks (1966) reviewed Van Tets' work favorably, but J. Nelson (1967) pointed out some apparent errors, particularly in the displays of the boobies.

The adaptations for feeding and locomotion in *A. anhinga* and *Phalacrocorax auritus* were analyzed by Owre (1967). The differences in their ecology, osteology, myology, and external morphology caused him to maintain anhingas and cormorants in separate families.

The Mallophaga of tropicbirds and frigatebirds are most like those of the procellariids, and those of the tropicbirds and procellariids are also related to those of the charadriiforms, according to Timmermann (1965). He concluded that *Phaethon*, *Fregata*, the tubenoses and the shorebirds (especially Laridae) are related, but that the Mallophaga do not suggest a close relationship between the tubenoses and the other totipalmate birds.

Tyler (1969) was unable to distinguish among the tropicbirds, frigatebirds, pelicans, boobies, cormorants, or anhingas on the basis of numerous eggshell characters, except that the pelicans have more shell nitrogen than the others.

Sibley and Ahlquist (1972) reviewed most of the publications cited in this section and summarized them:

1. If the Pelecaniformes are considered as a group, most opinions have supported a relationship to the Ciconiiformes, next to the Charadriiformes, Falconiformes and Procellariiformes and, to a lesser extent, to the Anseriformes. The Sphenisciformes, Gruiformes and Gaviiformes were also mentioned by at least one author.

2. *Fregata* and *Phaethon* are separated from the other pelecaniform birds in a large percentage of the cited papers. *Fregata* has been suggested as a relative of the Charadriiformes, Falconiformes and Procellariiformes. *Phaethon* is most often thought to be allied to the Charadriiformes (especially Laridae) and also to the Procellariiformes.

Our evaluation of the evidence reviewed suggests that the Pelecaniformes is a diverse group but that there is no clear indication that any of the presently included genera are more closely related to the members of some other order than to other pelecaniforms" (pp. 69–70).

Sibley and Ahlquist (1972) compared the electrophoretic patterns of the egg-white proteins of the six groups of totipalmate birds. We found the following (summarized from pp. 70–71):

1. The patterns of the cormorants, anhingas, and boobies are much alike and differ from those of the other groups.

2. Pelicans are somewhat like the boobies in some parts of their patterns.

3. The tropicbird pattern differs from the taxa noted above, but is generally similar to that of *Fregata*, although these two also differ in details. The tropicbirds and frigatebirds seem to be the most aberrant members of the group and they may be more closely related to some other order.

We concluded (1972:71) that "By comparison with most other orders of birds the differences among the egg-white protein patterns of the subgroups of the Pelecaniformes are large. . . . they can be considered to be modifications of a single ancestral pattern type and the differences may reflect the large genetic gaps which have developed during their long evolutionary history. *Phaethon* and *Fregata* seem to be the most aberrant . . . genera. They may be more closely related to . . . some other order . . . but we propose no modifications of the presently accepted arrangement. Neither do we believe that this question has yet been settled beyond all doubt."

Olson (1977) described *Limnofregata* from the Lower Eocene of Wyoming and assigned it to the Fregatidae. He noted that "If salt glands were present in *Limnofregata*, they would have to have been inside the orbit, as in all other Pelecaniformes" (p. 9). Differences and similarities between the skeletons of *Fregata*, *Limnofregata*, and the other pelecaniforms were described and Olson concluded that the evidence supported the phylogeny of Lanham (1947), "who treated the Phaethontes and Fregatae as being primitive within the order, to be followed by the more specialized families of the Pelecani. This is in contrast to such classifications as those of Peters (1931) and Wetmore (1960) where the frigatebirds are placed in a terminal position, separated from the Phaethontes by the Pelecani—a sequence that cannot be justified by the facts available now" (p. 29).

Saiff (1978) studied the middle ear region of the "Pelecaniformes and Ciconiiformes" and concluded that *Balaeniceps* is more closely related to "the Pelecaniformes than [to] the Ciconiiformes" and that *Phaethon* "shows . . . resemblances to Procellariiformes (but is quite distinct from them)." He considered the "other Pelecaniformes" to be distinct from the Procellariiformes, but concluded that the middle-ear morphology supported a "close relationship between Pelecaniformes (aside from *Phaethon*) and Ciconiiformes."

Cracraft (1985) conducted a "phylogenetic analysis" to

evaluate the monophyly of the Pelecaniformes and to determine interfamilial relationships within the order. A total of 52 characters was subjected to a numerical cladistic analysis. Pelecaniform monophyly was highly corroborated, with 12 postulated synapomorphies supporting the hypothesis. Within the pelecaniforms, the phaethontids are the sister-group of the remaining families, which are divided into two lineages, the fregatids on the one hand and the pelecanids, sulids, and phalacrocoracids (including anhingids) on the other. Within the latter clade, sulids, and phalacrocoracids are each other's closest relatives. This pattern of . . . relationships was strongly corroborated by the data.

This study also presents . . . evidence that pelecaniforms and procellariiforms are sister-taxa, although this hypothesis requires further analysis. Evidence supporting a relationship between pelecaniforms and ciconiiforms is . . . considered insufficient to warrant acceptance.

The hypothesis that the Whale-headed Stork (*Balaeniceps rex*) has a relationship to one or more pelecaniform taxa was . . . rejected. The characters said to indicate a close relationship are interpreted here to be convergences that arose as mechanical responses to similarities in feeding behavior.

Cracraft's 52 characters included 44 structural traits, mostly skeletal, and eight behavioral characters. These were scored for three character states (primitive, and two derived states) and placed in a matrix for comparisons among 11 families and two subfamilies of the pelecaniforms, procellariiforms, penguins, loons, grebes, and *Balaeniceps*. Trees were generated from the matrix and a classification developed, as follows:

Order Pelecaniformes
  Suborder Phaethontes
      Family Phaethontidae
  Suborder Steganopodes
    Infraorder Fregatae
      Family Fregatidae
    Infraorder Pelecani
      Superfamily Pelecanoidea
       Family Pelecanidae
      Superfamily Suloidea
      Family Sulidae
      Family Phalacrocoracidae
        Subfamily Phalacrocoracinae
        Subfamily Anhinginae

Cracraft (1985:849–851) concluded with a defense of cladistics and a critique of other methods, including DNA-DNA hybridization, and of other studies, including those of Cottam (1957) on *Balaeniceps* and Saiff (1978) on the middle ear.

Van Tets et al. (1988) compared the skeletal elements of boobies (*Sula*) and gannets (*Morus*) and concluded that the "differences confirm that *Sula* and *Morus* are generically distinct." They also described a fossil, *Sula tasmani*, from Lord Howe and Norfolk islands.

Warheit et al. (1989) compared the number of scleral ossicles in the eyes of 44 species of pelecaniforms. They found that *Phaethon*, *Fregata*, and *Pelecanus* "retain the primitive 15 ossicles per ring" but *Phalacrocorax*, *Anhinga*, and the Sulidae have had "a derived reduction to 12 or 13 ossicles. Within the Sulidae, *Sula* (*sensu stricto*) exhibits a further reduction to 10 ossicles." They concluded that these patterns of ossicle reduction are consistent with both the monophyletic and polyphyletic hypotheses of pelecaniform relationships.

Siegel-Causey (1988) "undertook a phylogenetic analysis of the Recent taxa of Phalacrocoracidae using qualitative osteological characters." He recognized "at least 35 species" (37 species in Table 1, p. 892) divided into two subfamilies, the Phalacrocoracinae (cormorants) with four genera and 17 species, and the Leucocarboninae (shags) with five genera and 20 species. He was unable to resolve the relationship of the anhingas to the cormorants.

Siegel-Causey (1989) examined the pneumatization of the cranium in the cormorants and found different patterns between the typical cormorants ("Phalacrocoracinae") and the shags ("Leucocarboninae"). He noted the position of "the nasal gland depression on the dorsal surface of the frontal" bone, and that "the absence of pneumatized bone within the frontal gland depression allows the nasal gland to fit within the orbit which is otherwise occupied by the eyes."

Support for the polyphyly of the traditional Pelecaniformes has come from a study by Jerold M. Lowenstein (pers. comm.), who used the immunological technique of radioimmuno assay to compare the proteins in the eggshells of birds. He obtained his material from eggshell fragments of *Pelecanus erythrorhynchos*, *Phalacrocorax auritus albociliatus*, *P. a. floridanus*, *Sula leucogaster*, *Phaethon aethereus*, *Fregata magnificens*, and the Horned Owl (*Bubo virginianus*). The Horned Owl was included as the "outgroup" representative. The two subspecies of the Double-crested Cormorant were the closest pair with an "immunological distance" (ID) of 9. The Brown Booby (*Sula*) was next closest to the cormorants at an ID of 19. Thus, the cormorants and the booby clustered together, as also shown by the DNA hybridization data, but the other taxa were more widely scattered. The frigatebird and tropicbird were at ID 24 from the cormorant-booby cluster, and ID 22 from one another. The pelican was at ID 26 from all the other taxa, while the Horned Owl was at ID 24 from the other taxa. Lowenstein notes that these values indicate that *Pelecanus* is not closely related to any of the other pelecaniform taxa. The results were so unexpected that Lowenstein assumed that the material must have been degraded and he did not publish his data.

The DNA Hybridization Evidence (Figs. 149–154, 166–170, 175–176, 339, 340, 356, 366–368)

The UPGMA dendrograms, based on corrected $\Delta T_{50}H$ values, suggest that the traditional order Pelecaniformes is polyphyletic, although the taxa previously placed in the group are members of our order Ciconiiformes, suborder Ciconii, and infraorder Ciconiides. Thus, the waterbird assemblage (our Ciconiides) seems to consist of a radiation that began more recently than had been assumed in the past. The Ciconiides branched from the Falconides at $\Delta T_{50}H$ 16.4, which we tentatively date as early Tertiary. The grebe lineage (parvorder Podicipedida) branched from the other members of the Ciconiides at Δ 14.9, and the tropicbird clade (parvorder Phaethontida) branched at Δ 14.0 (Fig. 366). The Sulida and Ciconiida diverged at Δ 13.3.

At Δ 12.1 the Sulida split into the lineages that produced the Suloidea and the Phalacrocoracoidea, and at Δ 11.0 the Anhingidae and Sulidae diverged (Fig. 366). It is surprising that the anhingas cluster with the boobies, rather than with the cormorants, but this pattern suggests that the common ancestor of the Suloidea and Phalacrocoracoidea was morphologically similar to the cormorants and anhingas, and that the boobies and gannets diverged from the ancestral condition. This situation is similar to that of the barbets and toucans in which the New World barbets are more closely related to the toucans than to the Old World barbets (see Piciformes).

The other members of the traditional order Pelecaniformes are members of our parvorder Ciconiida. The Pelecanoidea includes the pelicans and the Shoebill (*Balaeniceps*) in the family Pelecanidae, and the frigatebirds (Fregatidae) cluster with the other members of the Procellarioidea (penguins, loons, and tubenoses). The details of the branching pattern of the Ciconiida are discussed in a following section.

The melting curves introduce complications, presumably due to the effects of delayed maturity on the average rate of genomic evolution.

Fig. 149 (*Phaethon*) has an excellent homoduplex with a T_m ca. 87°C. The closest heteroduplex to *Phaethon* is the Royal Albatross, a species that does not begin to breed until 8–11 years old (Table 16). In view of the evidence in many other sets of melting curves, it seems apparent that the relative position of the Royal Albatross curve is due, in part, to the effects of delayed maturity. The rest of the sequence of curves, with approximate ages at maturity in parentheses, is: frigatebird (4), pelican (4), loon (2–3), gannet (4), booby (4), egret (1–2), anhinga (4?), godwit (2), cormorant (4), and grebe (2). Thus, most of the driver species begin to breed at ca. 3–4 years of age. If we ignore the albatross, the sequence of heteroduplex curves is as listed above, with the frigatebird the closest to *Phaethon*, followed by the pelican, etc. The spread among these curves is not large; all intersect with the single-stranded DNA axis between 10% and 25%, and the $\Delta T_{50}H$ between *Phaethon* and *Fregata* is ca. 12.5, *Pelecanus* ca. 13, *Sula* 15, and *Phalacrocorax* ca. 16.5, a range of ca. 4.0. These taxa could all be on the same branch relative to *Phaethon*, or on different branches at similar distances.

Fig. 150 (*Sula*) presents another view of the pelecaniforms. *Morus*, as expected, is closest to *Sula*, with *Fregata*, *Anhinga*, stork, cormorant, Shoebill, pelican, tropicbird, and a duck progressively farther out. *Fregata* is ca. $\Delta T_{50}H$ 11 from *Sula*, *Pelecanus* is ca. Δ 14, *Phaethon* Δ 16. *Ciconia* begins to breed at ca. 4 years, about the same as most of the driver species in this set.

Fig. 151 (*Anhinga*) shows *Morus* and *Sula* as closest to *Anhinga*, with *Fregata* next, then a cormorant, stork, Shoebill, pelican, and tropicbird. Again, *Fregata* is close to the tracer and *Phaethon* is most distant, with *Pelecanus* farther from the homoduplex than the frigatebird or cormorant. The position of *Balaeniceps* next to *Pelecanus* in Figs. 150 and 151 suggests that these genera are equidistant from *Sula* and *Anhinga*.

Fig. 152 (*Phalacrocorax*) provides another view. The gannet and booby are closest to the cormorants, then *Fregata*, *Phaethon*, Royal Albatross, pelican, and stork. Thus, *Phaethon* is closer to *Phalacrocorax* than is *Pelecanus*, whereas in Fig. 151 the reverse was true relative to *Anhinga*, yet we can assume that *Anhinga* and *Phalacrocorax* are more closely related to one another (and to the sulids) than either is to any other taxon. Is this apparent anomaly due to different rates, experimental error, or some other cause?

Fig. 153 (*Phalacrocorax*) seems to change some of the relative positions noted in Fig. 152. The other cormorants, booby, and anhinga are in expected positions; *Fregata* is next; then a stork, shearwater, loon, pelican, heron, tropicbird, and grebe. Again the frigatebird is close to the tracer, the pelican and tropicbird are far out. Storks and tubenoses (shearwater) often cluster close to any tracer, presumably because of relatively slow rates of DNA evolution; they must be viewed as of uncertain relationship to the tracer taxon.

Fig. 154 (*Phalacrocorax*) includes two more delayed maturity taxa, *Cathartes* and *Grus*. Like the storks and tubenoses, the New World vultures and cranes tend to cluster close to widely different tracer species. We believe this indicates slow rates of DNA change due to delayed maturity.

These melting curves indicate that *Phaethon* is not closely related to the cormorants or the boobies, and that the cormorants, anhingas, boobies, and gannets form a clade. *Fregata* is a puzzle and it is considered further when Figs. 175–185 are discussed in a later section (Albatrosses, Petrels, etc.).

The FITCH tree (Fig. 340) reflects the situations noted in the melting curves. *Phaethon* is distant from the other taxa in Fig. 340, and *Diomedea* exhibits the expected short branch length. *Pelecanus* and *Balaeniceps* are sister taxa and *Sula*, *Anhinga*, and *Phalacrocorax* form a clade. But look at *Fregata*. The UPGMA tree places the frigatebirds with the tubenoses, but in the FITCH tree *Fregata* clusters with the boobies and cormorants, not with *Diomedea*. Distances from the common node are: *Phaethon*, 7.9; *Phalacrocorax*, 7.7; *Sula*, 6.7; *Anhinga*, 6.1; *Fregata*, 5.7; *Threskiornis*, 5.2; *Balaeniceps*, 5.0; *Pelecanus*, 4.8; *Diomedea*, 3.9. That is a ca. 50% difference from *Phaethon* to *Diomedea*. In view of the branch length differences it is interesting to note that the distance from *Fregata* to *Diomedea* in Fig. 339 is 9.5 units, whereas the distance from *Fregata* to *Anhinga*, which is the shortest branch in the cormorant clade, is 10.0 units.

The relationships suggested by the data discussed above differ from the traditional concept of the Pelecaniformes in some respects, but they are congruent with some of the other sources of evidence. Most other studies have also concluded that the tropicbirds and frigatebirds are the groups most distant from one another and from the other pelecaniform taxa, and that the boobies, anhingas, and cormorants cluster together. The frigatebirds have often been suggested as relatives of the tubenoses. The pelicans usually have been placed in the same group with the boobies, anhingas, and cormorants, but Cottam (1957) concluded that *Pelecanus* is related to the Shoebill (*Balaeniceps*), and Lowenstein's study, noted above, is congruent with the DNA evidence that the pelicans are not closely related to the other pelecaniforms.

This group may present the most complex and controversial questions in the avian phylogeny. Is it possible that the totipalmate foot, lack of an incubation patch, the intraorbital salt gland, and other shared characters either have evolved more than once or are primitive characters that have been lost in the other lineages of the Ciconiides? This explanation will be rejected as improbable by most morphologists, but it should be considered as an alternative hypothesis to the monophyly of the totipalmate birds. We urge that the possibility of polyphyly be tested by independent studies of both molecules and morphology. Whatever the correct answer may be, it will be instructive.

More on some of these questions below.

Herons, Hamerkop, Flamingos, Ibises, Shoebill, Pelicans, New World Vultures, and Storks

Order CICONIIFORMES
  Suborder Ciconii
    Infraorder Ciconiides
      Parvorder Ciconiida
        Superfamily Ardeoidea
          Family Ardeidae: Herons, Bitterns, Egrets
        Superfamily Scopoidea
          Family Scopidae: Hamerkop or Hammerhead
        Superfamily Phoenicopteroidea
          Family Phoenicopteridae: Flamingos
        Superfamily Threskiornithoidea
          Family Threskiornithidae: Ibises, Spoonbills
        Superfamily Pelecanoidea
          Family Pelecanidae
            Subfamily Balaenicipitinae: Shoebill
            Subfamily Pelecaninae: Pelicans
        Superfamily Ciconioidea
          Family Ciconiidae
            Subfamily Ciconiinae: Storks, Openbills, Adjutants, Jabiru
            Subfamily Cathartinae: New World Vultures

In virtually all previous classifications the long-legged, long-necked wading birds have been placed together in the Ciconiiformes, Ardeiformes, Herodiones, Grallatores, or Pelargi. Linnaeus (1758) included them in his order Grallae with the shorebirds and gruiforms; cranes and herons were in the genus *Ardea* in the Linnaean classification. Thus, the assumption has been that long legs and long necks indicate relationship and to some degree this has proved to be correct. The exceptions include the discoveries, first from morphological similarities and now supported by DNA comparisons, that the pelicans and the Shoebill are closely related, and that the New World vultures and storks are closely related.

The storks, ibises, flamingos, pelicans, herons, boobies, cormorants, and anhingas have

504

desmognathous palates, diastataxic wings, small colic caeca, and usually tracheo-bronchial syringes. These characters are also shared with other major groups of birds, hence they are primitive in the cladistic sense and of limited value as evidence of the relationships of sub-groups. The characters that help to define the various groups are as follows:

Family ARDEIDAE: 20/65. Herons occur in all temperate and tropical regions and on most islands. Pelvic muscles AXY, rarely XY (Garrod); 4 or 6 powder-down patches on sides of rump and on breast; aftershaft present; holorhinal; interorbital septum fenestrated; claw of middle toe pectinate; flexor tendons Type 1 or 7; tarsus scutellate in front, rarely reticulate; short web between outer and middle toes; hind toe at level of inner toe; lores bare; bill straight or slightly curved, with "tooth" near tip, often serrate near tip of maxilla; 19–20 cervical vertebrae, 6th elongate with modified articular surfaces that permit S-shaped curve of neck; 11 primaries; usually 12 rectrices, rarely 8 or 10; oil gland variable, generally small, bilobed, tufted in most species, *Cochlearius* differs in having a large, untufted oil gland; eggs greenish or pale blue; one coat of nestling down.

Family SCOPIDAE: 1/1. The Hamerkop or Hammerhead (*Scopus umbretta*) occurs in tropical Africa, Arabia, and Madagascar, mainly in swamps, marshes, and along streams. It has 16 cervical vertebrae; the furcula does not reach the crista sterni; pelvic muscles AXY; 10 primaries; 16 secondaries; 12 rectrices; no powder downs; lores feathered; no biceps slip; partial division of pectoralis primus; flexor tendons Type 1, with one or two vincula between the flexor hallucis and flexor communis; hallux incumbent; bases of inner and outer toes webbed; bill large, compressed, with decurved tip; culmen narrow and ridged, with the nasal groove extending the length of the bill; head crested; oil gland bilobed, tufted; solitary breeders; nest a large (one-meter diameter), enclosed structure of sticks, grass, and mud placed in the fork of a tree; 3–6 chalky white eggs; young nidicolous.

Family PHOENICOPTERIDAE: 1/5 (or 1/4 or 3/4 or 3/5). The living species of flamingos are usually divided into three genera: *Phoenicopterus* with one or two species, *ruber* and *chilensis*, if two are recognized; Lesser Flamingo (*Phoeniconaias minor*) of Africa; and the two South American species of *Phoenicoparrus*, *andinus* and *jamesi*. The DNA comparisons show that the five species are closely related and we include them in *Phoenicopterus*.

Flamingos seem to combine a mosaic of the characters of storks and ducks: long legs and necks, webbed feet, and a bill that is bent in the middle with fine, transverse lamellae on the inner surfaces of maxilla and mandible; the maxilla fits inside the mandible or rests on it. Occipital fontanelles present.

The pelvic muscle formula is BXY+; hallux small or absent; tarsus scutate; tibia mostly bare; carotids fuse near base into a single vessel, right root reduced; holorhinal, pervious, slit-like nares; large caeca; stork-like sternum with a large incision on each side; pterylosis stork-like; pelvis, other skeletal features, muscular characters, intestinal coiling, all stork-like; mandible with hooked posterior process, as in ibises; lores bare; tongue fleshy as in ducks; oil gland densely tufted, bilobed; primaries 11; secondaries 23–25; rectrices 12–16; cervical vertebrae 19; nidifugous young with two downy plumages; colonial breeders; nest is a mound of mud and stones with a depression in the top; one white egg.

Family THRESKIORNITHIDAE: 14/34. The ibises and spoonbills occur in the tropical and subtropical regions on all continents. The ibises have long, decurved bills, and the spoonbills a straight bill, spatulate at the tip. The pelvic muscle formula is ABXY+; nares impervious and schizorhinal; mandible with hooked posterior process; furcula not meeting the carina; sternum with two incisions on each side; 17–18 cervical vertebrae; 10 primaries; 12 rectrices; no powder downs; occipital fontanelles present; fly with neck extended; pterylosis as in storks; biceps slip present; plantar tendons connected by a vinculum; oil gland bilobed, tufted; colonial breeders; nest of sticks in tree; 2–5 eggs; nidicolous; two coats of nestling down.

Family PELECANIDAE, Subfamily BALAENICIPITINAE: 1/1. The Shoebill (*Balaeniceps rex*) occurs in the papyrus swamps of central Africa from the Central African Empire, northern Cameroon, southern Sudan, and eastern Zaire, to western Tanzania and northern Zambia. The enormous broad, hooked, bill is the most obvious character.

The pelvic muscle formula is AXY; interorbital septum complete; nares impervious; lores bare; 16–17 cervical vertebrae; furcula ankylosed to the crista sterni (as in *Pelecanus*); only right carotid; 11 primaries; 12 rectrices; 1 pair of large powder-down patches extending almost from shoulder to tail; oil gland small, large tuft, indistinctly bilobed; hind toe long; fore toes not webbed; syrinx heron-like, intrinsic muscles represented by a ligament; palate like that of *Scopus*; nest a cone of grass on floating vegetation or island; 1–3 eggs; downy, nidicolous young.

Family PELECANIDAE, Subfamily PELECANINAE: 1/8. The species of *Pelecanus* occur in the tropical and temperate regions of the world. The long bill, large gular pouch, and totipalmate feet are the most obvious external characters. As discussed above, the pelicans have been allied with the other totipalmate birds from the earliest classifications.

The pelvic muscle formula is AX; no ambiens; nares impervious; furcula ankylosed to crista sterni; single left carotid; flexor tendons Type 2; caeca small; syrinx tracheo-bronchial, no intrinsic muscles; cervical vertebrae 17; primaries 11; secondaries 29; rectrices 20–24; oil gland large, bilobed, tufted; colonial breeders in trees or on ground; 2–3 chalky white eggs; hatchlings naked, develop white, gray, or black down; nidicolous.

Family CICONIIDAE, Subfamily CATHARTINAE: 5/7. New World Vultures. See morphological characters and taxonomic history under the Diurnal Birds of Prey.

Family CICONIIDAE, Subfamily CICONIINAE. 6/19. The storks and jabirus are large wading birds. Most species have long, heavy, straight bills; the species of *Mycteria* have blunt, slightly decurved bills. Kahl (1979) recognized six genera and 17 species of ciconiines. They occur on all continents in tropical and temperate latitudes, but are absent from northern North America, New Zealand, and the islands of the Pacific Ocean.

Pelvic muscle formula AXY(+) (or XY+); ambiens feeble, absent in some; flexor tendons Type 1; nares holorhinal, pervious; sternum with one pair of notches; bills large, not hooked at tip; angle of mandible truncated; pectoralis muscle double; no biceps slip; 17–18 cervical vertebrae; 11 primaries, the outer vestigial (absent in *Anastomus*); 17–26 secondaries; 12 rectrices; no powder downs; hind toe elevated, short front toes webbed basally; middle claw not pectinate; syrinx tracheal or tracheo-bronchial, no intrinsic syringeal muscles; oil gland large, bilobed, tufted; fly with neck extended; colonial or solitary breeders; nest of sticks in tree, cliff, building; 3–5 eggs; nidicolous.

The taxonomic histories of the long-legged, long-necked waders are intertwined, and we will review them under two headings: Herons, Storks, Ibises, and Allies; and Flamingos. The New World vultures (Cathartinae) are reviewed with the Diurnal Birds of Prey, with which traditionally they have been associated. The Pelecaninae, Sulidae, Phalacrocoracidae, and Anhingidae have been reviewed in the previous section.

Historical Review of the Classification

HERONS, STORKS, IBISES, AND ALLIES

In this review "ciconiiform" will refer to the herons, storks, and ibises—essentially those groups traditionally included in the Ciconiiformes.

Nitzsch (1840) placed the herons and the Sunbittern (*Eurypyga*) in his "family Erodii." *Ciconia*, *Anastomus* (Openbill storks), *Ibis* (*Mycteria*), and *Scopus* differ from the Erodii in their pterylosis and were separated as the Pelargi. A third family, Hemiglottides, was composed of ibises and spoonbills which Nitzsch considered to be similar to the storks, plovers, and sandpipers.

Bartlett (1860, 1861) discovered the powder downs on the lower back of *Balaeniceps* and concluded that it is more closely allied to the herons than to the storks and pelicans. He also found the hind toes and viscera (stomach, liver, intestine) to be heron-like. However, Reinhardt (1860, 1862) regarded the Shoebill as most closely related to *Scopus* and placed both in a subfamily closer to the storks than to the herons.

W. K. Parker (1861) was impressed by skeletal similarities among *Balaeniceps*, *Scopus*, and *Cochlearius* (Boat-billed Heron) and concluded that they are closely related. He was also convinced of the ciconiiform affinities of *Balaeniceps*.

Huxley (1867) placed the herons and storks in his "Suborder Desmognathae, Group Pelargomorphae." He thought that the ibises and spoonbills are most closely related to the flamingos and that the herons and storks are more closely allied to the totipalmate birds (pelicans, cormorants, boobies, etc.).

The order Grallatores of Sundevall (1872, see 1889) corresponded to the Grallae of Linnaeus and was defined as containing birds with "The feet long, with the tibiae bare at the tip; the toes cleft." This group included the cohort Herodii (herons), cohort Pelargi (spoonbills, storks, ibises, Hamerkop, Shoebill), and other cohorts containing the shorebirds and gruiforms.

Garrod (1873d, 1874a) listed the cohorts in his order Ciconiiformes in the sequence: Pelargi (storks), Cathartidae, Herodiones, Steganopodes (totipalmate birds), Accipitres; thus expressing his belief in an alliance between the New World vultures and the storks.

Reichenow (1877) thought that *Balaeniceps* is ciconiiform and most closely related to *Scopus*, but also related to the storks. His diagram of the ciconiiforms has two main branches stemming from the ibises: one to the herons, the other to the storks. Although located next to the storks, *Balaeniceps* is pictured as an offshoot from *Scopus*, which itself is on a side branch of the heron lineage.

Sclater (1880b) placed his ciconiiform families (Ardeidae, Ciconiidae, Plataleidae) between the Steganopodes and the Anseres. Reichenow's (1882) order Gressores included the ibises (Ibidae), storks (Ciconidae), flamingos (Phoenicopteridae), Hamerkop (Scopidae), Shoebill (Balaenicipidae), and herons (Ardeidae). Stejneger (1885) recognized the same families but gave superfamily rank to the ibises and spoonbills in his order Herodii, and transferred the flamingos to his order Chenomorphae with the waterfowl (Anseriformes).

Beddard (1884:552) concluded that *Scopus* is intermediate between the storks and herons: "On myological grounds only it would be difficult to assign it definitely to either group, in fact, the only features in which this genus especially resembles the Herons and differs markedly from the Storks are the form of the syrinx and the air-sacs, while . . . the arrangement of the feather-tracts and the structure of the skeleton are more particularly Stork-like."

Beddard (1888a) concluded from skeletal comparisons that *Balaeniceps* is a typical stork. He stated that herons, storks, and *Balaeniceps* are extremely similar osteologically, with some herons having stork-like characters and some storks having heron-like characters.

Skeletal comparisons convinced Shufeldt (1889b) that the North American herons are closely related to one another. He placed the night herons in *Nycticorax* and the other herons in *Ardea*. The bitterns (*Botaurus*, including *Ixobrychus*) presumably would have been assigned to an adjacent subfamily.

The arrangement of the secondary coverts in the herons is most like that of the falconiforms, excluding *Sagittarius* and the New World vultures (Goodchild 1886). However, the Marabou Stork (*Leptoptilos*) is like the cathartines in this character. The spoonbills and ibises differ little from *Ciconia*, but the arrangement of these coverts in *Ibis* (*Mycteria*) is like that in the charadriiforms.

Fürbringer (1888) placed *Balaeniceps* and *Scopus* in monotypic families and assigned *Cochlearius* to the Ardeidae. The ciconiiforms were the "Gens Pelargo-Herodii" in his system, and he thought them to be related to the pelecaniforms and falconiforms, as well as to the flamingos.

In his "ancient Ardeino-Anserine assemblage" Seebohm (1889) included the suborders Plataleae (ibises, spoonbills) and Herodiones (herons, storks), placed between the Phoenicopteri and the Steganopodes (pelicans, etc.). He believed that the Shoebill and Hamerkop are storks, and that the Boat-bill (*Cochlearius*) is a heron. In his 1890 classification he divided the Aves into seven subclasses, 13 orders, and 36 suborders. One portion of this arrangement was as follows:

Subclass Coraciiformes
  Order Cathartes
    Suborder Cathartes (New World vultures)
Subclass Anseriformes
  Order Pelecano-Herodiones
    Suborder Steganopodes (totipalmate birds)
    Suborder Herodiones (herons, storks, *Scopus*, *Balaeniceps*)
    Suborder Plataleae (spoonbills, ibises)
  Order Lamellirostres
    Suborder Phoenicopteri (flamingos)
    Suborder Anseres (waterfowl)
    Suborder Palamedeae (screamers)

In 1895 Seebohm again changed his classification. The Herodiones, Anseres, and Steganopodes were treated as suborders of the Ciconiiformes, with the Ibididae, Scopidae, Ardeidae, and Ciconiidae as families in the Herodiones.

Gadow (1893:55) reviewed Seebohm's system and pronounced his arrangements retrogressive. Newton (1896:Intro. 103) scathingly denounced Seebohm and his classifications, and criticized Sharpe as a "disciple of Mr. Seebohm" for having used Seebohm's 1890 version as the basis of Sharpe's 1891 classification.

Sharpe's (1891) arrangement, which elicited Newton's ire, used an order Pelargiformes with suborders for the herons, storks, Shoebill, Hamerkop, spoonbills, and ibises; followed by the orders Phoenicopteriformes (flamingos), Anseriformes, Pelecaniformes, Cathartidiformes, and Accipitriformes. Obviously, Sharpe was trying to express several disparate ideas by placing the flamingos between the storks and waterfowl, and the New World vultures between the waterbird groups and the diurnal raptors. Sharpe's diagrams of these groups reflect his opinion that the ciconiiforms are allied to the flamingos and waterfowl in one direction, and to the New World vultures in another.

Gadow (1892) proposed the following arrangement:

ARDEIFORMES
    Steganopodes (totipalmate birds = "Pelecaniformes")
    Herodii
        Ardeidae (herons, Shoebill)
        Scopidae (Hamerkop)
    Pelargi
        Ciconiidae (storks, ibises, spoonbills)
        Phoenicopteridae (flamingos)
FALCONIFORMES
    Cathartae (New World vultures)
    Accipitres

In 1893 Gadow modified his classification:

CICONIIFORMES
    Steganopodes (totipalmate birds)
    Ardeae
        Ardeidae (herons, Shoebill)
        Scopidae (Hamerkop)
    Ciconiae
        Ciconiidae (storks)
        Ibidae (ibises, spoonbills)
    Phoenicopteri
        Phoenicopteridae (flamingos)
ANSERIFORMES
    Palamedeae (screamers)
    Anseres (waterfowl)
FALCONIFORMES
    Cathartae (New World vultures)
    Accipitres (diurnal birds of prey)

The recurrent themes in these arrangements are the alliances of the pelecaniforms to the ciconiiforms, of the flamingos to ciconiiforms and anseriforms, and of the New World vultures to ciconiiforms and falconiforms.

In the *Catalogue of Birds* Sharpe (1898) divided the ciconiiforms into two orders, Plataleae (ibises, spoonbills) and Herodiones (herons, Shoebill, Hamerkop, storks), followed by the order Steganopodes.

In the *Hand-List* (1899) Sharpe changed the classification again; the order Ardeiformes was divided into the suborders Plataleae (ibises, spoonbills), Ciconiae (storks), Scopi (Hamerkop), Balaenicipites (Shoebill), and Ardeae (herons), followed by the orders Phoenicopteriformes, Anseriformes, Pelecaniformes, Cathartidiformes, and Accipitriformes. Part of this sequence was adopted by Wetmore (1930, 1960).

Beddard (1898a) reviewed the morphology and taxonomic history of the ciconiiforms (his Herodiones) and recognized the families Scopidae, Ciconiidae, Ardeidae, Balaenicepidae (sic), Plataleidae, and Phoenicopteridae. He discussed the assertion "that there are likenesses between the Herodiones and the accipitrine birds" which "reduces itself to a comparison between the Herodiones . . . and the Cathartidae and *Serpentarius* [*Sagittarius*]" (pp. 442–443). Beddard noted two similarities between ciconiiforms and "these lower accipitrines," namely, the coiling pattern of the intestines and the lack of intrinsic syringeal muscles in storks and New World vultures. The first he ascribed to convergence, and the second "point of resemblance rests . . . upon mere negativity." He stated that the syringeal muscle loss in the two groups had occurred in different ways and that "there is . . . as much to be said for a derivation of the Accipitres from the crane as from the pelargine stock."

Shufeldt (1901d) was skeptical about the proposed alliances between the ciconiiforms and the pelecaniforms or falconiforms. He believed that the ciconiiforms are linked to the waterfowl via the spoonbills and flamingos, that the Ardeidae are the most distinctive group, and that the storks and ibises are closely allied via the Wood Stork (*Mycteria americana*).

Mitchell (1913) studied the anatomy of *Balaeniceps* and expressed doubt that anatomical characters are adequately understood as indicators of phyletic relationships. He weighted all characters equally and grouped the Shoebill with the storks, ibises, and *Scopus* in the suborder Ciconiae, and the herons in the suborder Ardeae. He considered this a temporary phenetic classification, not an expression of phylogeny.

Chandler (1916) found differences in feather structure between the stork-ibis group and the herons and placed them in two suborders in his Ciconiiformes, an order that also included the Steganopodes and the Phoenicopteri. He concluded: "The Ardeae, or at least the Ardeidae, seem to form an end branch from the ciconiid stem, being comparatively more specialized than the Ciconiae, and apparently not giving rise to any other orders or suborders. *Eurypyga*, and to a lesser extent, *Cariama*, have a feather structure which is so heron-like that the possibility of their inclusion in the Ardeae is strongly suggested. *Cursorius* likewise has a feather structure which strongly argues for its inclusion in this group" (p. 324). Chandler seems to have been unaware of the probability of convergence to explain such similarities.

From a study of the skull of *Balaeniceps*, Böhm (1930) concluded that it is a typical stork, convergent toward *Cochlearius* in the shape of the bill. He considered similarities to *Scopus* to be superficial.

E. Stresemann (1934) thought the ciconiiforms are most closely related to the pelecaniforms and falconiforms. Although he placed *Balaeniceps* and *Scopus* in monotypic families in his order Gressores, he believed them to be more closely related to the storks than to the herons; he assigned the Boat-billed Heron (*Cochlearius*) to the Ardeidae.

According to Szidat (1942) the trematodes of herons and storks are markedly different, those of herons suggesting a relationship to the falconiforms.

Hopkins (1942) found two genera of Mallophaga on *Scopus* that are also found on the charadriiforms. *Scopus* shares only one genus of feather mites with the storks, flamingos, and waterfowl. Hopkins suggested that (1) *Scopus* is a charadriiform which has secondarily acquired the mite from a stork, or (2) the ciconiiforms and charadriiforms had a common ancestor and that *Scopus* is an early offshoot from the shorebird branch.

Clay (1950) noted that of nine genera of Mallophaga found on ciconiiforms, three are common to the herons, storks, and ibises, but only one of them has been found on the Shoebill. She wrote: "One genus (*Ciconiphilus*) found on the Ciconiiformes is also found on *Cygnus* (Swans: Anseriformes) and another (*Ibidoecus*) characteristic of the Threskiornithidae (Ibises) is also found on *Aramus scolopaceus* (Limpkin: Gruiformes); a third genus (*Laemobothrion*) found on some Threskiornithidae is again found on the Rallidae (Rails), Psophiidae (Trumpeters), *Opisthocomus* (Hoatzin) and less closely related species on the Falconiformes (Birds of Prey). The distribution of these genera suggests that *Ciconiphilus* may be a straggler on the swans from the Ciconiiformes, *Ibidoecus* a straggler on *Aramus* from the Threskiornithidae and *Laemobothrion* a straggler on this latter superfamily from the Rallidae" (p. 435).

Mayr and Amadon (1951) included *Cochlearius* in the Ardeidae, *Balaeniceps* in the Ciconiidae, and felt that the Ciconiiformes may be related to the flamingos.

Bock (1956) revised the classification of the herons based on traditional characters (powder downs, plumes, general proportions, color pattern, and nesting habits) as follows:

Family Ardeidae
  Subfamily Botaurinae, Bitterns
  Subfamily Ardeinae
    Tribe Tigriornithini, Tiger Herons
    Tribe Nycticoracini, Night Herons, incl. *Cochlearius*
    Tribe Ardeini, Day Herons

Bock synonymized 18 of the genera recognized by Peters (1931), thus reducing the genera of herons from 33 to 15.

Adams (1955) compared the skeletons of *Nycticorax* and *Nyctanassa* and concluded that they should be retained as separate genera.

Humphrey and Parkes (1963) disagreed with Bock's proposal to merge *Syrigma* with *Nycticorax*. From field studies of behavior and voice, and an evaluation of molts, juvenal plumage, and structure of cervical vertebrae, they argued that *Syrigma* belongs in Bock's tribe Ardeini.

Eisenmann (1965) recommended that *Tigrisoma* should include only *lineatum*, *fasciatum* (including *salmoni*), and *mexicanum*.

Cottam (1957) conducted a comparative study of the skeletons of *Balaeniceps*, herons, storks, and pelecaniforms. She concluded that the Shoebill "could occupy a monotypic family in the order Pelecaniformes, possibly near the Pelecanidae" (p. 70). The main points supporting this conclusion were:

1. *Balaeniceps* has a well-developed hook at the tip of the premaxilla like *Pelecanus*, *Phalacrocorax*, *Fregata*, and the newly hatched chicks of *Sula*. A conspicuous groove running from the anterior edge of the nostril, flanking the culmen, to the cutting edge of the premaxilla beside the terminal hook is shared by *Balaeniceps*, *Pelecanus*, *Sula*, *Phalacrocorax*, and *Fregata*.

2. The nasal septum is ossified in *Balaeniceps*, the Pelecani, and the Fregatae; in

Balaeniceps, as in *Pelecanus*, the external nares are above the internal nares, with the nasal cavity situated ventrally between them.

3. The palatine bones of *Balaeniceps* are ankylosed along the midline, posterior to the internal nares. There is a broad ventral ridge above the suture, alongside of which lie depressions for the attachment of the pterygoid musculature. This condition is quite similar to that found in *Sula*, *Phalacrocorax*, and *Pelecanus* and also resembles that of *Fregata*.

4. *Balaeniceps*, the Pelecani, and *Fregata* each have a large lachrymal which meets the quadratojugal bar. In *Balaeniceps*, complete occlusion of the antorbital vacuity is achieved by fusion of the lachrymal with the maxilla; in the Pelecani, particularly *Sula*, and in the Fregatae there is a tendency toward reduction of the antorbital cavity.

5. While the jaw articulation in *Balaeniceps* resembles that of the Ardeidae in some respects, it agrees with that of the Fregatae and Pelecani in those aspects differing from the ciconiiform condition.

6. The hypocleideum of the furcula of *Balaeniceps* is fused to the keel of the sternum, as it is in *Fregata* and many specimens of *Pelecanus*.

7. The form of the first metatarsal in *Balaeniceps* and the presumed function of the first toe seems more like those of *Pelecanus* than like those of any of the ciconiiform birds.

Cottam's conclusions were ascribed to convergence by most avian systematists, but the DNA data support her conclusion that *Balaeniceps* is closely related to *Pelecanus*.

Wetmore (1960) admitted that *Cochlearius* superficially resembles the Black-crowned Night-Heron (*N. nycticorax*) but argued that *Cochlearius* differs from the typical herons in numerous characters of the skull, and that the "eyes, wood brown by day, at night reflect the jacklight with a faint orange sheen, which I have not observed in other herons" (p. 10). He concluded that "from long acquaintance I regard their characters [as] sufficient to maintain a separate family status." Here again, the emphasis is on differences to justify a higher categorical rank, rather than using similarities to provide evidence of phylogenetic relationships.

Meyerriecks (1960) studied the breeding behavior of four species of North American herons, compared them with six other species, and summarized the evolution of ardeid social behavior: "The probable course of social behavior in herons has been from the primitive solitary status exemplified by *Botaurus*, through a transitory semisocial phase (*Butorides* and *Ixobrychus*), to extreme, year around sociality, represented by *Leucophoyx*, *Bubulcus*, and *Nycticorax*. The night herons (*Nycticorax* and *Nyctanassa*) must have evolved their present highly social structure independently of such species as [*Egretta*] *thula* and *rufescens*, because they differ in numerous respects, both behavioral and structural."

The Ciconiiformes of Verheyen (1959a, 1960g) contained the suborders Ardeae, Scopi, Ciconiae, and Balaenicipites. He thought the storks are related to the flamingos and shorebirds through the ibises and spoonbills. *Balaeniceps* and some of the Ardeae were supposedly links to the pelecaniforms. *Cochlearius* was placed in a tribe in the Ardeidae. In 1961 Verheyen included only the Scopidae, Ciconiidae, and Threskiornithidae in his Ciconiiformes. He placed the Shoebill and the herons in the adjacent order Ardeiformes and, following Wetmore (1960), he recognized the Cochleariidae for the Boat-billed Heron.

With paper electrophoresis, Sibley (1960) compared the egg-white proteins of 17 species of herons, five ibises and spoonbills, a stork, and a flamingo. The herons, ibises, stork, and flamingo showed more similarities to one another than to any other order. The pattern of *Mycteria americana* showed "affinities to the herons and ibises and is similar to *Pelecanus*." The heron patterns also contained similarities to those of the loons, some pelecaniforms, and some charadriiforms.

Kahl and Peacock (1963) described the bill-snap reflex of the Wood Stork (*Mycteria americana*), which is a tactile method for locating and seizing prey in turbid water. Kahl (1966a) found that this method is also used by the Marabou Stork (*Leptoptilos crumeniferus*) and the Yellow-billed Stork (*Mycteria ibis*) when feeding in muddy water.

Kahl (1963) observed that heat-stressed storks pant rapidly and excrete watery feces on their legs ("urohidrosis"). He suggested that urohidrosis increases heat loss by evaporation. Urohidrosis occurs in storks and New World vultures, but not in *Scopus* or *Balaeniceps* (Kahl 1967a). When heat-stressed, *Scopus* pants rapidly and increases its respiratory rate and *Balaeniceps* flutters the gular region, as do pelicans and herons.

By controlled experiments Hatch (1970) showed that the body temperature of the Turkey Vulture (*Cathartes aura*) is reduced by urohidrosis or by putting water on the legs. The liquid excreted by a heat-stressed Turkey Vulture is 95% water by weight. Captive birds maintained without drinking water can excrete as much as 10 cc per hour, and 7.5 cc per hour will lower the body temperature 1°C.

Kahl (1967b) noted that *Scopus* flies buoyantly, unlike storks and herons, but like storks, it sometimes soars. On the ground it does not sit on its tarsi as do storks, and when resting in trees its legs are folded under the body and the breast touches the perch, unlike storks. *Scopus* does not use the bill-snap feeding method, but does employ foot-stirring like that of herons. The bill-clattering displays of storks and the stretch displays of herons have no counterparts in the Hamerkop and it lacks the habit of exchanging sticks during nest building, as do many other ciconiiforms.

Kahl (1964, 1966b) also studied the ecology and breeding biology of *Mycteria americana* and *Leptoptilos crumeniferus*, and the possible functions of the spread-wing postures of the storks (1971). He suggested that the presence of urohidrosis in storks, New World vultures, and at least one species of cormorant might indicate relationships.

Mainly from skeletal characters, Ligon (1967) emphasized the "extreme anatomical dissimilarities" between herons and storks and placed them in separate orders. Like several earlier authors (e.g., Garrod 1873d, 1874a) Ligon declared the New World vultures (Cathartinae) to be related to the storks and he included them in the same order. Unfortunately he did not make comparisons with other ciconiiform groups. The DNA comparisons support the stork-cathartine alliance.

Cracraft (1967) examined the skeleton of the Boat-billed Heron (*Cochlearius*), compared it with those of other herons, and concluded that it is most closely related to the night-herons.

Curry-Lindahl (1968, 1971) compared the breeding displays, feeding techniques, and other behavior patterns of various species of herons. He agreed with the relationships proposed by Bock (1956), with the following exceptions:

1. *Ixobrychus sturmii* is placed in monotypic *Ardeirallus*.
2. *Nycticorax pileatus* is placed in monotypic *Pilherodius*.

3. *Egretta alba* is placed in *Ardea*.

4. *Butorides virescens* and *striatus* are conspecific, as also are *Egretta garzetta* and *thula*, and *Ardea cinerea* and *herodias*.

Parkes (1955) also suggested the mergence of *Ardea herodias* and *A. cinerea*.

Vanden Berge (1970) examined the appendicular musculature of 21 ciconiiform genera representing all groups except the Scopidae. He found a lack of consistency in the muscle patterns, but thought that the ciconiiforms, including flamingos, are more similar to one another than any one is to the members of other orders. He rejected Ligon's (1967) decision to split the order, but agreed with Bock (1956) and Cracraft (1967) that *Cochlearius* is most similar to the night-herons.

Sibley and Ahlquist (1972) compared the electrophoretic patterns of the egg-white proteins of members of the ciconiiform groups, except *Balaeniceps*. They found the patterns of the 32 species of herons for which egg-white specimens were available to be uniform. *Cochlearius* fit the ardeid pattern. The storks and ibises differed slightly from the herons and from one another; *Scopus* agreed best with the storks. The flamingos were judged to be closer to the ciconiiforms than to any other group, but we also concluded, erroneously, that the Anseriformes are the closest relatives of the ciconiiforms. We saw "little or no evidence . . . to suggest a close relationship between the Ciconiiformes and either the Pelecaniformes or the Falconiformes."

Payne and Risley (1976) compared 33 osteological characters among 53 of the 62 species of herons and analyzed the results by phenetic and cladistic methods. In the Ardeidae they recognized four subfamilies: Ardeinae, day herons; Nycticoracinae, night-herons; Tigrisomatinae, tiger-herons; and Botaurinae, bitterns. They concluded that *Syrigma* and *Pilherodius* are distinct from other day herons; that *Zebrilus* is closest to the bitterns, not to the tiger-herons; that *Tigrosoma* species are more closely related to one another than any one is to the African *Tigriornis*; and that allopatric semispecies tend to be similar in the kinds of skeletal characters they examined. Among several changes in generic and tribal allocations, they placed *Cochlearius* in the Cochlearini of the Nycticoracinae.

Parkes (1978) reviewed the problems of generic and specific taxonomy in the ciconiiforms, but did not comment on higher-category relationships. He suggested that hybridization between captive birds should be used as evidence of genetic similarity, and listed a number of examples.

Olson (1978) supported Cottam's (1957) suggestion that the Shoebill is closely related to the pelicans, but Cracraft (1981:693, 1985) concluded that the similarities between the two taxa are convergences and that the Shoebill is the sister taxon of the herons. Feduccia (1977) argued that the Shoebill is a stork on the basis of similarities in their stapes, but Olson (1978:168) reported that Feduccia (pers. comm.) also found the same "unique derived condition of the stapes . . . closely approached in certain Pelecaniformes."

Olson (1978) declared that the traditional order Ciconiiformes is polyphyletic. He assigned the flamingos to the Charadriiformes, placed the ibises between the Charadriiformes and the Gruiformes, and proposed that the Shoebill, Hamerkop, storks, and pelecaniforms compose a "loosely interrelated" group. The herons were transferred to the Gruiformes, closest to the mesitornithids, the Sunbittern, and the Kagu.

Hancock and Elliott (1978) reviewed the biology and classification of the herons and presented an eclectic classification based mainly on those of Bock (1956), Curry-Lindahl (1971), and Payne and Risley (1976). Two subfamilies, Ardeinae and Botaurinae, were recognized, and the Boat-billed Heron was placed with *Nycticorax* and *Gorsachius* in the Nycticoracini of the Ardeinae.

Payne (1979) provided the classification of the herons for the revised edition of Peters' *Check-list of Birds of the World.* He based the arrangement on Payne and Risley (1976) with *Casmerodius* in *Ardea*, *Bubulcus* in *Egretta*, *Butorides* in *Ardeola*, and the species *magnificus*, *goisagi*, and *melanolophus* in *Nycticorax*, rather than *Gorsachius*.

Kahl (1979) developed a classification of the storks, based mainly on his observations of courtship behavior:

Order Ciconiiformes
  Suborder Ardeae: Herons
  Suborder Scopi
    Family Scopidae: Hamerkop
  Suborder Ciconiae
    Family Ciconiidae
        Tribe Mycteriini: *Mycteria* [*Ibis*], *Anastomus*
        Tribe Ciconiini: *Ciconia* [*Dissoura, Sphenorhynchus, Euxenura*]
        Tribe Leptoptilini: *Ephippiorhynchus* [*Xenorhynchus*], *Jabiru, Leptoptilos*
    Family Balaenicipitidae: *Balaeniceps*
    Family Threskiornithidae
      Subfamily Threskiornithinae: Ibises (12 genera)
      Subfamily Plataleinae: Spoonbills
Order Phoenicopteriformes: Flamingos

Cracraft (1981) placed the Ciconiiformes and Falconiformes in his "Division 3." In the Ciconiiformes he defined two lineages: (1) flamingos, storks, ibises; (2) herons and *Balaeniceps*. These two groups were considered to be the sister group of *Scopus*.

"The major skeletal elements of all 17 species of storks were analyzed using . . . multivariate statistics to assess the phenetic affinities within the . . . Ciconiidae" (Wood 1983). The results were similar to Kahl's classification, except that *Jabiru* was more similar to *Ephippiorhynchus* than suggested by Kahl's arrangement, and these two genera were phenetically more similar to *Ciconia* than to *Leptoptilos*. Wood (1983:95) presented a phenogram "derived from UPGMA clustering of average taxonomic distances" based on a transformation of the data in the 51 phenograms he had developed from various measurements of ten skeletal elements. This "average phenogram" had three major branches: (1) *Mycteria, Anastomus*; (2) *Ciconia, Ephippiorhynchus, Jabiru*; (3) *Leptoptilos*. 1 and 2 are sister groups, 3 is the sister group of 1+2.

Wood (1984) recoded Kahl's data on courtship behavior in "numerical (multi-state) form," made a phenetic analysis of them, and analyzed the congruence between Kahl's classification and his own, based on skeletal measurements. He concluded that "Similarities based on skeletal morphology are highly congruent with those recalculated from the behavioral data. The classification suggested by both sets of data is similar to that proposed by Kahl with the following changes: (1) *Jabiru* is included with *Ephippiorhynchus*; (2) *Ephippiorhynchus* is transferred into the Ciconiini" (p. 35).

The karyotypes of six species of storks were compared with those of *Balaeniceps*, flamingos, *Cochlearius*, several other herons, and ibises. The members of each group tended to share certain chromosomal characters, but also to have characters shared widely with other groups of birds. The storks and the Shoebill shared "a relatively high number of medium-sized to small biarmed chromosomes with the Ardeidae and the Threskiornithidae. Several characteristics in this group of chromosomes separate" the Shoebill from the storks (de Boer and van Brink 1982).

Hancock (1984) noted that *Casmerodius alba* [*albus*] *modesta* of southeast Asia has an aerial display and other characters like those of species of *Egretta*, but that the American form, *Casmerodius alba* [*albus*] *egretta*, has similarities to species of *Ardea*. He suggested that *modesta* might belong in *Egretta* and *egretta* in *Ardea*.

Hancock and Kushlan (1984) revised the classification of Hancock and Elliott (1978). They followed Payne (1979) for the sequence of taxa, his four subfamilies, and the recognition of the Cochleariini for the Boat-billed Heron. They retained *Bubulcus* and *Butorides*, and placed *Casmerodius* in *Egretta*, rather than in *Ardea*. In *Nycticorax* they placed the traditional species of night-herons, but kept *goisagi, magnificus*, and *melanolophus* in *Gorsachius*.

Sheldon (1987a) used DNA-DNA hybridization to compare the single-copy genomes of 13 species of herons and one ibis (*Plegadis*). He constructed a tree from T_m values and tested for differences in the rates of evolution along each branch. The rate for bittern (*Botaurus, Ixobrychus*) single-copy DNA was found to be ca. 25% faster, and the rate for *Cochlearis* and *Tigrisoma* ca. 19% slower, than that of the day herons and night-herons (e.g., *Ardea, Egretta, Nycticorax*). Sheldon (1987b) compared the single-copy DNAs of 31 species or subspecies of herons and *Plegadis*, constructed a phylogeny from the ΔT_m values, and analyzed the results. He found that the traditional distinction between day herons and night-herons is primarily adaptive and that the two grades are members of the same clade; *Syrigma* is closely related to *Egretta* and *Bubulcus* and *Casmerodius* are closely related to *Ardea*, but *Egretta* is not; bitterns are the sister taxon of the day herons and night-herons; *Cochlearis* and *Tigrisoma* are closest relatives and together form the sister group of the other ardeids. His results supported the linear arrangement of taxa in the classification of Payne and Risley (1976).

FLAMINGOS

One of the most controversial and long-standing problems in avian systematics has been the relationships of the flamingos. Sibley et al. (1969) reviewed the literature relating to the flamingo problem; here we cite studies concerning their phylogeny.

To Linnaeus (1758:139) *Phoenicopterus* was a member of his "Order IV. Grallae," followed by the spoonbills in *Platalea*; the American storks in *Mycteria* and *Tantalus*; and the herons, cranes, White Stork, Black Stork, and ibises in *Ardea*.

Some early classifications placed the flamingos with the waterfowl because of the webbed feet and lamellate bill, e.g., Merrem (1813) and Wagler (1827). Others placed them near the web-footed charadriiforms.

Nitzsch (1840) isolated the flamingos in the "family Odontoglossae." He found their pterylosis to be most similar to those of *Ciconia* and *Tantalus* (*Mycteria*). Gray (1849) placed the Phoenicopteridae next to the Anatidae in his order Anseres, which contained all birds with palmately webbed feet.

Huxley (1867:460) concluded that "the genus *Phoenicopterus* is so completely intermediate between the anserine birds on the one side, and the storks and herons on the other, that it can be ranged with neither of these groups, but must stand as the type of a division by itself." Huxley thus became one of the first to adopt an essentially neutral position in the debate, a position still espoused by those who assume that living groups can be links or intermediates between other living groups. This is a logical impossibility because a phylogeny is a dichotomously branching structure.

The pelvic muscle formula and presence of caeca, aftershaft, and two carotids caused Garrod (1873d, 1874a) to place the flamingos with the thick-knees, Secretary-bird, and seriemas in the Otididae of his order Galliformes. This heterogeneous assemblage demonstrates the nonsense that can emerge from blind dependence on a few morphological characters that have been accepted as definitive of major groups.

Sclater (1880b) considered the flamingos to represent an order intermediate between the ciconiiforms and anseriforms. He commented: "The Herodiones (Pelargomorphae of Huxley) come very naturally, I think, between the Pelicans and the Ducks. In the 'Nomenclator' [Sclater and Salvin 1873] they are divided into four families—Ardeidae, Ciconiidae, Plataleidae, and Phoenicopteridae. I have, however, lately come to the conclusion that the last-named group should not be included in the Herodiones, although as Nitzsch has told us, the pterylosis is completely Stork-like, and occupies a middle place between *Ciconia* and *Tantalus*. Prof. Huxley says 'the genus *Phoenicopterus* is so completely intermixed between the Anserine birds on the one side, and the Storks and Herons on the other, that it can be ranged with neither of these groups, but must stand as a division by itself.' In this opinion I am not quite disposed to agree, and propose to use Nitzsch's appropriate term 'Odontoglossae' to designate the order" (p. 405).

Reichenow (1882) included the flamingos as a family in his order Gressores (Ciconiiformes) with no obvious ties to the waterfowl. Stejneger (1885) sought the middle ground by placing the flamingos in his order Chenomorphae (Anseriformes), but agreed that they are also related to the herons. Among the characters he noted as shared by flamingos and waterfowl are the elongated nasals and lachrymals, narrow frontal bones, presence of grooves for the supraorbital glands, basipterygoid processes, shape of furcula and scapulae, lamellate beak, palmate feet, and 14 rectrices.

Fürbringer (1888) was not convinced of a relationship between flamingos and waterfowl. He placed the flamingos in the "suborder Ciconiiformes" next to the "Pelargo-Herodii" (storks, herons), some distance from the Anseriformes.

From a study of five species of storks, seven anseriforms, and a Greater Flamingo (*P. ruber*), Weldon (1883) concluded that "while the skull and larynx of *Phoenicopterus*, together with its webbed feet and the characters of its bill, undoubtedly connect it with the Lamellirostres [Anseriformes], yet the rest of its organs—its air-cells, its muscles, its alimentary canal, its vertebral column, and the characters of its wing bones—show close relationship with the Storks." Seeking safety in neutrality, he placed the flamingos in their own order, as Huxley (1867) had done.

The pterylography, osteology, myology, and internal anatomy of *Phoenicopterus* convinced Gadow (1877) that flamingos are ciconiiforms, most closely allied to storks and spoonbills. In 1889 he pointed out that the pattern of intestinal convolutions also relate flamingos to storks, and that they share no intestinal features with the waterfowl except small caeca. In 1892 Gadow allied the Phoenicopteridae with the Ciconiidae in the Pelargi of his Ardeiformes, but in 1893 he placed the flamingos in their own suborder, Phoenicopteri, following the storks and ibises (Ciconiae) in the Ciconiiformes. He noted several similarities to the waterfowl and concluded that the Anseriformes and Ciconiiformes are linked by the Anhimidae (screamers) and the flamingos.

Seebohm (1889) concluded from a study of the skeleton that flamingos are intermediate between ducks and herons and closely related to the "Palamedeae" (screamers) and ibises. He ranked these groups as suborders in his "Ardeino-Anserine" order. He soon (1890a) changed his mind and recognized an order Lamellirostres, containing the suborders Phoenicopteri, Anseres, and Palamedeae, placed next to the Pelecano-Herodiones. In 1895 he changed again, erecting an order Ciconiiformes with suborders Herodiones, Anseres, and Steganopodes. The Anseres contained the Anatidae, Phoenicopteridae, and Palamedeidae.

Flamingos have an arrangement of secondary coverts similar to that of spoonbills and storks (except *Leptoptilos*), but the arrangement in herons and bitterns resembles that in the waterfowl and birds of prey (Goodchild 1891). Wray (1887) noted that most birds have six remiges originating on the metacarpus, but that flamingos, storks, and grebes have seven; thus these are the only birds with 12 primaries. W. DeW. Miller (1924a:317) argued that these three groups have 11 true primaries, plus the "remicle." The homology of the remicle (true primary or primary covert) remains uncertain. See Sibley (1970:42–43) and Stresemann and Stephan (1968a,b) for a discussion of the origin and significance of the remicle.

Parker (1889a) observed that the carpals, metacarpals, and phalanges of flamingos are more similar to those of ibises than to those of geese.

Shufeldt (1889c) thought flamingos are most like ibises in their skeletons, but 12 years later (1901e) decided that they are equally related to waterfowl and ciconiiforms and placed them in a separate order, the Odontoglossae.

Sharpe (1891) adopted the neutral position by placing the Phoenicopteriformes between the Pelargiformes and Anseriformes, which included the screamers as the suborder Palamedeae).

In the *Catalogue of Birds* Salvadori (1895) placed the suborders Palamedeae (screamers), Phoenicopteri (flamingos), and Anseres (waterfowl) in the Order Chenomorphae, which he defined: "This Order, the name of which has been proposed by Huxley, comprises all those Carinate birds which combine at least the following two characters:—Palate desmognathous; young covered with down and able to run or swim in a few hours after hatching. The other common characters of the group are:—Neck long, without apteria; oil-gland tufted; wings aquintocubital [diastataxic]; rhamphotheca with ceroma; nares pervious; maxillo-palatines coalesced across the middle line; mandible much produced and curved upwards behind its articulation with the quadrate; flexor perforans digitorum leading to all three anterior digits, but not to the hallux; ambiens muscle present. Eggs white.—Range cosmopolitan. Habits aquatic" (p. 1).

In the *Hand-List* Sharpe (1899) changed some of the names, but used his earlier (1891) arrangement with the Phoenicopteriformes between the ciconiiforms ("Ardeiformes") and the screamers ("Palamedeiformes"), followed by the Anseriformes. Note: the Palamedeiformes were omitted from volume 1 of the *Hand-List*, but an errata sheet in volume 2 directed their insertion on p. 205 of volume 1.

Beddard (1898a) reviewed and evaluated the anatomical evidence and concluded that the flamingos are related to the ciconiiforms and that resemblances to the waterfowl are merely superficial. He placed the Phoenicopteridae in his order Herodiones.

Mitchell (1901a) agreed with earlier studies of the intestinal tract, noting that the flamingos are most like the spoonbills in this respect. The only similarity to the waterfowl is the well-developed caecum, a condition related to diet.

Chandler (1916) noted that flamingo feathers are like those of anseriforms and unlike those of ciconiiforms, in (1) the shape and size of barbules, (2) form of ventral teeth on the proximal and distal barbules, (3) form of ventral and dorsal cilia on the distal barbules, (4) presence and form of the ventral barbicels of the outer proximal barbs.

Stresemann (1934) placed the order Phoenicopteri between the orders Steganopodes (totipalmate birds) and Gressores (ciconiiforms). He considered the flamingos to be "aberrant storks" and attributed similarities to the waterfowl to convergence. Wetmore (1930 to 1960) and Peters (1931) placed the flamingos in a suborder in their Ciconiiformes.

Howard (1950) thought the Upper Cretaceous *Parascaniornis* and Lower Paleocene *Scaniornis* show evidence of relationships to both herons and flamingos. She considered the Lower Cretaceous *Gallornis* to be anseriform, but the material is too fragmentary to offer solid clues to relationships. In 1955 Howard described *Telmabates antiquus* based on a fairly complete postcranial skeleton (Lower Eocene, Argentina) and placed it in the Telmabatidae, which she thought was ancestral to flamingos. In her opinion, *Telmabates* resembles the anseriforms and the fossil genus *Palaelodus*. She suggested that a separate order be recognized for the Telmabatidae, Palaelodidae, and Phoenicopteridae.

Berlioz (1950) included the flamingos in a suborder in his Anseriformes. Mayr and Amadon (1951) noted the conflicting evidence of the relationships of the flamingos and put them in the order Phoenicopteri between the Gressores (ciconiiforms) and Anseres, because "They may be related to both."

The great length of the intestine of flamingos is probably related to their diet and the large caeca in flamingos and waterfowl may be due to convergence, according to Ridley (1954).

Glenny (1945a, 1953a, 1955) found that all anseriforms and most ciconiiforms have the bicarotid (A–1) arrangement of arteries in the neck. Some herons have the B–1 condition in which a single carotid enters the hypapophyseal canal, but it is supplied by paired vessels of equal size from the left and right common carotids. *Balaeniceps* has the B–4-s condition in which the right carotid alone enters the hypapophyseal canal, a unique condition in the ciconiiforms, which Glenny used to assign the Shoebill to a monotypic family. The flamingos and some herons share the B–2-s carotid pattern which Glenny interpreted as evidence of relationship, but the carotid arrangement is variable among the ciconiiforms. For example, *Ardea herodias* has both the A–1 and B–1 conditions, and *Botaurus lentiginosus* has both B–1 and B–2-s. Hence, the flamingos could have evolved their B–2-s pattern from the basic A–1 found in both ciconiiforms and anseriforms.

Jenkin's (1957) study of the feeding mechanism of flamingos found that the shape of the bill, size of the jaws, and configuration of the mandibular joints are correlated with the pumping and filtering processes of feeding. The filtering apparatus of flamingos seems to be more specialized than those of the waterfowl or the Openbill Stork (*Anastomus*), although Jenkin believed that both inherited it from a common ancestor. The bend in the flamingo bill probably developed later in evolution, as it does during ontogeny. The straight, goose-like bill of the hatchling flamingo may seem to support these opinions, but the young of ciconiiforms with specialized bills, such as the spoonbills, also have straight bills like those of flamingo chicks.

Hopkins (1942, 1949), Clay (1950, 1957), and Rothschild and Clay (1952) agreed that the Mallophaga support a flamingo-anseriform relationship. Flamingos are parasitized by three genera of feather mites (*Anaticola, Anatoecus, Trinoton*) which are found otherwise only on the Anseriformes. The ciconiiforms are parasitized by different genera from those of flamingos and anseriforms. The flamingos share the mallophagan genus *Colpocephalum* with both ciconiiforms and anseriforms, but this genus occurs widely on other groups of birds.

Mayr (1957) and the parasitologist von Keler (1957) argued that the occurrence of similar feather mites on flamingos and waterfowl is probably due to recent transfer from the waterfowl to the flamingos. E. Stresemann (1959) agreed and reaffirmed his belief that the flamingos are most closely related to the ciconiiforms. Ash (1960) stressed that Mallophaga are poorly known systematically as well as ecologically.

Baer (1957) found that the cestode parasites of flamingos are most like those of the Charadriiformes, thus adding further confusion to the significance of parasites as indicators of host phylogeny.

Sibley (1960) found consistent differences between the electrophoretic patterns of the egg-white proteins of ciconiiforms and anseriforms. In a series of comparisons, carried out for various periods of separation, the pattern of the Lesser Flamingo (*Phoeniconaias* [*Phoenicopterus*] *minor*) consistently resembled that of the Great Blue Heron (*Ardea herodias*) more than it did that of the Georgian Teal [Yellow-billed Pintail] (*Anas georgica*). The similarity extended to other ciconiiforms (e.g., *Mycteria americana*), and Sibley concluded that the flamingos are related more closely to the ciconiiforms than to the anseriforms. Although electrophoretic patterns are often of doubtful value in questions of this kind, this particular example merits attention as a valid indication of relationship because the patterns of the two groups involved differ greatly, but are consistently similar among species within each group.

Verheyen (1959a, 1960g, 1961) found many characters suggesting an alliance between flamingos and the Ciconiiformes and Anseriformes. In his classification he gave the flamingos ordinal rank between the other two orders.

Although Wetmore (1956:3, 1960:10) thought that the flamingos resemble both Anseriformes and Ciconiiformes he placed them as a suborder in the latter group because this "course remains justified when the fossil genera *Palaelodus* and *Elornis* of the upper Eocene to Miocene of western Europe are considered."

The carotenoid pigment canthaxanthin occurs in the feathers of flamingos, the Scarlet Ibis (*Guara rubra*) [*Eudocimus ruber*], and the Roseate Spoonbill (*Platalea* [*Ajaia*] *ajaja*) (D. L. Fox 1962a–c; Fox and Hopkins 1966a,b; Fox et al. 1965, 1967). However, Brush (1967) found the same pigment in the Scarlet Tanager (*Piranga olivacea*), a passerine. It is possible that the biosynthetic pathways and enzymes involved in the synthesis of this pigment in flamingos and ciconiiforms are alike, and that those in the tanager differ from them, but until this is demonstrated the taxonomic value of this character must be regarded as unreliable.

Mainardi (1962a) prepared antisera against the red cells of a flamingo, a stork, a heron, an ibis, and three species of waterfowl. From the serological reactions he observed, Mainardi concluded that flamingos are equally distant from ciconiiforms and anseriforms and that the three groups are related. In 1963 he proposed a phylogenetic tree, based on immunological and fossil evidence, in which the waterfowl branched first from a common stem and later the flamingos and ciconiiformes diverged.

Sibley et al. (1969) reviewed the literature on the structure, fossil record, behavior, parasites, life history, and protein comparisons involving flamingos and concluded that most evidence is conflicting and difficult to interpret. They presented new data from comparisons of hemoglobins and egg-white proteins which led them to agree with Mainardi (1963). They recommended that the flamingos be placed in a suborder, Phoenicopteri, in the Ciconiiformes, and that the Ciconiiformes and Anseriformes be placed adjacent to one another as in Wetmore (1960).

The starch gel electrophoretic patterns of the hemoglobins of two species of flamingos were compared with those of other groups of birds (Sibley et al. 1969, plus unpublished data). The flamingo patterns resembled those of some ciconiiforms, the boobies, screamers, and some anseriforms; i.e., they were ambiguous. However, the tryptic peptides of the hemoglobins indicated greater similarity between flamingos and ciconiiforms than between flamingos and anseriforms.

Feduccia (1977b, 1978) and Olson and Feduccia (1980a,b) argued that the Eocene fossil *Presbyornis* is proof that the flamingos were derived from charadriiforms, not from ciconiiforms or anseriforms. The abstract from Olson and Feduccia (1980a) summarizes their evidence and argument:

Previous evidence supposedly showing a relationship between flamingos and either storks (Ciconiiformes) or ducks (Anseriformes) is re-examined in light of the recent hypothesis deriving flamingos from shorebirds of the order Charadriiformes. Anatomical characters used to indicate relationship between flamingos and storks are shown to consist entirely of primitive "non-anseriform" traits found in several other orders, including Charadriiformes. Most of the presumed anseriform characters of flamingos also occur in the Charadriiformes, as do all of the characters of flamingos that do not occur in either Ciconiiformes or Anseriformes. The distinctive life history and behavior of flamingos is demonstrated as being very similar to that of the Recurvirostridae . . . particularly the Australian Banded Stilt (*Cladorhynchus leucocephalus*), but is unlike that of storks or ducks. The appendicular myology of *Cladorhynchus* is described and is found to be quite similar to that of flamingos, whereas neither is close to storks. The thigh muscle M. iliotibialis medialis, heretofore considered unique to flamingos, was discovered in *Cladorhynchus* but not in other Recurvirostridae. Evidence from osteology, natal down, oology, and internal parasites strongly supports a charadriiform derivation of flamingos; pterylosis does not contradict such a relationship; and knowledge of the early evolution of flamingos and Anseriformes offers a logical explanation for their sharing similar mallophagan parasites. The earliest certain flamingo, from the early Middle Eocene of Wyoming, is described herein as a new monotypic genus and species that was intermediate in size and morphology between the Recurvirostridae and modern flamingos. Other aspects of paleontology of flamingos are discussed. Evolutionary steps in the development of filter feeding in birds are outlined. The structure of the feeding apparatus of flamingos is shown to be entirely different from that of the Anseriformes, but is strikingly convergent towards that of baleen whales. Morphological and behavioral precursors for filter feeding are shown to occur in the Charadriiformes but not in the Ciconiiformes. Flamingos (Phoenicopteridae) clearly belong in the order Charadriiformes, suborder Charadrii, immediately following the Recurvirostridae.

Many previous studies, and our DNA comparisons, support a phylogeny that is incompatible with the conclusions of Olson and Feduccia.

Jacob and Hoerschelmann (1985) compared the composition of the waxy secretions of the uropygial glands of the flamingos with those of other groups. They concluded that "this composition indicates relationships of the flamingos to wading birds (Charadriiformes), especially to the gulls (Laridae), to ducks (Anseriformes) and loons (Gaviiformes). It is, therefore, supposed that all of them are of common origin. The flamingos, however, should not be combined with one of these orders. The three genera [of flamingos] . . . cannot be distinguished by their preen wax composition. With the exception of *Ph. jamesi*, which diverges from all the remaining species, an identical type of wax occurs in all flamingos. The small qualitative and quantitative differences confirm the close relation between *Ph. ruber ruber* and *Ph. ruber roseus* as well as between them and *Ph. chilensis*."

The preen gland waxes are clearly primitive characters that reveal little or nothing about the relationships of the flamingos.

The karyotype of the flamingos is "identical to those found in . . . all Cathartidae . . . all Gruidae . . . and some Columbidae" (de Boer and van Brink 1982).

The DNA Hybridization Evidence (Figs. 155–175, 340–342, 356, 366–368)

The UPGMA dendrograms (Figs. 356, 366–368) suggest that the sequence of branchings in the Parvorder Ciconiida, from oldest to youngest was: Ardeoidea, Scopoidea, Phoenicopteroidea, Threskiornithoidea, Pelecanoidea, Ciconioidea, Procellarioidea. These branches occurred between Δ $T_{50}H$ 12.4 (Ardeoidea) and 10.9 (Procellarioidea). The branches were so close together that their actual sequence is uncertain and it would be equally appropriate to represent them as a polychotomous branching at ca. Δ $T_{50}H$ 11.6. This is suggested in the classification by assigning all of them to the rank of superfamilies, but using the small average differences as the basis for their sequence in the hierarchy.

The herons (Ardeidae) have been thought to be related to the storks and the DNA evidence agrees, although it indicates that the two groups are distinct. The herons branched at Δ 12.4, and the stork-condor clade at Δ 10.9 (Fig. 367). The herons, Hamerkop, flamingos, ibises, storks, and the Shoebill-pelican clade are the descendants of a common ancestor. Each of these clusters is the result of a radiation that probably began in isolation from its nearest relatives, flourished, and spread widely when it found an unoccupied ecological niche to exploit. They retain the imprint of their common ancestor in their morphological and genetic similarities.

The Hamerkop (*Scopus umbretta*) has been assigned to various groups, but usually in the vicinity of the storks, ibises, herons, and the Shoebill. The DNA evidence agrees; *Scopus* seems to be the only surviving member of a lineage that branched from the other members of this cluster at Δ 11.9 (Fig. 367).

The controversies concerning the relationships of the flamingos have been discussed above. The DNA evidence shows that the flamingos are neither anseriforms nor charadriiforms; they are related to the other members of the heron-ibis-stork cluster, as repeatedly proposed in the past. The flamingo clade branched from its nearest living relatives at Δ 11.5, which was probably in the early Tertiary. Fossils assigned to the ancestry of the flamingos before the Eocene must be regarded with the suspicion that convergence accounts for any similarities to modern flamingos. The DNA evidence shows that the living flamingos are closely related to one another; the largest $\Delta T_{50}H$ value between any two species is 1.2 (*Phoenicopterus* to *Phoeniconaias* and *Phoenicoparrus*), thus the living species probably have diverged from one another within the past 5–6 MY. By our criteria, the living species may be included in *Phoenicopterus*.

The ibises (Threskiornithidae) branched at Δ 11.1. There may be a split within the Threskiornithidae between the South American genera (*Mesembrinibis*, *Theristicus*, *Cercibis*) and the other genera in Fig. 367, most of which are Old World in distribution. If this division proves consistent two tribes may be recognized, Theristicini for the Neotropical taxa, and Threskiornithini for the others.

The next branch, at Δ 10.9, produced two living clades, the Procellarioidea and the Pelecanoidea. The procellarioids are discussed in the following section. The Pelecanoidea and Ciconioidea diverged at Δ 10.1. The Pelecanidae includes the pelicans (*Pelecanus*) and the Shoebill (*Balaeniceps*), which diverged at Δ 7.4. The Ciconiidae includes the New World vultures (Cathartinae) and the storks (Ciconiinae), which diverged at Δ 8.1 (Fig. 367).

After two centuries of being misplaced among the falconiforms it is clear that the New World vultures shared a most recent common ancestor with the storks. The substantial morphological evidence in support of this conclusion is reviewed under the Falconiformes. The relationships among the living species of cathartines are surprisingly close. By our criteria for assigning categories, *Sarcoramphus* and *Gymnogyps* could be included with the Andean Condor in *Vultur* (Linnaeus 1758:86). Brodkorb (1964) used Vulturidae, based on Illiger (1811), for the family. *Coragyps* is the most distant from the others at Δ 3.0, but *Coragyps atratus* and *Cathartes aura* have hybridized in the wild (McIlhenny 1937, Gray 1958).

The above discussion, based on corrected $\Delta T_{50}H$ distance values, seems neat and complete; but is it? UPGMA assumes that the rates of evolution are equal along all branches of the tree and produces a dendrogram with branches of equal length. When rates are equal, or nearly so, UPGMA produces an accurate picture of the data. As foregoing sections have emphasized, there are substantial rate differences among the groups of non-passerines, correlated with the age at first breeding. The effects of rate differences show up in the melting curves and the FITCH trees.

Fig. 155 (*Ardea*) includes representatives of several subgroups of our order Ciconiiformes. Only *Gallus* is outside the ciconiiform cluster. Reference to the UPGMA tree (Fig. 356) shows that *Ardea* may be expected to be about equidistant from the penguin (Spheniscidae), ibis (Threskiornithidae), *Cathartes* (Ciconiidae), and shearwater (Procellariidae); the cormorant (Phalacrocoracidae) and grebe (Podicipedidae) should be next, then the gull (Laridae), and the crane (Gruidae). The melting curves repeat this sequence for most of the taxa, but the crane is closer to the heron than are the grebe and the gull. We suggest that this is due to the effect of delayed maturity in the cranes, which begin to breed at an average age of 4–5 years. The Herring Gull matures at 4 years. What then about the Turkey Vulture, which probably delays breeding until 5–6 years old? Does its position reflect delayed maturity? Or have we been influenced by the morphological evidence of a close relationship between New World vultures and storks? Penguins and ibises also delay breeding; are their curves closer to the homoduplex than their relative branching times would indicate if we knew them? These are questions we cannot answer with confidence. We suspect that the UPGMA dendrogram is neither completely wrong nor completely right, but we do not know just how wrong. It will take additional experiments, designed to explore these questions, to provide the answers.

In Fig. 156 (*Ardea*) it is not surprising to find two storks closest to the heron homoduplex curve; herons and storks are related and storks have delayed maturity. That a gannet (*Morus*) should be next is also not surprising, for the UPGMA tree indicates that the Sulidae are next-door neighbors, their lineage having branched from that of the herons at $\Delta T_{50}H$ 13.3, and the sulids begin to breed at an average age of four years. A loon comes next and the ancestor of the Gaviidae branched from the heron lineage at Δ 12.4, as part of the clade that includes the groups from the Hamerkop to the tubenoses. By the same logic the pelican and flamingo are in their expected positions. In foregoing sections, the tropicbirds have been shown to be an isolated group with no close relatives; the bustard might be expected to be farther out than the sandpiper (*Tringa*), but bustards begin to breed at age 2–3, the sandpipers at two years. *Fulica* and *Anas* raise no questions.

Thus, by invoking different average genomic rates and allowing for experimental errors, we can explain, or explain away, the sequence of the curves in Fig. 156. Is the explanation correct? In part it certainly is; in part it may be wrong, but it can't be seriously wrong because all of these taxa (except *Anas*) are members of the same order in our classification.

Fig. 157 (*Gorsachius*) poses no problems. The storm-petrel, shearwater, and the two loons are in reasonable positions because all are expected to be about equidistant from a heron, if we refer to the UPGMA tree. The two grebes are in their expected relative position, and so are the anseriforms and galliforms. This set demonstrates that it is possible to obtain congruence among different expressions of the data if the taxa are chosen to do so. This was not the reason Fig. 157 was chosen, but it illustrates the point.

Fig. 158 (*Botaurus*) shows the tight clustering of the herons and the relative position of an ibis. Compare the relative position of *Botaurus* to the genera in Fig. 158 with the close relationships indicated between *Ardea* and *Casmerodius* in Fig. 155, and between *Gorsachius* and *Egretta* in Fig. 157. The bitterns are well separated from the other herons, and *Tigrosoma* is the most distant from *Botaurus*. Sheldon (1987a), using the FITCH program, found that *Botaurus* has the fastest relative rate, and *Tigrosoma* one of the slowest rates, among the herons. He calculated that the bittern lineage has evolved at an average rate ca. 25% faster than the typical heron rate, and that *Tigrisoma* has evolved ca. 19% slower than the average heron rate. *Tigrisoma lineatum* attains its adult plumage in ca. 5 years, but in captivity it laid eggs twice yearly (Rossi 1958). Many birds begin to breed in immature plumages, so it is not certain that *Tigrisoma* does not breed before 5 years of age.

Fig. 159 (*Scopus*) shows the relatively large distances between the Hamerkop and its nearest relatives, storks, ibises, herons, and flamingos.

Fig. 160 (*Phoenicopterus ruber*) suggests that the storks and ibises are closer to the flamingos than are the herons, avocets, and gulls. This agrees with traditional ideas and with the UPGMA tree, but the storks and ibises are delayed maturity groups and the relative positions of their curves may be deceptive. However, the gulls begin to breed at 3–4 years of age, the herons ca. 2 years, and the flamingos 2–3 years. The storks mature at an average of 4 years and the ibises at 2–3, but the curves of the Marabou Stork and the Glossy Ibis are virtually identical. We see no reason to suspect that these curves are not arrayed in a sequence that reflects the degrees of genetic relationship between the flamingo tracer and the driver taxa. We submit that the storks and ibises are more closely related to the flamingos than are the herons, gulls, or avocets.

Fig. 161 (*Phoenicopterus minor*) shows the close relationships among four of the five species of flamingos. This is confirmed by Figs. 162 and 163, which include all five species. The positions of *Gymnogyps*, *Coragyps*, *Ciconia*, and *Anastomus* in Fig. 161 suggest that the New World vultures are as closely related to the flamingos as are the storks. This is also indicated in the UPGMA tree. However, the New World vultures are among the groups with the most advanced ages at first breeding, ca. 6–8 years. The storks mature at 2–7 years. The fairly close clustering of all the driver curves in this set indicates that all of them are about the same distance from the flamingos. We interpret the melting curves as evidence that the New World vultures and the storks are equidistant from the flamingos, and about the same distance from the ibises, pelicans, and herons.

Fig. 162 (*Phoenicopterus chilensis*) suggests again that the storks and ibises are close to the flamingos, but in this set the stilts and avocets are closer to the flamingo than are the herons. Could the position of the stork and ibis be due to slower rates? Might the stilts and avocets be the closest relatives of the flamingos, as proposed by Olson and Feduccia (1980a)? These are possibilities to be considered, but in Fig. 131 the Banded Stilt (*Cladorhynchus*) is much closer to *Himantopus*, *Haematopus*, *Vanellus*, and *Eudromias*, than it is to the flamingo in Fig. 162. In Fig. 130, the avocet and stilts are the closest taxa to the oystercatcher tracer.

The anomalous aspect of Fig. 162 is that the herons are more distant from the flamingo than are the stilts and avocet. Is this a rate difference? Herons mature at 1–2 years, plovers at 1–4 years, average ca. 2 years; stilts and avocets are modified plovers so we may assume that they begin to breed at ca. 2 years of age. This seems like a doubtful explanation for the difference between the positions of the heron curves and those of the stilts and avocet. Experimental error is always a convenient escape, but when two related species behave like these herons it is not a safe escape. We leave it at that.

Fig. 163 (*Phoenicopterus andinus*) again shows the close relationships among the flamingos and, again, the storks and ibises are closest to the flamingo tracer and the stilts, avocet, and a plover cluster together. If *Cladorhynchus* is especially close to the flamingos, then so are the avocets and plovers—and all other charadriiforms.

Fig. 164 (*Threskiornis*) shows the distances between *Threskiornis* and several other ibis genera, and the virtually equal distances from the ibises to the Shoebill, New World vulture, storks, pelican, and the Hamerkop.

Fig. 165 (*Plegadis*) contains no surprises. Beyond the ibises, the storks are next, the flamingo and Hamerkop next, and the heron is farthest out.

In Fig. 166 (*Balaeniceps*) the question of the relationships of the Shoebill is examined. Is it most closely related to the storks or to the pelicans? Because the storks and pelicans seem to be members of rather closely related sister groups, the question is not easy to answer, but the evidence seems to favor the Shoebill-pelican alliance. We made several experimental sets involving the Shoebill, storks, pelican, and many other taxa. Using the facilities of the Microsoft EXCEL program, we combined four experimental sets, based on the same *Balaeniceps* tracer preparation, in various combinations. Fig. 166 is a summary of these data. If the Shoebill is not more closely related to the pelicans than to the storks, our data have not been able to detect the closest relative of the Shoebill. Pelicans and storks begin to breed at 4 years of age, thus it is unlikely that a rate difference accounts for their relative positions in Fig. 166.

Fig. 167 (*Pelecanus*) presents the reciprocal of Fig. 166 for the pelican-Shoebill relationship. The other taxa include a stork and the genera of the traditional Pelecaniformes. Unless rate differences can explain the relative positions of the curves, we must conclude that the pelicans are more closely related to the Shoebill than to the frigatebirds, boobies, anhingas, cormorants, and tropicbirds.

Fig. 168 (*Pelecanus*) includes the Shoebill, a stork, a petrel, penguin, loon, cormorant, booby, scolopacid, and a grebe. Again, unless rate differences provide a better explanation, the pelican is closer to the Shoebill than to the cormorant and booby. We may assume that the stork, petrel, and penguin are species with rate slowdowns correlated with delayed maturity, and the pelican will still be closest to the Shoebill. The boobies and cormorants begin to breed at ca. age 4, as do the pelicans, storks, and some penguins. The petrels mature at ca. 5–6 years. Thus, these taxa may be assumed to have been evolving at about the same average rates, so their relative positions should be unaffected by rate differences.

Fig. 169 (*Pelecanus*) compares the pelican with members of various groups. That a Turkey Vulture should be closest is not surprising because it has delayed maturity (6–8 years) and, from other evidence, is related to the pelicans. The other taxa provide additional perspective about the relationships of the pelicans. The hawk, owl, and bustard are birds with moderately delayed maturity; the others are mostly birds that begin to breed at age one year and belong to groups that are not involved in the problem of the relationships of the Shoebill and the pelicans.

Fig. 170 (*Pelecanus*) is somewhat redundant, but provides more evidence in support of the idea that the pelicans are not closely related to the other totipalmate birds. We do not reject the possibility that our data may be wrong, but we have no reason to think that they are. We hope to test these controversial results with additional experiments; for now we consider it probable that the traditional Pelecaniformes is a polyphyletic group.

Fig. 171 (*Gymnogyps*) presents an interesting set of curves. The position of the albatross is probably due to a combination of fairly close relationship to the California Condor, plus the effect of the delayed maturity in *Diomedea*. The storks and Old World vultures also do not begin to breed until ca. 4–6 years old, thus all of the curves (except that of *Milvago*) are those of birds with delayed maturity. *Gymnogyps* begins to breed at 6–8 years of age, thus the effect is magnified because the tracer and most of the drivers are delayed-maturity species. The main point of this set is to show that the New World vultures are not as closely related to the Old World vultures as they are to the storks and tubenoses. We think it does so.

Fig. 172 (*Sarcoramphus*) clusters closely with the other New World vultures, but in this set the Old World vulture is at about the same distance as the tubenose and storks. Note the position of *Circus*, an accipitrine hawk, closely related to the Old World vultures. *Circus* probably begins to breed at ca. 2 years of age, the Old World vultures at 5–7 years. We might assume that the Old World vultures would occupy the same relative position as that of *Circus*, if they bred at earlier ages, but the tubenoses and storks are also delayed-maturity birds. We favor the idea that the New World vultures are more closely related to storks than to Old World vultures, but the data are not always as clear as we would like.

In Fig. 173 (*Cathartes*), the two storks are slightly closer to the Turkey Vulture than is *Sarcogyps*, but all three are about equidistant from the tracer at the 50% level. This set of melting curves provides evidence of the effects of rate differences, as well as of relative branching times.

Fig. 174 (*Mycteria*) provides a view of the relationships between the Yellow-billed Stork and three other genera of storks, a New World vulture, ibises, Shoebill, flamingo, pelican, and the Hamerkop. The positions of the curves are somewhat modified by differences in average genomic rates, but the evidence of close relationships among these species is clear. The Andean Condor delays breeding until ca. 8 years old; its curve may be closer to the stork tracer than are the curves of the ibises because of the slow rate of DNA evolution in the New World vultures.

The FITCH tree (Fig. 341) affirms the evidence in the melting curves that the five species of flamingos are closely related. The distance from *Ciconia* to the basal node of the flamingos is 9.1; from *Cladorhynchus* it is 10.9. We have found no evidence that the flamingos are more closely related to the stilts than they are to any member of the Charadrii.

We conclude that the herons, Hamerkop, flamingos, ibises, Shoebill, pelicans, New World vultures, and storks are more closely related to one another than any of them is to another group. The differences in average genomic rates of DNA evolution, correlated with age at first breeding, complicate the interpretation of the data, but we are unable to present an alternative that better fits the evidence. We also believe that additional experiments designed to test the validity of our conclusions are warranted; we are not satisfied that our data are without errors.

We conclude that the Shoebill and the pelicans are sister taxa, that the storks and New World vultures are sister taxa, and that the traditional order Pelecaniformes is polyphyletic. This may be the most controversial conclusion of our entire study and we expect it to be disbelieved.

Albatrosses, Petrels, Shearwaters, Diving-Petrels, Penguins, Loons, and Frigatebirds

Order CICONIIFORMES
  Suborder Ciconii
    Infraorder Ciconiides
      Parvorder Ciconiida
        Superfamily Procellarioidea
          Family Fregatidae: Frigatebirds
          Family Spheniscidae: Penguins
          Family Gaviidae: Loons or Divers
          Family Procellariidae
            Subfamily Hydrobatinae: Storm-Petrels
            Subfamily Procellariinae: Petrels, Shearwaters, Diving-Petrels
            Subfamily Diomedeinae: Albatrosses

A relationship between the penguins and the procellariids has long been accepted. The loons have sometimes been placed with, or near, the procellariids, although a loon-grebe alliance has been more common. The frigatebirds usually have been placed with the pelecaniforms, but they share several morphological characters with the procellariids and some classifications have placed the Fregatidae in, or near, the traditional order Procellariiformes.

The families listed above differ in many morphological characters, but the Procellariidae, Spheniscidae, and Gaviidae share the following: schizognathous palate, two carotids, holorhinal nares, palmate feet, two nestling downs. These are primitive characters shared with many other groups, hence of little value as evidence of relationship. The characters of the families follow:

Family FREGATIDAE: 1/5. Tropical and subtropical seas and islands. Long, hooked, robust beak; large, naked, inflatable gular pouch; long, pointed wings; long, deeply forked tail; interdigital webs reduced to basal portion of toes; nails long, claw-like; middle toe pectinate on inner margin. Desmognathous; A+; flexor tendons Type 2; diastataxic; impervious nares;

528

small caeca; tracheo-bronchial syrinx; 11 primaries; 12 rectrices; 14–15 cervical vertebrae; oil gland indistinctly bilobed, tufted; single white egg; nidicolous young.

Family SPHENISCIDAE: 6/17. The penguins occur in the southern hemisphere, principally Antarctic and sub-Antarctic coasts and islands, including southern Australia, New Zealand, South America, and Africa. The Galapagos Penguin (*Spheniscus mendiculus*) is the northernmost species.

Feathers scale-like, distributed over entire body, no apteria, aftershaft present; during adult molt the old feathers are pushed out on the tips of the new feathers as they grow; forelimbs modified as flippers; wing bones flattened and more or less fused with little movement between them; scapula broad and large; coracoid large; legs far posterior; patella large; tarsometatarsus short and the elements incompletely fused in living species; sternum and pectoral muscles large; beak long, laterally compressed; biceps brachii absent (unique to penguins); no expansor secundariorum; skull bones not solidly fused; skeleton not pneumatic. Some of these characters are obviously related to the "flying under water" adaptations of the penguins as wing-propelled divers. Such characters have been used by Wetmore (1960) and others to elevate the group to the rank of a superorder, the Impennes.

The pelvic muscle formula is ABX+; flexor tendons Type 4, but there are variations in some species (Beddard 1898a:397); nares impervious; two lateral notches in sternum; small caeca; tongue and roof of mouth covered with papillae; cervical vertebrae 15; rhamphotheca complex and molted; four toes directed forward; oil gland densely tufted, bilobed.

Family GAVIIDAE: 1/5. Northern Holarctic. Large, strictly aquatic; legs set far back; feet palmate; tarsi compressed; patella fused to tibia; beak long, sharp; large supraorbital glands. ABCDX+; flexor tendons Types 2 and 4; pervious nares; caeca short; one lateral sternal notch; syrinx tracheo-bronchial; aftershaft; 11 primaries; 22–23 secondaries; 16–18 rectrices; 14–15 cervical vertebrae; no basipterygoid processes; oil gland densely tufted, deeply bilobed; two olivaceous eggs with darker marks; nidifugous. The two sets of nestling downs develop from the same papillae, the first pushed out by the growth of the second, as in adult penguins.

Family PROCELLARIIDAE: 24/115. Species of procellariids range over the oceans, islands, and coasts of most of the world. Their nostrils are enclosed in tube-like structures on the upper or lateral surface of the bill and this feature defines the group; their monophyly has never been doubted. The pelvic muscles are variable: ABXY+ in *Oceanites*, *Pelagodroma*, and *Garrodia*; ABXY in *Fregetta*; AX+ in *Bulweria*; AX in *Pelecanoides*; ABX in all others. Flexor tendons Type 4; diastataxic; impervious nares; caeca small or absent; oil gland densely tufted, bilobed; hallux small or absent; sternal notches variable; syrinx bronchial to tracheo-bronchial; mature down over entire body; nidicolous.

The Procellariidae of our classification is equivalent to the order Procellariiformes of many traditional classifications and the three subfamilies often have been recognized as families. In the following accounts "tubenoses" and "procellariids" refer to the taxa in the "Procellariiformes" of Wetmore (1960).

The review of the classification of the Procellariidae is presented here. Reviews of the Spheniscidae and Gaviidae are presented in following sections. The review of the Fregatidae is included with those of the totipalmate birds, the traditional Pelecaniformes.

Historical Review of the Classification

Linnaeus (1758) included *Procellaria* and *Diomedea* in his order Anseres, with the waterfowl, auks, pelicans, loons, gulls, and other web-footed birds. Similar assemblages were used by many of his successors. Nitzsch (1840) placed the tubenoses between the gulls and the ducks, and Gray (1845) thought they might be allied to the gulls, penguins, and auks.

Coues (1864, 1866a) produced the first important monograph of the group, although his work was criticized for being based on an inadequate series of specimens and for his lack of first-hand field knowledge. The classification proposed by Coues follows:

Family Procellariidae
   Subfamily Procellariinae
      Group Procellariaeae: Storm-Petrels
      Group Puffineae: Shearwaters
      Group Fulmareae: Fulmars
      Group Aestrelateae: Petrels (*Pterodroma*)
      Group Prioneae: Prions
   Subfamily Diomedeinae: Albatrosses
   Subfamily Halodrominae: Diving-Petrels

Huxley (1867) included the Procellariidae with the Laridae, Colymbidae (loons and grebes), and Alcidae in his "Cecomorphae," followed by the "Spheniscomorphae" (penguins). Huxley recognized the single family Procellariidae for all the tubenoses and separated it from the other members of the Cecomorphae by the greater expansion of the maxillo-palatines, a stronger ventral bend in the anterior portion of the vomer, and a larger ascending process of the palatine so that it ankylosed with the vomer. Huxley felt that the Giant Petrel, *Procellaria gigas* (*Macronectes giganteus*), is intermediate between gulls and albatrosses, and he saw similarities among the tubenoses, cormorants, and pelicans.

Sundevall (1872, see 1889:225) placed the "Toes webbed" birds together as the "Order Natatores," with the procellariids in "Cohort 4. Tubinares," the penguins in "Cohort 5. Impennes," and the auks, loons, and grebes in "Cohort 2. Pygopodes." Other "cohorts" contained the other web-footed groups. Thus, Sundevall regressed to the Linnaean arrangement.

Garrod (1873d, 1874a) included the tubenoses, loons, grebes, penguins, and ducks in his "Anseriformes," and Sclater (1880b) placed his order "Tubinares" between the "Gaviae" (gulls) and "Pygopodes" (loons, grebes, auks).

In Stejneger's (1885) classification the tubenoses followed the gulls in the order "Cecomorphae," which also included the Alcidae, Heliornithidae (sungrebes), Gaviidae, and Podicipedidae.

Forbes's (1882g) classification divided the tubenoses into the Oceanitidae (storm-petrels) and Procellariidae (all others). The albatrosses were separated in a subfamily, but the diving-petrels were given only generic distinction (*Pelecanoides*) in the Procellariinae.

Garrod (1881) included *Pelecanoides* in his "Oestrelatinae" because it has a semi-tendinosus muscle; this subfamily also contained the albatrosses, shearwaters, petrels, etc. Garrod changed his earlier opinion by suggesting that the herons and storks are the closest allies of the procellariids.

Fürbringer (1888) placed the tubenoses in the "Procellariiformes" between the

"Steganopodes" (frigatebirds, pelicans, cormorants, tropicbirds) and the "Aptenodytiformes" (penguins).

Seebohm (1890a) thought that the tubenoses belong between the galliforms and penguins, fairly close to the gulls, but far from the pelicans, herons, storks, and their allies. In Sharpe's (1891) classification the tubenoses were placed between the penguins and the auks. He thought that a slightly more distant relationship to the gulls was possible, but that the herons, storks, and pelicans are far from the procellariids.

Gadow (1892, 1893) placed the procellariids between the penguins and the "Ardeiformes" (pelicans, herons, storks), and far from the charadriiforms, including the gulls.

In the *Catalogue of Birds* Salvin (1896:340) reviewed the history of the classification of the "Order Tubinares" but did not express an opinion about their relationships. He divided the Tubinares into the Procellariidae (storm-petrels), Puffinidae (shearwaters, petrels, fulmars, prions), Pelecanoididae (diving petrels), and Diomedeidae (albatrosses).

Coues (1897) revised his 1864 and 1866a classification to produce the following arrangement:

Order Tubinares
    Family Diomedeidae
    Family Procellariidae
        Subfamily Fulmarinae
        Subfamily Puffininae
        Subfamily Procellariinae
        Subfamily Oceanitinae
    Family Pelecanoididae

In the *Hand-List* Sharpe (1899) expressed his opinions about the relationships of the procellariids by the sequence of the adjacent groups: Sphenisciformes, Procellariiformes, Alciformes, Lariformes, Charadriiformes. This arrangement reflects previous ideas based on external morphology, for example, the web-footed groups placed together and the auks and penguins near the tubenoses because of their similarities to the diving-petrels. Sharpe followed the family divisions of Salvin (1896) in his Procellariiformes.

In Pycraft's (1899a) classification only two families, Diomedeidae (albatrosses) and Procellariidae (all others), were recognized. Godman (1907–10) monographed the group and used Salvin's (1896) arrangement.

In the feather structure of the procellariids Chandler (1916) found "unmistakable resemblances to the Colymbiformes, especially the loons." He thought that *Diomedea* was the most specialized of the tubenoses and that a "primitive" member of the group may have given rise to the Ciconiiformes through the Pelecaniformes.

In a review of the tubenoses, Loomis (1918) was influenced by the works of Coues, Salvin, and Godman, and made few changes for his classification. He did not discuss the relationships of the tubenoses to other groups and, in 1923, he presented a classification nearly identical to that adopted by Wetmore (1960).

Lowe (1925a) made comparisons only within the tubenosed groups, using characters of the quadrate and adjacent bones to divide them into two families; Oceanitidae for the smaller petrels, and Procellariidae for the albatrosses, diving petrels, and shearwaters.

E. Stresemann (1934) accepted a relationship between procellariids and penguins, but was uncertain about their relationships to other groups.

In his classifications of the tubenosed groups, Mathews (1934; 1935; 1936a,b; 1937) carried generic splitting to the extreme by recognizing 52 genera for about 75 species placed in the usual four families. In 1948 Mathews swung to the other extreme and lumped the same species into 12 genera.

Fleming (1941) considered the probable evolution of the six species of *Pachyptila*, and Voous (1949) examined the relationships and evolution of the fulmars.

Simpson (1946) supported the relationship between penguins and petrels, and Mayr and Amadon (1951) noted that "the penguins are related to the petrels and less closely to the Steganopodes." (pelecaniforms).

Lanham (1947), in a study of the pelecaniforms, noted their diversity, but concluded that the traditional Pelecaniformes is a natural order. However, he thought that their nearest relatives are the Procellariidae (traditional Procellariiformes).

Kuroda (1954) developed a classification of the tubenosed groups based on skeletal and other morphological characters, and on an analysis of adaptations to aerial and aquatic propulsion. His most relevant conclusions were:

1. The albatrosses, from skull structure and manner of flight, seem to be related to the more volant members of the "Puffinae" (e.g., *Calonectris*).

2. The storm-petrels (Hydrobatidae) appear to be closely allied to the fulmars, petrels, and shearwaters.

3. The diving-petrels form a distinctive and primitive group that shares some skeletal and anatomical characters with both the "Hydrobatidae" and "Procellariidae."

4. Principally on skull characters, the gadfly-petrels (*Pterodroma*) are more similar to the fulmars and prions (Fulmarinae) than they are to the other groups.

Kuroda suggested that the tubenosed taxa descended from aquatic ancestors and he did not question the evidence for a relationship with the penguins. To Kuroda, two skeletal characters in the procellariids suggested descent from diving ancestors: (1) well-developed dorsal vertebral hypophyses, providing additional attachment for the M. longus collis anticus, enabling more powerful movement of the neck; (2) the processus rotularis of the tibia, which provides a larger area for the insertion of the thigh muscles, important in swimming. Kuroda suggested that this "is a remarkable characteristic of the Pygopodes [loons, grebes], shared only by the Tubinares, providing probably their remote relationship in the early Cretaceous" (p. 38).

Verheyen (1958c) recognized the Diomedeidae, Procellariidae, and Hydrobatidae in his order Procellariiformes. He believed the similarities between the diving-petrels and the auks are due to close relationship, not to convergence (1958d, 1961), and claimed that his comparisons of skeletal measurements showed that the Common Diving-Petrel (*Pelecanoides urinator*) and the Dovekie (*Alle alle*, Alcinae) are similar in 65% of 105 skeletal characters. As additional evidence of their relationship Verheyen noted that both groups have a simultaneous molt of the primaries. This molt pattern also occurs in many other aquatic birds, including ducks, loons, rails, grebes, flamingos, and anhingas, and is clearly an adaptive response to certain aspects of living in an aquatic habitat, not evidence of phylogeny.

Verheyen (1961:17) disagreed with Cain (1959:314) and Wetmore (1960:6) in their allocation of *Pelecanoides* to the "Procellariiformes." He noted: "How can we agree when the necessary information to verify the suggested relationships between the Diving Petrels and the Procellariiformes is completely lacking in their papers?"

In his final classification, Verheyen (1961) stated that although he believed the auks and their allies to be the nearest relatives of the procellariids, "they are more distantly allied with the Sphenisciformes." He placed the three orders "Sphenisciformes, Procellariiformes, Alciformes" together in the "superorder Hygrornithes."

Sibley (1960) found that the egg-white proteins of six species of procellariids had similar electrophoretic patterns, with a general resemblance to those of pelicans, herons, shorebirds, and ducks, "although clearly different from all of these."

The electrophoretic pattern of the eye lens proteins of the Fulmar (*Fulmarus glacialis*) was compared with those of various other groups by Gysels (1964a). He did not see evidence of a relationship to the penguins, and decided that the pattern was of the "charadriiform type." The presence of glycogen in the lens was interpreted as an advanced character that showed that *Fulmarus* is not one of the lower non-passerines. Gysels concluded: 1. *Fulmarus* is not a procellariiform, but belongs in the Charadriiformes. 2. The entire "order Procellariiformes" belongs next to the Charadriiformes. 3. The "Procellariiformes" are polyphyletic, with some members closest to the shorebirds.

Sibley and Brush (1967) rejected Gysels' conclusions because their studies of avian eye lens proteins revealed a tendency for rapid denaturation and similar electrophoretic properties among all birds.

In a study of procellariid Mallophaga, Timmermann (1965) rebutted the critics of the use of parasites as evidence of host relationships, and discussed the problems of interpretation. His conclusions concerning the tubenoses were:

1. *Pelecanoides* is a procellariiform (p. 197–198).

2. The tubenoses are most closely related to the Charadriiformes, and both *Phaethon* and *Fregata* are also related to the procellariids (pp. 203–207).

3. There is no support for a relationship between the tubenoses and the ciconiiforms or falconiforms.

4. A penguin-tubenose alliance is not supported by the Mallophaga or the tapeworms. Although penguins and petrels have a similar tapeworm fauna (Baer 1954a,b; 1955; 1957), whales are also hosts to the same tapeworm genera (p. 209).

Timmermann (1965:203–204) cited Verheyen (1960b) in support of his decision that the tubenoses are related to *Phaethon* and to the charadriiforms, particularly the gulls (*Larus*).

Brown and Fisher (1966) used paper electrophoresis to compare the serum proteins and hemoglobins of several procellariids. They found that the serum proteins of *Diomedea*, *Puffinus*, and *Pterodroma* are distinguishable, although species of the same genus seem identical. Albatross hemoglobins differed in the concentration of both components from those of the other genera examined.

Hamlet and Fisher (1967) reported minor variations in the air sacs of *Diomedea immutabilis*, *Puffinus pacificus*, and *Puffinus nativitatis*. Albatrosses have pneumatic connections to the ribs and coracoids; their absence in the petrels seems to be due to their smaller size.

Tyler (1969) compared the eggshell structures of 16 species of tubenoses, representing all major groups, and found no important differences in the total true shell nitrogen, the histological staining of different shell layers, and other aspects. Tyler found that the egg shells of penguins have a typical shell cover that is lacking from the shells of procellariids.

Sibley and Ahlquist (1972) compared the electrophoretic patterns of the egg-white proteins of seven species of albatrosses; 17 petrels, shearwaters, and fulmars; six species of storm-petrels; and two diving-petrels. The patterns of all species were remarkably uniform with only minor variations. The procellariid pattern is most similar to those of the penguins, and somewhat similar to those of the loons. It is also similar to those of the Charadriiformes, and resemblances to the patterns of *Fregata*, *Phaethon*, and *Pelecanus* were noted.

From all sources of evidence, Sibley and Ahlquist (1972:64) concluded that the "Procellariiformes are . . . monophyletic . . . appear to be allied to the Sphenisciformes, and . . . may be related to some or all of the following groups: Charadriiformes, *Gavia*, *Fregata*, *Phaethon*, *Pelecanus*."

Cracraft (1981) placed the penguins, loons, grebes, tubenoses, and pelecaniforms in his "Division 1" and argued for their monophyly on the basis of undefined skeletal and other characters. He noted that the albatrosses and frigatebirds "are exceedingly similar" in cranial morphology, "but the shared characters extend to the postcranial skeleton as well." He placed loons and grebes in the "Gaviiformes" and argued for their close relationship to one another and to the penguins.

Olson (1982) dismissed Cracraft's argument: "Not a single synapomorphy is advanced to justify 'Division 1' as a monophyletic group."

The DNA Hybridization Evidence (Figs. 175–185, 342, 356, 368)

The Procellarioidea branched from the Ciconioidea at Δ T$_{50}$H 10.9. The Fregatidae (Δ 10.7) may have been the next lineage to diverge, followed by the Spheniscidae at Δ 10.4 and the Gaviidae and Procellariidae at Δ 10.0 (Figs. 356, 368). These divergences presumably occurred over a short period of time and the exact branching sequence is uncertain. The branches may be represented as a multifurcation in the dendrogram, but we used the small differences in average delta values to place the four families in sequence in the Procellarioidea.

The subdivision of the Procellariidae into three subfamilies is indicated by the DNA comparisons. The Hydrobatinae diverged from the Procellariinae and Diomedeinae at Δ 7.9 and the Procellariinae and Diomedeinae diverged at Δ 7.3. It may be possible to recognize two subfamilies for the storm-petrels, but we defer this decision until more species can be compared. The diving-petrels could be placed in a tribe, as also could the Giant Petrel (*Macronectes*) (Fig. 368).

In Fig. 175 (*Fregata*) the penguin is closest to *Fregata*; this may reflect a correct relative position or the effect of delayed maturity in *Fregata* and *Spheniscus*—or both. The positions of *Sula*, *Anhinga*, and *Phalacrocorax* may present a problem. There is ample evidence (Figs. 150–154) that the boobies, anhingas, and cormorants form a clade; therefore we expect them to cluster together relative to any tracer, but in Fig. 175 *Sula* is separated from *Anhinga* and *Phalacrocorax* by an ibis, loon, flamingo, and pelican. All of these taxa have delayed maturity so we are denied the use of this refuge. The four intervening taxa are closely related to one another and to *Fregata*, and it seems possible that *Sula* is closer to *Fregata* than might be expected from the curves in Figs. 150–154. Of course, the answer is that we don't have an answer, just a question. *Phaethon* is in its usual position at the outer edge.

Fig. 176 (*Fregata*) provides some interesting opportunities for speculation. That the Royal Albatross should be closest to almost any tracer is not a surprise; it begins to breed at 8–11 years of age. The petrel, penguin, stork, and ibis sequence may be explained by the usual combination of delayed breeding and close relationships among these groups. However, the next four—storm-petrel, condor, loon, diving-petrel—require some thought. The condor may be explained by virtue of its age (6–8 years) at maturity, plus the evidence that it is a modified stork and the Ciconiidae are not far from the Fregatidae. The loon, we believe, is also a member of the Procellarioidea, so it is only a minor problem. The diving-petrels begin to breed at 2 years, the youngest among the tubenoses, and the storm-petrel (4–6 years) is not far from *Daption*. Thus, we can find reasons for this sequence of taxa, but the best explanation may be that all are quite closely related and, given some degree of error in all experiments, the precise relative positions are not important. *Egretta* and *Aechmophorus* are where we expect them to be.

In Fig. 177 (*Spheniscus*) the frigatebird swaps places with the penguin in Fig. 175; reciprocity is to be expected, admired, and applauded. The next several curves more or less repeat what we saw in Fig. 176; petrel, loon, New World vulture, booby, heron. The remaining curves are about where expected from other evidence. The crane is a delayed-maturity species, but the cranes are farther from the penguins than are the herons. The positions of the curves of the grebe, moorhen, woodpecker, *Gallus*, and Ostrich are in a predictable sequence. They give perspective to the set and lend support to the evidence that the penguins, frigatebirds, petrels, and loons are closely related to one another and to the New World vultures.

In Fig. 178 (*Spheniscus*) the frigatebird, petrel, and loon cluster together closest to the penguin tracer; the additional out-groups (bustard, grebe, pigeon, parrot, kingfisher, cuckoo, woodpecker, passerine, Ostrich) show that there is a great range of distances from the Procellarioidea to other groups.

Fig. 179 (*Eudyptula*) shows the range among the penguins and tubenoses from the smallest penguin as the tracer species to one of the largest penguins, followed by an albatross, three petrels, a storm-petrel, and a diving-petrel. It seems probable that the sequence of the tubenose genera is related to their ages at maturity: the albatross (ca. 5–7 years) to the diving-petrel (ca. 2 years), the others in between in positions and ages at first breeding.

Fig. 180 (*Gavia*) indicates that the loons are more closely related to the tubenoses and penguins than they are to the grebes. Even allowing for the effects of different ages at maturity, the evidence is clear. Loons mature at ca. 2–3 years, grebes average 2 years, medium-sized albatrosses 4–7 years, penguins average ca. 4 years. There is some variation among the two albatrosses and two penguins in Fig. 180, but all four cluster closely together relative to the loon tracer, as do the two grebes.

Fig. 181 (*Oceanodroma*) presents a sequence of melting curves that is determined by the combination of relationship and age at maturity. The storm-petrel tracer is itself a delayed breeder (4–6 years); the albatross and shearwater are delayed breeders and also tubenoses. The diving-petrel, another tubenose, matures at 2 years, but is next in the sequence ahead of the large Black-necked Stork which probably begins to breed at ca. 4–7 years of age. *Fregata* is next, related to the tubenoses and maturing at ca. 4 years, followed by the King Vulture (6–8 years) and among the closer relatives of the tubenoses. Then there is a small gap at the mid-range of the curves, followed by the four accipitrids with the loon among them. The position of the loon is farther out than expected, but it is difficult to evaluate in the context of the taxa in Fig. 181. Loons mature at 2–3 years; the large eagles and Old World vultures at 5–6 years. This may be enough to account for the situation. *Haliastur* and *Leucopternis* probably mature at ca. 2 years; in comparison with them, the loon curve is not far from its expected place.

Fig. 182 (*Lugensa*) presents a range of procellarioids and four species of the traditional pelecaniforms. It is interesting that the *Puffinus* and the *Pelecanoides* are so close together, with the *Diomedea* farther out. This seems to represent the triumph of relationship over rate slowdown due to delayed breeding. The other taxa are in their expected positions except for *Phaethon* and *Phalacrocorax*. Judging from their behavior in other experiments, we might have expected *Phaethon* to be the outermost and the cormorant to be even closer to the anhinga and booby; perhaps this is the triumph of experimental error over relationship.

Fig. 183 (*Pelecanoides*) is of special interest for it uses the tubenose that breeds at the youngest age (2 years) as the tracer, and the three petrels (*Lugensa, Pterodroma, Macronectes*) are closer to the homoduplex than is the albatross, and the two storm-petrels are still farther out. We believe this set reveals the true relationships among these taxa relative to *Pelecanoides*, in spite of differences in average genomic rates. The diving-petrels are closest to the typical petrels, next to the albatrosses, and farthest from the storm-petrels. The positions of the two penguins are as expected. The UPGMA tree shows this pattern of branching (Fig. 368).

Fig. 184 (*Diomedea epomophora*). The Royal is one of the largest albatrosses with an age at maturity of 8–11 years. It is virtually equidistant to most of the taxa in Fig. 184, with the other tubenoses and a penguin closest to the homoduplex curve. It is interesting to note that the diving-petrel and the penguin are at about the same distance from the albatross. The other taxa are mostly delayed-maturity species and the King Vulture is a next-door neighbor of the tubenoses. The position of the pelican seems far out, but we have no ready explanation for this modest departure from expectations which is unlikely to have great significance. We have not claimed perfection, just progress.

Fig. 185 (*Diomedea immutabilis*). The Laysan Albatross begins to breed at 7 years of age. The purpose of Fig. 185 is to show that *Fregata* is more closely related to the tubenoses than to the pelecaniforms. Since our evidence indicates that *Pelecanus* is also close to the tubenoses, its position is as expected. The cormorant, booby, and tropicbird are more distant. The same pattern is present in the UPGMA tree.

The FITCH tree (Fig. 342) links the tubenoses, penguins, and loons, but shows *Fregata* as the sister group of *Phalacrocorax*. Is it possible that this is the correct phylogeny? Or is it the result of the effects of experimental error and different rates of DNA evolution? The branch lengths tell a different story; from *Phalacrocorax* to *Fregata* it is 12 distance units, but from *Fregata* to *Pterodroma* it is 9.8 units. It is also 9.8 units from *Fregata* to *Gavia*, 10.2 from *Fregata* to *Spheniscus*, 9.1 from *Fregata* to *Diomedea*, and 11.9 from *Fregata* to *Ardea*. Thus, *Fregata* is closer to all other taxa in Fig. 342 than it is to *Phalacrocorax*. The position of *Fregata* relative to *Phalacrocorax* may be due to poor reciprocity in some of the *Fregata* comparisons. *Fregata* has been a problem in some of the melting curves and its relationships must be regarded as uncertain. We believe that it is closer to the tubenoses than to the cormorants, but this is one of the questions that should be examined by additional experiments.

Most of the internodal distances in Fig. 342 are short; the basal nodes could be collapsed into a polychotomy without changing the tree. This is what makes the resolution of the entire complex of the Ciconiides so difficult and it may indicate that these groups diverged from one another during a relatively brief period of time.

We conclude that the tubenoses, penguins, loons, and probably the frigatebirds are more closely related to one another than any one of them is to another group. We also conclude that the relationships of the frigatebirds require further study. The differences in average rates of genomic evolution, correlated with ages at first breeding, affect the positions of melting curves and the branch lengths in the FITCH tree. These phenomena complicate the interpretation of the data.

Penguins

Family SPHENISCIDAE: 6/17. The principal questions about the relationships of penguins are: 1. Did they have flying ancestors? 2. To which living group are they most closely related?

Historical Review of the Classification

Linnaeus (1758:132) included the Jackass Penguin (*Spheniscus demersus*) in his genus *Diomedea* as "*Diomedea demersa*," described as "alis impennibus, pedibus tetradactylis. Penguin pedibus nigris." The only other species in *Diomedea* was the Wandering Albatross, *D. exulans*. This seems to be a remarkable recognition of the relationship between tubenoses and penguins, but Linnaeus also included the species "*demersus*" in his genus *Phaethon* (p. 135), described as "alis impennibus, rostro mandibulis edentulis, digito postico distincto. Penguin." He also referred to this tropicbird-penguin combination on page 132, under *Diomedea demersa*, which was further described as "*Statura Phaethontis demersi, sed rostrum divertissimum*."

Illiger (1811) placed *Aptenodytes* in his family "Impennes" of the order "Natatores." Cuvier (1817) included *Aptenodytes* in the same family as the loons, grebes, and auks, and Wagler (1827) assigned the penguins to a group ("Autarchoglossae") with the loons, grebes, auks, kiwis, and the Dodo! It is apparent that the penguins presented special problems to the early systematists as they have to their successors.

Nitzsch (1840) included the penguins in his Pygopodes with the loons, grebes, and auks because he realized that their unique pterylosis is an adaptation to their marine habitat, not evidence of an independent origin.

Gray (1849) placed the penguins in his Anseres, with most of the other swimming birds. His belief that they are closely related to the auks is indicated by their position in his classification between the "Uridae" (murres) and the "Alcidae" (auks, puffins).

538

Huxley (1867:430) noted: "In the Gulls, the Divers, the Grebes, the Auks, and the Penguins, the bones which form the roof of the mouth have the same general arrangement and form as in the Plovers. But they are devoid of basipterygoid processes; and in the Penguins the pterygoids become much flattened above downwards." Huxley placed the penguins in the "Spheniscomorphae" among the schizognathous birds, and was impressed by their similarities to the auks (Alcinae), in particular to the flightless Great Auk (*Pinguinus impennis*).

Sundevall (1872, see 1889:225) placed all the web-footed birds in his "Order Natatores," which he noted as equivalent to the "Anseres" of Linnaeus, and the "Steganopodes of the older authors." Sundevall introduced the Natatores: "Toes webbed. By no other character need we define this order." The penguins were placed in "Cohort 5. Impennes," between "Cohort 4. Tubinares" and "Cohort 6. Lamellirostres." The latter included the flamingos and the ducks, geese, and swans.

The pelvic muscle formula of penguins is ABX+ (Garrod 1873d, 1874a), a condition shared by most procellariids as well as by many other birds. Garrod included the penguins in his "Cohort Anseres" with the ducks, loons, and grebes. Sclater (1880b) gave the penguins ordinal rank as the Impennes between his Pygopodes (loons, grebes, auks) and the Crypturi (tinamous). Reichenow (1882) placed the penguins in his order Urinatores with the loons, grebes, and auks.

From an anatomical study of the penguins Watson (1883:232) concluded that "they form the surviving members of a group which had early diverged from the primitive avian stem, but . . . when the separation took place the members . . . [were] so far diverged from the primitive ornithoscelidian form as to be possessed of anterior extremities, which instead of forming organs of terrestrial, had become transformed into organs adapted to aerial progression, in other words, into true wings."

Watson would not speculate about the closest living relatives of the penguins, but noted that they seem close to the "Palmipedes," i.e., the web-footed birds, surely a safe opinion.

Stejneger (1885) emphasized the differences between the penguins and other birds and placed them in the superorder Impennes, a treatment to be followed by Wetmore (1951, 1960) many years later. Menzbier (1887) separated the penguins as the Eupodornithes, one of his four subdivisions of the class Aves. He suggested that penguins may have had a reptilian ancestry separate from that of other birds.

Fürbringer (1888) brought the penguins and the procellariids into proximity, although he did not claim that they are closely related. In his classification the two groups are listed in sequence as the Aptenodytiformes and Procellariiformes. Fürbringer considered the similarities of the penguins to the loons and grebes to be superficial, i.e., convergent, not due to close relationship.

Gadow (1889:311–312) noted that the patterns of the intestinal convolutions in the penguins "possess undeniable characters in common with the Pygopodes [loons, grebes], Steganopodes [pelicans, etc.], and Tubinares [tubenoses]; they are on the whole orthocoelous, but the extreme length of their gut thrown into numerous straight and oblique, or quite irregular convolutions, renders comparison very difficult. They have probably branched off very early from the main orthocoelous stock in the Antarctic region, and thus have had time to assume, through intense specialization, those pseudo primitive characters in their whole organization which now separate the few surviving forms from the rest of birds."

Gadow (1893) concluded that the penguins are closest to the tubenoses, but also felt that a distant relationship to the loons and grebes was possible.

Seebohm expressed several opinions about the relationships of the penguins. First (1888b), from their skeletal peculiarities, he seemed convinced that their nearest allies are the loons and grebes, but in a classification two years later (1890a), the penguins appear as the order Impennes between the order Tubinares and the Gaviae (gulls and terns) of the order Gallo-Grallae. In 1895, he accepted the theory that the penguins had evolved from flying ancestors and noted: "To give them time to metamorphose their wings into paddles so completely as they have done, it must be assumed that their isolation occurred at a very early date, sufficiently early to warrant us in regarding the Penguins as the survivors of a group of birds whose isolation dates back far enough to entitle them to hold rank as a subclass."

In this statement, Seebohm expressed his opinion that categorical rank should be based on the time of origin, an idea that Hennig (1966) was to espouse many years later. Seebohm's statement also assumed a direct relationship between time and degree of morphological divergence.

Sharpe (1891:71) placed the order Sphenisciformes between the Colymbiformes (loons) and the Procellariiformes, followed by the Alciformes and Lariformes, thus preserving some of the old web-footed assemblage. In his diagrams (Plates X, XII) representing his concept of relationships, Sharpe placed the penguins (as the "Impennes") nearest the groups listed above, but not especially close to any one of them. In a footnote (p. 71) Sharpe diagnosed the Sphenisciformes: "Palate schizognathous; first digit of manus fused with the second in the adult; scapula very broad, not differing very much in size from the keel of the sternum; three metatarsal bones of tarsus very short and separated from each other throughout by deep grooves; bones of forearm all flattened. . . . Spinal feather-tract not defined on nape; none of the wing-feathers differentiated in quills."

Of the penguins Newton (1896:Intro. 111) wrote: "There is perhaps scarcely a feather or a bone which is not diagnostic, and nearly every character hitherto observed points to a low morphological rank. The title of an Order can scarcely be refused to the *Impennes*." Here again the definition of categorical rank is associated with specialized morphology, rather than with phylogenetic relationship; the conferring of a title becomes the reward for the possession of highly derived structural characters.

Beddard (1898a) placed the penguins between the extinct Hesperornithes (large, flightless diving birds from the Cretaceous of North America) and the Steganopodes (pelicans, etc.), while Pycraft (1898c) found the penguins to be osteologically most like the tubenoses, with less resemblance to the loons and grebes.

In the *Catalogue of Birds* Ogilvie-Grant (1898:623) placed the "Order Impennes" next to the "Order Alcae" (auks). He gave an extensive diagnosis and references to many papers on the anatomy of the group.

In the *Hand-List*, Sharpe (1899) used the sequence: grebes, loons, Hesperornithiformes, penguins, tubenoses, auks, gulls; each in a different order. The penguins were in the order Sphenisciformes, family Spheniscidae.

Ameghino (1905) described many fossil birds from Patagonia, and thought that the ancestors of the penguins progressed through a flightless terrestrial stage before becoming aquatic. He concluded that the early Tertiary penguins were more specialized than Recent

Journal of Comparative Physiology 1985 v.155(3)p.373-80

Proceedings of the Nutritional Society March 95 v.54 p.367/75

Newsweek Aug 11, 1997 v.130 p.6 p.62

Science News Jan 25, 1997 v.151 n4 p.52 Microfilm

◯ Nature, Jan 23, 1997 v.385 n6614 p.304   Q1.5383

Science News, April 24, 93 269-71 microfilm Q1.5385

Bound ◯ Journal of Exp. Biology v.154 Nov 90 P.397-405

Q H301.J68   New York Times (Late NY Edition) July 29, 97 PC4

Bound ◯ Nature v.388 July 3 97 P.64-7
Q1.N2

✗ Audobon v.98 Nov/Dec 96 p.62-9 Board QL671.A82

① Journal of Exp. Bio v.199 Oct 96 2215-23

ordered ✗ American Journal of Physiology v.266 April 94 pt 2 PK131g

Science News v.145 Jan 15 94 P.47 -microfilm Q1.576

ordered? Animal Behaviour v.32 Aug 84 p.952

Nature v.310 Aug 16, 84 p.545

Database: Expanded Academic ASAP
Subject: penguins
Library: UNC Asheville

Source: Nature, Jan 23, 1997 v385 n6614 p304(2).

Title: Energy saving in huddling penguins.

Author: Andre Ancel, Henk Visser, Yves Handrich, Dirkjan Masman and Yvon
Le Maho

Abstract: Huddling in groups among penguins enables the animals to
conserve sufficient energy to survive the Antarctic winter while incubating
eggs. This was concluded in a study of penguins in the Pointe Geologie
colony in Adele Land, wherein 36 male penguins were weighed, blood samples
taken and injected with deuterated water to be able to monitor body-water
loss. By huddling, males were found to be able to maintain a metabolic rate
25% below that of an individual bird at thermoneutrality. Those that were
isolated and unable to huddle failed to survive the long fast required for
successful incubation.

Subjects: Penguins — Behavior
Animals — Wintering

RN: A19465077

--- End ---

species, particularly in their relatively longer and more fused tarsometatarsi, hence they could not be the ancestors of living penguins.

Wiman (1905) thought that the early Tertiary penguins were more like other carinate birds than are modern penguins. He noted some points of similarity to the procellariids, but drew no taxonomic conclusions.

Chandler (1916:298) concluded that penguins were derived from extinct, toothed, aquatic birds (e.g., *Hesperornis*) because "the uniform distribution of feathers, the absence of specialized remiges and of under wing coverts with a reversed position, and the simple structure of both their pennaceous and their downy barbules, all point to their low systematic position."

E. Stresemann (1934) considered the "Tubinares" to be the closest relatives of the "Sphenisci" and cited the following as evidence: wing-propelled divers [diving-petrels] in the Tubinares; a tracheal septum in both groups; many similarities in the alimentary tract; reduction of M. biceps brachii; egg color; slow embryonic and post-embryonic development; two sets of down in the plumage sequence; geographical distribution. Stresemann thought that the evidence of relationships to other orders was still questionable.

Wetmore (1930) and Peters (1931) placed the order Sphenisciformes after the ratites and tinamous and before the loons, grebes, and tubenoses. However, following Lowe (see below), Wetmore (1934, 1940, 1951, 1960) elevated the penguins as the superorder Impennes at the beginning of his list of living "Neornithes." To justify this allocation Wetmore (1951:2) wrote: "The question of the weight to be given the peculiarities of uniform pterylosis, extreme specialization of the wing as a flipper for submarine progression, and incomplete fusion in the metatarsal elements, as well as such other details as erect posture in standing and walking and the anatomical adjustments involved, found in the penguins, is one that has merited careful review. It seems reasonable after this examination to retain the Impennes as a superorder, at least until we have further evidence through fossils as to their line of evolution."

Here again is the insoluble dilemma posed by trying to erect a classification that takes account of both phylogeny and morphological specialization in the assignment of categorical ranks.

A study by Virchow (1931) indicated that the specializations in the vertebral column and hind limbs are related to underwater propulsion. Walking upright, or tobogganing on snow using wings and feet, is correlated with the adaptations for swimming. An osteological study by Boas (1933) supported an alliance between penguins and procellariids.

Lowe (1933a, 1939a) asserted that penguins had an origin separate from that of other carinates, and that the ancestors of the penguins were flightless. His evidence, somewhat paraphrased, was:

1. The lack of apteria, proliferation of feathers over the body and wings, and failure of the remiges to differentiate from coverts are primitive features. Perhaps each feather corresponds to a scale of the ancestral reptile. In *Aptenodytes* (Emperor and King penguins) the first two rows of feathers above the rear edge of the wing are probably homologous to the median and greater underwing coverts. The third row of feathers are the remiges. This is a primitive feature because it is the embryonic condition of carinate flying birds, as shown by Wray (1887). In adults of carinate birds the remiges grow out over the ventral coverts.
2. Since the structure of the wing bones in early penguin embryos is like that of the adult, and

there is no approach to the embryonic carinate condition, the penguins must have had a distinct ancestry.

3. Miocene penguins are similar to modern forms with no suggestion of being intermediate to a presumed flying ancestor, thus proving that penguins did not have a flying ancestor.

4. The tarso-metatarsus of Penguins . . . is absolutely unique in the class Aves; a similar modification is conspicuous in the bipedal Dinosaurs (*Ceratosaurus* Upper Jurassic), and it may be that the physiological factors which led to the same morphological results in the two categories of animals concerned may imply an inheritance from a common ancestor, and not merely and only the convergent effects of similar habits. Thus the tendency to stand really upright may be inherited from a common ancestor, as may be the morphological and physiological details by which that habit finds expression (1933a:513).

5. The arrangement of certain muscles (rectus abdominis, pars abdominalis of the pectoralis major), the lack of pneumaticity in the bones, and other characters are primitive.

Lowe's arguments were full of speculation and special pleading to support his hypothesis, in spite of evidence to the contrary. His own evidence (item 1 above) opposes a separate ancestry for the penguins since it is unlikely that convergence would produce identical feather arrangements in embryos and adults derived from separate reptilian lineages.

Gregory (1935) pointed out that the characters used by Lowe in arguing for a separate reptilian ancestry for the penguins could be better understood as adaptations to life in the water. He noted the similarities in the wings of penguins to those of flying birds: "It is in the entire pectoral girdle, however, that the penguins retain the most convincing evidence of derivation from completely flying carinate birds. Here are essentially the same outstandingly avian characters of the blade-like scapula, the well developed furcula, the elongate coracoids, the foramen triosseum, the well developed carina and the enormous sternum. With all this the penguins merely fly under water instead of in the air."

Lowe's arguments based on fossils were also questioned by Gregory, who noted that all avian orders are distinguishable by the early Tertiary, and therefore that it is unwise to claim that similarities between Miocene or Eocene penguins and modern species proves great antiquity or suggests an evolutionary history distinct from that of other birds.

Murphy (1935:16) disagreed with Lowe's interpretations of the pterylographic evidence: "The feather arrangement along the hind edge of the wing is . . . persistently embryonic, but it does not follow that this is phylogenetically primitive. On the contrary, the condition is one that would almost necessarily be restored with the reduction of large flight-quills to the size of undifferentiated coverts." The reduction in size and the increase in the number of the remiges in penguins is clearly an adaptation for underwater propulsion.

Murphy and Harper (1921) and Murphy (1936:776) suggested that the similarities in morphology and life history between the penguins and the diving-petrels showed that a bird with characters like those of the procellariids could have been an intermediate stage in the evolution of penguins.

Simpson (1946) reviewed the fossil penguins and speculated on the origin of the group. He criticized Lowe, charging that his interpretation of the fossil record suffered from polemics: "The species singled out by Lowe to represent Miocene penguin morphology seem to me to be the most specialized and aberrant members of the group" (p. 43). On the affinities of the penguins, Simpson (1946:84) stated: "Excepting only the wing and the tarsometatarsus, the recent penguin skeleton is remarkably like that of many flying carinates and particularly of the Procellariiformes, as has been repeatedly noticed and can be confirmed by comparisons of almost any two genera of the two groups. If this similarity were a coincidence or due wholly to convergence, the Miocene penguins might be no less similar to the Procellariiformes but surely would not be expected to be more similar. The fact that they are more similar, even though in slight degree, is good supporting evidence that their remote ancestry was indeed like, if not identical with, that of the Procellariiformes."

It seemed reasonable to Simpson that the ancestors of penguins were aerial oceanic birds which, as an intermediate stage, adopted submarine as well as aerial flight. In the final stage, represented by penguins, exclusive submarine flight replaced aerial flight.

Marples (1952) and Simpson (1957, 1959, 1965, 1970, 1976) have described additional fossil penguins, especially from Australia and New Zealand. These forms extend the record to the lower or middle Eocene, but do not add to the evidence of the origin or ancestry of the penguins.

Howard (1950) accepted Simpson's conclusions, as also did Mayr and Amadon (1951): "penguins are related to the petrels and less closely to the Steganopodes."

Crompton (1953) found the development of the chondrocranium in the Jackass Penguin (*Spheniscus demersus*) to be typically avian, and agreed with Simpson (and others) that the tubenoses are the closest relatives of the penguins.

Penguins have a Type A–1 carotid artery pattern, a Type A coracoid artery, and Type 1 thoracic artery (Glenny 1944a, 1947a, 1955), as in the loons, most procellariids, many Charadriiformes, and several other groups.

Verheyen (1958e, 1961) argued that there is no conclusive evidence that penguins were derived from flying ancestors and considered them to be distantly allied to the kiwis on one hand and to the shearwaters and auks on the other. In his final classification Verheyen (1961) placed the penguins in an order beside the "Procellariiformes" in his superorder Hygrornithes.

Storer (1960a:61) agreed with Wetmore (quoted above) that the "differences between penguins and other birds are sufficient to merit the erection of a superorder for the penguins, yet phylogenetic evidence could justify placing these birds next to the petrels"—here again, the conflict between phylogeny and specialized morphology in the assignment of categorical rank.

The paper electrophoretic patterns of the egg-white proteins of *Spheniscus demersus* neither supported nor denied a relationship to the procellariids (Sibley 1960).

In the Little Blue Penguin (*Eudyptula minor*), Kinsky (1960) observed that the "nostrils of small chicks are tubular, with large, nearly round apertures. The tubes start to recede during the sixth week of age and the openings start flattening. This change is completed within one week, and at the age of 43 days the slit-like nostrils of the adult bird have formed." This structure is probably homologous to the tubiform nostrils of the procellariids and provides additional evidence of common ancestry.

Meister's (1962) histological study of the long bones of penguins disclosed differences from those of other birds in the general structure, disposition of marrow, and arrangement of the Haversian system. These characters are probably related to underwater swimming and flightlessness and reveal nothing about affinities.

Simonetta (1963) observed that the cranial morphology and kinesis of penguins are most similar to those of loons and grebes.

Gysels (1964) compared the eye lens proteins of *Spheniscus humboldti* with those of other birds, but found no evidence of a relationship to the procellariids. Remarkably, he suggested that the closest relative of the penguins is the Common Murre (*Uria aalge*), but not the other members of the Alcinae. This opinion was based on the alleged similarity of the immunoelectrophoretic patterns and the lack of glycogen in the lenses of *Spheniscus* and *Uria*, a primitive character according to Gysels. Glycogen was present in the eye lens of the Fulmar (*Fulmarus glacialis*), the only procellariid studied, and in those of charadriiforms other than *Uria*. Clearly, these observations are not evidence of phylogenetic relationships.

Tyler (1965) examined the fine structure of the egg shells of several species of penguins and found some differences among them in total shell nitrogen plotted against shell thickness.

Feeney et al. (1966) compared the electrophoretic and immunoelectrophoretic properties of the egg-white proteins of the Adelie Penguin (*Pygoscelis adeliae*) with those of other birds. The anti-penguin antiserum reacted strongly with the egg-white proteins of a shearwater, an albatross, a grebe, and a duck, but relatively weakly with those of the Domestic Fowl and a cassowary.

Allison and Feeney (1968) reported comparisons of the serum proteins of three species of penguins, but the results had no bearing on the phylogeny of the group.

Margoliash and his associates (Chan and Margoliash 1966, Chan et al. 1963, Margoliash et al. 1963) determined the amino acid sequences of the cytochromes *c* of several birds, including that of the King Penguin (*Aptenodytes patagonica*). The sequence of the chicken is more similar to that of the penguin than to those of the duck or pigeon. These data are too limited to be used as the basis for proposals about phylogeny.

Sibley and Ahlquist (1972) compared the electrophoretic patterns of the egg-white proteins of 10 of the 17 species of penguins with those of many other groups of birds. We concluded "that the penguin patterns are more like those of the Procellariiformes than those of any other group."

The DNA Hybridization Evidence

The DNA hybridization evidence has been discussed above. The penguin lineage branched from the loon-tubenose clade at $\Delta T_{50}H$ 10.4 (Fig. 368). If we use a calibration constant of $\Delta T_{50}H$ 1.0 = 4.5 million years, this divergence occurred ca. 47 MYA. The earliest known fossil penguins are from the lower to middle Eocene, about 45–50 MYA (Marples 1952, Simpson 1976). Although the divergence could have been earlier, the DNA dating of ca. 47 MYA is in good agreement with the fossil evidence. Our calibration has been doubted by Helm-Bychowski and Wilson (1986) who believe it to be in error "by a factor of almost 2." However, if we use a calibration constant of half our 4.5 value, say, 2.25, the divergence between penguins and procellariids would be only 22–23 MYA. Since there are fossil penguins dated at 45–50 MYA it seems clear that our calibration in this case is reasonably concordant with the fossil record.

Loons or Divers

Superfamily Procellarioidea
  Family Gaviidae: Loons or Divers

Family GAVIIDAE: 1/5. The five species of *Gavia* occur in the northern parts of the northern hemisphere. *Gavia stellata* is circumpolar in breeding distribution; *arctica* breeds in the Eurasian Arctic and western Alaska; *pacifica* in eastern Siberia, Alaska, and Canada; *immer* breeds in North America, Greenland, and Iceland; and *adamsii* in northern Russia, Siberia, western Alaska, and western arctic Canada. *G. stellata* and *pacifica* are sometimes considered to be conspecific, but they are sympatric in eastern Siberia.

The generic name of the loons has had a complex history because of errors in the identification of the type species. During the last century, *Gavia* was sometimes applied to one or more species of gulls; for example, in the second edition of the A.O.U. checklist (1895) "*Gavia alba*" was the name of the Ivory Gull (*Pagophila eburnea*), and the loons were placed in *Urinator*. The generic name *Colymbus* was also used for the loons, until it was determined that it was actually based on the Great Crested Grebe. In many publications of the nineteenth century the loons were placed in the "Order Colymbiformes, Family Colymbidae, genus *Colymbus*, for example in the *Hand-List* (Sharpe 1899:115). J. A. Allen (1897:312) and Coues (1903:1047) established the validity of *Gavia* as the type genus of the Gaviidae, but the confusion continued for many years until, in 1956, the International Commission on Zoological Nomenclature placed *Gavia* Forster 1788 on the Official List of Generic Names in Zoology (Storer 1979:135).

Throughout most of their taxonomic history the loons and grebes (Podicipedidae) have been considered to be closely related. Thus, they have been treated together and, for convenience, we will follow this tradition. Although loons and grebes are superficially similar they are not closely related. Loons are members of the penguin-tubenose group and the grebes seem to have no close living relatives. Some of the anatomical differences between loons and grebes are given in Table 20.

TABLE 20. Some Anatomical Differences between Loons and Grebes

Loons	Grebes
Hind process of mandible long	Process short or absent
Dorsal apterium only on neck	Only on back
Sternotracheal musculature symmetrical	Assymmetrical
Both carotids present	Only left carotid
Cervical vertebrae 14 or 15	Cervical vertebrae 17–21
Dorsal vertebrae free	Dorsal vertebrae fused
Sternum twice as long as wide, posterior border notched	Broad and short, notched each side, plus a triangular middle notch
11 primaries	12 primaries
Patella lacking	Large, pyramidal patella
Hypotarsus ridged, terminating in triangular, open area	Hypotarsus complex, with canals and grooves
Anterior toes webbed	All toes lobate
Tongue with large patch of spinous processes at base	Tongue with single row of spinous processes

From Fürbringer 1888, Gadow and Selenka 1891, Pycraft 1899b, Gardner 1925, and Stolpe 1935.

Historical Review of the Classification

The association of the loons and grebes began with the early classifications. Linnaeus (1758:135) included species of both groups in *Colymbus*, one of the genera in his order Anseres. Illiger's (1811) family "Pygopodes" included *Colymbus*, the penguins, and the auks, and Cuvier (1817) used a similar arrangement.

Nitzsch (1840) also placed the loons, grebes, auks, and penguins together in the Pygopodes, because of similarities in pterylosis. Gray (1845) inserted the loons and grebes as adjacent families between the Anatidae (ducks, etc.) and Alcidae (auks, murres, puffins) in his order Anseres. Coues (1866b) examined the skeleton and musculature of the Common Loon "*Colymbus torquatus*" (*Gavia immer*), and concluded that it is closely related to the grebes and more distantly to the auks.

Huxley (1867) united the loons and grebes in the Colymbidae, which with the Alcidae, Procellariidae, and Laridae (gulls, terns) composed his "Cecomorphae." Huxley noted: "The Colymbidae appear to be closely connected on the one hand with the Gulls, and on the other, more remotely, but still really, with the Rails" (p. 458). (This sentence was not Huxley's best.)

In the "Cohort Pygopodes" of his order Natatores ("Toes webbed"), Sundevall (1872, see 1889) included the auks, loons, and grebes: the auks in "Fam. Alcariae," the loons in "Fam. Eudyptinae," the grebes in "Fam. Colymbinae."

In Garrod's (1873d, 1874a) system the loons and grebes are in adjacent families between the penguins and the tubenoses in his order Anseriformes, which also included the ducks, geese, and swans.

The order Pygopodes of Sclater (1880b) included the Colymbidae (loons and grebes), and Alcidae (auks). The Pygopodes were inserted between the Impennes (penguins) and the Tubinares (tubenoses).

Reichenow (1882) united the Spheniscidae, Alcidae, and Colymbidae in his order Urinatores, and Stejneger (1885) gave the loons and grebes separate families in his order Cecomorphae. This assemblage followed the penguins in his list and included the Heliornithidae (sungrebes), Alcidae, Laridae, and Procellariidae.

The suborder Podicipitiformes of Fürbringer (1888) included the loons and grebes in the "Gens Colymbo-Podicipites" with the Cretaceous, toothed Hesperornithes as the adjacent gens. In his phylogenetic tree this group is closest to the pelicans and waterfowl, and quite distant from the tubenoses, shorebirds (Charadriiformes), and penguins.

Seebohm vacillated about the relationships of the loons and grebes. He first noted (1888a:3) that "it is impossible . . . to regard the Grebes as nearly related to the Divers. . . . their palatine bones notwithstanding, there can be little doubt that Grebes are modified Ducks." This opinion was soon altered when Seebohm (1888b) decided that skeletal differences between loons and grebes are unimportant and he united the two groups in the same suborder. He dismissed a close relationship to the auks, but thought the loons and grebes are closely allied to the penguins. In his classification (1890a) the loons and grebes were combined as the Pygopodes, placed between the Fulicariae (rails) and Gallinae (galliforms) in the order Gallo-Grallae of the subclass Galliformes.

Sharpe (1891) assigned the loons and grebes to adjacent orders between his Heliornithiformes (only *Heliornis*, the Neotropical Sungrebe) and Sphenisciformes. Gadow (1893) found loons and grebes similar, but was unable to suggest close ties with other groups. He placed them as two suborders in his Colymbiformes near the beginning of his sequence, followed by the penguins (Sphenisciformes).

Goodchild (1891) found that the "Colymbidae" (presumably the loons and grebes) have an arrangement of the secondary coverts similar to that of the cranes, gulls, flamingos, ibises, and storks, among others. Such a widespread character is useless as the basis for assessing relationships.

In the *Catalogue of Birds* Ogilvie-Grant (1898) placed the Colymbidae (loons) and Podicipedidae in the order Pygopodes, between orders containing the totipalmate pelicaniforms and the auks. Beddard (1898a) also treated the loons and grebes as separate families in his order Colymbi but did not speculate on their nearest relatives. From skeletal comparisons, Pycraft (1899b) concluded that loons and grebes are related, but he did not consider them to be close to the auks or the gulls.

According to Shufeldt (1892, 1904a,b, 1914b) the loons and grebes form a natural group, perhaps derived from a *Hesperornis*-like ancestor. He considered the loons and grebes to be closely related and placed them in subfamilies in the Podicipidae, the only family in his order Pygopodes. Among their closest relatives Shufeldt named the auks and gulls.

In the *Hand-List*, Sharpe (1899) placed the grebes in the "Order Podicipedidiformes" followed by the loons in the "Order Colymbiformes," the Hesperornithiformes, Sphenisciformes, Procellariiformes, and Alciformes. Convergent similarities were still determining much of the classification.

Chandler (1916) wrote: "The feathers of grebes and loons are very highly specialized and differentiated, and show an almost perfectly intermediate position between penguins . . . and Procellariiformes. . . . in the breast feathers and down, loons come much nearer the Sphenisciformes than do grebes, and they are also more similar to the Procellariiformes. The grebes appear to represent a separate offshoot of the group, and have a condition of the breast feathers which is different from . . . any other birds except some of the Alcidae."

Gardner (1925) found that the tongue of loons differs from that of grebes, although they have similar food habits. The loons have a large patch of spinous processes at the base of the tongue, the grebes only a single posterior row.

Stolpe (1932, 1935) found the hind limb myology and osteology of loons and grebes to differ substantially and concluded that they are not more closely related to one another than each is to some other group. In the loons the cnemial crest of the tibiotarsus is formed by a projection of the tibia, in grebes by a fusion of the patella and tibia, and in *Hesperornis* by the patella alone. Stolpe also showed that the movement of the toes in swimming differs between loons and grebes. Prior to the recovery stroke, loons flex the toes without rotating them; grebes rotate the toes through a 90° arc while flexing them so that the longer mesial lobes trail and the shorter lateral lobes fold against the underside of the toe.

Stolpe's observations and conclusions had a major influence on subsequent ideas about the relationship between loons and grebes. Most authors accepted his discoveries as conclusive evidence that the similarities between loons and grebes are due to convergence. An exception was Cracraft (1982), whose study is discussed below.

Hudson (1937) noted that the pelvic muscle formula of the Common Loon (*Gavia immer*) is ABCDXV+; that of the Eared Grebe (*Podiceps nigricollis*) is BCX. The Eared Grebe lacks the M. semimembranosus, peroneus brevis, and M. flexor perforatus digiti II, which are present in the loon. However, Storer (1960b:704) found M. flexor perforatus digiti II "present and well developed" in the Pied-billed Grebe (*Podilymbus*). Loons and grebes agree in having the M. sartorius with an isolated insertion on the medial side of the head of the tibia, and in having the pars interna of the gastrocnemius two-headed, arising from a long line down the proximal half of the tibia.

E. Stresemann (1934) attributed the similarities between loons and grebes to convergence and saw no obvious ties between either group and other orders. Peters (1931) and Wetmore (1930, 1934, 1940, 1951, 1960) placed the loons and grebes in separate but adjacent orders.

Mayr and Amadon (1951:5) were aware of Stolpe's (1935) discoveries, but kept the loons and grebes as adjacent orders because "the grebes have been thought to be remote allies of the petrels, and since McDowell (oral communication) thinks that the loons may be a specialized offshoot of petrel stock, it is possible that the grebes and loons have some distant or indirect relationship."

The Oligocene fossil *Colymboides minutus* was considered to be intermediate between loons and grebes by Milne-Edwards (1867–71), and Howard (1950), who believed that "there is no doubt that the diving birds, the grebes and loons, stem from a common ancestor." However, Storer (1956) judged *Colymboides* to be a loon and noted: "The coracoid of loons is most similar to that of shorebirds and gulls, and birds of these groups also have two proximal foramina on the tarsometatarsus and three anterior hypotarsal canals. Thus, the loons may have their closest relationship with the great charadriiform complex" (p. 425).

Storer (1960b) emphasized the differences in the cnemial crest, pelvic musculature, and foot structure between loons and grebes. "The Hesperornithes, the loons and the grebes are outstanding examples of convergent evolution. In fact, I doubt that they even had a common swimming ancestor" (p. 701).

In 1971, Storer stated his opinion that "The various groups of foot-propelled diving birds have long been regarded as prime examples of convergence. Before this convergence was recognized, the loons and the grebes were placed in the same order near the beginning of most classifications. The reasoning was that these birds resembled (albeit superficially) the well-known early toothed diver, *Hesperornis*, of the Cretaceous. Now it seems certain that, in spite of having teeth, *Hesperornis* was the most specialized foot-propelled diver known. As it is also certain that the loons and grebes are unrelated to *Hesperornis* or to each other, there is no reason for keeping them together or near the beginning of a classification" (p. 5).

In his classification, Storer (1971) placed the loons (Gaviiformes) after the Charadriiformes and the grebes (Podicipediformes) next to the penguins (Sphenisciformes).

Brodkorb (1963b) proposed the new family Lonchodytidae in the Gaviiformes for *Lonchodytes estesi* and *L. pterygius* from the Upper Cretaceous of Wyoming. This was assumed to have extended the known antiquity of the loons, but Brodkorb did not comment on comparisons, except to *Gavia*.

Verheyen (1959c, 1961) thought the loons belong in the "Alciformes" with the auks and diving-petrels, and that the grebes are related to the sungrebes (Heliornithidae). He placed the grebes in a suborder in his order Ralliformes, between the cranes (Grues) and rails (Ralli). In his 1961 classification he gave the grebes ordinal rank between the Ralliformes and the Jacaniformes (jacanas, Sunbittern, Kagu, mesites).

The electrophoretic patterns of the egg-white proteins of loons and grebes contained "little to indicate a grebe-petrel relationship and not much to support a grebe-loon alliance. . . . other than showing that the grebes are surely monophyletic (which was not in doubt), the egg-white profiles give us little new information about their affinities" (Sibley 1960:231). The egg-white patterns of loons most closely resembled those of gulls, and Sibley placed "the Gaviiformes near the Charadriiformes rather than in their usual place near the grebes" (p. 234).

The presence of a cover (a layer of material above the cuticle) and lack of pigmentation in the egg shells of grebes separates them from those of loons (Tyler 1969). Tyler also found differences in the amounts and distribution of true shell nitrogen, and in histological staining. He did not find similarities between the egg shells of grebes and procellariids, and could not suggest possible relatives of either loons or grebes.

Sibley and Ahlquist (1972) compared the egg-white proteins of three species of loons and 10 of the 19 species of grebes. The electrophoretic patterns differed between the two groups and we concluded that "the loons and grebes are . . . probably more closely related to some other group than to each other. The closest living relatives of the loons seem to be the shorebirds (Charadriiformes); the closest relatives of the grebes remain uncertain."

Cracraft (1981) included the Gaviidae and Podicipedidae in the Gaviiformes and (1982) reported that

A cladistic analysis of the skeletons of loons . . . grebes . . . and the Cretaceous diving birds *Hesperornis* and *Baptornis*, supports the hypothesis that they form a monophyletic group (. . . the Gaviomorphae). . . . skeletal evidence also suggests that penguins . . . are the sister group of the Gaviomorphae.

Arguments that similarities of gaviomorph taxa represent convergence are not well founded. First, morphological differences among taxa do not constitute valid evidence against their monophyly. . . . Second, in no case has anyone supporting convergence presented a corroborated alternative phylogenetic hypothesis.

A close relationship among gaviomorphs, penguins, and apparently also the Procellariiformes and Pelecaniformes implies that a lineage of aquatic birds was established very early in avian history, presumably in the Early Cretaceous or Late Jurassic.

Cracraft (1982) reviewed the history of the debate about the relationships among the foot-propelled divers and cited six principal "similarities that are unique within birds, and therefore are interpretable as being derived within the Gavio-impennes" (p. 46). These six similarities are: "1. The similarity of the palate is unique within birds. . . . 2. The preacetabular ilium is relatively very short. . . . 3. The humerus of loons and grebes has a unique structure within birds. . . . 4. The femora of loons and grebes are distinctly curved. . . . 5. The tibiotarsus is compressed anteroposteriorly. . . . 6. On the tarsometatarsus . . . the metatarsal groove is strongly raised as a thin ridge relative to the internal margin."

Each of these six characters was described and figured. Cracraft discussed Stolpe's (1935) evidence and concluded that it "contains no relevant information bearing on the problem."

Cracraft, correctly in our view, pointed out that "An argument of nonrelationship must be based on showing that loons and grebes are related to other taxa and not to each other" and that "differences . . . do not provide a logical basis" for concluding that similarities are due to convergence. Although we disagree, in part, with Cracraft's conclusions, his logical argument is a model of phylogenetic reasoning.

Cracraft's classification (1982:37) provides a summary of his conclusions about the relationships of the loons and grebes:

Class Aves
    Subclass Neornithes
        Division 1
            Cohort Gavio-impennes
                Superorder Sphenisci
                    Order Sphenisciformes
                        Family Spheniscidae (Penguins)
                Superorder Gaviomorphae
                    Order Gaviiformes
                        Family Gaviidae (loons)
                        Family Podicipedidae (grebes)
                    Order Hesperornithiformes (extinct, toothed birds)
            Cohort Stegano-tubinares
                Order Procellariiformes (albatrosses, petrels)
                Order Pelecaniformes (pelicans, tropicbirds, frigatebirds, gannets, cormorants)

The DNA comparisons support a relationship among loons, penguins, and procellariids, but not a close relationship between loons and grebes. The errors in Cracraft's reconstruction of the phylogeny of the diving birds are due to the difficulties of interpreting morphological characters, not to the principles he used as the basis for his analysis. Unfortunately, logic cannot compensate for the limitations of the human eye as an instrument to extract the phylogenetic component from the mixture of functional and genealogical information in gross structures, such as bones.

The DNA Hybridization Evidence

The DNA hybridization evidence has been discussed above. The loon lineage diverged from a common ancestry with the tubenoses at Δ $T_{50}H$ 10.0 (Fig. 368). Their next nearest living relatives are the penguins, tubenoses, and frigatebirds. The grebe lineage diverged earlier (Δ 14.9) (Fig. 366). The grebes have no close living relatives.

Introduction to the Order Passeriformes: The Passerine Birds or Perching Birds

The order Passeriformes contains 5274 (58%) of the 9021 species of Recent birds listed by Bock and Farrand (1980), or 5712 (59%) of the 9672 species in 2057 genera recognized by Sibley and Monroe (1990). Most passerines are small land-dwelling birds that feed primarily on insects, seeds, fruit, or nectar. The largest species are the Australian lyrebirds (*Menura*) and the Raven (*Corvus corax*), the smallest are the bushtits (*Psaltriparus*) and the Pygmy Tit (*Psaltria exilis*).

Except for the syrinx in the suboscines (suborder Tyranni), the bill, and to some degree the feet, the passerines tend to be morphologically similar and their subdivision into categories below suborders has been difficult. Convergence has produced morphologically similar eco-types in different parts of the world, some of which have been placed in the same family. Conversely, some closely related but morphologically dissimilar species have been placed in separate families. Some aspects of these problems have been recognized for more than a century; for example, Sclater (1880b:345) was troubled by the "vexed question" of dividing the oscine passerines (suborder Passeri) into families and he suggested that "The difficulty here obviously arises from the fact that the Oscines are all very closely related to one another, and, in reality, form little more than one group, equivalent to other so-called families of birds. As, however, there are some 4700 species of Oscines known, it is absolutely necessary to sub-divide them; and the task of doing this in the most convenient and natural way is not an easy one."

However, Sclater was mistaken; the oscines are not "all very closely related to one another." The DNA comparisons show that there are two major groups (Corvida, Passerida) and evidence of subgroups has been found in the comparisons of their DNAs.

Gadow (1891a:252) was also deceived by the morphological similarities among the passerines when he wrote, "In talking of these 'families' we are apt to forget, or rather we never appreciate, the solemn fact that, strictly speaking, ʼll the Oscines together are of the rank of one family only!" Lucas (1894) deplored the fact that the passerines had often been split into numerous families, which he viewed as destroying even a semblance of equivalence between passerine and non-passerine families. Fürbringer (1888) recognized only two families of passerines, but later authors have divided the same group of species into 63 (E. Stresemann 1934), 50 (Mayr and Amadon 1951), 70 (Wetmore 1960), or 104 families (Wolters 1975–82).

Sclater, Gadow, Lucas, and Fürbringer were right about the difficulties, but the DNA-DNA comparisons have shown that the passerines are actually much more genetically diverse than their similar morphologies seemed to indicate, and we have found it necessary to divide them into 45 families based on the same criteria used for the non-passerines. Although the number of families we recognize is closer to the opinions of Stresemann and Mayr and Amadon than to that of Fürbringer, it will become apparent that the boundaries of some of our families differ from those of previous classifications. This is largely because our categories are more nearly equivalent to the degrees of evolutionary divergence they represent. Many of the families in previous classifications are represented by subfamilies or tribes in our system.

The classifications of passerine birds that have been in use during the recent past owe some of their features to tradition, and a complete analysis of the sources of their arrangements would require a detailed review of past systems. Such a review would reveal that there have been many opinions about virtually every aspect of avian systematics and that the relative stability between ca. 1910 and 1960 was preceded by more than a century of debate and dissension. The period of stability was not produced by the discovery of ultimate truth but by a consensus that the true phylogeny and the perfect classification could never be known, and that comparative studies "have failed us after nearly 200 years of efforts" (E. Stresemann 1959). Stresemann (1951, 1975) examined the development of all aspects of ornithology to 1950, and the earlier classifications were reviewed by Gadow (1893) and Newton (1896).

Since about 1960 a new period of debate has prevailed, fueled in part by the development of new methods of data production, for example the molecular techniques, and in part by new concepts and procedures for analyzing morphological characters, such as cladistics and numerical taxonomy. The resolution of these conflicts and the development of a new consensus are not yet in sight.

A Chronological Survey of Passerine Classification

The historical components in the passerine classifications proposed in this century can often be traced back to Linnaeus, Gmelin, Owen, Cuvier, Buffon, and other zoologists of the late eighteenth and early nineteenth centuries. Linnaeus (1758) placed his "Ordo Passeres" as the last group in his Aves and included within it the genera *Columba* (pigeons) and *Caprimulgus* (nightjars), as well as most of the passerines he knew. Some of the passerines he assigned to the "Picae" (e.g., *Corvus, Sitta, Certhia*), and the shrikes, jays, tyrant flycatchers, and bulbuls he placed in the "Accipitres."

The opinions of George Robert Gray were especially influential and still permeate traditional classifications of birds. Gray's *List of the Genera of Birds* (1840) was followed by several editions and culminated in the famous *Hand-List*, the final volume of which was published in 1871. Gray's classification of the passerines was based mainly on the bill and other external characters visible in museum skin specimens. Gray (1869, 1870) presented the following arrangement for the families of his Passeres. Some of the included taxa are listed:

PASSERES Fissirostres
    Caprimulgidae: Frogmouths, Oilbird, Goatsuckers
    Cypselidae: Swifts

Hirundinidae: Swallows
Coraciadae [sic]: Rollers
Eurylaimidae: Broadbills (except *Smithornis*)
Todidae: Todies
Momotidae: Motmots
Trogonidae: Trogons
Bucconidae: Puffbirds
Alcedinidae: Kingfishers
Meropidae: Bee-eaters
Galbulidae: Jacamars
PASSERES Tenuirostres
Upupidae: Hoopoes
Promeropidae: Sunbirds, Sugarbirds, Hawaiian Honeycreepers
Coerebidae: Neotropical Honeycreepers
Trochilidae: Hummingbirds
Meliphagidae: Honeyeaters
Anabatidae: Neotropical Ovenbirds, Sharpbill, Woodcreepers, Nuthatches, Sittellas, New Zealand
    Wrens
Certhiidae: *Certhia, Tichodroma, Salpornis, Climacteris, Rhabdornis*
Menuridae: Lyrebirds, *Orthonyx, Mohoua*
Pteroptochidae: Tapaculos
Troglodytidae: Wrens, some Babblers
PASSERES Dentirostres
Luscinidae: Old World Warblers, African Warblers, Australian "Warblers," Scrub-birds, Kinglets,
    Chats, Accentors, etc.
Paridae: Tits, Bushtits, *Panurus*, Gnatcatchers, etc.
Chamaeadae [sic]: Wrentit
Mniotiltidae: Wood Warblers (Parulini)
Motacillidae: Wagtails, Pipits, *Grallina, Enicurus, Seiurus, Ephthianura*
Turdidae: Thrushes, Mockingbirds, *Chaetops*
Hydrobatidae: Dippers
Eupetidae: *Eupetes, Mesites*
Pycnonotidae: Bulbuls, some Babblers, *Yuhina, Turnagra*, etc.
Dicruridae: Drongos, *Melaenornis*, etc.
Artamidae: Woodswallows, *Oriolia, Pseudochelidon*, etc.
Oriolidae: Old World Orioles, Bowerbirds
Pittidae: Pittas, *Philepitta*
Formicariidae: Antbirds, Gnatwrens, etc.
Aegithinidae: some Babblers, Leafbirds, etc.
Muscicapidae: *Peltops*, Monarchs, muscicapines, *Smithornis*, Australian "flycatchers," Cuckoo-
    shrikes, etc.
Tyrannidae: Tyrant Flycatchers
Ampelidae: Waxwings, Silky Flycatchers
Cotingidae: Cotingas, Becards, Manakins, Plantcutters
Vireonidae: Vireos, Shrike-Vireos, *Icteria, Dulus*
Laniidae: *Cracticus*, Whistlers, *Chasiempis*, true shrikes, *Prionops*, vangas, etc.
PASSERES Conirostres
Corvidae: *Strepera, Gymnorhina, Pityriasis*, Jays, Magpies, Crows, some New Zealand
    Wattlebirds, *Struthidea*
Paradiseidae: sexually dimorphic Birds of Paradise
Sturnidae: Manucodes, *Astrapia*, Starlings, Oxpeckers, some New Zealand Wattlebirds,
    Euryceros, etc.

Icteridae: New World Orioles (troupials, grackles, etc.)
Ploceidae: Weaverbirds, Waxbills
Tanagridae: Tanagers
Fringillidae: some Finches, some emberizines, *Passer, Paradoxornis*
Emberizidae: some Finches, some emberizines
Alaudidae: Larks
Colidae [sic]: Colies or Mousebirds
Musophagidae: Turacos
Opisthocomidae: Hoatzin

In Gray's publications it is possible to find the sources of some arrangements that have been copied by his successors to the present day; not all were wrong, but many were. Thus, Gray had a lasting influence, although his groupings and sequence of taxa were based on a few superficial characters. His *Hand-List* was followed because it covered all known species and was a convenient basis for arranging collections and organizing faunal works.

As additional characters were examined, the weaknesses in the older systems began to be revealed. Nitzsch (1840) studied the pterylography of many groups and Müller (1847, English trans. 1878) described the structure of the syrinx. Müller's work marks the beginning of the modern classification of passerine birds because his major subdivision into suboscines and oscines has survived and been supported by other sources of evidence, including DNA hybridization.

Baird (1858) followed Cabanis (1847) "in dividing the order *Insessores* into the suborders *Strisores, Clamatores,* and *Oscines.*" The *Strisores* included the Trochilidae, Cypselidae (swifts), and Caprimulgidae, and the *Clamatores* consisted of the Alcedinidae, Prionitidae (trogons), and Colopteridae (suboscines). The suborder *Oscines* contained the "singing birds." Baird's classification of the North American Oscines follows (vernacular names added):

Order Insessores
  Suborder Oscines
    Family Turdidae
      Subfamily Turdinae: Thrushes
      Subfamily Regulinae: Kinglets
      Subfamily Cinclinae: Dippers
    Family Sylvicolidae
      Subfamily Motacillinae: Wagtails, Pipits
      Subfamily Sylvicolinae: Wood Warblers (Parulini)
      Subfamily Tanagrinae: Tanagers
    Family Hirundinidae: Swallows
    Family Bombycillidae
      Subfamily Bombycillinae: Waxwings
      Subfamily Ptiliogonidinae: Phainopepla, Solitaires (*Myadestes*)
    Family Laniidae
      Subfamily Laniinae: Shrikes
      Subfamily Vireoninae: Vireos
    Family Liotrichidae
      Subfamily Miminae: Mockingbirds, Thrashers
      Subfamily Campylorhynchinae: Wrens
      Subfamily Troglodytinae: Wrens
      Subfamily Chamaeanae [sic]: Wrentit

Family Certhiadae [sic]
   Subfamily Certhianae: Creepers
   Subfamily Sittinae: Nuthatches
Family Paridae
   Subfamily Polioptilinae: Gnatcatchers
   Subfamily Parinae: Titmice, Chickadees, Bushtits
Family Dacnididae: Honeycreepers (Coerebidae)
Family Alaudidae: Larks
Family Fringillidae: Finches, Sparrows, Buntings, Grosbeaks
Family Icteridae: Troupials, Blackbirds
Family Corvidae: Crows, Jays, Magpies

By 1863 Cabanis and Heine (1850–63) had combined the ideas of Keyserling and Blasius (1839), Nitzsch, and Müller into a system that was similar to those of the recent past. The influence of the Darwinian revolution after 1859 stimulated numerous comparative anatomical studies by Huxley, Garrod, Forbes, Sundevall, Sclater, Fürbringer, Gadow, Seebohm, Parker, Newton, Shufeldt, Lucas, Beddard, and Pycraft. Many problems that were solved during this period have remained solved; others proved recalcitrant.

The first volume of what was to be "unquestionably the most important work on systematic ornithology that has ever been published" (Zimmer 1926:96) appeared in 1874. The *Catalogue of the Birds in the British Museum* was begun by Richard Bowdler Sharpe, who wrote 13 of the 27 volumes. The passerine volumes (3–15), written by Sharpe, Seebohm, Gadow, and P. L. Sclater, were published between 1877 and 1890. The *Catalogue* emphasized the descriptions of species and diagnoses of genera. Families and subfamilies were diagnosed and, in some instances, discussions of family-level relationships were presented. The influence of the *Catalogue* on later workers would be difficult to overestimate. It became, and to some extent remains, the point of departure for studies in avian systematics.

For the Passeriformes, Sharpe (1877:1) decided that

The system of classification for the higher groups of Passerine birds to be followed . . . will be that of . . . Garrod, who, after an exhaustive consideration of many points in their anatomy, has established his classification not on one, but on several characters. I am informed by him that he has devoted great attention to the characters given by Prof. Sundevall (Meth. Av. Tent. p. 1) and by Dr. Elliott Coues in the Introduction to the great work on North-American Birds, and that there are too many exceptions to be found to the characters laid down to render their diagnoses of the order comprehensive. . . . some characters propounded by the above-named ornithologists, as follows:—

Hallux stout, furnished with a larger claw than the other toes; greater coverts arranged in a single row, not reaching beyond the middle of the secondaries; sternum simple, with a single notch in the posterior margin.

In the present work, for the lower groups, it is proposed to follow, as far as possible, the divisions of Professor Sundevall's 'Tentamen,' without adopting their exact order. However modified the arrangement may be, this useful treatise will form the basis of my classification.

Sharpe also stated that he would include "several alterations proposed by Dr. Coues . . . the primary arrangement of the suborder as put forward by Prof. Garrod . . . and by Mr. Wallace . . . and, for American Passeres the labours of Prof. Baird and Mr. Ridgway . . . will be consulted." Thus, the classification was an eclectic arrangement from many sources, certain neither to please all nor to offend many.

Sharpe (1877) began the passerine classification in volume 3 of the *Catalogue* with the oscines and placed the suboscines in volume 14 (Sclater 1888). The following synopsis of the classification of the passerines in the *Catalogue of Birds* begins with the suboscines, as in most other classifications. The numbers of genera are from the *Catalogue*; the vernacular names have been added. Names in parentheses identify the placement indicated by the DNA comparisons.

Order Passeriformes
  Suborder Passeres
    Division Mesomyodi
      Subdivision Oligomyodae
          Fam. Tyrannidae: Tyrant Flycatchers, 77 genera
          Fam. Oxyrhamphidae: Sharpbill, 1 gen.
          Fam. Pipridae: Manakins, 19 gen., incl. *Schiffornis*
          Fam. Cotingidae: Cotingas, Becards, 29 gen.
          Fam. Phytotomidae: Plantcutters, 1 gen.
          Fam. Philepittidae: Asities, 1 gen.
          Fam. Pittidae: Pittas, 4 gen.
          Fam. Xenicidae: New Zealand Wrens, 2 gen.
          Fam. Eurylaemidae: Broadbills, 7 gen.
  Suborder Passeres
    I. Acromyodi
      a. *Passeres normales*
        Section A. Turdiformes
          Group I. Coliomorphae
            Fam. Corvidae: Crows, etc. 39 gen., incl. *Strepera*, *Struthidea*, *Picathartes*, *Falculea* ("vangid"), *Corcorax*, New Zealand Wattlebirds
            Fam. Paradiseidae: Birds of Paradise, 18 gen.
            Fam. Oriolidae: Old World Orioles, 2 gen.
            Fam. Dicruridae: Drongos, 11 gen., incl. *Irena*
            Fam. Prionopidae: 19 gen., incl. *Grallina* (monarch), *Tephrodornis* (malaconotine), *Eurocephalus* (laniid), *Poeoptera* (starling), *Leptopterus* ("vangid"), *Rectes* (*Pitohui* = pachycephaline), *Phaeornis* (turdine?), *Fraseria* (muscicapine), *Hemipus* (monarch?), *Bradyornis* (muscicapine), *Melaenornis* (muscicapine), *Hypocolius* (= ?), *Platylophus* (corvine), *Prionops* (malaconotine), *Euryceros* ("vangid" = malaconotine), and others
          Group II. Cichlomorphae
            Fam. Campophagidae [sic]: Cuckoo-shrikes, 10 gen.
            Fam. Muscicapidae: 69 gen., incl. *Microeca*, *Batis*, *Bias*, *Platysteira*, *Petroica*, *Smicrornis*, *Gerygone*, *Metabolus*, *Monachella*, *Poecilodryas*, *Hyliota*, *Todopsis*, *Chenorhamphus*, *Malurus*, *Rhipidura*, *Philentoma*, *Myiagra*, *Smithornis*, *Arses*, *Monarcha*, *Peltops*, *Pomarea*, etc. These genera include monarchs, fairy wrens, fantails, a cracticine, malaconotines, acanthizines, and a broadbill.
            Fam. Turdidae
              Subfam. Sylviinae: Old World Warblers, 7 gen.
              Subfam. Turdinae: Thrushes, 11 gen., incl. "chats"
            Fam. Timeliidae [sic]
              Subfam. Brachypodiinae: 27 gen., incl. *Aegithina*, *Chloropsis*, *Pycnonotus* and other bulbuls, *Irena*
              Subfam. Troglodytinae: Wrens, 18 gen., incl. *Cinclus* [Sharpe (1885:440) thought that *Polioptila* is closest to *Stenostira*.]
              Subfam. Miminae: Mockingbirds, etc. 12 gen., incl. *Donacobius*, *Rhodinocichla*

Subfam. Myiadectinae: Solitaires, 3 gen.
Subfam. Ptilonorhynchinae: Bowerbirds, 6 gen.
Subfam. Timeliinae: Babblers, etc., 164 genera, incl. *Turnagra, Myiophoneus, Brachypteryx, Alethe, Lamprolia, Copsychus, Sphenoeacus, Origma, Stipiturus, Amytis (Amytornis), Megalurus, Origma, Camaroptera, Apalis, Hylia, Prinia, Cisticola, Orthotomus, Acanthiza, Chamaea, Orthonyx, Cinclosoma, Eupetes, Drymodes, Psophodes, Pinarornis, Accentor (Prunella), Paradoxornis, Ephthianura*. These genera include thrushes, monarchs, malurids, cisticolids, pardalotids, eopsaltriids, a passerid (*Prunella*), meliphagids, etc.
Fam. Paridae
Subfam. Parinae: Titmice, 8 gen., incl. *Aegithalus* [sic] (incl. *Remiz*), *Auriparus, Sphenostoma, Aphelocephala, Mohoua, Panurus*
Subfam. Regulinae: Kinglets, 2 gen.
Fam. Laniidae
Subfam. Gymnorhininae: 3 gen., *Pityriasis, Cracticus, Gymnorhina*
Subfam. Malaconotinae: 11 gen., incl. "Vangidae," *Telophorus, Dryoscopus, Laniarius, Nicator, Nilaus, Neolestes*
Subfam. Pachycephalinae: 5 gen., incl. *Falcunculus, Oreoica, Eopsaltria, Pachycare*
Subfam. Laniinae: 4 gen., incl. *Urolestes, Corvinella*
Subfam. Vireoninae: Vireos, etc., 6 gen.
Group III. Certhiomorphae
Fam. Certhiidae
Subfam. Certhiinae: Creepers, 4 gen., incl. *Certhia, Salpornis, Tichodroma, Climacteris*
Subfam. Sittinae: Nuthatches, 3 gen., incl. *Sitta, Sittella (Daphoenositta), Hypositta* (a vanga)
Group IV. Cinnyrimorphae
Fam. Nectariniidae: Sunbirds, 8 gen., incl. *Neodrepanis*
Fam. Meliphagidae
Subfam. Myzomelinae: *Myzomela, Acanthorhynchus*
Subfam. Zosteropinae: *Zosterops, Melithreptus, Plectrorhynchus* (last two are meliphagids)
Subfam. Meliphaginae: Honeyeaters, 20 gen., incl. *Oedistoma, Promerops* (not meliphagids)
Section B. Fringilliformes
Fam. Dicaeidae: 19 gen., incl. Hawaiian Honeycreepers, *Pinaroloxias, Oreocharis, Pardalotus, Parmoptila, Pholidornis, Melanocharis, Rhamphocharis*
Fam. Hirundinidae: Swallows, 11 gen.
Fam. Ampelidae: Waxwings, Palm Chat, Silky Flycatchers, 5 gen.
Fam. Mniotiltidae: Wood Warblers, 21 gen.
Fam. Motacillidae: Wagtails, Pipits, 7 gen.
Fam. Coerebidae: Neotropical Honeycreepers, etc.
Subfam. Diglossinae: *Diglossa, Diglossopsis*
Subfam. Dacnidinae: 6 gen., *Oreomanes, Conirostrum, Xenodacnis, Hemidacnis, Dacnis, Certhidea* (geospizine)
Subfam. Coerebinae: 3 gen., *Chlorophanes, Certhiola, Coereba*
Subfam. Glossoptilinae: *Glossoptila (Euneornis*, a tanager)
Fam. Tanagridae: Tanagers, etc.
Subfam. Procniatidae: Swallow Tanager, *Procnias = Tersina*
Subfam. Euphoniinae: Euphonias, 4 gen.
Subfam. Tanagrinae: Tanagers, 32 gen.

Subfam. Lamprotinae: 2 gen.
Subfam. Phoenicophilinae: 2 gen.
Subfam. Pitylinae: 17 gen., incl. *Buarremon, Pezopetes, Arremon, Saltator,*
Orchesticus, Diucopis, Conothraupis, Lamprospiza. {Sclater (1886:253) noted:
"Under this head [Pityline Fringillirostres] I place the most Finch-like of the
Tanagers. . . . it is very difficult to decide where to draw the line between some
of these forms and the Ground-finches allied to *Pipilo.*"}
Fam. Icteridae: Troupials, Meadowlarks, etc., 29 gen.
Fam. Fringillidae: Finches, Sparrows, Goldfinches, etc., 97 gen., incl.
Catamblyrhynchus, Passer, Montifringilla, Petronia, Haplospiza, Spiza, Atlapetes,
Tiaris
Section C. Sturniformes
Fam. Artamidae: Woodswallows, incl. *Pseudochelidon*
Fam. Sturnidae: Starlings, 42 gen., incl. *Fregilupus, Buphagus*
Fam. Ploceidae: Weaverbirds, Waxbills, 62 gen.
Fam. Alaudidae: Larks, 21 gen.
b. *Passeres abnormales*
Fam. Atrichiidae: Scrub-birds, *Atrichornis*
Fam. Menuridae: Lyrebirds, *Menura*

By 1880, when Philip Lutley Sclater presented his *Remarks on the Present State of the Systema Avium*, the boundaries of the suborders and many of the families that would be used for the next century had been established. Sclater departed from Gray's system and acknowledged his debt to Müller, Nitzsch, Sundevall, Garrod, Huxley, and others. The classification developed by Stejneger (1885) was based on that of Sclater and was used by many later systematists.

In his two massive volumes on avian anatomy and classification, Fürbringer (1888) treated the passerines as a uniform group of two "Familiae," the "Pseudoscines" and the "Passeridae" in the "Pico-Passeres." This arrangement was ignored by his successors, thus Fürbringer had little effect on the classification of the Passeriformes. His implied alliance between the piciforms and passeriforms in the "Pico-Passeres" may have helped to foster this false relationship in later classifications.

At the Second International Ornithological Congress, held in Budapest in 1891, Sharpe delivered a peroration on recent attempts to classify birds. He reviewed the history of avian classification since Linnaeus, with critiques of the proposals of Huxley (1867), Garrod (1874a), Sclater (1880b), Reichenow (1882), Stejneger (1885), Fürbringer (1888), Seebohm (1890b), and several others. Sharpe's review was 90 pages long and he concluded it with his own "scheme of the linear arrangement of the Class 'Aves,' in accordance with the views propounded in the preceding pages." Extensive notes and diagnoses of morphological characters, nesting, eggs, voice, and behavior accompany Sharpe's classification. His arrangement of passerine groups follows:

Order Eurylaemi: Broadbills
Order Menurae: Lyrebirds
Order Passeriformes
Section A. Oscines
Corvidae: Crows, Jays, Magpies
Paradiseidae: Birds of Paradise
Ptilonorhynchidae: Bowerbirds

Sturnidae: Starlings
Eulabetidae: Glossy Starlings
Eurycerotidae: the vanga *Euryceros*
Dicruridae: Drongos
Oriolidae: Old World Orioles
Icteridae: Troupials (New World Orioles, etc.)
Ploceidae: Weaverbirds, etc.
Tanagridae: Tanagers
Coerebidae: Neotropical Honeycreepers
Fringillidae: Finches, etc.
Alaudidae: Larks
Motacillidae: Wagtails, Pipits
Mniotiltidae: Wood Warblers
Certhiidae: Creepers
Meliphagidae: Honeyeaters
Nectariniidae: Sunbirds
Dicaeidae: Flowerpeckers
Zosteropidae: White-eyes
Paridae: Tits
Regulidae: Kinglets
Laniidae: Shrikes
Artamidae: Woodswallows
Ampelidae: Waxwings, Silky Flycatchers
Vireonidae: Vireos and allies
Sylviidae: Old World Warblers
Turdidae: Thrushes
Cinclidae: Dippers
Troglodytidae: Wrens
Mimidae: Mockingbirds and Thrashers
Timeliidae [sic]: Babblers
Pycnonotidae: Bulbuls
Campophagidae [sic]: Cuckoo-shrikes
Muscicapidae: Old World Flycatchers
Hirundinidae: Swallows
Section B. Oligomyodae
Tyrannidae: Tyrant Flycatchers
Oxyrhamphidae: Sharpbill (*Oxyruncus*)
Pipridae: Manakins
Cotingidae: Cotingas
Phytotomidae: Plantcutters
Philepittidae: Asities
Pittidae: Pittas
Xeniscidae [sic]: New Zealand Wrens
Section C. Tracheophonae
Dendrocolaptidae: Woodcreepers
Formicariidae: Antbirds
Pteroptochidae: Tapaculos
Section D. Atrichiidae: Scrub-birds

Gadow (1893) gave detailed attention to the non-passerines but, like Fürbringer, he viewed the passerines as morphologically uniform. He subdivided the suboscines on the basis of syringeal and other anatomical characters, discussed the classifications proposed by some of his predecessors, and presented the following arrangement (1893:301–302):

Legion Coraciomorphae
  Order Passeriformes
    Suborder Passeres anisomyodi
      (Subclamatores)
        Family Eurylaimidae: Broadbills
      (Clamatores)
        Family Pittidae: Pittas, Asities (incl. Philepittidae)
        Family Xenicidae: New Zealand Wrens (Acanthisittidae)
        Family Tyrannidae: Tyrant Flycatchers, Manakins, Sharpbill, Cotingas, Tityras
        Family Formicariidae: Antbirds, Ovenbirds, Woodcreepers
        Family Pteroptochidae: Tapaculos, Gnateaters
    Suborder Passeres diacromyodi
      (Suboscines)
        Family Menuridae
          Subfamily Atrichiinae: Scrub-birds
          Subfamily Menurinae: Lyrebirds
      (Oscines)

Gadow (1893:279–280) discussed the oscines, noting that "The subdivision of the oscines into families is still completely inadequate" (transl.). He listed 28 families of oscines, based on, but not identical to, the groups recognized by Sharpe and others in volumes 3–13 of the *Catalogue of Birds*. Gadow (1893:280) also noted some aspects of the classifications of Sclater (1880b) and Sundevall (1872) and commented that "These six or seven groups recognized by Sundevall, Sclater and Sharpe . . . are not based on morphological or phylogenetic grounds because, for the oscines, the methods of bill-wing-foot systematics are still being used. An important reason for the imperfect classification is intrinsically historical. Ornithology is a European science; European birds were designated as the types of families and the exotic forms were then somehow inserted in or between these families. With few exceptions, the European forms are considered to be the most highly evolved members of the oscines, while especially the Australian taxa are placed in the lower ranks. Also, American ornithologists consider their songbirds to be only highly evolved forms" (transl.).

Gadow urged that extensive research on the complete morphologies of all groups, including those of Australia and Indo-Malaya, be undertaken. He concluded that "The key to the mysteries of the songbirds lies in the Australian region of the Earth; from there they have occupied the habitats of the entire world" (p. 282, transl.). Gadow was remarkably prophetic in this statement, as the DNA comparisons have shown (Sibley and Ahlquist 1985a).

By 1900 the broad outlines of avian classification seemed fairly clear, but many problems remained. Robert Ridgway claimed no originality for his classification of the birds of North and Middle America (1901–11), but he noted that

The imperfection of our knowledge concerning the internal structure of many groups of birds, however, makes an entirely satisfactory classification impossible at the present time, and that here adopted must therefore be considered as provisional only. An entirely sound classification of birds is a matter of the future, requiring vastly extended investigations in the field of avian anatomy and the expenditure of an enormous amount of time and labor in elaborating the results. The matter of determining the limits of families and genera among birds is one of great difficulty especially among the Passeres; partly because such groups are often not clearly defined, but also because the material necessary for determining such questions is not always available. The question of what constitutes a "family" or a "genus" being involved, and, moreover, one concerning which there is much difference of opinion among systematists, the author's views may be stated, in order to make clear the principles which have been his guide in the present work. . . .

Accepting evolution as an established fact—and it is difficult to understand how anyone who has studied the subject seriously can by any possibility believe otherwise—there are no "hard and fast lines," no gaps, or "missing links" in the chain of existing animal forms except as they are caused by the extinction of certain intermediate types; therefore, there can be no such group as a family or genus (nor any other for that matter) unless it is cut off from other groups by the existence of such a gap; because unless thus isolated it can not be defined, and therefore has no existence in fact. These gaps being very unequally distributed, it necessarily follows that the groups thus formed are very unequal in value; sometimes alternate links in the chain may be missing; again, several in continuous sequence are gone, while occasionally a series of several or even numerous links may be intact. It thus happens that some family or generic groups seem very natural or homogeneous, because the range of generic or specific variation is not great and there is no near approach to the characters of another coordinate group, while others seem very artificial or heterogeneous because among the many generic or specific forms none seem to have dropped out, and therefore, however great the range of variation in structural details, no division into trenchant groups is practicable—not because extreme division would result, but simply because there can be no proper definition of groups which do not exist. In short, no group, whether of generic, family, or higher rank, can be valid unless it can be defined by characters which serve to distinguish it from every other (1901:vii–viii).

Thus, Ridgway attributed the difficulties associated with the classification of passerines to the relative lack of gaps resulting from the extinction of intermediate types, and to the unequal distribution of such gaps. To Ridgway it was the completeness of the record that caused the problems. Ridgway's explanation of the source of the problem sounds strange today, but his volumes remain as useful as when they were published.

Ridgway's "monumental work . . . is a detailed, taxonomic monograph . . . indispensable to the systematist of North and Middle American ornithology" (Zimmer 1926:525). Some of the planned volumes on the non-passerines have not yet been written, but Ridgway himself wrote the first eight. Parts 1–5 cover the Passeriformes and provide detailed descriptions of all species. Ridgway presented the criteria for his classification of North and Middle American passerines, included citations to previous works, and discussed the taxonomic problems he encountered. He pointed out the weaknesses in the taxonomic characters he used, and provided reasons for his allocations of species and genera to higher categories. Ridgway's diagnoses and discussions remain among the most complete available and he recorded the discrepancies and difficulties in numerous footnotes.

After Sharpe and his collaborators had completed the *Catalogue*, he began work on a *Hand-List of the Genera and Species of Birds*. Volumes 3–5 (1901, 1903, 1909) contain the passerines and Sharpe noted that "The task of compiling a list of the known species of Birds becomes very difficult when the Passeriformes are approached. . . . Apart from the work involved in picking up the threads since the 'Catalogue' was finished, the question of Classification presents grave difficulties. . . . A good deal of sterling work has been done during recent years, but we are still far from a satisfactory system as regards the Passerine birds" (1901:v).

Sharpe mainly followed the classification used in the *Catalogue*, but he also had the advice of a number of colleagues who were acknowledged in the introductions to the three volumes of the *Hand-List* (1901, 1903, 1909) containing the passerines. Thus, the classification in the *Hand-List* represents a consensus among avian systematists at the beginning of this century, as follows:

Order Eurylaemiformes
      Family Eurylaemidae: Broadbills
Order Menuriformes
      Family Menuridae: Lyrebirds
Order Passeriformes
  Suborder Mesomyodi
     Division Tracheophonae
      Family Pteroptochidae: Tapaculos
      Family Conopophagidae: Gnateaters
      Family Formicariidae: Antbirds
      Family Dendrocolaptidae: Woodcreepers, Ovenbirds
     Division Oligomyodae
      Family Tyrannidae: Tyrant Flycatchers
      Family Oxyrhamphidae: Sharpbill (Oxyruncidae)
      Family Pipridae: Manakins, incl. *Schiffornis*
      Family Cotingidae: Cotingas, Tityras, Becards, *Lipaugus*, *Attila*, etc.
      Family Phytotomidae: Plantcutters
      Family Pittidae: Pittas
      Family Philepittidae: Asities
      Family Xenicidae: New Zealand Wrens (Acanthisittidae)
  Suborder Acromyodi
    (*Passeres Abnormales*)
      Family Atrichornithidae: Scrub-birds
    (*Passeres Normales*)
      Family Hirundinidae: Swallows
      Family Muscicapidae: 93 genera, incl. *Muscicapa*, *Batis*, *Microeca*, *Petroica*, *Gerygone*, *Hyliota*, *Polioptila*, *Smithornis*, *Todopsis*, *Rhipidura*, *Monarcha*, *Peltops*
      Family Campophagidae [sic]: Cuckoo-shrikes
      Family Pycnonotidae: Bulbuls, incl. *Aegithina*, *Irena*, *Chloropsis*, *Tylas*
      Family Timeliidae [sic]: Babblers, incl. *Orthonyx*, *Cinclosoma*, *Hylacola*, *Psophodes*, *Calamanthus*, *Cinclorhamphus*, *Bowdleria*, *Bernieria*, *Ifrita*, *Amaurocichla*, *Lamprolia*, *Yuhina*, *Panurus*, *Paradoxornis*
      Family Troglodytidae: Wrens
      Family Cinclidae: Dippers
      Family Mimidae: Mockingbirds, Thrashers, Catbirds, incl. *Donacobius*, *Rhodinocichla*
      Family Turdidae: Thrushes, incl. *Turnagra*, *Erithacus*, *Accentor* (*Prunella*), *Ephthianura*, *Zeledonia*
      Family Sylviidae: Old World Warblers, incl. *Sylvia*, *Cisticola*, *Eremiornis*, *Origma*, *Acanthiza*, *Sericornis*, *Apalis*, *Neomixis*, *Pholidornis*, *Hylia*, *Prinia*, *Malurus*, *Amytornis*
      Family Vireonidae: Vireos, Peppershrikes, Shrike-vireos
      Family Ampelidae: Waxwings, Silky Flycatchers, Palm Chat
      Family Artamidae: Woodswallows, incl. *Pseudochelidon*
      Family Vangidae: Vangas, except *Aerocharis* (*Euryceros*) and *Hypositta*
      Family Prionopidae: a heterogeneous assemblage incl. *Grallina*, *Hemipus*, *Tephrodornis*, *Fraseria*, *Horizorhinus*, *Eurocephalus*, *Clytorhynchus*, *Rhectes* (*Pitohui*), *Sigmodus*, *Platylophus*, *Pinarolestes* (*Colluricincla*), *Hypocolius*

Family Aerocharidae: *Aerocharis* (*Euryceros*)
Family Laniidae: Shrikes, incl. *Pityriasis, Cracticus, Malaconotus, Laniarius, Pachycephala, Oreoica, Falcunculus, Eopsaltria*
Family Paridae: Titmice, incl. *Remiz, Auriparus, Sphenostoma, Aegithalos, Aphelocephala*
Family Chamaeidae: Wrentit
Family Regulidae: Kinglets
Family Sittidae: Nuthatches, incl. *Sitta, Hypositta, Daphoenositta*
Family Certhiidae: Creepers, incl. *Certhia, Salpornis, Tichodroma, Rhabdornis, Climacteris*
Family Zosteropidae: White-eyes
Family Dicaeidae: Flowerpeckers, incl. *Pardalotus, Oreocharis, Melanocharis, Rhamphocharis*, etc.
Family Nectariniidae: Sunbirds, incl. *Neodrepanis*
Family Promeropidae: Sugarbirds
Family Meliphagidae: Honeyeaters
Family Mniotiltidae: Wood Warblers, incl. *Certhidea*
Family Drepanididae: Hawaiian Honeycreepers
Family Motacillidae: Wagtails and Pipits
Family Alaudidae: Larks
Family Catamblyrhynchidae: Plush-capped Finch or Plushcap
Family Fringillidae: Buntings, Finches, Sparrows
Family Coerebidae: Neotropical Honeycreepers
Family Procniatidae: Swallow Tanager (*Tersina*)
Family Tanagridae: Tanagers
Family Ploceidae: Weaverbirds, *Vidua*, Waxbills
Family Icteridae: Troupials, Meadowlarks, Grackles, etc.
Family Sturnidae: Starlings
Family Eulabetidae: Glossy Starlings, incl. *Falculea* (a vanga), *Heterolocha* (Huia), *Creadion* (*Philesturnus*)
Family Paramythiidae: *Paramythia*
Family Buphagidae: Oxpeckers
Family Oriolidae: Old World Orioles
Family Dicruridae: Drongos
Family Paradiseidae: Birds of Paradise
Family Ptilonorhynchidae: Bowerbirds, incl. *Loria, Macgregoria, Loboparadisea, Cnemophilus*
Family Corvidae: Crows, Jays, Magpies, incl. *Corcorax*

Most of these family names have survived in later classifications, although their sequence in the list and the included genera may have been modified. It is apparent that the *Hand-List* was a major influence on the development of the eclectic classifications of Alexander Wetmore, Erwin Stresemann, and other avian systematists of the past 75 years.

Alexander Wetmore's classification of the birds of the world went through five revisions from 1930 to 1960. In the last version (1960:16) he introduced the Passeriformes as follows:

This order, with more living species than all the others combined . . . presents many difficult problems in logical arrangement. The major groups are clear, whether we rank them as suborders or superfamilies being a matter of opinion. But the limits and status of numerous families contained in these larger categories are uncertain since the internal anatomy is known for so few kinds that details of difference are poorly understood. Superficial resemblances, on the other hand, are so obvious in many cases that they cause confusion. Under the circumstances it continues to seem appropriate to me to accept the family grouping that has been current for many years, except in those cases where acceptable studies clearly indicate change. Supposition in these matters has led to various proposals for changes, some part of which undoubtedly will prove correct. It is equally probable that a part, possibly the considerably larger part, may prove to be unfounded when details are more clearly known. If change is accepted under these circumstances it may prove unwarranted, necessitating further shift, perhaps a return to the original status. Since this can only prove confusing I prefer the conservative course.

Wetmore's "conservative course" dominated the classification of birds, especially in the United States, from 1930 to the publication of the sixth edition of the American Ornithologists' Union *Check-list of North American Birds* (1983), which departed in but a few places from the Wetmore arrangement. However, this conservatism has been justified because most of the proposals for change, as Wetmore (and E. Stresemann 1959) noted, have not been clearly better than the traditional classifications of the passerines. In the original format, Wetmore's (1960) classification of the passerines follows:

Order Passeriformes, Perching Birds.
　Suborder Eurylaimi, Broadbills.
　　Family Eurylaimidae, Broadbills.
　Suborder Tyranni, Ovenbirds, Woodhewers, and Allies.
　　Superfamily Furnarioidea, Ovenbirds, Woodhewers, and Allies.
　　Family Dendrocolaptidae, Woodhewers.
　　　　Furnariidae, Ovenbirds.
　　　　Formicariidae, Ant-thrushes.
　　　　Conopophagidae, Antpipits.
　　　　Rhinocryptidae, Tapaculos.
　　Superfamily Tyrannoidea, Tyrant Flycatchers, Pittas, and Allies.
　　Family Cotingidae, Cotingas.
　　　　Pipridae, Manakins.
　　　　Tyrannidae, Tyrant Flycatchers.
　　　　Oxyruncidae, Sharpbills.
　　　　Phytotomidae, Plantcutters.
　　　　Pittidae, Pittas.
　　　　Acanthisittidae, New Zealand Wrens.
　　　　Philepittidae, Asities, False Sunbirds.
　Suborder Menurae, Lyrebirds.
　　Family Menuridae, Lyrebirds.
　　　　Atrichornithidae, Scrubbirds.
　Suborder Passeres, Songbirds.
　　Family Alaudidae, Larks.
　　　　Hirundinidae, Swallows.
　　　　Dicruridae, Drongos.
　　　　Oriolidae, Old World Orioles.
　　　　Corvidae, Crows, Magpies, Jays.
　　　　Cracticidae, Bell Magpies, Australian Butcher-birds.
　　　　Grallinidae, Magpie-larks.
　　　　Ptilonorhynchidae, Bowerbirds.
　　　　Paradisaeidae, Birds of Paradise.
　　　　Paridae, Titmice.
　　　　Sittidae, Nuthatches.
　　　　Hyposittidae, Coralbilled Nuthatches.
　　　　Certhiidae, Creepers.

Paradoxornithidae, Parrotbills, Suthoras.
Chamaeidae, Wrentits.
Timaliidae, Babblers.
Campephagidae, Cuckoo-shrikes.
Pycnonotidae, Bulbuls.
Chloropseidae, Leafbirds.
Cinclidae, Dippers.
Troglodytidae, Wrens.
Mimidae, Thrashers, Mockingbirds.
Turdidae, Thrushes.
Zeledoniidae, Wrenthrushes.
Sylviidae, Old World Warblers.
Regulidae, Kinglets.
Muscicapidae, Old World Flycatchers.
Prunellidae, Accentors.
Motacillidae, Wagtails, Pipits.
Bombycillidae, Waxwings.
Ptilogonatidae, Silky Flycatchers.
Dulidae, Palmchats.
Artamidae, Woodswallows.
Vangidae, Vanga Shrikes.
Laniidae, Shrikes.
Prionopidae, Woodshrikes.
Cyclarhidae, Peppershrikes.
Vireolaniidae, Shrike-vireos.
Callaeidae, Wattled Crows, Huias, Saddlebacks.
Sturnidae, Starlings.
Meliphagidae, Honey-eaters.
Nectariniidae, Sunbirds.
Dicaeidae, Flowerpeckers.
Zosteropidae, White-eyes.
Vireonidae, Vireos.
Coerebidae, Honeycreepers.
Drepanididae, Hawaiian Honeycreepers.
Parulidae, Wood Warblers.
Ploceidae, Weaverbirds.
Icteridae, Blackbirds, Troupials.
Tersinidae, Swallowtanagers.
Thraupidae, Tanagers.
Catamblyrhynchidae, Plushcapped Finches.
Fringillidae, Grosbeaks, Finches, Buntings.

A comparison between the passerine families of Sharpe's *Hand-List* and those of Wetmore (1960) reveals many similiarities. Sharpe recognized 63 families, Wetmore 70; Wetmore recognized 12 families not distinguished by Sharpe, and Sharpe used six that Wetmore did not. The suboscine groupings are essentially identical, except that Wetmore split Sharpe's Dendrocolaptidae by recognizing the Furnariidae.

Although Wetmore (1960) changed the sequence of oscine families, certain clusters were transferred intact from the *Hand-List*; for example, the nectar feeders (Meliphagidae, Nectariniidae, Dicaeidae, Zosteropidae) and the shrike-like groups (Artamidae, Vangidae, Laniidae, Prionopidae).

That Wetmore derived his passerine classification, in part, from the *Hand-List* is also apparent from his 1930 classification in which he recognized the Paramythiidae, the Aerocharidae, and a separate family for the "glossy starlings" (Eulabetidae of Sharpe, Graculidae of Wetmore). Ridgway (1901–11) and the earlier editions of the A.O.U. checklist also may have influenced Wetmore's ideas about passerine classification. His classification was admittedly eclectic, as indicated by the statements of Wetmore and Miller (1926).

Wetmore's classification of the oscines (Passeres) was a list of 54 groups he called families. Supposedly related families were placed next to, or near, one another, and the sequence was intended to express a gradient from primitive to advanced, with the corvine groups at the beginning and the New World nine-primaried oscines at the end.

Wetmore's classification was especially influential in North America, in large part because he and Waldron DeWitt Miller were assigned the task, in 1924, of drawing "up a new scheme of classification down to and including genera and subgenera" for use in the fourth edition of the A.O.U. checklist (1931). This classification "down to families and subfamilies, was published in 'The Auk' for July 1926, pp. 337–346" (A.O.U. 1931:iv).

Thus, Wetmore's (1930) classification of the birds of the world began as an assignment by Witmer Stone, chairman of the committee to prepare the fourth edition of the A.O.U checklist. In 1939 Wetmore became chairman of the checklist committee and directed the preparation and publication of the fifth edition (1957). The fourth and fifth editions were adopted as the official classification of North American birds which was used in almost all publications and for the arrangement of museum collections. At least three generations of North American ornithologists learned and accepted the Wetmore system for the birds of the world.

In Europe, Erwin Stresemann's scientific competence and authoritarian personality influenced all aspects of ornithology between about 1925 and his death in 1972. Stresemann's (1934) classification of the Passeriformes recognized 63 families, the same number used by Sharpe in the *Hand-List*. Although many of Stresemann's groups, and their sequence, are similar to Sharpe's arrangement, it is also possible to see the influence of Gadow (1893) and possibly of Wetmore (1930). Stresemann (1959:269–270) recorded the procedure he used to develop his classification: "Survival of the fittest will decide which of the many competing theories will prevail. Only one can finally survive. Each revisor attempts to shorten the struggle by acting as a selective factor. When he has to synthesize a modern system of birds he is forced to choose a single one among many conflicting theories, often without having the opportunity of examining thoroughly the arguments of the different authors. I myself have painfully experienced the feelings of a taxonomic compiler, for I developed (1934) an eclectic system of bird classification some 25 years ago. While doing so, I made a few mistakes, as I now realize. Has not the experience of others been the same?"

Thus, Stresemann, like so many others, simply assembled the components of his classification of passerines from the works of his predecessors, some of whom had produced original evidence, while others had merely exercised their intuition to choose among previous ideas. Stresemann (1959:269) was fully aware of the process when he wrote: "Variation is the consequence of the individuality of those who work on the same topic. Zoologists differ in their philosophical background, in the extent of their knowledge, in their thoroughness, and in their gift of combination. This variability is certainly displayed to a high degree by the avian systematists. What Max Fürbringer has written about them, will forever remain true: 'At various times a few fortunate individuals have existed who were gifted with such an acute insight that it revealed to them intuitively, one might say instinctively, this or that systematic relation among related forms without the necessity of laborious investigation.' At the other extreme there have been some poor devils who did wrong whatever they did and who were completely lost without methodology."

Stresemann's intuition was certainly as good as any, and probably better than most, but his classification reveals that he possessed no special sense that permitted him to avoid the powerful influence of tradition, even when wrong, or to exercise a gift of "acute insight." He denigrated those "who were completely lost without methodology" but there is no evidence that he, or any other, has been able to discern "instinctively, this or that systematic relationship . . . without . . . laborious investigation."

Stresemann's (1934) classification of the passerines follows:

Order Passeres
    Suborder Desmodactylae
        Family Eurylaemidae: Broadbills
    Suborder Eleuterodactylae [sic]
      Division Mesomyodae or Clamatores
        Superfamily Haploophonae
           Family Acanthisittidae: New Zealand Wrens
           Family Philepittidae: Asities
           Family Pittidae: Pittas
           Family Tyrannidae: Tyrant Flycatchers, Sharpbill
           Family Pipridae: Manakins
           Family Cotingidae: Cotingas, Tityras, Becards
           Family Phytotomidae: Plantcutters
        Superfamily Tracheophonae
           Family Conopophagidae: Gnateaters
           Family Pteroptochidae: Tapaculos
           Family Formicariidae: Antbirds
           Family Dendrocolaptidae: Woodcreepers, Ovenbirds
      Division Diacromyodae
        Superfamily Suboscines
           Family Atrichornithidae: Scrub-birds
           Family Menuridae: Lyrebirds
        Superfamily Oscines
           Family Alaudidae: Larks
           Family Hirundinidae: Swallows
           Family Campephagidae: Cuckoo-shrikes, *Aegithina*
           Family Pycnonotidae: Bulbuls, *Irena*
           Family Motacillidae: Wagtails, Pipits
           Family Cinclidae: Dippers
           Family Troglodytidae: Wrens
           Family Mimidae: Mockingbirds, Thrashers
           Family Turdidae: Thrushes, Chats
           Family Timaliidae: Babblers, incl. *Bernieria, Orthonyx*
           Family Sylviidae: Old World Warblers, incl. *Malurus*
           Family Muscicapidae: Old World Flycatchers, incl. *Peltops, Rhipidura, Monarcha, Microeca,* etc.
           Family Pachycephalidae: Whistlers

Family Prionopidae: Helmetshrikes
Family Laniidae: Shrikes, incl. *Laniarius, Malaconotus*
Family Vangidae: Vangas
Family Artamidae: Woodswallows
Family Pseudochelidonidae: *Pseudochelidon*
Family Dulidae: Palm Chat
Family Bombycillidae: Waxwings, Silky Flycatchers
Family Sturnidae: Starlings
Family Oriolidae: Old World Orioles
Family Dicruridae: Drongos
Family Cracticidae: Australian Magpies, etc.
Family Corvidae: Crows, Jays, etc. incl. *Corcorax*
Family Paradisaeidae: Birds-of-Paradise, Bowerbirds
Family Picathartidae: Bald Crows
Family Paradoxornithidae: Suthoras, incl. *Panurus*
Family Paridae: Titmice, incl. *Aegithalos*
Family Sittidae: Nuthatches, incl. *Daphoenositta*
Family Hyposittidae: Coral-billed Nuthatch
Family Certhiidae: Creepers, incl. *Climacteris, Tichodroma*
Family Nectariniidae: Sunbirds
Family Hyliidae: *Hylia, Pholidornis*
Family Chalcopariidae: *Chalcoparia (Anthreptes)*
Family Meliphagidae: Honeyeaters, incl. *Promerops*
Family Dicaeidae: Flowerpeckers, incl. *Pardalotus, Oreocharis, Paramythia*
Family Zosteropidae: White-eyes
Family Vireonidae: Vireos, Shrike-Vireos, Peppershrikes
Family Prunellidae: Accentors
Family Mniotiltidae: Wood Warblers, incl. *Rhodinocichla*
Family Tanagridae: Tanagers
Family Tersinidae: Swallow Tanager
Family Fringillidae: Finches, Carduelines, Buntings
Family Ploceidae: Weavers, Waxbills, *Passer*
Family Drepanididae: Hawaiian Honeycreepers
Family Coerebidae: Neotropical Honeycreepers
Family Diglossidae: *Diglossa*
Family Icteridae: Troupials, Oropendolas, Grackles, Caciques, Meadowlarks, etc.

Ernst Mayr, one of the most influential ornithologists and evolutionists of this century, was a student of Stresemann. Mayr had collected birds in New Guinea in 1928–30 and had studied the museum collections of Southwest Pacific birds in Europe. In 1931 he joined the staff of the American Museum of Natural History to curate and study the large collection of the Whitney South Sea Expeditions and the Rothschild collection. Mayr published a series of papers on the systematics of the birds of New Guinea and the Pacific islands, including a *List of New Guinea Birds* (1941). His classic book, *Systematics and the Origin of Species* (1942), included many examples based on his studies of Southwest Pacific birds.

In 1951, Mayr and Dean Amadon published a classification of Recent birds that developed "during the course of incorporating the Rothschild Collection of birds with the general collection of the American Museum of Natural History, [when] an attempt was made to arrive at a natural arrangement for each family or other unit. This often led to rather detailed studies or to intensive efforts to determine the correct position of difficult genera. . . . [We] incorporated the work of others whenever known to us and have included the non-passerine groups, although few changes are made from the now well-established sequence of Wetmore (1934, followed by Peters). Indeed we have throughout attempted to make no changes from the established sequence except when they are clearly indicated by recent evidence."

Mayr and Amadon departed somewhat more from Wetmore's arrangement for the passerines by placing the "Crows and Australian Crow-like Birds" at the end of the Oscines, and in the recognition of many subfamilies and tribes. They also assembled the "flycatchers," "warblers," babblers, thrushes, mockingbirds, wrens, and dippers into a large, heterogeneous family "Muscicapidae" based largely on the opinion of Hartert (1910) that these "Primitive Insect Eaters" were so much alike that they could not be separated, hence they should be assumed to be related. This family included many Australo-Papuan oscines, now known to be only convergently similar to their Afro-Eurasian ecological counterparts (Sibley and Ahlquist 1985a).

Wetmore's classification had been adopted by James Lee Peters for his *Check-list of Birds of the World*, and it was used for the non-passerines (volumes 1–6, 1931–51) and for part of the suboscines in volume 7 (1951). Peters died in 1952.

In 1953 Ernst Mayr was appointed to a professorship at Harvard University and moved to the Museum of Comparative Zoology. With the assistance of James C. Greenway, Jr., Mayr assumed responsibility for the continuation of the Peters' Check-list. Peters had enlisted the help of John T. Zimmer for the New World suboscine groups to be covered in volume 8, and Melvin A. Traylor, Jr., agreed to edit the volume, which was published in 1979. In the meantime, volume 9 had been prepared with the help of several collaborators and edited by Mayr and Greenway (1960), who elected to abandon the Wetmore sequence in favor of what came to be known as the "Basel sequence," because it was drafted by a committee during the 11th International Ornithological Congress in Basel, Switzerland, in 1954. As described by Mayr and Greenway (1956): "At the XI International Ornithological Congress at Basel, Dr. Stresemann proposed that a committee be appointed which would recommend to the editors of ornithological journals a standardized sequence of the families of Passerine birds. Dr. Stresemann pointed out that some editors follow Hartert, others Sharpe's Handlist, others the sequence of the AOU [Wetmore's sequence], and still others the recently proposed sequence of Mayr and Amadon (1951). If a reader wants to find a given family in an article, he may have to look either at the beginning or in the middle or at the end depending on the particular sequence adopted by the respective editor."

Thus, it seems that the idea that a classification should reflect the phylogeny had been abandoned in favor of a uniform arrangement for the convenience of editors and readers. The committee consisted of G. C. A. Junge, J. Berlioz, G. Dementiev, E. Mayr, R. E. Moreau, F. Salomonsen, and E. Stresemann. They "voted unanimously in favor of the sequence" which lists the larks and swallows first, followed by the "Old World Insect-eaters and Relatives," the "New World Insect-eaters and finches," and the "crows, birds of paradise, and associated families." The "more peculiar and isolated families, as well as the Old World Nectar-eaters, are grouped irregularly within this broad framework" (Mayr and Greenway 1956). The sequence approved by the committee follows:

Alaudidae
Hirundinidae

Motacillidae
Campephagidae
Pycnonotidae
Irenidae
Laniidae
Prionopidae (incl. *Pityriasis*)
Vangidae
Bombycillidae (Waxwings, Silky Flycatchers, Palm Chat)
Cinclidae
Troglodytidae
Mimidae
Prunellidae
Muscicapidae (Thrushes, Babblers, Flycatchers, Warblers)
Paridae
Sittidae (incl. *Hypositta*, *Neositta*)
Certhiidae (incl. all "creepers")
Dicaeidae
Nectariniidae
Zosteropidae
Meliphagidae
Emberizidae (incl. Buntings, Cardinals, Tanagers)
Parulidae
Drepaniidae [sic]
Vireonidae (incl. *Vireolanius*, *Cyclarhis*)
Icteridae
Fringillidae (Fringillinae and Carduelinae)
Estrildidae
Ploceidae
Sturnidae
Oriolidae
Dicruridae
Callaeidae
Artamidae
Cracticidae
Ptilonorhynchidae
Paradisaeidae
Corvidae

Wetmore (1957) responded to the Basel sequence by noting that "certain basic data either have been overlooked or have not been accorded sufficient weight." He was referring to the structure of the head of the humerus. "In the Corvidae, the internal tuberosity . . . overhangs the pneumatic fossa from which the rather large foramen leads into the hollow shaft." This contrasts with the condition in such groups as the "Fringillidae, Thraupidae, and Icteridae" in which "the internal tuberosity has a bladelike form" that "tends to divide the concavity into two irregular parts." The condition in the Corvidae is like that in the suboscines and at least some non-passerines. Wetmore argued that these facts favored the placement of the "crows and their allies . . . near the beginning of the oscinine families." The DNA hybridization data and the one versus two fossae are highly correlated.

Amadon (1957) suggested that the oscines represent "three broad levels of evolution" and he so divided them "from lower to higher" following the pattern of Wetmore's classification. Delacour and Vaurie (1957) recognized the three groups proposed by Amadon, with the crows and presumed allies near the beginning and the New World nine-primaried oscines at the end. Storer (1959) also supported the "crows first" sequence.

Mayr (1958) defended the Basel sequence and Mayr and Greenway (1960:vi–vii) noted that "There is no universally recognized sequence of Passerine families. The editors pledged themselves at the XI International Ornithological Congress at Basel to follow a sequence recommended by a special committee appointed by the President of the Congress. The sequence, adopted for volumes 9–15 follows the unanimous recommendations of this Committee (Mayr and Greenway, 1956, Breviora, no. 58). This is an arbitrary sequence, but not more so than other sequences proposed. It is essentially the sequence that has been used in the 19th century in most of the standard literature. In view of the accelerating pace of the study of comparative avian anatomy, serology and ethology, it is to be hoped that definite improvements in this sequence will be found in due time."

Cracraft (1981) included the orders Piciformes, Coliiformes, Coraciiformes, and Passeriformes in his "Division 9." His clusters of the subgroups of the Passeriformes were based largely on the work of others assembled into the following arrangement:

Order Passeriformes
  Suborder Tyranni
    Infraorder Eurylami
        Family Eurylaimidae
        Family Philepittidae
    Infraorder Pitti
        Family Pittidae
    Infraorder Furnarii
      Superfamily Furnarioidea
        Family Dendrocolaptidae
        Furnariidae
      Superfamily Formicarioidea
        Family Formicariidae
        Rhinocryptidae
    Infraorder Tyrannomorpha
      Superfamily Tyrannoidea
        Family Cotingidae
        Pipridae
        Phytotomidae
        Tyrannidae
        Oxyruncidae
  Suborder Passeres
        Family Acanthisittidae, *incertae sedis*
        Alaudidae, *incertae sedis*
        Hirundinidae, *incertae sedis*
    Infraorder Muscicapi
        Family Prunellidae, *incertae sedis*
        Motacillidae, *incertae sedis*
      Superfamily Muscicapoidea
        Family Muscicapidae (Muscicapinae, Turdinae)
        Cinclidae
        Mimidae
        Troglodytidae

Superfamily Sylvioidea
    Family Sylviidae (Sylviinae, Timaliinae, Monarchinae, Malurinae, Rhipidurinae,
        Pachycephalinae, Orthonychinae, Platysteirinae)
Infraorder Lanii
    Family Laniidae (Malaconotinae, Laniinae, incl. *Prionops*, *Pityriasis*)
        Vangidae
Infraorder Bombycilli
    Family Bombycillidae (Hypocoliinae, Dulinae, Bombycillinae, Ptilogonatinae)
Infraorder Sitti
    Family Certhiidae ("creepers" except *Salpornis*)
        Sittidae (Salpornithinae, Sittinae, Hyposittinae)
        Paridae (Parinae, Remizinae, Aegithalinae)
Infraorder Meliphagi
    Family Dicaeidae
        Nectariniidae
        Meliphagidae
        Zosteropidae
Infraorder Corvi
    Family Oriolidae, *incertae sedis*
        Dicruridae, *incertae sedis*
        Artamidae, *incertae sedis*
        Pycnonotidae, *incertae sedis*
        Irenidae, *incertae sedis*
        Campephagidae, *incertae sedis*
Superfamily Menuroidea
    Family Menuridae
        Atrichornithidae
Superfamily Corvoidea
    Family Grallinidae
        Corvidae
Superfamily Sturnoidea
  Infrasuperfamily Cractici
    Family Cracticidae
  Infrasuperfamily Sturni
    Family Sturnidae
        Callaeidae
        Paradisaeidae (Ptilonorhynchinae, Paradisaeinae)
Infraorder Passeromorpha
  Superfamily Passeroidea
    Family Passeridae
  Superfamily Ploceoidea
    Family Ploceidae
  Superfamily Estrildoidea
    Family Bubalornithidae
        Estrildidae (Poephilinae, Estrildinae, incl. Viduini)
Infraorder Fringilli
  Superfamily Vireonoidea
    Family Vireonidae
  Superfamily Emberizoidea
    Family Parulidae
        Thraupidae
        Emberizidae (Cardinalinae, Emberizinae, incl. Icterini, Carduelinae, incl.
          Drepanidini)

Olson (1982:735) dismissed Cracraft's "Division 9.—This is composed of . . . a group of taxa for which 'a precise hypothesis of . . . interrelationships has not been supported' (Cracraft 1981:701). This is all that is said for the monophyly of Division 9."

Joel Cracraft did his graduate work at Columbia University where Walter Bock was his major professor, but they came to hold disparate views about avian classification. Cracraft adopted the cladistic approach of the Hennigians at the American Museum of Natural History and Bock held to the evolutionist approach that was, and is, favored by *his* major professor at Harvard, Ernst Mayr. For the passerines, Bock (1982) suggested the following arrangement, but without strong convictions about many of the assignments.

Order Passeriformes
  Suborder Eurylaimi
    Family Eurylaimidae: Broadbills
    Family Philepittidae: Asities
    Family Pittidae: Pittas
    Family Xenicidae: New Zealand Wrens
  Suborder Furnarii
    Family Dendrocolaptidae: Woodcreepers
    Family Furnariidae: Ovenbirds
    Family Formicariidae: Antbirds
    Family Rhinocryptidae: Tapaculos
    Family Conopophagidae: Gnateaters
  Suborder Tyranni
    Family Cotingidae: Cotingas
    Family Phytotomidae: Plantcutters
    Family Pipridae: Manakins
    Family Tyrannidae: Tyrant Flycatchers
    Family Oxyruncidae: Sharpbill
  Suborder Menurae
    Family Menuridae: Lyrebirds
    Family Atrichornithidae: Scrubbirds
  Suborder Oscines
    (Subdivision "into superfamilies is poorly understood.")
    Family Alaudidae: Larks
    Family Hirundinidae: Swallows
    Family Pycnonotidae: Bulbuls
    Family Irenidae: Leafbirds, Fairy-bluebirds
    Family Campephagidae: Cuckooshrikes
    Family Muscicapidae: Old World Flycatchers
    Family Timaliidae: Babblers
    Family Sylviidae: Old World Warblers
    Family Turdidae: Thrushes
    Family Mimidae: Mockingbirds, Thrashers
    Family Troglodytidae: Wrens
    Family Cinclidae: Dippers
    Family Pachycephalidae: Whistlers or Thickheads
    Family Orthonychidae: Log-runners or Chowchillas
    Family Maluridae: Fairywrens, Thornbills, Grasswrens
    Family Prunellidae: Accentors or Dunnocks
    Family Motacillidae: Pipits, Wagtails
    Family Laniidae: Shrikes
    Family Prionopidae: Helmet-shrikes

Family Vangidae: Vangas
Family Pityriasididae: Bristlehead
Family Artamidae: Woodswallows
Family Bombycillidae: Waxwings, Silky-flycatchers, *Dulus*
Family Paridae: Chickadees, Titmice
Family Certhiidae: Northern Creepers
Family Sittidae: Nuthatches, Wallcreeper
Family Neosittidae: Sittellas
Family Climacteridae: Australo-Papuan Treecreepers
Family Dicaeidae: Flowerpeckers
Family Nectariniidae: Sunbirds, Spiderhunters
Family Meliphagidae: Honeyeaters
Family Zosteropidae: White-eyes
Family Vireonidae: Vireos
Family Drepanididae: Hawaiian Honeycreepers
Family Thraupidae: Tanagers
Family Parulidae: Wood Warblers
Family Catamblyrhynchidae: Plush-capped Finch
Family Zeledoniidae: Wren-thrush
Family Tersinidae: Swallow-tanager
Family Fringillidae: Finches
Family Emberizidae: Buntings, Sparrows, Cardinals
Family Icteridae: New World Orioles, Blackbirds, etc.
Family Ploceidae: Weaverbirds
Family Passeridae: Sparrows
Family Estrildidae: Waxbills, Grass Finches
Family Sturnidae: Starlings
Family Dicruridae: Drongos
Family Corvidae: Crows, Magpies, Jays
Family Cracticidae: Australian Magpies, Currawongs
Family Grallinidae: Magpie-larks
Family Callaeidae: Wattlebirds
Family Ptilonorhynchidae: Bowerbirds
Family Paradisaeidae: Birds of Paradise

Thus, Bock's classification of the oscines is a list of families, as was that of Wetmore (1960), but the sequence is the "crows last" arrangement favored by the Basel Committee and used by Mayr and Amadon (1951) and Mayr and Greenway (1956). As Wetmore did, Bock listed morphologically similar groups together, for example, the nectar-feeders, Old World insect-eaters, creepers, and nuthatches. However, throughout his comments, Bock expressed doubts about many of the groupings and the categorical levels of the classification. Bock (pers. comm.) notes that "this classification does not represent" his feelings on avian classification. It does, however, represent the kind of arrangement that emerges from an attempt to combine phylogeny with morphological specialization as criteria for the classification. In this case there is little evidence of phylogeny and substantial evidence that specialized morphologies dictated much of the arrangement.

Order Passeriformes

Order PASSERIFORMES: 1161/5712. The passerines are birds of small to medium size with an aegithognathous palate (except Conopophagidae, in which it is said to be schizognathous); hallux incumbent, large, directed backward; toes 2, 3, 4, directed forward, i.e., anisodactyl; digital formula 2-3-4-5; pelvic muscles AXY (AX in *Dicrurus*), ambiens absent; iliofemoralis externus usually absent, but present in some groups or as a "developmental anomaly" (Raikow 1982); M. pubo-ischio-femoralis divided into Pars cranialis and Pars caudalis (Raikow 1982); flexor tendons Type 7, except Eurylaimoidea and *Philepitta* wherein usually Type 1 (Olson 1971, Raikow 1982); two intrinsic muscles of hallux present, intrinsic muscles of digits 2, 3, 4, lacking, except for occasional vestige of extensor brevis digiti IV (Raikow 1982); full set of eight extrinsic digital muscles present (Raikow 1982); caeca short and non-functional; oil gland naked, indistinctly or distinctly bilobed, papilla moderately or well developed, gland varying in shape and size, no consistent morphological differences between or among any taxa (D. W. Johnston 1988:235); no basipterygoid processes; nasal glands minute (except *Phytotoma*?); only left carotid, B-4-s of Glenny (except paired carotids in *Pseudocalyptomena* and possibly other broadbills); cervical vertebrae 14 in most, 15 in Eurylamoidea; atlas perforated; metasternum usually two-notched, rarely four-notched; biceps slip absent; expansor secundariorum often present (Berger 1956, Raikow 1982), not lacking as reported by Beddard (1898a) and Ridgway (1901); tensor propatagialis brevis tendon present (Raikow 1982); hypocleideum present (except *Menura*); primaries usually 10, the outermost frequently small and concealed; primaries 11 in *Menura, Atrichornis*, most broadbills (10 in *Calyptomena*), furnarioids, some Passeri; secondaries usually 9 (10 in *Menura*); eutaxic; usually 12 rectrices, 10 in some, 16 in *Menura*, and only 6 rectrices in the furnariine genus *Sylviorthorhynchus* and the malurid genus *Stipiturus*; wing coverts in three distinct series: lesser, middle, and greater; aftershaft absent except in the New Zealand Wrens (Acanthisittidae) and the Passeri, in which it is small; downs only on apteria; powder downs only in *Artamus*; spermatozoa of distinctive structure with a spiral membrane around the darkly pigmented capital portion, a large acrosome, and occurring in "bundles" (McFarlane 1963, Henley et al. 1978, Feduccia 1979, Raikow 1982).

The molt of the remiges is uniform. The primaries are replaced from proximal to distal, i.e., descendant; secondaries from each end of the series toward secondary 5, i.e., convergent. The rectrices are replaced from the center toward the outside, i.e., centrifugal, except in *Certhia* in which the central pair is not lost until all the others have been replaced, as in the woodpeckers, a clearly convergent adaptation.

Raikow (1982) analyzed the distribution of 18 traditional morphological characters of the passerines as a test of their monophyly. He found that only five corroborate monophyly, namely, the aegithognathous palate, the "passerine" tensor propatagialis brevis, the bundled spermatozoa with coiled head and large acrosome, the enlarged hallux, and the Type 7 deep plantar tendons. Also in support of passeriform monophyly Raikow added new information from hind limb musculature, namely, the division of M. pubo-ischio-femoralis into Pars cranialis and Pars caudalis, and the loss of a set of intrinsic muscles of the forward digits in all passerines.

The largest passerine is the Greenland Raven (*Corvus corax principalis*), weighing up to 1700 grams. The lyrebirds (*Menura*) may be the next largest. The smallest is the Pygmy Tit (*Psaltria exilis*) of Java.

Incubation periods range from 11 to 21 days; *Menura* is exceptional with 35–40 days. Young hatched blind and helpless with sparse, mainly dorsal down. *Menura* has a heavy natal down at hatching.

Historical Review of the Classification

Since 1847, when Johannes Müller discovered the morphological complexity of the avian syrinx, the major subdivisions of the Passeriformes have been based, in part, on syringeal characters. Ames (1971) reviewed previous studies of the syrinx and made an extensive study of the syringes of the suboscines. W. E. Lanyon (1984, 1985, 1986, 1988a,b,c) used syringeal characters in phylogenetic studies of the tyrant flycatchers.

Mayr and Amadon (1951) and Wetmore (1960) recognized four suborders: Eurylaimi (broadbills), Tyranni (New World suboscines, pittas, New Zealand wrens, philepittas), Menurae (lyrebirds, scrub-birds), Oscines or Passeres ("songbirds"). Ames (1971:153) added a fifth suborder, Furnarii, but Olson (1971) recognized only three suborders—Tyranni, Menurae, Oscines—and placed the broadbills in the Tyranni because of similarities to the cotingas.

Olson (1971) found that the lyrebirds have a ball-and-socket jaw articulation like that of the oscines and unlike that of the suboscines. Although he retained the suborder Menurae, Olson expressed the "opinion that they will ultimately be found to be closer to the Oscines than to the Tyranni."

The validity of subordinal rank for the lyrebirds was challenged by Sibley (1974) and Feduccia (1975a), both of whom concluded that the lyrebirds are oscines. The DNA-DNA data support this conclusion and show that the lyrebirds are most closely related to the scrub-birds (*Atrichornis*) and next most closely related to the bowerbirds (Ptilonorhynchidae), and that the Australo-Papuan treecreepers (Climacteridae) are the sister group of the lyrebird, scrub-bird, bowerbird clade (Sibley et al. 1984b). Feduccia and Olson (1982) concluded that the lyrebirds and bowerbirds are not closely related.

The DNA Hybridization Evidence

The DNA-DNA data indicate that the four or five "suborders" noted above are not of equal categorical rank. We divide the Passeriformes into two suborders, the Tyranni for the suboscines and the Passeri for the oscines. These two groups are distinguished by morphological characters as well as DNA-DNA distance measures. They diverged at $\Delta T_{50}H$ 19.7. The Passeriformes diverged from the non-passerine clade composed of the Columbiformes, Gruiformes, and Ciconiiformes at Δ 21.6.

Old World Suboscines

Suborder Tyranni: 291/1151.
    Infraorder Acanthisittides
        Family Acanthisittidae: New Zealand Wrens
    Infraorder Eurylaimides
        Superfamily Pittoidea
            Family Pittidae: Pittas
        Superfamily Eurylaimoidea
            Family Eurylaimidae: Broadbills
            Family Philepittidae: Asities (*inc. sedis*)
    Infraorder/Family *inc. sedis*, *Sapayoa aenigma*

Family ACANTHISITTIDAE

2(3)/4(7–8). New Zealand Wrens. The three living, one recently extinct, and three (or four) subfossil species of New Zealand "wrens" may be the only known members of what may have been a more widely distributed group. The Rifleman (*Acanthisitta chloris*) occurs commonly on the two main islands, on Stewart Island, and on some of the offshore islands. It is a small bird that creeps over trunks and branches in nuthatch fashion. The other three species, placed in *Xenicus*, are the Rock Wren, Bush Wren, and the extinct Stephen Island Wren or Stephens Wren. Millener (1988) described the new genus *Pachyplichas* to include two subfossil species, *jagmi* and *yaldwyni*, from South Island Late Pleistocene–Holocene cave sediments and Holocene dune sands. He noted that a third subfossil acanthisittid species had been discovered, and supported the resurrection of *Traversia* for the extinct *lyalli* (Stephens Wren).

Historical Review of the Classification

Blyth (1849) seems to have been the first to use "Xenicidae" as the family name for the New Zealand wrens. Sundevall (1872) used "Acanthisittinae" (sic) as the family name, and Forbes

(1882f) proposed "Xenicidae," apparently in ignorance of the publications of Blyth and Sundevall. The correct family name for the group is in some doubt.

Forbes (1882f) found that the acanthisittid syrinx is located in the bronchi (haploophone) and lacks intrinsic muscles, a condition otherwise known only in some of the suboscines. Ames (1971) confirmed Forbes's observations and noted that "The syrinx shows a unique combination of cartilaginous fusion and lack of intrinsic musculature. These two peculiar genera show no clear relationship to any New World tyrannoid group" (p. 155).

There has been confusion about the syringeal musculature in the Acanthisittidae. For example, Beddard (1898a:181) described "The syrinx of *Xenicus* as . . . typically mesomyodian. The last few tracheal rings are consolidated into a large box, to the top of which the intrinsic muscles (small and median in insertion) are attached." Pycraft (1905a) also found what he thought to be an intrinsic syringeal muscle that "ends, in the form of very degenerate fibrous tissue, on the third bronchial ring." Forbes had reported that these fibers terminated before reaching the top of the "syringeal box." Ames (1971) showed that the muscle described by Beddard and Pycraft is the extrinsic M. tracheolateralis and that there are no intrinsic syringeal muscles in either *Acanthisitta* or *Xenicus*.

Forbes (1882f) thought that the haploophone syrinx allied the New Zealand wrens to the cotingas, manakins, tyrants, pittas, and philepittas, but Pycraft (1905a) placed the Acanthisittidae close to the ovenbirds (Furnariidae) because of their schizorhinal nares and slender maxillo-palatines. Pycraft suggested that the New Zealand wrens should be placed between the manakins (Pipridae) and the tracheophones (New World ovenbirds, antbirds, etc.).

Fürbringer (1888) included *Xenicus* in his "Oligomyodi" with *Pitta* and the New World tyrannoids, and suggested that the wide geographic distribution of the "Oligomyodi" attests to their extreme age and accounts for their anatomical diversity.

Sclater (1888:450) reviewed Forbes's study and concluded that the New Zealand wrens are "more nearly allied to the *Pittidae* than to any other Passerine form yet known. But they have only 10 rectrices instead of 12—the normal Passerine number, and the scutellation of the tarsus is different." Sclater placed the "Xenicidae" between the Pittidae and the Eurylaimidae, but Gadow (1893) inserted the group between the Pittidae and the Tyrannidae.

Pycraft (1905a) studied the anatomy of *Acanthisitta* and described the unique structure of the ear opening, which is a "narrow horizontal slit" behind the eye that gives access to a pocket-like chamber extending downward to the opening of the auditory meatus. Pycraft also concluded that the skull of *Acanthisitta* "appears to agree most nearly with that of the Synallaxine birds" (p. 615) and its "nearest allies . . . are the Furnariidae. . . . the same form of the maxillopalatine processes and the schizorhinal nares is present in all the Furnariidae" and in *Acanthisitta*. However, Pycraft decided that the peculiar features of the New Zealand wrens prevented their inclusion in the Furnariidae, but justified the formation of a separate family.

Based on the osteology of the tracheophone passerines Pycraft (1906b) included the "Xenicidae" in his suborder Tracheophonae with the New World Formicariidae, Dendrocolaptidae, Furnariidae, and Conopophagidae. However, the New Zealand wrens have a haploophone, not a tracheophone, syrinx, so Pycraft placed them "at the bottom of the tracheophone stem, the members of which split up into holorhinal and schizorhinal types" (p. 157). Thus, in spite of several discrepancies, Pycraft viewed the Acanthisittidae as "more or less nearly related" to the "Synallaxiinae," one of his subfamilies of the Neotropical Furnariidae.

Forbes and Pycraft agreed only that the New Zealand wrens are not oscines and that they should be placed in a separate family, but Forbes thought them to be related to the New World tyrannoids, the Old World pittas, and perhaps to the philepittas of Madagascar, while Pycraft allied them to the furnarioids.

Since 1906 the opinions of Forbes and Pycraft have been variously interpreted. Mathews (1927) divided the four species into three families and placed them between the Pittidae and the Atrichornithidae. Wetmore (1930, 1960) placed the New Zealand wrens between the Pittidae and the Philepittidae, following the New World tyrannoids. E. Stresemann (1934) recognized a "Superfamily Haploophonae" for the Acanthisittidae, Pittidae, Philepittidae, and the New World tyrannoids. Oliver (1945) observed that the vomer of *Acanthisitta* is distinctive in form and unlike that of *Pitta*, although the "maxillopalatines are entire in both genera."

Mayr and Amadon (1951:12) viewed the external similarities between the New Zealand wrens and some of the Neotropical "Tracheophonae," for example, *Conopophaga*, as due to convergence and placed the "Xenicidae" in the "Tyrannoidea (Haploophonae)" with the pittas, philepittas, and New World tyrannoids, thus following Forbes and Stresemann. Berndt and Meise (1960) followed previous authors and associated the "Xenicidae" with these same groups.

Sibley (1970) found the electrophoretic pattern of the egg-white proteins of *Acanthisitta* to differ "in many ways from those of the New World suboscine groups," suggested that the true relatives might be the oscines, and concluded that the total evidence indicated "that it is improbable that the Eurylaimidae, Acanthisittidae and Pittidae are closely related to one another." Ames (1971) concluded that the New Zealand wrens "show no clear relationship to any New World tyrannoid group."

Feduccia (1975a) found that *Acanthisitta* has a columella (stapes) which is "typically oscine, but with a shaft relatively more robust" than those of undoubted oscines. He concluded that "additional *new* evidence will be needed to draw conclusions of the relationships of the New Zealand wrens" and suggested "that their closest living relatives are to be found among the oscines." With reference to the New Zealand wrens Feduccia (1975b) wrote that although "possession of the primitive condition of the stapes . . . does not prove . . . oscine affinities, it suggests that they are not close allies of the modern suboscines, or at least would have had to evolve before the derived stapes type." He concluded that "it is improbable that *Acanthisitta* is a suboscine." In 1977 Feduccia extended his study of the avian stapes and concluded that "the oscines and suboscines could not have shared a common ancestor." This startling proposal caused him to declare the Acanthisittidae to be oscines and he speculated that the ancestors of the oscines might be "the primitive piciforms" or some group "intermediate between cor-aciiform and piciform birds."

Feduccia's (1977) "new model" of passerine phylogeny was soon questioned by Feduccia and his colleagues (Henley et al. 1978) from studies of the structure and bundling of spermatozoa and (Feduccia 1979) electron microscopical studies of the stapes in several groups. Their discoveries caused Feduccia to retreat from his earlier conclusions and to state that "it now seems . . . more probable that the order Passeriformes is monophyletic" although the "oscines and suboscines are very distinctive groups . . . separated by a broad and ancient evolutionary gulf."

Although Feduccia himself discovered the flaws in his new model of the passerine birds, he left the New Zealand wrens among the oscines. However, Feduccia cast doubt on the significance of the stapes as a clue to relationships and showed (1975a) that the stapes of *Acanthisitta* actually differs from those of all other groups of birds.

Wolters (1975–82) assigned the New Zealand wrens to their own suborder, Acanthisittae, placed between the suboscine Tyranni and the oscine suborder Passeres, and Mayr (1979) indicated his uncertainty by placing the Pittidae, Philepittidae, and Acanthisittidae in a "Suborder Incertae Sedis" between the New World Tyranni and the Australian Menurae. Sibley (1974), Feduccia (1975a), and Sibley and Ahlquist (1985a) have provided evidence that the lyrebirds (*Menura*) are oscines.

Raikow (1984) studied the hind limb myology and commented on the phylogeny of the New Zealand wrens. He concluded that the "Simplification of the intrinsic muscles of the pes confirms the monophyly of the family. Syringeal anatomy excludes them from the oscine radiation [and] hindlimb muscles corroborate the ideas of Feduccia (based on stapedial anatomy) and Sibley et al. (based on DNA hybridization) that they are outside of the suboscine radiation as they lack various derived states of different suboscine groups. Loss of M. flexor perforatus digiti IV places them as the sister group of the oscines in contrast to the DNA studies which place them as the sister group of the suboscines. The consensus . . . is that they form an ancient, isolated lineage arising near the base of the great passeriform radiation."

Millener (1988) reviewed the literature on the osteology of the Acanthisittidae, provided a list of their familial characteristics, and described various aspects of their anatomy. As noted above, he also described a new genus and two new species of subfossil acanthisittids.

The taxonomic history of the New Zealand wrens demonstrates the difficulties encountered in the attempts to determine the phylogeny and relationships of birds from morphological characters. From 1882 to 1975 there was a consensus that the Acanthisittidae are suboscines, although there was a wide range of opinion about just where they fit into the system. Feduccia expanded the arena to include the oscines, but the lack of confidence in any of the opinions is indicated by Mayr's assignment of the group to the limbo of "incertae sedis" in 1979. Raikow (1984) had to rely on the loss of a part of one flexor muscle to assign them to the oscine side of the ancient branch between the Tyranni and the Passeri. After a century of study and debate it was only possible to say that the Acanthisittidae are passerine birds of uncertain affinities.

The DNA Hybridization Evidence

The single-copy DNA of *Acanthisitta chloris* was compared with the DNAs of 57 other passerine species and two non-passerines (Sibley et al. 1982). From a study of the New World suboscines (Sibley and Ahlquist 1985b) there are two delta values between the driver DNA of *A. chloris* and the tracer DNAs of a tyrant flycatcher (*Myiarchus tyrannulus*) (17.5) and a tapaculo (*Scytalopus femoralis*) (18.2). Thus, there are 18 Δ $T_{50}H$ values between the New Zealand Rifleman and the New World + Old World suboscines which average 17.9, ± 0.2 SE, ± 0.63 SD. We have used 17.9 as the value for the divergence node of the Acanthisittides from the other suboscines. The Acanthisittidae seem to be the relict survivors of an ancient lineage, the ancestor of which may have occurred more widely prior to the separation of New Zealand from Australia (Fleming 1975:16).

The geological evidence indicates that the Tasman Sea between Australia and New

Zealand began to open ca. 80 MYA. If the ancestor of the Acanthisittidae was similar to the surviving species it is doubtful that it would have crossed more than a narrow strait of open water, thus we may assume that the isolation of the Acanthisittidae from the other suboscines began ca. 80 MYA. This may provide another calibration event, which yields a constant of Δ $T_{50}H$ 1.0 = 4.5 million years (80/17.9), thus nearly the same as for the Ostrich-rhea (80/17.1 = 4.7), the Old World–New World barbets (75/16.5 = 4.5), and the Old World–New World suboscines (75/15.8 = 4.7) which were, presumably, divided by the opening of the Atlantic Ocean. We use 75 MYA for the barbets and suboscines because, presumably, their ancestors were volant species. These calibrations are tentative and subject to correction. They are based on several assumptions, any one or all of which may be in error.

An alternative explanation may be suggested, namely, that the New Zealand wren lineage has been evolving about twice as fast as those of the Ostrich and rheas. If so, the divergence at Δ $T_{50}H$ 17.9 may have occurred ca. 40 MYA, or about the same time that the ancestor of the kiwis invaded New Zealand. If so, the New Zealand wren ancestor may have crossed the northern Tasman Sea via the island arcs and volcanic islands caused by the collision between the Australian and Pacific tectonic plates.

The comparisons between *A. chloris* and the 41 oscines provide evidence of the relative uniformity of the average genomic rate of DNA evolution in the order Passeriformes. The 41 comparisons range from 18.6 to 21.7, and average Δ $T_{50}H$ 19.8, ±0.13 SE, ±0.8 SD. Of the 41 oscines, 25 are members of the parvorder Corvida and 16 are of the parvorder Passerida. Relative to *Acanthisitta* the 25 Corvida average Δ $T_{50}H$ 19.5, ±0.1 SE, ±0.7 SD, range = 18.6–21.0. The 16 Passerida average 20.3, ±0.2 SE, ±0.7 SD, range = 19.2–21.7. Thus, the two ranges overlap from 19.2 to 21.0, and the two averages differ by Δ 0.8, although the average Δ $T_{50}H$ between the Corvida and the Passerida, based on 700 comparisons, is 12.8. The average of 89 DNA-DNA hybrids between the Tyranni and the Passeri is Δ $T_{50}H$ 19.7 (Fig. 369).

Fig. 186 (*Acanthisitta*) had a poor tracer, but it shows that *Acanthisitta* is equidistant from the Passeri and Tyranni, and far from the non-passerines. The spread among the heteroduplex curves of the passerines lacks evidence of a closer relationship to either of the suborders.

Fig. 343, the FITCH tree, shows the acanthisittids as the sister group of the other passerines. The KITSCH tree (Fig. 344) places the acanthisittids as the sister group of the suboscines as in the UPGMA tree (Fig. 369). The KITSCH tree has a relatively poor goodness-of-fit and this clustering may reflect a rate slowdown in all these groups.

We conclude that the acanthisittids are the survivors of an ancient passerine lineage with no close living relatives. We include them in the suborder Tyranni because they are not oscines (Passeri), but it is possible that they should be assigned to a third suborder as the sister group of the Tyranni and Passeri.

Family PITTIDAE

1/31. Pittas. Most of the species of pittas occur in southeast Asia; one or more extend to India, southern China, southern Japan, the Philippines, Solomon Islands, Bismarck Archipelago, New Guinea, and Australia. One species occurs in Africa. The number of species varies among authors and most recent classifications place all species in the genus *Pitta*, although Wolters (1975–82:168–169) recognized six genera. The DNA comparisons also suggest that subdivision of the family and the genus *Pitta* may be justified.

Pittas are ground-dwellers, usually in thick tropical forest or scrubland. They eat small animals (insects, worms), and build a large oven-shaped nest of grass and leaves, with a side entrance, on or near the ground; 4–5 white eggs with purple, red, etc. markings.

Plumages of both sexes are colorful; wings and tail short; bill stout; tarsi long with the podotheca entire in front and smooth (bilaminate planta tarsi). Temporal fossae extend across the occipital region of the skull, nearly meeting in the midline; syrinx bronchial (haploophone), lacks intrinsic muscles (Ames 1971:82). These characters define the pittas, but yield few clues to their relationships.

Historical Review of the Classification

The entire tarsal envelope of the pittas caused Sundevall (1872, see 1889:50) to place them in the "Fam. Eucichlinae," near the thrushes and dippers in his "Cohort Cichlomorphae; Phalanx Ocreatae." Garrod (1876f) showed that the pittas are mesomyodian suboscines and Sclater (1888) placed the Pittidae between the Philepittidae and the "Xenicidae" (Acanthisittidae), followed by the broadbills ("Eurylaemidae"). Sclater's classification assembled the Old World and New World mesomyodian groups into a single cluster, as follows:

Order Passeriformes
  Suborder Passeres
    Division Mesomyodi
      Subdivision Oligomyodae
        Family Tyrannidae, Tyrant Flycatchers
        Family Oxyrhamphidae, Sharpbill
        Family Pipridae, Manakins
        Family Cotingidae, Cotingas
        Family Phytotomidae, Plantcutters
        Family Philepittidae, Asities
        Family Pittidae, Pittas
        Family Xenicidae, New Zealand Wrens
        Family Eurylaemidae, Broadbills

Sclater (1888:1–2) defined the Mesomyodi as having the "Intrinsic muscles of the voice-organ affixed at or near the middle of the bronchial semi-rings," and the Oligomyodae as having the "Lower end of trachea not modified; syrinx as in the *Oscines*, but with a lesser number of singing-muscles." Sclater recognized the broadbills (Eurylaemidae) as distinctive ("plantar vinculum retained; manubrium not forked") and accepted (p. 455) their separation as the "Desmodactyli" of Forbes (1880a), but placed them with the "other Oligomyodian Passeres, instead of after the *Tracheophonae*" because it "seems more convenient."

Thus, the broadbills were set apart, but the first eight groups listed above were placed together in the classifications of many later authors. Sharpe (1901) used the same grouping for his "Oligomyodae" and Ridgway (1907:328–329) placed them together as the "Haploophonae" of his superfamily Mesomyodi, noting that "The Mesomyodi are chiefly American and mostly Neotropical, only three families (Xenicidae, Philepittidae, Pittidae) occurring in the eastern hemisphere." Wetmore (1930, 1960), Mayr and Amadon (1951), and others continued what had become another traditional assemblage of groups of uncertain affinities. However, the doubts expressed by Sibley (1970), Ames (1971), and Feduccia (1975a) caused Traylor (1979:ix) to place the Pittidae, Philepittidae, and Acanthisittidae "as a group *incertae sedis* since they are evidently no more nearly related to the Tyrannoidea than to the Furnarioidea, and quite possibly should have been next to or in the Eurylaimi."

Sibley and Ahlquist (1985b) placed the Pittidae, Eurylaimidae, and Philepittidae in the infraorder Eurylaimides, the sister taxon of the Tyrannides, containing the New World suboscines. From his study of the hind-limb musculature Raikow (1987:42) concluded that the "Pittidae is monophyletic and is the sister taxon of a clade that includes the Philepittidae and Eurylaimidae," and that the "Pittidae, Philepittidae, and Eurylaimidae constitute a monophyletic group within a larger clade that also includes the New World suboscines."

The DNA Hybridization Evidence

The DNA comparisons show that the pitta lineage diverged from that of the broadbills at $\Delta T_{50}H$ 12.1. The pitta-broadbill clade branched from the New World suboscines (Tyrannides) at Δ 15.8. Within the Pittidae the DNA delta values reveal some large genealogical distances between species. *Pitta baudii* of Borneo is $\Delta T_{50}H$ 9.6 from the other three species in Fig. 371. In our classification taxa Δ 9–11 apart are placed in separate families. *P. versicolor* (Moluccas, Lesser Sundas, Timor, Sumba, northern Australia) is Δ 7.5 from *P. brachyura* (India) and *P. guajana* (Malaysia, Java, Sumatra, Borneo), thus separable as subfamilies. We do not propose to recognize subdivisions of the Pittidae at this time, because we have the DNAs of so few species and have made few comparisons among those available. However, the DNA comparisons indicate that the superficial uniformity of the pittas conceals a substantial amount of genetic diversity.

Fig. 187 (*Pitta*) shows the large gap between *Pitta versicolor* and *P. guajana*, and the relative positions of the broadbills, Tyranni, New Zealand wrens, and Passeri.

Fig. 343 (FITCH) and Fig. 344 (KITSCH) agree in the placement of the pittas and broadbills on the same branch relative to the New World suboscines (Tyrannides).

We conclude that the pittas are a monophyletic group, most closely related to the broadbills.

Family EURYLAIMIDAE

8/14. Broadbills. The broadbills occur in the tropics of southeast Asia, from the Himalayan foothills of India and Nepal, southern China, and the Philippines, to Sumatra, Java, and Borneo. Two genera and three (or four) species occur in Africa.

The tendon of the flexor hallucis is connected by a vinculum to the tendon of the flexor profundus, thus Type 1; toes 3 and 4 joined basally; podotheca with scutes anteriorly and small, six-sided scales posteriorly; 15 cervical vertebrae; 12 rectrices; two carotids in *Pseudocalyptomena*, and possibly others; main leg artery the ischiatic. Nest pendant, pear-shaped, with side opening, a tail of material below may be several feet long; usually over water; eggs usually 2–4, up to 6, variously colored and marked in different species.

The typical broadbills have a broad head, large eyes, broad flat bills, and 11 primaries; plumages distinctively and brightly colored. Mainly insectivorous, larger species also eat lizards, frogs, etc.

The green broadbills (*Calyptomena*) have a smaller bill partly covered by a long tuft of antrorse loral plumes; 10 primaries; plumages are mostly green, males with black markings. Mainly, or entirely, frugivorous.

Historical Review of the Classification

In early classifications the broadbills were often allied with the rollers, trogons, or caprimulgiforms. Wallace (1856) suggested that they are the Old World representatives of the New World cotingas. Gray (1869–71) placed the broadbills near the coraciiforms and trogons. The pterylosis (Nitzsch 1840) and the sternum (Sclater 1872) were reported to be passerine.

Sundevall (1872, see 1889:130) placed the broadbills with some of the cotingas in his "Fam. Rupicolinae or Syndactylae," because they have "the toes joined for some distance." Garrod (1877a, 1878b), Forbes (1880a), and Pycraft (1905b) also found evidence that the broadbills are passerines. Garrod (1877b) discovered the plantar vinculum, which was long thought to be unique to the broadbills, but Raikow (1987) has found it in *Philepitta*. Forbes (1880a) confirmed Garrod's observations on the plantar vinculum and described the syrinx in two genera. Forbes (1880b) found several similarities between broadbills and *Philepitta*, but kept them separate because he believed that the plantar vinculum was unique to the broadbills. Sclater (1888:454) reviewed the evidence for the relationships of the broadbills in the *Catalogue of Birds*:

Family IX. EURYLAEMIDAE

The Eurylaemidae . . . until recently have been usually referred to the neighbourhood of *Coracias*, and considered to be non-Passerine. Nitzsch, in his celebrated 'Pterylography,' first showed that the pterylosis of *Eurylaemus* is that of the Passeres; and Blanchard subsequently figured the sternum, and proved that this is also of the Passerine form, although the manubrium sterni is unforked, contrary to . . . the case in the typical Passeres.

In 1877 Garrod further showed that the palate . . . is truly Passerine, but that they differ . . . from all other known Passeres in the structure of the foot. The tendon of the *flexor longus hallucis* sends out a strong vinculum to join the tendon of the *flexor profundus digitorum*, as . . . in nearly all non-Passerine birds in which a hallux is developed.

In 1880 Forbes . . . gave us accurate descriptions of the trachea . . . [and] proved . . . that the *Eurylaemidae* are Mesomyodians of the non-Tracheophonine division. But . . . [from] the plantar vinculum and . . . non-forked manubrium sterni, Forbes concluded that . . . the *Eurylaemidae* ought to form a main division of the Passeres . . . under the title "Desmodactyli," while all other Passeres should be denominated "Eleutherodactyli."

Seebohm (1890b) adopted Sclater's suggestion and separated the "Eurylaimi" as a suborder of the Passeriformes, an arrangement that was to be followed in many classifications for most of the next century. Gadow (1893) thought the broadbills are related to the pittas, but he isolated the "Eurylaemidae" as the only member of his "Subclamatores." Fürbringer (1902) demonstrated the limitations of his methods when he concluded from a study of the pectoral girdle that the broadbills are closest to the woodpeckers and swifts, but not to the rollers.

Pycraft (1905b), after a study of the skeleton, musculature, pterylosis, and syrinx, supported Fürbringer, in part, and disagreed, in part, with Forbes. Pycraft thought the broadbills are most closely related to the cotingas and should be considered a subfamily of the Cotingidae. Incredibly, at the same time, he thought it possible that the broadbills would prove to be related to the goatsuckers and the swifts. The branching pattern of such a tree is impossible to imagine. Obviously, Pycraft believed that similarity always indicates relationship.

It had been assumed that the African genus *Smithornis* was a muscicapine flycatcher until Bates (1914) noted that it lacks the syringeal muscles of the oscines and has a plantar vinculum. Lowe (1924b) confirmed Bates's observations and later (1931c) showed that the rare *Pseudocalyptomena graueri* of eastern Zaire is also a broadbill.

In the *Hand-List* Sharpe (1901) placed the "Order Eurylaemiformes" at the beginning of the passerine groups and followed Sclater (1888) in recognizing the subfamilies Calyptomeninae and Eurylaeminae. The "Eurylaemiformes" were followed in sequence by the "Menuriformes" and "Passeriformes." Thus, the broadbills were set apart from the other passerines, and the idea that they are primitive has been accepted in all recent classifications. Raikow (1987:2–4) reviewed the taxonomic history of the broadbills:

For many years the broadbills have occupied a rather special place in passerine systematics. Because they possess certain characters thought to be primitive within the Passeriformes they have been regarded as being the most primitive passerine birds, and have usually been classified apart for this reason. The idea that they are primitive has permeated the literature and has been accepted uncritically by those who classify and write about birds. In fact, this idea is based upon very little concrete evidence. The idea began with Garrod (1876:508), whose . . . definition of the Passeriformes included a point first noted by Sundevall (see Nicholson 1889), namely that the deep plantar tendons, the tendons of M. flexor hallucis longus (FHL) and M. flexor digitorum longus (FDL), are not connected by a vinculum. These tendons are interconnected in various ways among birds . . . and the formal recognition of various types by Gadow (1893–1896) led to their being given an exaggerated importance as taxonomic characters. . . . Shortly after thus defining the Passeriformes Garrod (1877) withdrew this character from the diagnosis after finding a vinculum in three species of broadbills. He believed that "either Sundevall's character no longer holds, or the Eurylaemidae are not Passeres" and chose the former alternative on the basis of other evidence. Garrod believed that the vinculum was a retained primitive character and suggested . . . that it provided a basis for separating the Eurylaimidae from the other passerines. Forbes (1880b) formalized this idea by dividing the order into the Desmodactyli, containing only the broadbills, and the Eleutherodactyli, with all other passerines. The Desmodactyli were defined as having retained the plantar vinculum and having the manubrium sterni unforked, the Eleutherodactyli as having lost the vinculum and having the manubrium generally strongly forked. Ridgway (1901:14) . . . added . . . that in the Desmodactyli the hallux is weak, while in the Eleutherodactyli it is the strongest toe. In association with the plantar tendons he characterized the eurylaimid foot as being "syndactyle," and that of other passerines as . . . "eleutherodactyle" or "schizopelmous." Finally he claimed that the Desmodactyli have 15 cervical vertebrae, and the Eleutherodactyli fourteen. Lowe (1931) made a distinction between the form of the joint between the quadrato-jugal and the quadrate in eurylaimids and . . . some other passerines.

This subordinal division, under various names, has been retained in most classifications until very recently, in association with the idea that the eurylaimids are morphologically distinctive and primitive. These ideas were widely accepted until Olson (1971) reexamined them. Olson found that the spina externa is forked in *Smithornis*, as Bates (1914) and Lowe (1924) had . . . reported, and that an unforked spina externa occurs in the Philepittidae (Ames 1971) and in some species of *Procnias* (Cotingidae). *Smithornis* has fourteen cervical vertebrae as . . . noted by Lowe (1931). Olson (1971) could not detect the "weakness" of the hallux referred to by Ridgway (1901), and neither can I. Olson also found the "eurylaimid-type" quadrato-jugal/quadrate articulation in a variety of suboscines. He concluded that only the plantar vinculum . . . sets the Eurylaimidae apart from other passerine birds. Considering this to be an inadequate basis for subordinal separation, Olson (1971) placed the Eurylaimidae next to the Philepittidae within a suborder Tyranni containing all passerine birds except the Oscines and Menurae. He suggested further that they may be closely related to the Cotingidae, an idea also explored by Pycraft (1905).

Recent workers have similarly demoted the broadbills. . . . Cracraft (1981) grouped the Eurylaimidae and Philepittidae as an Infraorder Eurylaimi at the same level as the Pitti, Furnarii, and Tyrannomorpha. Sibley et al. (1982) saw them as the sister group of the Pittidae, with a provisional relationship to the Philepittidae, which they did not study.

From his study of the hind-limb musculature Raikow (1987) concluded that "The Eurylaimidae is probably monophyletic, but there is a surprising lack of solid evidence for this hypothesis in the form of unequivocal morphological synapomorphies. A radiation within the Eurylaimidae is suggested, with evolving characters that include the development of extreme syndactyly, the enlargement of the bill to the 'broadbill' configuration, and numerous changes in the hind limb muscles. Some of these . . . provide excellent evidence for designating clades."

Raikow also concluded that the Philepittidae is the sister taxon of the Eurylaimidae, and that the Pittidae is the sister group of the philepittid-eurylaimid clade.

The DNA Hybridization Evidence

The DNA comparisons show that the broadbills branched from the pittas at $\Delta T_{50}H$ 12.1. The broadbill-pitta clade (infraorder Eurylaimides) diverged from the New World suboscines (infraorder Tyrannides) at Δ 15.8, as indicated above under the Pittidae. The FITCH and KITSCH analyses (Figs. 343, 344) agree with this arrangement.

The divergence between the Green Broadbill (*Calyptomena viridis*) and the genera *Eurylaimus* and *Cymbirhynchus* occurred at Δ 10.8. Our data for the broadbills are incomplete, hence we defer subdivision of the Eurylaimidae, although it seems probable that a family Calyptomenidae is separable.

Thus, the DNA hybridization evidence agrees well with Raikow's conclusions based on morphological characters.

Fig. 188 (*Calyptomena*) does not agree with the relative positions of the curves in Fig. 187, in that *Furnarius* is closer to *Calyptomena* than is *Pitta*. We think that the relative positions in Fig. 187 are more likely to reflect the actual relationships, and we have no simple explanation for the position of *Furnarius* in Fig. 188. Further comparisons are obviously indicated.

Family PHILEPITTIDAE

2/4. Asities and False Sunbirds. The philepittids are confined to Madagascar. *Philepitta*, the asities, and *Neodrepanis*, the false sunbirds, are quiet, usually solitary forest dwellers that feed on fruit and insects. *Neodrepanis*, which has a long, decurved bill and a tubular tongue, also takes nectar. It was long thought to be a true sunbird (Nectariniinae).

The philepittids have 12 rectrices; tarsus covered with rectangular scutes disposed in regular series; syrinx encircled by heavy uppermost bronchial ring; plumage sexually dimorphic.

Raikow (1987) studied the hind-limb musculature of the philepittids and discovered that *Philepitta castanea* has a plantar vinculum, as in the broadbills. He concluded that the philepittids are the sister group of the broadbills. Since we have been unable to obtain the DNA of any philepittid, we can offer no evidence from DNA comparisons. The following review of the taxonomic history of the Philepittidae is based on that of Raikow (1987).

Historical Review of the Classification

In early classifications the two genera were never placed together. *Philepitta* was considered to be an oscine, related to the starlings (Bonaparte 1850), the pittas (Gray 1869), or the birds of paradise (Sharpe 1870). Sundevall (1872, see 1889:132) placed *Philepitta* ("*Paictes*") in the monotypic "Fam. Paictinae," next to the "Thamnophilinae" (antbirds) with his "Oscines Scutelliplantares," a group that included other New World suboscines and the lyrebirds (*Menura*).

Milne-Edwards and Grandidier (1879) placed *Philepitta* next to the Nectariniidae apparently, as Forbes (1880b) suggested, because the eye wattles and bifid tongue resemble those of *Neodrepanis* which, at that time, was thought to be a sunbird.

Forbes (1880b) found the syrinx of *Philepitta* to be mesomyodian and haploophone, thus not oscinine, but similar to those of the broadbills. He noted that the slightly bifid manubrium sterni is like that of the broadbills, and that the pterylosis resembles that of the broadbills more than that of the pittas. Forbes did not detect the plantar vinculum in *Philepitta* and believed that the broadbills were the only group of passerines to possess this structure.

The suboscine affinities of *Philepitta* were supported by Pycraft (1907b), who cited skeletal evidence to include it with the broadbills, cotingas, and manakins in the "Eurylaimi."

Neodrepanis was described by Sharpe (1875b) and considered to be a sunbird by Milne-Edwards and Grandidier (1879). Gadow (1884) placed *Neodrepanis* in the Nectariniidae, but Sharpe (1885:2), in a footnote to the "Family Dicaeidae," stated that "I am firmly convinced that *Neodrepanis*, from Madagascar, placed by Capt. Shelley and Dr. Gadow (Cat. B. vol. ix, p. 2) in the *Nectariniidae*, is really a member of the family *Dicaeidae*."

Shelley (1900) suggested that *Neodrepanis* might be an oscine/suboscine link, and Sharpe (1909:34), in the *Hand-List*, assigned it to the subfamily Neodrepaninae of the Nectariniidae, immediately following the Dicaeidae.

Philepitta remained in the Philepittidae, and *Neodrepanis* in the Nectariniidae, until Amadon (1951) showed that *Neodrepanis* is neither a sunbird nor an oscine. The outer (10th) primary is long, while in sunbirds and most other oscines it is quite short; the hyporhachis is reduced as in *Philepitta*, not long as in sunbirds; the tarsal scutes are as in *Philepitta*, and unlike the oscine condition. Most important, the syrinx of *Neodrepanis* is mesomyodian, lacks intrinsic muscles, and has large external membranes, as in *Philepitta*. The tongue of *Neodrepanis* is tubular, but differs from that of the sunbirds. Amadon (1951) concluded that *Neodrepanis* is closely related to *Philepitta* but, in 1979, he recommended that they be placed in separate subfamilies. Wolters (1975–82:168) placed the two genera in separate families.

Ames (1971) confirmed the similarities in the syringes of the two genera, noted differences in some aspects, and placed the Philepittidae and Eurylaimidae in the suborder Eurylaimi.

Most recent classifications recognize the Philepittidae and place it with the suboscines, close to the broadbills.

Raikow (1987) compared the hind-limb muscles of *Philepitta* and *Neodrepanis* with those of broadbills, pittas, and New Zealand wrens (Acanthisittidae). As noted above, he found a plantar vinculum in *P. castanea*, although not in *N. coruscans*, interpreted this discovery as evidence of relationship between *Philepitta* and the broadbills, and concluded that the "Philepittidae is monophyletic and the sister group of the Eurylaimidae."

In the absence of DNA comparisons, we accept Raikow's conclusion, noting that his other conclusions about the relationships among the Old World suboscines are generally congruent with our DNA hybridization evidence. Raikow (1987:42) noted that his "proposed . . . phylogeny [was] compared to one suggested by C. G. Sibley and co-workers from their studies on DNA hybridization. Although not identical, the results of the two studies are so similar that the agreement cannot be attributed to chance. Given the unrelated nature of the data used in these different studies, the correspondence between their results must be due to their independent determination of an approximation of the true historical phylogeny. The relationships proposed in both investigations differ markedly from those in earlier, more traditional studies."

New World Suboscines

Infraorder Tyrannides
  Parvorder Tyrannida
    Family Tyrannidae
      Subfamily Pipromorphinae: Mionectine Flycatchers
      Subfamily Tyranninae: Tyrant Flycatchers
      Subfamily Tityrinae
        Tribe Schiffornithini: *Schiffornis*
        Tribe Tityrini: Tityras, Becards
      Subfamily Cotinginae: Cotingas, Plantcutters, Sharpbill
      Subfamily Piprinae: Manakins
  Parvorder Thamnophilida
    Family Thamnophilidae: Typical Antbirds
  Parvorder Furnariida
    Superfamily Furnarioidea
      Family Furnariidae
        Subfamily Furnariinae: Ovenbirds
        Subfamily Dendrocolaptinae: Woodcreepers
    Superfamily Formicarioidea
      Family Formicariidae: Ground Antbirds
      Family Conopophagidae: Gnateaters
      Family Rhinocryptidae: Tapaculos

The DNA-DNA hybridization comparisons show that the New World suboscine groups, which we place in the infraorder Tyrannides, are more closely related to one another than any one of them is to any Old World group. Figs. 369–373 depict the phylogeny of the living suboscine groups.

    We agree with Sibley (1970:115) and Ames (1971:155) that this group should be restricted to the New World members of Wetmore's (1960) Tyrannoidea. The Old World Pittidae, Eurylaimidae, Philepittidae, and Acanthisittidae are not closely related to the New World suboscines. The two lineages diverged at $\Delta T_{50}H$ 15.8.

Parvorder TYRANNIDA

146/537. Tyrants, Becards, Cotingas, and Manakins. The syringeal characters of the Tyrannida are exceptionally variable, and Ames (1971:152) concluded that "the Tyrannoidea cannot be defined on the basis of the syrinx. Certain syringeal characters . . . appear to be useful at about the family and subfamily levels in the New World Tyrannoidea."

All Tyrannida have a two-notched sternum with little variation (Heimerdinger and Ames 1967:20). Sclater (1888) and Ridgway (1907) defined some of the tyrannoid groups on the basis of foot structure and tarsal scutellation which Snow (1975:21) summarized as follows:

Pipridae: Tarsus exaspidean; second phalanx of outer toe wholly united with that of middle toe.

Cotingidae: Tarsal scutellation of various types, but never exaspidean; second phalanx of outer and middle toes not united.

Tyrannidae: Tarsus exaspidean; neither outer nor inner toe united to middle toe by more than the basal part of the first phalanx.

Snow then noted that "the difficulty has been that a too rigid application of these criteria leads to the probable misplacement of a few genera; but no better criteria have been suggested, and recent anatomical studies have shown great variability within all three families, so that it is unlikely that clear-cut morphological criteria will be found."

Snow's conclusion indicates that we cannot trust these characters to define the monophyletic clusters within the Tyrannida.

Family TYRANNIDAE: 146/537.

Subfamily PIPROMORPHINAE: 8/53. Mionectine Flycatchers.
Subfamily TYRANNINAE: 91/340. Tyrant Flycatchers.
Subfamily TITYRINAE: 4/23. Tityras and Becards.

The tyrants range from Alaska and Canada to Central America, the Caribbean islands, all of South America, the Falklands, and the Galapagos islands. The mionectines occur in wooded areas from southern Mexico to Bolivia and northern Argentina. Members of the Tityrinae range from southern Arizona and Mexico to northern Argentina; one species occurs on Jamaica.

Including the taxa that may belong to the Pipromorphinae (see below) Traylor (1977) recognized 374 species of tyrant flycatchers in 88 genera, divided into three subfamilies: Elaeniinae, Fluvicolinae, and Tyranninae. He transferred *Attila*, *Pseudattila*, *Casiornis*, *Laniocera*, and *Rhytipterna* from the Cotingidae to the Tyrannidae on the recommendations of Ames (1971) and Snow (1973). Traylor left *Lipaugus* in the Cotingidae but agreed with Ames et al. (1968) that *Corythopis* is a tyrannid.

The DNA data agree with these proposals for the taxa we have been able to study, namely, *Attila*, *Rhytipterna*, *Lipaugus*, and *Corythopis*.

Traylor (1977:136) "tentatively allied" the Tityrinae (*Tityra, Pachyramphus, Platypsaris*) "to the Tyrannidae only because their crania more nearly resemble those of Tyrannids than those of Cotingids." Snow (1979) placed the Tityrinae at the end of his Tyrannidae.

The morphological definition of the Tyrannidae and the separation of tyrants, becards, cotingas, and manakins are difficult because, as noted above, the characters usually employed are variable and discordant. Ames (1971:157–158) described the tyrant flycatchers (our Tyranninae) as:

the most diverse of suboscine families. Although the "typical" tyrannid could be described as a small olive bird with a flat, slightly hooked bill and strong rictal bristles, there are more atypical forms than typical ones. Usually the tarsus is exaspidean and the toes lack syndactyly. . . . In all of their external characters the Tyrannidae are so variable that taxonomic boundaries and relationships within the family and with other families are often difficult to determine.

With few exceptions the tyrannid syrinx is characterized by the presence of an intrinsic muscle, M. obliquus ventralis, and internal cartilages. Rarely, a second intrinsic muscle, M. obliquus lateralis, is present. Outside the traditional limits of the Tyrannidae (as revised by Hellmayr 1927) M. obliquus ventralis and internal cartilages occur in the New World Tyranni, separately or together, only in *Oxyruncus*, *Corythopis*, the manakin *Ilicura* and a few members of the Cotingidae.

Ames (1971:158–163) distinguished seven groups "each with a high degree of syringeal homogeneity and with certain features not found elsewhere in the family." An eighth group, with six subgroups, contains genera of uncertain relationships, including *Mionectes*, *Pipromorpha*, and *Corythopis*. The becards (*Pachyramphus*, *Platypsaris*) were noted by Ames (1971:163) as having "several tyrannid features of the syrinx that are not found in the more typical members of the Cotingidae." Ames thought it likely that the becards are "tyrannids" rather than "cotingids."

Warter (1965) found the skulls of the becards to be similar to those of tyrannine flycatchers and proposed that the Tityrinae be made a subfamily of the Tyrannidae, a conclusion accepted by Traylor (1977) and adopted by Snow (1979).

McKitrick (1985) considered the monophyly of the Tyrannidae in the light of nine traditional morphological characters. Of these only three (internal cartilages of the syrinx; m. obliquus ventralis, a syringeal muscle; enlarged femoral artery) were considered to be derived for the tyrants and none supported monophyly of the Tyrannidae of Traylor (1977, 1979). The principal genera that one or more of these characters associated with the tyrannids are *Iodopleura*, *Pachyramphus*, and *Tityra* (usually considered to be cotingas); *Oxyruncus* (monotypic family Oxyruncidae); and the manakins *Piprites*, *Sapayoa*, *Tyranneutes*, *Neopipo*, *Neopelma*, and *Schiffornis*. It is interesting that of those genera, *Pachyramphus*, *Tityra*, and *Schiffornis* cluster with some tyrannids on the basis of our DNA comparisons and the others (except *Oxyruncus*) contain small species which do not fit easily into any of the traditional groups. Our DNA comparisons suggest that *Sapayoa aenigma* is an isolated species of uncertain affinities, which is discussed below.

The DNA hybridization data support the morphological evidence of a relationship between the becards (Tityrinae) and the tyrants (Tyranninae). Figs. 372 and 373 show the divergence node at $\Delta T_{50}H$ 8.7.

The genus *Schiffornis*, usually placed with the manakins, clusters with the Tityrinae on the basis of DNA comparisons. The branch from the becard clade is at $\Delta T_{50}H$ 6.7. This allocation is tentative because we had only a small amount of *Schiffornis* DNA, and the delta values to some of the older nodes are not concordant with the data from other taxa.

Prum and Lanyon (1989) made a cladistic analysis of 19 morphological characters "to investigate the phylogeny of the *Schiffornis* group, a monophyletic assemblage of six genera . . . currently placed in three different tyrannoid families." The six genera are *Schiffornis*, *Laniisoma*, *Iodopleura*, *Laniocera*, *Xenopsaris*, and *Pachyramphus*. The monophyly of these taxa was supported by "two syringeal synapomorphies," and data from cranial morphology, plumages, and nest structure were also analyzed. The conclusions of this study agreed in part with our DNA hybridization evidence, but we lacked DNAs of some of the genera so the comparison is incomplete. The electrophoretic data of S. M. Lanyon (1985) "do not support the monophyly of the *Schiffornis* group."

Family TYRANNIDAE, Subfamily COTINGINAE: 28/69. Snow (1973) recognized 27 genera and 79 species in his Cotingidae, but in 1979 he transferred the becards to the Tyrannidae, as the subfamily Tityrinae. In 1982, Snow recognized 25 genera and 65 species of cotingas. Sibley et al. (1984a) added *Oxyruncus* and the three species of *Phytotoma* to the Cotinginae.

The cotingas range from Mexico through Central and South America to northeastern Argentina and Paraguay. Cotingas vary in size from that of a kinglet (*Regulus*) to that of a crow (*Corvus*); they are exceptionally variable in color and external appearance with such extreme types as the umbrella birds (*Cephalopterus*), bellbirds (*Procnias*), and cocks-of-the-rock (*Rupicola*). The tiny Kinglet Calyptura (*Calyptura cristata*) has the size and coloration of a small manakin, but "its allocation to the Cotingidae is based on its tarsal scutellation and foot structure which are typical for cotingas: its tarsus is pycnaspidean . . . and its toes are free. . . . Its allocation to the cotingas has always been accepted, but its remoteness from the rest of the family in nearly all external characters supports the view that the cotingas may be an association of diverse phylogenetic lines that arose from the primitive tyranniform stock before the main lines leading to the flycatchers and manakins were recognizable" (Snow 1982:39).

This discussion, and the uncertainties expressed in it, reflect the difficulties involved in determining genealogical relationships from morphological characters. The book by Snow (1982) provides a review of the cotingas, their characters, taxonomic problems, life histories, and distribution.

The DNA-DNA data support the inclusion in the Cotinginae of such morphologically diverse genera as *Pipreola*, *Lipaugus*, *Rupicola*, *Cephalopterus*, *Procnias*, and *Ampelion*.

The Sharpbill (*Oxyruncus cristatus*) has usually been placed in the Tyrannidae or in a monotypic family. Sibley et al. (1984a) compared the single-copy DNA of *Oxyruncus* with the DNAs of other tyrannoids and found it to be a cotinga, not a tyrant flycatcher. We include it in the subfamily Cotinginae.

Since 1888, when Sclater defined the tyrannoid groups, the cotingas have been viewed as having various types of tarsal scutellation, but never exaspidean, as in *Oxyruncus*. That the Sharpbill is a cotinga is supported by several characters in addition to the DNA hybridization evidence. *Oxyruncus* thus provides another example of the lack of congruence between tarsal scutellation and phylogenetic relationships in the suboscines.

Stiles and Whitney (1983) presented observations on the behavior of the Sharpbill but offered no suggestions concerning its relationships.

The plantcutters (*Phytotoma*) usually have been placed in a monotypic family, although clearly related to the cotingas. Küchler (1936) studied the pterylosis, external morphology, skeleton, syrinx, and alimentary tract of *P. rara* and concluded that *Phytotoma* is a cotinga. It has a pycnaspidean tarsal envelope, as do many cotingas, and the main artery of the leg is the sciatic, as in *Rupicola*. Ames (1971:156) noted the "evident similarity of the syrinx of *Phytotoma* to that of some cotingas (particularly *Heliochera*)" (*Ampelion*).

Lanyon and Lanyon (1989) used electrophoretic, syringeal, and osteological characters to assess the affinities of *Phytotoma*. They concluded that the plantcutters can be placed within the cotingine genus *Ampelion*. To "recognize the distinctiveness of the plantcutters" they "split *Ampelion* into the previously recognized genera *Ampelion*, *Doliornis*, and *Zaratornis*" and "recommended placement of these taxa (seven species) within the family Phytotomidae."

Although we do not have DNA hybridization data for the plantcutters, it seems clear that they are members of the cotingine radiation. Morphologically *Phytotoma* is even more like typical cotingas than is *Oxyruncus*, which is clearly a cotinga. We therefore include *Phytotoma* in the Cotinginae.

Family TYRANNIDAE, Subfamily PIPRINAE: 15/52. The manakins occur from southeastern Mexico to southeastern Brazil, northeastern Argentina, southeastern Paraguay, Bolivia, and Peru. Most manakins are small, short-winged, short-tailed birds with small bills, broad at the base, with a terminal hook on the maxilla. Most are sexually dimorphic, and the males of some species display in "courts." Only the females incubate.

Ames (1971:157) found considerable variation in the syringes of seven genera and noted that *Piprites* has a syrinx similar to that of the small tyrannids *Myiobius* and *Terenotriccus*. Other manakins show little similarity to either tyrannids or cotingas. Ames found that *Schiffornis*, the large, so-called "Thrush-like Manakin," has a syrinx "quite like that of the cotinga *Lipaugus*. . . . *Schiffornis* is unique among manakins . . . in possessing internal cartilages, but the manakins are so heterogeneous in syringeal structure that I have come to expect almost anything."

W. E. Lanyon (pers. comm.) has found that, in addition to *Schiffornis*, the genera *Sapayoa*, *Piprites*, *Tyranneutes*, and *Neopelma* have internal cartilages. The "typical" manakins lack these cartilages. All tyrannines have internal cartilages, and their presence in *Schiffornis*, which we find is most closely related to the becards, suggests that these other genera, which also have been considered to be manakins, may be either tyrannines or tityrines. Lanyon examined 18 of the 25 genera of cotingas recognized by Snow (1982) and found no internal cartilages in their syringes. Ames (1971:37) reported "a pair of very small . . . internal cartilages" in *Iodopleura*, a genus considered by Snow (1982) to be a cotinga. However, Ames (1971:156) noted that "The cotinga genus *Iodopleura* would appear from syringeal structure to be allied to the Tyrannidae."

Snow (1975:21) noted that *Manacus*, *Pipra*, *Chiroxiphia*, and a few smaller genera "are a well-defined group" but that *Schiffornis*, *Sapayoa*, and *Piprites* are "especially problematical" and their "allocation to the Pipridae [is] uncertain. . . . all show some affinity to the cotingas or tyrant-flycatchers and are unspecialized in the direction of the typical manakins" (p. 24). Thus, in addition to *Schiffornis*, there are other "manakins" that may belong in the Tityrinae or the Tyranninae.

The DNA hybridization data include 22 $\Delta T_{50}H$ values between manakins and cotingas that average 8.5, SE = 0.04, SD = 0.2. We therefore place the two groups as sister subfamilies in the Tyrannidae.

Family TYRANNIDAE, Subfamily PIPROMORPHINAE: 8/53. The DNA comparisons reveal some new (and controversial) facets of the phylogeny of the tyrannoids and confirm certain proposals made by others. One surprise was evidence that a lineage branched from the other tyrannoids before the radiation of the typical tyrants, becards, cotingas, and manakins began. This group, which we (Sibley and Ahlquist 1985b) designated as the family "Mionectidae," must be based on the genus *Pipromorpha*, having been established by Bonaparte in 1853 and used again by Wolters (1977:192, see Wolters 1975–82). Although the pipromorphine lineage branched from the tyrannines at $\Delta T_{50}H$ 9.4, and therefore meets our criteria for a family, we recognize the subfamily Pipromorphinae as the sister group of the other subfamilies of the Tyrannidae.

The Pipromorphinae may include, at least, *Mionectes* (includes *Pipromorpha*), *Leptopogon*, *Pseudotriccus*, *Corythopis*, *Hemitriccus*, (including *Idioptilon*), *Todirostrum*, *Poecilotriccus*, and *Taeniotriccus*. These genera are among those placed in the Elaeniinae by Traylor (1977:177). Traylor included *Pipromorpha* in *Mionectes*.

The DNA evidence indicates that the other genera in Traylor's Elaeniinae for which we have DNA data are indeed closer to *Elaenia* than to *Sayornis* or *Myiarchus*, which represent Traylor's Fluvicolinae and Tyranninae, respectively. These include *Camptostoma*, *Phaeomyias*, *Suiriri*, *Tyrannulus*, *Myiopagis*, *Mecocerculus*, *Anairetes*, and *Euscarthmus*. The DNA data are equivocal about several other genera in Traylor's Elaeniinae, viz., *Lophotriccus*, *Atalotriccus*, *Cnipodectes*, *Rhynchocyclus*, and *Platyrinchus*. However, the DNA data agree with the genera Traylor assigned to his Fluvicolinae and Tyranninae, except for some for which our data do not indicate a clear choice. Thus, it seems likely that the Pipromorphinae are so convergently similar to the true elaeniines that they are difficult to separate by the characters used by Traylor. However, Ames (1971:162) noted that *Mionectes* and *Pipromorpha* have a "peculiar syringeal structure," and Traylor (1977:151–159) discussed some of the genera that we assign to the Pipromorphinae and noted several characters that seem to set them apart from the typical elaeniine tyrants. For example, *Leptopogon* and *Mionectes* build nests "unlike the nests of any Elaeniine flycatcher" and they share the unusual behavioral trait of "single-wing flicking" (Monroe 1968:277). As Traylor noted, these characters cannot be fully evaluated because they are unknown for many genera.

The same problem afflicts the DNA evidence. We lack DNAs of many genera, and it would be necessary to "label" the DNAs of several more to clarify the boundaries of the Pipromorphinae. The divergence of the Pipromorphinae and the Tyranninae at $\Delta T_{50}H$ 9.4 is based on 47 DNA hybrids. Most of the pipromorphines share the Type I nasal septum defined by Warter (1965; see Traylor 1977:182), and most of them belong to the group that Warter (1965) called the "primitive tyrannids." W. E. Lanyon (pers. comm.) examined a large number of genera and found the "primitive nasal capsule" in *Corythopis*, *Myiornis*, *Tachuris*, *Tolmomyias*, some species of *Myiopagis*, *Todirostrum*, *Platyrinchus*, *Onychorhynchus*, *Oncostoma*, *Rhynchocyclus*, *Hemitriccus*, *Lophotriccus*, *Poecilotriccus*, *Cnipodectes*, and possibly *Leptopogon*, but not *Mionectes*! From a study of syringeal anatomy, W. E. Lanyon (1988a:16) rejected our definition of the Pipromorphinae (= Mionectidae = Corythopinae) because the assemblage we defined "implies that syringeal internal cartilages are primitive for all tyrannoids and subsequently were lost in all cotingas and true manakins. Also included among related genera, according to Sibley and Ahlquist, are *Pseudotriccus* and *Corythopis*, two other genera in my *Elaenia* assemblage. Most unsettling in this report is the fact that *Hemitriccus* and *Todirostrum* were designated members of this early radiation, while the DNA data were found to be 'equivocal' on such clearly related genera as *Lophotriccus* and *Atalotric-cus*. . . . Until there is additional support for this novel hypothesis, I favor the more parsimonious interpretation that the internal cartilages shared by all tyrant flycatchers are indeed evidence for common ancestry, and that *Mionectes* and *Leptopogon* are bona fide members of the tyrant lineage."

Lanyon's evidence and arguments may be correct, but we defer further discussion until our data can be re-evaluated and additional experiments conducted. The Tyrannida, however they may be split into families and subfamilies, are the result of a Neotropical radiation; all are closely related and there is a reasonable probability that the distribution of any morphological character is not precisely coterminal with natural clusters.

The DNA Hybridization Evidence

The melting curves provide another view of the relationships among the members of the Tyrannida and between them and other groups of birds. Fig. 189 (*Mionectes*) includes comparisons between *Mionectes* and five genera we assign to the Pipromorphinae, plus two genera of the Tyranninae. There is no large gap between the two groups, but *Elaenia* and *Sayornis* are the most distant from *Mionectes*.

In Fig. 190 (*Mionectes*) *Leptopogon* is closest to the homoduplex with three tyrannines, a piprine, and a tityrine (*Pachyramphus*) farther out.

The relative position of the curve of *Sapayoa aenigma* is of special interest. When first noted it was assumed to be caused by an aberrant DNA sample, although the melting curve seemed normal. However, in several other experiments *Sapayoa* is in this same position in relation to other tracer taxa (Figs. 193, 197, 198, 200). *Sapayoa* was not used as a tracer so it is uncertain whether its position in the melting curves is normal or due to experimental error.

Fig. 191 (*Mionectes*) shows the relative positions of the curves of several representatives of the Tyranni (manakin, cotinga, gnateater, antpitta, ovenbird, antbird), a broadbill, lyrebird, and a thrasher. The positions of the taxa are as expected, except for that of *Thamnophilus* beyond *Calyptomena*. However, they are close together and the average $\Delta T_{50}H$ difference between their nodes in the UPGMA tree is 2.0. The position of the *Menura* curve may be influenced by a rate slowdown in the lyrebirds, which have an average age at first breeding of ca. 3–4 years (Table 16).

Fig. 192 (*Myiarchus*) places *Corythopis* (Pipromorphinae) and *Pipreola* (Cotinginae) equidistant from the homoduplex, with members of the other groups of the Tyrannides clustered about equidistant from *Myiarchus*. This agrees with the UPGMA tree.

Fig. 193 (*Myiarchus*) shows the relative positions of the tyrannid subfamilies to the tyrannine tracer, with the enigmatic *Sapayoa* far out. *Todirostrum* and *Leptopogon*, which we place in the Pipromorphinae, cluster with the manakins, cotingas, and *Schiffornis*, not with *Pitangus* and *Sayornis*. Whatever may be the correct answer to the question of the Pipromorphinae, it is clear that they form a group separate from the Tyranninae.

Fig. 194 (*Myiarchus*). Again, *Leptopogon* clusters with *Pipreola*, not with *Elaenia* and *Empidonax*. The curve of *Acanthisitta* beyond those of *Corvus* and *Turdus* is viewed as evidence of its isolated position, not as evidence that it is an oscine.

Fig. 195 (*Oxyruncus*). This is only a fair experiment, but the closest curves to that of the

Sharpbill homoduplex are those of two cotingas, followed by a becard, tyrant, manakin, two tyrants, ovenbird, and an antbird. The *Furnarius* and *Thamnophilus* curves provide perspective. The larger cotingas may have delayed maturity (*Procnias* at ca. 3 years, Table 16) with a correlated slower average rate of DNA evolution, but *Pipreola* is smaller than *Rupicola* and its curve is the closest to that of *Oxyruncus*.

Fig. 196 (*Pipreola*) shows the close relationship between cotingas and tyrants, with the tapaculos, gnateaters, furnariids, and antbirds more distant.

Fig. 197 (*Pipreola*) shows the clustering of *Rupicola, Querula,* and *Cephalopterus* relative to *Pipreola*, suggesting that the three genera may form a subgroup within the Cotinginae. The becard, *Schiffornis*, and the manakin are distinct from the cotingas. The position of *Sapayoa*, between *Calyptomena* and *Pitta*, suggests that *Sapayoa* is as distant from the Tyrannides as are the Eurylaimides. If this is true, *Sapayoa* may be the only known representative of a previously unidentified higher taxon.

Fig. 198 (*Pachyramphus*) shows the tityrine cluster, with *Schiffornis*, manakins, cotingas, Sharpbill, and *Mionectes* farther out. Again, there is *Sapayoa*.

Fig. 199 (*Pachyramphus*) provides additional evidence that the Tyranninae and Pipromorphinae are on the same branch relative to the Tityrinae, and that the Formicariidae, Furnariidae (*Schizoeaca*), and Thamnophilidae are more distant.

Fig. 200 (*Pipra*) shows the clustering of tityrines, *Schiffornis,* cotingas, and tyrannines relative to the manakins, with *Sapayoa* in its puzzling place. The position of *Schiffornis* indicates that it is not a manakin.

Fig. 201 (*Pipra*) shows two clusters relative to the Piprinae: the closest group consists of a tityra, cotinga, tyrant, becard, and a pipromorphine; the second cluster includes members of the Thamnophilida and Furnariida.

Fig. 345 (FITCH) was constructed from data in Sibley and Ahlquist (1985b). This tree is mostly congruent with the UPGMA tree (Figs. 371–373). Note that *Schiffornis* clusters with the tityra-becard group (*Pachyramphus*), and the large distance between the pipromorphines (*Mionectes*) and the typical tyrants (*Elaenia, Sayornis, Myiarchus*). The small internodal distance leading to the manakins (*Pipra*) of 0.08 units is not significant, and that leading to the cotinga clade (*Pipreola*) of 0.15 is only marginally so. Thus, it may be appropriate to assume a trichotomy to the cotinga, manakin, and flycatcher clades. The uniformity of the branch lengths in this tree compared with many of the non-passerine trees is noteworthy. Among the Tyrannida the shortest branch from the base of the tree is the 6.6 units to *Pipra*, which is 84% of the longest distance of 7.8 units to *Mionectes*. This amount of variation may not indicate differences in rates.

We conclude that the relationships among the subfamilies of the Tyrannidae are appropriately represented by the classification and that the melting curves are mainly congruent with the UPGMA dendrograms. The relationships of *Sapayoa aenigma* remain to be determined.

Parvorders THAMNOPHILIDA and FURNARIIDA

Typical Antbirds, Ovenbirds, Woodcreepers, Ground Antbirds, Gnateaters, and Tapaculos. The DNA comparisons reveal that the "Furnarioidea" of Wetmore (1960) is more complex than previously thought. The typical antbirds (Thamnophilidae) are the descendants of one branch of a dichotomy at $\delta T_{50}H$ 13.5. The sister branch produced the living groups we place in the Furnarioidea and Formicarioidea. The latter includes the ground antbirds (Formicariidae), gnateaters (Conopophagidae), and tapaculos (Rhinocryptidae). The DNA hybridization data for these groups are congruent with the variations in the sternal notches described by Heimerdinger and Ames (1967), the characters of *Conopophaga* and *Corythopis* (Ames et al. 1968), and the syringeal characters studied by Ames (1971).

Parvorder FURNARIIDA

Superfamily FURNARIOIDEA: 66/280.Ovenbirds and Woodcreepers. Ames (1971: 153) found that the members of his suborder Furnarii (our parvorder Furnariida) "share an elaborate syringeal form not found elsewhere. No structures even remotely resembling the Membrana trachealis and Processus vocalis are found in other passerines."

Family FURNARIIDAE, Subfamily FURNARIINAE: 53/231. Ovenbirds or Horneros. Vaurie (1980) recognized 34 genera and ca. 214 species of ovenbirds, or horneros. They range from central Mexico south through Central and South America to Tierra del Fuego and the Falkland Islands.

Morphologically and ecologically the ovenbirds may be the most diverse avian subfamily yet recognized. They occur in all habitats from sea level to the puna zone in the Andes. Their adaptive radiation has produced morphotypes that converge on larks, wheatears, nuthatches, thrushes, thrashers, wrens, and dippers. Most of the species are small to medium in size among passerines, and they tend to be dull colored, often in shades of brown.

The syringes of the ovenbirds and woodcreepers (Furnarioidea) have two pairs of intrinsic muscles, thus, they differ from the members of the Formicarioidea (ground antbirds, gnateaters, tapaculos), which have either one pair or no intrinsic muscles.

The syringes of the ovenbirds (except *Geositta*) differ from those of the woodcreepers in their lack of horns on the Processi vocales (Ames 1971:154).

Garrod (1877a) described the nares in the ovenbirds as schizorhinal, a reference to the shape of the long nasal opening that extends posteriad from the naso-frontal hinge. Feduccia (1973) found considerable variation in the bony nares in ovenbirds and termed them pseudoschizorhinal in most species because they are not as deeply slit as the "true" schizorhinal condition in the Charadrii. Feduccia noted that the nares of some philydorine ovenbirds tend toward holorhiny, as in the woodcreepers.

Family FURNARIIDAE, Subfamily DENDROCOLAPTINAE: 13/49. Woodcreepers. The woodcreepers (or woodhewers) range from northern Mexico to northern Argentina, Bolivia, and Peru. They tend to be larger than the ovenbirds, from 20 to 40 cm long, and are mostly olive or rufous brown, often streaked or barred below. The shafts of the rectrices are usually stiffened, and most species forage in a manner convergently similar to the Northern creepers (*Certhia*) or to the woodpeckers (Marchant 1964).

The woodcreepers also differ from the ovenbirds by having horns on the Processi vocales of the syrinx (Ames 1971:154), and holorhinal nares. However, *Geositta*, an otherwise typical ovenbird, has large horns on the Processi vocales.

Feduccia (1973) compared several anatomical characters and the electrophoretic patterns of the hemoglobins of ovenbirds and woodcreepers. He concluded that they are "very closely related groups" and that "the group of ovenbirds most closely related to the wood-hewers is the subfamily Philydorinae." Feduccia found four genera that he considered to be intermediates between ovenbirds and woodcreepers.

The DNA hybridization data agree with the morphological evidence of the close relationship between ovenbirds and woodcreepers. The two groups diverged at $\Delta T_{50}H$ 6.6. They could be considered to be either tribes or subfamilies in the family Furnariidae.

Parvorder FURNARIIDA, Superfamily FORMICARIOIDEA: 20/92. Ground Antbirds, Gnateaters, and Tapaculos. The three families we recognize in the Formicarioidea share at least two derived morphological structures, namely, a distinctive syrinx and a four-notched sternum. These synapomorphies are congruent with the DNA hybridization data. As noted above, the traditional antbird family Formicariidae of Wetmore (1960) was a diphyletic composite of the "ground antbirds" and the "typical antbirds."

Family FORMICARIIDAE: 7/56. Ground Antbirds. The number and pattern of the notches and fenestra in the posterior border of the sternum in the suboscines were studied by Heimerdinger and Ames (1967). Two principal types, two-notched and four-notched, were found, with considerable variation in each. Most "antbirds" have a two-notched sternum, but the "ground-antbirds," including *Pittasoma*, *Grallaricula*, and *Grallaria*, have a four-notched sternum, or a tendency toward that condition. Other than these only the sternum of *Conopophaga* tends to be four-notched, and those of the rhinocryptids are consistently so. All other suboscines have two-notched sterna. Feduccia and Olson (1982:19–20) commented on these characters.

Ames (1971:154) discovered that the

antbirds may be divided into two groups on the basis of syringeal morphology. The majority . . . "typical antbirds," are distinguished by having one pair of intrinsic syringeal muscles, a very small Processus, and M. sternotrachealis bifurcate near its insertion. Examples . . . are *Taraba*, *Dysithamnus*, *Thamnophilus*, and *Myrmotherula*. The second group, the "ground antbirds", is characterized by the absence of intrinsic syringeal muscles, a large Processus, and a simple M. sternotrachealis. To this group belong *Grallaria*, *Chamaeza*, *Formicarius*, and *Conopophaga*. Long-legged terrestrial birds, they appear to be intermediate between the Formicariidae [our Thamnophilidae] and the Rhinocryptidae.

Such intermediacy is suggested by the presence of a four-notch metasternum, classically a rhinocryptid character, in some species of *Grallaria* and in *Pittasoma* (Heimerdinger and Ames 1967).

The morphological characters and DNA-DNA measurements are congruent in several respects. The $\Delta T_{50}H$ distances from *Formicarius* to *Chamaeza* (9.7, 10.1) and *Grallaria* (10.7, 10.9) could support the recognition of a subfamily or even another family. We prefer to leave the classification as presented above until the DNAs of additional genera can be compared to delineate the boundaries of clusters within the formicarioid families. As we presently understand the Formicariidae it includes, at least, *Formicarius*, *Chamaeza*, *Grallaria*, *Grallaricula*, and *Pittasoma*. Feduccia and Olson (1982:19–20) came to virtually the same conclusion, based on morphological characters. They noted variations in some of the skeletal characters. It is probable that *Myrmornis*, *Myrmothera*, *Hylopezus*, and *Thamnocharis* are also members of the "ground antbird" group, which thus contains 56 species, as noted above. The other 44 genera of antbirds are members of the Thamnophilidae.

Family CONOPOPHAGIDAE: 1/8. Gnateaters. The eight species of gnateaters (*Conopophaga*), and the members of the genus *Corythopis*, often have been placed together in the family Conopophagidae. The gnateaters are small, long-legged, short-tailed birds with short, rounded wings. Most of the species have a post-ocular stripe of elongate, usually white, feathers. They are terrestrial insectivores that live in the tropical and temperate forests of South America from Colombia, Surinam, and Brazil, south to northeastern Argentina, southern Paraguay, Bolivia, and Peru.

Ames et al. (1968) reviewed the taxonomic history of the group and, primarily on the basis of sternal and syringeal characters, recommended that *Conopophaga* be transferred to the Formicariidae and placed near *Grallaria*. The genus *Corythopis*, which had long been associated with *Conopophaga*, was moved to the "Tyrannidae."

The DNA data indicate that the rhinocryptid-conopophagid clade branched from the formicariid lineage at Δ T$_{50}$H 11.4, and the conopophagids branched from the rhinocryptids at Δ 10.7. We recognize the Conopophagidae and Rhinocryptidae as families since they diverged between Δ T$_{50}$H 9 and 11. However, we have not placed *Grallaria* in a family apart from the Formicariidae, although its lineage diverged from that of *Formicarius* at Δ T$_{50}$H 10.8. This is an inconsistency in the application of our criteria for defining categories, but until the DNAs of additional formicarioid genera can be compared we think it best to refrain from further splitting of the Formicariidae. The DNA data testify to the long history of these taxa and explain the distribution of their distinctive morphological characters.

Family RHINOCRYPTIDAE: 12/28. Tapaculos. The 26 to 28 species of tapaculos were placed in 11 or 12 genera by Peters (1951) and Meyer de Schauensee (1966). Most of the rhinocryptids are ground-dwellers and they occur in a wide range of habitats from Costa Rica to Patagonia, and from sea level to ca. 4000 meters in the Andes. They vary in size from that of a small wren to that of a large thrush and tend to run rather than fly (Sick 1964b).

The opercula that cover the nostrils are the basis for the name of the type genus, and all rhinocryptids have a four-notched sternum (Heimerdinger and Ames 1967). "In their syrinx the rhinocryptids possess a simple M. sternotrachealis and a dorsally originating intrinsic muscle. One genus, *Telodromas*, lacks the intrinsic muscle, its syrinx being much like those of *Formicarius* and *Grallaria*. The tapaculos are outwardly similar to the short-tailed, long-legged, ground-living antbirds which they resemble in syringeal structure" (Ames 1971:154).

Ames et al. (1968:24) noted that the pterylosis of the ventral tract in the rhinocryptids is "unique within passerines; the one exception to this is *Melanopareia maranonicus* whose pterylosis is very similar to several genera of Formicariidae."

The DNA hybridization data show that the tapaculos are formicarioids and the sister group of the Conopophagidae. The excellent congruence between the morphological characters and the DNA comparisons is apparent.

Parvorder THAMNOPHILIDA

Family THAMNOPHILIDAE: 45/188 Typical Antbirds. The "typical antbirds" occur from southern Mexico to northern Argentina, Bolivia, and Peru. Some species associate with army ants, but most do not.

As noted above, the thamnophilids have a two-notched sternum and a syrinx with one pair of intrinsic muscles, a small Processus, and a bifurcate M. sternotrachealis.

The Furnariida and the Thamnophilida are separated by a large phylogenetic gap. The node at $\Delta T_{50}H$ 13.5 is the average of 107 DNA-DNA hybrids.

Heimerdinger and Ames (1967) and Ames (1971) discovered the morphological distinctions between the ground antbirds and the typical antbirds, and correctly associated the former with *Conopophaga* and the rhinocryptids. The DNA data support their conclusions and make it possible to reconstruct the phylogeny. The congruence between the morphological and molecular evidence argues for the correctness of the phylogeny presented herein.

The DNA Hybridization Evidence

The UPGMA dendrograms (Figs. 369–372) have been referred to above. The melting curves in Fig. 202 (*Furnarius*) include representatives of some of the groups in the Tyrannides. The furnariids are in expected positions, the tapaculo is closer to the homoduplex than is the gnateater, which does not agree with the UPGMA dendrogram, although the branches are not far apart. As expected, the tyrannids cluster with one another.

Fig. 203 (*Conopophaga*) is quite distant from all heteroduplex curves and the sequence of curves does not agree completely with the UPGMA tree, but the tapaculo is close to the gnateater tracer, and the tyrannids are most distant.

Fig. 204 (*Scytalopus*) had a poor tracer, but the sequence of curves agrees fairly well with the UPGMA tree.

Fig. 205 (*Liosceles*) also had a poor tracer. The relative positions of the curves indicate that the furnariids are closest to the tapaculos, as did Fig. 204. The tyrannids and thamnophilids are most distant, as in the UPGMA tree.

The FITCH tree (Fig. 345) agrees with the melting curves and with the UPGMA trees. The ovenbirds (*Furnarius*) and woodcreepers (*Dendrocolaptes*) cluster together, as do the two tapaculos (*Liosceles, Scytalopus*), the gnateater (*Conopophaga*), and the ground-antbird (*Formicarius*). The typical antbird (*Thamnophilus*) is distant from the genera listed above.

We conclude that the ovenbirds, woodhewers, gnateaters, and tapaculos are more closely related to one another than any one of them is to the tyrannids or thamnophilids. When considered in combination with the data for the Tyrannidae, it is clear that the New World suboscines must be an ancient radiation that occurred while South America was isolated from other continents during the Tertiary. The Tyrannides are next most closely related to the Eurylaimides; the divergence at $\Delta T_{50}H$ 15.8 may have been a result of the opening of the Atlantic in the late Cretaceous, but this is speculation without evidence.

The Oscines or Songbirds: Suborder Passeri (Passeres)

The Passeri have a diacromyodian syrinx (the intrinsic syringeal muscles are attached to both ends of the bronchial half rings). Most oscines have more than three pairs of intrinsic syringeal muscles, but the lyrebirds (*Menura*) have three pairs and the scrub-birds (*Atrichornis*) have three, plus a few fibers representing a fourth pair (Sibley 1974:73). The DNA-DNA evidence indicates that these departures from the condition in the other oscines are derived states that evolved after the lyrebird–scrub-bird clade branched from the other Passeres.

In our classification the suborder Passeri contains 4561 species in 870 genera. Bock and Farrand (1980) counted 4177 species in 823 genera. Sharpe (1901, 1903, 1909) recognized 49 families in his suborder "Acromyodi," or 50 if the Menuridae is included. E. Stresemann (1934) recognized 49 families, Mayr and Amadon (1951) 36 families, Mayr and Greenway (1956) 40, Amadon (1957) 42, Delacour and Vaurie (1957) 39, Wetmore (1960) 54, and Wolters (1975–82) 91. We include the same taxa in 35 families, but we recognize many of the families of other classifications as subfamilies and tribes, and at least eight families not usually defined (Sibley and Ahlquist 1982e–h, 1985a,c; Sibley et al. 1984b, 1988).

Beecher (1953b) developed a phylogeny of the oscines based mainly on the jaw musculature and other characters of the head. He proposed some radical changes in the traditional concepts of oscine relationships which were not widely accepted. Mayr (1955) acknowledged the importance of Beecher's work, but was critical of his assumptions about the significance of the characters used and the logic of Beecher's arguments. Some of Beecher's conclusions agree with the DNA data, others do not. We will refer to his work throughout this section.

The Major Subdivisions of the Passeri

Suborder PASSERI (Oscines)
  Parvorder Corvida (formerly Corvi)
    Superfamily Menuroidea
    Superfamily Meliphagoidea
    Superfamily Corvoidea

Parvorder Passerida (formerly Muscicapae)
  Superfamily Muscicapoidea (formerly Turdoidea)
  Superfamily Sylvioidea
  Superfamily Passeroidea (formerly Fringilloidea)

The DNA data reveal two major groups within the Passeri which we recognize as the parvorders Corvida and Passerida, each subdivided into three superfamilies. In some previous publications these parvorders have been called "Corvi" and "Muscicapae." The Corvida and Passerida diverged at $\Delta T_{50}H$ 12.8. Most of the living Corvida are confined to Australasia and it seems apparent that the group originated and radiated in Australia because the oldest elements occur today only, or mainly, in Australia and New Guinea. These are the members of the superfamilies Menuroidea and Meliphagoidea, and most of the Corvoidea.

The superfamily Menuroidea includes the Menuridae (lyrebirds, scrub-birds), and Ptilonorhynchidae (bowerbirds). Sibley et al. (1984b) assigned the Climacteridae (tree-creepers) to the Menuroidea. We discuss this group below and question this assignment.

The Meliphagoidea is composed of the Maluridae (fairywrens, emuwrens, grasswrens), the Meliphagidae (honeyeaters), and the Pardalotidae (pardalotes, scrubwrens, thornbills, whitefaces, bristlebirds).

The Corvoidea includes the families Eopsaltriidae (Australo-Papuan "robins"), Irenidae (fairy-bluebirds, leafbirds), Orthonychidae (logrunners), Pomatostomidae (Australo-Papuan babblers), Laniidae (true shrikes: *Lanius, Corvinella, Eurocephalus*), Vireonidae (vireos, greenlets, shrike-vireos, peppershrikes), Corvidae (quail-thrushes, whipbirds, Australian Chough, Apostlebird, sittellas, *Mohoua, Finschia*, shrike-tits, *Oreoica, Rhagologus*, whistlers, shrike-thrushes, crows, jays, magpies, birds-of-paradise, *Melampitta*, currawongs, wood-swallows, Bornean Bristlehead, *Peltops*, orioles, cuckoo-shrikes, fantails, drongos, monarchs, magpie-larks, ioras, bushshrikes, helmetshrikes, *Batis, Platysteira*, vangas). The relationships of the Callaeatidae (New Zealand wattlebirds) are uncertain.

Many of the groups traditionally recognized as families are reduced to subfamilies or tribes.

The sister group of the Corvida, the parvorder Passerida, probably originated in Africa or Eurasia. Since the Corvida are oscines it is clear that they did not diverge from a South American suboscine group. The Passerida includes all of the oscine groups not members of the Corvida.

As Australia drifted closer to Asia during the Tertiary, representatives of some of the groups of Corvida dispersed to Asia and radiated there and in other parts of the world. In a reciprocal movement a few members of the Passerida have colonized Australia and New Guinea from Asia. The ancestor of the Vireonidae originated in Australia and may have reached South America via Antarctica.

Schodde (1975) listed 324 species of Australian passerines, of which 16 were introduced. Many of the 308 species occurring naturally may be defined as endemic, and ca. 242 (79%) qualify as "old endemics," i.e., they belong to lineages that almost certainly originated and radiated in Australia and New Guinea. In Schodde's list (1975) they are members of the Menuridae, Atrichornithidae, Muscicapidae, Orthonychidae, Timaliidae, Maluridae, Acanthizidae, Neosittidae, Climacteridae, Meliphagidae, Ephthianuridae, Pardalotidae, Paradisaeidae, Corcoracidae, Grallinidae, Artamidae, and Cracticidae.

There are ca. 433 species of passerines recorded from New Guinea and tropical Australia (Peckover and Filewood 1976) and at least 221 (51%) qualify as old endemics. There is some overlap between the species of Australia and New Guinea but at least 400 (57%) of the more than 700 species of Australo-Papuan passerines are old endemics. Beehler and Finch (1985) list 345 species of passerines from New Guinea. Approximately 274 (79%) of them are old endemics.

The determination of the taxonomic relationships of these birds, and their arrangement in a classification reflecting their phylogeny, has proved to be especially difficult. Convergent morphological characters have resulted in the clustering of Australo-Papuan species with groups based on European, Asian, and African types, thus obscuring the true relationships of the old endemic taxa. This problem has long been recognized (e.g., Storr 1958; Mayr 1963; Sibley 1970, 1974, 1976a,b; Schodde 1975; Schodde and McKean 1976; Boles 1979) but the available methods were often unsuccessful in differentiating between similarities due to common ancestry and those due to convergence.

Parvorder Corvida

Superfamily MENUROIDEA

Family MENURIDAE: 2/4. Lyrebirds and Scrub-birds.
Family PTILONORHYNCHIDAE: 7/20. Bowerbirds.

The two species of lyrebirds occur in forested areas of eastern Australia. Albert's Lyrebird (*Menura alberti*) is restricted to a small area in southeastern Queensland and northeastern New South Wales; the Superb Lyrebird (*M. novaehollandiae*) is fairly common from northeastern New South Wales, south to northeastern Victoria. It has been introduced in Tasmania.

The Superb Lyrebird was described by Latham (1802) from specimens taken near Sydney in 1798. The lyrebirds were often placed with the galliforms until Gould (1853) disposed of the galliform theory by describing the nest and the single egg. From 1853 to 1873 *Menura* was assigned to various places within the Passeriformes.

Garrod (1873d) proposed the arrangement that was to be accepted without serious debate for the next century. He based his classification on the thigh muscles at the higher levels, and on the plantar tendons, syringeal muscles, and arteries of the thigh for the subdivision of the Passeri. Garrod associated *Menura* with *Atrichornis* as the "Acromyodi Abnormales," and placed them next to the oscines, the "Acromyodi Normales." The syringeal differences between the two groups were the basis for Garrod's arrangement. Various categorical levels and relative positions in classifications were proposed during the next century, but in all arrangements *Menura* and *Atrichornis* were separated from the other passerines as the "Pseudoscines" (Sclater 1880b, Fürbringer 1888), the "Menuroideae" (Stejneger 1885), the "Menurae" (Sharpe 1891), the "Menuriformes" (Mathews 1927), or some other group name. Wetmore (1960) and Mayr and Amadon (1951) placed the "suborder Menurae" between the suboscines and the oscines. The consensus became that *Menura* and *Atrichornis* are aberrant, "primitive suboscines" whose nearest relatives are unknown.

Sibley (1974) reviewed the taxonomic history of the lyrebirds, including the anatomical, behavioral, and life history evidence pertinent to their relationships, and presented electrophoretic comparisons between the egg-white proteins of *Menura*, bowerbirds, and other groups of oscines and suboscines. Sibley (1974:78) interpreted "the total evidence to indicate that *Menura* is more closely related to the bowerbirds than to the birds-of-paradise" and recommended "that the suborder Menurae be dropped and that the Menuridae be placed next to the Ptilonorhynchidae in the suborder Passeres."

Feduccia (1975a) found that *Menura* has the "primitive" type of stapes typical of the oscines and concluded "that lyrebirds are oscine, and are likely close to the bowerbird–bird-of-paradise assemblage." The suboscines have a "derived" stapes "with an expanded bulbous footplate."

Although Feduccia (1975a) had concluded that *Menura* is an oscine, and not closely related to the New World suboscines, Feduccia and Olson (1982) interpreted certain similar anatomical characters as evidence of a relationship between the New World suboscine family Rhinocryptidae and the lyrebirds. The stapes of the rhinocryptid genus *Melanopareia* is of the "primitive" type, thus differing from those of "all other members of the suborder Tyranni for which the stapes is known." They also suggested that skeletal differences between *Menura* and the bowerbirds proved that the two groups are unrelated.

Morphological similarities do not always indicate genetic relationship, and morphological differences do not prove lack of relationship. The rhinocryptids are members of the New World suboscine suborder Tyranni; the lyrebirds are members of the oscine suborder Passeri. They are as far apart genealogically as any suboscine is from any oscine.

The relationships of the endemic New Zealand "thrush" (*Turnagra capensis*) were reviewed by Olson et al. (1983). Previous authors had assigned this species to several families including the Turdidae, Callaeatidae, Ptilonorhynchidae, and the monotypic Turnagridae. Olson et al. (1983) examined the external structure, pterylosis, myology, and osteology and concluded that *Turnagra* "belongs in the bird-of-paradise/bowerbird assemblage and is not closely related to the Pachycephalinae. *Turnagra* appears to be the most primitive member of this assemblage, sharing similarities both with the paradisaeid subfamily Cnemophilinae and with the Ptilonorhynchidae." Since *Turnagra* is probably extinct we cannot expect to obtain its DNA, but the DNA hybridization evidence that the bowerbirds and birds-of-paradise are not closely related suggests that *Turnagra* may be most closely related to one of these two groups, but not to both.

Raikow (1985a) compared the limb musculature of the Noisy Scrub-bird (*Atrichornis clamosus*) with that of the Superb Lyrebird (*Menura novaehollandiae*). He concluded that "The appendicular myology strongly corroborates the close affinity" of these two genera, but that the "limb muscle characters neither corroborate nor refute the hypothesis" that the lyrebirds are most closely related to the bowerbirds. Raikow found that the "Menurae possess a number of distinctive myological conditions not otherwise known in passerines, and therefore it is impossible to suggest another group with which they might share a more recent common ancestry than with the bowerbirds" (1985a:221–222).

Rich et al. (1985) compared the skeletons of *Atrichornis* and *Menura* with one another and with the descriptions of the skeletons of the Rhinocryptidae by Feduccia and Olson (1982). Rich et al. (1985:165) noted that "a suite of characters shared by *Menura* and *Atrichornis*, hitherto used to relate the Menurae to the Rhinocryptidae, are also shared by several other genera of birds from a variety of families. We suggest that these characters indicate convergence towards a terrestrial lifestyle and should not be used to indicate phylogenetic proximity."

Bock and Clench (1985) summarized the results of a morphological study of the Noisy Scrub-bird (*A. clamosus*) and concluded that *Atrichornis* and *Menura* are each other's closest relatives and form a monophyletic group of unknown affinities within the oscines.

The DNA-DNA measurements support the conclusion of Sibley (1974) that the lyrebirds and scrub-birds are most closely related to the bowerbirds, thus disagreeing with the conclusion of Feduccia and Olson (1982) that the lyrebirds and bowerbirds are unrelated. The Menuridae and Ptilonorhynchidae diverged at Δ $T_{50}H$ 9.9, *Menura* and *Atrichornis* diverged at Δ 7.8, and the divergence between the Passeri (including the Menuroidea) and the Tyranni (including the Rhinocryptidae) occurred at Δ 19.7.

THE BOWERBIRD–BIRD-OF-PARADISE RELATIONSHIP

"Their colorful plumage, bizarre courtship habits, and restriction to the Australian-Papuan region are usually cited as evidence for close affinities between these groups; indeed, until recently, the birds of paradise and the bower birds were usually placed in the same family or subfamily, the belief being that a sharp dividing line could not be drawn between typical birds of paradise, such as *Paradisaea*, and typical bower birds, such as *Ptilonorhynchus*" (Bock 1963b:91).

Stonor (1936, 1937, 1938) studied the skull morphology and other characters of these groups and concluded (1937) that they are not closely related to one another. Stonor (1937) advocated separate families for the two groups and contended that the bowerbirds are an isolated family with no close relationship to any other oscine family. Bock (1963b) reviewed previous studies and compared the skulls of all genera of bowerbirds and birds-of-paradise. Bock stated that "Although the bower birds are morphologically quite distinct from the true birds of paradise, they are related to them through the cnemophilines" (p. 122), and he concluded that "The Paradisaeidae and the Ptilonorhynchidae are assumed to be closely related, which is supported, although not fully proven, by the cranial evidence" (p. 124). Bock (1963b:117–118) made "the assumption" that the two groups "have both evolved from the same immediate common ancestor, and are, hence, more closely allied to one another than to any other group of passerine birds." He decided that "they should be maintained as separate families because their morphological differences are sufficient to justify familial status under the present concepts of passerine classification" (p. 118).

Although Sibley (1974:78) had concluded that *Menura* is more closely related to the bowerbirds than to the birds-of-paradise, he thought that "all three groups are members of a single natural cluster."

Thus, it was a surprise to find that the DNA-DNA data show that the bowerbirds and birds-of-paradise are not closely related. Instead, the birds-of-paradise are members of the superfamily Corvoidea and are most closely related to the Australo-Papuan magpies, currawongs, and butcherbirds (Artamini) (Δ 6.0), the Old World orioles and cuckoo-shrikes (Oriolini) (Δ 6.0), and the crows, jays, and magpies (Corvini) (Δ 6.2), as indicated in Figs. 369 and 370. The lineages leading to the bowerbirds and birds-of-paradise diverged at Δ $T_{50}H$ 11.7. Each group has many relatives more closely related to it than they are to one another.

Family CLIMACTERIDAE

2/7. Australo-Papuan Treecreepers. Six species of treecreepers occur in Australia and one (*placens*) in New Guinea. They are similar in form, coloration, and behavior to the Northern Hemisphere tree-creepers (*Certhia*), the Philippine creepers (*Rhabdornis*), and the Afro-Asian Spotted Creeper (*Salpornis*), and various combinations of these genera have been associated in traditional classifications, e.g., Wetmore (1960) placed these genera in the Certhiidae. Mayr and Amadon (1951) expressed their uncertainty, but placed *Salpornis*, *Rhabdornis*, *Climacteris*, and the Wallcreeper (*Tichodroma*) in the subfamily "Salporninae" of the Sittidae, and only *Certhia* in the Certhiidae. Some recent authors have isolated *Climacteris* in the family Climacteridae (e.g., Greenway 1967, Schodde 1975).

Although recognized as an old endemic Australo-Papuan group, the relationships of the Climacteridae within that assemblage have remained uncertain. Mayr (1963) suggested that the color pattern of *Climacteris* "is least unlike" those of *Acanthiza*, *Sericornis*, and *Gerygone*, and the honeyeaters were favored as their closest relatives by C. J. O. Harrison (1969c) and S. A. Parker (1982).

Orenstein (1977) conducted an extensive behavioral study of the treecreepers, including comparisons with the other "creepers" and "nuthatches." He found *Climacteris* to be distinctive in many ways, and concluded that "separate family status . . . seems warranted, but the question of its affinities still remains" (p. 223). Orenstein noted that "the presence of m. 'iliofemoralis externus' in *Climacteris* suggests an affinity with the Paradisaeidae, Ptilonorhynchidae and Callaeidae, which according to the leg-muscle dissections of S. R. Borecky (pers. comm.) appear to form a complex with the Grallinidae and Cracticidae, and possibly other families of presumed sturnid derivation."

The only relevant part of this statement is that *Climacteris* shares the named muscle with the bowerbirds. As discussed above, the bowerbirds and birds-of-paradise are not closely related. The affinities of the New Zealand wattlebirds (Callaeatidae) are unknown, and the starlings (Sturnidae) are members of the parvorder Passerida (Sibley and Ahlquist 1984b), thus they were not involved in the ancestry of the groups mentioned by Orenstein.

Orenstein (1977:224–228) questioned the characters used by Harrison (1969c) as evidence of a relationship between treecreepers and honeyeaters, and concluded that "*Climacteris* may represent a distinct branch of a major Australian radiation, sharing characteristics of meliphagids, acanthizids and birds of paradise." The DNA evidence shows that the Meliphagidae and "Acanthizidae" (Pardalotidae) are members of the superfamily Meliphagoidea, and the "Paradisaeidae" (Corvidae, Corvinae, Paradisaeini) are members of the Corvoidea, thus indicating that the characters used by Orenstein as the basis for his conclusion are primitive in the sense of Hennig (1966), and therefore of limited value for the determination of the relationships of the treecreepers.

The DNA Hybridization Evidence

The DNA data produced a surprising answer for they suggest that the treecreepers are the descendants of the oldest known branch in the Menuroidea at $\Delta T_{50}H$ 10.4 (Sibley et al. 1984b).

Climacteris is morphologically distinct from the lyrebirds and bowerbirds, although it is similar to *Atrichornis* in size, coloration, bill shape, and nasal opercula. These superficial characters may mean little but they suggest that a search for additional anatomical evidence might be fruitful.

One character, possibly unique to the treecreepers, is their syndactylous foot structure. Anterior digits two and three are bound together by skin to the end of the first phalanx on digit two, and digits three and four are joined to the base of the third phalanx on digit four. This condition of the forward toes apparently allows them to act in concert with the hallux as the birds creep on the trunks and branches of trees.

Sibley et al. (1984b) recognized the genus *Cormobates* for *leucophaea* and *placens*, and *Climacteris* for *picumnus*, *rufa*, *melanura*, *erythrops*, and *affinis*.

The Δ $T_{50}H$ distance values from and to *Climacteris* and other groups of Australo-Papuan oscines indicated that the treecreepers are most closely related to the bowerbirds; 21 comparisons gave an average Δ $T_{50}H$ of 10.4; for comparisons with the Meliphagoidea, 33 delta values averaged 12.1; for the Corvoidea, 46 delta values averaged 11.9. When the 79 values to the Meliphagoidea and Corvoidea were combined, the average was 12.0. Eight delta values between *Climacteris* and members of the Passerida averaged 13.6. These data convinced us that the Climacteridae are most closely related to the bowerbirds, hence also to the lyrebirds and scrub-birds. We therefore assigned the Climacteridae to the Menuroidea.

The melting curves and the new evidence of the correlation between age at maturity and the average rate of genomic evolution suggest that we may have been misled by the delta values.

Fig. 206 (*Menura*) had a poor tracer, but the curves seem to be good. The two lyrebirds are close together, as expected, the scrub-bird is next, and three bowerbirds follow, with three birds-of-paradise, a crow, and the Green Broadbill completing the sequence. We conclude from these curves that the scrub-birds and bowerbirds are more closely related to the lyrebirds than are the other taxa in the set.

Fig. 207 (*Ptilonorhynchus*) had a good tracer; the four species of bowerbirds show their close affinities and the Superb Lyrebird is next in line, followed by a bird-of-paradise, then the other lyrebird (*M. alberti*), two more birds-of-paradise, and a crow. These sets include only the species involved in the question of the closest relatives of the bowerbirds: lyrebirds or birds-of-paradise? We conclude that the bowerbirds are closer to the lyrebirds than to the birds-of-paradise, but it is clear that the differences are not great.

Fig. 208 (*Climacteris*) addresses the question of the relationships of the treecreepers. The two closest heteroduplex curves to the homoduplex are bowerbirds, then the two lyrebirds, followed by two members of the Meliphagoidea (*Gerygone*, *Conopophila*), and the Common Tree-Creeper (*Certhia familiaris*). It is clear that *Climacteris* is not closely related to *Certhia*, thus disposing of this question. It also seems likely that *Climacteris* is closer to the bowerbirds and lyrebirds than to the members of the Meliphagoidea.

Fig. 209 (*Climacteris*) has a good tracer and the two species of *Climacteris* show that the curves are good. The next nearest curve is a bowerbird, followed by a whistler (Corvoidea), a monarch (Corvoidea), a crow (Corvoidea), an Australo-Papuan babbler (Corvoidea), Logrunner (Corvoidea), fantail (Corvoidea), Australian robin (Corvoidea), and two members of the Meliphagoidea (*Acanthiza*, *Malurus*). From these curves we must conclude that *Climacteris* is more closely related to the Corvoidea than to the Meliphagoidea, but what about the bowerbirds? Here we must consider the possibility that different rates of DNA evolution may be complicating the picture. It is known that Superb Lyrebird males do not develop full lyrate tails until they are at least 2–5, and possibly 6 or 7, years of age (Table 16; Lill 1985). Females are thought to commence breeding much earlier. Thus, lyrebirds may be expected to have a relatively slower average genomic rate than the small species of the Meliphagoidea and Corvoidea. We have found no information about the age at maturity of bowerbirds.

More complications. *Climacteris* species are communal breeders, but *Cormobates* species breed as single pairs (Orenstein 1985). Communal breeders tend to begin to breed later in life than do single-pair species. Thus, we may assume (or speculate) that *Climacteris* species have delayed maturity. These facts and assumptions suggest that the curves of the lyrebirds may be closer to the homoduplexes in Fig. 208 than would be the curves of a species that begins to breed at one or two years of age, such as many of the Meliphagoidea and Corvoidea. If *Chlamydera* is a delayed breeder, it is possible that its melting curve in Fig. 209 is closer to *Climacteris* because it is evolving more slowly than *Pachycephala*, for example.

The FITCH tree in Fig. 346 shows that the Menuroidea have shorter branches, and presumably slower rates of genomic evolution, than the members of the Meliphagoidea (*Pardalotus* to *Malurus*). It is unclear why the lyrebirds and bowerbirds do not cluster as a group and the problem is complicated by too few comparisons involving *Menura*. When *Climacteris* is used as a driver the distances tend to be large, as indicated by its position in Fig. 346.

Although our present data indicate that the climacterids are most closely related to the lyrebirds and bowerbirds, we suggest that a re-examination of the relationships of the Climacteridae is appropriate.

We conclude that the bowerbirds and lyrebirds are more closely related to one another than either is to any other group, and that the relationships of the Climacteridae remain uncertain.

Superfamily MELIPHAGOIDEA 63/276.

Family MALURIDAE: 5/26.

Subfamily MALURINAE: 4/18.
  Tribe MALURINI: 3/15. Fairywrens, Treewrens, Russetwrens.
  Tribe STIPITURINI: 1/3. Emuwrens.
Subfamily AMYTORNITHINAE: 1/8. Grasswrens.

Most recent classifications of Australian passerines place the Australo-Papuan fairywrens and their closest relatives in the family Maluridae. The Australian malurids usually consist of eight species of fairywrens (*Malurus*), two species of emuwrens (*Stipiturus*), and eight species of grasswrens (*Amytornis*) (Parker in Schodde 1975). In New Guinea, Rand and Gilliard (1968) and Peckover and Filewood (1976) listed one species each of *Malurus*, *Clytomyias*, and *Chenorhamphus*, and two species of *Todopsis*.

Schodde and Weatherly (1982a) proposed a modified classification of the Maluridae in which they recognized 26 species in five genera, as follows:

1. Treewrens. One species, *Sipodotus* (*Todopsis*) *wallacii*.

2. Fairywrens. 14 species of *Malurus*, including "*Todopsis*" *cyanocephala* and "*Chenorhamphus*" *grayi*.

3. Russetwrens. *Clytomyias insignis*.

4. Grasswrens. Eight species of *Amytornis*.

5. Emuwrens. Two species of *Stipiturus*.

Schodde and Weatherly (1982b) described *Malurus campbelli* as a new species from New Guinea. Beehler and Finch (1985) followed Schodde and Weatherly (1982a), but treated *M. campbelli* as a subspecies of *grayi*.

The relationships of the malurids to other groups of passerines are not obvious from external morphology, and during the past century various arrangements have been proposed. The most frequent has been to place the malurids with the Old World warblers in the Sylviidae, a family that has included almost any small, thin-billed, mainly insectivorous, ten-primaried oscine having an unspotted juvenal plumage. The malurids were considered to be sylviids by Sharpe (1903), R.A.O.U. Checklist Committee (1926), Mathews (1927–30), Berlioz (1950), Beecher (1953b), Berndt and Meise (1960), and Wetmore (1960). Some of these authors recognized a subfamily or tribe containing taxa in addition to the Australo-Papuan species. For example, Beecher (1953b) included *Gerygone*, *Petroica*, *Calamanthus*, and *Sericornis* of Australasia, and *Vitia* and *Lamprolia* of Fiji in his Malurini, which he considered to be a tribe in the Cisticolinae of the Sylviidae. Berndt and Meise (1960) also included *Vitia* and *Gerygone*, plus *Acanthiza*, *Ephthianura*, etc. in their Malurinae.

Another frequent arrangement merges several groups of "primitive insect-eaters" into a family, Muscicapidae, following Hartert (1910), who was unable to separate the muscicapine and monarchine flycatchers, the sylviines, babblers, and thrushes from one another. Mayr and Amadon (1951) used the Muscicapidae in this broad sense, and included within it the "Malurinae" for 85 species of "Australian Warblers," including several New Zealand and Polynesian taxa.

C. J. O. Harrison and Parker (1965) proposed that *Malurus*, *Stipiturus*, the New Guinea malurids, and the Fijian Silktail (*Lamprolia*) are babblers and should be placed in the Timaliidae. The malurids were considered to be timaliids because they share some behavioral characteristics, and *Lamprolia* because Beecher (1953b) had included it in his Malurini. Harrison (1969a) found an interscapular apterium in the dorsal tract of the six malurine genera and concluded that this linked them together, but excluded *Lamprolia*. Harrison (1969a) also suggested that the behavior of *Amytornis* is like that of the babblers and, since Harrison and Parker (1965) had "shown that the behaviour of *Malurus* . . . was like that of babblers," all six genera "should be regarded as an Australasian subfamily or tribe of the babblers, Timaliidae."

The suggestion by Harrison and Parker (1965) and Harrison (1969a) that the malurids are babblers is clearly wrong, and it illustrates the difficulties involved in the interpretation of behavioral and morphological characters as clues to genealogical relationships.

The genus *Sylvia* and a few other genera are closely related to the babblers (Sibley and Ahlquist 1980, 1982b, 1985a,c, 1985d), and *Lamprolia* is a monarch (Olson 1980; Sibley and Ahlquist 1985a:9, Fig. 3).

Several classifications have included a family Maluridae, but the compositions have varied, although all have included the true malurids. Serventy and Whittell (1967) added the Australian "warblers" such as *Gerygone*, *Acanthiza*, *Sericornis*, *Aphelocephala*, *Dasyornis*, etc. Condon (1969) added only *Dasyornis*, but Macdonald (1973) and Parker (in Schodde 1975) restricted the Maluridae to the true members. McGill (1970) reviewed various classifications and declined to choose among them, but S. A. Parker (1971), in his review of McGill's book, favored a Maluridae composed of the typical genera.

The DNA Hybridization Evidence (Figs. 210, 211, 346, 374, 375)

The single-copy tracer DNA of the Variegated Fairywren (*Malurus lamberti*) was compared with the driver DNAs of two other species of *Malurus*, one *Stipiturus*, one *Amytornis*, and members of the Pardalotidae, Meliphagidae, Eopsaltriidae, a bowerbird, fantail, monarchs, whistlers, sittellas, quail-thrush, bird-of-paradise, muscicapines, and typical sylviids, including *Sylvia* and *Phylloscopus* (Sibley and Ahlquist 1982h).

The results are summarized in Figs. 374, 375. It is apparent that the Maluridae includes only the fairywrens, emuwrens, and grasswrens; that the sister group of the malurids is the meliphagid-pardalotid clade; that the Corvoidea and Menuroidea of the Corvida are the next nearest lineages; and that the Passerida, which includes the Sylviidae and the Muscicapinae, is the sister group of the Corvida. Thus, the malurids are not closely related to the sylviids or the muscicapines; they are members of the old endemic element of the Australo-Papuan oscine radiation.

The melting curves in Fig. 210 (*Malurus*) show the same relationships described above.

Family MELIPHAGIDAE

42/182. Honeyeaters, Australian Chats. Most of the species of honeyeaters occur in Australia and New Guinea and the group obviously originated and radiated in Australia. The present range includes New Zealand, many South Pacific islands, Hawaii, Polynesia (east to Samoa and Tonga), and Micronesia. One species occurs on Bali, another in the Bonin Islands. *Cleptornis marchei*, of Saipan Island, is a zosteropid, not a meliphagid.

Most of the meliphagids are nectarivores and the "most striking family character is the brush-tongue . . . in its structure notably different from that in other groups with similar habits. The tongue is prolonged and protrusible; the basal part is curled up on each side, forming two long grooves; the distal part is deeply cleft into four parts, which on their edges are delicately frayed and together form the 'brush' which licks up the nectar. In spite of much variation and secondary changes the basic characters of the tongue are present in all members of the family" (Salomonsen in Thomson 1964:374).

Nectar-adapted tongues have evolved in several groups of the Passeri, including the Nectariniidae (sunbirds, flowerpeckers, sugarbirds), Paramythiidae (tit berrypeckers), Melanocharitidae (berrypeckers), Zosteropidae (white-eyes), Timaliini (babblers), *Chloropsis* (leafbirds), Thraupini (tanagers), Drepanidini (Hawaiian honeycreepers), Estrildinae (*Zonaeginthus oculatus*), *Artamus* (wood-swallows), Parulini (wood warblers), Icterini (troupials), and some Ploceinae (weaverbirds). For some of these groups there is merely a tendency, in a few species, toward a nectar-adapted tongue, but it is clear that convergence has produced such tongues in many groups of oscine passerines.

In many classifications the nectarivorous groups have been placed together, either as members of a single family, or next to one another in a linear list. For example, Wetmore (1960) listed the Meliphagidae, Nectariniidae, Dicaeidae, and Zosteropidae in sequence. Mayr and Amadon (1951) included the same groups under the heading of "Old World Nectar Eaters," but expressed their uncertainties about the actual relationships among them. For reviews of some of the literature see Sibley (1970:81) and Sibley and Ahlquist (1974).

A persistent problem in the classification of nectarivorous birds concerns the southern African genus *Promerops*, the sugarbirds, which have been thought to be allied to the meliphagids by some authors. This problem is discussed under the Nectariniidae.

The DNA Hybridization Evidence (Figs. 211–214, 346–348, 374)

The Meliphagidae, including *Ephthianura* and *Ashbyia*, consists of the species long accepted as Australasian honeyeaters. The lineage branched from the pardalotid clade at Δ $T_{50}H$ 9.2. The honeyeaters are the most numerous, in species and individuals, of the old endemic groups of Australo-Papuasia, and it seems clear that the group originated and radiated in Australia and New Guinea.

The DNA data indicate that the Australian chats, *Ephthianura* and *Ashbyia*, are more closely related to such typical honeyeaters as *Ramsayornis*, *Prosthemadera*, *Anthochaera*, *Phylidonyris*, and *Entomyzon* than are such unquestionable meliphagids as *Certhionyx* and *Myzomela*. Evidence that *Ephthianura* and *Ashbyia* are honeyeaters has also been reported by Sibley (1970:73, 1976b:566) and S. A. Parker (1973).

Fig. 211 (*Anthochaera*). The Red Wattlebird is a meliphagid, and these melting curves show that the honeyeaters are more closely related to such corvoid genera as *Acanthiza*, *Corcorax*, *Grallina*, and *Corvus* than to the nectariniid genus *Dicaeum*.

Fig. 212 (*Anthochaera*) shows that *Ephthianura* and *Ashbyia* are honeyeaters, and indicates the relative positions of the Pardalotidae and Maluridae to the Meliphagidae.

Fig. 213 (*Anthochaera*) shows that the honeyeaters are more closely related to the other corvoids (*Corvus*, *Piezorhynchus*) than to the passeroids (*Parus* to *Motacilla*). The sunbirds are members of the Passeroidea.

Fig. 214 (*Ephthianura*) shows that the Australian chats (*Ephthianura*, *Ashbyia*) are honeyeaters, as are the Tui and the Western Spinebill.

Family PARDALOTIDAE

16/68. Australo-Papuan Warblers and allies. In previous publications we have used Acanthizidae for this family, but Pardalotidae has priority. Fig. 375 shows the branching sequence of some of the genera we include in the Pardalotidae.

The pardalotes (*Pardalotus*) have usually been viewed as relatives of the flowerpeckers (Dicaeini), which are members of the Nectariniidae of the parvorder Passerida. The bristlebirds (*Dasyornis*) are also members of the Pardalotidae. We recognize the subfamilies Pardalotinae (1/4), Dasyornithinae (1/3), and Acanthizinae (14/61).

The Acanthizinae are not related to the Sylviidae, but are members of an old endemic Australo-Papuan group that includes *Acanthiza* (thornbills), *Sericornis* (scrubwrens), *Acanthornis* (Scrubtit), *Crateroscelis* (mouse-babblers), *Oreoscopus* (Fernwren), *Chthonicola* (Speckled Warbler), *Hylacola* (heathwrens), *Pyrrholaemus* (Redthroat), *Calamanthus* (fieldwrens), *Smicrornis* (weebills), *Gerygone* (Australian warblers), *Aphelocephala* (whitefaces), *Origma* (Rock Warbler), and *Pycnoptilus* (Pilotbird).

Schodde (1975) included *Acanthornis*, *Hylacola*, *Pyrrholaemus*, *Calamanthus*, and *Chthonicola* in *Sericornis*. The DNA distance values do not support the inclusion of all these taxa in a single genus, but our limited data do not provide the basis for a conclusion about their generic relationships. However, our data suggest that the genera that Schodde (1975) included in *Sericornis* form a tribe Sericornithini (10/26) that is separable from the Acanthizini (4/35) at Δ T$_{50}$H 5.0, as shown in Fig. 375.

Olson (1987) assigned the Papuan genus *Amalocichla* to the "Acanthizidae" on the basis of characters of the humerus, external morphology, and habits.

Some of these relationships were vaguely suggested by the electrophoretic patterns of the egg-white proteins (Sibley 1976b:567).

The DNA Hybridization Evidence (Figs. 215–218, 346, 369, 374, 375)

We lack the DNAs of such genera as *Vitia*, *Cichlornis*, and *Ortygocichla*, but we doubt that these will prove to be sylviids. However, the New Caledonian Grassbird (*Megalurulus mariei*) is probably a member of the sylviid cluster that includes *Megalurus* (incl. *Bowdleria* of New Zealand), *Eremiornis*, and *Cincloramphus*.

Fig. 215 (*Pardalotus*) shows that *Pardalotus* is more closely related to the other corvoid genera (*Sericornis* to *Malurus*) than to the passeroids (*Prionochilus*, *Zosterops*, *Dicaeum*). *Pardalotus*, *Prionochilus*, and *Dicaeum* have usually been placed together in a family Dicaeidae. The DNA evidence shows that *Dicaeum* and *Prionochilus* are nectariniids (Passerida) and the pardalotes are members of the Corvida. *Zosterops* is a member of the Sylvioidea.

Fig. 215 (*Sericornis*) shows the relationships among some of the genera of the Pardalotidae (*Sericornis* to *Acanthiza*), and between the Pardalotidae and the Meliphagidae (*Ephthianura*), Maluridae (*Amytornis*), and Sylviidae (*Eremiornis*). *Eremiornis* is one of the few true sylviids confined to Australia.

Fig. 217 (*Acanthiza*) shows that the Pardalotidae (*Acanthiza*, *Sericornis*) are distant from the Corvidae (*Dendrocitta*, *Terpsiphone*), but more closely related to the corvids than to the members of the Passerida (*Toxostoma* to *Turdus*).

Fig. 218 (*Acanthiza*) shows the relationships between the pardalotids (*Acanthiza*, *Smicrornis*) and representatives of other groups of the Corvida (*Paradisaea* to *Climacteris*). Note that *Climacteris* and *Menura* are closest to one another, suggesting that they are equidistant from *Acanthiza*. This is relevant to the discussion above concerning the relationships of the Climacteridae. From this observation there is no evidence that *Menura* is evolving significantly more slowly than *Climacteris*.

The FITCH tree in Fig. 346 includes members of the principal groups of the Meliphagoidea. The branching pattern agrees with that of the UPGMA tree in Figs. 369, 374, and 375.

We conclude that the Pardalotidae are more closely related to other members of the Corvida than to any member of the Passerida, including the Nectariniidae. The Pardalotidae are one of the old endemic groups of Australia and New Guinea; their closest relatives are the honeyeaters, malurids, and corvoids. They are not closely related to the Sylviidae.

Superfamily CORVOIDEA

155/794. The Corvoidea includes the remaining old endemics of Australia and New Guinea, plus several groups presumably derived from corvoid ancestors that emigrated from Australia and radiated elsewhere, namely, the crows and ravens (*Corvus*), magpies (*Pica*), jays (e.g., *Garrulus*, *Cyanocitta*), etc. (Corvini); the orioles and cuckoo-shrikes (Oriolini); the bush-shrikes, helmetshrikes, and vangas (Malaconotinae); ioras (Aegithininae), vireos (Vireonidae), true shrikes (Laniidae), and the fairy-bluebirds and leafbirds (Irenidae).

The New Zealand wattlebirds (Callaeatidae) may also be corvoids, but we lack DNA of this group.

Family EOPSALTRIIDAE: 14/46. Australo-Papuan Robins and Flycatchers. The first branch in the corvoid phylogeny separated the ancestor of the Eopsaltriidae from that of the other corvoid groups at Δ T$_{50}$H 10.6 (Fig. 375). The FITCH tree (Fig. 347) also places the *Eopsaltria* as the first branch in the Corvoidea.

The Eopsaltriidae includes, at least, *Eopsaltria*, *Petroica*, *Melanodryas*, *Microeca*, *Tregellasia*, *Poecilodryas*, *Drymodes*, *Heteromyias*, *Monachella*, *Peneothello*, and *Pachycephalopsis*. *Eopsaltria* also occurs on New Caledonia and *Petroica* also occurs on many South Pacific islands, east to Samoa and Fiji. These genera are not related to the true thrushes (Turdinae), the Old World flycatchers (Muscicapinae), or the true babblers (Timaliini) (Sibley and Ahlquist 1980; 1982b,e; 1985a). Some other Australasian genera may be members of the Eopsaltriidae, but we lack their DNAs.

The scrub-robins (*Drymodes*) were usually considered to be thrushes or babblers by various authors. Sibley and Ahlquist (1982e) reviewed the taxonomic history of *Drymodes* and compared its DNA with those of the groups pertinent to the question of its relationships. *Drymodes* clustered with *Eopsaltria*, *Poecilodryas*, *Microeca*, and other members of the Corvoidea, and was distant from all members of the Passerida, including turdines and timaliines.

Syvanen (1987) suggested that "horizontal gene flow" between species, possibly as "virally mediated gene transfers," may account for the seeming conflict between morphological evidence and DNA hybridization evidence in the case of *Drymodes* and the sittellas (*Daphoenositta*). That this is erroneous is clear because *Drymodes* is morphologically unlike the thrushes and the sittellas differ in numerous ways from the nuthatches (*Sitta*). The problem has never been to find differences but to find evidence linking the Australo-Papuan endemics to their true relatives. Although "horizontal transfer" has been demonstrated to occur in a few cases, mainly in microorganisms, the percentage of the genome of a bird that would be affected by viral transfer from another species would be infinitesimal and the effect on the melting behavior (and delta values) of single-copy avian DNA would not be detectable.

Ames (1975) found a characteristic formation of the syringeal muscles in turdine thrushes and muscicapine flycatchers, which he called the "turdine thumb." This structure is not present in the Australo-Papuan robins and flycatchers (Eopsaltriidae). C. J. O. Harrison (1976) found that *Drymodes* lacks the turdine thumb and concluded that *Drymodes* "ought not to be included in either the typical thrushes, Turdinae, or the typical flycatchers, Muscicapini, but this evidence does not indicate where the true affinities lie." The DNA evidence agrees with the findings of Ames and Harrison, and shows that *Drymodes* is an eopsaltriid.

Fig. 219 (*Drymodes*) shows that *Drymodes* is more closely related to *Eopsaltria*, *Heteromyias*, and *Microeca* than to other members of the Corvida (*Monarcha* to *Xanthotis*), and that it is far from *Erithacus*, a member of the Passerida (Muscicapidae, Saxicolini).

Family IRENIDAE: 2/10. Fairy-bluebirds, Leafbirds. The fairy-bluebirds (*Irena*) occur in the lowlands of southern and southeastern Asia from India to Indonesia, southern China, and the Philippines. The Philippine form, *cyanogaster*, may be conspecific with *I. puella*. The eight species of leafbirds (*Chloropsis*) also occur in southeast Asia from India and southern China to Indonesia and the Philippines.

The fairy-bluebirds and leafbirds usually have been thought to be closely related to the ioras (*Aegithina*), but the DNA evidence reveals that the ioras (Aegithininae: Corvidae) are the sister group of the bushshrikes, helmetshrikes, and vangas at Δ T$_{50}$H 7.0. *Irena* and *Chloropsis* form the family Irenidae which is the sister group of the clade that includes the Orthonychidae, Pomatostomidae, Laniidae, Vireonidae, and Corvidae. The divergence between these families and the Irenidae was at Δ 10.2 (Fig. 375). The FITCH tree (Fig. 347) confirms the isolated position of *Irena*, but places it closer to the clade that includes *Vireo* and *Lanius* than to the clade that includes *Orthonyx* and *Pomatostomus*.

Fig. 220 (*Irena*) shows the relationship between *Irena* and *Chloropsis*, with other members of the Corvidae (*Colluricincla* to *Cracticus*) more distant. The curves of *Picathartes* and *Chaetops* are equidistant from that of *Irena*, suggesting that these two genera might be on the same branch of the tree. Additional evidence for this will be discussed below in connection with Figs. 251–253.

Fig. 221 (*Chloropsis*) shows the reciprocal position of the curve of *Irena*, and the relative distances to other genera of Corvida.

Family ORTHONYCHIDAE: 1/2. Logrunner and Chowchilla. The two species of *Orthonyx* occur in New Guinea and eastern Australia. They have been assigned to various families, most often to the Timaliidae or the Orthonychidae, usually accompanied by several other genera of uncertain affinities. For example, Deignan (1964) included eight Australo-Papuan genera in the subfamily Orthonychinae of the Muscicapidae, and Schodde (1975) combined *Orthonyx*, *Psophodes*, and *Cinclosoma* in his Orthonychidae. It is clear that *Orthonyx* has been a taxonomic puzzle.

The DNA comparisons show that the orthonychid lineage branched from the other corvoid lineages at Δ 10.0 (Fig. 375); we recognize the family Orthonychidae.

Family POMATOSTOMIDAE: 1/5. Australo-Papuan Babblers. The five species of *Pomatostomus* (including *Garritornis*), occur in Australia and New Guinea. Although usually thought to be timaliine babblers they are actually the descendants of an early branch in the Corvoidea and, therefore, they are Australo-Papuan old endemics. They are not related to the Sylviinae, which includes the true babblers (Timaliini).

The ancestor of the Pomatostomidae branched from the lineage that produced the living Corvidae at Δ 9.6 (Fig. 375). The FITCH tree (Fig. 347) indicates that *Pomatostomus* and *Orthonyx* are closest relatives. This may be true, but additional evidence is needed to confirm this possibility.

Family LANIIDAE: 3/30. True Shrikes. During the Tertiary Australia drifted north-ward. Possibly ca. 20–30 MYA, the ancestor of the Laniidae emigrated from Australia, probably to Asia. This event is recorded in the divergence between the Vireonidae and Laniidae at Δ T$_{50}$H 9.1 in Fig. 376. *Corvinella* and *Eurocephalus* occur only in Africa; *Lanius* probably radiated first in Africa and Eurasia and arrived more recently in North America, where *L. ludovicianus* ranges to southern Mexico.

Fig. 222 (*Lanius*) shows the nearest relatives of the Laniidae, including the vireos; all members of the Corvoidea.

Fig. 223 (*Lanius*) also includes members of the Corvoidea.

Fig. 224 (*Lanius*) shows the relationship of *Lanius* to several corvoid taxa, and the relative position of the Passerida (*Bombycilla* to *Melospiza*). The Malaconotinae (*Tephrodornis*, *Tchagra*), often included in the Laniidae, are farther from *Lanius* than are the drongos, orioles, and cuckoo-shrikes. Note that *Vireo* clusters with the Corvida, not with the Passerida.

Family VIREONIDAE: 4/51. Vireos, Greenlets, Peppershrikes, Shrike-Vireos. The 31 species of *Vireo* occur primarily in North America, but several species occur on Caribbean islands; one species has a subspecies in Bermuda, and two species occur as far south as Argentina. The 14 species of Neotropical greenlets (*Hylophilus*) are primarily South American; three occur in Central America, and one reaches southern Mexico. The four species of shrike-vireos (*Vireolanius*) range from southern Mexico to Bolivia, and the two species of peppershrikes (*Cyclarhis*) occur from southern Mexico to Uruguay.

Opinions about the relationships of the vireos have focused mainly on the Laniidae and the New World nine-primaried oscines, particularly the wood warblers (Parulini). The vireos have been thought to be related to the shrikes because the shrike-vireos have a shrike-like bill with a hooked tip and a subterminal notch in the maxillary tomium. The other vireonids have smaller, but similar, bills. The principal reason for placing the Vireonidae with the New World nine-primaried oscines has been the small size and coloration of the species of *Vireo*, and the tendency toward the reduction of the outer (10th) primary.

Sibley and Ahlquist (1982c) reviewed the taxonomic history of the vireos and compared the single copy tracer DNA of the Red-eyed Vireo (*V. olivaceus*) with the DNAs of other vireonids and with members of the Corvida and Passerida. The members of the Vireonidae clustered together with $\Delta T_{50}H$ values of 4.2 or less, the Corvida were between 7.5 and 9.4 (average 8.4; 8.8 in Fig. 376, based on 127 comparisons), and the Passerida from 10.7 to 13.5, average 12.0 (12.8 in Fig. 369).

Johnson et al. (1988) used starch gel electrophoresis to analyze the variation at 29 genetic loci in 20 species of four genera of the Vireonidae. Comparisons among the species demonstrated large genetic differences between some of the members of *Vireo* and *Hylophilus*, but the authors concluded that all vireonids could be included in a single subfamily. They also compared the vireonids with a corvid (*Pica pica*) and two species of paruline wood warblers (Emberizinae: Parulini), and agreed with Sibley and Ahlquist (1982c) that there is "a closer alliance of the vireos with the Corvidae than with the Emberizidae (specifically, the Parulinae)."

Thus, the family Vireonidae is a member of the Corvoidea. It is possible that the divergence from the Australian corvoids occurred as much as 30–40 MYA because the geological evidence indicates that the connection between South America and Antarctica was broken ca. 38–40 MYA. However, Johnson et al. (1988:443) estimated the corvid-vireonid split as ca. 16 MYA based on the genetic distance value between the two groups. Both estimates are tentative and subject to correction. Since all four genera occur in South America it seems likely that the group radiated there during the latter part of the Tertiary and that *Vireo* invaded North America after the establishment of the land connection via Central America in the Pliocene, ca. 5 MYA.

Fig. 225 (*Vireo*) shows the relationship of *Vireo* to *Cyclarhis* and *Hylophilus*, next to the corvids (*Pica*, *Coracina*), with the Passerida (*Phainopepla* to *Geothlypis*) most distant. These curves show that the vireos are not related to the wood warblers (Parulini: *Geothlypis*).

Fig. 347, the FITCH tree, places *Vireo* and *Pachycephala* as closest relatives among the taxa in this tree. This may be correct, but our data include few comparisons between these groups and additional data are needed to confirm or deny this possibility.

Family CORVIDAE: 127/647. Quail-thrushes, whipbirds, Australian White-winged Chough, Apostlebird, sittellas, New Zealand *Mohoua*, whistlers, shrike-tits, Crested Bellbird, pitohuis, shrike-thrushes, crows, jays, magpies, choughs, nutcrackers, birds-of-paradise, currawongs, Australian magpies, Australo-Papuan butcherbirds, wood-swallows, *Peltops*, Bornean Bristlehead, orioles, cuckoo-shrikes, fantails, drongos, monarchs, magpie-larks, ioras, bushshrikes, helmetshrikes, vangas, etc.

Possibly the most interesting and surprising result of the DNA comparisons of Australo-Papuan taxa is the discovery that the corvine birds of the world originated in Australia, and that most of them are still there or in nearby areas. The large assemblage listed above must be included in the family Corvidae if we are to observe the principle of categorical equivalence, but we must violate the principle of coordinate ranking for sister groups to avoid an excessive number of categorical ranks. To maintain the hierarchical relationship between the phylogeny and the classification we have used the principles of "subordination and sequencing" proposed by Nelson (1973) and discussed in chapter 16. The resulting classification reduces several morphologically distinctive groups to subfamilies and tribes but it is a reasonably accurate reflection of the phylogeny. If we were to inflate the ranks so that tribes became families the entire hierarchy would have to shift so much that some of the groups traditionally recognized as orders would become classes.

Subfamily CINCLOSOMATINAE: 6/15. The Cinclosomatinae includes the quail-thrushes (*Cinclosoma*), the three species of Papuan jewel-babblers (*Ptilorrhoa*), the Malaysian Rail-babbler (*Eupetes*), and the whipbirds and wedgebills (*Psophodes*). Sibley and Monroe (1990) assigned the Ifrit (*Ifrita kowaldi*) to this subfamily, but expressed doubt about its affinities. It may be a malurid. Deignan (1964) included most of these genera in the Orthonychinae (Muscicapidae) and Beehler and Finch (1985) followed Deignan. Peckover and Filewood (1976) list *Melampitta*, *Orthonyx*, *Androphobus*, and *Ifrita* in the Cinclosomatidae. We know that *Orthonyx* and *Melampitta* do not belong in this group, but we lack DNAs of *Androphobus* and *Ifrita*. The Cinclosomatinae branched from the other corvids at Δ T$_{50}$H 8.2 (Fig. 376).

Fig. 226 (*Cinclosoma*) shows the close relationship between *Cinclosoma* and *Ptilorrhoa*, with other members of the Corvida at greater distances from the homoduplex. The UPGMA tree (Fig. 376) and the KITSCH tree (Fig. 348) place *Cinclosoma* as the first branch in the Corvidae. The FITCH tree (Fig. 347) has *Cinclosoma* as the first branch of a clade that includes the Corvidae, Vireonidae, Laniidae, and Irenidae. This suggests that the Cinclosomatidae might be recognized as the sister group of these four families. This is a hypothesis to be tested by additional comparisons.

Subfamily CORCORACINAE: 2/2. White-winged Chough and Apostlebird. The White-winged Chough (*Corcorax*) and the Apostlebird (*Struthidea*) are closely related (Δ 4.4, Fig. 376). The Magpie-lark (*Grallina*) was often thought to be related to *Corcorax* and *Struthidea* because all three build mud nests and are Australian endemics (Amadon 1950b). *Grallina* is a monarch (Fig. 377).

The Corcoracinae diverged from the Pachycephalinae at Δ T$_{50}$H 7.8 (Fig. 376). The FITCH tree (Fig. 347) and the KITSCH tree (Fig. 348) cluster *Struthidea* next to *Corvus* and *Paradisaea*. The branches in this region of the phylogeny are close together, but are based on large numbers of comparisons. Although the stepwise branching pattern in Fig. 376 may not be statistically justified, we prefer to depict them as the average delta values indicate, rather than to merge several adjacent branches into a multifurcation. This does not change their taxonomic status, which is based on the $\Delta T_{50}H$ values.

Fig. 227 (*Struthidea*) shows the relationship between the Apostlebird and the Australian Chough, with other members of the Corvoidea next in the sequence, and the two bowerbirds (Menuroidea) farthest out. Note that *Grallina* is not close to *Struthidea*.

Subfamily PACHYCEPHALINAE: 14/59. The Pachycephalinae includes the sittellas (*Daphoenositta*), the endemic New Zealand Whitehead, Yellowhead, and Brown Creeper (*Mohoua*), the whistlers or thickheads (*Pachycephala*), shrike-thrushes (*Colluricincla*), Crested Bellbird (*Oreoica*), shrike-tits (*Falcunculus*), pitohuis (*Pitohui*), and the Mottled Whistler (*Rhagologus*). *Pachycare* of New Guinea and *Hylocitrea* of Celebes are, presumably, also members of this subfamily, but we lack their DNAs.

Most of the pachycephalines occur only in Australia and/or New Guinea, but members of the *Pachycephala pectoralis* group extend from Java and the Moluccas to Tasmania, the Loyalty Islands, New Caledonia, Tonga, Samoa, and Fiji (Galbraith 1956). The *P. caledonica* superspecies in Sibley and Monroe (1990) includes the *pectoralis* complex. The endemic New Zealand genera *Mohoua* and *Finschia* have been merged into *Mohoua* and we recognize the tribe Mohouini (1/3) (Sibley and Ahlquist 1987a).

The nuthatch-like sittellas (*Daphoenositta*) are the descendants of the earliest branch in the Pachycephalinae (Δ 6.9, Fig. 376) and we place them in the tribe Neosittini (1/2). Their nests, eggs, and immature plumages are similar to those of *Pachycephala*, which caused S. A. Parker (1982) to suggest that the sittellas "may have arisen . . . from the ancestors of the Pachycephalidae." Thus, the DNA evidence is congruent with the characters noted by Parker. The superficially similar nuthatches (*Sitta*) are members of the parvorder Passerida, super-family Sylvioidea (Sibley and Ahlquist 1982f,g).

The tribe Falcunculini (3/3) includes the shrike-tits (*Falcunculus*), the Crested Bellbird (*Oreoica*), and the New Guinea genus *Rhagologus*. The Pachycephalini (9/51) includes the whistlers (*Pachycephala*) and the shrike-thrushes (*Pitohui, Colluricincla*).

Fig. 228 (*Daphoenositta*) shows the relationship between the sittellas and *Pachycephala*, with other members of the Corvoidea next in line, and the lyrebird farthest away. Although the delayed maturity in *Menura* has caused a slowdown in the rate of DNA evolution (see Fig. 346), it is not obvious in these curves.

Fig. 229 (*Mohoua*) has a poor tracer, but the curves show the relationship of *Mohoua* to the pachycephalines (*Oreoica, Colluricincla, Falcunculus, Pachycephala*), with the monarchs, fantails, scrubwrens, and eopsaltriids more distant.

Fig. 230 (*Mohoua*) also shows the relationship between the New Zealand *Mohoua* and the corvids (*Rhagologus* to *Rhipidura*), with the meliphagoid *Acanthiza* next, and the two members of the Passerida (*Acrocephalus, Phylloscopus*) farthest away.

Fig. 231 (*Pachycephala*) includes five species of the Pachycephalinae (*Pachycephala* to *Falcunculus*), a monarch, and the more distant *Eopsaltria*.

The different clustering methods differ in the placement of the pachycephalines, but all put them close to the Corvinae and Dicrurinae. The FITCH tree (Fig. 347) places *Vireo* on the same clade as *Pachycephala*.

Subfamily CORVINAE: 56/297. Crows, jays, magpies, choughs, nutcrackers, birds-of-paradise, Australian magpies, currawongs, butcherbirds, wood-swallows, *Peltops*, Bornean Bristlehead, Old World orioles, cuckoo-shrikes.

The Corvinae includes six groups traditionally ranked as families: Corvidae, Paradisaeidae, Artamidae, Cracticidae, Oriolidae, and Campephagidae. That these groups should be so closely related is surprising but their most recent common ancestor diverged at $\Delta T_{50}H$ from the Dicrurinae, Aegithininae, and Malaconotinae (Figs. 377, 378).

The tribe Corvini includes the same taxa as the traditional Corvidae, namely, the ca. 25 genera and 117 species of crows, jays, magpies, nutcrackers, choughs, etc. Of these only the genus *Corvus* occurs in Australia and the close relationship between the Australian *C. mellori* and other species of *Corvus* outside of Australia (Fig. 378, *brachyrhynchos, albus*) indicates that the Australian species of *Corvus* are the descendants of recent colonists that have returned to the land of their ancestors.

The Paradisaeini includes only the birds-of-paradise (17/45). The earliest known branch produced a lineage represented today by the Lesser Melampitta (*Melampitta lugubris*) of New Guinea. This clade branched from the other birds-of-paradise at $\Delta T_{50}H$ 4.6 (Fig. 378). The forecrown feathers of the Lesser Melampitta are plush-like and iridescent, as in some other birds-of-paradise (Sibley and Ahlquist 1987b). The Greater Melampitta (*M. gigantea*), is one of the rarest New Guinea birds; only six specimens are known. Diamond (1983) described its plumage characters and compared the two species. Adults of both species seem to be all black; the young have areas of brown feathers. The size difference is indicated by their weights: 40–50 grams in *lugubris*, ca. 200 grams in *gigantea*. Diamond reported on some aspects of the behavior of *gigantea*, including its roosting and nesting in cavities in the walls of limestone sinkholes. The remiges and rectrices are stiffened, possibly serving to support the birds as they scurry up the rock faces of the narrow sinkholes. The flight feathers of specimens are worn, suggesting this explanation for their structure. It is not certain that the Greater Melampitta is closely related to the much smaller, common Lesser Melampitta, but we think it most probable that they are congeners (Sibley and Ahlquist 1987b).

The sexually monomorphic manucodes branched from the lineage that produced the dimorphic taxa at Δ 3.6 (Fig. 378), and the dimorphic taxa are closely related to one another. Between *Ptiloris paradiseus* and six other dimorphic genera the $\Delta T_{50}H$ values range from 0.8 to 1.2, indicating that these "genera" diverged from one another within the recent past. By our criteria all could be assigned to a single genus and it is not surprising that at least ten of the dimorphic genera have hybridized and produced viable offspring (Mayr 1942:260). The distinctive male plumages and displays evolved in response to sexual selection and selection against hybridization, and are additional evidence of their close relationships, not of phylogenetic diversity (Sibley 1957). Diamond (1972) proposed that the 20 genera of birds-of-paradise usually recognized could be reduced to 10. The DNA data suggest that even more "lumping" is justified.

Our tribe Artamini (6/24) is synonymous with all, or most, of the taxa placed in the Cracticidae of many authors. It includes the wood-swallows (*Artamus*), the currawongs (*Strepera*), Australian magpies (*Gymnorhina*), butcherbirds (*Cracticus*), *Peltops* of New Guinea, and the Bornean Bristlehead (*Pityriasis gymnocephala*). *Artamus* branched from the lineage leading to the other genera at Δ 4.9, and the Artamidae have been recognized as a monotypic family in all recent classifications. *Pityriasis* was placed with *Cracticus* and *Gym-*

norhina from its discovery in 1835 until recent years when some authors have placed it in the "Prionopidae." It is only Δ 4.4 (Fig. 378) from the other artamines. (The value of 4.1 in Ahlquist et al. 1984 was based only on one-directional comparisons.) The Papuan genus *Peltops* is also an artamine at Δ 3.5 from the typical genera. It usually has been thought to be a monarch (Sibley and Ahlquist 1984c).

Price and Emerson (1988) reported the occurrence of closely related species of the mallophagan genus *Menacanthus* on *Strepera versicolor* and on species of the traditional family Corvidae (our Corvini).

The tribe Oriolini (8/111) includes the Old World orioles ("Oriolidae") and the cuckoo-shrikes ("Campephagidae"). It was another surprise to discover that these two morphologically distinctive groups are so closely related. They diverged from one another at Δ T$_{50}$H 4.8. The orioles and cuckoo-shrikes in Australia and New Guinea are probably recent colonists.

Fig. 232 (*Corvus*) shows the relationships between *Corvus*, a jay, two birds-of-paradise, *Gymnorhina* (Artamini), a bowerbird, a honeyeater, and a New World suboscine tyrant flycatcher (*Pitangus*). The relative positions of the birds-of-paradise and the bowerbird support other evidence that these two groups are not closely related to one another, and that the Paradisaeini is closest to the Corvini and Artamini.

Fig. 233 (*Ptiloris*) depicts the relationships among three of the tribes of the Corvinae (Paradisaeini, Corvini, Artamini), and their relationship to the Menuroidea (bowerbirds and lyrebirds). This set of curves should settle the debate about whether the birds-of-paradise are more closely related to the corvids or to the bowerbirds. Indirectly, it also indicates that the bowerbirds and lyrebirds are closely related; at least they are shown to be equidistant from the bird-of-paradise homoduplex.

Fig. 234 (*Melampitta*) shows that the Lesser Melampitta is closer to the birds-of-paradise (*Manucodia*) than to the other corvoid groups represented. Fig. 235 includes additional comparisons between *Melampitta* and other groups. The same tracer was used in both experiments and *Manucodia* is closest to *Melampitta*. Once more, note the positions of *Chlamydera*, *Menura*, and *Climacteris*. The fact that they cluster together when compared to *Melampitta* does not prove that they are closely related to one another, only that they are equidistant from the homoduplex, which is true of closely related taxa.

Fig. 236 (*Peltops*) shows that *Peltops* is a member of the Artamini, and closely related to other members of the Corvidae.

Fig. 237 (*Peltops*) provides additional comparisons between *Peltops* and members of the Corvidae. The position of the Bornean Bristlehead is of special interest; this species was assigned to the Artamini by Ahlquist et al. (1984) on the basis of DNA hybridization evidence.

Fig. 238 (*Campephaga*) shows that the cuckoo-shrikes are members of the Corvidae, most closely related to the Old World orioles, birds-of-paradise, and artamines.

Subfamily DICRURINAE: 21/164. Fantails, drongos, monarchs, magpie-larks. Species of the Dicrurinae occur in Australia, New Guinea, many Pacific islands, southern Asia, and Africa. We have DNA hybridization data for *Monarcha*, *Arses*, *Myiagra*, *Hypothymis*, *Philentoma*, *Metabolus*, *Terpsiphone*, *Trochocercus*, *Lamprolia*, and *Chasiempis*, showing that all are monarchs. The only muscicapine flycatcher occurring in either Australia or New Guinea is *Muscicapa griseisticta*, which breeds in eastern Asia and is a winter visitor to New Guinea.

The magpie-larks, *Grallina cyanoleuca* and *G. bruijni*, are also monarchs. *G. cyanoleuca*, at Δ T$_{50}$H 2.9 from *Monarcha*, is barely a separate genus and is as close to *Monarcha* as are *Lamprolia* (3.3), *Trochocercus* (3.1), or *Chasiempis* (2.6) (Fig. 377). The monarchs are placed in the tribe Monarchini (18/98).

The drongos, *Dicrurus* and *Chaetorhynchus*, are an average Δ T$_{50}$H of 5.0 from *Monarcha* and *Grallina*. We place the drongos in the tribe Dicrurini (2/24).

The fantails (*Rhipidura*) are the sister group of the other monarchines from which they diverged at Δ 6.1. We recognize the tribe Rhipidurini (1/42).

Fig. 239 (*Rhipidura*) shows the distances between the Rhipidurini and the Monarchini (*Arses*, *Piezorhynchus*), Pachycephalinae (*Pachycephala*), Cinclosomatinae (*Cinclosoma*, *Falcunculus*), Pomatostomidae, and Eopsaltriidae (*Melanodryas*, *Monachella*).

Fig. 240 (*Monarcha*) shows that the paradise-flycatchers are monarchs, and that the Corvida (*Pomatostomus* to *Gerygone*) can be distinguished from the Passerida (*Turdus* to *Erithacus*). In some sets the members of these two groups overlap because of the variation in experimental error.

Fig. 241 (*Monarcha*) provides additional perspective on the relationships among the corvoids (*Grallina* to *Artamus*), the distance to the meliphagoids (*Xanthotis*), and to the Passerida (*Alophoixus* to *Acrocephalus*). The tight cluster of the three genera of the Passerida indicates equal branch lengths from *Monarcha* to three families of the Passerida: Pycnonotidae, Zosteropidae, and Sylviidae.

Fig. 242 (*Grallina*) shows that the Magpie-lark is most closely related to the monarchs, not to *Struthidea* and *Corcorax*. Note the out-group positions of *Orthonyx* (Orthonychidae) and *Monachella* (Eopsaltriidae).

Subfamily AEGITHININAE: 1/4. Ioras. The ioras occur in southeastern Asia from India and southern China to Indonesia and the Philippines. They often have been associated with the Irenidae, but the DNA comparisons indicate that they are the sister group of the Malaconotinae with the divergence at Δ T$_{50}$H 7.0 (Fig. 377; also see Figs. 347, 348). Fig. 243 (*Aegithina*) shows that *Aegithina* is more closely related to the monarchs, bushshrikes, drongos, and vireos, than to the fairy-bluebirds (*Irena*) and leafbirds (*Chloropsis*).

Subfamily MALACONOTINAE: 27/106. Bushshrikes, Boubous, Gonoleks, Tchagras, Puffbacks, Brubrus, Chatshrike, Helmetshrikes, Wattle-eyes, *Batis*, Woodshrikes, Philentomas, Vangas.

The African bushshrikes have long been recognized as different from the Laniidae and various treatments have been used to indicate the distinction. For example, White (1962:13) placed most of the bushshrikes in the Malaconotinae of the Laniidae. Benson et al. (1971:278) erected the family Malaconotidae to include *Nilaus*, *Dryoscopus*, *Tchagra*, *Laniarius*, *Malaconotus* (including *Telophorus*), "and perhaps *Lanioturdus*." They placed *Batis* and *Platysteira* in the "Monarchinae" of the "Muscicapidae."

Traylor (1970) discussed the African "Muscicapidae" and placed *Bias*, *Pseudobias*, *Batis*, and *Platysteira* in the "Platysteirinae," and *Erythrocercus*, *Elminia*, *Trochocercus*, and *Terpsiphone* in the "Monarchinae." *Melaenornis*, *Fraseria*, *Muscicapa*, *Myioparus*, *Humblotia*, and *Newtonia* were assigned to the "Muscicapinae." Traylor lumped *Dioptrornis*, *Bradornis*, *Empidornis*, and *Sigelus* in *Melaenornis*.

The DNA comparisons provide the basis for an intriguing hypothesis. About 30–35

MYA ($\Delta T_{50}H$ 7.2, Fig. 377) the ancestral species of the malaconotine and aegithinine lineages emigrated from Australia (or New Guinea), which by then had drifted quite close to Asia. Apparently this ancestral lineage branched soon thereafter ($\Delta T_{50}H$ 7.0). One branch produced the Aegithininae, the other soon divided again (Δ 6.5), and one of these branches dispersed to Africa, radiated there, and became the Malaconotini (8/48). The ancestor of some elements of the other branch (Vangini, 19/58) remained in southern Asia (*Philentoma, Tephrodornis*); the ancestor of others (*Platysteira, Batis, Prionops*) dispersed to Africa. Ca. 15–20 MYA (Δ 5.4) the ancestor of the vangas arrived in Madagascar and radiated there to produce the remarkably diverse 13 species traditionally placed in the "Vangidae." If this seems unlikely, consider the radiation of the 22 species of Hawaiian honeycreepers (Drepanidini) which, from a cardueline finch ancestor, probably achieved their present diversity in less than 15 million years (Sibley and Ahlquist 1982a).

The details of this narrative may be wrong, and the branches based on fewer than five DNA-DNA hybrids may be off by several percent, but we suggest (1) that the major branches are essentially correct, (2) that the African bushshrikes and the Malagasy vangas were derived from Australo-Papuan corvine ancestors, and (3) that the Malaconotinae is the sister group of the Dicrurinae.

The inclusion of *Batis, Platysteira*, and *Philentoma* in the Malaconotinae, rather than in the Monarchinae, is based on the $\Delta T_{50}H$ values (Fig. 377) and some unpublished comparisons with *Monarcha guttulus. Batis* (*capensis, molitor, senegalensis*) is Δ 5.9 (N = 6) from *Prionops + Leptopterus*, and Δ 6.6 (N = 4) from *Telophorus + Laniarius*, but *Batis capensis* is Δ 7.2 (N = 2) from *Monarcha guttulus. Platysteira* (*cyanea, castanea*) is Δ 6.4 (N = 3) from *Prionops + Leptopterus*, and Δ 6.6 (N = 1) from *Telophorus*, but *P. cyanea* is Δ 7.4 from *M. guttulus. Philentoma* (*velatum, pyrhopterum*) is Δ 5.7 (N = 2) from *Prionops + Leptopterus*, and 6.6 (N = 1) from *Telophorus*, but *P. pyrhopterum* is Δ 7.5 (N = 2) from *M. guttulus*.

Tephrodornis usually has been assumed to be a cuckoo-shrike ("Campephagidae" is our Oriolini), but the DNA data show it to be a member of the bushshrike tribe Vangini. Beecher (1953b:296–300) suggested that *Tephrodornis* is related to the "Prionopinae" on the basis of jaw musculature and other characters and he proposed that the entire "shrike assemblage," including the vangas, originated from the Australo-Papuan Monarchinae.

Raikow et al. (1980) studied the appendicular myology of the "Laniidae" as defined by Rand (1960), including the true shrikes, the bushshrikes, and the Bornean Bristlehead (*Pityriasis gymnocephala*). They concluded (p. 150) that these taxa constitute "a poorly defined assemblage" and, although they found "No evidence to refute the hypothesis of monophyly," they obtained "only weak and uncertain corroborating evidence" to support monophyly. They decided that the "practical course is to retain the family [Laniidae] as a taxonomic unit, with the recognition that it is still not rigorously demonstrated to be a clade." Raikow et al. (1980) divided the "Laniidae" into four subfamilies: Malaconotinae for the "bush-shrikes," Laniinae for *Lanius* and *Corvinella*, Prionopinae for *Prionops* and *Eurocephalus*, and Pityriasinae for *Pityriasis*. Concerning *Pityriasis* they stated that "The limb musculature strongly supports its inclusion in the Laniidae, and indicates that it is the primitive sister taxon of the Prionopinae."

Reference to Figs. 376 and 377 reveals a few congruencies, and several discrepancies, between the proposals of Raikow et al. (1980) and the DNA-based phylogeny. The DNA comparisons agree with Raikow et al. concerning the close relationship between *Lanius* and *Corvinella*. They do not agree with an association of *Eurocephalus* with *Prionops*, or with the exclusion of *Prionops* from the Malaconotinae. Neither did Raikow et al. discover that *Batis*, *Platysteira*, *Philentoma*, *Tephrodornis*, and the "Vangidae" are members of the Malaconotinae. This is not surprising, since they did not consider these taxa as relevant to the problem, but it indicates a weakness in a procedure that bases a hypothesis of groups on a previous classification of uncertain validity, and does not include a search for all possible relatives of each taxon.

The inclusion of *Pityriasis* in the Laniidae as "the primitive sister taxon of the Prionopinae," based on the limb musculature, indicates a more serious difficulty with the method used by Raikow et al. (1980). As they noted, "The enigmatic Bornean Bristlehead has been placed by previous workers in several different families." However, the relationship of *Pityriasis* to the Australo-Papuan genera *Cracticus*, *Gymnorhina*, and *Strepera* had been suggested frequently from its discovery in 1835 until as recently as 1953 (Beecher 1953b:298, Hachisuka 1953). It would have been logical to include comparisons with these taxa in any study involving *Pityriasis*.

Ahlquist et al. (1984) and Sibley and Ahlquist (1984c) have compared the DNA of *Pityriasis* with a wide array of passerine taxa and it is clear that the Bornean Bristlehead is an artamine (Corvidae: Corvinae: Artamini), not a laniid. Thus, the Artamini is composed of *Cracticus*, *Strepera*, *Gymnorhina*, *Pityriasis*, *Artamus*, and *Peltops*. The conclusion of Raikow et al. (1980) that the limb musculature of *Pityriasis* "strongly supports its inclusion in the Laniidae" suggests that the characters they were using are primitive for a larger cluster than the taxa they examined.

Fig. 244 (*Prionops*) shows the two groups of shrikes: *Prionops* plus *Laniarius* to *Malaconotus* are malaconotines; *Corvinella* to *Lanius* are laniids.

Fig. 245 (*Prionops*) shows that *Batis* is close to the malaconotines and this is also shown by Figs. 247, 249, and 250. The relative distances from *Prionops* to other corvoid taxa are also indicated.

Fig. 246 (*Telophorus*). *Telophorus*, another malaconotine, provided a better homoduplex than *Prionops* and Fig. 246 also shows the gap between the bushshrikes and the true shrikes, plus the difference (relative to *Telophorus*) between *Aegithina* and the Irenidae (*Chloropsis*, *Irena*).

Fig. 247 (*Telophorus*) shows that *Batis* is closer to *Telophorus* than are the other taxa in this set, and indicates the distant positions of *Orthonyx* and *Eopsaltria* relative to the bushshrikes. In Fig. 246 the Irenidae were in about the same position as *Orthonyx* and *Eopsaltria* in Fig. 247. These distances are reflected in the classification.

Fig. 248 (*Telophorus*) shows that *Platysteira* is also a malaconotine, indicates the relative positions of several corvoid taxa, and shows the distant positions of *Acanthiza* (Meliphagoidea) and *Menura* (Menuroidea).

Fig. 249 (*Laniarius*) includes seven genera of malaconotines (*Laniarius* to *Prionops*), three species of *Lanius*, and a bulbul (Passerida).

Fig. 250 (*Cyanolanius*). The Blue Vanga, often placed in *Leptopterus*, was collected in the Comoro Islands. The vangas of Madagascar have radiated into a group of 14 species, including the nuthatch-like *Hypositta*, the sickle-billed *Falculea*, and the Helmetbird (*Eu-*

ryceros) with an enormous, arched bill. The vangas have been treated as a family, Vangidae, by all recent authors, and we assumed that *Cyanolanius* would be distant from all other passerines, but it clustered with the helmetshrikes. Benson (1985) notes that "In the hand, some species [of vangas] recall bush-shrikes Malaconotinae . . . or even wood-swallows Artamidae." He also notes that most species "are strongly gregarious (as are Prionopidae)." Thus, it seems that the vangas represent a rather recent invasion of Madagascar from Africa, not an ancient relict group. Another possibility is that *Cyanolanius* is a recent immigrant from Africa and that it is not closely related to the vangas of Madagascar.

Genera *Incertae Sedis*. There are at least six Papuan genera of uncertain affinities: *Loria*, *Cnemophilus*, *Macgregoria*, *Ifrita*, *Androphobus*, and *Amalocichla*. Most or all of these may be members of the Corvida, but we lack their DNAs. Olson (1987) assigned *Amalocichla* to the "Acanthizidae."

Family CALLAEATIDAE: 3/3. New Zealand Wattlebirds. The Kokako (*Callaeas cinerea*), Saddleback (*Creadion carunculatus*), and the extinct Huia (*Heterolocha acutirostris*) are (or were) endemic to New Zealand. We lack the DNA of any member of this group. It is placed here *incertae sedis*.

Garrod (1872a) suggested that "*Neomorpha*" (*Heterolocha*) may be related to the starlings and icterines, which he thought were members of the same family, Sturnidae. Garrod believed that the relationship between the Huia and the Sturnidae was "very intimate" and "would place it at the head of that family."

In the *Catalogue of Birds*, Sharpe (1877:142–145) placed the New Zealand wattlebirds in the Corvidae, between *Picathartes* and "*Falculia*" (*Falculea*, a vanga). *Struthidea* and *Strepera* were also assigned to the Corvidae.

Gadow (1888c) suggested that "if a Satin Bird, *Ptilonorhynchus* could be induced to marry a Piping Crow, *Gymnorhina*, their offspring might . . . become a *Glaucopsis*" (*Callaeas*). Note: *Glaucopis* and *Glaucopsis* are synonyms of *Callaeas*.

In the *Hand-List* Sharpe (1909:544) placed *Heterolocha* and *Creadion* in the Eulabetidae (glossy starlings), and "*Glaucopis*" (*Callaeas*) in the Corvidae (p. 627). E. Stresemann (1934) did not mention the wattlebirds in his systematic list. Stonor (1942) allied the three wattlebird genera in the "Callaeidae" on the basis of the reduced keel on the sternum, reduced flight powers, large legs, and presence of the mouth wattles. He concluded that the wattlebirds "appear to be an offshoot from the same stock that gave rise to the Starlings and their immediate allies."

Mayr and Amadon (1951:31) reviewed the evidence, concluded that the "Callaeidae" are not allied to the Sturnidae, and placed them between the bowerbirds and the Australian mud-nest builders ("Grallinidae"). Wetmore (1960:20) noted that Stonor had separated the wattlebirds as the "Callaeidae" and listed the family between the Vireolaniidae and the Sturnidae.

Williams (1976) reviewed the evidence of the affinities of the "Callaeatidae" and concluded that he was "unwilling to hazard an opinion" because the evidence so far presented "does not make any of the alternatives seem a plausible choice."

Parvorder *incertae sedis*, Family PICATHARTIDAE: 2/4. In this position, on the boundary between the Corvida and the Passerida, we place two genera, *Picathartes* and *Chaetops*, each with two species. *Picathartes*, the rockfowl of West Africa, have long been a puzzle, but they have usually been placed in the Corvidae or the Timaliidae. *Chaetops*, the rock-jumpers of South Africa, sometimes considered a single species, has also been placed in the Timaliidae, or in the Turdidae. To our knowledge, the two genera have never been thought to be closely related.

The DNAs of both genera were used in comparisons, but they were omitted from the UPGMA tree, as were others. In our classification (Sibley et al. 1988) we placed *Picathartes* in the Timaliini, but did not mention *Chaetops*.

The melting curves revealed an unexpected result when three experiments were analyzed with the EXCEL program.

Fig. 251 (*Chaetops*) has a poor tracer, but it shows that the closest taxon to *Chaetops* is *Picathartes*, and the heteroduplex curves include representatives of the Corvida and Passerida which are intermixed, although four members of the Corvida are the next closest to *Chaetops* after *Picathartes*.

Fig. 252 (*Picathartes*) shows a rather tight cluster of heteroduplex curves composed of a mixture of Corvida and Passerida, including *Corvus* and two babblers, *Pellorneum* and *Trichastoma*.

Fig. 253 (*Picathartes*) also includes a mixture of Corvida and Passerida, with *Corvus* closest to *Picathartes*, but with members of the two parvorders intermixed. A babbler (*Turdoides*) is among the more distant heteroduplex curves.

In Fig. 266 (*Sitta*), *Picathartes* is nearly as far from the nuthatch homoduplex as is *Corvus*. It is impossible to decide whether the *Picathartes* curve should go with the Passerida or with the *Corvus*.

In Fig. 287 (*Sylvia*), *Picathartes* is in the same relative position as in Fig. 266—between several Passerida and *Vireo* and *Corvus*. This set may be interpreted as suggesting a borderline position for *Picathartes* because its curve is actually between the two groups, and *Sylvia* is closely related to the babblers, of which there are four genera among the heteroduplexes (*Stachyris*, *Chamaea*, *Leiothrix*, *Turdoides*).

In Fig. 288 (*Hippolais*), *Picathartes* is again at the outer fringe of a series of species of Passerida, next to *Pomatostomus*, a member of the Corvida, and superimposed on the curve of *Troglodytes*, a member of the Passerida.

From the DNA comparisons we conclude, cautiously, that *Picathartes* and *Chaetops* may be one another's closest relatives, and that their lineage may have branched from that of the other Corvida soon after the divergence between the Corvida and the Passerida.

Some additional information is available from comparisons of the heads of the humeri of both species of *Picathartes* and both species of *Chaetops*, with representatives of several groups of the Corvida and Passerida. The humerus of *Picathartes* is typically corvine. It has a single deep pneumatic fossa with a large trabeculated opening into the hollow shaft of the bone. The humerus of *Picathartes* is ca. 40 mm in length; that of *Chaetops* is ca. 28 mm long. The humerus of *Chaetops* has a single cup-shaped fossa, but it is not pneumatic; the fossa does not communicate with the hollow shaft. Where a second fossa would be in a typical member of the Passerida is a relatively flat area without an indentation. The capital shaft ridge between this area and the fossa is low, but obvious. In general, the head of the humerus of *Chaetops* is more like that of the corvine Scrub Jay (*Aphelocoma coerulescens*) than that of such members of the Passerida as the California Thrasher (*Toxostoma redivivum*), European Starling (*Sturnus vulgaris*), and Yellow-headed Blackbird (*X. xanthocephalus*). The humerus of the meliphagid *Entomyzon cyanotis* is typically corvine and pneumatic, but otherwise it is similar to that of *Chaetops*. We know, from previous study of the humeri of many passerines, that in the smaller species of the Corvida the fossa is not always pneumatic. Thus, *Picathartes* has a corvine humeral head and that of *Chaetops* is more like that of the Corvida than that of the Passerida.

We conclude that *Picathartes* is a member of the Corvida and that *Chaetops* is probably a member of the Corvida. We suggest that these two genera may be one another's closest relatives, but that additional DNA comparisons should be completed before a definite conclusion is reached. We place these genera in the Picathartidae but in the limbo of "Parvorder *incertae sedis*" until additional evidence is available.

Parvorder Passerida

Parvorder PASSERIDA: 639/3456. All oscine passerines that are not members of the Corvida belong to the parvorder Passerida. The two parvorders diverged from a common ancestor at Δ $T_{50}H$ 12.8 (Fig. 369), probably in the Eocene or Oligocene. The oldest known passerine fossils are from the upper Oligocene of France. By their "osteological characteristics they differ from the primitive passerines [suboscines] . . . and correspond to advanced passerines of the Oscines suborder" (Mourer-Chauvire et al. 1989). During the middle and upper Tertiary, while the Corvida were radiating in Australia and New Guinea, the Passerida were radiating and dispersing in Eurasia, Africa, and North America. South America was isolated from the other continents until the late Tertiary and, presumably, the only passerines in South America during this time were the New World suboscines (Tyrannides). Members of the Passerida probably colonized South America in the Miocene when the ancestor of the Cardinalini, Icterini, and Thraupini diverged from the other Emberizinae ca. 15–25 MYA (Δ $T_{50}H$ 5.8) (Fig. 384).

The long period of geographic separation between the Corvida and the Passerida provided numerous opportunities for convergent evolution to produce ecological counterparts, especially between the endemic Corvida of Australo-Papuasia and the Passerida of Africa and Eurasia. The taxonomic results are recorded in the many examples of polyphyletic groups that have been proposed during the past 200 years, and which are still to be found in current classifications. The DNA-DNA hybridization evidence revealed the branching pattern of the passerine phylogeny and the extent of convergence between the two main subdivisions of the Passeri. No other discovery based on the DNA hybridization evidence has solved more problems in avian systematics than the recognition of the two parvorders of the suborder Passeri.

We divide the Passerida into three superfamilies: Muscicapoidea, Sylvioidea, and Passeroidea.

Superfamily MUSCICAPOIDEA

113/610. The Muscicapoidea includes the Bombycillidae (waxwings, silky flycatchers, Palm Chat), Cinclidae (dippers), Muscicapidae (thrushes, muscicapine flycatchers, chats), and the Sturnidae (starlings, mynas, mockingbirds, thrashers, American catbirds).

Family BOMBYCILLIDAE

5/8. Waxwings, silky flycatchers, Palm Chat. The three species of waxwings occur in the Northern Hemisphere and the four species of silky flycatchers range from the southwestern U.S. (*Phainopepla*) and Mexico to Panama. The Palm Chat occurs only on the island of Hispaniola in the Lesser Antilles.

Sharpe (1885:212, 1903:259), and most other authors before 1900, placed the waxwings, silky flycatchers, and the Palm Chat in the "Ampelidae," but Ridgway (1904:113) divided them into the Bombycillidae (waxwings), Ptilogonatidae (silky flycatchers), and Dulidae (Palm Chat). Wetmore (1930, 1960) followed this treatment in his classifications, but Delacour and Amadon (1949) and Delacour and Vaurie (1957) placed the three groups as subfamilies in the Bombycillidae and included the Grey Hypocolius (*Hypocolius ampelinus*) of southwest Asia in a fourth subfamily. Mayr and Amadon (1951) also included *Hypocolius* in the Bombycillidae, and associated the Artamidae with the Bombycillidae under the "Waxwings and Wood Swallows." Amadon (1956) was uncertain about the relationship between *Hypocolius* and the waxwings, and Greenway (1960:373) noted that the allocation of *Hypocolius* to the Bombycillidae "is tentative. Actual relationship of this peculiar species . . . yet to be established." Greenway (1960:373) also questioned the "status and true relationships" of *Dulus*, which he placed in the monotypic family Dulidae.

From a study of the coloration, nesting, food habits, skeleton, certain muscles, and the digestive tract, Arvey (1951) concluded that the waxwings, silky flycatchers, and the Palm Chat are closely related and should be included in the same family. Arvey did not examine *Hypocolius*. Beecher (1953b) interpreted his study of the jaw muscles as indicating that the waxwings, silky flycatchers, Palm Chat, and *Hypocolius* are related to one another and to the cuckoo-shrikes and bulbuls. Bock (1962) noted that the humeral fossa is single in the "Bombycillidae (including *Dulus*)" and also in the Artamidae. Sibley (1970:77) thought that the electrophoretic patterns of the egg-white proteins appears "to support a relationship between *Bombycilla* and *Phainopepla* but not between these and *Dulus*." Sibley (1973) noted similarities between the egg-white protein patterns of *Phainopepla* and the turdine genus *Myadestes* and suggested that the silky flycatchers "are more closely related to *Myadestes* than to any other genus."

These often conflicting opinions demonstrate that there has been no consensus about the relationships of the taxa mentioned as members of the Bombycillidae. We have confirmed Bock's observation (1962) of a single humeral fossa in the bombycillids, one of the few exceptions to the general rule of two fossae in the Passerida and one in the Corvida.

The DNA Hybridization Evidence

The tracer DNAs of *Bombycilla*, *Phainopepla*, and *Dulus* have been compared with one another and with a large array of driver DNAs from other passerines. The DNA of *Hypocolius* has not been available. The results show that the waxwings and silky flycatchers diverged at Δ 5.2, and that the Palm Chat lineage diverged from the waxwing–silky flycatcher clade at Δ 6.6 (Fig. 379). The FITCH tree (Fig. 349) shows that the Bombycillidae cluster more closely with the other Muscicapoidea than with the Sylvioidea or Corvoidea. The Bombycillidae branched from the other muscicapoid groups at Δ 10.6. We recognize three tribes: Dulini (1/1), Ptilogonatini (3/4), and Bombycillini (1/3).

We place the Hypocoliidae in the Sylvioidea, following the Pycnonotidae. This is a tentative assignment pending DNA comparisons.

Fig. 254 (*Phainopepla*) shows that *Dulus* and *Bombycilla* are the closest relatives of *Phainopepla*. The other taxa in Fig. 254 represent the major groups of the Passeri. Although the waxwings have a single humeral fossa, the DNA hybridization comparisons place the Bombycillidae in the Passerida. In Fig. 254 *Corvus*, the only member of the Corvida in this set, is the most distant from the homoduplex. The relative positions of the heteroduplex curves suggest that the Bombycillidae are closer to the Sylvioidea and Passeroidea than to the Muscicapoidea, but the average delta value is 10.6 to the Muscicapoidea, and 11.7 to the Sylvioidea and Passeroidea. The Bombycillidae may not be in their correct position in the dendrogram, but it seems likely that they are members of the Passerida. The waxwing lineage may have branched from the lineage of the Passerida soon after the divergence between the Corvida and the Passerida.

Family CINCLIDAE

1/5. Dippers. Species of *Cinclus* occur in Eurasia, western North America, Central America, and South America in the mountains south to northwestern Argentina.

The wrens and/or the thrushes usually have been thought to be the closest relatives of the dippers, although Shufeldt (1882) erroneously concluded from an osteological study that the paruline genus *Seiurus* is also close to *Cinclus*. The "booted" tarsal envelope and a spurious tenth primary are the principal characters that have been cited as evidence of a relationship between dippers and thrushes. This alliance has long been accepted (e.g., Baird 1864, Coues 1884, Sharpe 1891, Shufeldt 1904b, Stejneger 1905). Ridgway (1904:676) favored a relationship to the thrushes and the wrens, and viewed the wrens as possibly the closer relatives. In all of the more recent classifications (e.g., Wetmore 1960) the dippers have been placed near the thrushes and usually not far from the wrens. These two groups have been the allies most consistently proposed and there have been no important disagreements.

Mayr and Amadon (1951), following Hartert (1910), combined a large array of "primitive insect eaters" in the "Muscicapidae," in which they included the dippers as the "subfamily Cinclinae," because "we do not feel that the characters of *Cinclus*, consisting chiefly of adaptations for its aquatic accomplishments, merit more than subfamily rank." Their "Cinclinae" followed the "Troglodytinae, Miminae, Turdinae," thus agreeing with the traditional ideas about the relationships of *Cinclus*. Sibley (1970:66) concluded that "the egg white evidence supports a dipper-thrush alliance" but that "the differences between . . . *Cinclus* and . . . the wrens are so numerous that it seems unlikely that they are closely related." The sixth edition of the A.O.U. checklist (1983:537) placed the Cinclidae following the Troglodytidae, but noted that "The relationships of this family are uncertain."

The DNA Hybridization Evidence

Comparisons between *Cinclus* tracer DNA and the DNAs of other passerines show that the dipper lineage branched from the other muscicapoids at $\Delta T_{50}H$ 9.7 (Fig. 379). We therefore recognize the monotypic family Cinclidae, which is the sister group of the muscicapid-sturnid clade. The FITCH tree (Fig. 349) shows *Cinclus* branching from the muscicapid clade before the starling-mockingbird branch. The wrens (Troglodytinae) are members of the superfamily Sylvioidea, thus similarities between wrens and dippers must be due to convergence, not recent common ancestry.

Fig. 255 (*Cinclus*) shows that the dippers are about equidistant from the muscicapid-sturnid cluster (*Mimus* to *Catharus*), with the babbler, wren, and corvoids (*Corvus, Terpsiphone*) progressively more distant.

Family MUSCICAPIDAE

69/449. Thrushes, muscicapine flycatchers, chats. In several publications we have used "Turdidae" for this group, but priority favors *Muscicapa* as the type genus of the family. Our Muscicapidae does not include the Australo-Papuan flycatchers, monarchs, etc., often placed in a large cluster under this family name. We recognize two subfamilies in the Muscicapidae: Turdinae and Muscicapinae.

Subfamily TURDINAE: 22/179. Typical thrushes. The "typical thrushes" include *Turdus, Zoothera, Hylocichla, Catharus, Myadestes, Monticola, Chlamydochaera*, and several other genera, but not *Zeledonia, Drymodes*, or the "chat-like thrushes" such as *Erithacus, Saxicola, Oenanthe*, etc. The true thrushes occur over most of the world. The Song Thrush (*Turdus philomelos*) and the Eurasian Blackbird (*T. merula*) have been introduced into New Zealand. *Amalocichla* of New Guinea has often been considered to be a thrush, but we lack its DNA and view its status as *incertae sedis*. Olson (1987) assigned *Amalocichla* to the "Acanthizidae."

The three species of bluebirds (*Sialia*) occur in North America. Their lineage branched from that of the other turdines at $\Delta T_{50}H$ 8.0, which could provide the basis for the recognition of a separate subfamily (Fig. 379).

Subfamily MUSCICAPINAE: 47/270. Our Muscicapinae differs from most treatments of the group in that it includes mainly African and Eurasian taxa. We lack the DNAs of several genera and cannot assign them to a higher category. For example, *Bias, Megabyas*, and *Pseudobias* have usually been placed in the Muscicapidae, but they may be related to *Batis* and the other malaconotines of Africa. We recognize two tribes, Muscicapini (17/115) for the muscicapine flycatchers, and Saxicolini (30/155) for the muscicapine chats, including *Saxicola, Erithacus, Oenanthe, Luscinia, Cossypha, Phoenicurus*, etc.

Historical Review of the Classification

The thrushes have been placed in the same family with the sylviine warblers and muscicapine flycatchers, or in an adjacent family, by virtually all authors during the past century (e.g., Seebohm 1881, Seebohm and Sharpe 1898–1902, Pycraft 1905c, Hartert 1910, Mayr and Amadon 1951, Ripley 1952). Many have favored an arrangement that associates the thrushes with the babblers, mockingbirds, wrens, dippers, and accentors, often as subfamilies in the same family. Hartert (1910) included these groups, plus the Old World flycatchers, in a large family "Muscicapidae," and his influence is still apparent. For example, the sixth edition of the A.O.U. checklist (1983) includes the Sylviinae, Muscicapinae, Monarchinae, Turdinae, and Timaliinae in the "Muscicapidae." Hartert's "Muscicapidae," as we have noted before, is a polyphyletic assemblage that includes members of both parvorders and most of the superfamilies of the Passeri. In fact, the Muscicapidae of some classifications has included members of all six superfamilies when the Climacteridae has been assumed to be allied to the Certhiinae.

Hartert's proposal grew out of his frustration with the difficulties involved in separating the groups of oscines that seemed to merge imperceptibly through intermediate species from one group to the next. He wrote (1910:469, transl.): "In my opinion it is impossible to separate the families Muscicapidae, Sylviidae and Turdidae. The so-called muscicapids merge gradually into the so-called turdids. . . . What one cannot classify may be considered to be a timaliid. . . . So far as we know the separation of the above-named pseudo-families by anatomical characters is as little possible as by external characters."

In his Muscicapidae Hartert (1910) included the muscicapine and monarchine flycatchers, the sylviine warblers, the babblers, and the thrushes. As adjacent families he recognized the Accentoridae (Prunellinae) and the Troglodytidae, in which he placed the wrens and the dippers.

Hartert's arrangement apparently was derived from that of Seebohm and Sharpe (1898–1902), and it became the basis for that of Mayr and Amadon (1951) which, in turn, was the foundation of the "Basel sequence" adopted by a committee that met during the 11th International Ornithological Congress of 1954, in Basel, Switzerland. One of the "Actions of the Committee" was that "For the reasons stated by Hartert" the Turdidae, Sylviidae, and Muscicapidae "should be combined in a single family" (Mayr and Greenway 1956:7). The Muscicapidae, as approved by the Basel Committee and adopted by the editors of the Peters' *Check-list of Birds of the World*, included the following subfamilies (Mayr and Greenway 1956:8):

Turdinae (incl. *Zeledonia*)
Timaliinae (incl. *Chamaea*)
Paradoxornithinae
Polioptilinae (incl. *Rhamphocaenus* and *Microbates*)
Sylviinae (incl. *Regulus*, *Leptopoecile*, *Lophobasileus*)
Malurinae
Muscicapinae
Monarchinae
Pachycephalinae

These groups include members of both parvorders and five of the six superfamilies of the Passeri. The seven members of the Basel Committee were the most experienced and knowledgeable avian systematists in the world and their predecessors had been trying to resolve the phylogeny of these groups for over a century. If the DNA hybridization evidence has now provided the correct pattern of their relationships, why were these affinities not apparent from the evidence available in 1954? The following summary of some of the characters of these groups may answer this question. The data are from various sources, including Sharpe (1879), Seebohm (1881), Gadow (1893), Hartert (1910), Ridgway (1904, 1907), Witherby et al. (1940–41), Ripley (1952), and Beecher (1953b). Sibley (1970:69) summarized these data, including the humeral fossa conditions proposed by Bock (1962). We have examined the condition of the humeral fossa in all subgroups of the Passeri and have found that the following taxa have the double condition typical of the Passerida.

All members of the following groups have ten primaries, the outer of variable development, and they share many characters common to all members of the Passeri. The following family names identify the traditional groups recognized by most ornithologists in 1954.

Turdidae: Juvenal plumage usually spotted; tarsus typically "booted" except lower portion, and sometimes scutellate in young birds; single molt (all species?); rictal bristles variable; jaw muscles similar to those of Mimidae and Cinclidae; humeral fossa double.

Sylviidae: Juvenal plumage unspotted; tarsus usually scutellate; double molt frequently present; rictal bristles variable; jaw muscles most similar to those of Muscicapidae and Pycnonotidae and not differing importantly from those of the Turdidae, Sturnidae, or Hirundinidae; humeral fossa now known to be double.

Muscicapidae: Juvenal plumage usually spotted; tarsus scutellate; usually a single molt; strong rictal bristles; jaw muscles similar to those of Sylviidae and Turdidae; humeral fossa double.

Timaliidae: Juvenal plumage unspotted; tarsus scutellate; usually a single molt; rictal bristles present; jaw muscles similar to those of Sylviidae, Motacillidae, Alaudidae, and several other groups; humeral fossa double.

Mimidae: Juvenal plumage unspotted; tarsus scutellate; single molt; rictal bristles present; jaw muscles as in Turdidae; humeral fossa double.

Cinclidae: Juvenal plumage spotted (Stejneger 1905); tarsus "booted"; single molt; rictal bristles absent; jaw muscles similar to those of the Turdidae and several other groups; humeral fossa double.

Troglodytidae: Juvenal plumage unspotted; tarsus scutellate; single molt; rictal bristles absent or vestigial; jaw muscles similar to those of *Certhia*, *Parus*, *Sitta*, and *Malurus*; humeral fossa double.

Prunellidae: Juvenal plumage unspotted; tarsus scutellate in front with some scales more or less fused; single molt, rictal bristles absent; jaw muscles similar to those of Turdidae; humeral fossa double.

The humeral fossa data were not available in 1954 and the jaw muscle characters of Beecher (1953b) had been criticized by Mayr (1955). Beecher's (1953b) phylogeny was flawed because he placed the Sylviidae and Timaliidae in separate superfamilies. (The DNA hybridization data reveal the Sylviini and Timaliini to be sister tribes in the Sylviinae.) The value of tarsal scutellation as a taxonomic character has been questioned by Pycraft (1906b), Blaszyk (1935), Plotnick and Pergolani de Costa (1955), and Rand (1959), among others, and the development of rictal bristles is correlated with food habits. There was no basis for assigning more weight to some characters than others, thus, the attributes of these "families" presented a chaotic mixture with no clear guides to relationships. However, from the vantage point of the DNA evidence, we now can see certain consistencies in the characters listed above; for example, spotted juvenal plumages and booted tarsi occur in the Muscicapidae and

Cinclidae as defined by the DNA comparisons. Other congruencies may be expected to emerge from appropriate comparisons.

After the conclusions of the Basel Committee were published (Mayr and Greenway 1956) a consensus developed that the "primitive insect eaters" to be included in the "Muscicapidae" were the Old World flycatchers (including the Australo-Papuan flycatchers, monarchs, whistlers, etc.), thrushes, sylviine warblers, Australo-Papuan "warblers" (e.g., thornbills, fairywrens, etc.), and babblers. Included, or adjacent, groups were the mockingbirds and thrashers, wrens, dippers, accentors, and wagtails and pipits. Many recent classifications (e.g., Vaurie 1959, Berndt and Meise 1960, Storer 1971, Voous 1977) have included such a grouping. Voous (1985) attempted to find a consensus by developing an eclectic arrangement. Under the heading of "Primitive Insect Eaters" he listed the Cinclidae, Troglodytidae, Mimidae, Prunellidae, Turdidae, Sylviidae, Muscicapidae, Rhipiduridae, Monarchidae, Pachycephalidae, Timaliidae, and Aegithalidae. This was followed by a group of "Old Australian Endemics" composed of the Maluridae, Acanthizidae (including Mohouinae), Ephthianuridae, Neosittidae, and Climacteridae. This arrangement was a compromise between traditional classifications and the results as of 1984 of our DNA hybridization studies (Voous 1985:x).

The convergently similar members of the Australo-Papuan Corvida and the Afro-Eurasian Passerida have presented the most difficult problems in the classification of the muscicapoid and sylvioid Passeri. The association of superficially similar but genetically unrelated ecotypes in such polyphyletic taxa as the "Muscicapidae" of many classifications has obscured the zoogeographic and phylogenetic histories of many oscine taxa. The result is a classical example of the difficulties encountered in using morphological characters to determine the boundaries of monophyletic clusters of convergently similar species.

We had hoped that it might be possible to abandon the family name "Muscicapidae" to terminate the confusion that is certain to accompany its continued use (Sibley and Ahlquist 1980, 1985a). Unfortunately, that is not possible without violating the spirit, if not the rules, of nomenclature. We hope that the application of "Muscicapidae" as a family name will henceforth take account of the evidence presented here. See also the comments by Mayr and Cottrell (1986:v–vii).

The DNA Hybridization Evidence

The Muscicapidae consists of two subfamilies: Turdinae, including the "typical thrushes," and Muscicapinae, including the muscicapine flycatchers (Muscicapini, 17/115) and the chat-like thrushes or chats (Saxicolini, 30/155). The chats have been thought to be most closely related to the turdine thrushes because they tend to have booted tarsi and to look and behave like small turdines. The DNA comparisons show that the muscicapine flycatchers and saxicoline chats are more closely related to one another than either is to any other group. The Muscicapini forage in flycatcher fashion; the Saxicolini feed on the ground on insects and other items, thus they are ecologically more similar to the turdines than to their closest relatives, the Muscicapini.

The turdine-muscicapine divergence occurred at $\Delta T_{50}H$ 8.8. The muscicapine-saxicoline dichotomy occurred at $\Delta 7.0$.

The Muscicapidae is the sister group of the Sturnidae and they diverged at Δ 9.1 (Fig. 379).

Fig. 256 (*Turdus*) shows that the typical thrushes (*Turdus* to *Catharus*) cluster together, with the solitaire (*Myadestes*) and *Alethe* more distant. We include these genera in our Turdinae. The chats and muscicapines (*Cyornis* to *Cossypha*) are next, followed by the Western Bluebird (*Sialia mexicana*). *Hypothymis* and *Rhipidura* are members of the Corvida. The position of *Sialia* is of special interest. The bluebirds have nearly always been placed in the Turdidae, usually with the typical thrushes, but the DNA evidence is somewhat equivocal concerning their relationships. The UPGMA clustering emphasizes the greater distances obtained when *Sialia* is used as a driver and places them as a sister group of the thrushes and muscicapines. The FITCH tree (Fig. 349) allies *Sialia* with the typical thrushes. Sibley and Monroe (1990) include *Sialia* in the Turdinae.

Fig. 257 (*Myadestes*) suggests that the solitaires are closer to *Catharus* than to *Zoothera*. The saxicolines (*Myrmecocichla*, *Cyornis*) are next in the sequence, then *Bombycilla*, two sylvioids (*Sylvia*, *Certhia*), a passeroid, and a corvoid (*Lanius*). The position of *Bombycilla* supports its allocation to the Passerida rather than to the Corvida.

Fig. 258 (*Sialia*) shows the close relationship among the three species of bluebirds, and the relative distances from the sturnines, mimines, and saxicolines. The three bombycillids cluster together beyond the muscicapid-sturnid group.

Fig. 259 (*Sialia*) shows that the bluebirds are about as distant from the turdine thrushes as from the saxicolines and sturnids. Sibley and Monroe (1990) include *Monticola* and *Myiophonus* in the Turdinae, but they are clearly separated from *Turdus* and *Zoothera*. This is shown in Fig. 379.

Fig. 260 (*Erithacus*) shows the close relationship between the chats (*Erithacus*, *Myrmecocichla*, *Phoenicurus*) and the muscicapine flycatchers (*Rhinomyias*, *Cyornis*, *Muscicapa*), compared with the turdine (*Catharus*). The three Corvida (*Philentoma*, *Monarcha*, *Terpsiphone*) are well separated from the Passerida. This set demonstrates that the monarch flycatchers are not closely related to the muscicapine flycatchers.

Fig. 261 (*Erithacus*) provides additional information about the relationships between the saxicoline chats (*Erithacus*) and other groups of Passerida, with the two members of the Corvida, *Vireo* and *Meliphaga*, as the out-groups.

We conclude that the traditional Muscicapidae of Hartert (1910), followed by many subsequent authors, does not reflect the phylogeny of the passerines. The DNA hybridization evidence presents a radically different pattern of relationships summarized in our classification. The Muscicapidae includes only the turdine thrushes, muscicapine flycatchers, and saxicoline chats of the parvorder Passerida, superfamily Muscicapoidea.

Family STURNIDAE: 38/148.

Tribe STURNINI: 27/114. Starlings, Mynas, Oxpeckers.
Tribe MIMINI: 11/34. Mockingbirds, Thrashers, American Catbirds.
The Sturnini are confined to the Old World, the Mimini to the New World. The starlings usually have been thought to be related to the crows and other members of the corvoid assemblage, or to the New World troupials (Icterini) and/or the Old World weaverbirds

(Ploceinae). The mockingbirds and thrashers have been viewed as relatives of the thrushes (Turdidae) and/or the wrens (Troglodytidae).

Evidence of a relationship between the starlings and mockingbirds had been reported by Beecher (1953b) and Stallcup (1961). In 1980 we compared the DNAs of sturnines and mimines in a study based on 153 DNA-DNA hybrids among 18 oscine genera used as tracers (Sibley and Ahlquist 1980). Among our conclusions was the following statement. (DNAs of the cited genera were used in the 1980 study). "The thrushes, muscicapine flycatchers, mockingbirds, starlings, and dippers are members of a monophyletic assemblage. a) Within this group the muscicapine flycatchers (*Muscicapa, Melaenornis, Niltava, Rhinomyias*) are closely related to the chat-like thrushes (*Erithacus, Erythropygia, Phoenicurus, Luscinia, Cossypha, Pogonocichla, Myrmecocichla, Copsychus*). b) The starlings (*Sturnus, Onychognathus, Spreo, Ampeliceps, Aplonis*) are closest to the mockingbirds and thrashers (*Mimus, Dumetella, Toxostoma, Oreoscoptes*. c) The turdine thrushes include *Turdus, Catharus, Hylocichla, Zoothera* and *Myadestes*. d) *Cinclus* is closer to the thrushes, flycatchers, starlings and mockingbirds than to the wrens."

A Distance Wagner tree (Farris 1972) based on the DNA hybridization data showed *Mimus* and *Sturnus* to be more closely related to one another than to any other taxon, and they clustered with the thrushes, muscicapine flycatchers, saxicoline chats and dippers.

The same pattern emerged from a more extensive study of the passerines (Sibley and Ahlquist 1985d) in which the mimine-sturnine relationship was based on the same data as in the 1980 paper, but additional data pertaining to other passerine groups were included. The following is based on Sibley and Ahlquist (1984b).

Diversity and Distribution

Amadon (1962) recognized 111 species of starlings in 26 genera, approximately evenly divided between Africa and Asia. Three species of *Sturnus* occur in Europe and *Aplonis* reaches Australia and many southwest Pacific islands. Most starlings nest in cavities but *Aplonis metallica* builds a pendant, globular nest with a side entrance and *Acridotheres ginginianus* digs a nest hole in an earthen bank. The color of starling eggs varies from white to green or blue-green, some are unmarked, others have reddish or brownish markings.

Davis and Miller (1960) recognized 31 species in 13 genera in the "family Mimidae," including the Black-capped Donacobius (*Donacobius atricapillus*) which Miller (1964) noted as having the voice and habits of a wren (Troglodytinae). Clench et al. (1982) concluded that *Donacobius* actually is a wren, which is consistent with several DNA comparisons. Kiltie and Fitzpatrick (1984) place *Donacobius* near *Campylorhynchus*. In Tables 1–3 of Sibley and Ahlquist (1984b), *Donacobius* clusters with the Sylvioidea, including the wrens, not with the mimines in the Turdoidea. The A.O.U. checklist committee (1983) transferred *Donacobius* to the Troglodytidae.

Most of the mockingbirds and thrashers occur from southern Canada and the United States to the West Indies and Central America. With the exclusion of *Donacobius* only *Mimus* occurs in South America.

All mimines build open, cup-shaped nests usually placed in bushes or trees. The Pearly-eyed Thrasher (*Margarops fuscatus*) places its "bulky, cup-shaped nest . . . in a bush or tree, cavity of a tree, or on the side of cave or cliff" and the Trembler (*Cinclocerthia ruficauda*) builds its nest "in a cavity of a tree or tree fern, or at the base of a palm frond" (Bond 1971:169–170). Egg colors are blue or green with various amounts of spotting or streaking.

Thus, the eggs and nests are variable, but do not oppose a relationship between the two groups.

Taxonomic History

Opinions about the relationships of the starlings have ranged widely, but most of the classifications of the past 130 years have placed the starlings close to the crows and their allies, including the birds-of-paradise, the Old World orioles, and the drongos. A relationship to the corvoid groups was advocated by Sharpe (1890, 1891), Reichenow (1914), E. Stresemann (1934), Stonor (1938), Delacour and Vaurie (1957), and Bock (1963b).

A relationship to the corvoids and the New World troupials (Icterini) was indicated in the classifications of Bonaparte (1850), Gray (1870), Sundevall (1872), Sclater (1880b), the early A.O.U. checklists (1886, 1895, 1910), Shufeldt (1889a), and Coues (1896).

The corvoids and ploceines were viewed as starling relatives by Reichenow (1882), von Boetticher (1931), Amadon (1943, 1956), Mayr and Amadon (1951), Mayr and Greenway (1956, 1962), Storer (1971), and Voous (1977).

Wallace (1874) associated the starlings with the weaverbirds, woodswallows, and larks as "Sturnoid Passeres." W. K. Parker (1875a) reported similarities between the skulls of the Celebean Myna (*Enodes*) and a Song Thrush (*Turdus philemelos*), but decided that the myna was more shrike-like and possibly related to the birds-of-paradise and the drongos (*Dicrurus*).

Stejneger (1885) placed the starlings with the corvids and meliphagids, which may have influenced Wetmore (1930, 1951, 1960), who listed the starlings near the meliphagids, although far from the Corvidae. Wetmore (1960) also placed the New Zealand wattlebirds (Callaeatidae), the shrike-vireos (*Vireolanius*), and the shrikes (Laniidae) near the starlings. His influence on the A.O.U. checklists of 1931, 1957, and 1983 is apparent. In the 1983 list the Sturnidae is between the Laniidae and Meliphagidae, far from the Corvidae.

Sharpe (1890:1) declared that the starlings are "undoubtedly allied" to the Corvidae and repeated this emphatic opinion in his extensive review of avian classification (1891:85).

Amadon (1943, 1956) reviewed the genera of starlings and, as possible relatives (1956:9), suggested the Oriolidae, Vangidae, and Dicruridae, with the Prionopidae, Cracticidae, Paradisaeidae, and Corvidae as less likely relatives. He also noted that the Ploceidae might be related to the starlings, as von Boetticher (1931) had suggested. Mayr and Amadon (1951) included the Sturnidae in a group of "Weaverbirds, Starlings and Associated Families," which included the Ploceidae, Oriolidae, and Dicruridae, followed by the Corvidae and their allies. This arrangement was also used by Mayr and Greenway (1956, 1962).

Berndt and Meise (1960) placed the starlings between the Ploceidae and Fringillidae and Bock (1963b) suggested that the birds-of-paradise and bowerbirds may have been derived from the starlings. Voous (1977:382) placed the Sturnidae between the Corvidae and Passeridae and noted that "the Ploceidae may probably be their closest relatives." Voous (1985:xvi) included the Sturnidae in the "Starlings, Weaverbirds and Allies" with the Passeridae, Ploceidae, Estrildidae, and Viduidae.

Thus, there has been no consensus about the relationships of the starlings. Among the groups suggested as their closest relatives are members of both parvorders and three of the six superfamilies which we recognize in our DNA-based classification. The alleged relationship between starlings and corvids seems to have been based on the similar shape of the bill in starlings, some corvines, and Old World orioles and on the black plumages of some starlings and some corvines. It appears that the most influential character has been tradition, with most authors adopting the opinions of previous authors.

The taxonomic history of the mockingbirds and thrashers ("Mimidae") has been relatively simple. Most authors have placed them with or near the thrushes; some have allied them to the wrens. They were considered to be thrushes by Bonaparte (1850), Gray (1869), Coues (1896), Ridgway (1907), Beecher (1953b, 1978), Morioka (1967), and Gulledge (1975). Of these authors, only Beecher (1953b) compared mockingbirds and thrushes with starlings, and he found several similarities, as noted below.

Baird (1858, following Cabanis 1850) removed the Miminae from the Turdidae and placed it with the babblers, wrens, and Wrentit (*Chamaea*) in the "Liotrichidae" (Timaliidae). He noted that "the Miminae have a Thrush-like appearance, which has caused them to be placed by most authors among the *Turdidae*." However, he concluded that "it is very difficult to draw the line between this sub-family and the wrens; the chief difference lies in the larger size and bristled gape." In 1864 Baird reversed himself and reinstated the Miminae as a subfamily of the Turdidae.

Stejneger (1883) believed that the mockingbirds are closely related to the wrens. This opinion was adopted by the A.O.U. checklist committees of 1886 and 1895 which treated the mockingbirds as a subfamily of the Troglodytidae, and the checklist committee of 1910 which listed the wrens and mockingbirds as adjacent families. Lucas (1888) forged a compromise when he suggested that "the Miminae hold a somewhat intermediate position between the Wrens and the Thrushes" and thus provided the basis for one of the most frequent linear arrangements in lists, viz., Troglodytidae, Mimidae, Turdidae. This pattern was followed by Wetmore (1930, 1951, 1960), Stresemann (1934), Mayr and Amadon (1951), Mayr and Greenway (1956, 1960), Amadon (1957), Delacour and Vaurie (1957), Berndt and Meise (1960), Storer (1971), and Voous (1977). The A.O.U. checklist committee of 1983 placed the "Mimidae" between the polyphyletic family "Muscicapidae" (which includes the thrushes) and the "Prunellidae." Voous (1985:xv) listed the Troglodytidae, Mimidae, Prunellidae, and Turdidae in his sequence of families of "Primitive Insect Eaters." Thus, as for the starlings, there has been no consensus about the relationships of the mockingbirds, although an alliance to the thrushes has been reasonably consistent.

Morphological Evidence

Beecher (1953b) compared the jaw musculature, the ectethmoid plate, and other characters of the head region in a quest for evidence of phylogenetic relationships among the oscines. In the starlings he found the jaw muscle pattern to be "similar to that of the Turdinae in complex M3b" and that the palate resembles that of the Turdinae. He found the jaw muscle pattern, bill, palate, and tongue of the mockingbirds to be similar to those of the thrushes. The starlings, mockingbirds, and thrushes have a double ectethmoid foramen, thus differing from the corvoid groups in which it is single. Beecher noted that "the double ectethmoid foramen and the muscle differences suggest that the supposed affinity of the Miminae to the babblers and wrens is the result of convergence. The Miminae may stem from the Turdinae" (p. 282). Thus, Beecher was probably the first to suggest a fairly close relationship among the thrushes, mockingbirds, and starlings.

In the suboscines and the corvoid groups (crows, birds-of-paradise, Old World orioles, drongos, woodswallows, etc.) there is one tricipital fossa in the head of the humerus which usually opens into the hollow shaft of the bone via a trabeculated opening. Such a fossa is said to be pneumatic because it permits a connection from the air sac system to the hollow humerus. In the other oscines (our parvorder Passerida) there are usually two fossae which are not pneumatic. The starlings have two complete fossae or, in *Eulabes* (*Gracula*), the beginning of a second fossa, according to Bock (1962). *Sturnus* has two fossae, as in the mockingbirds and thrushes. We have found that the tricipital fossa is consistently single in the Corvida and double in about 90% of the Passerida. The double condition in the starlings is inconsistent with a close relationship between them and the Corvidae.

W. E. Lanyon (pers. comm.) found syringeal characters that unite mimines, sturnines, and turdines and distinguish them from the corvines. Lanyon examined the stained cartilaginous syringeal elements in these groups, as follows: Mimines (*Dumetella*, *Mimus*, *Cinclocerthia*, *Margarops*); Turdines (*Catharus*, *Turdus*, *Copsychus*); Sturnines (*Sturnus*, *Aplonis*, *Scissirostrum*, *Cinnyricinclus*); and Corvines (*Dendrocitta*, *Crypsirina*, *Cyanocorax*, *Cyanocitta*, *Perisoreus*, *Pica*, *Calocitta*, *Corvus*). Lanyon noted that "The only character complex that varies in any significant way among these four samples is the size of the pessulus . . . and the positional relationship of the ventral ends of the A3 elements to the pessulus. In *Dumetella*, *Catharus*, and *Sturnus*, the ventral ends of the left and right A3's do not meet, but rather are separated by the comparatively wide pessulus, which is continuous with the fused A4's. But in *Dendrocitta* [a corvid] the pessulus is so narrow that the ventral ends of the A3's nearly touch each other medially. I can separate all eight of the corvid specimens on the basis of this character complex. I would not be able, with certainty, to distinguish between turdids, mimids, and sturnids, however."

Warner (1972:385) also observed these differences between the corvoids and the starlings and thrushes.

These morphological characters do not prove that mockingbirds and starlings are one another's closest living relatives, but they suggest that it is unlikely that the starlings are more closely related to the corvoids than to the mimines and turdines.

Serological Evidence

Stallcup (1961) used the precipitin technique to compare the saline-soluble tissue proteins of 17 genera representing 15 of the families of oscines recognized in the 1957 A.O.U. checklist. Among the taxa in this study were the Corvini, represented by the Blue Jay (*Cyanocitta cristata*); Troglodytinae, Carolina Wren (*Thryothorus ludovicianus*); Mimini, Northern Mockingbird (*Mimus polyglottos*) and Brown Thrasher (*Toxostoma rufum*); Turdinae, American Robin (*Turdus migratorius*); and Sturnini, Common Starling (*Sturnus vulgaris*).

Antisera were prepared against tissue extracts from these species and comparisons were made with representatives of 11 or 12 other oscine families. The results were presented in two tables and a series of diagrams, and Stallcup offered the following interpretations of the precipitin measurements.

1. "Members of several families are more like *Cyanocitta* than is *Sturnus*" (p. 51).

2. "*Thryothorus* does not resemble closely the members tested of the families Mimidae, Turdidae, and Regulidae" (p. 52).

3. "On the basis of the serological data, there is some justification for assuming relationship between the mimids and thrushes, although the serological resemblance of . . . these two families is not as great as that between *Toxostoma* and *Sturnus*" (p. 52).

4. "The serological data present no clear idea as to the species most like . . . *Turdus*. The species that show greatest serological correspondence to *Turdus* are *Sturnus*, *Dendroica*, *Parus*, and *Mimus*. It would seem, therefore . . . that the turdids and mimids are related. There are other species . . . that show greater serological correspondence to *Turdus* than does *Mimus*. *Sturnus* is a notable example" (pp. 52–53). Note: Stallcup was considering only the question of the relationship between mimines and turdines in these comments. Thus he did not attempt to explain the reactions between the antiserum against *Turdus* with *Dendroica* and *Parus*. In other tests *Dendroica* was most like *Spiza* and *Agelaius*, and *Parus* was most like *Cyanocitta* and *Turdus*. The degrees of relationship indicated in these comparisons with *Parus* were lower (82%, 79%) than those between *Turdus* and *Sturnus* (92%, 86%).

5. "Serologically, *Sturnus* seems to be most like *Toxostoma*" (p. 54). The *Sturnus-Toxostoma* reactions were 92% and 91%, thus among the higher values in the experiments.

There are some internal discrepancies in Stallcup's data which are characteristic of serological comparisons in which several rabbits are used to produce antisera. As Stallcup noted (1961:49), this explains the unequal reciprocals in some of the tests. However, Stallcup's data reveal a close serological relationship between starlings and mimines with the thrushes nearby and the corvids and wrens at a considerable distance away.

The DNA Hybridization Evidence

Fig. 379 shows the UPGMA tree of the Sturnidae and Turdidae. Sibley and Ahlquist (1984b) present tables of $\Delta T_{50}H$ values and other details. In Fig. 379, the Sage Thrasher (*Oreoscoptes montanus*) is closer to *Mimus* than to the typical thrashers (*Toxostoma*). Gulledge (1975) came to the same conclusion.

Fig. 262 (*Lamprotornis*) shows the clustering of the sturnines and mimines relative to the thrushes, with *Corvus* as the most distant taxon. This one set of curves indicates that the mockingbirds and thrashers are more closely related to the starlings than to the thrushes, and that the starlings are more closely related to mockingbirds, thrashers, and thrushes than to the corvids.

Fig. 263 (*Lamprotornis*) includes heteroduplex curves of additional passerine taxa; the thrasher (*Toxostoma*) is closer to the starlings than is any other member of the Passerida, and the three Corvida (*Artamus*, *Lanius*, *Vireo*) are the farthest from the starling tracer.

Fig. 264 (*Sturnus*) includes additional taxa, with the Northern Mockingbird and Grey Catbird clustering with the starling *Aplonis*, the sunbird (*Arachnothera*, a member of the Passerida) next, five species of the Corvida (*Paradisaea* to *Lanius*) next, and the suboscine cotinga, *Gymnodera*, farthest out. These relative positions are as represented in our classification.

Fig. 265 (*Toxostoma*) provides reciprocal comparisons between a thrasher tracer, two mimines, three starlings, three muscicapids (*Rhinomyias* to *Ficedula*), a waxwing, and two wrens. The relative positions of these curves again show the close relationship between mimines and sturnines, and the distant position of the wrens compared to the Mimini.

The FITCH tree (Fig. 349) shows the close relationship between *Sturnus* and *Mimus*, and their relationship to the thrushes, with *Corvus* and *Sylvia* more distant.

We conclude that the starlings (Sturnini) and mockingbirds (Mimini) are one another's closest relatives, that the thrushes and muscicapine flycatchers (Muscicapidae) are their next nearest relatives, that the wrens are not closely related to the Mimini, and that the corvids are as distant from the starlings as are any and all of the members of the parvorder Corvida.

The firmly held belief in a starling-corvid relationship was the result of an early assignment of the two groups to adjacent positions in classifications that became a tradition as successors accepted and perpetuated the arrangement. There was never any solid evidence for this idea, but tradition is a powerful force when faith takes precedence over facts.

A Possible History of the Starling-Mockingbird Connection

The present breeding distributions of the Mimini are far south of the Bering Strait and the north Atlantic, and among the Sturnini only *Sturnus vulgaris* breeds in northern Europe and Iceland (Voous 1960). In North America the introduced *S. vulgaris* rarely breeds as far north as central Alaska (Kessel and Gibson 1978). However, during the late Oligocene and early Miocene there were emergent land connections between Europe and North America and the climate in the northern hemisphere was considerably milder than today. Eldholm and Thiede (1980) concluded that "connections by shallow water and possibly emerged, or locally emerged, continent existed to the Middle Oligocene between Greenland and Svalbard [Spitsbergen] and to the Pliocene on the Faeroe-Iceland Ridge." Gradstein and Srivastava (1980) noted that relatively warm Atlantic waters occurred in the Labrador Sea in the Eocene and that "less warm Atlantic water influence prevailed in Oligocene and Miocene time but it was not until late Miocene time that there is evidence of a cold Labrador Current hugging the Canadian shelves." Similarly, Wolfe (1980) found evidence of a mixed broad-leaved deciduous forest at high latitudes in the northern hemisphere during the Oligocene and Miocene with no evidence of glaciation until "late in the Neogene."

It thus seems probable that the common ancestor of the starlings and mockingbirds was able to spread over the northern hemisphere in the Miocene and that the increasingly severe boreal climate in the late Neogene (2–12 MYA) pushed the two populations southward and out of contact. If this is correct it indicates a calibration constant of $\Delta T_{50}H$ 1.0 = ca. 2 MY (12/5.7). Earlier (Sibley and Ahlquist 1984b) we used the constant based on the Ostrich-rhea divergence (Δ 1.0 = 4.5 MY), but the ratites do not begin to breed until 2–5 years of age. If the average rate of genomic evolution is correlated with age at first breeding we should expect to find that birds that breed at 1–2 years of age have a faster rate than those that delay breeding until older. This example is speculative, but it suggests that the correct constant for passerines that begin to breed when one or two years old may be closer to Δ 1.0 = 2–3 MY than to Δ 1.0 = 4–5 MY.

Superfamily SYLVIOIDEA

199/1195. The Sylvioidea includes the Sittidae (nuthatches, Wallcreeper), Certhiidae (Northern tree-creepers, Spotted Creeper, wrens, Verdin, gnatcatchers, gnatwrens), Paridae (penduline tits, titmice, chickadees), Aegithalidae (long-tailed tits, bushtits), Hirundinidae (swallows, martins), Regulidae (kinglets, goldcrests), Pycnonotidae (bulbuls, greenbuls), Cisticolidae (African warblers), Zosteropidae (white-eyes, silvereyes), and Sylviidae (leaf warblers, grass warblers, sylviine warblers, babblers, Wrentit). The Hypocoliidae is included in the Sylvioidea, but we lack DNA of *Hypocolius* and do not know its true relationships.

Family SITTIDAE

2/25. Nuthatches and Wallcreeper. In most parts of the world there is at least one species of passerine bird that forages on the surfaces of the trunks and branches of trees, or on the faces of rocks and cliffs. These "scansorial" birds are the nuthatches and creepers, based on the Linnaean genera *Sitta* and *Certhia* of Eurasia and North America. Morphologically and behaviorally similar species in other parts of the world were associated with *Sitta* and *Certhia* in early classifications, and these assemblages have persisted in virtually all arrangements to the present. Thus, any species convergently similar to European *Sitta* or *Certhia* has been associated with one or the other of these two genera, and the scansorial species often have been placed together in the same family. The following brief review reveals some of the roots of the problem.

Gray (1869:164) assembled several groups of thin-billed birds into his family Anabatidae, including suboscines and oscines. In his "Subfam. VI. Sittinae" Gray (p. 181) included the true nuthatches (*Sitta*), the Coral-billed Nuthatch of Madagascar (*Hypositta*, a vanga), the sittellas of Australia and New Guinea (*Daphoenositta*, corvids), and the New Zealand wrens (Acanthisittidae, suboscines). Gray's family Certhiidae included the Northern tree-creepers (*Certhia*); *Caulodromus* (*Rimator*), a babbler; the Spotted Creeper (*Salpornis*); the Wallcreeper (*Tichodroma*); *Climacteris*, the Australo-Papuan treecreepers which we think are menuroids; and *Rhabdornis*, the Philippine creepers, of uncertain affinities.

Sundevall (1872, see 1889:108) placed the "Certhiinae, Sittinae," and "Acanthisittinae" in "Cohort 4. Certhiomorphae, or Scansores." Sharpe (1877:3), who followed Sundevall's classification for many groups, diagnosed the "Group Certhiomorphae" in "Section A. Turdiformes," to contain the nuthatches and creepers. Gadow (1883a:322) followed Sharpe and placed the "Family Certhiidae," composed of the Certhiinae and the Sittinae, in the Certhiomorphae. Gadow's "Certhiinae" included *Tichodroma*, and his "Sittinae" included *Sitta*, *Sittella* (*Daphoenositta*), and *Hypositta* (a vanga). Sharpe (1903:346) gave family status to the Sittidae and Certhiidae, with the genera *Sitta*, *Dendrophila* (*Sitta*), *Neositta*, *Hypositta*, and *Daphoenositta* in the Sittidae. Wetmore (1930, 1960) maintained three families, in sequence, "Sittidae, Hyposittidae, Certhiidae," but Mayr and Amadon (1951:23) viewed the Sittidae "as we conceive it" to be a "scrap basket." They "tentatively" suggested the following subfamilies: Salporninae (*Salpornis*, *Rhabdornis*, *Climacteris*, and *Tichodroma*), Sittinae (*Sitta*, *Neositta*, and *Daphoenositta*), and Hyposittinae ("The coral-billed 'nuthatch' of Madagascar is another puzzling bird").

Greenway (1967) included *Sitta*, *Daphoenositta*, and *Tichodroma* in his Sittidae, but indicated his doubts about the relationships of *Daphoenositta* in a footnote: "The relationships of this taxon are obscure." Löhrl (1964) concluded from behavioral studies that *Tichodroma* is related to *Sitta*, not to *Certhia*.

Thus, for the Sittidae, the problem has been to discover which of the "nuthatch-like" birds are truly related to *Sitta*, and which are only convergently similar.

The Coral-billed Nuthatch (*Hypositta corallirostris*) of Madagascar was associated with *Sitta* in all classifications, but its relationship to the true nuthatches was sometimes doubted. Beecher (1953b:298) was one of the few who departed from the majority view when he declared that "*Hypositta* differs from typical vangids only in having the lacrymal fused and is not close to Sittidae internally" and "*Hypositta* . . . seems to be a vangid" (p. 319). Dorst (1960a) stated emphatically that *Hypositta* is closely related to the Sittidae, but soon changed his mind and declared that *Hypositta* is a vangid, and not related to *Sitta* (1960b). Greenway (1967:124) placed *Hypositta* in the limbo of "Genus Incertae Sedis" and noted that "Although often accorded familial rank, or treated as a subfamily of the Sittidae, now considered, probably correctly, to be a vangid by some authors (e.g., Dorst 1960)." Note: Greenway cited the wrong paper by Dorst, i.e., Dorst 1960a, but it was in his second paper in 1960 (1960b) that Dorst concluded that *Hypositta* is a vanga. Sibley and Ahlquist (1982f) made the same mistake.

The present consensus is that *Hypositta* is a vanga. Although we have been unable to obtain its DNA, we place it with the vangas in the Corvidae: Malaconotinae: Vangini.

The DNA Hybridization Evidence

The Australo-Papuan sittellas (*Daphoenositta*) are superficially similar to *Sitta* in external appearance and behavior, so it is not surprising that they have been thought to be related to the true nuthatches. However, the species of *Sitta* nest in holes in trees or crevices in rocks, and their 6–10 eggs are white with reddish spots (Löhrl 1985). The sittellas build "an extremely beautiful well-camouflaged deep cup; of flakes of bark and lichens, bound with spiders' web and moulded to resemble bulge of wood; usually in upright fork of living or dead branch. . . . Eggs: 3; blue-white to grey-white, speckled and blotched glossy black, olive-brown; many faint grey underlying markings in zone at large end" (Pizzey 1980:310).

DNA-DNA comparisons show that the sittellas are members of the old endemic Australo-Papuan assemblage that includes the whistlers, shriketits, and Crested Bellbird (Sibley and Ahlquist 1982f, 1985a). We place them in the Corvidae: Pachycephalinae: Neosittini.

The only genera in the Sittidae are *Sitta* with 24 species, and *Tichodroma* with one species. Their lineages diverged at $\Delta T_{50}H$ 9.0 (Fig. 380). We place them in the subfamilies Sittinae and Tichodrominae (not Tichodromadinae, as in Sibley et al. 1988). The sittid clade branched from their sister group, the Certhiidae, at Δ 10.0. *Sitta pygmaea* is Δ 5.0 from *S. carolinensis* in Fig. 380. This suggests that generic and tribal subdivisions may be appropriate when the DNAs of additional species of sittids are obtained and compared.

Fig. 266 (*Sitta*) shows the relationship between *Sitta* and *Tichodroma*: not close relatives, but apparently closest relatives. *Certhia* and other sylvioids follow, with *Picathartes* at the outer limit just inside *Corvus*.

Fig. 267 (*Sitta*) includes additional taxa with the sylvioids closest to *Sitta*, muscicapoids next, and passeroids farthest out.

Family CERTHIIDAE

22/97. The Certhiidae includes the Northern Hemisphere tree-creepers (*Certhia*) and the Spotted Creeper (Certhiinae, 2/7); the wrens (Troglodytinae, 16/75); and the Verdin (*Auriparus flaviceps*), gnatcatchers (*Polioptila*), and gnatwrens (*Rhamphocaenus*, *Microbates*) (Polioptilinae, 4/15).

The wrens obviously originated and radiated in the New World, as did the Polioptilinae. *Certhia* is Holarctic in distribution and may have originated in the Old World, where there are five species. In the New World there is certainly one species *(Certhia familiaris)* and possibly two if *Certhia americana* is a good species (Sibley and Monroe 1990). The Verdin usually has been placed in the Paridae, or with the Old World penduline tits in the Remizidae (e.g., Snow 1967, A.O.U. 1983). The gnatcatchers and gnatwrens usually have been thought to be sylviine warblers. Rand and Traylor (1953) suggested that the Neotropical gnatwrens are related to *Macrosphenus* of Africa, rather than to *Polioptila*, but the DNA evidence indicates that the similarities between the gnatwrens and *Macrosphenus* are due to convergence, not close relationship.

The genus *Donacobius* was thought to be related to the mockingbirds and thrashers, but Clench et al. (1982) concluded that it is a wren, which is supported by our DNA comparisons. Kiltie and Fitzpatrick (1984) suggested that *Donacobius* is closest to *Campylorhynchus*. See comments about the relationships of the wrens under the family Sturnidae, above.

Beecher (1953b:317) found the "Creepers (Certhiidae)" to have a jaw muscle pattern "similar to that of the wrens" and to have "other internal characters as in wrens." He considered *Certhia* to be the "most specialized form" and *Rhabdornis*, *Salpornis*, and *Tichodroma* to be "primitive members of the group, but *Climacteris* . . . to be an endemic Australian timaliid genus." Beecher (1953b:319) noted several characters that "seem to link the creepers to the wrens, and the wall-creeper *Tichodroma* suggests a transition between creepers and nuthatches."

The Certhiinae, in our classification, includes only *Certhia* and *Salpornis*, but the "Certhiidae" of previous authors has often admitted other creepers, namely, the Philippine creepers (*Rhabdornis*) and the Australo-Papuan treecreepers (*Climacteris*, *Cormobates*). Even when these groups have been assigned to separate families or subfamilies they have been associated in the sequence of groups in a classification. For example, Greenway (1967) placed the Salpornithinae in the Certhiidae, and recognized the Rhabdornithidae and Climacteridae as adjacent families. His uncertainty about their relationships was indicated by footnotes: "The relationships of this taxon are obscure."

The DNA Hybridization Evidence

As discussed above (family Climacteridae) the Australo-Papuan treecreepers are members of the parvorder Corvida, superfamily Menuroidea, and are only convergently similar to the Certhiinae (Sibley et al. 1984b).

The Afro-Asian Spotted Creeper (*Salpornis spilonotus*) is the closest relative of *Certhia*; the two lineages branched at Δ T$_{50}$H 8.7 (Fig. 380). We lack the DNA of *Rhabdornis* and there seems to be no definitive evidence concerning its relationships.

The certhiine lineage branched from that of the wrens and polioptilines at Δ T$_{50}$H 9.0, and the Troglodytinae and Polioptilinae diverged at Δ 8.2. *Auriparus* branched from the other polioptilines at Δ 5.2. The *Rhamphocaenus-Microbates* lineage diverged from the gnat-catchers at Δ 4.7. See Fig. 380.

Fig. 268 (*Certhia*) shows *Microbates*, a wren, and a gnatcatcher as closest to *Certhia*. Next is a bushtit (Aegithalidae) and a chickadee (Paridae), followed by the Verdin which we place in the Certhiidae. (See following figures for more on this question.) The positions of the curves of *Sitta* and *Climacteris* show that the nuthatches are not as close to *Certhia* as are the wrens (etc.), and that the Climacteridae are far distant from the Certhiidae.

Fig. 269 (*Salpornis*) shows the relationship between the Wallcreeper and *Certhia*, a wren next, then a sylviid, starling, sylviid, etc., with a honeyeater (Corvida) as the outermost curve.

Fig. 270 (*Thryomanes*) includes eight species of wrens, a starling, mockingbird, and crow. The gap between the wrens and the mockingbird shows that these groups are not close relatives. The melting curves are always progressively compressed from the homoduplex, so the proximity of the starling and mockingbird curves to that of the crow does not mean that they are closely related to one another, only that both are distant from the wren tracer.

Fig. 271 (*Thryomanes*) shows that the gnatcatchers are closest to the wrens, *Certhia* and *Auriparus* are next, then a cluster formed of *Cinclus*, *Chamaea*, *Oreoscoptes*, and *Parus*, with the honeyeater (Corvida) and the cotinga (suboscine) in their expected relative positions.

Fig. 272 (*Polioptila*) shows the close relationship between the gnatcatchers, the gnat-wrens, and the Verdin, with the wrens and *Certhia* next, then the kinglet, parid, aegithalid, and the thrush (*Myadestes*). These relative positions are reflected in the UPGMA tree (Fig. 380).

Family PARIDAE

7/65. Penduline Tits, Titmice, Chickadees. The Paridae includes the penduline tits (*Anthoscopus*, *Remiz*) and the titmice and chickadees (*Parus*). We recognize two subfamilies, Remizinae (4/12) and Parinae (3/53).

The Paridae has often been the repository for any small, fluffy-plumaged, ten-primaried oscine, including the titmice, long-tailed tits, bushtits, kinglets, etc. Gadow (1883a) included *Parus*, *Acredula* (*Aegithalos*, *Psaltriparus*), *Auriparus*, *Panurus*, *Regulus*, and several other genera in his Paridae. His doubts about the relationships of some of these genera were expressed in several places, for example, a footnote (p. 3): "*Panurus* does not belong to the Paridae, but perhaps to the Fringillidae."

E. Stresemann (1923) called attention to the complete post-juvenal molt in *Aegithalos*, *Psaltriparus*, *Psaltria*, *Panurus*, and *Paradoxornis*. *Aegithalos*, *Psaltriparus*, and *Psaltria* share certain cranial characters, nest structure, and naked hatchlings, but *Parus* differs in these aspects. Delacour (1944) speculated that a "line of relationships" extends from the sunbirds (Nectariniidae) to the Dicaeidae, which in turn are allied to *Remiz* and through *Remiz* to *Aegithalos*, although he believed that *Remiz*, *Aegithalos*, and their allies are so different from

Parus that they should not be in the same family with *Parus*. It would be difficult to construct a phylogeny that would represent such a tangle of presumed relationships.

Mayr and Amadon (1951) divided the Paridae into three subfamilies—Parinae, Remizinae, and Aegithalinae—but Mayr and Greenway (1956) did not subdivide the Paridae. Vaurie (1957a) objected to this arrangement and advocated the recognition of three families: Paridae, Remizidae, and Aegithalidae. Vaurie (1957a:2) also noted that "Mr. Jean Delacour, who for a long period has been giving much thought to a classification of the passerine birds, tells me that in his opinion the penduline, long-tailed and true titmice represent three full families. He would place the Aegithalidae between the Paradoxornithinae on one side and the Paridae on the other in a sequence of families. He considers that the Paradoxornithinae are but a subfamily of the Muscicapidae, allied within this family to the Timaliinae, and would place in the Paridae only the true titmice. The Remizidae, which do not seem to be related at all to the Aegithalidae or Paridae, would then be placed next to the Dicaeidae."

Beecher (1953b) placed *Remiz*, *Auriparus*, and *Anthoscopus* in the Paridae, and Fiedler (1951) concluded from a study of the jaw musculature that the Paridae are close to the Paradoxornithidae. From behavioral comparisons, Löhrl (1964) suggested that *Aegithalos* and *Psaltriparus* should be the occupants of the Aegithalidae, apart from the Paridae, and Snow (1967) recognized the Aegithalidae, Remizidae (including *Auriparus*), and Paridae. The A.O.U. (1983) recognized the Paridae for *Parus*, the Remizidae for *Auriparus*, and the Aegithalidae for *Psaltriparus*, but noted that "The families Remizidae and Aegithalidae were formerly included in the Paridae; their true relationships are uncertain, so they are placed after the Paridae pending new evidence" (p. 512).

The relationship between the morphologically similar Black-capped Chickadee (*Parus atricapillus*) and Carolina Chickadee (*Parus carolinensis*) of the eastern United States was examined by Mack et al. (1986) using restriction enzyme analyses of mtDNA. They found "substantial genetic divergence" in which 11 of 14 enzymes "produced fragment patterns that distinguish the two chickadees." For the same pair of species, Braun and Robbins (1986) found "little or no differentiation at 35 presumed genetic loci" in proteins compared by starch gel electrophoresis. *Parus gambeli*, also known to hybridize with *P. atricapillus*, differed from *atricapillus* at 3 loci.

The DNA Hybridization Evidence

The DNA comparisons show that *Parus* and *Anthoscopus* represent a lineage that branched from the sittid-certhiid clade at Δ 10.8. Their sister group includes the swallows and the long-tailed tits (Aegithalidae), from which they diverged at Δ 10.6. Thus, the tit-like external morphology of the Paridae and Aegithalidae may be the primitive condition retained in these two groups, but greatly modified in the Hirundinidae. However, see remarks below under the Aegithalidae. The Remizinae and Parinae diverged at Δ 8.6 (Fig. 380).

Anthoscopus of Africa is sometimes included in *Remiz*, and *Melanochlora* and *Sylviparus* are presumably members of the Parinae. We lack the DNAs of *Remiz*, *Psaltria*, *Cephalopyrus*, *Melanochlora*, and *Sylviparus*.

Fig. 273 (*Parus*) shows that *Anthoscopus* is closest to *Parus*, with *Sylvia*, *Turdoides*, *Certhia*, and *Regulus* next in the sequence. The position of *Aegithalos* indicates that the long-tailed tits and bushtits are not closely related to *Parus*. The curve of *Prunella* places the Passeroidea in relation to the other curves of species of sylvioids.

Fig. 274 (*Parus*) includes members of other passeroid groups, with the corvoid Grey Jay as the outermost curve. Note that the Bushtit curve is farther from *Parus* than those of the waxwing, gnatcatcher, and starling, although all these are clustered. The point is that the Aegithalidae are separable from the Paridae.

Family AEGITHALIDAE

3/8. Long-tailed Tits and Bushtits. The taxonomic history of the Aegithalidae has been reviewed above. The five species of long-tailed tits (*Aegithalos*) occur in Eurasia, the Bushtit (*Psaltriparus minimus* incl. *melanotis*) occurs in western North America from southwestern Canada to Guatemala, east to the Rocky Mountains and central Texas. The ancestor of the Bushtit may have entered North America from Asia via the Bering land bridge in the late Miocene, ca. 10–12 MYA. This is suggested by the divergence between *Aegithalos* and *Psaltriparus* at $\Delta T_{50}H$ 5.0. The Aegithalidae diverged from the other sylvioids at Δ 10.4 (Fig. 380).

We lack the DNA of *Psaltria exilis* of Java which is usually placed in the Aegithalidae. Its affinities should be regarded as unknown, but we include it in the Aegithalidae for the present.

Fig. 275 (*Aegithalos*) has a poor tracer, but it shows that *Psaltriparus* is closest to *Aegithalos* among the taxa in this set. This set of curves illustrates the effect of an excess of short-stranded fragments in the tracer DNA.

The FITCH tree (Fig. 350) shows that the close branches between the sylvioid groups in Fig. 380 can be distinguished. A statistical analysis of the delta values showed that the sylvioid lineages are separable at a high level of confidence (Sibley et al. 1987).

Family HIRUNDINIDAE

14/89. Swallows and Martins. In the earliest classifications the swallows were associated with the swifts, but this confusion was resolved more than a century ago. See discussion and review under the Swifts and Hummingbirds.

Sundevall (1872, see 1889) placed the "Family Hirundininae" in his "Cohort 6. Chelidonomorphae" and recognized only the genus *Hirundo* for all species. Sharpe (1885:85) introduced the Family Hirundinidae: "The Swallows were for many years associated with the swifts . . . to which in outward form and habits of life they much assimilate. That the resemblance is strictly external has been shown by the researches of many comparative anatomists, and the fundamental differences between the two families have been well pointed out by the late Professor Garrod (Zoologist, 1877, p. 217). The Swallows therefore may be described as a family of Broad-billed Passeres (*Oscines latirostres* of recent authors) with nine primaries. They approach in many respects the Flycatchers (*Muscicapidae*), of which the genera *Hemichelidon* and *Artomyias* display a definite Swallow-like appearance."

The distinctive adaptations of the swallows as aerial insectivores set them apart from all other oscines, and the structures of their tarsi and syringes are unique. The short tarsus is sharply ridged behind, a condition described as acutiplantar, and the syrinx has "more or less complete bronchial rings, as compared with half rings with a membrane across the inner face" in all other oscines (Thomson 1964:790). The complete bronchial rings have been described as primitive among the oscines but, as Ames (1971:164) pointed out, "The features that distinguish the syrinx in the Hirundinidae (double bronchial elements) were almost certainly not found in the syrinx of the ancestral oscine and must be considered adaptive modifications of unknown value. Although the . . . swallows do represent [a] distinct and probably early offshoot . . . of the main oscine stem . . . the term 'primitive' is inappropriate as applied to their syrinx." Thus, the specialized syrinx is a derived character which evolved after the swallow lineage diverged from the common ancestor last shared with the other sylvioids.

The well-defined characters of the swallows have been the basis for setting them apart as a family of the Passeri, although there have been various suggestions concerning their relationships to other oscines, e.g., Sharpe (1885), as cited above. In 1901, Sharpe placed the swallows as the first group in his "Passeres Normales" (oscines), followed by the Muscicapidae, and nearly all subsequent authors have used this sequence.

Wetmore (1930, 1960) began his list of oscine families with the larks and swallows and the same pattern was followed by E. Stresemann (1934:851), Mayr and Amadon (1951), Mayr and Greenway (1956), Delacour and Vaurie (1957), Amadon (1957), Peters (1960), Voous (1977), and A.O.U. (1983). The adjacent groups often have been the Motacillidae, Campephagidae, or Dicruridae. Berndt and Meise (1960) placed the Hirundinidae between the Zosteropidae and Bombycillidae, and Wolters (1980) inserted the swallows after the starlings, at the end of his sequence. Beecher (1953b) suggested a derivation from the Muscicapidae with affinities to the Sturnidae, Sylviidae, and Turdidae, and Sibley (1970) noted similarities between the electrophoretic patterns of the egg-white proteins of swallows, sylviids, and muscicapids.

Thus, the swallows have long been recognized as a distinctive group, but there has been little consensus about their relationships to other oscines.

The DNA Hybridization Evidence

Tracer DNAs of the Bank Swallow, or Sand Martin (*R. riparia*), and the Barn Swallow (*Hirundo rustica*) were compared with the driver DNAs of other oscines representing both parvorders and the three superfamilies of the Passerida. The results indicate that the swallows are members of the Sylvioidea and that their lineage branched from those of the other sylvioids at Δ 10.1 (Sibley and Ahlquist 1982i, and Fig. 380). We recognize the family Hirundinidae (14/89) and the subfamily Hirundininae (13/87). Although we lack DNA of the river martins (*Pseudochelidon*) we recognize the subfamily Pseudochelidoninae (1/2).

Fig. 276 (*Hirundo*) shows the relationship of the swallows to the sylvioids (*Sylvia*, *Pycnonotus*), but members of the other groups of the Passeri are only slightly more distant, suggesting that the swallows are a distinct group without close relatives. The corvoids (*Lanius*, *Xanthotis*) provide the outer bound of the set of curves.

Fig. 277 (*Riparia*) shows the clustering of the five species of swallows, and the gap between them and other Passeri. As in Fig. 276, the sylvioids are the closest taxa to the swallows.

Family REGULIDAE

1/6. Kinglets or Goldcrests. The kinglets, like the parids and some other groups, are small, fluffy-plumaged, ten-primaried oscines, but *Regulus* has at least one distinctive morphological character: "Nostrils basal, with an oval opening in front of a coriaceous groove, indistinctly operculated, covered with a small stiff and peculiarly shaped feather" (Gadow 1883a:79).

The small feather covering the nostrils has been the basis for placing the species of *Regulus* in a subfamily or family usually within, or adjacent to, the Paridae or the Sylviidae. *Leptopoecile*, *Lophobasileus*, and *Sylviparus* sometimes have been included in the same group with *Regulus*.

Gadow (1883a) placed the Regulinae in the Paridae, and Sharpe (1903) inserted the Regulidae after the Paridae and Chamaeidae and before the Sittidae. Wetmore (1930, 1960) placed the Regulidae between his Sylviidae and Muscicapidae. Mayr and Amadon (1951) included *Regulus* in the Sylviinae: Sylviini of the Muscicapidae, and noted that "*Regulus* agrees so well with some species of *Phylloscopus* as to leave little doubt that it is a sylviid adapted to boreal coniferous forests. More doubt exists as regards the central Asiatic *Lophobasileus* and *Leptopoecile*. These little birds suggest *Regulus*, but might be related to titmice, notably *Aegithalos*. We follow custom in leaving them near *Regulus* and *Phylloscopus*. Their mossy ground nest favors this assignment" (p. 19).

The A.O.U. checklist committee (1983) also included *Regulus* in the Muscicapidae: Sylviinae: Sylviini, following *Phylloscopus*. Thus, there has been a consensus that the kinglets are related to the sylviines.

The DNA Hybridization Evidence

The DNA comparisons indicate that *Regulus* branched from a common ancestor with other sylvioid lineages at Δ 9.7 (Fig. 380). The branches between adjacent lineages of the Sylvioidea are mostly close to one another, some only 0.2 or 0.3 Δ units apart. Figs. 17 and 350 show that these differences, although small, may be statistically significant. These branches may be represented as a multifurcation in the dendrogram, but that does not change the taxonomic status of each of the groups.

Fig. 278 (*Regulus*) agrees with other evidence that the kinglets are closest to *Phylloscopus* and the other sylviids.

Family PYCNONOTIDAE

21/137. Bulbuls, Greenbuls. The bulbuls and greenbuls occur in Africa and Asia. Morphological characters usually ascribed to the Pycnonotidae include short tarsi, numerous rictal bristles, abundant rump plumage, and a patch of bristle-like feathers in the nape region.

The fairy-bluebirds (*Irena*), ioras (*Aegithina*), and leafbirds (*Chloropsis*) are sometimes included in the Pycnonotidae, sometimes placed in separate monotypic families, or combined in the "Irenidae," "Aegithinidae," or "Chloropseidae." The uncertainty about the relationships of the bulbuls to these three genera, and of the fairy-bluebirds, ioras, and leafbirds to one another and to other passerines, has been a feature of all previous classifications. The DNA hybridization evidence shows that *Irena*, *Chloropsis*, and *Aegithina* are members of the corvoid radiation in the Corvida, thus not related to the bulbuls.

Sundevall (1872, see 1889:72) placed the "Families" "Pycnonotinae" and "Phyllornithinae" (*Chloropsis*) between the waxwings ("Ampelidinae") and the "Oriolinae," followed by the woodswallows ("Artaminae") and cuckoo-shrikes ("Campophaginae"). Sharpe (1881) placed the bulbuls, leafbirds, ioras, and *Irena* in the subfamily "Bradypodinae" of the "Timeliidae," followed by the wrens ("Troglodytinae"), in which he included the dippers (*Cinclus*). In the *Hand-List* Sharpe (1901, 1903) inserted the family Pycnonotidae between the "Campophagidae" and the "Timeliidae" followed by the Troglodytidae and Cinclidae. Sharpe's arrangement is reflected in Wetmore's (1960) classification which includes the sequence Timaliidae, Campephagidae, Pycnonotidae, Chloropseidae, Cinclidae, Troglodytidae.

Delacour (1943a) reviewed the older literature and revised the genera and species of bulbuls. He suggested that the bulbuls are not closely related to the Old World flycatchers, thrushes, babblers, sylviids, or the other groups often placed in the "Muscicapidae" of Hartert (1910) and others. Delacour and Vaurie (1957) listed the Pycnonotidae between the Campephagidae and Irenidae, near the waxwings.

Mayr and Amadon (1951) suggested that the "bulbuls are among the more primitive appearing of Old World song birds. They may be related to the Campephagidae, but a few, such as *Nicator*, resemble some of the bush shrikes (Laniidae: Malaconotinae), though perhaps only superficially." They included the Pycnonotidae, Irenidae, and Campephagidae under the heading of "Bulbuls and Allies." This arrangement was adopted in the Basel sequence (Mayr and Greenway 1956) and in Peters (1960).

The association of the bulbuls and cuckoo-shrikes is a feature of virtually all classifications proposed during the past century, but evidence for this alliance seems not to exist. It is likely that their similar geographic distributions and the custom of placing the two groups together, which began long ago, constitute the only "characters" they have in common. Since the cuckoo-shrikes are members of the Corvida, and the bulbuls of the Passerida, their presumed close relationship is revealed as a false idea that persisted because of the power of tradition and the lack of evidence to the contrary.

The DNA Hybridization Evidence

The DNA comparisons show that the Pycnonotidae, including the shrike-like *Nicator*, are the living members of a lineage that branched from the other sylvioids at Δ 9.5. Their closest relatives are the Regulidae, Cisticolidae, Zosteropidae, and Sylviidae (Fig. 380).

Fig. 279 (*Pycnonotus*) shows the relative distances from *Pycnonotus* to several muscicapids. In Figs. 269, 276, and 284 *Pycnonotus* clusters with the members of the Passerida, not with the honeyeaters (Corvida). In Fig. 281 *Pycnonotus* clusters with the sylviids.

We conclude that the bulbuls are members of the Sylvioidea and are not related to the cuckoo-shrikes, Irenidae, or other members of the Corvida as so often proposed in the past.

Family *inc. sedis* HYPOCOLIIDAE

1/1. The Grey Hypocolius (*Hypocolius ampelinus*) breeds in the Tigris-Euphrates valley in Iraq and southwestern Arabia, and wanders more widely in winter. It has usually been assigned to a position near the waxwings (Bombycillidae) in recent classifications. Its affinities are uncertain and we lack its DNA. We place it here without evidence that it is related to the adjacent groups.

Family CISTICOLIDAE

14/119. African Warblers. DNA comparisons among the genera traditionally placed in the Sylviidae revealed the existence of several distinct groups, including one cluster composed of genera endemic to Africa or of obvious African origin. Six genera have been identified as members of this group by DNA comparisons, namely, *Cisticola*, *Prinia*, *Hypergerus*, *Camaroptera*, *Eminia*, and *Apalis*. Of these, only the first two include species that occur outside Africa. The other genera included in the Cisticolidae are thought to be closely related to those listed above. The cisticolid lineage branched from the other sylvioids at $\Delta T_{50}H$ 9.4 (Fig. 381).

White (1962:653) treated several genera together that he noted "are sometimes called Grass Warblers, viz., *Cisticola*, *Incana*, *Scotocerca*, and *Prinia*. They comprise 50 species." White also dealt with a group of "indigenous African warblers" (p. 695):

Apalis: 16 species, several . . . much polytypic variation.
Artisornis: very close to the Asiatic *Orthotomus*, and might even be treated as identical with it.
Scepomycter: 1 species, of rather uncertain affinities.
Drymocichla: *Eminia*, *Hypergerus*, *Bathmocercus*: all monotypic.
Camaroptera: 7 species. [including] *Calamonastes*.
Euryptila: monotypic and of uncertain affinities.
Eremomela: 9 species.
Sylvietta: 9 species.
Hemitesia: monotypic.
Macrosphenus: 4 species.
Graueria and *Amaurocichla*: both monotypic, and the latter of very uncertain affinities.
Parisoma: 5 species. *P. buryi* is of uncertain affinities and may not belong to this
    genus . . . affinities of *Parisoma* to other warblers are not clear, and it may well be closely related
    to *Sylvia*.
Hylia and *Pholidornis*: monotypic and of uncertain affinities.

Of these we have DNA hybridization evidence that *Parisoma* is a sylviine (see below), and that *Sylvietta* is ca. $\Delta T_{50}H$ 9.0 from the cisticolids. *Sylvietta* is only Δ 7.5 from *Sphenoeacus mentalis*, thus it is not a cisticolid.

We also have DNA evidence that *Seicercus*, *Sphenoeacus*, *Bradypterus*, and *Chloropeta* are Δ 9.0–9.5 from *Cisticola*. White (1960) associated *Bradypterus*, *Schoenicola*, *Chloropeta*, and *Sphenoeacus* with *Sylvia*, *Phylloscopus*, *Locustella*, *Lusciniola*, *Acrocephalus*, and *Hippolais*. We have DNA evidence linking most of these genera to *Sylvia*. (Note: *Seicercus* and *Phylloscopus* are sometimes regarded as congeneric.)

Hall and Moreau (1970:161) reported that "Forbes-Watson felt that *Incana* was closer to *Prinia* than to *Cisticola* but it reminded him of *Apalis* and *Camaroptera* as well."

Hall and Moreau (1970:204) noted that "*Hylia* and the very dissimilar *Pholidornis* show flattening of the epibranchial horns of the hyoid apparatus—a character of the sunbirds—and have consequently often been placed in that family. Chapin preferred . . . to transfer *Hylia* to the warblers, though he admitted that 'its firm plumage, rather strong bill and well-developed nasal operculum are somewhat exceptional' in the warblers. He records that it has a harsh and sunbird-like call-note and also a whistle, and its nest is a globular structure hidden in forks of bushes (not suspended like a sunbird's). It is apparent that *Hylia* has some characters which are atypical of sunbirds and others that are atypical of warblers. Until further anatomical evidence is forthcoming we regard it (and *Pholidornis*) as a species of uncertain family."

Hall and Moreau (1970:204) summarized their review of the warblers of Africa:

The intensity of . . . speciation in Africa is well illustrated by the warblers, of which we recognize about 150 African species, almost a third [in] a single genus, *Cisticola*. Only six of the warbler species range outside Africa . . . the most notable being *Cisticola juncidis*.

The warblers also contain a relatively high percentage of species, and even genera, of uncertain affinities. This is partly due to the lack of definitive "warbler" characters and is aggravated by inadequate knowledge of their anatomy and, in several species, of juvenile plumages, nests and eggs. Even among some of the better-known genera, such as *Prinia, Apalis, Camaroptera*, there is room for a re-assessment of generic characters. Elucidation of affinities might be assisted by systematic investigation . . . of several small anatomical characters, three of which are mentioned incidentally in the discussions— ossification of leg tendons, detected in some cisticolas but not others: a peculiarity of nostril, used as a generic character for *Scepomycter* and found also in *Bathmocercus*: flattened epibranchial horns of the hyoids, which are regarded as typical of the sunbirds but are found also in *Hylia prasina*, a species sometimes included in the warblers.

We conclude that there is acceptable evidence that the Cisticolidae includes, at least: *Cisticola, Prinia, Hypergerus, Camaroptera, Eminia, Apalis, Incana,* and *Scotocerca*. We can also be certain that the following African genera are not cisticolids: *Parisoma, Seicercus, Sphenoeacus, Bradypterus, Chloropeta,* and *Sylvietta*. We regard the affinities of the remaining genera as unknown. Sibley and Monroe (1990) include *Parisoma* in *Sylvia*.

The DNA Hybridization Evidence

Fig. 280 (*Cisticola*) shows the close relationships among *Cisticola, Prinia, Hypergerus, Apalis,* and *Camaroptera*, and their distinct cluster relative to the cluster of the sylviids (*Megalurus* to *Sylvia*). The tight cluster of the sylviids indicates that they are on a separate branch of the tree from that of the cisticolids.

Fig. 281 (*Cisticola*) shows that the cisticolids are distinct from the other sylvioid families: Sylviidae, Pycnonotidae, Zosteropidae, Hirundinidae, Certhiidae, Aegithalidae, Sittidae, Paridae.

Fig. 282 (*Prinia*) shows the clustering of the cisticolids (*Prinia, Cisticola, Hypergerus, Camaroptera*) relative to the sylviids (*Phylloscopus* to *Cincloramphus*), and the out-group position of *Gerygone*, an Australian acanthizine (Corvida: Pardalotidae) often placed in the Sylviidae in the past.

We conclude that the Cisticolidae is a distinct group of sylvioid genera of African origin. The cisticolid lineage branched from its nearest relatives at $\Delta T_{50}H$ 9.4, thus meeting the criteria for a family.

Family ZOSTEROPIDAE

13/96. White-eyes, Silvereyes, and *Cleptornis*. The Zosteropidae are small oscines with a reduced, or absent, outer (10th) primary; slender, usually straight or slightly decurved bills;

operculate nostrils; and a bifid, protractile tongue each half of which is laciniate in many species. The wings are short, the tail short and square. The tarsi have a few scales in front and the outer toes are partly united. The plumage tends to be yellowish or greenish above and whitish, brownish, or gray below. Most of the 96 species have a circumorbital ring of white feathers. The sexes are alike.

Moreau (1957) described the variation in the African species and noted that the white-eyes "are a tropical passerine family, with a range over the whole of the Ethiopian Region and eastwards, through the islands of the Indian Ocean and India to Japan, the central Pacific and Australasia. There is . . . a gap of over a thousand miles . . . between about 50°E. and 66°E., across eastern Arabia, Persia and Baluchistan."

Mees (1957:3) noted that "The Zosteropidae constitute a natural family of the Passeres, of uncertain relationships, though generally they are placed in the neighbourhood of the Dicaeidae and the Nectariniidae because of their somewhat similar way of living." Mees (1957, 1961, 1969) reviewed the Indo-Australian white-eyes.

The brush-tipped nectarivorous tongue has been the basis for placing the white-eyes with or near the other nectar-feeding groups, such as the Meliphagidae and Nectariniidae, although the nine-primaried wing and general appearance caused Sundevall (1872, see 1889:81) to include *Zosterops* in his "Fam. 46. Dendroecinae" with *Dicaeum*, some of the New World wood warblers (Parulini), and the Neotropical honeycreepers *Conirostrum*, *Dacnis*, etc. (Thraupini).

Gadow (1884) introduced the "Cinnyrimorphae" as forming a "tolerably natural group, as far as the *Nectariniidae* and *Meliphagidae* proper are concerned. With regard to the *Zosteropinae*, their degree of relationship with the *Meliphagidae* is doubtful, and they might, perhaps, with more propriety be ranged with the *Dicaeidae*, which, in all probability, have very little to do with the Cinnyrimorphae *sensu strictori*."

In spite of his doubts, Gadow (1884:146) placed the subfamily "Zosteropinae" in the Meliphagidae, and included two genera of true meliphagids, *Melithreptus* and *Plectorhynchus* (*Plectorhyncha*). The two honeyeaters apparently were included in the Zosteropinae because they have short first primaries, a squarish tail, and relatively short bills.

The white-eyes and flowerpeckers (Dicaeinae) have been associated because the latter have a small or vestigial tenth primary and, in some genera, a tongue adapted for nectar feeding.

In the *Hand-List* Sharpe (1909) placed only the white-eyes in the Zosteropidae, but the subsequent groups were the Dicaeidae, Nectariniidae, Promeropidae, and Meliphagidae. Thus, based on convergent similarities, another false tradition was established.

Wetmore (1930, 1960) used the sequence Meliphagidae, Nectariniidae, Dicaeidae, Zosteropidae; E. Stresemann (1934) listed Meliphagidae, Dicaeidae, and Zosteropidae. In the "Old World Nectar Eaters" Mayr and Amadon (1951) included the Dicaeidae, Nectariniidae, Meliphagidae, and Zosteropidae, but they expressed their doubts: "The relationships of the Zosteropidae remain to be discovered. Since some of them are somewhat specialized for feeding on nectar, they may . . . be left in the vicinity of the Meliphagidae and Dicaeidae" (p. 27).

"The Old World Nectar-Feeder Assemblage" recognized by Beecher (1953b:290) included the "sunbirds, flower-peckers, and white-eyes [which] share many internal characters with the Pycnonotinae. . . . They could have arisen from the Sylviinae close to the bulbul stem; but the serrate-tipped mandibles of sunbirds and flowerpeckers may be forecast in such a bulbul as *Andropadus*, and it is relatively easy to derive the plumage types of the whole assemblage from bulbuls. All have the ninth primary long and the tenth short, the ectethmoid truncate, lacrymal fused, and a large palatine salivary gland. . . . the bulbul *Phyllastrephus zosterops* resembles white-eyes in plumage. . . . Anatomically, white-eyes are nothing but warblers (or bulbuls) adapted for nectar-feeding."

Thus, Beecher found evidence of the relationship among bulbuls, sylviines, and white-eyes but, by including the sunbirds and flowerpeckers in the same assemblage, he also demonstrated the difficulties involved in the interpretation of morphological characters as clues to phylogeny.

The Basel sequence (Mayr and Greenway 1956) included the traditional arrangement: Dicaeidae, Nectariniidae, Zosteropidae, Meliphagidae, which was also used in volume 12 of the *Check-list of Birds of the World* (Paynter 1967). Delacour and Vaurie (1957), Berndt and Meise (1960), and Wolters (1975–82) also placed the nectar-feeders together.

With reference to *Cleptornis marchei* of Saipan Island, Pratt et al. (1987:287) noted that "Until now, this species has been classified as an aberrant honeyeater (Meliphagidae). Pratt's hypothesis, based on behavioral, ecological, and zoogeographical considerations, that the 'Golden Honeyeater' is really a white-eye (Zosteropidae) has . . . been confirmed by biochemical studies in the laboratory of C. G. Sibley (in litt.) at the Yale Peabody Museum. . . . Among the white-eyes, *Cleptornis* appears closest to *Rukia*."

The DNA Hybridization Evidence

The DNA comparisons show that the Zosteropidae are sylvioids and that the white-eye lineage branched at Δ 9.1 (Fig. 381). Since the Meliphagidae is a family of the parvorder Corvida, the Nectariniidae (including the Dicaeini) is a family of the Passeroidea, and the Zosteropidae of the Sylvioidea, it is apparent that the morphological similarities among these groups are due to convergence, not most recent common ancestry.

The white-eyes of the Caroline Islands (Yap, Truk, Ponape) have been placed in the genus *Rukia*, described by Mees (1969:225) as "Large slender-billed white-eyes, mainly characterized by their aberrant coloration, which is brownish, not greenish. Bill and legs are also of unusual coloration. . . . The eye-ring can be almost complete (*R. oleaginea*), developed under the eye only (*R. ruki*) or virtually absent."

Comparisons between the tracer DNA of *Zosterops lateralis* of Australia and the Olive White-eye (*Rukia oleaginea*) of Yap Island produced a Δ $T_{50}H$ of 1.5, while *Z. pallida* of South Africa was Δ 2.4 from *Z. lateralis*, and *Z. palpebrosus* of southeast Asia was Δ 2.2 from *lateralis*. It seems reasonable to include the species *oleaginea* in *Zosterops* (as *Z. oleagineus*).

The "Golden Honeyeater" (*Cleptornis marchei*) occurs only on the islands of Saipan and Agiguan in the Mariana Islands of Micronesia. From its original description by Oustalet (1889), until the note by Pratt et al. (1987:287; see above), it was assigned to the Meliphagidae. We compared the tracer DNA of *Cleptornis* with four species of *Zosterops* (*pallidus*, *palpebrosus*, *lateralis*, *oleagineus*), several meliphagids, and other oscines. *Cleptornis* is Δ $T_{50}H$

3.0 from *Zosterops*, but ca. Δ 13.0 from the meliphagids, as would be expected if *Cleptornis* is a member of the Passerida. The Δ 3.0 from *Zosterops* shows that the Golden Honeyeater is actually a member of the Zosteropidae.

Baker (1951) reviewed what was known about *Cleptornis*, including the structure of the nest, which is hung from a fork of a branch, and the pale blue eggs with rufous spotting. The nests of white-eyes are also hung from forks, and their eggs are plain pale blue. The plumage of *Cleptornis* is mostly bright yellow, with a pale yellow orbital ring. The bill is relatively long, and decurved, with the culmen 18–20 mm in length. The bills of three species of *Rukia* range from 20–24 mm (Baker 1951:330). The tail of *Cleptornis* is longer (56–66 mm) than that of *Rukia* (41–57), but wings and tarsi are essentially identical in length in the two.

Baker (1951:304) noted: "Not only is it remarkable that the Golden Honey-eater has become established on a single island in a rather closely associated chain of islands, but it is also difficult to determine from where the bird came. It seemingly has no close relatives in the Micronesian area. Oustalet (1895:202) points out that one has to go to New Guinea, Moluccas, Australia, Fiji, Samoa, and Tonga in order to find related forms. . . ., *Timeliopsis* of New Guinea has some resemblances to *Cleptornis*, although the coloration is different. *Timeliopsis* has a similar bill, but has a longer tail and longer wing; the shortness of the wing in *Cleptornis* is not unusual since other insular forms also exhibit this characteristic."

Since *Cleptornis* is a white-eye it is easy to understand its confinement to Saipan and Agiguan in the southern Mariana Islands. There are populations of a typical white-eye, *Zosterops conspicillatus,* on Saipan, Tinian, Rota, and Guam. Only on Saipan are there two species. The sympatry of *Cleptornis* and *Z. conspicillatus saypani* on Saipan may be a case of double invasion, in which the ancestor of *Cleptornis* arrived first and differentiated before the more widespread *conspicillatus* arrived. Whatever may be the explanation for the two species on Saipan, *Cleptornis* now has close relatives on adjacent islands that would tend to impede its ability to expand its range.

Baker (1951:330) noted that "*Rukia palauensis* . . . was described under the generic name *Cleptornis* by Reichenow. This generic allocation was not followed by subsequent authors; Stresemann proposed the generic name *Megazosterops* in 1930, and Mayr (1944:7) placed this white-eye in the genus *Rukia* along with other large white-eyes." Mees (1969:233) retained *Megazosterops* for *palauensis* because he was not convinced that it "is closer related to *Rukia* than to other members of the Zosteropidae."

It seems apparent that if *Rukia* and *Megazosterops* are true white-eyes, there are no obvious morphological reasons to exclude *Cleptornis* from the Zosteropidae.

Fig. 283 (*Cleptornis*) leaves no doubt about the relationships of *Cleptornis*. These melting curves also show the distinctness of the Nectariniidae (*Anthreptes* to *Nectarinia*) and the Meliphagidae (*Phylidonyris* to *Myzomela*). The convergent similarities among these three groups caused them to be placed next to one another in virtually all classifications until the DNA hybridization evidence revealed their true affinities.

Fig. 284 (*Cleptornis*) shows that the white-eyes are more closely related to the sylviids, cisticolids, and bulbuls than to the nectariniids (*Promerops*), melanocharitids (*Melanocharis*), or meliphagids (*Anthochaera, Plectorhyncha*).

We conclude that the Zosteropidae is a sylvioid family; that *Cleptornis* is a zosteropid; and that the Zosteropidae, Nectariniidae, and Meliphagidae represent independently evolved lineages whose morphological similarities are due to convergence, not to recent common ancestry.

Family SYLVIIDAE

101/552. Leaf Warblers, Grassbirds, Songlarks, and Babblers. The taxonomic history of the Sylviidae provides many lessons for the systematist. All of the villains are present: convergence, tradition, misinterpretation of characters, attempts to solve problems by subdivision and by incorporation—each pitfall has trapped one or more able and zealous ornithologists. Although the DNA comparisons have solved some of the problems, they also present new ones that we cannot solve because of the lack of the necessary material.

No doubt it is possible to trace some of the confusion to the earliest attempts to classify birds, but we begin with Sharpe's comments (1879:6) concerning the classification of the "Cichlomorphae," the "Thrush-like Passeres, the difficulties in classifying which are not likely to be exaggerated by any one who attempts the task. As already stated in this work, the system of classification here adopted is founded on that of the late Prof. Sundevall, who, however, admits . . . that the divisions he proposes for the Cichlomorphae are purely artificial."

Sharpe went on to describe the difficulties and to define the families of the "Cichlomorphae." The Turdidae, which included the "Sylviinae," was characterized as follows: "Bill slender, but rather wide and depressed; *wing long and flat, with a very small bastard primary not more than half the length of the second*, the latter generally longer than the secondaries. Composed of birds *generally migratory*."

It was Seebohm (1881) who had to wrestle with the "Turdidae" in the *Catalogue of Birds* and he was not happy with Sharpe's definition, which he considered to be

an artificial one. It consists of birds belonging to two distinct families, which are separated from each other by structural characters of greater importance (i.e., extending in all probability to a remoter geological period) than those which divide either of them from the *Muscicapidae* and the *Timeliidae*, as defined in the classification referred to. Under these circumstances I have endeavoured to meet the difficulty by making two provisional subfamilies, which I characterize as follows:—

Sylviinae. The young in first plumage differ very slightly in colour from the adult, both being generally unspotted both above and below, and the difference being confined to the shade or degree of colour, which is generally most conspicuous on the underparts. In the rare instances in which the upper parts are spotted in the adult, the spots are less conspicuous in the young birds. In the first autumn before migration, if a partial moult takes place, it is simply a renewal of certain feathers by feathers of the same colour, so that, in winter, birds of the year are generally easily recognizable by a difference of shade in the colour, especially in that of the underparts. This difference, however, is lost in the complete moult which takes place in both adult and young in spring, a moult which usually takes place in March shortly before the spring migration begins. In autumn . . . a second annual complete moult takes place in adult birds. The autumn plumage is usually intermediate in colour between the spring plumage and that of the bird of the year. Curiously enough, this peculiarity in the colour of the immature bird, and in the subsequent moults which the plumage undergoes, is correlated with the existence of scutellations on the front of the tarsus.

Seebohm's description of the "Turdinae" followed, with the differences in the juvenal plumage (spotted), molts (one only), and a "plain tarsus" (booted) described. Seebohm's observations were cogent and correct, and he concluded with a remarkably prescient statement that describes essentially what the DNA comparisons have revealed: "When sufficient facts have accumulated to make a classification of the Passeres possible, it is probable that the *Muscicapidae* and the *Timeliidae* will be all or most of them absorbed in the families *Turdidae* and *Sylviidae*, each of which may again be subdivided into Turdine, Timeliine, and Muscicapine groups of genera or subfamilies."

Seebohm (1881:2–3) included only seven genera in his "Subfamily Sylviinae:" *Sylvia*, *Phylloscopus*, *Hypolais* (sic), *Acrocephalus*, *Locustella*, *Lusciniola*, and *Cettia*.

Between 1881 and 1903, the concept of the boundaries of the "Sylviidae" changed radically. Seebohm and Sharpe (1898–1902) monographed the Turdidae and proposed modifications of the classification of the thrushes and their real, or presumed, relatives. In the *Hand-List* Sharpe (1903) included 76 genera in his Sylviidae, including nine Australian endemics we now know to be members of the parvorder Corvida, and others of uncertain affinities. This heterogeneous compilation may have set the stage for the confusion that was to follow.

Because of his conviction that "it is impossible to separate the families Muscicapidae, Sylviidae and Turdidae," Hartert (1910) placed the muscicapine and monarchine flycatchers, the sylviine warblers, the babblers, and the thrushes together in his version of the "Muscicapidae." (See above under the family Muscicapidae for details.) Hartert's enlarged "Muscicapidae" was expanded by subsequent authors until it became the "Primitive Insect Eaters" of Mayr and Amadon (1951) and part of the Basel sequence (Mayr and Greenway 1956). This group came to include representatives of both parvorders, including members of the Meliphagoidea, Corvoidea, Muscicapoidea, and Sylvioidea, with associated "families" representing the Passeroidea. Until recently, this polyphyletic assemblage was used in many publications, e.g., A.O.U. 1983. The results of our DNA hybridization studies were accepted in volume 11 of the *Check-list of Birds of the World* (Mayr and Cottrell 1986) in which separate families for the Sylviidae, Muscicapidae, Maluridae, Acanthizidae, Monarchidae, and Eopsaltriidae were recognized.

As indicated above, we have found that the babblers, the "Timaliidae" of many authors, are closely related to the sylviines. The taxonomic history of the babblers is as complex as that of any group of birds, and a brief review will add some interesting examples to the catalog of opinions and guesses that have constituted many of the "characters" of avian systematics.

Sundevall's "Fam. 14. Brachypteryginae" (1872, see 1889:57) was one of the families in his "Phalanx Brevipennes" of the "Cohort Cichlomorphae," and it included some of the genera still placed in the Timaliidae or Timaliinae of recent authors, including *Timalia*, *Pellorneum*, *Alcippe*, and *Garrulax*. Other "families" of the Brevipennes, characterized by having short wings, long scutellate tarsi, a large outer primary, and soft, lax plumage, included the Acanthizinae, Cisticolinae, Malurinae, Aegithininae, Copsychinae, Crateropodinae, Troglodytinae, Toxostominae, and several others. The genera contained in some of these groups make the implied alliances even more surprising.

Sharpe based his classification on that of Sundevall, and his treatment of the "Timeliidae" required two volumes of the *Catalogue of Birds* (1881, 1883). In the introduction to the first volume (1881), Sharpe noted that "the large family *Timeliidae*, or Babbling-Thrushes, a group which is largely represented in the Old World . . . contains only a few members in the

American continents. Five subfamilies have been described in the present volume . . . the Bulbuls, the Wrens, the Mocking-Thrushes, the Solitaires, and the Bower-birds. The total number of species . . . is 407."

In the introduction to the second volume (1883) Sharpe recorded the addition of 687 species, making a total of 1094. The first volume included 66 genera, the second 161, a total of 227 genera, with an average of 4.8 species per genus. Sharpe did not use trinomials, thus his "species" included many forms which, today, would be considered subspecies.

In the second volume only the subfamily "Timeliinae" was added to the first five because Sharpe (1883:1) considered "it impossible to divide the birds hitherto referred or allied to the typical *Timeliidae* into well-defined or definable subfamilies or groups." Sharpe then stated that his views about the classification proposed in the 1881 volume had changed, and "that the family, as at present constituted, contains many forms which are not real *Timeliidae*." He therefore arranged the "remaining forms under groups of one subfamily." The result was ten groups, some of which still contained "many forms which are not real" babblers. Among the members of Sharpe's Timeliinae were several thrushes, *Lamprolia* (a monarch), *Stipiturus* (Maluridae), *Apalis* (and other genera we assign to the Cisticolidae), *Acanthiza* (Pardalotidae), *Chamaea* (the Wrentit, which *is* a babbler, see below), *Orthonyx* (Orthonychidae), and the "Accentores" (*Prunella*, Passeridae, plus *Ephthianura*, Meliphagidae). Clearly, the Timeliidae was a waste basket into which Sharpe had dumped a large number of taxa whose affinities he could not determine, and he knew it.

By 1903, Sharpe had revised his ideas about the Timeliidae, which was reduced to 576 species in 122 genera and six subfamilies: Crateropodinae, Timeliinae, Brachypteryginae, Sibiinae, Liotrichinae, and Paradoxornithinae. Non-babbler genera were still present, but the bulbuls, wrens, mockingbirds, thrushes, bowerbirds, accentors, *Ephthianura*, and many others had been removed to other families. However, the vicissitudes of the babblers were far from over.

Pycraft (1905c) proposed a "turdiform" group to include part of the Timaliidae, plus the bulbuls, mockingbirds, thrushes, sylviids, paruline wood warblers, kinglets, dippers, wrens, larks, and wagtails. Five years later came Hartert's (1910) proposal to combine the babblers, thrushes, Old World flycatchers, and sylviids in the "Muscicapidae," which we have noted in several places, especially under the Muscicapidae.

Hartert's flawed treatment was the basis for that of Delacour (1946), who defined the subfamily Timaliinae on the basis of external form, habitat, behavior, voice, juvenal plumage, and food habits. Delacour concluded that the babblers are closest to the Sylviinae and that it is extremely difficult to distinguish between them. In Delacour's classification the "Muscicapidae" included the Timaliinae, Turdinae, Sylviinae, Muscicapinae, Pachycephalinae, and Cinclosomatinae. He divided the Timaliinae into five tribes: Turdoidini, Chamaeini, Timaliini, Pomatorhini, and Pellorneini. The Wrentit (*Chamaea*) and the Bearded Tit (*Panurus*) were placed in the Chamaeini, which Delacour proposed as the link between the babblers and the "Aegithalinae-Parinae" and then, in a sequential series, to the Remizidae, Dicaeidae, and Nectariniidae. In 1950, Delacour commented on several babbler genera and erected a sixth tribe, Picathartini, for *Picathartes* of West Africa, which he thought to be closest to the Turdoidini. Delacour and Amadon (1951) also commented on *Picathartes* and the evidence linking it to the Timaliidae, rather than to the Corvidae or Sturnidae.

Mayr and Amadon (1951) adopted Delacour's classification for the 282 species they placed in the "Subfamily Timaliinae" of the "Muscicapidae." They commented:

The babblers or Timaliinae have long been a "scrap basket" for genera that did not fit well into the Turdinae or Sylviinae. Delacour's (1946) revision brought a semblance of order into this group, but even so he was obliged to set aside a section for "aberrant genera." To the five tribes that he set up, a sixth, the Picathartini, including only . . . *Picathartes*, is to be added. . . . This genus has usually been placed in the Corvidae, where it surely does not belong.

We agree with Delacour in placing the wren-tit, *Chamaea*, of California in the tribe Chamaeini of the Timaliinae. This bird appears to be very closely allied to the genus *Moupinia* of China.

A number of genera of the Australo-Papuan region (*Eupetes, Cinclosoma, Orthonyx, Psophodes, Ifrita, Androphobus,* and *Melampitta*) do not fit well in the Timaliinae but may for the time being be left as a tribe, the Cinclosomatini of that subfamily. Some may consider them as nearer to the Turdinae. These seven genera do not comprise a homogeneous group; *Psophodes*, as noted elsewhere, may belong to the Pachycephalini. *Cinclorhamphus*, sometimes associated with this group, we tentatively place in the Malurinae" (p. 18).

We now know, from DNA comparisons, that the Wrentit is indeed a babbler (Sibley and Ahlquist 1982b), but that most, and perhaps all, of the Australo-Papuan genera listed above are not babblers but are members of the parvorder Corvida (Sibley and Ahlquist 1985a). It also seems likely that *Picathartes* is a member of the Corvida; see discussion under Parvorder *incertae sedis*, family Picathartidae, above.

Beecher (1953b) interpreted his jaw muscle comparisons as supporting Delacour's revision, although he placed the babblers in the "superfamily Timalioidea" and the sylviids in the "Sylvioidea," thus splitting the Passeri into two groups, which the DNA data show to be tribes in the Sylviinae! Beecher thought that his "Cisticolinae" was a link between his "Timalioidea" and the "Sylvioidea." Beecher (1953b:321) believed the Timaliidae "to be a microcosm of the Timalioidea as well as the stem group from which its specialized families arose (the transitional Cisticolinae is as much a subfamily of Timaliidae as of Sylviidae). The best check on the evidence that the Timaliidae has given rise to shrike groups is seen in the existence of timaliine shrikes (*Pteruthius, Laniellus*). A good check on timaliid origin for other groups is seen in the occurrence of timaliine larks (*Cinclorhamphus*) in Australia where true larks do not occur. Similar examples are seen in what I interpret as timaliine titmice (*Parisoma, Myioparus*), creepers (*Climacteris*), and nuthatches (*Neositta*)."

Beecher erred in stating that true larks do not occur in Australia. The Australasian Lark or Bush-Lark (*Mirafra javanica*) is native to Australia and New Guinea, as well as widespread in southeastern Asia. We now know, from DNA comparisons, that *Climacteris* and *Neositta* (*Daphoenositta*) are members of the Corvida, and that *Parisoma* and *Cincloramphus* are sylviids. (Note: The correct spelling is "*Cincloramphus*," not "*Cinclorhamphus*.")

Beecher had considered the jaw musculature of *Picathartes* to be similar to that of *Corvus* (*fide* Delacour and Amadon 1951:61), but he later (1953b:313) agreed with Delacour and Amadon "as to its timaliine status."

Mayr and Greenway (1956) included the Timaliinae, including *Chamaea*, as one of nine subfamilies in their "Muscicapidae," the others being the Turdinae, Paradoxornithinae, Polioptilinae, Sylviinae, Malurinae, Muscicapinae, Monarchinae, and Pachycephalinae. They gave family status to the Cinclidae, Troglodytidae, and Mimidae, thus departing from Mayr and Amadon (1951).

Delacour and Vaurie (1957) also included nine subfamilies in their Muscicapidae, differing from Mayr and Amadon (1951) only by including *Paradoxornis* in the Timaliinae and by recognizing the Rhipidurinae for the fantails. Amadon (1957) made adjacent families of the Timaliidae, Muscicapidae, Sylviidae, Turdidae, Mimidae, and Troglodytidae. Wetmore (1960) retained the families of his earlier lists, with two sequences of families that include the groups under discussion: (1) Paradoxornithidae, Chamaeidae, Timaliidae; (2) Cinclidae, Troglodytidae, Mimidae, Turdidae, Zeledoniidae, Sylviidae, Regulidae, Muscicapidae.

Simmons (1963) thought the behavior of certain babblers "does not suggest a particularly close affinity with the thrush assemblage" and cited some seemingly typical babbler genera that do not exhibit the behavioral attributes he ascribed to the group. For the Wrentit, Simmons concluded that "the behaviour evidence for the Wren-tit's being classed as a babbler is overwhelming."

Also based on behavior, Harrison and Parker (1965) proposed that *Malurus* and certain other genera be placed in the Timaliidae rather than in the Muscicapidae. They also thought that the Timaliidae "appear to have close affinities, through *Paradoxornis*, with the long-tailed tits, Aegithalidae; and possibly through these to the penduline tits, Remizidae, and the true tits, Paridae, assuming that the assemblage of the three latter groups, now usually combined within the Paridae, is not polyphyletic."

The history of the classification of the sylviine warblers and timaliine babblers provides additional evidence of the difficulties that seem to afflict every attempt to extract phylogenetic information from morphological characters. Although Seebohm (1881) had found valid characters that define and separate the sylviids and the turdids, other arguments prevailed. Sharpe was not truly interested in higher-category classification and his reliance on Sundevall's strange ideas of relationships repeatedly led him astray. Later workers copied from Sharpe and compounded his errors with more of their own.

Hartert (1910) apparently believed that because he had difficulty in telling members of certain groups apart, they must be closely related. The influence of his erroneous concept of the "Muscicapidae" survives in most recent classifications and has been repeated many times. (Discussion under family Muscicapidae.)

The idea that different living groups can be linked to one another via other living groups, examples of which are cited above, reveals another source of confusion about phylogeny that has affected many of the classifications proposed during the past century. Beecher's statement (1953b:321) that "the transitional Cisticolinae is as much a subfamily of Timaliidae as of Sylviidae" is an extreme example, especially remarkable because he placed the Sylviidae and Timaliidae in separate superfamilies. This is surprising because Beecher (1953b:320) also wrote that "Few ornithologists appeared to realize that a linear series is not classification at all. Evolution is basically a process of divergence, and those who judged the thrushes, crows, or finches to be the most specialized groups were each right and each wrong. In a branching phyletic tree—the simplest expression of relationships so far as they may be inferred from morphology—all three, equally, are terminal groups. Lacking a phylogenetic tree, there was no classification, only a list of families."

It seems that Beecher had a clear and correct understanding of the relationship between phylogeny and classification, but that he, like so many others, was defeated by the complexities of morphology. Beecher was aware of the results to be expected from adaptive radiation, namely, that closely related taxa may occupy different ecological niches and have superficially different characters. He wrote that "the classifications based on superficial external characters laid great stress on bill resemblance, forgetful of the evolutionary prerequisite that new lines, diverging from an ancestral stock, must be *differently adapted*. Thus they failed . . . to group families naturally and had no basis for detecting numerous cases of convergence. This gave an erroneous picture of oscinine evolution" (p. 320).

Beecher's failure to discover the elements of the phylogeny of the oscines, in spite of his understanding of the evolutionary process, is further evidence that morphology does not provide simple clues to the genealogical history of birds. The cladists will argue that unless their procedures are followed the correct phylogeny cannot be determined; the fallacy of this argument is to be found in Cracraft's (1981) classification, which was based on Hennigian principles and procedures.

The DNA Hybridization Evidence

The DNA data show that the family Sylviidae is not closely related to the Muscicapidae, but that these two families belong to lineages that diverged at Δ 11.7, probably ca. 20–30 MYA. The branch between the Sylvioidea and the Muscicapoidea is actually older than that between the Sylvioidea and Passeroidea at Δ $T_{50}H$ 11.1 (Fig. 369).

The DNA comparisons reveal that the Sylviidae consists of at least four subfamilies: Acrocephalinae (36/221), Megalurinae (10/21), Garrulacinae (2/54), and Sylviinae (53/256).

The acrocephalines are the descendants of the earliest branch at Δ 8.9, and the megalurines diverged from the garrulacines plus sylviines at Δ 8.2. The Garrulacinae and Sylviinae diverged at Δ 7.9. The Sylviinae is divided into three tribes.

The Acrocephalinae includes *Phylloscopus*, *Seicercus*, *Hippolais*, *Acrocephalus*, *Orthotomus*, *Sylvietta*, and *Sphenoeacus*. These genera divided into two groups at Δ 8.7, with the divergence between the first two and the last five. Under our system of assigning categories these two groups could be ranked as subfamilies, but we defer further subdivision until more genera of sylviids can be examined.

The Megalurinae includes *Megalurus* (including *Bowdleria*), *Eremiornis*, and *Cincloramphus*. The last two occur only in Australia; *Megalurus* extends to southern and eastern Asia. The Fernbird ("*Bowdleria*" *punctata*) is a *Megalurus* which is endemic to New Zealand (Sibley and Ahlquist 1987a). We lack the DNAs of other genera that may be members of the Megalurinae. Among these are several genera that occur on islands in the southwest Pacific, for example, *Megalurulus* of New Caledonia.

The genus *Garrulax* has often been noted as distinctive and the DNA comparisons place it as the sister group of the Sylviinae with the branch at Δ 7.9. We recognize the Garrulacinae. *Babax* is assigned to the Garrulacinae, but we lack its DNA.

The Sylviinae consists of the tribes Sylviini (1/22), Chamaeini (1/1), and Timaliini (51/233). The Sylviini includes only *Sylvia* (including *Parisoma*). Our data include only *subcaeruleum*, formerly in *Parisoma*. Vaurie (1957b) restricted *Parisoma* to *subcaeruleum*, *boehmi*, *layardi*, and *lugens*. He reviewed previous opinions and assigned "*leucomelaena* (and probably *buryi*) to *Sylvia*" and "*griseigularis* and *plumbeum* to the flycatchers." Clancey

(1957) recommended the transfer of *plumbeum* to *Myioparus* "adjacent to *Muscicapa*." We follow Sibley and Monroe (1990) by including *Parisoma* in *Sylvia*.

Assuming the DNA evidence is correct, Seebohm's prediction of 1881 has come true. The babblers (Timaliini) are so closely related to *Sylvia* that they form the sister tribe of the Sylviini; they diverged at Δ 7.5 (Fig. 381).

The tracer DNAs of the Wrentit (*Chamaea fasciata*), the Short-tailed Jungle Babbler (*Trichastoma malaccense*), the Garden Warbler (*Sylvia borin*), and the Lesser Whitethroat (*Sylvia curruca*) were compared with the driver DNAs of several species of timaliine babblers, sylviine warblers, and other passerine taxa (Sibley and Ahlquist 1982b). Species of the following genera of "babblers" were used in the comparisons: *Chamaea*, *Trichastoma*, *Alcippe*, *Kenopia*, *Pellorneum*, *Turdoides*, *Stachyris*, *Malacopteron*, *Macronous*, and *Garrulax*. *Actinodura* was included in separate comparisons. For the Sylviini, we used *Sylvia atricapilla*, *S. curruca*, *S. borin*. Other sylviid genera were *Acrocephalus* and *Phylloscopus*. Other groups represented included members of the Paridae, Certhiidae, Regulidae, Muscicapidae, Aegithalidae, Sturnidae, Nectariniidae, Motacillinae, Passerinae, Fringillidae, Vireonidae, Laniidae, Dicrurinae, Meliphagidae, and Tyrannidae.

The results of these and subsequent comparisons indicate that *Chamaea* is a babbler and that its lineage branched from the sylviines and timaliines at Δ 7.2. In Fig. 381 the *Chamaea* branch is actually 7.2 from the sylviines and 7.5 from the timaliines. These differences may not reflect the exact branching sequence among these three taxa, but it seems likely that the Wrentit diverged from its Asian relatives about 15–20 MYA.

Presumably, the ancestor of the Wrentit entered North America via the Bering land bridge. Some of the delta values in Sibley and Ahlquist (1982b) have been slightly modified by additional data. For example, the early study did not reveal the divergence between the Sylviini and the Timaliini; instead, the warblers and babblers appeared to be members of a single monophyletic cluster.

The babbler genera listed above cluster together with Δ values of less than 7.2 (Fig. 381). Our data for the species of *Sylvia* are incomplete and the delta values between some of the species are large enough to suggest splitting the genus. At this time we conclude only that *Sylvia* is most closely related to the babblers, and that *Parisoma* is a synonym of *Sylvia*.

Fig. 285 (*Sylvia*) shows the close relationship between the sylviines, timaliines, and acrocephalines, with the aegithalids, certhiids, sittids, and regulids next, and the thornbill (Corvida: Pardalotidae) farthest out. As discussed above, the thornbills were among the endemic Australian groups often included in the Sylviidae in the past.

Fig. 286 (*Sylvia*) shows that *Parisoma*, represented by *subcaeruleum*, is a *Sylvia*. The outer cluster includes members of the Timaliini (*Turdoides*), Acrocephalinae (*Phylloscopus*, *Melocichla*, *Sylvietta*), and Cisticolidae (*Eminia*, *Prinia*, *Cisticola*).

Fig. 287 (*Sylvia*) shows the close relationship between *Sylvia* and the babblers (*Stachyris* to *Turdoides*) and to the Australian sylviid *Cincloramphus*. *Picathartes* lies between the cluster of Passerida and the two members of the Corvida (*Vireo*, *Corvus*). The relationships of *Picathartes* are discussed above under the Picathartidae, in which Fig. 287 is cited.

Fig. 288 (*Hippolais*) also shows the relationship between the sylviids and the babblers, although *Hippolais* is a member of the Acrocephalinae (Fig. 381). *Sylvia* clusters with the two babblers (*Pomatorhinus*, *Yuhina*), and other members of the Sylvioidea (*Psaltriparus* to *Sitta*) cluster. From other evidence we would expect the curve of *Troglodytes* to be close to that of *Certhia*, but the curves of *Troglodytes* and *Picathartes* are superimposed. The *Picathartes* curve is where we find it in other sets, so it seems likely that the *Troglodytes* curve is aberrant, although it looks normal. The Australian babbler, *Pomatostomus*, is in its expected position as a member of the Corvida, not related to the timaliine babblers.

Fig. 289 (*Phylloscopus*) shows the relationship of the tracer to *Acrocephalus* and *Sylvia*, with representatives of other sylvioid groups next in the sequence of curves.

Fig. 290 (*Megalurus*) shows that the New Zealand Fernbird ("*Bowdleria*") is actually a *Megalurus*, and that the Australian genera *Eremiornis* and *Cincloramphus* are sylviids, not members of the old endemic Corvida of Australia and New Guinea, as are the two malurids, *Malurus* and *Stipiturus*.

Fig. 291 (*Megalurus*) shows that *Megalurus* is closer to the Cisticolidae than to the members of the Corvida (*Mohoua* to *Lichmera*).

Fig. 292 (*Cincloramphus*) shows that the Australian genera *Cincloramphus* and *Eremiornis* are members of the Megalurinae of the Sylviidae. The old endemic Australo-Papuan Corvida (*Lichmera* to *Malurus*) are in their expected outgroup positions.

Fig. 293 (*Melocichla*). *Melocichla* occurs in Africa. The melting curves show the relationship between *Melocichla* and *Sphenoeacus*, with *Sylvietta* next. These three genera we place in the Acrocephalinae. *Camaroptera* and *Cisticola* are cisticolids, *Cincloramphus* and *Megalurus* are megalurines, *Polioptila* and *Regulus* are sylvioids, and *Gerygone* is an Australian endemic member of the Corvida.

Fig. 294 (*Turdoides*) shows the close relationship of the babblers to *Sylvia*, with *Phylloscopus* and other sylvioids (*Certhia* to *Anthoscopus*) next. The Australian old endemic babbler, *Pomatostomus*, is the outermost curve. These curves show that the timaliine babblers are most closely related to the sylviines, and that the Pomatostomidae of Australia and New Guinea are not timaliine babblers.

Fig. 350, the FITCH tree, is the analysis of 15 clusters of taxa comprising the Sylvioidea. The similarity to the UPGMA tree is apparent, especially the closely spaced series of steps from *Sylvia* to *Hirundo* from essentially the same baseline. The nearly equal branch lengths suggest that the branches occurred over a short space of time. The pattern indicates the relationship of the Zosteropidae to the Old World warblers and confirms the distinction between *Regulus* and *Phylloscopus*. The relationship of the swallows to the other sylvioids is indicated, as is the distinction between the Aegithalidae and the Paridae. The cluster consisting of *Certhia*, *Polioptila*, and *Thryomanes* confirms the composition of the Certhiidae and its relationship to the Sittidae.

Superfamily PASSEROIDEA

327/1651. The Passeroidea includes six families: Alaudidae, Paramythiidae, Melanocharitidae, Nectariniidae, Passeridae, and Fringillidae. Wetmore (1960) divided approximately the same species into 14 families, and Wolters (1975–82) used 23 families. Figs. 369 and 382–385 diagram the phylogeny of the Passeroidea as indicated by DNA-DNA hybridization.

The Passeroidea diverged from the Sylvioidea at $\Delta T_{50}H$ 11.1, ca. 20–30 MYA.

Family ALAUDIDAE

17/91. Larks. Most of the species of larks occur in Africa and Eurasia. One widespread species, the Horned Lark or Shore Lark (*Eremophila alpestris*), has also colonized the New World, and the Australasian Lark (*Mirafra javanica*) occurs in Australia and New Guinea.

The larks differ from other oscines in lacking an ossified syringeal pessulus and having "latiplantar" tarsi (rounded behind). The tarsi have scutes on the posterior surface, as well as on the anterior, and the hallux tends to be long and nearly straight, an adaptation related to their terrestrial habits.

The larks have been considered a distinct group with no close relatives since Keyserling and Blasius (1839) noted the latiplantar tarsus. The syringeal and tarsal characters have been viewed as primitive by many avian systematists and cited as the basis for assigning the larks a position near the beginning of the sequence of oscine families. These characters define the Alaudidae, but they are derived conditions that evolved after the larks diverged from the other passeroids at $\Delta T_{50}H$ 10.4 (Fig. 382).

Sharpe (1877:1–3) adopted the arrangement of the families of Passeres proposed by Wallace (1874), but by 1890 he had "learned that the classification adopted in 1877 is somewhat artificial" and was distressed to find that one result was that "the *Alaudidae* find themselves separated from the *Motacillidae*" (1890:1). However, he followed the original arrangement and the Alaudidae were placed after the Ploceidae in volume 13 of the *Catalogue of Birds*. In the *Hand-List* (1909) Sharpe remedied what he had viewed as an error by placing the Alaudidae following the Motacillidae.

Another traditional idea has been that the swallows, like the larks, are primitive, and should also be placed near the beginning of the sequence of oscine families. (See above under the Hirundinidae.) Thus, the larks and swallows became associated and the Motacillidae, following Sharpe, were thought to be allied to the larks. This trio appears in the classifications of the Basel sequence (Mayr and Greenway 1956) and of Delacour and Vaurie (1957), but not in Mayr and Amadon (1951) or Wetmore (1960). Referring to the Motacillidae, Delacour and Vaurie (1957:4) noted that "This family is placed next to the Larks in many lists. It is dubious, however, that the Pipits and Wagtails are closely related to the Larks."

Some classifications placed the larks near the emberizines or ploceines because some larks have finch-like bills and, in some genera, the tenth primary is reduced to a rudiment, or to the nine-primaried condition. For example, Berlioz (1950:1040) advocated an alliance of the Alaudidae with the Fringillidae and Ploceidae on one hand and to the Motacillidae on the other, and he rejected the conventional position of the larks at the beginning of the Passeres. Berlioz was a member of the Basel Committee and he raised the question, as reported by Mayr and Greenway (1956:6): "Should this family [Alaudidae], currently listed near the beginning of the Oscines, be transferred nearer to the Emberizidae, a position which it held in some of the older classifications?" The answer was: "This is not advisable. The Alaudidae are a very peculiar family. They differ from all other Acromyiodean Passeres by having not only the front but also the back of the tarsus scutellate and in having the pessulus rudimentary. This indicates that the larks may not be closely related to any of the other families. Since they are not specialized to any great extent they are probably best placed near the head of the list. Two functional characters, the heavy bill in some of the seed-eating genera, and the reduction in the number of primaries, cannot be considered evidence for relationship to the finches."

The sequence of the oscine families that emerged from the deliberations of the Basel Committee was agreed to by all except Berlioz, who "stated that he still preferred a placement of the Alaudidae near the Emberizidae" (Mayr and Greenway 1956:8). The Basel sequence has the Alaudidae as the first family, followed by Hirundinidae, Motacillidae, Campephagidae, etc.

Beecher (1953b:314) interpreted his jaw muscle data as indicating an origin of the larks "from the Cisticolinae close to the pipits, monarchs, and parrotbills." This was challenged by Mayr (1955:42) as "highly dubious."

Wetmore (1930, 1960) consistently placed the Alaudidae and Hirundinidae at the beginning of his list of oscine families, and the A.O.U. checklist (1983) continued the tradition.

In almost any book about birds published in this century, the larks and swallows are the first two families in the sequence of oscines. This is another instructive example of the power of tradition, and of the difficulties involved in the interpretation of morphological characters as indicators of phylogeny.

The DNA Hybridization Evidence

The DNA comparisons are clear and simple. The larks are the living descendants of the earliest branch in the passeroid tree at $\Delta T_{50}H$ 10.4. The family Alaudidae is, therefore, the sister group of the other passeroid families. The specialized syringeal and tarsal characters are thereby revealed as derived, not primitive; i.e., they evolved after the lark lineage branched from the other passeroids.

Fig. 295 (*Eremophila*) shows the four genera of larks to be diverse, with *Ammomanes* at Δ 8.0 from *Eremophila* in Fig. 382. In Fig. 295, the next taxa beyond *Ammomanes* are *Ploceus* and *Nectarinia*, then other Passerida. The swallow (*Riparia*) is among the most distant taxa from *Eremophila*. It seems that Berlioz was about right in his objection at the meeting of the Basel Committee in 1954.

THE NECTARIVOROUS PASSEROIDEA

The taxonomic history of the nectar-feeding passeroids is complex. We have found it necessary to recognize three families: Paramythiidae, Melanocharitidae, and Nectariniidae. In the past the species we include in the first two families were sometimes placed in the Meliphagidae, the Dicaeidae, or the Nectariniidae.

The taxonomic history of the nectar-feeding passerines is complex because unrelated taxa have been placed together on the basis of their convergently similar tongues. Thus, as discussed above under the Meliphagidae and Zosteropidae, members of different higher categories have been assembled into the same, or adjacent, families or subfamilies. This confusion continues to the present, in spite of wide recognition of the high probability of convergence in feeding structures in birds.

Sundevall (1872, see 1889:110) defined his "Cohort 5. Cinnyrimorphae, or *Tubilingues*" as having "The tongue long, extensile, affording a suctorial tube." In his "Fam. 1. Arbelorhininae" he placed some of the Neotropical honeycreepers which came to be called the "Coerebidae," and which the DNA data show to be nectar-feeding tanagers. Sundevall's "Fam. 2. Drepanidinae" contained the Hawaiian honeycreepers, now known to be nectarivorous cardueline finches (Sibley and Ahlquist 1982a), and "Fam. 3. Nectariniinae" seems to have included the same species we now place in the subfamily Nectariniinae, based on DNA comparisons. "Fam. 4. Meliphaginae" included *Promerops* of southern Africa, and most of the meliphagid honeyeaters; a few genera of meliphagids were placed in "Fam. 5. Philedoninae." Sundevall (1872, see 1889:81) placed the flowerpeckers (our Dicaeini) and *Zosterops* in the "Dendroecinae" of his "Cichlomorphae" because they have only nine primaries. This group also included the New World paruline wood warblers and some of the Neotropical honeycreepers. The "Pardalotinae," which were to be wrongly associated with the flowerpeckers in many later classifications, were also placed in the "Cichlomorphae."

The passerine classification used by Sharpe (1877:1–3) in the *Catalogue of Birds* was an eclectic mixture based on Sundevall, Wallace (1874), and Garrod (1876f). Sharpe recognized a "Group Cinnyrimorphae" characterized by "Tongue extensile" in his "Section A. Turdiformes." The task of describing the "Cinnyrimorphae" for the *Catalogue* fell to Gadow (1884), who noted that "The Cinnyrimorphae seem to form a tolerably natural group, as far as the *Nectariniidae* and *Meliphagidae* proper are concerned. With regard to the *Zosteropinae*, their degree of relationship with the *Meliphagidae* is doubtful, and they might, perhaps, with more propriety be ranged with the *Dicaeidae*, which, in all probability, have very little to do with the Cinnyrimorphae *sensu strictiori*" (p. vii). A more hedged and reluctant statement is hard to imagine.

Gadow's Nectariniidae included eight genera which, except for the philepittid *Neodrepanis*, are currently considered to be nectariniids. *Zosterops*, *Promerops*, and *Oedistoma* were placed in the Meliphagidae.

Sharpe (1885) treated the Dicaeidae under "Section B. Fringilliformes," defined as having a "Wing with *nine* primaries, the first [outer] of which is fully developed and usually very long." In a footnote (p. 1) Sharpe cited *Pardalotus* and *Prionochilus* as "exceptions in the family *Dicaeidae*" to this definition, but which "could not be divorced from the rest of the Flower-peckers without doing violence to the general arrangement of the family."

Sharpe's (1885) "Dicaeidae" was a remarkable mixture. In addition to *Dicaeum* and *Prionochilus*, which are certainly flowerpeckers, it included *Oreocharis* and *Rhamphocharis*, which are paramythiids; *Melanocharis* (including *Urocharis* and *Pristorhamphus*), a melanocharitid; *Parmoptila* (including *Lobornis*), an African estrildine; *Pholidornis*, also African, of uncertain affinities; the Hawaiian honeycreepers (Drepanidini), which are cardueline finches; *Pinaroloxias*, the Cocos Island Finch, which is either an emberizine or a tanager; and *Pardalotus* (the pardalotes or diamondbirds), an Australian meliphagoid genus related to the thornbills (*Acanthiza*).

In the *Hand-List* Sharpe (1909) gave the Hawaiian honeycreepers their own family and removed *Pholidornis* and *Parmoptila* from the Dicaeidae. The remaining genera were *Dicaeum* (including three generic names that became synonyms of *Dicaeum*); *Oreocharis*, *Prionochilus*, *Melanocharis*, *Urocharis* (a synonym of *Melanocharis* for the species *longicauda*), *Pristorhamphus*, *Rhamphocharis* (including *Eafa*), and *Pardalotus*. Sharpe (1909:545) erected the family Paramythiidae for *Paramythia montium* and placed it between the Eulabetidae (glossy starlings) and the Buphagidae (oxpeckers).

Sharpe (1909) retained *Neodrepanis* in the Nectariniidae and the monotypic Promeropidae was placed between the Nectariniidae and the Meliphagidae.

Mayr (1941) included *Toxorhamphus* in the Meliphagidae and placed *Melanocharis*, *Rhamphocharis*, *Oreocharis*, and *Paramythia* in the Dicaeidae.

Delacour (1944) considered the sunbirds to be a compact, well-characterized group with natural affinities to the Dicaeidae, and through them to *Remiz* and *Aegithalos*. He noted that the Zosteropidae "likewise resemble the sunbirds, though less markedly" (p. 19). Mayr and Amadon (1947) discussed the possible relationships of the Old World nectarivores and, although agreeing with Delacour that the sunbirds and flowerpeckers may be related, declined to render a strong opinion. Under the "Old World Nectar Feeders" Mayr and Amadon (1951:25) discussed the relationships of the Dicaeidae, Nectariniidae, Meliphagidae, and Zosteropidae. (See comments above under the latter two families.) Concerning the Dicaeidae, Mayr and Amadon noted that

The primitive fruit-eating dicaeid genus *Melanocharis* of New Guinea has a great resemblance to certain genera of Meliphagidae (*Timeliopsis*, *Oedistoma*). Since the latter have a highly specialized tongue and that of *Melanocharis* is unspecialized (Mayr and Amadon 1947), this resemblance may not indicate affinity.

Another moot affinity of the flowerpeckers is with the birds placed by us in the subfamily Remizinae of the Paridae. The genus *Cephalopyrus* of the Himalayas could be an intermediate.

Finally, one may mention . . . the resemblance of certain flowerpeckers to the Bombycillidae in appearance, fondness for mistletoe berries, gregarious habits, and other details of behavior.

About the Nectariniidae, Mayr and Amadon (1951:25–26) wrote:

The sunbirds . . . are evidently relatives of the Dicaeidae, highly specialized for nectar feeding. The tongue is quite similar in the nectar-feeding . . . flowerpeckers, and both build a similar pensile nest. Though more specialized as regards plumage and . . . tongue, sunbirds do not show the progressive loss of the tenth primary culminating in the nine-primaried condition of such dicaeid genera as *Pardalotus* and many species of *Dicaeum*.

The Dicaeidae are best represented in Australia, Papua, the East Indies, and the Philippines, and do not reach Africa; almost the reverse is true of the Nectariniidae.

The curious African genera, *Pholidornis* and *Parmoptila*, formerly associated with the Dicaeidae or Nectariniidae, are considered by Chapin (1917) to be aberrant, thin-billed Ploceidae, with which we agree.

The African species *Hylia prasina* has usually been placed in the Sylviinae and may be an aberrant member of that group. Bates (1930, p. 447) figured the hyoid bones of this species, which he found to be flattened like those of a sunbird. The tenth primary is rather larger than in typical sunbirds. He placed *Hylia* in a separate family but thought it was allied to the Nectariniidae. Serle (1949, p. 212), among others, found its habits and call notes to suggest those of a sunbird, though the song is more musical. The nest is more or less globular, not much like that of a sunbird. *Hylia* may be a primitive sunbird. Chapin considers this possible but not established.

Beecher (1953b:290) placed the sunbirds, flowerpeckers, and white-eyes together and considered them to be "sylvioid nectar feeders" (p. 321) derived from the "Pycnonotinae" of his Sylviidae.

Salomonsen (1967) revised the Dicaeidae and included *Melanocharis*, *Rhamphocharis*, *Prionochilus*, *Dicaeum*, *Oreocharis*, *Paramythia*, and *Pardalotus*. Of these, *Pardalotus* is clearly not a passeroid; it is a member of the Corvoidea in the Pardalotinae of the Pardalotidae. Rand (1967a) included *Anthreptes*, *Hypogramma*, *Nectarinia*, *Aethopyga*, and *Arachnothera* in his Nectariniidae.

Rand and Gilliard (1968) placed *Oedistoma pygmaeum* and three species of *Toxorhamphus* in the Meliphagidae, and *Melanocharis* (5 species), *Rhamphocharis crassirostris*, *Oreocharis arfaki*, and *Paramythia montium* in the Dicaeidae.

Peckover and Filewood (1976) placed *Toxorhamphus novaeguineae* and *T. poliopterus* in the Nectariniidae, *Oedistoma pygmaeum* and *Oedistoma* (*Toxorhamphus*) *iliolophum* in the Meliphagidae, and the five species of *Melanocharis*, *Rhamphocharis*, *Oreocharis*, and *Paramythia* in the Dicaeidae.

Beehler and Finch (1985) placed *Melanocharis*, *Rhamphocharis*, *Oreocharis*, and *Paramythia* in the Dicaeidae, and *Toxorhamphus* (2 species) and *Oedistoma* (2 species) in the Meliphagidae.

These confusing transfers and revisions make it apparent that the relationships of the New Guinea species of nectar-feeding passeroids are unclear. The DNA data have sorted out some of the problems, but we lack the DNAs of a few of the taxa involved in these questions. Following is our present assessment.

Family PARAMYTHIIDAE: 2/2. The Crested Berrypecker, *Paramythia montium*, and the Tit Berrypecker, *Oreocharis arfaki*, are the only known members of this family. Both are confined to New Guinea. The nest of *Paramythia* was described by Rand and Gilliard (1968:585) as more like that of *Melanocharis* than like the nests of the flowerpeckers, *Dicaeum*. Diamond (1972:404–405) found *Oreocharis* only above 4700 feet and *Paramythia* in the "high altitude stunted mossy forest, from timberline down to 9,500 ft (Mt. Michael) and on the very summit (8,165 ft) of Mt. Karimui. Most of its altitudinal range lies above that of its smaller relative *Oreocharis arfaki*." Both species feed mainly on fruit in the mid to upper story of the forest.

Although *Paramythia* and *Oreocharis* differ in several respects, Salomonsen (1961:3) noted that the bill of *Paramythia* "is essentially like that of *Oreocharis*. The flanks are supplied with distinct filoplumes, as in *Oreocharis*. The color pattern . . . bears a remarkable resemblance to that of the male *Oreocharis*. Common to the two genera are the black head and throat, the green, contrasting upper parts and wings, the bluish tail, and the yellow under tail coverts. The main difference in coloration is the exchange of yellow with blue on the abdomen, breast, and cheeks in *Paramythia*."

Salomonsen also believed that the contrasting light terminal spots on the remiges of *Oreocharis* "undoubtedly indicate relationship" to *Pardalotus*. The paramythiid and melanocharitid lineages diverged at $\Delta T_{50}H$ 9.3 (Fig. 383).

Fig. 296 (*Paramythia*) shows the close relationship between *Paramythia* and *Oreocharis*, and the more distant positions of *Toxorhamphus*, *Melanocharis*, *Promerops*, *Nectarinia*, and *Dicaeum*. *Pardalotus* and *Melidectes* are members of the Australo-Papuan old endemic Corvida.

Family MELANOCHARITIDAE: 3/10. The five species of *Melanocharis* and *Rhamphocharis crassirostris* are called berrypeckers and the species of *Toxorhamphus* are the longbills. *Toxorhamphus pygmaeum*, usually placed in *Oedistoma*, is known as the Pygmy Honeyeater or Pygmy Longbill.

Salomonsen (1960) considered *Melanocharis* and *Rhamphocharis* to be the most primitive members of the Dicaeidae, citing as evidence the "rather simple" structure of the tongue, the booted tarsus, and the well-developed tenth primary. He also believed that *Rhamphocharis* is closely related to *Melanocharis* based on their common possession of a "large outer (tenth) primary, serrated edges of the bill, white marks on rectrices, comparatively long tail (of similar relative size as in *M. longicauda*), pale slate-colored underparts in male (of about the same shade as in *M. versteri*), and pronounced sexual dimorphism in color pattern as well as in size, the females being considerably larger than the males" (p. 17). He went on to note that "*Rhamphocharis* differs from *Melanocharis* mainly in its much longer and more slender bill and in the color pattern of the plumage, especially that of the female."

We have DNA from four of the five species of *Melanocharis*, lacking only *M. arfakiana* (which is known from only two specimens), and from the monotypic *Rhamphocharis crassirostris*. The DNA comparisons show that *versteri* and *longicauda* are most closely related at Δ 2.0 (Fig. 383). *Rhamphocharis* and *M. striativentris* are about the same distance from *versteri* (2.6 and 2.8, respectively), so they probably belong to the same sister group. *M. nigra* is the most distant at Δ 3.7. This arrangement is corroborated by such features as plumage pattern and color, body proportions, degree of geographic differentiation, etc.

The coverage of species and quality of the data are such that a revision of the genera may be suggested. *Melanocharis* (Sclater 1858) would apply to *nigra* since this was the first species described (by Lesson in 1830). *Rhamphocharis* (Salvadori 1876) could be used for *crassirostris* and *striativentris*, having priority over *Neneba* (De Vis 1897). This leaves *versteri* and *longicauda*, for which *Pristorhamphus* (Finsch 1876) is the earliest available name. We include *Rhamphocharis* in *Melanocharis* as in Fig. 383 and Sibley and Monroe (1990).

There has been a great deal of confusion about the relationships of the species placed in *Toxorhamphus* and *Oedistoma*. Diamond (1972:352) described the ecological differences between the species of these two genera and concluded that *iliolophus* should be assigned to *Oedistoma*. He noted that *T. poliopterus* and *T. novaeguineae* "live mainly in the understory and do not visit flowering trees" and that they occupy mutually exclusive altitudinal ranges. The species *pygmaeum* and *iliolophum* are more alike in their ecological preferences and spend more time in flowering trees and the upperstory of the forest. Diamond assigned *pygmaeum* and *iliolophum* to *Oedistoma* in the Meliphagidae. *Melanocharis*, *Rhamphocharis*, *Oreocharis*, and *Paramythia* were placed in the Dicaeidae.

The DNA evidence shows that all these genera are passeroids, hence none is a meliphagid. The species *iliolophus* and *novaeguineae* diverged at Δ 2.8 which, according to our criteria, could be used as the basis for assigning them to different genera. Thus, the recognition of *Oedistoma* for *iliolophum* is supported, although we lack the DNA of *O. pygmaeum*. The branch between the Toxorhamphini (2/4) and the Melanocharitini (1/6) was at Δ 5.6 (Fig. 383).

Fig. 297 (*Melanocharis*) shows the close relationship between *Melanocharis* and *Toxorhamphus*, with the nectariniids (*Promerops*, *Dicaeum*) more distant, and the two members of the Corvida (*Phylidonyris*, *Pardalotus*) as the most distant. This set of curves shows that *Melanocharis* and *Toxorhamphus* are more closely related to the sunbirds than to the honeyeaters.

Fig. 298 (*Toxorhamphus*) confirms the close relationship between *Toxorhamphus* and *Melanocharis*. It also shows that *Toxorhamphus* is closer to *Promerops*, sunbirds, *Dicaeum*, and *Zosterops* than to the honeyeaters (*Myzomela*, *Plectorhyncha*).

Family NECTARINIIDAE: 8/169. Sunbirds, Spiderhunters, Flowerpeckers, Sugarbirds. The taxonomic history of the sunbirds and their allies has been discussed above. The history of the African sugarbirds (*Promerops*) is treated below.

Subfamily PROMEROPINAE: 1/2. African Sugarbirds.

Subfamily NECTARINIINAE: 7/167. Sunbirds, Spiderhunters.

We recognize two subfamilies, Promeropinae and Nectariniinae, with two tribes, Dicaeini (2/44) and Nectariniini (5/123), in the Nectariniinae.

Promerops is confined to southern Africa. The sunbirds of the genera *Anthreptes*, *Hypogramma*, and *Nectarinia* occur over all of Africa, Madagascar, and offshore islands, across the Middle East to India, southeast Asia, the Philippines, Indonesia, New Guinea, the Solomon Islands, and the Bismarck Archipelago. The widespread species *Nectarinia jugularis* occurs in northeastern Australia. The sunbirds and spiderhunters of the genera *Aethopyga* and *Arachnothera* occur in southeast Asia from India and southeastern China to the Philippines and Indonesia.

The flowerpeckers (*Prionochilus*, *Dicaeum*) range from India, Sri Lanka, southwestern China, and southeast Asia to the Philippines, Indonesia, New Guinea, New Britain, New Ireland, the Solomon Islands, and Australia.

The Promeropinae diverged from the Nectariniinae at Δ 8.5; the Dicaeini and Nectariniini diverged at Δ 6.3 (Fig. 383).

Fig. 299 (*Nectarinia*) shows that the sunbirds are closest to the flowerpeckers (*Prionochilus*), and that the accentors (*Prunella*), sugarbirds (*Promerops*), longbills (*Toxorhamphus*), icterines (*Psarocolius*), and berrypeckers (*Melanocharis*) cluster together, with the honeyeater (*Lichenostomus*) well outside this group.

Fig. 300 (*Nectarinia*) depicts the relative distances between the sunbird homoduplex and members of the Passerida (to *Sylvia*), with the Corvida outermost.

Fig. 301 (*Nectarinia*) includes additional members of the Passerida, with two meliphagids (*Myzomela*, *Meliphaga*) as the most distant. The distinctness of the Nectariniidae from the Meliphagidae is shown by all of these sets of melting curves. It is also clear that the sugarbirds (*Promerops*) are members of the Passerida, not of the Corvida.

THE RELATIONSHIPS OF THE SUGARBIRDS, *Promerops*.

The relationships of few avian genera have been the subject of more debate and speculation than those of *Promerops*, the sugarbirds of southern Africa. The Cape Sugarbird (*P. cafer*) occurs in the *Protea* and heath zone of the mountains of southern Cape Province, South Africa. Gurney's Sugarbird (*P. gurneyi*) ranges from eastern Cape Province through Natal to northeastern Transvaal, with an isolated population in the mountains of eastern Zimbabwe and adjacent Mozambique. The two species are closely related and might be considered subspecies, but they come into contact in eastern Cape Province and seem to remain distinct. Skead (1964) reported that both species "have been found occupying the same patch of *Protea lacticolor*" in the eastern Amatole Mountains, and that both nest there. A specimen from this area, taken in 1904, may be a hybrid. Skead concluded that "they are two good species," and they are treated as such by the Southern African Ornithological Society (1980). We have compared the DNAs of the two *Promerops* and they differ by ca. δ $T_{50}H$ 0.5, indicating a divergence within the past one to two million years (Fig. 383).

The sugarbirds feed on insects and nectar, especially of the proteas, and build open, cup-shaped nests, unlike the closed, pensile nests of the sunbirds (McLachlan and Liversidge 1978:535).

Promerops obviously evolved in Africa, but in the structure of its tongue, nest construction, and some aspects of behavior, it resembles the Australasian honeyeaters (Meliphagidae). In other characters the sugarbirds are similar to the sunbirds (Nectariniini).

Taxonomists have responded to these conflicting sources of evidence in three principal ways: (1) by placing *Promerops* in the Meliphagidae, (2) by placing it in the Nectariniidae, or (3) by placing it in the monotypic family Promeropidae. In 1974 we (Sibley and Ahlquist 1974) concluded, from comparisons of the electrophoretic patterns of the egg-white proteins, that *Promerops* is most closely related to the starlings (Sturnini), thus adding a fourth proposal. It is now obvious that this was an error; the DNA evidence supports the inclusion of the Promeropinae in the Nectariniidae.

"*Promerops* and its relationships have caused problems since its earliest days. Linnaeus placed it first in the genus *Upupa* of the hoopoes without having a specimen to back his decision. Later he was to err again by describing it as *Merops* of the bee-eaters from a drawing. . . . Two years later Brisson realized the mistake and changed the name to *Promerops*" (Skead 1967:246).

Thus, by 1760 the sugarbirds had already been moved around and finally assigned to their own genus. Layard (1867) placed the sugarbirds and the sunbirds in the Promeropidae, but Sharpe, as the editor of a later edition of Layard's book (Layard and Sharpe 1875–84), included *Promerops* in the Nectariniidae.

Gadow (1883b) studied the "suctorial apparatus" of the nectar feeding "Tenuirostres" and discovered that the tongues of the meliphagids are "protractile, bifid, each half broken up into numerous stiff horny fibres, so as to form a brush" (Gadow 1884:127). He also decided that the tongue of *Promerops* seems to be more similar to that of the meliphagids than to that of the sunbirds, whose tongue he described as "long, protractile, ending in a tube anteriorly bifid" (1884:1). Gadow (1884:282) placed *Promerops* in the Meliphaginae among typical honeyeaters, but Sharpe (1909) compromised by inserting the Promeropidae between the Nectariniidae and the Meliphagidae.

Knowlton (1909:802) assigned *Promerops* to the Nectariniidae, but noted that "there is still some doubt as to the propriety of including . . . *Promerops* in this family." Reichenow (1914) also placed the sugarbirds with the sunbirds.

The tongues of the meliphagids and *Promerops* were compared by Scharnke (1931, 1932), who discussed the similarities and suggested that unless one had further knowledge of the two groups he would certainly assign the sugarbirds to the Meliphagidae. However, Scharnke (1932) concluded that the similar tongues in the honeyeaters and sugarbirds are due to convergence and that there is actually no evidence to support a close relationship between the two groups. Scharnke's conclusion was influenced by the plumage characters of *Promerops* and by its geographical isolation in southern Africa. He proposed that the family Promeropidae be recognized.

Salomonsen (1933) disagreed with Scharnke and cited evidence based on comparisons of the alimentary canal, feeding habits, plumage pattern, nests, and eggs to support his contention that *Promerops* is a meliphagid. To explain the zoogeographic problem Salomonsen suggested that *Promerops* and *Protea* were more widespread in the past and have become restricted to southern Africa.

E. Stresemann (1934) accepted Salomonsen's opinion and included *Promerops* in the Meliphagidae in his classification. Wetmore (1940, 1951, 1960), White (1963), and many others have also assigned the sugarbirds to the Meliphagidae. Delacour (1944) accepted Salomonsen's conclusion, but Dorst (1952:192) agreed with Scharnke. Mayr and Amadon (1951) recorded their uncertainty by stating that "We leave *Promerops* as a subfamily of the Meliphagidae, but we feel that its similarity may, after all, be parallelism." Beecher (1953b) concluded that *Promerops* is a meliphagid and proposed that "the Ploceidae arose from the Promeropinae or Cisticolinae in Africa."

Moreau (1966:110) stated the zoogeographic case against a close relationship between the sugarbirds and honeyeaters:

As regards the sugarbirds . . . there seems to be no objection, in either their morphology or their habits as described by Broekhuysen (1959), to putting them with the Meliphagidae . . . as Mayr and Amadon have done. But some reluctance to accept this classification must be felt, because the geographical difficulties are great. The Meliphagidae are typically an Australo-Papuan family, with no other extension westward except that a single species reaches the island of Bali, just east of Java. The admission of *Promerops* into the Meliphagidae gives this family a range that is unique. Clearly, to account for the present situation three possibilities suggest themselves: (1) movement direct across the Indian Ocean; (2) expansion of the ancestral stock round the Indian Ocean, with subsequent enormous extinction in intermediate areas; (3) convergence. I think the first of these possibilities most unlikely and I favour the last. . . . Provisionally I keep the Promeropidae as a family.

Clancey (1964) "tentatively included . . . the former family Promeropidae . . . in the Meliphagidae," but Skead (1967) emphasized the high probability of convergence in tongue structure, plus the geographical hiatus, and retained the Promeropidae.

Liversidge (in Skead 1967) compared the tongues and feeding methods of sugarbirds, sunbirds, and honeyeaters, as follows:

Similarities between *Promerops* and meliphagids.
 1. Superficial resemblances of the tongues.
 2. Tongue tip divided into four sections.
Differences between *Promerops* and meliphagids.
 1. Muscles do not reach bifurcation of tongue.
 2. Anterior muscles lateral, not ventral.
 3. Entire tip of cuticle.
 4. Tongue and hyoid musculature different.
 5. Cuticle divided along entire tongue, not only at tip.
 6. Presence of inner, undivided horny layer, grooved in shape.
 7. Tongue grooved along entire length.
 8. Tongue stiffened at tip, making licking of nectar impossible.
Similarities between *Promerops* and nectariniids.
 1. Greater portion of tongue tubular and composed of horny cuticle.
 2. Sucking of nectar.

Differences between *Promerops* and nectariniids.
1. Tongue with brush-like horny tips in *Promerops*.
2. Tubular portion not entirely circular.
3. Lack of suction cavity in basal portion of tongue.
4. Different method of sucking, i.e., less movement of tongue.

Bock (1985) dismissed Liversidge's comparisons as inaccurate and misleading.

Rand (1967b) pointed out that the tongue of *Promerops* differs from those of the meliphagids in that "only the two outer parts of the tip are frayed to give the brush tip. The two centered elements are not frayed and appear as if modified for probing." The differences noted by Rand are clearly visible in the drawings in Scharnke's paper which were reproduced by Delacour (1944), Dorst (1952), and Rand (1967b). Rand listed eight families of oscines in which nectar-feeding tongues have evolved, apparently independently, namely: "Meliphagidae, Nectariniidae, Dicaeidae, Zosteropidae, Chloropseidae, Timaliidae, Coerebidae, and Drepanididae." Rand (1967b) also noted that the "Parulidae and Icteridae have members with a tendency toward a nectar-adapted tongue." To these may be added the genus *Artamus* (Corvinae: Artamini) (McKean 1969), and the Australian estrildine *Zonaeginthus oculatus* (V. Ziswiler, pers. comm.). Many species of oscines that feed to some degree on nectar do not have specially modified tongues. For example, Short and Horne (1978) reported that at least 16 species of ploceines have been observed feeding on nectar.

Although Salomonsen had been one of the advocates of the meliphagid theory of sugarbird affinities, he retreated to neutrality by 1967, as recorded in a footnote (1967:449) referring to *Promerops*: "Probably represents a separate family (Promeropidae)." Hall and Moreau (1970), McLachlan and Liversidge (1978), and the Southern African Ornithological Society (1980) also adopted the neutral position by recognizing the Promeropidae.

Gill (1971) discovered that the Blue-naped Sunbird (*Hypogramma hypogrammicum*) of southeast Asia has a tongue that differs from those of other sunbirds, but resembles those of *Promerops* and the meliphagids. "The tongue of most sunbird species is for the major part of its length a closed tube formed by inward rolling and meeting of the edges. . . . The tongue tip is split and bitubular, but lacks elaborate fimbriation" (p. 485). The tongue of *Hypogramma* is non-tubular and the tip is quadrifid and brush-tipped, thus similar to that of *Promerops*. Gill concluded that "certainly *Promerops*' quadrifid tongue structure is of even less value now than before as a taxonomic character indicating relationship with the Meliphagidae."

In 1974 we concluded that *Promerops* "is a specialized starling" (Sibley and Ahlquist 1974). We are now certain that this was an error, caused by our misinterpretation of the electrophoretic patterns of the egg-white proteins. However, a re-examination of the figures in the 1974 paper reveals that the patterns of *Promerops* are more similar to those of *Nectarinia* than to those of *Meliphaga*.

Olson and Ames (1984) described a structure in the syrinx of *Promerops* that they considered a homolog of the "turdine thumb" (Ames 1975) of the thrushes. From this evidence they concluded that *Promerops* is a member of the "Turdidae-Muscicapidae" complex.

The most recent advocate of a meliphagid origin for *Promerops* is Bock (1985), who bases his conclusion primarily on detailed comparisons of the corneous tongues and tongue musculature of *Promerops*, sunbirds, and honeyeaters. Bock presented critical reviews of previous studies and stated his intention to test whether *Promerops* is a member of the Nectariniidae or of the Meliphagidae. He also considered it possible that *Promerops* "is closely allied to some other passerine family and best included in that family, or that *Promerops* is sufficiently distant to be placed in a monotypic family with affinities to a passerine group other than the Nectariniidae or the Meliphagidae."

In his comparisons, Bock assumed that *Toxorhamphus* is a meliphagid genus, but our DNA comparisons show that it is a passeroid (Melanocharitidae) related to the Nectariniidae. Thus, it is interesting that Bock found that "a major distinction exists between the tongue morphology of *Toxorhamphus* and that of the remaining genera of the Meliphagidae." Bock found "no important . . . resemblances between the tongues of the nectariniids and that of *Promerops*" and concluded that the two are not homologous, but that "the tongue of *Promerops* shares many detailed points of resemblance with meliphagid tongues"—assuming that *Toxorhamphus* is a meliphagid.

In the tongue musculature, Bock found that *Promerops* shares many similarities with both sunbirds and honeyeaters, and that "*Promerops* shows some resemblances to various meliphagid genera in tongue muscle structure. The most striking one is insertion of the M. hypoglossus anterior on the basihyale in *Promerops* and *Oedistoma*. *Toxorhamphus* is the only meliphagid that has an elongated M. stylohyoideus arising from the roof of the braincase similar to that . . . in *Promerops*; this similarity may be of independent origin." Bock argued that "similarities" indicate that *Promerops* must be a meliphagid, but the most similar "meliphagids" are *Toxorhamphus* and *Oedistoma*, both of which are not meliphagids but melanocharitids, and therefore related far more closely to the Nectariniidae than to the Meliphagidae. Bock concluded that "*Promerops* is a member of the Meliphagidae and the structure of the corneous tongue supports it strongly." Thus, the evidence for this conclusion is based on a misidentification of *Toxorhamphus* and *Oedistoma* as meliphagids, rather than as near relatives of the sunbirds. Therefore, Bock's data actually support a relationship between *Promerops* and the sunbirds, not the honeyeaters.

Bock (1985:374) commented on the paper by Olson and Ames (1984) and disputed their conclusion that *Promerops* is a member of the turdid-muscicapid complex.

The DNA Hybridization Evidence

The DNA comparisons show that the promeropine lineage diverged from the other nectariniids at Δ 8.5 (Fig. 383).

If *Promerops* were more closely related to the Meliphagidae than to the Nectariniidae, the divergence between the sugarbirds and honeyeaters would be less than δ 12.8, which is the node between the Corvida and the Passerida. Instead, *Promerops* is 8.5 from the Nectariniidae, 9.6 from the Melanocharitidae, 9.8 from the Passeridae, 10.0 from the Fringillidae, 10.4 from the Alaudidae, and less than 12.8 from all other members of the Passerida. It is ca. 12.8 from all members of the Corvida, including the Meliphagidae. Unless one can falsify the DNA hybridization method, the conclusion must be that *Promerops* is a member of the Passerida: Passeroidea: Nectariniidae. We place it in the subfamily Promeropinae of the Nectariniidae.

Fig. 302 (*Promerops*) confirms the delta values. The two species of *Promerops* are closely related to one another, and the cluster of the nectariniids and melanocharitids (*Nectarinia* to *Melanocharis*) is obviously closer to *Promerops* than are the two honeyeaters (*Lichenostomus*, *Phylidonyris*).

Family PASSERIDAE: 57/386.

Subfamily PASSERINAE: 4/36. Sparrows, Rock Sparrows, Snowfinches.
Subfamily MOTACILLINAE: 5/65. Wagtails and Pipits.
Subfamily PRUNELLINAE: 1/13. Accentors, Hedge-sparrows.
Subfamily PLOCEINAE: 17/117. Weaverbirds.
Subfamily ESTRILDINAE: 30/155. Waxbills, Mannikins, Widowbirds, etc.

The Passeridae obviously originated in the Old World, probably in Africa. The Passerinae and Motacillinae occur widely in Africa and Eurasia; the Prunellinae in Eurasia; the Ploceinae in Africa, Arabia, and southern Asia. The Estrildinae range from Africa to southern Asia and Australia. Except for man-made introductions, only the pipits (*Anthus*) have colonized the New World. The passerid lineage branched from that of the nectariniids at $\Delta T_{50}H$ 9.8, ca. 20–30 MYA (Figs. 382, 383).

Sundevall (1872, see 1889) based his classification on external characters, so it is not surprising that he assembled the finch-billed passerines into his "Cohort 2. CONIROSTRES." The ten primaried "Ploceinae . . . Viduinae . . . Accentorinae" were placed together as "Decempennatae," and the nine-primaried "Amplipalatales" included the "Chloridinae" (Carduelinae) and the "Fringillinae" (*Fringilla*, *Passer*, etc.). The "Arctipalatales" contained the "Loxiinae" (crossbills), "Emberizinae" (*Emberiza*, plus longspurs, *Phrygilus*, etc.), "Zonotrichinae" [New World taxa only, including Bobolink, cowbirds, most of the emberizines, *Junco*, *Chondestes* etc., *Tiaris*, *Sicalis* (a tanager), etc.], "Pitylinae" (including *Geospiza*, *Oryzoborus*, *Cardinalis*, *Saltator*), and "Arremoninae" (including *Arremon*, *Pipilo*, etc.). The conirostral "Simplicirostres" were divided into the "Tachyphoninae, Thraupinae, and Tanagrinae," which included the remainder of the tanagers. The "Motacillinae" were placed in "Cohort 1. CICHLOMORPHAE," with other nine-primaried "Thrush-like Oscines" assigned to five other "families" which included the paruline wood warblers, flowerpeckers, several tanagers, and the pardalotes.

Sharpe (1883:648) placed the "Accentores" as "Group X" in his huge and heterogeneous grab bag, the "Timeliidae," but he did not believe that the accentors are related to the babblers: "The position of the *Accentors* in the Order *Passeriformes* is by no means easy to define; they certainly have no relations with the *Timeliidae*, as they possess a very small first [outer] primary. Mr. Seebohm, however, has not admitted them into his volume of the *Turdidae*, and in his latest work, the 'History of British Birds,' he has placed them with the *Paridae*, although . . . they should, in my opinion, have been associated with other families. I follow Mr. Salvin . . . in placing *Ephthianura* with *Accentor*, to which it is most closely allied in external form, although the habits of the birds and the colour of their eggs differ *in toto*."

Sharpe did not reveal with which "other families" the accentors should have been associated, and the Australian genus *Ephthianura* is now known to be a honeyeater.

Sharpe (1885:457) introduced the Motacillidae: "This family contains only the Wagtails and Pipits, and is the best-defined of all the nine-quilled Passeres, as the inner secondary quills are elongated so as to be nearly as long as the primaries. In this respect they resemble the Larks (*Alaudidae*), to which they also bear a great likeness in the formation of the feet. The *Alaudidae*, however, have the hinder aspect of the tarsus scutellated and have a small bastard primary, so tiny, however, as in general to escape observation. The Wagtails and Pipits have no bastard primary at all."

Sharpe said only that the motacillids "resemble," or bear a "likeness," to the larks, and he also pointed out several differences, but his comments may have been the beginning of the association of the Alaudidae and Motacillidae in some of the classifications of the next century. The larks came to be placed at the beginning of the sequence of oscine groups, and the Motacillidae were sometimes placed nearby, e.g., Mayr and Greenway (1956).

Sharpe (1888) dealt with the "Fringillidae," which included some of the genera we now know to be members of the Passeridae. In his "Fringillinae," Sharpe included *Passer, Petronia*, and *Montifringilla*. The latter included the species currently admitted to the genus, plus those now placed in the cardueline genus *Leucosticte*.

E. Bartlett (1889) suggested that the starlings (Sturnidae) and the weaverbirds (Ploceinae) are related, and this may have influenced Sharpe (1890) to place the weavers in the "Sturniformes," but there is no mention of Bartlett's work in volume 13 of the *Catalogue* in which Sharpe (1890) treated "Section C. Sturniformes" of the suborder Passeres: "The classification adopted in the third volume of the present work . . . for the arrangement of the *Passeriformes* was principally that of Mr. Wallace (Ibis, 1874, p. 409), with certain modifications. During the sixteen years . . . since . . . we have learned that the classification adopted in 1877 is somewhat artificial. . . . the [section] treated in the present volume seems to be the most unnatural. The starlings are divorced from the *Corvidae*, to which they are undoubtedly allied; the *Artamidae* may be a Sturnine family, but of that I am not yet assured; the *Alaudidae* find themselves separated from the *Motacillidae*, and the *Ploceidae* from the *Fringillidae* and *Icteridae*."

We now know that the starlings are not closely related to the Corvidae (including *Artamus*), and that the motacillines have closer relatives than the larks, but Sharpe was right in his association of the weaverbirds with the "Fringillidae and Icteridae." However, in volume 13 (1890) of the *Catalogue*, the "Ploceidae" were inserted between the Sturnidae and Alaudidae. The widowbirds and the estrildines, plus *Philetairus* and *Plocepasser*, were placed in the "Viduinae," and the other passerids in the "Ploceinae," an arrangement that was based mainly on the length of the outer primary. Sharpe (1890:198) provided a "Key to the Subfamilies": "A. With the first primary very small and falcate, attenuated towards the end; this first primary never reaching beyond the primary coverts, and generally falling conspicuously short of the latter . . . 1. VIDUINAE. B. With the first primary large, generally obtuse at the end, and extending beyond the primary-coverts . . . 2. PLOCEINAE."

The Passeridae and Fringillidae were also separated by the size of the outer primary; in the Passeridae the 10th primary is on the dorsal side of the wing and usually relatively large, but in the Fringillidae it is absent or very small, and concealed on the ventral side of the wing. The passerids with small outer primaries (e.g., *Passer*) were, therefore, sometimes placed in the Fringillidae.

In volume 4 of the *Hand-List* Sharpe (1903) placed the "Accentorinae" in the Turdidae after the "Turdinae" and followed by the monotypic "Ephthianurinae." Clearly, Sharpe thought that the accentors were related to the thrushes, and this association was to be debated frequently in the future. *Ephthianura* is a meliphagid.

In volume 5 (1909) of the *Hand-List*, Sharpe placed the following groups in sequence: Mniotiltidae (Parulini), Drepanididae, Motacillidae, Alaudidae, Catamblyrhynchidae, Fringillidae, Coerebidae, Procniatidae (*Tersina*), Tanagridae, Ploceidae, Icteridae. We place these groups in the Alaudidae, Passeridae, and Fringillidae of the Passeroidea. Thus, Sharpe recognized most of the members of the passeroid clade, although he did not include the Nectariniidae or the Prunellinae (accentors), and he believed the Icteridae to be closely related to the Sturnidae, which followed the Icteridae in his list.

In Sharpe's classification most of the genera were assigned to the same families or subfamilies that would be accepted today. Some of the exceptions included his placement of the Galapagos Warbler Finch (*Certhidea*) with the paruline wood warblers in the "Mniotiltidae," and *Passer* and *Petronia* in the Fringillidae.

As in the *Catalogue*, Sharpe (1909) divided the Ploceidae into the "Viduinae" and "Ploceinae."

Shelley (1905) placed the long-tailed ploceines in his "Viduinae," including the bishop-birds (*Euplectes* = *Coliuspasser*) in which all twelve rectrices are long, while in *Vidua* only the two middle pairs are elongate. Reichenow (1914) included the estrildines, widowbirds, and bishopbirds in his "Spermestinae," but did not associate *Vidua* with *Euplectes*.

Chapin (1917) reviewed the classification of the weaverbirds, examined the characters used to classify them, and presented the first modern classification of the Ploceidae. He noted that the size of the outer primary is misleading as the basis for subdividing the weaverbirds, and introduced the presence of nestling mouth-markings to define the estrildines. Chapin defined two types of mouth-markings, the domino and horseshoe patterns, and he placed in the Estrildinae only species whose nestlings have mouth-markings, even if they also have a long outer primary.

Chapin found that the ploceines, estrildines, *Passer*, *Pinicola*, and *Paroaria* are alike in skeletal characters, but that *Textor* (*Bubalornis*) differs from these in both cranial and sternal structure. Chapin separated the buffalo-weavers (*Bubalornis*, *Dinemellia*) as the "Textoridae" on the basis of the skeletal characters, plus their unusual nest structure, long outer (10th) primary, spotted eggs, lack of nestling mouth-markings, tarsal scutellation, and the unique phalloid organ in *Bubalornis*. He placed the ploceines and estrildines in the Ploceidae, with the waxbills, widowbirds, and *Pholidornis* in the Estrildinae, and the typical weavers, *Sporopipes*, *Histurgops*, *Plocepasser*, *Philetairus*, and *Euplectes* (*Coliuspasser*) in the Ploceinae. Chapin considered the long tail feathers in the widowbirds and bishopbirds to be the result of convergence, not close relationship.

Sushkin (1924, 1925, 1927) presented the results of his studies on the anatomy and classification of the weaverbirds. He concluded (1927) that *Passer*, *Petronia*, and *Montifringilla*, are related to one another and should form the Passerinae in the Ploceidae. He cited skeletal structure, similarities in the palatal surface of the rhamphotheca, a complete post-juvenal molt, and nest structure in support of his proposal.

As evidence of relationships, Sushkin favored the pattern of ridges and furrows on the palatal surface of the bill sheath, but he also considered the tarsal scutellation and several skeletal elements. He recognized the unusual characters of *Bubalornis*, but chose to expand the

Ploceidae to include the Bubalornithinae, Plocepasserinae (including *Plocepasser*, *Pseudonigrita*, *Histurgops*, *Philetairus*), Passerinae, Sporopipinae, Estrildinae, and Ploceinae.

Sushkin (1927:23) also made the strange suggestion that some characters of the suboscine plantcutters (*Phytotoma*) "may seem to entitle [*Phytotoma*] to an ancestral relation to *Bubalornis*," but he also noted the many ways these genera differ. Sushkin thought the Passerinae are closer to the Ploceinae than to the Estrildinae, that *Vidua* is an estrildine, and that *Sporopipes* is closer to the ploceines and estrildines than to the Passerinae.

Neunzig (1928, 1929) suggested that *Pyromelana* and *Coliuspasser* are closely related to *Vidua*, to which Chapin (1929) responded with a vigorous reaffirmation of his belief that the viduines are closely related to the estrildines and that *Pyromelana* and *Coliuspasser* are ploceines. Chapin (1929:482) reported that *Vidua*, unlike most passerines, has a row of lesser upper secondary coverts. Morlion (1964) reported two rows of these coverts in *Vidua*, and Zeidler (1966:123, fig. 17) found an apparently homologous row of seven small, downy feathers in *Passer*. Sibley (1970:87–88) reviewed the condition of these coverts in the ploceid groups and concluded that "Each group differs from the others and the assignment of homologies is uncertain. *Vidua* seems to be most like *Passer* and least like the Estrildinae. . . . it is impossible to interpret their taxonomic value."

Chapin (1929:482) noted that *Vidua* differs from the estrildines and most ploceines in having a first lower greater primary covert, as do most oscines. *Passer* also has this covert (Zeidler 1966:fig. 10).

Von Boetticher (1931) suggested that the Ploceidae and Sturnidae are related and that *Bubalornis* on the ploceid side and *Buphagus* on the sturnid side are the primitive members of their respective families and closest to one another. Von Boetticher also suggested that the nine-primaried oscines, including the Motacillidae and Dicaeidae, were derived from the ploceid-sturnid complex. In these comments we see again the impossible idea that some living species are primitive members of their families and can be links between related groups, and that living taxa can be derived from other living taxa. The idea of a ploceid-sturnid relationship is not supported by the DNA data, which places them as members of different superfamilies.

Delacour and Edmond-Blanc (1933–34) revised *Euplectes* and *Vidua* and proposed that the Viduinae be placed in the Ploceidae. Delacour (1944) revised the Estrildinae and concluded that the nearest relatives of the estrildines are the viduines and that these groups evolved from the Sporopipinae. Delacour also stated that he was "inclined to think that the Ploceidae are really nearer to the Sturnidae than to the Fringillidae" (p. 73) because of their nesting habits, although the starlings are mostly hole-nesters and the weavers build a woven, enclosed nest. Delacour suggested that these nest types are more similar to one another than either is to the usual open nest of fringillids. Delacour (1943b:71) placed *Anomalospiza* in the Ploceinae and proposed that *Pholidornis* should be placed near *Hylia* in the Hyliidae between the Zosteropidae and Nectariniidae, thus following Bates (1930). Paynter (1967:208) placed *Hylia* and *Pholidornis* in the Sylviidae.

Fiedler (1951) interpreted his comparisons of jaw muscles as evidence of a relationship between the Fringillidae and Ploceinae, but Beecher (1953b) placed them some distance apart. Beecher considered his Ploceidae (incl. Viduinae, Passerinae) to be quite different from the Estrildidae in their jaw musculature, and suggested that "The Estrildidae seem . . . to have arisen from the Meliphaginae or Cisticolinae in Australia, while the Ploceidae arose from the Promeropinae or Cisticolinae in Africa" (p. 303).

From a study of cranial and palatal characters, Tordoff (1954a) concluded that the Estrildinae are most closely related to the Carduelinae. He included these two groups in the Ploceidae with the Bubalornithinae, Passerinae, Ploceinae, and Viduinae. Stallcup (1954), from a study of pelvic musculature and serological comparisons of muscle and soft organ proteins, concluded that the carduelines cannot be distinguished from the New World finches and tanagers, and that the major features of the leg muscles of carduelines are like those of ploceids. Stallcup also reported that the carduelines are serologically separable from the cardinals, emberizines, and tanagers. According to Stallcup (1954:204), the carduelines show more serological similarity to the estrildines than to the New World nine-primaried oscines, and the estrildines are more like the New World groups than are the carduelines. Stallcup's data are ambiguous, but he concluded that a family Carduelidae, containing the Estrildinae and Carduelinae, was justified, thus, in part, following Tordoff.

In 1954, Chapin accepted a treatment of the weavers more like that of Sushkin (1927) in which the Bubalornithinae were placed in the Ploceidae. Chapin suggested that the Viduinae are close to the estrildines, and not to *Euplectes*.

Bock (1960) showed that the palatine process has little or no value in showing relationships among passerine families and used his data to argue against a close relationship between carduelines and estrildines. Raikow (1978) found no evidence of a close relationship between carduelines and estrildines in the limb muscles, and included the Carduelinae in the Fringillidae.

Steiner (1955) stressed the differences between the typical ploceines and the waxbills, and argued for the recognition of the latter as the family Spermestidae. Wolters (1957, 1960), although primarily concerned with generic and specific limits, placed the Viduinae in the Estrildidae.

Mainardi (1958b) reviewed the conclusions of Beecher, Tordoff, and Stallcup, added his own serological comparisons of red cell antigens, and concluded that the Estrildinae and Passerinae are closely related and that the Emberizinae are most closely related to *Fringilla*. He stated that the "Carduelinae are intermediate between Estrildinae and Passerinae on one side, and Emberizinae and *Fringilla* on the other" (p. 336). Mainardi also presented some electrophoretic patterns of the hemoglobins of these groups which he believed agreed with his serological data.

White and Moreau (1958) placed the waxbills in the Estrildidae and doubted the inclusion of the Sporopipinae in the Ploceidae, but "pending further studies of *Sporopipes*" (p. 141) they included it in the Ploceinae. Wolters (1966) placed *Sporopipes* closest to the Estrildinae.

Crook (1958) studied the behavior of *Bubalornis* and decided that his observations, plus anatomical characters, supported the recognition of the family Bubalornithidae, but he had no information on *Dinemellia*.

Steiner (1960) based a revision of the "Spermestidae" (Estrildinae) primarily on the mouth-markings of nestlings and reaffirmed his belief that the waxbills should be separated in their own family. He discussed the relationships of the widowbirds and concluded that the Viduinae should be placed in the Ploceidae, because their similarities to estrildines are due to mimicry of the host waxbills, not to close relationship.

Friedmann (1960) reviewed the literature on the parasitic weavers and concluded that the widowbirds are most closely related to the estrildines but, because they have a number of characters not shared with ploceines or estrildines, they should be separated as the Viduinae in the Ploceidae. Friedmann (p. 8) questioned whether there is a valid basis for keeping the Ploceidae separate from the Fringillidae, noting that "In view of the general acceptance of the muscicapine-sylviine-turdine assemblage in one family, it appears that a similar amalgamation may be justified here." Friedmann thought that this was more appropriate than to follow Steiner's suggestion to place the waxbills in the Estrildidae.

Wolters (1960) placed the Viduinae in the Estrildidae, while Nicolai (1961) found that the widowbirds have ploceine-like elements in their vocalizations. Friedmann (1962) criticized the papers by Steiner (1960), Wolters (1960), and Nicolai (1961), and defended his opinion (1960) that the viduines are closest to the estrildines and that both groups should be placed in the Ploceidae.

Collias and Collias (1964) studied the evolution of nest-building in the weaverbirds and concluded that their observations supported Chapin's (1917) classification. After consultations with Chapin and Friedmann, Collias and Collias developed a "diagram of relationships" that includes the Bubalornithinae, Passerinae, Plocepasserinae, Ploceinae, Sporopipinae, Estrildinae, and Viduinae in the Ploceidae. They were uncertain about the relationships of the Passerinae and Sporopipinae; the nests of the Passerinae "did not bear any close resemblance to those of the other subfamilies" (p. 118). The nests of the buffalo-weavers are most like those of the Plocepasserinae, that of *Dinemellia* being similar to the nest of *Plocepasser mahali*, and the nests of the Ploceinae are also most like those of plocepasserines. Estrildine nests vary greatly but are most like that of *Sporopipes*. Wolters (1966), as noted above, placed *Sporopipes* closest to the estrildines.

From a detailed study of the breeding behavior of the viduines, Nicolai (1964) concluded that "In their courtship, in the innate song elements, in the seasonal alteration of breeding plumage and cryptic dress, and in their plumage characters the Viduinae reveal themselves as close relatives of the Euplectinae, a subfamily of the weaverbirds (Ploceidae)" (p. 201).

Zisweiler (1964, 1965, 1967a) concluded from a study of feeding behavior, bill, skull, jaw muscles, the horny palate, and the digestive tract that the Viduinae are related to the Ploceidae and are closest to the *Euplectes* group, thus agreeing with Nicolai (1964). Zisweiler proposed the division of the Ploceidae into a *Euplectes* group and a *Ploceus* group, and supported Steiner's separation of the waxbills as the Estrildidae. Moreau (1967) pointed out that *Passer* dust-bathes but the Ploceinae do not, contrary to the reference in Ficken and Ficken (1966:652).

Pocock (1966) reported on the occurrence of certain foramina in the posterior wall of the orbit, and suggested that the Passeridae should be recognized. However, subsequent comparisons of many more taxa showed that "the foramina defined by Pocock actually exhibit a continuum and that they are of doubtful taxonomic value at any level" (Sibley 1970:91–92).

Zisweiler (1967b) compared the seed-opening mechanism, the horny palate, and the alimentary canal of *Montifringilla nivalis* with these structures in other seed-eating passerines. He concluded that *Montifringilla* is most like the Ploceidae and should be placed, with *Passer*, in the Passerinae.

Sibley (1970:96) concluded from electrophoretic comparisons of the egg-white proteins that (1) the Ploceinae and Estrildinae are more closely related to one another than to any other group, and should be placed in the same family; (2) the carduelines are related to the other fringillids and are not especially close to the estrildines; (3) *Passer* is not as close to the estrildines and ploceines as they are to one another, and not as close to the New World nine-primaried fringillids as they are to one another; (4) the family Passeridae should probably be recognized, but *Montifringilla* may be closest to the Ploceidae; (5) the viduines may be related to the Ploceidae but *Passer* and the emberizines are possible relatives; (6) *Bubalornis* is probably closest to the Ploceidae, and *Philetairus* may be closer to *Passer* than to the Ploceidae.

Poltz and Jacob (1974) analyzed the chemical structure of the uropygial gland secretion from 18 species, including emberizines, fringillines, carduelines, ploceines, and *Passer*. They found that the uropygial waxes of *Passer* are of "the same type as . . . for Emberizidae and Fringillidae" and quite different from those of *Ploceus* and *Quelea*. They noted that "This may be a convergent property. Waxes of the same type were detected in the preen gland lipids of the Cuckoo (*Cuculus canorus*) and Barn Owl (*Tyto alba*). There is, however, the possibility that the sparrows are actually closer related to the Fringillidae and Emberizidae than to the Ploceids." Jacob (1978:199) summarized: "Fringillidae and Emberizidae including *Passer domesticus* and *Passer montanus* are clearly separated from Ploceidae. The Estrildinae and Viduinae are closely related to Ploceinae. It should be noted that *Cinclus cinclus* possesses a very similar uropygial gland wax." These, and other results of the interesting work by these authors, indicate that the preen gland lipids are subject to convergence and cannot be assumed to reflect phylogenetic relationships in every instance. This is also true for other biochemical data based on comparisons of low molecular weight "secondary substances."

Bentz (1979) compared the limb musculature among species representing the various groups of weavers, waxbills, and sparrows and concluded that the families Ploceidae and Estrildidae should be recognized. In the Ploceidae Bentz included the Passerinae, Ploceinae, and Bubalornithinae; in the Estrildidae he included the Poephilinae, Viduinae, Lonchurinae, and Estrildinae. In his Passerinae, Bentz included *Plocepasser*, *Pseudonigrita*, *Philetairus*, *Passer*, *Petronia*, *Montifringilla*, and *Sporopipes*. He found that "*Philetairus*, *Sporopipes*, and *Plocepasser* are myologically good members of the Passerinae but appear to be more closely related to each other than to *Passer* and the other members of the subfamily" (p. 23).

Bock and Morony (1978) found a "unique skeletal structure—the preglossale—in the tongue of the passerine finches" (p. 122) and proposed that "*Passer*, *Montifringilla* and *Petronia* . . . should be classified as a distinct family, the Passeridae" (p. 145). Although the presence of the preglossale in these genera may be taken as evidence of their close relationship, it does not automatically provide the basis for the separation of these genera as "a distinct family." The structure may have been present in the common ancestor of the three genera, but not in the ancestors of the other passerid lineages, or it may have been present in the ancestors of all of the passerid lineages, but lost in all but the Passerinae. These questions can be answered by determining the condition in the other living passerid lineages. The structure of the tongue in the insectivorous Motacillinae and the relatively omnivorous Prunellinae would be of particular interest.

Ziswiler (1979) provided the answers to some of the questions posed above when he described the various stiffening devices that have evolved in the tongues of seed-eating fringillids that "squeeze seeds out of the shell by using their tongue to support and orientate the seed while it is being husked." The emberizines "use a fat tissue and blood sinuses to stiffen their tongue, *Passer* and *Montifringilla*, both ploceids, have developed a neomorph, the Praeglossale . . . and the estrildids stiffen their tongue by swelling enormous venous sinuses, which are fixed both to the Ossa entoglossa and to the Os hypentoglossum, a neomorph bone. These . . . prove that each of the three bird families became granivorous independently of the others."

The DNA Hybridization Evidence

The DNA comparisons offer a relatively simple picture of the Passeridae, with some aspects that agree with the groups defined above, plus the unexpected addition of the Motacillinae and Prunellinae.

Following the nectariniid-passerid divergence at Δ 9.8, the passerid branch divided at Δ 8.5. One branch was the ancestor of the Passerinae, including *Passer* and *Petronia*, for which we have DNA data, and we accept the evidence for the inclusion of *Montifringilla*. The other branch soon divided again at Δ 8.3, and one of these lineages gave rise to the Motacillinae; the other divided at Δ 7.9 and one branch became the Prunellinae. The other lineage divided at Δ 6.9 into the lineages that produced the living Estrildinae and Ploceinae (Fig. 382).

These divergences were so close together that we cannot be certain of the exact sequence of the branchings, but it is probable that they all occurred within a period of about five million years, ca. 20 and 25 MYA. They may be represented as a multifurcation in the dendrogram.

In earlier studies (Sibley and Ahlquist 1981b,c) we presented somewhat different arrangements of the passerid subgroups, although their relationships to one another were apparent. The above narrative is based on more complete data (Sibley and Ahlquist 1985a,c).

Fig. 303 (*Passer*) shows that *Ploceus*, *Prunella*, and *Agelaius* are about equidistant from *Passer*, with *Nectarinia* next, then members of the Muscicapoidea (and presumably other Passerida). The Corvida are represented by a honeyeater.

Fig. 304 (*Passer*) confirms that *Petronia* is closely related to *Passer*, and that the ploceines (*Ploceus*, *Philetarius*) are closer to *Passer* than are the estrildines (*Nigrita*, *Vidua*); *Turdus* shows the relative position of the Muscicapoidea to the Passeroidea.

Fig. 305 (*Motacilla*) shows that the wagtails and pipits are more closely related to the Ploceinae (*Quelea*) and Passerinae (*Passer*) than to the Fringillidae (*Melospiza*, *Dendroica*), the Nectariniidae, Sylviidae (*Parus*), Turdidae, or the Corvida (*Vireo*, *Meliphaga*).

Fig. 306 (*Ploceus*) shows the relationship of the weaverbirds to the sunbirds (*Nectarinia*), *Passer,* and other groups of the Passerida, with the three Corvida (*Vireo*, *Corvus*, *Lichenostomus*) as the distant out-groups.

Fig. 307 (*Vidua*) shows that the viduines are closest to the estrildines and ploceines, and that *Motacilla* and *Passer* are closer to *Vidua* than are the fringillids or alaudids.

The melting curves indicate that the Passeridae includes the sparrows (*Passer*), rocksparrows, wagtails, pipits, accentors, weavers, waxbills, and whydahs (widow-birds, indigobirds).

The FITCH tree, Fig. 351, includes members of the Passeroidea, except the Fringillidae. With minor differences it agrees with the UPGMA tree (Figs. 369, 382, and 383). Two major radiations are evident: (1) the cluster that includes the granivorous and insectivorous weaverbirds and allies plus the wagtails and accentors; (2) the nectarivores with one clade composed of the sunbirds, flowerpeckers, and sugarbirds, and the other of the Papuan endemics, *Paramythia*, *Melanocharis*, and *Toxorhamphus*. The larks (*Alauda*) are the sister group of the Nectariniidae, Melanocharitidae, Paramythiidae, Passeridae, and Fringillidae.

Family FRINGILLIDAE: 240/993.

Subfamily PEUCEDRAMINAE: 1/1. Olive Warbler.
Subfamily FRINGILLINAE: 39/169. Old World Finches.
    Tribe FRINGILLINI: 1/3. Chaffinches, Brambling.
    Tribe CARDUELINI: 20/136. Goldfinches, Crossbills, etc.
    Tribe DREPANIDINI: 18/30. Hawaiian Honeycreepers
Subfamily EMBERIZINAE: 200/823. New World 9-Primaried Oscines.
    Tribe EMBERIZINI: 32/156. Buntings, Longspurs, Towhees, etc.
    Tribe PARULINI: 25/115. Wood Warblers, incl. *Zeledonia*.
    Tribe CARDINALINI: 13/42. Cardinals.
    Tribe ICTERINI: 26/97. Troupials, Meadowlarks, Grackles, etc.
    Tribe THRAUPINI: 104/413. Tanagers, Neotropical Honeycreepers, Swallow Tanager, Plushcap, Seedeaters, Tanager-finches.

The Fringillidae is the sister group of the nectariniid-passerid clade; the divergence occurred at Δ 10.0, probably ca. 25–35 MYA (Fig. 384).

The DNA comparisons indicate that *Peucedramus taeniatus*, the Olive Warbler, is the sister taxon of the entire nine-primaried oscine clade. Its taxonomic history is discussed below. The Fringillinae probably originated and radiated in the Old World, the Emberizinae in the New World.

Taxonomic History

Sundevall (1872, see 1889) placed the wood warblers (Parulini) in his "Cohort Cichlomorphae" as part of "Phalanx 6. Novempennatae," which he called the "Thrush-like Oscines." The parulines were divided among four "families": Dendroecinae, which included *Dicaeum* and *Zosterops*, as well as several paruline genera (e.g., *Dendroica*, *Geothlypis*), and four genera of Neotropical honeycreepers ("coerebids"), which we place in the Thraupini; the Setophaginae included only parulines, but the Icteriinae (based on *Icteria*) and the Hemithraupinae were composed of parulines and thraupines.

In "Phalanx 2. Amplipalatales" of the "Cohort Conirostres" Sundevall (1872, see 1889) placed the carduelines in the "Chloridinae" and the fringillines plus *Passer* and *Petronia* in the "Fringillinae." He defined the Chloridinae as having nine primaries and being "remarkable for the palate being more broadly and deeply arched, with three elevated slender lines widely separated one from another." These "elevated slender lines" were the palatal ridges used by Sushkin (1929a) as evidence for a relationship between the carduelines and the Hawaiian honeycreepers.

Sundevall's "Phalanx 3. Arctipalatales" of the "Cohort Conirostres" included nine-primaried, finch-like birds, "for the most part American;" the Loxiinae for the crossbills; Emberizinae and Zonotrichinae for emberizines, plus the icterine bobolinks and cowbirds, and some tangers; Pitylinae for *Geospiza*, *Cardinalis*, and several emberizines; Arremoninae for

Pipilo, Buarremon, and several others; Cissopinae for the Magpie Tanager (*Cissopis*). In "Phalanx 4. Simplicirostres" Sundevall placed the "families" Tachyphoninae, Rhamphocelinae, Thraupinae, and Tanagrinae, all composed of tanagers.

In "Cohort 3. Coliomorphae . . . Phalanx 1. Novempennatae," Sundevall distributed the Icterini among the Chalcophaninae, Agelaeinae, and Icterinae (based on *Icterus*). The Neotropical honeycreepers and the Hawaiian honeycreepers were assigned by Sundevall to "Cohort 5. Cinnyrimorphae" and placed in the Arbelorhininae and Drepanidinae.

Thus, Sundevall scattered the closely related members of the Fringillidae among four cohorts and 21 families. The shape of the bill, position of the nostrils, rictal bristles, structure of the tongue, number of primaries, shapes of wings and tail, and structure of the feet were the principal beak-feather-foot characters used by Sundevall to define his groups.

Wallace (1874) based his arrangement of the oscines on the structure of the wing. He divided the Passeri into three series according to the number of primaries and the degree of development of the outermost. The "Tanagroid Passeres" were defined as "Wing with 9 primaries, the first [outer] of which is fully developed and very long." In this group Wallace placed the "Motacillidae, Mniotiltidae [Parulini], Coerebidae, Drepanidae, Dicaeidae, Ampelidae [Bombycillidae], Hirundinidae, Tanagridae, Fringillidae, and Icteridae." In the "Sturnoid Passeres," defined as "Wing with 10 primaries, the first of which is rudimentary," he placed the "Ploceidae, Sturnidae, Artamidae, and Alaudidae." Note the association of the Ploceidae and Artamidae with the Sturnidae, an arrangement that has persisted in some classifications.

Sclater (1880b) reviewed the "present state of the Systema Avium" and commented on several classifications, including those of Sundevall and Wallace. Sclater objected to Wallace's arrangement of the Passeres because "it separates some very nearly allied forms far too widely. The 'spurious primary' which Mr. Wallace relies upon to divide his Tanagroids and Sturnoids is not even a *generic* character. . . . Mr. Wallace puts the Alaudidae amongst his Sturnoids; but in some larks . . . the spurious primary is altogether wanting. The Ploceidae and Fringillidae, which are barely distinguishable as families, fall under different heads, as do the Sturnidae and Icteridae. Yet there cannot be a doubt as to the intimate connexion of the two last-named families. In my opinion Sundevall's groups of the Oscines are therefore far more naturally conceived."

Although certainly aware of Sclater's criticism of Wallace's classification, Sharpe (1885:1) began volume 10 of the *Catalogue of Birds* as follows:

Order II. PASSERIFORMES
Suborder I. PASSERES
Section B. Fringilliformes. (Nine-Quilled Passeres.)
Wing with *nine* primaries, the first of which is fully developed and usually very long.
Cf. Wallace, Ibis, 1874, p. 410.

The families which Mr. Wallace has arranged in his Series B, Tanagroid Passeres, do not fall easily into a linear series. The *Motacillidae* ally the group with the Larks (*Alaudidae*). . . . The *Dicaeidae* cannot be separated from the *Nectariniidae* . . . and some of the aberrant genera, such as *Rhamphocharis*, exhibit a great likeness to some of the *Meliphagidae*. The *Mniotiltidae*, or American Warblers, lead through the *Coerebidae* to the *Tanagridae*, and thence to the *Fringillidae*. The Chatterers (*Ampelidae*) [Bombycillidae] and the Swallows (*Hirundinidae*) are, as Mr. Wallace has remarked, difficult to locate; but the

Ampelidae may be arranged somewhere near *Pardalotus*; and the nearest allies of the Swallows really seem to be the Flycatchers, which approach them closely through the genera *Hemichelidon, Artomyias*, and others.

Sharpe then presented a diagram in which he "attempted to indicate the natural arrangement of the Nine-quilled Passeres as well as their affinities to families not belonging to this section" (p. 2).

Thus, from Wallace's classification, based largely on the number of primaries, the New World nine-primaried oscine cluster was emerging. However, Wallace's "Tanagroid Passeres" also included the "Motacillidae, Dicaeidae, Ampelidae, and Hirundinidae" which introduced complications. Sharpe was impaled on the sharp-horned dilemma of convergence and adaptive radiation, coupled with the limitations imposed by a single defining character.

Sharpe (1885:2) did not follow Wallace in all respects for he placed the Hawaiian honeycreepers (Drepanidini) in his "Dicaeidae," which also included *Pardalotus* and several other genera that are not flowerpeckers. Sharpe's "Mniotiltidae" included only the New World wood warblers (Parulini), thus establishing the boundaries of that group that have remained stable to the present.

Volume 11 of the *Catalogue* included the "Tanagridae, Coerebidae, and Icteridae" and was written by P. L. Sclater (1886), who had a long interest in the tanagers and extensive experience in the Neotropics. In his Introduction, Sclater expressed his opinions about the relationships of the three New World families assigned to him:

The Coerebidae I consider to be nearly allied to the Tanagridae; and it is indeed somewhat difficult to separate them by external characters. They appear to perform the same functions in Nature in the Neotropical Region as the Nectariniidae and Dicaeidae in the tropics of the Old World. The Tanagridae are also very closely allied to the Fringillidae, and are in fact fruit- and insect-eating Finches. They come in very naturally between the Mniotiltidae and Coerebidae on the one side, and the Fringillidae on the other. But whether the Icteridae should immediately follow the Tanagridae in a natural series is, I think, a little open to question. To my mind, the Icteridae, although their outer primary is entirely aborted, present many points of alliance with the Sturnidae; and it would therefore be better, I think, to place them *after* the Fringillidae, and in the immediate neighborhood of the former family. But, under Mr. Wallace's system of arrangement of the Oscines according to the number of their primaries, which has been adopted in this part of the Catalogue of Birds, the Icteridae do very well in their present situation.

Thus, while Sclater recognized the close relationship between the tanagers and Neotropical honeycreepers, the convergent similarities of the starlings and troupials (Icterini) continued to lead him astray.

Sclater's Coerebidae included the Neotropical honeycreepers and the Galapagos Warbler Finch, *Certhidea*, about which Sclater noted that "Its true place is perhaps a little uncertain, but it seems to come nearest to *Conirostrum* and *Dacnis*." He divided the Coerebidae into four subfamilies.

Sclater was the tanager expert and his "Tanagridae" agrees with recent treatments of the "Thraupidae" or "Thraupinae," with a few discrepancies. For example, in his "Pitylinae" he placed *Buarremon* (*Atlapetes*), *Arremon, Pezopetes, Saltator*, and *Pitylus*. The A.O.U. (1983) assigned the first three to the Emberizinae, the last two to the Cardinalinae. It is not certain to which group these, and several other genera, actually belong.

Sclater's Icteridae contained the same taxa currently viewed as members of the "Icteridae" (our Icterini). He included the Bobolink (*Dolichonyx*) and the cowbirds (*Molothrus*) in the "Agelaeinae," one of his five subfamilies.

The "Fringillidae" were introduced by Sharpe (1888:1) in volume 12 of the *Catalogue*:

> The present volume . . . treats of the *Fringillidae*, a family closely allied to the *Tanagridae* . . . and also connected through the Buntings with the Larks (*Alaudidae*).
>
> No one has as yet propounded a satisfactory classification of the *Fringillidae*, the difficulty consisting in the complete connection which exists between the various genera of Finches and Buntings; and such ornithologists only who have not entered into a detailed study of this family will speak of the Finches, Buntings, and their allies as if they constituted well-defined families. Any one who has worked upon a large or small fragment of the family must acknowledge that the definition of the genera is difficult and the recognition of subfamilies almost impossible. The *Fringillidae* naturally group themselves into three divisions—Grosbeaks, Finches, and Buntings; but numerous forms connect them, being referable to the confines of any of the three groups. Thus *Cardinalis* will probably be found from its osteology to be a Bunting with the aspect of a Grosbeak; while *Urocynchramus* is certainly a Bunting with the aspect of a Rose-Finch, or, if it be preferred, a Rose-Finch with the bill of a Bunting.
>
> Every division of the family is therefore to be accepted on the score of convenience rather than having a foundation of solid structural characters; and it would not be unreasonable to treat the whole family as constituting one great genus *Fringilla*, with various sections or subgenera, as was once done for the family *Picidae* by the late Professor Sundevall.

With this admission of defeat before he started, Sharpe proceeded to divide the Fringillidae into three subfamilies:

Coccothraustinae: *Geospiza*, some carduelines, grosbeaks, *Cardinalis*, *Loxigilla*, *Catamblyrhynchus* (a tanager), *Volatinia* (tanager), and several others.

Fringillinae: chaffinches, the remaining carduelines, and the Passerinae; *Petronia*, *Passer*, *Montifringilla*.

Emberizinae: *Urocynchramus*, *Atlapetes*, *Haplospiza* (tanager), *Diuca* (tanager), and the genera currently placed in the "Emberizidae" in most classifications (our Emberizini).

In his *Manual of North American Birds* (1887), Robert Ridgway followed the classification of the first edition of the *Check-List of North American Birds* (A.O.U. 1886). In the order Passeres Ridgway (1887) recognized 21 North American families, as follows: Cotingidae, Tyrannidae, Alaudidae, Corvidae, Sturnidae, Icteridae, Fringillidae, Tanagridae, Hirundinidae, Ampelidae, Laniidae, Vireonidae, Coerebidae, Mniotiltidae, Motacillidae, Cinclidae, Troglodytidae, Certhiidae, Paridae, Sylviidae, and Turdidae. This sequence includes the traditional alliances among the Corvidae, Sturnidae, and Icteridae; Laniidae and Vireonidae; Cinclidae, Troglodytidae, and Certhiidae; and the position of the thrushes at the end of the series.

In 1901 Ridgway introduced a cosmopolitan element into the systematics of New World birds with the publication of the first volume of *The Birds of North and Middle America*. Baird, Coues, Stejneger, and other North American ornithologists had been cited by Sharpe and his collaborators in the *Catalogue*, but Ridgway extended the coverage into the Neotropics, considered the classification of the higher categories on a global scale, and described each species in much the same way that Sharpe had used. Ridgway (1901:vii) stated that the classification he had adopted "is essentially that of the most recent and advanced authorities, with such minor modifications as in the judgment of the present author seem desirable." The authorities named on pages 6–7 included Gadow (1893), Beddard (1898a), Fürbringer (1888), Newton (1896), and Stejneger (1885).

Ridgway's 1901 classification added the Catamblyrhynchidae, Procniatidae (*Tersina*), Ptiliogonatidae [sic], Dulidae, Sittidae, Chamaeidae, Mimidae, and Ploceidae.

Ridgway began with the Fringillidae because "owing to inadequate facilities for properly arranging the larger birds in the National Museum collection these are not available for study, and . . . it became necessary either to begin with the smaller birds, already systematically arranged, or else postpone the work indefinitely." Sharpe must have sympathized with this universal complaint—he had to work in a dark basement.

Ridgway (1901:24) defined the Fringillidae:

Conirostral, "nine-primaried," acutiplantar Oscines, with the commissure distinctly and more or less abruptly angulated or deflexed basally, or else with the mandibular rami less than one-fifth as long as gonys, the mandibular tomium distinctly elevated (often angulated, sometimes toothed) post-medially, thence distinctly (usually abruptly) deflected to the rictus; rictal bristles obvious, usually distinct.

The above brief and in many respects unsatisfactory diagnosis covers the extreme variations in certain external structural details among a very large assemblage of species arbitrarily considered as forming the family Fringillidae. As here limited the family includes the whole of the Fringillidae as treated by Dr. Sharpe in the twelfth volume of the Catalogue of the Birds in the British Museum (the latest authority on the group), only the genus *Catamblyrhynchus* being withdrawn, with the addition of the genera *Pyrrhocoma*, *Pezopetes*, *Buarremon*, *Arremon*, *Diucopis*, *Conothraupis*, *Oreothraupis* (?), *Saltator*, and "*Pitylus*," which Dr. Sclater, in the eleventh volume of the same work (and elsewhere), has placed among the Tanagridae.

The group most closely related to the Fringillidae is, of course, that called Tanagridae, or at least certain members of the latter, which possibly is, even after the above-mentioned eliminations, too comprehensive. . . . As commonly understood and accepted, the two supposed families are clearly purely artificial, and the arbitrary line that has usually been drawn between them is manifestly far out of place, the Tanagridae having been made to include forms (those mentioned above) which are unquestionably fringilline in their relationships.

Ridgway continued with this theme for several pages, including a critique of Sharpe's three subfamilies as "unnatural groups." Ridgway (p. 28) then tried to solve the problem by further subdivision of the Fringillidae into 18 "groups." The first four, Coccothrausteae, Loxiae, Pyrrhulae, Fringillae, included the carduelines, plus *Passer*. The other 14 groups contained the emberizines, cardinalines, and some of the genera we have recently identified as finch-billed tanagers, e.g., *Haplospiza*, *Sicalis*, *Oryzoborus*, and *Volatinia*.

Ridgway recognized the family Catamblyrhynchidae for the Plushcap, *Catamblyrhynchus diadema*, which he noted as "Usually placed in the Fringillidae" (p. 19). This monotypic family was accepted by Sharpe (1909) and by many later authors, including Wetmore (1930, 1960) and Hellmayr (1938).

In Part 2 of his opus, Ridgway (1902) included the "Tanagridae—The Tanagers; Icteridae—The Troupials; Coerebidae—The Honey Creepers; Mniotiltidae—The Wood Warblers." The Tanagridae were diagnosed as: "Non-granivorous (frugivorous and insectivorous), conirostral, 'nine-primaried,' acutiplantar Oscines, with the commissure not abruptly angulated or deflexed basally, and with the mandibular tomium not distinctly angulated (never toothed) subbasally. As stated under the head of family Fringillidae, the division here made (like all preceding ones) between the Tanagers and the Finches is an arbitrary one.

The Tanagridae, as here restricted, are without doubt a more or less artificial group, and I am doubtful as to whether the fruit-eating *Euphoniae* (genera *Euphonia*, *Pyrrhuphonia*, and *Chlorophonia*) should not be separated from the others as a distinct family. This question, however, can only be settled after the internal structure of all the genera has been carefully studied."

Here again the expressions of uncertainty are coupled with the faith that if only the "internal structure" could be studied, all could be set right. The assumption was that external characters are adaptive and variable, but that the internal anatomy holds the key to phylogeny; besides, this pious hope provided a way out of a dilemma by postponing the decision but permitting the author to proceed with the real task before him: describing the species of North and Middle American birds.

The species that Ridgway included in his Tanagridae are still accepted as members of the Thraupidae, Thraupinae, or Thraupini.

Ridgway (1902:169) defined the Icteridae as: "Nine-primaried, conirostral, acutiplantar Oscines without obvious rictal bristles." He continued with a description of the variations in the shape of the bill and other external characters, and noted that "The absence of obvious rictal bristles is the only external character that I am able to discover which will serve to distinguish the Icteridae, as a group, from the Fringillidae. It is true that none of the Icteridae have the bill notched . . . but neither do many genera of the Fringillidae" (p. 171). This was followed by a list of several characters in which the two groups agree, and by a discussion of the differences between the Icteridae and other oscine families. Ridgway concluded: "Although so nearly allied to the Fringillidae that only a single external character seems available for its diagnosis, the Icteridae nevertheless constitute a well-circumscribed group, there being not a single genus whose proper reference to it can be seriously questioned." The proof of this last statement is found in the genera Ridgway placed in his Icteridae; all are still accepted as members of the group, whether as Icteridae, Icterinae, or Icterini.

Ridgway (1902:374) diagnosed the Coerebidae as: "Small slender-, acute-, or hook-billed 'nine-primaried' acutiplantar Oscines with the tongue deeply incised (bifid or trifid) and fringed or brushy at tip; transpalatine processes much reduced, forming minute spikes or points; interpalatine spur abortive, or small; palatines produced backward over pterygoids."

For the skeletal characters Ridgway cited Lucas (1894) and continued with a discussion of the variations in bill shape and other external characters. Ridgway (pp. 374–375) quoted Sclater's (1886) diagnosis of the Coerebidae, and commented that it is "not possible to give a satisfactory diagnosis of the Family Coerebidae since the internal structure . . . remains practically unknown." Ridgway (p. 375) cited Lucas (1894) and wrote:

So far as the typical genera, *Coereba*, *Glossiptila* [*Euneornis*], and *Cyanerpes* are concerned, Mr. Lucas finds them to represent a well-circumscribed group, of uncertain affinities, though apparently more nearly related to the Australasian family Meliphagidae (Honey-eaters) than to the American families Mniotiltidae and Tanagridae, usually held to be the nearest relatives of the Coerebidae. The gist of Mr. Lucas's conclusions is as follows:

(1) "As groups of birds are constituted the Coerebidae are certainly sufficiently distinct to stand apart, and the gap between them and the Mniotiltidae seems widest, although this may be due to a tendency on my part to place considerable weight on the general pattern of the palate."

(2) "That the members of the Coerebidae do not form a homogeneous group, but contains at least three well-marked types."

Lucas (1894) examined:

Representatives of the Mniotiltidae, Meliphagidae, Drepanididae, Tanagridae, and Fringillidae . . . in the hope that the affinities of the Coerebidae might be made apparent; and I am compelled to confess that, on the whole, the result has been unsatisfactory, and that the examination of a considerable number of specimens has rather lessened my hopes that anatomical, and especially osteological, characters may be relied upon to show relationship among the passeres.

Of course one trouble lies in the fact that the so-called families of passeres, at least very many of them, are not families at all, or not the equivalents of the families of other groups of vertebrates. It is my belief that any group of vertebrates to be of family rank should be capable of skeletal diagnosis, and this test applied to the passeres reduces them to a family or two, as has been done by Huxley and Fürbringer.

In spite of his frustration, Lucas (1894) proceeded to describe and compare various characters of the "Coerebidae" and:

To sum up: In their . . . palate the Coerebidae differ from the Mniotiltidae and resemble . . . Drepanididae and some Tanagridae.

In their tongue the Coerebidae are markedly different from the Mniotiltidae . . . largely a difference of degree rather than of kind. They differ *in toto* from the Tanagridae, are quite distinct from the Drepanididae, and find their nearest homologue in *Acanthorhynchus* [a meliphagid]. . . . there are three distinct types of tongue among the Coerebidae and . . . no comparison can be made with them . . . as a group.

As groups of birds are constituted the Coerebidae are certainly sufficiently distinct to stand apart, and the gap between them and the Mniotiltidae seems widest. . . .

The relationship with the tanagers is not very close, although such short-billed forms as *Chlorophanes* and *Dacnis* . . . might bring the two groups a little closer.

In size, form, pterylosis, structure of tongue, and pattern of convolutions of alimentary canal, there is a strong resemblance between *Coereba* and *Acanthorhynchus*, and so far the two forms exhibit a most interesting case of parallelism. . . . but . . . there is a striking dissimilarity. . . . in *Acanthorhynchus* the palatines run outside the palatal process of the premaxillary instead of along the inner side, as in passerine birds generally.

Thus, from Lucas's study of "internal anatomy" there emerged a series of conflicting statements that merely added to the confusion about the affinities of the Coerebidae. Sclater had argued for a close relationship between the honeycreepers and tanagers, but Lucas denied it. Ridgway (1902:377), having reviewed Lucas's results, found himself "very doubtful as to the naturalness of the group known as the Coerebidae," but he recognized the Coerebidae, as have most of his successors.

Ridgway (1902:425) diagnosed the wood warblers, "Mniotiltidae," as:

Slender-billed or flat-billed "nine-primaried" acutiplantar *Oscines*, with neither the tertials nor hind claw elongated [to exclude Motacillidae] nor the tongue deeply cleft nor laciniate at tip [to exclude Coerebidae].

Bill usually slender-conoidal, sometimes rather stout, rarely short-subulate; if slender-cuneate with acute tip, not strongly, if at all, decurved terminally, and tail not longer than distance from bend of wing to tips of secondaries [to exclude *Conirostrum*]; if depressed, with triangular vertical profile, the rictal bristles strongly developed . . . and tail rounded; if comparatively stout, decidedly compressed with culmen decidedly convex, the tip of maxilla not uncinate and without distinct subterminal tomial notch [to exclude nine-primaried Vireonidae]. Tongue moderately slender, with tip but slightly bifid or fimbriate. Skull with interpalatine process well developed; trans-palatine process short, bluntly angular; palatines not produced backward over pterygoids.

This diagnosis was clearly developed by first deciding which species were to be placed in the Mniotiltidae, then setting up characters to include them and exclude all others. This is supported by Ridgway's own words following those above (1902:426): "In addition to the forms which are usually referred to the Mniotiltidae (see Sharpe 1885 . . .) it seems best to place here the following genera, withdrawn from other groups: *Certhidea* and *Ateleodacnis* (probably also *Conirostrum*), from the Coerebidae; *Hemispingus*, from Tanagridae, and *Rhodinocichla*, from Mimidae. This transfer seems to be necessary in order to render possible anything like a satisfactory diagnosis of the Mniotiltidae, Coerebidae, and Tanagridae, as separate groups."

Certhidea is now called the Galapagos Warbler Finch, thus either an emberizine or a thraupine. *Rhodinocichla* is still an enigma; the A.O.U. (1983) placed it in the "Thraupinae" with the note: "Systematic position uncertain; may be related to the 'paruline' genus *Granatellus*."

Ridgway discussed other species of uncertain relationships and, except for the two genera noted above, all of his "mniotiltids" are still considered to be parulids or parulines.

Ridgway's classification became the accepted arrangement in North America and Sharpe (1909) adopted most of it for the *Hand-List*. In a footnote (pp. 188–189), Sharpe made complimentary references to Ridgway's first volume and to Hartert's (1903) *Die Vögel der Palaearktischen Fauna*, as sources of new ideas about the classification of the Fringillidae. As one example, Sharpe (1909:188) accepted the "Catamblyrhynchidae" based on Ridgway (1901:19).

In the *Hand-List*, Sharpe (1909) used the sequence: Mniotiltidae, Drepanididae, Motacillidae, Alaudidae, Catamblyrhynchidae, Fringillidae, Coerebidae, Procniatidae [*Tersina*], Tanagridae, Ploceidae, Icteridae, Sturnidae. This indicates his continued belief in a relationship between the wagtails and the larks, and among the weavers, troupials, and starlings.

Sharpe removed the Hawaiian honeycreepers from the Dicaeidae to their own family, "Drepanididae." With the wood warblers (Mniotiltidae) he included the Galapagos Warbler Finch (*Certhidea*), which had been assigned to the Coerebidae in the *Catalogue* (vol. 11). Otherwise the Mniotiltidae of the *Hand-List* contained the genera currently considered to be parulines. The Swallow Tanager, *Procnias* (*Tersina*), was placed in the monotypic "Procniatidae."

The Fringillidae of the *Hand-List* included 139 genera versus 99 in the *Catalogue* (vol. 12). Some of the difference is due to generic splitting, but Sharpe (apparently following Ridgway) also transferred several genera from Sclater's Tanagridae to the Fringillidae, for example, *Pitylus*, *Saltator*, *Arremon*, *Atlapetes*, *Buarremon*, and *Pezopetes*. The cardinal grosbeaks (our Cardinalini), the recently identified tanager-finches—e.g., *Sicalis*, *Volatinia*, *Diuca*, *Catamenia*, *Oryzoborus*, and *Haplospiza* (Sibley and Ahlquist 1985d:115, Bledsoe 1988b)—the ploceine *Anomalospiza*, and the three genera of the Passerinae were members of Sharpe's Fringillidae in the *Hand-List*. The "Coerebidae" remained the same as in the *Catalogue*, but *Glossoptila* became *Euneornis*.

The Icteridae of the *Hand-List* seems to be identical in coverage to Sclater's treatment in the *Catalogue* (1886), although Sclater used 29 genera and Sharpe 33.

The New World nine-primaried oscines were treated in the *Catalogue of Birds of the Americas and the Adjacent Islands* by Hellmayr (1935, 1936, 1937, 1938). Part 8 (1935) included the Coerebidae and Compsothlypidae, the latter being the New World wood warblers (our Parulini), previously called the Mniotiltidae and soon to become the Parulidae, as dictated by the rules of zoological nomenclature.

Hellmayr's interest was in species and subspecies, and he followed Ridgway for the higher categories. For example, in the Preface to Part 9 (1936:iii), Hellmayr noted relative to the tanagers: "The limits of this family, which is very closely related to the finches, are much disputed among ornithologists, and the assignment of certain genera to one group rather than to the other is largely arbitrary, owing to the absence of information as to their anatomical structure. For the sake of convenience the author has closely followed the late Robert Ridgway's definition of the family."

Hellmayr (1936:1) followed Ridgway (1907:880) for the change of the generic name of the Swallow Tanager to *Tersina* from *Procnias*, thus the family became Tersinidae. The tanager family became the Thraupidae, and included *Rhodinocichla* because (Hellmayr 1936:354, footnote) Clark (1913) considered it to be a tanager most closely related to *Mitrospingus*.

In Part 10 (1937) Hellmayr covered the Icteridae, and in Part 11 (1938) the Ploceidae, Catamblyrhynchidae, and Fringillidae. In the preface to Part 11, Hellmayr wrote: "The arrangement of the finches [Fringillidae] . . . is purely tentative, though it is mainly based on the scheme advanced by the late Peter Sushkin (*The Auk*, 42, pp. 259–261, 1925), according to the characters of the bony palate in the North American genera. The ultimate allocation of many neotropical groups depends, however, on the study of their anatomy, and in the absence of such data the author has been forced to rely on external features and analogy. In many cases it remains clearly an open question whether certain common characters are the expression of natural affinity or merely the result of secondary adaptation through secondary development."

Once again the reference to prior authority, the uncertainty, and the faith that "anatomy" would provide the "ultimate allocation" of taxa.

Hellmayr divided his Fringillidae into the Richmondeninae for the "Cardinals and Allies," which included *Saltator* and *Spiza*; Geospizinae, including *Certhidea* (*fide* Sushkin 1929b); Fringillinae, for *Fringilla*; Carduelinae, including several emberizines, plus *Catamenia*, *Oryzoborus*, *Volatinia*, and *Sicalis*, which we now know from DNA hybridization data are tanagers; Emberizinae, including *Diuca* and *Haplospiza*, which are tanagers, and others that may be tanagers.

THE RELATIONSHIPS OF THE OLIVE WARBLER (*Peucedramus taeniatus*)

The Olive Warbler was considered to be a paruline wood warbler from its discovery until 1962, when William George concluded, from a study of the hyoid apparatus and other characters, that it could be a sylviine warbler. Webster (1962) disagreed and, from skin and skull characters, argued that it must be a wood warbler. The A.O.U. checklist (1983:640) noted: "Systematic position uncertain; this genus may prove to be sylviine (Muscicapidae) rather than paruline."

The nest of the Olive Warbler is similar to that of a kinglet (*Regulus*) or gnatcatcher (*Polioptila*), and the nestlings deposit their droppings around the rim of the nest, as do cardueline finches. These characters suggested that the Olive Warbler might not be a paruline, but it has nine primaries, thus it is an unlikely candidate for membership in the Sylviidae. The

DNA comparisons reveal that *Peucedramus* is, apparently, the only living descendant of the earliest branch in the fringillid clade; i.e., it is the sister taxon of the other members of the Fringillidae! This conclusion is tentative and additional studies should be conducted. See below for the DNA evidence.

THE RELATIONSHIPS OF THE CHAFFINCHES, *Fringilla*

The relationship of *Fringilla* to other finches has produced considerable debate. The principal questions are: (1) what other group, e.g., carduelines or emberizines, is closest to *Fringilla*, and (2) how should these groups be classified?

Sushkin (1924) decided that "the family Fringillidae, as judged by the characters exhibited by the bony palate, the syrinx, and the external features of the horny palate, proves to consist of three distinct divisions which may be named the Cardueline, the Passerine, and the Emberizine." The Cardueline division "may be divided into three branches as follows: (a) includes, as far as one can judge from the genera examined, only one genus—*Fringilla*; (b), which is purely American, comprises the Cardinaline section (*Richmondena, Cyanocompsa, Oryzoborus*); while (c), mainly Palaearctic and Ethiopian, includes the rest, viz., *Carduelis, Carpodacus*, and *Coccothraustes*." Sushkin also stated that "the Cardueline division is more closely related to the Ploceo-Passerine group than to the Emberizinae; and the Drepanididae seem to present another related group." Sushkin proposed the following classification:

Superfamily Emberizoidei
  Icteridae
  Coerebidae
  Tanagridae
  Emberizidae
Superfamily Fringilloidei
  Fringillidae (Fringillinae, Cardinalinae, Carduelinae)
  Ploceidae (Passerinae, Ploceinae, Viduinae)
  Drepanididae

Sushkin (1925) again presented his classification with the Fringillidae composed as above. The evidence was not detailed, but the close relationship of *Fringilla* and the carduelines has been confirmed by many other studies. However, the carduelines are especially close to the Hawaiian honeycreepers, a suggestion that Sushkin (1929a) also made. The key feature in Sushkin's evidence was the pattern of ridges and furrows on the palatal surface of the rhamphotheca in which *Fringilla* and the carduelines are alike, and in which the emberizines differ from them. Ziswiler (1965) confirmed Sushkin's observations. Other aspects of Sushkin's arrangement have been shown to be incorrect.

The *Fringilla*-cardueline alliance has been supported by jaw muscle comparisons (Fiedler 1951, Beecher 1953b) and behavioral similarities (Mayr et al. 1956, Andrew 1956, Marler 1957, Andrew 1961).

Tordoff (1954a,b) disagreed; from his study of the bony palate and other cranial characters, he concluded that *Fringilla* is related to the emberizines, and that the carduelines are closest to the estrildines. These proposals were accepted by Mayr (1955) but rejected by Bock (1960), and Tordoff himself soon abandoned this viewpoint (pers. comm.).

Bock (1960) concluded from a study of the palatine process of the premaxilla in the Passeri that "the presence of an unfused palatine process in *Fringilla* and its apparent absence in the carduelines does not necessarily mean that the two groups are unrelated, as supposed by Tordoff" and that "in several aspects of the bony palate and jaw musculature, *Fringilla* is intermediate between the emberizine and cardueline finches, but is closer to the carduelines." Bock saw no "indications of a relationship between the carduelines plus *Fringilla* and the ploceids or estrildids, as advanced by Tordoff," but he thought that "it does seem reasonable to suggest that the emberizine finches gave rise to the carduelines through a *Fringilla*-like group" (p. 477).

Ziswiler (1964) compared the feeding behaviors, bills, skulls, jaw muscles and their innervation, and the horny palates of seed-eating birds (1965), and concluded that *Fringilla* is related to the carduelines. From a study of the anatomy and histology of the alimentary canal in seed-eating passerines, Ziswiler (1967a) concluded that the "Fringillidae, Pyrrhuloxiidae, Ploceidae, and Estrildidae" each had "an origin independent of" one another and probably had "arisen from different ancestors." He proposed placing *Fringilla* and the carduelines in separate subfamilies in the Fringillidae.

Ackermann (1967) used "numerical taxonomy" to compare a large number of skeletal measurements of *Passer*, *Fringilla*, and six carduelines. He found *Fringilla* and the carduelines most similar, but concluded that numerical taxonomic methods are of doubtful value in avian systematics.

C. J. O. Harrison (1966) interpreted similarities of plumage color and pattern as evidence of a close relationship between *Fringilla* and *Carduelis*.

Mainardi (1957a,c) used a serological method to compare the red cell proteins of *Fringilla* with those of several carduelines. He concluded that the European Goldfinch (*C. carduelis*) is intermediate between the Greenfinch (*C. chloris*) and Chaffinch, but the results were flawed because Mainardi's "serological distance" was 8 units between the Siskin (*C. spinus*) and the Goldfinch and 2.8 between Greenfinch and Goldfinch, but only 1.4 between Goldfinch and Chaffinch. Mainardi (1957b) also compared the electrophoretic behavior of the hemoglobins of three species of *Carduelis* and four other carduelines with that of *Fringilla*. He found that *Fringilla* hemoglobin produces two bands close together; in the carduelines the bands are farther apart.

Mainardi (1958b) interpreted serological comparisons of red blood cell proteins as evidence of a close estrildine-passerine relationship, and a close emberizine-*Fringilla* relationship, with the carduelines between the two clusters. However, Mainardi found that the hemoglobins of the carduelines and emberizines are alike and that they differ from those of *Fringilla*. He concluded that his data supported Tordoff (1954a) and Stallcup (1954), who thought that the carduelines and estrildines are closely related.

Mainardi (1961) extended his serological comparisons to additional groups of passerines and concluded that "the Carduelines represent the bridge between *Fringilla* and the ploceids." However, he made no comparisons with emberizines and his conclusions were predicated on the assumption that the corvines are primitive and that *Fringilla* is "more primitive than the Ploceids."

The records of bird hybrids in A. P. Gray (1958) were utilized by Mainardi (1960a) as the basis for a "degree of affinity" value among species of passerines. He concluded that

Fringilla is closest to the carduelines because it has been reported to hybridize with *Chloris*, *Pyrrhula*, and *Serinus*.

Sibley (1970:102–103) reported on two Greenfinch-Chaffinch hybrids, produced in captivity and obtained alive. The hybrids showed their parentage in their plumages, and the electrophoretic patterns of their hemoglobins were intermediate between those of the parental species. From several sources of evidence, Sibley (1970:115) concluded that "it is highly probable that the carduelines are related to the other Fringillidae and are not especially close to the Estrildinae" and that "it is probable that *Fringilla* is more closely related to the carduelines than to any other group."

THE RELATIONSHIPS OF THE HAWAIIAN HONEYCREEPERS, *Drepanidini*

We recognize 18 genera and 30 species; the A.O.U. checklist committee (1983) recognized 28 species in 16 genera, arranged in three tribes of the Drepanidinae in the Fringillidae. Several possible generic mergers were noted.

The drepanidines are characterized by a remarkable array of bill types, from the finch-like bills of *Psittirostra*, *Melamprosops*, and *Ciridops*, and the slender bills of *Loxops*, *Himatione*, and *Palmeria*, to the parrot-like beak of *Pseudonestor* and the long, decurved bills of *Hemignathus* and *Drepanis*. This variation prompted early taxonomists to distribute the species among several families, including the finches, flowerpeckers, and honeyeaters. Later, it became obvious that these birds are closely related to one another and, as in the Galapagos finches, that a single ancestral species had given rise to the entire group (Amadon 1950a, Raikow 1977b, Sibley and Ahlquist 1982a).

The identity of the ancestor has produced much speculation, but the drepanidines are nine-primaried oscines, so their origin must have been within that group. Gadow (1891a) considered only nectar-feeding taxa as possible ancestors and decided that the Neotropical honeycreepers ("coerebids") must be the closest relatives of Hawaiian honeycreepers, and that the tangers are also related to them. However, Gadow also noted that the drepanidines share characters of the horny palate with the carduelines.

Lucas (1894) suggested that the tongues of the Hawaiian honeycreepers could have been derived from that of the New World troupial genus *Icterus* or that of the paruline *Dendroica*. Sushkin (1929a) proposed the carduelines as the closest relatives because of similarities in the bills, skulls, and horny palates. Amadon (1950a) reviewed the earlier proposals and concluded that the "coerebids" or tangers had provided the ancestor. Beecher (1953b) found the jaw musculature of *Psittirostra* to be like that of the carduelines, and noted "the striking similarity of the Hawaiian finches to the cardueline finches in all but plumage" but concluded that the similarities are due to "parallel development from . . . thraupine stock" (p. 312).

Bock (1960:477) argued that the carduelines are the most probable "ancestral drepaniids" because there are no anatomical characters that preclude the relationship and because the carduelines include species more capable of colonizing the Hawaiian Islands than do any of the other groups that have been suggested. Bock (1972) also found that the tongue apparatus of *Ciridops* resembles that of the carduelines, not that of the "coerebines." Sibley (1970) also supported the carduelines as the most likely ancestors, based on electrophoretic comparisons of the egg-white proteins.

Raikow (1976, 1977a) studied the limb musculature and concluded (1977b:116) that the drepanidines "arose from a single founder species," which "was a primitive member of the Carduelines." Raikow suggested that this ancestor was a typical finch similar to the living *Psittirostra* and that the "nectar-feeding habits arose in Hawaii and are merely convergent with similar conditions in other families of birds."

Sibley and Ahlquist (1982a) compared the DNAs of the pertinent groups and supported a close relationship between the Carduelini and the Drepanidini (see the DNA evidence, below).

Johnson et al. (1989) used starch gel electrophoresis to compare 36 protein loci in nine species of Hawaiian honeycreepers, two species of carduelines, and two emberizines. They concluded that the drepanidines "are more similar genetically to the two species of emberizids than to the two species of carduelines, a result that conflicts with a recent consensus of opinion based on morphologic and other biochemical data."

THE RELATIONSHIPS WITHIN THE EMBERIZINAE

An impressive array of evidence indicates that the groups we place in the Emberizinae are closely related to one another. The DNA comparisons, discussed below, confirm the previous evidence, and reveal the phylogeny of the groups. There are several studies that have influenced the arrangement of these groups in recent classifications.

Beecher (1951, 1953b) argued that the "Coerebidae" should be divided between the warblers and tanagers, with *Ateleodacnis*, *Coereba*, and *Conirostrum* placed in the "Coerebini" of the Parulidae, and *Chlorophanes*, *Cyanerpes*, *Dacnis*, *Diglossa*, *Euneornis*, *Hemidacnis*, and *Iridophanes* placed in the "Dacnini" of the "Thraupinae." Meyer De Schauensee (1966:454) objected and Wetmore (1960) declined to "dismember the Coerebidae without further study," but most ornithologists embraced this proposal as the solution to the problem of the Coerebidae. It was adopted by Paynter and Storer (1970) for the Peters' checklist, although they recorded their reservations (p. ix).

The A.O.U. (1983) placed *Coereba* in the Coerebinae of the Emberizidae, with the note: "Formerly considered, along with several genera now treated as thraupine or emberizine, in a distinct family, the Coerebidae; presently considered a distinct monotypic subfamily close to the Parulinae." *Conirostrum* was placed in the Thraupinae of the Emberizidae, with the note: "Affinities uncertain, possibly emberizine if not thraupine."

Also in the Thraupinae: "The genera *Dacnis*, *Chlorophanes* and *Cyanerpes*, formerly placed in the family Coerebidae, are now considered to be thraupines related to the genus *Tangara*."

As we note below, the DNA evidence indicates that all of these genera are nectarivorous tanagers, but that they are not one another's closest relatives within the Thraupini.

Tersina has been separated in a monotypic family, subfamily, or tribe because of its convergently swallow-like morphology and behavior, although clearly recognized as a tanager. This is an example of the assignment to a higher category of a taxon that is morphologically specialized, but for which there is no evidence that it represents a lineage that shared a common ancestor with all members of the group from which it is separated, in this case the other tanagers. *Tersina* is a specialized tanager, but it is not the sister group of all other tanagers.

The "Wren-thrush," *Zeledonia coronata*, was long believed to be a thrush, or to be closely related to the thrushes. It was assigned to the Zeledoniidae, next to the Turdidae, by

Ridgway (1907) and its turdine affinities were seldom questioned, although it was recognized as an aberrant genus. Sibley (1968) compared the electrophoretic patterns of the egg-white proteins of *Zeledonia* and other passerines, and reviewed the morphological evidence. The egg-white protein patterns indicated that *Zeledonia* is not a thrush, but could be a nine-primaried oscine. Morphologically it is a wood warbler. Sibley (1970) placed the Zeledoniini next to the Parulini in his classification of the Emberizinae. The A.O.U (1983:638) placed *Zeledonia* in the Parulinae, noting that it is "now regarded as a paruline."

It seems apparent that *Zeledonia* is closest to the paruline genus *Basileuterus*; in fact, it may be regarded as a terrestrial species of that genus. Since we lack its DNA we continue to recognize *Zeledonia*, but not the Zeledoniini.

The Yellow-breasted Chat (*Icteria virens*) has usually been placed with the wood war-blers, but it has seemed aberrant in comparison with the typical members of the Parulini. For example, the A.O.U. (1983:639) placed *Icteria* in the Parulinae, but noted: "Allocation of the genus is in doubt; it may not be a paruline." Sibley and Ahlquist (1982d) compared the tracer DNA of *Icteria* with the DNAs of other passerines and showed that it is a paruline warbler.

The vireos (Vireonidae) were, until recently, usually thought to be related to the wood warblers. We have discussed their relationships above, under the Corvoidea: Vireonidae.

The DNA Hybridization Evidence

In general, the DNA evidence supports the close relationships among the members of this family that have been apparent from morphology, but the DNA data reveal many details, some never before suspected. The phylogeny developed from the DNA comparisons explains some of the problems that plagued avian systematists in the past.

The fringillid clade branched from the passerid-nectariniid clade at Δ $T_{50}H$ 10.0, perhaps ca. 25–30 MYA (Fig. 369). As noted above, the oldest known dichotomy in the Fringillidae led to the lineage represented by the Olive Warbler (*Peucedramus taeniatus*) on one branch, and the fringilline-emberizine clade on the other. This node, at Δ $T_{50}H$ 7.8, appears to establish the position of *Peucedramus*, but this answer is so unexpected that further studies should be made. We place it in the monotypic subfamily Peucedraminae, and suggest that a search be made for other possible members of this group.

The Fringillinae diverged from the Emberizinae at Δ 6.9, and the fringilline-cardueline branch occurred at Δ 5.9. The Drepanidini-Carduelini divergence was at Δ 4.3 (Fig. 384).

The Emberizini branched at Δ 6.0 from the other tribes of the emberizine clade, and the Parulini diverged next at Δ 5.8. The Cardinalini-Icterini clade diverged at Δ 5.5 from the Thraupini, and from one another at Δ 5.3 (Figs. 384, 385).

Fig. 308 (*Fringilla*) shows that the carduelines (*Leucosticte* to *Pinicola*) are the closest relatives of the chaffinches. The emberizines are next, with the passerids (*Passer*, *Motacilla*) and nectariniids at about the same distance, and the larks just beyond. The starling curve forms the out-group for this set. The curves agree well with the UPGMA tree in Fig. 369.

Fig. 309 (*Carduelis*) shows the cluster of the carduelines (*Carduelis* to *Pinicola*), then a tight cluster at the 50% single-stranded level includes *Icterus*, *Ploceus*, and *Fringilla*, with *Emberiza* just beyond, and the nectariniid *Hypogramma* next. *Zosterops* shows the relative position of the Sylvioidea and *Vireo* represents the Corvida.

Fig. 310 (*Viridonia*). The *Viridonia* homoduplex is so close to the *Vestiaria* hetero-duplex that generic separation of these two species is questionable. The carduelines (*Car-duelis*, *Loxia*) form a tight cluster, closest to *Viridonia*, and testify to the cardueline-drepanidine alliance. The out-group cluster includes a nectar-feeding tanager (*Cyanerpes*), a troupial (*Icterus*), two more tanagers, a wood warbler, and an emberizine. This set of curves should settle the question of the closest relatives of the Hawaiian honeycreepers.

Fig. 311 (*Viridonia*) includes representatives of some of the groups in Fig. 310, and adds more distant taxa: *Turdus* of the Muscicapoidea, and two members of the Corvida, a crow and a honeyeater.

Fig. 312 (*Peucedramus*) shows the large distances between the Olive Warbler and the taxa that have been suggested as its closest relatives. The closest cluster includes a sunbird, a cardueline, an icterine, two parulines, and an emberizine. Three sylviines form the next cluster (*Sylvia* to *Thryothorus*), with *Vireo* as the out-group, representing the Corvida. It seems clear that *Peucedramus* is closer to the Fringillidae than to the Sylviidae, but it appears to be equidistant from all fringillids, hence we have assigned it to a monotypic subfamily as the sister group of the other fringillids.

Fig. 313 (*Spizella*) shows the relationships between the emberizine tracer and other Passerida. The other member of the Emberizini (*Melospiza*) is closest, the other Emberizinae (*Tersina*, *Agelaius*, *Dendroica*) are next, then the two carduelines, the ploceine (*Plocepasser*), sunbird, and the sylvioid (*Polioptila*).

Fig. 314 (*Pooecetes*) shows some of the relationships among the emberizines. *Pooecetes*, *Atlapetes*, and *Junco* are Emberizini; *Cacicus* is an icterine; *Diuca* to *Piranga* are tanagers (Thraupini); and the cardinaline is the farthest out.

Fig. 315 (*Pooecetes*) includes a nectarivorous tanager, *Diglossa*; *Ploceus* and *Nec-tarinia* indicate the relative positions of the weavers and sunbirds; and the Certhiidae are represented by a wren.

Fig. 316 (*Calcarius*) demonstrates the cohesion of the Emberizinae: *Psarocolius* (Ict-erini), *Tachyphonus* and *Catamblyrhynchus* (Thraupini), *Pooecetes* (Emberizini), and *Den-droica* (Parulini). *Pooecetes* is expected to be closest to *Calcarius*, but note the spread among the curves at the lower temperatures (60–75°C), and the tight cluster at 80°C, at the 50% single-stranded level. The spread at the lower temperatures reflects variation in the percentage of short fragments in the driver DNAs. The two *Calcarius* curves were produced from two samples from the same preparation, yet they differ slightly.

Fig. 317 (*Dendroica*) also shows small differences between samples of the same prepa-ration. Note that the three curves of *Dendroica striata* differ slightly at the lower temperatures, but are superimposed at 85°C.

Fig. 318 (*Icterus*) compares the icterine tracer with two other icterines (*Cacicus*, *Leistes*), a thraupine, emberizine, paruline, cardinaline, nectariniid, parid, lark, starling, and a vireo. The parid is closer to the fringillid tracer than is the lark, but the Alaudidae average Δ $T_{50}H$ 10.4 from the Fringillidae and the Paridae average Δ 11.1 from the Fringillidae (Figs. 382, 383). The difference between the two curves is within the usual range of experimental error and by making many comparisons and averaging the delta values it is possible to compensate for this kind of variation.

Fig. 319 (*Cardinalis*). The four emberizines (*Tachyphonus* to *Myioborus*) cluster tightly relative to the cardinal; the three passerids (*Motacilla* to *Taeniopygia*) and the sunbird are next; then the lark, *Melanocharis*, and the sylvioid white-eye. Again, the berrypecker would be expected to cluster with the sunbird, but Fig. 383 shows that these branches are close together.

Fig. 320 (*Nephelornis*). The tracer is a tanager and the other two tanagers are closest to it. *Viridonia* is a Hawaiian honeycreeper, a member of the Fringillinae. The curves agree quite well with the branching pattern in Fig. 369.

Fig. 321 (*Nephelornis*) shows that the finch-billed tanagers (*Diuca, Catamblyrhynchus, Sicalis, Volatinia*) cluster with the flower-piercer and the typical tanager (*Tachyphonus*). The cardinal, paruline, icterine, and emberizine cluster, and the cardueline (*Loxia*) is the out-group.

Fig. 322 (*Tachyphonus*) shows the relative positions of some of the emberizine tribes to the tanager tracer. After the Swallow Tanager, the icterine (*Psarocolius*) is closest and the paruline and emberizine are equidistant from *Tachyphonus*. The tight clustering of the Black-poll Warbler and Vesper Sparrow indicates that the Parulini and Emberizini are on the same branch relative to the tanager, and on a different branch from that of the Icterini. It is unlikely that different average rates of genomic evolution are involved in the differences among these groups; all may be assumed to be evolving at the same rate.

Fig. 323 (*Sicalis*) shows that the finch-billed tanagers (*Sicalis, Volatinia, Emberizoides, Diuca, Oryzoborus, Poospiza*) cluster with the typical tanagers (*Tachyphonus, Piranga*), with the emberizine, cardinaline, and fringilline next in sequence.

Fig. 324 (*Catamblyrhynchus*). The Plushcap has often been placed in a monotypic family, but the DNA hybridization comparisons showed that it is a tanager. The heteroduplex curves from *Chlorornis* to *Dubusia* are those of tanagers, again showing the clustering of typical tanagers with a conebill, the Swallow Tanager, and a finch-billed tanager (*Sicalis*). The paruline, icterine, and passerid are in their expected positions.

The UPGMA trees and the FITCH tree (Fig. 352) agree in detail and support the evidence in the melting curves. We conclude that the DNA data indicate, or suggest, that:

1. The Olive Warbler is the descendant of the earliest branch in the Fringillidae.
2. The carduelines and drepanidines are closely related.
3. The Fringillini is the sister group of the Carduelini plus the Drepanidini.
4. The Cardinalini and Icterini are sister groups.
5. The Cardinalini-Icterini clade is the sister group of the Thraupini.
6. The tanager tribe Thraupini includes the "coerebid" honeycreepers, the Swallow Tanager, the Plush-capped Finch or Plushcap, and most (or all) of the tanager-finches, which have been assumed to be members of the Emberizini because of their bill shapes. It may be that, with few exceptions, the finch-billed Emberizinae of South America are members of the Thraupini, not of the Emberizini.

Historical Geography: Patterns of Distribution in Space and Time

The present distributions of birds and other organisms are the results of past events of at least two kinds: vicariance and dispersal. Vicariance refers to presently disjunct distributions of related organisms caused by the appearance of a barrier that split the range of the common ancestral species. Dispersal involves the extension of the range of a species over a pre-existing barrier.

The vicariance model predicts that if we could find a single group of organisms that (1) had a primitive cosmopolitan distribution (i.e., whose ancestors were worldwide in distribution), (2) had responded (by speciating) to every geological or ecological vicariance event that occurred (i.e., to every barrier that appeared) after the origin of its ancestors, (3) had undergone no extinction, and (4) had undergone no dispersal, we could, by reconstructing the interrelationships of its members, arrive at a detailed description of the history in space of the ancestral biota of which the ancestors of the group were a part. Since we would also have arrived at a detailed description of the world from the time of the first speciation event within the group to the present, we could, by correlating the sequence of branching points thus reconstructed with the sequence of events indicated by studies in historical geology, arrive at a chronology of the biogeographic events.

    That extant distribution patterns are diverse, and do not all obviously correspond to each other in every detail, is evidence that at least criteria (2)–(4) do not always prevail in nature. Since under the vicariance model sympatry (the occurrence of taxa in the same area) is evidence of dispersal, the fact that we find numerous sympatric taxa at any given locality is evidence that dispersal has occurred. The fossil record provides abundant evidence that extinction has occurred. Finally, the fact that within any biota some taxa are very widespread, and others very localized, is evidence that not all members of a biota need respond (by speciating) to every vicariance event.

    Clearly, then, neither dispersal nor vicariance explanations can be discounted a priori as irrelevant for any particular group of organisms, and it might seem that the ideal method of biogeographic analysis would be one that allows us to choose objectively between these two types of explanations for particular groups (Nelson and Platnick 1981:46–47).

    Thus, evidence of phylogenetic relationships and patterns of distribution in space and time are the basis for hypotheses about vicariance and dispersal events of the past. For this study the evidence consists of the dendrograms and melting curves produced by DNA-DNA

699

comparisons and the approximate datings of divergence events based on the calibration of the avian DNA clock (or clocks). We will attempt to explain only those branching events or patterns that seem to have an obvious relationship to some dated geological event or with fossils whose identity and age are not in doubt.

Some Major Geological Events of the Past 150 Million Years

The avian lineage diverged from a reptilian ancestor in the Jurassic, probably about 160–175 MYA. Fossils of *Archeopteryx*, the oldest certain bird, are dated as late Jurassic (Brodkorb 1971, L. D. Martin 1985), thus ca. 145–150 MYA, according to the geological time scale of Harland et al. (1982). "In the late Jurassic all the southern continents (South America, Africa, India, Australia and Antarctica) were joined to form the supercontinent Gondwanaland. By the end of the Cretaceous these continents had rifted apart and India had already drifted about 1200 km northwards, being then separated from southward-drifting Antarctica by about 4000 km of new ocean crust, Africa had separated from Antarctica by about 2800 km, South America was still in contact with Antarctica and Australia may have separated by about 200 km from Antarctica (Smith et al, 1981; Cande & Mutter 1982). The evidence revealing the pathways and timing of this dispersal ('flight from the pole') of the southern continents is preserved in the palaeomagnetic 'stripe' anomalies in the crust of the ocean floor that formed between the separating continents" (Audley-Charles 1987).

The History of the Atlantic Ocean

It is generally agreed that Africa and South America were a continuous land area until the early Cretaceous, ca. 120–130 MYA. When Gondwana began to break up, a rift first opened in the south and spread northward until a complete separation between the two continents developed. The details of the process, and the dating of the final separation that would have formed a barrier to terrestrial vertebrates, are uncertain and controversial.

Van Andel et al. (1977) used the evidence from sediment and biostratigraphic data from approximately 400 deep-sea drilling cores to reconstruct the depositional history of the South Atlantic during the last 125 MY. They concluded that "During its early history the South Atlantic consisted of a narrow rift divided by the Rio Grande Rise–Walvis Ridge barrier into a restricted northern and an open (to the southern oceans) southern basin. Free circulation of surface water between the southern ocean and the North Atlantic became possible late in the Mesozoic or in the early Cenozoic, and deep circulation (below 3 km depth) paths were open from north to south by the early Cenozoic. . . . In the late Cretaceous the South Atlantic became part of the world ocean system and global events have overshadowed local ones since that time" (p. 651).

Thus, until at least the Late Cretaceous, ca. 75–80 MYA, there may have been a land or shallow-water connection between the North and South Atlantic across the Walvis–Rio Grande ridge system. A deep-water connection was established in the Late Cretaceous, ca. 70 MYA, or later.

Emery and Uchupi (1984) reviewed the massive literature on the geology of the Atlantic and concluded that sea-floor spreading in the South Atlantic began 119–129 MYA near the southern end of the Cape Basin when the Falkland Plateau began to separate from southern Africa. By 90 MYA (Turonian, Middle Cretaceous) there was a wedge-shaped basin between southern Africa and southern South America, and a deep-water passageway between the South and North Atlantic oceans. There were also east-west trending barriers across the South Atlantic. The Falkland-Agulhas Plateau formed a barrier in the south, and the Walvis Ridge–Rio Grande Plateau–Torres Ridge divided the middle South Atlantic between what is now Angola and southern Brazil. The Walvis Ridge, now submerged, is about 2000 km long. By the late Cretaceous (Campanian, 83–73 MYA) the separation was wide between Africa and South America (Emery and Uchupi 1984:273–275, 559–581, 804–834).

Dingle et al. (1983:2) date the beginning of continental drift as ca. 127 MYA, and the final separation of the Falkland Plateau from the southern tip of Africa as 100 MYA.

Rand and Mabesoone (1982) presented "new evidence . . . to support the old but practically discarded idea that the separation of . . . South America and Africa, was delayed in the middle portion" until the Late Cretaceous. They examined the evidence from geology and fossils and postulated a "land bridge connecting the Brazilian Bulge and Nigeria." This proposal is controversial but Rand and Mabesoone (1982:181) concluded that the information available from geophysics, sedimentology, paleontology, and oceanography indicates the following:

(1) All authors agree that during the opening of the South Atlantic one or more barriers impeded the free circulation of deep ocean water as well as permitting the exchange of benthic organisms and plants between . . . South America and Africa.

(2) No general agreement was reached about where the barriers existed and when they disappeared.

(3) Considering the . . . position of northeastern Brazil . . . the authors believe that at least a partially submerged land bridge must have existed between northeastern Brazil and western Africa until the end of the Cretaceous. The island chain on the Rio Grande Rise–Walvis Ridge in the south might have existed, too, but the evidence is much more in favour of the land bridge in the northeast of Brazil.

A summary of these sources suggests that the opening of the Atlantic began in the south ca. 120 MYA, and a land connection between Africa and South America that would have permitted at least some terrestrial vertebrates to cross between the continents probably persisted until 80 MYA, and possibly until 70 MYA.

We have assumed that the divergence between the lineages that produced the living Ostrich and rheas was caused by the opening of the Atlantic and we assigned a date of ca. 80 MYA to that event (Sibley and Ahlquist 1981a). Since the $\Delta T_{50}H$ between the Ostrich and the Greater Rhea is 17.1 (17.4 in Sibley and Ahlquist 1985c) the calibration factor is $\Delta 1.0 = 4.7$ MY (80/17.1). This may be close to the correct factor for birds that begin to breed at 2–4 years of age, at least we have no evidence to the contrary.

Another possible vicariant event caused by the opening of the Atlantic is the split between the Neotropical cuckoos (Crotophagidae, Neomorphidae, Opisthocomidae) and the Old World cuckoos (Centropodidae, Cuculidae) at $\Delta 17.6$. The members of the New World family Coccyzidae are more closely related to the Old World families ($\Delta 14.5$) than to the Neotropical families, thus they may have reached the New World via a northern route. That cuckoos were in South America at least 60 MYA is indicated by a Paleocene fossil from Brazil reported by R. F. Baird and P. V. Rich (pers. comm.).

The History of Antarctica, Australia, New Guinea, New Zealand, India, and Southeast Asia

In the early Cretaceous Africa and South America were in broad contact but sea-floor spreading was beginning to separate them in the South Atlantic, as described above. The southern tip of South America was virtually in contact with western Antarctica via the islands of the Scotia Arc, but there was a wide seaway between Africa and Antarctica. Australia was in contact with eastern Antarctica, and what would become western New Zealand was part of Antarctica. Most of northern and central Australia was covered by water. India was a large island between Africa and Australia, separated from Africa, Antarctica, and Australia by open water. Madagascar lay between southeastern Africa and southern India. New Guinea was not yet emergent.

At 120 MYA the Tethys Ocean between Australia and Asia was wide and contained a series of Gondwana fragments that had rifted from the northern Australian continental margin in the early Jurassic. These islands drifted rapidly northward, collided with southeastern Asia in the late Jurassic and early Cretaceous, and became southern Tibet, Burma, the Thai-Malay peninsula, Borneo, Sumatra, western Sulawesi (Celebes), western Java, and several other islands. The blocks that became southern Tibet, Burma, and the Thai-Malay peninsula were above sea level during the Jurassic and early Cretaceous, and Sumatra was probably emergent from the late Cretaceous to the Eocene. By 60 MYA southern Tibet was in contact with Asia. Timor and New Guinea remained on the Australian continental margin (Audley-Charles 1983, 1987).

Sea-floor spreading anomalies indicate that Australia began to rift from Antarctica between 110 and 90 MYA. Until ca. 43 MYA the rate of separation was slow (ca. 9 mm/yr or 5 km/MY), but by 60–55 MYA Australia was mostly above sea level and moving northward away from Antarctica (Cande and Mutter 1982). By 40–30 MYA the Gondwana fragment islands in the Tethys Ocean formed a stepping-stone connection between Australia–New Guinea and southeastern Asia, and Australia was widely separated from Antarctica. Ca. 15 MYA Australia–New Guinea collided with the southeast Asian volcanic arcs, producing new volcanic and collision islands which form part of the present archipelagos of Australasia (Audley-Charles 1983, 1987).

The evidence from fossil pollen and plants in Australia, and present plant distribution in Malaysia, indicates that there was a land area between Asia and Australia from which Gondwana plants were able to disperse in both directions during the early Tertiary, ca. 65–50 MYA. There is also geological evidence that emergent land areas were present during the Cretaceous and early Tertiary on the continental fragments rifted from Australia–New Guinea in the Jurassic (Audley-Charles 1987).

About 80 MYA the New Zealand continental fragment, including the Campbell Plateau, split from Antarctica, and the Tasman Sea south of the Lord Howe Rise began to open, separating New Zealand from Australia. This movement continued until ca. 65–60 MYA. Today the narrowest portion of the Tasman Sea, between Tasmania and the southern end of New Zealand, is about 1500 km wide.

The central and southern portions of the Tasman Sea are deep, but the Lord Howe Rise extends as a submarine ridge northwest from New Zealand toward northeastern Australia (Hayes and Ringis 1973). New Zealand is composed of a western portion derived from

Antarctica, and an eastern portion of uncertain origin, possibly a "terrane" that was originally part of a "Pacific continental/archipelago which later fragmented" (Craw 1985:6).

India and Madagascar probably separated from Antarctica, Australia, and Africa in the late Jurassic or early Cretaceous, ca. 140 MYA. India then began a northward drift, which at times was more rapid than any other continental movement yet known, 35–175 mm per year. India and Madagascar were in contact until the late Cretaceous (90–80 MYA), and the Seychelles separated from India in the early Paleocene, ca. 65–60 MYA. India collided with Asia in the Eocene, ca. 50 MYA (Norton and Sclater 1979, Whitmore 1981, Audley-Charles 1987).

The Drake Passage between southern South America and Antarctica began to open in the late Eocene to early Oligocene, ca. 40–38 MYA, thus forming a water barrier between the two continents. To account for the fossil record of marsupials and condylarths, Colbert (1981) advocates a connection between South America and Antarctica from the late Cretaceous to the early Paleocene, ca. 80–65 MYA.

The geological record provides the basis for several speculations about the history of birds. The most interesting example concerns the origin and evolution of the old endemic passerines of Australia and New Guinea. The DNA data indicate that the members of the parvorder Corvida probably radiated in Australo-Papuasia during the Tertiary. The geological evidence suggests that the ancestor of the Corvida may have reached Australia as early as 50–65 MYA, when Gondwana plants dispersed in both directions via a land area between Asia and Australia, or ca. 30–40 MYA when the Gondwana fragment islands in the Tethys Ocean provided a stepping-stone bridge from southeast Asia. The divergence between the Corvida and Passerida at $\Delta T_{50}H$ 12.8 will fit the 30–40 MYA dating if we assume that passerines that begin to breed at one year of age are evolving about twice as fast as the ratites. If $\Delta 1.0 = 2.3$ or 2.4 MY, $\Delta 12.8 = 30$–32 MY. In some publications (e.g., Sibley and Ahlquist 1985a) we assumed that the divergence between the Corvida and Passerida occurred ca. 55–60 MYA, based on the ratite calibration, but this seems less likely than the more recent date. All of these datings are tentative and subject to correction.

There are at least two groups of special interest relative to New Zealand: the moas and kiwis, and the New Zealand wrens (Acanthisittidae). The kiwis diverged from the Emu-cassowary clade at $\Delta T_{50}H$ 9.5. Assuming that they evolved at the Ostrich-rhea rate of $\Delta 1.0 = 4.7$ MY, the divergence occurred ca. 45 MYA. At this time there were emergent islands in the Tethys Ocean (noted above) and, possibly, an island arc between northern Australia, New Caledonia, and New Zealand (Holloway 1979). The ancestor of the moas and kiwis could have taken several million years to make the crossing and may have been able to walk most of the way as volcanic and collision islands arose and were eroded away.

The New Zealand wrens diverged from the other suboscines at $\Delta 17.9$. Sibley et al. (1982) used the ratite rate of DNA evolution to calculate a divergence time of ca. 80 MYA, which equates with the opening of the Tasman Sea between Australia and New Zealand. If, instead, we use the tentative passerine rate of $\Delta 1.0 = 2.3$ MY, the divergence occurred ca. 40–42 MYA. Thus, the ancestor of the acanthisittids may have crossed the northern Tasman Sea via the same island chain used by the moa-kiwi ancestor. If the ancestor was as sedentary as the living species it is unlikely that it flew across the Tasman Sea as did the Silvereye (*Zosterops lateralis*) in the 1850's and 1860's (Falla et al. 1979:206).

There seem to be no obvious ornithogeographic relationships that must be explained by the movement of India. Relationships between African and southern Asian birds may be explained by the land contact across the Middle East. Sahni (1984) presented evidence for a dispersal corridor between India, Africa, and Madagascar ca. 80–65 MYA as India drifted close to eastern Africa.

Madagascar contains several endemic bird groups and it has been assumed that they represent ancient divergences. However, the only group for which we have DNA hybridization data, the vangas (*Cyanolanius*), have proved to be closely related to the bushshrikes of Africa (*Prionops*) and India (*Tephrodornis*), at Δ 5.4. This divergence may have occurred as recently as 12 MYA.

It is difficult to explain the geographic history of the Vireonidae. The DNA evidence shows that they diverged from a common ancestor shared with a cluster of endemic Australo-Papuan taxa at Δ 8.8, and from the Laniidae at Δ 9.1. There may be no difference between these values, although both are the averages of more than 100 comparisons. These divergences probably occurred ca. 20–25 MYA.

It seems likely that the Vireonidae radiated in South America because all four living genera occur there today, but only *Vireo* occurs north of Mexico. This suggests that the ancestor entered South America via Antarctica, but the Drake Passage was a wide water barrier by 25 MYA. Unless the time calibration is grossly in error we must assume that the ancestral vireonid reached South America from Australia by crossing the Drake Passage.

There are several other sister-group pairs of taxa between Australia and South America. These include the megapodes and cracids (Δ 19.8), Magpie Goose (*Anseranas*) and screamers (Anhimidae) (Δ 12.4), Plains-wanderer (*Pedionomus*) and seed-snipe (Thinocoridae) (Δ 10.8), and possibly the Old World suboscines (Eurylaimides) and New World suboscines (Tyrannides) (Δ 15.8).

The Bering Land Bridge

A land connection between Asia and North America apparently existed in the Bering Strait area from the Mesozoic until a few thousand years ago, but "the *utilization* of this bridge by terrestrial organisms has been controlled primarily by climate, such as warm interglacials or warm periods that extended poleward like that of the medial Miocene" (McKenna 1983:468).

The Bering Strait has not been a barrier to waterbirds or long-distance migrants, but the ancestors of at least two small, sedentary passerines probably dispersed from Asia to North America via the Bering Bridge. The Bushtit (*Psaltriparus minumus*) is the sister taxon of the long-tailed tits (*Aegithalos*) of Eurasia (Δ 5.0), and the Wrentit (*Chamaea fasciata*) is the sister taxon of the sylviine warblers and timaliine babblers (Δ 7.2, 7.5). These divergences could have occurred in the Miocene, ca. 11–16 MYA, assuming that Δ 1.0 = 2.3 MY.

The Interamerican Interchange

South America was an island continent from the time it broke its connection with Africa in the Cretaceous (ca. 80 MYA) and from Antarctica in the late Eocene or early Oligocene (ca. 35–40 MYA), until the Pliocene, ca. 3–5 MYA when the Panamanian gap was closed. Vuilleumier (1985) reviewed the literature and analyzed the evidence "from distribution patterns of families and genera of both Recent and fossil" land and freshwater non-passerines in relation to connections between North and South America. He did not examine the origins of groups.

The DNA comparisons provide new evidence that bears on the origins of New World taxa and the relationships between North and South America.

SOUTH AMERICA-AFRICA.

The Ostrich-rhea connection and the cuckoos have been discussed above. Other groups that might have an African–South American connection include the barbets, the trogons, and possibly the sungrebes. The New World barbets diverged from the African barbets at Δ 11.5. There is no evidence that this was a result of the opening of the Atlantic; the connection may have been via North America. The New World trogons diverged from the African trogons at Δ 7.4, and from the Asian trogons at Δ 6.6. These branches probably occurred in the Cenozoic, long after the opening of the Atlantic. Thus, again, it is unlikely that a trans-Atlantic crossing between Africa and South America can be invoked to explain these relationships.

The neotropical Sungrebe (*Heliornis*) has been thought to be related to the African Finfoot (*Podica*) and the Asian Finfoot (*Heliopais*). The DNA data show that *Heliornis* is closely related to the Limpkin (*Aramus*) (Δ 4.5). We lack DNAs of *Podica* and *Heliopais*, but there are several morphological differences between *Heliornis* and the two Old World genera (Brooke 1984) and *Heliornis* may be more closely related to *Aramus* than to *Podica* and *Heliopais*. This question is moot until we can compare the DNAs of all three genera.

The New World quail (Odontophoridae) probably originated in South America and they have usually been placed with the Phasianidae. The DNA evidence shows that the odontophorids branched from the Phasianidae and Numididae at Δ 15.1. This large genetic gap indicates an ancient branch but the geography of the divergence is not clear.

SOUTH AMERICA–AUSTRALIA.

The cracid-megapode, screamer-*Anseranas*, and seed-snipe–*Pedionomus* sister-group pairs have been discussed above. There may be other taxon pairs between South America and Australia, but they are not immediately obvious.

SOUTH AMERICA–NORTH AMERICA.

The New World suboscines (Tyrannides) radiated in South America and have dispersed to Central America and southern North America during the late Cenozoic. The Cotinginae have reached the southwestern United States and a few species of the Tyranninae occur as far north as Alaska in summer.

The Vireonidae radiated in South America and the genus *Vireo* is widespread in North America. The corvines (Corvini) originated in Australia, dispersed to Eurasia and across the Bering Strait to colonize North America. Since the Pliocene two genera of jays (*Cyanolyca*, *Cyanocorax*) have dispersed to South America. The dippers (*Cinclus*) dispersed from Eurasia to North America and then to South America.

The nine-primaried oscines (Emberizinae) are composed of two clusters. The Emberizini and Parulini apparently radiated in North America; the Thraupini, Cardinalini, and Icterini in South America. The DNA evidence shows that the finch-billed nine-primaried taxa of South America are members of the Thraupini, not of the Emberizini. The branches among these groups are close together and recent, but the finch-billed nine-primaried oscines of South America cluster with the typical tanagers, not with the buntings, longspurs, and North American sparrows.

Fig. 18. Ostrich x Brown Kiwi, Emu, Greater Rhea, Turkey Vulture, Glossy Ibis, Jackass Penguin, Chilean Tinamou, Karoo Bustard, Wood Duck, American Coot, Domestic Fowl

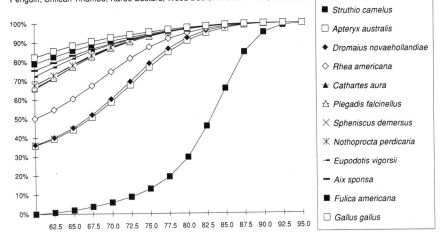

Fig. 19. Greater Rhea x Southern Cassowary, Brown Kiwi, Emu, Ostrich, Chilean Tinamou, Mallard, Domestic Fowl

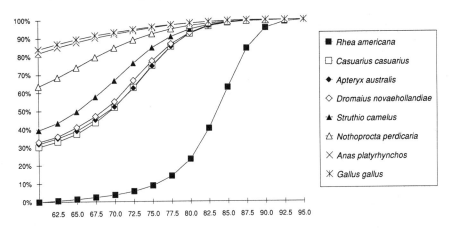

Fig. 20. Emu x Southern Cassowary, Brown Kiwi, Greater Rhea, Ostrich, Chilean Tinamou, Domestic Fowl

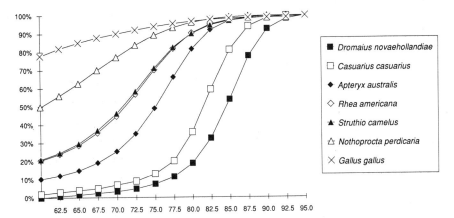

Fig. 21. Emu x Southern Cassowary, Brown Kiwi, Turkey Vulture, Jackass Penguin, Yellow-billed Stork, Karroo Bustard, Horned Screamer, Canada Goose, American Coot, Domestic Fowl, White-tailed Ptarmigan

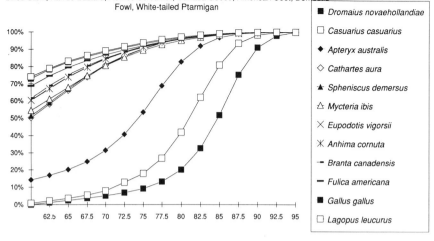

- ■ *Dromaius novaehollandiae*
- □ *Casuarius casuarius*
- ◆ *Apteryx australis*
- ◇ *Cathartes aura*
- ▲ *Spheniscus demersus*
- △ *Mycteria ibis*
- ✕ *Eupodotis vigorsii*
- ✳ *Anhima cornuta*
- ➖ *Branta canadensis*
- ▬ *Fulica americana*
- ■ *Gallus gallus*
- □ *Lagopus leucurus*

Fig. 22. Southern Cassowary x Emu, Brown Kiwi, Ostrich, Greater Rhea, Brushland Tinamou, Elegant Crested-Tinamou, Horned Screamer, Canada Goose, Turkey, Silver Pheasant

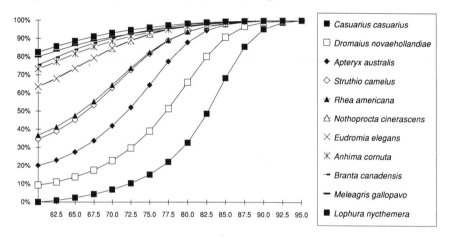

- ■ *Casuarius casuarius*
- □ *Dromaius novaehollandiae*
- ◆ *Apteryx australis*
- ◇ *Struthio camelus*
- ▲ *Rhea americana*
- △ *Nothoprocta cinerascens*
- ✕ *Eudromia elegans*
- ✳ *Anhima cornuta*
- ➖ *Branta canadensis*
- ▬ *Meleagris gallopavo*
- ■ *Lophura nycthemera*

Fig. 23. Brown Kiwi x Southern Cassowary, Emu, Ostrich, Greater Rhea, Brushland Tinamou, Elegant Crested-Tinamou, Magpie Goose, Canada Goose, Wood Duck, Silver Pheasant, Domestic Fowl

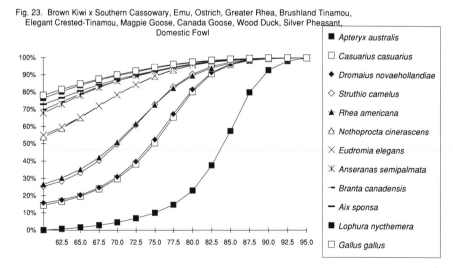

- ■ *Apteryx australis*
- □ *Casuarius casuarius*
- ◆ *Dromaius novaehollandiae*
- ◇ *Struthio camelus*
- ▲ *Rhea americana*
- △ *Nothoprocta cinerascens*
- ✕ *Eudromia elegans*
- ✳ *Anseranas semipalmata*
- ➖ *Branta canadensis*
- ▬ *Aix sponsa*
- ■ *Lophura nycthemera*
- □ *Gallus gallus*

Fig. 24. Chilean Tinamou x Little Tinamou, Elegant Crested-Tinamou, Emu, Brown Kiwi, Ostrich, Greater Rhea, Turkey Vulture, Jackass Penguin, American Coot, Canada Goose, Silver Pheasant

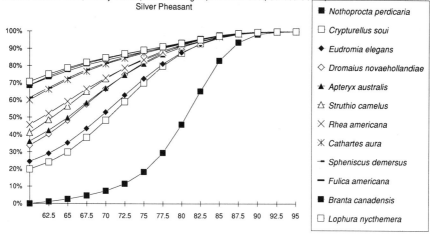

- ■ *Nothoprocta perdicaria*
- □ *Crypturellus soui*
- ◆ *Eudromia elegans*
- ◇ *Dromaius novaehollandiae*
- ▲ *Apteryx australis*
- △ *Struthio camelus*
- ✕ *Rhea americana*
- ✳ *Cathartes aura*
- ⇀ *Spheniscus demersus*
- ─ *Fulica americana*
- ■ *Branta canadensis*
- □ *Lophura nycthemera*

Fig. 25. Domestic Fowl x Natal Francolin, Indian Peafowl, Silver Pheasant, Turkey, White-tailed Ptarmigan, Helmeted Guineafowl, Crested Bobwhite, Speckled Chachalaca, Black Curassow, Australian Brush-turkey, Northern Pintail, Mute Swan

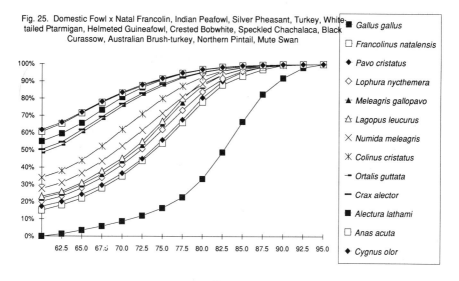

- ■ *Gallus gallus*
- □ *Francolinus natalensis*
- ◆ *Pavo cristatus*
- ◇ *Lophura nycthemera*
- ▲ *Meleagris gallopavo*
- △ *Lagopus leucurus*
- ✕ *Numida meleagris*
- ✳ *Colinus cristatus*
- ⇀ *Ortalis guttata*
- ─ *Crax alector*
- ■ *Alectura lathami*
- □ *Anas acuta*
- ◆ *Cygnus olor*

Fig. 26. Domestic Fowl x Indian Peafowl, Turkey, Helmeted Guineafowl, Crested Bobwhite, Black Curassow, Australian Brush-turkey, Mute Swan, Marabou Stork, Hartlaub's Turaco, Common Moorhen, Ostrich

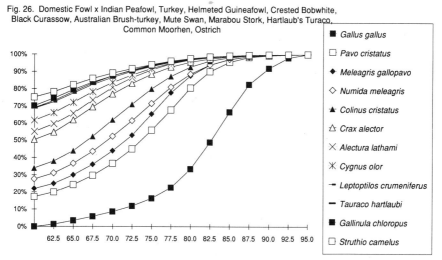

- ■ *Gallus gallus*
- □ *Pavo cristatus*
- ◆ *Meleagris gallopavo*
- ◇ *Numida meleagris*
- ▲ *Colinus cristatus*
- △ *Crax alector*
- ✕ *Alectura lathami*
- ✳ *Cygnus olor*
- ⇀ *Leptoptilos crumeniferus*
- ─ *Tauraco hartlaubi*
- ■ *Gallinula chloropus*
- □ *Struthio camelus*

Fig. 27. Natal Francolin x Cape Francolin, Rock Partridge, Indian Peafowl, Brown Quail, Domestic Fowl, Blue Grouse, Crested Guineafowl, Mountain Quail, Crested Bobwhite, Black Curassow, Wattled Brush-turkey

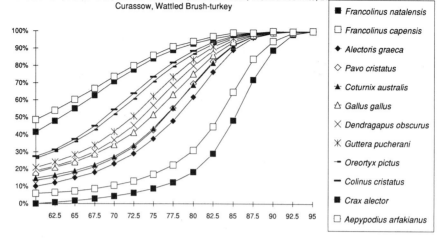

- ■ *Francolinus natalensis*
- □ *Francolinus capensis*
- ◆ *Alectoris graeca*
- ◇ *Pavo cristatus*
- ▲ *Coturnix australis*
- △ *Gallus gallus*
- ✕ *Dendragapus obscurus*
- ✳ *Guttera pucherani*
- ⚊ *Oreortyx pictus*
- ▬ *Colinus cristatus*
- ■ *Crax alector*
- □ *Aepypodius arfakianus*

Fig. 28. Natal Francolin x Plain Chachalaca, Australian Brush-turkey, Magpie Goose, Horned Screamer, Cape Teal, Royal Albatross, Brent Goose, Black Bustard, Ostrich, Chilean Tinamou

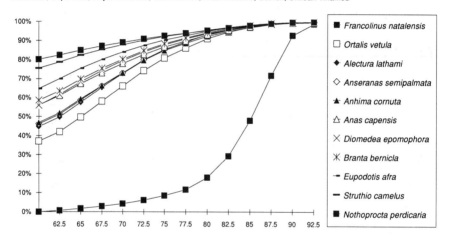

- ■ *Francolinus natalensis*
- □ *Ortalis vetula*
- ◆ *Alectura lathami*
- ◇ *Anseranas semipalmata*
- ▲ *Anhima cornuta*
- △ *Anas capensis*
- ✕ *Diomedea epomophora*
- ✳ *Branta bernicla*
- ⚊ *Eupodotis afra*
- ▬ *Struthio camelus*
- ■ *Nothoprocta perdicaria*

Fig. 29. Helmeted Guineafowl x Crested Guineafowl, Indian Peafowl, Natal Francolin, Turkey, Red-breasted Partridge, Blue Grouse, Mountain Quail, Crested Bobwhite, Black Curassow, Andean Guan, Wattled Brush-turkey

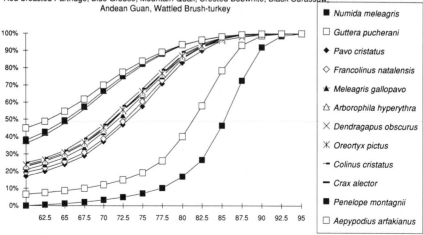

- ■ *Numida meleagris*
- □ *Guttera pucherani*
- ◆ *Pavo cristatus*
- ◇ *Francolinus natalensis*
- ▲ *Meleagris gallopavo*
- △ *Arborophila hyperythra*
- ✕ *Dendragapus obscurus*
- ✳ *Oreortyx pictus*
- ⚊ *Colinus cristatus*
- ▬ *Crax alector*
- ■ *Penelope montagnii*
- □ *Aepypodius arfakianus*

Fig. 30. Helmeted Guineafowl x Sickle-winged Guan, Wattled Brush-turkey, Horned Screamer, Mute Swan, Blue Crane, Kori Bustard, Red-knobbed Coot, Ostrich, Brown Kiwi, Common Buttonquail, Red-chested Buttonquail

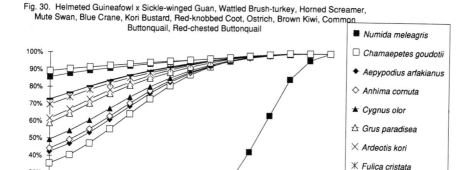

- ■ *Numida meleagris*
- □ *Chamaepetes goudotii*
- ◆ *Aepypodius arfakianus*
- ◇ *Anhima cornuta*
- ▲ *Cygnus olor*
- △ *Grus paradisea*
- ✕ *Ardeotis kori*
- ✳ *Fulica cristata*
- ⟶ *Struthio camelus*
- ▬ *Apteryx australis*
- ■ *Turnix sylvatica*
- □ *Turnix pyrrhothorax*

Fig. 31. Helmeted Guineafowl x Trinidad Piping-Guan, Wattled Brush-turkey, Grey-headed Albatross, Marabou Stork, Shoebill, Gentoo Penguin, Egyptian Vulture, Striated Heron, Cape Gannet, Little Grebe, Greater Kestrel

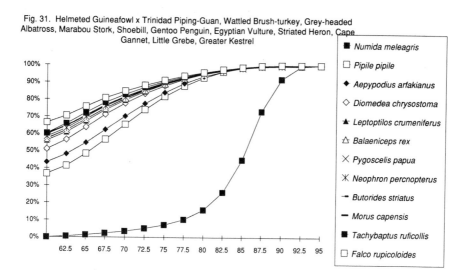

- ■ *Numida meleagris*
- □ *Pipile pipile*
- ◆ *Aepypodius arfakianus*
- ◇ *Diomedea chrysostoma*
- ▲ *Leptoptilos crumeniferus*
- △ *Balaeniceps rex*
- ✕ *Pygoscelis papua*
- ✳ *Neophron percnopterus*
- ⟶ *Butorides striatus*
- ▬ *Morus capensis*
- ■ *Tachybaptus ruficollis*
- □ *Falco rupicoloides*

Fig. 32. Helmeted Guineafowl x African Scops-Owl, Double-banded Sandgrouse, Common Sandpiper, Tambourine Dove, Pale-billed Hornbill, Red-faced Mousebird, Grey Woodpecker, Cape Robin-Chat, Red-bellied Parrot, Levaillant's Cuckoo

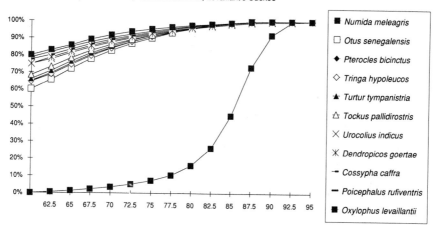

- ■ *Numida meleagris*
- □ *Otus senegalensis*
- ◆ *Pterocles bicinctus*
- ◇ *Tringa hypoleucos*
- ▲ *Turtur tympanistria*
- △ *Tockus pallidirostris*
- ✕ *Urocolius indicus*
- ✳ *Dendropicos goertae*
- ⟶ *Cossypha caffra*
- ▬ *Poicephalus rufiventris*
- ■ *Oxylophus levaillantii*

Fig. 33. Scaled Quail x Mountain Quail, Rock Partridge, Common Quail, Indian Peafowl, Helmeted Guineafowl, Turkey, Natal Francolin, Blue Grouse, Andean Guan, Australian Brush-turkey

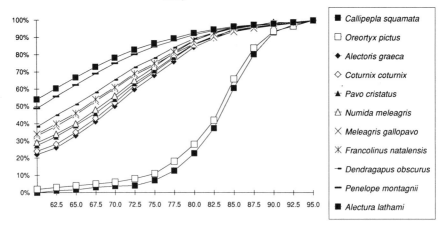

- ■ *Callipepla squamata*
- □ *Oreortyx pictus*
- ◆ *Alectoris graeca*
- ◇ *Coturnix coturnix*
- ▲ *Pavo cristatus*
- △ *Numida meleagris*
- ✕ *Meleagris gallopavo*
- ✳ *Francolinus natalensis*
- ⁻ *Dendragapus obscurus*
- ▬ *Penelope montagnii*
- ■ *Alectura lathami*

Fig. 34. White-winged Guan x Trinidad Piping-Guan, Speckled Chachalaca, Helmeted Guineafowl, Australian Brush-turkey, Natal Francolin, Turkey, Mute Swan, Black Vulture, Marabou Stork, Black Bustard, Common Moorhen, Ostrich

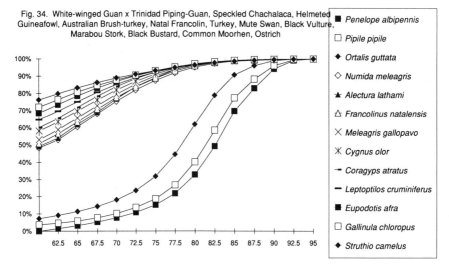

- ■ *Penelope albipennis*
- □ *Pipile pipile*
- ◆ *Ortalis guttata*
- ◇ *Numida meleagris*
- ▲ *Alectura lathami*
- △ *Francolinus natalensis*
- ✕ *Meleagris gallopavo*
- ✳ *Cygnus olor*
- ⁻ *Coragyps atratus*
- ▬ *Leptoptilos cruminiferus*
- ■ *Eupodotis afra*
- □ *Gallinula chloropus*
- ◆ *Struthio camelus*

Fig. 35. Mallard x Wood Duck, Canada Goose, Spotted Whistling-Duck, Magpie Goose, Horned Screamer, Ostrich, Greater Rhea

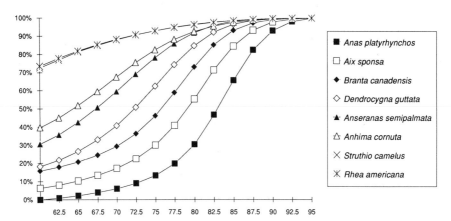

- ■ *Anas platyrhynchos*
- □ *Aix sponsa*
- ◆ *Branta canadensis*
- ◇ *Dendrocygna guttata*
- ▲ *Anseranas semipalmata*
- △ *Anhima cornuta*
- ✕ *Struthio camelus*
- ✳ *Rhea americana*

Fig. 36. Mallard x Wedge-tailed Eagle, Shikra, Brolga, Black Bustard, Black Vulture, Eurasian Kestrel, Common Moorhen, Common Bronzewing, Ruddy Ground-Dove

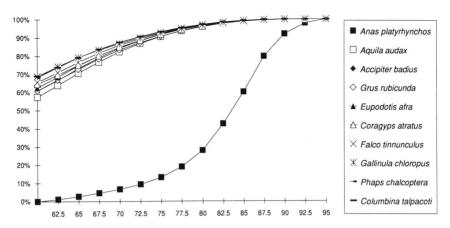

- ■ *Anas platyrhynchos*
- □ *Aquila audax*
- ◆ *Accipiter badius*
- ◇ *Grus rubicunda*
- ▲ *Eupodotis afra*
- △ *Coragyps atratus*
- ✕ *Falco tinnunculus*
- ✴ *Gallinula chloropus*
- ━ *Phaps chalcoptera*
- ━ *Columbina talpacoti*

Fig. 37. Gadwall x Northern Pintail, Muscovy Duck, White-winged Scoter, Wood Duck, Mute Swan, Canada Goose, Ruddy Duck, Spotted Whistling-Duck, Magpie Goose, Southern Screamer, Greater Flamingo, Australian Brush-turkey

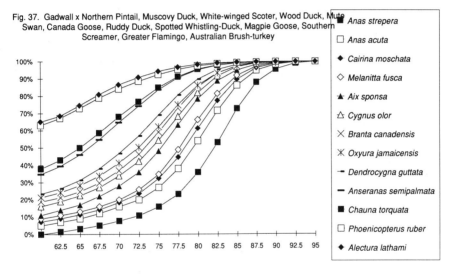

- ■ *Anas strepera*
- □ *Anas acuta*
- ◆ *Cairina moschata*
- ◇ *Melanitta fusca*
- ▲ *Aix sponsa*
- △ *Cygnus olor*
- ✕ *Branta canadensis*
- ✴ *Oxyura jamaicensis*
- ━ *Dendrocygna guttata*
- ━ *Anseranas semipalmata*
- ■ *Chauna torquata*
- □ *Phoenicopterus ruber*
- ◆ *Alectura lathami*

Fig. 38. Horned Screamer x Southern Screamer, Magpie Goose, Spotted Whistling-Duck, Mallard, Ruddy Duck, Australian Brush-turkey, Andean Guan, Trinidad Piping-Guan, Domestic Fowl

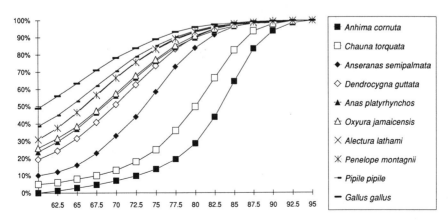

- ■ *Anhima cornuta*
- □ *Chauna torquata*
- ◆ *Anseranas semipalmata*
- ◇ *Dendrocygna guttata*
- ▲ *Anas platyrhynchos*
- △ *Oxyura jamaicensis*
- ✕ *Alectura lathami*
- ✴ *Penelope montagnii*
- ━ *Pipile pipile*
- ━ *Gallus gallus*

714

Fig. 39. Northern Screamer x Southern Screamer, Ruddy Duck, Gadwall, Greater Flamingo, White-winged Guan, Marabou Stork, Blue Crane, Black-crowned Night-Heron, Red-throated Caracara, Horned Grebe, Greater Rhea

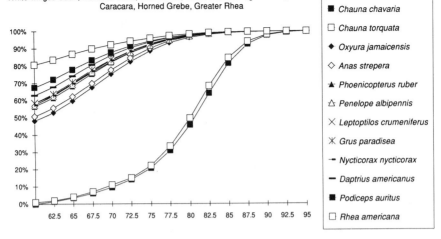

- ■ *Chauna chavaria*
- □ *Chauna torquata*
- ◆ *Oxyura jamaicensis*
- ◇ *Anas strepera*
- ▲ *Phoenicopterus ruber*
- △ *Penelope albipennis*
- ✕ *Leptoptilos crumeniferus*
- ✳ *Grus paradisea*
- ⌒ *Nycticorax nycticorax*
- ─ *Daptrius americanus*
- ■ *Podiceps auritus*
- □ *Rhea americana*

Fig. 40. Magpie Goose x Southern Screamer, Northern Screamer, Spotted Whistling-Duck, Ruddy Duck, Gadwall, Yellow-billed Stork, Greater Flamingo, Black Curassow, Australian Brush-turkey, Great Blue Heron, Domestic Fowl

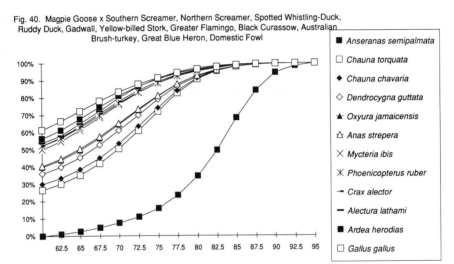

- ■ *Anseranas semipalmata*
- □ *Chauna torquata*
- ◆ *Chauna chavaria*
- ◇ *Dendrocygna guttata*
- ▲ *Oxyura jamaicensis*
- △ *Anas strepera*
- ✕ *Mycteria ibis*
- ✳ *Phoenicopterus ruber*
- ⌒ *Crax alector*
- ─ *Alectura lathami*
- ■ *Ardea herodias*
- □ *Gallus gallus*

Fig. 41. Common Buttonquail x Red-legged Seriema, Grey-breasted Seedsnipe, Common Black-headed Gull, African Jacana, Kori Bustard, Limpkin, Common Moorhen, Sandhill Crane

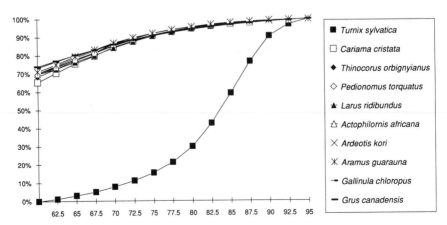

- ■ *Turnix sylvatica*
- □ *Cariama cristata*
- ◆ *Thinocorus orbignyianus*
- ◇ *Pedionomus torquatus*
- ▲ *Larus ridibundus*
- △ *Actophilornis africana*
- ✕ *Ardeotis kori*
- ✳ *Aramus guarauna*
- ⌒ *Gallinula chloropus*
- ─ *Grus canadensis*

Fig. 42. Hairy Woodpecker x Downy Woodpecker, Gila Woodpecker, Northern Flicker, Black-spotted Barbet, Lilac-breasted Roller, Swallow-wing, Wreathed Hornbill, White-throated Bee-eater, White-tipped Sicklebill, American Crow

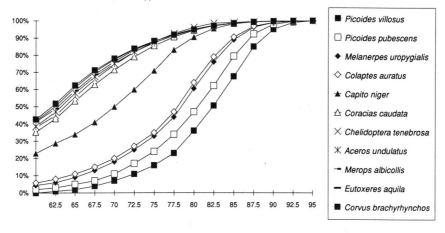

- ■ *Picoides villosus*
- □ *Picoides pubescens*
- ◆ *Melanerpes uropygialis*
- ◇ *Colaptes auratus*
- ▲ *Capito niger*
- △ *Coracias caudata*
- ✕ *Chelidoptera tenebrosa*
- ✳ *Aceros undulatus*
- ⟶ *Merops albicollis*
- ▬ *Eutoxeres aquila*
- ■ *Corvus brachyrhynchos*

Fig. 43. Hairy Woodpecker x Northern Flicker, Speckled Tinkerbird, White-eared Jacamar, Sacred Kingfisher, Blue-crowned Motmot, Black-nest Swiftlet, Speckled Mousebird, Chestnut-breasted Cuckoo, Yellow-bellied Elaenia, Eurasian Hoopoe

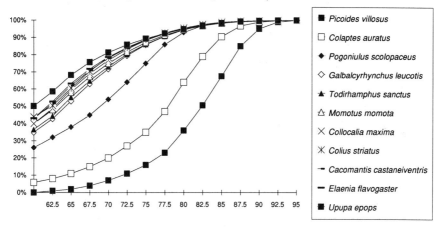

- ■ *Picoides villosus*
- □ *Colaptes auratus*
- ◆ *Pogoniulus scolopaceus*
- ◇ *Galbalcyrhynchus leucotis*
- ▲ *Todirhamphus sanctus*
- △ *Momotus momota*
- ✕ *Collocalia maxima*
- ✳ *Colius striatus*
- ⟶ *Cacomantis castaneiventris*
- ▬ *Elaenia flavogaster*
- ■ *Upupa epops*

Fig. 44. Spotted Honeyguide x Scaly-throated Honeyguide, Lesser Honeyguide, Malaysian Honeyguide, Golden-tailed Woodpecker, Olivaceous Piculet, Red-billed Toucan, Black-spotted Barbet, Black-collared Barbet, Blue-throated Barbet

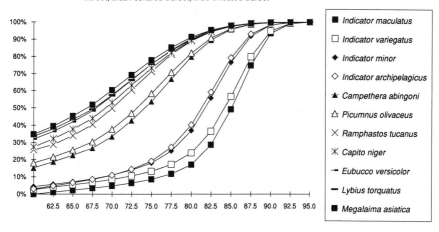

- ■ *Indicator maculatus*
- □ *Indicator variegatus*
- ◆ *Indicator minor*
- ◇ *Indicator archipelagicus*
- ▲ *Campethera abingoni*
- △ *Picumnus olivaceus*
- ✕ *Ramphastos tucanus*
- ✳ *Capito niger*
- ⟶ *Eubucco versicolor*
- ▬ *Lybius torquatus*
- ■ *Megalaima asiatica*

Fig. 45. Blue-throated Barbet x Red-throated Barbet, Choco Toucan, Double-toothed Barbet, Yellow-fronted Tinkerbird, Black-spotted Barbet, Hairy-breasted Barbet, Malaysian Honeyguide, Chestnut Woodpecker

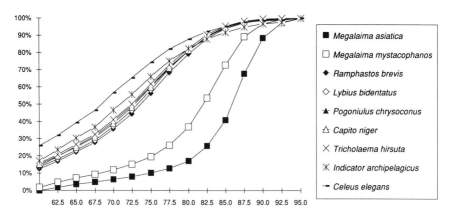

■ *Megalaima asiatica*

□ *Megalaima mystacophanos*

◆ *Ramphastos brevis*

◇ *Lybius bidentatus*

▲ *Pogoniulus chrysoconus*

△ *Capito niger*

✕ *Tricholaema hirsuta*

✖ *Indicator archipelagicus*

➤ *Celeus elegans*

Fig. 46. Lettered Aracari x Collared Aracari, Emerald Toucanet, Choco Toucan, Versicolored Barbet, Scarlet-crowned Barbet, Hairy-breasted Barbet, Red-crowned Barbet, Double-toothed Barbet, Malaysian Honeyguide, Chestnut Woodpecker

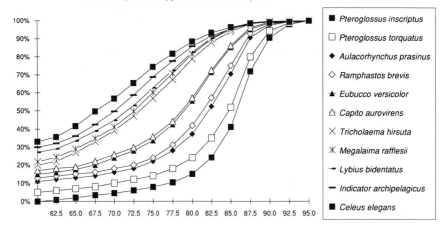

■ *Pteroglossus inscriptus*

□ *Pteroglossus torquatus*

◆ *Aulacorhynchus prasinus*

◇ *Ramphastos brevis*

▲ *Eubucco versicolor*

△ *Capito aurovirens*

✕ *Tricholaema hirsuta*

✖ *Megalaima rafflesii*

➤ *Lybius bidentatus*

— *Indicator archipelagicus*

■ *Celeus elegans*

Fig. 47. Green-tailed Jacamar x White-eared Jacamar, White-chested Puffbird, Swallow-wing, Belted Kingfisher, Spotted Honeyguide, Red-billed Toucan, Black-spotted Barbet, Greyish Piculet, Golden-naped Barbet, Black-collared Barbet

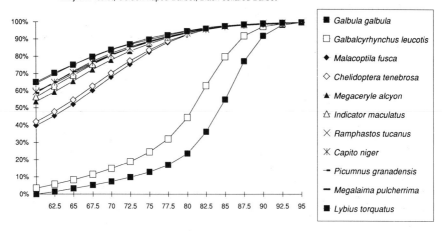

■ *Galbula galbula*

□ *Galbalcyrhynchus leucotis*

◆ *Malacoptila fusca*

◇ *Chelidoptera tenebrosa*

▲ *Megaceryle alcyon*

△ *Indicator maculatus*

✕ *Ramphastos tucanus*

✖ *Capito niger*

➤ *Picumnus granadensis*

— *Megalaima pulcherrima*

■ *Lybius torquatus*

Fig. 48. Green-tailed Jacamar x Bluish-fronted Jacamar, Collared Puffbird, Dollarbird, Little Green Bee-eater, Helmeted Hornbill, Collared Trogon, Black-backed Kingfisher, Speckled Mousebird, Red-throated Barbet, Green Jay, Green Woodhoopoe

■ *Galbula galbula*
□ *Galbula cyanescens*
◆ *Bucco capensis*
◇ *Eurystomus orientalis*
▲ *Merops orientalis*
△ *Buceros vigil*
✕ *Trogon collaris*
✳ *Ceyx erithacus*
⌐ *Colius striatus*
— *Megalaima mystacophanos*
■ *Cyanocorax yncas*
□ *Phoeniculus purpureus*

Fig. 49. Green-tailed Jacamar x Coppery-chested Jacamar, Moustached Puffbird, Knysna Turaco, Picazuro Pigeon, Croaking Ground-Dove, Guira Cuckoo, Common Cuckoo, Crimson Rosella, Mealy Parrot, Ivory-billed Aracari

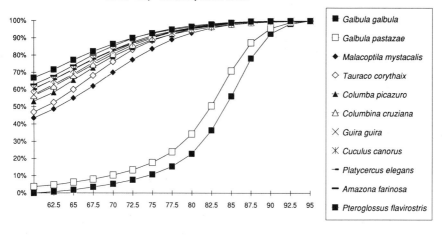

■ *Galbula galbula*
□ *Galbula pastazae*
◆ *Malacoptila mystacalis*
◇ *Tauraco corythaix*
▲ *Columba picazuro*
△ *Columbina cruziana*
✕ *Guira guira*
✳ *Cuculus canorus*
⌐ *Platycercus elegans*
— *Amazona farinosa*
■ *Pteroglossus flavirostris*

Fig. 50. White-chested Puffbird x Moustached Puffbird, Yellow-billed Nunbird, Collared Puffbird, Brown Nunlet, Swallow-wing, Yellow-billed Jacamar, Green-tailed Jacamar, Giant Kingfisher, Green Kingfisher

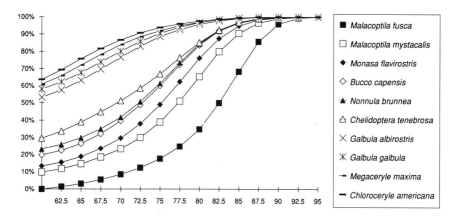

■ *Malacoptila fusca*
□ *Malacoptila mystacalis*
◆ *Monasa flavirostris*
◇ *Bucco capensis*
▲ *Nonnula brunnea*
△ *Chelidoptera tenebrosa*
✕ *Galbula albirostris*
✳ *Galbula galbula*
⌐ *Megaceryle maxima*
— *Chloroceryle americana*

Fig. 51. Rufous Hornbill x Helmeted Hornbill, Black-and-white Casqued-Hornbill, Malabar Pied Hornbill, Blyth's Hornbill, Indian Roller, European Bee-eater, White-throated Kingfisher, Broad-billed Tody, Common Scimitar-bill, Eurasian Hoopoe

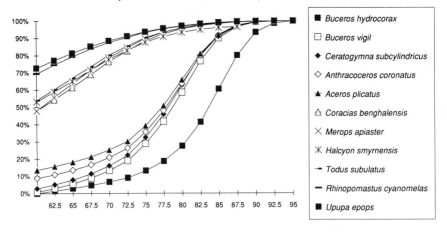

- ■ *Buceros hydrocorax*
- □ *Buceros vigil*
- ◆ *Ceratogymna subcylindricus*
- ◇ *Anthracoceros coronatus*
- ▲ *Aceros plicatus*
- △ *Coracias benghalensis*
- ✕ *Merops apiaster*
- ✳ *Halcyon smyrnensis*
- ⚊ *Todus subulatus*
- ▬ *Rhinopomastus cyanomelas*
- ■ *Upupa epops*

Fig. 52. Southern Ground-Hornbill x Rhinoceros Hornbill, Dollarbird, Ringed Kingfisher, Blue-crowned Motmot, Narina Trogon, White-throated Bee-eater, Yellow-billed Jacamar, Collared Puffbird, Green Woodhoopoe, Common Scimitar-bill, Eurasian Hoopoe

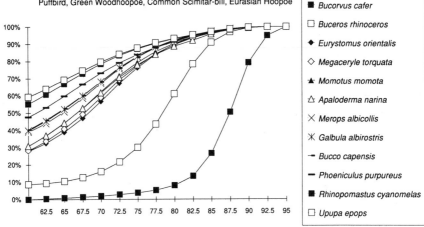
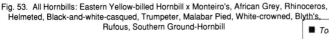

- ■ *Bucorvus cafer*
- □ *Buceros rhinoceros*
- ◆ *Eurystomus orientalis*
- ◇ *Megaceryle torquata*
- ▲ *Momotus momota*
- △ *Apaloderma narina*
- ✕ *Merops albicollis*
- ✳ *Galbula albirostris*
- ⚊ *Bucco capensis*
- ▬ *Phoeniculus purpureus*
- ■ *Rhinopomastus cyanomelas*
- □ *Upupa epops*

Fig. 53. All Hornbills: Eastern Yellow-billed Hornbill x Monteiro's, African Grey, Rhinoceros, Helmeted, Black-and-white-casqued, Trumpeter, Malabar Pied, White-crowned, Blyth's, Rufous, Southern Ground-Hornbill

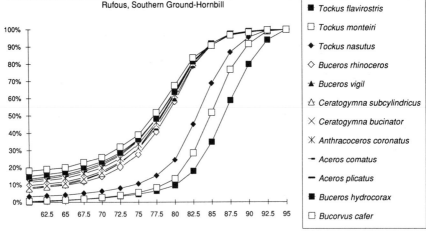

- ■ *Tockus flavirostris*
- □ *Tockus monteiri*
- ◆ *Tockus nasutus*
- ◇ *Buceros rhinoceros*
- ▲ *Buceros vigil*
- △ *Ceratogymna subcylindricus*
- ✕ *Ceratogymna bucinator*
- ✳ *Anthracoceros coronatus*
- ⚊ *Aceros comatus*
- ▬ *Aceros plicatus*
- ■ *Buceros hydrocorax*
- □ *Bucorvus cafer*

Fig. 54. Green Woodhoopoe x Common Scimitar-bill, African Olive Pigeon, Alpine Swift, Cockatiel, Black-nest Swiftlet, Chestnut-fronted Macaw, White-whiskered Hermit, Yellow Bishop, Tyrian Metaltail, Rufous-breasted Antthrush

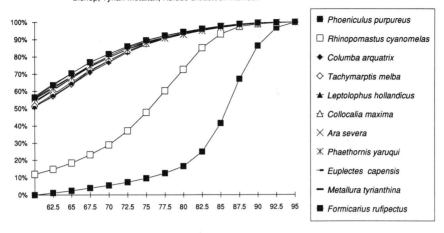

■ *Phoeniculus purpureus*
□ *Rhinopomastus cyanomelas*
◆ *Columba arquatrix*
◇ *Tachymarptis melba*
▲ *Leptolophus hollandicus*
△ *Collocalia maxima*
✕ *Ara severa*
✳ *Phaethornis yaruqui*
� *Euplectes capensis*
— *Metallura tyrianthina*
■ *Formicarius rufipectus*

Fig. 55. Green Woodhoopoe x Common Scimitar-bill, Eurasian Hoopoe, Red-billed Hornbill, Swallow-wing, Narina Trogon, Green-tailed Jacamar, Spotted Honeyguide, Golden-tailed Woodpecker, Red-headed Barbet, Black-collared Barbet

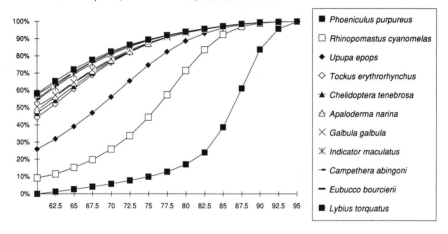

■ *Phoeniculus purpureus*
□ *Rhinopomastus cyanomelas*
◆ *Upupa epops*
◇ *Tockus erythrorhynchus*
▲ *Chelidoptera tenebrosa*
△ *Apaloderma narina*
✕ *Galbula galbula*
✳ *Indicator maculatus*
➤ *Campethera abingoni*
— *Eubucco bourcierii*
■ *Lybius torquatus*

Fig. 56. Narina Trogon x Black-tailed Trogon, Diard's Trogon, Grey Go-away-bird, Hartlaub's Turaco, Pied Kingfisher, Green-tailed Jacamar, Speckled Mousebird, , Brown Jacamar, Red-faced Mousebird, Collared Puffbird, Black-streaked Puffbird

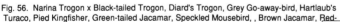

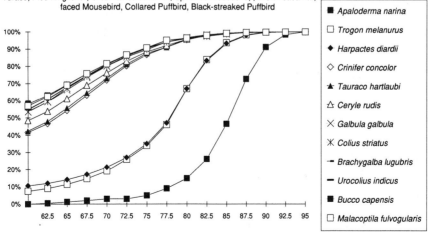

■ *Apaloderma narina*
□ *Trogon melanurus*
◆ *Harpactes diardii*
◇ *Crinifer concolor*
▲ *Tauraco hartlaubi*
△ *Ceryle rudis*
✕ *Galbula galbula*
✳ *Colius striatus*
➤ *Brachygalba lugubris*
— *Urocolius indicus*
■ *Bucco capensis*
□ *Malacoptila fulvogularis*

Fig. 57. Narina Trogon x Whitehead's Trogon, African Scops-Owl, Barn Owl, Marbled Frogmouth, European Nightjar, Yellow-crowned Parrot, Little Swift, White-bellied Swiftlet, Barred Becard, Lewin's Honeyeater, Brown Inca

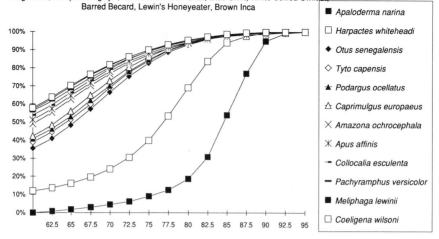

- ■ *Apaloderma narina*
- □ *Harpactes whiteheadi*
- ◆ *Otus senegalensis*
- ◇ *Tyto capensis*
- ▲ *Podargus ocellatus*
- △ *Caprimulgus europaeus*
- ✕ *Amazona ochrocephala*
- ✳ *Apus affinis*
- ⌐ *Collocalia esculenta*
- ▬ *Pachyramphus versicolor*
- ■ *Meliphaga lewinii*
- □ *Coeligena wilsoni*

Fig. 58. Narina Trogon x Collared Trogon, Large Green-Pigeon, Hoatzin, Guira Cuckoo, Groove-billed Ani, Channel-billed Cuckoo, Dideric Cuckoo, Lesser Cuckoo, Jamaican Lizard-Cuckoo, Dwarf Cuckoo, Little Cuckoo

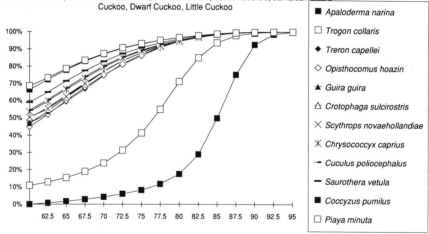

- ■ *Apaloderma narina*
- □ *Trogon collaris*
- ◆ *Treron capellei*
- ◇ *Opisthocomus hoazin*
- ▲ *Guira guira*
- △ *Crotophaga sulcirostris*
- ✕ *Scythrops novaehollandiae*
- ✳ *Chrysococcyx caprius*
- ⌐ *Cuculus poliocephalus*
- ▬ *Saurothera vetula*
- ■ *Coccyzus pumilus*
- □ *Piaya minuta*

Fig. 59. Scarlet-rumped Trogon x Red-naped Trogon, Collared Trogon, Narina Trogon, Short-eared Owl, Common Nighthawk, Lilac-breasted Roller, Hartlaub's Turaco, Black-and-white Casqued Hornbill, Sacred Kingfisher, Rock Pigeon, Swallow-wing

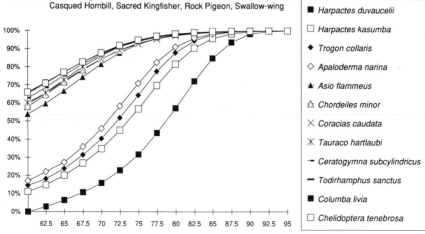

- ■ *Harpactes duvaucelii*
- □ *Harpactes kasumba*
- ◆ *Trogon collaris*
- ◇ *Apaloderma narina*
- ▲ *Asio flammeus*
- △ *Chordeiles minor*
- ✕ *Coracias caudata*
- ✳ *Tauraco hartlaubi*
- ⌐ *Ceratogymna subcylindricus*
- ▬ *Todirhamphus sanctus*
- ■ *Columba livia*
- □ *Chelidoptera tenebrosa*

Fig. 60. Lilac-breasted Roller x Woodland Kingfisher, Red-throated Bee-eater, Blue-crowned Motmot, Trumpeter Hornbill, Narina Trogon, Black-tailed Trogon, Red-naped Trogon, Blue-eared Kingfisher, Red-faced Mousebird

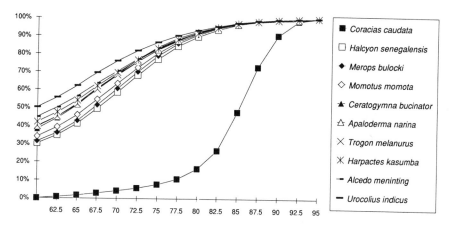

Fig. 61. Lilac-breasted Roller x Indian Roller, Dollarbird, Red-bearded Bee-eater, Little Green Bee-eater, Blue-crowned Motmot, Narrow-billed Tody, Wreathed Hornbill, Pale-billed Hornbill, Green Woodhoopoe, Common Scimitar-bill

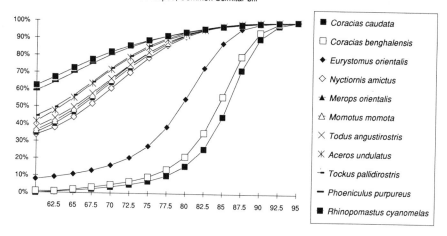

Fig. 62. Lilac-breasted Roller x Dollarbird, Large Green-Pigeon, Laughing Dove, Senegal Parrot, Chestnut-collared Swift, Blue-and-yellow Macaw, Chimney Swift, Ruby-throated Hummingbird, Great Grey Shrike, House Finch

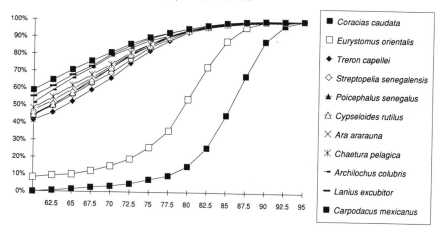

Fig. 63. Lilac-breasted Roller x Indian Roller, Dollarbird, Green-tailed Jacamar, Coppery-chested Jacamar, Collared Puffbird, Brown Nunlet, Fine-spotted Woodpecker, Spotted Honeyguide, Scarlet-crowned Barbet, Channel-billed Toucan

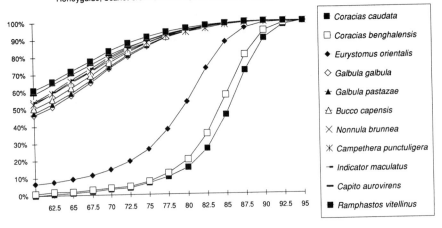

- ■ *Coracias caudata*
- □ *Coracias benghalensis*
- ◆ *Eurystomus orientalis*
- ◇ *Galbula galbula*
- ▲ *Galbula pastazae*
- △ *Bucco capensis*
- ✕ *Nonnula brunnea*
- ✳ *Campethera punctuligera*
- ➝ *Indicator maculatus*
- — *Capito aurovirens*
- ■ *Ramphastos vitellinus*

Fig. 64. Blue-crowned Motmot x Rufous-capped Motmot, Broad-billed Motmot, Turquoise-browed Motmot, Pied Kingfisher, Broad-billed Tody, Indian Roller, Helmeted Hornbill, Narina Trogon, Swallow-wing, Green Woodhoopoe, Eurasian Hoopoe

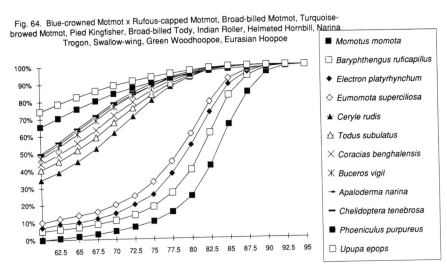

- ■ *Momotus momota*
- □ *Baryphthengus ruficapillus*
- ◆ *Electron platyrhynchum*
- ◇ *Eumomota superciliosa*
- ▲ *Ceryle rudis*
- △ *Todus subulatus*
- ✕ *Coracias benghalensis*
- ✳ *Buceros vigil*
- ➝ *Apaloderma narina*
- — *Chelidoptera tenebrosa*
- ■ *Phoeniculus purpureus*
- □ *Upupa epops*

Fig. 65. Blue-crowned Motmot x Rufous-capped Motmot, Turquoise-browed Motmot, Grey-headed Kingfisher, Broad-billed Tody, Dollarbird, Malachite Kingfisher, Little Green Bee-eater, Southern Ground-Hornbill, Collared Puffbird, Whitehead's Trogon

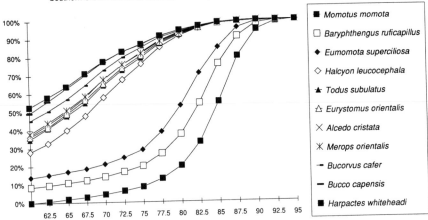

- ■ *Momotus momota*
- □ *Baryphthengus ruficapillus*
- ◆ *Eumomota superciliosa*
- ◇ *Halcyon leucocephala*
- ▲ *Todus subulatus*
- △ *Eurystomus orientalis*
- ✕ *Alcedo cristata*
- ✳ *Merops orientalis*
- ➝ *Bucorvus cafer*
- — *Bucco capensis*
- ■ *Harpactes whiteheadi*

Fig. 66. Broad-billed Tody x Indian Roller, Grey-headed Kingfisher, Blue-crowned Motmot, European Bee-eater, Helmeted Hornbill, Collared Trogon, Green-tailed Jacamar, Eurasian Hoopoe

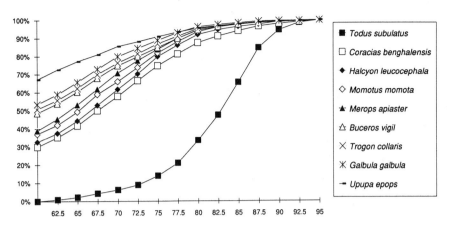

■ *Todus subulatus*

□ *Coracias benghalensis*

◆ *Halcyon leucocephala*

◇ *Momotus momota*

▲ *Merops apiaster*

△ *Buceros vigil*

✕ *Trogon collaris*

✳ *Galbula galbula*

– *Upupa epops*

Fig. 67. Ringed Kingfisher x Giant Kingfisher, Pied Kingfisher, Green Kingfisher, Blue-crowned Motmot, Broad-billed Tody, Indian Roller, Red-throated Bee-eater, White-eared Jacamar, Rufous Hornbill, Green Woodhoopoe, Eurasian Hoopoe

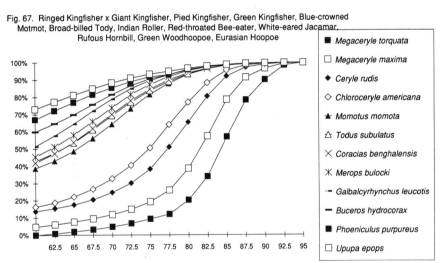

■ *Megaceryle torquata*

□ *Megaceryle maxima*

◆ *Ceryle rudis*

◇ *Chloroceryle americana*

▲ *Momotus momota*

△ *Todus subulatus*

✕ *Coracias benghalensis*

✳ *Merops bulocki*

– *Galbalcyrhynchus leucotis*

— *Buceros hydrocorax*

■ *Phoeniculus purpureus*

□ *Upupa epops*

Fig. 68. Ringed Kingfisher x Belted Kingfisher, Pied Kingfisher, Green-and-rufous Kingfisher, Rufous-collared Wood-Kingfisher, Woodland Kingfisher, Common Paradise-Kingfisher, Half-collared Kingfisher, African Pygmy Kingfisher, Black-backed Kingfisher

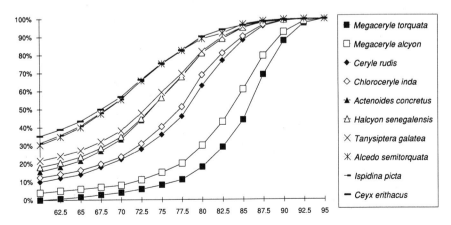

■ *Megaceryle torquata*

□ *Megaceryle alcyon*

◆ *Ceryle rudis*

◇ *Chloroceryle inda*

▲ *Actenoides concretus*

△ *Halcyon senegalensis*

✕ *Tanysiptera galatea*

✳ *Alcedo semitorquata*

– *Ispidina picta*

— *Ceyx erithacus*

Fig. 69. Half-collared Kingfisher x Black-backed Kingfisher, African Pygmy Kingfisher, Blue-winged Kookaburra, Hook-billed Kingfisher, Woodland Kingfisher, Pied Kingfisher, Common Paradise-Kingfisher, Giant Kingfisher, American Pygmy Kingfisher

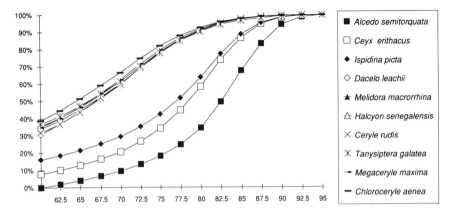

Fig. 70. Blue-throated Bee-eater x Little Green Bee-eater, White-throated Bee-eater, Red-throated Bee-eater, Dollarbird, Broad-billed Motmot, Grey-headed Kingfisher, White-eared Jacamar, Trumpeter Hornbill, Narina Trogon, Courol

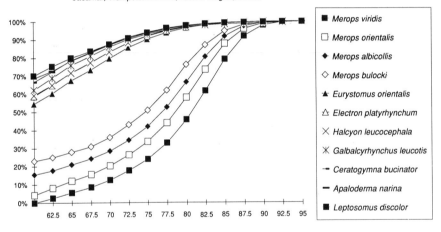

Fig. 71, Blue-throated Bee-eater x Little Green Bee-eater, Lilac-breasted Roller, Common Paradise-Kingfisher, Scarlet-rumped Trogon, Rufous-capped Motmot, Bluish-fronted Jacamar, Rhinoceros Hornbill, Lesser Honeyguide, Double-toothed Barbet

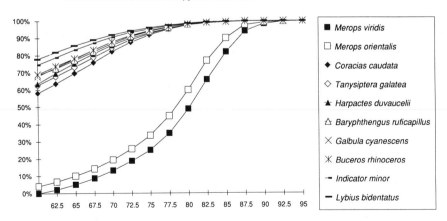

Fig. 72. Red-faced Mousebird x Speckled Mousebird, Spotted Eagle-Owl, Marbled Frogmouth, Grey-Go-away-bird, Asian Barred Owlet, Knysna Turaco, Barn Owl, Pauraque, Oilbird, Lesser Cuckoo, Dideric Cuckoo

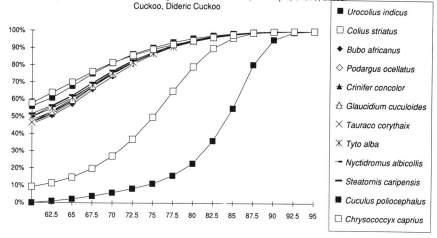

- ■ *Urocolius indicus*
- □ *Colius striatus*
- ◆ *Bubo africanus*
- ◇ *Podargus ocellatus*
- ▲ *Crinifer concolor*
- △ *Glaucidium cuculoides*
- ✕ *Tauraco corythaix*
- ✳ *Tyto alba*
- ⊶ *Nyctidromus albicollis*
- ━ *Steatornis caripensis*
- ■ *Cuculus poliocephalus*
- □ *Chrysococcyx caprius*

Fig. 73. Red-faced Mousebird x Blue-naped Mousebird, Speckled Mousebird, Indian Roller, Lesser Treeswift, Trumpeter Hornbill, Narina Trogon, Fork-tailed Palm-Swift, Sparkling Violet-ear Hummingbird

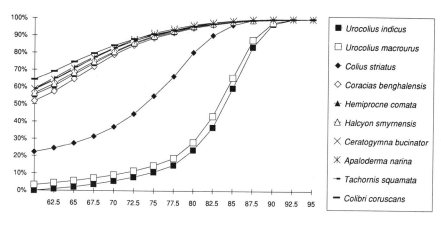

- ■ *Urocolius indicus*
- □ *Urocolius macrourus*
- ◆ *Colius striatus*
- ◇ *Coracias benghalensis*
- ▲ *Hemiprocne comata*
- △ *Halcyon smyrnensis*
- ✕ *Ceratogymna bucinator*
- ✳ *Apaloderma narina*
- ⊶ *Tachornis squamata*
- ━ *Colibri coruscans*

Fig. 74. Red-faced Mousebird x Speckled Mousebird, Indian Roller, African Collared-Dove, Trumpeter Hornbill, White-throated Kingfisher, Senegal Parrot, Collared Puffbird, Lesser Honeyguide, Rainbow Bee-eater, Chestnut Woodpecker, Eurasian Hoopoe

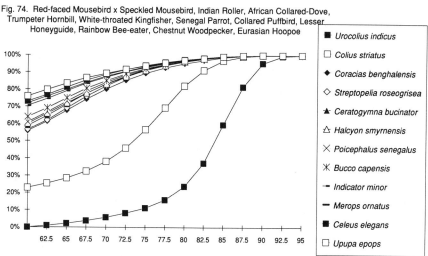

- ■ *Urocolius indicus*
- □ *Colius striatus*
- ◆ *Coracias benghalensis*
- ◇ *Streptopelia roseogrisea*
- ▲ *Ceratogymna bucinator*
- △ *Halcyon smyrnensis*
- ✕ *Poicephalus senegalus*
- ✳ *Bucco capensis*
- ⊶ *Indicator minor*
- ━ *Merops ornatus*
- ■ *Celeus elegans*
- □ *Upupa epops*

726

Fig. 75. Red-faced Mousebird x Kerguelen Petrel, Chilean Flamingo, Long-winged Harrier, Cape Gannet, Blue Crane, Snowy Egret, Wattled Lapwing, Horned Grebe, Kori Bustard, American Kestrel

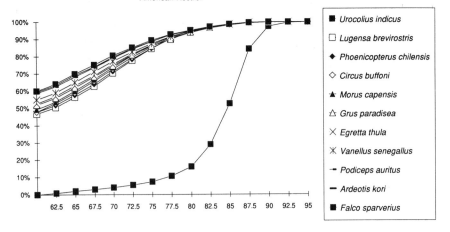

- ■ *Urocolius indicus*
- □ *Lugensa brevirostris*
- ◆ *Phoenicopterus chilensis*
- ◇ *Circus buffoni*
- ▲ *Morus capensis*
- △ *Grus paradisea*
- ✕ *Egretta thula*
- ✶ *Vanellus senegallus*
- ⇀ *Podiceps auritus*
- — *Ardeotis kori*
- ■ *Falco sparverius*

Fig. 76. Lesser Cuckoo x Red-chested Cuckoo, Shining Bronze-Cuckoo, Brush Cuckoo, Asian Koel, Pied Cuckoo, Yellow-billed Cuckoo, Smooth-billed Ani, Squirrel Cuckoo, Greater Roadrunner, Guira Cuckoo

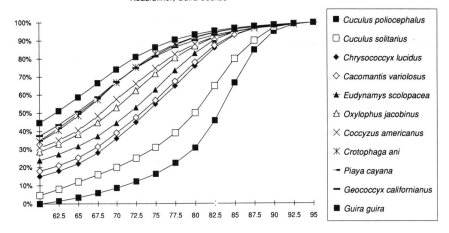

- ■ *Cuculus poliocephalus*
- □ *Cuculus solitarius*
- ◆ *Chrysococcyx lucidus*
- ◇ *Cacomantis variolosus*
- ▲ *Eudynamys scolopacea*
- △ *Oxylophus jacobinus*
- ✕ *Coccyzus americanus*
- ✶ *Crotophaga ani*
- ⇀ *Piaya cayana*
- — *Geococcyx californianus*
- ■ *Guira guira*

Fig. 77. Lesser Cuckoo x Yellow-billed Cuckoo, Indian Scops-Owl, Common Nighthawk, African Grass-Owl, Oilbird, Blue Ground-Dove, White-tipped Dove, Senegal Parrot, Chestnut-fronted Macaw, Speckled Mousebird

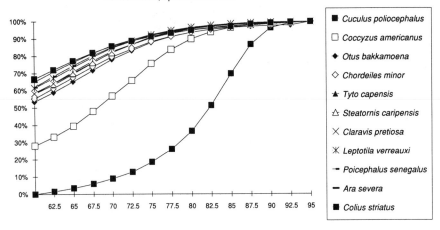

- ■ *Cuculus poliocephalus*
- □ *Coccyzus americanus*
- ◆ *Otus bakkamoena*
- ◇ *Chordeiles minor*
- ▲ *Tyto capensis*
- △ *Steatornis caripensis*
- ✕ *Claravis pretiosa*
- ✶ *Leptotila verreauxi*
- ⇀ *Poicephalus senegalus*
- — *Ara severa*
- ■ *Colius striatus*

Fig. 78. Lesser Cuckoo x Purple-crested Turaco, Diard's Trogon, Helmeted Hornbill, White-throated Bee-eater, Green-tailed Jacamar, Malaysian Honeyguide, Buff-necked Woodpecker, Emerald Toucanet, Blue-throated Barbet

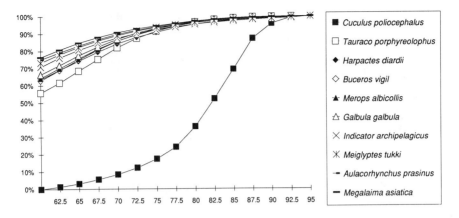

Fig. 79. Hoatzin x Guira Cuckoo, Smooth-billed Ani, Common Cuckoo, Dideric Cuckoo, Greater Roadrunner, Australian Brush-turkey, Black Curassow, Domestic Fowl

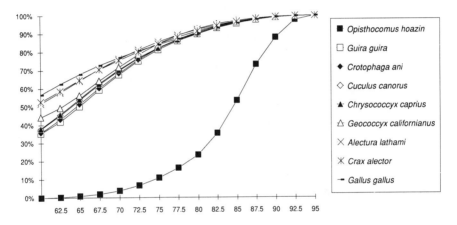

Fig. 80. Smooth-billed Ani x Greater Ani, Guira Cuckoo, Greater Roadrunner, Red-chested Cuckoo, Asian Koel, Black-eared Cuckoo, Yellow-billed Cuckoo, Squirrel Cuckoo, Jamaican Lizard-Cuckoo, Purple-crested Turaco

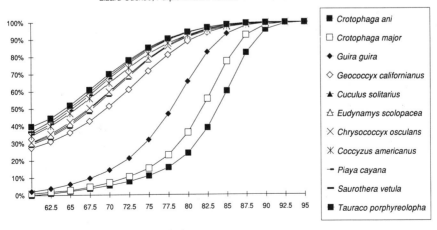

728

Fig. 81. Smooth-billed Ani x Guira Cuckoo, Channel-billed Cuckoo, Hartlaub's Turaco, Indian
Roller, Black-tailed Trogon, Amazon Kingfisher, Turquoise-browed Motmot, Green-tailed
Jacamar, Speckled Mousebird, Fine-spotted Woodpecker, Channel-billed Toucan

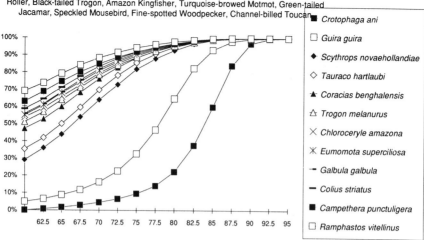

Fig. 82. Smooth-billed Ani x Guira Cuckoo, Double-banded Plover, Western Marsh-Harrier,
Purple-crested Turaco, Snowy Egret, Swinhoe's Snipe, Croaking Ground-Dove, Yellow-
crowned Parrot, Chinese Francolin

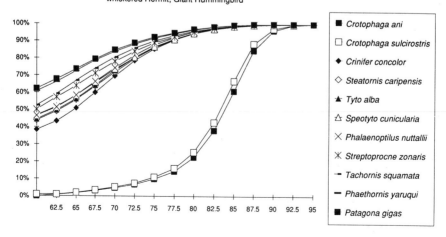

Fig. 83. Smooth-billed Ani x Groove-billed Ani, Grey Go-away-bird, Oilbird, Barn Owl,
Burrowing Owl, Common Poorwill, White-collared Swift, Fork-tailed Palm-Swift, White-
whiskered Hermit, Giant Hummingbird

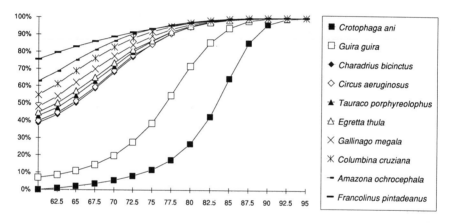

Fig. 84. Greater Roadrunner x Greater Ani, Guira Cuckoo, Black-bellied Malkoha, Dideric Cuckoo, Chestnut-breasted Cuckoo, Jamaican Lizard-Cuckoo, Grey Go-away-bird, Dwarf Cuckoo, Little Cuckoo

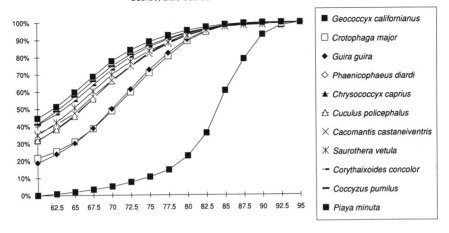

- ■ Geococcyx californianus
- □ Crotophaga major
- ◆ Guira guira
- ◇ Phaenicophaeus diardi
- ▲ Chrysococcyx caprius
- △ Cuculus policephalus
- ✕ Cacomantis castaneiventris
- ✳ Saurothera vetula
- ⊸ Corythaixoides concolor
- — Coccyzus pumilus
- ■ Piaya minuta

Fig. 85. Blue-and-yellow Macaw x Chestnut-fronted Macaw, Orange-chinned Parakeet, Senegal Parrot, Pink Cockatoo, Wompoo Fruit-Dove, Tambourine Dove, Ruddy Quail-Dove, African Olive Pigeon, Mourning Dove

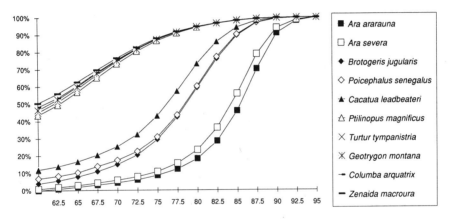

- ■ Ara ararauna
- □ Ara severa
- ◆ Brotogeris jugularis
- ◇ Poicephalus senegalus
- ▲ Cacatua leadbeateri
- △ Ptilinopus magnificus
- ✕ Turtur tympanistria
- ✳ Geotrygon montana
- ⊸ Columba arquatrix
- — Zenaida macroura

Fig. 86. Blue-and-yellow Macaw x Pink Cockatoo, Western Marsh-Harrier, Egyptian Vulture, Chinese Goshawk, Eastern Screech-Owl, Mountain Caracara, Barn Owl, Osprey, Merlin, Collared Falconet

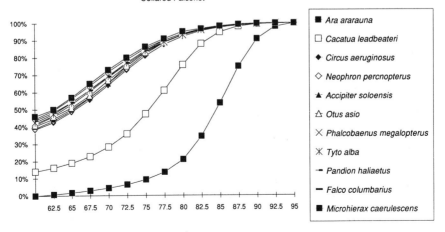

- ■ Ara ararauna
- □ Cacatua leadbeateri
- ◆ Circus aeruginosus
- ◇ Neophron percnopterus
- ▲ Accipiter soloensis
- △ Otus asio
- ✕ Phalcobaenus megalopterus
- ✳ Tyto alba
- ⊸ Pandion haliaetus
- — Falco columbarius
- ■ Microhierax caerulescens

Fig. 87. Blue-and-yellow Macaw x Oilbird, White-tailed Nightjar, Knysna Turaco, Hartlaub's Turaco, Little Swift, Chimney Swift, Asian Koel, Pied Cuckoo, Rufous-breasted Hermit, Band-tailed Barbthroat

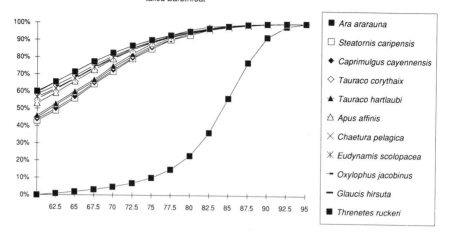

- ■ *Ara ararauna*
- ☐ *Steatornis caripensis*
- ◆ *Caprimulgus cayennensis*
- ◇ *Tauraco corythaix*
- ▲ *Tauraco hartlaubi*
- △ *Apus affinis*
- ✕ *Chaetura pelagica*
- ✻ *Eudynamis scolopacea*
- ⇀ *Oxylophus jacobinus*
- — *Glaucis hirsuta*
- ■ *Threnetes ruckeri*

Fig. 88. Blue-and-yellow Macaw x Chestnut-fronted Macaw, Pale-headed Rosella, Andean Condor, Black Vulture, King Vulture, Turkey Vulture, Blue-crowned Motmot, Diard's Trogon, Pale-billed Hornbill, Speckled Mousebird, Golden-collared Toucanet

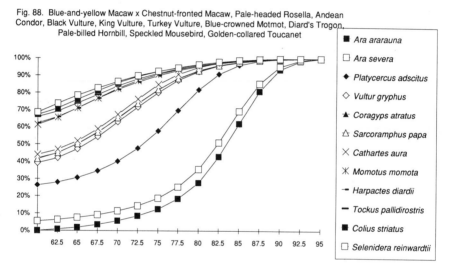

- ■ *Ara ararauna*
- ☐ *Ara severa*
- ◆ *Platycercus adscitus*
- ◇ *Vultur gryphus*
- ▲ *Coragyps atratus*
- △ *Sarcoramphus papa*
- ✕ *Cathartes aura*
- ✻ *Momotus momota*
- ⇀ *Harpactes diardii*
- — *Tockus pallidirostris*
- ■ *Colius striatus*
- ☐ *Selenidera reinwardtii*

Fig. 89. Pink Cockatoo x Galah, Cockatiel, Rainbow Lorikeet, Port Lincoln Ringneck, Cobalt-winged Parakeet, Yellow-crowned Parrot, Meyer's Parrot, Merlin, African Grass-Owl

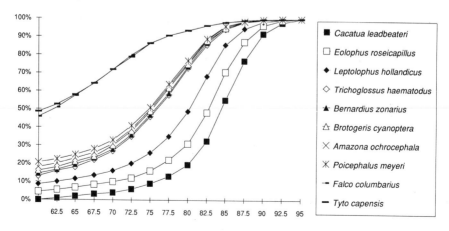

- ■ *Cacatua leadbeateri*
- ☐ *Eolophus roseicapillus*
- ◆ *Leptolophus hollandicus*
- ◇ *Trichoglossus haematodus*
- ▲ *Bernardius zonarius*
- △ *Brotogeris cyanoptera*
- ✕ *Amazona ochrocephala*
- ✻ *Poicephalus meyeri*
- ⇀ *Falco columbarius*
- — *Tyto capensis*

Fig. 90. Little Swift x Black-nest Swiftlet, Chimney Swift, Common Nighthawk, Lilac-breasted
Roller, White-tipped Sicklebill, Rock Pigeon, Sacred Kingfisher, Senegal Parrot, Speckled
Mousebird, Black-billed Cuckoo, Hairy-breasted Barbet

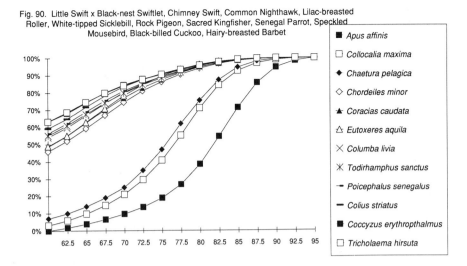

- ■ Apus affinis
- ☐ Collocalia maxima
- ◆ Chaetura pelagica
- ◇ Chordeiles minor
- ▲ Coracias caudata
- △ Eutoxeres aquila
- ✕ Columba livia
- ✴ Todirhamphus sanctus
- ⌐ Poicephalus senegalus
- ▬ Colius striatus
- ■ Coccyzus erythropthalmus
- ☐ Tricholaema hirsuta

Fig. 91. Chimney Swift x White-bellied Swiftlet, Little Swift, Brown-backed Needletail, Chestnut-
collared Swift, White-collared Swift, Lesser Treeswift, Australian Owlet-Nightjar, Pauraque,
Oilbird, Ruby-throated Hummingbird, Red-billed Emerald

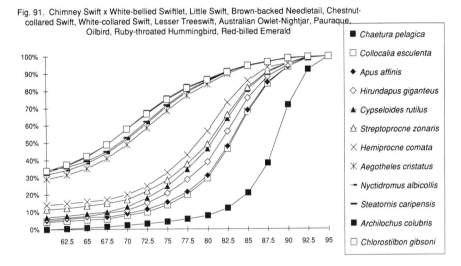

- ■ Chaetura pelagica
- ☐ Collocalia esculenta
- ◆ Apus affinis
- ◇ Hirundapus giganteus
- ▲ Cypseloides rutilus
- △ Streptoprocne zonaris
- ✕ Hemiprocne comata
- ✴ Aegotheles cristatus
- ⌐ Nyctidromus albicollis
- ▬ Steatornis caripensis
- ■ Archilochus colubris
- ☐ Chlorostilbon gibsoni

Fig. 92. Chimney Swift x Lesser Treeswift, Rufous-tailed Hummingbird, Rock Pigeon, Chestnut-
fronted Macaw, Speckled Mousebird, Green Broadbill, Horned Lark, Banded Pitta, Spot-
breasted Woodpecker, Choco Toucan

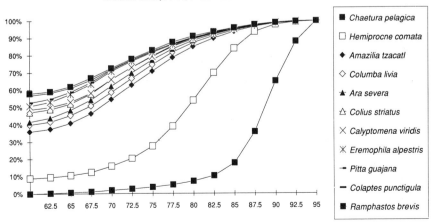

- ■ Chaetura pelagica
- ☐ Hemiprocne comata
- ◆ Amazilia tzacatl
- ◇ Columba livia
- ▲ Ara severa
- △ Colius striatus
- ✕ Calyptomena viridis
- ✴ Eremophila alpestris
- ⌐ Pitta guajana
- ▬ Colaptes punctigula
- ■ Ramphastos brevis

Fig. 93. Chimney Swift x White-bellied Swiftlet, Straw-necked Ibis, California Condor, Yellow-billed Stork, Blue Crane, Brown Booby, Pelagic Cormorant, Hartlaub's Turaco, Smooth-billed Ani, Lesser Cuckoo, Purple Swamphen

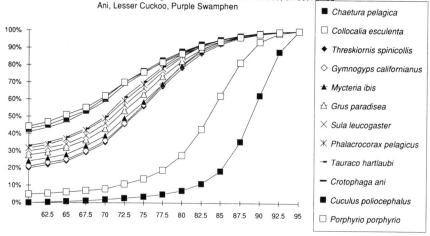

Legend:
- ■ *Chaetura pelagica*
- □ *Collocalia esculenta*
- ◆ *Threskiornis spinicollis*
- ◇ *Gymnogyps californianus*
- ▲ *Mycteria ibis*
- △ *Grus paradisea*
- ✕ *Sula leucogaster*
- ✳ *Phalacrocorax pelagicus*
- — *Tauraco hartlaubi*
- — *Crotophaga ani*
- ■ *Cuculus poliocephalus*
- □ *Porphyrio porphyrio*

Fig. 94. Chimney Swift x Lesser Treeswift, Shy Albatross, Swainson's Hawk, Common Loon, Buffy Fish-Owl, Eastern Screech-Owl, Large-tailed Nightjar, African Grass-Owl, New Zealand Grebe, Common Poorwill

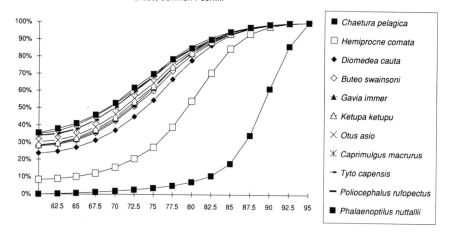

Legend:
- ■ *Chaetura pelagica*
- □ *Hemiprocne comata*
- ◆ *Diomedea cauta*
- ◇ *Buteo swainsoni*
- ▲ *Gavia immer*
- △ *Ketupa ketupu*
- ✕ *Otus asio*
- ✳ *Caprimulgus macrurus*
- — *Tyto capensis*
- — *Poliocephalus rufopectus*
- ■ *Phalaenoptilus nuttallii*

Fig. 95. Rufous-tailed Hummingbird x Cinnamon Hummingbird, White-vented Plumeleteer, Giant Hummingbird, Brown Inca, White-tailed Hillstar, Green-tailed Trainbearer, Buff-tailed Sicklebill, Rufous-breasted Hermit, Tawny-bellied Hermit

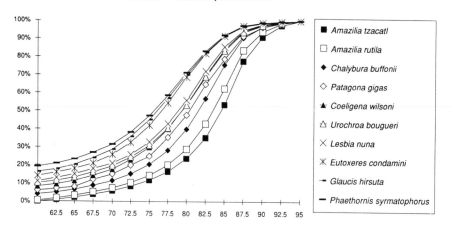

Legend:
- ■ *Amazilia tzacatl*
- □ *Amazilia rutila*
- ◆ *Chalybura buffonii*
- ◇ *Patagona gigas*
- ▲ *Coeligena wilsoni*
- △ *Urochroa bougueri*
- ✕ *Lesbia nuna*
- ✳ *Eutoxeres condamini*
- — *Glaucis hirsuta*
- — *Phaethornis syrmatophorus*

Fig. 96. Rufous-tailed Hummingbird x Sapphire-vented Puffleg, Rainbow-bearded Thornbill, White-tailed Goldenthroat, Lesser Treeswift, Black-nest Swiftlet, Alpine Swift, Australian Owlet-Nightjar, White-tailed Nightjar, Oilbird

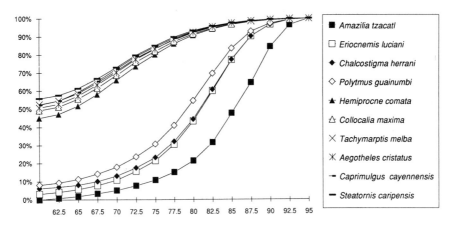

■ *Amazilia tzacatl*
□ *Eriocnemis luciani*
◆ *Chalcostigma herrani*
◇ *Polytmus guainumbi*
▲ *Hemiprocne comata*
△ *Collocalia maxima*
✕ *Tachymarptis melba*
✖ *Aegotheles cristatus*
⊸ *Caprimulgus cayennensis*
— *Steatornis caripensis*

Fig. 97. Rufous-tailed Hummingbird x Lesser Treeswift, Chimney Swift, Common Bronzewing, European Turtle-Dove, Chestnut-fronted Macaw, Yellow-crowned Parrot, Dusky Myzomela, Speckled Mousebird, Banded Pitta, Choco Toucan, Olivaceous Piculet

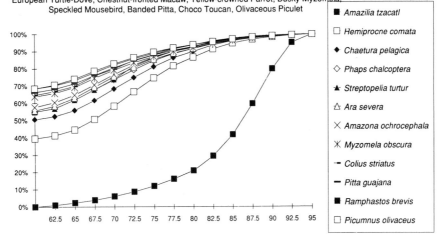

■ *Amazilia tzacatl*
□ *Hemiprocne comata*
◆ *Chaetura pelagica*
◇ *Phaps chalcoptera*
▲ *Streptopelia turtur*
△ *Ara severa*
✕ *Amazona ochrocephala*
✖ *Myzomela obscura*
⊸ *Colius striatus*
— *Pitta guajana*
■ *Ramphastos brevis*
□ *Picumnus olivaceus*

Fig. 98. Rufous-tailed Hummingbird x Tawny-bellied Hermit, Shy Albatross, Lesser Frigatebird, Common Loon, Swainson's Hawk, Long-whiskered Owlet, Large-tailed Nightjar, African Grass-Owl, Red-footed Falcon, White-throated Nightjar

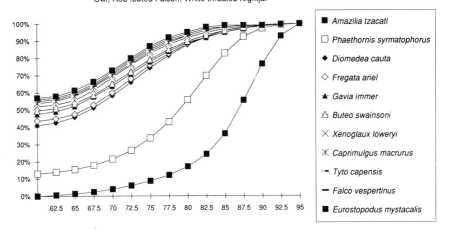

■ *Amazilia tzacatl*
□ *Phaethornis syrmatophorus*
◆ *Diomedea cauta*
◇ *Fregata ariel*
▲ *Gavia immer*
△ *Buteo swainsoni*
✕ *Xenoglaux loweryi*
✖ *Caprimulgus macrurus*
⊸ *Tyto capensis*
— *Falco vespertinus*
■ *Eurostopodus mystacalis*

734

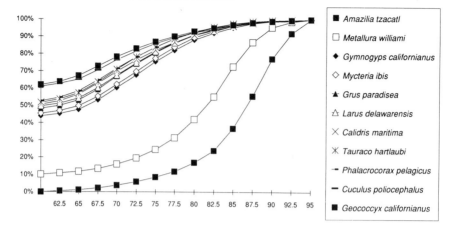

Fig. 99. Rufous-tailed Hummingbird x Viridian Metaltail, California Condor, Yellow-billed Stork, Blue Crane, Ring-billed Gull, Purple Sandpiper, Hartlaub's Turaco, Pelagic Cormorant, Lesser Cuckoo, Greater Roadrunner

- ■ *Amazilia tzacatl*
- □ *Metallura williami*
- ◆ *Gymnogyps californianus*
- ◇ *Mycteria ibis*
- ▲ *Grus paradisea*
- △ *Larus delawarensis*
- ✕ *Calidris maritima*
- ✳ *Tauraco hartlaubi*
- ⌐ *Phalacrocorax pelagicus*
- ▬ *Cuculus poliocephalus*
- ■ *Geococcyx californianus*

Fig. 100. Purple-crested Turaco x Spotted Eagle-Owl, Eastern Screech-Owl, Whip-poor-will, Australian Owlet-Nightjar, African Olive Pigeon, Vinaceous Dove, Senegal Parrot, Orange-chinned Parakeet, Common Cuckoo, Green Broadbill, Northern Mockingbird

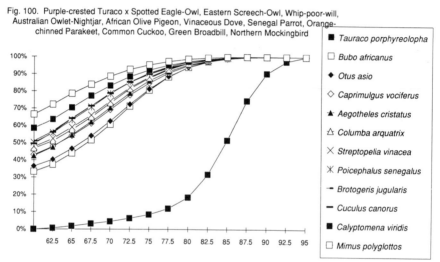

- ■ *Tauraco porphyreolopha*
- □ *Bubo africanus*
- ◆ *Otus asio*
- ◇ *Caprimulgus vociferus*
- ▲ *Aegotheles cristatus*
- △ *Columba arquatrix*
- ✕ *Streptopelia vinacea*
- ✳ *Poicephalus senegalus*
- ⌐ *Brotogeris jugularis*
- ▬ *Cuculus canorus*
- ■ *Calyptomena viridis*
- □ *Mimus polyglottos*

Fig. 101. Purple-crested Turaco x Lilac-breasted Roller, Brown Jacamar, European Bee-eater, Trumpeter Hornbill, Scaly-throated Honeyguide, Crimson-rumped Toucanet, Grey Woodpecker, Black-collared Barbet

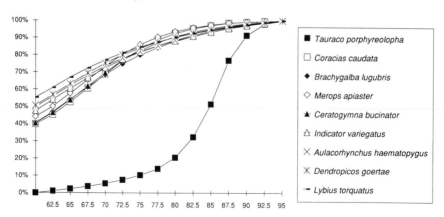

- ■ *Tauraco porphyreolopha*
- □ *Coracias caudata*
- ◆ *Brachygalba lugubris*
- ◇ *Merops apiaster*
- ▲ *Ceratogymna bucinator*
- △ *Indicator variegatus*
- ✕ *Aulacorhynchus haematopygus*
- ✳ *Dendropicos goertae*
- ⌐ *Lybius torquatus*

Fig. 102. Great Grey Owl x Barred Owl, Crested Owl, Buffy Fish-Owl, Snowy Owl, Great Horned Owl, Short-eared Owl, Andean Pygmy-Owl, Burrowing Owl, African Grass-Owl, Barn Owl

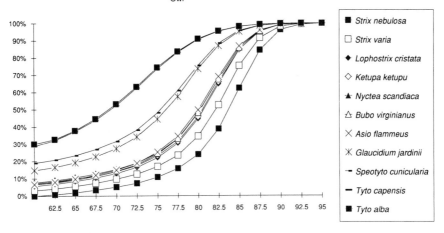

Fig. 103. Great Grey Owl x Mottled Owl, Barn Owl, Knysna Turaco, Pauraque, Oilbird, Marbled Frogmouth, Spotted Nightjar, Common Poorwill, Australian Owlet-Nightjar

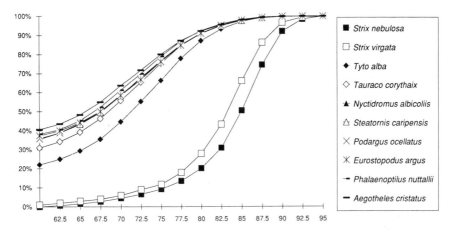

Fig. 104. Australian Owlet-Nightjar x Common Potoo, Marbled Frogmouth, White-throated Nightjar, Oilbird, Large-tailed Nightjar, Pauraque, Common Poorwill, Lesser Nighthawk, Javan Frogmouth

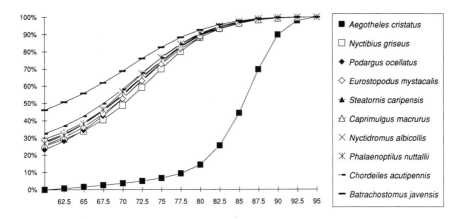

Fig. 105. Tawny Frogmouth x Marbled Frogmouth, Javan Frogmouth, Common Potoo, Spotted Nightjar, Pauraque, Oilbird, European Nightjar, Purple-crested Turaco, Australian Owlet-Nightjar

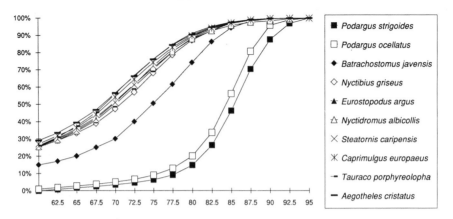

- ■ *Podargus strigoides*
- □ *Podargus ocellatus*
- ◆ *Batrachostomus javensis*
- ◇ *Nyctibius griseus*
- ▲ *Eurostopodus argus*
- △ *Nyctidromus albicollis*
- ✕ *Steatornis caripensis*
- ✳ *Caprimulgus europaeus*
- ⌐ *Tauraco porphyreolopha*
- — *Aegotheles cristatus*

Fig. 106. Oilbird x Common Potoo, Pauraque, European Nightjar, Lesser Nighthawk, Tawny Frogmouth, Burrowing Owl, Australian Owlet-Nightjar, Little Swift, Rock Pigeon, Pallid Cuckoo, Song Sparrow

- ■ *Steatornis caripensis*
- □ *Nyctibius griseus*
- ◆ *Nyctidromus albicollis*
- ◇ *Caprimulgus europaeus*
- ▲ *Chordeiles acutipennis*
- △ *Podargus strigoides*
- ✕ *Speotyto cunicularia*
- ✳ *Aegotheles cristatus*
- ⌐ *Apus affinis*
- — *Columba livia*
- ■ *Cuculus pallidus*
- □ *Melospiza melodia*

Fig. 107. Common Nighthawk x Lesser Nighthawk, Pauraque, European Nightjar, Common Potoo, Barn Owl, Oilbird, Hartlaub's Turaco, Burrowing Owl, Tawny Frogmouth, Australian Owlet-Nightjar, Banded Imperial-Pigeon, Little Swift

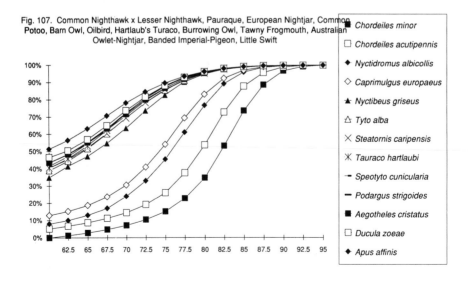

- ■ *Chordeiles minor*
- □ *Chordeiles acutipennis*
- ◆ *Nyctidromus albicollis*
- ◇ *Caprimulgus europaeus*
- ▲ *Nyctibeus griseus*
- △ *Tyto alba*
- ✕ *Steatornis caripensis*
- ✳ *Tauraco hartlaubi*
- ⌐ *Speotyto cunicularia*
- — *Podargus strigoides*
- ■ *Aegotheles cristatus*
- □ *Ducula zoeae*
- ◆ *Apus affinis*

Fig.108. Whip-poor-will x Chuck-will's-widow, Pauraque, White-tailed Nightjar, European
Nightjar, Common Nighthawk, Square-tailed Nightjar, Spotted Nightjar, Common Potoo, Oilbird,
Tawny Frogmouth

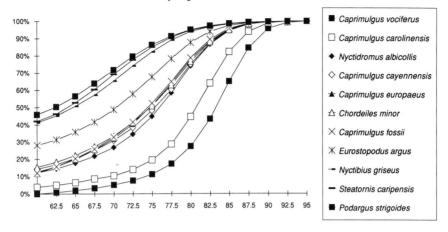

Fig. 109. Whip-poor-will x Chuck-will's-widow, Spotted Nightjar, Crested Owl, Great Grey Owl,
Great Horned Owl, Barn Owl, Common Potoo, Oilbird, Tawny Frogmouth, Javan Frogmouth

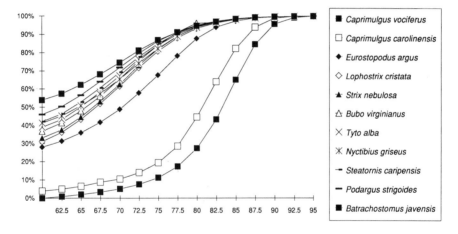

Fig. 110. Mourning Dove x Ring-necked Dove, White-headed Pigeon, Squatter Pigeon, New
Zealand Pigeon, Wompoo Fruit-Dove, White-tailed Lapwing, Spotted Sandgrouse, Black-faced
Sandgrouse, Common Snipe, Grey-breasted Seedsnipe

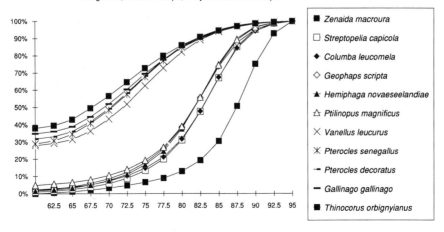

738

Fig. 111. Mourning Dove x European Turtle-Dove, Rock Pigeon, Africań Scops-Owl, Common Nighthawk, Andean Pygmy-Owl, Lesser Treeswift, Little Swift, Speckled Mousebird, White-whiskered Hermit

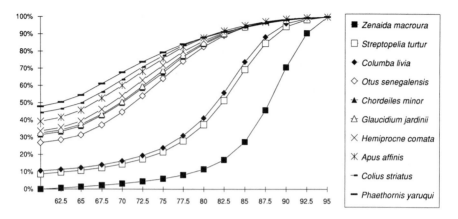

Fig. 112. Sunbittern x Blue Crane, Limpkin, Red-legged Seriema, Sungrebe, Black Bustard, Grey-winged Trumpeter, Takahe, Plains-wanderer, Common Buttonquail

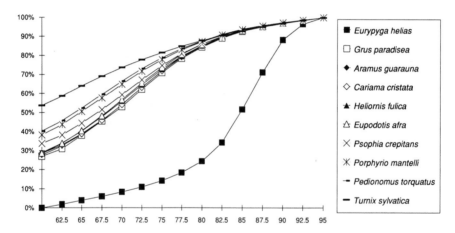

Fig. 113. Karroo Bustard x Black Bustard, Black-bellied Bustard, Kori Bustard, Blue Crane, Grey Crowned-Crane, Limpkin, Sungrebe, Grey-winged Trumpeter, Sunbittern, White-breasted Waterhen, Red-knobbed Coot

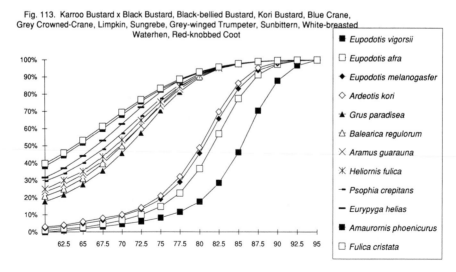

Fig. 114. Karroo Bustard x Yellow-billed Stork, Common Loon, Cape Gannet, Blue Crane, Great Blue Heron, Red-billed Tropicbird, Western Grebe, Double-crested Cormorant, Sunbittern, Red-knobbed Coot

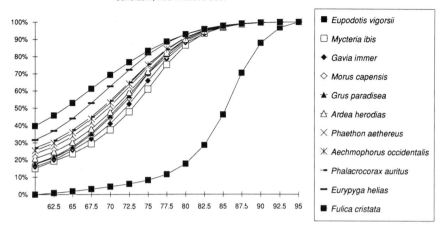

- ■ *Eupodotis vigorsii*
- □ *Mycteria ibis*
- ◆ *Gavia immer*
- ◇ *Morus capensis*
- ▲ *Grus paradisea*
- △ *Ardea herodias*
- ✕ *Phaethon aethereus*
- ✳ *Aechmophorus occidentalis*
- ▬ *Phalacrocorax auritus*
- ▬ *Eurypyga helias*
- ■ *Fulica cristata*

Fig. 115. Red-crested Bustard x Kori Bustard, Jackass Penguin, Common Loon, Limpkin, Blue Crane, Red-legged Seriema, Sungrebe, Little Grebe, Grey-winged Trumpeter, Sunbittern, Plains-wanderer

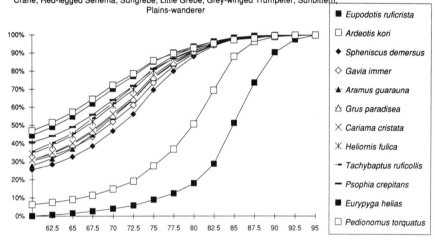

- ■ *Eupodotis ruficrista*
- □ *Ardeotis kori*
- ◆ *Spheniscus demersus*
- ◇ *Gavia immer*
- ▲ *Aramus guarauna*
- △ *Grus paradisea*
- ✕ *Cariama cristata*
- ✳ *Heliornis fulica*
- ▬ *Tachybaptus ruficollis*
- ▬ *Psophia crepitans*
- ■ *Eurypyga helias*
- □ *Pedionomus torquatus*

Fig. 116. Sandhill Crane x Blue Crane, Limpkin, Sungrebe, Grey-winged Trumpeter, Red-legged Seriema, Kori Bustard, Clapper Rail, Sunbittern, Plains-wanderer, Kagu, Common Buttonquail

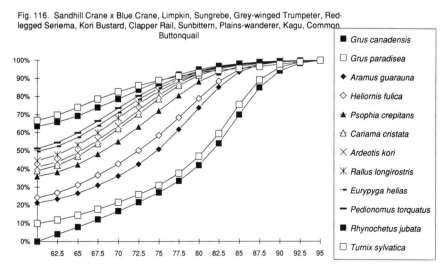

- ■ *Grus canadensis*
- □ *Grus paradisea*
- ◆ *Aramus guarauna*
- ◇ *Heliornis fulica*
- ▲ *Psophia crepitans*
- △ *Cariama cristata*
- ✕ *Ardeotis kori*
- ✳ *Rallus longirostris*
- ▬ *Eurypyga helias*
- ▬ *Pedionomus torquatus*
- ■ *Rhynochetus jubata*
- □ *Turnix sylvatica*

Fig. 117. Limpkin x Sungrebe, Brolga, Sandhill Crane, Grey-winged Trumpeter, Red-legged Seriema, Kori Bustard, Clapper Rail, Sunbittern, Wattled Jacana

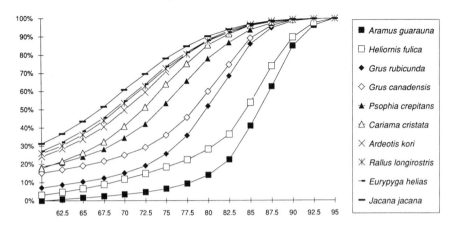

Fig. 118. Limpkin x Brolga, Grey-headed Albatross, Royal Albatross, Shy Albatross, Manx Shearwater, Sacred Ibis, Black-capped Petrel, Iceland Gull, Kori Bustard, Baillon's Crake, Plains-wanderer

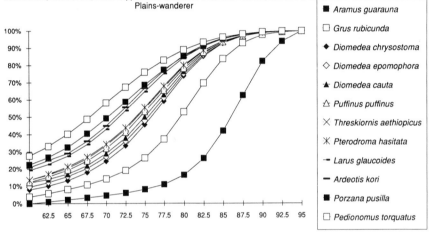

Fig. 119. Sungrebe x Limpkin, Brolga, Black Crowned-Crane, Grey-winged Trumpeter, Clapper Rail, Red-crested Bustard, Common Snipe, Plains-wanderer, Rufous-bellied Seedsnipe, Comb-crested Jacana

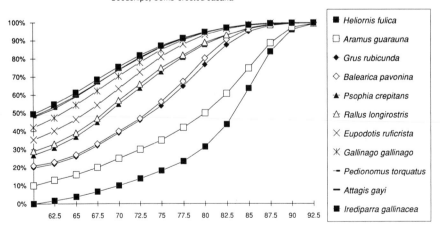

Fig. 120. Grey-winged Trumpeter x Brolga, Limpkin, Sungrebe, Red-legged Seriema, Black Bustard, White-breasted Waterhen, Sunbittern, Greater Painted-snipe, Plains-wanderer, Common Buttonquail

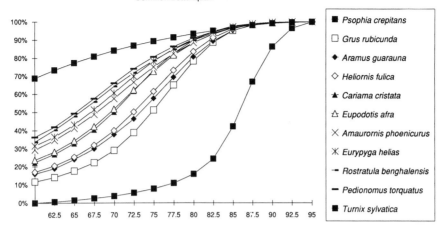

Legend (Fig. 120):
- ■ Psophia crepitans
- □ Grus rubicunda
- ◆ Aramus guarauna
- ◇ Heliornis fulica
- ▲ Cariama cristata
- △ Eupodotis afra
- ✕ Amaurornis phoenicurus
- � Eurypyga helias
- ➙ Rostratula benghalensis
- ━ Pedionomus torquatus
- ■ Turnix sylvatica

Fig. 121. Red-legged Seriema x Sarus Crane, Grey Crowned-Crane, Limpkin, Karroo Bustard, Sungrebe, Grey-winged Trumpeter, Sunbittern, Plains-wanderer, Common Moorhen, Common Buttonquail

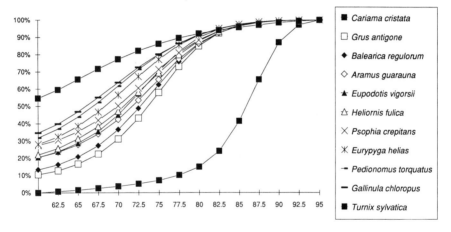

Legend (Fig. 121):
- ■ Cariama cristata
- □ Grus antigone
- ◆ Balearica regulorum
- ◇ Aramus guarauna
- ▲ Eupodotis vigorsii
- △ Heliornis fulica
- ✕ Psophia crepitans
- ✳ Eurypyga helias
- ➙ Pedionomus torquatus
- ━ Gallinula chloropus
- ■ Turnix sylvatica

Fig. 122. Purple Swamphen x Takahe, Azure Gallinule, Baillon's Crake, Watercock, American Coot, Plains-wanderer, Horned Screamer, Black Curassow, Wattled Brush-turkey, Helmeted Guineafowl

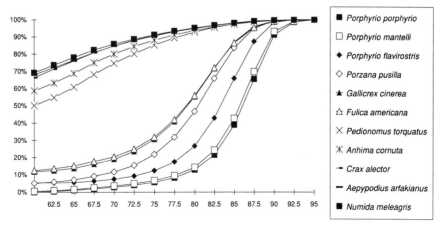

Legend (Fig. 122):
- ■ Porphyrio porphyrio
- □ Porphyrio mantelli
- ◆ Porphyrio flavirostris
- ◇ Porzana pusilla
- ▲ Gallicrex cinerea
- △ Fulica americana
- ✕ Pedionomus torquatus
- ✳ Anhima cornuta
- ➙ Crax alector
- ━ Aepypodius arfakianus
- ■ Numida meleagris

Fig. 123. Double-banded Sandgrouse x Black-faced Sandgrouse, Spotted Sandgrouse, Crab
Plover, Black-faced Sheathbill, Ruddy Quail-Dove, Large Green-Pigeon, Mourning Dove, White-
breasted Waterhen, Paradise Shelduck, Helmeted Guineafowl

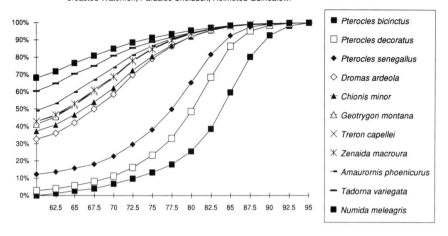

Fig. 124. Black-faced Sandgrouse x Double-banded Sandgrouse, Jackass Penguin, Turkey
Vulture, Yellow-billed Stork, Red-backed Hawk, Black-winged Stilt, Grey Plover, Herring Gull,
Hartlaub's Turaco, New Zealand Pigeon, Pallid Cuckoo

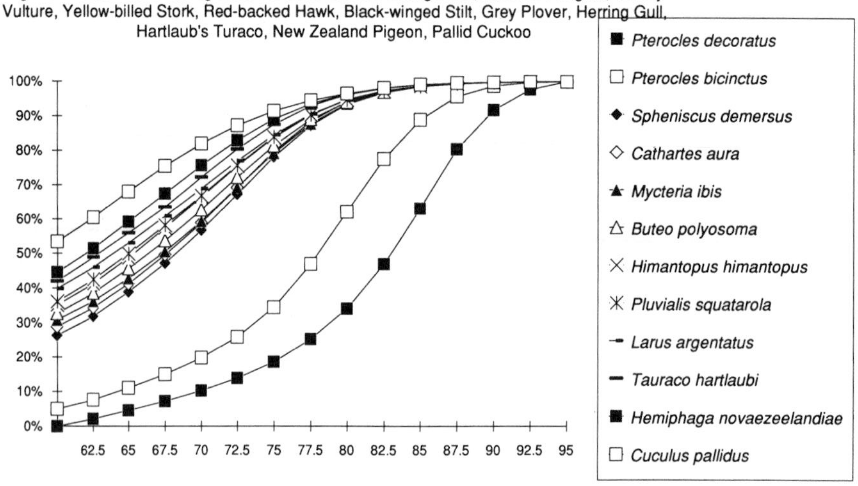

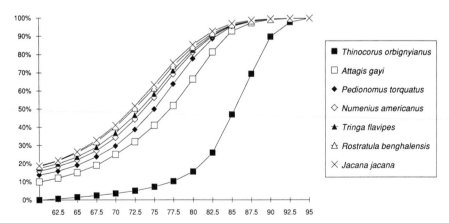

Fig. 125. Grey-breasted Seedsnipe x Rufous-bellied Seedsnipe, Plains-wanderer, Long-billed
Curlew, Lesser Yellowlegs, Greater Painted-snipe, Wattled Jacana

Fig. 126. Plains-wanderer x Grey-breasted Seedsnipe, Rufous-bellied Seedsnipe, Upland Sandpiper, Marbled Godwit, Greater Painted-snipe, Comb-crested Jacana

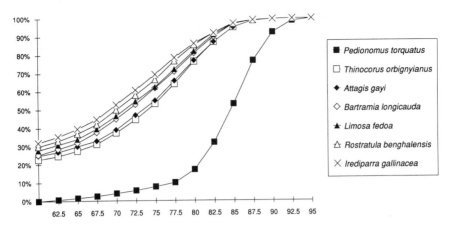

■ Pedionomus torquatus

□ Thinocorus orbignyianus

◆ Attagis gayi

◇ Bartramia longicauda

▲ Limosa fedoa

△ Rostratula benghalensis

✕ Irediparra gallinacea

Fig. 127. Least Sandpiper x Giant Snipe, Water Thick-knee, Crab Plover, Wattled Jacana, Greater Painted-snipe, Least Seedsnipe, Plains-wanderer, American Avocet, Australian Pratincole, Black-faced Sheathbill

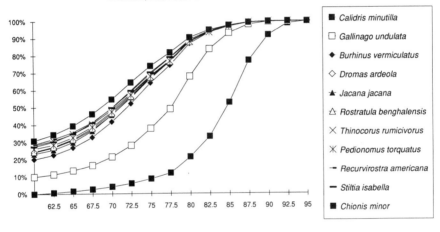

■ Calidris minutilla

□ Gallinago undulata

◆ Burhinus vermiculatus

◇ Dromas ardeola

▲ Jacana jacana

△ Rostratula benghalensis

✕ Thinocorus rumicivorus

✖ Pedionomus torquatus

— Recurvirostra americana

— Stiltia isabella

■ Chionis minor

Fig. 128. Greater Painted-snipe x Wattled Jacana, Marbled Godwit, Wood Sandpiper, Plains-wanderer, Least Seedsnipe, Pintail Snipe

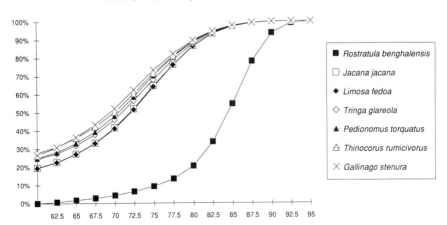

■ Rostratula benghalensis

□ Jacana jacana

◆ Limosa fedoa

◇ Tringa glareola

▲ Pedionomus torquatus

△ Thinocorus rumicivorus

✕ Gallinago stenura

744

Fig. 129. Comb-crested Jacana x African Jacana, Wattled Jacana, Marbled Godwit, Greater
Painted-Snipe, Short-billed Dowitcher, Least Seedsnipe, Upland Sandpiper, Lesser Yellowlegs,
Plains-wanderer, American Woodcock

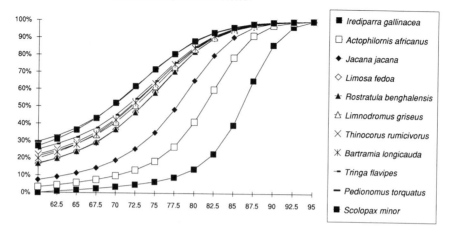

Fig. 130. Variable Oystercatcher x Black Oystercatcher, American Avocet, Banded Stilt, Black-
winged Stilt, Puna Plover, Southern Lapwing, Peruvian Thick-knee, Double-banded Courser,
Australian Pratincole, Grey-breasted Seedsnipe

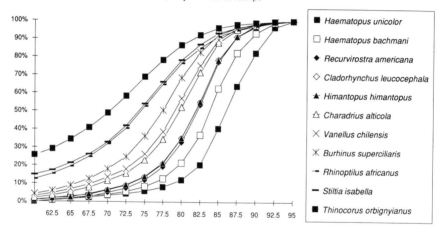

Fig. 131. Banded Stilt x White-headed Stilt, Variable Oystercatcher, Black Oystercatcher,
Crowned Lapwing, Eurasian Dotterel, Crab Plover, Water Thick-knee, Long-billed Curlew,
Australian Pratincole, Oriental Pratincole

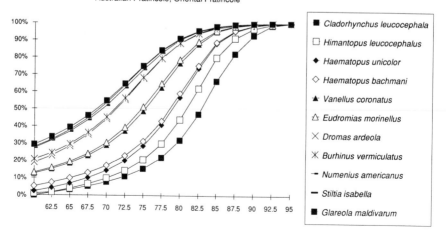

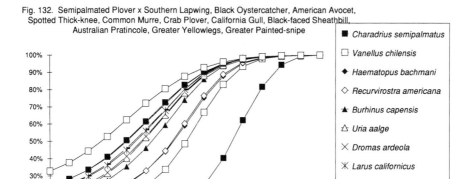

Fig. 132. Semipalmated Plover x Southern Lapwing, Black Oystercatcher, American Avocet, Spotted Thick-knee, Common Murre, Crab Plover, California Gull, Black-faced Sheathbill, Australian Pratincole, Greater Yellowlegs, Greater Painted-snipe

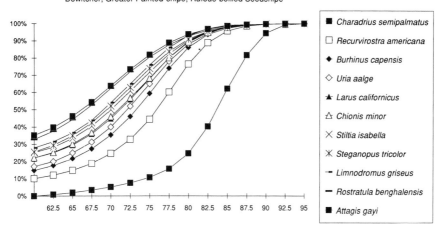

Fig. 133. Semipalmated Plover x American Avocet, Spotted Thick-knee, Common Murre, California Gull, Black-faced Sheathbill, Australian Pratincole, Wilson's Phalarope, Short-billed Dowitcher, Greater Painted-snipe, Rufous-bellied Seedsnipe

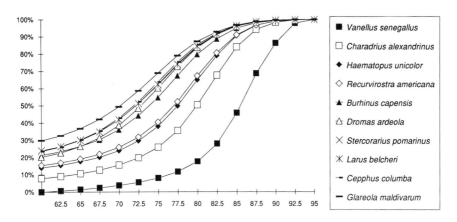

Fig. 134. Wattled Lapwing x Snowy Plover, Variable Oystercatcher, American Avocet, Spotted Thick-knee, Crab Plover, Pomarine Jaeger, Band-tailed Gull, Pigeon Guillemot, Oriental Pratincole

Fig. 135. Wattled Lapwing x White-tailed Lapwing, Puna Plover, Banded Stilt, Black-winged
Stilt, American Avocet, Crab Plover, Black-faced Sheathbill

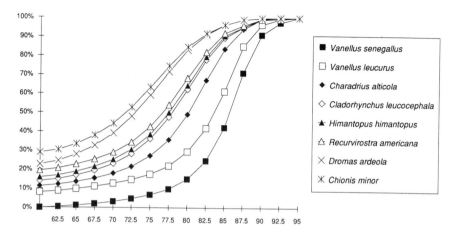

- ■ *Vanellus senegallus*
- □ *Vanellus leucurus*
- ◆ *Charadrius alticola*
- ◇ *Cladorhynchus leucocephala*
- ▲ *Himantopus himantopus*
- △ *Recurvirostra americana*
- ✕ *Dromas ardeola*
- ✳ *Chionis minor*

Fig. 136. Crab Plover x Oriental Pratincole, Great Black-backed Gull, Pigeon Guillemot, Red-
necked Avocet, Peruvian Thick-knee, Black Oystercatcher, Banded Stilt, Semipalmated Plover,
Black-faced Sheathbill

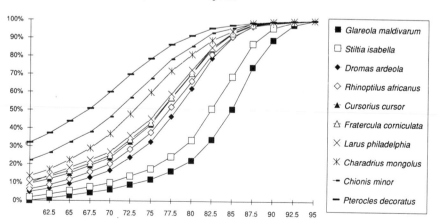

- ■ *Dromas ardeola*
- □ *Glareola maldivarum*
- ◆ *Larus marinus*
- ◇ *Cepphus columba*
- ▲ *Recurvirostra novaehollandiae*
- △ *Burhinus superciliaris*
- ✕ *Haematopus bachmani*
- ✳ *Cladorhynchus leucocephala*
- – *Charadrius semipalmatus*
- – *Chionis minor*

Fig. 137. Oriental Pratincole x Australian Pratincole, Crab Plover, Double-banded Courser,
Cream-colored Courser, Horned Puffin, Bonaparte's Gull, Mongolian Plover, Black-faced
Sheathbill, Black-faced Sandgrouse

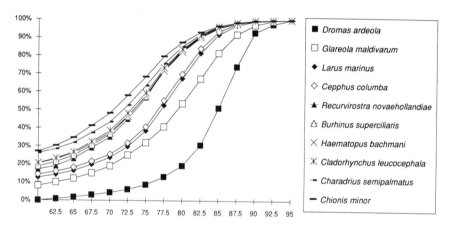

- ■ *Glareola maldivarum*
- □ *Stiltia isabella*
- ◆ *Dromas ardeola*
- ◇ *Rhinoptilus africanus*
- ▲ *Cursorius cursor*
- △ *Fratercula corniculata*
- ✕ *Larus philadelphia*
- ✳ *Charadrius mongolus*
- – *Chionis minor*
- – *Pterocles decoratus*

Fig. 138. Common Tern x Black Tern, Herring Gull, California Gull, Pomarine Jaeger, Horned Puffin, Crab Plover, Spotted Thick-knee, American Avocet, Semipalmated Plover, Semipalmated Sandpiper, Black-faced Sheathbill

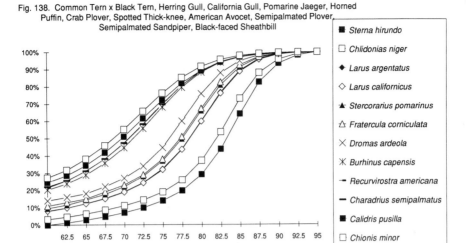

- ■ *Sterna hirundo*
- □ *Chlidonias niger*
- ◆ *Larus argentatus*
- ◇ *Larus californicus*
- ▲ *Stercorarius pomarinus*
- △ *Fratercula corniculata*
- ✕ *Dromas ardeola*
- ✳ *Burhinus capensis*
- ⌐ *Recurvirostra americana*
- — *Charadrius semipalmatus*
- ■ *Calidris pusilla*
- □ *Chionis minor*

Fig. 139. Red-backed Hawk x Red-tailed Hawk, Shikra, Osprey, Secretary-bird, Turkey Vulture, Black Vulture, Great Horned Owl, Barn Owl, American Kestrel, Chestnut-fronted Macaw

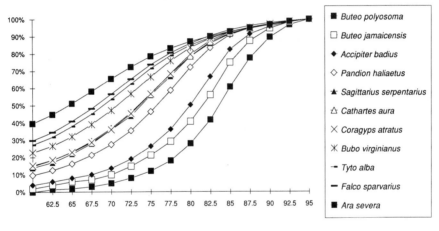

- ■ *Buteo polyosoma*
- □ *Buteo jamaicensis*
- ◆ *Accipiter badius*
- ◇ *Pandion haliaetus*
- ▲ *Sagittarius serpentarius*
- △ *Cathartes aura*
- ✕ *Coragyps atratus*
- ✳ *Bubo virginianus*
- ⌐ *Tyto alba*
- — *Falco sparvarius*
- ■ *Ara severa*

Fig. 140. Red-backed Hawk x Red-tailed Hawk, Shikra, Osprey, Secretary-bird, Turkey Vulture, Sooty Shearwater, Grey Crowned-Crane, Great Horned Owl, Black-crowned Night-Heron, Herring Gull, American Kestrel, Chestnut-fronted Macaw

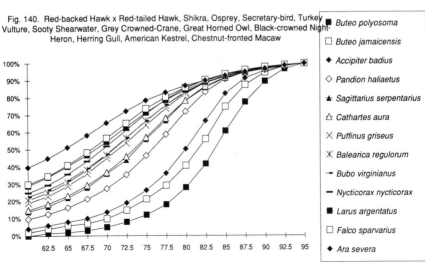

- ■ *Buteo polyosoma*
- □ *Buteo jamaicensis*
- ◆ *Accipiter badius*
- ◇ *Pandion haliaetus*
- ▲ *Sagittarius serpentarius*
- △ *Cathartes aura*
- ✕ *Puffinus griseus*
- ✳ *Balearica regulorum*
- ⌐ *Bubo virginianus*
- — *Nycticorax nycticorax*
- ■ *Larus argentatus*
- □ *Falco sparvarius*
- ◆ *Ara severa*

Fig. 141. Northern Harrier x Chestnut-flanked Sparrowhawk, White-backed Vulture, Egyptian Vulture, Lammergeier, Black Vulture, King Vulture, Laughing Falcon, Collared Forest-Falcon, Yellow-headed Caracara, Collared Falconet, Merlin

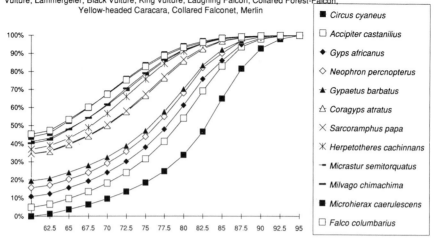

- ■ *Circus cyaneus*
- □ *Accipiter castanilius*
- ◆ *Gyps africanus*
- ◇ *Neophron percnopterus*
- ▲ *Gypaetus barbatus*
- △ *Coragyps atratus*
- ✕ *Sarcoramphus papa*
- ✳ *Herpetotheres cachinnans*
- ⇀ *Micrastur semitorquatus*
- — *Milvago chimachima*
- ■ *Microhierax caerulescens*
- □ *Falco columbarius*

Fig. 142. Northern Harrier x Lammergeier, Andean Condor, Morepork, Spotted Eagle-Owl, African Grass-Owl, Brown Falcon, Cockatiel, Senegal Parrot, Mealy Parrot

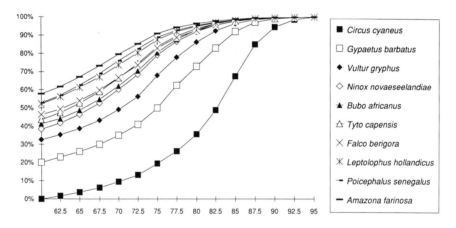

- ■ *Circus cyaneus*
- □ *Gypaetus barbatus*
- ◆ *Vultur gryphus*
- ◇ *Ninox novaeseelandiae*
- ▲ *Bubo africanus*
- △ *Tyto capensis*
- ✕ *Falco berigora*
- ✳ *Leptolophus hollandicus*
- ⇀ *Poicephalus senegalus*
- — *Amazona farinosa*

Fig. 143. Lammergeier x Lappet-faced Vulture, Red-headed Vulture, Crested Serpent-Eagle, Common Buzzard, Andean Condor, King Vulture, Yellow-billed Stork, Secretary-bird, Marabou Stork, Red-throated Caracara, American Kestrel

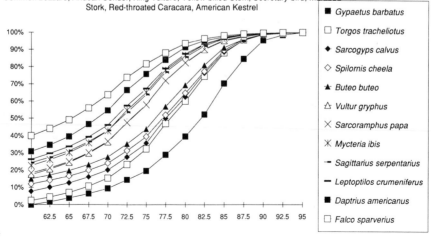

- ■ *Gypaetus barbatus*
- □ *Torgos tracheliotus*
- ◆ *Sarcogyps calvus*
- ◇ *Spilornis cheela*
- ▲ *Buteo buteo*
- △ *Vultur gryphus*
- ✕ *Sarcoramphus papa*
- ✳ *Mycteria ibis*
- ⇀ *Sagittarius serpentarius*
- — *Leptoptilos crumeniferus*
- ■ *Daptrius americanus*
- □ *Falco sparverius*

Fig. 144. American Kestrel x New Zealand Falcon, Collared Falconet, Red-throated Caracara, Laughing Falcon, Collared Forest-Falcon, Andean Condor, Lammergeier, Osprey, Verreaux's Eagle, Pearl Kite

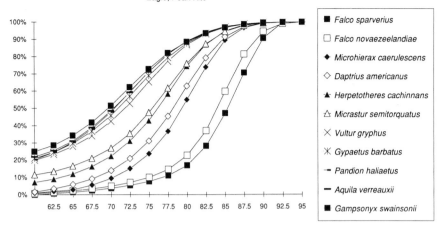

Fig. 145. Red-throated Caracara x Yellow-headed Caracara, Mountain Caracara, Collared Falconet, Laughing Falcon, Red-footed Falcon, Collared Forest-Falcon, White-backed Vulture, Short-toed Snake-Eagle, Wedge-tailed Eagle, Osprey

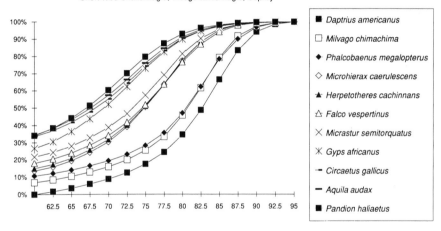

Fig. 146. Western Grebe x Horned Grebe, Jackass Penguin, Red-throated Loon, Laysan Albatross, Sharp-tailed Ibis, South American Tern, Great Blue Heron, European Nightjar

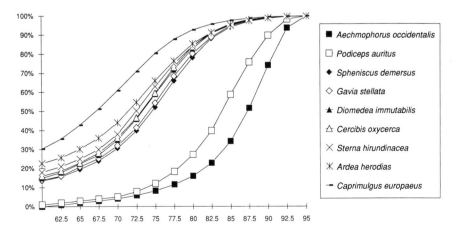

750

Fig. 147. Western Grebe x Horned Grebe, Jackass Penguin, Yellow-billed Stork, Turkey Vulture, Sooty Shearwater, American White Pelican, Red-backed Hawk, Red-throated Loon, Brolga, Gadwall

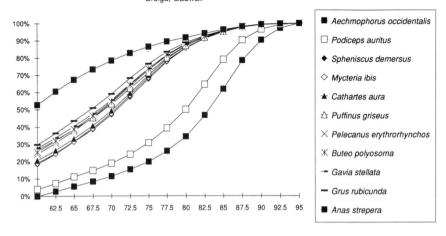

- ■ *Aechmophorus occidentalis*
- □ *Podiceps auritus*
- ◆ *Spheniscus demersus*
- ◇ *Mycteria ibis*
- ▲ *Cathartes aura*
- △ *Puffinus griseus*
- ✕ *Pelecanus erythrorhynchos*
- ✖ *Buteo polyosoma*
- ⌐ *Gavia stellata*
- ▬ *Grus rubicunda*
- ■ *Anas strepera*

Fig. 148. Western Grebe x Jackass Penguin, Yellow-billed Stork, Turkey Vulture, Leach's Storm-Petrel, Cape Gannet, Common Loon, Red-billed Tropicbird, Great Blue Heron, Herring Gull, Red-knobbed Coot, Chilean Tinamou

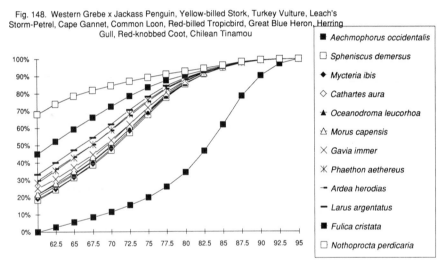

- ■ *Aechmophorus occidentalis*
- □ *Spheniscus demersus*
- ◆ *Mycteria ibis*
- ◇ *Cathartes aura*
- ▲ *Oceanodroma leucorhoa*
- △ *Morus capensis*
- ✕ *Gavia immer*
- ✖ *Phaethon aethereus*
- ⌐ *Ardea herodias*
- ▬ *Larus argentatus*
- ■ *Fulica cristata*
- □ *Nothoprocta perdicaria*

Fig. 149. Red-billed Tropicbird x Royal Albatross, Great Frigatebird, Pink-backed Pelican, Common Loon, Cape Gannet, Brown Booby, Snowy Egret, African Darter, Bar-tailed Godwit, Pelagic Cormorant, Western Grebe

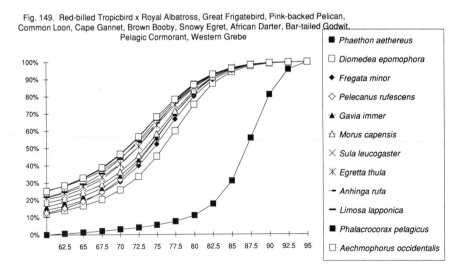

- ■ *Phaethon aethereus*
- □ *Diomedea epomophora*
- ◆ *Fregata minor*
- ◇ *Pelecanus rufescens*
- ▲ *Gavia immer*
- △ *Morus capensis*
- ✕ *Sula leucogaster*
- ✖ *Egretta thula*
- ⌐ *Anhinga rufa*
- ▬ *Limosa lapponica*
- ■ *Phalacrocorax pelagicus*
- □ *Aechmophorus occidentalis*

Fig. 150. Masked Booby x Cape Gannet, Great Frigatebird, African Darter, White Stork, Double-crested Cormorant, Shoebill, American White Pelican, Red-billed Tropicbird, White-backed Duck

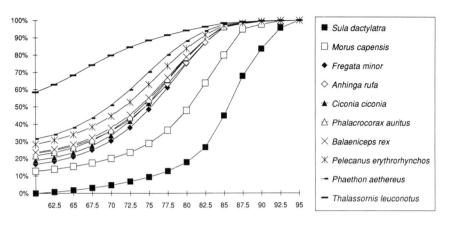

Fig. 151. African Darter x Cape Gannet, Masked Booby, Lesser Frigatebird, Pelagic Cormorant, White Stork, Shoebill, American White Pelican, Red-billed Tropicbird

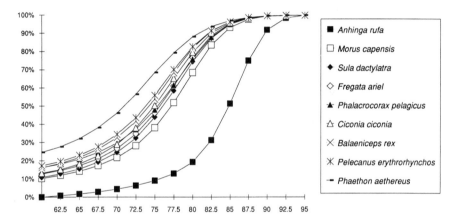

Fig. 152. Double-crested Cormorant x Pelagic Cormorant, Long-tailed Cormorant, Cape Gannet, Blue-footed Booby, Lesser Frigatebird, Red-billed Tropicbird, Royal Albatross, Brown Pelican, Yellow-billed Stork

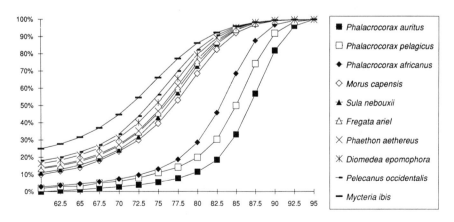

Fig. 153. Double-crested Cormorant x Great Cormorant, Masked Booby, African Darter, Great Frigatebird, Yellow-billed Stork, Sooty Shearwater, Common Loon, Great White Pelican, Great Blue Heron, Red-billed Tropicbird, Western Grebe

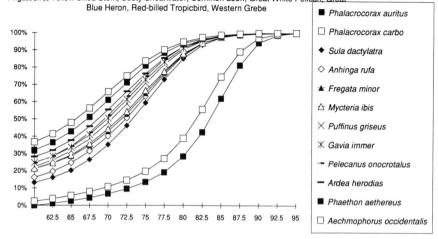

■ *Phalacrocorax auritus*
□ *Phalacrocorax carbo*
◆ *Sula dactylatra*
◇ *Anhinga rufa*
▲ *Fregata minor*
△ *Mycteria ibis*
✕ *Puffinus griseus*
✹ *Gavia immer*
╺ *Pelecanus onocrotalus*
━ *Ardea herodias*
■ *Phaethon aethereus*
□ *Aechmophorus occidentalis*

Fig. 154. Double-crested Cormorant x Great Cormorant, Masked Booby, African Darter, Great Frigatebird, Yellow-billed Stork, Turkey Vulture, American White Pelican, Brolga, Red-billed Tropicbird, Herring Gull, Horned Grebe

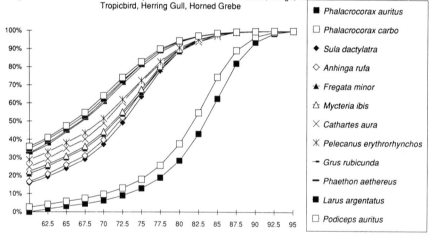

■ *Phalacrocorax auritus*
□ *Phalacrocorax carbo*
◆ *Sula dactylatra*
◇ *Anhinga rufa*
▲ *Fregata minor*
△ *Mycteria ibis*
✕ *Cathartes aura*
✹ *Pelecanus erythrorhynchos*
╺ *Grus rubicunda*
━ *Phaethon aethereus*
■ *Larus argentatus*
□ *Podiceps auritus*

Fig. 155. Great Blue Heron x Great Egret, Jackass Penguin, Glossy Ibis, Great Frigatebird, Turkey Vulture, Sooty Shearwater, Double-crested Cormorant, Brolga, Western Grebe, Herring Gull, Domestic Fowl

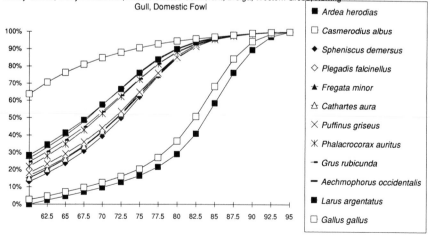

■ *Ardea herodias*
□ *Casmerodius albus*
◆ *Spheniscus demersus*
◇ *Plegadis falcinellus*
▲ *Fregata minor*
△ *Cathartes aura*
✕ *Puffinus griseus*
✹ *Phalacrocorax auritus*
╺ *Grus rubicunda*
━ *Aechmophorus occidentalis*
■ *Larus argentatus*
□ *Gallus gallus*

Fig. 156. Great Blue Heron x Yellow-billed Stork, White Stork, Cape Gannet, Common Loon, American White Pelican, Greater Flamingo, Red-billed Tropicbird, Karroo Bustard, Lesser Yellowlegs, Red-knobbed Coot, Gadwall

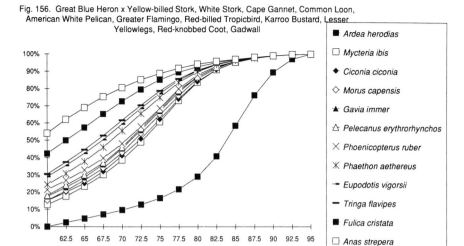

- ■ *Ardea herodias*
- □ *Mycteria ibis*
- ◆ *Ciconia ciconia*
- ◇ *Morus capensis*
- ▲ *Gavia immer*
- △ *Pelecanus erythrorhynchos*
- ✕ *Phoenicopterus ruber*
- ✳ *Phaethon aethereus*
- ⟶ *Eupodotis vigorsii*
- ▬ *Tringa flavipes*
- ■ *Fulica cristata*
- □ *Anas strepera*

Fig. 157. White-backed Night-Heron x Snowy Egret, Wilson's Storm-Petrel, Sooty Shearwater, Red-throated Loon, Common Loon, Horned Grebe, New Zealand Grebe, Mute Swan, Bufflehead, Black Curassow, Natal Francolin

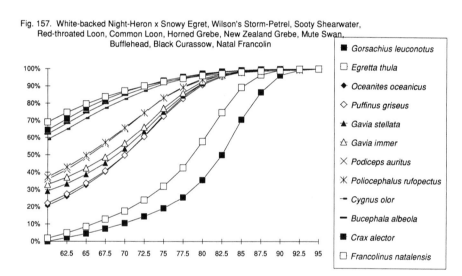

- ■ *Gorsachius leuconotus*
- □ *Egretta thula*
- ◆ *Oceanites oceanicus*
- ◇ *Puffinus griseus*
- ▲ *Gavia stellata*
- △ *Gavia immer*
- ✕ *Podiceps auritus*
- ✳ *Poliocephalus rufopectus*
- ⟶ *Cygnus olor*
- ▬ *Bucephala albeola*
- ■ *Crax alector*
- □ *Francolinus natalensis*

Fig. 158. American Bittern x Cattle Egret, Little Blue Heron, White-backed Night-Heron, Black-crowned Night-Heron, Great Blue Heron, Green Heron, Whistling Heron, Rufescent Tiger-Heron, Glossy Ibis

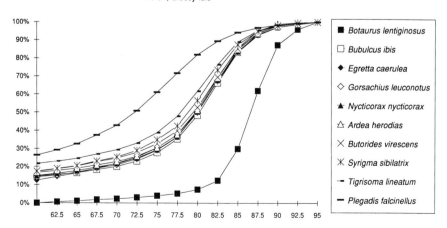

- ■ *Botaurus lentiginosus*
- □ *Bubulcus ibis*
- ◆ *Egretta caerulea*
- ◇ *Gorsachius leuconotus*
- ▲ *Nycticorax nycticorax*
- △ *Ardea herodias*
- ✕ *Butorides virescens*
- ✳ *Syrigma sibilatrix*
- ⟶ *Tigrisoma lineatum*
- ▬ *Plegadis falcinellus*

Fig. 159. Hamerkop x Marabou Stork, Buff-necked Ibis, Slaty Egret, Lesser Flamingo

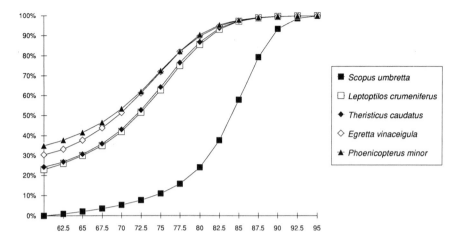

Fig. 160. Greater Flamingo x Lesser Flamingo, Yellow-billed Stork, Marabou Stork, Glossy
Ibis, Black-crowned Night-Heron, Great Egret, American Avocet, California Gull, Magpie
Goose, Northern Screamer, Domestic Fowl

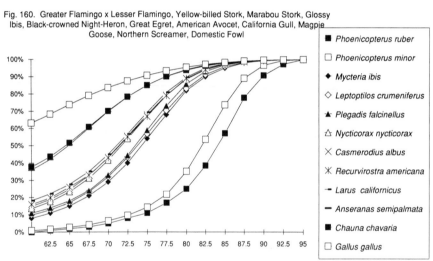

Fig. 161. Lesser Flamingo x Greater Flamingo, Chilean Flamingo, Puna Flamingo, California
Condor, Black Vulture, Black Stork, African Openbill, Sharp-tailed Ibis, Shoebill, American
White Pelican, African Spoonbill

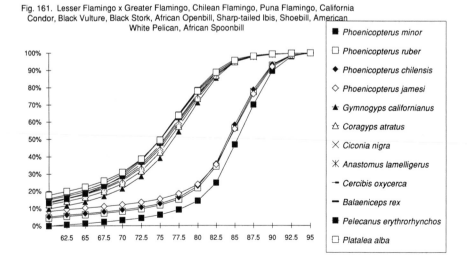

Fig. 162. Chilean Flamingo x Andean Flamingo, Lesser Flamingo, Wood Stork, Sacred Ibis, Black-winged Stilt, American Avocet, Banded Stilt, Little Blue Heron, Yellow-crowned Night-Heron

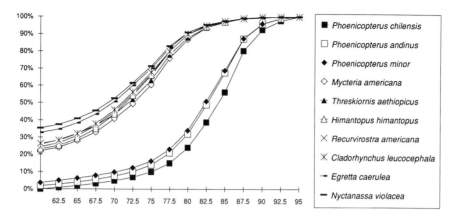

Fig. 163. Andean Flamingo x Puna Flamingo, Lesser Flamingo, Chilean Flamingo, Black Stork, Sacred Ibis, Black-winged Stilt, Banded Stilt, White-headed Stilt, American Avocet, Double-banded Plover

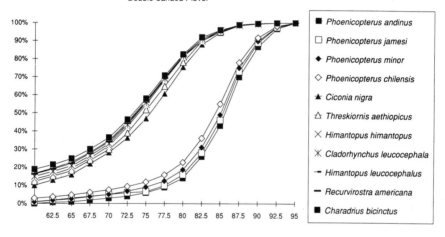

Fig. 164. Straw-necked Ibis x Sacred Ibis, Yellow-billed Spoonbill, Hadada Ibis, Buff-necked Ibis, Shoebill, King Vulture, Marabou Stork, Yellow-billed Stork, American White Pelican, Hamerkop

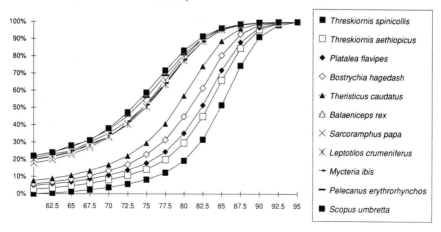

Fig. 165. Glossy Ibis x Straw-necked Ibis, African Spoonbill, Hadada Ibis, Sharp-tailed Ibis, Green Ibis, Black-necked Stork, African Openbill, Chilean Flamingo, Hamerkop, Great Blue Heron

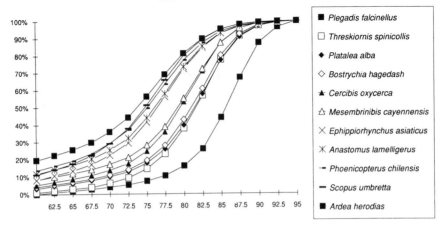

■ Plegadis falcinellus
□ Threskiornis spinicollis
◆ Platalea alba
◇ Bostrychia hagedash
▲ Cercibis oxycerca
△ Mesembrinibis cayennensis
✕ Ephippiorhynchus asiaticus
✕ Anastomus lamelligerus
— Phoenicopterus chilensis
— Scopus umbretta
■ Ardea herodias

Fig. 166. Shoebill x American White Pelican, White Stork, Yellow-billed Stork, Lesser Flamingo

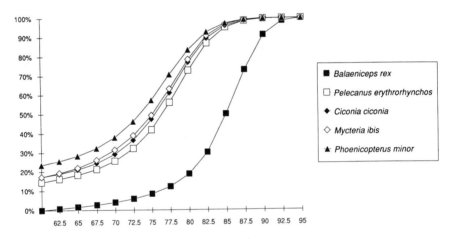

■ Balaeniceps rex
□ Pelecanus erythrorhynchos
◆ Ciconia ciconia
◇ Mycteria ibis
▲ Phoenicopterus minor

Fig. 167. American White Pelican x Shoebill, Black-necked Stork, Great Frigatebird, Cape Gannet, Masked Booby, African Darter, Double-crested Cormorant, Red-billed Tropicbird

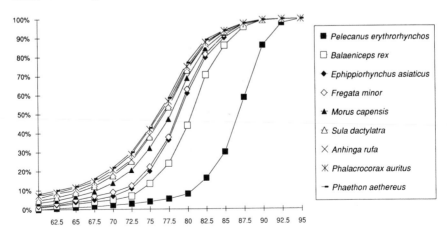

■ Pelecanus erythrorhynchos
□ Balaeniceps rex
◆ Ephippiorhynchus asiaticus
◇ Fregata minor
▲ Morus capensis
△ Sula dactylatra
✕ Anhinga rufa
✕ Phalacrocorax auritus
— Phaethon aethereus

Fig. 168. American White Pelican x Shoebill, Yellow-billed Stork, Cape Petrel, Jackass Penguin, Common Loon, Great Cormorant, Masked Booby, Bar-tailed Godwit, Western Grebe

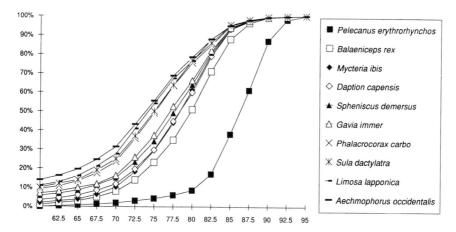

Fig. 169. American White Pelican x Turkey Vulture, Red-backed Hawk, Great Horned Owl, Karroo Bustard, Oilbird, American Kestrel, Rock Pigeon, Red-knobbed Coot, Southern Screamer, Gadwall, Domestic Fowl

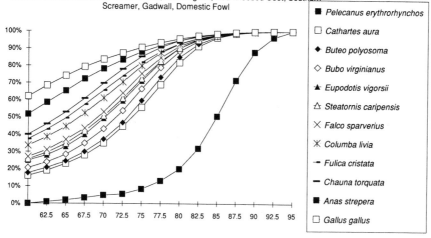

Fig. 170. American White Pelican x Jackass Penguin, Sooty Shearwater, Common Loon, Masked Booby, Brolga, Magnificent Frigatebird, Double-crested Cormorant, Red-billed Tropicbird, Horned Grebe, Greater Yellowlegs

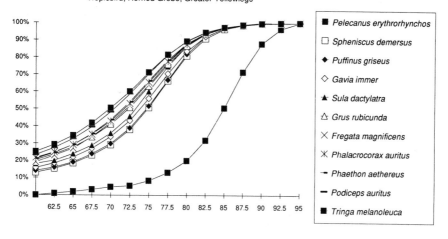

758

Fig. 171. California Condor x Black Vulture, Buller's Albatross, Marabou Stork, Fork-tailed Storm-Petrel, White-backed Vulture, White Stork, Egyptian Vulture, Yellow-headed Caracara

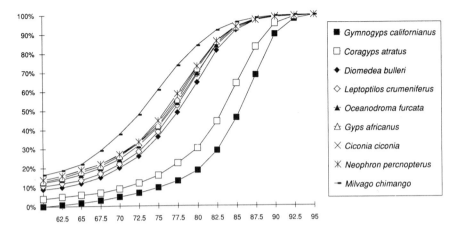

- ■ *Gymnogyps californianus*
- □ *Coragyps atratus*
- ◆ *Diomedea bulleri*
- ◇ *Leptoptilos crumeniferus*
- ▲ *Oceanodroma furcata*
- △ *Gyps africanus*
- ✕ *Ciconia ciconia*
- ✳ *Neophron percnopterus*
- — *Milvago chimango*

Fig. 172. King Vulture x Andean Condor, Black Vulture, Turkey Vulture, Fork-tailed Storm-Petrel, Egyptian Vulture, Marabou Stork, White Stork, Northern Harrier, Red-throated Caracara, Great Egret

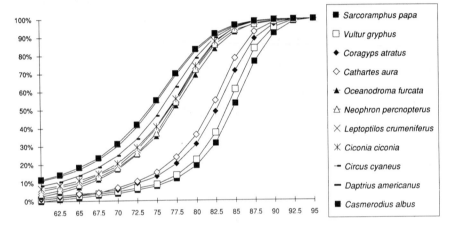

- ■ *Sarcoramphus papa*
- □ *Vultur gryphus*
- ◆ *Coragyps atratus*
- ◇ *Cathartes aura*
- ▲ *Oceanodroma furcata*
- △ *Neophron percnopterus*
- ✕ *Leptoptilos crumeniferus*
- ✳ *Ciconia ciconia*
- — *Circus cyaneus*
- — *Daptrius americanus*
- ■ *Casmerodius albus*

Fig. 173. Turkey Vulture x King Vulture, White Stork, Yellow-billed Stork, Red-headed Vulture, Masked Booby, American White Pelican, Great Blue Heron

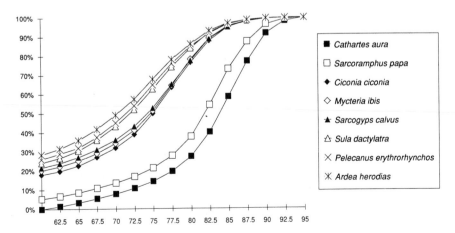

- ■ *Cathartes aura*
- □ *Sarcoramphus papa*
- ◆ *Ciconia ciconia*
- ◇ *Mycteria ibis*
- ▲ *Sarcogyps calvus*
- △ *Sula dactylatra*
- ✕ *Pelecanus erythrorhynchos*
- ✳ *Ardea herodias*

Fig. 174. Yellow-billed Stork x Marabou Stork, Black-necked Stork, Jabiru, Andean Condor, Green Ibis, Shoebill, Yellow-billed Spoonbill, Hadada Ibis, Lesser Flamingo, American White Pelican, Hamerkop

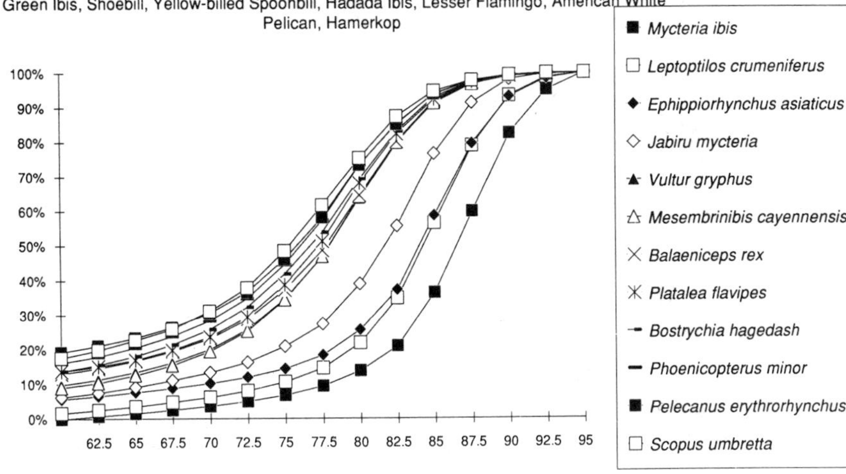
100%
90%
80%
70%
60%
50%
40%
30%
20%
10%
0%
62.5 65 67.5 70 72.5 75 77.5 80 82.5 85 87.5 90 92.5 95
Mycteria ibis
Leptoptilos crumeniferus
Ephippiorhynchus asiaticus
Jabiru mycteria
Vultur gryphus
Mesembrinibis cayennensis
Balaeniceps rex
Platalea flavipes
Bostrychia hagedash
Phoenicopterus minor
Pelecanus erythrorhynchus
Scopus umbretta

Fig. 175. Great Frigatebird x Magnificent Frigatebird, Jackass Penguin, Red-footed Booby, Buff-necked Ibis, Common Loon, Greater Flamingo, Pink-backed Pelican, African Darter, Double-crested Cormorant, Great Blue Heron, White-tailed Tropicbird

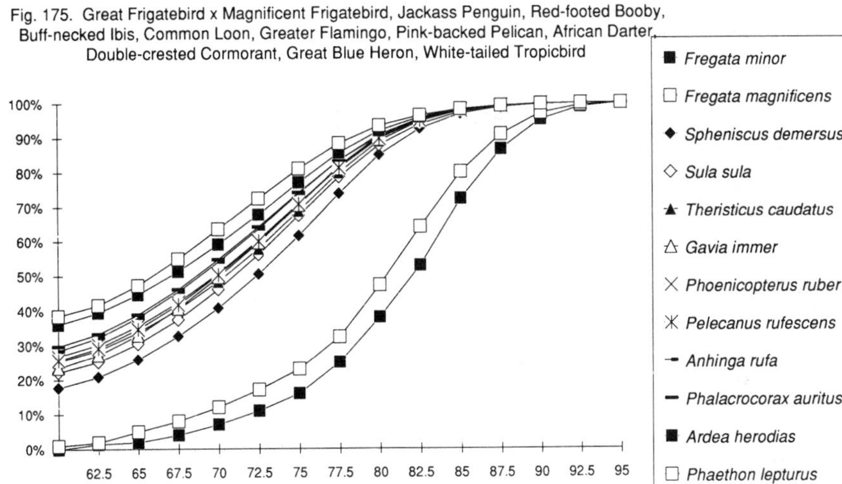
100%
90%
80%
70%
60%
50%
40%
30%
20%
10%
0%
62.5 65 67.5 70 72.5 75 77.5 80 82.5 85 87.5 90 92.5 95
Fregata minor
Fregata magnificens
Spheniscus demersus
Sula sula
Theristicus caudatus
Gavia immer
Phoenicopterus ruber
Pelecanus rufescens
Anhinga rufa
Phalacrocorax auritus
Ardea herodias
Phaethon lepturus

Fig. 176. Magnificent Frigatebird x Royal Albatross, Cape Petrel, Jackass Penguin, White Stork, Sharp-tailed Ibis, Fork-tailed Storm-Petrel, Andean Condor, Common Loon, Common Diving-Petrel, White-faced Heron, Western Grebe

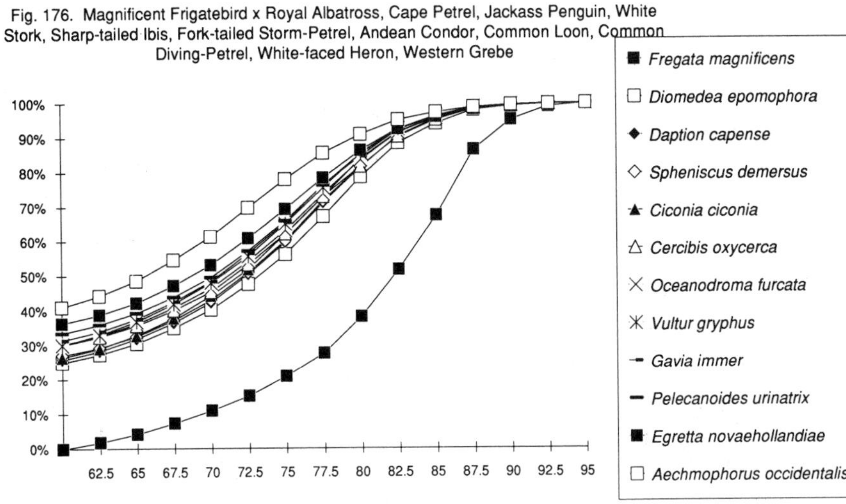
100%
90%
80%
70%
60%
50%
40%
30%
20%
10%
0%
62.5 65 67.5 70 72.5 75 77.5 80 82.5 85 87.5 90 92.5 95
Fregata magnificens
Diomedea epomophora
Daption capense
Spheniscus demersus
Ciconia ciconia
Cercibis oxycerca
Oceanodroma furcata
Vultur gryphus
Gavia immer
Pelecanoides urinatrix
Egretta novaehollandiae
Aechmophorus occidentalis

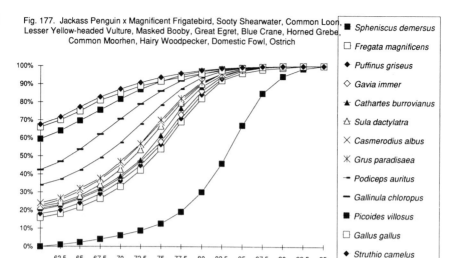

Fig. 177. Jackass Penguin x Magnificent Frigatebird, Sooty Shearwater, Common Loon, Lesser Yellow-headed Vulture, Masked Booby, Great Egret, Blue Crane, Horned Grebe, Common Moorhen, Hairy Woodpecker, Domestic Fowl, Ostrich

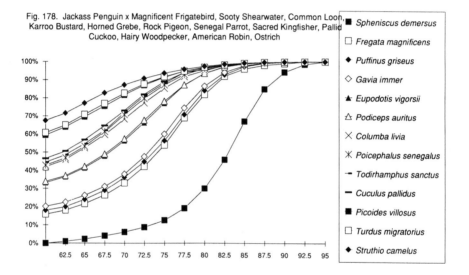

Fig. 178. Jackass Penguin x Magnificent Frigatebird, Sooty Shearwater, Common Loon, Karroo Bustard, Horned Grebe, Rock Pigeon, Senegal Parrot, Sacred Kingfisher, Pallid Cuckoo, Hairy Woodpecker, American Robin, Ostrich

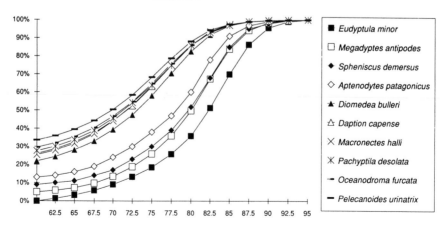

Fig. 179. Little Penguin x Yellow-eyed Penguin, Jackass Penguin, King Penguin, Buller's Albatross, Cape Petrel, Hall's Giant Petrel, Antarctic Prion, Fork-tailed Storm-Petrel, Common Diving-Petrel

Fig. 180. Red-throated Loon x Grey-headed Albatross, Shy Albatross, Adelie Penguin, Jackass Penguin, Western Grebe, New Zealand Grebe

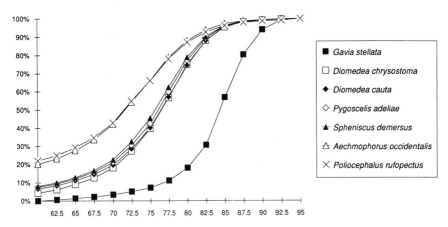

- ■ *Gavia stellata*
- □ *Diomedea chrysostoma*
- ◆ *Diomedea cauta*
- ◇ *Pygoscelis adeliae*
- ▲ *Spheniscus demersus*
- △ *Aechmophorus occidentalis*
- ✕ *Poliocephalus rufopectus*

Fig. 181. Fork-tailed Storm-Petrel x Grey-headed Albatross, Sooty Shearwater, Common Diving-Petrel, Black-necked Stork, Lesser Frigatebird, King Vulture, Crested Serpent-Eagle, Red-headed Vulture, Red-throated Loon, Brahminy Kite, White Hawk

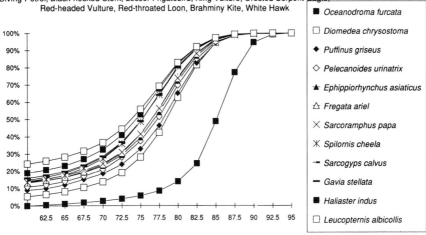

- ■ *Oceanodroma furcata*
- □ *Diomedea chrysostoma*
- ◆ *Puffinus griseus*
- ◇ *Pelecanoides urinatrix*
- ▲ *Ephippiorhynchus asiaticus*
- △ *Fregata ariel*
- ✕ *Sarcoramphus papa*
- ✷ *Spilornis cheela*
- ⁃ *Sarcogyps calvus*
- — *Gavia stellata*
- ■ *Haliaster indus*
- □ *Leucopternis albicollis*

Fig.182. Kerguelen Petrel x Manx Shearwater, Common Diving-Petrel, Grey-headed Albatross, Fork-tailed Storm-Petrel, Gentoo Penguin, Lesser Frigatebird, Red-throated Loon, Masked Booby, African Darter, Red-billed Tropicbird, Pelagic Cormorant

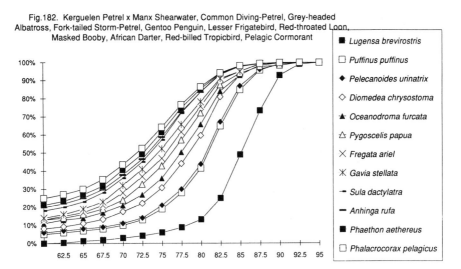

- ■ *Lugensa brevirostris*
- □ *Puffinus puffinus*
- ◆ *Pelecanoides urinatrix*
- ◇ *Diomedea chrysostoma*
- ▲ *Oceanodroma furcata*
- △ *Pygoscelis papua*
- ✕ *Fregata ariel*
- ✷ *Gavia stellata*
- ⁃ *Sula dactylatra*
- — *Anhinga rufa*
- ■ *Phaethon aethereus*
- □ *Phalacrocorax pelagicus*

Fig. 183. Common Diving-Petrel x South Georgian Diving-Petrel, Kerguelen Petrel, Black-capped Petrel, Hall's Giant Petrel, Shy Albatross, Fork-tailed Storm-Petrel, Wilson's Storm-Petrel, Jackass Penguin, King Penguin

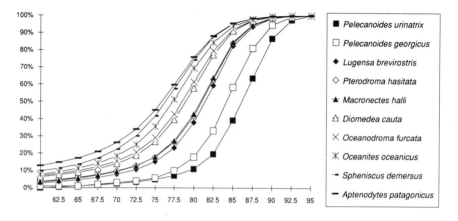

Fig. 184. Royal Albatross x Trindade Petrel, Ringed Storm-Petrel, Jackass Penguin, Common Diving-Petrel, King Vulture, Lesser Frigatebird, Marabou Stork, Shoebill, American White Pelican

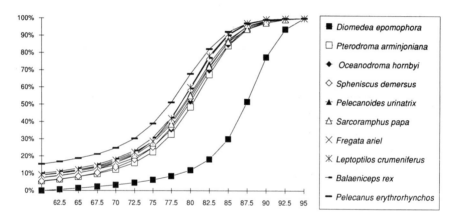

Fig. 185. Laysan Albatross x Lesser Frigatebird, Great Frigatebird, American White Pelican, Pelagic Cormorant, Brown Booby, Red-billed Tropicbird

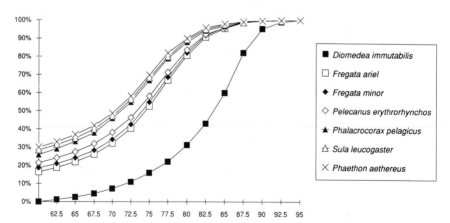

Fig. 186. New Zealand Rifleman x Great Bowerbird, Amazonian Umbrellabird, Blue-crowned
Manakin, Paradise Riflebird, Green Broadbill, White-fronted Honeyeater, Blue-headed Pitta,
House Sparrow, Noisy Pitta, Sacred Kingfisher, Downy Woodpecker

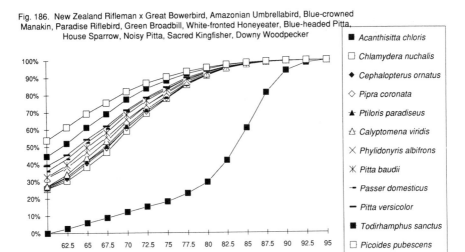

- ■ *Acanthisitta chloris*
- ☐ *Chlamydera nuchalis*
- ◆ *Cephalopterus ornatus*
- ◇ *Pipra coronata*
- ▲ *Ptiloris paradiseus*
- △ *Calyptomena viridis*
- ✕ *Phylidonyris albifrons*
- ✳ *Pitta baudii*
- ⊸ *Passer domesticus*
- — *Pitta versicolor*
- ■ *Todirhamphus sanctus*
- ☐ *Picoides pubescens*

Fig. 187. Noisy Pitta x Banded Pitta, Green Broadbill, Chestnut-crowned Foliage-gleaner,
Rusty-margined Flycatcher, New Zealand Rifleman, Lincoln's Sparrow, American Robin

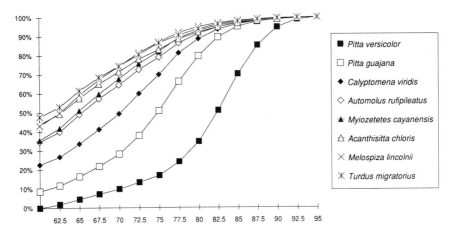

- ■ *Pitta versicolor*
- ☐ *Pitta guajana*
- ◆ *Calyptomena viridis*
- ◇ *Automolus rufipileatus*
- ▲ *Myiozetetes cayanensis*
- △ *Acanthisitta chloris*
- ✕ *Melospiza lincolnii*
- ✳ *Turdus migratorius*

Fig. 188. Green Broadbill x Rufous Hornero, Indian Pitta, Lewin's Honeyeater, New Zealand
Rifleman, Great Thrush, Eurasian Skylark

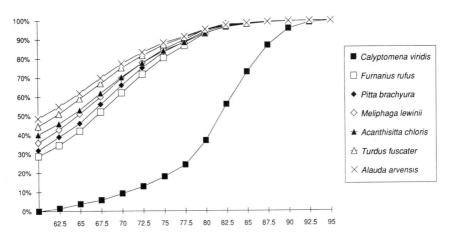

- ■ *Calyptomena viridis*
- ☐ *Furnarius rufus*
- ◆ *Pitta brachyura*
- ◇ *Meliphaga lewinii*
- ▲ *Acanthisitta chloris*
- △ *Turdus fuscater*
- ✕ *Alauda arvensis*

Fig. 189. Olive-striped Flycatcher x Streak-necked Flycatcher, Ochre-bellied Flycatcher, Slaty-capped Flycatcher, Rufous-headed Pygmy-Tyrant, Stripe-necked Tody-Tyrant, Ringed Antpipit, Common Tody-Flycatcher, Mountain Elaenia, Eastern Phoebe

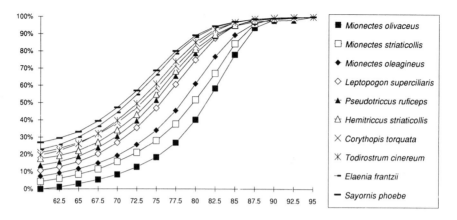

Fig. 190. Olive-striped Flycatcher x Slaty-capped Flycatcher, Mountain Elaenia, Dusky-capped Flycatcher, Least Flycatcher, Swallow-tailed Manakin, White-winged Becard, Broad-billed Sapayoa

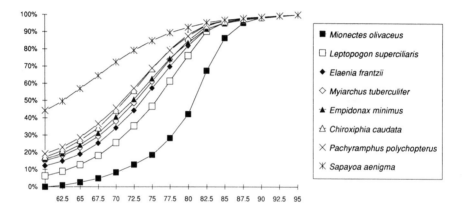

Fig. 191. Olive-striped Flycatcher x Slaty-capped Flycatcher, Golden-headed Manakin, Green-and-black Fruiteater, Rufous Gnateater, Chestnut-crowned Antpitta, Rufous Hornero, Green Broadbill, Plain-winged Antshrike, Albert's Lyrebird, Long-billed Thrasher

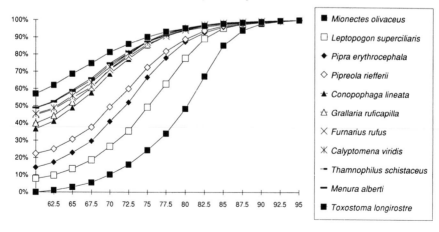

Fig. 192. Brown-crested Flycatcher x Ringed Antpipit, Barred Fruiteater, Rufous-vented Tapaculo, Rufous Gnateater, White-flanked Antwren, Spot-crowned Woodcreeper, Spot-winged Antshrike, White-chinned Thistletail, Tawny Antpitta

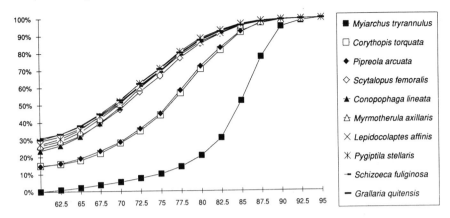

Fig. 193. Brown-crested Flycatcher x Short-crested Flycatcher, Great Kiskadee, Eastern Phoebe, Common Tody-Flycatcher, Sepia-capped Flycatcher, Blue-backed Manakin, Barred Fruiteater, Thrush-like Schiffornis, Broad-billed Sapayoa

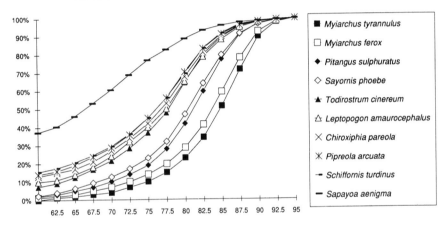

Fig. 194. Brown-crested Flycatcher x Mountain Elaenia, Least Flycatcher, Slaty-capped Flycatcher, Barred Fruiteater, Green Broadbill, Little Raven, Clay-colored Thrush, New Zealand Rifleman

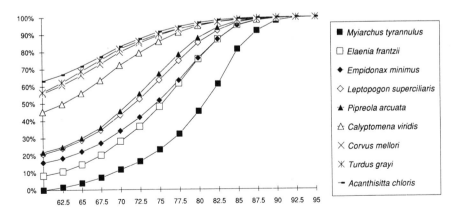

766

Fig. 195. Sharpbill x Barred Fruiteater, Andean Cock-of-the-rock, Pink-throated Becard, Bright-rumped Attila, Golden-headed Manakin, Greyish Mourner, Brown-crested Flycatcher, Rufous Hornero, Plain-winged Antshrike

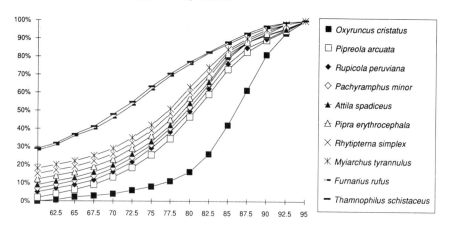

Fig. 196. Barred Fruiteater x Plum-throated Cotinga, White-crested Spadebill, Common Tody-Flycatcher, Pied Water-Tyrant, Ringed Antpipit, Rufous-vented Tapaculo, Chestnut-crowned Gnateater, Barred Woodcreeper, Rufous-capped Antthrush

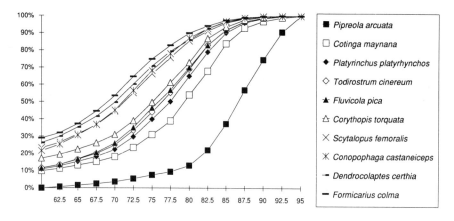

Fig. 197. Barred Fruiteater x Green-and-black Fruiteater, Andean Cock-of-the-rock, Purple-throated Fruitcrow, Amazonian Umbrellabird, Barred Becard, Thrush-like Schiffornis, White-collared Manakin, Green Broadbill, Broad-billed Sapayoa, Noisy Pitta

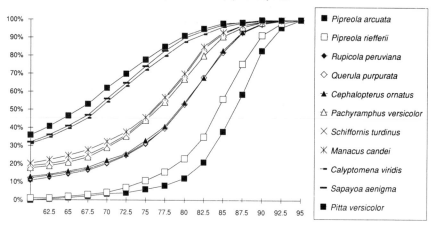

Fig. 198. White-winged Becard x Pink-throated Becard, Black-tailed Tityra, Thrush-like
Schiffornis, Yellow-crested Manakin, Amazonian Umbrellabird, Blue-backed Manakin, Bare-
throated Bellbird, Sharpbill, Olive-striped Flycatcher, Broad-billed Sapayoa

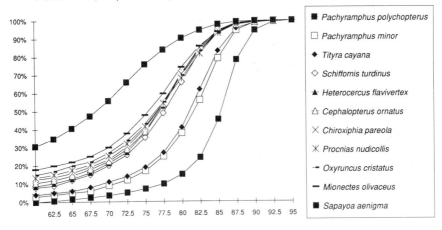

■ *Pachyramphus polychopterus*

□ *Pachyramphus minor*

◆ *Tityra cayana*

◇ *Schiffornis turdinus*

▲ *Heterocercus flavivertex*

△ *Cephalopterus ornatus*

✕ *Chiroxiphia pareola*

✸ *Procnias nudicollis*

⌐ *Oxyruncus cristatus*

▬ *Mionectes olivaceus*

■ *Sapayoa aenigma*

Fig. 199. White-winged Becard x Rufous Mourner, Short-crested Flycatcher, Eastern Phoebe,
Sepia-capped Flycatcher, Olive-striped Flycatcher, Common Tody-Flycatcher, Rufous-breasted
Antthrush, White-chinned Thistletail, Barred Antshrike

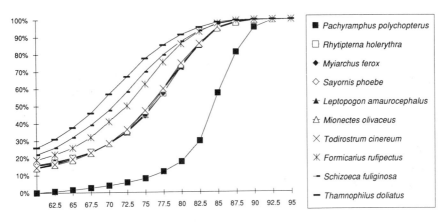

■ *Pachyramphus polychopterus*

□ *Rhytipterna holerythra*

◆ *Myiarchus ferox*

◇ *Sayornis phoebe*

▲ *Leptopogon amaurocephalus*

△ *Mionectes olivaceus*

✕ *Todirostrum cinereum*

✸ *Formicarius rufipectus*

⌐ *Schizoeca fuliginosa*

▬ *Thamnophilus doliatus*

Fig. 200. Golden-headed Manakin x Blue-crowned Manakin, Striped Manakin, White-bearded
Manakin, White-winged Becard, Black-tailed Tityra, Purple-throated Fruitcrow, Lesser Elaenia,
Thrush-like Schiffornis, Broad-billed Sapayoa

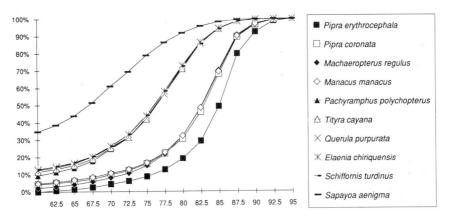

■ *Pipra erythrocephala*

□ *Pipra coronata*

◆ *Machaeropterus regulus*

◇ *Manacus manacus*

▲ *Pachyramphus polychopterus*

△ *Tityra cayana*

✕ *Querula purpurata*

✸ *Elaenia chiriquensis*

⌐ *Schiffornis turdinus*

▬ *Sapayoa aenigma*

Fig. 201. Golden-headed Manakin x Andean Cock-of-the-rock, Masked Tityra, Bare-throated Bellbird, Rufous Mourner, Barred Becard, Ringed Antpipit, Rufous-vented Tapaculo, Rufous Hornero, Rufous Gnateater, Plain-winged Antshrike

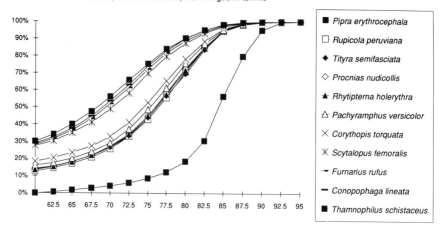

■ *Pipra erythrocephala*

□ *Rupicola peruviana*

◆ *Tityra semifasciata*

◇ *Procnias nudicollis*

▲ *Rhytipterna holerythra*

△ *Pachyramphus versicolor*

✕ *Corythopis torquata*

✳ *Scytalopus femoralis*

⁻ *Furnarius rufus*

— *Conopophaga lineata*

■ *Thamnophilus schistaceus*

Fig. 202. Rufous Hornero x Stout-billed Cinclodes, Dark-breasted Spinetail, Barred Woodcreeper, Rufous-vented Tapaculo, Rufous Gnateater, Golden-headed Manakin, Brown-crested Flycatcher, Barred Fruiteater

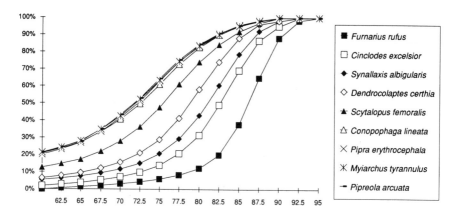

■ *Furnarius rufus*

□ *Cinclodes excelsior*

◆ *Synallaxis albigularis*

◇ *Dendrocolaptes certhia*

▲ *Scytalopus femoralis*

△ *Conopophaga lineata*

✕ *Pipra erythrocephala*

✳ *Myiarchus tyrannulus*

⁻ *Pipreola arcuata*

Fig. 203. Chestnut-crowned Gnateater x Rufous Gnateater, White-fringed Antwren, Rufous-vented Tapaculo, Plain Antvireo, Plain Xenops, White-chinned Woodcreeper, Tawny Antpitta, Plain-winged Antshrike, Rufous-tailed Tyrant, Plum-throated Cotinga

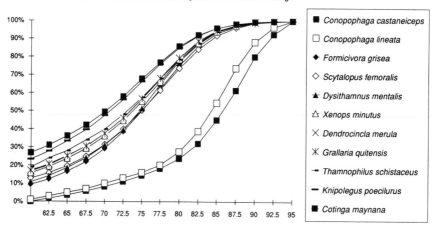

■ *Conopophaga castaneiceps*

□ *Conopophaga lineata*

◆ *Formicivora grisea*

◇ *Scytalopus femoralis*

▲ *Dysithamnus mentalis*

△ *Xenops minutus*

✕ *Dendrocincla merula*

✳ *Grallaria quitensis*

⁻ *Thamnophilus schistaceus*

— *Knipolegus poecilurus*

■ *Cotinga maynana*

Fig. 204. Brown-rumped Tapaculo x Rusty-belted Tapaculo, Stout-billed Cinclodes, Straight-billed Woodcreeper, Rufous-breasted Antthrush, White-cheeked Antbird, Plain Antvireo, White-winged Becard, Green-and-black Fruiteater, Olive-striped Flycatcher

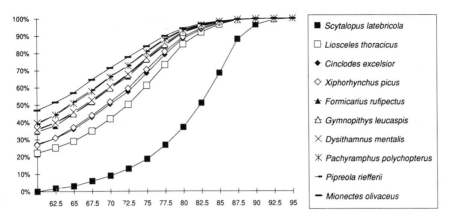

Fig. 205. Rusty-belted Tapaculo x Brown-rumped Tapaculo, Spotted Barbtail, Rufous Hornero, Jet Antbird, Golden-headed Manakin, Rufous-breasted Antthrush, White-winged Becard, Barred Antshrike, Green-and-black Fruiteater, Eastern Phoebe

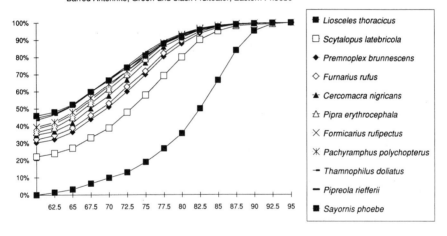

Fig. 206. Superb Lyrebird x Albert's Lyrebird, Noisy Scrub-bird, Great Bowerbird, Green Catbird, Satin Bowerbird, Ribbon-tailed Astrapia, Little Raven, King-of-Saxony Bird-of-paradise, Lesser Bird-of-paradise, Green Broadbill

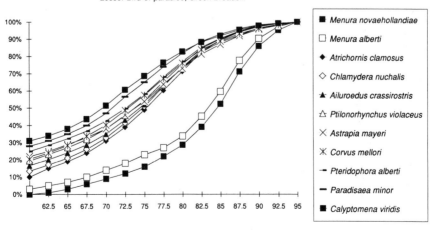

Fig. 207. Satin Bowerbird x Spotted Bowerbird, White-eared Bowerbird, Green Catbird,
Superb Lyrebird, Ribbon-tailed Astrapia, Albert's Lyrebird, Brown Sicklebill, King-of-Saxony
Bird-of-paradise, Slender-billed Crow

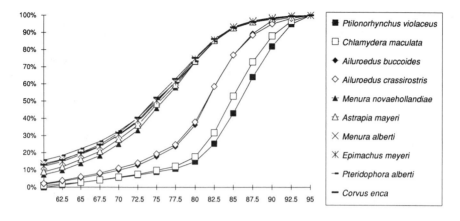

Fig. 208. Rufous Treecreeper x Brown Treecreeper, Spotted Bowerbird, Green Catbird,
Albert's Lyrebird, Superb Lyrebird, Satin Bowerbird, Western Gerygone, Grey Honeyeater,
Common Tree-Creeper

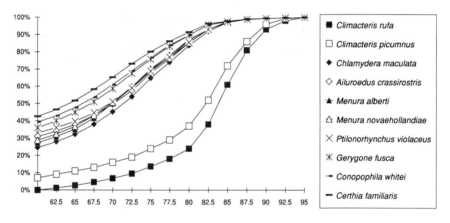

Fig. 209. Rufous Treecreeper x Brown Treecreeper, Spotted Bowerbird, Rufous Whistler,
Shining Monarch, Little Raven, White-browed Babbler, Logrunner, Willie Wagtail, Yellow-
rumped Thornbill, Hooded Robin, Splendid Fairywren

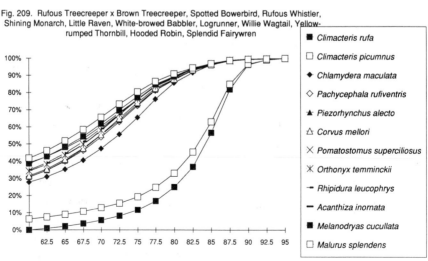

Fig. 210. Variegated Fairywren x Southern Emuwren, Thick-billed Grasswren, White-fronted
Honeyeater, Western Thornbill, White-faced Robin, Ashy Robin, Malaysian Flycatcher,
Orphean Warbler, Oriental White-eye

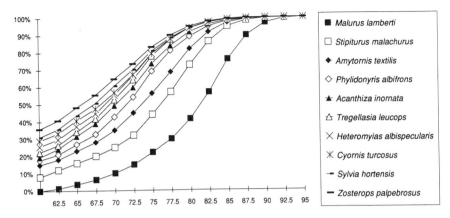

Fig. 211. Red Wattlebird x Little Wattlebird, White-plumed Honeyeater, Dusky Myzomela,
Yellow-rumped Thornbill, White-winged Chough, Magpie-lark, Little Raven, Olive-crowned
Flowerpecker

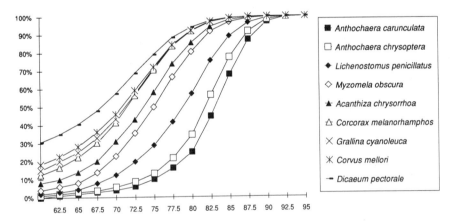

Fig. 212. Red Wattlebird x Tui, Gibberbird, White-fronted Chat, Yellow-rumped Thornbill,
Rufous Bristlebird, Large Scrubwren, Southern Emuwren, White-shouldered Fairywren, Thick-
billed Grasswren

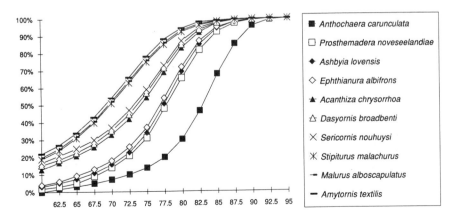

Fig. 213. Red Wattlebird x Singing Honeyeater, Little Raven, Shining Monarch, Great Tit, European Starling, Chestnut-winged Babbler, Clapper Lark, Dark-eyed Junco, White Wagtail

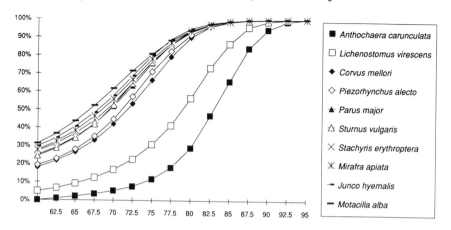

- ■ *Anthochaera carunculata*
- □ *Lichenostomus virescens*
- ◆ *Corvus mellori*
- ◇ *Piezorhynchus alecto*
- ▲ *Parus major*
- △ *Sturnus vulgaris*
- ✕ *Stachyris erythroptera*
- ✳ *Mirafra apiata*
- – *Junco hyemalis*
- — *Motacilla alba*

Fig. 214. White-fronted Chat x Gibberbird, Tui, Western Spinebill, Western Thornbill, Southern Whiteface, Cinnamon Quail-thrush, White-faced Robin, Logrunner

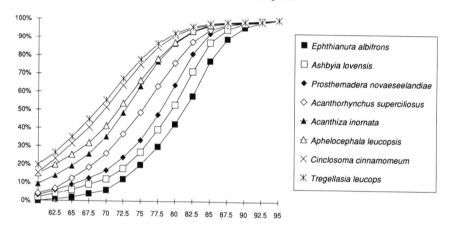

- ■ *Ephthianura albifrons*
- □ *Ashbyia lovensis*
- ◆ *Prosthemadera novaeseelandiae*
- ◇ *Acanthorhynchus superciliosus*
- ▲ *Acanthiza inornata*
- △ *Aphelocephala leucopsis*
- ✕ *Cinclosoma cinnamomeum*
- ✳ *Tregellasia leucops*

Fig. 215. Striated Pardalote x White-browed Scrubwren, Yellow-rumped Thornbill, White-plumed Honeyeater, Golden Whistler, Varied Sittella, Splendid Fairywren, Yellow-breasted Flowerpecker, Oriental White-eye, Orange-bellied Flowerpecker

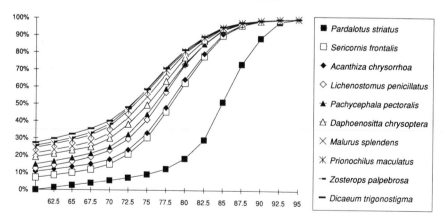

- ■ *Pardalotus striatus*
- □ *Sericornis frontalis*
- ◆ *Acanthiza chrysorrhoa*
- ◇ *Lichenostomus penicillatus*
- ▲ *Pachycephala pectoralis*
- △ *Daphoenositta chrysoptera*
- ✕ *Malurus splendens*
- ✳ *Prionochilus maculatus*
- – *Zosterops palpebrosa*
- — *Dicaeum trigonostigma*

Fig. 216. White-browed Scrubwren x Large Scrubwren, Rusty Mouse-warbler, Southern Whiteface, Western Gerygone, Redthroat, Western Thornbill, White-fronted Chat, Thick-billed Grasswren, Spinifex-bird

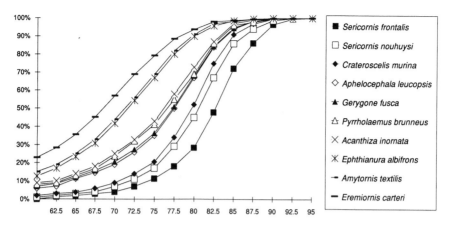

■ Sericornis frontalis

□ Sericornis nouhuysi

◆ Crateroscelis murina

◇ Aphelocephala leucopsis

▲ Gerygone fusca

△ Pyrrholaemus brunneus

✕ Acanthiza inornata

✳ Ephthianura albifrons

� Amytornis textilis

— Eremiornis carteri

Fig. 217. Yellow-rumped Thornbill x White-browed Scrubwren, Sunda Treepie, Asian Paradise-Flycatcher, Curve-billed Thrasher, Great Tit, Carolina Wren, Yellow-vented Bulbul, Arrow-marked Babbler, Corn Bunting, Purple Martin, American Robin

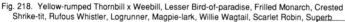
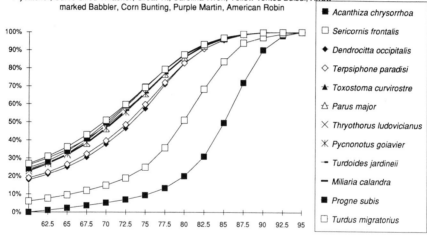

■ Acanthiza chrysorrhoa

□ Sericornis frontalis

◆ Dendrocitta occipitalis

◇ Terpsiphone paradisi

▲ Toxostoma curvirostre

△ Parus major

✕ Thryothorus ludovicianus

✳ Pycnonotus goiavier

➤ Turdoides jardineii

— Miliaria calandra

■ Progne subis

□ Turdus migratorius

Fig. 218. Yellow-rumped Thornbill x Weebill, Lesser Bird-of-paradise, Frilled Monarch, Crested Shrike-tit, Rufous Whistler, Logrunner, Magpie-lark, Willie Wagtail, Scarlet Robin, Superb Lyrebird, Rufous Treecreeper

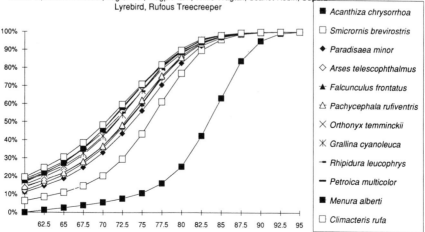

■ Acanthiza chrysorrhoa

□ Smicrornis brevirostris

◆ Paradisaea minor

◇ Arses telescophthalmus

▲ Falcunculus frontatus

△ Pachycephala rufiventris

✕ Orthonyx temminckii

✳ Grallina cyanoleuca

➤ Rhipidura leucophrys

— Petroica multicolor

■ Menura alberti

□ Climacteris rufa

Fig. 219. Southern Scrub-Robin x Eastern Yellow Robin, Ashy Robin, Lemon-bellied Flyrobin, Spot-winged Monarch, Brown Whistler, Crested Bellbird, Chestnut Quail-thrush, Willie Wagtail, Rusty Mouse-warbler, Tawny-breasted Honeyeater, European Robin

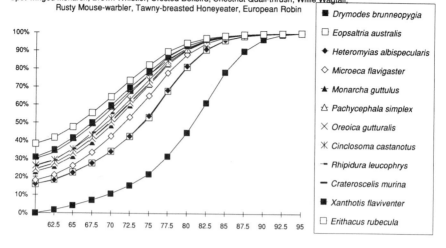

- ■ *Drymodes brunneopygia*
- □ *Eopsaltria australis*
- ◆ *Heteromyias albispecularis*
- ◇ *Microeca flavigaster*
- ▲ *Monarcha guttulus*
- △ *Pachycephala simplex*
- ✕ *Oreoica gutturalis*
- ✳ *Cinclosoma castanotus*
- ⚊ *Rhipidura leucophrys*
- ⚊ *Crateroscelis murina*
- ■ *Xanthotis flaviventer*
- □ *Erithacus rubecula*

Fig. 220. Asian Fairy-bluebird x Greater Green Leafbird, Rufous Shrike-thrush, Glossy-mantled Manucode, Rufous Whistler, Sunda Treepie, Black Butcherbird, White-necked Rockfowl, Rufous Rock-jumper

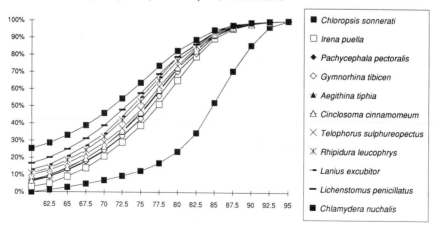

- ■ *Irena puella*
- □ *Chloropsis sonnerati*
- ◆ *Colluricincla megarhyncha*
- ◇ *Manucodia atra*
- ▲ *Pachycephala rufiventris*
- △ *Dendrocitta occipitalis*
- ✕ *Cracticus quoyi*
- ✳ *Picathartes gymnocephalus*
- ⚊ *Chaetops frenatus*

Fig. 221, Greater Green Leafbird x Asian Fairy-bluebird, Golden Whistler, Black-backed Magpie, Common Iora, Cinnamon Quail-thrush, Sulphur-breasted Bushshrike, Willie Wagtail, Great Grey Shrike, White-plumed Honeyeater, Great Bowerbird

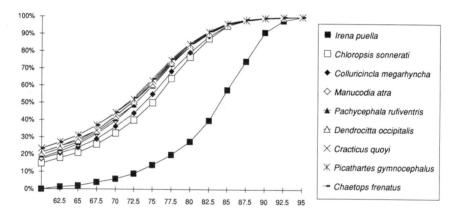

- ■ *Chloropsis sonnerati*
- □ *Irena puella*
- ◆ *Pachycephala pectoralis*
- ◇ *Gymnorhina tibicen*
- ▲ *Aegithina tiphia*
- △ *Cinclosoma cinnamomeum*
- ✕ *Telophorus sulphureopectus*
- ✳ *Rhipidura leucophrys*
- ⚊ *Lanius excubitor*
- ⚊ *Lichenstomus penicillatus*
- ■ *Chlamydera nuchalis*

Fig. 222. Great Grey Shrike x Grey Cuckoo-shrike, Pied Currawong, White-shouldered Triller, Small Minivet, Black Butcherbird, Olive-backed Oriole, Common Woodshrike, Black-and-crimson Oriole, White-eyed Vireo, Rufous-browed Peppershrike

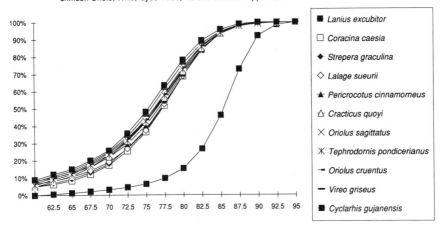

Fig. 223. Great Grey Shrike x Ribbon-tailed Astrapia, Pied Crow, Greater Racket-tailed Drongo, Bornean Whistler, Cinnamon Quail-thrush, Common Iora, White-throated Fantail, Logrunner, Western Yellow Robin, Asian Fairy-bluebird

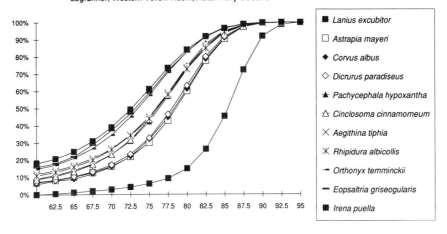

Fig. 224. Red-backed Shrike x Loggerhead Shrike, Greater Racket-tailed Drongo, Black-naped Oriole, Black-faced Cuckoo-shrike, Common Woodshrike, Black-crowned Tchagra, Red-eyed Vireo, Cedar Waxwing, European Starling, Himalayan Bulbul, Song Sparrow

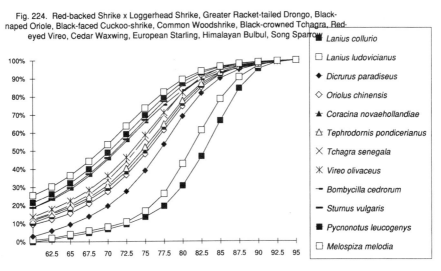

Fig. 225. Red-eyed Vireo x Rufous-browed Peppershrike, Scrub Greenlet, Black-billed Magpie, Black-faced Cuckoo-shrike, Phainopepla, Olive Sunbird, House Sparrow, Cape Weaver, White Wagtail, Common Yellowthroat

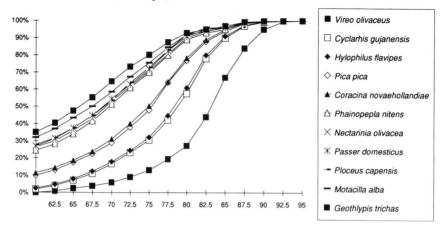

■ *Vireo olivaceus*
□ *Cyclarhis gujanensis*
◆ *Hylophilus flavipes*
◇ *Pica pica*
▲ *Coracina novaehollandiae*
△ *Phainopepla nitens*
✕ *Nectarinia olivacea*
✳ *Passer domesticus*
⁃ *Ploceus capensis*
— *Motacilla alba*
■ *Geothlypis trichas*

Fig. 226. Cinnamon Quail-thrush x Chestnut-backed Jewel-babbler, Crested Shrike-tit, Chirruping Wedgebill, Golden Whistler, Black-backed Magpie, Varied Sittella, Paradise Riflebird, Little Raven, Hooded Robin

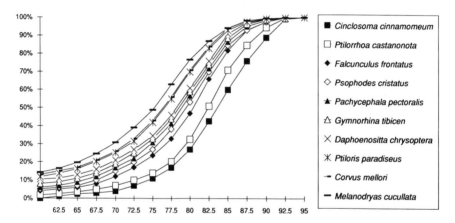

■ *Cinclosoma cinnamomeum*
□ *Ptilorrhoa castanonota*
◆ *Falcunculus frontatus*
◇ *Psophodes cristatus*
▲ *Pachycephala pectoralis*
△ *Gymnorhina tibicen*
✕ *Daphoenositta chrysoptera*
✳ *Ptiloris paradiseus*
⁃ *Corvus mellori*
— *Melanodryas cucullata*

Fig. 227. Apostlebird x White-winged Chough, Island Monarch, Pied Currawong, Glossy-mantled Manucode, Magpie-lark, Black-faced Cuckoo-shrike, Varied Sittella, Olive-backed Oriole, Great Bowerbird, White-eared Catbird

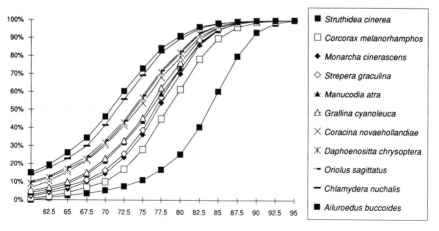

■ *Struthidea cinerea*
□ *Corcorax melanorhamphos*
◆ *Monarcha cinerascens*
◇ *Strepera graculina*
▲ *Manucodia atra*
△ *Grallina cyanoleuca*
✕ *Coracina novaehollandiae*
✳ *Daphoenositta chrysoptera*
⁃ *Oriolus sagittatus*
— *Chlamydera nuchalis*
■ *Ailuroedus buccoides*

Fig. 228. Varied Sittella x Golden Whistler, Chirruping Wedgebill, Island Monarch, Cinnamon
Quail-thrush, Black-faced Cuckoo-shrike, Logrunner, Rufous Babbler, White-browed
Scrubwren, Rufous Bristlebird, Superb Lyrebird

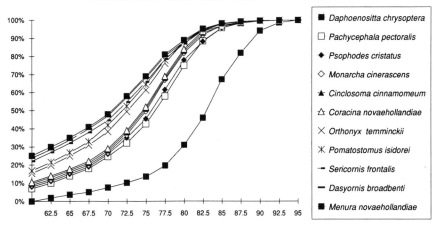

Fig. 229. Whitehead x Pipipi, Crested Bellbird, Grey Shrike-thrush, Crested Shrike-tit, Rufous
Whistler, Yap Monarch, White-throated Fantail, White-browed Scrubwren, Eastern Yellow
Robin

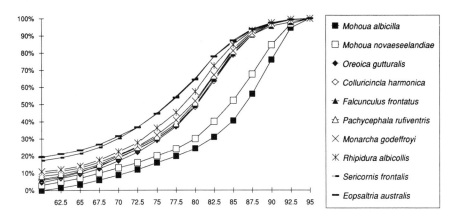

Fig. 230. Pipipi x Whitehead, Mottled Whistler, Grey Shrike-thrush, Frilled Monarch, Truk
Monarch, Rufous Whistler, Maroon-breasted Philentoma, White-throated Fantail, Chestnut-
rumped Thornbill, Clamorous Reed-Warbler, Arctic Warbler

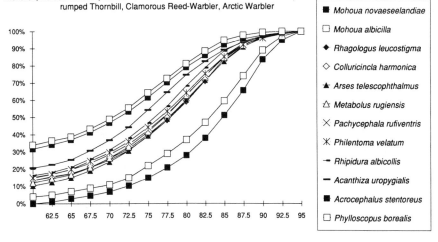

Fig. 231. Golden Whistler x Bornean Whistler, Rusty Pitohui, Grey Shrike-thrush, Mottled Whistler, Crested Shrike-tit, Island Monarch, Eastern Yellow Robin

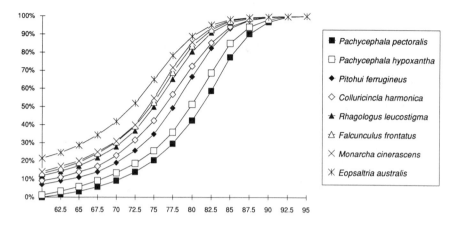

- ■ *Pachycephala pectoralis*
- □ *Pachycephala hypoxantha*
- ◆ *Pitohui ferrugineus*
- ◇ *Colluricincla harmonica*
- ▲ *Rhagologus leucostigma*
- △ *Falcunculus frontatus*
- ✕ *Monarcha cinerascens*
- ✳ *Eopsaltria australis*

Fig. 232. Little Raven x Mexican Jay, Brown Sicklebill, Glossy-mantled Manucode, Black-backed Magpie, Great Bowerbird, White-plumed Honeyeater, Great Kiskadee

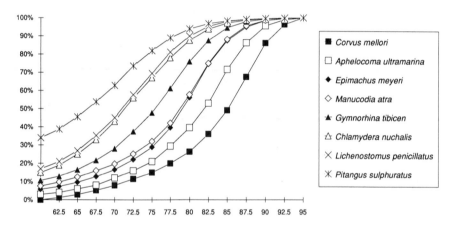

- ■ *Corvus mellori*
- □ *Aphelocoma ultramarina*
- ◆ *Epimachus meyeri*
- ◇ *Manucodia atra*
- ▲ *Gymnorhina tibicen*
- △ *Chlamydera nuchalis*
- ✕ *Lichenostomus penicillatus*
- ✳ *Pitangus sulphuratus*

Fig. 233. Paradise Riflebird x Brown Sicklebill, King Bird-of-paradise, Slender-billed Crow, White-browed Wood-swallow, Grey Currawong, Satin Bowerbird, Green Catbird, Spotted Bowerbird, Superb Lyrebird

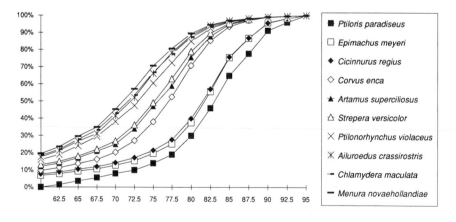

- ■ *Ptiloris paradiseus*
- □ *Epimachus meyeri*
- ◆ *Cicinnurus regius*
- ◇ *Corvus enca*
- ▲ *Artamus superciliosus*
- △ *Strepera versicolor*
- ✕ *Ptilonorhynchus violaceus*
- ✳ *Ailuroedus crassirostris*
- ‒ *Chlamydera maculata*
- — *Menura novaehollandiae*

Fig. 234. Lesser Melampitta x Glossy-mantled Manucode, Black-faced Monarch, Little Raven,
Magpie-lark, Grey Butcherbird, Grey Fantail, Southern Boubou, Olive-backed Oriole,
Logrunner, Asian Fairy-bluebird

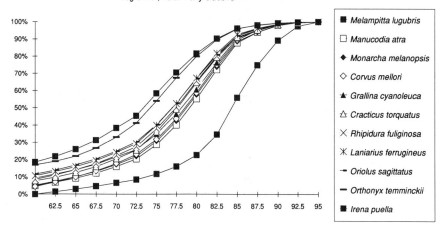

Fig. 235. Lesser Melampitta x Eastern Whipbird, Rufous Whistler, Masked Shrike, White-eyed
Vireo, White-eyed Robin, Chestnut-rumped Thornbill, Spotted Bowerbird, Superb Lyrebird,
Rufous Treecreeper

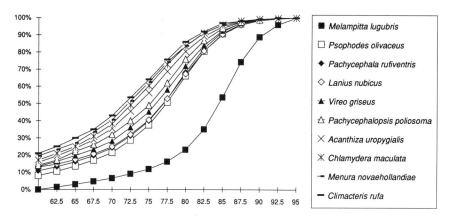

Fig. 236. Mountain Peltops x Pied Currawong, White-browed Wood-swallow, Large
Woodshrike, Small Minivet, Pied Triller, Island Monarch, Olive-backed Oriole, Magpie-lark

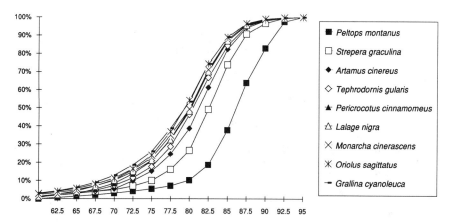

Fig. 237. Mountain Peltops x Bornean Bristlehead, White-shouldered Triller, Rufous Whistler, King-of-Saxony Bird-of-paradise, Black-naped Oriole, Rufous Fantail, White-faced Robin, Yellow-rumped Thornbill

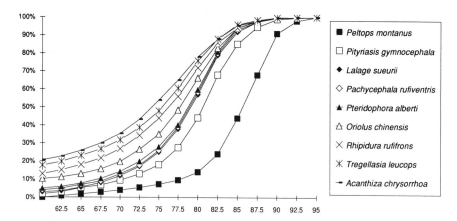

Fig. 238. Red-shouldered Cuckoo-shrike x Purple-throated Cuckoo-shrike, Grey Cuckoo-shrike, White-shouldered Triller, Small Minivet, African Black-headed Oriole, Paradise Riflebird, Pied Currawong, Black-faced Wood-swallow, Little Raven

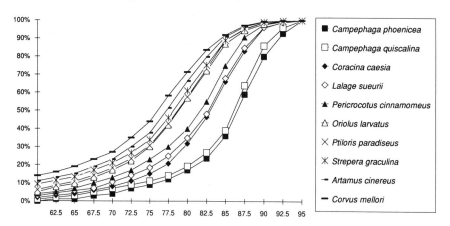

Fig. 239. Willie Wagtail x Spotted Fantail, Northern Fantail, Frilled Monarch, Shining Monarch, Golden Whistler, Cinnamon Quail-thrush, Crested Shrike-tit, White-browed Babbler, Hooded Robin, Torrent Robin

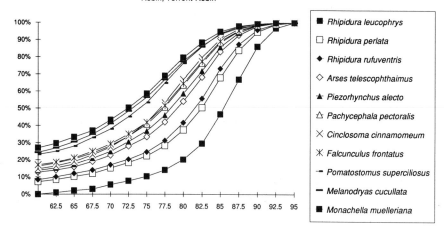

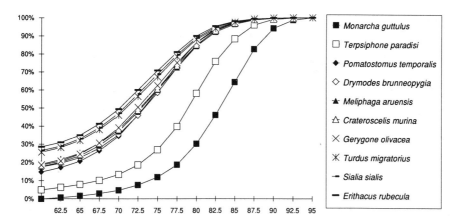

Fig. 240. Spot-winged Monarch x Asian Paradise-Flycatcher, Grey-crowned Babbler, Southern Scrub-Robin, Puff-backed Honeyeater, Rusty Mouse-warbler, White-throated Gerygone, American Robin, Eastern Bluebird, European Robin

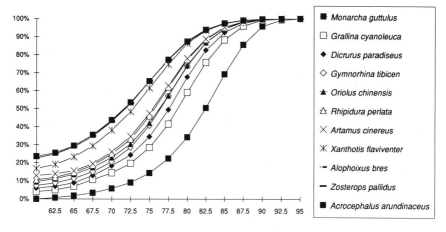

Fig. 241. Spot-winged Monarch x Magpie-lark, Greater Racket-tailed Drongo, Black-backed Magpie, Black-naped Oriole, Spotted Fantail, Black-faced Wood-swallow, Tawny-breasted Honeyeater, Grey-cheeked Bulbul, Pale White-eye, Great Reed-Warbler

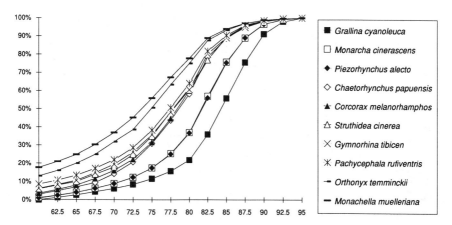

Fig. 242. Magpie-lark x Island Monarch, Shining Monarch, Pygmy Drongo, White-winged Chough, Apostlebird, Black-backed Magpie, Rufous Whistler, Logrunner, Torrent Robin

782

Fig. 243. Common Iora x Maroon-breasted Philentoma, Cape Batis, Southern Boubou, Large Woodshrike, Greater Racket-tailed Drongo, Black-naped Monarch, Magpie-lark, Solitary Vireo, Greater Green Leafbird, Asian Fairy-bluebird

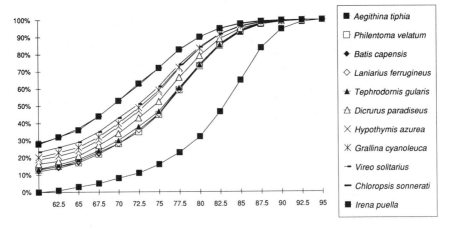

Legend:
- ■ Aegithina tiphia
- □ Philentoma velatum
- ◆ Batis capensis
- ◇ Laniarius ferrugineus
- ▲ Tephrodornis gularis
- △ Dicrurus paradiseus
- × Hypothymis azurea
- ✳ Grallina cyanoleuca
- – Vireo solitarius
- — Chloropsis sonnerati
- ■ Irena puella

Fig. 244. White Helmetshrike x Southern Boubou, Brubru, Brown-crowned Tchagra, Olive Bushshrike, Fiery-breasted Bushshrike, Yellow-billed Shrike, White-crowned Shrike, Red-backed Shrike, Tiger Shrike

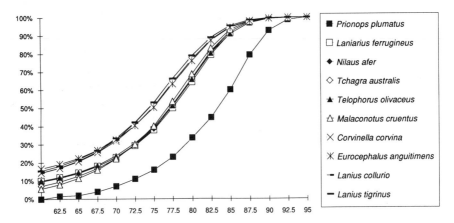

Legend:
- ■ Prionops plumatus
- □ Laniarius ferrugineus
- ◆ Nilaus afer
- ◇ Tchagra australis
- ▲ Telophorus olivaceus
- △ Malaconotus cruentus
- × Corvinella corvina
- ✳ Eurocephalus anguitimens
- – Lanius collurio
- — Lanius tigrinus

Fig. 245. White Helmetshrike x Senegal Batis, Fork-tailed Drongo, Ribbon-tailed Astrapia, Sunda Treepie, Asian Paradise-Flycatcher, Black-whiskered Vireo, White-eyed Vireo

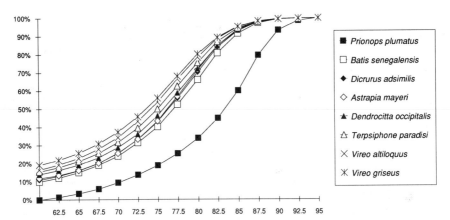

Legend:
- ■ Prionops plumatus
- □ Batis senegalensis
- ◆ Dicrurus adsimilis
- ◇ Astrapia mayeri
- ▲ Dendrocitta occipitalis
- △ Terpsiphone paradisi
- × Vireo altiloquus
- ✳ Vireo griseus

Fig. 246. Olive Bushshrike x Sulphur-breasted Bushshrike, Southern Boubou, Brubru, Black-backed Puffback, Common Iora, White Helmetshrike, Yellow-billed Shrike, Great Grey Shrike, Greater Green Leafbird, Asian Fairy-bluebird

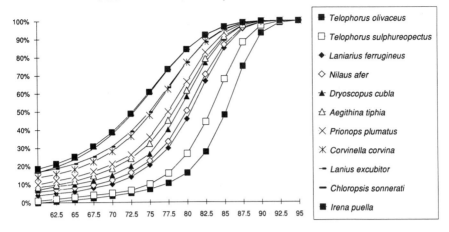

- ■ *Telophorus olivaceus*
- □ *Telophorus sulphureopectus*
- ◆ *Laniarius ferrugineus*
- ◇ *Nilaus afer*
- ▲ *Dryoscopus cubla*
- △ *Aegithina tiphia*
- ✕ *Prionops plumatus*
- ✳ *Corvinella corvina*
- → *Lanius excubitor*
- — *Chloropsis sonnerati*
- ■ *Irena puella*

Fig. 247. Olive Bushshrike x Cape Batis, Magnificent Riflebird, Bornean Whistler, Fork-tailed Drongo, Cinnamon Quail-thrush, Sunda Treepie, African Crested-Flycatcher, White-throated Fantail, Logrunner, Western Yellow Robin

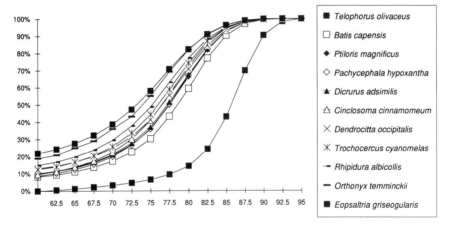

- ■ *Telophorus olivaceus*
- □ *Batis capensis*
- ◆ *Ptiloris magnificus*
- ◇ *Pachycephala hypoxantha*
- ▲ *Dicrurus adsimilis*
- △ *Cinclosoma cinnamomeum*
- ✕ *Dendrocitta occipitalis*
- ✳ *Trochocercus cyanomelas*
- → *Rhipidura albicollis*
- — *Orthonyx temminckii*
- ■ *Eopsaltria griseogularis*

Fig. 248. Olive Bushshrike x Sulphur-breasted Bushshrike, Four-colored Bushshrike, Brown-throated Wattle-eye, Maroon-breasted Philentoma, Rufous Whistler, Apostlebird, Magpie-lark, Black-naped Monarch, Chestnut-rumped Thornbill, Superb Lyrebird

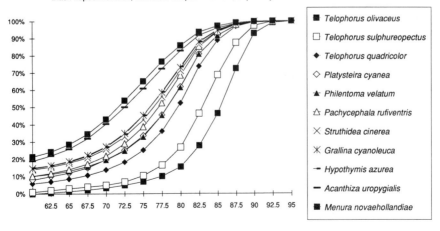

- ■ *Telophorus olivaceus*
- □ *Telophorus sulphureopectus*
- ◆ *Telophorus quadricolor*
- ◇ *Platysteira cyanea*
- ▲ *Philentoma velatum*
- △ *Pachycephala rufiventris*
- ✕ *Struthidea cinerea*
- ✳ *Grallina cyanoleuca*
- → *Hypothymis azurea*
- — *Acanthiza uropygialis*
- ■ *Menura novaehollandiae*

Fig. 249. Common Gonolek x Brown-crowned Tchagra, Black-backed Puffback, Cape Batis, Sulphur-breasted Bushshrike, Fiery-breasted Bushshrike, White Helmetshrike, Red-backed Shrike, Great Grey Shrike, Loggerhead Shrike, Yellow-spotted Nicator

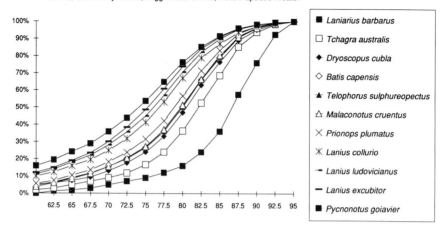

Fig. 250. Blue Vanga x Large Woodshrike, White Helmetshrike, Cape Batis, Brubru, Northern Puffback, Woodchat Shrike, Red-backed Shrike, Great Grey Shrike, Common Fiscal

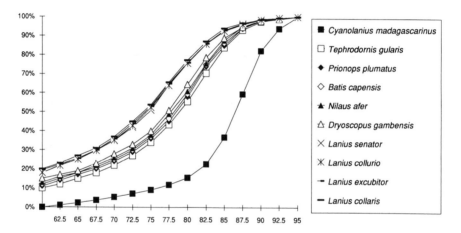

Fig. 251. Rufous Rock-jumper x White-necked Rockfowl, White-eyed Robin, Pied Crow, Dark-throated Oriole, Apostlebird, Red-shouldered Glossy-Starling, Grey Catbird, Southern Scrub-Robin, Cedar Waxwing, Great Bowerbird, Logrunner

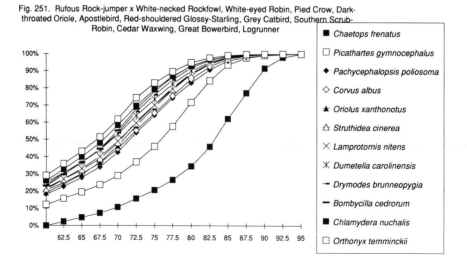

Fig. 252. White-necked Rockfowl x Lesser Swamp-Warbler, Black-capped Babbler, Slender-billed Crow, Orphean Warbler, Red-backed Shrike, Black-chested Prinia, Ferruginous Babbler

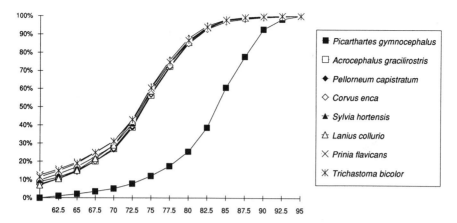

Fig. 253. White-necked Rockfowl x Slender-billed Crow, Green-headed Sunbird, Black-billed Magpie, Red-shouldered Cuckoo-shrike, Orphean Warbler, Fiery-breasted Bushshrike, Arrow-marked Babbler, Yellow-vented Bulbul, Red-capped Robin-Chat

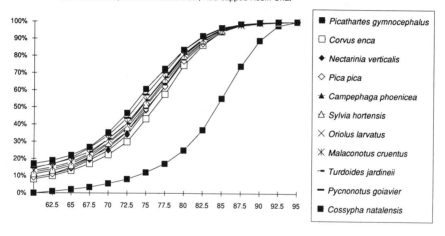

Fig. 254. Phainopepla x Palm Chat, Cedar Waxwing, Bewick's Wren, Cape Weaver, Black-tailed Gnatcatcher, Eastern Bluebird, American Dipper, American Robin, American Crow

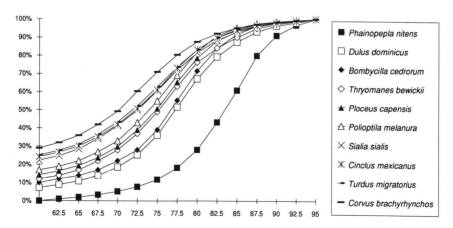

Fig. 255. American Dipper x Northern Mockingbird, Sunda Blue Flycatcher, American Robin, Swainson's Thrush, Short-tailed Babbler, Musician Wren, American Crow, Asian Paradise-Flycatcher

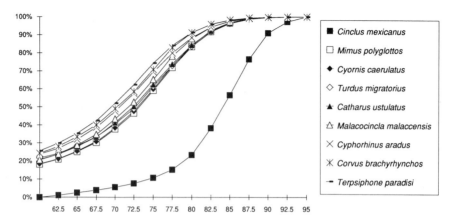

- Cinclus mexicanus
- Mimus polyglottos
- Cyornis caerulatus
- Turdus migratorius
- Catharus ustulatus
- Malacocincla malaccensis
- Cyphorhinus aradus
- Corvus brachyrhynchos
- Terpsiphone paradisi

Fig. 256. American Robin x Orange-headed Thrush, Veery, Wood Thrush, Townsend's Solitaire, Brown-chested Alethe, Malaysian Flycatcher, Grey-chested Jungle-Flycatcher, Red-capped Robin-Chat, Western Bluebird, Black-naped Monarch, Willie Wagtail

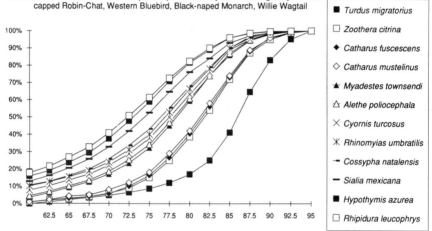

- Turdus migratorius
- Zoothera citrina
- Catharus fuscescens
- Catharus mustelinus
- Myadestes townsendi
- Alethe poliocephala
- Cyornis turcosus
- Rhinomyias umbratilis
- Cossypha natalensis
- Sialia mexicana
- Hypothymis azurea
- Rhipidura leucophrys

Fig. 257. Townsend's Solitaire x Andean Solitaire, Veery, Orange-headed Thrush, Southern Anteater-Chat, Malaysian Flycatcher, Cedar Waxwing, Orphean Warbler, Common Tree-Creeper, House Sparrow, Tiger Shrike

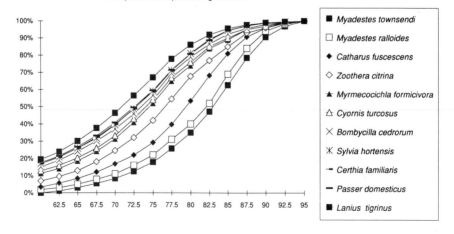

- Myadestes townsendi
- Myadestes ralloides
- Catharus fuscescens
- Zoothera citrina
- Myrmecocichla formicivora
- Cyornis turcosus
- Bombycilla cedrorum
- Sylvia hortensis
- Certhia familiaris
- Passer domesticus
- Lanius tigrinus

Fig. 258. Eastern Bluebird x Mountain Bluebird, Western Bluebird, Red-winged Starling, European Starling, Rufous-chested Flycatcher, Grey Catbird, Curve-billed Thrasher, Malaysian Flycatcher, Cedar Waxwing, Palm Chat, Phainopepla

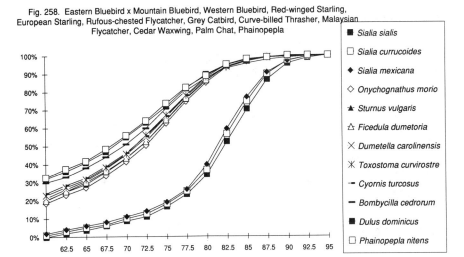

- ■ Sialia sialis
- □ Sialia currucoides
- ◆ Sialia mexicana
- ◇ Onychognathus morio
- ▲ Sturnus vulgaris
- △ Ficedula dumetoria
- ✕ Dumetella carolinensis
- ✳ Toxostoma curvirostre
- ━ Cyornis turcosus
- ━ Bombycilla cedrorum
- ■ Dulus dominicus
- □ Phainopepla nitens

Fig. 259. Eastern Bluebird x Western Bluebird, Mountain Bluebird, Orange-headed Thrush, Cape Thrush, Yellow-eyed Thrush, Maranon Thrush, Cocoa Thrush, Mountain Rock-Thrush, Sunda Whistling-Thrush

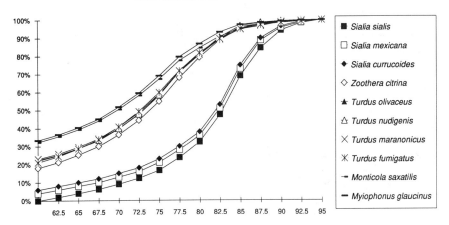

- ■ Sialia sialis
- □ Sialia mexicana
- ◆ Sialia currucoides
- ◇ Zoothera citrina
- ▲ Turdus olivaceus
- △ Turdus nudigenis
- ✕ Turdus maranonicus
- ✳ Turdus fumigatus
- ━ Monticola saxatilis
- ━ Myiophonus glaucinus

Fig. 260. European Robin x Grey-chested Jungle-Flycatcher, Sunda Blue Flycatcher, Southern Anteater-Chat, Common Redstart, Spotted Flycatcher, Swainson's Thrush, Rufous-winged Philentoma, Spot-winged Monarch, Asian Paradise-Flycatcher

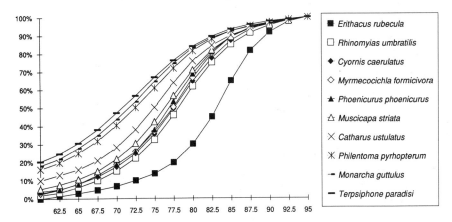

- ■ Erithacus rubecula
- □ Rhinomyias umbratilis
- ◆ Cyornis caerulatus
- ◇ Myrmecocichla formicivora
- ▲ Phoenicurus phoenicurus
- △ Muscicapa striata
- ✕ Catharus ustulatus
- ✳ Philentoma pyrhopterum
- ━ Monarcha guttulus
- ━ Terpsiphone paradisi

Fig. 261. European Robin x Cape Robin-Chat, Eastern Bluebird, Swainson's Thrush, Grey Catbird, Andean Solitaire, Olive Sunbird, House Sparrow, Cedar Waxwing, Red-eyed Vireo, Puff-backed Honeyeater

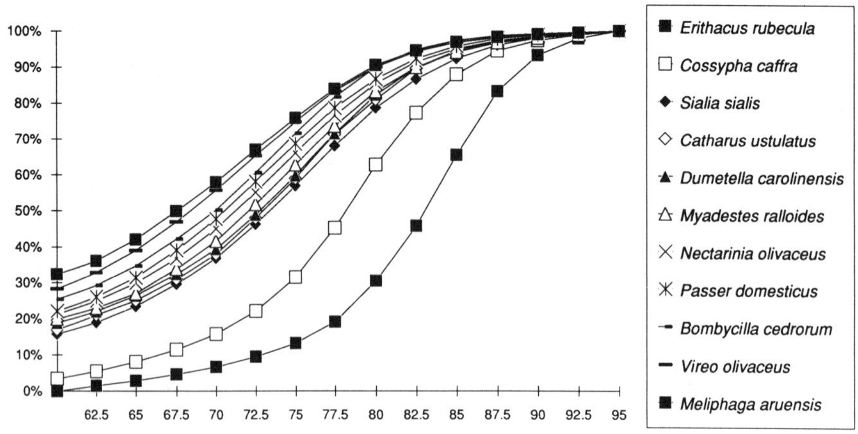
100%
90%
80%
70%
60%
50%
40%
30%
20%
10%
0%
62.5 65 67.5 70 72.5 75 77.5 80 82.5 85 87.5 90 92.5 95
Erithacus rubecula
Cossypha caffra
Sialia sialis
Catharus ustulatus
Dumetella carolinensis
Myadestes ralloides
Nectarinia olivaceus
Passer domesticus
Bombycilla cedrorum
Vireo olivaceus
Meliphaga aruensis

Fig. 262. Red-shouldered Glossy-Starling x Spotless Starling, Wattled Starling, Singing Starling, Long-billed Thrasher, Northern Mockingbird, Grey Catbird, Mountain Rock-Thrush, Veery, Nightingale, American Dipper, Little Raven

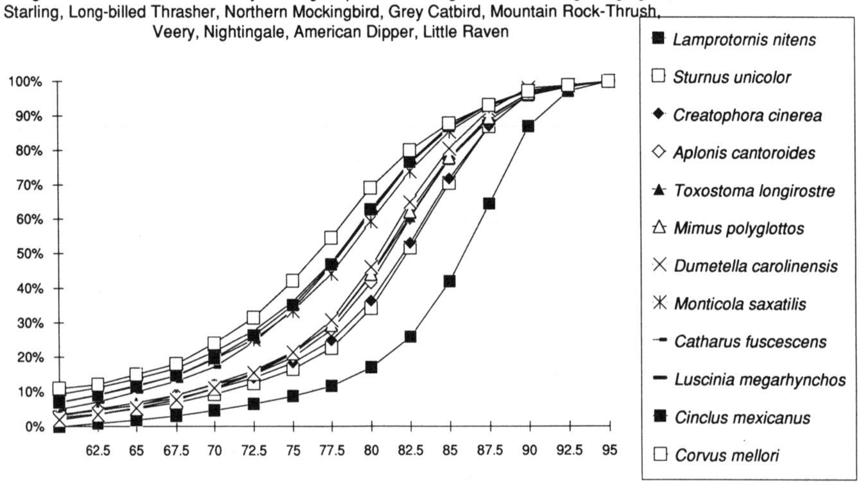
100%
90%
80%
70%
60%
50%
40%
30%
20%
10%
0%
62.5 65 67.5 70 72.5 75 77.5 80 82.5 85 87.5 90 92.5 95
Lamprotornis nitens
Sturnus unicolor
Creatophora cinerea
Aplonis cantoroides
Toxostoma longirostre
Mimus polyglottos
Dumetella carolinensis
Monticola saxatilis
Catharus fuscescens
Luscinia megarhynchos
Cinclus mexicanus
Corvus mellori

Fig. 263. Red-shouldered Glossy-Starling x Spotless Starling, Long-billed Thrasher, Village Weaver, Yellow-vented Bulbul, Black-capped Chickadee, Horned Lark, White-browed Wood-swallow, Great Grey Shrike, White-eyed Vireo

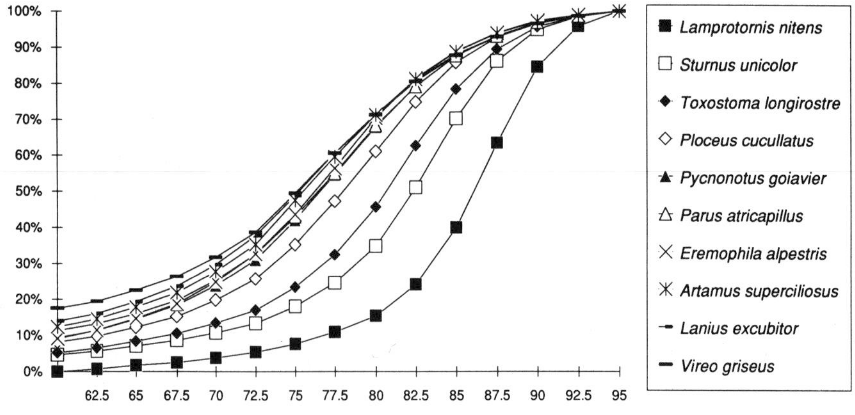
100%
90%
80%
70%
60%
50%
40%
30%
20%
10%
0%
62.5 65 67.5 70 72.5 75 77.5 80 82.5 85 87.5 90 92.5 95
Lamprotornis nitens
Sturnus unicolor
Toxostoma longirostre
Ploceus cucullatus
Pycnonotus goiavier
Parus atricapillus
Eremophila alpestris
Artamus superciliosus
Lanius excubitor
Vireo griseus

Fig. 264. European Starling x Singing Starling, Northern Mockingbird, Grey Catbird, Little Spiderhunter, Lesser Bird-of-paradise, American Crow, Willie Wagtail, Red-eyed Vireo, Loggerhead Shrike, Bare-necked Fruitcrow

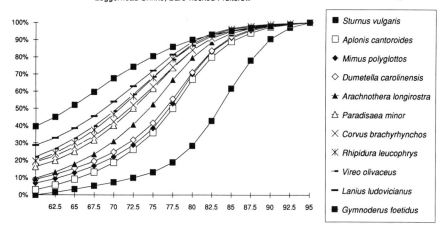

- ■ *Sturnus vulgaris*
- □ *Aplonis cantoroides*
- ◆ *Mimus polyglottos*
- ◇ *Dumetella carolinensis*
- ▲ *Arachnothera longirostra*
- △ *Paradisaea minor*
- ✕ *Corvus brachyrhynchos*
- ✳ *Rhipidura leucophrys*
- ➝ *Vireo olivaceus*
- — *Lanius ludovicianus*
- ■ *Gymnoderus foetidus*

Fig. 265. Long-billed Thrasher x Northern Mockingbird, Grey Catbird, Red-shouldered Glossy-Starling, Hill Myna, Wattled Starling, Grey-chested Jungle-Flycatcher, Townsend's Solitaire, Rufous-chested Flycatcher, Cedar Waxwing, Carolina Wren, Musician Wren

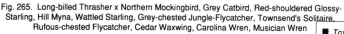

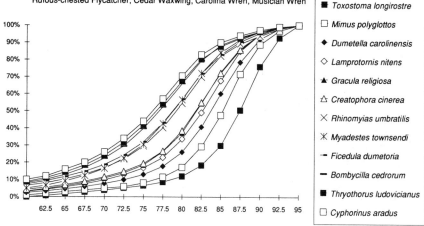

- ■ *Toxostoma longirostre*
- □ *Mimus polyglottos*
- ◆ *Dumetella carolinensis*
- ◇ *Lamprotornis nitens*
- ▲ *Gracula religiosa*
- △ *Creatophora cinerea*
- ✕ *Rhinomyias umbratilis*
- ✳ *Myadestes townsendi*
- ➝ *Ficedula dumetoria*
- — *Bombycilla cedrorum*
- ■ *Thryothorus ludovicianus*
- □ *Cyphorinus aradus*

Fig. 266. White-breasted Nuthatch x Wallcreeper, Common Tree-Creeper, Tropical Gnatcatcher, Black-capped Chickadee, House Wren, Verdin, Bushtit, Orphean Warbler, White-necked Rockfowl, Pied Crow

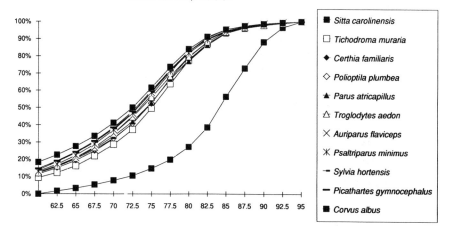

- ■ *Sitta carolinensis*
- □ *Tichodroma muraria*
- ◆ *Certhia familiaris*
- ◇ *Polioptila plumbea*
- ▲ *Parus atricapillus*
- △ *Troglodytes aedon*
- ✕ *Auriparus flaviceps*
- ✳ *Psaltriparus minimus*
- ➝ *Sylvia hortensis*
- — *Picathartes gymnocephalus*
- ■ *Corvus albus*

Fig. 267. White-breasted Nuthatch x Common Tree-Creeper, Lesser Whitethroat, Tufted Titmouse, Spotless Starling, White-browed Shortwing, Rufous-chested Flycatcher, American Robin, American Dipper, Hedge Accentor, House Sparrow

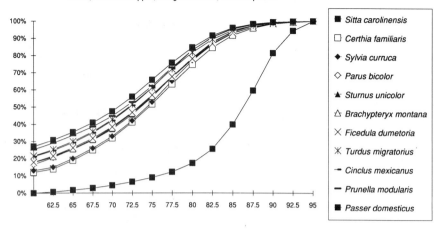

■ Sitta carolinensis
☐ Certhia familiaris
◆ Sylvia curruca
◇ Parus bicolor
▲ Sturnus unicolor
△ Brachypteryx montana
✕ Ficedula dumetoria
✳ Turdus migratorius
— Cinclus mexicanus
— Prunella modularis
■ Passer domesticus

Fig. 268. Common Tree-Creeper x Tawny-faced Gnatwren, House Wren, Tropical Gnatcatcher, Bushtit, Black-capped Chickadee, Verdin, Orphean Warbler, White-breasted Nuthatch, Rufous Treecreeper

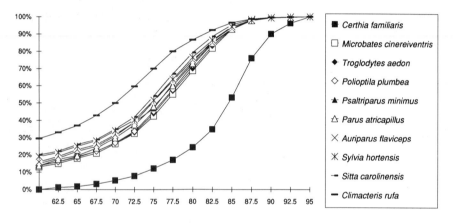

■ Certhia familiaris
☐ Microbates cinereiventris
◆ Troglodytes aedon
◇ Polioptila plumbea
▲ Psaltriparus minimus
△ Parus atricapillus
✕ Auriparus flaviceps
✳ Sylvia hortensis
— Sitta carolinensis
— Climacteris rufa

Fig. 269. Spotted Creeper x Common Tree-Creeper, Carolina Wren, Sedge Warbler, Common Myna, Orphean Warbler, Silvereye, Olive-winged Bulbul, Brown Scrub-Robin, American Goldfinch, Brown Honeyeater

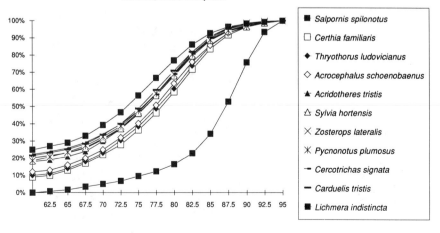

■ Salpornis spilonotus
☐ Certhia familiaris
◆ Thryothorus ludovicianus
◇ Acrocephalus schoenobaenus
▲ Acridotheres tristis
△ Sylvia hortensis
✕ Zosterops lateralis
✳ Pycnonotus plumosus
— Cercotrichas signata
— Carduelis tristis
■ Lichmera indistincta

Fig. 270. Bewick's Wren x Carolina Wren, House Wren, Sepia-brown Wren, Grey-breasted Wood-Wren, Musician Wren, Cactus Wren, Southern Nightingale-Wren, European Starling, Northern Mockingbird, American Crow

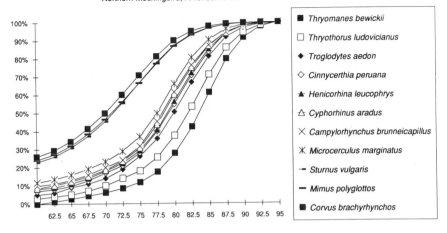

- ■ *Thryomanes bewickii*
- □ *Thryothorus ludovicianus*
- ◆ *Troglodytes aedon*
- ◇ *Cinnycerthia peruana*
- ▲ *Henicorhina leucophrys*
- △ *Cyphorhinus aradus*
- ✕ *Campylorhynchus brunneicapillus*
- ✳ *Microcerculus marginatus*
- ⌐ *Sturnus vulgaris*
- ▬ *Mimus polyglottos*
- ■ *Corvus brachyrhynchos*

Fig. 271. Bewick's Wren x House Wren, Black-tailed Gnatcatcher, Common Tree-Creeper, Verdin, American Dipper, Wrentit, Sage Thrasher, Tufted Titmouse, Fuscous Honeyeater, Bare-necked Fruitcrow

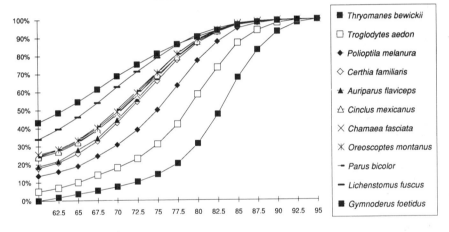

- ■ *Thryomanes bewickii*
- □ *Troglodytes aedon*
- ◆ *Polioptila melanura*
- ◇ *Certhia familiaris*
- ▲ *Auriparus flaviceps*
- △ *Cinclus mexicanus*
- ✕ *Chamaea fasciata*
- ✳ *Oreoscoptes montanus*
- ⌐ *Parus bicolor*
- ▬ *Lichenstomus fuscus*
- ■ *Gymnoderus foetidus*

Fig. 272. Black-tailed Gnatcatcher x Tawny-faced Gnatwren, Long-billed Gnatwren, Verdin, House Wren, Common Tree-Creeper, Musician Wren, Golden-crowned Kinglet, Black-capped Chickadee, Bushtit, Andean Solitaire

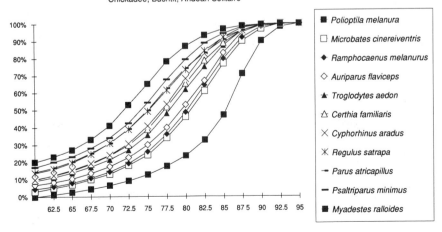

- ■ *Polioptila melanura*
- □ *Microbates cinereiventris*
- ◆ *Ramphocaenus melanurus*
- ◇ *Auriparus flaviceps*
- ▲ *Troglodytes aedon*
- △ *Certhia familiaris*
- ✕ *Cyphorhinus aradus*
- ✳ *Regulus satrapa*
- ⌐ *Parus atricapillus*
- ▬ *Psaltriparus minimus*
- ■ *Myadestes ralloides*

792

Fig. 273. Black-capped Chickadee x Great Tit, Southern Penduline-Tit, Orphean Warbler, Arrow-marked Babbler, Common Tree-Creeper, Golden-crowned Kinglet, Black-tailed Gnatcatcher, Long-tailed Tit, Hedge Accentor

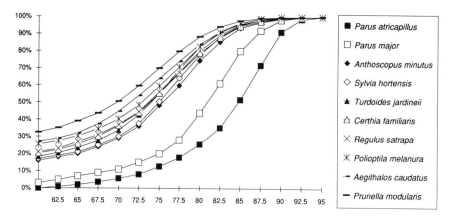

- ■ *Parus atricapillus*
- □ *Parus major*
- ◆ *Anthoscopus minutus*
- ◇ *Sylvia hortensis*
- ▲ *Turdoides jardineii*
- △ *Certhia familiaris*
- ✕ *Regulus satrapa*
- ✻ *Polioptila melanura*
- ⊸ *Aegithalos caudatus*
- — *Prunella modularis*

Fig. 274. Black-capped Chickadee x Great Tit, Red-billed Leiothrix, Black-chested Prinia, Cedar Waxwing, Tropical Gnatcatcher, Spotless Starling, Bushtit, American Robin, Orphean Warbler, Grey Jay

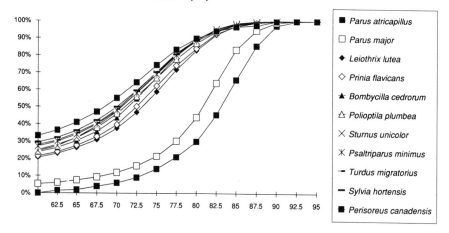

- ■ *Parus atricapillus*
- □ *Parus major*
- ◆ *Leiothrix lutea*
- ◇ *Prinia flavicans*
- ▲ *Bombycilla cedrorum*
- △ *Polioptila plumbea*
- ✕ *Sturnus unicolor*
- ✻ *Psaltriparus minimus*
- ⊸ *Turdus migratorius*
- — *Sylvia hortensis*
- ■ *Perisoreus canadensis*

Fig. 275. Long-tailed Tit x Bushtit, Chestnut-winged Babbler, Great Tit, Garden Warbler, Tropical Gnatcatcher, Red-breasted Nuthatch, Carolina Wren, Common Tree-Creeper, Willow Warbler, Southern Penduline-Tit

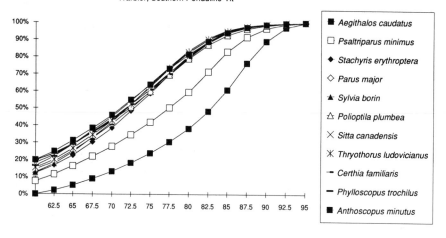

- ■ *Aegithalos caudatus*
- □ *Psaltriparus minimus*
- ◆ *Stachyris erythroptera*
- ◇ *Parus major*
- ▲ *Sylvia borin*
- △ *Polioptila plumbea*
- ✕ *Sitta canadensis*
- ✻ *Thryothorus ludovicianus*
- ⊸ *Certhia familiaris*
- — *Phylloscopus trochilus*
- ■ *Anthoscopus minutus*

Fig. 276. Barn Swallow x Sand Martin, Lesser Whitethroat, Himalayan Bulbul, Horned Lark, European Starling, White Wagtail, House Wren, Song Sparrow, Red-backed Shrike, Tawny-breasted Honeyeater

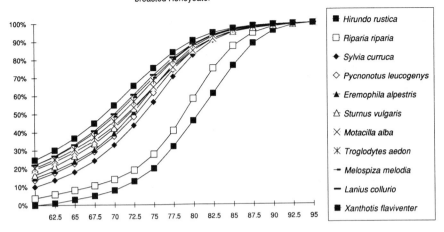

Fig. 277. Sand Martin x Purple Martin, Barn Swallow, Northern Rough-winged Swallow, South African Swallow, Oriental White-eye, Orphean Warbler, Yellow Bishop, Arrow-marked Babbler, Black-chested Prinia, Black-throated Accentor

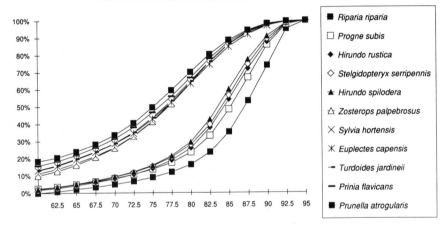

Fig. 278. Ruby-crowned Kinglet x Golden-crowned Kinglet, Willow Warbler, Garden Warbler, Great Tit, Tinkling Cisticola, Long-billed Gnatwren, Long-tailed Tit

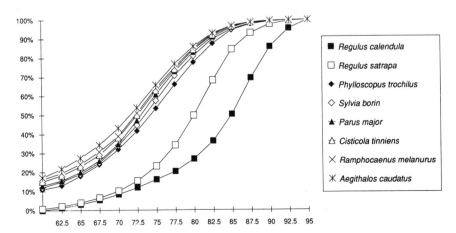

Fig. 279. Yellow-vented Bulbul x Olive-winged Bulbul, Common Bristlebill, Cape Robin-Chat, Brown-chested Alethe, Grey-chested Jungle-Flycatcher, Malaysian Flycatcher, Wattled Starling, Spotless Starling, Sunda Whistling-Thrush

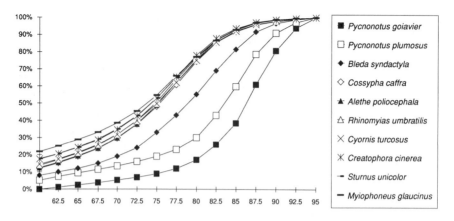

- ■ *Pycnonotus goiavier*
- □ *Pycnonotus plumosus*
- ◆ *Bleda syndactyla*
- ◇ *Cossypha caffra*
- ▲ *Alethe poliocephala*
- △ *Rhinomyias umbratilis*
- ✕ *Cyornis turcosus*
- ✱ *Creatophora cinerea*
- ╼ *Sturnus unicolor*
- ▬ *Myiophoneus glaucinus*

Fig. 280. Rattling Cisticola x Tinkling Cisticola, Rufous-fronted Prinia, Oriole Warbler, Bar-throated Apalis, Grey-backed Camaroptera, Little Grassbird, Arctic Warbler, Yellow-breasted Warbler, African Sedge-Warbler, Rufous-vented Warbler

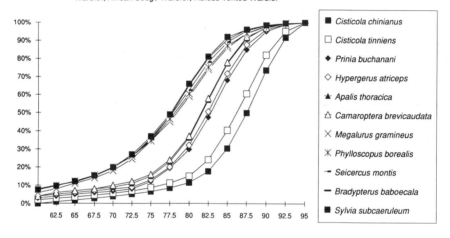

- ■ *Cisticola chinianus*
- □ *Cisticola tinniens*
- ◆ *Prinia buchanani*
- ◇ *Hypergerus atriceps*
- ▲ *Apalis thoracica*
- △ *Camaroptera brevicaudata*
- ✕ *Megalurus gramineus*
- ✱ *Phylloscopus borealis*
- ╼ *Seicercus montis*
- ▬ *Bradypterus baboecala*
- ■ *Sylvia subcaeruleum*

Fig. 281. Rattling Cisticola x Tinkling Cisticola, Orphean Warbler, Willow Warbler, Yellow-vented Bulbul, Arrow-marked Babbler, Yap Olive White-eye, Barn Swallow, Common Tree-Creeper, Long-tailed Tit, Red-breasted Nuthatch, Southern Penduline-Tit

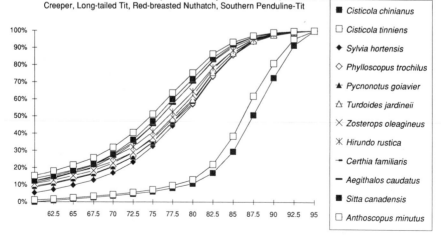

- ■ *Cisticola chinianus*
- □ *Cisticola tinniens*
- ◆ *Sylvia hortensis*
- ◇ *Phylloscopus trochilus*
- ▲ *Pycnonotus goiavier*
- △ *Turdoides jardineii*
- ✕ *Zosterops oleagineus*
- ✱ *Hirundo rustica*
- ╼ *Certhia familiaris*
- ▬ *Aegithalos caudatus*
- ■ *Sitta canadensis*
- □ *Anthoscopus minutus*

Fig. 282. Black-chested Prinia x Rufous-fronted Prinia, Rattling Cisticola, Oriole Warbler, Green-backed Camaroptera, Willow Warbler, Rufous-vented Warbler, Spinifex-bird, African Scrub-Warbler, Rufous Songlark, Western Gerygone

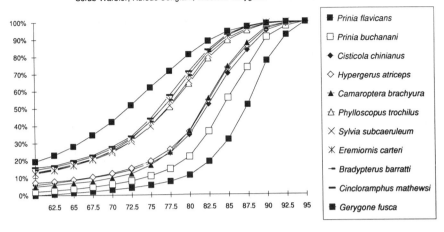

- ■ *Prinia flavicans*
- □ *Prinia buchanani*
- ◆ *Cisticola chinianus*
- ◇ *Hypergerus atriceps*
- ▲ *Camaroptera brachyura*
- △ *Phylloscopus trochilus*
- ✕ *Sylvia subcaeruleum*
- ✳ *Eremiornis carteri*
- ▬ *Bradypterus barratti*
- ▬ *Cincloramphus mathewsi*
- ▰ *Gerygone fusca*

Fig. 283. Golden White-eye x Oriental White-eye, Yap Olive White-eye, Collared Sunbird, Grey-breasted Spiderhunter, Olive-crowned Flowerpecker, Green-headed Sunbird, White-fronted Honeyeater, Singing Honeyeater, Red-headed Myzomela

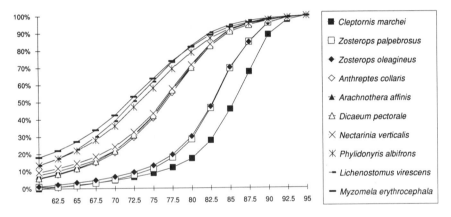

- ■ *Cleptornis marchei*
- □ *Zosterops palpebrosus*
- ◆ *Zosterops oleagineus*
- ◇ *Anthreptes collaris*
- ▲ *Arachnothera affinis*
- △ *Dicaeum pectorale*
- ✕ *Nectarinia verticalis*
- ✳ *Phylidonyris albifrons*
- ▬ *Lichenostomus virescens*
- ▬ *Myzomela erythrocephala*

Fig. 284. Golden White-eye x Silver-eye, Orphean Warbler, Willow Warbler, Lazy Cisticola, Yellow-vented Bulbul, Gurney's Sugarbird, Lemon-breasted Berrypecker, Little Wattlebird, Striped Honeyeater

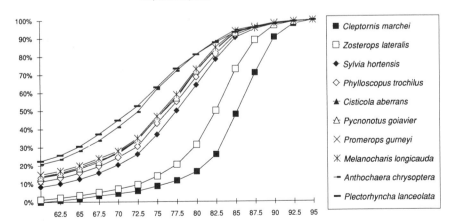

- ■ *Cleptornis marchei*
- □ *Zosterops lateralis*
- ◆ *Sylvia hortensis*
- ◇ *Phylloscopus trochilus*
- ▲ *Cisticola aberrans*
- △ *Pycnonotus goiavier*
- ✕ *Promerops gurneyi*
- ✳ *Melanocharis longicauda*
- ▬ *Anthochaera chrysoptera*
- ▬ *Plectorhyncha lanceolata*

Fig. 285. Orphean Warbler x Arrow-marked Babbler, Willow Warbler, Lesser Swamp-Warbler, Spinifex-bird, Long-tailed Tit, Common Tree-Creeper, House Wren, White-breasted Nuthatch, Golden-crowned Kinglet, Yellow-rumped Thornbill

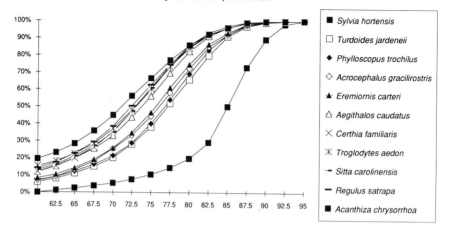

Fig. 286. Orphean Warbler x Lesser Whitethroat, Rufous-vented Warbler, Arrow-marked Babbler, Arctic Warbler, Moustached Grass-Warbler, Grey-capped Warbler, Green Crombec, Black-chested Prinia, Tinkling Cisticola

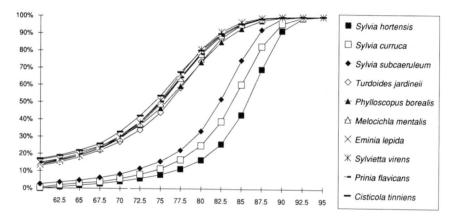

Fig. 287. Orphean Warbler x Chestnut-winged Babbler, Wrentit, Willow Warbler, Red-billed Leiothrix, Brown Babbler, Brown Songlark, White-necked Rockfowl, Black-whiskered Vireo, American Crow

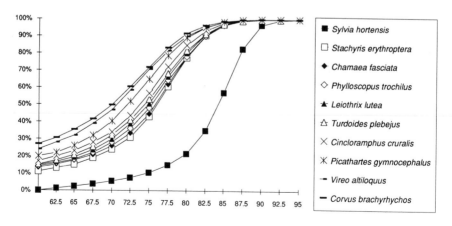

Fig. 288. Melodious Warbler x Chestnut-backed Scimitar-Babbler, Formosan Yuhina, Lesser Whitethroat, Bushtit, Black-capped Chickadee, Common Tree-Creeper, Red-breasted Nuthatch, House Wren, White-necked Rockfowl, White-browed Babbler

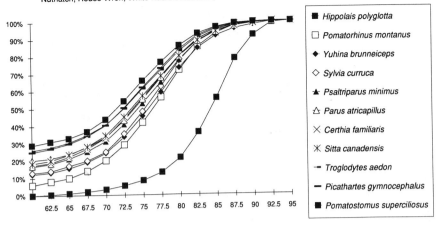

- ■ *Hippolais polyglotta*
- □ *Pomatorhinus montanus*
- ◆ *Yuhina brunneiceps*
- ◇ *Sylvia curruca*
- ▲ *Psaltriparus minimus*
- △ *Parus atricapillus*
- ✕ *Certhia familiaris*
- ✳ *Sitta canadensis*
- ⚊ *Troglodytes aedon*
- ⚊ *Picathartes gymnocephalus*
- ■ *Pomatostomus superciliosus*

Fig. 289. Willow Warbler x Arctic Warbler, Sedge Warbler, Garden Warbler, Great Tit, Long-billed Gnatwren, Rattling Cisticola, Musician Wren, Common Tree-Creeper

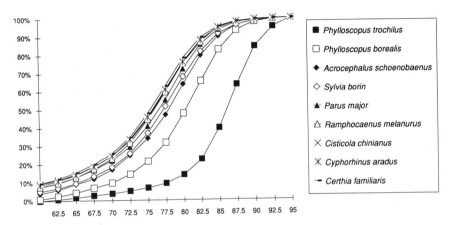

- ■ *Phylloscopus trochilus*
- □ *Phylloscopus borealis*
- ◆ *Acrocephalus schoenobaenus*
- ◇ *Sylvia borin*
- ▲ *Parus major*
- △ *Ramphocaenus melanurus*
- ✕ *Cisticola chinianus*
- ✳ *Cyphorhinus aradus*
- ⚊ *Certhia familiaris*

Fig. 290. Fernbird x Little Grassbird, Spinifex-bird, Brown Songlark, Rufous Songlark, Arctic Warbler, Clamorous Reed-Warbler, Lazy Cisticola, Purple-backed Fairywren, Southern Emuwren

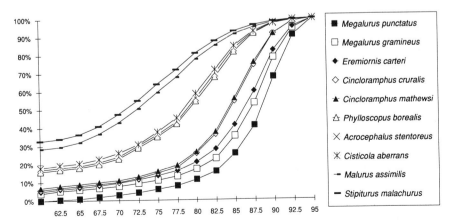

- ■ *Megalurus punctatus*
- □ *Megalurus gramineus*
- ◆ *Eremiornis carteri*
- ◇ *Cincloramphus cruralis*
- ▲ *Cincloramphus mathewsi*
- △ *Phylloscopus borealis*
- ✕ *Acrocephalus stentoreus*
- ✳ *Cisticola aberrans*
- ⚊ *Malurus assimilis*
- ⚊ *Stipiturus malachurus*

798

Fig. 291. Fernbird x Little Grassbird, Yellow-bellied Prinia, Orphean Warbler, Whitehead,
Golden Whistler, Shining Monarch, Grey Fantail, Scarlet Robin, Brown Honeyeater

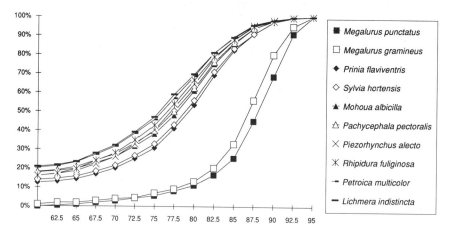

- ■ *Megalurus punctatus*
- □ *Megalurus gramineus*
- ◆ *Prinia flaviventris*
- ◇ *Sylvia hortensis*
- ▲ *Mohoua albicilla*
- △ *Pachycephala pectoralis*
- ✕ *Piezorhynchus alecto*
- ✳ *Rhipidura fuliginosa*
- ✚ *Petroica multicolor*
- ▬ *Lichmera indistincta*

Fig. 292. Brown Songlark x Rufous Songlark, Little Grassbird, Spinifex-bird, Lesser Swamp-
Warbler, Orphean Warbler, Brown Honeyeater, Great Bowerbird, Yellow-rumped Thornbill,
Splendid Fairywren

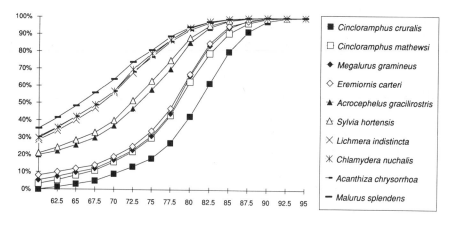

- ■ *Cincloramphus cruralis*
- □ *Cincloramphus mathewsi*
- ◆ *Megalurus gramineus*
- ◇ *Eremiornis carteri*
- ▲ *Acrocephelus gracilirostris*
- △ *Sylvia hortensis*
- ✕ *Lichmera indistincta*
- ✳ *Chlamydera nuchalis*
- ✚ *Acanthiza chrysorrhoa*
- ▬ *Malurus splendens*

Fig. 293. Moustached Grass-Warbler x Cape Grass-Warbler, Green Crombec, Tinkling
Cisticola, Brown Songlark, Little Grassbird, Black-tailed Gnatcatcher, Ruby-crowned Kinglet,
White-throated Gerygone

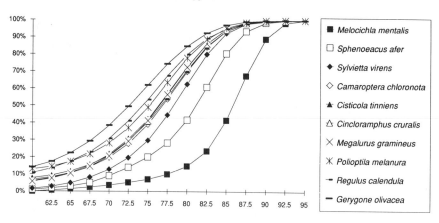

- ■ *Melocichla mentalis*
- □ *Sphenoeacus afer*
- ◆ *Sylvietta virens*
- ◇ *Camaroptera chloronota*
- ▲ *Cisticola tinniens*
- △ *Cincloramphus cruralis*
- ✕ *Megalurus gramineus*
- ✳ *Polioptila melanura*
- ✚ *Regulus calendula*
- ▬ *Gerygone olivacea*

Fig. 294. Arrow-marked Babbler x Chestnut-winged Babbler, Orphean Warbler, Willow Warbler, Common Tree-Creeper, Long-tailed Tit, Red-breasted Nuthatch, Southern Penduline-Tit, White-browed Babbler

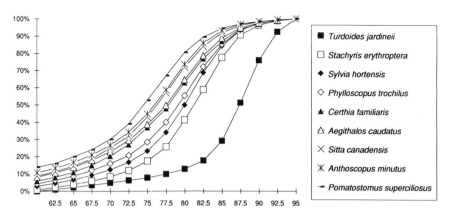

- ■ *Turdoides jardineii*
- □ *Stachyris erythroptera*
- ◆ *Sylvia hortensis*
- ◇ *Phylloscopus trochilus*
- ▲ *Certhia familiaris*
- △ *Aegithalos caudatus*
- ✕ *Sitta canadensis*
- ✱ *Anthoscopus minutus*
- — *Pomatostomus superciliosus*

Fig. 295. Horned Lark x Crested Lark, Clapper Lark, Desert Lark, Village Weaver, Green-headed Sunbird, Orphean Warbler, Sand Martin, American Robin

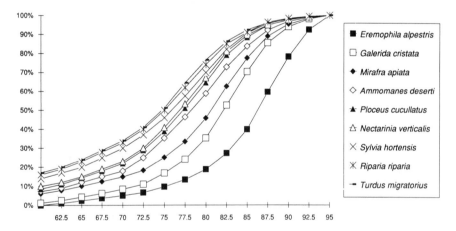

- ■ *Eremophila alpestris*
- □ *Galerida cristata*
- ◆ *Mirafra apiata*
- ◇ *Ammomanes deserti*
- ▲ *Ploceus cucullatus*
- △ *Nectarinia verticalis*
- ✕ *Sylvia hortensis*
- ✱ *Riparia riparia*
- — *Turdus migratorius*

Fig. 296. Crested Berrypecker x Tit Berrypecker, Grey-winged Longbill, Green-crowned Longbill, Plumed Longbill, Spotted Berrypecker, Cape Sugarbird, Green-headed Sunbird, Olive-crowned Flowerpecker, Striated Pardalote, Belford's Melidectes

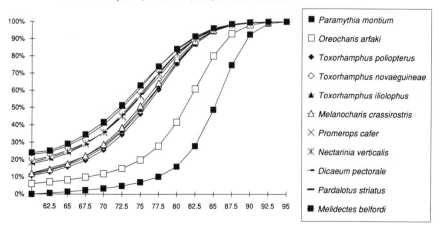

- ■ *Paramythia montium*
- □ *Oreocharis arfaki*
- ◆ *Toxorhamphus poliopterus*
- ◇ *Toxorhamphus novaeguineae*
- ▲ *Toxorhamphus iliolophus*
- △ *Melanocharis crassirostris*
- ✕ *Promerops cafer*
- ✱ *Nectarinia verticalis*
- — *Dicaeum pectorale*
- — *Pardalotus striatus*
- ■ *Melidectes belfordi*

Fig. 297. Fan-tailed Berrypecker x Lemon-breasted Berrypecker, Streaked Berrypecker, Grey-winged Longbill, Plumed Longbill, Cape Sugarbird, Olive-crowned Flowerpecker, White-fronted Honeyeater, Striated Pardalote

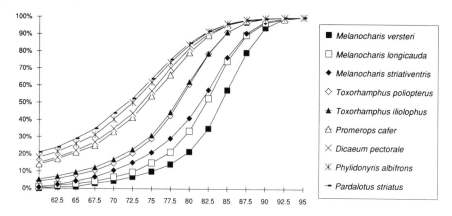

Fig. 298. Plumed Longbill x Green-crowned Longbill, Lemon-breasted Berrypecker, Fan-tailed Berrypecker, Cape Sugarbird, Brown-throated Sunbird, Scarlet Sunbird, Olive-crowned Flowerpecker, Yap Olive White-eye, Dusky Myzomela, Striped Honeyeater

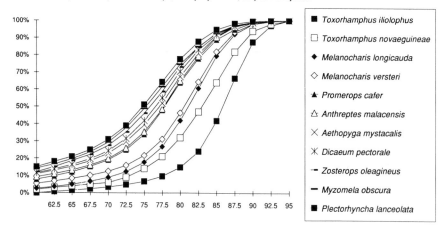

Fig. 299. Green-headed Sunbird x Collared Sunbird, Crimson Sunbird, Yellow-breasted Flowerpecker, Black-throated Accentor, Cape Sugarbird, Plumed Longbill, Russet-backed Oropendola, Lemon-breasted Berrypecker, White-plumed Honeyeater

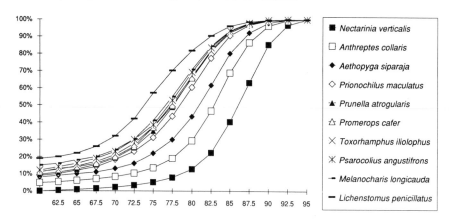

Fig. 300. Green-headed Sunbird x Purple-naped Sunbird, Orange-bellied Flowerpecker, Cape Sugarbird, Yellow Bishop, Hedge Accentor, Orphean Warbler, Little Raven

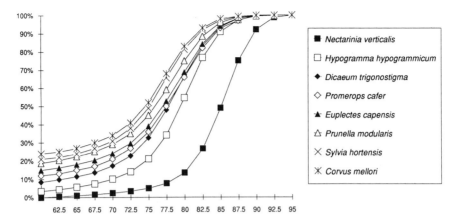

- ■ *Nectarinia verticalis*
- □ *Hypogramma hypogrammicum*
- ◆ *Dicaeum trigonostigma*
- ◇ *Promerops cafer*
- ▲ *Euplectes capensis*
- △ *Prunella modularis*
- ✕ *Sylvia hortensis*
- ✳ *Corvus mellori*

Fig. 301. Green-headed Sunbird x Purple-naped Sunbird, Plumed Longbill, Chestnut-shouldered Petronia, Oriental White-eye, White-breasted Nuthatch, American Dipper, Dusky Myzomela, Lewin's Honeyeater

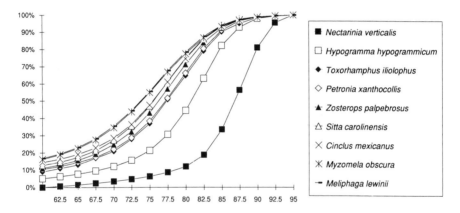

- ■ *Nectarinia verticalis*
- □ *Hypogramma hypogrammicum*
- ◆ *Toxorhamphus iliolophus*
- ◇ *Petronia xanthocollis*
- ▲ *Zosterops palpebrosus*
- △ *Sitta carolinensis*
- ✕ *Cinclus mexicanus*
- ✳ *Myzomela obscura*
- ‒ *Meliphaga lewinii*

Fig. 302. Cape Sugarbird x Gurney's Sugarbird, Olive Sunbird, Brown-throated Sunbird, Scarlet Sunbird, Olive-crowned Flowerpecker, Yellow-breasted Flowerpecker, Plumed Longbill, Fan-tailed Berrypecker, White-plumed Honeyeater, White-fronted Honeyeater

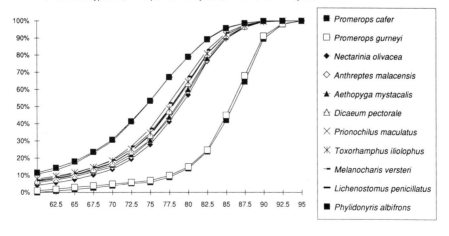

- ■ *Promerops cafer*
- □ *Promerops gurneyi*
- ◆ *Nectarinia olivacea*
- ◇ *Anthreptes malacensis*
- ▲ *Aethopyga mystacalis*
- △ *Dicaeum pectorale*
- ✕ *Prionochilus maculatus*
- ✳ *Toxorhamphus iliolophus*
- ‒ *Melanocharis versteri*
- ‒ *Lichenostomus penicillatus*
- ■ *Phylidonyris albifrons*

Fig. 303. House Sparrow x Village Weaver, Black-throated Accentor, Red-winged Blackbird, Olive Sunbird, European Starling, Red-capped Robin-Chat, White-plumed Honeyeater

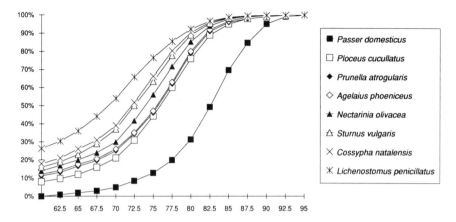

- ■ *Passer domesticus*
- □ *Ploceus cucullatus*
- ◆ *Prunella atrogularis*
- ◇ *Agelaius phoeniceus*
- ▲ *Nectarinia olivacea*
- △ *Sturnus vulgaris*
- ✕ *Cossypha natalensis*
- ✳ *Lichenostomus penicillatus*

Fig. 304. House Sparrow x Grey-headed Sparrow, Chestnut-shouldered Petronia, Bush Petronia, Village Weaver, Sociable Weaver, Grey-headed Negrofinch, Pin-tailed Whydah. American Robin

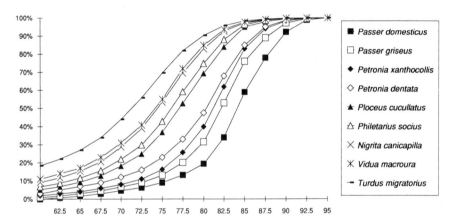

- ■ *Passer domesticus*
- □ *Passer griseus*
- ◆ *Petronia xanthocollis*
- ◇ *Petronia dentata*
- ▲ *Ploceus cucullatus*
- △ *Philetarius socius*
- ✕ *Nigrita canicapilla*
- ✳ *Vidua macroura*
- ‑ *Turdus migratorius*

Fig. 305. White Wagtail x Yellow Wagtail, Brown Tree-Pipit, Red-billed Quelea, House Sparrow, Swamp Sparrow, Magnolia Warbler, Olive Sunbird, Tufted Titmouse, American Robin, Red-eyed Vireo, Puff-backed Honeyeater

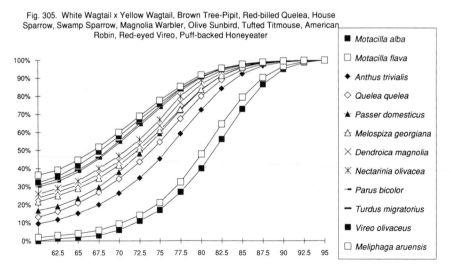

- ■ *Motacilla alba*
- □ *Motacilla flava*
- ◆ *Anthus trivialis*
- ◇ *Quelea quelea*
- ▲ *Passer domesticus*
- △ *Melospiza georgiana*
- ✕ *Dendroica magnolia*
- ✳ *Nectarinia olivacea*
- ‑ *Parus bicolor*
- — *Turdus migratorius*
- ■ *Vireo olivaceus*
- □ *Meliphaga aruensis*

Fig. 306. Cape Weaver x Olive Sunbird, House Sparrow, Swamp Sparrow, Cedar Waxwing, Horned Lark, European Starling, Pale White-eye, Garden Warbler, Red-eyed Vireo, American Crow, Fuscous Honeyeater

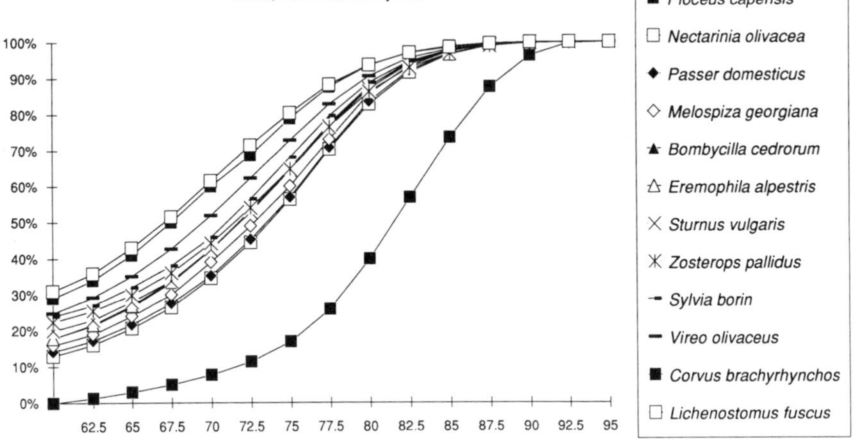
100%
90%
80%
70%
60%
50%
40%
30%
20%
10%
0%
62.5 65 67.5 70 72.5 75 77.5 80 82.5 85 87.5 90 92.5 95
Ploceus capensis
Nectarinia olivacea
Passer domesticus
Melospiza georgiana
Bombycilla cedrorum
Eremophila alpestris
Sturnus vulgaris
Zosterops pallidus
Sylvia borin
Vireo olivaceus
Corvus brachyrhynchos
Lichenostomus fuscus

Fig. 307. Pin-tailed Whydah x Queen Whydah, Red-billed Firefinch, Black-necked Weaver, White-browed Sparrow-Weaver, Sociable Weaver, Scaly Weaver, Yellow Wagtail, Mossie, Chaffinch, Eurasian Skylark

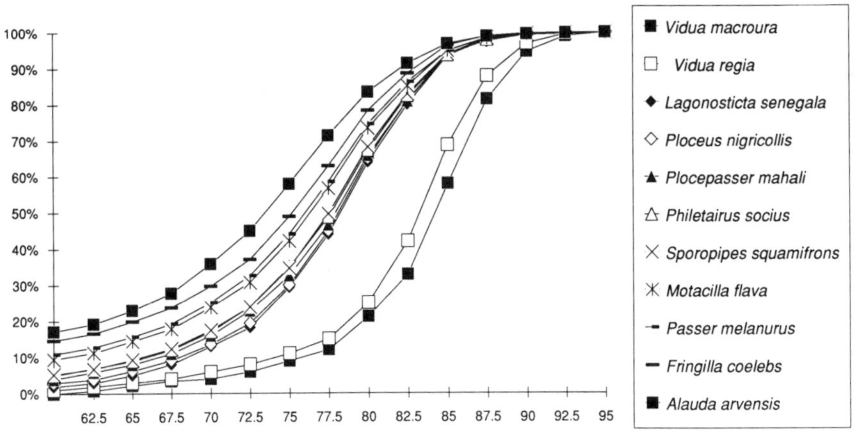
100%
90%
80%
70%
60%
50%
40%
30%
20%
10%
0%
62.5 65 67.5 70 72.5 75 77.5 80 82.5 85 87.5 90 92.5 95
Vidua macroura
Vidua regia
Lagonosticta senegala
Ploceus nigricollis
Plocepasser mahali
Philetairus socius
Sporopipes squamifrons
Motacilla flava
Passer melanurus
Fringilla coelebs
Alauda arvensis

Fig. 308. Chaffinch x Arctic Rosy Finch, House Finch, Pine Grosbeak, Northern Cardinal, Blackpoll Warbler, Dead Sea Sparrow, Rock Bunting, White Wagtail, Green-headed Sunbird, Desert Lark, Spotless Starling

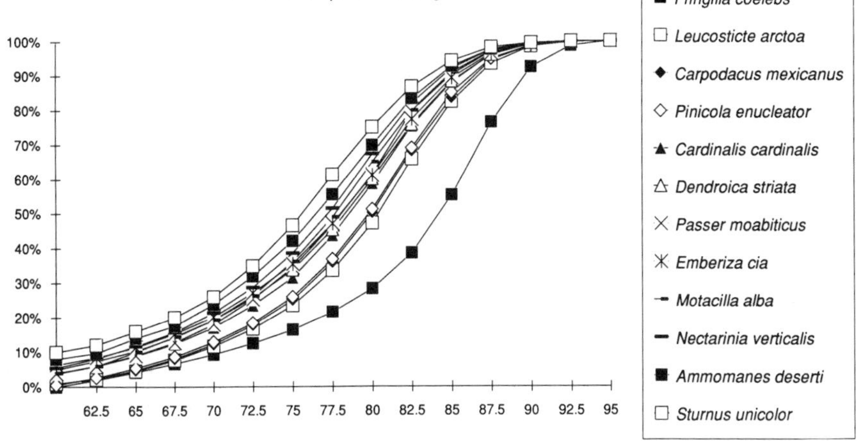
100%
90%
80%
70%
60%
50%
40%
30%
20%
10%
0%
62.5 65 67.5 70 72.5 75 77.5 80 82.5 85 87.5 90 92.5 95
Fringilla coelebs
Leucosticte arctoa
Carpodacus mexicanus
Pinicola enucleator
Cardinalis cardinalis
Dendroica striata
Passer moabiticus
Emberiza cia
Motacilla alba
Nectarinia verticalis
Ammomanes deserti
Sturnus unicolor

804

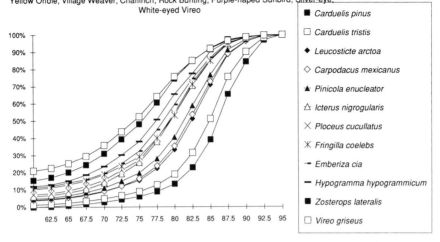

Fig. 309. Pine Siskin x American Goldfinch, Arctic Rosy Finch, House Finch, Pine Grosbeak, Yellow Oriole, Village Weaver, Chaffinch, Rock Bunting, Purple-naped Sunbird, Silver-eye, White-eyed Vireo

- Carduelis pinus
- Carduelis tristis
- Leucosticte arctoa
- Carpodacus mexicanus
- Pinicola enucleator
- Icterus nigrogularis
- Ploceus cucullatus
- Fringilla coelebs
- Emberiza cia
- Hypogramma hypogrammicum
- Zosterops lateralis
- Vireo griseus

Fig. 310. Common Amakihi x Iiwi, American Goldfinch, Eurasian Siskin, Red Crossbill, Red-legged Honeycreeper, Orchard Oriole, Scrub Tanager, Silver-beaked Tanager, Common Yellowthroat, Lincoln's Sparrow

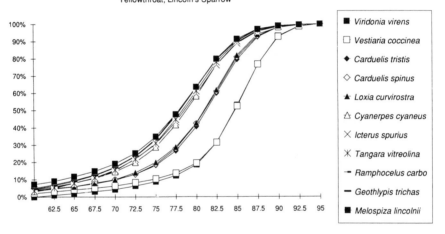

- Viridonia virens
- Vestiaria coccinea
- Carduelis tristis
- Carduelis spinus
- Loxia curvirostra
- Cyanerpes cyaneus
- Icterus spurius
- Tangara vitreolina
- Ramphocelus carbo
- Geothlypis trichas
- Melospiza lincolnii

Fig. 311. Common Amakihi x Apapane, Red Crossbill, Pine Grosbeak, American Redstart, Red-legged Honeycreeper, Bananaquit, Northern Cardinal, American Robin, American Crow, Puff-backed Honeyeater

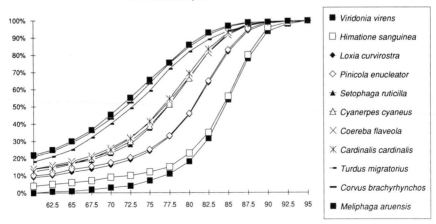

- Viridonia virens
- Himatione sanguinea
- Loxia curvirostra
- Pinicola enucleator
- Setophaga ruticilla
- Cyanerpes cyaneus
- Coereba flaveola
- Cardinalis cardinalis
- Turdus migratorius
- Corvus brachyrhynchos
- Meliphaga aruensis

Fig. 312. Olive Warbler x Green-headed Sunbird, Arctic Rosy Finch, Yellow-hooded Blackbird, Three-striped Warbler, Seaside Sparrow, Slate-throated Redstart, Orphean Warbler, Ruby-crowned Kinglet, Carolina Wren, White-eyed Vireo

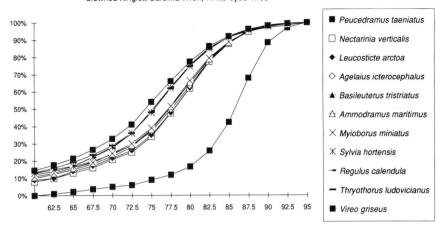

- ■ *Peucedramus taeniatus*
- □ *Nectarinia verticalis*
- ◆ *Leucosticte arctoa*
- ◇ *Agelaius icterocephalus*
- ▲ *Basileuterus tristriatus*
- △ *Ammodramus maritimus*
- ✕ *Myioborus miniatus*
- ✖ *Sylvia hortensis*
- ➤ *Regulus calendula*
- — *Thryothorus ludovicianus*
- ■ *Vireo griseus*

Fig. 313. American Tree Sparrow x Swamp Sparrow, Swallow Tanager, Red-winged Blackbird, Black-throated Green Warbler, Arctic Rosy Finch, Pine Siskin, White-browed Sparrow-Weaver, Green-headed Sunbird, Tropical Gnatcatcher

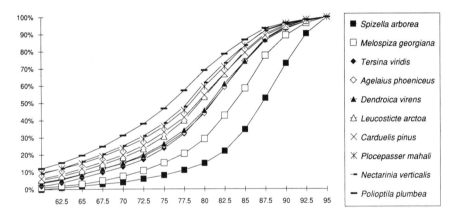

- ■ *Spizella arborea*
- □ *Melospiza georgiana*
- ◆ *Tersina viridis*
- ◇ *Agelaius phoeniceus*
- ▲ *Dendroica virens*
- △ *Leucosticte arctoa*
- ✕ *Carduelis pinus*
- ✖ *Plocepasser mahali*
- ➤ *Nectarinia verticalis*
- — *Polioptila plumbea*

Fig. 314. Vesper Sparrow x White-winged Brush-Finch, Dark-eyed Junco, Yellow-rumped Cacique, Common Diuca-Finch, Swallow Tanager, Grassland Yellow-Finch, Slaty Finch, Plushcap, Pardusco, Summer Tanager, Northern Cardinal

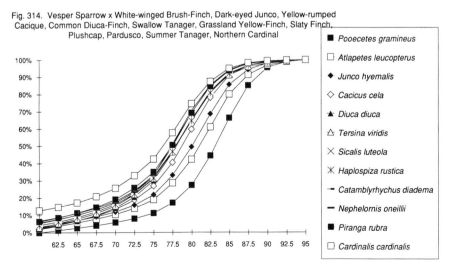

- ■ *Pooecetes gramineus*
- □ *Atlapetes leucopterus*
- ◆ *Junco hyemalis*
- ◇ *Cacicus cela*
- ▲ *Diuca diuca*
- △ *Tersina viridis*
- ✕ *Sicalis luteola*
- ✖ *Haplospiza rustica*
- ➤ *Catamblyrhynchus diadema*
- — *Nephelornis oneillii*
- ■ *Piranga rubra*
- □ *Cardinalis cardinalis*

Fig. 315. Vesper Sparrow x Black-throated Sparrow, Orchard Oriole, Glossy Flower-Piercer,
Blackpoll Warbler, Village Weaver, Olive Sunbird, Sepia-brown Wren

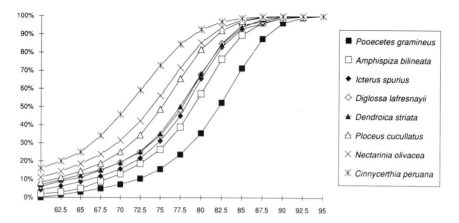

- ■ *Pooecetes gramineus*
- □ *Amphispiza bilineata*
- ◆ *Icterus spurius*
- ◇ *Diglossa lafresnayii*
- ▲ *Dendroica striata*
- △ *Ploceus cucullatus*
- ✕ *Nectarinia olivacea*
- ✳ *Cinnycerthia peruana*

Fig. 316. Lapland Longspur x Lapland Longspur, Russet-backed Oropendola (2), White-lined
Tanager (2), Plushcap (2), Vesper Sparrow (2), Blackpoll Warbler (2)

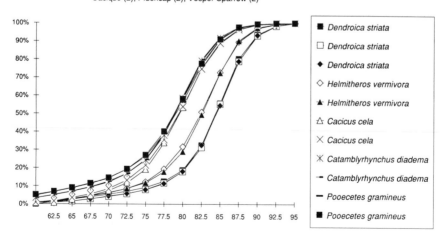

- ■ *Calcarius lapponicus*
- □ *Calcarius lapponicus*
- ◆ *Psarocolius angustifrons*
- ◇ *Psarocolius angustifrons*
- ▲ *Tachyphonus rufus*
- △ *Tachyphonus rufus*
- ✕ *Catamblyrhynchus diadema*
- ✳ *Catamblyrhynchus diadema*
- ⁃ *Pooecetes gramineus*
- ⁃ *Pooecetes gramineus*
- ■ *Dendroica striata*
- □ *Dendroica striata*

Fig. 317. Blackpoll Warbler x Blackpoll Warbler (2), Worm-eating Warbler (2), Yellow-rumped
Cacique (2), Plushcap (2), Vesper Sparrow (2)

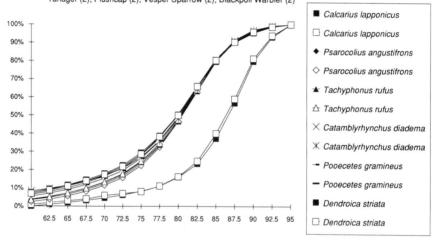

- ■ *Dendroica striata*
- □ *Dendroica striata*
- ◆ *Dendroica striata*
- ◇ *Helmitheros vermivora*
- ▲ *Helmitheros vermivora*
- △ *Cacicus cela*
- ✕ *Cacicus cela*
- ✳ *Catamblyrhynchus diadema*
- ⁃ *Catamblyrhynchus diadema*
- ⁃ *Pooecetes gramineus*
- ■ *Pooecetes gramineus*

Fig. 318. Yellow Oriole x Solitary Cacique, Red-breasted Blackbird, White-lined Tanager, Dark-eyed Junco, Slate-throated Redstart, Northern Cardinal, Green-headed Sunbird, Black-capped Chickadee, European Skylark, Spotless Starling, White-eyed Vireo

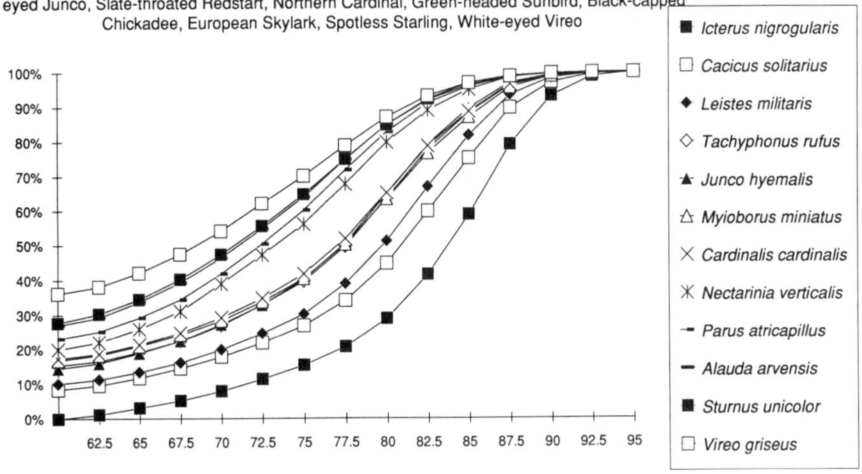
100%
90%
80%
70%
60%
50%
40%
30%
20%
10%
0%
62.5 65 67.5 70 72.5 75 77.5 80 82.5 85 87.5 90 92.5 95
Icterus nigrogularis
Cacicus solitarius
Leistes militaris
Tachyphonus rufus
Junco hyemalis
Myioborus miniatus
Cardinalis cardinalis
Nectarinia verticalis
Parus atricapillus
Alauda arvensis
Sturnus unicolor
Vireo griseus

Fig. 319. Northern Cardinal x White-lined Tanager, Orchard Oriole, Vesper Sparrow, Slate-throated Redstart, White Wagtail, House Sparrow, Zebra Finch, Purple-naped Sunbird, Desert Lark, Lemon-breasted Berrypecker, Yap Olive White-eye

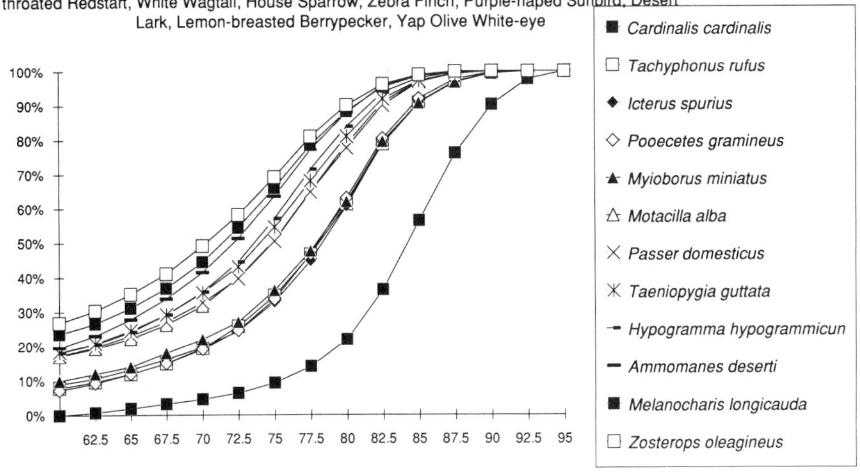
100%
90%
80%
70%
60%
50%
40%
30%
20%
10%
0%
62.5 65 67.5 70 72.5 75 77.5 80 82.5 85 87.5 90 92.5 95
Cardinalis cardinalis
Tachyphonus rufus
Icterus spurius
Pooecetes gramineus
Myioborus miniatus
Motacilla alba
Passer domesticus
Taeniopygia guttata
Hypogramma hypogrammicun
Ammomanes deserti
Melanocharis longicauda
Zosterops oleagineus

Fig. 320. Pardusco x Magpie Tanager, Rufous-crested Tanager, Northern Cardinal, Vesper Sparrow, White Wagtail, Common Amakihi, Olive Sunbird, Mossie, Golden-crowned Kinglet, White-eyed Vireo

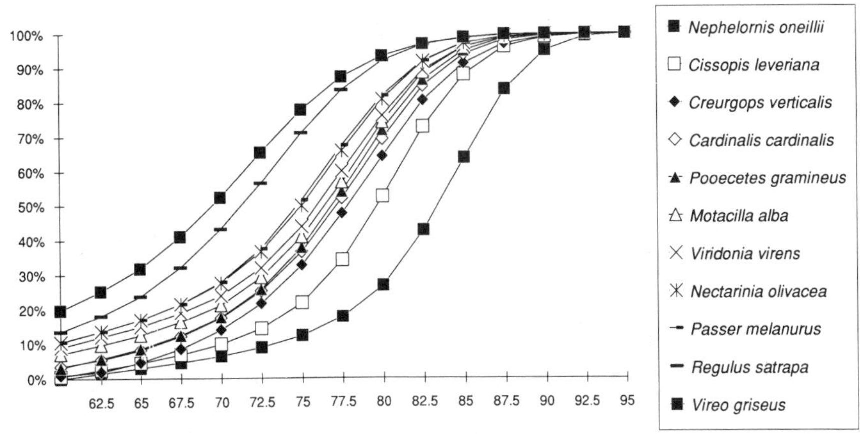
100%
90%
80%
70%
60%
50%
40%
30%
20%
10%
0%
62.5 65 67.5 70 72.5 75 77.5 80 82.5 85 87.5 90 92.5 95
Nephelornis oneillii
Cissopis leveriana
Creurgops verticalis
Cardinalis cardinalis
Pooecetes gramineus
Motacilla alba
Viridonia virens
Nectarinia olivacea
Passer melanurus
Regulus satrapa
Vireo griseus

808

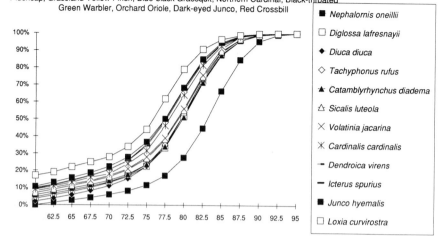

Fig. 321. Pardusco x Glossy Flower-piercer, Common Diuca-Finch, White-lined Tanager, Plushcap, Grassland Yellow-Finch, Blue-black Grassquit, Northern Cardinal, Black-throated Green Warbler, Orchard Oriole, Dark-eyed Junco, Red Crossbill

- ■ *Nephalornis oneillii*
- ☐ *Diglossa lafresnayii*
- ◆ *Diuca diuca*
- ◇ *Tachyphonus rufus*
- ▲ *Catamblyrhynchus diadema*
- △ *Sicalis luteola*
- ✕ *Volatinia jacarina*
- ✳ *Cardinalis cardinalis*
- ⌐ *Dendroica virens*
- ━ *Icterus spurius*
- ■ *Junco hyemalis*
- ☐ *Loxia curvirostra*

Fig. 322. White-lined Tanager x Swallow Tanager (2), Russet-backed Oropendola (2), Blackpoll Warbler (2), Vesper Sparrow (2)

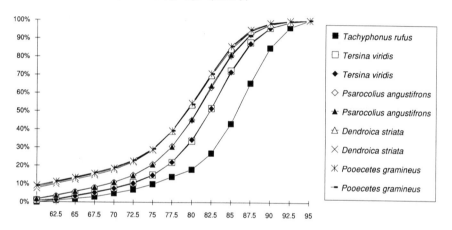

- ■ *Tachyphonus rufus*
- ☐ *Tersina viridis*
- ◆ *Tersina viridis*
- ◇ *Psarocolius angustifrons*
- ▲ *Psarocolius angustifrons*
- △ *Dendroica striata*
- ✕ *Dendroica striata*
- ✳ *Pooecetes gramineus*
- ⌐ *Pooecetes gramineus*

Fig. 323. Grassland Yellow-Finch x Blue-black Grassquit, White-lined Tanager, Wedge-tailed Grass-Finch, Common Diuca-Finch, Lesser Seed-Finch, Summer Tanager, Ringed Warbling-Finch, Vesper Sparrow, Northern Cardinal, Chaffinch

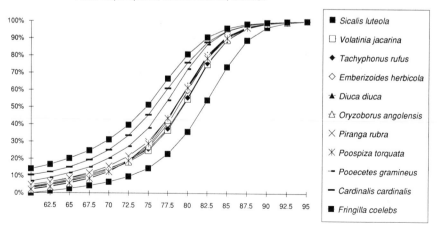

- ■ *Sicalis luteola*
- ☐ *Volatinia jacarina*
- ◆ *Tachyphonus rufus*
- ◇ *Emberizoides herbicola*
- ▲ *Diuca diuca*
- △ *Oryzoborus angolensis*
- ✕ *Piranga rubra*
- ✳ *Poospiza torquata*
- ⌐ *Pooecetes gramineus*
- ━ *Cardinalis cardinalis*
- ■ *Fringilla coelebs*

Fig. 324. Plushcap x Grass-green Tanager, Pardusco, Cinereous Conebill, Grassland Yellow-Finch, White-lined Tanager, Swallow Tanager, Buff-breasted Mountain-Tanager, Mourning Warbler, Orchard Oriole, Mossie

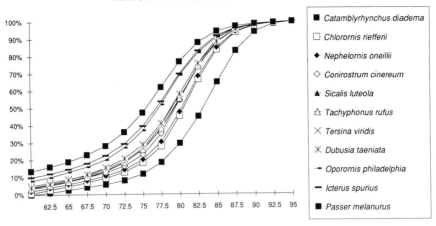

810

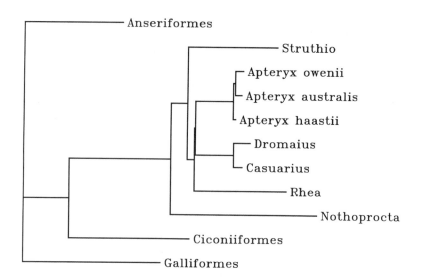

FITCH
Sum of squares = 2.99507
Average percent standard deviation = 6.78808
Examined 153 trees

Between	And	Length
Galliformes	1	13.44859
1	Anseriformes	9.60927
1	2	4.45684
2	3	9.94096
3	4	1.61553
4	Struthio	8.62856
4	5	0.69851
5	7	0.08508
7	8	3.62504
8	9	0.20434
9	Apteryx owenii	0.75896
9	A. australis	0.60958
8	A. haastii	0.25335
7	6	3.70526
6	Dromaius	1.59077
6	Casuarius	0.82933
5	Rhea	8.88994
3	Nothoprocta	14.17599
2	Ciconiiformes	11.81258

```
Nothoprocta    0.00  3 23.01  8 24.24  8 19.41  8 19.30  1 20.50  6 20.50  1 20.50  1
              41.45  8 34.60  4 35.43  7
Struthio      25.26  9  0.00  7 20.09  8 15.80  8 14.00  2 15.31  8 15.30  1 12.60  1
              38.42  9 35.18 10 32.88 14
Rhea          25.29  9 17.52  9  0.00  6 14.16  9 13.23  3 13.25 10 13.20  1 14.20  1
              38.18  5 34.87  7 33.64  8
Dromaius      24.08  8 14.33  7 15.56  7  0.00  3  2.35  6  9.51  7  9.50  1  8.70  1
              31.40  5 30.20  1 28.80  1
Casuarius     24.67  6 15.00  1 10.30  1  3.20  1  0.00  1 10.10  1  8.90  1  8.90  1
              33.10  3 29.54  5 28.80  1
Apteryx       23.93  3 12.64  9 13.15 11 10.19 11  8.90 11  0.00  4  1.97  8  1.27  5
australis     35.13  3 32.30  1 27.81  9
A. owenii     24.00  1 12.60  1 13.20  1 10.20  1  8.90  1  1.16  8  0.00  1  1.10  5
              35.10  1 32.30  1 27.80  1
A. haastii    24.20  1 12.58  4 14.18  4  8.74  5  8.70  1  1.02 14  1.31  9  0.00  4
              35.10  1 32.30  1 27.80  1
Galliformes   50.42  5 38.97  6 42.25  4 38.40  4 39.15  2 37.50  3 37.50  1 37.50  1
               0.00 11 23.51 36 29.37 58
Anseriformes  38.68  4 31.62  6 33.78  6 30.21  7 31.80  1 33.67  6 33.70  1 33.70  1
              22.78 55  0.00  9 26.18 53
Ciconiiformes 35.40  1 32.90  1 33.60  1 28.80  1 28.80  1 27.80  1 27.80  1 27.80  1
              29.40  1 26.20  1  0.00  1
```

FIGURE 325. FITCH tree of relationships among ratite birds and tinamous. The analyses were made using the Fitch-Margoliash algorithm of Felsenstein's (1989) PHYLIP 3.2 package of computer programs and plotted using the PLOTGRAM program of PHYLIP. For figs. 325–352 three items are shown: the input data matrix, a table of branch lengths for the tree, and the tree itself. Data matrices are either complete or folded. For each cell in the matrix the average distance (delta $T_{50}H$) is given to two decimals. This is followed by the number of comparisons which were averaged for that cell. The table gives the distances among the nodes and terminal taxa as taken from the computer output, the number of trees examined, and the goodness-of-fit statistics (sum of squares and average percent standard deviation) for the best tree. The branch lengths of the tree are proportional to the distances given in the table. Some data have been pooled. For example the tinamou comparisons involved three experiments with a *Nothoprocta* tracer, but several genera of tinamous were used as drivers. The Galliformes, Anseriformes, and Ciconiiformes are as defined in this book and include comparisons among all tracers and drivers within each group.

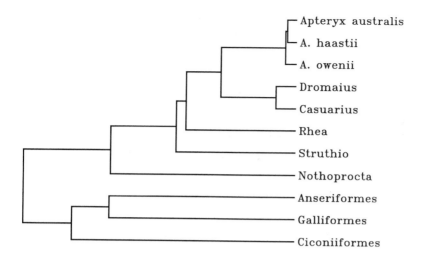

Sum of squares = 6.766
Average percent standard deviation = 10.20293
Examined 512 trees

FROM	TO	LENGTH	TIME
9	*Apteryx australis*	0.53340	16.88396
9	*A. haastii*	0.53340	16.88396
10	9	0.11012	16.35055
10	*A. owenii*	0.64352	16.88396
8	10	4.01274	16.24044
7	*Dromaius*	1.21005	16.88396
7	*Casuarius*	1.21005	16.88396
8	7	3.44621	15.67391
6	8	2.15485	12.22770
6	*Rhea*	6.81111	16.88396
5	6	0.60298	10.07285
5	*Struthio*	7.41409	16.88396
4	5	4.03826	9.46987
4	*Nothoprocta*	11.45235	16.88396
3	4	5.43161	5.43161
1	Anseriformes	11.52893	16.88396
1	Galliformes	11.52893	16.88396
2	1	2.30250	5.35503
2	Ciconiiformes	13.83142	16.88396
3	2	3.05253	3.05253

FIGURE 326. KITSCH tree of the same taxa as in Fig. 325. KITSCH is the Fitch-Margoliash algorithm modified to assume uniform rates of genetic change among lineages, thus the branches are equal in length. The results of KITSCH clustering are similar, but not always identical, to those obtained by UPGMA. The data matrix is given in Fig. 325.

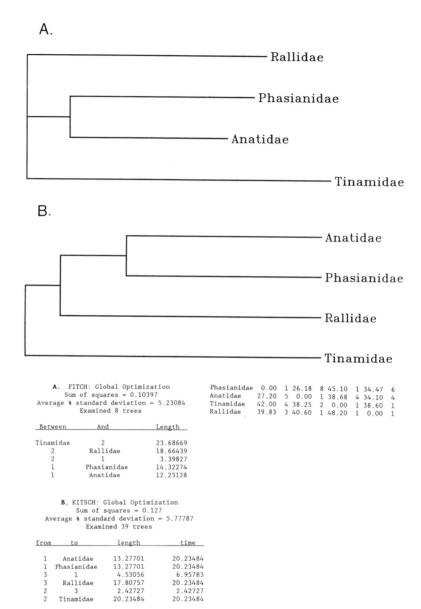

A. FITCH: Global Optimization
Sum of squares = 0.10397
Average % standard deviation = 5.23084
Examined 8 trees

Between	And	Length
Tinamidae	2	23.68669
2	Rallidae	18.66439
2	1	3.39827
1	Phasianidae	14.32274
1	Anatidae	12.23128

B. KITSCH: Global Optimization
Sum of squares = 0.127
Average % standard deviation = 5.77787
Examined 39 trees

from	to	length	time
1	Anatidae	13.27701	20.23484
1	Phasianidae	13.27701	20.23484
3	1	4.53056	6.95783
3	Rallidae	17.80757	20.23484
2	3	2.42727	2.42727
2	Tinamidae	20.23484	20.23484

Phasianidae	0.00	1	26.18	8	45.10	1	34.47	6
Anatidae	27.20	5	0.00	1	38.68	4	34.10	4
Tinamidae	42.00	4	38.25	2	0.00	1	38.60	1
Rallidae	39.83	3	40.60	1	48.20	1	0.00	1

FIGURE 327. Relationships among Tinamidae, Phasianidae, Anatidae, and Rallidae. (A) is the FITCH tree and (B) is the KITSCH tree derived from the same data matrix.

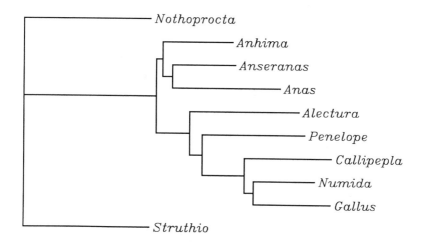

```
                 FITCH                    Gallus       0.00  1
        Sum of squares = 0.22010          Numida      12.81 10  0.00  4
Average percent standard deviation = 1.88717  Callipepla  16.02 11 14.68  4  0.00  1
        Examined 120 trees                Penelope    21.27 10 19.64  7 22.20  4  0.00  1
                                          Alectura    23.43  7 21.58  6 22.87  3 20.72  8  0.00  4
  Between         And          Length     Anhima      22.64  7 21.37  3 23.17  3 20.74 16 20.69  7  0.00  4
                                          Anseranas   25.97  3 20.40  1 22.43  1 22.46  5 21.10  2 12.44  5
Struthio          1           11.67036    Anas        26.06  8 26.69  7 26.35  1 23.87  3 24.73  7 17.58 24 15.78  9  0.00  3
   1          Nothoprocta     11.73964    Nothoprocta 41.08  8 43.60  1 40.20  1 37.33  3 36.87  3 30.95  2 32.90  1 33.65  4
   1              6           12.28774                 0.00  3
   6              8            0.59410    Struthio    41.79  9 38.96  5 40.80  1 34.80  2 35.90 11 31.85  2 30.65  2 36.31  7
   8          Anhima           6.43505                23.41 66  0.00  7
   8              7            0.89015
   7          Anseranas        5.81663
   7              Anas         9.96337
   6              5            3.08930
   5          Alectura        10.10270
   5              4            1.16408
   4          Penelope         9.48133
   4              3            3.88518
   3          Callipepla       8.07477
   3              2            0.84438
   2              Numida       5.66965
   2              Gallus       7.14035
```

FIGURE 328. FITCH tree of relationships among the Craciformes, Galliformes, and Anseriformes. Values were pooled as follows: *Anhima* = all Anhimidae; *Anseranas* = *Anseranas* only; *Anas* = all Anatidae; *Alectura* = all Megapodiidae; *Penelope* = all Cracidae; *Callipepla* = all Odontophoridae; *Numida* = all Numididae; *Gallus* = all Phasianidae.

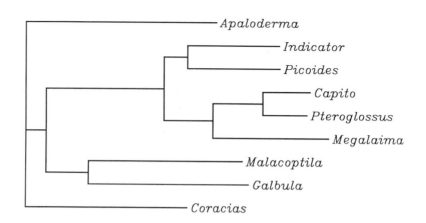

```
           FITCH                    Coracias     0.00  3 21.02  6 22.12  4 23.32  9 28.90  1 28.75  2 29.10  1 28.70  2
      Sum of squares = 0.62143                   26.50  2
Average percent standard deviation = 4.72797  Apaloderma  22.10  1  0.00  5 24.93  6 25.96  9 28.90  1 28.90  1 28.90  1 28.60  1
          Examined 91 trees                     25.00  1
                                   Galbula      22.70  3 24.97  6  0.00  5 19.83 16 29.50  4 27.90  7 28.60  4 28.09  8
                                                27.12  6
Between        And          Length  Malacoptila 21.02  4 24.00  7 17.46  9  0.00  4 27.82  4 26.74  7 27.50  5 25.87  7
                                                26.72  6
Coracias        1          9.71337  Megalaima   29.00  1 28.90  1 29.50  1 27.80  1  0.00  1 12.37  7 13.12  4 16.30  1
   1        Apaloderma     11.44813              14.70  1
   1            3           1.24165  Pteroglossus 28.80 1 28.90  1 27.90  1 26.70  1 12.30  4  0.00  1  6.00  4 16.40  1
   3            6           7.04476              14.40  1
   6            7           1.42412  Capito      29.10  1 28.90  1 25.55  2 26.60  2 12.76  7  5.31 14  0.00  2 15.64  7
   7        Indicator       5.49067              14.72  4
   7        Picoides        5.53069  Picoides    23.00  1 24.50  1 22.20  2 23.05  2 16.65  4 15.70  3 16.50  1  0.00  2
   6            4           2.96199              10.40  1
   4            5           2.98436  Indicator   23.17  3 25.02  5 25.84  5 26.37  9 17.63  6 15.77  7 16.55  2 11.11  8
   5        Capito          2.81718               0.00  5
   5        Pteroglossus    2.61899
   4        Megalaima       6.90551
   3            2           2.55147
   2        Malacoptila     9.22010
   2        Galbula         9.61336
```

FIGURE 329. FITCH tree of relationships among the Piciformes and Galbuliformes. Values were pooled as follows: *Apaloderma* = all Trogonidae; *Indicator* = all Indicatoridae; *Picoides* = all Picidae; *Capito* = New World barbets; *Pteroglossus* = toucans; *Megalaima* = *Megalaima* only; *Malacoptila* = all Bucconidae; *Galbula* = all Galbulidae; *Coracias* = all Coraciidae. The Lybiidae are not included because none was labeled.

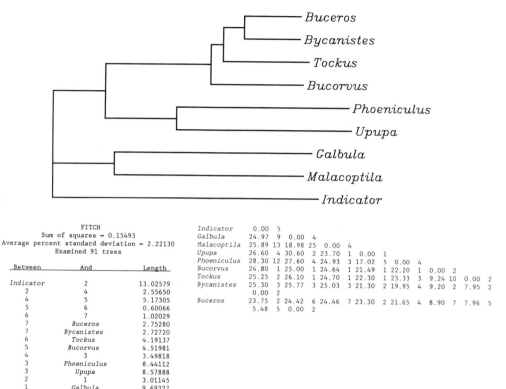

FITCH
Sum of squares = 0.15493
Average percent standard deviation = 2.22130
Examined 91 trees

Between	And	Length
Indicator	2	13.02579
2	4	2.55650
4	5	5.17305
5	6	0.60066
6	7	1.02029
7	Buceros	2.75280
7	Bycanistes	2.72720
6	Tockus	4.19137
5	Bucorvus	4.51981
4	3	3.49818
3	Phoeniculus	8.44112
3	Upupa	8.57888
2	1	3.01145
1	Galbula	9.69327
1	Malacoptila	9.28673

```
Indicator    0.00  5
Galbula     24.97  9  0.00  4
Malacoptila 25.89 13 18.98 25  0.00  4
Upupa       26.60  4 30.60  2 23.70  1  0.00  1
Phoeniculus 28.30 12 27.60  4 24.93  3 17.02  5  0.00  4
Bucorvus    24.80  1 25.00  1 24.64  1 21.49  1 22.20  1  0.00  2
Tockus      25.25  2 26.10  1 24.70  1 22.30  1 23.33  3  9.24 10  0.00  2
Bycanistes  25.30  3 25.77  3 25.03  3 21.30  2 19.95  4  9.20  2  7.95  2
             0.00  2
Buceros     23.75  2 24.42  6 24.46  7 23.30  2 21.65  4  8.90  7  7.96  5
             5.48  5  0.00  2
```

FIGURE 330. FITCH tree of relationships among the Bucerotiformes and Upupiformes. Data pooled for taxa not included in Fig. 329 as follows: *Buceros, Bycanistes, Tockus,* and *Bucorvus* include only members of those genera. *Phoeniculus* includes comparisons to *Rhinopomastus.*

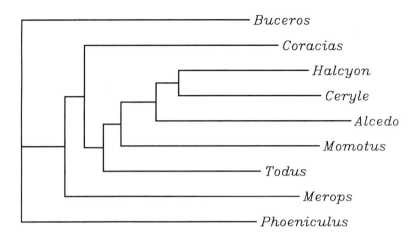

FITCH
Sum of squares = 0.15493
Average percent standard deviation = 2.22130
Examined 91 trees

Between	And	Length
Indicator	2	13.02579
2	4	2.55650
4	5	5.17305
5	6	0.60066
6	7	1.02029
7	Buceros	2.75280
7	Bycanistes	2.72720
6	Tockus	4.19137
5	Bucorvus	4.51981
4	3	3.49818
3	Phoeniculus	8.44112
3	Upupa	8.57888
2	1	3.01145
1	Galbula	9.69327
1	Malacoptila	9.28673

Coracias	0.00	4	17.65	4	18.60	2	21.07	3	19.90	2	19.20	5	19.03	6	
	23.43	3	21.74	8											
Halcyon	20.03	3	0.00	2	13.02	4	15.61	1	15.89	1	18.48	4	21.65	4	
	24.17	3	23.50	4											
Ceryle	20.07	3	11.94	8	0.00	2	17.16	5	19.90	2	18.58	4	21.60	5	
	26.30	1	23.23	3											
Alcedo	21.07	1	15.61	11	15.95	8	0.00	1	18.03	1	20.75	1	26.30	1	
	23.40	1	23.40	1											
Todus	15.75	2	15.89	8	16.55	8	18.03	3	0.00	2	16.78	5	18.47	7	
	22.90	1	20.60	5											
Momotus	19.73	3	16.85	4	17.32	8	20.75	2	19.10	4	0.00	2	20.17	6	
	21.36	1	22.78	5											
Merops	22.63	3	24.55	4	24.78	4	26.30	1	25.40	1	24.04	5	0.00	2	
	23.60	1	25.20	1											
Phoeniculus	22.60	2	23.40	2	23.40	2	24.00	2	23.90	1	23.80	2	23.87	3	
	0.00	3	23.45	12											
Buceros	22.72	4	26.60	2	24.30	2	24.90	1	24.90	1	26.80	3	21.87	3	
	18.17	6	0.00	4											

FIGURE 331. FITCH tree of relationships among some members of the Coraciiformes. Data pooled for taxa not included in Figs. 329 and 330 as follows: *Halcyon* = all Alcedinidae; *Ceryle* = all Cerylidae; *Alcedo* = all Dacelonidae; *Momotus* = all Momotidae; *Todus* = all Todidae; *Merops* = all Meropidae.

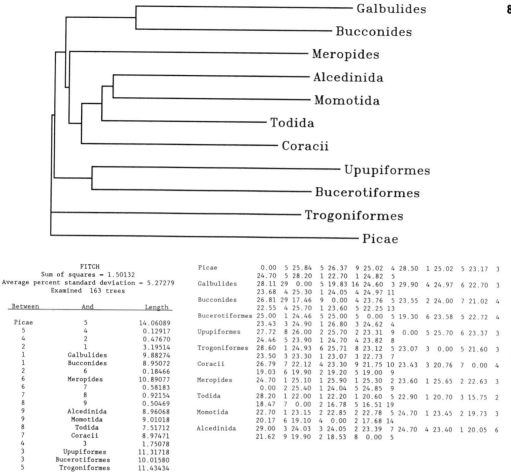

FITCH
Sum of squares = 1.50132
Average percent standard deviation = 5.27279
Examined 163 trees

Between	And	Length
Picae	5	14.06089
5	4	0.12917
4	2	0.47670
2	1	3.19514
1	Galbulides	9.88274
1	Bucconides	8.95072
2	6	0.18466
6	Meropides	10.89077
6	7	0.58183
7	8	0.92154
8	9	0.50469
9	Alcedinida	8.96068
9	Momotida	9.01018
8	Todida	7.51712
7	Coracii	8.97471
4	3	1.75078
3	Upupiformes	11.31718
3	Bucerotiformes	10.01580
5	Trogoniformes	11.43434

```
Picae          0.00  5 25.84  5 26.37  9 25.02  4 28.50  1 25.02  5 23.17  3
              24.70  5 28.20  1 22.70  1 24.82  5
Galbulides    28.11 29  0.00  5 19.83 16 24.60  3 29.90  4 24.97  6 22.70  3
              23.68  4 25.30  1 24.05  4 24.97 11
Bucconides    26.81 29 17.46  9  0.00  4 23.76  5 23.55  2 24.00  7 21.02  4
              22.55  4 25.70  1 23.60  5 22.25 13
Bucerotiformes 25.00  1 24.46  5 25.00  5  0.00  5 19.30  6 23.58  5 22.72  4
              23.43  3 24.90  1 26.80  3 24.62  4
Upupiformes   27.72  8 26.00  2 25.70  2 23.31  9  0.00  5 25.70  6 23.37  3
              24.46  5 23.90  1 24.70  4 23.82  8
Trogoniformes 28.60  1 24.93  6 25.71  8 23.12  5 23.07  3  0.00  5 21.60  3
              23.50  3 23.30  1 23.07  3 22.73  7
Coracii       26.79  7 22.12  4 23.30  9 21.75 10 23.43  3 20.76  7  0.00  4
              19.03  6 19.90  2 19.20  5 19.00  9
Meropides     24.70  1 25.10  1 25.90  1 25.30  2 23.60  1 25.65  2 22.63  3
               0.00  2 25.40  1 24.04  5 24.85  9
Todida        28.20  1 22.00  1 22.20  1 20.60  5 22.90  1 20.70  3 15.75  2
              18.47  7  0.00  2 16.78  5 16.51 19
Momotida      22.70  1 23.15  2 22.85  2 22.78  5 24.70  1 23.45  2 19.73  3
              20.17  6 19.10  4  0.00  2 17.68 14
Alcedinida    29.00  3 24.03  3 24.05  2 23.39  7 24.70  4 23.40  1 20.05  6
              21.62  9 19.90  2 18.53  8  0.00  5
```

FIGURE 332. FITCH tree of relationships among parvclasses Picae and Coraciae. Data pooled within the taxa named.

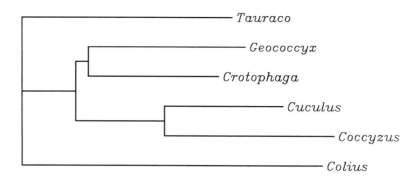

```
           FITCH                    Coccyzus    0.00  3 20.90  1 19.18  6 13.30 10 24.95  4 31.40  1
   Sum of squares = 0.39146         Geococcyx  20.77  6  0.00  1 13.85  4 18.55  8 19.80  2 26.70  1
Average percent standard deviation = 5.55191  Crotophaga 19.00  5 14.00  1  0.00  4 16.54 10 18.84  7 26.70  2
        Examined 28 trees          Cuculus    15.21  7 18.15  2 17.87  6  0.00  6 22.60  9 28.83  3
                                    Tauraco    29.08  4 19.80  1 22.53  3 22.95 13  0.00  4 27.73  3
   Between      And        Length   Colius     25.10  1 25.40  1 25.70  1 25.86  5 22.05  2  0.00  6

   Colius        1        14.61375
     1         Tauraco    10.20109
     1           3         2.64633
     3           4         0.60993
     4        Geococcyx    7.58351
     4        Crotophaga   6.29598
     3           2         4.30258
     2         Cuculus     5.74186
     2         Coccyzus    8.22403
     4        Crotophaga   6.33375
```

FIGURE 333. FITCH tree of relationships among members of the Cuculiformes. Data pooled as follows: *Tauraco* = all Musophagiformes; *Geococcyx* = *Geococcyx* only; *Crotophaga* = *Crotophaga* and *Guira; Cuculus* = Old World cuckoos; *Coccyzus* = *Coccyzus, Saurothera,* and *Piaya; Colius* = all Coliiformes.

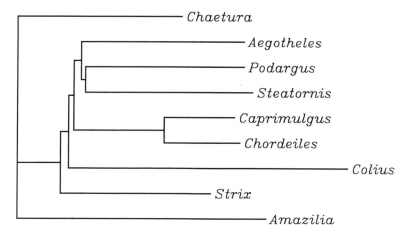

```
            FITCH
    Sum of squares = 0.50374
Average percent standard deviation = 4.13934
       Examined 113 trees

Between        And          Length

Amazilia        2          12.83984
   2         Chaetura        8.46319
   2            5            2.23751
   5            4            0.41793
   4            3            0.26073
   3            1            0.37809
   1         Aegotheles      8.36997
   1            6            0.22206
   6          Podargus       8.15966
   6         Steatornis      8.59585
   3            7            4.65484
   7         Caprimulgus     3.61623
   7         Chordeiles      3.89874
   4           Colius       14.36890
   5            Strix        7.74040
```

```
Chordeiles   0.00  1  7.03  3 17.50  1 18.10  1 18.50  1 15.40  2 22.25  2
            24.80  1 23.60  1
Caprimulgus  8.17  3  0.00  5 17.43  3 18.22  4 18.15  2 16.19 18 20.90  5
            25.40  5 22.55  2
Steatornis  18.60  2 18.40  2  0.00  2 19.20  2 19.50  1 18.02  6 22.45  2
            24.90  1 23.40  1
Podargus    16.50  2 16.10  6 15.67  3  0.00  1 17.00  2 17.90  1 20.00  1
            25.60  1 23.10  1
Aegotheles  17.20  2 16.77  9 16.83  3 16.48  4  0.00  1 18.70  1 18.00  1
            23.10  1 23.90  1
Strix       17.55  4 17.61 10 16.82  4 17.88  4 18.70  2  0.00  6 19.42  6
            23.32  6 22.90  3
Chaetura    19.27  3 18.69  7 19.80  2 20.05  2 18.00  1 17.91 10  0.00  6
            21.33 33 23.97  3
Amazilia    23.83  3 23.96  7 23.25  2 25.55  2 23.10  1 22.56  9 21.24 14
             0.00  6 29.97  3
Colius      23.07  3 23.77  3 23.10  3 23.13  3 23.87  3 21.80  8 26.59 13
            29.61  9  0.00  6
```

FIGURE 334. FITCH tree of relationships among Strigiformes. *Aegotheles, Podargus, Steatornis, Caprimulgus,* and *Chordeiles* indicate values for those genera used as tracers and drivers. Pooled data as follows: *Chaetura* = all swifts; *Amazilia* = all hummingbirds; *Strix* = all owls.

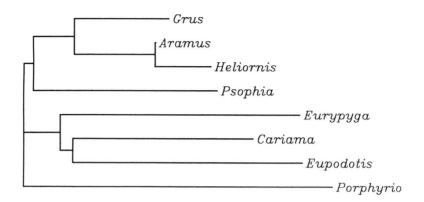

```
                FITCH                    Porphyrio  0.00  6 23.40  2 22.08  8 20.30  1 20.23  3 18.13  3 18.47  3 17.14 10
      Sum of squares = 1.26842           Eurypyga  20.69  7  0.00  2 16.64  5 16.35  2 17.80  1 16.70  2 16.45  2 15.22  5
Average percent standard deviation = 7.82793  Eupodotis 22.52  6 20.43  3  0.00  4 16.60  1 19.13  3 17.60  3 16.47  3 16.89  7
          Examined 72 trees              Cariama  20.36  7 17.00  2 15.13  6  0.00  2 16.00  1 14.80  2 13.95  2 13.54  5
                                         Psophia  18.30  5 18.80  1 16.50  5 15.90  1  0.00  3 13.45  2 12.50  1 12.14  5
   Between      And      Length          Heliornis 15.98  4 16.70  1 17.30  5 15.70  1 14.00  1  0.00  2  4.45  2  9.44  5
                                         Aramus   16.37  9 17.30  1 15.24  9 13.80  1 11.80  1  1.75  2  0.00  5  6.79  8
  Porphyrio       3      11.53444        Grus     17.38 13 16.77  3 15.06  8 14.00  1 11.13  3  8.87  3  5.57  3  0.00  5
       3          4       0.36533
       4          6       1.52496
       6        Grus      3.52316
       6          5       3.01301
       5        Aramus    0.02009
       5        Heliornis 2.09155
       4        Psophia   6.86978
       3          1       1.36771
       1        Eurypyga  8.95289
       1          2       0.47676
       2        Cariama   6.73612
       2        Eupodotis 8.57266
```

FIGURE 335. FITCH tree of the relationships among the Gruiformes. Comparisons among the genera as named except for following pooled values: *Grus* = all cranes; *Eupodotis* = all bustards; *Porphyrio* = all rails.

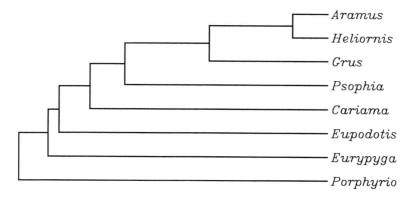

```
                         KITSCH
                  Sum of squares = 2.847
        Average percent standard deviation = 11.72710
                     Examined 247 trees

        FROM        TO          LENGTH          TIME

         6        Aramus        1.05582        9.24219
         6        Heliornis     1.05582        9.24219
         7          6           2.49013        8.18637
         7        Grus          3.54595        9.24219
         5          7           2.52050        5.69624
         5        Psophia       6.06644        9.24219
         4          5           1.04537        3.17574
         4        Cariama       7.11181        9.24219
         3          4           0.92940        2.13037
         3        Eupodotis     8.04121        9.24219
         2          3           0.32668        1.20097
         2        Eurypyga      8.36789        9.24219
         1          2           0.87429        0.87429
         1        Porphyrio     9.24219        9.24219
```

FIGURE 336. KITSCH tree of the relationships of the same taxa as in Fig. 335. The data matrix is given in Fig. 335.

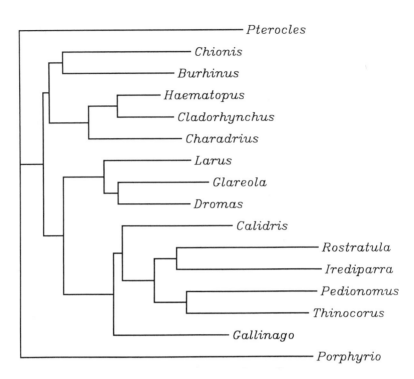

FITCH
Sum of squares = 4.36900
Average percent standard deviation = 7.26400
Examined 388 trees

Between	And	Length
Porphyrio	12	12.83174
12	Pterocles	9.83176
12	6	1.03111
6	9	0.26811
9	11	0.60322
11	Chionis	5.64059
11	Burhinus	4.89758
9	7	1.74132
7	8	1.26317
8	Haematopus	1.87361
8	Cladorhynchus	2.46393
7	Charadrius	4.06961
6	10	0.87309
10	14	1.79674
14	Larus	3.81147
14	13	0.62492
13	Glareola	3.96870
13	Dromas	3.14285
10	5	2.20871
5	4	0.39011
4	Calidris	4.82353
4	2	1.39518
2	3	0.99134
3	Rostratula	6.18083
3	Irediparra	6.31917
2	1	1.42178
1	Pedionomus	5.69221
1	Thinocorus	5.33293
5	Gallinago	5.04657

```
Porphyrio      0.00  4 24.30  2 23.20  3 23.47  3 26.50  1 22.27  3 22.90  6
              18.75  2 17.80  1 19.80  1 18.45  2 18.00  1 22.00  1 22.40  1
              22.50  1 22.04  7
Pedionomus    27.20  2  0.00  3 11.19  8 14.52  4 14.10  2 14.70  5 12.92 14
              17.20  1 18.10  1 16.80  1 16.80  1 15.50  1 20.10  1 22.40  3
              22.60  1 16.60  3
Thinocorus    23.20  1 10.45  2  0.00  3 13.80  5 13.40  1 14.23  3 12.52 15
              16.70  2 16.50  3 16.00  1 16.00  1 15.30  1 18.00  1 22.00  1
              17.40  1 16.25  2
Irediparra    23.50  1 15.80  1 14.26  5  0.00  3 12.50  2 14.58  5 13.81 15
              16.65  4 16.80  3 16.55  2 17.05  2 17.50  1 17.80  1 22.90  1
              17.30  1 16.33  4
Rostratula    26.50  2 14.00  1 14.00  3 12.50  3  0.00  2 14.92  5 13.69 12
              16.75  2 17.20  1 16.30  1 17.20  1 17.40  1 18.70  1 21.60  1
              16.40  1 16.54  5
Gallinago     22.30  1 12.40  1 15.15  4 15.43  3 16.60  1  0.00  3 13.88 14
              12.87  3 12.43  3 11.90  1 11.65  2 11.20  1 14.10  1 16.85  2
              13.00  1 12.10  9
Calidris      26.55  2 14.00  1 13.94  5 13.85  4 13.50  3  7.62  8  0.00  9
              14.32  7 14.26  7 14.40  5 15.10  4 13.50  1 15.52  4 19.00  1
              14.85  2 12.96 35
Charadrius    22.35  2 18.50  1 18.43  3 18.60  4 16.77  3 16.35  4 14.12 17
               0.00  7  8.16  8  8.36  5 11.53  6 12.13  3 12.93  3 17.10  1
              14.65  4 13.01 39
Cladorhynchus 17.80  1 18.30  1 18.70  2 19.30  1 17.50  1 17.90  2 13.77  6
               7.58 10  0.00  3  4.15  2 11.00  4 11.60  1 13.00  1 17.00  1
              14.15  2 12.89  8
Haematopus    19.80  1 16.80  1 16.90  2 18.07  3 17.00  1 15.17  3 13.63  6
               6.57  6  4.39  8  0.00  4 10.09  7 11.10  2 12.10  1 15.80  1
              11.70  3 11.99  7
Burhinus      18.40  1 20.60  1 18.85  2 19.20  1 17.90  1 17.90  2 15.10  6
              11.50  7 10.72  5  9.90  2  0.00  3 10.10  1 11.30  1 16.80  1
              14.30  2 12.63  6
Dromas        18.00  1 16.80  1 17.80  2 17.53  3 17.40  1 14.66  5 13.12 10
              12.30  6 12.07  6 11.88  4 11.87  3  0.00  3 13.00  1 16.00  1
               7.70  3  7.90  3
Chionis       22.00  1 20.10  1 18.05  2 18.37  3 18.00  1 16.15  2 14.82  4
              12.30  6 11.34  5 10.90  3 10.43  6 13.00  1  0.00  3 17.40  1
              13.80  3 12.18 10
Pterocles     22.80  2 27.80  1 22.67  3 22.93  4 21.60  1 22.65  2 19.08  4
              17.13  3 17.00  3 15.80  1 16.80  2 16.00  1 17.40  1  0.00  5
              19.60  3 18.10  3
Glareola      22.50  1 22.60  1 17.40  1 17.30  1 16.40  1 14.40  1 13.60  3
              12.90  4 12.60  3 11.93  3 12.63  3  6.67  3 13.60  1 17.66  5
               0.00  3  8.36 34
Larus         22.30  1 16.60  1 16.20  1 16.07  1 16.70  1 12.10  1 13.19 18
              11.82 17 12.50  1 12.00  1 12.00  1  8.00  1 14.50  1 18.10  1
               8.40  1  0.00  7
```

FIGURE 337. FITCH tree of relationships among the shorebirds. For *Pedionomus, Rostratula, Gallinago, Haematopus, Burhinus, Dromas, Chionis,* and *Pterocles* comparisons involve only those genera. Samples pooled as follows: *Porphyrio* = all rails; *Thinocorus* = all Thinocoridae; *Irediparra* = all Jacanidae; *Calidris* = all Tringinae; *Charadrius* = all Charadriinae; *Cladorhynchus* = all Recurvirostrini; *Glareola* = all Glareolidae; *Larus* = all Laridae.

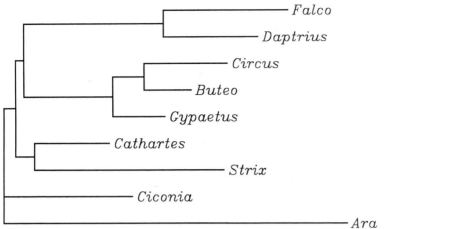

```
       FITCH: Global Optimization        Circus     0.00  4  4.60  2  6.23  7 19.13 10 16.67  6 12.17  6 13.50  1 16.50 10
         Sum of squares = 1.55370                   22.71 10
Average percent standard deviation = 6.67223  Buteo      5.00  1  0.00  3  4.75  2 13.70  3 14.48  4 10.60  4 10.47  3 14.20  6
          Examined 191 trees                        21.37  3
                                          Gypaetus   5.15  2  6.10  1  0.00  2 17.50  1 13.77  3  9.26  5 10.90  5 12.90  1
  Between      And        Length                    18.50  1
                                          Falco     15.58  5 15.34  5 14.75  2  0.00  4  7.87  9 13.45  4 15.20  4 17.84  5
  Ara          1          12.52144                   22.50  3
  1            5           0.43417       Daptrius   14.55  2 14.80  6 13.30  1  8.06  9  0.00  3 13.90  5 13.90  1 17.73 10
  5            3           0.30394                   22.01 10
  3            4           5.09310       Cathartes  9.52  5  9.56  7  8.67 18 13.62 11 11.71 13  0.00 14  8.55 24 14.95  2
  4            Falco       4.52660                   17.60  1
  4            Daptrius    3.43614       Ciconia   11.20  1 14.10  1 10.80  2 15.75  2 13.90  1  8.71 15  0.00  6 11.95  4
  3            6           3.24826                   17.23  3
  6            7           1.14749       Strix      13.90  2 13.90  5 12.93  3 16.70  4 15.70  4  8.90  5 11.90  1  0.00  6
  7            Circus      3.01751                   20.15  6
  7            Buteo       1.70144       Ara        18.70  1 18.80  4 18.47  3 21.30  4 19.88  6 17.58  5 17.20  1 19.74  9
  6            Gypaetus    1.89237                    0.00  7
  5            2           0.68214
  2            Cathartes   2.73678
  2            Strix       6.91439
  1            Ciconia     4.70105
```

FIGURE 338. FITCH tree of relationships among the birds of prey. Values pooled as follows: *Falco* = species of *Falco* only; *Daptrius* = all caracaras; *Circus* = *Circus* only; *Buteo* = *Buteo* and *Accipiter* only; *Gypaetus* = all Old World vultures; *Cathartes* = all New World vultures; *Strix* = all owls; *Ciconia* = all storks; *Ara* = all parrots.

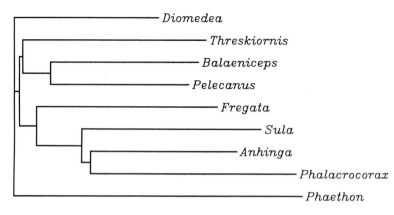

FITCH
Sum of squares = 1.89476
Average percent standard deviation = 7.25481
Examined 91 trees

Between	And	Length
Phaethon	7	7.87777
7	Diomedea	3.92866
7	4	0.13939
4	6	0.09048
6	Threskiornis	4.99855
6	5	0.74624
5	Balaeniceps	4.04805
5	Pelecanus	3.78319
4	1	0.46334
1	Fregata	4.94382
1	3	1.23441
3	Sula	4.90055
3	2	0.24079
2	Anhinga	4.00732
2	Phalacrocorax	5.62728

```
Phaethon       0.00  3 12.56  5 15.13  3 15.30  1 14.50  4 13.28  5 12.40  2
              13.10  6 10.80  3
Fregata       14.58  5  0.00  5 12.73  7 12.93  3 10.86  9 10.98 11 11.70  1
              10.42  4  9.80  3
Phalacrocorax 15.75  4 11.27  6  0.00  6 10.62  4 10.34 11 13.27 12 12.00  1
              11.90  4 10.80  3
Anhinga       13.90  1  9.47  3  9.26  8  0.00  2  8.62  4 11.30  5 10.60  1
               9.20  2  9.15  2
Sula          16.50  1 11.36  5 12.08  6 11.70  1  0.00  3 13.07  6 12.50  1
              12.02 10 11.30  1
Pelecanus     12.08  6  9.59 14 11.65 18 10.98  5 10.52 19  0.00 12  7.42  9
               9.02 16  7.00  2
Balaeniceps   13.20  1  9.56  5 12.76  5 12.60  1 11.49  7  8.53  7  0.00  4
              10.00 12  8.40  1
Threskiornis  13.60  1 11.33  3 13.50  3 12.80  1 11.40  3 11.40  5 10.10  1
               0.00  4 10.43  3
Diomedea      12.88  4  9.35 12 12.13  6  9.15  1 11.25  6  9.91  7  8.40  1
               8.43  3  0.00  6
```

FIGURE 339. FITCH tree of relationships among the traditional pelecaniforms and some allies. *Diomedea* = all albatrosses; *Threskiornis* = all ibises; *Sula* = *Sula* and *Morus*. For the remaining taxa only congeners were pooled.

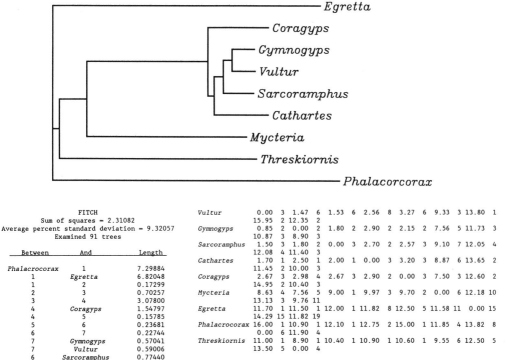

```
          FITCH                    Vultur        0.00  3  1.47  6  1.53  6  2.56  8  3.27  6  9.33  3 13.80  1
   Sum of squares = 2.31082                     15.95  2 12.35  2
Average percent standard deviation = 9.32057    Gymnogyps     0.85  2  0.00  2  1.80  2  2.90  2  2.15  2  7.56  5 11.73  3
          Examined 91 trees                     10.87  3  8.90  3
                                                Sarcoramphus  1.50  3  1.80  2  0.00  3  2.70  2  2.57  3  9.10  7 12.05  4
   Between        And        Length             12.08  4 11.40  3
                                                Cathartes     1.70  1  2.50  1  2.00  1  0.00  3  3.20  3  8.87  6 13.65  2
Phalacrocorax      1          7.29884           11.45  2 10.00  3
   1            Egretta       6.82048           Coragyps      2.67  3  2.98  4  2.67  3  2.90  2  0.00  3  7.50  3 12.60  2
   1               2          0.17299           14.95  2 10.40  3
   2               3          0.70257           Mycteria      8.63  4  7.56  5  9.00  1  9.97  3  9.70  2  0.00  6 12.18 10
   3               4          3.07800           13.13  3  9.76 11
   4            Coragyps      1.54797           Egretta      11.70  1 11.50  1 12.00  1 11.82  8 12.50  5 11.58 11  0.00 15
   4               5          0.15785           14.29 15 11.82 19
   5               6          0.23681           Phalacrocorax 16.00  1 10.90  1 12.10  1 12.75  2 15.00  1 11.85  4 13.82  8
   6               7          0.22744            0.00  6 11.90  4
   7            Gymnogyps     0.57041           Threskiornis 11.00  1  8.90  1 10.40  1 10.90  1 10.60  1  9.55  6 12.50  5
   7            Vultur        0.59006           13.50  5  0.00  4
   6            Sarcoramphus  0.77440
   5            Cathartes     1.38616
   3            Mycteria      4.06199
   2            Threskiornis  5.02095
```

FIGURE 340. FITCH tree of relationships among Cathartidae and other groups. *Egretta* = all herons; *Mycteria* = all storks; *Threskiornis* = all ibises. For the remaining taxa only congeners were pooled.

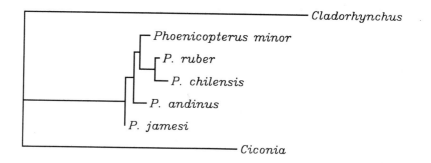

FITCH
Sum of squares = 5.80166
Average percent standard deviation = 18.05370
Examined 45 trees

Between	And	Length
Ciconia	1	6.02043
1	Cladorhynchus	7.94569
1	2	2.89137
2	3	0.22828
3	5	0.15809
5	Phoenicopterus minor	0.26050
5	4	0.41995
4	P. ruber	0.11080
4	P. chilensis	0.35585
3	P. andinus	0.35041
2	P. jamesi	0.00000

Ciconia	0.00	1	14.65	4	8.70	1	10.60	1	11.60	1	9.30	2	10.30	1
Cladorhynchus	12.10	1	0.00	1	9.40	1	11.90	1	12.90	1	13.00	2	13.00	1
Phoenicopterus jamesi	8.66	5	9.35	2	0.00	1	0.56	5	1.03	6	0.84	7	0.80	5
P. andinus	10.60	4	11.92	5	0.59	7	0.00	1	1.58	5	1.47	6	0.97	6
P. chilensis	11.60	4	12.87	3	1.48	6	1.50	1	0.00	1	0.73	10	1.47	6
P. ruber	9.14	7	11.98	5	0.77	6	1.50	1	0.37	7	0.00	1	0.80	4
P. minor	9.27	7	10.92	5	0.73	6	0.58	6	0.83	7	0.86	9	0.00	1

FIGURE 341. FITCH tree of relationships among the flamingos. *Cladorhynchus* = all Recurvirostrini; *Ciconia* = all storks.

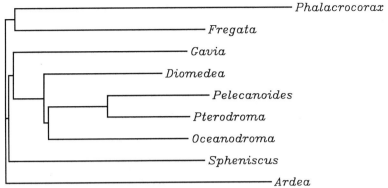

FITCH: Global Optimization
Sum of squares = 1.44170
Average percent standard deviation = 5.72414
Examined 185 trees

Between	And	Length
Ardea	3	6.84877
3	1	0.24814
1	Phalacrocorax	7.12554
1	Fregata	4.88737
3	2	0.08170
2	4	0.12399
4	Gavia	4.46504
4	5	0.79706
5	Diomedea	3.01821
5	6	0.11343
6	7	1.51209
7	Pelecanoides	2.62058
7	Pterodroma	2.11449
6	Oceanodroma	3.58296
2	Spheniscus	5.04567

Pelecanoides	0.00	2	4.79	8	7.37	6	8.03	4	9.90	4	9.00	1	10.05	2
	11.40	1	12.26	5										
Pterodroma	4.60	3	0.00	2	7.30	7	7.80	5	8.92	6	10.60	2	9.23	3
	11.60	1	11.78	5										
Diomedea	7.38	4	6.47	18	0.00	3	7.10	8	8.50	8	9.30	4	9.35	12
	10.40	2	11.69	12										
Oceanodroma	7.53	3	6.93	10	6.54	7	0.00	2	8.37	6	9.70	2	8.73	3
	12.10	1	12.10	1										
Spheniscus	11.50	2	10.52	20	9.46	9	10.96	5	0.00	7	10.60	2	10.00	4
	12.44	15	14.73	7										
Gavia	9.00	2	8.81	16	8.05	12	9.12	5	9.35	15	0.00	8	9.34	5
	11.70	6	11.82	12										
Fregata	12.00	1	10.26	8	9.80	3	11.00	2	9.64	5	11.50	2	0.00	5
	13.37	3	12.43	13										
Ardea	12.00	2	11.61	23	10.25	8	12.08	5	11.31	9	12.50	5	11.76	7
	0.00	7	14.29	15										
Phalacrocorax	12.20	1	11.72	4	10.80	3	12.10	1	11.78	5	13.15	2	11.27	6
	13.82	8	0.00	6										

FIGURE 342. FITCH tree of relationships among the Fregatidae, Spheniscidae, Gaviidae, and Procellariidae. *Pterodroma* = Procellariinae except *Pelecanoides; Oceanodroma* = all Hydrobatinae; *Spheniscus* = all Spheniscidae; *Ardea* = all herons. For other taxa only congeners were pooled.

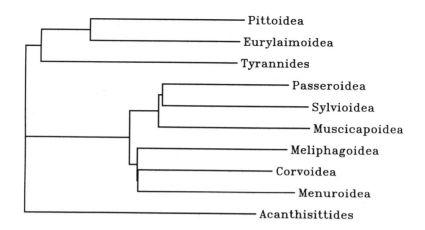

FITCH: Global optimization
Sum of squares = 0.17268
Average percent standard deviation = 0.64243
Examined 260 trees

Between	And	Length
Acanthisittides	2	9.28287
2	3	0.62459
3	1	1.98932
1	Pittoidea	6.13923
1	Eurylaimoidea	5.97077
3	Tyrannides	7.86562
2	6	4.23696
6	7	1.13170
7	8	0.15476
8	Passeroidea	5.03992
8	Sylvioidea	5.84008
7	Muscicapoidea	6.06103
6	4	0.31303
4	Meliphagoidea	5.97411
4	5	0.03481
5	Corvoidea	5.34319
5	Menuroidea	6.25681

```
Acanthisittides  0.00
Pittoidea       18.39   9  0.00
Eurylaimoidea   18.02   8 12.11  11  0.00
Tyrannides      17.41  11 16.00  18 15.82  18  0.00
Menuroidea      19.80   3 19.40   1 19.20   2 19.50   1  0.00
Meliphagoidea   19.53   7 17.10   1 16.30   1 19.30   1 12.28  51  0.00
Corvoidea       19.47  16 17.70   1 19.20   3 19.20   6 11.60 191 11.35 293
                 0.00
Muscicapoidea   20.07   3 20.20   2 19.93   3 19.91  10 14.10   2 13.23  20
                12.91 198  0.00
Sylvioidea      20.31   7 20.10   1 18.90   1 19.40   2 13.75  16 13.60  83
                12.86 194 11.95 167  0.00
Passeroidea     20.21   8 19.55   2 20.50   2 19.80   1 12.10   1 12.54  70
                11.91 135 11.38 129 10.88 383  0.00
```

FIGURE 343. FITCH tree of relationships among the higher categories of passerine birds. Data pooled within the named taxa.

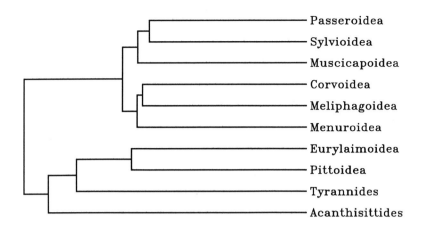

```
              KITSCH: Global optimization
                 Sum of squares = 1.618
       Average percent standard deviation = 2.78118
                   Examined 425 trees

     FROM        TO          LENGTH        TIME

       9      Passeroidea      5.44000     9.79477
       9      Sylvioidea       5.44000     9.79477
       8          9            0.40391     4.35477
       8      Muscicapoidea    5.84391     9.79477
       7          8            0.52615     3.95086
       6      Corvoidea        5.67500     9.79477
       6      Meliphagoidea    5.67500     9.79477
       5          6            0.19042     4.11977
       5      Menuroidea       5.86542     9.79477
       7          5            0.50463     3.92935
       4          7            3.42472     3.42472
       2      Eurylaimoidea    6.05500     9.79477
       2      Pittoidea        6.05500     9.79477
       3          2            1.89949     3.73977
       3      Tyrannides       7.95449     9.79477
       1          3            0.98531     1.84028
       1    Acanthisittides    8.93980     9.79477
       4          1            0.85497     0.85497
```

FIGURE 344. KITSCH tree of the same taxa as in Fig. 343. The data matrix is given in Fig. 343.

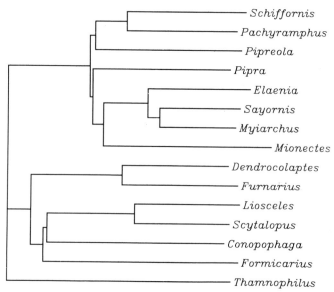

```
              FITCH
       Sum of squares = 1.33599
Average percent standard deviation = 4.24612
          Examined 351 trees

  Between          And          Length

Thamnophilus        6           6.67522
    6               7           2.45601
    7               9           0.15221
    9              10           0.93070
   10           Schiffornis     3.53841
   10           Pachyramphus    3.27364
    9           Pipreola        4.33295
    7               8           0.08117
    8           Pipra           4.07809
    8              11           0.31973
   11              13           1.30536
   13           Elaenia         3.04740
   13              12           0.35554
   12           Sayornis        2.39783
   12           Myiarchus       2.27011
   11           Mionectes       4.99134
    6               4           0.71149
    4               5           2.67056
    5           Dendrocolaptes  3.16372
    5           Furnarius       3.44940
    4               1           0.37915
    1               3           0.11354
    3               2           2.59477
    2           Liosceles       3.12662
    2           Scytalopus      2.82076
    3           Conopophaga     5.27036
    1           Formicarius     5.80637
```

```
Thamnophilus   0.00  1 12.55  2 12.70  3 12.80  1 12.96  5 12.98  9 12.90  3
              13.40  1 12.87  3 13.25  2 13.40  1 13.50  1 13.10  1 13.30  1
              13.50  1
Conopophaga   13.14  5  0.00  1 10.20  1 11.20  1 10.95  2 11.92  4 12.20  3
              13.33  3 13.60  1 13.70  1 12.90  1 11.80  1 13.00  1 13.70  1
              13.67  1
Scytalopus    13.43 26 10.68  6  0.00  1  5.80  3 11.46 13 12.14 14 12.35  4
              13.60  2 13.22  4 13.77  3 14.25  2 14.30  1 14.50  1 13.30  2
              13.75  2
Liosceles     13.66 16 11.20  2  6.20  2  0.00  1 11.53 10 12.12  5 12.30  3
              14.50  1 13.80  1 14.70  1 14.60  1 14.30  1 13.10  1 14.70  1
              13.90  1
Formicarius   13.94 27 11.42  4 11.20  4 11.30  1  0.00  1 12.60  7 12.53  3
              14.40  1 13.55  2 13.65  2 14.10  1 14.10  1 13.50  1 13.70  1
              13.30  1
Furnarius     13.43  6 12.40  1 10.50  1 12.10  1 12.30  1  0.00  1  6.68 12
              14.30  1 13.80  1 14.15  2 13.70  1 13.00  1 14.25  2 14.40  1
              14.70  1
Dendrocolaptes 13.35 4 12.20  1  9.40  1 11.20  1 10.10  1  6.57 18  0.00  1
              14.30  1 13.60  2 13.50  2 13.70  1 12.50  1 13.75  2 13.60  1
              13.20  1
Mionectes     14.73  3 14.90  1 13.16  1 14.50  1 13.57  3 14.17  3 13.65  2
               0.00  1  9.38  3  9.73  3  9.60  2 10.70  1  9.47  7  9.50  5
               9.14  7
Pipra         14.90  1 14.60  1 14.30  1 13.80  1 13.60  1 14.20  1 14.40  1
              10.08  5  0.00  1  8.39 13  8.72  5  9.00  2  8.12  9  9.37  3
               9.05  4
Pipreola      13.20  1 14.10  1 13.20  1 14.70  1 14.50  1 14.27  2 14.40  1
              10.42  5  8.60 11  0.00  1  9.90  3 10.20  1  9.22  9  9.55  4
               9.92  5
Pachyramphus  14.90  1 12.90  1 14.20  1 14.60  1 11.80  1 13.70  1 13.70  1
               9.73  7  8.53  6  8.62 10  0.00  1  7.70  1  8.95  6  9.00  4
               8.96  4
Schiffornis   13.50  1 12.90  1 14.30  1 14.30  1 14.10  1 13.40  1 12.50  1
              10.58  4  8.77 15  8.17  7  6.70  6  0.00  1 10.57  3  9.60  1
               9.30  1
Myiarchus     13.93  7 13.67  3 13.05  2 13.00  1 14.50  1 13.87  6 14.17  3
               8.40 10  8.09 14  8.49 12  7.88  6  8.70  1  0.00  1  4.44 14
               5.52 10
Sayornis      13.30  1 13.70  1 13.30  1 14.70  1 14.40  1 13.60  1
               9.08  6  8.42  6  8.73  9  8.79  7 10.60  1  4.87 19  0.00  1
               5.44  7
Elaenia       13.50  1 13.70  1 13.70  1 13.90  1 13.30  1 14.70  1 13.20  1
               9.56  9  8.83  3  9.00  3  8.78  4  9.10  1  6.12 12  5.78 12
               0.00  1
```

FIGURE 345. FITCH tree of relationships among some New World suboscine birds. For *Schiffornis, Liosceles, Scytalopus,* and *Conopophaga* only congeners were pooled. Others pooled as follows: *Pachyramphus* = *Pachyrampus, Platypsaris, Tityra; Pipreola* = all cotingas; *Pipra* = all manakins except *Sapayoa; Elaenia* = *Elaenia, Capsiempis, Mecocerculus, Phaeomyias, Anairetes, Camptostoma, Euscarthmus, Myiopagis, Tyrannulus; Sayorinis* = *Sayornis, Contopus, Empidonax, Ochthoeca, Agriornis, Gubernetes, Knipolegus, Machetornis, Fluvicola, Muscigralla, Pyrocephalus, Sublegatus; Myiarchus* = *Myiarchus, Rhytipterna, Megarhynchus, Myiozetetes, Attila, Pitangus, Myiodynastes, Tyrannus; Mionectes* = *Mionectes, Leptopogon, Pseudotriccus, Idioptilon, Todirostrum, Corythopis; Furnarius* = Furnariinae; *Dendrocolaptes* = Dendrocolaptinae; *Formicarius* = *Formicarius, Chamaeza, Grallaria; Thamnophilus* = Thamnophilidae.

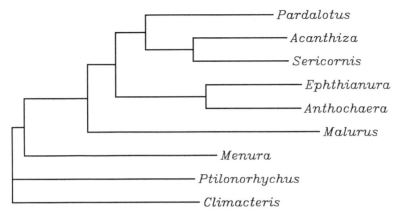

```
FITCH: Global optimization
         Sum of squares = 0.37726
Average percent standard deviation = 4.13165
              Examined 161 trees

  Between          And          Length

Climacteris         2           4.85136
     2              1           0.31481
     1              3           1.65881
     3              5           0.72766
     5              6           0.77987
     6          Pardalotus      3.30023
     6              7           1.22603
     7          Acanthiza       2.42841
     7          Sericornis      2.46409
     5              4           2.33432
     4          Ephthianura     2.47630
     4          Anthochaera     2.46362
     3           Malurus        6.00832
     1           Menura         4.98725
     2        Ptilonorhynchus   4.72994
```

```
Climacteris     0.00  4 12.25  2  9.44 14 10.54  5 12.22 12 12.15  2 12.30  2
                12.32  5 12.05  6
Malurus         12.20  1  0.00  2 12.70  1 13.40  1 11.20  2 11.40  1 10.98  6
                11.80  1 10.40  3
Ptilonorhychus  10.90  2 13.40  2  0.00  5  9.88 10 12.63  3 11.80  1 12.30  1
                11.90  1 12.40  2
Menura          10.50  1 12.70  1  9.95  6  0.00  2 11.55  2 11.60  1 11.70  1
                11.70  1 11.70  1
Anthochaera     12.20  1 11.87  7 12.45  2 13.80  1  0.00  4  5.07  6  9.72  6
                 9.40  1 10.17  6
Ephthianura     12.20  1 12.17  3 11.00  1 12.30  1  4.80  5  0.00  2  9.90  1
                 8.80  1  9.65  2
Sericornis      11.30  1 11.43  3 11.90  1 11.70  1  9.47  3  8.75  2  0.00  4
                 6.80  1  5.18  8
Pardalotus      10.80  1 10.90  1 11.90  1 11.70  1  8.45  6  8.85  2  6.84  5
                 0.00  2  7.04  7
Acanthiza       10.90  1 10.80  1 12.00  1 11.70  1  8.89 16  9.40  6  4.63  7
                 7.40  1  0.00  4
```

FIGURE 346. FITCH tree of relationships among the Menuroidea and Meliphagoidea. Pooling as follows: *Pardalotus* = Pardalotinae; *Acanthiza* = Acanthizini; *Sericornis* = Sericornithini; *Ephthianura* = Ephthianura and *Ashbyia*; *Anthochaera* = Anthochaera, Acanthagenys, Phylidonyris, Lichmera, Melilestes, Meliphaga, Melithreptus, Entomyzon; *Malurus* = Malurinae; *Menura* = Menuridae; *Ptilonorhynchus* = Ptilonorhynchidae; *Climacteris* = Climacteridae.

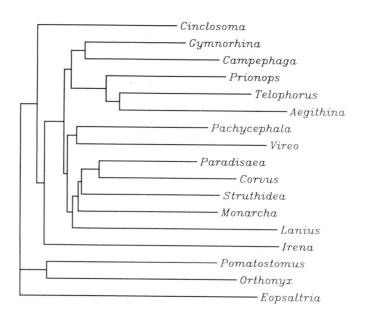

```
        FITCH: Global optimization
          Sum of squares = 5.31924
Average percent standard deviation = 6.24937
              Examined 987 trees

    Between        And           Length

Eopsaltria         1            5.86233
    1              3            0.40546
    3          Cinclosoma       3.42534
    3              5            0.19649
    5              4            0.47401
    4             14            0.17154
   14             15            0.33199
   15          Gymnorhina       2.47249
   15          Campephaga       3.31029
   14             10            0.86265
   10          Prionops         2.94637
   10              9            0.32419
    9          Telophorus       3.24239
    9          Aegithina        4.12483
    4              8            0.08909
    8              7            0.22542
    7          Pachycephala     3.23356
    7          Vireo            4.67544
    8              6            0.13097
    6             12            0.13766
   12             11            0.07887
   11             13            0.43732
   13          Paradisaea       2.40935
   13          Corvus           3.38137
   11          Struthidea       3.41493
   12          Monarcha         3.44782
    6          Lanius           5.05061
    5          Irena            5.78712
    1              2            0.66604
    2          Pomatostomus     4.20599
    2          Orthonyx         4.68185
```

```
Eopsaltria   0.00  4 11.40  1 10.00  1 11.15  2 12.20  1 11.40  1 10.32  4
             9.80  1 10.80  9 12.90  1 12.40  1 10.70  1 10.21 15 12.40  1
             9.75  2 11.10  1 11.30  3
Irena       11.40  3  0.00  7 11.40  2 12.30  1 11.32 10 11.21 14 10.10  2
            10.20  1 10.17  6  9.87  3  9.60  8 10.31  8 10.56  7 10.92  8
             9.87  3  9.94 20 10.28  5
Orthonyx    11.32  6 11.40  1  0.00  2 10.70  1 11.90  1 11.00  1  9.84  5
             9.80  1 10.33  6 13.30  1 11.60  1  9.50  1 10.20  5 10.40  1
            10.00  1 10.40  1 10.10  1
Pomatostomus 10.75 2 12.30  1  7.90  1  0.00  2 12.40  1 11.60  1  8.43  6
             9.15  2  8.65  6 12.50  1 11.70  1  9.80  1  9.30  3 11.40  1
             9.45  2 10.50  1  9.70  1
Lanius      12.20  1 12.53  3 11.90  1 12.40  1  0.00  6  9.82  4  9.40  1
             8.05  2  8.83  6  9.50  1  9.34 11  9.42 12  8.41  8  8.93  6
             8.82  5  8.82 14  8.76  7
Vireo       11.40  1 12.70  3 11.00  1 11.60  3 10.10  8  0.00  7  8.54  5
             8.45  2  7.91  9  9.35  2  9.53  3  9.08  4  8.68 24  8.86 15
             7.99  8  8.28 13  8.89  9
Cinclosoma  10.50  1 10.10  1  8.25  2  8.20  2  9.40  1  8.50  1  0.00  2
             8.35  2  7.57  7 10.10  1  9.00  1  7.90  1  8.80  1  8.90  2
             8.15  2  8.57  3  7.80  4
Struthidea   9.80  2 10.10  1  8.40  1  9.20  1  8.10  1  8.40  1  7.67  6
             0.00  3  7.21  9  9.70  1  8.80  1  7.90  1  7.11 10  6.80  2
             7.67  3  8.74  5  7.84  5
Pachycephala 10.56 37 10.20 1 10.30  2 10.52  5  8.80  1  7.90  1  7.62 12
             7.15  2  0.00 11  9.00  1  8.00  1  7.40  3  7.80 25  7.00  1
             7.25  2  7.55  4  8.10  2
Aegithina   12.86  5 12.01  8 13.30  1 12.50  1 11.28  5 10.17  9 10.10  1
             9.65  2  8.95  4  0.00  4  7.38 19  7.49 17  9.33  7 10.30  1
             9.20  1  9.59  9  7.60  3
Telophorus  12.40  1 12.38  5 11.60  1 11.70  1 10.20 14  9.85  6  9.00  1
             8.75  2  8.04  8  7.25  2  0.00  8  7.15 13  9.12 12  8.92  6
             8.33  6  8.27 18  7.06  9
Prionops    10.70  1 10.02  5  9.50  1  9.80  1  8.98 16  9.33  9  7.85  2
             7.90  1  7.52  5  6.65  2  6.18 18  0.00  6  8.08 18  7.63  6
             7.22  6  7.08 13  7.25 11
Monarcha    10.52 24  9.40  1  9.60  2  9.25  6  9.10  1  8.70  1  7.37  7
             6.52  5  6.58 21  9.30  1  9.10  1  7.38  4  0.00  6  6.65  2
             6.55  4  7.08  8  6.87  7
Corvus      11.57  3 11.60  2 11.30  1 11.40  1  8.00  1  8.60  1 11.23  3
             8.80  2  7.20  6 10.00  1  6.80  1  9.05  2  7.25 13  0.00  6
             6.19  9  8.64  7  8.25  9
Paradisaea  10.51 13 10.95  2  9.92  4  9.38  4  8.58  5  8.58  6  7.21 11
             5.90  9  7.02 10  7.50  1  7.43  3  7.50  1  6.51 17  5.53 11
             0.00  9  6.30  7  6.07 11
Campephaga  11.10  1  8.50  1 10.30  1 10.50  1 10.17  3  9.20  3  7.63  3
             6.90  1  6.75  2  9.60  1  8.90  3  8.87  3  8.24 10  8.40  4
             7.65  2  0.00  3  7.23 10
Gymnorhina  10.26  5  7.87  2  9.65  2  8.80  1  8.14  8  8.25  2  6.69  7
             6.82  6  6.25 12  7.60  1  6.68  9  6.29  8  6.85 26  6.67 10
             5.64  7  5.54 35  0.00 10
```

FIGURE 347. FITCH tree of relationships among members of the Corvoidea. Pooling as follows: *Eopsaltria* = Eopsaltriidae; *Irena* = *Irena* and *Chloropsis*; *Lanius* = *Lanius, Corvinella, Eurocephalus*; *Vireo* = Vireonidae; *Cinclosoma* = Cinclosomatinae; *Struthidea* = *Struthidea* and *Corcorax*; *Pachycephala* = Pachycephalinae; *Telophorus* = Malaconotini; *Prionops* = Vangini; *Monarcha* = Dicrurinae; *Corvus* = Corvini; *Paradisaea* = Paradisaeini; *Campephaga* = Oriolini; *Gymnorhina* = Artamini. Species in *Orthonyx, Pomatostomus,* and *Aegithina* were pooled.

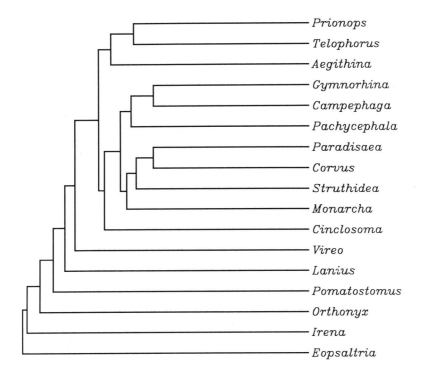

```
              KITSCH: Global rearrangements
                 Sum of squares = 11.134
        Average percent standard deviation = 9.04152
                  Examined 1567 trees

     FROM       TO          LENGTH        TIME

      11     Prionops       3.25997      5.34191
      11     Telophorus     3.25997      5.34191
      10        11          0.42688      2.08194
      10     Aegithina      3.68685      5.34191
       9        10          0.23413      1.65506
      16     Gymnorhina     2.89139      5.34191
      16     Campephaga     2.89139      5.34191
      15        16          0.42129      2.45052
      15     Pachycephala   3.31268      5.34191
      13        15          0.19973      2.02924
      14     Paradisaea     2.89536      5.34191
      14     Corvus         2.89536      5.34191
       8        14          0.32415      2.44655
       8     Struthidea     3.21951      5.34191
      12         8          0.17743      2.12240
      12     Monarcha       3.39695      5.34191
      13        12          0.11546      1.94497
       7        13          0.29830      1.82950
       7     Cinclosoma     3.81071      5.34191
       9         7          0.11028      1.53121
       5         9          0.44158      1.42093
       5     Vireo          4.36256      5.34191
       3         5          0.18833      0.97935
       3     Lanius         4.55089      5.34191
       6         3          0.21872      0.79102
       6     Pomatostomus   4.76961      5.34191
       4         6          0.24857      0.57231
       4     Orthonyx       5.01818      5.34191
       2         4          0.24162      0.32373
       2     Irena          5.25979      5.34191
       1         2          0.08212      0.08212
       1     Eopsaltria     5.34191      5.34191
```

FIGURE 348. KITSCH tree of the taxa as in Fig. 347. The data matrix is given in Fig. 347.

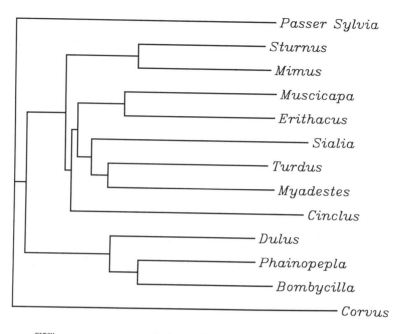

```
                                              Muscicapa   0.00  1  7.22  6  8.93  3 10.00  1  9.80  1 10.60  1  9.90  1
            FITCH                                        10.70  1 11.30  1 10.80  1 10.70  1 11.55  2 13.76  6
     Sum of squares = 1.26463                  Erithacus   6.25  6  0.00  1  9.42  4  9.50  1  8.60  1  9.75  1 10.80  1
Average percent standard deviation = 4.25956             11.40  1 11.30  1 10.20  1 10.30  1 11.76 11 12.70  8
          Examined 231 trees                   Turdus      8.54 10  8.70 10  0.00  1  7.30  3 10.60  4  9.20  1 10.40  1
                                                         11.20  2  9.40  1  8.80  7  8.52  4 11.77 10 13.02 43
  Between        And          Length           Myadestes   8.41  8  8.71  8  7.21  7  0.00  1 11.05  2  9.00  2 10.50  3
                                                         10.25  2 10.07  3  9.85  4 10.08  4 11.38 13 12.75  4
Corvoidea       1             7.25442          Sialia      9.82  6  9.18  9  8.42 23  8.80  3  0.00  1 10.13  3 12.45  2
  1        Passeroidea                                   12.33  3 11.80  3  9.81  7 10.28  8 11.75  4 13.34  5
           +Sylvioidea        5.76667          Cinclus     9.73  3  9.75  2  9.45  4 11.00  1 12.30  1  0.00  1 10.90  1
  1             4             0.26064                    12.70  1 11.00  1 10.80  1 10.90  2 11.95  8 13.38  6
  4             10            0.86381          Bombycilla 11.30  2 10.80  1 12.20  1 12.60  1 13.10  1 11.80  1  0.00  1
 10             11            1.60977                     4.90  1  7.10  1 10.95  2 11.35  2 11.54 12 13.22  4
 11          Sturnus          2.80116          Phainopepla 10.70 1  9.60  1 11.60  1 11.95  2 11.00  1 11.20  1  7.00  1
 11          Mimus            2.93613                     0.00  1  6.30  1  9.90  1 11.30  1 10.27  6 12.77  3
 10             5             0.13835          Dulus      11.30  1 11.30  1  9.40  1  8.90  1  9.80  1 11.00  1  6.70  1
  5             8             0.13383                     6.50  1  0.00  1 10.50  3 10.65  2 11.59 13 13.00  1
  8             9             1.05221          Sturnus     8.74  5  8.60  3  8.52  5  8.60  2  9.20  2  9.95  2 10.80  2
  9          Muscicapa        3.34793                    10.90  1  9.90  1  0.00  1  5.71 18 11.53 23 12.75 30
  9          Erithacus        3.31758          Mimus       8.43  3  8.73  3  8.95  6  9.25  4 10.57  3  9.85  2 10.25  2
  8             6             0.31209                     10.63  3 10.53  3  5.76 22  0.00  1 11.33 33 12.81 12
  6          Sialia           4.80843          Passeroidea 11.60 1 11.80  1 11.40  1 11.80  1 12.00  1 11.50  1
  6             7             0.37445          +Sylvioidea 10.30 1 11.60  1 11.50  1 11.30  1  0.00  1 13.16 37
  7          Turdus           3.54337          Corvoidea  13.70  1 12.70  1 13.00  1 12.80  1 13.30  1 13.40  1 13.20  1
  7          Myadestes        3.69317                     12.80  1 13.00  1 12.80  1 12.80  1 12.92 49  0.00  0
  5          Cinclus          5.17664
  4             3             1.89915
  3          Dulus            3.21183
  3             2             0.63205
  2          Phainopepla      2.59644
  2          Bombycilla       2.99417
```

FIGURE 349. FITCH tree of relationships among the Muscicapoidea. The following were pooled: *Passer Sylvia* = Passeroidea and Sylvioidea; *Sturnus* = starlings; *Mimus* = mockingbirds; *Muscicapa* = *Muscicapa, Niltava, Rhinomyias, Ficedula*; *Erithacus* = *Erithacus, Luscinia, Cossypha, Copsychus*; *Turdus* = *Turdus, Catharus, Hylocichla, Zoothera, Chlamydochaera*; *Corvus* = Corvoidea. Other comparisons limited to genera indicated.

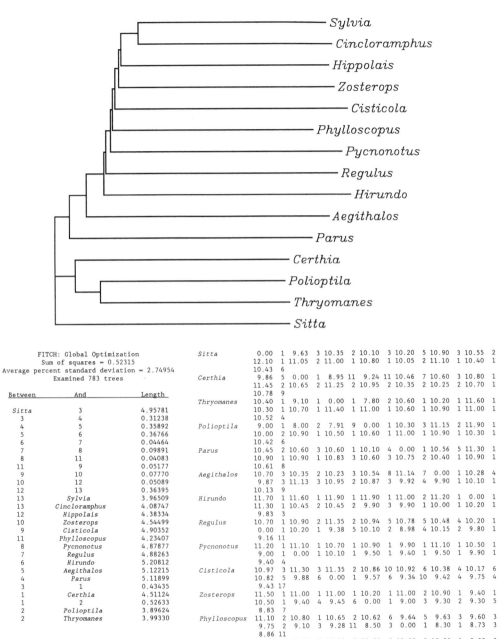

```
FITCH: Global Optimization          Sitta        0.00  1  9.63  3 10.35  2 10.10  3 10.20  5 10.90  3 10.55  2
      Sum of squares = 0.52315                   12.10  1 11.05  2 11.00  1 10.80  1 10.05  2 11.10  1 10.40  1
Average percent standard deviation = 2.74954     10.43  6
          Examined 783 trees          Certhia      9.86  5  0.00  1  8.95 11  9.24 11 10.46  7 10.60  3 10.80  1
                                                  11.45  2 10.65  2 11.25  2 10.95  2 10.35  2 10.25  2 10.70  1
Between        And          Length              10.78  9
                                      Thryomanes  10.40  1  9.10  1  0.00  1  7.80  2 10.60  1 10.20  1 11.60  1
Sitta          3          4.95781                10.30  1 10.70  1 11.40  1 11.00  1 10.60  1 10.90  1 11.00  1
3              4          0.31238                10.52  4
4              5          0.35892     Polioptila   9.00  1  8.00  2  7.91  9  0.00  1 10.30  1 11.15  2 11.90  1
5              6          0.36766                10.00  2 10.90  1 10.50  1 10.60  1 11.00  1 10.90  1 10.30  1
6              7          0.04464                10.42  6
7              8          0.09891     Parus       10.45  2 10.60  3 10.60  1 10.10  4  0.00  1 10.56  5 11.30  1
8              11         0.04083                10.90  1 10.90  1 10.83  3 10.60  3 10.75  2 10.40  1 10.90  1
11             9          0.05177                10.61  8
9              10         0.07770     Aegithalos  10.70  3 10.35  2 10.23  3 10.54  8 11.14  7  0.00  1 10.28  4
10             12         0.05089                 9.87  3 11.13  3 10.95  2 10.87  3  9.92  4  9.90  1 10.10  1
12             13         0.36395                10.13  9
13             Sylvia     3.96509     Hirundo     11.70  1 11.60  1 11.90  1 11.90  1 11.00  2 11.20  1  0.00  1
13             Cincloramphus  4.08747            11.30  1 10.45  2 10.45  2  9.90  3  9.90  1 10.00  1 10.20  1
12             Hippolais  4.38334                 9.83  3
10             Zosterops  4.54499     Regulus     10.70  1 10.90  2 11.35  2 10.94  5 10.78  5 10.48  4 10.20  1
9              Cisticola  4.90352                 0.00  1 10.20  1  9.38  5 10.10  2  8.98  4 10.15  2  9.80  1
11             Phylloscopus  4.23407             9.16 11
8              Pycnonotus  4.87877    Pycnonotus  11.20  1 11.10  1 10.70  1 10.90  1  9.90  1 11.10  1 10.50  1
7              Regulus    4.88263                 9.00  1  0.00  1 10.10  1  9.50  1  9.40  1  9.50  1  9.90  1
6              Hirundo    5.20812                 9.40  4
5              Aegithalos  5.12215    Cisticola   10.97  3 11.30  3 11.35  2 10.86 10 10.92  6 10.38  4 10.17  6
4              Parus      5.11899                10.82  5  9.88  6  0.00  1  9.57  6  9.34 10  9.42  4  9.75  4
3              1          0.43435                 9.43 17
1              Certhia    4.51124     Zosterops   11.50  1 11.00  1 11.00  1 10.20  1 11.00  2 10.90  1  9.40  1
1              2          0.52633                10.50  1  9.40  4  9.45  6  0.00  1  9.00  3  9.30  2  9.30  5
2              Polioptila  3.89624                8.83  7
2              Thryomanes  3.99330    Phylloscopus 11.10  2 10.80  1 10.65  2 10.62  6  9.64  5  9.63  3  9.60  3
                                                  9.75  2  9.10  3  9.28 11  8.50  3  0.00  1  8.30  1  8.73  3
                                                  8.86 11
                                      Hippolais   11.05  2 10.50  2 10.90  1 10.87  3 10.57  3 10.20  1  9.97  3
                                                 10.10  1  9.50  2  9.40 11  9.05  2  8.56  5  0.00  1  8.65  4
                                                  8.57 11
                                      Cincloramphus 11.10 1 10.80 1 11.00 1 10.35 2 10.86 10 10.40 1 10.20 1
                                                 10.05  2  9.90  1  9.28 11  8.95  4  8.78  4  9.10  3  0.00  1
                                                  7.93  9
                                      Sylvia      11.13  3 10.78  4 10.62  5 10.71 15 10.54  8 10.38  6  9.92  5
                                                  9.71  9  9.43  3  9.41 10  8.81  7  8.75 17  8.96  7  8.20  8
                                                  0.00  1
```

FIGURE 350. FITCH tree of relationships among the Sylvioidea. The following were pooled: *Certhia* = *Certhia* and *Salpornis*; *Thryomanes* = wrens; *Polioptila* = *Polioptila, Ramphocaenus, Microbates*; *Aegithalos* = *Aegithalos* and *Psaltriparus*; *Hirundo* = swallows; *Pycnonotus* = bulbuls; *Cisticola* = *Cisticola* and *Prinia*; *Zosterops* = white-eyes including *Cleptornis*; *Hippolais* = *Hippolais* and *Acrocephalus*; *Cincloramphus* = *Cincloramphus, Megalurus, Eremiornis, Bowdleria*; *Sylvia* = *Sylvia* plus the typical babblers. For *Sitta, Parus, Regulus* and *Phylloscopus* congeners were pooled.

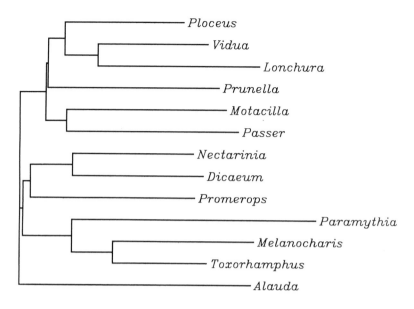

```
Alauda       0.00  4 11.00  1  9.90  1 13.30  1  9.88  1 10.30  1  9.30  1
            10.52  4 10.53  3 10.75  2 11.10  2 10.15  1  9.46 13
Melanocharis 11.00  1  0.00  3  5.92 10  9.96  1  9.85  4 10.33  6  9.37  1
            11.20  1 11.50  1 11.10  1 11.00  1 10.70  1 10.00  2
Toxorhamphus  9.90  2  5.05  4  0.00  3  9.32  1  8.03  3  9.15  4  8.44  9
             9.63  3  9.93  3  9.30  1  9.10  1  9.16  1  8.37  3
Paramythia   13.30  1  9.96  5  9.32  4  0.00  2 10.90  3 11.95  4 11.22  6
            12.70  1 12.40  1 12.30  1 12.20  1 10.50  1 10.50  1
Promerops    9.88  6  9.48  4  8.73  3 10.90  1  0.00  5  8.42  4  7.73 18
             9.65  6 10.13  6  9.10  4  8.90  3  9.10  1  8.09  9
Dicaeum      8.90  1  8.95  1  8.80  1 11.95  1  8.42  1  0.00  1  5.36  5
             8.90  1  8.70  1  8.90  1  8.90  1 10.30  1  7.70  1
Nectarinia  10.90  1  9.55  2  8.98  4 11.37  1  8.30  3  7.22  5  0.00  3
             9.42  4  9.70  1  9.03  3  8.80  3  9.00  1  8.92  4
Passer      10.50  1 11.20  1  9.60  1 13.00  1  9.80  1  9.60  1  9.70  1
             0.00  2  9.43  6  7.40  1  7.60  1 10.10  1  8.15  8
Lonchura    11.40  1 11.50  1  9.90  1 12.40  1 10.10  1  8.70  1  9.70  1
            10.10  1  0.00  2 10.50  1  9.70  1  6.60  1  8.03  8
Motacilla   11.60  1 11.10  1  9.30  1 12.30  1  9.10  1  8.90  1  9.10  1
             8.70  1 10.50  1  0.00  2  8.60  4  8.00  1  7.68  4
Prunella    10.90  1 11.00  1  9.10  1 12.20  1  8.90  1  8.90  1  8.70  2
             8.85  2  9.70  3  8.60  4  0.00  2  7.90  1  7.16  5
Vidua       10.15  4 10.70  1  9.20  1 10.50  1  9.10  1 10.30  1  9.35  2
             8.44  9  6.47 11  7.95  4  7.90  2  0.00  3  6.17 15
Ploceus      9.80  1 10.00  1  8.40  1 10.50  1  8.10  1  7.70  1  7.80  1
             7.83  3  7.17  3  7.10  2  7.20  1  6.20  1  0.00  4
```

FIGURE 351. FITCH tree of relationships among the Passeroidea except Fringillidae. The following were pooled: *Alauda* = larks; *Paramythia* = *Paramythia* and *Oreocharis; Dicaeum* = *Dicaeum* and *Prionochilus; Nectarinia* = sunbirds; *Passer* = *Passer* and *Petronia; Lonchura* = Estrildini; *Motacilla* = *Motacilla* and *Anthus; Ploceus* = Ploceinae. For *Melanocharis, Toxorhampus, Promerops, Prunella,* and *Vidua* only congeners were pooled.

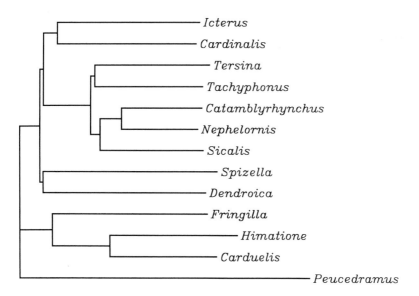

```
            FITCH                    Peucedramus   0.00  7 9.65  2 8.94  9 8.90  1 8.57  3 8.72  8 8.81 24 8.73  3
      Sum of squares = 0.61203                     8.20  2 9.10  1 9.70  1 9.40  2 8.80  1
Average percent standard deviation = 3.50920  Fringilla     9.60  1 0.00  1 5.79  7 6.50  1 6.83  3 6.95  2 6.55  2 6.70  2
            Examined 245 trees                      6.85  2 6.85  1 6.60  1 6.50  1 6.40  1
                                           Carduelis     8.90  1 6.60  1 0.00  1 4.30  1 6.90  1 6.95  2 7.55  2 7.50  2
  Between        And         Length                 6.90  1 6.80  1 7.00  1 6.80  1 6.50  1
                                           Himatione     8.90  1 6.50  1 4.33  6 0.00  2 8.10  1 7.05  2 7.48  5 7.70  1
Peucedramus        3        5.37931                 7.35  2 7.20  1 7.50  1 7.65  2 7.40  2
    3              7        0.37769        Cardinalis    8.60  1 6.80  1 7.40  2 7.90  1 0.00  2 5.10  5 6.22  5 6.10  5
    7              5        0.06816                 5.70  1 5.20  1 4.90  1 5.40  2 5.53  3
    5              4        0.25989        Icterus       8.70  1 7.30  1 7.20  1 7.10  1 5.40  3 0.00  4 6.02 15 6.64 12
    4           Icterus     2.63561                 6.10  2 5.70  1 5.98  6 6.36  5 6.30  1
    4          Cardinalis   2.56897        Dendroica     8.80  1 7.30  2 7.20  2 7.20  1 6.07  3 5.81 18 0.00  4 6.32 22
    5             10        0.88548                 6.50  1 6.14  7 5.90  1 6.30  1
   10             11        0.07605        Spizella      8.70  1 7.30  3 7.43  6 8.20  1 6.32  6 6.15 24 6.17 22 0.00  6
   11           Tersina     2.11843                 6.30  5 6.18  5 6.12  4 6.11  7 6.25  2
   11          Tachyphonus  1.99234        Sicalis       8.20  1 7.20  2 7.30  2 7.40  1 5.95  2 5.70  2 6.10  2 6.35  8
   10              8        0.17552                 0.00  2 3.70  2 3.95  2 4.10  2 4.50  2
    8              9        0.39570        Nephelornis   9.90  1 7.10  1 6.90  3 7.50  1 5.85  2 5.80  2 6.20  2 6.35  2
    9       Catamblyrhynchus 1.48160                3.20  1 0.00  3 3.10  1 4.00  2 4.10  1
    9          Nephelornis  1.40531        Catamblyrhynchus 9.60  1 6.20  1 6.55  2 7.50  1 5.80  2 6.00  6 6.03  7 6.07  3
    8           Sicalis     1.90188                 4.00  2 2.80  2 0.00  3 3.90  1 4.30  2
    7              6        0.05891        Tachyphonus   9.40  1 6.50  1 7.40  1 7.60  1 5.90  1 5.71 11 6.26 11 6.39 12
    6           Spizella    3.22710                 4.06  7 4.25  2 4.20  1 0.00  4 4.28  6
    6           Dendroica   3.01610        Tersina       8.80  1 7.50  1 7.30  2 7.40  1 6.05  2 6.15  2 6.40  3 6.45  4
    3              1        0.61071                 4.50  1 4.20  1 4.20  1 3.90  4 0.00  3
    1           Fringilla   2.87039
    1              2        1.07092
    2           Himatione   2.35515
    2           Carduelis   1.97051
```

FIGURE 352. FITCH tree of relationships within the Fringillidae. The following were pooled: *Icterus* = Icterini; *Spizella* = Emberizini; *Dendroica* = Parulini; *Himatione* = Drepanidini; *Carduelis* = Carduelini. For *Cardinalis, Tersina, Tachyphonus, Catamblyrhynchus, Nephelornis, Sicalis, Fringilla,* and *Peucedramus* only congeners were pooled.

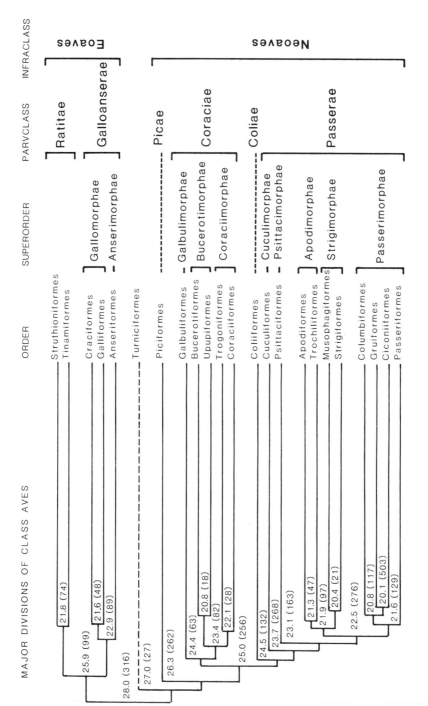

FIGURE 353. Major divisions of class Aves determined by average linkage (UPGMA) clustering of DNA-DNA hybridization distances. NOTE: In Figs. 353–385 the values at each node are the mean delta $T_{50}H$ followed in parentheses by the number of delta values averaged.

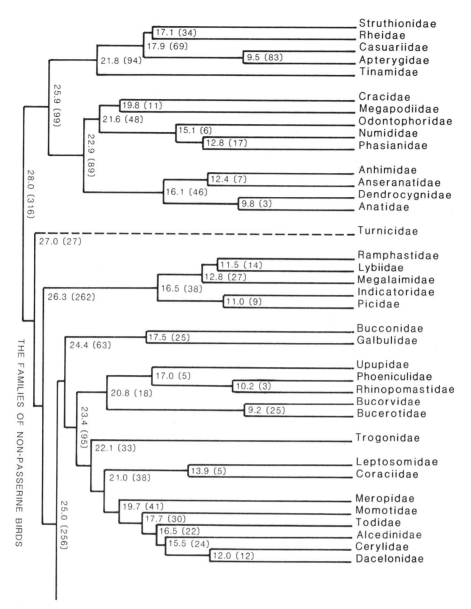

FIGURE 354. Families of non-passerine birds determined by average linkage (UPGMA) clustering. Struthionidae to Dacelonidae are shown. This figure links to Fig. 355.

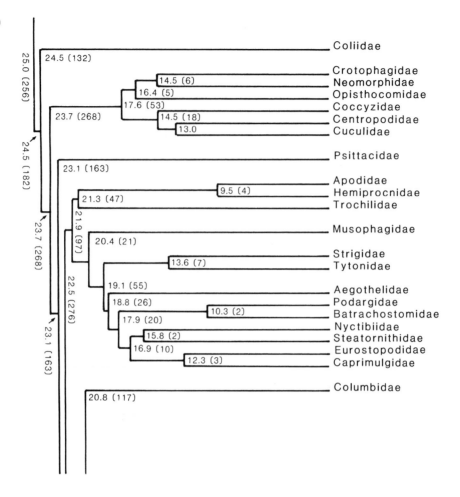

FIGURE 355. Families of non-passerine birds determined by average linkage (UPGMA) clustering. Coliidae to Columbidae are shown. This figure links to Figs. 354 and 356.

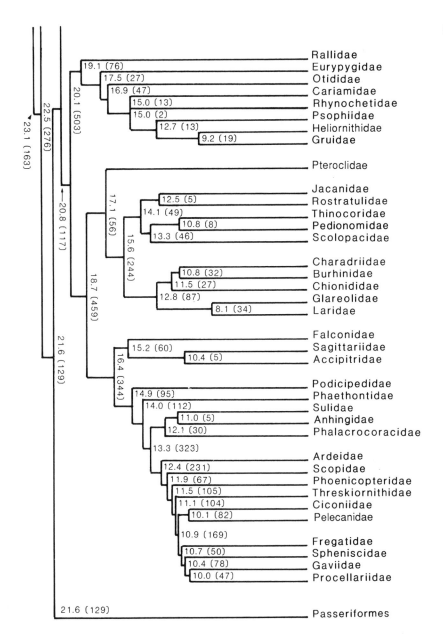

FIGURE 356. Families of non-passerine birds determined by average linkage (UPGMA) clustering. Rallidae to Procellariidae are shown. This figure links to Fig. 355.

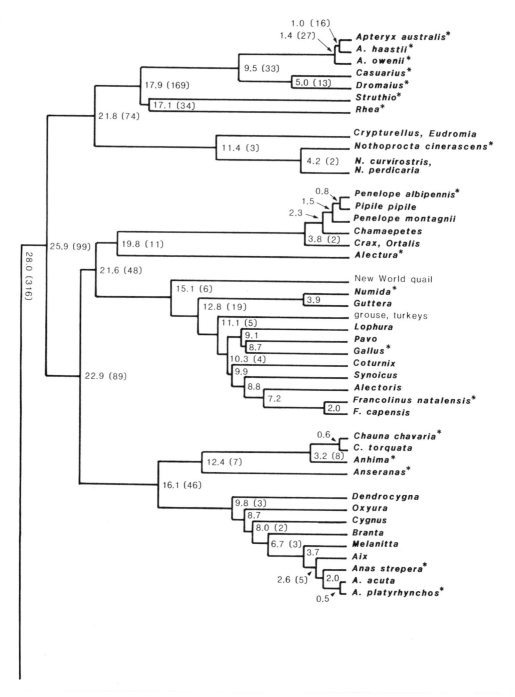

FIGURE 357. Relationships among members of the parvclasses Ratitae and Galloanserae determined by average linkage (UPGMA) clustering. Figs. 357–368 show the non-passerines and link to one another. In Figs. 357–385 the asterisks* after the scientific names of the birds indicate the species used as tracers.

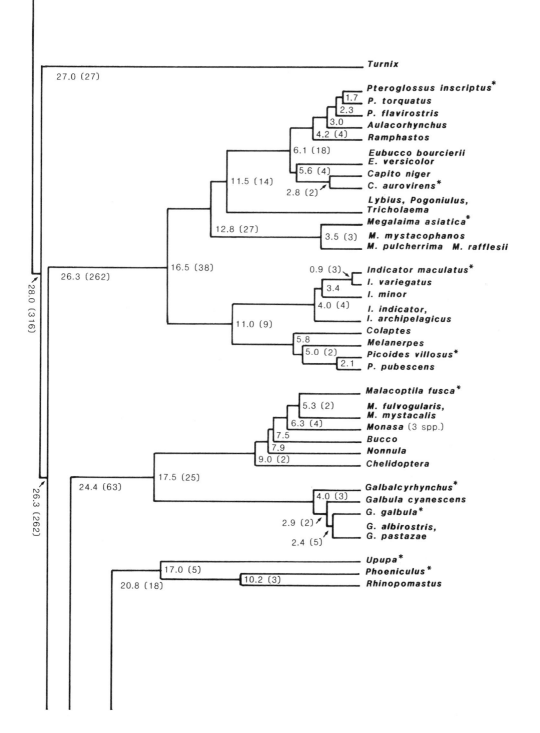

FIGURE 358. Relationships among members of the Piciformes, Galbuliformes, and Upupiformes as determined by average linkage (UPGMA) clustering.

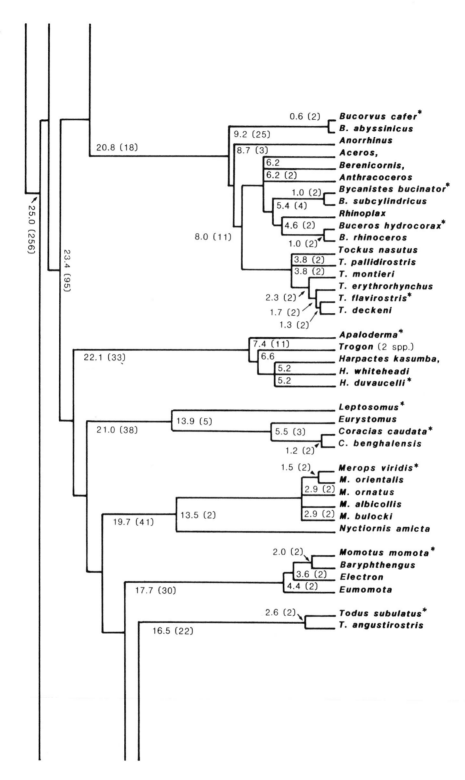

FIGURE 359. Relationships among members of the Bucerotiformes, Trogoniformes, and Coraciiformes (Coraciidae, Meropidae, Momotidae, and Todidae) determined by average linkage (UPGMA) clustering.

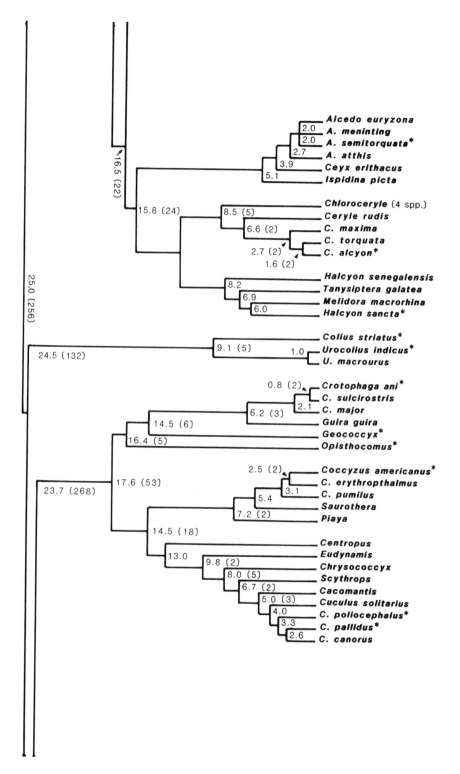

FIGURE 360. Relationships among members of the Coraciiformes (Alcedinidae, Dacelonidae, and Cerylidae), Coliiformes, and Cuculiformes determined by average linkage (UPGMA) clustering.

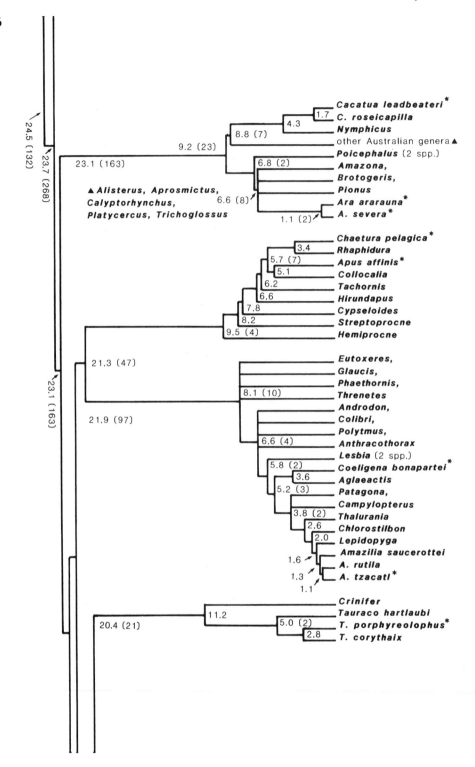

FIGURE 361. Relationships among the Psittaciformes, Apodiformes, Trochiliformes, and Musophagiformes determined by average linkage (UPGMA) clustering.

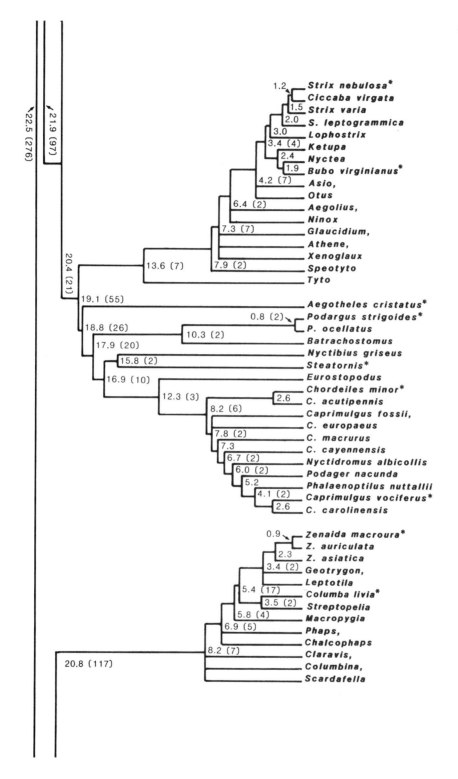

FIGURE 362. Relationships among members of the Strigiformes and Columbiformes determined by average linkage (UPGMA) clustering.

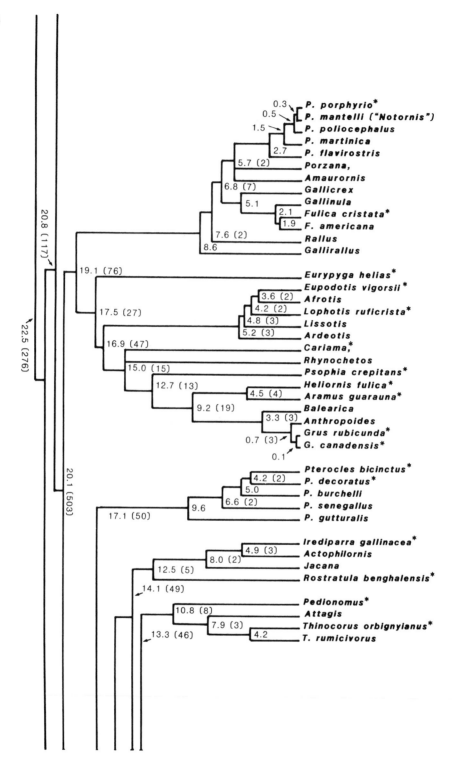

FIGURE 363. Relationships among members of the Gruiformes and Ciconiiformes (Pteroclidae, Jacanidae, Rostratulidae, and Thinocoridae) determined by average linkage (UPGMA) clustering.

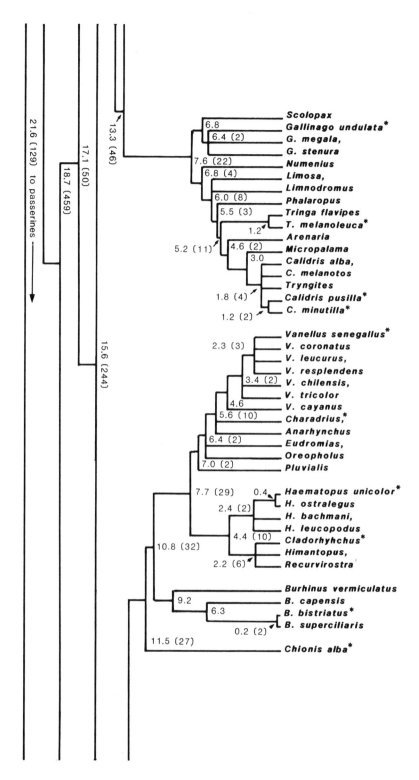

FIGURE 364. Relationships among members of the Ciconiiformes (Scolopacidae, Charadriidae, Burhinidae, and Chionididae) determined by average linkage (UPGMA) clustering.

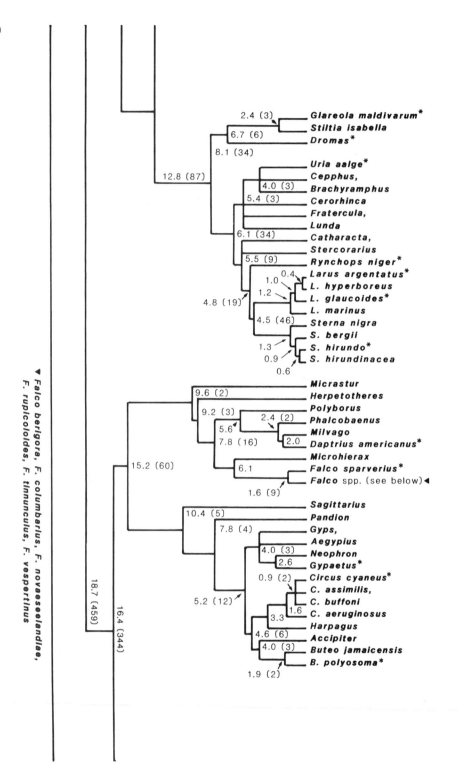

FIGURE 365. Relationships among some members of the Ciconiiformes (Glareolidae, Laridae, Falconidae, Sagittariidae, and Accipitridae) determined by average linkage (UPGMA) clustering.

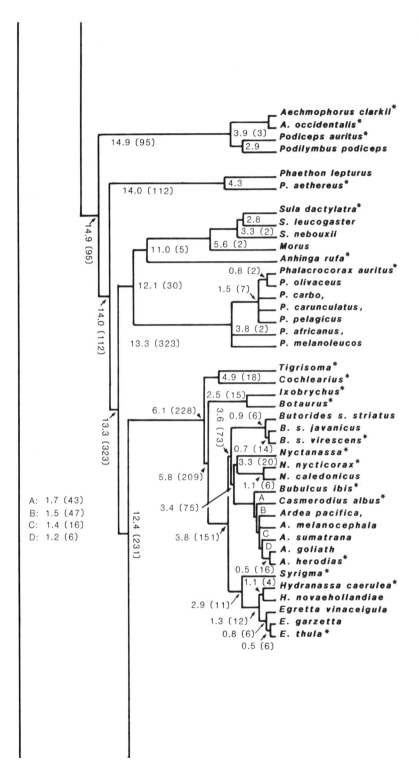

FIGURE 366. Relationships among some members of the Ciconiiformes (Podicipedidae, Phaethontidae, Sulidae, Anhingidae, Phalacrocoracidae, and Ardeidae) determined by average linkage (UPGMA) clustering.

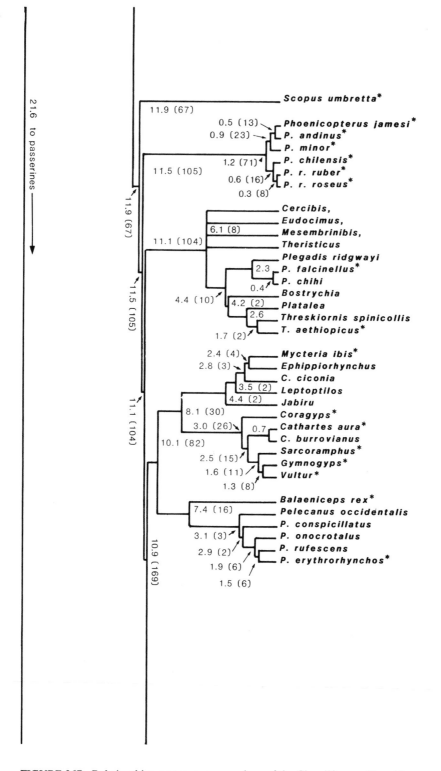

FIGURE 367. Relationships among some members of the Ciconiiformes (Scopidae, Phoenicopteridae, Threskiornithidae, Ciconiidae, and Pelecanidae) determined by average linkage (UPGMA) clustering.

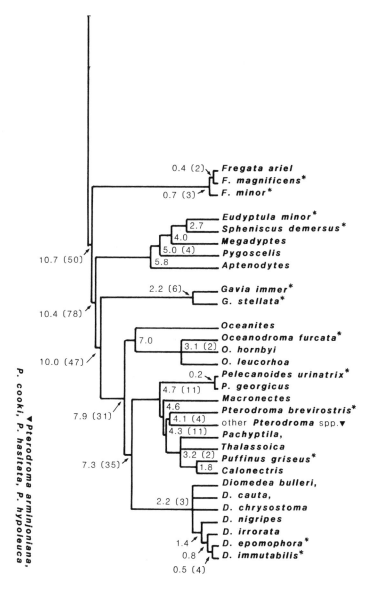

FIGURE 368. Relationships among members of the Procellarioidea (Fregatidae, Spheniscidae, Gaviidae, and Procellariidae) determined by average linkage (UPGMA) clustering. This concludes the non-passerines. Note that the line across the bottom of the figure represents the node to the Passeriformes at delta 21.6.

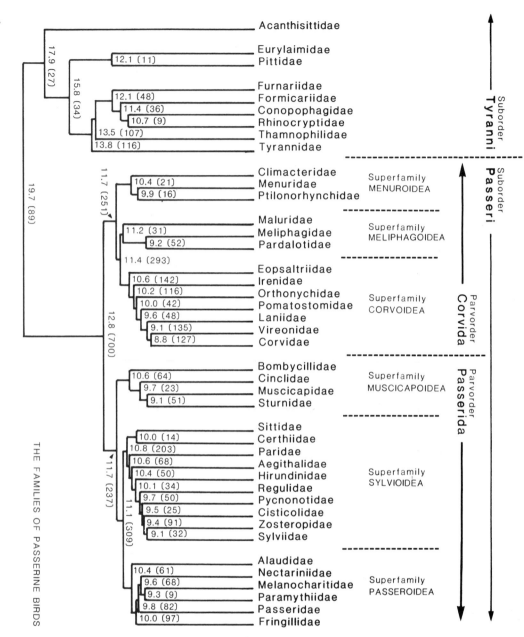

FIGURE 369. Families of passerine birds determined by average linkage (UPGMA) clustering of DNA-DNA hybridization distances.

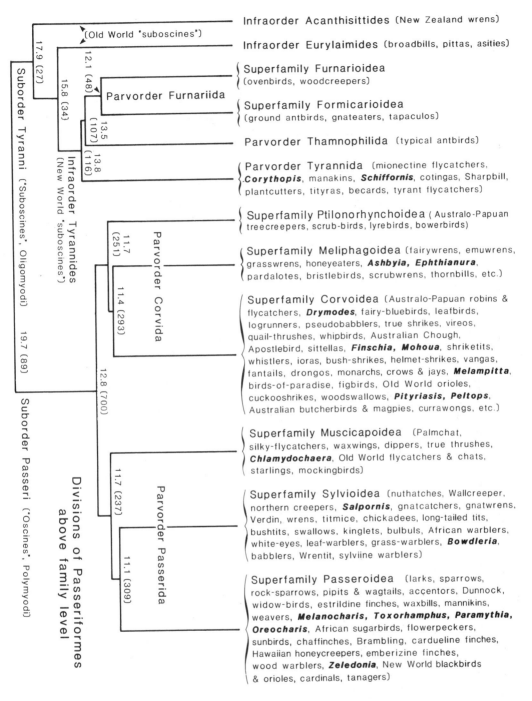

Infraorder Acanthisittides (New Zealand wrens)

(Old World "suboscines")

Infraorder Eurylaimides (broadbills, pittas, asities)

Superfamily Furnarioidea
(ovenbirds, woodcreepers)

Parvorder Furnariida

Superfamily Formicarioidea
(ground antbirds, gnateaters, tapaculos)

Parvorder Thamnophilida (typical antbirds)

Parvorder Tyrannida (mionectine flycatchers,
Corythopis, manakins, *Schiffornis*, cotingas, Sharpbill,
plantcutters, tityras, becards, tyrant flycatchers)

Superfamily Ptilonorhynchoidea (Australo-Papuan
treecreepers, scrub-birds, lyrebirds, bowerbirds)

Superfamily Meliphagoidea (fairywrens, emuwrens,
grasswrens, honeyeaters, *Ashbyia*, *Ephthianura*,
pardalotes, bristlebirds, scrubwrens, thornbills, etc.)

Superfamily Corvoidea (Australo-Papuan robins &
flycatchers, *Drymodes*, fairy-bluebirds, leafbirds,
logrunners, pseudobabblers, true shrikes, vireos,
quail-thrushes, whipbirds, Australian Chough,
Apostlebird, sittellas, *Finschia, Mohoua*, shriketits,
whistlers, ioras, bush-shrikes, helmet-shrikes, vangas,
fantails, drongos, monarchs, crows & jays, *Melampitta*,
birds-of-paradise, figbirds, Old World orioles,
cuckooshrikes, woodswallows, *Pityriasis, Peltops*,
Australian butcherbirds & magpies, currawongs, etc.)

Superfamily Muscicapoidea (Palmchat,
silky-flycatchers, waxwings, dippers, true thrushes,
Chlamydochaera, Old World flycatchers & chats,
starlings, mockingbirds)

Superfamily Sylvioidea (nuthatches, Wallcreeper,
northern creepers, *Salpornis*, gnatcatchers, gnatwrens,
Verdin, wrens, titmice, chickadees, long-tailed tits,
bushtits, swallows, kinglets, bulbuls, African warblers,
white-eyes, leaf-warblers, grass-warblers, *Bowdleria*,
babblers, Wrentit, sylviine warblers)

Superfamily Passeroidea (larks, sparrows,
rock-sparrows, pipits & wagtails, accentors, Dunnock,
widow-birds, estrildine finches, waxbills, mannikins,
weavers, *Melanocharis, Toxorhamphus, Paramythia,
Oreocharis*, African sugarbirds, flowerpeckers,
sunbirds, chaffinches, Brambling, cardueline finches,
Hawaiian honeycreepers, emberizine finches,
wood warblers, *Zeledonia*, New World blackbirds
& orioles, cardinals, tanagers)

17.9 (27)

12.1 (48)

15.8 (34)

13.5 (107)

13.8 (116)

Suborder Tyranni ("Suboscines", Oligomyodi)

Infraorder Tyrannides (New World "suboscines")

11.7 (251)

11.4 (293)

Parvorder Corvida

12.8 (700)

19.7 (89)

11.7 (237)

Parvorder Passerida

11.1 (309)

Suborder Passeri ("Oscines", Polymyodi)

Parvorder Tyrannides

Divisions of Passeriformes above family level

FIGURE 370. Divisions of the Passeriformes above the family level determined by average linkage (UPGMA) clustering.

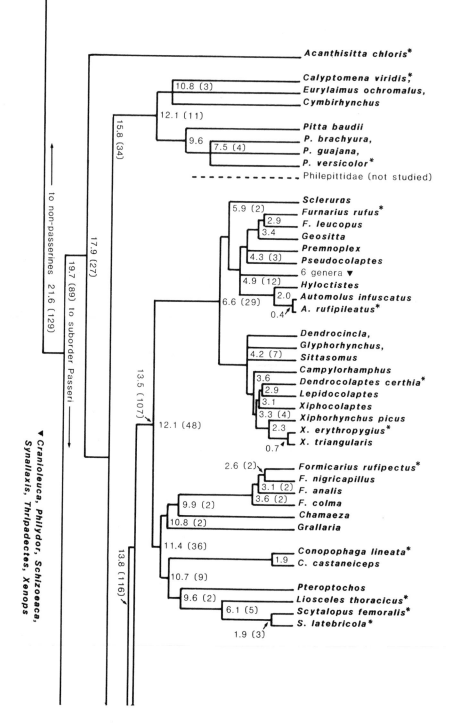

FIGURE 371. Relationships among Acanthisittidae, Eurylaimidae, Pittidae, Furnariidae, Formicariidae, Conopophagidae, and Rhinocryptidae determined by average linkage (UPGMA) clustering. The dendrograms of the passerines (Figs. 371–385) link to one another, and to the non-passerines at delta 21.6. Asterisks* indicate the species used as tracers.

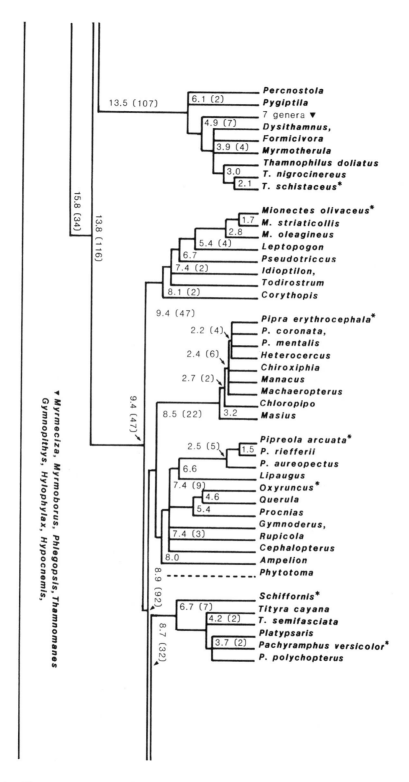

FIGURE 372. Relationships among some members of the Tyrannidae determined by average linkage (UPGMA) clustering.

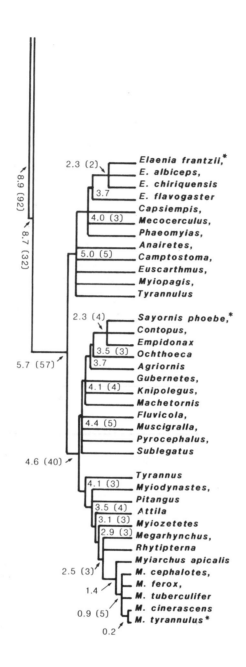

FIGURE 373. Relationships among some members of the Tyrannidae determined by average linkage (UPGMA) clustering.

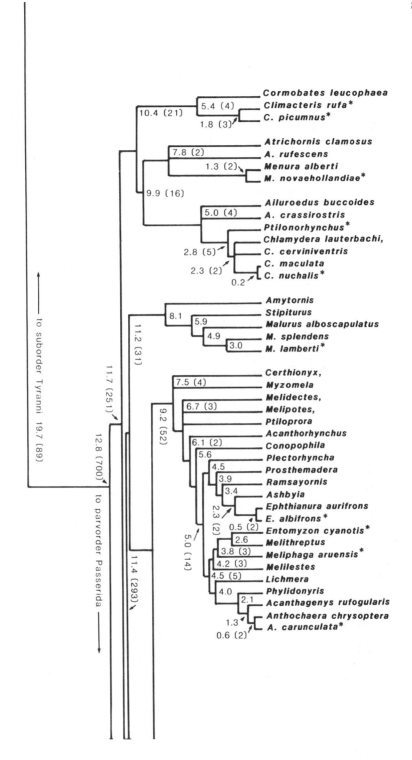

FIGURE 374. Relationships among the Climacteridae, Menuridae, Ptilonorhynchidae, Maluridae, and Meliphagidae determined by average linkage (UPGMA) clustering.

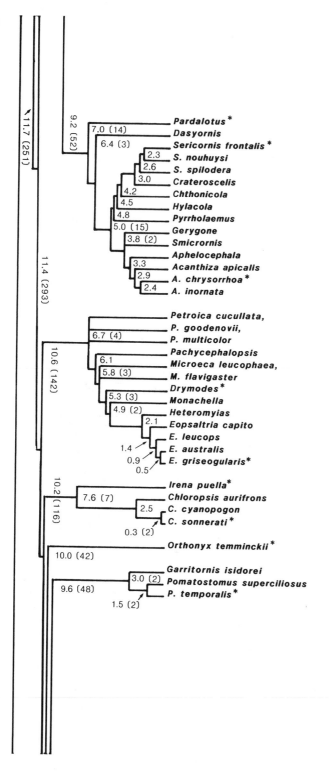

FIGURE 375. Relationships among the Pardalotidae, Eopsaltriidae, Irenidae, Orthonychidae, and Pomatostomidae determined by average linkage (UPGMA) clustering.

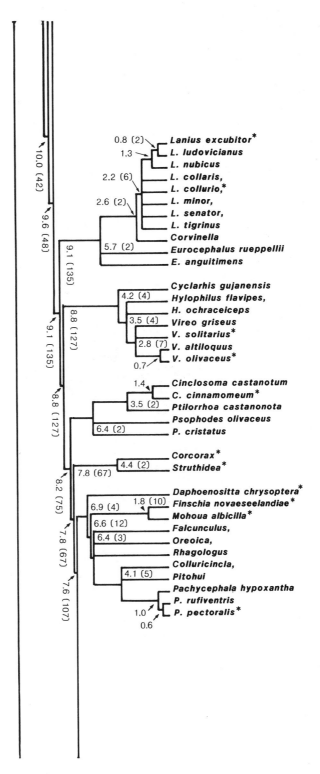

FIGURE 376. Relationships among the Laniidae, Vireonidae, and Corvidae (Cinclosomatinae, Corcoracinae, and Pachycephalinae) determined by average linkage (UPGMA) clustering.

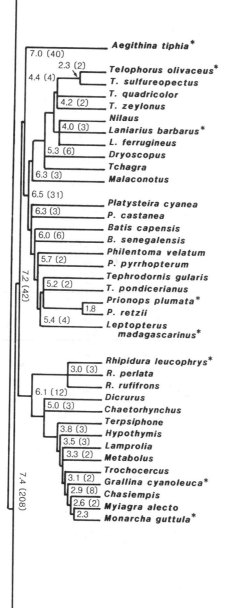

FIGURE 377. Relationships among members of the Corvidae (Aegithininae, Malaconotinae, and Dicrurinae) determined by average linkage (UPGMA) clustering.

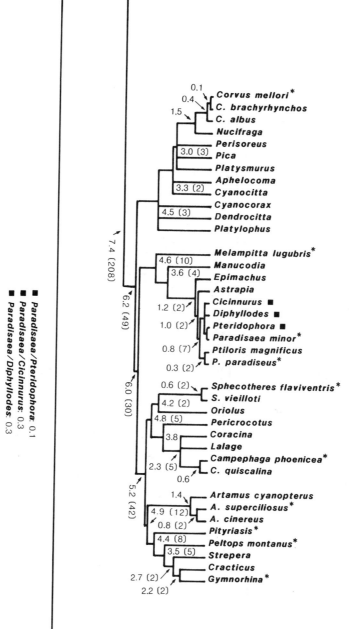

FIGURE 378. Relationships among members of the Corvidae: Corvinae determined by average linkage (UPGMA) clustering.

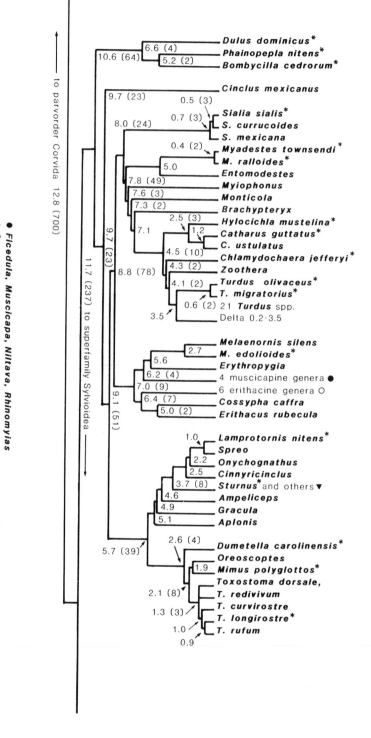

FIGURE 379. Relationships among the Muscicapoidea determined by average linkage (UPGMA) clustering.

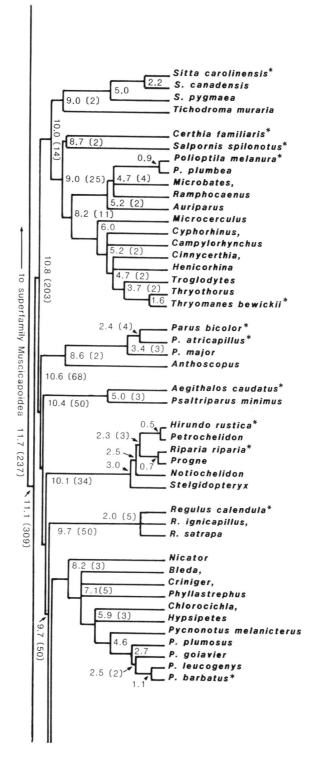

FIGURE 380. Relationships among the Sylvioidea (Sittidae, Certhiidae, Paridae, Aegithalidae, Hirundinidae, Regulidae, and Pycnonotidae) determined by average linkage (UPGMA) clustering.

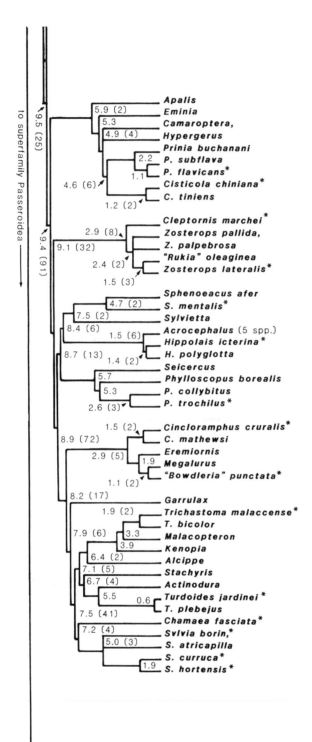

FIGURE 381. Relationships among the Sylvioidea (Cisticolidae, Zosteropidae, and Sylviidae) determined by average linkage (UPGMA) clustering.

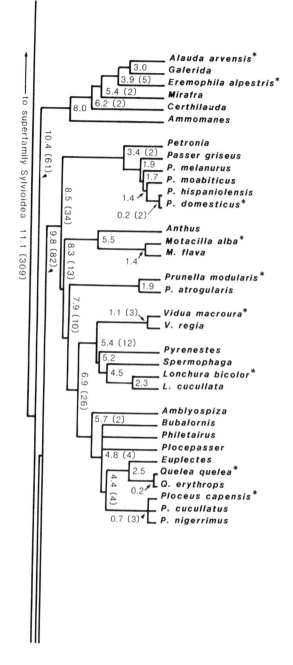

FIGURE 382. Relationships among the Passeroidea (Alaudidae and Passeridae) determined by average linkage (UPGMA) clustering.

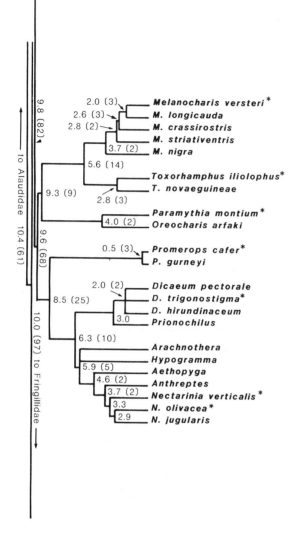

FIGURE 383. Relationships among the Passeroidea (Melanocharitidae, Paramythiidae, and Nectariniidae) determined by average linkage (UPGMA) clustering.

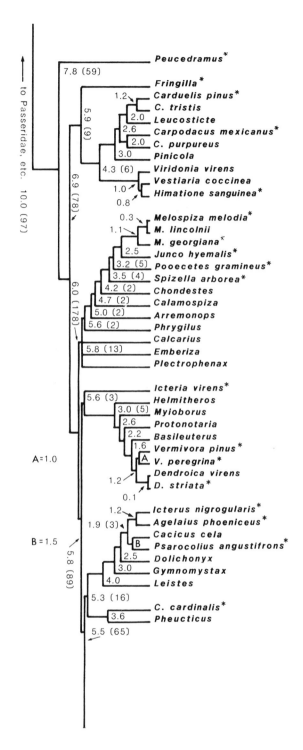

FIGURE 384. Relationships among some members of the Fringillidae determined by average linkage (UPGMA) clustering.

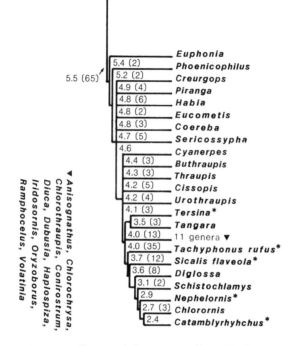

FIGURE 385. Relationships among some members of the Fringillidae determined by average linkage (UPGMA) clustering.

Literature Cited

Abbott, L. A., F. A. Bisby, and D. J. Rogers. 1985. Taxonomic analysis in biology. Columbia Univ. Press, New York.

Abelson, J. 1979. RNA processing and the intervening sequence problem. Ann. Rev. Biochem. 48:1035–1069.

Ackerman, A. 1967. Quantitative Untersuchungen an körnerfressenden Singvögeln. J. für Orn. 108:430–473.

Adams, R. L. P., R. H. Burdon, A. M. Campbell, D. P. Leader, and R. M. S. Smellie. 1981. The biochemistry of the nucleic acids. Ninth ed. Chapman and Hall, London and New York.

Adams, T. 1955. Comparative osteology of the night herons. Condor 57:55–60.

Ahlquist, J. E. 1974a. The relationships of the shorebirds. Ph.D. diss., Yale Univ.

Ahlquist, J. E. 1974b. Godwits, curlews, and tringine sandpipers: new evidence challenges old classifications. Discovery 10:14–25. Peabody Museum, Yale Univ.

Ahlquist, J. E., F. H. Sheldon, and C. G. Sibley. 1984. The relationships of the Bornean Bristlehead (*Pityriasis gymnocephala*) and the Black-collared Thrush (*Chlamydochaera jefferyi*). J. für Orn. 125:129–140.

Ahlquist, J. E., A. H. Bledsoe, J. T. Ratti, and C. G. Sibley. 1987a. Divergence of the single-copy DNA sequences of the Western Grebe (*Aechmophorus occidentalis*) and Clark's Grebe (*A. clarkii*), as indicated by DNA-DNA hybridization. Postilla 200, 7 pp., Peabody Mus. Nat. Hist., Yale Univ., New Haven, Conn.

Ahlquist, J. E., A. H. Bledsoe, F. H. Sheldon, and C. G. Sibley. 1987b. DNA hybridization and avian systematics. Auk 104:556–563.

Ainley, D. G., R. E. LeResche, and W. J. L. Sladen. 1983. Breeding biology of the Adelie Penguin. Univ. Calif. Press, Berkeley.

Alberts, B., D. Bray, J. Lewis, M. Raff, K. Roberts, and J. D. Watson. 1983. Molecular biology of the cell. Garland Publ. Co., New York.

Allen, J. A. 1897. The proper generic name of the loons. Auk 14:312.

Allen, J. A. 1908. The case of *Strix* vs. *Aluco*. Auk 25:288–291.

Allen, J. A. 1910. Richard Bowdler Sharpe. Auk 27:124–129.

Allen, R. P. 1942. The Roseate Spoonbill. Research Rept. No. 2, Natl. Audubon Soc., New York.

Allen, S., and I. Gibson. 1972. Genome amplifications and gene expression in the ciliate macronucleus. Biochem. Genet. 6:293–313.

Allison, R. G., and R. E. Feeney. 1968. Penguin blood serum proteins. Arch. Biochem. Biophys. 124:548–555.

Alonso, S., A. Minty, Y. Bourlet, and M. Buckingham. 1986. Comparison of three actin-coding sequences in the mouse; evolutionary relationships between the actin genes of warm-blooded vertebrates. J. Mol. Biol. 23:11–22.

Alston, R. E., and B. L. Turner. 1963. Biochemical systematics. Prentice-Hall, Englewood Cliffs, New Jersey.

Alt, F. W., R. Kellems, J. Bertino, and R. T. Schimke. 1978. Selective multiplication of dihydrofolate reductase genes in methotrexate resistant variants of cultured murine cells. J. Biol. Chem. 253:1357–1370.

Altenburg, L. C., M. J. Getz, and G. G. Saunders. 1975. ^{125}I in molecular hybridization experiments. Pp. 325–342 in Methods in cell biology, vol. 10. D. M. Prescott, ed. Academic Press, New York.

Altman, S. 1984. Aspects of biochemical catalysis. Cell 36:237–239.

Altmann, R. 1889. Ueber nucleosäuren. Arch. Anat. Physiol. 524–536.

Alvarez del Toro, M. 1971. On the biology of the American Finfoot in southern Mexico. Living Bird 10:79–88.

Amadon, D. 1943. The genera of starlings and their relationships. Amer. Mus. Novit. 1247:1–16.

Amadon, D. 1950a. The Hawaiian honeycreepers (Aves, Drepaniidae). Bull. Amer. Mus. Nat. Hist. 95:151–262.

Amadon, D. 1950b. Australian mud nest builders. Emu 50:123–127.

Amadon, D. 1951. Le pseudo-souimanga de Madagascar. L'Oiseau et R.F.O. 21:59–63.

Amadon, D. 1956. Remarks on the starlings, family Sturnidae. Amer. Mus. Novit. 1803:1–41.

Amadon, D. 1957. Remarks on the classification of the perching birds [order Passeriformes]. Proc. Zool. Soc. Calcutta, Mookerjee Mem. Vol., pp. 259–268.

Amadon, D. 1962. Family Sturnidae. Pp. 75–121 in Check-list of birds of the world, vol. 15. E. Mayr and J. C. Greenway, Jr., eds. Mus. Comp. Zool., Cambridge, Mass.

Amadon, D. 1977. Notes on the taxonomy of vultures. Condor 79:413–416.

Amadon, D. 1979. Family Philepittidae. Pp. 330–331 in Check-list of birds of the world, vol. 8. M. A. Traylor, Jr., ed. Mus. Comp. Zool., Cambridge, Mass.

Amadon, D., and J. Bull. 1988. Hawks and owls of the world. Proc. West. Found. Vert. Zool. 3:295–357.

Ameghino, F. 1905. Enumeración de los impennes fosiles de Patagonia y de la isla Seymour. Anal. Mus. Nac. Hist. Natur. Buenos Aires, Ser. 3, 6:97–167.

American Ornithologists' Union. 1886. Code of nomenclature and check-list of North American birds. Amer. Orn. Union, New York.

American Ornithologists' Union. 1895. Check-list of North American birds. 2nd ed. Amer. Orn. Union, New York.

American Ornithologists' Union. 1910. Check-list of North American birds. 3rd ed. Amer. Orn. Union, New York.

American Ornithologists' Union. 1931. Check-list of North American birds. 4th ed. Amer. Orn. Union, Lancaster, Penn.

American Ornithologists' Union. 1957. Check-list of North American birds. 5th ed. Port City Press, Baltimore, Maryland.

American Ornithologists' Union. 1983. Check-list of North American birds. 6th ed. Allen Press, Lawrence, Kansas.

American Ornithologists' Union. 1985. Thirty-fifth supplement to the American Ornithologists' Union check-list of North American birds. Auk 102:680–686.

Ames, P. L. 1971. The morphology of the syrinx in passerine birds. Bull. Peabody Mus. Nat. Hist. 37:1–194.

Ames, P. L. 1975. The application of syringeal morphology to the classification of the Old World insect eaters (Muscicapidae). Bonn. Zool. Beitr. 26:107–134.

Ames, P. L., M. A. Heimerdinger, and S. L. Warter. 1968. The anatomy and systematic position of the antpipits *Conopophaga* and *Corythopis*. Postilla 114:1–32.

Anderson, D. M., and W. R. Folk. 1976. Iodination of DNA. Studies of the reaction and iodination of papovavirus DNA. Biochemistry 15:1022–1030.

Anderson, D. M., R. H. Scheller, J. W. Posakony, L. B. McAllister, S. G. Trabert, C. Beall, R. J. Britten, and E. H. Davidson. 1981. Repetitive sequences of the sea urchin genome. Distribution of members of specific repetitive families. J. Mol. Biol. 145:5–28.

Anderson, J. E., M. Ptashne, and S. C. Harrison. 1987. Structure of the repressor-operator complex of bacteriophage 434. Nature 326:846–852.

Anderson, S. A., A. T. Bankier, B. G. Barrell, H. H. L. DeBruijn, A. R. Coulson, J. Drouin, I. C. Eperon, D. P. Nierlich, B. A. Roe, F. Sanger, P. H. Schreier, H. J. H. Smith, R. Staden, and I. G. Young. 1981. Sequence and organization of the human mitochondrial genome. Nature 290:457–465.

Andrew, R. J. 1956. Intention movements of flight in certain passerines, and their use in systematics. Behaviour 10:179–204.

Andrew, R. J. 1961. The displays given by passerines in courtship and reproductive fighting: a review. Ibis 103a:315–348.

Angerer, R. C., E. H. Davidson, and R. J. Britten. 1975. DNA sequence organization in the mollusc *Aplysia californica*. Cell 6:29–39.

Angerer, R. C., E. H. Davidson, and R. J. Britten. 1976. Single-copy DNA and structural gene sequence relationships among four sea urchin species. Chromosoma 56:213–226.

Antonov, A. S. 1986. Molecular analysis of plant DNA genomes: conserved and diverged DNA sequences. Pp. 171–183 *in* DNA systematics, vol. 2: Plants. S. K. Dutta, ed. CRC Press, Inc., Boca Raton, Florida.

A.O.U., abbreviation for American Ornithologists' Union.

Appert, O. 1970. Zur Biologie einiger Kua-Arten Madagaskars (Aves, Cuculi). Zool. Jahrb. Syst. 97:424–453.

Appert, O. 1980. Erste Farbaufnahmen der Rachenzeichnung junger Kuas von Madagaskar (Cuculi, Couinae). Orn. Beobachter 77:85–101.

Appert, O. 1985. Zur Biologie der Mesitornithiformes (Nakas oder "Stelzenrallen") Madagaskars und erste fotographische Dokumente von vertreten der Ordnung. Orn. Beobachter 82:31–54.

Arnheim, N. 1983. Concerted evolution of multigene families. Pp. 38–61 *in* Evolution of genes and proteins. M. Nei and R. K. Koehn, eds. Sinauer Assoc., Sunderland, Mass.

Arnheim, N., and A. C. Wilson. 1967. Quantitative immunological comparison of bird lysozymes. J. Biol. Chem. 242:3951–3956.

Arnheim, N., E. M. Prager, and A. C. Wilson. 1969. Immunological comparisons of chicken, quail, and pheasant lysozymes. J. Biol. Chem. 244:2085–2094.

Arrighi, F. E., J. Bergendahl, and M. Mandel. 1968. Isolation and characterization of DNA from fixed cells and tissues. Exp. Cell Res. 50:47–53.

Arscott, P. G., G. Lee, V. A. Bloomfield, and D. F. Evans. 1989. Scanning tunnelling microscopy of Z-DNA. Nature 339:484–486.

Arthur, R. R., and N. A. Straus. 1978. DNA-sequence organization in the genome of the domestic chicken (*Gallus domesticus*). Can. J. Biochem. 56:257–263.

Arvey, M. D. 1951. Phylogeny of the waxwings and allied birds. Publ. Univ. Kansas Mus. Nat. Hist. 3:473–530.

Ash, J. S. 1960. A study of the Mallophaga of birds with particular reference to their ecology. Ibis 102:93–110.

Astbury, W. T., and F. C. Bell. 1938. X-ray study of thymonucleic acid. Nature 141:747–748.

Atkin, N. B., G. Mattinson, W. Beçak, and S. Ohno. 1965. The comparative DNA content of 19 species of placental mammals, reptiles, and birds. Chromosoma 17:1–10.

Attardi, G., H. Parnas, M.-I. H. Hwang, and B. Attardi. 1966. Giant-size rapidly labeled nuclear ribonucleic acid and cytoplasmic messenger ribonucleic acid in immature duck erythrocytes. J. Mol. Biol. 20:145–182.

Audley-Charles, M. G. 1983. Reconstruction of eastern Gondwanaland. Nature 306:48–50.

Audley-Charles, M. G. 1987. Dispersal of Gondwanaland: relevance to evolution of the angiosperms. *In* Biogeography of the Malay Archipelago. T. C. Whitmore, ed. Clarendon Press, Oxford.

Averkina, R. F., N. G. Andreyeva, and N. N. Kartashev. 1965. Immunological peculiarities of some alciform birds and their taxonomic role [in Russian]. Zool. Zh. (Moscow) 44:1690–1700.

Avery, O. T., C. M. MacLeod, and M. McCarty. 1944. Studies on the chemical nature of the substance inducing transformation of pneumococcal types. J. Exper. Med. 79:137–158.

Avise, J. C. 1986. Mitochondrial DNA and the evolutionary genetics of higher animals. Phil. Trans. Roy. Soc. London B 312:325–342.

Avise, J. C., and C. F. Aquadro. 1982. A comparative summary of genetic distances in the vertebrates. Pp. 151–185 *in* Evol. Biol., vol. 15. M. Hecht, B. Wallace, G. Prance, eds. Plenum Press, New York.

Avise, J. C., and C. F. Aquadro. 1987. Malate dehydrogenase isozymes provide a phylogenetic marker for the Piciformes (woodpeckers and allies). Auk 104:324–328.

Avise, J. C., and R. A. Lansman. 1983. Polymorphism of mitochondrial DNA in populations of higher animals. Pp. 147–164 *in* Evolution of genes and proteins. M. Nei and R. K. Koehn, eds. Sinauer Assoc., Sunderland, Mass.

Avise, J. C., and W. S. Nelson. 1989. Molecular genetic relationships of the extinct Dusky Seaside Sparrow. Science 243:646–648.

Avise, J. C., and N. C. Saunders. 1984. Hybridization and introgression among species of sunfish (*Lepomis*): analysis by mitochondrial DNA and allozyme markers. Genetics 108:237–255.

Avise, J. C., C. Giblin-Davidson, J. Laerm, J. C. Patton, and R. A. Lansman. 1979a. Mitochondrial DNA clones and matriarchal phylogeny within and among geographic populations of the pocket gopher, *Geomys pinetis*. Proc. Natl. Acad. Sci. USA 76:6694–6698.

Avise, J. C., R. A. Lansman, and R. O. Shade. 1979b. The use of restriction endonucleases to measure mitochondrial DNA sequence relatedness in natural populations. I. Population structure and evolution in the genus *Peromyscus*. Genetics 92:279–295.

Avise, J. C., J. F. Shapira, S. W. Daniel, C. F. Aquadro, and R. A. Lansman. 1983.

Mitochondrial DNA differentiation during the speciation process in *Peromyscus*. Mol. Biol. Evol. 1:38–56.

Avise, J. C., E. Bermingham, L. G. Kessler, and N. C. Saunders. 1984a. Characterization of mitochondrial DNA variability in a hybrid swarm between subspecies of bluegill sunfish (*Lepomis macrochirus*). Evolution 38:931–941.

Avise, J. C., J. E. Neigel, and J. Arnold. 1984b. Demographic influences on mitochondrial DNA lineage survivorship in animal populations. J. Mol. Evol. 20:99–105.

Avise, J. C., G. S. Helfman, N. C. Saunders, and L. S. Hales. 1986. Mitochondrial DNA differentiation in North American eels: population genetic consequences of an unusual life history pattern. Proc. Natl. Acad. Sci. USA 83:4350–4354.

Baba, M. L., L. L. Darga, and M. Goodman. 1982. Recent advances in molecular evolution of the primates. Pp. 6–27 *in* Advanced views in primate biology. A. B. Chiarelli and R. S. Corruccini, eds. Springer-Verlag, Berlin.

Bachmann, K., O. B. Goin, and C. J. Goin. 1972a. Nuclear DNA amounts in vertebrates. Pp. 419–450 *in* Evolution of Genetic Systems, H. H. Smith, ed., Brookhaven Symp. Biol., vol. 23. Gordon and Breach, New York.

Bachmann, K., B. A. Harrington, and J. P. Craig. 1972b. Genome size in birds. Chromosoma 37:405–416.

Baer, J. G. 1954a. Révision taxonomique et étude biologique des Tetrabothriidae parasites d'oiseaux de haute mer et de mammifères marins. Univ. Neuchâtel, Mém., Ser. in-Quarto 1:1–123.

Baer, J. G. 1954b. Quelques considerations sur la spécificité parasitaire. Rev. Parasitol. 15:253–258.

Baer, J. G. 1955. Facteurs écologiques et spécificité parasitaire. Proc. 11th Intl. Orn. Congr. 293–295.

Baer, J. G. 1957. Répartition et endémicité des cestodes chez les reptiles, oiseaux et mammifères. Pp. 270–292 *in* Prem. Symp. sur la spécificité parasitaire des parasites de vertébrés. J. G. Baer, ed. Univ. Neuchâtel.

Bailey, V. 1928. A hybrid scaled × Gambel's quail from New Mexico. Auk 45:210.

Baird, S. F. 1858. Birds. With the co-operation of John Cassin and George N. Lawrence. Vol. 9, Part 2 *in* Reports of explorations and surveys, to ascertain the most practicable and economic route for a railroad from the Mississippi River to the Pacific Ocean. B. Tucker, Printer, Washington, D.C.

Baird, S. F. 1864. Review of American birds. Pt. 1. Smithson. Misc. Coll. 181:1–450.

Baker, C. M. A., and H. C. Hanson. 1966. Molecular genetics of avian proteins—VI. Evolutionary implications of blood proteins of eleven species of geese. Comp. Biochem. Physiol. 17:997–1006.

Baker, R. H. 1951. The avifauna of Micronesia, its origin, evolution, and distribution. Univ. Kansas Publ. Mus. Nat. Hist. 3:1–359.

Ball, R. M. Jr., S. Freeman, F. C. James, E. Bermingham, and J. C. Avise. 1988. Phylogeographic population structure of Red-winged Blackbirds assessed by mitochondrial DNA. Proc. Natl. Acad. Sci. USA 85:1558–1562.

Banks, R. C., and N. K. Johnson. 1961. A review of North American hybrid hummingbirds. Condor 63:3–28.

Banks, R. C., and L. W. Walker. 1964. A hybrid scaled × Douglas quail. Wilson Bull. 76:378–380.

Banzhaf, W. 1929. Die Vorderextremität von *Opisthocomus cristatus* (Vieillot). Z. Morph. Okol. Tiere 16:113–233.

Barker, W. C., and M. O. Dayhoff. 1976. Immunoglobulins and related proteins. Pp. 165–190 *in* Atlas of protein sequence and structure. Vol. 5. Natl. Biomed. Res. Found., Silver Springs, Maryland.

Barnikol, H. A. 1951. Über einige Gesetzmässigkeitein im Aufbau der motorischen Trigeminusäste bei Vögeln. Anat. Anz. 98:217–223.

Barnikol, H. A. 1953. Vergleichend anatomische und taxonomisch phylogenetische Studien am Kopf der Opisthocomiformes, Musophagidae, Galli, Columbae und Cuculi. Ein Beitrag zum Opisthocomus-Problem. Zool. Jahrb. Syst. 8l:487–526, 17 figs.

Barnikol, H. A. 1954. Zur morphologie des Nervus trigeminus der Vögel unter besonderer Berücksichtigung der Accipitres, Cathartidae, Striges und Anseriformes. Z. Wiss. Zool. 157:285–332.

Barrows, B. 1885. Accipitres. Pp. 260–348 *in* The standard natural history, Vol. 4, Birds. John S. Kingsley, ed. S. E. Cassino, Boston.

Bartlett, A. D. 1860. Note on the *Balaeniceps rex*. Proc. Zool. Soc. London 1860 (28):461.

Bartlett, A. D. 1861. On the affinities of *Balaeniceps*. Proc. Zool. Soc. London 1861:131–134.

Bartlett, A. D. 1962. Note on the habits and affinities of the kagu (*Rhinochetus jubatus*). Proc. Zool. Soc. London 1862:218–219.

Bartlett, A. D. 1866. Notes on the breeding of several species of birds in the Society's gardens during the year 1865. Proc. Zool. Soc. London 1866:76–79.

Bartlett, E. 1877. Remarks on the affinities of *Mesites*. Proc. Zool. Soc. London 1877:292–293.

Bartlett, E. 1889. A monograph of the weaverbirds, Ploceidae, and arboreal and terrestrial finches, Fringillidae. Spottiswoode and Co., London.

Bates, G. L. 1914. Some facts bearing on the affinities of *Smithornis*. Ibis 56:495–502.

Bates, G. L. 1918. The reversed under wing-coverts of birds and their modifications, as exemplified in the birds of West Africa. Ibis 60:529–583.

Bates, G. L. 1930. Handbook of the birds of West Africa. John Bale, Sons and Danielsson, London.

Baumel, J. J., editor. 1979. Nomina anatomica avium. Academic Press, London.

Bautz, E. K., and F. A. Bautz. 1964. The influence of non-complementary bases on the stability of ordered polynucleotides. Proc. Natl. Acad. Sci. USA 52:1478–1481.

Beauchamp, R. S., J. Pasternak, and N. A. Straus. 1979. Characterization of the free living nematode *Panagrellus silusiae*: absence of short period interspersion. Biochemistry 18:245–250.

Beçak, W., M. L. Beçak, H. R. S. Nazareth, and S. Ohno. 1964. Close karyological kinship between the reptilian suborder Serpentes and the class Aves. Chromosoma 15:606–617.

Bedard, J. 1969. Adaptive radiation in Alcidae. Ibis 111:189–198.

Beddard, F. E. 1884. A contribution to the anatomy of *Scopus umbretta*. Proc. Zool. Soc. London 1884:543–553.

Beddard, F. E. 1885. On the structural characters and classification of the cuckoos. Proc. Zool. Soc. London 1885:168–187.

Beddard, F. E. 1886a. On the syrinx and other points in the anatomy of the Caprimulgidae. Proc. Zool. Soc. London. 1886:147–153.

Beddard, F. E. 1886b. On some points in the anatomy of *Chauna chavaria*. Proc. Zool. Soc. London 1886:178–181.

Beddard, F. E. 1888a. On certain points in the visceral anatomy of *Balaeniceps rex*, bearing upon its affinities. Proc. Zool. Soc. London 1888:284–290.

Beddard, F. E. 1888b. On the classification of the Striges. Ibis 30:335–344.

Beddard, F. E. 1889a. Contributions to the anatomy of the hoatzin (*Opisthocomus cristatus*) with particular reference to the structure of the wing in the young. Ibis 31:283–293.

Beddard, F. E. 1889b. On certain points in the anatomy of the Accipitres, with reference to the affinities of *Polyboroides*. Proc. Zool. Soc. London 1889:77–82.

Beddard, F. E. 1889c. Contribution to the anatomy of picarian birds—Part 1. On some points in the structure of the hornbills. Proc. Zool. Soc. London 1889:587–594.

Beddard, F. E. 1889d. On the anatomy of Burmeister's cariama (*Chunga burmeisteri*). Proc. Zool. Soc. London 1889:594–602.

Beddard, F. E. 1890a. On the structure of *Psophia* and on its relations to other birds. Proc. Zool. Soc. London 1890:329–341.

Beddard, F. E. 1890b. On the anatomy of *Podica senegalensis*. Proc. Zool. Soc. London 1890:425–443.

Beddard, F. E. 1890c. On *Photodilus badius*, with remarks on its systematic position. Ibis 32:293–304.

Beddard, F. E. 1893a. General characters and anatomy of the Coraciidae. *In* A monograph of the Coraciidae by H. E. Dresser. Publ. by author, Farnborough, Kent.

Beddard, F. E. 1893b. On the osteology, pterylosis and muscular anatomy of the American fin-foot (*Heliornis surinamensis*). Ibis 35:30–40.

Beddard, F. E. 1896a. A contribution to the knowledge of the anatomy of *Rynchops*. Proc. Zool. Soc. London 1896:299–303.

Beddard, F. E. 1896b. Contributions to the anatomy of picarian birds—Part II. A note upon the pterylosis of the barbets and toucans. Proc. Zool. Soc. London 1896:555–557.

Beddard, F. E. 1896c. Contributions to the anatomy of picarian birds—Part III. On some points in the anatomy of the kingfishers. Proc. Zool. Soc. London 1896:603–606.

Beddard, F. E. 1898a. The structure and classification of birds. Longmans, Green and Co., London.

Beddard, F. E. 1898b. On the anatomy of an Australian cuckoo, *Scythrops novae-hollandiae*. Proc. Zool. Soc. London 1898:44–49.

Beddard, F. E. 1901a. On the anatomy of the radiated fruit-cuckoo (*Carpococcyx radiatus*). Ibis 43:200–214.

Beddard, F. E. 1901b. Notes on the anatomy of picarian birds. No. IV. On the skeletons of *Bucorvus cafer* and *B. abyssinicus*; with notes on other hornbills. Proc. Zool. Soc. London 1901:16–24.

Beddard, F. E. 1901c. Notes upon the anatomy and systematic position of *Rhynchaea*. Proc. Zool. Soc. London 1901(2):587–596.

Beddard, F. E. 1902a. Notes upon the osteology of *Aramus scolopaceus*. Ibis 44:33–54.

Beddard, F. E. 1902b. On the syrinx and other points in the structure of *Hierococcyx* and some allied genera of cuckoos. Ibis 44:599–608.

Beddard, F. E. 1911. On the alimentary tract of certain birds and on the mesenteric relations of the intestinal loops. Proc. Zool. Soc. London 1911:47–93.

Beddard, F. E., and P. C. Mitchell. 1894. On the anatomy of *Palamedea cornuta*. Proc. Zool. Soc. London 1894:536–557.

Beddard, F. E., and F. G. Parsons. 1893. On certain points in the anatomy of parrots bearing on their classification. Proc. Zool. Soc. London 1893:507–514.

Beebe, C. W. 1909. A contribution to the ecology of the adult hoatzin. Zoologica 1:45–66.

Beebe, C. W. 1914. Preliminary pheasant studies. Zoologica 1:261–285.

Beebe, C. W. 1918–1922. A monograph of the pheasants. 4 vols. H. F. and G. Witherby, London.

Beebe, T. P., Jr., T. E. Wilson, D. F. Ogletree, J. E. Katz, R. Balhorn, M. B. Salmeron, and W. J. Siekhaus. 1989. Direct observation of native DNA structures with the scanning tunneling microscope. Science 243:370–372.

Beecher, W. J. 1951. Convergence in the Coerebidae. Wilson Bull. 63:274–287.

Beecher, W. J. 1953a. Feeding adaptations and systematics in the avian order Piciformes. J. Wash. Acad. Sci. 43:293–299.

Beecher, W. J. 1953b. A phylogeny of the oscines. Auk 70:270–333.

Beecher, W. J. 1978. Feeding adaptations and evolution in the starlings. Bull. Chicago Acad. Sci. 11:269–298.

Beehler, B. M., and B. W. Finch. 1985. Species-checklist of the birds of New Guinea. Austr. Orn. Monogr. No. 1. Royal Austr. Orn. Union, Moonee Ponds, Victoria.

Beeman, R. W. 1987. A homoeotic gene cluster in the red flour beetle. Nature 327:247–249.

Belford, H. S., and W. F. Thompson. 1979. Single-copy DNA homologies and the phylogeny of *Atriplex*. Carnegie Inst. Wash. Yearbook 78:217–223.

Belford, H. S., W. F. Thompson, and D. B. Stein. 1982. DNA hybridization techniques for the study of plant evolution. Pp. 1–18 *in* Phytochemistry and Angiosperm Phylogeny. D. A. Young and D. S. Siegler, eds. Praeger Publ., New York.

Bellairs, A. d'A. 1964. Palate. Pp. 591–592 *in* A new dictionary of birds. A. L. Thomson, ed. Nelson, London.

Bellairs, A. d'A., and C. R. Jenkin. 1960. The skeleton of birds. Pp. 241–300 *in* Biology and comparative physiology of birds, Vol. 1. A. J. Marshall, ed. Academic Press, New York.

Bellchambers, T. P. 1916. Notes on the Mallee Fowl *Leipoa ocellata rosinae*. South Australian Ornithologist 2:134–140.

Bendich, A. J., and E. T. Bolton. 1967. Relatedness among plants as measured by the DNA agar technique. Plant Physiol. 42:959–967.

Bendich, A. J., and B. J. McCarthy. 1970a. Ribosomal RNA homologies among distantly related organisms. Proc. Natl. Acad. Sci. USA 65:349–356.

Bendich, A. J., and B. J. McCarthy. 1970b. DNA comparisons among barley, oats, rye, and wheat. Genetics 65:545–565.

Bennett, M. D. 1972. Nuclear DNA content and minimum mitotic time in herbaceous plants. Proc. Roy. Soc. London Ser. B. 181:109–135.

Bennett, M. D., and J. B. Smith. 1976. Nuclear DNA amounts in angiosperms. Phil. Trans. Roy. Soc. London B274:227–274.

Benson, C. W. 1985. Vanga. P. 619 *in* A dictionary of birds. B. Campbell and E. Lack, eds. T. and A. D. Poyser, Calton, England.

Benson, C. W., R. K. Brooke, R. J. Dowsett, and M. P. S. Irwin. 1971. The birds of Zambia. Collins, London.

Bentz, G. D. 1979. The appendicular myology and phylogenetic relationships of the Ploceidae and Estrildidae (Aves: Passeriformes). Bull. Carnegie Mus. Nat. Hist. 15:1–25.

Benveniste, R. E. 1985. The contributions of retroviruses to the study of mammalian evolution. Pp. 359–417 *in* Molecular evolutionary genetics. R. J. MacIntyre, ed. Plenum, New York.

Benveniste, R. E., and G. J. Todaro. 1974. Evolution of type C viral genes. I. Nucleic acid from baboon type C virus as a measure of divergence among primate species. Proc. Natl. Acad. Sci. USA 71:4513–4518.

Benveniste, R. E., and G. J. Todaro. 1975. Evolution of type C viral genes: preservation of ancestral murine type C viral sequences in pig cellular DNA. Proc. Natl. Acad. Sci. USA 72:4090–4094.

Benveniste, R. E., and G. J. Todaro. 1976. Evolution of type C viral genes: evidence for an Asian origin of man. Nature 261:101–108.

Benveniste, R. E., R. Callahan, C. J. Sherr, V. Chapman, and G. J. Todaro. 1977. Two distinct endogenous type C viruses isolated from the asian rodent *Mus cervicolor*: conservation of virogene sequences in related rodent species. J. Virology 21:849–862.

Berger, A. J. 1952. The comparative functional morphology of the pelvic appendage in three genera of Cuculidae. Amer. Midl. Nat. 47:513–605.

Berger, A. J. 1953a. The pterylosis of *Coua caerulea*. Wilson Bull. 65:12–17.

Berger, A. J. 1953b. On the locomotor anatomy of the Blue Coua, *Coua caerulea*. Auk 70:49–83.

Berger, A. J. 1954. The myology of the pectoral appendage of three genera of American cuckoos. Misc. Publ. Univ. Mich. Mus. Zool. No. 85:1–35.

Berger, A. J. 1955. On the anatomy and relationships of glossy cuckoos of the genera *Chrysococcyx*, *Lampromorpha*, and *Chalcites*. Proc. U.S. Natl. Mus. 103:585–597.

Berger, A. J. 1956. The appendicular myology of the Pygmy Falcon (*Polihierax semitorquatus*). Amer. Midl. Nat. 55:326–333.

Berger, A. J. 1959. Leg-muscle formulae and systematics. Wilson Bull. 71:93–94.

Berger, A. J. 1960. Some anatomical characters of the Cuculidae and the Musophagidae. Wilson Bull. 72:60–104.

Berlioz, J. 1950. Systematique. Pp. 845–1055 *in* Traité de Zoologie, vol. 15. Oiseaux. P. P. Grassé, ed. Masson et Cie., Paris.

Berman, S. L., and R. J. Raikow. 1982. The hindlimb musculature of the mousebirds (Coliiformes). Auk 99:41–57.

Bermingham, E., and J. C. Avise. 1986. Molecular zoogeography of freshwater fishes in the southeastern United States. Genetics 113:939–965.

Bermingham, E., T. Lamb, and J. C. Avise. 1986. Size polymorphism and heteroplasmy in the mitochondrial DNA of lower vertebrates. Jour. Heredity 77:249–252.

Bernardi, G. 1965. Chromatography of nucleic acids on hydroxyapatite. Nature 206:779–783.

Berndt, R., and W. Meise, editors. 1962. Naturgeschichte der Vögel. Vol. 2. Franckh'sche Verlags., Stuttgart. 679 pp.

Berry, S. J. 1985. Insect nucleic acids. Pp. 219–253 *in* Comprehensive insect physiology, biochemistry, and pharmacology, vol. 10. G. A. Kerkut and L. I. Gilbert, eds. Pergamon Press, New York.

Berthold, A. A. 1831. Beiträge zur Anatomie, Zootomie und Physiologie. Dieterich, Göttingen. 265 pp.

Bianchi, N. O., C. Redi, C. Garagna, E. Capanna, and M. G. Manfredi Romanini. 1983. Evolution of the genome size in *Akodon* (Rodentia, Cricetidae). J. Mol. Evol. 19:362–370.

Billberg, G. J. 1828. Aves. Synopsis faunae scandinaviae, vol. 1 (2). Holmiae. 208 pp.

Birstein, V. J. 1982. Structural characteristics of genome organization in amphibians: differential staining of chromosomes and DNA structure. J. Mol. Evol. 18:73–91.

Bishop, K. D., and C. B. Frith. 1979. A small collection of eggs of birds-of-paradise at Baiyer River Sanctuary, Papua New Guinea. Emu 79:140–141.

Blackburn, D. G. 1984. From whale toes to snake eyes: comments on the reversibility of evolution. Syst. Zool. 33:241–245.

Blake, E. R. 1979. Order Tinamiformes. Pp. 12–47 *in* Check-list of birds of the world. Vol. 1, second edition. E. Mayr and G. W. Cottrell, eds. Mus. Comp. Zool., Cambridge, Mass.

Blanford, W. T. 1870. Observations on the geology and zoology of Abyssinia, made during the progress of the British expedition to that country in 1867–68. Macmillan, London. 487 pp.

Blaszyk, P. 1935. Untersuchungen über die Stammesgeschichte der Vogelschuppen und Federn und über Abhangigkeit ihrer Ausbildung am Vogelfuss von der Funktion. Gegenbaur's Morph. Jahrb. 75:483–521, 522–567.

Bledsoe, A. H. 1987. DNA evolutionary rates in nine-primaried passerine birds. Mol. Biol. Evol. 4:559–571.

Bledsoe, A. H. 1988a. A phylogenetic analysis of postcranial skeletal characters of the ratite birds. Annals Carnegie Mus. 57:73–90.

Bledsoe, A. H. 1988b. Nuclear DNA evolution and phylogeny of the New World nine-primaried oscines. Auk 105:504–515.

Bledsoe, A. H., and F. H. Sheldon. 1989. The metric properties of DNA-DNA hybridization dissimilarity measures. Syst. Zool. 38:93–105.

Bloomfield, V. A., D. M. Crothers, and I. Tinoco, Jr. 1974. Physical chemistry of nucleic acids. Harper and Row, New York.

Blyth, E. 1840. Birds, Pp. 154–267 *in* Georges Cuvier's The animal kingdom, English transl. of 2nd ed., rev. William S. Orr, London.

Blyth, E. 1842. Notes on various Indian and Malayan birds, with descriptions of some presumed new species. J. Asiatic Soc. Bengal 11:160–195.

Blyth, E. 1849. Catalogue of the birds in the museum of the Asiatic Society. Baptist Mission Press, Calcutta.

Boas, J. E. V. 1933. Kreuzbein, Becken und Plexus Lumbosacralis der Vögel. Mem. Acad. Roy. Sci. Lett. Danemark Sec. Sci., 9th Ser., 5(1). 74 pp.

Bock, C. E. 1970. The ecology and behavior of the Lewis woodpecker (*Asyndesmus lewis*). Univ. Calif. Publ. Zool. 92. 91 pp.

Bock, W. J. 1956. A generic review of the family Ardeidae (Aves). Amer. Mus. Novit. 1779:1–49.

Bock, W. J. 1958. A generic review of the plovers (Charadriinae, Aves). Bull. Mus. Comp. Zool., 118(2). 97 pp.

Bock, W. J. 1960. The palatine process of the premaxilla in the Passeres. Bull. Mus. Comp. Zool. 122:361–488.

Bock, W. J. 1962. The pneumatic fossa of the humerus in the Passeres. Auk 79:425–443.

Bock, W. J. 1963a. The cranial evidence for ratite affinities. Pp. 39–54 *in* Proc. 13th Intl. Orn. Congress, Amer. Orn. Union.

Bock, W. J. 1963b. Relationships between the birds of paradise and the bower birds. Condor 65:91–125.

Bock, W. J. 1964. The systematic position of the Australian dotterel, *Peltohyas australis*. Emu 63:383–403.

Bock, W. J. 1972. Morphology of the tongue apparatus of *Ciridops anna* (Drepanididae). Ibis 114:61–78.

Bock, W. J. 1973. Philosophical foundations of classical evolutionary classification. Syst. Zool. 22:375–392.

Bock, W. J. 1982. Aves. Pp. 967–1015 *in* Synopsis and classification of living organisms. S. R. Parker, ed. McGraw-Hill, New York.

Bock, W. J. 1985. Relationships of the sugarbird (*Promerops*; Passeriformes, ?

Meliphagidae). Pp. 349–374 *in* Proc. Intl. Congr. African Vertebrates. K.-L. Schuchmann, ed. Mus. Koenig, Bonn.

Bock, W. J., and M. H. Clench. 1985. Morphology of the Noisy Scrub-bird, *Atrichornis clamosus* (Passeriformes: Atrichornithidae): systematic relationships and summary. Rec. Austral. Mus. 37:243–254.

Bock, W. J., and J. Farrand, Jr. 1980. The number of species and genera of Recent birds: a contribution to comparative systematics. Amer. Mus. Novit. 2703:1–29.

Bock, W. J., and A. McEvey. 1969a. Osteology of *Pedionomus torquatus* (Aves: Pedionomidae) and its allies. Proc. Roy. Soc. Victoria 82:187–232.

Bock, W. J., and A. McEvey. 1969b. The radius and relationship of owls. Wilson Bull. 81:55–68.

Bock, W. J., and W. DeW. Miller. 1959. The scansorial foot of the woodpeckers, with comments on the evolution of perching and climbing feet in birds. Amer. Mus. Novit. 1931.

Bock, W. J., and J. J. Morony, Jr. 1978. Relationships of the passerine finches (Passeriformes: Passeridae). Bonn. Zool. Beitr. 29:122–147.

Boetticher, H. von. 1931. Die verwandtschaftlich-systematische Stellung der Webervögel (Ploceidae) zu den Finkenvögeln (Fringillidae) und Staren (Sturnidae). Senckenbergiana 13:147–153.

Boetticher, H. von. 1934. Kurze phylogenetisch-systematische Uebersicht der regenpfeiferartigen Vögel (Charadriiformes) und ihrer nächsten naturlichen Verwandten nach dem heutigen Stand unserer Kenntnisse. Kocsag (Budapest) 7:1–25.

Boetticher, H. von. 1940 [1941]. Bemerkungen zur Systematik der Anatiden. Verh. Orn. Gesell. Bayern 22:160–165.

Boetticher, H. von. 1942. Über die Einteilung der Familie der Entenvögel (Anatidae) in Unterfamilien und Sektionen. Zool. Anz. 140:37–48.

Boetticher, H. von. 1943a. Die phylogenetisch-systematische Stellung von *Anseranas*. Zool. Anz. 142:55–58.

Boetticher, H. von. 1943b. Gedanken über die systematische Stellung einiger Papageien. Zool. Anz. 143:191–200.

Boetticher, H. von. 1954. Note sur la classification des vanneaux. L'Oiseau R.F.O. 24:175–179.

Boetticher, H. von. 1964. Papageien. A. Ziemsen, Wittenberg.

Boetticher, H. von, and W. Eichler. 1951. Parasitophyletische Studien zur Ornithosystematik. I. Die Acidoproctidae der Anseres. Zool. Garten 19:121–126.

Boetticher, H. von, and W. Eichler. 1954. Parasitophyletische Studien zur Ornithosystematik. II. Die Verteilung der Degeeriellidae und Falcolipeuridae bei den Accipitres. Biol. Zentralbl. 73:212–221.

Bogusz, D., C. A. Appleby, J. Landsmann, E. S. Dennis, M. J. Trinick, and W. J. Peacock. 1988. Functioning haemoglobin genes in non-nodulating plants. Nature 331:178–180.

Böhm, M. 1930. Über den Bau des jungendlichen Schädels von *Balaeniceps rex* nebst Bemerkungen über dessen systematische Stellung und über das Gaumenskelet der Vögel. Z. Morph. Okol. Tiere 17:677–718.

Böker, H. 1929. Flugvermögen und Kropf bei *Opisthocomus cristatus* und *Stringops habroptilus*. Morph. Jahrb. (Leipzig) 63:152–207.

Boles, W. E. 1979. The relationships of the Australo-Papuan flycatchers. Emu 79:107–110.

Bolton, E. T., and A. Bendich. 1965. Interactions of nucleic acids. Plant nucleic acids. Carnegie Inst. Wash. Yearbook 64:314–316.

Bolton, E. T., and B. J. McCarthy. 1962. A general method for the isolation of RNA complementary to DNA. Proc. Natl. Acad. Sci. USA 48:1390–1397.

Bonaparte, C. L. 1850. Conspectus generum avium. E. J. Brill.

Bonaparte, C. L. 1853. Classification ornithologique par séries. C. R. Acad. Sci. Paris 37:641–647.

Bond, J. 1971. Birds of the West Indies. Houghton-Mifflin, Boston.

Bonner, J., W. T. Garrard, J. Gottesfeld, D. S. Holmes, J. S. Sevall, and M. Wilkes. 1974. Functional organization of the mammalian genome. Cold Spring Harbor Symp. Quant. Biol. 38:303–310.

Bonner, T. I., D. J. Brenner, B. R. Neufeld, and R. J. Britten. 1973. Reduction in the rate of DNA reassociation by sequence divergence. J. Mol. Biol. 81:123–135.

Bonner, T. I., R. Heineman, and G. J. Todaro. 1980. Evolution of DNA sequences has been retarded in Malagasy primates. Nature 286:420–423.

Bonner, T. I., R. Heineman, and G. J. Todaro. 1981. A geographical factor involved in the evolution of the single-copy DNA sequences of primates. Pp. 293–300 in Evolution today, Proc. 2nd Intl. Congr. Syst. Evol. Biol. G. G. E. Scudder and J. L. Reveal, eds. Hunt Inst. Botanic. Document., Carnegie-Mellon Univ., Pittsburgh, Penn.

Borst, P., and D. R. Greaves. 1987. Programmed gene rearrangements altering gene expression. Science 235:658–667.

Botchan, M., and J. D. Watson. 1978. Chromatin. Cold Spring Harbor Symp. Quant. Biol., Vol. 42. Cold Spring Harbor, New York.

Bottjer, P. D. 1983. Systematic relationships among the Anatidae: an immunological study with a history of anatid classification and a system of classification. Ph.D. diss., Yale Univ., New Haven, Conn.

Bowen, W. W. 1927. Remarks on the classification of the Pteroclididae. Amer. Mus. Novit. 273. 12 pp.

Bozzoni, I., and E. Beccari. 1978. Clustered and interspersed repetitive DNA sequences in four amphibian species with different genome size. Biochim. Biophys. Acta 520:245–252.

Braun, M. J., and M. B. Robbins. 1986. Extensive protein similarity of the hybridizing chickadees Parus atricapillus and P. carolinensis. Auk 103:667–675.

Breathnach, R., and P. Chambon. 1981. Organization and expression of eukaryotic split genes coding for proteins. Ann. Rev. Biochem. 50:349–383.

Brenner, D. J., G. R. Fanning, K. E. Johnson, R. V. Citarella, and S. Falkow. 1969. Polynucleotide sequence relationships among members of Enterobacteriaceae. J. Bacteriol. 98:637–650.

Brenner, D. J., A. G. Steigerwalt, D. P. Falcao, D. P. Weaver, and G. R. Fanning. 1976. Characterization of Yersinia enterocolitica and Yersinia pseudotuberculosis by deoxyribonucleic acid hybridization and by biochemical reactions. Intl. J. Syst. Bacteriol. 26:180–194.

Brereton, J. le G. 1963. Evolution within the Psittaciformes. Pp. 499–517 in Proc. 13th Intl. Orn. Congr., Amer. Orn. Union.

Brereton, J. le G., and K. Immelmann. 1962. Head-scratching in the Psittaciformes. Ibis 104:169–175.

Brisson, M. J. 1760. Ornithologie ou methode contenant la division des oiseaux . . . Imprimeur du Roi, Paris. 6 vols.

British Ornithologists' Union. 1952. Check-list of the birds of Great Britain and Ireland. Brit. Orn. Union, London.

Britten, R. J. 1971. Sequence complexity, kinetic complexity, and genetic complexity. Carnegie Inst. Wash. Yearbook 69:503–506.

Britten, R. J. 1972. DNA sequence interspersion and a speculation about evolution. Pp. 80–94 *in* Evolution of genetic systems, H. H. Smith, ed. Gordon and Breach, New York.

Britten, R. J. 1986. Rates of DNA sequence evolution differ between taxonomic groups. Science 231:1393–1398.

Britten, R. J., and E. H. Davidson. 1969. Gene regulation for higher cells: a theory. Science 165:349–357.

Britten, R. J., and E. H. Davidson. 1971. Repetitive and non-repetitive DNA sequences and a speculation on the origins of evolutionary novelty. Quart. Rev. Biol. 46:111–138.

Britten, R. J., and E. H. Davidson. 1976. DNA sequence arrangement and preliminary evidence on its evolution. Federation Proc. 35:2151–2157.

Britten, R. J., and E. H. Davidson. 1985. Hybridisation strategy. Pp. 3–15 *in* Nucleic acid hybridisation. B. D. Hames and S. J. Higgins, eds. IRL Press, Oxford and Washington, D.C.

Britten, R. J., and D. E. Kohne. 1966. Nucleotide sequence repetition in DNA. Carnegie Inst. Wash. Yearbook 65:78–106.

Britten, R. J., and D. E. Kohne. 1967. Repeated nucleotide sequences. Carnegie Inst. Wash. Yearbook 66:73–88.

Britten, R. J., and D. E. Kohne. 1968. Repeated sequences in DNA. Science 161:529–540.

Britten, R. J., and R. B. Roberts. 1971. The probability of occurrence of accidental sequence homologies. Carnegie Inst. Wash. Yearbook 69:501–503.

Britten, R. J., and J. Smith. 1970. A bovine genome. Carnegie Inst. Wash. Yearbook 68:378–386.

Britten, R. J., and M. Waring. 1965. "Renaturation" of the DNA of higher organisms. Carnegie Inst. Wash. Yearbook 64:316–321.

Britten, R. J., D. E. Graham, and M. Henerey. 1972. Sea urchin repeated and single-copy DNA. Carnegie Inst. Wash. Yearbook 71:270–273.

Britten, R. J., D. E. Graham, and B. R. Neufeld. 1974. Analysis of repeating DNA sequences by reassociation. Pp. 363–418 *in* Methods in Enzymology, vol. 29, L. Grossman and K. Moldave, eds. Academic Press, London and New York.

Britten, R. J., A. Cetta, and E. H. Davidson. 1978. The single copy DNA sequence polymorphism of the sea urchin *Strongylocentrotus purpuratus*. Cell 15:1175–1186.

Britten, R. J., T. J. Hall, Z. Lev, G. P. Moore, A. S. Lee, T. L. Thomas, and E. H. Davidson. 1979. Examples of evolution and expression in the sea urchin genome. Pp. 219–227 *in* Eukaryotic gene regulation. Academic Press, New York.

Britten, R. J., W. F. Baron, D. B. Stout, and E. H. Davidson. 1988. Sources and evolution of human *Alu* repeated sequences. Proc. Natl. Acad. Sci. USA 85:4770–4774.

Britten, R. J., D. B. Stout, and E. H. Davidson. 1989. The current source of human *Alu* retroposons is a conserved gene shared with Old World monkey. Proc. Natl. Acad. Sci. USA 86:3718–3722.

Brock, G. T. 1937. The morphology of the Ostrich chondrocranium. Proc. Zool. Soc. London, 107B:225–243.

Brodkorb, P. 1960. The skeleton and systematic position of *Gampsonyx*. Auk 77:88–89.

Brodkorb, P. 1963a. Catalogue of fossil birds. Part 1 (Archaeopterygiformes through Ardeiformes). Bull. Florida State Mus., Biol. Sci. 7:179–293.

Brodkorb, P. 1963b. Birds from the Upper Cretaceous of Wyoming. Pp. 55–70 *in* Proc. 13th Intl. Orn. Congr., Amer. Orn. Union.

Brodkorb, P. 1964. Catalogue of fossil birds. Part 2 (Anseriformes through Galliformes). Bull. Florida State Mus., Biol. Sci. 8:195–335.

Brodkorb, P. 1971. Origin and evolution of birds. Pp. 19–55 *in* Avian biology. D. S. Farner and J. R. King, eds. Academic Press, New York.

Brodkorb, P. 1976. Discovery of a Cretaceous bird, apparently ancestral to the orders Coraciiformes and Piciformes (Aves: Carinatae). Smithson. Contrib. Paleobiol. 27:67–73.

Broekhuysen, G. J. 1959. The biology of the Cape Sugarbird *Promerops cafer* (L.). Ostrich (suppl.) 3:180–221.

Brooke, R. K. 1970. Taxonomic and evolutionary notes on the subfamilies, tribes, genera and subgenera of the swifts (Aves: Apodidae). Durban Mus. Novitates 9:13–24.

Brooke, R. K. 1984. Taxonomic subdivisions within the Heliornithidae. Ostrich 55:171–173.

Brooks, R. R., and P. C. Huang. 1972. Redundant DNA of *Neurospora crassa*. Biochem. Genet. 6:41–49.

Brown, D. D., and I. Dawid. 1968. Specific gene amplification in oocytes. Science 160:272–280.

Brown, D. D., and K. Sugimoto. 1973. 5S DNAs of *Xenopus laevis* and *Xenopus mulleri*: evolution of a gene family. J. Mol. Biol. 78:397–415.

Brown, L. 1980. The African Fish Eagle. Purnell, Cape Town, South Africa.

Brown, L., and D. Amadon. 1968. Eagles, hawks, and falcons of the world. McGraw-Hill, New York. 2 vols.

Brown, L. E., and H. I. Fisher. 1966. Electrophoretic study of blood proteins of some procellariiform birds. Auk 83:111–116.

Brown, P. C., R. N. Johnston, and R. T. Schimke. 1983. Approaches to the study of mechanisms of selective gene amplification in cultured mammalian cells. Pp. 197–212 *in* Gene structure and regulation in development. S. Subtelny and F. C. Kafatos, eds. Alan R. Liss, Inc., New York.

Brown, R. G. B., N. G. B. Jones, and D. J. T. Hussell. 1967. The breeding behaviour of Sabine's gull, *Xema sabini*. Behaviour 28:110–140.

Brown, W. M. 1983. Evolution of animal mitochondrial DNA. Pp. 62–88 *in* Evolution of genes and proteins. M. Nei and R. K. Koehn, eds. Sinauer Assoc., Sunderland, Mass.

Brown, W. M., E. M. Prager, and A. C. Wilson. 1982. Mitochondrial DNA sequences of primates: tempo and mode of evolution. J. Mol. Evol. 18:225–239.

Brownell, E. 1983. DNA/DNA hybridization studies of muroid rodents: symmetry and rates of molecular evolution. Evolution 37:1034–1051.

Brownlee, S. 1987. The lords of the flies. Discover 8(4):26–40.

Bruning, D. 1985. Buttonquail. Pp. 76–77 *in* A dictionary of birds. B. Campbell and E. Lack, eds. T. and A. D. Poyser, Ltd., Calton, England.

Bruns, G. P., S. Fischer, and B. A. Lowy. 1965. A study of the synthesis and interrelationships of ribonucleic acids in duck erythrocytes. Biochim. Biophys. Acta 95:280–290.

Brush, A. H. 1967. Pigmentation in the scarlet tanager, *Piranga olivacea*. Condor 69:549–559.

Brush, A. H. 1979. Comparison of egg-white proteins: effect of electrophoretic conditions. Biochem. Syst. Evol. 7:155–165.

Bryan, P. N., and O. H. J. Destree. 1983. Activation and function of chromatin. Pp. 43–70 *in* Genes: structure and expression. A. M. Kroon, ed. Horizons in Biochem. Biophys., vol. 7. John Wiley and Sons, New York.

Buchholz, H. 1986. Die Höhle eines Spechtvögels aus dem Eozän von Arizona, USA (Aves, Piciformes). Verh. Naturwiss. Ver. Hamburg N.F. 28:5–25.

Bump, G., and J. W. Bump. 1969. A study of the Spotted Tinamous and the Pale Spotted Tinamous of Argentina. Wildlife Rept. No. 120, U.S. Dept. Interior, Fish and Wildlife Service, Washington, D.C.

Bunemann, P. 1971. The recovery of trees from measures of dissimilarity. Pp. 387–396 *in* Mathematics in the archeological and historical sciences. F. R. Hodson, D. G. Kendall, and P. Tautu, eds. Edinburgh Univ. Press, Edinburgh.

Bürglin, T. R., M. Finney, A. Coulson, and G. Ruvkun. 1989. *Caenorhabditis elegans* has scores of homoeobox-containing genes. Nature 341:239–243.

Buri, R. O. 1900. Zur Anatomie des Flügels von *Micropus melba* und einigen anderen Coracornithes, zugleich Beitrag zur Kenntnis der systematischen Stellung der Cypselidae. Jenaische Z. Naturwiss. 33:361–610.

Burlingame, R. W., W. E. Love, B.-C. Wang, R. Hamlin, N.-H. Xuong, and E. N. Moudrianakis. 1985. Crystallographic structure of the octameric histone core of the nucleosome at a resolution of 3.3 A. Science 228:546–553.

Burr, H. E., and R. T. Schimke. 1980. Intragenomic DNA sequence homologies in the chicken and other members of the Class Aves: DNA re-association under reduced stringency conditions. J. Mol. Evol. 15:291–307.

Burt, W. H. 1929. Pterylography of certain North American woodpeckers. Univ. Calif. Publ. Zool. 30:427–442.

Burt, W. H. 1930. Adaptive modifications in the woodpeckers. Univ. Calif. Publ. Zool. 32:455–524.

Burton, P. J. K. 1971. Some observations on the splenius capitis muscle of birds. Ibis 113:19–28.

Burton, P. J. K. 1984. Anatomy and evolution of the feeding apparatus in the avian orders Coraciiformes and Piciformes. Bull. Brit. Mus. (Nat. Hist.), Zool. Ser. 47:331–443.

Bush, G. L. 1975. Modes of animal speciation. Ann. Rev. Ecol. Syst. 6:339–364.

Bush, G. L., S. M. Case, A. C. Wilson, and J. L. Patton. 1977. Rapid speciation and chromosomal evolution in mammals. Proc. Natl. Acad. Sci. USA 74:3942–3946.

Cabanis, J. 1847. Ornithologische Notizen. Archiv Naturgesch. 13:186–256, 308–352.

Cabanis, J. 1850. Museum Heineanum. Part I. Gut St. Burchard, Halberstadt.

Cabanis, J., and F. Heine. 1850–63. Museum Heineanum, Halberstadt.

Caccone, A., G. D. Amato, and J. R. Powell. 1987. Intraspecific DNA divergence in *Drosophila*: A study on parthenogenetic *D. mercatorum*. Mol. Biol. Evol. 4:343–350.

Caccone, A., and J. R. Powell. 1987. Molecular evolutionary divergence among North American cave crickets. II. DNA-DNA hybridization. Evolution 41:1215–1238.

Caccone, A., and J. R. Powell. 1989. DNA divergence among hominoids. Evolution 43:925–942.

Caccone, A., R. DeSalle, and J. R. Powell. 1988. Calibration of the change in thermal stability of DNA duplexes and degree of base-pair mismatch. J. Mol. Evol. 27:212–216.

Cade, T. J. 1982. The falcons of the world. Collins, London.

Cade, T. J., and L. I. Greenwald. 1966. Drinking behavior of mousebirds in the Namib Desert, southern Africa. Auk 83:126–128.

Cade, T. J., and G. L. Maclean. 1967. Transport of water by adult sandgrouse to their young. Condor 69:323–343.

Cade, T. J., J. Willoughby, and G. L. Maclean. 1966. Drinking behavior of sandgrouse in Namib and Kalahari deserts, Africa. Auk 83:124–126.

Cain, A. J. 1954. Subdivisions of genus *Ptilinopus* (Aves, Columbae). Bull. Brit. Mus. (Natur. Hist.), Zool. 2:267–284.

Cain, A. J. 1959. Taxonomic concepts. Ibis 101:302–318.

Cairns, J., G. S. Stent, and J. D. Watson. 1966. Phage and the origins of molecular biology. Cold Spring Harbor Lab. Quant. Biol. Cold Spring Harbor, New York.

Campbell, A. 1983. Transposons and their evolutionary significance. Pp. 258–279 in Evolution of genes and proteins. M. Nei and R. K. Koehn, eds. Sinauer Assoc., Sunderland, Mass.

Cande, S. C., and J. C. Mutter. 1982. A revised identification of the oldest sea-floor spreading anomalies between Australia and Antarctica. Earth and Planetary Sci. Letters 58:151–160.

Canfield, R. E. 1963a. Peptides derived from tryptic digestion of egg white lysozyme. J. Biol. Chem. 238:2691–2697.

Canfield, R. E. 1963b. The amino acid sequence of egg white lysozyme. J. Biol. Chem. 238:2698–2707.

Canfield, R. E., and C. B. Anfinsen. 1963. Chromatography of pepsin and chymotrypsin digests of egg white lysozyme on phosphocellulose. J. Biol. Chem. 238:2684–2690.

Carus, J. V. 1868–75. II. Classe. Aves, Vögel. Pp. 191–367 in his Handbuch der Zoologie, vol. 1. W. Engelmann, Leipzig.

Catterall, J. F., J. P. Stein, P. Kristo, A. R. Means, and B. W. O'Malley. 1980. Primary sequence of ovomucoid messenger RNA as determined from cloned complementary DNA. J. Cell Biol. 87:480–487.

Catzeflis, F. M., F. H. Sheldon, J. E. Ahlquist, and C. G. Sibley. 1987. DNA-DNA hybridization evidence of the rapid rate of muroid rodent DNA evolution. Mol. Biol. Evol. 4:242–253.

Catzeflis, F. M., E. Nevo, J. E. Ahlquist, and C. G. Sibley. 1989. Relationships of the chromosomal species in the Eurasian mole rats of the *Spalax ehrenbergi* group as determined by DNA-DNA hybridization, and an estimate of the spalacid-murid divergence time. J. Mol. Biol. 29:223–232

Cavalier-Smith, T. 1982. Skeletal DNA and the evolution of genome size. Ann. Rev. Biophys. Bioeng. 11:273–302.

Cavalier-Smith, T., editor. 1985. The evolution of genome size. Wiley-Interscience, New York.

Cavalier-Smith, T. 1987. Eukaryotes with no mitochondria. Nature 326:332–333.

Cavalli-Sforza, L. L., and A. W. F. Edwards. 1967. Phylogenetic analysis: models and estimation procedures. Evolution 32:550–570.

Cech, T. R. 1986. RNA as an enzyme. Sci. Amer. 255:64–75.

Cech, T. R. 1987. The chemistry of self-splicing RNA and RNA enzymes. Science 236:1532–1539.

Cech, T. R., and J. E. Hearst. 1975. An electron microscopic study of mouse foldback DNA. Cell 5:429–446.

Cech, T. R., and J. E. Hearst. 1976. Organization of highly repeated sequences in mouse main-band DNA. J. Mol. Biol. 100:227–256.

Cech, T. R., A. Rosenfeld, and J. E. Hearst. 1973. Characterization of the most rapidly renaturing sequences in mouse main-band DNA. J. Mol. Biol. 81:299–325.

Chamberlin, M. E., R. J. Britten, and E. H. Davidson. 1975. Sequence organization in *Xenopus* DNA studied by the electron microscope. J. Mol. Biol. 96:317–333.

Chambon, P. 1978. Summary: The molecular biology of the eukaryotic genome is coming of age. Pp. 1209–1234 in Chromatin. M. Botchan and J. D. Watson, eds. Cold Spring Harbor Symp. Quant. Biol., Vol. 42. Cold Spring Harbor, New York.

Chambon, P., F. Perrin, K. O'Hare, J. L. Mandel, J. P. LePennec, M. LeMeur, A. Krust, R.

Heilig, P. Gerlinger, F. Gannon, M. Cochet, R. Breathnach, and C. Benoist. 1979. Structure and expression of ovalbumin and closely related chicken genes. Pp. 259–279 *in* Eucaryotic gene regulation. Academic Press, New York.

Chan, S. K., and E. Margoliash. 1966. Amino acid sequence of chicken heart cytochrome *c*. J. Biol. Chem. 241:507–515.

Chan, H.-C., W. T. Ruyechan, and J. G. Wetmur. 1976. In vitro iodination of low complexity nucleic acids without chain scission. Biochemistry 15(25):5487–5490.

Chan, S. K., S. B. Needleman, J. W. Stewart, O. F. Walasek, and E. Margoliash. 1963. Amino acid sequences of various cytochromes *c*. Federation Proc. 22:658.

Chandler, A. C. 1916. A study of the structure of feathers, with reference to their taxonomic significance. Univ. Calif. Publ. Zool. 13:243–446.

Chang, C. P., and T. J. Mabry. 1973. The constitution of the Order Centrospermae: rRNA-DNA hybridization studies among βlain-and anthocyanin-producing families. Biochem. Syst. 1:185–190.

Chang, C.-T., T. C. Hain, J. R. Hutton, and J. G. Wetmur. 1974. Effects of microscopic and macroscopic viscosity on the rate of renaturation of DNA. Biopolymers 13:1847–1858.

Chapin, J. P. 1917. The classification of the weaver-birds. Bull. Amer. Mus. Nat. Hist. 37:243–280.

Chapin, J. P. 1929. Nomenclature and systematic position of the paradise whydahs. Auk 46:474–484.

Chapin, J. P. 1954. The birds of the Belgian Congo. Part IV. Bull. Amer. Mus. Nat. Hist. 75B. 846 pp.

Chapman, F. M. 1938. Life in an air castle: nature studies in the tropics. Appleton-Century, New York. 250 pp.

Chapman, R. W., J. C. Stephens, R. A. Lansman, and J. C. Avise. 1982. Models of mitochondrial DNA transmission genetics and evolution in higher eukaryotes. Genet. Res. Cambridge 40:41–57.

Chargaff, E. 1950. Chemical specificity of nucleic acids and mechanism of their enzymatic degradation. Experientia 6:201–209.

Cheke, A. S. 1985. Dodo. P. 152 *in* A dictionary of birds. B. Campbell and E. Lack, eds. T. and A. D. Poyser, Calton, England.

Chooi, W. Y. 1971. Variation in nuclear DNA content in the genus *Vicia*. Genetics 68:195–211.

Chubb, C. 1916. Order Opisthocomiformes. Pp. 51–64 *in* The birds of British Guiana, based on the collection of Frederick Vavasour McConnell, vol. 1. B. Quaritch, London.

Clancey, P. A. 1957. The systematic position of *Parisoma plumbeum*. Ibis 99:512–513.

Clancey, P. A. 1964. The birds of Natal and Zululand. Oliver and Boyd, Edinburgh and London.

Clark, G. A., Jr. 1960. Notes on the embryology and evolution of the megapodes (Aves: Galliformes). Postilla 45. 7 pp.

Clark, G. A., Jr. 1964a. Ontogeny and evolution in the megapodes (Aves: Galliformes). Postilla 78. 37 pp.

Clark, G. A., Jr. 1964b. Life histories and the evolution of megapodes. Living Bird 3:149–167.

Clark, H. L. 1894(1895). The pterylography of certain American goatsuckers and owls. Proc. U.S. Natl. Mus. 17:551–572.

Clark, H. L. 1898(1899). The feather-tracts of North American grouse and quail. Proc. U.S. Natl. Mus. 21:641–653.

Clark, H. L. 1901a. The pterylosis of *Podargus*: with notes on the pterylography of the Caprimulgi. Auk 18:167–171.

Clark, H. L. 1901b. The classification of birds. Auk 18:370–381.

Clark, H. L. 1902a. Are hummingbirds cypseloid or caprimulgoid? Science 15:108–109.

Clark, H. L. 1902b. Communication. Condor 4:75–76.

Clark, H. L. 1906. The feather tracts of swifts and hummingbirds. Auk 23:68–91.

Clark, H. L. 1913. Notes on the Panama thrush-warbler. Auk 30:11–15.

Clark, H. L. 1918. Notes on the anatomy of the Cuban Trogon. Auk 35:286–289.

Clay, T. 1947. The systematic position of the Musophagi as indicated by their mallophagan parasistes. Ibis 89:654–656.

Clay, T. 1950. A preliminary survey of the distribution of Mallophaga (feather lice) on the Class Aves (birds). J. Bombay Nat. Hist. Soc. 49:430–443.

Clay, T. 1951. The Mallophaga and relationships within the Falconiformes. Ibis 93(4):628.

Clay, T. 1953. Revisions of the genera of Mallophaga. I. The *Rallicola*-complex. Proc. Zool. Soc. London 123:563–587.

Clay, T. 1957. The Mallophaga of birds. Pp. 120–158 *in* Premier Symp. sur la spécificité parasitaire des parasites de Vertébrés. Int. Union Biol. Sci.(B) 32. Univ. Neuchâtel.

Clay, T. 1958. Revisions of Mallophaga genera. *Degeeriella* from the Falconiformes. Bull. Brit. Mus. (Nat. Hist.), Entomol. 7:121–207.

Clegg, M. T. 1987. Plant molecular evolution. Amer. Nat. 130 (supplement) S1-S100 (Preface plus 5 chapters).

Clench, M. H., J. L. Gulledge, and K. C. Parkes. 1982. The Black-capped Donacobius is a wren, not a mimid. Abstracts, 100th meeting Amer. Orn. Union.

Cockrum, E. L. 1952. A check-list and bibliography of hybrid birds in North America north of Mexico. Wilson Bull. 64:140–159.

Cody, M. L. 1971. Ecological aspects of reproduction. Pp. 461–512 *in* Avian biology, vol. 1. D. S. Farner and J. R. King, eds. Academic Press, New York.

Cohn, J. M. W. 1968. The convergent flight mechanism of swifts (Apodi) and hummingbirds (Trochili) (Aves). Ph.D. diss. Univ. of Michigan, Ann Arbor, Michigan.

Colbert, E. H. 1981. The distribution of tetrapods and the breakup of Gondwana. Pp. 277–282 *in* Gondwana five. Proc. 5th Intl. Gondwana Symp. M. M. Cresswell and P. Vella, eds. A. A. Balkema, Rotterdam.

Colless, D. H. 1967. The phylogenetic fallacy. Syst. Zool. 16:289–295.

Collias, N. E., and E. C. Collias. 1964. Evolution of nestbuilding in the weaverbirds (Ploceidae). Univ. Calif. Publ. Zool. 73:1–162.

Commorford, S. L. 1971. Iodination of nucleic acids in vitro. Biochemistry 10:1993–2000.

Compton, L. V. 1932. A probable hybrid between the California Quail and the Texas Bobwhite. Condor 34:48.

Compton, L. V. 1938. The pterylosis of the Falconiformes with special attention to the taxonomic position of the osprey. Univ. Calif. Publ. Zool. 42:173–211.

Condon, H. T. 1969. A handlist of the birds of South Australia. 3rd ed., revised. South Australian Ornith. Assoc.

Corbin, K. W. 1967. Evolutionary relationships in the avian genus *Columba* as indicated by ovalbumin tryptic peptides. Evolution 21:355–368.

Corbin, K. W. 1968. Taxonomic relationships of some *Columba* species. Condor 70:1–13.

Cornay, J.-E. 1847. Considérations générales sur la classification des oiseaux, fondée sur la considération de l'os palatin antérieur. Revue Zool. Soc. Cuvierienne (Paris) 10:360–369.

Cottam, P. A. 1957. The Pelecaniform characters of the skeleton of the Shoebill Stork, *Balaeniceps rex*. Bull. Brit. Mus. (Nat. Hist.) Zool. 5:49–72.

Cotter, W. B., Jr. 1957. A serological analysis of some anatid classifications. Wilson Bull. 69:291–300.

Cottrell, G. W. 1968. The genera of puffbirds. (Bucconidae). Breviora 285. 5 pp.

Coues, E. 1864. A critical review of the family Procellaridae: Part I., embracing the Procellarieae, or stormy petrels. Part II., embracing the Puffinae. Proc. Acad. Nat. Sci. Philadelphia 16:72–91, 116–144.

Coues, E. 1866a. A critical review of the family Procellariidae: Part III; embracing the Fulmareae. Part IV; embracing the Aestrelateae and the Prioneae. Part V; embracing the Diomedeinae and the Halodrominae. With a general supplement. Proc. Acad. Nat. Sci. Philadelphia 18:25–33, 134–172, 172–197.

Coues, E. 1866b. The osteology of the *Colymbus torquatus*; with notes on its myology. Mem. Boston Soc. Natur. Hist. 1(2):131–172.

Coues, E. 1868. A monograph of the Alcidae. Proc. Acad. Nat. Sci. Philadelphia 20:3–81.

Coues, E. 1872. Key to North American birds. 1st edition. Estes and Lauriat, Boston.

Coues, E. 1874. Birds of the Northwest: A handbook of the ornithology of the region drained by the Missouri River and its tributaries. Misc. Publ. No. 3, Dept. Interior, U.S. Geol. Surv. Territories. Govt. Printing Office, Washington, D.C.

Coues, E. 1879 (1880). Third instalment of American ornithological bibliography. Bull. U.S. Geol. Geogr. Surv. Terr. 5:521–1072.

Coues, E. 1884. Key to North American birds. 2nd edition. Estes and Lauriat, Boston.

Coues, E. 1896. Key to North American birds. 4th edition. Estes and Lauriat, Boston.

Coues, E. 1897. Remarks on certain Procellariidae. Auk 14:314–315.

Coues, E. 1900. *Strix* vs. *Aluco*. Auk 17:65–66.

Coues, E. 1903. Key to North American birds. 5th ed. Dana Estes and Co., Boston.

Cowie, D. B. 1964. Lysogeny and DNA homology. Carnegie Inst. Wash. Yearbook 63:380–387.

Cowie, D. B., and R. J. Avery. 1971. Bacteriophage DNAs. Carnegie Inst. Wash. Yearbook 67:528–536.

Cowie, D. B., and A. D. Hershey. 1965. Multiple sites of interaction with host-cell DNA in the DNA of phage λ. Proc. Natl. Acad. Sci. USA 53:57–62.

Cowie, D. B., and B. J. McCarthy. 1963. Homology between bacteriophage λ DNA and *E. coli* DNA. Proc. Natl. Acad. Sci. USA 50:537–543.

Cracraft, J. 1967. On the systematic position of the boat-billed heron. Auk 84:529–533.

Cracraft, J. 1971. The relationships and evolution of the rollers: families Coraciidae, Brachypteraciidae, and Leptosomatidae. Auk 88:723–752.

Cracraft, J. 1972. The relationships of the higher taxa of birds: problems in phylogenetic reasoning. Condor 74:379–392.

Cracraft, J. 1973. Systematics and evolution of the Gruiformes (Class Aves). 3. Phylogeny of the suborder Grues. Bull. Amer. Mus. Nat. Hist. 151:1–128.

Cracraft, J. 1974. Phylogeny and evolution of the ratite birds. Ibis 116:494–521.

Cracraft, J. 1976. The species of moas (Aves: Dinornithidae). Pp. 189–205 *in* Collected papers in avian paleontology honoring the 90th birthday of Alexander Wetmore. S. L. Olson, ed. Smithson. Contrib. Paleobiol. 27. 211 pp.

Cracraft, J. 1980. Phylogenetic theory and methodology in avian paleontology: a critical appraisal. Contrib. Sci. Nat. Hist. Mus. Los Angeles County 330:9–16.

Cracraft, J. 1981. Toward a phylogenetic classification of the recent birds of the world (Class Aves). Auk 98:681–714.

Cracraft, J. 1982. Phylogenetic relationships and monophyly of loons, grebes, and hesperornithiform birds, with comments on the early history of birds. Syst. Zool. 31:35–56.

Cracraft, J. 1985. Monophyly and phylogenetic relationships of the Pelecaniformes: a numerical cladistic analysis. Auk 102:834–853.

Cracraft, J. 1986. The origin and early diversification of birds. Paleobiology 12:383–399.

Crain, W. R., F. C. Eden, W. R. Pearson, E. H. Davidson, and R. J. Britten. 1976a. Absence of short period interspersion of repetitive and non-repetitive sequences in the DNA of *Drosophila melanogaster*. Chromosoma 56:309–326.

Crain, W. R., E. H. Davidson, and R. J. Britten. 1976b. Contrasting patterns of DNA sequence arrangement in *Apis mellifera* (honeybee) and *Musca domestica* (housefly). Chromosoma 59:1–12.

Cramp, S. (ed.) 1985. The birds of the western palearctic. Vol. 4. Oxford Univ. Press.

Cramp, S., and K. E. L. Simmons (eds.). 1977. Handbook of the birds of Europe, the Middle East, and North Africa. Vol. 1. Oxford Univ. Press.

Cramp, S., and K. E. L. Simmons (eds.). 1980. Handbook of the birds of Europe, the Middle East, and North Africa. Vol. 2. Oxford Univ. Press.

Cramp, S., and K. E. L. Simmons (eds.). 1982. Handbook of the birds of Europe, the Middle East, and North Africa. Vol. 3. Oxford Univ. Press.

Craw, R. C. 1985. Classic problems of southern hemisphere biogeography re-examined. Zeitschr. Zool. Syst. Evol.-forsch. 23:1–10.

Crick, F. 1979. Split genes and RNA splicing. Science 204:264–271.

Crome, F. H. J. 1976. Some observations on the biology of the cassowary in northern Queensland. Emu 76:8–14.

Crompton, A. W. 1953. The development of the chondrocranium of *Spheniscus demersus* with special reference to the columella auris of birds. Acta Zool. 34:71–146.

Crook, J. H. 1958. Etudes sur le comportement social de *Bubalornis a. albirostris* (Vieillot). Alauda 26:161–195.

Crothers, D. M., and M. Fried. 1982. Transmission of long-range effects in DNA. Cold Spring Harbor Symp. Quant. Biol. 47:263–269.

Crothers, D. M., N. R. Kallenbach, and B. H. Zimm. 1965. The melting transition of low-molecular weight DNA: theory and experiment. J. Mol. Biol. 11:802–820.

Crowe, T. M. 1978. The evolution of guinea-fowl (Galliformes, Phasianidae, Numidinae) taxonomy, phylogeny, speciation and biogeography. Ann. South African Mus. 76(2):43–136.

Crowe, T. M., and A. A. Crowe. 1985. The genus *Francolinus* as a model for avian evolution and biogeography in Africa: I. Relationships among species. Pp. 207–240 *in* Proc. Intl. Symp. African Vertebrates. K.-L. Schuchmann, ed. Mus. Koenig, Bonn.

Croxall, J. P., and A. J. Gaston. 1988. Patterns of reproduction in high-latitude northern- and southern-hemisphere seabirds. Pp. 1176–1194 *in* Proc. 19th Intl. Orn. Congr. H. Ouellet ed. Univ. of Ottawa Press, Ottawa.

Cumley, R. W., and L. J. Cole. 1942. Differentiation of Old and New World species of the genus *Columba*. Amer. Nat. 76:570–581.

Cumley, R. W., and M. R. Irwin. 1944. The correlation between antigenic composition and geographic range in the Old or New World of some species of *Columba*. Amer. Nat. 78:238–256.

Cunningham, O. 1870. Notes on some points in the anatomy of three kingfishers (*Ceryle stellata*, *Dacelo gigas*, and *Alcedo ispida*). Proc. Zool. Soc. London 1870:280–283.

Curry-Lindahl, K. 1968. Hagrärs (Ardeidae) taxonomi belyst av etologiska studier. En preliminär redogörelse. Var Fagelvärld 27:289–308.

Curry-Lindahl, K. 1971. Systematic relationships in herons (Ardeidae), based on comparative studies of behaviour and ecology. Ostrich, Suppl. 9:53–70.

Curtis, S. E., and M. T. Clegg. 1984. Molecular evolution of chloroplast DNA sequences. Mol. Biol. Evol. 1:291–301.

Cuvier, G. 1817. Les oiseaux. Pp. 290–540 *in his* Le règne animal . . . , vol. 1. Deterville, Paris.

Dandanell, G., P. Valentin-Hanson, J. E. L. Larsen, and K. Hammer. 1987. Long-range cooperativity between gene regulatory sequences in a prokaryote. Nature 325:823–826.

Daniels, G. R., and P. L. Deininger. 1983. A second major class of Alu family repeated DNA sequences in a primate genome. Nucleic Acids Res. 11:7595–7610.

Darnell, J. E., Jr. 1982. Variety in the level of gene control in eukaryotic cells. Nature 297:365–371.

Darnell, J. E., Jr. 1983. The processing of RNA. Sci. Amer. 249:90–100.

Darnell, J. E., Jr. 1985. RNA. Sci. Amer. 253:68–78.

Darwin, C. 1857. Letter to T. H. Huxley, Sept. 26, 1857. P. 104 *in* More letters of Charles Darwin, vol. 1. F. Darwin, ed. Appleton, New York.

Darwin, C. 1859. On the origin of species by means of natural selection. John Murray, London. 502 pp.

Davidson, E. H. 1982. Evolutionary change in genomic regulatory organization: speculations on the origins of novel biological structure. Pp. 65–84 *in* Evolution and Development. J. T. Bonner, ed. Springer-Verlag, Berlin.

Davidson, E. H., and R. J. Britten. 1973. Organization, transcription, and regulation in the animal genome. Quart. Rev. Biol. 48:565–613.

Davidson, E. H., and R. J. Britten. 1979. Regulation of gene expression: possible role of repetitive sequences. Science 204:1052–1059.

Davidson, E. H., and J. W. Posakony. 1982. Repetitive sequence transcripts in development. Nature 297:633–635.

Davidson, E. H., B. R. Hough, M. Chamberlin, and R. J. Britten. 1971. Sequence repetition in the DNA of *Nassaria (Ilyanassa) obsoleta*. Devel. Biol. 25:445–463.

Davidson, E. H., B. R. Hough, C. S. Amenson, and R. J. Britten. 1973. General interspersion of repetitive with non-repetitive sequence elements in the DNA of *Xenopus*. J. Mol. Biol. 77:1–23.

Davidson, E. H., D. E. Graham, B. R. Neufeld, M. E. Chamberlin, C. S. Amenson, B. R. Hough, and R. J. Britten. 1974. Arrangement and characterization of repetitive sequence elements in animal DNAs. Cold Spring Harbor Symp. Quant. Biol. 38:295–301.

Davidson, E. H., G. A. Galau, R. C. Angerer, and R. J. Britten. 1975a. Comparative aspects of DNA organization in metazoa. Chromosoma 51:253–259.

Davidson, E. H., B. R. Hough, W. H. Klein, and R. J. Britten. 1975b. Structural genes adjacent to interspersed repetitive DNA sequences. Cell 4:217–238.

Davidson, E. H., W. H. Klein, and R. J. Britten. 1977. Sequence organization in animal DNA and a speculation on hnRNA as a coordinate regulatory transcript. Devel. Biol. 55:69–84.

Davies, S. J. J. F. 1961. The orientation of pecking in very young magpie geese *Anseranas semipalmata*. Ibis 103a:277–283.

Davies, S. J. J. F. 1962a. The response of the magpie goose to aerial predators. Emu 62:51–55.

Davies, S. J. J. F. 1962b. The nest-building behaviour of the magpie goose *Anseranas semipalmata*. Ibis 104:147–157.

Davies, S. J. J. F. 1963. Aspects of the behaviour of the magpie goose *Anseranas semipalmata*. Ibis 105:76–98.

Davies, S. J. J. F. 1976. The natural history of the Emu in comparison with that of other ratites. Pp. 109–120 *in* Proc. 16th Intl. Orn. Congr. H. J. Frith and J. H. Calaby, eds. Australian Acad. Sci., Canberra.

Davies, S. J. J. F., and H. J. Frith. 1964. Some comments on the taxonomic position of the magpie goose *Anseranas semipalmata* (Latham). Emu 63:265–272.

Davis, B. D. 1980. Frontiers of the biological sciences. Science 209:78–89.

Davis, D. E. 1940a. Social nesting habits of the smooth-billed ani. Auk 57:179–218.

Davis, D. E. 1940b. Social nesting habits of *Guira guira*. Auk 57:472–484.

Davis, J., and A. H. Miller. 1960. Family Mimidae. Pp. 440–458 *in* Check-list of birds of the world, vol. 9. E. Mayr and J. C. Greenway, Jr., eds. Mus. Comp. Zool., Cambridge, Mass.

Davis, M. B. 1973. Labeling of DNA with ^{125}I. Carnegie Inst. Wash. Yearbook 72:217–221.

Dawson, W. L. 1920. An oological revision of the Alciformes. J. Mus. Comp. Oology (Santa Barbara, Calif.) 1:7–14.

DeBeer, G. R. 1937. The development of the vertebrate skull. Oxford Univ. Press, London. 552 pp.

DeBeer, G. R. 1954. "*Archeopteryx lithographica*." Brit. Mus., London.

DeBeer, G. R. 1956. The evolution of ratites. Bull. Brit. Mus. (Nat. Hist.) Zool. 4:57–76.

DeBeer, G. R. 1964. Phylogeny of the ratites. Pp. 681–685 *in* A new dictionary of birds. A. L. Thomson, ed. Nelson, London.

de Boer, L. E. M. 1980. Do the chromosomes of the kiwi provide evidence for a monophyletic origin of the ratites? Nature 287:84–85.

de Boer, L. E. M., and J. M. van Brink. 1982. Cytotaxonomy of the Ciconiiformes (Aves), with karyotypes of eight species new to cytology. Cytogenet. Cell Genet. 34:19–34.

Degen, E. 1894. On some of the main features in the evolution of the bird's wing. (With notes by W. P. Pycraft.) Bull. Brit. Orn. Club 2:vii–xxxiii.

Degens, P. O. 1983a. Hierarchical cluster methods as maximum likelihood estimators. Pp. 249–253 *in* Numerical taxonomy, J. Felsenstein, ed. Springer-Verlag, Berlin.

Degens, P. O. 1983b. Hierarchische Clusteranalyse. Approximation und Agglomeration. Pp. 189–202 *in* Automatisierung in der Klassifikation. I. Dahlberg and M. R. Shrader, eds. Indeks Verlag, Frankfurt.

Degens, P. O. 1985. Ultrametric approximation to distances. Computational Statistics Quarterly 2:93–101.

Degens, P. O., and B. Lausen. 1986. Statistical analysis of the reconstruction of phylogenies with DNA-DNA hybridization data. Res. Rept. No. 86/6. Dept. of Statistics, Univ. of Dortmund.

Degens, P. O., W. Vach, B. Lausen, U. Halekoh, and A. Terhaar. 1986. Die Average-Linkage-Methode bei gewichten Datensatzen mit fehlenden Messungen. Tech. Rept. No. 86/2. Dept. of Statistics, Univ. of Dortmund.

Deignan, H. G. 1964. Check-list of birds of the world. Vol. 10. E. Mayr and R. A. Paynter, Jr., eds. Mus. Comp. Zool., Cambridge, Mass.

Deininger, P. L., and C. W. Schmid. 1976. Thermal stability of human DNA and chimpanzee DNA heteroduplexes. Science 194:846–848.

Deininger, P. L., and C. W. Schmid. 1979. A study of the evolution of repeated DNA sequences in primates and the existence of a new class of repeated sequences in primates. J. Mol. Biol. 127:437–460.

Delacour, J. 1936. Note sur la classification des Anatidés. L'Oiseau R.F.O. 6:366–379.

Delacour, J. 1938. La systématique des Anatidés et leurs moeurs. Proc. 8th Intl. Orn. Congr. 225–242.

Delacour, J. 1943a. A revision of the genera and species of the family Pycnonotidae (bulbuls). Zoologica 28:17–28.

Delacour, J. 1943b. A revision of the subfamily Estrildinae of the family Ploceidae. Zoologica 28:69–86.

Delacour, J. 1944. A revision of the family Nectariniidae (sunbirds). Zoologica 29:17–38.

Delacour, J. 1946. Les timaliinés. L'Oiseau R.F.O. 16:7–36.

Delacour, J. 1950. Les timaliinés. Additions et modifications. L'Oiseau R.F.O. 20:186–191.

Delacour, J. 1951a. The pheasants of the world. Country Life Ltd., London. 347 pp.

Delacour, J. 1951b. The significance of the number of toes in some woodpeckers and kingfishers. Auk 68:49–51.

Delacour, J. 1954. Waterfowl of the world, vol. 1. Country Life Ltd., London. 284 pp.

Delacour, J., and D. Amadon. 1949. The relationships of *Hypocolius*. Ibis 91:427–429.

Delacour, J., and D. Amadon. 1951. The systematic position of *Picathartes*. Ibis 93:60–62.

Delacour, J., and M. F. Edmond-Blanc. 1933–34. Monographie des veuves (Revision des genres *Euplectes* et *Vidua*). L'Oiseau R.F.O. (N.S.) 4:52–110.

Delacour, J., and E. Mayr. 1945. The family Anatidae. Wilson Bull. 57:3–55.

Delacour, J., and E. Mayr. 1946. Supplementary notes on the family Anatidae. Wilson Bull. 58:104–110.

Delacour, J., and C. Vaurie. 1957. A classification of the oscines (Aves). Contrib. Sci., Los Angeles County Mus. 16:1–6.

Demain, A. 1981. Industrial microbiology. Science 214:987–995.

DeMay, I. S. 1940. A study of the pterylosis and pneumaticity of the screamer. Condor 42:112–118.

Denhardt, D. T. 1966. A membrane filter technique for the detection of complementary DNA. Biochem. Biophys. Research Commun. 23:641–646.

De Queiroz, K., and D. A. Good. 1988. The scleral ossicles of *Opisthocomus* and their phylogenetic significance. Auk 105:29–35.

DeVis, C. W. 1897. Diagnoses of thirty-six new or little-known birds from British New Guinea. Ibis 39:371–392.

Diamond, J. M. 1972. Avifauna of the eastern highlands of New Guinea. Publ. Nuttall Orn. Club, No. 12. Cambridge, Mass.

Diamond, J. M. 1983. *Melampitta gigantea*: possible relation between feather structure and underground roosting habits. Condor 85:85–91.

Diaz, M. O., G. Barsacchi-Pilone, K. A. Mahon, and J. G. Gall. 1981. Transcript from both strands of a satellite DNA occur on lampbrush chromosome loops of the Newt *Notophthalmus*. Cell 24:649–659.

DiBerardino, M. A., N. J. Hoffner, and L. D. Etkin. 1984. Activation of dormant genes in specialized cells. Science 224:946–952.

Dickerson, R. E. 1971. The structure of cytochrome *c* and the rates of molecular evolution. J. Mol. Evol. 1:26–45.

Dickerson, R. E. 1983a. Base sequence and helix structure variation in *B* and *A* DNA. J. Mol. Biol. 166:419–441.

Dickerson, R. E. 1983b. The DNA helix and how it is read. Sci. Amer. 249(6):94–111.

Dickerson, R. E., H. R. Drew, B. N. Conner, R. M. Wing, A. V. Fratini, and M. L. Kopka. 1982. The anatomy of A-, B-, and Z-DNA. Science 216:475–485.

Dingle, R. V., W. G. Siesser, and A. R. Newton. 1983. Mesozoic and Tertiary geology of southern Africa. A. A. Balkema, Rotterdam. 575 pp.

Dittmann, D. L., R. M. Zink, and J. A. Gerwin. 1989. Evolutionary genetics of phalaropes. Auk 106:326–331.

Doerfler, W. 1983. DNA methylation and gene activity. Ann. Rev. Biochem. 52:93–124.

Doolittle, R. F. 1979. Protein evolution. Pp. 1–118 in The Proteins. Vol. 4. H. Neurath and R. L. Hill, eds. Academic Press, New York.

Doolittle, W. F. 1987. The origin and function of intervening sequences in DNA: a review. Amer. Nat. 130:915–928.

Dorst, J. 1950. Contribution à l'étude du plumage des Trogonidés. Bull. Mus. Nat. Hist. (Paris) 2e Ser. 22:693–699.

Dorst, J. 1952. Contribution à l'etude de la langue des Meliphagidés. L'Oiseau R.F.O. 22:185–214.

Dorst, J. 1960a. Considérations sur les passereaux de la famille des vangidés. Pp. 173–177 in Proc. 12th Intl. Orn. Congr., G. Bergman, K. O. Donner, L. Von Haartman, eds. Tilgmannin Kirjapaino, Helsinki.

Dorst, J. 1960b. A propos des affinités systématique de deux oiseaux malgaches: Tylas eduardi et Hypositta corallirostris. L'Oiseau R.F.O. 30:259.

Dorst, J., and J.-L. Mougin. 1979. Order Pelecaniformes. Pp. 155–193 in Check-list of birds of the world, vol. 1, second edition. E. Mayr and G. W. Cottrell, eds. Mus. Comp. Zool., Cambridge, Mass.

Doty, P., B. B. McGill, and S. A. Rice. 1959a. The properties of sonic fragments of deoxyribose nucleic acid. Proc. Natl. Acad. Sci. USA 44:432–438.

Doty, P., H. Boedtker, J. R. Fresco, R. Haselkorn, and M. Litt. 1959b. Secondary structure in nucleic acids. Proc. Natl. Acad. Sci. USA 45:482–499.

Doty, P., J. Marmur, J. Eigner, and C. Schildkraut. 1960. Strand separation and specific recombination in deoxyribonucleic acids: physical chemical studies. Proc. Natl. Acad. Sci. USA 46:461–476.

Douglas, M. E., and J. C. Avise. 1982. Speciation rates and morphological divergence in fishes: tests of gradual versus rectangular modes of evolutionary change. Evolution 36:224–232.

Dowsett, A. P. 1983. Closely related species of Drosophila can contain different libraries of middle repetitive DNA sequences. Chromosoma 88:104–108.

Dresser, H. E. 1884–86. A monograph of the Meropidae, or family of the bee-eaters. Publ. by the author, London. 144 pp.

Dresser, H. E. 1893. A monograph of the Coraciidae, or the family of the rollers. Publ. by the author, Farnborough, Kent.

Dubinin, V. B. 1958. Parasitological criteria in avian systematics [in Russian]. Uchenye Zapiski Moscow Univ. 197:241–259.

Dubochet, J., and M. Noll. 1978. Nucleosome arcs and helices. Science 202:280–286.

Dubois, A. 1902–04. Synopsis avium. Nouveau manuel d'ornithologie. H. Lamertin, Brussels. 2 vols.

Durrer, H., and W. Villiger. 1966. Schillerfarben der Trogoniden. Eine elektronenmikroskopische Untersuchung. J. für Orn. 107:1–26.

Dwight, J., Jr. 1900. The moult of the North American Tetraonidae (quails, partridges and grouse). Auk 17:34–51, 143–166.

Dwight, J., Jr. 1925. The gulls (Laridae) of the world; their plumages, moults, variations, relationships and distribution. Bull. Amer. Mus. Nat. Hist. 52:63–408.

Dyson, F. 1985. Origins of life. Cambridge Univ. Press.

Easteal, S. 1988. Rate constancy of globin gene evolution in placental mammals. Proc. Natl. Acad. Sci. USA 85:7622–7626.

Eden, F. C. 1980. A cloned chicken DNA fragment includes two repeated DNA sequences with remarkably different genomic organizations. J. Biol. Chem. 255:4854–4863.

Eden, F. C., and J. P. Hendrick. 1978. Unusual organization of DNA sequences in the chicken. Biochemistry 17:5838–5844.

Eden, F. C., J. P. Hendrick, and S. S. Gottlieb. 1978. Homology of single copy and repeated sequences in chicken, duck, Japanese quail, and ostrich DNA. Biochemistry 17:5113–5121.

Eden, F. C., A. M. Musti, and D. A. Sobieski. 1981. Clusters of repeated sequences of chicken DNA are extensively methylated but contain specific undermethylated regions. J. Mol. Biol. 48:129–151.

Efstradiatis, A., W. R. Crain, R. J. Britten, and E. H. Davidson. 1976. DNA sequence organization in the lepidopteran *Antheraea pernyi*. Proc. Natl. Acad. Sci. USA 73:2289–2293.

Eichler, W. 1955. Wirtsspezifität der Parasiten und Evolution der Wirte. Proc. 11th Intl. Orn. Congr. 303–308.

Eisenmann, E. 1965. The tiger-herons (*Tigrisoma*) of Argentina. El Hornero (Buenos Aires) 10:225–234.

Eldholm, O., and J. Thiede. 1980. Cenozoic continental separation between Europe and Greenland. Palaeogeo. Palaeoclim. Palaeoec. 30:243–259.

Eldredge, N., and J. Cracraft. 1980. Phylogenetic patterns and the evolutionary process. Columbia Univ. Press, New York.

Elliot, D. G. 1878. A study of the Pteroclidae or family of the sand-grouse. Proc. Zool. Soc. London 1878:223–264.

Elliot, D. G. 1885. Opisthocomi, Gallinae, Pterocletes, Columbae. Pp. 196–259 *in* J. S. Kingsley, ed. The standard natural history, vol. 4, Birds. S. E. Cassino, Boston.

Ellis, J. J. 1985. Species and varieties in the *Rhizopus arrhizus–Rhizopus oryzae* group as indicated by their DNA complementarity. Mycologia 77:243–247.

Elzanowski, A. 1977. Skulls of *Gobipteryx* (Aves) from the Upper Cretaceous of Mongolia. Results of the Polish-Mongolian palaeontological expeditions. Part 7. Palaeon. Polon. 37:153–165.

Emery, K. O., and E. Uchupi. 1984. The geology of the Atlantic ocean. Springer Verlag, Berlin. 1050 pp.

Entingh, T. D. 1970. DNA hybridization in the genus *Drosophila*. Genetics 66:55–68.

Epplen, J. T., M. Leipoldt, W. Engel, and J. Schmidtke. 1978. DNA sequence organization in avian genomes. Chromosoma 69:307–321.

Epplen, J. T., U. Diedrich, M. Wagenmann, J. Schmidtke, and W. Engel. 1979. Contrasting DNA sequence organisation patterns in sauropsidian genomes. Chromosoma 75:199–214.

Ertl, H. H., L. E. Feinendegen, and H. J. Heiniger. 1970. Iodine-125, a tracer in cell biology: physical properties and biological aspects. Phys. Med. Biol. 15:447–456.

Evans, I. J., A. M. James, and S. R. Barnes. 1983. Organization and evolution of repeated DNA sequences in closely related plant genomes. J. Mol. Biol. 170:803–826.

Falla, R. A., R. B. Sibson, and E. G. Turbott. 1979. The new guide to the birds of New Zealand and outlying islands. Collins, Auckland and London.

Farmer, J. J. III, et al. (14 co-authors). 1985. Biochemical identification of new species and biogroups of Enterobacteriaceae isolated from clinical specimens. J. Clin. Microbiol. 21:46–76.

Farris, J. S. 1972. Estimating phylogenetic trees from distance matrices. Amer. Nat. 106:645–668.

Fedoroff, N. V. 1984. Transposable genetic elements in maize. Sci. Amer. 250(6):85–90, 95–98.

Feduccia, A. 1973. Evolutionary trends in the Neotropical ovenbirds and woodhewers. Ornith. Monogr. No. 13, pp. 1–69. Amer. Orn. Union, Washington, D.C.

Feduccia, A. 1974. Morphology of the bony stapes in New and Old World suboscines: new evidence for common ancestry. Auk 91:427–429.

Feduccia, A. 1975a. Morphology of the bony stapes in the Menuridae and Acanthisittidae: evidence for oscine affinities. Wilson Bull. 87:418–420.

Feduccia, A. 1975b. Morphology of the bony stapes (columella) in the Passeriformes and related groups: evolutionary implications. Misc. Publ. No. 63, Univ. Kansas Mus. Nat. Hist.

Feduccia, A. 1975c. The bony stapes in the Upupidae and Phoeniculidae: new evidence for common ancestry. Wilson Bull. 87:416–417.

Feduccia, A. 1976. Morphology of the bony stapes in *Philepitta* and *Neodrepanis*: new evidence for suboscine affinities. Auk 93:169–170.

Feduccia, A. 1977a. A model for the evolution of perching birds. Syst. Zool. 26:19–31.

Feduccia, A. 1977b. Hypothetical stages in the evolution of modern ducks and flamingos. J. Theoretical Biol. 67:715–721.

Feduccia, A. 1978. *Presbyornis* and the evolution of ducks and flamingos. Amer. Scientist 66:298–304.

Feduccia, A. 1979. Comments on the phylogeny of perching birds. Proc. Biol. Soc. Wash. 92:689–696.

Feduccia, A., and L. D. Martin. 1976. The Eocene zygodactyl birds of North America (Aves: Piciformes). Smithson. Contrib. Paleobiol. 27:101–110.

Feduccia, A., and S. L. Olson. 1982. Morphological similarities between the Menurae and the Rhinocryptidae, relict passerine birds of the southern hemisphere. Smithson. Contrib. Zool. No. 366. 22 pp.

Feeney, R. E., D. T. Osuga, S. B. Lind, and H. T. Miller. 1966. The egg-white proteins of the Adelie penguin. Comp. Biochem. Physiol. 18:121–130.

Felsenfeld, G. 1985. DNA. Sci. Amer. 253:58–67.

Felsenstein, J. 1984. The statistical approach to inferring phylogenetic trees and what it tells us about parsimony and compatibility. Pp. 169–191 *in* Cladistics: perspectives on the reconstruction of evolutionary history. T. Duncan and T. F. Stuessy, eds. Columbia Univ. Press, New York.

Felsenstein, J. 1987. Estimation of hominoid phylogeny from a DNA hybridization data set. J. Mol. Evol. 123–131.

Felsenstein, J. 1989. PHYLIP 3.2 manual. Univ. Calif. Herbarium, Berkeley, Calif.

Ferris, S. D., A. C. Wilson, and W. M. Brown. 1981a. Evolutionary tree for apes and humans based on cleavage maps of mitochondrial DNA. Proc. Natl. Acad. Sci. USA 78:2432–2436.

Ferris, S. D., W. M. Brown, W. S. Davidson, and A. C. Wilson. 1981b. Extensive polymorphism in the mitochondrial DNA of apes. Proc. Natl. Acad. Sci. USA 78:6319–6323.

Ferris, S. D., R. D. Sage, and A. C. Wilson. 1982. Evidence from mtDNA sequences that common laboratory strains of inbred mice are descended from a single female. Nature 295:163–165.

Ficken, R. W., and M. S. Ficken. 1966. A review of some aspects of avian field ethology. Auk 83:637–661.

Fiedler, W. 1951. Beiträge zur Morphologie der Kiefermuskulatur der Oscines. Zool. Jahrb. (Anatomie) 7:235–288.

Field, K. G., G. J. Olsen, D. J. Lane, S. J. Giovannoni, M. T. Ghiselin, E. C. Raff, N. R. Pace, and R. A. Raff. 1988. Molecular phylogeny of the animal kingdom. Science 239:748–753.

Finsch, O. 1867–68. Die Papageien. E. J. Brill, Leiden. 2 vols.

Finsch, O. 1876. On *Pristorhamphus versteri*, a new genus and species of bird from the Arfak Mountains, New Guinea. Proc. Zool. Soc. London 1875:641–642.

Firtel, R. A., and J. Bonner. 1972. Characterization of the genome of the cellular slime mold, *Dictyostelium discoideum*. J. Mol. Biol. 66:339–361.

Fisher, H. I. 1939. Pterylosis of the black vulture. Auk 56:407–410.

Fisher, H. I. 1942. The pterylosis of the Andean condor. Condor 44:30–32.

Fisher, H. I. 1943. The pterylosis of the king vulture. Condor 45:69–73.

Fisher, H. I. 1944. The skulls of the cathartid vultures. Condor 46:272–296.

Fisher, H. I. 1946. Adaptations and comparative anatomy of the locomotive apparatus of New World vultures. Amer. Midl. Nat. 35:545–727.

Fisher, H. I. 1947. The skeletons of recent and fossil *Gymnogyps*. Pacific Sci. 1:227–236.

Fitch, W. M. 1976. Molecular evolutionary clocks. Pp. 160–178 *in* Molecular Evolution, F. J. Ayala, ed. Sinauer Associates, Sunderland, Mass.

Fitch, W. M., and E. Margoliash. 1967. The construction of phylogenetic trees. Science 155:279–284.

Fitzinger, L. 1856–65. Über das System und die Charakteristik der natürlichen Familien der Vögel. Kaiserl. Akad. Wiss. (Wien), (Math.-Naturwiss. Classe) Sitzsber. 21:277–318; 46(1):194–240; 5l(2):285–322.

Fjeldså, J. 1976. The systematic affinities of sandgrouse, Pteroclididae. Vidensk. Meddr. Dansk Naturh. Foren. 139:179–243.

Flavell, R. B., and W. F. Thompson. 1983. Cytosine methylation and the activity of ribosomal RNA genes in wheat. Carnegie Inst. Wash. Yearbook 82:12–15.

Fleming, C. A. 1941. The phylogeny of the prions. Emu 4l:134–155.

Fleming, C. A. 1975. The geological history of New Zealand and its biota. Pp. 1–86 *in* Biogeography and ecology of New Zealand and its biota. G. Kuschel, ed. W. Junk, The Hague.

Flieg, G. M. 1971. Tytonidae × Strigidae cross produces fertile eggs. Auk 88:178.

Forbes, W. A. 1879. On the systematic position of the genus *Lathamus* of Lesson. Proc. Zool. Soc. London 1879:166–174.

Forbes, W. A. 1880a. Contributions to the anatomy of passerine birds. II. On the syrinx and other points in the anatomy of the Eurylaemidae. Proc. Zool. Soc. London 1880:380–386.

Forbes, W. A. 1880b. Contributions to the anatomy of passerine birds. IV. On some points in the structure of *Philepitta*, and its position amongst the Passeres. Proc. Zool. Soc. London 1880:387–391.

Forbes, W. A. 1880c. On some points in the structure of *Nasiterna* bearing on its affinities. Proc. Zool. Soc. London 1880:76–77.

Forbes, W. A. 1880d. On the anatomy of *Leptosoma discolor*. Proc. Zool. Soc. London 1880:465–475.

Forbes, W. A. 1880e. Remarks on Dr. Gadow's papers on the digestive system of birds. Ibis 22:234–237.

Forbes, W. A. 1881a. Notes on the anatomy and systematic position of the jacanas (Parridae). Proc. Zool. Soc. London 1881:639–647, 3 figs.

Forbes, W. A. 1881b. On the conformation of the thoracic end of the trachea in the "ratite" birds. Proc. Zool. Soc. London 1881:778–788; 836–837.

Forbes, W. A. 1881c. Note on the structure of the palate in the Trogons (Trogonidae). Proc. Zool. Soc. London 1881(1882):836–837, 1 fig.

Forbes, W. A. 1881d. On the contributions to the anatomy and classification of birds made by the late Prof. Garrod, F.R.S. Ibis 23:1–32.

Forbes, W. A. 1882a. Note on the gall-bladder and some other points in the anatomy of the Toucans and Barbets (Capitonidae). Proc. Zool. Soc. London 1882:94–96.

Forbes, W. A. 1882b. Description of the pterylosis of *Mesites*, with remarks on the position of that genus. Proc. Zool. Soc. London 1882:267–271.

Forbes, W. A. 1882c. On some points in the anatomy of the todies (Todidae), and on the affinities of that group. Proc. Zool. Soc. London 1882:442–540.

Forbes, W. A. 1882d. Note on some points in the anatomy of an Australian duck (*Biziura lobata*). Proc. Zool. Soc. London 1882:455–458, 2 figs.

Forbes, W. A. 1882e. Contributions to the anatomy of passerine birds. Part V. On the structure of the genus *Orthonyx*. Proc. Zool. Soc. London 1882:544–546.

Forbes, W. A. 1882f. Contributions to the anatomy of passerine birds. Part 6. On *Xenicus* and *Acanthisitta* as types of a new family (Xenicidae) of mesomyodean Passeres from New Zealand. Proc. Zool. Soc. London 1882:569–571.

Forbes, W. A. 1882g. Report on the anatomy of the petrels (Tubinares), collected during the voyage of H.M.S. Challenger. *In* Great Britain and Ireland, Challenger Office: Report on the scientific results of the voyage of H.M.S. Challenger 1873–76, Zool. 4(11). 64 pp.

Forbes-Watson, A. 1967. Observations at a nest of the cuckoo-roller *Leptosomus discolor*. Ibis 109:425–430.

Forshaw, J. M. 1969. Australian parrots. Lansdowne Press, Melbourne. 306 pp.

Forshaw, J. M. 1973. Parrots of the world. Lansdowne Press, Melbourne.

Fouquet, H., B. Bierweiler, and H. W. Sauer. 1974. Reassociation kinetics of nuclear DNA from *Physarum polycephalum*. Eur. J. Biochem. 44:407–410.

Fox, D. L. 1962a. Carotenoids of the scarlet ibis. Comp. Biochem. Physiol. 5:31–43.

Fox, D. L. 1962b. Metabolic fractionation, storage and display of carotenoid pigments by flamingoes. Comp. Biochem. Physiol. 6:1–40.

Fox, D. L. 1962c. Carotenoids of the roseate spoonbill. Comp. Biochem. Physiol. 6:305–310.

Fox, D. L., and T. S. Hopkins. 1966. Comparative metabolic fractionation of carotenoids in three flamingo species. Comp. Biochem. Physiol. 17:841–856.

Fox, D. L., T. S. Hopkins, and D. B. Zilversmit. 1965. Blood carotenoids of the roseate spoonbill. Comp. Biochem. Physiol. 14:641–649.

Fox, D. L., V. E. Smith and A. A. Wolfson. 1967. Carotenoid selectivity in blood and feathers of Lesser (African), Chilean and Greater (European) flamingos. Comp. Biochem. Physiol. 23:225–232.

Fox, G. E., E. Stackebrandt, R. B. Hespell, J. Gibson, J. Maniloff, T. A. Dyer, R. S. Wolfe, W. E. Balch, R. S. Tanner, L. J. Magrum, L. B. Zablen, R. Blakemore, R. Gupta, L. Bonen, B. J. Lewis, D. A. Stahl, K. R. Luehrsen, K. N. Chen, and C. R. Woese. 1980. The phylogeny of prokaryotes. Science 209:457–463.

Frank, G. H. 1954. The development of the chondrocranium of the ostrich. Ann. Univ. Stellenbosch 30A:179–248.

Frank-Kamenetskii, M. 1986. A simple solution to the stability of the double helix? Nature 324:305.

Franklin, R., and R. G. Gosling. 1953a. The structure of thymonucleate fibres. I. The influence of water content. Acta Crystallographica 6:673–677.

Franklin, R., and R. G. Gosling. 1953b. The structure of sodium thymonucleate fibres. II. The cylindrically symmetrical Patterson function. Acta Crystallographica 6:678–685.

Freifelder, D. 1983. Molecular biology. Science Books International, Boston, Mass.

Friant, M. 1945a. Les os carpiens du nandou (Rhea). C. R. Acad. Sci. Paris 221:641–643.

Friant, M. 1945b. Développement et interprétation de la ceinture scapulaire du nandou (Rhea). C. R. Acad. Sci. Paris 221:711–713.

Friant, M. 1946. Le procoracoide des oiseaux. C. R. Acad. Sci. Paris 222:153–155.

Friant, M. 1947. La position systématique des Anhimae groupe aviaire sud-américain. C. R. Acad. Sci. Paris 224:592–593.

Friant, M. 1959. Quelques caractères du squelette chez les oiseaux de la sous-classe des Ratites. Acta Anat. 39:300–328.

Friday, A. E. 1981. Hominoid evolution: the nature of biochemical evidence. Pp. 1–23 in Aspects of human evolution. Symp. Soc. Study Human Biol., vol. 21. C. B. Stringer, ed. Taylor and Francis, London.

Friedburg, E. C. 1985. DNA repair. Freeman, New York.

Friedlander, G., J. W. Kennedy, E. S. Macias, and J. M. Miller. 1981. Nuclear and radio-ochemistry. 3rd edition. J. Wiley, New York.

Friedmann, H. 1930. The caudal molt of certain coraciiform, coliiform and piciform birds. Proc. U.S. Natl. Mus. 77:1–6.

Friedmann, H. 1950. The birds of North and Middle America. Bull. U.S. Natl. Mus. 50, pt. 11. 793 pp.

Friedmann, H. 1955. Recent revisions in classification and their biological significance. Pp. 23–43 in Recent studies in avian biology, A. Wolfson, ed. Univ. of Illinois Press, Urbana.

Friedmann, H. 1960. The parasitic weaverbirds. Bull. U.S. Natl. Mus. 223:1–196.

Friedmann, H. 1962. The problem of the Viduinae in the light of recent publications. Smithson. Misc. Coll. 145(3):1–10.

Frisch, O. von. 1969. Zur Jugend Entwicklung und Ethologie des Spiessflughuhns (*Pterocles alchata*). Bonn. Zool. Beitr. 20:130–144.

Frisch, O. von. 1970. Zur Brutbiologie und Zucht des Spiessflughuhns (*Pterocles alchata*) in Gefangenshaft. J. für Orn. 111:189–195.

Frith, H. J. 1962. The Mallee-Fowl. Angus and Robertson, Sydney.

Frith, H. J. 1964a. The downy young of the freckled duck, *Stictonetta naevosa*. Emu 64:42–47.

Frith, H. J. 1964b. Taxonomic relationships of *Stictonetta naevosa* (Gould). Nature 202:1352–1353.

Frith, H. J., and S. J. J. F. Davies. 1961. Ecology of the magpie goose, *Anseranas semi-*

palmata Latham (Anatidae). Commonwealth Sci. Industr. Res. Organ., Wildlife Res. 6:91–141.

Fruton, J. S. 1972. Molecules and Life. Wiley-Interscience, New York.

Fry, C. H. 1969. The evolution and systematics of bee-eaters (Meropidae). Ibis 111:557–592.

Fry, C. H. 1980. The origin of Afrotropical kingfishers. Ibis 122:57–74.

Fry, C. H. 1984. The bee-eaters. Buteo Press, Vermillion, South Dakota.

Fry, K., and W. Salser. 1977. Nucleotide sequences of HS-α satellite DNA from kangaroo rat *Dipodomys ordii* and characterization of similar sequences in other rodents. Cell 12:1069–1084.

Fry, K., R. Poon, P. Whitcombe, J. Idriss, W. Salser, J. Mazrimas, and F. Hatch. 1973. Nucleotide sequence of HS-β satellite DNA from kangaroo rat *Dipodomys ordii*. Proc. Natl. Acad. Sci. USA 70:2642–2646.

Fürbringer, M. 1888. Untersuchungen zur Morphologie und Systematik der Vögel. Vols. 1, 2. 1751 pp. Von Holkema, Amsterdam.

Fürbringer, M. 1889. Einige Bemerkungen über die Stellung von Stringops und den eventuellen Herd der Entstehung der Papageien, sowie über den systematischen Platz von Jynx. J. für Orn. 37:236–245.

Fürbringer, M. 1902. Zur vergleichenden Anatomie des Brustschulterapparates und der Schultermuskeln. Part 5. Jena Z. für Naturwiss. 36:289–736.

Gadow, H. 1876. Ueber das Verdauungssystem der Vögel. J. für Orn. 24:163–173.

Gadow, H. 1877. Anatomie des *Phoenicopterus roseus* Pall. und seine Stellung in System. J. für Orn. 25:382–397.

Gadow, H. 1879. Versuch einer vergleichenden Anatomie des Verdauungssystemes der Vögel. Jena Z. Naturwiss. 13:92–171, 339–403.

Gadow, H. 1882. On some points in the anatomy of *Pterocles*, with remarks on its systematic position. Proc. Zool. Soc. London 1882:312–332.

Gadow, H. 1883a. Catalogue of the birds in the British Museum. Vol. 8. Brit. Mus., London.

Gadow, H. 1883b. On the suctorial apparatus of the Tenuirostres. Proc. Zool. Soc. London 1883:62–69.

Gadow, H. 1884. Catalogue of the Passeriformes . . . in the British Museum. Vol. 9. Brit. Mus., London.

Gadow, H. 1888a. The morphology of birds. [Review of Fürbringer 1888.] Nature 39:150–152, 177–181.

Gadow, H. 1888b. Remarks on the numbers and on the phylogenetic development of the remiges of birds. Proc. Zool. Soc. London 1888:655–667.

Gadow, H. 1888c. Remarks on p. 4 *in* A history of the birds of New Zealand, 2nd edition, vol. 1, by W. L. Buller. Publ. by W. L. Buller, London.

Gadow, H. 1889. On the taxonomic value of the intestinal convolutions in birds. Proc. Zool. Soc. London 1889:303–316.

Gadow, H. 1891a. Further remarks on the relationships of the Drepanididae. Pp. 251–257 *in* Aves Hawaiiensis: the birds of the Sandwich Islands. S. B. Wilson and A. H. Evans, eds. R. H. Porter, London.

Gadow, H. 1891b. Notes on the structure of *Pedionomus torquatus*, with regard to its systematic position. Rec. Australian Mus. 1:205–211.

Gadow, H. 1891c. Vögel. I. Anatomischer Theil. *In* Bronn's Klassen und Ordnungen des Thier-Reichs, vol. 6(4). 1008 pp. C. F. Winter, Leipzig. [Also cited as Gadow and Selenka 1891, see below.]

Gadow, H. 1892. On the classification of birds. Proc. Zool. Soc. London 1892:229–256.

Gadow, H. 1893. Vögel. II. Systematischer Theil. *In* Bronn's Klassen und Ordnungen des Thier-Reichs, vol. 6(4). 303 pp. C. F. Winter, Leipzig.

Gadow, H. 1894. Muscular system. Pp. 602–620 *in* A dictionary of birds, Part 3. A. Newton, ed. Adam and Charles Black, London.

Gadow, H. 1895. Untitled. Ibis 37:299–300.

Gadow, H. 1898. A classification of vertebrata Recent and extinct. Adam and Charles Black, London.

Gadow, H., and E. Selenka. 1891. Vögel. I. Anatomischer Theil. *In* Bronn's Klassen und Ordnungen des Thier-Reichs, vol. 6(4). 1008 pp. C. F. Winter, Leipzig.

Galau, G. A., M. E. Chamberlin, B. R. Hough, R. J. Britten, and E. H. Davidson. 1976. Evolution of repetitive and nonrepetitive DNA. Pp. 200–224 *in* Molecular Evolution. F. J. Ayala, ed. Sinauer Assoc., Sunderland, Mass.

Galbraith, I. C. J. 1956. Variation, relationships and evolution in the *Pachycephala pectoralis* superspecies (Aves, Muscicapidae). Bull. Brit. Mus. (Nat. Hist.) 4:133–222.

Gall, J. G., and D. D. Atherton. 1974. Satellite DNA sequences in *Drosophila virilis*. J. Mol. Biol. 85:633–644.

Gardner, L. L. 1925. The adaptive modifications and the taxonomic value of the tongue in birds. Proc. U.S. Natl. Mus. 67:1–49.

Garrod, A. H. 1872a. Notes on the anatomy of the Huia bird (*Heterolocha gouldi*). Proc. Zool. Soc. London 1872:643–647.

Garrod, A. H. 1872b. Note on the tongue of the psittacine genus *Nestor*. Proc. Zool. Soc. London 1872 (1873):787–789.

Garrod, A. H. 1873a. On the value in classification of a peculiarity in the anterior margin of the nasal bones of certain birds. Proc. Zool. Soc. London 1873:33–38.

Garrod, A. H. 1873b. On the carotid arteries of birds. Proc. Zool. Soc. London 1873:457–472.

Garrod, A. H. 1873c. On some points in the anatomy of *Steatornis*. Proc. Zool. Soc. London 1873:526–535.

Garrod, A. H. 1873d. On certain muscles of the thigh of birds and on their value in classification. Part I. Proc. Zool. Soc. London 1873:626–644.

Garrod, A. H. 1874a. On certain muscles of birds and their value in classification. Part II. Proc. Zool. Soc. London 1874:111–124.

Garrod, A. H. 1874b. On some points in the anatomy of the Columbae. Proc. Zool. Soc. London 1874:249–259.

Garrod, A. H. 1874c. On the "showing-off" of the Australian bustard (*Eupodotis australis*). Proc. Zool. Soc. London 1874:471–473.

Garrod, A. H. 1874d. On some points in the anatomy of the parrots which bear on the classification of the suborder. Proc. Zool. Soc. London 1874:586–598, 1 pl.

Garrod, A. H. 1875. On the disposition of the deep plantar tendons in different birds. Proc. Zool. Soc. London 1874:339–348.

Garrod, A. H. 1876a. On a peculiarity in the carotid arteries, and other points in the anatomy, of the ground-hornbill (*Bucorvus abyssinicus*). Proc. Zool. Soc. London 1876:60–61.

Garrod, A. H. 1876b. On the anatomy of *Chauna derbiana* and on the systematic positions of the screamers (Palamedeidae). Proc. Zool. Soc. London 1876:189–200.

Garrod, A. H. 1876c. On the anatomy of *Aramus scolopaceus*. Proc. Zool. Soc. London 1876:275–277.

Garrod, A. H. 1876d. Notes on the anatomy of *Plotus anhinga*. Proc. Zool. Soc. London 1876:335–345.

Garrod, A. H. 1876e. Notes on the anatomy of the Colies (*Colius*). Proc. Zool. Soc. London 1876:416–419.

Garrod, A. H. 1876f. On some anatomical characters which bear upon the major subdivisions of the passerine birds. I. Proc. Zool. Soc. London 1876:506–519.

Garrod, A. H. 1877a. Notes on the anatomy of passerine birds. III. Proc. Zool. Soc. London 1877:523–526.

Garrod, A. H. 1877b. Notes on the anatomy of passerine birds. II. Proc. Zool. Soc. London 1877:447–452.

Garrod, A. H. 1877c. Notes on the anatomy and systematic position of the genera *Thinocorus* and *Attagis*. Proc. Zool. Soc. London 1877:413–418.

Garrod, A. H. 1877d. On the anatomical characters distinguishing the swallow and the swift. Zoologist 1:217–220.

Garrod, A. H. 1878a. On the systematic position of the Momotidae. Proc. Zool. Soc. London 1878:100–102.

Garrod, A. H. 1878b. Notes on the anatomy of passerine birds. IV. Proc. Zool. Soc. London 1878:143.

Garrod, A. H. 1878c. Note on points in the anatomy of Levaillant's darter (*Plotus levaillanti*). Proc. Zool. Soc. London 1878:679–681.

Garrod, A. H. 1878d. Notes on the anatomy of *Indicator major*. Proc. Zool. Soc. London 1878:930–935.

Garrod, A. H. 1879a. Notes on points in the anatomy of the Hoatzin (*Opisthocomus cristatus*). Proc. Zool. Soc. London 1879:109–114.

Garrod, A. H. 1879b. On the conformation of the thoracic extremity of the trachea in the class Aves. Part I. The Gallinae. Proc. Zool. Soc. London 1879:354–380.

Garrod, A. H. 1881. Notes on the anatomy of *Pelecanoides* (*Puffinuria*) *urinatrix*. Pp. 521–522 *in* The collected scientific papers of the late Alfred Henry Garrod. W. A. Forbes, ed. R. H. Porter, London.

Gaunt, S. J., J. R. Miller, D. J. Powell, and D. Duboule. 1986. Homoeobox gene expression in mouse embryos varies with position by the primitive streak stage. Nature 324:662–664.

Gehring, W. J. 1985. The homeo box: a key to the understanding of development? Cell 40:3–5.

Gehring, W. J. 1987. Homeo boxes in the study of development. Science 236:1245–1252.

Gellert, M., and H. Nash. 1987. Communication between segments of DNA during site-specific recombination. Nature 325:401–404.

George, J. C., and A. J. Berger. 1966. Avian myology. Academic Press, New York.

George, U. 1969. Über das Tränken der Jungen und andere Lebensäusserungen des Senegal-Flughuhns. *Pterocles senegallus*, in Marokko. J. für Orn. 110:181–191.

George, U. 1970. Beobachtungen an *Pterocles senegallus* und *Pterocles coronatus* in der Nordwest-Sahara. J. für Orn. 111:175–188.

Gerbe, Z. 1877. Sur les plumes du vol et leur mue. Bull. Soc. Zool. France 2:289–291.

Gharrett, A. J., R. C. Simon, and J. D. McIntyre. 1977. Reassociation and hybridization properties of DNAs from several species of fish. Comp. Biochem. Physiol. 56B:81–85.

Ghiselin, M. T. 1984. Narrow approaches to phylogeny: a review of nine books of cladism. Oxford Surv. Evol. Biol. 1:209–222.

Giebel, C. G. A. 1861. Zur Naturgeschichte des surinamischen Wasserhuhnes (*Podoa surinamensis*). Z. Gesamm. Naturwiss. 18:424–437.

Gilbert, W. 1986. The RNA world. Nature 319:618.

Gill, F. B. 1971. Tongue structure of the sunbird *Hypogramma hypogrammica*. Condor 73:485–486.

Gillespie, D. 1977. Newly evolved repeated sequences in primates. Science 196:889–891.

Gillespie, D., and S. Spiegelman. 1965. A quantitative assay for the DNA/RNA hybrids immobilized on a membrane. J. Mol. Biol. 12:829–842.

Gillespie, J. H. 1984a. Molecular evolution over the mutational landscape. Evolution 38:1116–1129.

Gillespie, J. H. 1984b. The molecular clock may be an episodic clock. Proc. Natl. Acad. Sci. 81:8009–8013.

Ginatulin, A. A., and L. K. Ginatulina. 1979. Molecular structure of the genome in vertebrates. *In* Evolutionary studies: parallelism and convergence. V. A. Krassilov, ed. Vladivostok.

Ginatulin, A. A., L. K. Ginatulina, and N. N. Vorontsov. 1983. Genome analysis of ground squirrels of the genus *Citellus* (Rodentia, Sciuridae) II. DNA sequence organization. Genetica 62:117–128.

Ginatulina, L. K., A. A. Ginatulin, E. A. Lyapunova, and N. N. Vorontsov. 1982. Genome analysis of ground squirrels of the genus *Citellus* (Rodentia, Sciuridae) I. DNA reassociation kinetics and genome size of eight species. Genetica 59:211–221.

Gingerich, P. D. 1976. Evolutionary significance of the Mesozoic toothed birds. Smithson. Contrib. Paleobiol. 27:23–33.

Glaus, K. R., H. P. Zassenhaus, H. S. Fechheimer, and P. S. Perlman. 1980. Avian mtDNA: structure, organization, and evolution. Pp. 131–135 *in* The organization and expression of the mitochondrial genome. A. M. Kroon and C. Saccone, eds. North Holland Publ., Amsterdam.

Glenny, F. H. 1942a. Arteries in the heart region of the kiwi. Auk 59:225–228.

Glenny, F. H. 1942b. Main arteries in the region of the neck and thorax of the Australian cassowary. Canad. J. Res. 20:363–367.

Glenny, F. H. 1943a. A systematic study of the main arteries in the region of the heart, Aves VI. Trogoniformes, Part 1. Auk 60:235–239.

Glenny, F. H. 1943b. A systematic study of the main arteries in the region of the heart. Aves X. Strigiformes, Part 1. Trans. Roy. Can. Inst. 24:233–239.

Glenny, F. H. 1944a. A systematic study of the main arteries in the region of the heart. Aves V. Sphenisciformes, Part 1. Ohio J. Sci. 44:28–30.

Glenny, F. H. 1944b. A systematic study of the main arteries in the region of the heart. Aves VIII. Anseriformes, Part 1. Canad. J. Res. 22:17–35.

Glenny, F. H. 1945a. A systematic study of the main arteries in the region of the heart. Aves XIII. Ciconiiformes, Part 1. Amer. Midl. Nat. 33:449–454.

Glenny, F. H. 1945b. A systematic study of the main arteries in the region of the heart. Aves XIV. Gruiformes, Part 1. Auk 62:266–269.

Glenny, F. H. 1945c. A systematic study of the main arteries in the region of the heart. Aves VI. Trogoniformes, Part 2. Auk 62:408–409.

Glenny, F. H. 1947a. A systematic study of the main arteries in the region of the heart. Aves V. Sphenisciformes, Part 2. Ohio J. Sci. 51:347–352.

Glenny, F. H. 1947b. A systematic study of the main arteries in the region of the heart. Aves XIV. Gruiformes, Part 2. Auk 64:407–410.

Glenny, F. H. 1951. A systematic study of the main arteries in the region of the heart. Aves XVIII. Psittaciformes, Part 1. Ohio J. Sci. 51:347–352.

Glenny, F. H. 1953a. A systematic study of the main arteries in the region of the heart. Aves XIII. Ciconiiformes, Part 2. Ohio J. Sci. 53:347–348.

Glenny, F. H. 1953b. A systematic study of the main arteries in the region of the heart. Aves XX. Caprimulgiformes, Part 1. Ohio J. Sci. 53:356–357.

Glenny, F. H. 1955. Modifications of pattern in the aortic arch system of birds and their phylogenetic significance. Proc. U.S. Natl. Mus. 104 (3346):525–621.

Glenny, F. H. 1957. A revised classification of the Psittaciformes based on the carotid artery arrangement patterns. Ann. Zool. (Agra) 2:47–56.

Glenny, F. H. 1965. Main cervical and thoracic arteries of some flightless birds. Ann. Zool. (Agra) 5:1–8.

Glenny, F. H. 1967. Main arteries in the neck and thorax of three sun grebes (Heliornithidae). Auk 84:431–432.

Glutz von Blotzheim, U. 1958. Zur Morphologie und Ontogenese von Schultergurtel, Sternum und Becken von *Struthio*, *Rhea* und *Dromiceius*. Rev. Suisse de Zool. 65:609–772.

Godman, F. DuC. 1907–10. A monograph of the petrels (Order Tubinares). Witherby, London. 381 pp.

Goeldi, E. A. 1896. A cigana (*Opisthocomus cristatus*), resenha ornithológica. Bol. Mus. Paraense Hist. Nat. (Pará) 1:167–184.

Goin, O. B., C. J. Goin, and K. Bachmann. 1968. DNA and amphibian life history. Copeia 1968:532–540.

Goldberg, R. B., W. R. Crain, J. V. Ruderman, G. P. Moore, T. R. Barnett, R. C. Higgins, R. A. Galfand, G. A. Galau, R. J. Britten, and E. H. Davidson. 1975. DNA sequence organization in the genomes of five marine invertebrates. Chromosoma 51:225–251.

Goodchild, J. G. 1886. Observations on the disposition of the cubital coverts in birds. Proc. Zool. Soc. London 1886:184–203.

Goodchild, J. G. 1891. The cubital coverts of the Euornithae in relation to taxonomy. Proc. Roy. Physical Soc. Edinb. 11:317–333.

Goodman, M., M. L. Weiss, and J. Czelusniak. 1982a. Molecular evolution above the species level: branching pattern, rates, and mechanisms. Syst. Zool. 31:376–399.

Goodman, M., A. E. Romero-Herrera, H. Dene, J. Czelusniak, and R. E. Tashian. 1982b. Amino acid sequence evidence on the phylogeny of primates and other eutherians. Pp. 115–191 *in* Macromolecular sequences in systematic and evolutionary biology. M. Goodman, ed. Plenum Press, New York.

Goodman, M., D. A. Tagle, D. H. A. Fitch, W. Bailey, J. Czelusniak, B. F. Koop, P. Benson, and J. L. Slightom. 1990. Primate evolution at the DNA level and a classification of hominoids. J. Mol. Evol. 30:260–266.

Goodman, N. C., S. C. Gulati, R. Redfield, and S. Spiegelman. 1973. Room-temperature chromatography of nucleic acids on hydroxylaptite columns in the presence of formamide. Analytical Biochem. 52:286–299.

Goodwin, D. 1958. Remarks on the taxonomy of some American doves. Auk 75:330–334.

Goodwin, D. 1959a. Taxonomic notes on the American ground doves. Auk 76:510–515.

Goodwin, D. 1959b. Taxonomy of the genus *Columba*. Bull. Brit. Mus. (Nat. Hist.) 6: 1–23.

Goodwin, D. 1960. Taxonomy of the genus *Ducula*. Ibis 102:526–535.

Goodwin, D. 1964. Some aspects of taxonomy and relationships of barbets (Capitonidae). Ibis 106:198–220.

Goodwin, D. 1965. Remarks on drinking methods of some birds. Avicult. Mag. 71:76–80.

Goodwin, D. 1967. Pigeons and doves of the world. Brit. Mus. (Nat. Hist.), London.

Goodwin, D. 1983. Pigeons and doves of the world. 3rd ed. Cornell Univ. Press, Ithaca, New York.

Gould, J. 1853. Nest and egg of *Menura alberti*. Illustr. London News, March 19, 1853. Report of meeting of Zool. Soc. of London.

Gould, S. J. 1985. A clock of evolution. Nat. Hist. 94(4):12–25.

Grabowski, P. J., and P. A. Sharp. 1986. Affinity chromatography of splicing complexes: U2, U5, and U4 + U6 small nuclear ribonucleoprotein particles in the spliceosome. Science 233:1294–1299.

Gradstein, F. M., and S. P. Srivastava. 1980. Aspects of Cenozoic stratigraphy and paleoecology of the Labrador Sea and Baffin Bay. Palaeogeo., Palaeoclim., Palaeoecol. 30:261–295.

Graham, D. E., B. R. Neufeld, E. H. Davidson, and R. J. Britten. 1974. Interspersion of repetitive and non-repetitive DNA sequences in the sea urchin genome. Cell 1:127–137.

Grajal, A., S. D. Strahl, R. Parra, M. G. Dominguez, and A. Neher. 1989. Foregut fermentation in the Hoatzin, a neotropical leaf-eating bird. Science 245:1236–1238.

Gray, A. P. 1958. Bird hybrids. Tech. Commun. 13, Commonwealth Bureau Animal Breed. Genet. Commonwealth Agric. Bur., Farnham Royal, Bucks., England. 390 pp.

Gray, G. R. 1840. A list of the genera of birds. R. and J. Taylor, London.

Gray, G. R. 1844–49. The genera of birds. 3 vols. R. and J. Taylor, London.

Gray, G. R. 1869–71. Hand-list of genera and species of birds. 3 vols. Trustees, Brit. Mus., London.

Greenway, J. C., Jr. 1960. Check-list of birds of the world. Vol. 9. E. Mayr and J. C. Greenway, Jr., eds. Mus. Comp. Zool., Cambridge, Mass.

Greenway, J. C., Jr. 1967. Check-list of birds of the world. Vol. 12. R. A. Paynter, Jr., ed. Mus. Comp. Zool., Cambridge, Mass.

Gregory, W. K. 1935. Remarks on the origins of the ratites and penguins. Proc. Linnean Soc. New York 1933/1934, No. 45/46:1–18.

Grimes, L. G. 1980. Observations of group behaviour and breeding biology of the Yellow-billed Shrike *Corvinella corvina*. Ibis 122:166–192.

Grimmer, J. L. 1962. Strange little world of the hoatzin. Natl. Geogr. Mag. 122:391–401.

Grivell, L. A. 1986. Deciphering divergent codes. Nature 324:109–110.

Grula, J. W., T. J. Hall, J. A. Hunt, T. D. Giugni, G. J. Graham, E. H. Davidson, and R. J. Britten. 1982. Sea urchin DNA sequence variation and reduced interspecies differences of the less variable sequences. Evolution 36:665–676.

Gueho, E., J. Tredick, and H. J. Phaff. 1985. DNA relatedness among species of *Geotrichum* and *Dipodascus*. Canadian J. Bot. 63:961–966.

Guéron, M., M. Kochoyan, and J.-L. Leroy. 1987. A single mode of DNA base-pair opening drives imino proton exchange. Nature 328:89–92.

Guerrier-Takada, C., and S. Altman. 1984. Catalytic activity of an RNA molecule prepared by transcription in vitro. Science 223:285–286.

Guerrier-Takada, C., K. Gardiner, T. Marsh, N. Pace, and S. Altman. 1983. The RNA moiety of ribonuclease P is the catalytic subunit of the enzyme. Cell 35:849–857.

Gulledge, J. L. 1975. A study of phenetic and phylogenetic relationships among the mockingbirds, thrashers and their allies. Ph.D. diss., City Univ. New York.

Guntert, M. 1981. Morphologische Untersuchungen der adaptiven Radiation des Verdauungstraktes bei Papageien (Psittaci). Zool. Jahrb. Anat. 106:471–526.

Gutierrez, R. J., R. M. Zink, and S. Y. Yang. 1983. Genic variation, systematic, and biogeographic relationships of some galliform birds. Auk 100:33–47.

Gysels, H. 1964a. Bidrage tot de Systematiek van de Vogels, aan de hand van de elektroforese in agar van de oplosbare lens-en spierproteïnen. Natuurwet. Tijdschr. 46:43–178.

Gysels, H. 1964b. A biochemical evidence for the heterogeneity of the family Psittacidae. Bull. Soc. Roy. Zool. Anvers 33:29–41.

Gysels, H. 1970. Some ideas about the phylogenetic relationships of the Tinamiformes, based on protein characters. Acta Zool. Pathol. Antverp 50:3–13.

Gysels, H., and M. Rabaey. 1962. Taxonomic relationships of *Afropavo congensis* Chapin 1936 by means of biochemical techniques. Bull. Soc. Zool. Anvers 26:72–85.

Gysels, H., and M. Rabaey. 1964. Taxonomic relationships of *Alca torda*, *Fratercula arctica* and *Uria aalge* as revealed by biochemical methods. Ibis 106:536–540.

Hachisuka, The Marquess. 1938. Classification and distribution of the game birds. Proc. 9th Intl. Orn. Congr. 177–182.

Hachisuka, The Marquess. 1953. The affinities of *Pityriasis* of Borneo. Proc. 7th Pacific Sci. Congr. 4:67–69.

Hackett, S. J. 1989. Effects of varied electrophoretic conditions on detection of evolutionary patterns in the Laridae. Condor 91:73–90.

Haffer, J. 1968. Über die Flügel und Schwanzmauser columbianischer Piciformes. J. für Orn. 109:157–171.

Hake, S., and V. Walbot. 1980. The genome of *Zea mays*, its organization and homology to related grasses. Chromosoma (Berl.) 79:251–270.

Hall, B. K. 1984. Developmental mechanisms underlying the formation of atavisms. Biol. Rev. 59:89–124.

Hall, B. P., and R. E. Moreau. 1970. An atlas of speciation in African passerine birds. Brit. Mus., London.

Hall, T. J., J. W. Grula, E. H. Davidson, and R. J. Britten. 1980. Evolution of sea urchin non-repetitive DNA. J. Mol. Evol. 16:95–110.

Halstead, L. B. 1982. Evolutionary trends and the phylogeny of the Agnatha. Pp. 159–196 *in* Problems of phylogenetic reconstruction. K. A. Joysey and A. E. Friday, eds. Academic Press, New York.

Hamlet, M. P., and H. I. Fisher. 1967. Air sacs of respiratory origin in some procellariiform birds. Condor 69:586–595.

Hanai, R., and A. Wada. 1988. The effects of guanine and cytosine variation on dinucleotide frequency and amino acid composition in the human genome. J. Mol. Evol. 27:321–325.

Hanawalt, P. C., E. C. Friedberg, and C. F. Fox. 1978. DNA repair mechanisms. Academic Press, New York.

Hanawalt, P. C., P. K. Cooper, A. K. Ganesan, and C. A. Smith. 1979. DNA repair in bacteria and mammalian cells. Ann. Rev. Biochem. 48:783–836.

Hancock, J. 1984. Aerial stretch display of the eastern race of the Great White Egret *Egretta alba*. Ibis 126:92–94.

Hancock, J., and H. Elliott. 1978. The herons of the world. Harper and Row, New York.

Hancock, J., and J. Kushlan. 1984. The herons handbook. Harper and Row, New York.

Hanham, A., and M. J. Smith. 1980. Sequence homology of the single-copy DNA of salmon. Comp. Biochem. Physiol. 65B:333–338.

Hanke, B., and G. Niethammer. 1955. Zur morphologie und histologie des oesophagus von *Thinocorus orbignyanus*. Bonn. Zool. Beitr. 6:207–211.

Harford, A. G. 1977. The organization of DNA sequences in polytene chromosomes of *Drosophila*. Pp. 315–338 *in* Chromatin and chromosome structure. H. J. Li and R. A. Eckhardt, eds. Academic Press, New York.

Hargitt, E. 1890. Catalogue of the birds in the British Museum. Vol. 18:1–597. Brit. Mus., London.

Harland, W. B., A. V. Cox, P. G. Llewellyn, C. A. G. Pickton, A. G. Smith, and R. Walters. 1982. A geologic time scale. Cambridge Univ. Press.

Harpold, M. M., and S. P. Craig. 1978. The evolution of non-repetitive DNA in sea urchins. Differentiation 10:7–11.

Harris, M. P. 1967. The biology of oystercatchers *Haematopus ostralegus* on Skokholm Island, S. Wales. Ibis 109:180–193.

Harris, M. P. 1969. Age at breeding and other observations on the Waved Albatross *Diomedea irrorata*. Ibis 111:97–98.

Harris, M. P. 1973. The biology of the Waved Albatross *Diomedea irrorata* of Hood Island, Galapagos. Ibis 115:483–510.

Harris, S. E., J. M. Rosen, A. R. Means, and B. W. O'Malley. 1975. Use of a specific probe for ovalbumin mRNA to quantitate estrogen induced gene transcripts. Biochemistry 14:2072–2080.

Harrison, C. J. O. 1960. Signal plumage and phylogenic relationship in some doves. Bull. Brit. Orn. Club 80:134–140.

Harrison, C. J. O. 1966. Plumage pattern and colour relationships of the genera *Carduelis* and *Fringilla*. Bull. Brit. Orn. Club 86:41–47.

Harrison, C. J. O. 1969a. The affinities of the blue wren genus *Malurus* and related genera: with special reference to the grass-wren genus *Amytornis*. Emu 69:1–8.

Harrison, C. J. O. 1969b. The nesting habits of sittellas and nuthatches. Emu 69:106–107.

Harrison, C. J. O. 1969c. The possible affinities of the Australian treecreepers of the genus *Climacteris*. Emu 69:161–168.

Harrison, C. J. O. 1969d. Additional information on the carpometacarpal process as a taxonomic character. Bull. Brit. Orn. Club 89:27–29.

Harrison, C. J. O. 1976. The syrinx of the Southern Scrub-robin *Drymodes brunneipygia*. Emu 76:154.

Harrison, C. J. O., and S. A. Parker. 1965. The behavioural affinities of the Blue Wrens of the genus *Malurus*. Emu 65:103–113.

Harrison, L. 1915. Mallophaga from *Apteryx*, and their significance; with a note on the genus *Rallicola*. Parasitology 8:88–100.

Harrison, L. 1916a. Bird parasites and bird phylogeny. Bull. Brit. Orn. Club 36:49–52.

Harrison, L. 1916b. Bird-parasites and bird-phylogeny. Ibis 58:254–263.

Hartert, E. 1892. Catalogue of the birds in the British Museum. Vol. 16. Brit. Mus., London.

Hartert, E. 1903. Die Vögel der Paläarktischen Fauna. Vol. 1 (in parts). R. Friedlander, Berlin.

Hartert, E. 1910. Die Vögel der Paläarktischen Fauna. R. Friedlander, Berlin.

Hartl, D. L., and D. E. Dykhuizen. 1985. The neutral theory and the molecular basis of preadaptation. Pp. 107–124 *in* Population genetics and molecular evolution. T. Ohta and K. Aoki, eds. Japan Soc. Press, Tokyo, and Springer-Verlag, Berlin.

Hartl, D. L., D. E. Dykhuizen, and A. M. Dean. 1985. Limits of adaptation: the evolution of selective neutrality. Genetics 111:655–674.

Harvey, P. H., and R. M. Zammuto. 1985. Patterns of mortality and age at first reproduction in natural populations of mammals. Nature 315:319–320.

Haseltine, W. A. 1983. Ultraviolet light repair and mutagenesis revisited. Cell 33:13–17.

Hatch, D. E. 1970. Energy conserving and heat dissipating mechanisms of the turkey vulture. Auk 87:111–124.

Hatch, F. T., and J. A. Mazrimas. 1970. Satellite DNAs in the kangaroo rat. Biochem. Biophys. Acta 224:291–294.

Hatch, F. T., and J. A. Mazrimas. 1974. Fractionation and characterization of satellite DNAs of the kangaroo rat (*Dipodomys ordii*). Nucl. Acids Res. 1:559–575.

Hatch, F. T., A. J. Bodner, J. A. Mazrimas, and D. H. Moore II. 1976. Satellite DNA and cytogenetic evolution. DNA quantity, satellite DNA and karyotypic variations in kangaroo rats (Genus *Dipodomys*). Chromosoma 58:155–168.

Hawke, J. P., A. C. McWorther, A. G. Steigerwalt, and D. J. Brenner. 1981. Int. J. Syst. Bacteriol. 31:396–400.

Hayes, D. E., and J. Ringis. 1973. Seafloor spreading in the Tasman Sea. Nature 243:454–458.

Hayes, F. M., E. H. Lilly, R. L. Ratliff, D. A. Smith, and D. L. Williams. 1970. Thermal transitions in mixtures of polydeoxyribonucleotides. Biopolymers 9:1105–1117.

Hecht, M. K., and J. L. Edwards. 1977. The methodology of phylogenetic inference above the species level. Pp. 3–51 *in* Major patterns in vertebrate evolution. M. K. Hecht, P. C. Goody, and B. M. Hecht, eds. Plenum Press, New York.

Heimerdinger, M. A., and P. L. Ames. 1967. Variation in the sternal notches of suboscine passeriform birds. Postilla 105:1–44.

Heinroth, O. 1911. Beiträge zur Biologie namentlich Ethologie und Psychologie der Anatiden. Proc. 5th Intl. Orn. Congr. 589–702.

Heinroth, O., and M. Heinroth. 1921–26. Die Vögel Mitteleuropas. Vol. 1. Hugo Bermühler, Berlin. 339 pp.

Hellmayr, C. E. 1927. Catalogue of birds of the Americas. Part 5. Field Mus. Nat. Hist., Publ. 242, Zool. Ser., No. 13, Chicago.

Hellmayr, C. E. 1935. Catalogue of birds of the Americas. Part 8. Field Mus. Nat. Hist., Publ. 347, Zool. Ser., No. 13, Chicago.

Hellmayr, C. E. 1936. Catalogue of birds of the Americas. Part 9. Field Mus. Nat. Hist., Publ. 365, Zool. Ser., No. 13, Chicago.

Hellmayr, C. E. 1937. Catalogue of birds of the Americas. Part 10. Field Mus. Nat. Hist., Publ. 381, Zool. Ser., No. 13, Chicago.

Hellmayr, C. E. 1938. Catalogue of birds of the Americas. Part 11. Field Mus. Nat. Hist., Publ. 430, Zool. Ser., No. 13, Chicago.

Hellmayr, C. E., and B. Conover. 1949. Catalogue of the birds of the Americas. Part 1, No. 4. Field Mus. Nat. Hist., Publ. 634, Zool. Ser. No. 13, Chicago.

Helm-Bychowski, K. M., and A. C. Wilson. 1986. Rates of nuclear DNA evolution in pheasant-like birds: evidence from restriction maps. Proc. Natl. Acad. Sci. USA 83:688–692.

Hendrickson, H. T. 1969. A comparative study of the egg white proteins of some species of the avian order Gruiformes. Ibis 111:80–91.

Henley, C., A. Feduccia, and D. P. Costello. 1978. Oscine spermatozoa: a light and electron microscopy study. Condor 80:41–48.

Hennig, W. 1950. Grundzüge einer Theorie der Phylogenetischen Systematik. Deutscher Zentralverlag, Berlin.

Hennig, W. 1966. Phylogenetic systematics. Univ. Illinois Press, Urbana. 263 pp.

Hennig, W., and P. M. B. Walker. 1970. Variations in the DNA from two rodent families (Cricetidae and Muridae). Nature 225:915–919.

Hershey, A. D., and M. Chase. 1952. Independent functions of viral protein and nucleic acid in growth of bacteriophage. J. Gen. Physiol. 36:39–56.

Hertwig, O. 1885. Das Problem der Befruchtung und der Isotropie des Eies, eine Theorie der Vererbung. Jenaische Zeitschr. für Med. und Naturwissenschaft 18:276–318.

Hewett-Emmett, D., P. J. Venta, and R. E. Tashian. 1982. Features of gene structure, organization, and expression that are providing unique insights into molecular evolution and systematics. Pp. 357–405 *in* Macromolecular sequences in systematic and evolutionary biology. M. Goodman, ed. Plenum Press, New York.

Hilder, V. A., G. A. Dawson, and M. T. Vlad. 1983. Ribosomal 5S genes in relation to C-value in amphibians. Nucleic Acids Res. 11:2381–2390.

Hinegardner, R. 1968. Evolution of cellular DNA content in teleost fishes. Amer. Nat. 102:517–523.

Hinegardner, R. 1974a. Cellular DNA content of the mollusca. Comp. Biochem. Physiol. 47A:447–460.

Hinegardner, R. 1974b. Cellular DNA content of the echinodermata. Comp. Biochem. Physiol. 49B:219–226.

Hinegardner, R. 1976. Evolution of genome size. Pp. 179–199 *in* Molecular evolution. F. J. Ayala, ed. Sinauer Assoc., Sunderland, Mass.

Hinegardner, R., and D. E. Rosen. 1972. Cellular DNA content and the evolution of teleost fishes. Amer. Nat. 106:621–644.

Ho, C. Y.-K., E. M. Prager, A. C. Wilson, D. T. Osuga, and R. E. Feeney. 1976. Penguin evolution: protein comparisons demonstrate phylogenetic relationship to flying aquatic birds. J. Mol. Evol. 8:271–282.

Hofer, H. 1945. Untersuchungen über den Bau des Vogelschädels, besonders über den der Spechte und Steisshühner. Zool. Jahrb., Abt. Anat. 68:127.

Hofer, H. 1955. Neuere Untersuchungen zur Kopfmorphologie der Vögel. Pp. 104–137 *in* Proc. 11th Intl. Orn. Congr. A. Portmann and E. Sutter, eds. Birkhauser Verlag, Basel and Stuttgart.

Holland, P. W. H., and B. L. M. Hogan. 1986. Phylogenetic distribution of Antennapedia-like homoeo boxes. Nature 321:251–253.

Holliday, R. 1987. The inheritance of epigenetic defects. Science 238:163–170.

Holliday, R. 1989. A different kind of inheritance. Sci. Amer. 260:60–73.

Holloway, J. D. 1979. A survey of the Lepidoptera, biogeography and ecology of New Caledonia. W. Junk, The Hague.

Holman, J. A. 1961. Osteology of living and fossil New World quails (Aves, Galliformes). Bull. Florida State Mus. Biol. Sci. 6:131–233.

Holman, J. A. 1964. Osteology of gallinaceous birds. Quart. J. Florida Acad. Sci. 27:230–252.

Holmes, R. T., and F. A. Pitelka. 1964. Breeding behavior and taxonomic relationships of the curlew sandpiper. Auk 81:362–379.

Holmgren, N. 1955. Studies on the phylogeny of birds. Acta Zool. 36:243–328.

Holyoak, D. T. 1973. Comments on taxonomy and relationships in the parrot subfamilies Nestorinae, Loriinae and Platycercinae. Emu 73:157–176.

Homberger, D. G. 1980. Funktionell-Morphologische Untersuchungen zur Radiation der Ernährungs- und Trinkmethoden der Papageien (Psittaci). Bonn. Zool. Monogr. 13:1–192.

Honacki, J. H., K. E. Kinman, and J. W. Koeppl, eds. 1982. Mammal species of the world. Assoc. Syst. Coll., Lawrence, Kansas.

Hopkins, G. H. E. 1942. The Mallophaga as an aid to the classification of birds. Ibis 84:94–106.

Hopkins, G. H. E. 1949. Some factors which have modified the phylogenetic relationship between parasite and host in the Mallophaga. Proc. Linnean Soc. London 161:37–39.

Hori, H., B.-L. Lim, and S. Osawa. 1985. Evolution of green plants as deduced from 5S rRNA sequences. Proc. Natl. Acad. Sci. USA 82:820–823.

Houde, P. 1986. Ostrich ancestors found in the northern hemisphere suggest new hypothesis of ratite origins. Nature 324:563–565.

Houde, P. 1988. Paleognathous birds from the early Tertiary of the Northern Hemisphere. Nuttall Orn. Club, Cambridge, Mass.

Howard, H. 1950. Fossil evidence of avian evolution. Ibis 92:1–21.

Howard, H. 1955. A new wading bird from the Eocene of Patagonia. Amer. Mus. Novit. 1710:1–25.

Howard, H. 1964a. Fossil Anseriformes. Pp. 233–326 *in* The waterfowl of the world, vol. 4. J. Delacour, ed. Country Life, Ltd., London.

Howard, H. 1964b. A species of the "pigmy goose," *Anabernicula*, from the Oregon Pleistocene, with a discussion of the genus. Amer. Mus. Novit. 2200. 14 pp.

Howell, T. R., and G. A. Bartholomew. 1962. Temperature regulation in the Red-tailed Tropic Bird and the Red-footed Booby. Condor 64:6–18.

Howell, T. R., and G. A. Bartholomew. 1969. Experiments on nesting behavior of the Red-tailed Tropicbird, *Phaethon rubricauda*. Condor 71:113–119.

Hoyer, B. H., and R. B. Roberts. 1967. Studies of nucleic acid interactions using DNA-agar. Pp. 425–479 *in* Molecular genetics, pt. II. H. Taylor, ed. Academic Press, New York.

Hoyer, B. H., B. J. McCarthy, and E. T. Bolton. 1964. A molecular approach in the systematics of higher organisms. Science 144:959–967.

Hoyer, B. H., N. W. van de Velde, M. Goodman, and R. B. Roberts. 1972. Examination of hominoid evolution by DNA sequence homology. J. Hum. Evol. 1:645–649.

Hoyer, B. H., N. R. Rice, and N. W. van de Velde. 1973. Sonication of DNA to produce fragments suitable for reassociation experiments. Carnegie Inst. Wash. Yearbook 72:214–217.

Hudson, G. E. 1937. Studies on the muscles of the pelvic appendage in birds. Amer. Midl. Nat. 18:1–108.

Hudson, G. E. 1948. Studies on the muscles of the pelvic appendage in birds. II: The heterogeneous order Falconiformes. Amer. Midl. Nat. 39:102–127.

Hudson, G. E., and P. J. Lanzillotti. 1964. Muscles of the pectoral limb in Galliform birds. Amer. Midl. Nat. 71:1–113.

Hudson, G. E., P. J. Lanzillotti, and G. D. Edwards. 1959. Muscles of the pelvic limb in Galliform birds. Amer. Midl. Nat. 61:1–67.

Hudson, G. E., R. A. Parker, J. Van den Berge, and P. J. Lanzillotti. 1966. A numerical analysis of the modifications of the appendicular muscles in various genera of gallinaceous birds. Amer. Midl. Nat. 76:1–73.

Hudson, G. E., K. M. Hoff, J. Van den Berge, and E. C. Trivette. 1969. A numerical study of the wing and leg muscles of Lari and Alcae. Ibis 111:459–524.

Hudson, P. J. 1985. Population parameters for the Atlantic Alcidae. Pp. 233–261 *in* The Atlantic Alcidae. D. N. Nettleship and T. R. Birkhead, eds. Academic Press, London.

Hudspeth, M. E. S., W. E. Timberlake, and R. B. Goldberg. 1977. DNA sequence organization in the water mold *Achlya*. Proc. Nat. Acad. Sci., USA, 74:4332–4336.

Hüe, F., and R.-D. Etchécopar. 1957. Les Ptéroclidides. L'Oiseau R.F.O. 27:35–58.

Hull, D. L. 1970. Contemporary systematic philosophies. Ann. Rev. Ecol. Syst. 1:19–54.

Hull, D. L. 1988. Science as a process. Univ. of Chicago Press, Chicago.

Hulselmans, J. L. J. 1962. The comparative myology of the pelvic limb of *Afropavo congensis* Chapin 1936. Bull. Soc. Roy. Zool. Anvers 26:25–61.

Humphrey, P. S. 1958. Classification and systematic position of the eiders. Condor 60:129–135.

Humphrey, P. S., and K. C. Parkes. 1963. Plumages and systematics of the whistling heron (*Syrigma sibilatrix*). Pp. 84–90 *in* Proc. 13th Intl. Orn. Congr., Amer. Orn. Union.

Hunt, J. A., and H. A. Carson. 1983. Evolutionary relationships of four species of Hawaiian Drosophila as measured by DNA reassociation. Genetics 104:353–364.

Hunt, J. A., T. J. Hall, and R. J. Britten. 1981. Evolutionary distances in Hawaiian Drosophila measured by DNA reassociation. J. Mol. Evol. 17:361–367.

Husain, K. Z. 1958. Subdivisions and zoogeography of the genus *Treron* (green fruit-pigeons). Ibis 100:334–348.

Hutchinson, J., R. K. J. Narayan, and H. Rees. 1980. Constraints on the composition of supplementary DNA. Chromosoma 78:137–145.

Huxley, T. H. 1867. On the classification of birds; and on the taxonomic value of the modifications of certain of the cranial bones observable in that class. Proc. Zool. Soc. London 1867:415–472.

Huxley, T. H. 1868. On the classification and distribution of the Alectoromorphae and Heteromorphae. Proc. Zool. Soc. London 1868:294–319.

Hwu, H. R., J. W. Roberts, E. H. Davidson, and R. J. Britten. 1986. Insertion and/or deletion of many repeated DNA sequences in human and higher ape evolution. Proc. Natl. Acad. Sci. USA 83:3875–3879.

Illiger, J. K. W. 1811. Prodromus systematis Mammalium et Avium. 301 pp. C. Salfeld, Berlin.

Ingold, J. L., J. C. Vaughn, S. I. Guttman, and L. R. Maxson. 1989. Phylogeny of the cranes (Aves: Gruidae) as deduced from DNA-DNA hybridization and albumin micro-complement fixation analyses. Auk 106:595–602.

Irwin, M. R. 1932. Dissimilarities between antigenic properties of red blood cells of dove hybrid and parental genera. Proc. Soc. Exp. Biol. Med. New York 29:850–851.

Isenberg, I. 1979. Histones. Ann. Rev. Biochem. 48:159–191.

Jackson, I. J., P. Schofield, and B. Hogan. 1985. A mouse homoeo box gene is expressed during embryogenesis and in adult kidney. Nature 317:745–748.

Jacob, F., and J. Monod. 1961. Genetic regulatory mechanisms in the synthesis of proteins. J. Mol. Biol. 3:318–356.

Jacob, J. 1978. Uropygial gland secretions and feather waxes. Pp. 165–211 *in* Chemical Zoology. Academic Press, New York.

Jacob, J., and H. Hoerschelmann. 1985. Klassifizierung der Flamingos (Phoenicopteriformes) durch vergleichende Analyse von Bürzeldrüsensekreten. Z. Zool. Syst. Evolut.-forsch. 23:49–58.

Jacobs, H. T., J. W. Posakony, J. W. Grula, J. W. Roberts, J.-H. Xin, R. J. Britten, and E. H. Davidson. 1983. Mitochondrial DNA sequences in the nuclear genome of *Strongylocentrotus purpuratus*. J. Mol. Biol. 165:609–632.

Jannett, F. J., Jr. 1975. "Hip glands" of *Microtus pennsylvanicus* and *M. longicaudus* (Rodentia: Muridae), voles "without" hip glands. Syst. Zool. 24:171–175.

Jantzen, H. 1973. Change of genome expression during development of *Acanthamoeba castellanii*. Arch. Mikrobiol. 91:163–178.

Jeffreys, A. J., and R. A. Flavell. 1977. The rabbit β-globin gene contains a large insert in the coding sequence. Cell 12:1097–1108.

Jehl, J. R., Jr. 1968a. Relationships in the Charadrii (shorebirds): a taxonomic study based on color patterns of the downy young. Mem. San Diego Soc. Natur. Hist. 3: 1–54.

Jehl, J. R., Jr. 1968b. The systematic position of the surfbird, *Aphriza virgata*. Condor 70:206–210.

Jeikowski, H. 1974. Der Übergang von der diastataxischen zur eutaxischen Flügelfederanordnung bei *Halcyon*. J. für Orn. 115:152–180.

Jelinek, W. R., and C. W. Schmid. 1982. Repetitive sequences in eukaryotic DNA and their expression. Ann. Rev. Biochem. 51:813–844.

Jenkin, P. M. 1957. The filter-feeding and food of flamingos (Phoenicopteri). Trans. Roy. Soc. London, Phil. Ser. B, 240:401–493.

Johnsgard, P. A. 1960a. Pair-formation mechanisms in *Anas* (Anatidae) and related genera. Ibis 102:616–618.

Johnsgard, P. A. 1960b. Comparative behavior of the Anatidae and its evolutionary implications. Wildfowl Trust, 11th Ann. Rep. (1958–59):31–45.

Johnsgard, P. A. 1960c. A quantitative study of sexual behavior of mallards and black ducks. Wilson Bull. 72:135–155.

Johnsgard, P. A. 1960d. Hybridization in the Anatidae and its taxonomic implications. Condor 62:25–33.

Johnsgard, P. A. 1960e. Classification and evolutionary relationships of the sea ducks. Condor 62:426–433.

Johnsgard, P. A. 1960f. The systematic position of the ringed teal. Bull. Brit. Orn. Club 80:165–167.

Johnsgard, P. A. 1961a. The taxonomy of the Anatidae—A behavioral analysis. Ibis 103a:71–85.

Johnsgard, P. A. 1961b. The systematic position of the marbled teal. Bull. Brit. Orn. Club 81:37–43.

Johnsgard, P. A. 1961c. The sexual behavior and systematic position of the hooded merganser. Wilson Bull. 73:227–236.

Johnsgard, P. A. 1961d. Tracheal anatomy of the Anatidae and its taxonomic significance. Wildfowl Trust, 12th Ann. Rep. (1959–60):58–69.

Johnsgard, P. A. 1961e. Breeding biology of the magpie goose. Wildfowl Trust, 12th Ann. Rep. (1959–60):92–103.

Johnsgard, P. A. 1961f. Evolutionary relationships among the North American mallards. Auk 78:3–43.

Johnsgard, P. A. 1962. Evolutionary trends in the behaviour and morphology of the Anatidae. Wildfowl Trust, 13th Ann. Rep. (1960–61):130–148.

Johnsgard, P. A. 1963. Behavioral isolation mechanisms in the family Anatidae. Proc. 13th Intl. Orn. Congr. 531–543.

Johnsgard, P. A. 1964. Comparative behavior and relationships of the eiders. Condor 66:113–129.

Johnsgard, P. A. 1965a. Observations on some aberrant Australian Anatidae. Wildfowl Trust, 16th Ann. Rep. (1963–64):73–83.

Johnsgard, P. A. 1965b. Handbook of waterfowl behavior. Cornell Univ. Press, Ithaca, New York.

Johnsgard, P. A. 1966a. Behavior of the Australian musk duck and blue-billed duck. Auk 83:98–110.

Johnsgard, P. A. 1966b. The biology and relationships of the torrent duck. Wildfowl Trust, 17th Ann. Rep. (1964–65):66–74.

Johnsgard, P. A. 1967. Observations on the behaviour and relationships of the white-backed duck and the stiff-tailed ducks. Wildfowl Trust, 18th Ann. Rep. (1965–66):98–107.

Johnsgard, P. A. 1968a. Some putative mandarin duck hybrids. Bull. Brit. Orn. Club 88:140–148.

Johnsgard, P. A. 1968b. Waterfowl: their biology and natural history. Univ. of Nebraska Press, Lincoln.

Johnsgard, P. A. 1970. A summary of intergeneric New World quail hybrids, and a new intergeneric hybrid combination. Condor 72:85–88.

Johnsgard, P. A. 1971. Experimental hybridization of the New World quail (Odontophorinae). Auk 88:264–275.

Johnsgard, P. A. 1973. Grouse and quails of North America. Univ. of Nebraska Press, Lincoln.

Johnsgard, P. A. 1983. Cranes of the world. Indiana Univ. Press, Bloomington.

Johnsgard, P. A. 1986. The pheasants of the world. Oxford Univ. Press, New York.

Johnson, N. K., R. M. Zink, and J. A. Marten. 1988. Genetic evidence for relationships in the avian family Vireonidae. Condor 90:428–445.

Johnson, N. K., J. A. Marten, and C. J. Ralph. 1989. Genetic evidence for the origin and relationships of Hawaiian honeycreepers (Aves: Fringillidae). Condor 91:379–396.

Johnston, D. W. 1988. A morphological atlas of the avian uropygial gland. Bull. Brit. Mus. Nat. Hist. (Zool.) 54(5):199–259.

Johnston, R. F. 1961. The genera of American ground doves. Auk 78:372–378.

Johnston, R. F. 1962. The taxonomy of pigeons. Condor 64:69–74.

Jollie, M. 1953. Are the Falconiformes a monophyletic group? Ibis 95:369–371.

Jollie, M. 1976. A contribution to the morphology and phylogeny of the Falconiformes. Part 1. Evol. Theory 1:285–298.

Jollie, M. 1977a. A contribution to the morphology and phylogeny of the Falconiformes. Part 2. Evol. Theory 2:115–208.

Jollie, M. 1977b. A contribution to the morphology and phylogeny of the Falconiformes. Part 3. Evol. Theory 2:209–300.

Jollie, M. 1977c. A contribution to the morphology and phylogeny of the Falconiformes. Part 4. Evol. Theory 3:1–141.

Jones, K. W. 1970. Chromosomal and nuclear location of mouse satellite DNA in individual cells. Nature 225:912–915.

Jordan, R. A., and R. W. Brosemer. 1974. Characterization of DNA from bee species. J. Insect Physiol. 20:2513–2520.

Judin, K. A. 1965. Phylogeny and classification of Charadriiformes [in Russian]. Fauna USSR, Aves, Ser. 1,2(1), n.s. 91. Acad. of Sci., Moscow and Leningrad.

Judson, H. F. 1979. The Eighth Day of Creation. Simon and Schuster, New York.

Kahl, M. P. 1963. Thermoregulation in the wood stork, with special reference to the role of the legs. Physiol. Zool. 36:141–151.

Kahl, M. P. 1964. Food ecology of the wood stork (*Mycteria americana*) in Florida. Ecol. Monogr. 34:97–117.

Kahl, M. P. 1966a. Comparative ethology of the Ciconiidae. Part 1. The Marabou Stork, *Leptoptilos crumeniferus* (Lesson). Behaviour 27:76–106.

Kahl, M. P. 1966b. A contribution to the ecology and reproductive biology of the marabou stork (*Leptoptilos crumeniferus*) in East Africa. J. Zool. (London) 148:289–311.

Kahl, M. P. 1967a. Behavioural reactions to hyperthermia in *Scopus umbretta* and *Balaeniceps rex*. Ostrich 38:27–30.

Kahl, M. P. 1967b. Observations on the behaviour of the Hamerkop *Scopus umbretta* in Uganda. Ibis 109:25–32.

Kahl, M. P. 1971. Spread-wing postures and their possible functions in the Ciconiidae. Auk 88:715–722.

Kahl, M. P. 1979. Family Ciconiidae. Pp. 245–252 *in* Check-list of birds of the world. Vol. 1, second edition. E. Mayr and G. W. Cottrell, eds. Mus. Comp. Zool., Cambridge, Mass.

Kahl, M. P., and L. J. Peacock. 1963. The bill-snap reflex: a feeding mechanism in the American wood stork. Nature 199:505–506.

Kaneda, M., I. Kato, N. Tominga, K. Titani, and K. Narita. 1969. The amino acid sequence of quail lysozyme. J. Biochem. 66:747–749.

Kaplan, N. O. 1965. Evolution of dehydrogenases. Pp. 243–277 *in* Evolving genes and proteins. V. Bryson and H. J. Vogel, eds. Academic Press, New York.

Kato, I., W. J. Kohr, and M. J. Laskowski, Jr. 1978. Evolution of avian ovomucoids. Pp. 197–206 *in* Regulatory proteolytic enzymes and their inhibitors, vol. 47. S. Magnusson, M. Ottesen, B. Foltman, K. Dana, and H. Neurath, eds. Pergamon Press, Oxford.

Kaup, J. J. 1859. Monograph of the Strigidae. Trans. Zool. Soc. London 4:201–260.

Kawaguchi, Y., H. Honda, J. Taniguchi-Morimura, and S. Iwasaki. 1989. The codon CUG is read as serine in an asporogenic yeast *Candida cylindracea*. Nature 341:164–166.

Kear, J. 1973. The Magpie Goose *Anseranas semipalmata* in captivity. Intl. Zoo Yearbook 13:28–32.

Kedrova, O. S., N. S. Vladychenskaya, and A. S. Antonov. 1983. A comparison of the Alligator Gar genome with genomes of certain other fishes. Molec. Biol. 17:307–314. Transl. from Molekulyarnaya Biol. 17:383–391. Plenum, New York.

Keith, S., C. W. Benson, and M. P. S. Irwin. 1970. The genus *Sarothrura* (Aves, Rallidae). Bull. Amer. Mus. Nat. Hist. 143:1–84.

Keler, St. von. 1957. Über die Deszendenz und die Differenzierung der Mallophagen. Z. Parasitenkunde 18:55–160.

Kemp, A. C. 1979. A review of the hornbills: biology and radiation. Living Bird 17:105–135.

Kemp, A. C., and T. M. Crowe. 1985. The systematics and zoogeography of Afrotropical hornbills (Aves: Bucerotidae). Pp. 279–324 *in* Proc. Intl. Symp. African Vertebrates. K.-L. Schuchmann, ed. Museum Koenig, Bonn.

Kennell, D. E. 1971. Principles and practices of nucleic acid hybridization. Progress Nucleic Acid Res. Mol. Biol. 11:259–301.

Kessel, B., and D. G. Gibson. 1978. Status and distribution of Alaska birds. Studies Avian Biol. No. 1. Cooper Orn. Soc.

Kessler, L. G., and J. C. Avise. 1984. Systematic relationships among waterfowl (Anatidae) inferred from restriction endonuclease analysis of mitochondrial DNA. Syst. Zool. 33:370–380.

Kessler, L. G., and J. C. Avise. 1985a. A comparative description of mitochondrial DNA differentiation in selected avian and other vertebrate genera. Mol. Biol. Evol. 2:109–125.

Kessler, L. G., and J. C. Avise. 1985b. Microgeographic lineage analysis by mitochondrial genotype: variation in the cotton rat (*Sigmodon hispidus*). Evolution 39:831–837.

Keyserling, A. G. von, and J. H. Blasius. 1839. Ueber ein zoologisches Kennzeichnen der Ordnung der Sperlingsarten-oder Singvögel. Wiegmann Archiv. für Naturgesch. Pt. 1:332–334.

Khoury, G., and P. Gruss. 1983. Enhancer elements. Cell 33:313–314.

Kiltie, R. A., and J. W. Fitzpatrick. 1984. Reproduction and social organization of the Black-capped Donacobius (*Donacobius atricapillus*) in southeastern Peru. Auk 101:804–811.

Kimura, M. 1968. Evolutionary rate at the molecular level. Nature 217:624–626.

Kimura, M. 1983a. The neutral theory of molecular evolution. Pp. 208–233 *in* Evolution of genes and proteins. M. Nei and R. K. Koehn, eds. Sinauer Assoc., Sunderland, Mass.

Kimura, M. 1983b. The neutral theory of molecular evolution. Cambridge Univ. Press.

King, J. L., and T. H. Jukes. 1969. Non-Darwinian evolution: random fixation for selectively neutral alleles. Science 164:788–798.

Kingsbury, D. T. 1967. Deoxyribonucleic acid homologies among species of the genus *Neisseria*. J. Bacteriol. 94:870–874.

Kingsley, J. S. 1885. Psittaci. Pp. 349–367 *in* The standard natural history, vol. 4, birds. J. S. Kingsley, ed. S. E. Cassino, Boston.

Kinsky, F. C. 1960. The yearly cycle of the northern blue penguin (*Eudyptula minor novaehollandiae*) in the Wellington harbour area. Dominion Mus. (New Zealand) Record 3:145–218.

Kitto, G. B., and A. C. Wilson. 1966. Evolution of malate dehydrogenase in birds. Science 153:1408–1410.

Klein, W. H., T. L. Thomas, C. Lai, R. H. Scheller, R. J. Britten, and E. H. Davidson. 1978. Characteristics of individual repetitive sequence families in the sea urchin genome studied with cloned repeats. Cell 14:889–900.

Klug, A., and P. J. G. Butler. 1983. The structure of nucleosomes and chromatin. Pp. 1–41 *in* Genes: structure and expression. A.M. Kroon, ed. John Wiley and Sons, New York.

Klug, A., J. T. Finch, and T. J. Richmond. 1985. Crystallographic structure of the octamer histone core of the nucleosome. Science 229:1109–1110.

Knowlton, F. H. 1909. Birds of the world. R. Ridgway, ed. Henry Holt and Co., New York. 873 pp.

Kohne, D. E. 1970. Evolution of higher-organism DNA. Quart. Rev. Biophysics 33:327–375.

Kohne, D. E. 1971. Pattern of DNA acquisition during evolution. Carnegie Inst. Wash. Yearbook 69:485–488.

Kohne, D. E., and R. J. Britten. 1971. Hydroxyapatite techniques for nucleic acid reassociation. Pp. 500–512 *in* Procedures in nucleic acid research, vol. 2. G. L. Cantoni and D. R. Davies, eds. Harper and Row, New York.

Kohne, D. E., J. A. Chiscon, and B. H. Hoyer. 1971. Nucleotide sequence change in non-repeated DNA during evolution. Carnegie Inst. Wash. Yearbook 69:488–501.

Kohne, D. E., J. A. Chiscon, and B. H. Hoyer. 1972. Evolution of primate DNA sequences. J. Human Evol. 1:627–644.

Kohne, D. E., S. A. Levison, and M. J. Byers. 1977. Room temperature method for increasing the rate of DNA reassociation by many thousand-fold: the phenol emulsion reassociation technique. Biochemistry 16:5329–5341.

Kolata, G. 1980. Genes in pieces. Science 207:392–393.

Kolata, G. 1982. New theory of hormones proposed. Science 215:1383–1284.

Kollar, E. J., and C. Fisher. 1980. Tooth induction in chick epithelium: expression of quiescent genes for enamel synthesis. Science 207:993–995.

König, C. 1982. Zur systematischen Stellung der Neuweltgeier (Cathartidae). J. für Orn. 123:259–267.

Koop, B. F., D. A. Tagle, M. Goodman, and J. L. Slightom. 1989. A molecular view of primate phylogeny and important systematic and evolutionary questions. Mol. Biol. Evol. 6:580–612.

Kornberg, R. D. 1974. Chromatin structure: a repeating unit of histones and DNA. Science 184:868–871.

Kossel, A. 1885. Zur Kenntniss der Eiweisfaulniss. I. Ueber die Bildung des Indols und Skatols. Ber. Deutsche Chem. Gesell. 18:79–81.

Kossel, A. 1893. Ueber die Nucleinsäure. Arch. Anat. Physiol. 157:380.

Kossel, A., and A. Neumann. 1893. Ueber das Thymin, ein Spaltungsprodukt der Nuclein-säure. Ber. Deutsche Chem. Gesell. 26:2753–2756.

Kossel, A., and A. Neumann. 1894. Darstellung und Spaltungsprodukts der Nucleinsäure (Adenylsäure). Ber. Deutsche Chem. Gesell. 27:2221.

Krajewski, C. 1989. Phylogenetic relationships among cranes (Gruiformes: Gruidae) based on DNA hybridization. Auk 106:603–617.

Krampitz, G., K. Kreisler, and R. Faust. 1974. Über die Aminosäuren-Zusammensetzung morphologischer Eischalen-Fraktionen von Ratitae. Biomineralisation Forschungsber. 7:1–13.

Krassowsky, S. K. 1936. Zur morphologie der Spechtschädel. Anat. Anz. 82:112–128.

Krieger, D. T. 1983. Brain peptides: what, where, and why? Science 222:975–985.

Kroon, A. M. editor. 1983. Genes: structure and expression. Vol. 7, Horizons in biochem-istry and biophysics. E. Quagliariello and F. Palmieri, series eds. Wiley and Sons, New York.

Küchler, W. 1936. Anatomische Untersuchungen an *Phytotoma rara* Mol. J. für Orn. 84:352–362.

Kükenthal, W., and T. Krumbach, editors. 1927–34. Aves. *In* Handbuch der Zoologie. Vol. 7, part 2. Walter de Gruyter, Berlin. 899 pp. [Also see E. Stresemann 1934.]

Kurochkin, E. N. 1968. Locomotion and morphology of the pelvic extremities in swimming and diving birds. [In Russian.] Acad. Sci. Ukranian SSR, Inst. Zool., Moscow.

Kurochkin, E. N. 1988. Cretaceous Mongolian birds and their significance for the study of bird phylogeny. English summary *in* Fossil reptiles and birds of Mongolia. Trans. Joint Soviet-Mongolian Paleo. Exped. 34:108. Nauka, Moscow.

Kuroda, Nagahisa. 1954. On the classification and phylogeny of the order Tubinares, particu-larly the shearwaters (*Puffinus*), with special considerations on their osteology and habit differentiation. Herold Co. Ltd., Tokyo.

Kuroda, Nagamichi. 1967. Psittacidae of the world [in Japanese]. Orn. Soc. Japan, Tokyo.

Kurtzman, C. P., H. J. Phaff, and S. A. Meyer. 1983. Nucleic acid relatedness among yeasts. Pp. 139–166 *in* Yeast genetics: fundamental and applied aspects. J. F. T. Spencer, D. M. Spencer, and A. R. W. Smith, eds. Springer Verlag, New York.

Lack, D. 1956a. The species of *Apus*. Ibis 98:34–62.

Lack, D. 1956b. A review of the genera and nesting habits of swifts. Auk 73:1–32.

Lack, D. 1966. Population studies of birds. Oxford Press, London.

Lack, D. 1968. Ecological adaptations for breeding in birds. Methuen, London.

Laerm, J., J. C. Avise, J. C. Patton, and R. A. Lansman. 1982. Genetic determination of the status of an endangered pocket gopher in Georgia. J. Wildlife Manag. 46:513–518.

Lahue, R. S., K. G. Au, and P. Modrich. 1989. DNA mismatch correction in a defined system. Science 245:160–164.

Laird, C. D. 1971. Chromatid structure: relationship between DNA content and nucleotide sequence diversity. Chromosoma 32:378–406.

Laird, C. D., and B. J. McCarthy. 1968. Magnitude of interspecific nucleotide sequence variability in *Drosophila*. Genetics 60:303–322.

Laird, C. D., B. L. McConaughy, and B. J. McCarthy. 1969. Rate of fixation of nucleotide substitutions in evolution. Nature 224:149–154.

Lake, J. A. 1986. In defense of bacterial phylogeny. Nature 321:657–658.

Lake, J. A. 1988. Origin of the eukaryotic nucleus determined by rate-invariant analysis of rRNA sequences. Nature 331:184–186.

Lamb, T., and J. C. Avise. 1986. Directional introgression of mitochondrial DNA in a hybrid population of tree frogs: the influence of mating behavior. Proc. Natl. Acad. Sci. USA 83:2526–2530.

Lambrecht, K. 1933. Handbuch der Palaeornithologie. Gebrüder Borntraeger, Berlin. 1024 pp.

Landsmann, J., E. S. Dennis, T. J. V. Higgins, C. A. Appleby, A. A. Kortt, and W. J. Peacock. 1986. Common evolutionary origin of legume and non-legume plant haemoglobins. Nature 324:166–168.

Lang, C. 1956. Das cranium der Ratiten mit besonderer Berücksichtigung von *Struthio camelus*. Z. Wiss. Zool. 159:165–224.

Lanham, U. N. 1947. Notes on the phylogeny of the Pelecaniformes. Auk 64:65–70.

Lansman, R. A., R. O. Shade, J. F. Shapira, and J. C. Avise. 1981. The use of restriction endonucleases to measure mitochondrial DNA sequence relatedness in natural populations. III. Techniques and potential applications. J. Mol. Evol. 17:214–226.

Lansman, R. A., J. C. Avise, C. F. Aquadro, J. F. Shapira, and S. W. Daniel. 1983a. Extensive genetic variation in mitochondrial DNA's among geographic populations of the deer mouse, *Peromyscus maniculatus*. Evolution 37:1–16.

Lansman, R. A., J. C. Avise, and M. D. Huettel. 1983b. Critical experimental test of the possibility of "paternal leakage" of mitochondrial DNA. Proc. Natl. Acad. Sci. USA 80:1969–1971.

Lanyon, S. M. 1985. Molecular perspective on higher-level relationships in the Tyrannoidea (Aves). Syst. Zool. 34:404–418.

Lanyon, S. M., and W. E. Lanyon. 1989. The systematic position of the plantcutters, *Phytotoma*. Auk 106:422–432.

Lanyon, S. M., and R. M. Zink. 1987. Genetic variation in piciform birds: monophyly and generic and familial relationships. Auk 104:724–732.

Lanyon, W. E. 1984. A phylogeny of the kingbirds and their allies. Amer. Mus. Novit. 2797:1–28.

Lanyon, W. E. 1985. A phylogeny of the myiarchine flycatchers. Pp. 361–380 *in* Neotropical Ornithology. P. A. Buckley, M. S. Foster, E. S. Morton, R. S. Ridgely, and F. G. Buckley, eds. Ornith. Monogr. No. 36, Amer. Orn. Union, Washington, D.C.

Lanyon, W. E. 1986. A phylogeny of the thirty-three genera in the *Empidonax* assemblage of tyrant flycatchers. Amer. Mus. Novit. 2846:1–64.

Lanyon, W. E. 1988a. A phylogeny of the thirty-two genera in the *Elaenia* assemblage of tyrant flycatchers. Amer. Mus. Novit. 2914:1–57.

Lanyon, W. E. 1988b. The phylogenetic affinities of the flycatcher genera *Myiobius* Darwin and *Terenotriccus* Ridgway. Amer. Mus. Novit. 2915:1–11.

Lanyon, W. E. 1988c. A phylogeny of the flatbill and tody-tyrant assemblage of tyrant flycatchers. Amer. Mus. Novit. 2923:1–41.

Larson, S. 1955. Tertiary and Pleistocene differentiation in the suborder Charadrii [in Swedish, English summary]. Var Fagelvärld 14:65–78.

Larson, S. 1957. The suborder Charadrii in Arctic and boreal areas during the Tertiary and Pleistocene: a zoogeographic study. Acta Vertebratica 1:1–84.

LaRue, J. M., and J. C. Speck. 1970. Turkey egg white lysozyme. Preparation of the crystalline enzyme and investigation of the amino acid sequence. J. Biol. Chem. 245:1985–1991.

Latham, J. 1802. General Synopsis of Birds, supplement II. Leigh, Sotheby and Son, London.

Lausen, B. 1987. Zur Beurteilung der Rekonstruktion phylogenetischer Stammbaume anhand genetischer Distanzen. Doctoral diss., Univ. of Dortmund.

Lausen, B., and P. O. Degens. 1986. Variance estimation and the reconstruction of phylogenies. Pp. 306–314 in Die Klassifikation und ihr Umfeld. P. O. Degens, H.-J. Hermes, and O. Opitz, eds. Indeks Verlag, Frankfurt.

Lausen, B., and W. Vach. 1986. Estimation, graphical representation and judgement of evolutionary trees in expert systems. Pp. 61–74 in Expert systems in statistics. R. Haux, ed. Fischer, Stuttgart.

Layard, E. L. 1867. The birds of South Africa. Longman, Green, New York.

Layard, E. L., and R. B. Sharpe. 1875–84. The birds of South Africa (revised). B. Quaritch, London.

Lee, C. H., and J. G. Wetmur. 1972a. Independence of length and temperature effects on the rate of helix formation between complementary ribopolymers. Biopolymers 11:549–561.

Lee, C. H., and J. G. Wetmur. 1972b. On the kinetics of helix formation between complementary ribohomopolymers and deoxyribohomopolymers. Biopolymers 11:1485–1487.

Lee, G., P. A. Arscott, V. A. Bloomfield, and D. F. Evans. 1989. Scanning tunnelling microscopy of nucleic acids. Science 244:475–477.

Lee, Y. C., and R. Montgomery. 1962. Glycopeptides from ovalbumin: the structure of the peptide chains. Arch. Biochem. Biophys. 97:9–17.

Lee, Y. M., D. J. Friedman, and F. J. Ayala. 1985. Superoxide dismutase: an evolutionary puzzle. Proc. Natl. Acad. Sci. USA 82:824–828.

Lemmrich, W. 1931. Der Skleralring der Vögel. Jena Z. Naturwiss. 65:513–586.

Lesson, R.-P. 1830. Catalogue des oiseaux recueillis dans l'expédition de La Coquille, avec la description de plusiers genres nouveaux et d'un grand nombre d'espèces inédites. Pp. 614–735 in Voyage autor du monde . . . sur la Corvette . . . La Coquille . . . 1822, 1823, 1824 et 1825. Zoologie, by R.-P. Lesson and P. Garnot, vol. 1, pp. 1–735. Arthus Bertrand, Libraire-Editeur.

Lesson, R.-P. 1831. Traité d'ornithologie. Vol. 1. Levrault, Paris.

Levene, P. A. 1909. Über die Hefenucleosäure. Biochem. Zeitschr. 17:120–131.

Levene, P. A., and W. A. Jacobs. 1912. On the structure of thymus nucleic acid. J. Biol. Chem. 12:411–420.

Levin, D. A., and A. C. Wilson. 1976. Rates of evolution in seed plants: net increase in diversity of chromosome numbers and species numbers through time. Proc. Natl. Acad. Sci. USA 73:2086–2090.

Lewin, B. 1980. Gene expression. 2nd. ed. Vol. 2. Eukaryotic chromosomes. John Wiley and Sons, New York.

Lewin, B. 1983. Genes. John Wiley and Sons, New York.

Lewin, R. 1986. Proposal to sequence the human genome stirs debate. Science 232:1598–1600.

Lewin, R. 1987. When does homology mean something else? Science 237:1570.

Lewis, J. 1989. Genes and segmentation. Nature 341:382–383.

Lewontin, R. C., and J. L. Hubby. 1966. A molecular approach to the study of genic heterozygosity in natural populations, II. Amount of variation and degree of heterozygosity in natural populations of Drosophila pseudoobscura. Genetics 54:595–609.

L'Herminier, F. J. 1827. Recherches sur l'appareil sternal des oiseaux, considéré sous le double rapport de l'ostéologie et de la myologie; suivies d'un essai sur la distribution de cette classe de vertébrés, basée sur la considération du sternum et de ses annexes. Ann. (Mem.) Soc. Linnéenne Paris 6:3–39.

Li, W.-H. 1983. Evolution of duplicate genes and pseudogenes. Pp. 14–37 *in* Evolution of genes and proteins. M. Nei and R. K. Koehn, eds. Sinauer Assoc., Sunderland, Mass.

Ligon, J. D. 1967. Relationships of the cathartid vultures. Occ. Papers, Univ. Michigan Mus. Zool. No. 651. 26 pp.

Lill, A. 1985. Lyrebird. Pp. 332–333 *in* A dictionary of birds. B. Campbell and E. Lack, eds. T. and A. D. Poyser, Calton, England.

Lilljeborg, W. 1866. Outline of a systematic review of the class of birds. Proc. Zool. Soc. London 1866:5–20.

Lima-de-Faria, A., U. Arnason, B. Widegren, J. Essen-Möller, M. Isaksson, E. Olsson, and H. Jaworska. 1984. Conservation of repetitive DNA sequences in deer species studied by Southern blot transfer. J. Mol. Evol. 20:17–24.

Linnaeus, C. 1758. Systema naturae per regna tria naturae. 10th edition, rev. 2 vols. L. Salmii, Holmiae.

Lint, K. C. 1960. Notes on breeding Andean Condors at San Diego Zoo. Intl. Zoo Yearbook 2:82.

Livesey, B. C. 1986. A phylogenetic analysis of Recent anseriform genera using morphological characters. Auk 103:737–754.

Lloyd, J. A., A. N. Lamb, and S. S. Potter. 1987. Phylogenetic screening of the human genome: identification of differentially hybridizing repetitive sequence families. Mol. Biol. Evol. 4:85–98.

Löhrl, H. 1964. Verhaltensmerkmale der Gattungen *Parus* (Meisen), *Aegithalos* (Schwanzmeisen), *Sitta* (Kleiber), *Tichodroma* (Mauerläufer) und *Certhia* (Baumläufer). J. für Orn. 105:153–181.

Löhrl, H. 1985. Nuthatch. Pp. 400–401 *in* A dictionary of birds. B. Campbell and E. Lack, eds. T. and A. D. Poyser, Calton, England.

Loomis, L. M. 1918. Expedition of the California Academy of Sciences to the Galapagos Islands, 1905–1906. XII. A review of the albatrosses, petrels, and diving petrels. Proc. Calif. Acad. Sci. Ser. 4, 2, pt. 2 (12).

Loomis, L. M. 1923. On the classification of the albatrosses, petrels, and diving petrels. Auk 40:596–602.

Lorenz, K. 1941. Vergleichende Bewegungstudien an Anatinen. J. für Orn. 89(Suppl. 3):194–293.

Low, G. C. 1931. The literature of the Charadriiformes from 1894–1928. 2nd ed. H. F. and G. Witherby, London.

Lowe, P. R. 1914. A note on the common ringed plover of the British Isles (*Charadrius hiaticola major* Seebohm), and on coloration as a factor in generic differentiation. Ibis 56:395–403.

Lowe, P. R. 1915a. Coloration as a factor in family and generic differentiation. Ibis 57:320–346.

Lowe, P. R. 1915b. Studies on the Charadriiformes. I. On the systematic position of the ruff (*Machetes pugnax*) and the semipalmated sandpiper (*Ereunetes pusillus*), together with a review of some osteological characters which differentiate the Eroliinae (dunlin group) from the Tringinae (redshank group). Ibis 57:609–616.

Lowe, P. R. 1915c. Studies on the Charadriiformes. II. On the osteology of the Chatham Island Snipe (*Coenocorypha pusilla* Buller). Ibis 57:690–716.

Lowe, P. R. 1916a. Studies on the Charadriiformes. III. Notes in relation to the systematic position of the sheath-bills (Chionididae). Ibis 58:122–155.

Lowe, P. R. 1916b. Studies on the Charadriiformes. IV. An additional note on the sheath-bills: some points in the osteology of the skull of an embryo of *Chionarchus "minor"* from Kerguelen. V. Some notes on the crab-plover (*Dromas ardeola* Paykull). Ibis 58:313–337.

Lowe, P. R. 1922. On the significance of certain characters in some charadriine genera, with a provisional classification of the order Charadriiformes. Ibis 64:475–495.

Lowe, P. R. 1923. Notes on the systematic position of *Ortyxelus*, together with some remarks on the relationships of the Turnicomorphs and the position of the seed-snipe (Thinocoridae) and Sandgrouse. Ibis 65:276–299.

Lowe, P. R. 1924a. On the anatomy and systematic position of the Madagascan bird *Mesites* (*Mesoenas*), with a preliminary note on the osteology of *Monias*. Proc. Zool. Soc. London 1924:1131–1152.

Lowe, P. R. 1924b. On the presence of broadbills in Africa. Proc. Zool. Soc. London 1924:279–291.

Lowe, P. R. 1925a. On the classification of the tubinares or petrels. Proc. Zool. Soc. London 1925 (1926):1433–1443.

Lowe, P. R. 1925b. (1) On the systematic position of the Jacanidae (Jacanás) with some notes on a hitherto unconsidered anatomical character of apparent taxonomic value. (2) A preliminary note on the classification of the Charadriiformes (Limicolae and Laro-Limicolae) based on this character, *viz.*, the morphology of the quadrato-tympanic articulation. Ibis 67:132–147.

Lowe, P. R. 1926. More notes on the quadrate as a factor in avian classification. Ibis 68:152–188.

Lowe, P. R. 1927. On the anatomy and systematic position of *Aechmorhynchus cancellatus* (Gmelin), together with some notes on the genera *Bartramia* and *Mesoscolopax;* the subfamily Limosinae; and the pterylosis of *Scolopax*. Ibis 69:114–132.

Lowe, P. R. 1928. Studies and observations bearing on the phylogeny of the ostrich and its allies. Proc. Zool. Soc. London 1928:185–247.

Lowe, P. R. 1930. On the relationships of the Aepyornithes to the other Struthiones as revealed by a study of the pelvis of *Mullerornis*. Ibis 72:470–490.

Lowe, P. R. 1931a. On the relations of the Gruimorphae to the Charadriimorphae and Rallimorphae, with special reference to the taxonomic position of Rostratulidae, Jacanidae, and Burhinidae (Oedicnemidae *olim*); with a suggested new order (Telmatomorphae). Ibis 73:491–534.

Lowe, P. R. 1931b. An anatomical review of the "waders" (Telmatomorphae), with special reference to the families, subfamilies, and genera within the suborders Limicolae, Grui-Limicolae and Lari-Limicolae. Ibis 73:712–771.

Lowe, P. R. 1931c. On the anatomy of *Pseudocalyptomena* and the occurrence of broadbills (Eurylaemidae) in Africa. Proc. Zool. Soc. London 100:445–461.

Lowe, P. R. 1933a. On the primitive characters of the penguins, and their bearing on the phylogeny of birds. Proc. Zool. Soc. London 1933:483–541.

Lowe, P. R. 1933b. Structural diversity in charadriine genera correlated with differences in colour-pattern. Ibis 75:112–129.

Lowe, P. R. 1935. On the relationship of the Struthiones to the dinosaurs and to the rest of the avian class, with special reference to the position of *Archaeopteryx*. Ibis 77:398–432.

Lowe, P. R. 1938. Some preliminary notes on the anatomy and the systematic position of *Afropavo congensis* Chapin. Proc. 9th Intl. Orn. Congr. 219–230. J. Delacour, ed. Rouen.

Lowe, P. R. 1939a. Some additional notes on Miocene penguins in relation to their origin and systematics. Ibis 81:281–296.

Lowe, P. R. 1939b. On the systematic position of the swifts (suborder Cypseli) and hummingbirds (suborder Trochili), with special reference to their relation to the order Passeriformes. Trans. Zool. Soc. London 24:307–348.

Lowe, P. R. 1942. Some additional anatomical factors bearing on the phylogeny of the Struthiones. Proc. Zool. Soc. London, Ser. 8, 112:1–20.

Lowe, P. R. 1943. Some notes on the anatomical differences obtaining between the Cuculidae and the Musophagidae, with special reference to the specialization of the oesophagus in *Cuculus canorus* Linnaeus. Ibis 85:490–515.

Lowe, P. R. 1944. An analysis of the characters of *Archaeopteryx* and *Archaeornis*. Were they reptiles or birds? Ibis 86:517–543.

Lowe, P. R. 1946. On the systematic position of the woodpeckers (Pici), honey-guides (*Indicator*), hoopoes and others. Ibis 88:103–127.

Lowe, P. R. 1948. What are the Coraciiformes? Ibis 90:572–582.

Lucas, F. A. 1886. The affinities of *Chaetura*. Auk 3:444–451.

Lucas, F. A. 1888. Notes on the osteology of the thrushes, Miminae, and wrens. Proc. U.S. Natl. Mus. 11:173–180.

Lucas, F. A. 1889. The main divisions of the swifts. Auk 6:8–13.

Lucas, F. A. 1894. Notes on the anatomy and affinities of the Coerebidae and other American birds. Proc. U.S. Natl. Mus. 17:299–312.

Lucas, F. A. 1895a. Additional characters of the Macropterygidae. Auk 12:155–157.

Lucas, F. A. 1895b. The deep plantars in the Trochilidae. Ibis 37:298–299.

Lucas, F. A. 1895c. Untitled. Ibis 37:300.

Lucas, F. A. 1899. Notes on the myology of *Hemiprocne zonaris*. Auk 16:77–78.

Lutz, H. 1942. Beitrag zur Stammesgeschichte der Ratiten. Vergleich zwischen Emu-Embryo und entsprechendem Carinatenstadium. Rev. Suisse Zool. 49:299–399.

Lydekker, R. 1891. Catalogue of the fossil birds in the British Museum (Nat. Hist.). Trustees, British Mus., London.

Lynch, J. F., and P. L. Ames. 1970. A new hybrid hummingbird, *Archilochus alexandri* × *Selasphorus sasin*. Condor 72:209–212.

Lyon, B. E., and P. L. Fogden. 1989. Breeding biology of the Sunbittern (*Eurypyga helias*) in Costa Rica. Auk 106:503–507.

Macdonald, J. D. 1973. Birds of Australia. A. H. and A. W. Reed, Sydney.

Macgregor, H. C., H. Horner, C. A. Owen, and I. Parker. 1973. Observations on centromeric heterochromatin and satellite DNA in salamanders of the genus *Plethodon*. Chromosoma 43:329–348.

Mack, A. L., F. B. Gill, R. Colburn, and C. Spolsky. 1986. Mitochondrial DNA: a source of genetic markers for studies of similar passerine bird species. Auk 103:676–681.

MacLean, G. L. 1967. Die systematische Stellung der Flughühner (Pteroclidae). J. für Orn. 108:203–217.

MacLean, G. L. 1969a. The sandgrouse—doves or plovers? J. für Orn. 110:104–107.

MacLean, G. L. 1969b. A study of seedsnipe in southern South America. Living Bird 8:33–80.

Madsen, C. S., K. P. McHugh, and S. R. de Kloet. 1988. A partial classification of waterfowl (Anatidae) based on single-copy DNA. Auk 105:452–459.

Mainardi, D. 1957a. Affinitá sierologiche e filogenesi nei fringillidi. Arch. Zool. Ital. 42:152–159.

Mainardi, D. 1957b. L'evoluzione nei fringillidi. Concordanza fra una "mappa sierologica" e i dati dell'analisi eletroforetica delle emoglobine. Ist. Lombardo, Rend. Sci. 92:180–186.

Mainardi, D. 1957c. Sulle possibilitá di ricavare una serie filetica da dati sull'affinitá sierologica. Ricerche sui fringillidi. Ist. Lombardo, Rend. Sci. 91:565–569.

Mainardi, D. 1958a. Immunology and chromatography in taxonomic studies on gallinaceous birds. Nature 182:1388–1389.

Mainardi, D. 1958b. La filogenesi nei fringillidi basata sui rapporti immunologici. Ist. Lombardo, Rend. Sci. B92:336–356.

Mainardi, D. 1959. Immunological distances among some gallinaceous birds. Nature 184:913–914.

Mainardi, D. 1960a. Dati di ibridologia per una sistematica dei fringillidi. Ist. Lombardo, Rend. Sci. B94:43–62.

Mainardi, D. 1960b. Immunological relationships of the peacock *Pavo cristatus*. Misc. Rep. Yamashina's Inst. Orn. Zool. 2 (15):130–132.

Mainardi, D. 1961. Distanze immunologiche tra alcune famiglie di passeriformi. Ist. Lombardo, Rend. Sci. B95:117–122.

Mainardi, D. 1962a. Immunological data on the phylogenetic relationships and taxonomic position of flamingos (Phoenicopteridae). Ibis 104:426–428.

Mainardi, D. 1962b. Studio immunogenetico sulla posizione tassonomica di *Melopsittacus undulatus*. Riv. Ital. Orn., Ser. 2, 32:136–140.

Mainardi, D. 1963. Immunological distances and phylogenetic relationships in birds. Proc. 13th Intl. Orn. Congr. 103–114.

Mainardi, D., and A. M. Taibel. 1962. Studio immunogenetico sulle parentele filogenetiche nell'ordine dei galliformi. Ist. Lombardo, Rend. Sci. B96:131–140.

Mandel, M., and J. Marmur. 1968. Use of ultraviolet absorbance-temperature profile for determining the guanine plus cytosine content of DNA. Pp. 195–206 *in* Methods in Enzymology, vol. 12B, L. Grossman and K. Moldave, eds. Academic Press, New York.

Manfredi Romanini, M. G. 1985. The nuclear content of desoxyribonucleic acid and some problems of mammalian phylogenesis. Mammalia 49:369–385.

Manger Cats-Kuenen, C. S. W. 1961. Casque and bill of *Rhinoplax vigil* (Forst.) in connection with the architecture of the skull. Konikl. Nederland. Verh. Akad. Wetensch., Afd. Natuurkunde 53(3):1–51.

Maniatis, T., S. Goodbourn, and J. A. Fischer. 1987. Regulation of inducible and tissue-specific gene expression. Science 236:1237–1245.

Maniatis, T., and R. Reed. 1987. The role of small nuclear ribonucleoprotein particles in pre-mRNA splicing. Nature 325:673–678.

Manning, G. S. 1983. Breathing and bending fluctuations in DNA modeled by an open-base-pair kink coupled to axial compression. Biopolymers 22:689–729.

Manning, J. E., C. W. Schmid, and N. Davidson. 1975. Interspersion of repetitive and nonrepetitive DNA sequences in the *Drosophila melanogaster* genome. Cell 4:141–155.

Marchalonis, J. J. 1977. Immunity in evolution. Harvard Univ. Press, Cambridge, Mass.

Marchant, S. 1964. Ovenbird. Pp. 571–574 *in* A new dictionary of birds, A. L. Thomson, ed. Nelson, London.

Margoliash, E. 1963. Primary structure and evolution of cytochrome *c*. Proc. Natl. Acad. Sci. USA 50:672–679.

Margoliash, E., S. B. Needleman, and J. W. Stewart. 1963. A comparison of the amino acid sequences of the cytochromes *c* of several vertebrates. Acta Chem. Scand. 17, Suppl. 1:250–256.

Marks, J., C. W. Schmid, and V. M. Sarich. 1989. DNA hybridization as a guide to phylogeny: relations of the Hominoidea. J. Hum. Evol. 17:769–786.

Marler, P. 1957. Specific distinctiveness in the communication signals of birds. Behaviour 11:13–19.

Marmur, J. 1961. A procedure for the isolation of deoxyribonucleic acid from microorganisms. J. Mol. Biol. 3:208–218.

Marmur, J., and P. Doty. 1959. Heterogeneity in deoxyribonucleic acids. Dependence on composition of the configurational stability of deoxyribonucleic acids. Nature 183:1427–1429.

Marmur, J., and P. Doty. 1961. Thermal denaturation of nucleic acids. J. Mol. Biol. 3:585–596.

Marmur, J., and P. Doty. 1962. Determination of the base composition of deoxyribonucleic acid from its thermal denaturation temperature. J. Mol. Biol. 5:109–118.

Marmur, J., S. Falkow, and M. Mandel. 1963a. New approaches to bacterial taxonomy. Ann. Rev. Microbiol. 17:329–372.

Marmur, J., R. Rownd, and C. L. Schildkraut. 1963b. Denaturation and renaturation of deoxyribonucleic acid. Pp. 231–300 *in* Progress in Nucleic Acid Research, vol. 1, J. N. Davidson and W. E. Cohn, eds. Academic Press, New York.

Marples, B. J. 1952. Early tertiary penguins of New Zealand. New Zeal. Geol. Surv., Paleon. Bull. 20:1–66.

Marples, B. J. 1953. Fossil penguins from the mid-Tertiary of Seymour Island. Falkland Is. Dependencies Surv., Sci. Rep. No. 5.

Marshall, C. H. T., and G. F. L. Marshall. 1871. A monograph of the Capitonidae or scansorial barbets. Publ. by authors, London.

Marshall, J. T., Jr. 1966. Relationships of certain owls around the Pacific. Bull. Siam Soc., Natur. Hist. 21:235–242.

Marshall, J. T., Jr. 1967. Parallel variations in North and Middle America screech-owls. Western Found. Vert. Zool. Monogr. No. 1.

Martin, L. D. 1985. Archeopteryx. Pp. 20–22 *in* A dictionary of birds. B. Campbell and E. Lack, eds. T. and A. D. Poyser, Calton, England.

Martin, R. 1904. Die vergleichende Osteologie der Columbiformes unter besonderer Berücksichtigung von *Didunculus strigirostris*. Zool. Jahrb. Syst. 20:167–352.

Martin, W. 1836. Untitled. Proc. Zool. Soc. London 1836(4):29–32.

Martinson, H. G. 1973a. The nucleic acid–hydroxylapatite interaction. I. Stabilization of native double-stranded deoxyribonucleic acid by hydroxylapatite. Biochemistry 12:139–145.

Martinson, H. G. 1973b. The nucleic acid–hydroxylapatite interaction. II. Phase transitions in the deoxyribonucleic acid–hydroxylapatite system. Biochemistry 12:145–150.

Martinson, H. G. 1973c. The basis of fractionation of single-stranded nucleic acids on hydroxylapatite. Biochemistry 12:2731–2736.

Martinson, H. G. 1973d. Role of the double-stranded nucleic acid backbone configuration in adsorption interactions. Biochemistry 12:2737–2746.

Martinson, H. G., and E. B. Wagenaar. 1974. Thermal elution chromatography and the resolution of nucleic acids on hydroxylapatite. Analytical Biochem. 61:144–154.

Marx, J. L. 1978. Gene structure: more surprising developments. Science 199:517–518.

Marx, J. L. 1985. A crystalline view of protein-DNA binding. Science 229:846–848.

Marx, J. L. 1988. Homeobox linked to gene control. Science 242:1008–1009.

Marx, J. L. 1989. Two cultures find common ground. Science 244:652–653.

Mathews, B. W. 1988. No code for recognition. Nature 335:294–295.

Mathews, G. M. 1910. On some necessary alterations in the nomenclature of birds. Novitates Zool. 17:492–503.

Mathews, G. M. 1927–30. Systema avium australasianarum. Brit. Orn. Union, London.

Mathews, G. M. 1934. A check-list of the order of Procellariiformes. Novitates Zool. 39:151–206.

Mathews, G. M. 1935. Addition to a check-list of the order Procellariiformes. Novitates Zool. 39:253.

Mathews, G. M. 1936a. Key to the order Procellariiformes. Emu 36:40–48.

Mathews, G. M. 1936b. Remarks on procellarian and puffinine petrels. Emu 36:91–98, 273–280.

Mathews, G. M. 1937. *Pachyptila*, or the prions. Emu 37:280–284.

Mathews, G. M. 1948. Systematic notes on petrels. Bull. Brit. Orn. Club 68:155–170.

Mathews, G. M., and T. Iredale. 1921. Orders Casuarii to Columbae. A manual of the birds of Australia, vol. 1. H. F. and G. Witherby, London. 279 pp.

Maurer, D. R., and R. J. Raikow. 1981. Appendicular myology, phylogeny, and classification of the avian order Coraciiformes (including Trogoniformes). Annals Carnegie Mus. 50:417–434.

Maxam, A. M., and W. Gilbert. 1980. Sequencing end-labelled DNA with base-specific chemical cleavages. Pp. 499–560 *in* Methods in enzymology, vol. 65. Academic Press, New York.

Maxson, L. R. 1984. Molecular probes of phylogeny and biogeography in toads of the widespread genus *Bufo*. Mol. Biol. Evol. 1:345–356.

May, W. 1962. Die Morphologie des Chondrocraniums und Osteocraniums eines Waldkauzembryos (*Strix aluco* L.). Z. Wiss. Zool. 166:134–202.

Mayr, E. 1941. List of New Guinea birds. Amer. Mus. Nat. Hist., New York.

Mayr, E. 1942. Systematics and the origin of species. Columbia Univ. Press, New York.

Mayr, E. 1944. Notes on some genera from the Southwest Pacific. Amer. Mus. Novit. 1269:1–8.

Mayr, E. 1945. The downy plumage of the Australian dabchick. Emu 44:231–233.

Mayr, E. 1955. Comments on some recent studies of song bird phylogeny. Wilson Bull. 67:33–44.

Mayr, E. 1957. Evolutionary aspects of host specificity among parasites of vertebrates. *In* Prem. Symp. sur la spécificité parasitaire des parasites de vertébrés. J. G. Baer, ed. Intl. Union Biol. Sci., Ser. B, No. 32.

Mayr, E. 1958. The sequence of songbird families. Condor 60:194–195.

Mayr, E. 1963. Comments on the taxonomic position of some Australian genera of songbirds. Emu 63:1–7.

Mayr, E. 1969. Principles of systematic zoology. McGraw-Hill, New York.

Mayr, E. 1979. Check-list of birds of the world. Vol. 8. M. A. Traylor, Jr., ed. Mus. Comp. Zool., Cambridge, Mass.

Mayr, E. 1981. Biological classification: toward a synthesis of opposing methodologies. Science 214:510–516.

Mayr, E., and D. Amadon. 1947. A review of the Dicaeidae. Amer. Mus. Novit. 1360:1–32.

Mayr, E., and D. Amadon. 1951. A classification of Recent birds. Amer. Mus. Novit. 1496:1–42.

Mayr, E., and G. W. Cottrell. 1986. Check-list of birds of the world. Vol. 11. Mus. Comp. Zool., Cambridge, Mass.

Mayr, E., and J. C. Greenway, Jr. 1956. Sequence of passerine families (Aves). Breviora 58:1–11.

Mayr, E., and J. C. Greenway, Jr. 1960. Check-list of birds of the world. Vol. 9. Mus. Comp. Zool., Cambridge, Mass.

Mayr, E., and J. C. Greenway, Jr. 1962. Check-list of birds of the world. Vol. 15. Mus. Comp. Zool., Cambridge, Mass.

Mayr, E., and R. A. Paynter, Jr. 1964. Check-list of birds of the world. Vol. 10. Mus. Comp. Zool., Cambridge, Mass.

Mayr, E., R. J. Andrew, and R. A. Hinde. 1956. Die systematische Stellung der Gattung *Fringilla*. J. für Orn. 97:258–273.

Mazrimas, J. A., and F. T. Hatch. 1972. A possible relationship between satellite DNA and the evolution of kangaroo rat species (genus *Dipodomys*). Nature New Biol. 240:102–105.

Mazrimas, J. A., and F. T. Hatch. 1977. Similarity of satellite DNA properties in the order Rodentia. Nucl. Acids Res. 4:3215–3227.

McCabe, R. A. 1954. Hybridization between the bob-white and scaled quail. Auk 71:293–297.

McCarthy, B. J., and E. T. Bolton. 1963. An approach to the measurement of genetic relatedness among organisms. Proc. Natl. Acad. Sci. USA 50:156–164.

McCarthy, B. J., and R. B. Church. 1970. The specificity of molecular hybridization reactions. Ann. Rev. Biochem. 39:131–150.

McCarty, M. 1985. The transforming principle. Norton, New York.

McClintock, B. 1952. Chromosome organization and gene expression. Cold Spring Harbor Symp. Quant. Biol. 16:13–47.

McClintock, B. 1965. The control of gene action in maize. Brookhaven Symp. Biol. 15:341–404.

McDowell, S. 1948. The bony palate of birds. Part I. The Palaeognathae. Auk 65:520–549.

McFarlane, R. W. 1963. The taxonomic significance of avian sperm. Proc. 13th Intl. Orn. Congr. 91–102.

McGill, A. R. 1970. Australian Warblers. Bird Observ. Club, Melbourne.

McGinnis, W., M. S. Levine, E. Hafen, E. Kuroiwa, and W. J. Gehring. 1984a. A conserved DNA sequence in homoetic genes of the *Drosophila* antennapedia and bithorax complexes. Nature 308:428–433.

McGinnis, W., A. L. Garber, J. Wirz, A. Kuroiwa, and W. J. Gehring. 1984b. A homologous protein-coding sequence in Drosophila homeotic genes and its conservation in other metazoans. Cell 37:403–408.

McGinnis, W., C. P. Hart, W. J. Gehring, and F. H. Ruddle. 1984c. Molecular cloning and chromosome mapping of a mouse DNA sequence homologous to homeotic genes of Drosophila. Cell 38:675–680.

McGowan, C. 1982. The wing musculature of the Brown Kiwi *Apteryx mantelli* and its bearing on ratite affinities. J. Zool. London 97:173–219.

McGowan, C. 1984. Evolutionary relationships of ratites and carinates: evidence from ontogeny of the tarsus. Nature 307:733–735.

McGowan, C. 1986. The wing musculature of the Weka (*Gallirallus australis*) a flightless rail endemic to New Zealand. J. Zool. London, Ser. A 210:305–346.

McIlhenny, E. A. 1937. Results of 1936 bird banding operations at Avery Island, Louisiana, with special references to sex ratios and hybrids. Bird Banding 8:117–121.

McKean, J. L. 1969. The brush tongue of Artamidae. Bull. Brit. Orn. Club 89:129–130.

McKenna, M. C. 1983. Holarctic landmass rearrangement, cosmic events, and Cenozoic terrestrial organisms. Ann. Missouri Botan. Garden 70:459–489.

McKitrick, M. C. 1985. Monophyly of the Tyrannidae (Aves): comparison of morphology and DNA. Syst. Zool. 34:35–45.

McLachlan, G. R., and R. Liversidge. 1978. Roberts Birds of South Africa. John Voelcker Bird Book Fund, Cape Town.

McReynolds, L., B. W. O'Malley, A. D. Nisbet, J. E. Fothergill, D. Givol, S. Fields, M. Robertson, and G. G. Brownlee. 1978. Sequence of chicken ovalbumin mRNA. Nature 273:723–728.

Meade-Waldo, E. G. B. 1896. Sand grouse breeding in captivity. Zoologist, 3rd Ser., 20:298–299.

Meade-Waldo, E. G. B. 1897. Sand grouse. Avicultural Mag. 3:171–180.

Meade-Waldo, E. G. B. 1906. Sandgrouse. Avicultural Mag. 12:219–222.

Meade-Waldo, E. G. B. 1922. Sand-grouse. Bull. Brit. Orn. Club 42:69–70.

Mebs, T. 1960. Untersuchungen über den Rhythmus der Schwingen und Schwanzmauser bei grossen Falken. J. für Orn. 101:175–194.

Mednikov, B. M. 1980. DNA × DNA hybridization in taxonomy. Pp. 447–476 in Biology Reviews (Physico-Chemical Aspects). Vol. 1. V. P. Skulachev, ed. Soviet Sci. Rev., Sect. D.

Mednikov, B. M., Y. S. Reshetnikov, and K. A. Savvaitova. 1977. Molecular DNA hybridization: an approach to disputable issues in fish taxonomy. Cybium 3e Série 1:111–119.

Mees, G. F. 1957. A systematic review of the Indo-Australian Zosteropidae (Part I). Zool. Verh. 35:1–204.

Mees, G. F. 1961. A systematic review of the Indo-Australian Zosteropidae (Part II). Zool. Verh. 50:1–168.

Mees, G. F. 1964. A revision of the Australian owls (Strigidae and Tytonidae). Zool. Verh. 65:3–62.

Mees, G. F. 1969. A systematic review of the Indo-Australian Zosteropidae (Part III). Zool. Verh. 102:1–390.

Meinertzhagen, R. 1964. Sandgrouse. Pp. 711–712 in A new dictionary of birds. A. L. Thomson, ed. Nelson, London.

Meise, W. 1963. Verhalten der straussartigen Vögel und Monophylie der Ratitae. Proc. 13th Intl. Orn. Congr. 115–125.

Meister, W. 1962. Histological structure of the long bones of penguins. Anat. Rec. 143:377–387.

Mendelssohn, H., and Y. Leshem. 1983. Observations on reproduction and growth of Old World vultures. Pp. 214–241 in Vulture biology and management. S. R. Wilbur and J. A. Jackson, eds. Univ. Calif. Press, Berkeley.

Menzbier, M. von. 1887. Vergleichende Osteologie der Pinguine in Anwendung zur Haupteintheilung der Vögel. Bull. Soc. Imp. Natur. Moscou 483–587.

Merrem, B. 1813. Tentamen systematis naturalis avium. Abh. Königel. (Preussische) Akad. Wiss. Berlin 1812–13 (1816) (Physikal.):237–259.

Meyer, T. E., M. A. Cusanovich, and M. D. Kamen. 1986. Evidence against use of bacterial amino acid sequence data for construction of all-inclusive phylogenetic trees. Proc. Natl. Acad. Sci. USA 83:217–220.

Meyer de Schauensee, R. 1966. The species of birds of South America. Acad. Nat. Sci. Phila., Livingston Publ. Co., Narberth, Penn.

Meyerowitz, E. M., and R. E. Pruitt. 1985. Arabidopsis thaliana and plant molecular genetics. Science 229:1214–1218.

Meyerriecks, A. J. 1960. Comparative breeding behavior of four species of North American herons. Nuttall Orn. Club Publ. No. 2, Cambridge, Mass.

Meyerriecks, A. J. 1966. Untitled. Auk 83:683–684.

Miescher, F. 1871. Ueber die chemische Zusammensetzung der Eiterzellen. Hoppe-Seyler's Med.-Chem. Untersuchungen 4:441–460.

Miescher, F. 1879. Die Histochemischen und Physiologischen Arbeiten. Vogel, Leipzig.

Mikhailov, K. E., and E. N. Kurochkin. 1988. The eggshells of Struthioniformes from the Palearctic and its position in the system of views on Ratitae evolution. English summary *in* Fossil reptiles and birds of Mongolia. Trans. Joint Soviet-Mongolian Paleo. Exped. 34:108–109. Nauka, Moscow.

Miklos, G. L. G., and A. C. Gill. 1982. Nucleotide sequences of highly repeated DNAs; compilation and comments. Genet. Res., Cambridge, 39:1–30.

Miksche, J. P., and Y. Hotta. 1973. DNA base composition and repetitious DNA in several conifers. Chromosoma 41:29–36.

Millener, P. R. 1988. Contributions to New Zealand's Late Quaternary avifauna. 1: *Pachyplichas*, a new genus of wren (Aves: Acanthisittidae), with two new species. J. Roy. Soc. New Zealand 18:383–406.

Miller, A. H. 1937. Structural modifications in the Hawaiian goose (*Nesochen sandvicensis*): a study in adaptive evolution. Univ. Calif. Publ. Zool. 42.

Miller, A. H. 1953. A fossil hoatzin from the Miocene of Colombia. Auk 70:484–489.

Miller, A. H. 1964. Mockingbird. Pp. 479–481 *in* A new dictionary of birds. A. L. Thomson, ed. Nelson, London.

Miller, A. H. 1965. The syringeal structure of the Asiatic owl *Phodilus*. Condor 67:536–538.

Miller, A. H., and H. I. Fisher. 1938. The pterylosis of the California condor. Condor 40:248–256.

Miller, A. H., and C. G. Sibley. 1941. A Miocene gull from Nebraska. Auk 58:563–566.

Miller, H. T., and R. E. Feeney. 1966. The physical and chemical properties of an immunologically cross-reacting protein from avian egg whites. Biochemistry 5:952–958.

Miller, S. J., and J. G. Wetmur. 1975. Physical properties of endonuclease S1 digestion products of DNA renaturation intermediates. Biopolymers 14:309–317.

Miller, W. DeW. 1912. A revision of the classification of the kingfishers. Bull. Amer. Mus. Nat. Hist. 31:239–311.

Miller, W. DeW. 1915. Notes on ptilosis, with special reference to the feathering of the wing. Bull. Amer. Mus. Nat. Hist. 34:129–140.

Miller, W. DeW. 1919. The deep plantar tendons in the puff-birds, jacamars and their allies. Auk 36:285–286.

Miller, W. DeW. 1920. The genera of ceryline kingfishers. Auk 37:422–429.

Miller, W. DeW. 1924a. Further notes on ptilosis. Bull. Amer. Mus. Nat. Hist. 50:305–331.

Miller, W. DeW. 1924b. Variations in the structure of the aftershaft and their taxonomic value. Amer. Mus. Novit. 140.

Milne-Edwards, A. 1867–71. Recherches anatomiques et paléontologiques pour servir à l'histoire des oiseaux fossiles de la France. 4 vols. V. Masson et Fils, Paris.

Milne-Edwards, A. 1878a. Remarques sur le genre *Mesites* et sur la place qu'il doit occuper dans la serie ornithologique. Ann. Sci. Natur., Ser. 6, 7(6). 13 pp.

Milne-Edwards, A. 1878b. Observations sur les affinités zoologiques du genre *Mesites*. C. R. Acad. Sci. (Paris) 86:1029–1031.

Milne-Edwards, A. 1878c. Observations sur les affinités zoologiques du genre *Phodilus* et description d'un nouveau genre de rapace nocturene. Mus. Hist. Nat. (Paris), Nouv. Arch., Ser. 2, 1:185–199.

Milne-Edwards, A., and A. Grandidier. 1879. Histoire naturelle des oiseaux. *In* Histoire physique, naturelle et politique de Madagascar. Vol. 12. A. Grandidier, ed. L'Imprimerie Nat., Paris.

Milon, P. 1952. Notes sur le genre *Coua*. L'Oiseau R.F.O. 22:75–90.

Mindell, D. P., and R. L. Honeycutt. 1989. Variability in transcribed regions of ribosomal DNA and early divergences in birds. Auk 106:539–548.

Mirsky, A. E., and H. Ris. 1949. Variable and constant components of chromosomes. Nature 163:666–667.

Mirsky, A. E., and H. Ris. 1951. The desoxyribonucleic acid content of animal cells and its evolutionary significance. J. Gen. Physiol. 34:451–462.

Mitchell, P. C. 1894. On the perforated flexor muscles in some birds. Proc. Zool. Soc. London 1894:495–498.

Mitchell, P. C. 1895. On the anatomy of *Chauna chavaria*. Proc. Zool. Soc. London 1895:350–358.

Mitchell, P. C. 1896a. On the intestinal tract of birds. Proc. Zool. Soc. London 1896:136–159.

Mitchell, P. C. 1896b. A contribution to the anatomy of the hoatzin (*Opisthocomus cristatus*). Proc. Zool. Soc. London 1896:618–628.

Mitchell, P. C. 1899. On so-called "quintocubitalism" in the wing of birds; with special reference to the Columbae, and notes on anatomy. J. Linnean Soc. London 27:210–236.

Mitchell, P. C. 1901a. On the intestinal tract of birds; with remarks on the valuation and nomenclature of zoological characters. Trans. Linnean Soc. London, 2nd Ser., Zool. 8:173–275.

Mitchell, P. C. 1901b. On the anatomy of gruiform birds; with special reference to the correlation of modifications. Proc. Zool. Soc. London 1901(1902)(2):629–655.

Mitchell, P. C. 1901c. On the anatomy of the kingfishers, with special reference to the conditions in the wing known as eutaxy and diastataxy. Ibis 43:97–123.

Mitchell, P. C. 1905. On the anatomy of limicoline birds; with special reference to the correlation of modifications. Proc. Zool. Soc. London 1905(2):155–169.

Mitchell, P. C. 1913. Observations on the anatomy of the shoebill (*Balaeniceps rex*) and allied birds. Proc. Zool. Soc. London 1913:644–703.

Mitchell, P. C. 1915. Anatomical notes on the gruiform birds *Aramus giganteus* Bonap., and *Rhinochetus kagu*. Proc. Zool. Soc. London 1915:413–423.

Mitchell, P. J., and R. Tjian. 1989. Transcriptional regulation in mammalian cells by sequence-specific DNA binding proteins. Science 245:371–378.

Mivart, St. G. 1877. On the axial skeleton of the Struthionidae. Trans. Zool. Soc. London 10:1–52.

Mivart, St. G. 1878. On the axial skeleton of the Pelecanidae. Trans. Zool. Soc. London 10:315–378.

Mivart, St. G. 1895. On the hyoid bone of certain parrots. Proc. Zool. Soc. London 1895:162–174.

Mivart, St. G. 1896a. On the hyoid bones of *Nestor meridionalis* and *Nanodes discolor*. Proc. Zool. Soc. London 1896:236–240.

Mivart, St. G. 1896b. A monograph of the lories, or brush-tongued parrots, composing the family Loriidae. R. H. Porter, London.

Miyamoto, M. M., J. L. Slightom, and M. Goodman. 1987. Phylogenetic relations of humans and African apes from DNA sequences in the psi eta-globin region. Science 238:369–373.

Miyazawa, Y., and C. A. Thomas, Jr. 1965. Nucleotide composition of short segments of DNA molecules. J. Mol. Biol. 11:223–237.

Mizuno, S., and H. C. Macgregor. 1974. Chromosomes, DNA sequences, and evolution in salamanders of the genus *Plethodon*. Chromosoma 48:239–296.

Mizuno, S., C. Andrews, and H. C. Macgregor. 1976. Interspecific "common" repetitive DNA sequences in salamanders of the genus *Plethodon*. Chromosoma 58:1–31.

Mlíkovsky, J. 1985. Towards a new classification of birds. Pp. 1145–1146 *in* Proc. 18th Intl. Orn. Congr. V. D. Ilyichev and V. M. Gavrilov, eds. Nauka, Moscow.

Moehring, P. H. G. 1752. Avium genera. G. G. Rump, Bremen.

Monroe, B. L., Jr. 1968. A distributional survey of the birds of Honduras. Orn. Monogr. No. 7. Amer. Orn. Union, Washington, D.C.

Moore, G. P., R. H. Scheller, E. H. Davidson, and R. J. Britten. 1978. Evolutionary change in the repetition frequency of sea urchin DNA sequences. Cell 15:649–660.

Moore, G. P., A. R. Moore, and L. I. Grossman. 1984. The frequency of matching sequences in DNA. J. Theor. Biol. 108:111–122.

Moreau, R. E. 1938. A contribution to the biology of the Musophagiformes, the so-called plantaineaters. Ibis 80:639–671.

Moreau, R. E. 1957. Variation in the western Zosteropidae (Aves). Bull. Brit. Mus. (Nat. Hist.) Zool. 4:311–433.

Moreau, R. E. 1958. Some aspects of the Musophagidae. Ibis 100:67–112; 238–270.

Moreau, R. E. 1964. Turaco. Pp. 842–844 *in* A new dictionary of birds. A. L. Thomson, ed. Nelson, London.

Moreau, R. E. 1966. The bird faunas of Africa and its islands. Academic Press, New York.

Moreau, R. E. 1967. Dust-bathing in Ploceidae? Ibis 109:445.

Morioka, H. 1967. Anatomy and relationships of thrushes, dippers, and wrens. Ph.D. diss., Univ. of Illinois, Urbana.

Moritz, C., and W. M. Brown. 1986. Tandem duplication of D-loop and ribosomal RNA sequences in lizard mitochondrial DNA. Science 233:1425–1427.

Morlion, M. 1964. Pterylography of the wing of the Ploceidae. Le Gerfaut 54:111–158.

Mourer-Chauviré, C., M. Hugueney, and P. Jonet. 1989. Découverte de passeriformes dans l'Oligocène supérieur de France. C. R. Acad. Sci. Paris 309(II):843–849.

Moynihan, M. 1955. Some aspects of reproductive behavior in the black-headed gull (*Larus ridibundus ridibundus* L.) and related species. Behaviour, Suppl. 4. 201 pp.

Moynihan, M. 1956. Notes on the behavior of some North American gulls. I. Aerial hostile behavior. Behaviour 10:126–178.

Moynihan, M. 1958a. Notes on the behavior of some North American gulls. II. Non-aerial hostile behavior of adults. Behaviour 12:95–182.

Moynihan, M. 1958b. Notes on the behavior of some North American gulls. III. Pairing behavior. Behaviour 13:112–130.

Moynihan, M. 1959a. Notes on the behavior of some North American gulls. IV. The ontogeny of hostile behavior and display patterns. Behaviour 14:214–239.

Moynihan, M. 1959b. A revision of the family Laridae (Aves). Amer. Mus. Novit. 1928:1–42.

Moynihan, M. 1962. Hostile and sexual behavior patterns of South American and Pacific Laridae. Behaviour, Suppl. 8, 365 pp.

Mudge, G. P. 1902. On the myology of the tongue of parrots, with a classification of the order, based upon the structure of the tongue. Trans. Zool. Soc. London 16:211–278.

Müller, J. P. 1845. Über die bisher unbekannten typischen Verscheidenheiten der Stimmorgane der Passerinen. Abh. Königl. (Preussische) Akad. Wiss. Berlin 1845. 1847:321–392, 405–406.

Müller, J. P. 1878. On certain variations in the vocal organs of the Passeres that have hitherto escaped notice. Transl. by J. Bell. A. H. Garrod, ed. Ray Soc., London. 74 pp., 7 pl.

Müller, P. L. S. 1776. Des ritters Carl von Linne. . . . Vollstandigen natursystems supplement- und register-band über alle sechs theile oder classer des thierreichs. G. N. Raspe, Nürnberg.

Murie, J. 1871. On the dermal and visceral structures of the kagu, sun-bittern, and boatbill. Trans. Zool. Soc. London 7:465–492.

Murie, J. 1872a. On the genus *Colius*, its structure and systematic position. Ibis 14:262–280.

Murie, J. 1872b. On the motmots and their affinities. Ibis 14:383–412.

Murie, J. 1872c. On the skeleton of *Todus*, with remarks as to its allies. Proc. Zool. Soc. London 1872:664–680.

Murie, J. 1873. On the Upupidae and their relationships. Ibis 15:181–211.

Murphy, R. C. 1935. Untitled. Proc. Linnaean Soc. New York 45–46:11–17.

Murphy, R. C. 1936. Oceanic birds of South America. Amer. Mus. Nat. Hist., New York. 2 vols.

Murphy, R. C., and F. Harper. 1921. A review of the diving petrels. Bull. Amer. Mus. Nat. Hist. 44:495–553.

Murray, M. G., D. L. Peters, and W. F. Thompson. 1981. Ancient repeated sequences in the pea and mung bean genomes and implications for genome evolution. J. Mol. Evol. 17:31–42.

Nagl, W. 1978. Endopolyploidy and polyteny in differentiation and evolution. Toward an understanding of quantitative and qualitative variation of nuclear DNA in ontogeny and phylogeny. North-Holland, Amsterdam.

Nei, M. 1975. Molecular population genetics and evolution. Frontiers of biology, vol. 40. A. Neuberger and E. L. Tatum, eds. North-Holland, Amsterdam.

Nei, M. 1987. Molecular evolutionary genetics. Columbia Univ. Press, New York.

Nei, M., F. Tajima, and Y. Tateno. 1983. Accuracy of estimated phylogenetic trees from molecular data. II. Gene frequency data. J. Mol. Evol. 19:153–170.

Nelson, G. J. 1973. Classification as an expression of phylogenetic relationships. Syst. Zool. 22:344–359.

Nelson, G. J., and N. Platnick. 1981. Systematics and biogeography. Columbia Univ. Press, New York.

Nelson, J. B. 1966. The breeding biology of the Gannet *Sula bassana* on the Bass Rock, Scotland. Ibis 108:584–626.

Nelson, J. 1967. Untitled. Auk 84:307–308.

Nelson, J. B. 1978. The Sulidae / gannets and boobies. Oxford Univ. Press.

Neunzig, R. 1928. Beiträge zur Kenntnis der Ploceiden. VII. Revision der Gattung *Steganura*. Zool. Anz. 78:177–190.

Neunzig, R. 1929. Zum Brutparasitismus der Viduinen. J. für Orn. 77:1–21.

Newton, A. 1868. Remarks on Prof. Huxley's proposed classification of birds. Ibis 10:85–96.

Newton, A. 1876. On the assignation of a type to Linnaean genera, with especial reference to the genus *Strix*. Ibis 18:94–105.

Newton, A. 1884. Ornithology. Pp. 1–50 *in* Encyclopaedia Britannica, 9th ed., vol. 18.

Newton, A. 1896. A dictionary of birds. Adam and Charles Black, London. 4 vols.

Newton, A., ed. 1871–74. Strigidae. Pp. 146–198 *in* William Yarrell's A history of British birds, vol. 1, 4th ed., rev. John Van Voorst, London.

Newton, A., and H. Gadow. 1893. A dictionary of birds. Vol. 1. Adam and Charles Black, London. (Also see Newton 1896.)

Nicholson, F. 1889. See Sundevall 1872.

Nicolai, J. 1961. Die Stimmen einiger Viduinen. J. für Orn. 102:213–214.

Nicolai, J. 1964. Der Brutparasitismus der Viduinae als ethologisches Problem. Z. für Tierpsych. 21:129–204.

Niethammer, J. 1964. Die Pigmentierung und das Farbmuster junger Haubentaucher (*Podiceps cristatus*). J. für Orn. 105:389–426.

Nitzsch, C. L. 1840. System der Pterylographie. E. Anton, Halle. 228 pp. Engl. trans. P. L. Sclater, ed., 1867, Ray Soc., London.

Nöhring, R. 1973. Erwin Stresemann. J. für Orn. 114:455–500.

Nolan, R. A., A. H. Brush, N. Arnheim, and A. C. Wilson. 1975. An inconsistency between protein resemblance and taxonomic resemblance: immunological comparison of diverse proteins from gallinaceous birds. Condor 77:154–159.

Nolan, V., Jr. 1978. The ecology and behavior of the Prairie Warbler (*Dendroica discolor*). Orn. Monogr. No. 26. Amer. Orn. Union, Washington, D.C.

Norton, I. O., and J. G. Sclater. 1979. A model for the evolution of the Indian Ocean and the breakup of Gondwanaland. J. Geophys. Res. 84:6803–6830.

Nuechterlein, G. L. 1981a. Variations and multiple functions of the advertising display of Western Grebes. Behaviour 76:289–317.

Nuechterlein, G. L. 1981b. Courtship behavior and reproductive isolation between Western Grebe morphs. Auk 98:335–349.

Nussinov, R. 1984. Strong doublet preferences in nucleotide sequences and DNA geometry. J. Mol. Evol. 20:111–119.

Nuttall, G. H. F. 1904. Blood immunity and blood relationships. Cambridge Univ. Press.

O'Donald, P. 1983. The Arctic Skua. Cambridge Univ. Press.

Ogilvie-Grant, W. R. 1889. On the genus *Turnix*. Ibis 31:446–475.

Ogilvie-Grant, W. R. 1892. Catalogue of the . . . Bucerotes and Trogones in the . . . British Museum. Vol. 17:347–502. Brit. Mus., London.

Ogilvie-Grant, W. R. 1893. Catalogue of the game birds . . . in the . . . British Museum. Vol. 22:1–585. Brit. Mus., London.

Ogilvie-Grant, W. R. 1898. Catalogue of the Steganopodes, Pygopodes, Alcae, and Impennes in . . . the British Museum. Vol. 26:329–653. Brit. Mus., London.

Ohama, T., T. Kumazaki, H. Hori, and S. Osawa. 1984. Evolution of multicellular animals as deduced from 5S rRNA sequences: a possible early emergence of the Mesozoa. Nucleic Acids Res. 12:5101–5108.

O'Hara, R. J. 1988. Diagrammatic classifications of birds, 1819–1901: views of the natural system in 19th-century British ornithology. Pp. 2746–2759 *in* Proc. 19th Intl. Orn. Congr., H. Ouellet, ed. Natl. Mus. Nat. Sci. Canada, Ottawa.

Ohmart, R. D. 1967. Comparative molt and pterylography in the quail genera *Callipepla* and *Lophortyx*. Condor 69:535–548.

Ohno, S., and N. B. Atkin. 1966. Comparative DNA values and chromosome complements of eight species of fishes. Chromosoma 18:455–466.

Ohno, S., C. Stenius, L. C. Christian, W. Beçak, and M. L. Beçak. 1964. Chromosomal uniformity in the avian subclass *Carinatae*. Chromosoma 15:280–288.

Ohta, T., and M. Kimura. 1971. On the constancy of the evolutionary rate of cistrons. J. Mol. Evol. 1:18–25.

Ohyama, K., and 12 co-authors. 1986. Chloroplast gene organization deduced from complete sequence of liverwort *Marchantia polymorpha* chloroplast DNA. Nature 322:572–574.

Olins, D. E., and A. L. Olins. 1978. Nucleosomes: the structural quantum in chromosomes. Amer. Scientist 66:704–711.

Oliver, W. R. B. 1945. Avian evolution in New Zealand and Australia. Emu 45:55–77, 119–152.

Olmo, E. 1973. Quantitative variations in the nuclear DNA and phylogenesis of the amphibia. Caryologia 26:43–68.

Olmo, E. 1976. Genome size in some reptiles. J. Exp. Zool. 195:305–310.

Olmo, E., and A. Morescalchi. 1975. Evolution of the genome and cell sizes in salamanders. Experientia 31:804–806.

Olson, S. L. 1970. Untitled. Bird Banding 41:258–259.

Olson, S. L. 1971. Taxonomic comments on the Eurylaimidae. Ibis 113:507–516.

Olson, S. L. 1973. A classification of the Rallidae. Wilson Bull. 85:381–416.

Olson, S. L. 1976. Oligocene fossils bearing on the origins of the Todidae and the Momotidae (Aves: Coraciiformes). Smithson. Contrib. Paleobiol. 27:111–119.

Olson, S. L. 1977. A Lower Eocene frigatebird from the Green River formation of Wyoming (Pelecaniformes: Fregatidae). Smithson. Contrib. Paleobiol. No. 35. 33 pp.

Olson, S. L. 1980. *Lamprolia* as part of a South Pacific radiation of monarchine flycatchers. Notornis 27:7–10.

Olson, S. L. 1982. A critique of Cracraft's classification of birds. Auk 99:733–739.

Olson, S. L. 1983. Evidence for a polyphyletic origin of the Piciformes. Auk 100:126–133.

Olson, S. L. 1985. The fossil record of birds. Pp. 79–238 *in* Avian biology, vol. 8. D. S. Farner, J. R. King, and K. C. Parkes, eds. Academic Press, New York.

Olson, S. L. 1987. The relationships of the New Guinean ground-robins *Amalocichla*. Emu 87:247–248.

Olson, S. L., and P. L. Ames. 1984. *Promerops* as a thrush, and its implications for the evolution of nectarivory in birds. Ostrich 55:213–218.

Olson, S. L., and A. Feduccia. 1980a. Relationships and evolution of flamingos (Aves:Phoenicopteridae). Smithson. Contrib. Zool. 316:1–73.

Olson, S. L., and A. Feduccia. 1980b. *Presbyornis* and the origin of the Anseriformes (Aves:Charadriomorphae). Smithson. Contrib. Zool. 323:1–24.

Olson, S. L., and D. W. Steadman. 1981. The relationships of the Pedionomidae (Aves: Charadriiformes). Smithsonian Contrib. Zool. 337.

Olson, S. L., K. C. Parkes, M. H. Clench, and S. R. Borecky. 1983. The affinities of the New Zealand passerine genus *Turnagra*. Notornis 30:319–336.

O'Malley, B. W., J. P. Stein, S. L. C. Woo, A. Dugaiczyk, J. F. Catterall, and E. C. Lai. 1979. A comparison of the sequence organization of the chicken ovalbumin and ovomucoid genes. Pp. 281–299 *in* Eucaryotic gene regulation. Academic Press, New York.

Orenstein, R. I. 1977. Morphological adaptations for bark foraging in the Australian treecreepers (Aves: Climacteridae). Univ. Microfilms Intl., Ann Arbor, Michigan.

Orenstein, R. I. 1985. Treecreeper (2). Pp. 608–609 *in* A dictionary of birds. B. Campbell and E. Lack, eds. T. and A. D. Poyser, Calton, England.

Ornstein, R. L., and J. R. Fresco. 1983. Correlation of T_m and sequence of DNA duplexes with ΔH computed by an improved empirical potential method. Biopolymers 22:1979–2000.

Orosz, J. M., and J. G. Wetmur. 1974. *In vitro* iodination of DNA. Maximizing iodination while minimizing degradation; use of buoyant density shifts for DNA-DNA hybrid isolation. Biochemistry 13:5467–5473.

Orr, R. T. 1963. Comments on the classification of swifts of the subfamily Chaeturinae. Proc. 13th Intl. Orn. Congr. 126–134.

Ostermann, R., and P. O. Degens. 1984a. Eigenschaften des Average-Linkage-Verfahrens anhand der Monte-Carlo-Studie. Pp. 108–114 *in* Anwendungen der Klassifikation: Datenanalyse und numerische Klassifikation. Indeks Verlag, Frankfurt.

Ostermann, R., and P. O. Degens. 1984b. Zur Beurteilung der Qualität des Average-Linkage-Verfahrens anhand verschiedener Ferlerverteilungen. Tech. Rept. No. 84/16. Dept. of Statistics, Univ. of Dortmund.

Ostermann, R., and P. O. Degens. 1985. Die Qualität des Average-Linkage-Verfahrens bei verschiedenen Fehlerverteilungen. EDV in Medizin und Biologie 16:91–96.

Osuga, D. T., and R. E. Feeney. 1968. Biochemistry of the egg-white proteins of the ratite group. Arch. Biochem. Biophys. 124:560–574.

Ottley, W. 1879. A description of the vessels of the neck and head in the ground-hornbill (*Bucorvus abyssinicus*). Proc. Zool. Soc. London 1879:461–467.

Oustalet, M. E. 1889. Sur la faune ornithologique des Iles Mariannes. Le Naturaliste, ser. 2, 3:260–261.

Oustalet, M. E. 1895. Les mammifères et les oiseaux des Iles Mariannes. Nouv. Arch. Hist. Nat. Paris, ser. 3, 7:141–228.

Ovenden, J. R., A. G. Mackinlay, and R. H. Crozier. 1987. Systematics and mitochondrial genome evolution of Australian rosellas (Aves: Platycercidae). Mol. Biol. Evol. 4:526–543.

Owen, R. 1866. Birds and mammals. On the anatomy of vertebrates, vol. 2. Longmans, Green, London.

Owre, O. T. 1967. Adaptations for locomotion and feeding in the anhinga and the double-crested cormorant. Orn. Monogr. No. 6. Amer. Orn. Union, Washington, D.C.

Padgett, R. A., M. M. Konarska, P. J. Grabowski, S. F. Hardy, and P. A. Sharp. 1984. Lariat RNA's as intermediates and products in the splicing of messenger RNA precursors. Science 225:898–903.

Palca, J. 1986. The numbers game. Nature 321:371.

Pardue, M. L., and J. G. Gall. 1970. Chromosomal localization of mouse satellite DNA. Science 168:1356–1358.

Parker, S. A. 1971. Review of "Australian Warblers" by A. R. McGill. 1970. Bird Obs. Club, Melbourne. Emu 71:90–91.

Parker, S. A. 1973. The tongues of *Ephthianura* and *Ashbyia*. Emu 73:19–20.

Parker, S. A. 1982. The relationships of the Australo-Papuan treecreepers and sittellas. S. Austral. Ornith. 28:197–200.

Parker, W. K. 1861. On the osteology of *Balaeniceps rex* (Gould). Trans. Zool. Soc. London 4:269–351.

Parker, W. K. 1863. On the systematic position of the crested screamer (*Palamedea chavaria*). Proc. Zool. Soc. London 1864:511–518.

Parker, W. K. 1864. On the osteology of gallinaceous birds and tinamous. Trans. Zool. Soc. London 5:149–241.

Parker, W. K. 1868. A monograph on the structure and development of the shoulder-girdle and sternum in the vertebrata. R. Hardwicke for the Ray Soc., London.

Parker, W. K. 1875a. On aegithognathous birds (Part I). Trans. Zool. Soc. London 9:289–352.

Parker, W. K. 1875b. On the morphology of the skull in the woodpeckers (Picidae) and wrynecks (Yungidae). Trans. Linnean Soc. London, 2nd Ser., Zool., 1(1):1–22.

Parker, W. K. 1889a. On the "manus" of *Phoenicopterus*. Ibis 31:183–185.

Parker, W. K. 1889b. On the osteology of *Steatornis caripensis*. Proc. Zool. Soc. London 1889:161–190.

Parker, W. K. 1889c. On the systematic position of the swifts (Cypselidae). Zoologist, 3rd Ser., 13:91–95.

Parker, W. K. 1891a. On the morphology of a reptilian bird, *Opisthocomus cristatus*. Trans. Zool. Soc. London 13:43–85.

Parker, W. K. 1891b. On the morphology of the Gallinaceae. Trans. Linnean Soc. London, Ser. 2, 5:213–244.

Parkes, K. C. 1955. Systematic notes on North American birds. Part I. The herons and ibises (Ciconiiformes). Ann. Carnegie Mus. 33:287–291.

Parkes, K. C. 1978. A review of the classification of the Ciconiiformes. Pp. 7–15 *in* Wading birds. A. Sprunt IV, J. C. Ogden, and S. Winckler, eds. Natl. Audubon Soc. Rept. No. 7. New York.

Parkes, K. C., and G. A. Clark, Jr. 1966. An additional character linking ratites and tinamous, and an interpretation of their monophyly. Condor 68:459–471.

Parsons, C. W. 1954. Note on the embryonic development of the hoatzin (*Opisthocomus hoazin*). Proc. Roy. Soc. Edinburgh B. 65:205–212.

Partridge, L., and P. H. Harvey. 1988. The ecological context of life history evaluation. Science 241:1449–1455.

Patterson, C. 1982. Morphological characters and homology. Pp. 21–74 *in* Problems of phylogenetic reconstruction. K. A. Joysey and A. E. Friday, eds. Academic Press, New York.

Patterson, C. 1988. Homology in classical and molecular biology. Mol. Biol. Evol. 5:603–625.

Payne, R. B. 1979. Family Ardeidae. Pp. 193–244 *in* Check-list of birds of the world. E. Mayr and G. W. Cottrell, eds. Mus. Comp. Zool., Cambridge, Mass.

Payne, R. B., and C. J. Risley. 1976. Systematics and evolutionary relationships among the herons (Ardeidae). Misc. Publ. Univ. Michigan Mus. Zool. 150:1–115.

Paynter, R. A., Jr., ed. 1967. Check-list of birds of the world. Vol. 12. Mus. Comp. Zool., Cambridge, Mass.

Paynter, R. A., Jr., and R. W. Storer. 1970. Check-list of birds of the world. Vol. 13. Mus. Comp. Zool., Cambridge, Mass.

Peacock, W. J., D. Brutlag, E. Goldring, R. Appels, C. W. Hinton, and D. L. Lindsley. 1974. The organization of highly repeated DNA sequences in *Drosophila melanogaster* chromosomes. Cold Spring Harbor Symp. Quant. Biol. 38:405–416.

Peakall, D. B. 1963. Egg-white proteins as an aid to avian systematics. Proc. 13th Intl. Orn. Congr. 135–140.

Pearson, W. R., J. R. Wu, and J. Bonner. 1978. Analysis of rat repetitive DNA sequences. Biochemistry 17:51–59.

Peckover, W. S., and L. W. C. Filewood. 1976. Birds of New Guinea and tropical Australia. A. H. and A. W. Reed, Sydney.

Pedersen, R. A. 1971. DNA content, ribosomal gene multiplicity, and cell size in fish. J. Exp. Zool. 177:65–78.

Pellegrini, M., W. E. Timberlake, and R. B. Goldberg. 1981. Electron microscopy of *Achlya* deoxyribonucleic acid sequence organization. Molec. Cell Biol. 1:136–143.

Perkins, R. 1964. The electrophoretic patterns of the serum proteins and hemoglobins of the genus *Larus*. Murrelet 45:26–28.

Perrin, J. 1875. On the myology of *Opisthocomus cristatus*. Trans. Zool. Soc. London 9:353–370.

Perutz, M. F. 1986. A bacterial haemoglobin. Nature 322:405.

Peterle, T. J. 1951. Intergeneric galliform hybrids: a review. Wilson Bull. 63:219–224.

Peters, J. L. 1931–51. Check-list of birds of the world. 7 vols: 1(1931), 2(1934), 3(1937), 4(1940), 5(1945), 6(1948), 7(1951). Mus. Comp. Zool., Cambridge, Mass.

Peters, J. L. 1960. Check-list of birds of the world. Vol. 9. E. Mayr and J. C. Greenway, Jr., eds. Mus. Comp. Zool., Cambridge, Mass.

Petrov, N. B., and V. V. Aleshin. 1983. Heterogeneity and homology of the repetitive and unique DNA sequences of dragonflies (Odonata, Insecta). Molec. Biol. 17:277–286. Transl. from Molekulyarnaya Biol. 17:345–355. Plenum, New York.

Piechocki, R. 1955. Über Verhalten, Mauser und Umfärbung einer gekäfigten Steppenweihe (*Circus macrourus*). J. für Orn. 96:327–336.

Piechocki, R. 1956. Über die Mauser eines gekäfigten Turmfalken (*Falco tinnunculus*). J. für Orn. 97:301–309.

Piechocki, R. 1963a. Über die Mauser eines gekäfigten Baumfalken (*Falco subbuteo*). Beitr. Vogelk. 9:69–77.

Piechocki, R. 1963b. Vorläufiges über die Mauser der Handschwingen beim Mäusebussard (*Buteo buteo*). J. für Orn. 104:182–184.

Pilbeam, D. 1983. Hominoid evolution and hominid origins. Pp. 43–61 *in* Recent advances in the evolution of the primates. C. Chagas, ed. Pontificae Acad. Scient. Scripta Varia 50. Vatican, Rome.

Pilbeam, D. 1985. Patterns of hominoid evolution. Pp. 51–59 *in* Ancestors—the hard evidence. E. Delson, ed. Alan R. Liss, New York.

Pinto, O. 1950. Da classificacao e nomenclatura dos suracuas brasileiros (Trogonidae). Sec. Agric., Dept. Zool. (Sao Paulo). Papéis Avulsos 9:89–136.

Pizzey, G. 1980. A field guide to the birds of Australia. Collins, Sydney.

Plotnick, R. 1956. Afinidad entre los géneros *Elanus* y *Gampsonyx* (Accipitridae, Aves). Rev. Invest. Agrícolas (Buenos Aires) 10:313–315.

Plotnick, R., and M. J. I. Pergolani de Costa. 1955. Clave de las familias de Passeriformes representadas en la Argentina. Rev. Invest. Agrícolas (Buenos Aires) 9:65–88.

Pocock, T. N. 1966. Contributions to the osteology of African birds. Proc. 2nd Pan-African Orn. Congr. 83–94.

Poltz, J., and J. Jacob. 1974. Bürzeldrüsensekrete bei Ammern (Emberizidae), Finken (Fringillidae) und Webern (Ploceidae). J. für Orn. 115:119–127.

Poplin, F. 1980. *Sylviornis neocaledoniae* n.g., n. sp. (Aves), ratite éteint de la Nouvelle-Calédonie. C. R. Acad. Sci. Paris 290:691–694.

Poplin, F., and C. Mourer-Chauviré. 1985. *Sylviornis neocaledoniae* (Aves, Galliformes, Megapodiidae), oiseau géant éteint de L'Ile des Pins (Nouvelle-Calédonie). Geobios 18:73–97.

Poplin, F., C. Mourer-Chauviré, and J. Evin. 1983. Position systematique et datation de *Sylviornis neocaledoniae*, Mégapode géant (Aves, Galliformes, Megapodiidae) éteint de la Nouvelle-Calédonie. C. R. Acad. Sci. Paris 297(II):301–304.

Porter, S. D., and M. Smith. 1986. Homoeo-domain homology in yeast MAT α 2 is essential for repressor activity. Nature 320:766–768.

Portugal, F. H., and J. S. Cohen. 1977. A century of DNA. M.I.T. Press, Cambridge, Mass.

Posakony, J. W., R. H. Scheller, D. M. Anderson, R. J. Britten, and E. H. Davidson. 1981. Repetitive sequences of the sea urchin genome. III. Nucleotide sequences of cloned repeat elements. J. Mol. Biol. 149:41–67.

Powell, J. R., A. Caccone, G. D. Amato, and C. Yoon. 1986. Rates of nucleotide substitutions in *Drosophila* mitochondrial DNA and nuclear DNA are similar. Proc. Natl. Acad. Sci. USA 83:9090–9093.

Prager, E. M., and A. C. Wilson. 1976. Congruency of phylogenies derived from different proteins. A molecular analysis of the phylogenetic position of cracid birds. J. Mol. Evol. 9:45–57.

Prager, E. M., and A. C. Wilson. 1980. Phylogenetic relationships and rates of evolution in birds. Pp. 1209–1214 *in* Proc. 17th Intl. Orn. Congr. R. Nöhring, ed. Deutschen Orn.-Gesellsch., Berlin.

Prager, E. M., A. C. Wilson, D. T. Osuga, and R. E. Feeney. 1976. Evolution of flightless land birds on southern continents: transferrin comparison shows monophyletic origin of ratites. J. Mol. Evol. 8:283–294.

Pratt, H. D., P. L. Bruner, and D. G. Berrett. 1987. The birds of Hawaii and the tropical Pacific. Princeton Univ. Press, Princeton, New Jersey.

Preisler, R. S., and W. F. Thompson. 1981a. Evolutionary sequence divergence within repeated DNA families of higher plant genomes. I. Analysis of reassociation kinetics. J. Mol. Evol. 17:78–84.

Preisler, R. S., and W. F. Thompson. 1981b. Evolutionary sequence divergence within repeated DNA families of higher plant genomes. II. Analysis of thermal denaturation. J. Mol. Evol. 17:85–93.

Prensky, W. 1976. The radioiodination of RNA and DNA to high specific activities. Pp. 121–152 *in* Methods in Cell Biology, vol. 13. D. M. Prescott, ed. Academic Press, New York.

Price, R. D., and K. C. Emerson. 1988. *Menacanthus dennisi* (Mallophaga: Menoponidae), a new species from the Grey Currawong (Passeriformes: Cracticidae) in South Australia. Florida Entomologist 71:202–204.

Prinzinger, G., and R. Prinzinger. 1985. Fleisch als Nährung von Gestreiften Mausvögeln im Freiland. J. für Orn. 126:442.

Prosser, J., M. Moar, M. Bobrow, and K. W. Jones. 1973. Satellite sequences in chimpanzee (*Pan troglodytes*). Biochim. Biophys. Acta 319:122–134.

Prum, R. O. 1988. Phylogenetic interrelationships of the barbets (Aves: Capitonidae) and toucans (Aves: Ramphastidae) based on morphology with comparisons to DNA-DNA hybridization. Zool. J. Linn. Soc. 92:313–343.

Prum, R. O., and W. E. Lanyon. 1989. Monophyly and phylogeny of the *Schiffornis* group (Tyrannoidea). Condor 91:444–461.

Ptashne, M. 1986. Gene regulation by proteins acting at a distance. Nature 322:697–701.

Ptashne, M. 1988. How eukaryotic transcriptional factors work. Nature 335:683–689.

Pukkila, P. J. 1975. Identification of the lampbrush chromosome loops which transcribe 5S ribosomal RNA in *Notophthalmus* (*Triturus*) *viridescens*. Chromosoma 53:71–89.

Pycraft, W. P. 1890. A contribution to the pterylography of birds' wings. Trans. Leiceister Lit. Phil. Soc. n.s., 2:123–144.

Pycraft, W. P. 1895. On the pterylography of the hoatzin, *Opisthocomus cristatus*. Ibis 37:345–373.

Pycraft, W. P. 1898a. A contribution towards our knowledge of the morphology of the owls. Part I. Pterylography. Trans. Linnean Soc. London, 2nd Ser., Zool., 7:223–275.

Pycraft, W. P. 1898b. Contributions to the osteology of birds. Part I. Steganopodes. Proc. Zool. Soc. London 1898:82–101.

Pycraft, W. P. 1898c. Contributions to the osteology of birds. Part II. Impennes. Proc. Zool. Soc. London 1898(1899):958–989.

Pycraft, W. P. 1899a. Contributions to the osteology of birds. Part III. Tubinares. Proc. Zool. Soc. London 1899:381–411.

Pycraft, W. P. 1899b. Contributions to the osteology of birds. Part IV. Pygopodes. Proc. Zool. Soc. London 1899(1900):1018–1046.

Pycraft, W. P. 1899c. Some facts concerning the so-called "Aquintocubitalism" in the bird's wing. J. Linnean Soc. London (Zool.) 27:236–256.

Pycraft, W. P. 1900. On the morphology and phylogeny of the Palaeognathae (Ratitae and Crypturi) and Neognathae (Carinatae). Trans. Zool. Soc. London 15:149–290.

Pycraft, W. P. 1901. Some points in the morphology of the palate of the Neognathae. J. Linnean Soc. London (Zool.) 28:343–357.

Pycraft, W. P. 1902. Contributions to the osteology of birds. Part V. Falconiformes. Proc. Zool. Soc. London 1902(1):277–320.

Pycraft, W. P. 1903a. On the pterylography of *Photodilus*. Ibis 45:36–48.

Pycraft, W. P. 1903b. A contribution towards our knowledge of the morphology of the owls. Part II. Osteology. Trans. Linnean Soc. London, Ser. 2, 9:1–46.

Pycraft, W. P. 1903c. Contributions to the osteology of birds. Part VI. Cuculiformes. Proc. Zool. Soc. London 1903(1):258–291.

Pycraft, W. P. 1905a. Some points in the anatomy of *Acanthidositta chloris*, with some remarks on the systematic position of the genera *Acanthidositta* and *Xenicus*. Ibis 47:603–621.

Pycraft, W. P. 1905b. Contributions to the osteology of birds. Part VII. Eurylaemidae; with remarks on the systematic position of the group. Proc. Zool. Soc. London 1905(2):30–56.

Pycraft, W. P. 1905c. On the systematic position of *Zeledonia coronata*, with some observations on the position of the Turdidae. Ibis 47:1–24.

Pycraft, W. P. 1906a. Notes on a skeleton of the musk-duck, *Biziura lobata*, with special reference to skeletal characters evolved in relation to the diving habits of this bird. J. Linnean Soc. London 29:396–407.

Pycraft, W. P. 1906b. Contributions to the osteology of birds. Part VIII. The "tracheophone" Passeres; with remarks on the families allied thereto. Proc. Zool. Soc. London 1906:133–159.

Pycraft, W. P. 1907a. On the anatomy and systematic position of the colies. Ibis 49:229–253.

Pycraft, W. P. 1907b. Contributions to the osteology of birds. Part IX. Tyranni; Hirundines; Muscicapae; Lanii, and Gymmorhines. Proc. Zool. Soc. London 1907:352–379.

Quelch, J. J. 1890. On the habits of the hoatzin (*Opisthocomus cristatus*). Ibis 32:327–335.

Radman, M., and R. Wagner. 1988. The high fidelity of DNA duplication. Sci. Amer. 259:40–46.

Raikow, R. J. 1975. The evolutionary reappearance of ancestral muscles as developmental anomalies in two species of birds. Condor 77:514–517.

Raikow, R. J. 1976. Pelvic appendage myology of the Hawaiian Honeycreepers (Drepanididae). Auk 93:774–792.

Raikow, R. J. 1977a. Pectoral appendage myology of the Hawaiian Honeycreepers (Drepanididae). Auk 94:331–342.

Raikow, R. J. 1977b. The origin and evolution of the Hawaiian Honeycreepers (Drepanididae). Living Bird 15:95–117.

Raikow, R. J. 1978. Appendicular myology and relationships of the New World nine-primaried oscines (Aves: Passeriformes). Bull. Carnegie Mus. Nat. Hist. 7:1–43.

Raikow, R. J. 1982. Monophyly of the Passeriformes: test of a phylogenetic hypothesis. Auk 99:431–445.

Raikow, R. J. 1984. Hindlimb myology and phylogenetic position of the New Zealand wrens. Abstract 446. Amer. Zool. 24(3).

Raikow, R. J. 1985a. Systematic and functional aspects of the locomotor system of the scrub-birds, *Atrichornis*, and Lyrebirds, *Menura* (Passeriformes: Atrichornithidae and Menuridae). Rec. Austral. Mus. 37:211–228.

Raikow, R. J. 1985b. Problems in avian classification. Current Ornithology 2:187–212. R. F. Johnston, ed. Plenum, New York.

Raikow, R. J. 1987. Hindlimb myology and evolution of the Old World suboscine passerine birds (Acanthisittidae, Pittidae, Philepittidae, Eurylaimidae). Ornith. Monogr. No. 41, Amer. Orn. Union, Washington, D.C.

Raikow, R. J. and J. Cracraft. 1983. Monophyly of the Piciformes: a reply to Olson. Auk 100:134–138.

Raikow, R. J., S. R. Borecky, and S. L. Berman. 1979. The evolutionary re-establishment of a lost ancestral muscle in the bowerbird assemblage. Condor 81:203–206.

Raikow, R. J., P. J. Polumbo, and S. R. Borecky. 1980. Appendicular myology and relationships of the shrikes (Aves: Passeriformes: Laniidae). Ann. Carnegie Mus. Nat. Hist. 49:131–152.

Rand, A. L. 1936. The distribution and habits of Madagascar birds. Bull. Amer. Mus. Nat. Hist. 72:143–499.

Rand, A. L. 1959. Tarsal scutellation of song birds as a taxonomic character. Wilson Bull. 71:274–277.

Rand, A. L. 1960. Check-list of birds of the world. Vol. 9. E. Mayr and J. C. Greenway, Jr., eds. Mus. Comp. Zool., Cambridge, Mass.

Rand, A. L. 1967a. Check-list of birds of the world. Vol. 12. R. A. Paynter, Jr., ed. Mus. Comp. Zool., Cambridge, Mass.

Rand, A. L. 1967b. The flower-adapted tongue of a timaliine bird and its implications. Fieldiana (Zool.) 51:53–61.

Rand, A. L., and E. T. Gilliard. 1968. Handbook of New Guinea birds. Natural History Press, Garden City, New York.

Rand, A. L., and M. A. Traylor, Jr. 1953. The systematic position of the genera *Ramphocaenus* and *Microbates*. Auk 70:334–337.

Rand, H. M., and J. M. Mabesoone. 1982. Northwestern Brazil and the final separation of South America and Africa. Palaeogeo. Palaeoclim. Palaeoecol. 38:163–183.

Randi, E., and F. Spina. 1987. An electrophoretic approach to the systematics of Italian gulls and terns (Aves, Laridae and Sternidae). Monitore Zool. Ital. (N.S.) 21:317–344.

Ratti, J. T. 1979. Reproductive separation and isolating mechanisms between sympatric dark- and light-phase Western Grebes. Auk 96:573–586.

Razin, A., and J. Friedman. 1981. DNA methylation and its possible biological roles. Prog. Nucl. Acid Res. Mol. Biol. 25:33–52.

R.A.O.U. Checklist Committee. 1926. The official checklist of the birds of Australia. 2nd edition. R.A.O.U., Melbourne.

Reeck, G. R., et al. 1987. Homology in proteins and nucleic acids: a terminology muddle and a way out of it. Cell 50:667.

Rees, H. 1974. DNA in higher plants. *In* Evolution of Genetic Systems. H. H. Smith, ed. Brookhaven Sympos. Biol., vol. 23. Gordon and Breach, New York.

Reichenow, A. 1877. Systematische Uebersicht der Schreitvögel (Gressores). J. für Orn. 25:113–171, 229–277.

Reichenow, A. 1881. Conspectus Psittacorum. Systematische Uebersicht aller bekannten Papageirarten. J. für Orn. 29:1–40, 113–177, 225–289, 337–398.

Reichenow, A. 1882. Die Vögel der Zoologischen Gärten. Vol. 1. L. A. Kittler, Leipzig. 278 pp.

Reichenow, A. 1913. Die Vögel. Handbuch der systematischen Ornithologie. Vol. 1. F. Enke, Stuttgart.

Reichenow, A. 1914. Die Vögel. Handbuch der systematischen Ornithologie. Vol. 2. F. Enke, Stuttgart.

Reinhardt, J. 1860. On the affinities of *Balaeniceps*. Proc. Zool. Soc. London 1860:377–380.

Reinhardt, J. 1862. Some remarks on the genus *Balaeniceps*. Ibis 4:158–175.

Rice, N. R. 1971a. Thermal stability of reassociated repeated DNA from rodents. Carnegie Inst. Wash. Yearbook 69:472–479.

Rice, N. R. 1971b. Some observations on interspersion of DNA sequences. Carnegie Inst. Wash. Yearbook 69:479–482.

Rice, N. R. 1971c. Reassociation profiles of rodent DNAs. Carnegie Inst. Wash. Yearbook 69:482–485.

Rice, N. R. 1971d. Differences in the DNA of closely related rodents. Carnegie Inst. Wash. Yearbook 70:366–369.

Rice, N. R. 1972. Change in repeated DNA in evolution. Pp. 44–79 *in* Brookhaven Symp. Biol. vol. 23. H. H. Smith, ed. Gordon and Breach, New York.

Rice, N. R. 1974. Single-copy relatedness among several species of the Cricetidae (Rodentia). Carnegie Inst. Wash. Yearbook 73:1098–1102.

Rice, N. R., and P. Esposito. 1973. Relatedness among several hamsters. Carnegie Inst. Wash. Yearbook 72:200–204.

Rice, N. R., and P. Paul. 1972. Reassociation of single-copy DNA sequences. Carnegie Inst. Wash. Yearbook 71:262–264.

Rice, N. R., and N. A. Straus. 1973. Relatedness of mouse satellite deoxyribonucleic acid to deoxyribonucleic acid of various *Mus* species. Proc. Natl. Acad. Sci. USA 70:3546–3550.

Rich, A. 1982. Right-handed and left-handed DNA: Conformational information in genetic material. Cold Spring Harbor Symp. Quant. Biol. 47:1–12.

Rich, A., A. Nordheim, and A. H-J. Wang. 1984. The chemistry and biology of left-handed Z-DNA. Ann. Rev. Biochem. 53:791–846.

Rich, P. V. 1979. The Dromornithidae, an extinct family of large ground birds endemic to Australia. Bur. Nat. Resources, Geol. and Geophys. Bull. No. 184.

Rich, P. V., and P. J. Haarhoff. 1985. Early Pliocene Coliidae (Aves, Coliiformes) from Langebaanweg, South Africa. Ostrich 56:20–41.

Rich, P. V., A. R. McEvey, and R. F. Baird. 1985. Osteological comparison of the scrub-birds, *Atrichornis*, and lyrebirds, *Menura* (Passeriformes: Atrichornithidae and Menuridae). Rec. Austral. Mus. 37:165–191.

Richdale, L. E. 1957. A population study of penguins. Oxford Univ. Press.

Ricklefs, R. E. 1972. Fecundity, mortality, and avian demography. Pp. 366–435 *in* Breeding biology of birds. D. S. Farner, ed. Natl. Acad. Sci. USA, Washington, D.C.

Ridgway, R. 1875. Outlines of a natural arrangement of the Falconidae. Bull. U.S. Geol. Surv. Terr., Ser. 2, No. 4:225–231.

Ridgway, R. 1887. A manual of North American birds. J. P. Lippincott, Philadelphia.

Ridgway, R. 1892. The humming birds. U.S. Natl. Mus., Rep. for 1890:253–383.

Ridgway, R. 1901. The birds of North and Middle America. Bull. U.S. Natl. Mus. 50(1):1–715.

Ridgway, R. 1902. The birds of North and Middle America. Bull. U.S. Natl. Mus. 50(2):1–834.

Ridgway, R. 1904. The birds of North and Middle America. Bull. U.S. Natl. Mus. 50(3):1–801.

Ridgway, R. 1907. The birds of North and Middle America. Bull. U.S. Natl. Mus. 50(4):1–973.

Ridgway, R. 1909. Hybridism and generic characters in the Trochilidae. Auk 26:440–442.

Ridgway, R. 1911. The birds of North and Middle America. Bull. U.S. Natl. Mus. 50(5):1–859.

Ridgway, R. 1914. The birds of North and Middle America. Bull. U.S. Natl. Mus. 50, pt. 6. 882 pp.

Ridgway, R., and H. Friedmann. 1941. The birds of North and Middle America. Bull. U.S. Natl. Mus. 50, pt. 9. 254 pp.

Ridley, M. W. 1954. Observations on the diet of flamingos. J. Bombay Nat. Hist. Soc. 52:5–7.

Riede, I., E. Jacob, and M. Renz. 1983. DNA sequence divergence in the *Drosophila virilis* group. Chromosoma 88:109–115.

Riggs, C. R. 1948. The family Eurypygidae: a review. Wilson Bull. 60:75–80.

Ripley, S. D. 1945. The barbets. Auk 62:542–563.

Ripley, S. D. 1946. The barbets—errata and addenda. Auk 63:452–453.

Ripley, S. D. 1952. The thrushes. Postilla 13:1–48.

Roberts, J. M., L. B. Buck, and R. Axel. 1983. A structure for amplified DNA. Cell 33:53–63.

Roberts, J. W., J. W. Grula, J. W. Posakony, R. Hudspeth, E. H. Davidson, and R. J. Britten. 1983. Comparison of sea urchin and human mtDNA: Evolutionary rearrangement. Proc. Natl. Acad. Sci. USA 80:4614–4618.

Roberts, L. 1988. Academy backs genome project. Science 239:725–726.

Robertson, M. 1988. Homoeo boxes, POU proteins and the limits to promiscuity. Nature 336:522–524.

Romero-Herrera, A. E., N. Lieska, M. Goodman, and E. L. Simons. 1979. The use of amino acid sequence analysis in assessing evolution. Biochimie 61:767–779.

Rossi, J. A. H. 1958. Contribución al conocimiento de la biología de la garza roja. Ser. Zool. 1(2), Facultad de Ciencias Exactas y Naturales. Univ. de Buenos Aires.

Roth, V. L. 1988. The biological basis of homology. Pp. 1–26 *in* Ontogeny and systematics. C. J. Humphries, ed. Columbia Univ. Press, New York.

Rothschild, M., and T. Clay. 1952. Fleas, flukes, and cuckoos: a study of bird parasites. Collins, London. 305 pp.

Rould, M. A., J. J. Perona, D. Söll, and T. A. Steitz. 1989. Structure of *E. coli* glutamyl-tRNA synthetase complexed with tRNA^{Gln} and ATP at 2.8 A resolution. Science 246:1135–1142.

Rowan, M. K. 1967. A study of the colies of southern Africa. Ostrich 38:63–115.

Ruiz-Carrillo, A., M. Affolter, and J. Renaud. 1983. Genomic organization of the genes coding for the six main histones sequence of the H5 gene. J. Mol. Biol. 170:843–859.

Rutgers, A., and K. A. Norris, eds. 1970. Encyclopaedia of aviculture. Vol. 1. Blandford Press, London.

Rylander, M. K. 1968. The electrophoretic patterns of the serum proteins of the genera *Erolia* and *Ereunetes* (family Scolopacidae). Murrelet 48:39–40.

Saenger, W. 1984. Principles of nucleic acid structure. Springer-Verlag, New York.

Saenger, W., W. N. Hunter, and O. Kennard. 1986. DNA conformation is determined by economics in the hydration of phosphate groups. Nature 324:385–388.

Saether, B-E. 1988. Pattern of covariation between life-history traits of European birds. Nature 331:616–617.

Sahni, A. 1984. Cretaceous-Paleocene terrestrial faunas of India: lack of endemism during drifting of the Indian plate. Science 226:441–443.

Saiff, E. 1978. The middle ear of the skull of birds: the Pelecaniformes and Ciconiiformes. Zool. J. Linnaean Soc. 63:315–370.

Salomonsen, F. 1933. Zur Systematik und Biologie von *Promerops*. Ornith. Monatsber. 41:37–40.

Salomonsen, F. 1960. Notes on flowerpeckers (Aves, Dicaeidae) 1. The genera *Melanocharis*, *Rhamphocharis*, and *Prionochilus*. Amer. Mus. Novit. 1990.

Salomonsen, F. 1961. Notes on flowerpeckers (Aves, Dicaeidae) 5. The genera *Oreocharis*, *Paramythia*, and *Pardalotus* (except the superspecies *Pardalotus striatus*). Amer. Mus. Novit. 2067.

Salomonsen, F. 1967. Check-list of birds of the world. Vol. 12. R. A. Paynter, Jr., ed. Mus. Comp. Zool., Cambridge, Mass.

Salser, W., S. Bowen, D. Browne, F. El Adli, N. Fedoroff, K. Fry, H. Heindell, G. Paddock, R. Poon, B. Wallace, and P. Whitcome. 1976. Investigation of the organization of mammalian chromosomes at the DNA sequence level. Federation Proc. 35:23–35.

Salvadori, T. 1876. Descrizione di cinquantotto nuove specie di uccelli, ed osservazioni intorno ad altre poco note, della Nuova Guinea e de altre Isole Papuane, raccolte dal Dr. Odoardo Beccari e dai cacciatori del Sig. A. A. Bruijn. Annali Mus. Civ. Storia Naturale Genova, vol. 7, ser. 1, pp. 896–976.

Salvadori, T. 1891. Catalogue of the Psittaci . . . in the British Museum. Vol. 20:1–658. Brit. Mus., London.

Salvadori, T. 1893. Catalogue of the Columbae . . . in the British Museum. Vol. 21:1–676. Brit. Mus., London.

Salvadori, T. 1895. Catalogue of the Chenomorphae . . . and Ratitae in . . . the British Museum. Vol. 27:1–636. Brit. Mus., London.

Salvin, O. 1896. Catalogue of the . . . Tubinares [petrels, albatrosses] in . . . the British Museum. Vol. 25:340–455. Brit. Mus., London. [See Saunders, H. 1896.]

Salvin, O., and E. Hartert. 1892. Catalogue of the Picariae . . . in the British Museum. Upupae and Trochili. Vol. 16:1–433. Brit. Mus., London.

Samols, D., and H. Swift. 1979. Genomic organization in the flesh fly, *Sarcophaga bullata*. Chromosoma 75:129–143.

Sanchez de Jiménez, E., J. L. González, J. L. Dominguez, and E. S. Saloma. 1974. Characterization of DNA from differentiated cells. Analysis of the chicken genomic complexity. Eur. J. Biochem. 45:25–29.

Sanderson, K. E. 1976. Genetic relatedness in the family Enterobacteriaceae. Ann. Rev. Microbiol. 30:327–349.

Sanft, K. 1960. Aves, Upupae Bucerotidae. Das Tierreich 76:1–174.

Sanger, F. 1981. Determination of nucleotide sequences in DNA. Bioscience Reports 1:3–18.

Sanger, F., G. M. Air, B. G. Barrell, N. L. Brown, A. R. Coulson, J. C. Fiddes, C. A. Hutchison III, P. M. Slocombe, and M. Smith. 1977. Nucleotide sequence of bacteriophage φ-X174. Nature 265:687–695.

Sanger, F., and H. Tuppy. 1951. The amino acid sequence of the phenylalanyl chain of insulin. Biochem. J. 49:463–481.

Santiago, L., and A. V. Rake. 1973. Rodent DNA reassociation kinetics. Biochem. Genet. 9:275–282.

Sarich, V. M. 1972. Generation time and albumin evolution. Biochem. Genet. 7:205–212.

Sarich, V. M., and J. E. Cronin. 1977. Generation length and rates of hominoid molecular evolution. Nature 269:354–355.

Sarich, V. M., and A. C. Wilson. 1967a. Rates of albumin evolution in primates. Proc. Natl. Acad. Sci. USA 58:142–148.

Sarich, V. M., and A. C. Wilson. 1967b. Immunological time scale for hominid evolution. Science 158:1200–1204.

Sarich, V. M., and A. C. Wilson. 1973. Generation time and genomic evolution in primates. Science 179:1144–1147.

Sarich, V. M., C. W. Schmid, and J. Marks. 1989. DNA hybridization as a guide to phylogeny: a critical analysis. Cladistics 5:3–32.

Saunders, H. 1896. Catalogue of the Gaviae [terns, gulls, skuas] in . . . the British Museum. Vol. 25:1–339. Brit. Mus., London. [See Salvin, O. 1896.]

Sawyer, J. R., and J. C. Hozier. 1986. High resolution of mouse chromosome: banding conservation between man and mouse. Science 232:1632–1635.

Schalow, H. 1886. Die Musophagidae. Monographische Studien. J. für Orn. 34:1–77.

Scharnke, H. 1931. Beiträge zur Morphologie und Entwicklungsgeschichte der Zunge der Trochilidae, Meliphagidae und Picidae. J. für Orn. 79:425–491.

Scharnke, H. 1932. Ueber den Bau der Zunge der Nectariniidae, Promeropidae und Drepanididae nebst Bemerkungen zur Systematik der blutenbesuchenden Passeres. J. für Orn. 80:114–123.

Scheller, R. H., D. M. Anderson, J. W. Posakany, L. B. McAllister, R. J. Britten, and E. H. Davidson. 1981. Repetitive sequences of the sea urchin genome. II. Subfamily structure and evolutionary conservation. J. Mol. Biol. 149:15–39.

Scherberg, N. H., and S. Refetoff. 1975. Radioiodine labeling of ribopolymers for special applications in biology. Pp. 343–359 *in* Methods in cell biology, vol. 10. D. M. Prescott, ed. Academic Press, New York.

Scherzinger, W. 1975. Breeding European owls. Avicultural Mag. 81:70–73.

Schifter, H. 1967. Beiträge zum Fortpflanzungsverhalten und zur Jugendentwicklung der Mausvögel (Coliidae). Zool. Jahrb. Syst., 94:68–181.

Schifter, H. 1985. Systematics and distribution of mousebirds (Coliidae). Pp. 325–347 *in* Proc. Intl. Symp. African Vertebrates. K.-L. Schuchmann, ed. Mus. Koenig, Bonn.

Schildkraut, C. L., and S. Lifson. 1965. Dependence of the melting temperature of DNA on salt concentration. Biopolymers 3:195–208.

Schildkraut, C. L., J. Marmur, and P. Doty. 1961. The formation of hybrid DNA molecules and their use in studies of DNA homologies. J. Mol. Biol. 3:595–617.

Schildkraut, C. L., K. L. Wierzchowski, J. Marmur, D. M. Green, and P. Doty. 1962. A study of base sequence homology among the T series of bacteriophages. Virology 18:43–55.

Schimke, R. T., ed. 1982. Gene amplification. Cold Spring Harbor Lab., Cold Spring Harbor, New York.

Schimke, R. T., R. J. Kaufman, F. W. Alt, and R. F. Kellems. 1978. Gene amplification and drug resistance in cultured murine cells. Science 202:1051–1055.

Schlegel, H. 1862. Oti and Striges. Mus. Hist. Nat. Pays-Bas (Leyden), Revue méthodique et critique des collections 2(11,12). 75 pp.

Schlegel, H. 1867. Urinatores. Mus. Hist. Nat. Pays-Bas (Leyden), Revue méthodique et critique des collections 6(33). 52 pp.

Schleif, R. 1987. Why should DNA loop? Nature 327:369–370.

Schleif, R. 1988a. DNA looping. Science 240:127–128.

Schleif, R. 1988b. DNA binding by proteins. Science 241:1182–1187.

Schleifer, K. H., and E. Stackebrandt. 1983. Molecular systematics of prokaryotes. Ann. Rev. Microbiol. 37:143–187.

Schmekel, L. 1962. Embryonale und frühe postembryonale Erythropoiese in Leber, Milz, Dottersack und Knochenmark der Vögel. Rev. Suisse Zool. 69:559–615.

Schmekel, L. 1963. Die embryonale Erythropoiese der Charadriiformes. Rev. Suisse Zool. 70:677–688.

Schmid, C. W., and P. L. Deininger. 1975. Sequence organization of the human genome. Cell 6:345–358.

Schmid, C. W., and W. R. Jelinek. 1982. The Alu family of dispersed repetitive sequences. Science 216:1065–1070.

Schmidtke, J., and I. Kandt. 1981. Single-copy DNA relationships between diploid and tetraploid teleostean fish species. Chromosoma 83:191–197.

Schmidtke, J., E. Schmitt, E. Matzke, and W. Engel. 1979. Non-repetitive DNA sequence divergence in phylogenetically diploid and tetraploid teleostean species of the family Cyprinidae and the order Isospondylii. Chromosoma 75:185–198.

Schnell, G. D. 1970a. A phenetic study of the suborder Lari (Aves) I. Methods and results of principal components analyses. Syst. Zool. 19:35–57.

Schnell, G. D. 1970b. A phenetic study of the suborder Lari (Aves) II. Phenograms, discussion, and conclusions. Syst. Zool. 19:264–302.

Schnell, G. D., and S. D. Wood. 1976. More on chicken-turkey-pheasant resemblances. Condor 78:550–553.

Schneuwly, S., R. Klemerz, and W. J. Gehring. 1987. Redesigning the body plan of *Drosophila* by ectopic expression of the homoeotic gene *Antennapedia*. Nature 325:816–818.

Schodde, R. 1975. Interim list of Australian songbirds. R.A.O.U., Melbourne.

Schodde, R., and J. L. McKean. 1976. The relations of some monotypic genera of Australian oscines. Pp. 530–541 *in* Proc. 16th Intl. Orn. Congr. H. J. Frith and J. H. Calaby, eds. Australian Acad. Sci., Canberra.

Schodde, R., and R. G. Weatherly. 1982a. The Fairywrens. A monograph of the family Maluridae. Lansdowne Editions, Melbourne.

Schodde, R., and R. G. Weatherly. 1982b. Campbell's Fairy-wren, a new species from New Guinea. Emu 82:380–309.

Schoonees, J. 1963. Some aspects of the cranial morphology of *Colius indicus*. Ann. Univ. Stellenbosch, Ser. A, 38:215–246.

Schultz, G. A., and R. B. Church. 1972. DNA base sequence heterogeneity in the order Galliformes. J. Exp. Zool. 179:119–128.

Sclater, P. L. 1858. On the zoology of New Guinea. J. of Proc. Linn. Soc. London (Zool.) 2:149–170.

Sclater, P. L. 1865a. Notes on the genera and species of Cypselidae. Proc. Zool. Soc. London 1865:593–617.

Sclater, P. L. 1865b. On the structure of *Leptosoma discolor*. Proc. Zool. Soc. London 1865:682–688.

Sclater, P. L. 1866a. Notes upon the American Caprimulgidae. Proc. Zool. Soc. London 1866:123–145.

Sclater, P. L. 1866b. Additional notes on the Caprimulgidae. Proc. Zool. Soc. London 1866:581–590.

Sclater, P. L. 1870. Note on the systematic position of *Indicator*. Ibis 12:176–180.

Sclater, P. L. 1872. Observations on the systematic position of the genera *Peltops*, *Eurylaemus*, and *Todus*. Ibis 24:177–180.

Sclater, P. L. 1879. Remarks on the nomenclature of the British owls, and on the arrangement of the order Striges. Ibis 21:346–352.

Sclater, P. L. 1880a. List of the certainly known species of Anatidae. Proc. Zool. Soc. London 1880:496–536.

Sclater, P. L. 1880b. Remarks on the present state of the systema avium. Ibis 22:340–350, 399–411.

Sclater, P. L. 1882. A monograph of the jacamars and puff-birds, or families Galbulidae and Bucconidae. R. H. Porter, London.

Sclater, P. L. 1886. Catalogue of the Passeriformes or perching birds in the collection of the British Museum. Vol. 11. Brit. Mus., London.

Sclater, P. L. 1888. Catalogue of the Passeriformes, or perching birds, in the collection of the British Museum. Vol. 14. Brit. Mus., London.

Sclater, P. L. 1890. Remarks on the fifth cubital remex of the wing in the Carinatae. Ibis 32:77–83.

Sclater, P. L. 1896. Obituary . . . Mr. H. Seebohm. Ibis 38:159–162.

Sclater, P. L., and O. Salvin. 1870. Synopsis of the Cracidae. Proc. Zool. Soc. London 1870:504–544.

Sclater, P. L., and O. Salvin. 1873. Nomenclator avium neotropicalium. London.

Sclater, P. L., and O. Salvin. 1876. A revision of the Neotropical Anatidae. Proc. Zool. Soc. London 1876:358–412.

Sclater, P. L., and G. E. Shelley. 1891. Catalogue of the birds of the British Museum. Vol. 19:122–208. Brit. Mus., London.

Sclater, W. L. 1924. Systema avium aethiopicarum. Part I. Brit. Orn. Union, London. 304 pp.

Seebohm, H. 1881. Catalogue of birds in the British Museum. Vol. 5, pt. 2. Brit. Mus., London.

Seebohm, H. 1888a. The geographical distribution of the family Charadriidae, or the plovers, sandpipers, snipes, and their allies. H. Southeran and Co., London. 524 pp.

Seebohm, H. 1888b. An attempt to diagnose the suborders of the great Gallino-Gralline group of birds, by the aid of osteological characters alone. Ibis 30:415–435.

Seebohm, H. 1889. An attempt to diagnose the suborders of the ancient Ardeino-Anserine assemblage of birds by the aid of osteological characters alone. Ibis 31:92–104.

Seebohm, H. 1890a. The classification of birds: an attempt to classify the subclasses, orders, suborders, and some of the families of existing birds. R. H. Porter, London.

Seebohm, H. 1890b. An attempt to diagnose the Pico-Passerine group of birds and the suborders of which it consists. Ibis 32:29–37.

Seebohm, H. 1890c. An attempt to diagnose the subclass Coraciiformes and the orders, suborders, and families comprised therein. Ibis 32:200–205.

Seebohm, H. 1895. Classification of birds; an attempt to diagnose the subclasses, orders, suborders, and families of existing birds. Supplement. R. H. Porter, London.

Seebohm, H., and R. B. Sharpe. 1898–1902. A monograph of the Turdidae. 2 vols. H. Sotheran and Co., London.

Segal, I. H. 1976. Biochemical calculations. 2nd ed. Wiley, New York.

Serle, W. 1949. Birds of Sierra Leone. Ostrich 20:114–126.

Serventy, D. L. 1956. Age at first breeding of the Short-tailed Shearwater *Puffinus tenuirostris*. Ibis 98:532–533.

Serventy, D. L., and H. M. Whittell. 1967. Birds of Western Australia. 4th ed. Lamb Publ., Perth.

Seth-Smith, D. 1906. Bird notes from the Zoological Gardens. Avicult. Mag. 12:285–286.

Shakked, Z., G. Guerstein-Guzikevich, M. Eisenstein, F. Frowlow, and D. Rabinovich. 1989. The conformation of the DNA double helix is dependent on its environment. Nature 342:456–460.

Shapiro, H. S. 1976. Distribution of purines and pyrimidines in deoxyribonucleic acids. Pp. 241–275 *in* Handbook of biochemistry and molecular biology, vol. 2. G. D. Fasman, ed. Chemical Rubber Co. Press, Cleveland, Ohio.

Shapiro, J. A., ed. 1983. Mobile genetic elements. Academic Press, New York.

Sharp, P. A. 1987. Splicing of messenger RNA precursors. Science 235:766–771.

Sharpe, R. B. 1868–71. A monograph of the Alcedinidae: or, family of kingfishers. Publ. by author, London.

Sharpe, R. B. 1870. Contributions to the ornithology of Madagascar. I. Proc. Zool. Soc. London 1870:384–401.

Sharpe, R. B. 1874. Catalogue of birds in the British Museum, vol. 1. Brit. Mus., London.

Sharpe, R. B. 1875a. Catalogue of birds in the British Museum, vol. 2. Brit. Mus., London.

Sharpe, R. B. 1875b. Contributions to the ornithology of Madagascar. IV. Proc. Zool. Soc. London 1875:70–78.

Sharpe, R. B. 1877. Catalogue of birds in the British Museum, vol. 3. Brit. Mus., London.

Sharpe, R. B. 1879. Catalogue of birds in the British Museum, vol. 4. Brit. Mus., London.

Sharpe, R. B. 1881. Catalogue of birds in the British Museum, vol. 6. Brit. Mus., London.

Sharpe, R. B. 1883. Catalogue of birds in the British Museum, vol. 7. Brit. Mus., London.

Sharpe, R. B. 1885. Catalogue of the Passeriformes . . . in the British Museum. Vol. 10. Brit. Mus., London.

Sharpe, R. B. 1888. Catalogue of birds in the British Museum, vol. 12. Brit. Mus., London.

Sharpe, R. B. 1890. Catalogue of birds in the British Museum, vol. 13. Brit. Mus., London

Sharpe, R. B. 1891. A review of recent attempts to classify birds. Proc. 2nd Intl. Orn. Congr., Budapest.

Sharpe, R. B. 1894. Catalogue of birds in the British Museum, vol. 23. Brit. Mus., London.

Sharpe, R. B. 1896. Catalogue of birds in the British Museum, vol. 24. Brit. Mus., London.

Sharpe, R. B. 1899. A hand-list of the genera and species of birds. Vol. 1. Brit. Mus., London.

Sharpe, R. B. 1900. A hand-list of the genera and species of birds. Vol. 2. Brit. Mus., London.

Sharpe, R. B. 1901. A hand-list of the genera and species of birds, vol. 3. Brit. Mus., London.

Sharpe, R. B. 1903. A hand-list of the genera and species of birds, vol. 4. Brit. Mus., London.

Sharpe, R. B. 1909. A hand-list of the genera and species of birds, vol. 5. Brit. Mus., London.

Sharpe, R. B., and W. R. Ogilvie-Grant. 1892. Catalogue of birds in the British Museum, vol. 17. Brit. Mus., London.

Sharpe, R. B., and W. R. Ogilvie-Grant. 1898. Catalogue of birds in the British Museum, vol. 26. Brit. Mus., London.

Sheldon, F. H. 1986. A study of the evolution and phylogeny of the herons (Ardeidae) using DNA-DNA hybridization. Ph.D. thesis, Yale Univ.

Sheldon, F. H. 1987a. Rates of single-copy DNA evolution in herons. Mol. Biol. Evol. 4:56–69.

Sheldon, F. H. 1987b. Phylogeny of herons estimated from DNA-DNA hybridization data. Auk 104:97–108.

Sheldon, F. H., and A. H. Bledsoe. 1989. Indexes to the reassociation and stability of solution DNA hybrids. J. Mol. Evol. 29:328–343.

Shelley, G. E. 1891. Catalogue of birds in the British Museum, vol. 19. Brit. Mus., London.

Shelley, G. E. 1896–1912. The birds of Africa. Vols. 1–5. R. H. Porter, London.

Shepherd, J. C. W., W. McGinnis, A. E. Carrasco, E. M. De Robertis, and W. J. Gehring. 1984. Fly and frog homoeo domains show homologies with yeast mating type regulatory proteins. Nature 310:70–71.

Sherr, C. J., R. E. Benveniste, and G. J. Todaro. 1978. Endogenous mink (*Mustela vison*) type C virus isolated from sarcoma virus-transformed mink cells. J. Virology 25:738–749.

Sherwood, S. W., and J. L. Patton. 1982. Genome evolution in pocket gophers (Genus *Thomomys*) II. Variation in cellular DNA content. Chromosoma 85:163–179.

Shields, G. F., and N. A. Straus. 1975. DNA-DNA hybridization studies of birds. Evolution 29:159–166.

Short, L. L. 1967. A review of the genera of grouse (Aves, Tetraoninae). Amer. Mus. Novit. 2289. 39 pp.

Short, L. L. 1970. The affinity of African with Neotropical woodpeckers. Ostrich, Suppl. 8:35–40.

Short, L. L. 1982. Woodpeckers of the world. Monogr. Ser. No. 4, Delaware Mus. Nat. Hist., Greenville, Delaware.

Short, L. L. 1985. Neotropical-Afrotropical barbet and woodpecker radiations: a comparison. Pp. 559–574 *in* Neotropical ornithology, Ornith. Monogr. No. 36. P. A. Buckley, M. S. Foster, E. S. Morton, R. S. Ridgely, and F. G. Buckley, eds. Amer. Orn. Union, Washington, D.C.

Short, L. L., and J. F. M. Horne. 1978. Nectar-feeding of some ploceine weavers. Scopus 2:53–58.

Short, L. L., and A. R. Phillips. 1966. More hybrid hummingbirds from the United States. Auk 83:253–265.

Shufeldt, R. W. 1881a. Osteology of *Speotyto cunicularia* var. *hypogaea*. Bull. U.S. Geol. Geogr. Surv. Terr. 6:87–117.

Shufeldt, R. W. 1881b. Osteology of the North American Tetraonidae. Bull. U.S. Geol. Geogr. Surv. Terr. 6:309–350.

Shufeldt, R. W. 1882. Notes upon the osteology of *Cinclus mexicanus*. Bull. Nuttall Orn. Club 7:213–221.

Shufeldt, R. W. 1883a. Remarks upon the osteology of *Phalacrocorax bicristatus*. Science 2:640–642, 822.

Shufeldt, R. W. 1883b. Osteology of the Cathartidae. Ann. Rep. U.S. Geol. Geogr. Surv. Terr. 12:727–806.

Shufeldt, R. W. 1884. Osteology of *Ceryle alcyon*. J. Anat. Physiol. 18:279–294.

Shufeldt, R. W. 1885a. On the coloration in life of the naked skin-tracts on the head of *Geococcyx californicus*. Ibis 27:286–288.

Shufeldt, R. W. 1885b. Contribution to the comparative osteology of the Trochilidae, Caprimulgidae, and Cypselidae. Proc. Zool. Soc. London 1885:886–915.

Shufeldt, R. W. 1886a. The skeleton in *Geococcyx*. J. Anat. Physiol. 20:244–266.

Shufeldt, R. W. 1886b. Osteological note upon the young of *Geococcyx californianus*. J. Anat. Physiol. 21:101–102.

Shufeldt, R. W. 1886c. Contributions to the anatomy of *Geococcyx californianus*. Proc. Zool. Soc. London 1886:466–491.

Shufeldt, R. W. 1886d. Additional notes upon the anatomy of the Trochili, Caprimulgi, and Cypselidae. Proc. Zool. Soc. London 1886:501–503.

Shufeldt, R. W. 1888a. Observations upon the osteology of the North American Anseres. Proc. U.S. Natl. Mus. 11:215–251.

Shufeldt, R. W. 1888b. Observations upon the osteology of the order Tubinares and Steganopedes. Proc. U.S. Natl. Mus. 11:253–315.

Shufeldt, R. W. 1888c. Observations upon the morphology of *Gallus bankiva* of India (including a complete account of its skeleton). J. Comp. Med. Surg. 9:343–376.

Shufeldt, R. W. 1888d. On the affinities of *Aphriza virgata*. J. Morphol. 2:311–340.

Shufeldt, R. W. 1888e. Observations on the pterylosis of certain Picidae. Auk 5:212–218.

Shufeldt, R. W. 1889a. Osteology of *Circus hudsonius*. J. Comp. Med. Surg. 10:126–159.

Shufeldt, R. W. 1889b. Osteological studies on the sub-family Ardeinae. Parts I and II. J. Comp. Med. Surg. 10:218–243, 287–317.

Shufeldt, R. W. 1889c. Note on the anserine affinities of the flamingoes. Science 14:224–225.

Shufeldt, R. W. 1889d. Notes on the anatomy of *Speotyto cunicularia hypogaea*. J. Morphol. 3:115–125.

Shufeldt, R. W. 1889e. Studies of the Macrochires, morphological and otherwise, with the view of indicating their relationships and defining their several positions in the system. J. Linnean Soc. London 20:299–394.

Shufeldt, R. W. 1891a. Notes on the classification of the pigeons. Amer. Nat. 25:157–158.

Shufeldt, R. W. 1891b. Some comparative osteological notes on the North American Kites. Ibis 33:228–232.

Shufeldt, R. W. 1891c. Contributions to the comparative osteology of Arctic and sub-Arctic waterbirds. Part IX. J. Anat. Physiol. 25:509–525.

Shufeldt, R. W. 1891d. On the question of saurognathism of the Pici, and other osteological notes upon that group. Proc. Zool. Soc. London 1891:122–129.

Shufeldt, R. W. 1891e. On the comparative osteology of the United States Columbidae. Proc. Zool. Soc. London 1891:194–196.

Shufeldt, R. W. 1892. Concerning the taxonomy of the North American pygopodes, based upon their osteology. J. Anat. Physiol. 26:199–203.

Shufeldt, R. W. 1893a. The Chionididae. A review of the opinions on the systematic position of the family. Auk 10:158–165.

Shufeldt, R. W. 1893b. Comparative notes on the swifts and humming-birds. Ibis 35:84–100.

Shufeldt, R. W. 1894a. Note on the shoulder girdle of the man-o'-war bird. Science 23:50.

Shufeldt, R. W. 1894b. On the osteology of certain cranes, rails, and their allies, with remarks upon their affinities. J. Anat. Physiol. 29:21–34.

Shufeldt, R. W. 1901a. On the systematic position of the sand grouse (*Pterocles; Syrrhaptes*). Amer. Nat. 35:11–16.

Shufeldt, R. W. 1901b. On the osteology and systematic position of the screamers (*Palamedea*: *Chauna*). Amer. Nat. 35:455–461.

Shufeldt, R. W. 1901d. Osteology of the herodiones. Ann. Carnegie Mus. 1:158–249.

Shufeldt, R. W. 1901e. Osteology of the flamingoes (Odontoglossae). Family: Phoenicopteridae. Sp. *P. ruber*. Ann. Carnegie Mus. 1:295–324.

Shufeldt, R. W. 1901f. On the osteology of the pigeons (Columbae). J. Morph. 17:487–514.

Shufeldt, R. W. 1901g. The osteology of the cuckoos (Coccyges). Proc. Amer. Phil. Soc. 40:4–51.

Shufeldt, R. W. 1902a. The osteology of the steganopodes. Mem. Carnegie Mus. 1:109–223.

Shufeldt, R. W. 1902b. Osteology of the psittaci. Ann. Carnegie Mus. 1:339–421.

Shufeldt, R. W. 1902c. Pterylosis of hummingbirds and swifts. Condor 4:47–48.

Shufeldt, R. W. 1903a. Osteology of the Limicolae. Ann. Carnegie Mus. 2:15–70.

Shufeldt, R. W. 1903b. On the osteology and systematic position of the kingfishers. (*Halcyones*.) Amer. Nat. 37:697–725.

Shufeldt, R. W. 1904a. On the osteology and systematic position of the Pygopodes. Amer. Nat. 38:13–49.

Shufeldt, R. W. 1904b. An arrangement of the families and the higher groups of birds. Amer. Nat. 38:833–857.

Shufeldt, R. W. 1909. Osteology of birds. Bull. Education Dept. No. 447 (New York State Mus. Bull. 130). 381 pp.

Shufeldt, R. W. 1914a. On the skeleton of the ocellated turkey (*Agriocharis ocellata*), with notes on the osteology of other Meleagridae. Aquila 21:1–52.

Shufeldt, R. W. 1914b. On the oology of the North American Pygopodes. Condor 16:169–180.

Shufeldt, R. W. 1914c. Contribution to the study of the "Tree-Ducks" of the genus *Dendrocygna*. Zool. Jahrb. Abt. Syst. Geogr. Biol. Tiere 38:1–70.

Shufeldt, R. W. 1915a. On the comparative osteology of the limpkin (*Aramus vociferus*) and its place in the system. Anat. Rec. 9:591–606.

Shufeldt, R. W. 1915b. Comparative osteology of certain rails and cranes, and the systematic positions of the supersuborders Gruiformes and Ralliformes. Anat. Rec. 9:731–750.

Shufeldt, R. W. 1918a. Notes on the osteology of the young of the hoatzin (*Opisthocomus cristatus*) and other points on its morphology. J. Morphol. 31:599–606.

Shufeldt, R. W. 1918b. The skeleton of the "kea parrot" of New Zealand (*Nestor notabilis*). Emu 18:25–43.

Shufeldt, R. W. 1922. On the skeleton of the wedge-tailed eagle (*Uroaetus audax*, Latham). Emu 21:295–306.

Sibley, C. G. 1956. The aftershaft in jacamars and puff-birds. Wilson Bull. 68:252–253.

Sibley, C. G. 1957. The evolutionary and taxonomic significance of sexual dimorphism and hybridization in birds. Condor 59:166–191.

Sibley, C. G. 1960. The electrophoretic patterns of avian egg-white proteins as taxonomic characters. Ibis 102:215–284.

Sibley, C. G. 1961. Hybridization and isolating mechanisms. Pp. 69–88 *in* Vertebrate speciation. W. F. Blair, ed. Univ. Texas Press, Austin.

Sibley, C. G. 1968. The relationships of the "wren-thrush," *Zeledonia coronata* Ridgway. Postilla 125:1–12.

Sibley, C. G. 1970. A comparative study of the egg-white proteins of passerine birds. Bull. Peabody Mus. Nat. Hist. 32:1–131.

Sibley, C. G. 1973. The relationships of the silky flycatchers. Auk 90:394–410.

Sibley, C. G. 1974. The relationships of the lyrebirds. Emu 74:65–79.

Sibley, C. G. 1976a. Protein evidence of the origin of certain Australian birds. Pp. 66–70 *in* Proc. 16th Intl. Orn. Congr. H. J. Frith and J. H. Calaby, eds. Austral. Acad. Sci., Canberra.

Sibley, C. G. 1976b. Protein evidence of the relationships of some Australian passerine birds. Pp. 557–570 *in* Proc. 16th Intl. Orn. Congr. H. J. Frith and J. H. Calaby, eds. Austral. Acad. Sci., Canberra.

Sibley, C. G., and J. E. Ahlquist. 1972. A comparative study of the egg-white proteins of nonpasserine birds. Bull. Peabody Mus. Nat. Hist. 39:1–276.

Sibley, C. G., and J. E. Ahlquist. 1973. The relationships of the Hoatzin. Auk 90:1–13.

Sibley, C. G., and J. E. Ahlquist. 1974. The relationships of the African sugarbirds (*Promerops*). Ostrich 45:22–30.

Sibley, C. G., and J. E. Ahlquist. 1980. The relationships of the "primitive insect eaters" (Aves: Passeriformes) as indicated by DNA × DNA hybridization. Pp. 1215–1220 *in* Proc. 17th Intl. Orn. Congr. R. Nöhring, ed. Deutsche Orn. Gesellsch, Berlin.

Sibley, C. G., and J. E. Ahlquist. 1981a. The phylogeny and relationships of the ratite birds as indicated by DNA-DNA hybridization. Pp. 301–335 *in* Evolution Today, Proc. Second Intl. Congr. Syst. Evol. Biol. G. G. E. Scudder and J. L. Reveal, eds. Hunt Inst. Botanic. Document., Pittsburgh, Penn.

Sibley, C. G., and J. E. Ahlquist. 1981b. The relationships of the Accentors (*Prunella*) as indicated by DNA-DNA hybridization. J. für Orn. 122:369–378.

Sibley, C. G., and J. E. Ahlquist. 1981c. The relationships of the wagtails and pipits (Motacillidae) as indicated by DNA-DNA hybridization. L'Oiseau R.F.O. 51:189–199.

Sibley, C. G., and J. E. Ahlquist. 1981d. Instructions for specimen preservation for DNA extraction: a valuable source of data for systematics. Newsletter Assoc. Syst. Coll. 9:44–45. Mus. Nat. Hist., Univ. Kansas, Lawrence, Kansas.

Sibley, C. G., and J. E. Ahlquist. 1982a. The relationships of the Hawaiian honeycreepers (Drepaninini) as indicated by DNA-DNA hybridization. Auk 99:130–140.

Sibley, C. G., and J. E. Ahlquist. 1982b. The relationships of the Wrentit (*Chamaea fasciata*) as indicated by DNA-DNA hybridization. Condor 84:40–44.

Sibley, C. G., and J. E. Ahlquist. 1982c. The relationships of the vireos (Vireoninae) as indicated by DNA-DNA hybridization. Wilson Bull. 94:114–128.

Sibley, C. G., and J. E. Ahlquist. 1982d. The relationships of the Yellow-breasted Chat (*Icteria virens*) and the alleged "slow-down" in the rate of macromolecular evolution in birds. Postilla 187:1–19. Peabody Mus. Nat. Hist., Yale Univ.

Sibley, C. G., and J. E. Ahlquist. 1982e. The relationships of the Australo-Papuan scrub-robins *Drymodes* as indicated by DNA-DNA hybridization. Emu 82:101–105.

Sibley, C. G., and J. E. Ahlquist. 1982f. The relationships of the Australo-Papuan sittellas *Daphoenositta* as indicated by DNA-DNA hybridization. Emu 82:173–176.

Sibley, C. G., and J. E. Ahlquist. 1982g. The relationships of the Australasian whistlers *Pachycephala* as indicated by DNA-DNA hybridization. Emu 82:199–202.

Sibley, C. G., and J. E. Ahlquist. 1982h. The relationships of the Australo-Papuan fairy-wrens *Malurus* as indicated by DNA-DNA hybridization. Emu 82:251–255.

Sibley, C. G., and J. E. Ahlquist. 1982i. The relationships of the swallows (Hirundinidae). J. Yamashina Inst. for Orn. 14(64/65):122–130.

Sibley, C. G., and J. E. Ahlquist. 1983. The phylogeny and classification of birds, based on the data of DNA-DNA hybridization. Current Orn. 1:245–292. R. F. Johnston, ed. Plenum Press, New York.

Sibley, C. G., and J. E. Ahlquist. 1984a. The phylogeny of the hominoid primates as indicated by DNA-DNA hybridization. J. Mol. Evol. 20:2–15.

Sibley, C. G., and J. E. Ahlquist. 1984b. The relationships of the starlings (Sturnidae: Sturnini) and the mockingbirds (Sturnidae: Mimini). Auk 101:230–243.

Sibley, C. G., and J. E. Ahlquist. 1984c. The relationships of the Papuan genus *Peltops*. Emu 84:181–183.

Sibley, C. G., and J. E. Ahlquist. 1985a. The phylogeny and classification of the Australo-Papuan passerine birds. Emu 85:1–14.

Sibley, C. G., and J. E. Ahlquist. 1985b. Phylogeny and classification of New World sub-oscine passerine birds (Passeriformes: Oligomyodi: Tyrannides). Pp. 396–428 *in* Neotropical Ornithology. P. A. Buckley, M. S. Foster, E. S. Morton, R. S. Ridgely, and F. G. Buckley, eds. Orn. Monogr. No. 36, Amer. Orn. Union, Washington, D.C.

Sibley, C. G., and J. E. Ahlquist. 1985c. The relationships of some groups of African birds, based on comparisons of the genetic material, DNA. Proc. Intl. Congr. African Vertebrates. K.-L. Schuchmann, ed. Mus. Koenig, Bonn.

Sibley, C. G., and J. E. Ahlquist. 1985d. The phylogeny and classification of the passerine birds, based on comparisons of the genetic material, DNA. Pp. 83–121 *in* Proc. 18th Intl. Orn. Congr. V. D. Ilyichev and V. M. Gavrilov, eds. Nauka, Moscow.

Sibley, C. G., and J. E. Ahlquist. 1986. Reconstructing bird phylogeny by comparing DNAs. Sci. Amer. 254:82–92.

Sibley, C. G., and J. E. Ahlquist. 1987a. The relationships of four species of New Zealand passerine birds. Emu 87:63–66.

Sibley, C. G., and J. E. Ahlquist. 1987b. The Lesser Melampitta is a bird of paradise. Emu 87:66–68.

Sibley, C. G., and J. E. Ahlquist. 1987c. Avian phylogeny reconstructed from comparisons of the genetic material, DNA. Pp. 95–121 *in* Molecules and morphology in evolution: conflict or compromise. C. Patterson, ed. Cambridge Univ. Press, London.

Sibley, C. G., and J. E. Ahlquist. 1987d. DNA hybridization evidence of hominoid phylogeny: results from an expanded data set. J. Mol. Evol. 26:99–121.

Sibley, C. G., and A. H. Brush. 1967. An electrophoretic study of avian eye-lens proteins. Auk 84:203–219.

Sibley, C. G., and C. Frelin. 1972. The egg white protein evidence of ratite affinities. Ibis 114:377–387.

Sibley, C. G., and B. L. Monroe, Jr. 1990. Distribution and taxonomy of the birds of the world. Yale Univ. Press, New Haven, Conn.

Sibley, C. G., K. W. Corbin, and J. E. Ahlquist. 1968. The relationships of the seed-snipe (Thinocoridae) as indicated by their egg white proteins and hemoglobins. Bonn. Zool. Beitr. 19:235–248.

Sibley, C. G., K. W. Corbin, and J. H. Haavie. 1969. The relationships of the flamingos as indicated by the egg white proteins and hemoglobins. Condor 71:155–179.

Sibley, C. G., K. W. Corbin, J. E. Ahlquist, and A. Ferguson. 1974. Birds. Pp. 89–176 *in* Biochemical and Immunological Taxonomy of Animals. C. A. Wright, ed. Academic Press, New York.

Sibley, C. G., G. R. Williams, and J. E. Ahlquist. 1982. The relationships of the New Zealand wrens (Acanthisittidae) as indicated by DNA-DNA hybridization. Notornis 29:113–130.

Sibley, C. G., S. M. Lanyon, and J. E. Ahlquist. 1984a. The relationships of the Sharpbill (*Oxyruncus cristatus*). Condor 86:48–52.

Sibley, C. G., R. Schodde, and J. E. Ahlquist. 1984b. The relationships of the Australo-Papuan treecreepers Climacteridae as indicated by DNA-DNA hybridization. Emu 84:236–241.

Sibley, C. G., J. E. Ahlquist, and F. H. Sheldon. 1987. DNA hybridization and avian phylogenetics: reply to Cracraft. Pp. 97–125 *in* Evol. Biol. vol. 21. M. K. Hecht, B. Wallace, and G. T. Prance, eds. Plenum, New York.

Sibley, C. G., J. E. Ahlquist, and B. L. Monroe, Jr. 1988. A classification of the living birds of the world based on DNA-DNA hybridization studies. Auk 105:409–423.

Sibley, C. G., J. A. Comstock, and J. E. Ahlquist. 1990. DNA hybridization evidence of hominoid phylogeny: a reanalysis of the data. J. Mol. Evol. 30:202–236.

Sick, H. 1964a. Hoatzin. Pp. 369–371 *in* A new dictionary of birds. A. L. Thomson, ed. Nelson, London.

Sick, H. 1964b. Rhea. Pp. 697–699 *in* A new dictionary of birds. A. L. Thomson, ed. Nelson, London.

Sick, H. 1964c. Tapaculo. Pp. 805–806 *in* A new dictionary of birds. A. L. Thomson, ed. Nelson, London.

Siegel-Causey, D. 1988. Phylogeny of the Phalacrocoracidae. Condor 90:885–905.

Siegel-Causey, D. 1989. Cranial pneumatization in the Phalacrocoracidae. Wilson Bull. 101:108–112.

Simeone, A., F. Mavilio, L. Bottero, A. Giampaolo, G. Russo, A. Faiella, E. Boncinelli, and C. Peschle. 1986. A human homoeo box gene specifically expressed in spinal cord during embryonic development. Nature 320:763–765.

Simmons, K. E. L. 1963. Some behaviour characters of the babblers (Timaliidae). Avicult. Mag. 69:183–193.

Simonetta, A. M. 1960. On the mechanical implications of the avian skull and their bearing on the evolution and classification of birds. Quart. Rev. Biol. 35:206–220.

Simonetta, A. M. 1963. Cinesi e morfologia del cranio negli uccelli non passeriformi. Studio su varie tendenze evolutive. Part 1. Arch. Zool. Ital. (Torino) 48:53–135.

Simonetta, A. M. 1968. Cinesi e morfologia del cranio negli uccelli non passeriformi. Studio su varie tendenze evolutive. Part II. Striges, Caprimulgiformes ed Apodiformes. Arch. Zool. Ital. (Torino) 52:1–36.

Simpson, G. G. 1944. Tempo and mode in evolution. Columbia Univ. Press, New York. 237 pp.

Simpson, G. G. 1946. Fossil penguins. Bull. Amer. Mus. Nat. Hist. 87:1–100.

Simpson, G. G. 1957. Australian fossil penguins, with remarks on penguin evolution and distribution. Rec. South Australian Mus. 13:51–70.

Simpson, G. G. 1959. A new fossil penguin from Australia. Proc. Roy. Soc. Victoria, N.S. 71:113–119.

Simpson, G. G. 1965. New record of a fossil penguin in Australia. Proc. Roy. Soc. Victoria 79:91–93.

Simpson, G. G. 1970. Miocene penguins from Victoria, Australia, and Chubut, Argentina. Mem. Natl. Mus. Victoria 31:17–23.

Simpson, G. G. 1976. Penguins. Yale Univ. Press, New Haven, Conn.

Simpson, S. F., and J. Cracraft. 1981. The phylogenetic relationships of the Piciformes (Class Aves). Auk 98:481–494.

Skead, C. J. 1964. Sugarbirds in the Amatole Mountains, King William's Town, Cape Province. Ostrich 35:236.

Skead, C. J. 1967. The sunbirds of southern Africa, also the sugarbirds, the white-eyes and the spotted creeper. South African Bird Book Fund, Cape Town.

Skutch, A. F. 1935. Helpers at the nest. Auk 52:257–273.

Skutch, A. F. 1959. Life history of the Groove-billed Ani. Auk 76:281–317.

Skutch, A. F. 1966. Life history notes on three tropical American cuckoos. Wilson Bull. 78:139–165.

Skutch, A. F. 1985. Toucan. Pp. 602–604 *in* A dictionary of birds. B. Campbell and E. Lack, eds. T. and A. D. Poyser, Calton, England.

Smith, A. B. 1988. Phylogenetic relationship, divergence times, and rates of molecular evolution for camarodont sea urchins. Mol. Biol. Evol. 5:345–365.

Smith, A. G., A. M. Hurley, and J. C. Briden. 1981. Phanerozoic paleocontinental world maps. Cambridge Univ. Press.

Smith, G. 1975. Systematics of parrots. Ibis 117:18–68.

Smith, M. 1979. The first complete nucleotide sequencing of an organism's DNA. Amer. Scientist 67:57–67.

Smith, M. J., R. J. Britten, and E. H. Davison. 1975. Studies on nucleic acid reassociation kinetics: reactivity of single-stranded tails in DNA-DNA renaturation. Proc. Natl. Acad. Sci. USA 72:4805–4809.

Smith, M. J., R. Nicholson, M. Stuerzl, and A. Lui. 1982. Single copy DNA homology in sea stars. J. Mol. Evol. 18:92–101.

Smith, M. W. 1988. Structure of vertebrate genes: a statistical analysis implicating selection. J. Mol. Evol. 27:45–55.

Sneath, P. H. A., and R. R. Sokal. 1973. Numerical taxonomy. W. H. Freeman and Co., San Francisco.

Snow, D. W. 1961. The natural history of the oilbird, *Steatornis caripensis*, in Trinidad, W.I. Part 1: general behavior and breeding habits. Zoologica (New York) 46:27–49.

Snow, D. W. 1962. The natural history of the oilbird, *Steatornis caripensis*, in Trinidad, W.I. Part 2. Population, breeding ecology and food. Zoologica (New York) 47:199–221.

Snow, D. W. 1967. Check-list of birds of the world. Vol. 12. R. A. Paynter, Jr. ed. Mus. Comp. Zool., Cambridge, Mass.

Snow, D. W. 1973. The classification of the Cotingidae (Aves). Breviora 409:1–27. Mus. Comp. Zool., Cambridge, Mass.

Snow, D. W. 1975. The classification of the manakins. Bull. Brit. Orn. Club 95:20–27.

Snow, D. W. 1979. Pipridae, Cotingidae. Pp. 245–308 *in* Check-list of birds of the world, vol. 8. M. A. Traylor, Jr., ed. Mus. Comp. Zool., Cambridge, Mass.

Snow, D. W. 1982. The cotingas. Brit. Mus. Nat. Hist., Oxford Univ. Press.

Snow, M. H. L. 1986. New data from mammalian homoeobox-containing genes. Nature 324:618–619.

Sohn, U.-I., K. H. Rothfels, and N. A. Straus. 1975. DNA: DNA hybridization studies in black flies. J. Mol. Evol. 5:75–85.

Sokal, R. R. 1985. The continuing search for order. Amer. Nat. 126:729–749.

Sokal, R. R., and C. D. Michener. 1958. A statistical method for evaluating systematic relationships. Univ. Kansas Sci. Bull. 38:1409–1438.

Sokal, R. R., and P. H. A. Sneath. 1963. Principles of Numerical Taxonomy. W. H. Freeman and Co., San Francisco.

Solignac, M., M. Monnerot, and J.-C. Mounolou. 1986. Mitochondrial DNA evolution in the *melanogaster* species subgroup of *Drosophila*. J. Mol. Evol. 23:31–40.

Sourdis, J., and C. Krimbas. 1987. Accuracy of phylogenetic trees estimated from DNA sequence data. Mol. Biol. Evol. 4:159–168.

Southern African Ornithological Society. 1980. Checklist of southern African birds. Southern African Orn. Soc., P. A. Clancey, ed. Sigma Press, Pretoria.

Southern, E. M. 1970. Base sequence and evolution of guinea pig α-satellite DNA. Nature 227:794–798.

Southern, E. M. 1974. Eukaryotic DNA. Pp. 101–139 *in* Biochemistry of Nucleic Acids. K. Burton, ed. MTP International Rev. of Science: Biochemistry Series 1,4. Butterworth, London, and University Park Press, Baltimore.

Sparrow, A. H., and A. F. Nauman. 1976. Evolution of genome size by DNA doublings. Science 192:524–529.

Sparrow, A. H., H. J. Price, and A. G. Underbrink. 1972. A survey of DNA content per cell and per chromosome of prokaryotic and eukaryotic organisms: some evolutionary considerations. Pp. 451–494 *in* Evolution of Genetic Systems. H. H. Smith ed., Brookhaven Symp. Biol., vol. 23. Gordon and Breach, New York.

Spradling, A. C., and G. M. Rubin. 1981. *Drosophila* genome organization: conserved and dynamic aspects. Ann. Rev. Genet. 15:219–264.

Springer, M. S., and J. A. W. Kirsch. 1989. Rates of single-copy DNA evolution in phalangeriform marsupials. Mol. Biol. Evol. 6:331–341.

Springer, M., and C. Krajewski. 1989. DNA hybridization in animal taxonomy: a critique from first principles. Quart. Rev. Biol. 64:291–318.

Stackebrandt, E., and C. R. Woese. 1981. The evolution of prokaryotes. Pp. 1–31 *in* Molecular and cellular aspects of microbial evolution. M. Carlile, I. Collins, and B. Moseley, eds. Soc. Gen. Microbiol. Symp. 32. Cambridge Univ. Press, Cambridge.

Stallcup, W. B. 1954. Myology and serology of the avian family Fringillidae. Publ. Mus. Nat. Hist. Univ. Kansas 8(2):157–211.

Stallcup, W. B. 1961. Relationships of some families of the suborder Passeres (songbirds) as indicated by comparisons of tissue proteins. J. Grad. Res. Center, Southern Methodist Univ. 29(1):43–65.

Stapel, S. O., J. A. M. Leunissen, M. Versteeg, J. Wattel, and W. W. de Jong. 1984. Ratites as oldest offshoot of avian stem—evidence from α-crystallin A sequences. Nature 311:257–259.

Starck, D. 1955. Die endokraniale Morphologie der Ratiten, besonders der Apterygidae und Dinornithidae. Morphol. Jahrb. 96:14–72.

Starck, D. 1959. Neuere Ergebnisse der vergleichenden Anatomie und ihre Bedeutung für die Taxonomie, erlautert an der Trigeminus-Muskulatur der Vögel. J. für Orn. 100:47–59.

Starck, D. 1960. Über ein Anlagerungsgelenk zwischen Unterkiefer und Schädel basis bei den Mausvögeln (Coliidae). Zool. Anz. 164:1–11.

Starck, D., and A. Barnikol. 1954. Beiträge zur Morphologie der Trigeminusmuskulatur der Vögel (besonders der Accipitres, Cathartidae, Striges und Anseres). Morph. Jahrb. 94:1–64.

Stebbins, G. L., and D. L. Hartl. 1988. Comparative evolution: latent potentials for anagenetic advance. Proc. Natl. Acad. Sci. USA 85:5141–5145.

Stefos, K. 1971. Heterochromatin distribution in the chromosomes of birds. Amer. Soc. Cell Biol., 11th annual meeting, abstracts p. 287.

Stefos, K., and F. E. Arrighi. 1974. Repetitive DNA of *Gallus domesticus* and its cytological locations. Exper. Cell Res. 83:9–14.

Stegmann, B. K. 1957a. Über die Eigenheiten des Fluges der Pterocliden [in Russian, German summary]. Zool. Zh. (Moscow) 36:1521–1529.

Stegmann, B. K. 1957b. Über einige Eigenheiten im Bau des Schultergürtels bei den Tauben und Flughühnern und die funktionelle Bedeutung der Clavicula bei den Vögeln [in Russian, German summary]. Bull. Soc. Nat. Moscou, Biol. 62:45–56.

Stegmann, B. K. 1958. Die phylogenetischen Beziehungen zwischen den Tauben und Flughühnern und die Stellung dieser Vögel im System [in Russian, German summary]. Bull. Soc. Nat. Moscou, Biol. 63:25–36.

Stegmann, B. K. 1959. Some structural peculiarities of the skull and vertebral column in pigeons and sand-grouses [in Russian, English summary]. Zool. Zh. (Moscow) 38:1049–1059.

Stegmann, B. K. 1968. Über die phyletischen Beziehungen zwischen Regenpfeifervögeln, Tauben und Flughühnern. J. für Orn. 109:441–445.

Stegmann, B. K. 1969. Über die systematische Stellung der Tauben und Flughühner. Zool. Jahrb., Syst., 96:1–51.

Stein, D. B., and W. F. Thompson. 1975. DNA hybridization and evolutionary relationships in three *Osmunda* species. Science 189:888–890.

Stein, D. B., and W. F. Thompson. 1979. Studies in the Osmundaceae: single-copy DNA comparisons. Carnegie Inst. Wash. Year Book 78:223–225.

Stein, D. B., W. F. Thompson and H. S. Belford. 1979. Studies on DNA sequences in the Osmundaceae. J. Mol. Evol. 13:215–232.

Stein, J. P., J. F. Catterall, P. Kristo, A. R. Means, and B. W. O'Malley. 1980. Ovomucoid intervening sequences specify functional domains and generate protein polymorphism. Cell 21:681–687.

Steinbacher, G. 1935. Funktionell-anatomische untersuchungen an Vogelfüssen mit Wendezehen und Rückzehen. J. für Orn. 83:214–282.

Steinbacher, J. 1937. Anatomische Untersuchungen über die systematische Stellung der Galbulidae und Bucconidae. Arch. Naturgesch., N.S., 6:417–515.

Steiner, H. 1916. Das Problem der Diastataxie des Vogelflügels. Vierteljahrsschr. Naturforsch. Ges. Zürich 61:488–502.

Steiner, H. 1918. Das Problem der Diastataxie des Vogelflügels. Jena. Z. Naturwiss. 55:221–496.

Steiner, H. 1936. Über die äussere Gestaltung eines fünfzehntägigen Embryos des Emus, *Dromiceius novae-hollandiae* (Lath.). Rev. Suisse Zool. 43:543–550.

Steiner, H. 1946. Zur Pterylose des afrikanischen Strausses, *Struthio camelus* L. Schweiz. Verh. Naturf. Ges. 126:158–159.

Steiner, H. 1955. Das Brutverhalten der Prachtfinken, Spermestidae, als Ausdruck ihres selbständigen Familiencharakters. Pp. 350–355 *in* Proc. 11th Intl. Orn. Congr.

Steiner, H. 1956. Die taxonomische und phylogenetische Bedeutung der Diastataxie des Vogelflügels. J. für Orn. 97:1–20.

Steiner, H. 1958. Nachweis der Diastataxie im Flügel von Emu und Kasuar, Ordnung Casuarii der Ratiten. Rev. Suisse Zool. 65:420–427.

Steiner, H. 1960. Klassifikation der Prachtfinken, Spermestidae, auf Grund der Rachenzeichnungen iherer Nestlinge. J. für Orn. 101:92–112.

Steitz, J. A. 1988. "Snurps." Sci. Amer. 258(6):56–63.

Stejneger, L. 1883. Remarks on the systematic arrangement of the American Turdidae. Proc. U.S. Nat. Mus. 5:449–483.

Stejneger, L. 1885. Birds. *In* The standard natural history, vol. 4. J. S. Kingsley, ed. S. E. Cassino, Boston.

Stejneger, L. 1905. The birds of the genus *Cinclus* and their geographical distribution. Smithson. Misc. Coll. 47:421–430.

Stephenson, E. C., H. P. Erba, and J. G. Gall. 1981. Histone gene clusters of the newt Notophthalmus are separated by long tracts of satellite DNA. Cell 24: 639–647.

Stiles, F. G., and B. Whitney. 1983. Notes on the behavior of the Costa Rican Sharpbill (*Oxyruncus cristatus frater*). Auk 100:117–125.

Stock, A. D., and T. D. Bunch. 1982. The evolutionary implications of chromosome banding pattern homologies in the bird order Galliformes. Cytogenet. Cell Genet. 34:136–148.

Stolpe, M. 1932. Physiologisch-anatomische Untersuchungen über die hintere Extremität der Vögel. J. für Orn. 80:161–247.

Stolpe, M. 1935. *Colymbus*, *Hesperornis*, *Podiceps*: ein Vergleich ihrer hinteren Extremität. J. für Orn. 83:115–128.

Stonehouse, B. 1985. Tropicbird. Pp. 610–611 *in* A dictionary of birds. B. Campbell and E. Lack, eds. T. and A. D. Poyser, Calton, England.

Stonor, C. R. 1936. The evolution and mutual relationships of some members of the Paradiseidae. Proc. Zool. Soc. London 1936:1177–1185.

Stonor, C. R. 1937. On the systematic position of the Ptilonorhynchidae. Proc. Zool. Soc. London 1937:107 (ser. B) 475–490.

Stonor, C. R. 1938. Some features of the variation of the birds of paradise. Proc. Zool. Soc. London 1938:417–481.

Stonor, C. R. 1942. Anatomical notes on the New Zealand wattled crow (*Callaeas*), with especial reference to its powers of flight. Ibis 84:1–18.

Storer, R. W. 1945a. Structural modifications in the hind limb in the Alcidae. Ibis 87:433–456.

Storer, R. W. 1945b. The systematic position of the murrelet genus *Endomychura*. Condor 47:154–160.

Storer, R. W. 1952. A comparison of variation, behavior and evolution in the sea bird genera *Uria* and *Cepphus*. Univ. Calif. Publ. Zool. 52:121–222.

Storer, R. W. 1956. The fossil loon, *Colymboides minutus*. Condor 58:413–426.

Storer, R. W. 1959. The arrangement of songbird families. Condor 61:152–153.

Storer, R. W. 1960a. The classification of birds. Pp. 57–93 *in* Biology and Comparative Physiology of Birds, vol. 1. A. J. Marshall, ed. Academic Press, New York.

Storer, R. W. 1960b. Evolution in the diving birds. Proc. 12th Intl. Orn. Congr. 694–707.

Storer, R. W. 1963a. Observations on the great grebe. Condor 65:279–288.

Storer, R. W. 1963b. Courtship and mating behavior and the phylogeny of the grebes. Pp. 562–569 *in* Proc. 13th Intl. Orn. Congr.

Storer, R. W. 1965. The color phases of the Western Grebe. Living Bird 4:59–63.

Storer, R. W. 1967a. The patterns of downy grebes. Condor 69:469–478.

Storer, R. W. 1967b. Observations on Rolland's grebe. El Hornero (Buenos Aires) 10:339–350.

Storer, R. W. 1969. The behavior of the horned grebe in spring. Condor 71:180–205.

Storer, R. W. 1971. Classification of birds. Pp. 1–18 *in* Avian Biology, vol. 1. D. S. Farner and J. R. King, eds. Academic Press, New York.

Storer, R. W. 1979. Order Podicipediformes. Pp. 140–155 *in* Check-list of birds of the world, vol. 1, second edition. E. Mayr and G. W. Cottrell, eds. Mus. Comp. Zool., Cambridge, Mass.

Storer, R. W., and G. L. Nuechterlein. 1985. An analysis of plumage and morphological characters of the two color forms of the Western Grebe (*Aechmophorus*). Auk 102:102–119.

Storr, G. M. 1958. On the classification of the Old World flycatchers. Emu 58:277–283.

Strahl, S. D. 1985. The behavior and socio-ecology of the hoatzin, *Opisthocomus hoazin*, in the llanos of Venezuela. Ph.D. diss., State Univ. New York, Albany.

Strasburger, E. 1909. The minute structure of cells in relation to heredity. Pp. 102–111 *in* Darwin and modern science. A. C. Steward, ed. Cambridge Univ. Press.

Strauch, J. G., Jr. 1978. The phylogeny of the Charadriiformes (Aves): a new estimate using the method of character compatibility analysis. Trans. Zool. Soc. London 34:263–345.

Strauch, J. G., Jr. 1985. The phylogeny of the Alcidae. Auk 102:520–539.

Straus, N. A. 1971. Comparative DNA renaturation kinetics in amphibians. Proc. Natl. Acad. Sci. USA 68:799–802.

Straus, N. A. 1976. Repeated DNA in eukaryotes. Pp. 3–29 *in* Handbook of Genetics, vol. 5. R. C. King, ed. Plenum Press, New York.

Stresemann, E. 1923. Ueber die systematische Stellung der Paradoxornithinae. Verhandl. Orn. Gesellsch. Bayern 15:387–390.

Stresemann, E. 1934. Aves. *In* Handbuch der Zoologie, vol. 7, part 2. W. Kükenthal and T. Krumbach, eds. 899 pp. Walter de Gruyter, Berlin.

Stresemann, E. 1951. Die Entwicklung der Ornithologie von Aristoteles bis zur Gegenwart. F. W. Peters, Berlin. 431 pp.

Stresemann, E. 1959. The status of avian systematics and its unsolved problems. Auk 76:269–280.

Stresemann, E. 1965. Die Mauser der Hühnervögel. J. für Orn. 106:58–64.

Stresemann, E. 1967. Inheritance and adaptation in moult. Pp. 75–80 *in* Proc. 14th Intl. Orn. Congr.

Stresemann, E. 1975. Ornithology from Aristotle to the present. Transl. by H. and C. Epstein. G. W. Cottrell, ed. Forward by E. Mayr. Harvard Univ. Press, Cambridge, Mass.

Stresemann, E., and D. Amadon. 1979. Order Falconiformes. Pp. 271–425 *in* Check-list of the birds of the world, vol. 1, second edition. E. Mayr and G. W. Cottrell, eds. Mus. Comp. Zool., Cambridge, Mass.

Stresemann, E., and B. Stephan. 1968a. Zahl und Zählung der Handschwingen bei den Honiganzeigern (Indicatoridae). J. für Orn. 109:221–222.

Stresemann, E., and B. Stephan. 1968b. Über das Remicle. J. für Orn. 109:315–322.

Stresemann, E., and V. Stresemann. 1966a. Die Mauser der Vögel. J. für Orn. 107:1–445.

Stresemann, E., and V. Stresemann. 1966b. Die Mauser der Schopfkuckucke (*Clamator*). J. für Orn. 110:192–204.

Stresemann, V. 1958. Sind die Falconidae ihrer Mauserweise nach eine einheitliche Gruppe? J. für Orn. 99:81–88.

Stresemann, V. 1959. The wing molt and systematic position of the genus *Gampsonyx*. Auk 76:360–361.

Stresemann, V., and E. Stresemann. 1960. Die Handschwingenmauser der Tagraubvögel. J. für Orn. 101:373–403.

Stresemann, V., and E. Stresemann. 1961a. Die Handschwingen-Mauser der Kuckucke (Cuculidae). J. für Orn. 102:317–352.

Stresemann, V., and E. Stresemann. 1961b. Die Handschwingen-Mauser der Eisvögel (Alcedinidae). J. für Orn. 102:439–455.

Strickland, H. E. 1843. On the structure and affinities of *Upupa*, Lin., and *Irrisor*, Lesson. Ann. Mag. Natur. Hist. 12:238–243.

Stryer, L. 1988. Biochemistry. 3rd ed. W. H. Freeman, New York.

Sturkie, P. D. 1954. Avian physiology. Cornell Univ. Press, Ithaca, New York.

Sturm, R. A., and W. Herr. 1988. The POU domain is a bipartite DNA-binding structure. Nature 336:601–604.

Sundevall, C. J. 1835. Ornithologiskt system. Kongliga Svenska Vetenskaps Akad. (Stockholm), Handlingar, n.s., 1835:43–130.

Sundevall, C. J. 1851. Om muskelbyggnaden i foglarnas extremiteter. Skandin. Naturforskarnes, Forhandl. 6:259–269.

Sundevall, C. J. 1872. Methodi naturalis avium disponendarum tentamen. Samson and Wallin, Stockholm. Eng. transl. by F. Nicholson, 1889. R. H. Porter, London.

Sundevall, C. J. 1889. Sundevall's tentamen. English translation of Sundevall 1872 by F. Nicholson. R. H. Porter, London.

Sushkin, P. P. 1899a. Zur Morphologie des Vogelskelets. I. Schädel von *Tinnunculus* [in Russian]. Nouv. Mem. Soc. Nat. Moscou 16(2)1–163. German summary in Zool. Zbl. (1897) 5:307–311.

Sushkin, P. P. 1899b. Beiträge zur Classification der Tagraubvögel mit Zugrundelegung der osteologischen Merkmale. Zool. Anz. 22:500–518.

Sushkin, P. P. 1900a. Systematische Ergebnisse osteologischer Untersuchungen einiger Tagraubvögel. Zool. Anz. 23:269–277.

Sushkin, P. P. 1900b. Weitere systematische Ergebnisse Vergleichend-osteologischer Untersuchungen der Tagraubvögel. Zool. Anz. 23:522–528.

Sushkin, P. P. 1905. Zur Morphologie des Vogelskelets. Vergleichende Osteologie der normalen Tagraubvögel (Accipitres) und die Fragen der Klassifikation. I. Grundeinteilung der Accipitres. II. Die Falken und ihre nächsten Verwandten [in Russian]. Nouv. Mem. Soc. Nat. Moscou 16(4):1–247.

Sushkin, P. P. 1924. On the Fringillidae and allied groups. Bull. Brit. Orn. Club 45:36–39.

Sushkin, P. P. 1925. The evening grosbeak (*Hesperiphona*), the only American genus of a Palaearctic group. Auk 42:256–261.

Sushkin, P. P. 1927. On the anatomy and classification of the weaver birds. Bull. Amer. Mus. Nat. Hist. 57:1–32.

Sushkin, P. P. 1929a. On the systematic position of the Drepaniidae. Pp. 379–381 *in* Proc. 6th Intl. Orn. Congr.

Sushkin, P. P. 1929b. On some peculiarities of adaptive radiation presented by insular faunae. *In* Proc. 6th Intl. Orn. Congr.

Sutter, E. 1956. Zur Flügel- und Schwanzmauser des Turmfalken (*Falco tinnunculus*). Orn. Beob. 53:172–182.

Sutton, W. D., and M. McCallum. 1972. Related satellite DNAs in the genus *Mus*. J. Mol. Biol. 71:633–656.

Swann, H. K. 1924–45. A monograph of the birds of prey (order Accipitres). Weldon and Wesley, London. 16 pts. (6–16 edited by Alexander Wetmore).

Swierczewski, E. V., and R. J. Raikow. 1981. Hind limb morphology, phylogeny, and classification of the Piciformes. Auk 98:466–480.

Syvanen, M. 1987. Molecular clocks and evolutionary relationships: possible distortions due to horizontal gene flow. J. Mol. Evol. 26:16–23.

Szarski, H. 1974. Cell size and nuclear DNA content in vertebrates. Intl. Rev. Cytol. 44:93–111.

Szecsi, A., and A. Dobrovolszky. 1983. Fusarium-fajok összehasonlito vizsgalata DNS:DNS hibridizacioval. Növénytermelés 32:289–297. English version in Mycopathologia (see next item).

Szecsi, A., and A. Dobrovolszky. 1985a. Phylogenetic relationships among *Fusarium* species measured by DNA reassociation. Mycopathologia 89:89–94.

Szecsi, A., and A. Dobrovolszky. 1985b. Genetic distance in fungus *Fusarium* measured by comparative computer analysis of DNA thermal denaturation profiles. Mycopathologia 89:95–100.

Szidat, L. 1942. Ueber die Beziehungen zwischen Parasitologie und Ornithologie. Vogelzug 13:17–35.

Tateno, Y., M. Nei, and F. Tajima. 1982. Accuracy of estimated phylogenetic trees from molecular data. I. Distantly related species. J. Mol. Evol. 18:387–404.

Taylor, W. P. 1909. An instance of hybridization in hummingbirds, with remarks on the weight of generic characters in the Trochilidae. Auk 26:291–293.

Temminck, C. J. 1820–40. Manuel d'ornithologie: ou tableau systematique des oiseaux qui se trouvent en Europe. 2nd ed., 4 vols. in 3. G. Dutour (v. 1–2), E. d'Ocagne (v. 3), and H. Cousin (v. 4), Paris.

Tereba, A., and B. J. McCarthy. 1973. Hybridization of ^{125}I-labeled ribonucleic acid. Biochemistry 12:4675–4679.

Teshima, I. 1972. DNA-DNA hybridization in blackflies (Diptera: Simuliidae). Canad. J. Zool. 50:931–940.

Thompson, D. W. 1899. On characteristic points in the cranial osteology of the parrots. Proc. Zool. Soc. London 1899:9–46.

Thompson, D. W. 1901. On the pterylosis of the giant humming-bird (*Patagona gigas*). Proc. Zool. Soc. London 1901:311–324.

Thompson, W. F., and M. G. Murray. 1981. The nuclear genome: structure and function. Pp. 1–81 *in* The biochemistry of plants. Vol. 6, Proteins and nucleic acids. A. Marcus, ed. Academic Press, New York.

Thomson, A. L., editor. 1964. A new dictionary of birds. Nelson, London. 928 pp.

Tilghman, S. M., D. C. Tiemeier, J. G. Seidman, B. M. Peterlin, M. Sullivan, J. V. Maizel, and P. Leder. 1978. Intervening sequence of DNA identified in the structural portion of a mouse β-globin gene. Proc. Natl. Acad. Sci. USA 75:725–729.

Timberlake, W. E. 1978. Low repetitive DNA content in *Aspergillus nidulans*. Science 202:973–975.

Timmermann, G. 1957a. Studien zu einer vergleichenden Parasitologie der Charadriiformes oder Regenpfeifervögel. Teil I: Mallophaga. Parasitologische Schriftenreihe, Heft 8, Gustav Fischer, Jena. 204 pp.

Timmermann, G. 1957b. Stellung und Gliederung der Regenpfeifervögel (Ordnung Charadriiformes) nach Massgabe des Mallophagologischen Befundes. Pp. 159–172 *in* Premier symposium sur la spécificité parasitaire des parasites de vertébrés. J. G. Baer, ed. Univ. Neuchâtel. Union Intl. Sci. Biol., Ser. B, vol. 32.

Timmermann, G. 1959. Drei neue Sturmvögelfederlinge. Zool. Anz. 162:148–153.

Timmermann, G. 1962. Die verwandtschaftlichen Affinitäten der Sturmvögel im Lichte der vergleichenden Parasitologie. Zeitschr. Parasitenkunde 22:100–101.

Timmermann, G. 1963. Fragen der Anatidensystematik in parasitologischer Sicht. Pp. 189–197 *in* Proc. 13th Intl. Orn. Congr.

Timmermann, G. 1965. Die Federlingsfauna der Sturmvögel und die Phylogenese des procellariiformen Vögelstammes. Abh. Naturwiss. Vereins Hamburg Verhandl., N.F., 8, Suppl. 249 pp.

Timmermann, G. 1969. Zur Frage der systematischen Stellung der Flughühner (Pteroclididae) in vergleichend-parasitologischer Sicht. J. für Orn. 110:103–104.

Tinbergen, N. 1959. Comparative studies of the behaviour of gulls (Laridae): a progress report. Behaviour 15:1–70.

Tlsty, T., P. C. Brown, R. Johnston, and R. T. Schimke. 1982. Enhanced frequency of generation of methotrexate resistance and gene amplification in cultured mouse and hamster cell lines. Pp. 231–238 *in* Gene Amplification. R. T. Schimke, ed. Cold Spring Harbor Lab., New York.

Tobler, H., K. D. Smith, and H. Ursprung. 1972. Molecular aspects of chromatin elimination in *Ascaris lumbricoides*. Devel. Biol. 27:190–203.

Toivonen, L. A., D. T. Crowe, R. J. Detrick, S. W. Klemann, and J. C. Vaughn. 1983. Ribosomal RNA gene number and sequence divergence in the diploid-tetraploid species pair of North America hylid tree frogs. Biochem. Genetics 21:299–308.

Tomioka, N., and M. Sugiura. 1983. The complete nucleotide sequence of a 16S ribosomal RNA gene from a blue-green alga, *Anacystis nidulans*. Mol. Gen. Genet. 191:46–50.

Tordoff, H. B. 1954a. A systematic study of the avian family Fringillidae based on the structure of the skull. Misc. Publ. Mus. Zool. Univ. Mich. No. 81:1–41.

Tordoff, H. B. 1954b. Relationships in the New World nine-primaried oscines. Auk 71:273–284.

Traylor, M. A., Jr. 1970. Notes on African Muscicapidae. Ibis 112:395–397.

Traylor, M. A., Jr. 1977. A classification of the tyrant flycatchers (Tyrannidae). Bull. Mus. Comp. Zool. 148:129–184.

Traylor, M. A., Jr. 1979. Family Tyrannidae. Pp. 1–245 *in* Check-list of birds of the world. Vol. 8. M. A. Traylor, Jr., ed. Mus. Comp. Zool., Cambridge, Mass.

Tyler, C. 1964. A study of the egg shells of the Anatidae. Proc. Zool. Soc. London 142:547–583.

Tyler, C. 1965. A study of the egg shells of the Sphenisciformes. J. Zool. 147:1–19.

Tyler, C. 1966. A study of the egg shells of the Falconiformes. J. Zool. 150:413–425.

Tyler, C. 1969. A study of the egg shells of the Gaviiformes, Procellariiformes, Podicipitiformes and Pelecaniformes. J. Zool. 158:395–412.

Tyler, C., and K. Simkiss. 1959. A study of the egg shells of ratite birds. Proc. Zool. Soc. London 133:201–243.

Tzagoloff, A. 1982. Mitochondria. Plenum Press, New York.

Uberbacher, E. C., and G. J. Bunick. 1985. Crystallographic structure of the octamer histone core of the nucleosome. Science 229:1112–1113.

Uberbacher, E. C., J. M. Harp, E. Wilkinson-Singley, and G. J. Bunick. 1986. Shape analysis of the histone octamer in solution. Science 232:1247–1249.

Udvardy, A., and P. Schedl. 1983. Structural polymorphism in DNA. J. Mol. Biol. 166:159–181.

Uhlenbeck, O., R. Harrison, and P. Doty. 1968. Some effects of non-complementary bases on the stability of helical complexes of polyribonucleotides. *In* Molecular Associations in Biology. Academic Press, New York.

Ullrich, R. C., K. A. Droms, J. D. Doyon, and C. A. Specht. 1980a. Characterization of DNA from the basidiomycete *Schizophyllum commune*. Exp. Mycology 4:123–134.

Ullrich, R. C., B. D. Kohorn, and C. A. Specht. 1980b. Absence of short-period repetitive-sequence interspersion in the basidiomycete *Schizophyllum commune*. Chromosoma 81:371–387.

Ullrich, R. C., and J. R. Raper. 1977. Evolution of genetic mechanisms in fungi. Taxon 26:169–179.

Vach, W., and P. O. Degens. 1986. Starting more robust estimation of ultrametrics. Pp. 239–246 *in* Die Klassifikation und ihr Umfeld. P. O. Degens, H.-J. Hermes, and O. Opitz, eds. Indeks Verlag, Frankfurt.

Van Andel, T. H., J. Thiede, J. G. Sclater, and W. W. Hay. 1977. Depositional history of the South Atlantic ocean during the last 125 million years. J. Geol. (Chicago) 85:651–698.

Vanden Berge, J. C. 1970. A comparative study of the appendicular musculature of the order Ciconiiformes. Amer. Midl. Nat. 84:289–364.

Van Tets, G. F. 1965. A comparative study of some social communication patterns in the Pelecaniformes. Orn. Monogr. No. 2. Amer. Orn. Union, Washington, D.C.

Van Tets, G. F., C. W. Meredith, P. J. Fullagar, and P. M. Davidson. 1988. Osteological differences between *Sula* and *Morus*, and a description of an extinct new species of *Sula* from Lord Howe and Norfolk islands, Tasman Sea. Notornis 35:35–57.

Van't Hoff, S., and A. H. Sparrow. 1963. A relationship between DNA content, nuclear volume, and minimum mitotic cycle time. Proc. Natl. Acad. Sci. USA 49:897–902.

Van Valen, L. 1973. A new evolutionary law. Evol. Theory 1:1–30.

Van Valen, L. 1974. Molecular evolution as predicted by natural selection. J. Mol. Biol. 3:89–101.

Van Valen, L. M. 1983. Similar, but not homologous. Nature 305:664.

Varley, J. M., H. C. MacGregor, and H. P. Erba. 1980a. Satellite DNA is transcribed on lampbrush chromosomes. Nature 283:686–688.

Varley, J. M., H. C. MacGregor, I. Nardi, C. Andrews, and H. P. Erba. 1980b. Cytological evidence of transcription of highly repeated DNA sequences during the lampbrush stage in *Triturus cristatus carnifex*. Chromosoma 80:289–307.

Vaurie, C. 1957a. Systematic notes on Peleartic birds. No. 28. The families Remizidae and Aegithalidae. Amer. Mus. Novit. 1853:1–21.

Vaurie, C. 1957b. Notes on the genus *Parisoma* and on the juvenal plumage and systematic position of *Parisoma plumbeum*. Ibis 99:120–122.

Vaurie, C. 1959. The birds of the Palearctic fauna. Order Passeriformes. H. F. and G. Witherby, London.

Vaurie, C. 1964. Systematic notes on the bird family Cracidae. No. 1: Geographical variation of *Ortalis canicollus* and *Penelope marail*. Amer. Mus. Novit. 2197. 8 pp.

Vaurie, C. 1965a. Systematic notes on the bird family Cracidae. No. 2: Relationships and geographical variation of *Ortalis vetula*, *Ortalis poliocephala*, and *Ortalis leucogastra*. Amer. Mus. Novit. 2222. 36 pp.

Vaurie, C. 1965b. Systematic notes on the bird family Cracidae. No. 3: *Ortalis guttata*, *Ortalis superciliaris*, and *Ortalis motmot*. Amer. Mus. Novit. 2232. 21 pp.

Vaurie, C. 1965c. Systematic notes on the bird family Cracidae. No. 4: *Ortalis garrula* and *Ortalis ruficauda*. Amer. Mus. Novit. 2237. 16 pp.

Vaurie, C. 1966a. Systematic notes on the bird family Cracidae. No. 5: *Penelope purpurascens*, *Penelope jacquacu*, and *Penelope obscura*. Amer. Mus. Novit. 2250. 23 pp.

Vaurie, C. 1966b. Systematic notes on the bird family Cracidae. No. 6: Review of nine species of *Penelope*. Amer. Mus. Novit. 2251. 30 pp.

Vaurie, C. 1967a. Systematic notes on the bird family Cracidae. No. 7: The genus *Pipile*. Amer. Mus. Novit. 2296. 16 pp.

Vaurie, C. 1967b. Systematic notes on the bird family Cracidae. No. 8. The genera *Aburria*, *Chamaepetes*, and *Penelopina*. Amer. Mus. Novit. 2299. 12 pp.

Vaurie, C. 1967c. Systematic notes on the bird family Cracidae. No. 9. The genus *Crax*. Amer. Mus. Novit. 2305. 20 pp.

Vaurie, C. 1967d. Systematic notes on the bird family Cracidae. No. 10. The genera *Mitu* and *Pauxi* and generic relationships of the Cracini. Amer. Mus. Novit. 2307. 20 pp.

Vaurie, C. 1968. Taxonomy of the Cracidae (Aves). Bull. Amer. Mus. Nat. Hist. 138:131–260.

Vaurie, C. 1980. Taxonomy and geographical distribution of the Furnariidae (Aves, Passeriformes). Bull. Amer. Mus. Nat. Hist. 166:1–357.

Verheyen, R. 1953. Bijdrage tot de osteologie en die systematiek der Anseriformes. Le Gerfaut 43 (Suppl.):373–456 (in Flemish) :457–497 (French transl.).

Verheyen, R. 1955a. Note sur la variabilité des caractères ostéologiques chez la Macreuse noire, *Melanitta nigra* (L.). Bull. Inst. Roy. Sci. Nat. Belgique 31(21). 19 pp.

Verheyen, R. 1955b. La systématique des Anseriformes basée sur l'osteologie comparée. Bull. Inst. Roy. Sci. Nat. Belgique 31(35–38). 72 pp.

Verheyen, R. 1955c. Contribution à la systématique des Piciformes basée sur l'anatomie comparée. Bull. Inst. Roy. Sci. Nat. Belgique 31(50–51). 43 pp.

Verheyen, R. 1955d. Analyse du potentiel morphologique et considérations sur la systématique des Coraciiformes (Wetmore 1934). Bull. Inst. Roy. Sci. Nat. Belgique 31(92–94). 51 pp.

Verheyen, R. 1956a. Les Striges, les Trogones et les Caprimulgi dans la systématique moderne. Bull. Inst. Roy. Sci. Nat. Belgique 32(3). 31 pp.

Verheyen, R. 1956b. Contribution à l'anatomie et a la systématique des touracos (Musophagi) et des coucous (Cuculiformes). Bull. Inst. Roy. Sci. Nat. Belgique 32(23). 28 pp.

Verheyen, R. 1956c. Note systématique sur *Opisthocomus hoazin* (St. Müller). Bull. Inst. Roy. Sci. Nat. Belgique 32(32). 8 pp.

Verheyen, R. 1956d. Contribution à l'anatomie et à la systématique des Galliformes. Bull. Inst. Roy. Sci. Nat. Belgique 32(42). 24 pp.

Verheyen, R. 1956e. Note sur l'anatomie et la classification des Coliiformes. Bull. Inst. Roy. Sci. Nat. Belgique 32(47). 7 pp.

Verheyen, R. 1956f. Analyse du potentiel morphologique et projet d'une nouvelle classification des Psittaciformes. Bull. Inst. Roy. Sci. Nat. Belgique 32(55). 54 pp.

Verheyen, R. 1956g. Note sur l'anatomie et la place des Kamichis (Anhimiformes) dans les systémes de classification. Le Gerfaut 46:215–221.

Verheyen, R. 1956h. Les colibris (Trochili) et les martinets (Apodi) sont-ils réellement apparentés? Le Gerfaut 46:237–252.

Verheyen, R. 1957a. Analyse du potential morphologique et projet de classification des Columbiformes (Wetmore 1934). Bull. Inst. Roy. Sci. Nat. Belgique 33(3). 42 pp.

Verheyen, R. 1957b. Contribution au démembrement de l'ordo artificiel des Gruiformes (Peters 1934). I. Les Ralliformes. Bull. Inst. Roy. Sci. Nat. Belgique 33(31). 44 pp.

Verheyen, R. 1957c. Contribution au démembrement de l'ordo artificiel des Gruiformes (Peters 1934). II. Les Cariamiformes. Bull. Inst. Roy. Sci. Nat. Belgique 33(39). 7 pp.

Verheyen, R. 1957d. Contribution au démembrement de l'ordo artificiel des Gruiformes (Peters 1934). III. Les Jacaniformes. Bull. Inst. Roy. Sci. Nat. Belgique 33(48). 19 pp.

Verheyen, R. 1958a. Contribution au démembrement de l'ordo artificiel des Gruiformes IV. Les Turniciformes. Bull. Inst. Roy. Sci. Nat. Belgique 34(2). 18 pp.

Verheyen, R. 1958b. Analyse du potentiel morphologique et projet d'une nouvelle classification des Charadriiformes. Bull. Inst. Roy. Sci. Nat. Belgique 34(18). 35 pp.

Verheyen, R. 1958c. Note sur la classification des Procellariiformes (Tubinares). Bull. Inst. Roy. Sci. Nat. Belgique 34(30). 22 pp.

Verheyen, R. 1958d. Contribution a la systématique des Alciformes. Bull. Inst. Roy. Sci. Nat. Belgique 34(45). 15 pp.

Verheyen, R. 1958e. Convergence ou paramorphogenese. Systématique et phylogénie des Manchots (Sphenisciformes). Le Gerfaut 48:43–69.

Verheyen, R. 1959a. Note sur la systématique de base des Lariformes. Bull. Inst. Roy. Sci. Nat. Belgique 35(9). 16 pp.

Verheyen, R. 1959b. Contribution à l'anatomie et a la systématique de base des Ciconiiformes (Parker 1868). Bull. Inst. Roy. Sci. Nat. Belgique 35(24). 34 pp.

Verheyen, R. 1959c. Révision de la systématique des Falconiformes. Bull. Inst. Roy. Sci. Nat. Belgique 35(37). 51 pp.

Verheyen, R. 1959d. Les plongeons (Gaviae) et les grèbes (Podicipitides) dans les systémes de classification. Bull. Inst. Roy. Sci. Nat. Belgique 35(44). 12 pp.

Verheyen, R. 1960a. Les tinamous dans les systémes ornithologiques. Bull. Inst. Roy. Sci. Nat. Belgique 36(1). 11 pp.

Verheyen, R. 1960b. Les Pelecaniformes et le paille-en-queue (*Phaethon*). Bull. Inst. Roy. Sci. Nat. Belgique 36(25). 18 pp.

Verheyen, R. 1960c. Considérations sur la colonne vertébrale des oiseaux (Non-Passeres). Bull. Inst. Roy. Sci. Nat. Belgique 36(42). 24 pp.

Verheyen, R. 1960d. Sur la valeur des indices ostéo métriques en ornithotaxonomie. Bull. Inst. Roy. Sci. Nat. Belgique 36(55). 27 pp.

Verheyen, R. 1960e. A propos de l'aptérisme chez les Carinates (Aves). Bull. Inst. Roy. Sci. Nat. Belgique 36(56). 7 pp.

Verheyen, R. 1960f. Outline of procedure in basic avian systematics. Le Gerfaut 50:223–230.

Verheyen, R. 1960g. Les nandous (Rheiformes) sont apparentés aux tinamous (Tinamidae/Galliformes). Le Gerfaut 50:289–293.

Verheyen, R. 1960h. Les kiwis (Apterygiformes) dans les systémes de classification. Bull. Soc. Roy. Zool. d'Anvers No. 15. 11 pp.

Verheyen, R. 1960i. Contribution à l'osteologie et à la systématique des Ratitae. Bull. Soc. Roy. Zool. d'Anvers No. 17. 19 pp.

Verheyen, R. 1960j. What are Ciconiiformes? Pp. 741–743 *in* Proc. 12th Intl. Orn. Congr.

Verheyen, R. 1961. A new classification for the non-passerine birds of the world. Bull. Inst. Roy. Sci. Nat. Belgique 37(27). 36 pp.

Verreaux, J., and O. Des Murs. 1860. Description d'oiseaux de la Nouvelle-Caledonie et indication des espèces déjà connues de ce pays. Rev. Mag. Zool., Ser. 2, 12:383–396, 431–443.

Vieillot, L. J. P. 1816. Analyse d'une nouvelle ornithologie élémentaire. Deterville, Paris. 70 pp.

Virchow, H. 1931. Wirbelsäule und Bein der Pinguine. Morph. Jahrb. 67:459–565.

Vladychenskaya, N. S., O. S. Kedrova, and N. B. Petrov. 1983. Genome structure in the Alligator Gar *Lepisosteus osseus* (Gandoidomorpha). Molec. Biol. 17:300–307. Transl. from Molekularynaya Biol. 17:373–382. Plenum, New York.

Vogel, F., M. Kopun, and R. Rathenberg. 1976. Mutation and molecular evolution. Pp. 13–33 *in* Molecular anthropology. M. Goodman and R. E. Tashian, eds. Plenum Press, New York.

Voipio, P. 1955. Muuttuva lintujen järjestelmää (Das veränderliche System des Vögel) [in Finnish, German summary]. Ornis Fennica 32:108–129.

Voous, K. H. 1949. The morphological, anatomical, and distributional relationship of the Arctic and Antarctic fulmars (Aves, Procellariidae). Ardea 37:113–122.

Voous, K. H. 1960. Atlas of European birds. English version. Nelson, London.

Voous, K. H. 1977. List of Holarctic bird species. Passerines. Ibis 119:223–250, 376–406.

Voous, K. H. 1985. Table of classification. Pp. xi–xvii *in* A dictionary of birds. B. Campbell and E. Lack, eds. T. and A. D. Poyser, Calton, England.

Vossbrinck, C. R., J. V. Maddox, S. Friedman, B. A. Debrunner-Vossbrinck, and C. R. Woese. 1987. Ribosomal RNA sequence suggests microsporidia are extremely ancient prokaryotes. Nature 326:411–414.

Vuilleumier, F. 1965. Relationships and evolution within the Cracidae (Aves, Galliformes). Bull. Mus. Comp. Zool. 134. 27 pp.

Vuilleumier, F. 1985. Fossil and Recent avifaunas and the interamerican interchange. Pp. 389–424 *in* The great American biotic interchange. F. G. Stehli and S. D. Webb, eds. Plenum, New York.

Wada, A. 1987. Automated high-speed DNA sequencing. Nature 325:771–772.

Wagler, J. G. 1827. Systema avium. Pt. 1. J. G. Cottae, Stuttgart and Tubingen. 411 pp.

Wagner, G. P. 1989. The biological homology concept. Ann. Rev. Ecol. Syst. 20:51–69.

Wahli, W., I. B. Dawid, G. U. Ryffel, and R. Weber. 1981. Vitellogenesis and the vitellogenin gene family. Science 212:298–304.

Wakabayashi, S., H. Matsubara, and D. A. Webster. 1986. Primary sequence of a dimeric bacterial haemoglobin from *Vitreoscilla*. Nature 322:481–483.

Walbot, V., and L. S. Dure III. 1976. Developmental biochemistry of cotton seed embryogenesis and germination. VII. Characterization of the cotton genome. J. Mol. Biol. 101:503–536.

Waldrop, M. M. 1989. The structure of the "second genetic code." Science 246:1122.

Wallace, A. R. 1856. Attempts at a natural arrangement of birds. Ann. Mag. Nat. Hist. 18:193–216.

Wallace, A. R. 1863. Who are the humming bird's relations? Zoologist, 1st Ser., 21:8486–8491.

Wallace, A. R. 1874. On the arrangement of the families constituting the Order Passeres. Ibis 22:406–416.

Wallace, D. C., and H. J. Morowitz. 1973. Genome size and evolution. Chromosoma 40:121–126.

Wang, L-H., S. Y. Tsai, R. G. Cook, W. G. Beattie, M-J. Tsai, and B. W. O'Malley. 1989.

COUP transcription factor is a member of the steroid receptor superfamily. Nature 340:163–166.

Warheit, K. I., D. A. Good, and K. de Queiroz. 1989. Variation in numbers of scleral ossicles and their phylogenetic transformations within the Pelecaniformes. Auk 106:383–388.

Waring, M. J., and R. J. Britten. 1966. Nucleotide sequence repetition: a rapidly reassociating fraction of mouse DNA. Science 154:791–794.

Warner, R. W. 1972. The anatomy of the syrinx in passerine birds. J. Zool., London 168:381–393.

Warter, S. L. 1965. The cranial osteology of the New World Tyrannoidea and its taxonomic implications. Ph.D. diss. Louisiana State Univ., Univ. Microfilms, Ann Arbor, Michigan.

Waterston, J. 1928. The Mallophaga of sand-grouse. Proc. Zool. Soc. London 1928:333–356.

Watson, J. D. 1968. The double helix. Athenaeum, New York.

Watson, J. D., and F. H. C. Crick. 1953. Molecular structure of nucleic acids. A structure for deoxyribose nucleic acid. Nature 171:737–738.

Watson, M. 1883. Report on the anatomy of the Spheniscidae collected during the voyage of H.M.S. Challenger. *In* Great Britain and Ireland, Challenger Office: Report on the scientific results of the voyage of H.M.S. Challenger 1873–76, Zool. 7(18). 244 pp.

Webb, M. 1957. The ontogeny of the cranial bones, cranial peripheral and cranial parasympathetic nerves, together with a study of the visceral muscles of *Struthio*. Acta Zool. (Stockholm) 38:81–203.

Webster, J. D. 1962. Systematic and ecologic notes on the Olive Warbler. Wilson Bull. 74:417–421.

Weiner, A. M., and R. A. Denison. 1982. Either gene amplification or gene conversion may maintain the homogeneity of the multigene family encoding human U1 small nuclear RNA. Cold Spring Harbor Symp. Quant. Biol. 47:1141–1149.

Weldon, W. F. R. 1883. On some points in the anatomy of *Phoenicopterus* and its allies. Proc. Zool. Soc. London 638–652.

Wells, R., and R. Sager. 1971. Denaturation and the renaturation kinetics of chloroplast DNA from *Chlamydomonas reinhardi*. J. Mol. Biol. 58:611–622.

Wells, R., H.-D. Royer, and C. P. Hollenberg. 1976. Non Xenopus-like DNA sequence organization in the *Chironomus tentans* genome. Mol. Gen. Genet. 147:45–51.

Werman, S. D., M. S. Springer, and R. J. Britten. 1990. Nucleic acids I: DNA-DNA hybridization. *In* Molecular systematics. D. M. Hillis and C. Moritz, eds. Sinauer Assoc., Sunderland, Mass.

Westheimer, F. H. 1986. Polyribonucleic acids as enzymes. Nature 319:534–536.

Westheimer, F. H. 1987. Why nature chose phosphates. Science 235:1173–1178.

Wetmore, A. 1914. A peculiarity in the growth of the tail feathers of the giant hornbill (*Rhinoplax vigil*). Proc. U.S. Natl. Mus. 47:497–500.

Wetmore, A. 1918. On the anatomy of *Nyctibius* with notes on allied birds. Proc. U.S. Natl. Mus. 54:577–586.

Wetmore, A. 1930. A systematic classification for the birds of the world. Proc. U.S. Natl. Mus. 76(24):1–8.

Wetmore, A. 1934. A systematic classification for the birds of the world, revised and amended. Smithson. Misc. Coll. 89(13):1–11.

Wetmore, A. 1938. A fossil duck from the Eocene of Utah. J. Paleont. 12:280–283.

Wetmore, A. 1940. A systematic classification for the birds of the world. Smithson. Misc. Coll. 99(7):1–11.

Wetmore, A. 1947. Nomenclature of the higher groups in swifts. Wilson Bull. 59:211–212.

Wetmore, A. 1951. A revised classification for the birds of the world. Smithson. Misc. Coll. 117(4):1–22.

Wetmore, A. 1956. A check-list of the fossil and prehistoric birds of North America and the West Indies. Smithson. Misc. Coll. 131(5). 105 pp.

Wetmore, A. 1957. The classification of the Oscine Passeriformes. Condor 59:207–209.

Wetmore, A. 1960. A classification for the birds of the world. Smithson. Misc. Coll. 139(11):1–37.

Wetmore, A., and W. DeW. Miller. 1926. The revised classification for the fourth edition of the A.O.U. check-list. Auk 43:337–346.

Wetmur, J. G. 1976. Hybridization and renaturation kinetics of nucleic acids. Ann. Rev. Biophys. Bioeng. 5:337–361.

Wetmur, J. G., and N. Davidson. 1968. Kinetics of renaturation of DNA. J. Mol. Biol. 31:349–370.

White, C. M. N. 1960. A check list of the Ethiopian Muscicapidae (Sylviinae). Part I. Occ. Papers Natl. Mus. Southern Rhodesia No. 24B:399–430.

White, C. M. N. 1962. A revised check list of African shrikes, orioles, drongos, starlings, crows, waxwings, cuckoo-shrikes, bulbuls, accentors, thrushes and babblers. Zambian Dept. of Game and Fisheries, Government Printer, Lusaka, Zambia.

White, C. M. N. 1963. A revised check list of African flycatchers, tits, tree creepers, sunbirds, white-eyes, honey eaters, buntings, finches, weavers and waxbills. Zambian Dept. of Game and Fisheries, Government Printer, Lusaka, Zambia.

White, C. M. N. 1965. A revised check list of African non-passerine birds. Zambian Dept. of Game and Fisheries, Government Printer, Lusaka, Zambia.

White, C. M. N., and R. E. Moreau. 1958. Taxonomic notes on the Ploceidae. Bull. Brit. Orn. Club 78:140–145, 157–163.

White, M. J. D. 1968. Models of speciation. Science 159:1065–1070.

White, M. J. D. 1969. Chromosomal rearrangements and speciation in animals. Ann. Rev. Genet. 3:75–98.

White, M. J. D. 1973. Animal cytology and evolution. 3rd edition. Cambridge Univ. Press.

White, M. J. D. 1978a. Chain processes in chromosomal speciation. Syst. Zool. 27:285–298.

White, M. J. D. 1978b. Modes of speciation. W. H. Freeman and Co., San Francisco. 454 pp.

Whitfield, P., and W. Bottomley. 1983. Organization and structure of chloroplast genes. Ann. Rev. Plant Physiol. 34:279–326.

Whitmore, T. C. 1981. Wallace's Line and plate tectonics. Clarendon Press, Oxford.

Wickens, M., and P. Stephenson. 1984. Role of the conserved AAUAAA sequence: four AAUAAA point mutants prevent messenger RNA 3′ end formation. Science 226:1045–1051.

Wickler, W. 1961. Über die Stammesgeschte und den taxonomischen Wert einer Verhaltensweisen der Vögel. Z. Tierpsychol. 18:320–342.

Wieder, R., and J. G. Wetmur. 1981. One hundred-fold acceleration of DNA renaturation rates in solution. Biopolymers 20:1537–1547.

Wieder, R., and J. G. Wetmur. 1982. Factors affecting the kinetics of DNA reassociation in phenol-water emulsion at high DNA concentrations. Biopolymers 21:665–677.

Wiley, E. O. 1981. Phylogenetics. John Wiley and Sons, New York.

Wilkes, M. M., W. R. Pearson, J-R. Wu, and J. Bonner. 1978. Sequence organization of the rat genome by electron microscopy. Biochemistry 17:60–69.

Wilkins, M. H. F., R. G. Gosling, and W. E. Seeds. 1951. Nucleic acid: an extensible molecule. Nature 167:759–760.

Williams, G. R. 1976. The New Zealand wattlebirds (Callaeatidae). Pp. 161–170 *in* Proc. 16th Intl. Orn. Congr. H. A. Frith and J. H. Calaby, eds. Austral. Acad. Sci., Canberra.

Willughby, F., and J. Ray. 1676. Ornithologiae libri tres. Royal Soc., London. 307 pp. (Eng. transl. 1678).

Wilson, A. C., and V. M. Sarich. 1969. A molecular time scale for human evolution. Proc. Natl. Acad. Sci. USA 63:1088–1093.

Wilson, A. C., N. O. Kaplan, L. Levine, A. Pesce, M. Reichlin, and W. S. Allison. 1964. Evolution of lactic dehydrogenases. Federation Proc. 23:1250–1266.

Wilson, A. C., G. L. Bush, S. M. Case, and M.-C. King. 1975. Social structuring of mammalian populations and rate of chromosomal evolution. Proc. Natl. Acad. Sci. USA 72:5061–5065.

Wilson, A. C., S. S. Carlson, and T. J. White. 1977. Biochemical evolution. Ann. Rev. Biochem. 46:573–639.

Wilson, E. B. 1895. An atlas of the fertilization and karyokinesis of the ovum. Macmillan, New York.

Wiman, C. 1905. Vorläufige Mitteilung über die alttertiären Vertebraten der Seymourinsel. Bull. Geol. Inst. Univ. Uppsala 6:247–252.

Witherby, H. F., F. C. R. Jourdain, N. F. Ticehurst, and B. W. Tucker. 1940–41. Handbook of British birds. 5 vols. H. F. and G. Witherby, London.

Woese, C. R. 1981. Archaebacteria. Sci. Amer. 244:98–122.

Wolfe, J. A. 1980. Tertiary climates and floristic relationships at high latitudes in the northern hemisphere. Palaeogeogr., Palaeoclim., Palaeoecol. 30:313–323.

Wolfe, K. H., P. M. Sharp, and W.-H. Li. 1989. Mutation rates differ among regions of the mammalian genome. Nature 337:283–285.

Wolters, H. E. 1957. Die Klassifikation der Weberfinken (Estrildidae). Bonn. Zool. Beitr. 8:90–129.

Wolters, H. E. 1960. Zur Systematik der Atlasfinken (Untergattung *Hypochera* der Gattung *Vidua*, Viduinae, Estrildidae, Aves). Bonn. Zool. Beiträge 1:19–25.

Wolters, H. E. 1966. On the relationships and generic limits of African Estrildinae. Ostrich Suppl. 6:75–81.

Wolters, H. E. 1975–82. Die Vogelarten der Erde. Paul Parey, Hamburg and Berlin. xx + 745 pp.

Wood, D. S. 1983. Phenetic relationships of the Ciconiidae (Aves). Annals Carnegie Mus. 52:79–112.

Wood, D. S. 1984. Concordance between classifications of the Ciconiidae based on behavioral and morphological data. J. für Orn. 125:25–37.

Woolfenden, G. E. 1961. Postcranial osteology of the waterfowl. Bull. Florida State Mus. 6:1–129.

Woolfenden, G. E., and J. W. Fitzpatrick. 1984. The Florida Scrub Jay: Demography of a cooperative-breeding bird. Princeton Univ. Press, Princeton, New Jersey.

Wray, R. S. 1887. On some points in the morphology of the wings of birds. Proc. Zool. Soc. London 1887:343–357.

Wright, C. A., ed. 1974. Biochemical and immunological taxonomy of animals. Academic Press, London and New York.

Wu, C.-I., and W.-H. Li. 1985. Evidence for higher rates of nucleotide substitution in rodents than in man. Proc. Natl. Acad. Sci. USA 82:1741–1745.

Wynshaw-Boris, A. J., and R. W. Hanson. 1983. Approaches to the study of hormonal regulation of gene expression. Pp. 171–203 *in* Genes: structure and expression. A. M. Kroon, ed. John Wiley and Sons, New York.

Yamashina, Y. 1952. Classification of the Anatidae based on the cyto-genetics. Papers Coordinat. Comm. Res. Genet. 3:1–34.

Young, B. D., and M. L. M. Anderson. 1985. Quantitative analysis of solution hybridisation. Pp. 47–71 *in* Nucleic acid hybridisation. B. D. Hames and S. J. Higgins, eds. IRL Press, Oxford and Washington, D.C.

Young, C. G. 1929. A contribution to the ornithology of the coastland of British Guiana. Ibis 71:1–38.

Zaug, A. J., and T. R. Cech. 1986. The intervening sequence RNA of *Tetrahymena* is an enzyme. Science 231:470–475.

Zavattari, E., and I. Cellini. 1956. La minuta architettura delle ossa degli uccelli e il suo valore nella sistematica dei grandi gruppi. Monit. Zool. Ital. 64:189–200.

Zeidler, K. 1966. Untersuchungen über Flügelbefiederung und Mauser des Haussperlings (*Passer domesticus* L.). J. für Orn. 107:113–153.

Zimmer, J. T. 1926. Catalogue of the Edward Ayer ornithological library. Field Mus. Nat. Hist., Publ. 240 (Zool. Ser., vol. 16). 2 vols.

Zimmerman, J. L., and R. B. Goldberg. 1977. DNA sequence organization in the genome of *Nicotiana tabacum*. Chromosoma 59:227–252.

Zimmerman, S. B. 1982. The three-dimensional structure of DNA. Ann. Rev. Biochem. 51:395–427.

Ziswiler, V. 1964. Neue Aspekte zur Systematik körnerfressender Singvögel. Verh. Schweiz. Naturforsch. Ges. 144:133–134.

Ziswiler, V. 1965. Zur Kenntnis des Samenöffnens und der Struktur des hörnernen Gaumens bei körnerfressenden Oscines. J. für Orn. 106:1–48.

Ziswiler, V. 1967a. Vergleichend morphologische Untersuchungen am Verdauungstrakt körnerfressender Singvögel zur Abklärung ihrer systematischen Stellung. Zool. Jahrb. Syst. 94:427–520.

Ziswiler, V. 1967b. Die taxonomische Stellung des Schneefinken *Montifringilla nivalis* (Linnaeus). Orn. Beobachter 64:105–110.

Ziswiler, V. 1979. Zungenfunktionen und Zungenversteifung bei granivoren Singvögeln. Rev. Suisse Zool. 86:823–831.

Zuckerkandl, E. 1976. Programs of gene action and progressive evolution. Pp. 387–447 *in* Molecular anthropology. M. Goodman and R. E. Tashian, eds. Plenum Press, New York.

Zuckerkandl, E., and L. Pauling. 1962. Molecular disease, evolution, and genic diversity. Pp. 189–225 *in* Horizons in Biochemistry. M. Kasha and B. Pullman, eds. Academic Press, New York. 604 pp.

Zuckerkandl, E., and L. Pauling. 1965. Evolutionary divergence and convergence in proteins. Pp. 97–166 *in* Evolving genes and proteins. V. Bryson and H. J. Vogel, eds. Academic Press, New York.

Zuckerkandl, E., G. Latter, and J. Jurka. 1989. Maintenance of function without selection: *Alu* sequences as "cheap genes." J. Mol. Evol. 29:504–512.

Zusi, R. L. 1962. Structural adaptations of the head and neck in the Black Skimmer, *Rynchops nigra*, L. Publ. Nuttall Orn. Club No. 3. 101 pp.

Zusi, R. L., and J. T. Marshall. 1970. A comparison of Asiatic and North American sapsuckers. Bull. Siam. Soc. Natur. Hist. 23:393–407.

Zusi, R. L., and R. W. Storer. 1969. Osteology and myology of the head and neck of the pied-billed grebes (*Podilymbus*). Misc. Publ. Univ. Michigan Mus. Zool. No. 139. 49 pp.

Zweibel, L. J., V. H. Cohn, D. R. Wright, and G. P. Moore. 1982. Evolution of single-copy DNA and the ADH gene in seven drosophilids. J. Mol. Evol. 19:62–71.

Index